Introduction to Comparative Government

Fourth Edition

Michael Curtis, General Editor
Rutgers University

Jean Blondel
European University Institute

Bernard E. Brown
City University of New York

Joseph Fewsmith
Boston University

Roger E. Kanet
University of Illinois at Champaign-Urbana

Donald Kommers
University of Notre Dame

Theodore McNelly
University of Maryland

Martin C. Needler
University of the Pacific

John S. Reshetar Jr.
University of Washington

Stephen Wright
Northern Arizona University

 LONGMAN

An imprint of Addison Wesley Longman, Inc.

New York • Reading, Massachusetts • Menlo Park, California • Harlow, England
Don Mills, Ontario • Sydney • Mexico City • Madrid • Amsterdam

Acquisitions Editor: Margaret Loftus
Project Coordination and Text Design: York Production Services
Cover Designer: Kay Petronio
Supplements Editor: Tom Kulesa
Art Coordination: York Production Services
Photo Researcher: Diane Kraut
Electronic Production Manager: Valerie Zaborski
Manufacturing Manager: Helene G. Landers
Electronic Page Makeup: York Production Services
Printer and Binder: R. R. Donnelley & Sons Company
Cover Printer: Phoenix Color Corp.

For permission to use copyrighted material, grateful acknowledgment is made to the copyright holders on p. 594, which is hereby made part of this copyright page.

Library of Congress Cataloging-in-Publication Data

Introduction to comparative government. Michael Curtis, general
    editor; Jean Blondel ... [et al.].—4th ed.
        p. cm.
    Includes bibliographical references and index.
    ISBN 0-673-99757-X
    1. Comparative government. I. Curtis, Michael, 1923–   .
II. Blondel, Jean, 1929–   .
JF51. I58   1996   96-25150
320.3—dc20   CIP

ISBN 0-673-99757-X

    34567890—DOC—9998

For
Alida & Steve
and
Cynthia & Howard
as a token
of my affection

BRIEF CONTENTS

DETAILED CONTENTS

PART 1

INDUSTRIAL DEMOCRACIES

CHAPTER 2   THE GOVERNMENT OF GREAT BRITAIN   *Michael Curtis*   **33**

Cʜᴀᴘᴛᴇʀ 3   THE GOVERNMENT OF FRANCE   *Jean Blondel*   105

CHAPTER 4   THE GOVERNMENT OF GERMANY   *Donald Kommers*   159

C HAPTER 5 THE GOVERNMENT OF JAPAN *Theodore McNelly* **228**

CHAPTER 6   A CHANGING EUROPE   *Michael Curtis*   281

PART 2   315

COMMUNIST AND POST-COMMUNIST SYSTEMS

CHAPTER 7   THE GOVERNMENT OF THE RUSSIAN FEDERATION

Roger E. Kanet and John S. Reshetar Jr.   **317**

P<small>ART</small> 3 _____ 449

THIRD WORLD COUNTRIES

C<small>HAPTER</small> 9   **THE GOVERNMENT OF INDIA**   *Bernard E. Brown*   **451**

CHAPTER 10   THE GOVERNMENT OF MEXICO   *Martin C. Needler*   501

CHAPTER 11   **THE GOVERNMENT OF NIGERIA**   *Stephen Wright*   **542**

CHAPTER 12   **CONCLUSION**   591

PREFACE

The fourth edition of this book provides an up-to-date introduction to comparative government and politics by examining the politics of some industrialized democratic countries (Great Britain, France, Germany, and Japan), Communist and former Communist countries (Russia and China), and three third world countries in different continents (India, Mexico, and Nigeria). Why have these nine countries been chosen to exemplify the politics, policies, and problems of democratic, past and present Communist systems, and developing third world countries? The reason is partly that these countries are of great historical or contemporary significance and have a wealth of political experience. The study of their political systems is interesting in itself and instructive for those wanting to understand the world in which we live. In addition, information about the politics of these countries often provides the main empirical data for the formulation of generalizations in comparative government. This fourth edition also includes a new chapter focusing on the dramatic changes taking place in both Western and Eastern Europe including the formation of the new European Union.

It should be understood that this book is not based on any narrow or rigid theoretical approach. Instead, the authors prefer that students should be exposed to alternative ways of comparing political systems. The first chapter, "Introduction," therefore proposes a number of alternative classifications of political systems and a general context that allows the nine systems to be compared in different ways.

Each instructor and student can choose the comparative approach that he or she thinks is the most helpful for understanding the whole or parts of political systems. This is particularly important since this new edition appears at a time of unusual flux in at least two of the major political systems in the book, Russia and China.

Both individually and collectively, the ten authors of the book owe intellectual debts to many colleagues who have given valuable advice and also to our students at different institutions. We also thank the various readers of earlier drafts of this manuscript, whose comments and suggestions improved the end result:

Donald Barry, Lehigh University
Richard E. Chard,
 State University of New York at Stony Brook
Mark Cichok, University of Texas at Arlington
Edward DeClair, Gettysburg College
Mark W. Delancy, University of South Carolina
Manoutchehr Eskandari-Qajar,
 Santa Barbara City College
Sumit Ganguly, Hunter College
William Garner, Southern Illinois University
Bertil L. Hanson, Oklahoma State University
Stephen P. Hoffman, Taylor University
Alana Jadel, North Carolina State University
Michael Levy, Southeast Missouri University
Frank Meyers,
 State University of New York at Stony Brook
Richard Piper, University of Tampa
Jonas Pontusson, Cornell University
George Romoser, University of New Hampshire
Nirvikar Singh, Delhi School of Economics
Dale Story, The University of Texas at Arlington
James White, University of North Carolina
Paul Wallace, University of Missouri–Columbia
Ife Williams, Savannah State College

Michael Curtis

CHAPTER 1

Introduction
Michael Curtis

WHY STUDY COMPARATIVE POLITICS AND GOVERNMENT?

Why should we study the political systems, behavior, and values of other countries? Why should we try to make comparisons between countries? A simple answer is that an essential part of being educated today is knowing something about the politics of foreign countries. For many there is also a fascination and intellectual excitement in the study of foreign systems and in the discovery of political ways of life different from our own.

Study of foreign political systems, or comparative politics, is useful for additional reasons. We can understand better our own system if we can appreciate its similarities to and differences from other systems. We can see, for example, and try to understand why the United States Supreme Court can declare legislation unconstitutional while the highest court in Britain cannot. We can observe that the central authorities in the Soviet Union up to 1991 controlled the republics making up that country to a greater degree than the U.S. federal government controls the states. In both cases we are led to general conclusions about the nature of power in the United States as well as in the other countries. Knowledge of the politics of foreign countries allows us both as citizens and as students to discuss and evaluate more intelligently U.S. policy and attitudes to those countries.

Study of different systems lets us compare the ways in which governments face similar problems and respond to them and to the needs and demands of their citizens. All societies deal with crucial matters such as health, control over the economy, management of production, or changes caused by new technology and by modernization. Students will be interested in the distinctive ways in which different societies deal with problems of this kind. We can learn both positive and negative lessons from experiences such as the National Health Service in Britain, government proposals for economic planning in France, workers' participation in industrial management in Germany, the cooperation of the state and the industrial sector in the development of technology in Japan, the problems of modernization in Communist countries or countries influenced by communism, or from the efforts of a changing, diverse society such as India to maintain a democratic form of government.

An effective comparison of systems must accurately describe and satisfactorily explain the similarities and differences of the systems being compared. The first step in this process is to understand how individual systems, or parts of those systems, function. From the specific information and understanding of the political institutions and the political processes of different countries, we may then pose questions of a more general nature. We can ask questions as to the extent and ways in which systems are democratic, their level of political development, their degree of stability or effectiveness in making decisions, or the manner in which political ideologies influence their policy.

To answer questions of this kind we need to decide on some criteria for analysis of the similarities and differences between countries. Such criteria, in turn, may often influence policy.

What criteria should be used to provide generalizations? Since Aristotle (384–322 B.C.) began the study of comparative politics, countless students have analyzed the nature and quality of political regimes. They have looked at the way the functions of government are performed and the relationship between rulers and ruled. Students have also examined the kinds of rules that exist and actions that are taken. They ask if the ruling groups are acting in their own interest or the interest of the whole community. They observe how much force and how much persuasion are being exercised.

The modern method of political science has sought to formulate general statements applicable to the large numbers of particular cases.[1] It argues that a necessary scientific approach means a search for generalizations, regularities of behavior, and—even more ambitiously—laws of the social and political process. The search for generalizations is necessary and, indeed, essential if comparative analysis is to be valuable, but it is not easy because of the multiplicity and diversity of human activities and because of the play of chance factors that affect the political process.[2]

In recent years two major additions have been made in the study of comparative politics. The area of interest was once largely limited to those few countries in Western Europe and the English-speaking world with highly developed institutions and a familiar history. These countries were the principal powers of the world; now there are over 180 nation-states. Students are, therefore, also interested in the politics of the newer nation-states, in which an increasing part of the world's population lives, and try to include these states within the scope of the generalizations about comparative politics. About 5 billion of the world's 5.6 billion population live in these states. Moreover, students are not content merely with descriptions of political institutions and constitutional arrangements; more attention is now paid to nongovernmental and social organizations and to the political behavior of individuals and groups.

This book takes these considerations into account. Each chapter deals with four essential aspects of the particular country in the following order:

1. *Factors that have helped shape political behavior*: historical background, geography, economic and social conditions, ethnic and caste groups, religious beliefs and ideologies.

2. *The political process*: the ways in which rulers are chosen, the role of political parties and interest groups, the manner in which individual citizens participate in politics.

3. *The major political institutions*: the way they exercise power, the interrelationship between them, and the restraints on them.

4. *Public policy*: certain basic functions performed by political institutions in all systems, such as maintaining internal order and external security, resolving the competitive demands of individuals and groups, raising expenditure to pay for services provided by government, regulating the behavior of citizens in differing ways.

The author of each of the country studies provides basic information about all these four aspects without the use of jargon or unhelpful methodologies so that the political system and its policies can be comprehensible.

With information and analysis of this kind, we can formulate generalizations that are the heart of comparative politics. Our nine countries can be used for that purpose in a variety of ways that include the following:

1. The nine countries can be compared on the basis of the various political, social, and economic problems they have encountered, and they can be compared according to their different paths to political development and modernity.

2. The three most important West European countries can be compared with the six non-Western countries. Questions can be raised about general differences in the nature and style of politics in Western and non-Western nations.

3. The two foremost past and present Communist countries—the Soviet Union-Russia and China—can be compared with the seven non-Communist countries and also with each other as differences and rivalries emerged between them.

4. The states created after World War II can be compared with the older states. India and Nigeria, two of the most important of the less developed countries, can illustrate the prob-

lems facing the newer nation-states in creating stable and effective political systems.

5. The liberal democratic countries can be compared with the nondemocratic countries. Thus, questions can be posed about why some countries are more likely to be democratic than others and what factors are likely to foster democratic systems.

6. The nine states illustrate different kinds of party systems—one, two, or multiparty—and the relations between those systems and governmental institutions and policy.

CLASSIFICATION OF SYSTEMS

Every political system is at once unique and different from all others and is in flux. Britain presents an interesting mixture of traditional and modern forms of organization and behavior. France, though an old state, has had its political continuity disrupted by frequent changes of system and internal divisions. The former Soviet Union was the first Communist system to be established; its ruling party controlled not only its own system but also the policies of Communist parties in other countries for many years, until the collapse of its system in 1990–1991. In China, the most populous Communist state, the vast majority of the people are peasants, not proletarians as Marxist theory suggests. Germany and Japan are prosperous democracies that were rapidly successful after the devastation and collapse of their systems from defeat in World War II; Japan now has the highest gross national product per capita of any industrialized country. India is the most populous state, emerging

from colonial rule after the war, that has remained essentially democratic in character. Nigeria, with a fifth of black Africans, has alternated between civilian rule and dominant military rule.

Since political systems do not fit neatly in rigid categories, all classification is at best partial and temporary. Nevertheless, classification serves to illuminate some politically meaningful similarities and dissimilarities. Of the many ways to classify political systems, a few are discussed here.

The Number and Kinds of Rulers

Aristotle is usually regarded as the father of comparative political analysis. His classification (see Table 1.1) was based on the number of people who participated in governing (one, few, or many); on the ethical quality of their rule, depending on whether it was in the general interest or in their self-interest (A or B); and on their socioeconomic status (C). Those regimes that served the interests of the ruling group only were perversions of the true constitutional forms.

Aristotle clearly preferred the aristocratic form (2A) because the mean and moderate were most desirable. Other classical theorists in ancient Rome thought that simple and moderate forms of government would degenerate and that stability depended on the existence of a "mixed state" with all the social classes either participating or being represented to some degree.

The Aristotelian theory has been useful in indicating the number and nature of the governing group. Modern democracies including the United States would be in category 3A. But

Table 1.1   THE ARISTOTELIAN DIVISION

Number of Rulers	A Rule in the General Interest	B Self-interest Rule	C Social Group
1. One	Monarchy	Tyranny	King
2. Few	Aristocracy	Oligarchy	The wealthy
3. Many	Polity or democracy	Ochlocracy	The poor

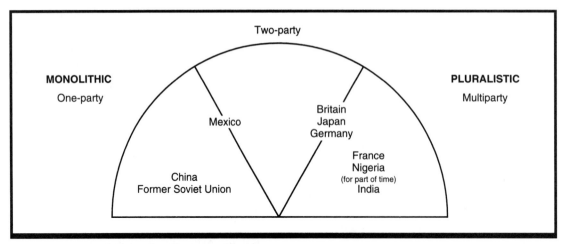

Figure 1.1   Monolithic, Pluralistic, and Party Systems

in all systems a relatively small number of people either rule or dominate the political process. This group is sometimes termed the political elite. The elite may remain closed to outsiders as in aristocratic systems or as in Communist, one-party, or military-dominated systems. In such a case the system is likely to be monolithic in that only a single or a limited political point of view is allowed. In other systems the elite is open to the emergence of individuals from a diversity of backgrounds and with different views. The elite then consists not of members of one group but of a number of groups and individuals competing for political power. Systems of this kind, which allow for choice among competing elite groups, are known as pluralistic (see Figure 1.1).

Political Culture

Anthropologists have used the concept of culture to provide a total picture of the life, actions, and beliefs of a community. For comparative politics the concept of political culture has been used to clarify those community-held beliefs, feelings, and values that influence political behavior. In each community there are sets of attitudes toward the political system. They will depend on knowledge of the way in which the system operates, its personnel, and its poli-

cies. They will also depend on the ability of people to participate in the political process and on the degree to which the system is accepted as legitimate (the right of rulers to exercise power).

In all countries the political values, norms, and behavior patterns, or political culture, are transmitted to present and future citizens. This political socialization is produced by a variety of agencies such as the family, school system, religious bodies, mass media, popular literature and art, fable, heroes, and popular mythology. In developed systems, such as the United States, the family has been thought of as the dominant factor in the process of socialization, though this view has been qualified.[3] Socialization can take place either unconsciously, such as by membership in a caste in India, or more deliberately, as in the communes in China or the kibbutzism in Israel. The impact of all these agencies of socialization varies according to changes in population, and according to social relations, technological innovation, and political events.[4]

Political Development

Attempts to classify systems according to stages of political development have been stimulated by the creation, since 1945, of a large number of states, now the majority in the world, all trying to establish viable political systems and modernize their economies and societies. One influential early theory of political leadership types was formulated by Max Weber, who classified societies as follows:[5]

Traditional: based on conformity of the people, rule on the basis of tradition or divine law by a monarch or aristocracy whose power is made legitimate by status or heredity. Examples of this type are Saudi Arabia and Thailand.

Charismatic: political leadership based on personal magnetism and devotion, and often exercised by a military leader or religious prophet. Examples here might be Egypt under Nasser, Cuba under Castro, and Indonesia under Sukarno.

Bureaucratic: a constitutional regime in which the legal rules are established and officials adhere to those rules and exercise authority according to known procedures. Most Western political systems are of this kind.

Economic and social modernization is relatively easy to define, but it is more difficult to define political development. Many recent studies compare two "ideal types" of societies—traditional and modern—to help explain economic, social, and political differences.[6]

Some of the comparisons made are the following:

1. In traditional societies the vast majority of the population is engaged in agriculture, which accounts for a large part of the gross national product (GNP) of the country. In modern societies, such as that of the United States, only a small percentage of the population works in agriculture, which accounts for a small part of the GNP; in the United States it is now under 3 percent. Instead, the population works in industry and, to an even larger degree, in providing services, which in some countries now account for the majority of the work force.

2. In traditional societies the chief social relationships are the family, the tribe, or the clan, from which the dominant values derive. In modern societies there is a more complex and diverse set of relationships. Individuals belong to a variety of different groups, such as trade unions, business associations, religious faiths, and political and social organizations. The chief values come from a wide variety of sources. Science and technology are significant factors, though religious and traditional values may still remain to some extent.

3. In traditional countries the population is less literate, on average much poorer, shorter-lived, and more rural than in modernized countries.

4. Politics in traditional countries have been less differentiated than in modern systems, where political functions are carried out by different categories of people and where political rule is justified by rational principles rather than by concepts like divine right or heredity.

The distinction between traditional and modern does not imply any judgment of inferiority or superiority regarding individuals or societies. Many traditional societies have pro-

---

Table 1.2   WORLD AT WORK: PERCENT IN OCCUPATIONS

Poor Countries	61% agriculture
	22% rural nonfarm and urban informal
	15% urban industry and services
Middle-Income Countries	29% agriculture
	18% rural nonfarm and urban informal
	46% wage employment in industry and services
Rich Countries	4% agriculture
	27% industry
	60% services

Source: World Development Report, 1995.

Table 1.3   OUR NINE COUNTRIES: POPULATION AND INCOME

| Country | Land Area (thousand km) | Population (million) | GDP Per Capita ($ thousand) | % Occupational Distribution men and women | | | | | |
| | | | | agriculture | | industry | | services | |
				w	m	w	m	w	m
Britain	244	57	18.1	1	3	15	42	84	55
China	9,561	1,187	0.3	74	67	17	19	10	14
France	547	57	23.1	3	4	20	46	77	49
Germany	356	80	24.1	6	5	33	54	60	40
India	3,288	880	0.3	78	64	10	15	12	20
Japan	378	124	29.3	7	4	29.3	38	65	58
Mexico	1,958	88	3.7	12	38	35	34	53	28
Nigeria	924	115	0.2	67	64	7	16	26	20
Russia	17,075	149	8.2	9	17	35	48	56	34
United States	9,373	257	23.3	1	4	17	40	81	56

duced significant cultures, elaborate political structures, and efficient administrative systems.

Factors such as greater industrialization, application of technology and science, economic growth leading to increases in gross national product and per capita income, more education for a larger part of the population, independence of women, increasing urbanization, improved transportation, and Western influence have disrupted traditional societies and changed the economic, social, and political structure in those countries as can be seen in Tables 1.2, 1.3, and 1.4.

Countries have taken different paths to modernity. In some cases the path has been Western-style democracy, in others fascism or

Table 1.4   POPULATION: AGE AND SEX STRUCTURES, 1995

| Country | Women Per 100 Men | % of Population under 15 | | % of Population over 60 | % of Population | | Women per 100 Men | |
		w	m		urban	rural	urban	rural
Britain	104	20	23	18	89	11	105	98
China	95	27	10	9	30	70	93	95
France	105	20	22	17	73	27	107	100
Germany	106	17	24	16	86	14	107	98
India	94	35	8	7	27	73	88	96
Japan	103	17	22	18	78	22	102	106
Mexico	101	36	7	6	75	25	103	94
Nigeria	102	47	5	4	39	61	95	106
Russian Federation	114	23	20	10	73	27	114	113
United States	105	22	19	14	76	24	107	98

Source: The World's Women, 1995.

communism, and in many of the newer countries different forms of nationalism and social change.

No exact correlation exists between economic and social change and political development. Earlier studies that tried to explain political development simply by trends in a society toward urbanization, industrialization, greater communication, and more education have now proved inadequate explanations of a complex process.

One important recent development is the economic growth of East Asia, particularly in the now-prosperous states of Indonesia, Japan, Taiwan, Malaysia, Singapore, South Korea, Thailand, and of Hong Kong. These countries have not had one economic model, but rather a mix of policies with varying state intervention. Moreover, most of these states are more authoritarian than democratic, with a combination of some democratic political framework with a one-party system and with strong controls over freedom of expression and public behavior.

All states have differing mixtures of traditional and modern elements and are at different stages of political development. There is no single way in which the process of political development occurs or any one group that is crucial in that process. Change was fostered in Japan by the aristocratic oligarchy, in Western Europe by commercial traders and capitalists, in Latin America by strong leaders, in revolutionary countries by leaders of a political party or movement, in some countries such as Morocco by traditional authorities, in some African countries by bureaucratic-military elites, and in other new countries such as Nigeria by a variety of groups and institutions.

In all countries the process of political development leads to certain changes, of which some important ones are usually the following:

1. A complex governmental structure in which different institutions and people perform different functions, such as legislative, executive, judicial, and military actions.

2. Attempts to integrate the whole community to achieve a coherent and stable system.

3. A claim to legitimacy of the ruling group based on a secular and more rational view of the right to rule.

4. A widening of political participation in some way to the whole population, which helps choose the ruling group.

5. The ability of government to manage tensions within the system and to implement policies.

Feature 1.1   Human Development, 1996

- Unprecedented development—rising life expectancy, falling infant mortality, increasing educational attainment, improved nutrition
- Global GDP about $22 trillion
- The developed countries have about 20 percent of world's population and 80 percent of its income, and consume about 70 percent of world's energy, 75 percent of its metals, 85 percent of its wood
- Manufacturing jobs have declined and service jobs have increased
- In the 1980s a number of military dictatorships ceded power to civilians, and one-party states had multiparty elections
- But political repression, torture, human rights violations continue in over 110 countries
- Ethnic clashes in about half the world's states
- Of the 82 armed conflicts in 1989–92, only 3 were between states; the rest were within individual states; most conflicts in developing countries
- Changes in family—more unwed mothers, increasing divorce, smaller households, feminization of poverty
- Women are 70 percent of world's poor, and nearly 70 percent of all illiterates
- Life expectancy is 76 in rich countries, 61 in poor countries

---

Feature 1.2 Africa

- Poorest continent in the world
- People were poorer at the end of the 1980s than at the beginning
- High birth rate and population increase
- Late 1980s, 3 multiparty democracies, and 30 military dictatorships or one-party states
- More multiparty elections in 1990s
- South Africa—GDP is 4 times the combined GDPs of the 10 other countries in southern Africa
- South Africa—11 official national languages: 22 percent have Zulu as first language
- Ethnic divisions in many countries
- About 2000 language groups, of which 50 are important

One recent suggestion, proposed by the UN Development Program in 1990, is to compare systems using an index of human development rather than relying simply on statistics of productivity or income. The three key indicators would be life expectancy and a healthy life; degree of literacy and knowledge; and purchasing power of individuals. The index compares the quality and welfare of societies by taking account of factors such as education, nutrition, social welfare, degree of inequality, cultural norms; social problems such as drugs, divorce, and homelessness; and extent of political participation and freedom.

Development is affected by many factors. These would include the different rates of economic growth, population increase (now about 2 percent in developing countries compared with 0.5 percent in industrial countries), degree of political stability, extent of ethnic or internal strife, the democratic or authoritarian nature of the political system, and the effect of world trade on a country.

In the developing countries as a whole, average life expectancy has increased by 16 years and adult literacy by 40 percent since 1960. Many of these countries have made striking gains in health and education, and have increased average income. Yet other developing countries have done poorly, and about one-quarter have actually suffered a fall in living standards. Poverty, especially in Africa, remains a serious problem for

more than 1 billion people, one-fifth of the world's population, many of whom lack primary health care and are illiterate. In the world as a whole, and in developing countries in particular, women still lag behind men in power, wealth, and opportunity, though there have been important changes in the lives of women over the last 20 years, as Table 1.5 and Feature 1.3 show.

Is there any correlation between human development and human freedom and civil liberties in societies? There does not appear to be an exact causal relation between the two, but it is clear that countries that rank high on the freedom index, based on compliance with international treaties and conventions of human rights, tend to rank high in human development. Comparison also shows that between 1985 and 1996 a number of countries became more democratic and enjoyed greater political freedom.

Men and Women

The lives of men and women differ in terms of their access to resources, health care, education, and professional opportunities. Great disparities still remain between the sexes in spite of recent progress toward equality.

1. Education Increasing numbers of women have been educated at the secondary level and beyond. Progress has been most rapid in Latin America, with a female literacy rate over 75 percent, and least in sub-Saharan Africa. In some areas women outnumber men in post-secondary schools.

2. Fertility Higher education, family planning, and the increase in the number of women who work have led to lower fertility for women in most parts of the world. During the 25 years between 1970 and 1995, average global fertility has declined from 6 to 4 births per woman (see Table 1.6).

3. Work Women are still less active economically than are men (see Table 1.7). While some 72–83 percent of men are economically active, only 58 percent (in East Asia) to 21 percent (in North Africa) of women are active.

Women rarely account for more than 1–2 percent of senior executive positions, but they are more numerous in the general category of administration and management. In the health and teaching professions, women are well rep-

resented, though usually at the lower levels of the status and wage hierarchy. Women are increasingly visible in the media as reporters and anchors but less well represented as program managers and senior editors. They are also less visible as Nobel Prize winners. Since 1901, when Nobel Prizes began to be awarded, women have received only 28 of the total 634, and 12 of those shared the prize with a man.

4. Power Women have rarely reached the highest levels of influence in the public and private sectors (see Table 1.8). In the 1990s, only 10 of the 191 countries in the world had women as heads of government. A larger number of women have been appointed to ministerial or subministerial positions. In the legislatures of the world, progress for women has been mixed and varies widely among regions. The average proportion of women in national parliaments in 1995 was 11.3 percent.

Feature 1.3 Women in Society and Politics, 1995

- Minority in world, 49.3 percent of population; a majority in developed areas
- Literacy rates increased, but illiteracy among women still high in much of Africa and in parts of Asia; in rural areas much higher illiteracy than in urban areas; women outnumber men in higher education in many developed regions
- Marrying later, fewer children; in developed regions 1.9 births per woman, in Africa 6
- Marriage less frequent and less stable; more divorce
- Households smaller in size
- More single-parent families; in developed countries women are the single parent in 75 percent of families
- Increase in percent of work force; now 40 percent in developed regions
- Work in different occupations than men, usually lower pay and status; in developing countries many work as unpaid family laborers in agriculture and household
- Earn less per hour than men, and earn less in general; often work part-time
- Major responsibility for household work and care of children
- Often work more hours than men; working time fluctuates widely because of domestic obligations and work outside the home
- Work in occupations that are losing status, while men dominate new occupations of higher status
- Underrepresented in production jobs in large cities; work mainly in professional, clerical, and especially service occupations, teaching, health
- Constitute 70 percent of world's poor
- Lack access to economic and political opportunities, including senior managerial jobs
- Very underrepresented in all political positions and offices

Table 1.5 GENDER COMPARISONS

Country	Life Expectancy 1992		1991 Education Females per 100 Males		Employment Female Share of Labor Force (%)
	f	m	primary	secondary	
Britain	79	73	96	96	39
China	71	68	86	72	43
France	81	73	94	106	40
Germany (West)	79	73	96	98	39
India	62	61	71	55	25
Japan	82	76	95	99	38
Mexico	74	67	94	92	27
Nigeria	54	50	76	74	34
Russian Federation	75	64	—	—	—
United States	80	73	95	95	41

Source: World Development Report, 1994.

Women have become influential in nongovernmental organizations (NGOs) at the grassroots, national, and international levels. Social issues previously largely ignored, such as violence against women and rights of choice, have entered the mainstream of public policy discussion.

Few women have risen to senior positions in politics. Only 24 women have been heads of state or government, half since 1990. In 1994, only 5 percent of the world's cabinet ministers were women, though women held over 15 percent of ministerial positions in 16 countries, and over 15 percent of subministerial positions in

Table 1.6 HOUSEHOLDS AND FAMILIES

Country	Average Household Size, 1990	% of Women-headed Households	Fertility Rate, 1990–1995	Abortion Allowed, 1994
Britain	2.5	25	1.9	Yes
China	4.0	—	2.2	Yes
France	2.5	22	1.8	Yes
Germany	2.3	30	1.5	No
India	5.5	—	3.9	No
Japan	3.0	17	1.7	Yes
Mexico	5.0	15	3.2	No
Nigeria	4.7	—	6.4	No
Russian Federation	2.8	—	2.0	Yes
United States	2.6	32	2.1	Yes

Source: The World's Women, 1995.

Table 1.7 ECONOMIC ACTIVITY

Country	% of Adults Employed 1994		Women as % of Labor Force, 1994	Women per 100 men in occupational groups, 1990						
	w	m		Professional, Technical	Administrative, Managerial	Clerical	Sales	Service	Agricultural	Production
Britain	46	77	39	78	49	318	181	195	109	18
China	70	87	43	82	13	35	88	107	92	56
France	44	70	41	71	10	180	94	219	48	18
Germany	45	76	39	—	—	—	—	—	—	—
India	28	84	24	26	2	7	7	22	45	15
Japan	50	78	40	72	9	150	62	118	91	42
Mexico	30	82	28	76	24	115	47	82	4	14
Nigeria	45	87	35	35	6	23	177	13	36	18
Russian Federation	55	78	45	—	—	—	—	—	—	—
United States	50	77	41	103	67	392	100	150	19	22

Source: The World's Women, 1995.

Table 1.8 WOMEN IN PUBLIC LIFE

Country	% of Parliamentary Seats Held by Women, 1994		Government Ministerial Positions, 1994		Subministerial Positions, 1994		Administrative and Managerial Workers 1985–1992
	upper house	lower house	total no.	% women	total no.	% women	% women
Britain	6	9	23	8.7	56	7.1	33
China	—	21	50	6.0	225	4.0	12
France	5	6	29	6.9	113	11.5	9
Germany	15	21	25	16.0	153	5.2	—
India	7	7	34	2.9	138	7.2	2
Japan	15	3	16	6.3	50	8.0	8
Mexico	5	8	20	5.0	60	5.0	19
Nigeria	—	—	34	2.9	18	11.1	6
Russian Federation	5	10	35	0	303	2.6	—
United States	7	11	22	13.6	264	26.1	40

Source: The World's Women, 1995.

23 countries. Women have been most prominent in social ministries (health, education, housing, and welfare) and in the law and justice departments. The role of women in parliaments has been mixed and varies widely among regions; it has declined in Eastern Europe after 1987 and in Asia but has increased in Africa and Latin America. Women's representation is strongest in Northern Europe, especially in the Nordic countries.

Feature 1.4 Women Elected Heads of State or Government in the Twentieth Century

PRESIDENTS

Argentina (1974–76), Bolivia (1979–80), Haiti (1991), Iceland (1980–), Ireland (1990–), Nicaragua (1990–), Philippines (1986–92), Sri Lanka (1994), Yugoslavia (1982–86)

PRIME MINISTERS

Bangladesh (1991–), Britain (1979–90), Burundi (1993), Canada (1993), Dominica (1980–), France (1991–92), India (1966–77), Israel (1969–74), Norway (1981, 1986–89, 1990–), Pakistan (1988–90, 1993–), Poland (1992–93), Portugal (1981–85), Rwanda (1993–94), Sri Lanka (1970–77, 1994–), Turkey (1993–1996)

Source: Division for the Advancement of Women of the United Nations Secretariat.

The Economic System

For some analysts, the chief characteristic of political systems is the nature of the economic system. Many socialists hold this view, but it is particularly important for Marxists, who stress the nature of the production process and the social or class relationships that are bound up with particular historical phases of that process. The Marxist philosophy of history differentiates five broad successive types of social relationship. It sees history as propelled by the struggles between classes, the essential conflict always being between those who own the means of production and those who do not. The state is seen as the reflection of the interests of the dominant economic class and the support of the interests of that class.

In contemporary capitalist systems, such as that of the United States, all organs of power would be seen mainly as organs of the capitalist class; opposing them would be Socialist or Communist systems.

There is an obvious connection among social relationships, the economic system, and political institutions. But there is no automatic correlation between an economic basis such as private ownership of property and political institutions or actions. Marxist theory has not taken account of the complexity and heterogeneity of modern societies and regimes in three main ways. First, nothing in Marxism effectively explains the considerable diversity of political forms that capitalist countries have taken or the mixture of public and private enterprise in those countries. Second, even at their zenith, Communist regimes were not a monolithic group (see p. 17). The acute disagreements and intermittent hostility between the Soviet and Chinese regimes reflected both ideological and tactical differences about communism as well as tension between two great rival powers. For almost 20 years, China referred to the Soviet Union as hegemonic, interested in worldwide expansion. Similarly, the dispute between China and Vietnam, based on different geopolitical interests and historical enmity, led to hostilities in 1979. Third, conflict in politics has resulted from many factors other than class differences. The most important of these, which have often been more meaningful for a political system than class are as follows:

1. *Religion*: Catholics and Protestants in Northern Ireland; Muslims and Hindus in Asia; Muslims and Christians or Jews (see Table 1.9). Most of the conflicts around the world in recent years have resulted from religious discord.

2. *Race*: Blacks and whites in South Africa; blacks and Asians in Uganda.

3. *Language*: English- and French-speaking populations in Canada; Flemish- and French-speaking populations in Belgium.

4. *Tribe*: Yorubas, Ibos, and Hausa-Fulanis in Nigeria.

5. *Caste*: The four major castes and thousands of subcastes in India.

6. *Nation*: Basques and Catalans in Spain; Serbs and Croats in former Yugoslavia; Kurds in Turkey and Iraq.

Constitutional Democracies

Many contemporary systems describe themselves as democratic. Self-description, however, is not always accurate. The "people's democracies" of Central and Eastern Europe or Yemen after World War II could more accurately be classified as forms of dictatorship.

Constitutional democracies have certain characteristics. There are free elections with competing candidates and a political opposition that is free to criticize the government. The press and other media are free and censorship is rare. People are able to write and speak as they like and to practice any religion they choose. Personal and civil rights are usually respected. A wide variety of unofficial associations exists and no single group or element in society is dominant. The military does not intervene in politics—loyally upholds the regime—and is under the control of the political leaders. Political change takes place by a peaceful process. The rule of law ensures impartial justice for all.

In all constitutional democracies, officials who make and enforce law are themselves subject to the law. All government actions must be

Table 1.9 Adherents of All Religions by Continental Areas, Mid–1993

Religion	Africa	Asia	Europe	Latin America	Northern America	Oceania	Former USSR	World
Christians	341,208,000	300,383,000	409,653,000	443,056,000	241,147,000	22,686,000	111,618,000	1,869,751,000
Roman Catholics	128,167,000	130,102,000	260,034,000	412,366,000	97,892,000	8,229,000	5,711,000	1,042,501,000
Protestants	91,070,000	85,764,000	73,206,000	17,550,000	97,176,000	7,537,000	10,071,000	382,374,000
Orthodox	29,771,000	3,847,000	35,777,000	1,793,000	6,062,000	577,000	95,733,000	173,560,000
Anglicans	28,013,000	744,000	32,629,000	1,322,000	7,404,000	5,734,000	1,000	75,847,000
Other Christians	64,187,000	79,926,000	8,007,000	10,025,000	32,614,000	609,000	102,000	195,470,000
Muslims	284,844,000	668,298,000	13,633,000	1,400,000	3,332,000	104,000	42,761,000	1,014,372,000
Nonreligious	2,578,000	721,113,000	57,542,000	18,444,000	24,718,000	3,572,000	84,907,000	912,874,000
Hindus	1,569,000	746,512,000	707,000	916,000	1,285,000	369,000	2,000	751,360,000
Buddhists	22,000	332,143,000	273,000	561,000	565,000	26,000	412,000	334,002,000
Atheists	336,000	167,217,000	16,669,000	3,343,000	1,336,000	549,000	52,402,000	241,852,000
Chinese folk religionists	14,000	140,661,000	60,000	76,000	123,000	21,000	1,000	140,956,000
New-Religionists	22,000	121,693,000	50,000	550,000	1,439,000	10,000	1,000	123,765,000
Tribal religionists	70,000,000	28,654,000	1,000	971,000	41,000	69,000	0	99,736,000
Sikhs	28,000	19,318,000	232,000	8,000	257,000	9,000	1,000	19,853,000
Jews	359,000	6,264,000	1,475,000	1,132,000	6,850,000	100,000	1,973,000	18,153,000
Shamanists	1,000	10,591,000	2,000	1,000	1,000	1,000	257,000	10,854,000
Confucians	1,000	6,204,000	2,000	2,000	26,000	1,000	2,000	6,230,000
Baha'is	1,591,000	2,774,000	91,000	830,000	370,000	79,000	7,000	5,742,000
Jains	56,000	3,847,000	15,000	4,000	4,000	1,000	0	3,927,000
Shintoists	0	3,332,000	1,000	1,000	1,000	1,000	0	3,336,800
Other religionists	461,000	12,714,000	1,475,000	3,701,000	491,000	4,000	337,000	19,183,000
Total Population	703,090,000	3,291,718,000	501,881,000	474,996,000	281,986,000	27,602,000	294,681,000	5,575,954,000

Source: 1994 Encyclopaedia Brittanica Book of the Year.

performed in a legal manner and can be controlled by appropriate authorities. These authorities may include the ordinary courts and the system of common law as in the United States and Britain, an elaborate code of law as in the German *Rechtsstaat*, or special administrative courts such as the *Conseil d'État* in France.

Constitutional democracies exist, with few exceptions, in the older and more developed political systems and in some countries influenced by them. Of the 5.8 billion people in the world, about 50 percent live under constitutional democracies, 40 percent in one-party or one-person regimes, and 8 percent in military regimes.

Authoritarian Systems

Authoritarian systems or dictatorships may exist because a country has no tradition or standard of constitutional behavior, because there is no general consensus about the desirability of freedom, or because a limited and closed elite dominates the political process. Dictatorship may result from the instability or ineffectiveness of a democratic government, from the desire to put a particular ideology into effect, or from the reaction to economic changes and instability or to defeat in war.

In authoritarian regimes political activity is controlled, all the media are subject to censorship, liberty is restricted, there is no legally recognized opposition, public criticism is rare, and parliamentary institutions are absent or meaningless. Power is exercised by small groups such as military leaders, party officials, bureaucrats, or religious figures. But economic activities can usually be pursued with some independence, a certain degree of cultural freedom is allowed, and voluntary internal and external travel is possible. A large number of modern regimes embody similar characteristics. In many Latin American countries in the past, political parties have been barred or suspended, the press has been censored, and opponents have been imprisoned arbitrarily.

Some authoritarian regimes are personal or party dictatorships supported by a considerable part of the population and interested in general social or economic reform. Such regimes may be based on a particular doctrine or may be more pragmatic and less doctrinaire, such as the Latin American populist systems that have been both nationalist and socially reformist.[7]

Of a different kind are the bureaucratic-authoritarian or authoritarian-corporativist regimes which appeared in Latin America in the 1960s.[8] They were dominated by technocrats, bureaucrats, and military personnel and were not based on labor's political support. Often the economies of the countries ruled by these regimes were dependent on foreign capital.

Other authoritarian regimes are military dictatorships. Throughout history the military has interested itself in politics, in exercising power, or in influencing political decisions. In past Asian or Middle Eastern regimes, there was little distinction between civil and military authority, the monarch was absolute ruler and controlled the army. The military has often intervened on behalf of politicians, usually those of a conservative disposition. Sometimes civilian political leaders themselves urge the intervention of the military or depend on the approval of the military, as in Turkey in 1908 and 1960. In some Latin American constitutions the military is given the task of guaranteeing the constitutional powers. Thirteen of the 19 Latin American countries were under some form of military rule in 1983. In 1991 there were none. Similarly, in every country in Central Africa, civilian governments are now in power, and the role of the military has been reduced.

Sometimes the military leadership, regarding itself as the most honest, most efficient, and most advanced organization in a nation, may turn out the politicians or civilian rulers it believes to be corrupt, misguided, or inefficient. It may do so where political instability results from irreconcilable political divisions or continual political crises, or when the nation has been humiliated by defeat in war.

Totalitarian Systems

The existence of some similar important features in the Communist regime of the Soviet Union under Stalin, the Fascist regime of Italy, and the Nazi regime of Germany led some analysts to suggest a new concept of totalitarianism.[9] This concept implies the existence of a

---

Feature 1.5 **Totalitarianism**

- Leadership by a single, dominant personality
- One-party system
- Comprehensive ideology based on class, race, or nation
- State control over the economy
- Monopoly control over the media
- Censorship
- Powerful secret police
- Terror
- Concentration camps

---

new twentieth-century type of system based on a dominant leader supported by a mass party acting on an aggressive ideology that explains and influences political actions.

According to this concept, a totalitarian system differs from an authoritarian regime in that it attempts to control behavior totally and subordinates all organizations and individuals to the ruling group. Whereas authoritarian regimes allow individuals and groups some independence of action, the central feature of totalitarian systems is that the state attempts to control the whole of society, minds as well as bodies, and to this end mobilizes the population, youth as well as adults.

As shown in Feature 1.5, the totalitarian system concentrates power in the hands of an individual or group. It eliminates all opposition parties, controls communication and the mass media, exercises control over the economy and over highly centralized planning, uses religion for its own purpose even though it is fundamentally irreligious, and makes deliberate use of terror as a controlling factor through the secret police, concentration or labor camps, and the completely amoral use of force. A single official ideology and a single party lead to the elimination of dissension, even within the one ruling party, and the refusal to allow any standard of morality other than that of the party or the leader.

The three regimes regarded as prime examples of the totalitarian model—Nazi Germany, Fascist Italy, and the Soviet Union under Stalin, if not after his death—did not embody all characteristics of the model to the same degree. Moreover, there was in reality less coherence and unity in decision making in these systems than is suggested in the model.[10] Nevertheless, despite the differences in ideology, purpose, and kind of support they obtained, these three regimes were similar in their ruthlessness and extreme dictatorial behavior, and they may be regarded as models of a particular kind of political system, which can be distinguished from authoritarian systems. Moreover, while authoritarian regimes have sometimes evolved into democracies as in the recent cases of Greece, Spain, and Portugal, no totalitarian system had done so until 1989.[11]

Communist and Non-Communist Systems

A classification of systems into Communist and non-Communist has been of great political significance in the making of U.S. foreign policy as well as for theoretical analysis. Communism today is purportedly based on the principles of Marxism-Leninism. From Karl Marx (1818–1883) is derived the belief, or ideology, that capitalism will be overthrown by a revolution of the proletariat, or working class, and be replaced by a classless Communist system after a transitional stage of socialism. In this system the guiding principle would be "from each according to his ability, to each according to his needs."

It was Lenin (1870–1924) who called for the creation of a highly centralized and disciplined revolutionary party to lead the proletariat. His principle of democratic centralism means in practice that all members of the party must adhere to central party policy. The Russian party, which successfully carried out the revolution in 1917, became the model for all Communist parties in both Communist and non-Communist systems.

In the Soviet Union the Communist party exercised control not only over the state and over industrial and agricultural production but also over all social organizations and all forms of communication. Under Stalin (1879–1953) this control was more complete than it was after his death.

For many years the Soviet Union controlled the policies of foreign Communist parties and the activities of regimes created in Eastern Europe after World War II. In the latter systems a Communist party based on Marxist-Leninist principles was the ruling group. All factories were nationalized and agriculture was largely under collective control. Communism was therefore regarded as a monolithic bloc with its center in Moscow.

Starting in the 1960s, the Communist movement began to fragment. The Communist parties in non-Communist systems such as Italy, Spain, and sometimes even France showed a degree of independence and were occasionally critical of the Soviet Union. Some of these parties—sometimes called Eurocommunist—declared that they believed in the democratic process and would allow free elections and abide by electoral decisions if they came to power.[12]

In 1948, Yugoslavia, under its Communist leader, Tito, refused to accept orders from the Soviet Union and was expelled from the international Communist movement. The most significant division in the Communist movement, however, was between the Soviet Union and China. In spite of their common claimed inheritance of Marxism-Leninism, the two countries were divided by ideological issues and rivalry for leadership of the international Communist movement, as well as by a dispute over their common border.

The last few years have seen dramatic changes in the former Soviet Union and in China, and the collapse of the Communist systems in Eastern Europe. These systems toppled when it became clear that the Soviet Union would no longer use force to maintain the monopoly of power and privileged position of their Communist rulers. The East European states have, at different speeds, introduced elements of a market economy, and some have moved to a more democratic regime.

The political and economic changes during the 1980s in the Soviet Union have stemmed from the policies of *glasnost* (openness) and

perestroika (restructuring) of the Soviet leader, Mikhail Gorbachev. But the policies were accompanied by violence, internal turmoil, civil war in some parts of the country, and an attempt to overthrow the leader in a coup in August 1991. Gorbachev, who had tried to preserve the Union, resigned in December 1991.

The stagnation of the Soviet economy, marked by scarcity of goods and inefficient modes of production and distribution, led to a call for a move from the centralized command economy under state control to a more market-oriented economy, in which controls would be reduced and individual farming and private business would be encouraged. Total control of resources was regarded as incompatible with the process of modernization and with a modern economy that requires the free flow of information and decentralized decision making.

During the *glasnost* period, one-party rule by the Communist party and democratic centralism gave way to looser political control, competition between different political groups and ideas, relaxation of censorship, open discussion and criticism of official policy, abandonment of Marxism-Leninism as the official creed, some contested elections, and the opening of borders to allow people to travel and emigrate. The Soviet Union has also disintegrated as a political structure, with the rise of nationalism in many of the republics—ethnic group assertion and religious enthusiasm. The republics have become independent states and the Soviet Union was replaced in December 1991 by the Commonwealth of Independent States, a grouping of most of the former republics in a loose alliance. The Russian Federation took over many of the functions of the former Soviet Union.

The former Communist systems are in different phases of transition to some other form of political system. Russia, under Boris Yeltsin in the 1990s, decentralized economic decision making for most of the economy and encouraged private ownership. Its new constitution, drafted in 1993, provides for a Russian Federation with democratic characteristics.

China today is difficult to categorize in any simple way. For 30 years under Mao Zedong, its totalitarian system controlled the economy, the life and movements of its citizens, the allocation

Feature 1.6

Eight Useful Classifications in Comparative Politics

- Number and kind of rulers
- Political culture
- Political development
- Economic systems
- Constitutional democracies
- Authoritarian systems
- Totalitarianism
- Communist, non-Communist, and Third World

of jobs, and decisions on production in agriculture and industry. The Communist Party, never more than 5 percent of the population—a disciplined, loyal, and secretive force—monopolize political power, the state activities, and the media. Since the late 1970s economic reforms have sparked rapid growth, increase in GNP, lessening of central control, strengthening of the influence of cities and provinces, and a considerable increase in the numbers of people employed in the private sector, which now accounts for a large part of industrial and other production in the country. Yet this liberalizing of the economy and growth of a competitive free market with free prices, stock markets, and private businesses is still accompanied by the authoritarian control of a single party, the Communist Party, with centralized decision making. If central economic planning no longer exists, central political control still does with some qualifications such as a freer process, multicandidate elections for the party's Central Committee, and elections for local people's congresses with competing candidates.

There has always been a further problem in the classification of systems as Communist or non-Communist. It neglects the large number of nations, now the majority in the world, that are neither Communist states nor Western democracies. Since the Bandung Conference of 1955, when 29 African and Asian nations met to discuss their common interests, a group now known as third world countries—most of which achieved political independence since 1945—emerged, with some exceptions, as nonaligned in conflicts between the other two groups.

Containing a majority of the world's population, these countries themselves vary considerably in wealth, ranging from oil-rich Saudi Arabia to impoverished Bangladesh, and in level of political development and importance. But all of them reject any form of colonialism, advocate political and economic independence, and stress the need for nation building.

The eight classifications of political systems that have been presented throw light on different aspects of political behavior or institutions in different nations (see Feature 1.6). Which one should the student use for analysis and comparison? The answer is twofold. Use the one that illuminates the largest number of features in a system: economic, social, and cultural as well as political. Or use that which is most helpful for understanding a particular issue: the claim to legitimacy of the rulers, the political culture, the relative power of institutions and their personnel, the degree of freedom, the stability or efficiency of the system, or the nature of domestic and foreign policies.

THE POLITICAL PROCESS

For comparative analysis it is useful to study the ways in which the electoral process works in different countries and the parties and groups that play a part in that process. Even nondemocratic countries hold elections, which supposedly demonstrate the solidarity of the people with the existing political leadership and are intended to promote consensus. But to be meaningful, elections must present voters with alternative candidates, parties, or issues from which to choose, and they must be fairly and honestly organized. Elections must also allow peaceful change of government, meaning that all will accept the electoral decision and that, at the same time, the minority will be permitted to oppose the policies of the successful majority.

Political development has meant that an increasing proportion of the population obtains the vote and that there is greater political equality. Gradually, disqualifications for representation based on religion, property, education, and sex are removed. Ownership of property and educational degrees are no longer necessary to vote, and in all but a few countries women are no longer excluded from suffrage. The minimum age limit of 21, once generally accepted, has recently been lowered in many countries.

People generally take part in political activities through membership in a party or interest group, as well as by voting. In a number of systems, opportunities are provided for direct political participation of the people in deciding some issues. The chief forms of such participation are referendums or plebiscites, approval of constitutions, initiatives presenting petitions or bills, and recall of elected officials. In addition to these devices, governments and politicians may take account of the views of citizens expressed in public opinion polls and change their policies or attitudes accordingly. Nevertheless, in all systems the extent of direct participation by any considerable part of the people is limited.

Functional Representation

Earlier assemblies consisted of representatives from the legally defined and hierarchical groups of "estates" into which society was divided. Gradually, in most countries, assemblies began to represent citizens as individuals rather than as members of groups and occupations.

The case for some form of functional representation is still argued by part of the Left, especially guild Socialists; by some pluralists who think representation should take account of occupational activity; and by those advocating a corporate system. (Corporatism, which has been prominent in Latin systems, is a system of interest representation in which certain occupational categories participate in official bodies.) The supporters of functional representation believe that geographically oriented parliaments and parties are not sufficiently representative of the economic interests of the community. In spite of the practical difficulty in selecting the functional groups to be represented and in deciding on the relative weight of the different occupations, a number of countries, including France and Germany, have set up various kinds of economic and social councils to represent interest groups. In most countries such councils have been limited to giving advice and possess

no real power. Moreover, interest groups have found that they are better able to influence political decisions through direct contacts with governments or parliaments or through membership in official advisory committees than through economic and social councils.

Not surprisingly, functional representation existed in some Communist systems. In the former Soviet Union the system of soviets, or councils, supposedly representative of the workers, was not very meaningful in reality. In the former Yugoslavia, however, the workers' councils in industry and the agricultural cooperatives were of some significance for a time. Yet, even there, the "workers' democracy," which was supposed to be responsive to the demands of workers in factories, was in fact controlled by the Communist Party.

Territorial Representation

There are many different methods of territorial representation, whether in single-member or multimember constituencies.

Single-Member Constituencies These are relatively small geographic areas, often approximately equal in population, which elect one representative. The usual method, as in the United States, is that the candidate with the highest number of votes wins—the plurality system. This has the virtue of simplicity, tends to limit the number of parties that win seats, and generally fosters a two-party system. One party may gain an absolute majority of seats. Logically, this electoral method can lead to the formation of strong single-party governments and make coalitions unnecessary.

But it is also a system that is mathematically inequitable. A candidate may win with a minority of the total votes cast for the various parties in the constituency, as shown in Table 1.10.

A majority in the legislature may represent a minority of the population, thus distorting national opinion. Minor parties are usually underrepresented because they receive a smaller percentage of seats than of votes cast for their candidates.

Other methods include a second-ballot system, as in France when no candidate has won

Table 1.10   CONSTITUENCY: MANHATTAN, EAST SIDE

Loftus	25,463
Harper	23,185
Collins	14,694
Michel	8,247

Loftus is the winner with 35.5 percent of the votes.

an overall majority at the first ballot, and the alternative-vote system, which allows for electors to rank the various candidates and for their preferences to be transferred from the lowest candidates until one candidate obtains a majority.

Multimember Constituencies There are areas in which a number of representatives are chosen by each voter. When this system is followed in its most extreme form, the whole country might be one constituency, as in Weimar Germany (1919–1933) and in Israel. The least extreme examples are constituencies that elect between two and five members, as in France during the Fourth Republic.

The most common electoral system in multimember areas is proportional representation (PR). Seats in the legislature are allocated to parties in proportion to their share of the electoral vote. A more accurate representation of electoral opinion is thus produced. But PR also produces or perpetuates a multiparty system, thereby usually making government coalitions of different parties necessary because it is extremely rare for one party to obtain an overall majority. Government is thus often less likely to be stable or effective than in the plurality system, though the Scandinavian countries are an exception in this regard. Italy, for example, has had 55 governments in 45 years. Every country using PR has at least four parties of some importance in its legislature. PR also allows small extremist parties to obtain representation.

What is the most desirable electoral system for a nation? The answer is that electoral systems are methods, not ends in themselves. Their value must be related to the political system as a whole. A single-member plurality system, such as the U.S. system, tends to reduce the number of parties. In Britain it has, with some qualification, allowed a strong government to emerge with a coherent policy. The PR method tends to lead to a multiparty system which accurately reflects electoral divisions; but it also tends to preserve those divisions and to make strong government less probable.

INTEREST GROUPS

Students of comparative politics examine the different kinds of interest groups and the various ways that such groups formulate demands, express political views, and make claims on government.

Pressure on rulers has always taken a variety of forms, ranging from riots, acts of violence, and rebellions to social movements, political parties, and peaceful presentation of petitions. What is distinctive in modern times is the powerful, sustained role of groups in getting or preventing action and in influencing decisions and policy. Interest groups are now necessary for the running of the modern state.

Interest groups are very diverse in character.[13] Many have a formal structure and organization, but some are informal. Some are temporary bodies organized for one specific purpose and often disband when that is achieved. Others are permanent organizations concerned with a continuing problem or issue. Some are concerned primarily with the interests of one part of society, while others are concerned with a common interest or a general problem relevant to the whole society or even to the international community. Some, such as ecological, civil rights, or women's groups, can be regarded as social movements.

The impact of groups depends on a number of factors:

1. The demands of the group and the way those demands are seen by the politicians and officials handling the issue.

2. The functions performed or planned by the state and the degree to which groups are consulted about those functions or can supply information about them.

3. The size, reputation, and cohesiveness of the group and the amount of money and energy it is prepared to expend on the issue.

4. The degree of concern of the members of the group about some particular problem.

This is not a complete list of the relevant factors, but it is helpful to analyze some of these factors when comparing interest groups.

POLITICAL PARTIES

An interest group is concerned with influencing decisions on a limited number of issues; a political party, in addition to this function, is also concerned with running candidates, contesting elections, and holding office. But it is sometimes easier to distinguish between them in theory than in practice. In Weimar Germany, the German Farmers' Party was essentially an interest group. In the United States, an antiabortion group became the Right-to-Life Party. In Britain, a close relationship exists between the Labour Party and the trade unions, which provide over five-sixths of the membership and about 80 percent of the financing of the party.

How then can we define a party? A starting point is to see it as a group of people who hold certain political beliefs in common or who are prepared to support official candidates of the party. Members of a party work together to win elections in order to gain and maintain political power. Parties struggle for power as well as to achieve certain policies and goals.

Parties have been compared in different ways. One interesting method, proposed by an author of this book, is to see them as being of three types: traditional, representative, and mobilizing.[14] Traditional parties reflect the social and economic control of a hereditary or an oligarchic elite and last until that control is ended. Representative parties, such as those in the United States, put forward the views of followers of the parties at a particular time. Mobilizing parties, such as the parties of the third world and most Communist parties until the late 1980s, aim at converting the population to a particular point of view.

The reason for the creation of parties and their main base varies widely as Table 1.11 shows.

POLITICAL INSTITUTIONS

All political systems carry out certain basic functions. Although these functions have been defined in different ways, it is still most useful for beginning students of comparative politics to think of them in the traditional language of legislative, executive, and judicial functions or powers. The legislative function involves discussion of public affairs and enactment of general rules and laws. The executive function involves the application of those general rules to specific cases and the formulation of policy based on

---

Table 1.11   THE MAIN BASES OF WORLD POLITICAL PARTIES

Main Basis	Party
Ideology	Communist, Nazi
Economic Interest	U.S. Republican Party, Lok Dal (Indian Farmers)
Religion	Muslim Brotherhood (Egypt), BJP (India)
Nationalism	Scottish National Party, Parti Quebecois
Ethnic	People's Progressive Party (Guyana), Tamil Federal Party (Sri Lanka)
Caste	Parts of the Indian Congress Party, Janata Dal
Specific Issue	Green Party (Germany)
Faction	Japanese Liberal Democratic Party, Italian Christian Democratic Party
Mobilization	TANU (Tanzania)

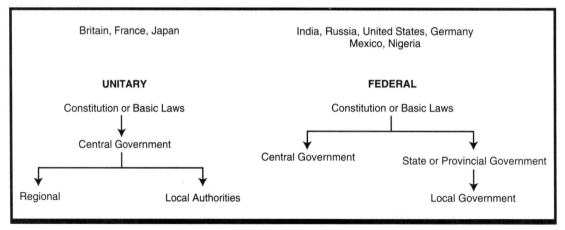

Figure 1.2   Unitary and Federal Systems: Division of Power

those rules. The judicial function involves resolution of disputes between individuals or between individuals and the state.

Constitutions usually determine what institutions are to carry out these functions as well as the extent and limit of their powers.[15] The interrelationship between functions and institutions depends on (1) whether the system is unitary or federal (see Figure 1.2), and (2) whether there is a separation or nonseparation of functions, or powers (which is the word usually used).

A unitary system is one in which a set of central institutions exercises authority as in Great Britain, China, or France. Local and regional authorities obtain their powers from the central authority, which can amend those powers if it desires.

A federal system is one in which powers are divided between a central government and state or provincial governments. Both levels of government have certain powers of their own derived from the constitution or interpretations of it. The states do not get their powers from the central government; power is shared between the central and state institutions. Federalism is thus more complex than a unitary system.

For comparison, the distinction between federal and unitary systems is useful, but modern trends in government have sometimes blurred the distinction. In many federal systems, such as that of the United States, the central institutions have grown stronger, while in

some unitary states, such as Britain and France, some decentralization of power has occurred to regions and local authorities.

The concept of separation of powers originated in the seventeenth and eighteenth centuries as a method of controlling excessive use of power by one group or institution. It involves the establishment of three separate institutions—a legislature, an executive, and a judiciary—each almost exclusively responsible for the exercise of its separate function. It may also entail separation of personnel by forbidding any person to be a member of more than one branch of government at the same time. The United States is a model of this concept of separation of powers.

In systems that do not embody a separation of powers, such as the British, the members of one institution, the executive, are also members of the legislature. The executive usually controls a majority of the legislature and, because of party discipline, can control the legislative process as well as decision making in general. This concentration of power has often led to strong government.

Again, it is important to remember that these are types of systems rather than exact reality. In all modern systems each institution exercises some functions associated with the other two institutions. Some degree of cooperation between the three institutions is necessary to perform the work of government. A separation of powers need not necessarily result in weak or stalemated government, which may result from a variety of other factors, such as political parties, a strong legislature, an active high court that declares legislation invalid, or the mores of political behavior.

THE POLITICAL EXECUTIVE

The executive branch of government is the major organ of modern political leadership. Its prominence reflects the increase in the activities of the state in domestic affairs and its special role in foreign policy.

The kind of executive branch found in a system is shaped by many factors. A useful beginning method of comparison is to examine the relationship between the executive and legislature. In nondemocratic systems, the executive is likely to have almost complete control over the legislature. In democratic systems, a more varied relationship exists. Four familiar types are the following:

1. *Cabinet government*: The classical model of this type is the British system, but Germany, Japan, and India also illustrate it in different ways. Political leadership is provided by the cabinet ministers, a small group of leaders of the party or parties headed by a prime minister who control a majority in the legislature, of which they are also members. The link between the executive and the legislature is crucial. The cabinet is collectively responsible to the legislature for political decisions, government policies, and legislative programs. Individual ministers are responsible for the conduct of their administrative departments and for their political actions.

2. *Presidential system*: The United States is the model for the presidential system, which has been imitated by many other countries. A single head of the executive, the popularly elected president, is both the political leader and the head of state, hence the major policymaker. The president appoints all the chief members of the government and executive agencies. The members of the cabinet are all subordinate and responsible to the president. Collective responsibility to the legislature does not exist. The present Fifth Republic of France is an interesting mixture of the presidential and cabinet systems.

3. *Assembly government*: In this type of system the legislature dominates the executive, which has little disciplined control over legislative and financial matters. The legislature is in many ways the real decision-making body in the system. The regimes most characteristic of this type were the French Third (1875–1940) and Fourth (1946–1958) Republics, with weak political executives, constant government instability—102 governments in the Third and 24 in the Fourth Republic—and few disciplined parties. The legislature saw itself, rather than the executive, as the true representative of the sovereignty of the people. The postwar Italian system has had similar features.

4. *Council government*: Systems of collective leadership are rare. The oldest example is the Federal Council of Switzerland. This political executive of seven, elected by the legislature, shares ministerial duties and administers the country. Communist systems have also experimented with this type. In the Soviet Union, after Stalin, collective leadership existed for short periods before an individual leader consolidated his political position.

LEGISLATURES AND ASSEMBLIES

Almost all political systems have legislative bodies or parliamentary assemblies of some kind, with members either elected or appointed. Their significance varies over time in an individual system as well as comparatively between one system and another. Assemblies play different roles and exercise functions of different kinds (see Tables 1.12 and 1.13).[16]

Assemblies have declined in power and prestige in most countries in recent years, the United States being the major exception. This decline has occurred for a number of reasons. Government functions and expenditures have greatly increased since World War II. The complexity of both internal and international affairs often prevents members of the legislature from fully understanding issues or having sufficient information about them because of the inadequate research facilities and staff available to them.

Table 1.12   Main Functions of Assemblies

Activity	Some Examples
Select head of state	Italy, Soviet Union
Approve head of government	Germany, Israel
Approve individual ministers of government	United States
Hold ministers accountable by motions of no confidence or censure	Britain, Italy
Impeach the executive	United States
Support the executive	Soviet Union
Pass legislation	Most systems
Debate	India, Switzerland
Question ministers	Canada, Netherlands
Hold committees of inquiry into government action	United States
Provide criticism as loyal opposition	Britain
Maintain financial control	United States
Act as ombudsman or parliamentary commissioner	Sweden, New Zealand

The executive can claim to be as representative of the people as is the legislature. The bureaucracy, or permanent administration, at the disposal of the executive has grown substantially in number and significance. The leaders of organized parties have dominated politics, and the mass media, especially television, have tended to concentrate on the personalities of the leaders. In the newer nations, the executive is usually viewed as the instrument through which modernization can most rapidly occur.

Parliaments are therefore no longer the dominant bodies in political life. Rarely do they control the legislative program, act as a watchdog over government spending and the financial process, or control ministerial behavior in any continuous real way. Democratic governments are created and normally fall as a result of electoral decisions, and only rarely as the result of parliamentary debate. The power of party organizations in generating political leadership and creating disciplined political forces has reduced the possibility of independent behavior on the part of parliamentarians once a party decision on an issue has been made.

PUBLIC POLICY

Comparison of what different countries do—their public policy—is as significant as comparison of the political culture, processes, ideas, or institutions already discussed. Public policy is in-

Table 1.13   Choice of Upper Chambers

Hereditary	House of Lords in Britain; about ⅔ of 1,200 peers are hereditary
Direct election	United States, Australia, Switzerland; often in federal states
Indirect election	France, by electoral college composed of National Assembly deputies, departmental councilors and city councils
Election by lower chamber	Norway, Iceland
Corporate election	Ireland, representatives of economic and social interests

evitably related to those other aspects of political systems and can only be explained in the context of the rest of the system. Only then can one attempt to answer such questions as why the United States does not have a national health insurance system while Germany has had one since 1883, or why it has traditionally been easier to get support for public housing in Western Europe than in the United States, or why the United States has been so far ahead of other countries in the development of a public education system extending to the whole population.[17]

Multiple Affairs of State

It is true of all countries that the role of government has grown in the twentieth century. The state is no longer limited, as in earlier times, largely to maintaining internal order and external defense, providing a minimum of basic services, and raising taxation to pay for these activities. Government has expanded for a wide variety of reasons: economic recession, war, social justice, help for the underprivileged, protection of minority rights, demands for the redistribution of income or wealth, and the ideas of social reformers.

States are now concerned with a mix of policies concerning social welfare, economic management, and protection of the environment. A substantial part of government budgets is spent on defense, either directly on the armed forces and weaponry or indirectly on research and the development of technology. But spending on social services is now the largest item in many budgets and continues to grow as people live longer and more is spent on pensions and hospitals.

In all states—liberal, socialist, conservative, or communist—there is some economic planning, though to considerably different degrees. Attempts are made to stimulate economic growth, to increase employment, to check inflation, to get a favorable balance of trade with foreign countries, and to regulate industry and other economic activities from mining coal to making cigarettes. Governments have recently become increasingly aware of ecological and aesthetic issues and of the need to improve the quality of life in their countries.

Governments are also faced with a variety of problems that may limit their capacity to act. In some countries a backlash has occurred against the rising cost of programs, which has necessitated both an increase of taxation to pay for them and a larger bureaucracy. A state may not be able to cope with all the demands made on it or with the increased expectations of citizens. Some observers have suggested that government may become "overloaded."[18] External factors, such as the very rapid increase in the price of oil in the 1970s, may accelerate the process of inflation and increase unemployment, causing further transfers of resources from a country.

Government spending accounts for a considerable part of the GDP of modern states—in Sweden it reached 68 percent of GDP—though countries differ in the size of welfare and health services, taxation policies, industrial policies, and public ownership. In spite of the fact that the world economy has now become a global system in which international trade and money flows affect interest rates and investment in different countries, the nation-state is still important for political and economic decisions.

A crucial economic and political factor is the increase in government spending (see Table 1.14). In the 24 OECD (Organization for Economic Cooperation and Development) countries that spending rose from 28.1 percent of GDP in 1960 to 43.8 percent in 1990. The main areas accounting for this growth were pensions, health care, unemployment benefits, and family support. Social security and health care costs both doubled within this 30 year period: the former from 7 percent to 15.4 percent, and the latter from 3.9 to 7.8 percent.

The largest single item in the increase is public pensions, which have doubled in 30 years and are now one-quarter of the increase in public expenditure. This results from three main factors: wider pension coverage, the rise in the number of elderly from 65 million to over 100 million, and increased pension benefits.

Why Do Public Policies Differ?

Political scientists differ in the importance given to political and other variables in explain-

Table 1.14 CENTRAL GOVERNMENT EXPENDITURE

Country	Defense		Education		Health		Housing, social security, welfare		Economic services		Other		Total Expenditure as % of GNP	
	1980	1993	1980	1993	1980	1993	1980	1993	1980	1993	1980	1993	1980	1993
Britain	13.8	9.9	2.4	3.3	13.5	14.0	30.0	32.5	7.5	6.6	32.9	33.7	38.2	43.4
China	—	16.4	—	2.2	—	0.4	—	0.2	—	39.5	41.3	—	9.2	—
France	7.4	6.0	8.6	7.0	14.8	16.1	46.8	45.5	6.8	5.0	15.6	20.4	39.3	45.5
Germany (FDR, 1980)	9.1	6.4	0.9	0.8	19.0	16.8	49.6	45.9	8.7	9.7	12.6	20.4	30.3	33.6
India	19.8	14.5	1.9	2.2	1.6	1.9	4.3	7.1	24.2	16.2	48.3	58.0	13.2	16.9
Japan	—	—	—	—	—	—	—	—	—	18.4	15.8	—	17.4	—
Mexico	2.3	2.4	18.0	13.9	2.4	1.9	18.5	13.0	31.2	13.4	27.6	55.5	17.4	17.9
Nigeria	—	—	—	—	—	—	—	—	—	—	—	—	—	—

Source: World Development Report, 1995.

ing the diversity of public policies. The following paragraphs look at some of the relevant factors without ranking them in order of importance.

Political Structure and Institutions The likelihood and kind of actions taken by the state will be affected by some of the factors discussed previously: a unitary or federal system, separation or nonseparation of powers, national or locally based parties, democratic or nondemocratic politics, the nature of the elite political group(s), and the qualities and interests of the civil service.

The Political Process Relevant here is whether political decisions are based on ideology or are more pragmatic and the result of bargaining, as in the United States. Public policies will also depend on the strength of interest groups and the nature of the party system.

The Prevailing Ideas in the Community Public policy will differ depending on whether the dominant ideas are those of liberalism, democratic socialism, communism, conservatism, nationalism, fascism, or anticolonialism. It is probable, for example, that Americans more than most peoples want the state to play a limited role.[19] Ideas, in turn, are partly a response to current social problems and to the external concerns of the country and its international role.

The Basic Elements of the Social System Factors such as the geography of a country, demographic and racial composition of the population, economic and occupational distribution, and the degree of literacy will affect policy. Some studies argue, for example, that factors like economic development, the age structure of the population, and the age of the social security system explain most of the differences in the social security expenditures in different countries.[20]

CONCLUSION

We have now reviewed the reasons why individual political systems should be studied and why comparisons are useful. We have looked at the various bases on which comparison may

proceed, at some major differences among systems, and at some major categories in which different systems may be analyzed. The reader is now invited to begin the challenging and exciting task of understanding a number of the major countries in the world and to compare their political systems in a meaningful way.

KEY TERMS

assembly government
authoritarian
bureaucracy
cabinet government
charismatic
communist
constitutional democracy
developing countries
elite
Eurocommunism
federal system
functional representation
glasnost
Mikhail Gorbachev
gross domestic product (GDP)
gross national product (GNP)
human development
interest groups
legitimacy
liberal
Marxism
modernization
multimember constituency
party system
perestroika
political culture
political development
political socialization
presidential system
proportional representation (PR)
separation of powers
single-member constituency
socialist
Stalin
Third World
totalitarian
unitary system

Further Readings

Budge, Ian, et al. *Parties, Policies and Democracy* (Boulder, CO: Westview, 1994)

Chazan, Naomi, et al. *Policies and Society in Contemporary Africa* (Boulder, CO: Rienner, 1992).

Dogan, Mattei, and Ali Kazancigil, eds. *Comparing Nations: Concepts, Strategies, Substance* (Cambridge: Blackwell, 1994).

Dogan, Mattei, and Dominique Pelassy. *How to Compare Nations: Strategies in Comparative Politics* (Chatham: Chatham House, 1984).

Duke, Lois L., ed. *Women in Politics: Outsiders or Insiders?* (Englewood Cliffs, NJ: Prentice-Hall, 1993).

Finer, S. E., et al. *Comparing Constitutions* (New York: Oxford University Press, 1995).

Githens, Marianne, et al. *Different Roles, Different Voices: Women and Politics in the United States and Europe* (New York: HarperCollins, 1994).

Harrop, Martin, ed. *Power and Policy in Liberal Democracies* (New York: Cambridge University Press, 1992).

Huntington, Samuel P. *The Third Wave: Democratization in the Late Twentieth Century* (Norman: University of Oklahoma Press, 1993).

Laver, Michael, and Norman Schofield. *Multiparty Government: The Politics of Coalition in Europe* (New York: Oxford University Press, 1990).

Lewis, Bernard. *Cultures in Conflict: Christians, Muslims, and Jews in the Age of Discovery* (New York: Oxford University Press, 1995).

Lijphart, Arend, ed. *Parliamentary versus Presidential Government* (New York: Oxford University Press, 1992).

Lijphart, Arend, et al. *Electoral Systems and Party Systems: A Study of 27 Democracies, 1945–90* (New York: Oxford University Press, 1994).

Linz, Juan J., and Arturo Valenzuela, eds. *Democracy, Presidential or Parliamentary: Does It Make a Difference?* (Baltimore: Johns Hopkins University Press, 1992).

Norton, Philip, ed. *Legislatures* (New York: Oxford University Press, 1990).

Pempel, T. J., ed. *Uncommon Democracies: The One-Party Dominant Regimes* (Ithaca: Cornell University Press, 1990).

Pierson, Christopher. *Socialism after Communism: The New Market Socialism* (Cambridge: Polity, 1995).

Rustow, Dankwart A., and K. P. Erickson, eds. *Comparative Political Dynamics: Global Research Perspectives* (New York: HarperCollins, 1991).

Sartori, Giovanni. *The Theory of Democracy Revisited* (Chatham: Chatham House, 1987).

Smith, Anthony D. *National Identity* (New York: Penguin, 1991).

Thompson, Richard. *Theories of Ethnicity: A Critical Appraisal* (New York: Greenwood, 1989).

Vanhanen, Tatu. *The Process of Democratization: A Comparitive Study of 147 States, 1980–1988* (New York: Crane Russack, 1990).

Wiarda, Howard, ed. *New Directions in Comparative Politics* (Boulder, CO: Westview, 1991).

Wilson, Graham. *Interest Groups* (Cambridge: Blackwell, 1990).

Zeigler, L. Harmon. *Political Parties in Industrial Democracies* (Ithasca: Peacock, 1993).

Notes

1. David Easton, *The Political System* (New York: Knopf, 1953), p. 55.
2. Albert O. Hirschman, *A Bias for Hope* (New Haven: Yale University Press, 1971), p. 27.
3. M. Kent Jennings and Richard G. Niemi, *The Political Character of Adolescence* (Princeton: Princeton University Press, 1974).
4. Gabriel A. Almond and Stephen J. Genco, "Clouds, Clocks, and the Study of Politics," *World Politics, 29,* no. 4 (July 1977), p. 495.
5. Max Weber, *From Max Weber,* in H. H. Gerth and C. W. Mills, eds. (New York: Oxford University Press, 1946).
6. Bernard E. Brown, *Government and Politics,* in John Wahlke et al., eds. (New York: Random House, 1966), pp. 214–216.
7. Gino Germani, *Authoritarianism, Fascism and National Popularism* (New Brunswick, NJ: Transaction, 1978).

8. David Collier, ed., *The New Authoritarianism in Latin America* (Princeton: Princeton University Press, 1979).

9. Carl Friedrich and Zbigniew Brzezinski, *Totalitarian Dictatorship and Autocracy* (New York: Praeger, 1961).

10. Michael Curtis, *Totalitarianism* (New Brunswick, NJ: Transaction, 1979).

11. Jeane J. Kirkpatrick, *Dictatorships and Double Standards* (New York: Simon and Schuster, 1982).

12. Bernard E. Brown, *Eurocommunism and Eurosocialism* (New York: Cyrco Press, 1979).

13. David Truman, *The Governmental Process* (New York: Knopf, 1951); Samuel Finer, *Anonymous Empire* (London: Pall Mall, 1958).

14. Jean Blondel, *Political Parties: A Genuine Case for Discontent?* (London: Wildwood House, 1978).

15. K. C. Wheare, *Modern Constitutions* (New York: Oxford University Press, 1963).

16. Jean Blondel, *Comparative Legislatures* (Englewood Cliffs, NJ: Prentice-Hall, 1973).

17. A. J. Heidenheimer, H. Heclo, and C. T. Adams, *Comparative Public Policy: The Politics of Social Choice in Europe and America* (New York: St. Martin's Press, 1975).

18. Michel Crozier, S. P. Huntington, and J. Watanuki, *The Crisis of Democracy: Report on the Governability of Democracies* (New York: New York University Press, 1975).

19. Anthony King, "Ideas, Institutions and the Policies of Governments: A Comparative Analysis," *British Journal of Political Science, 3,* no. 3 (July 1973), pp. 291–313.

20. Harold Wilensky, *The Welfare State and Equality* (Berkeley: University of California Press, 1975), pp. 27–28.

PART 1

Industrial Democracies

CHAPTER 2

The Government of Great Britain

Michael Curtis

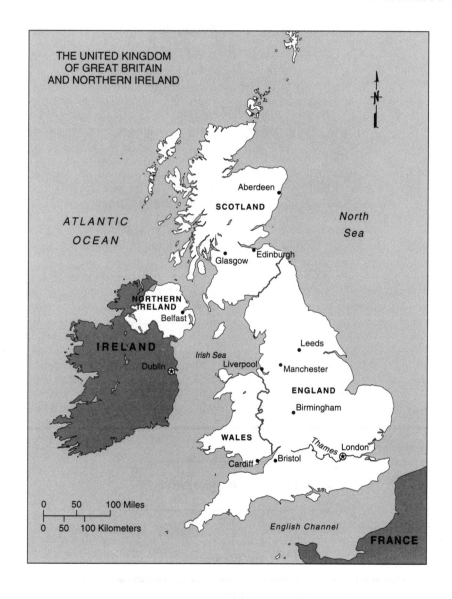

THE UNITED KINGDOM OF GREAT BRITAIN AND NORTHERN IRELAND

ATLANTIC OCEAN

SCOTLAND

Aberdeen

North Sea

Glasgow • Edinburgh

NORTHERN IRELAND

Belfast

IRELAND

Dublin

Irish Sea

Liverpool

Leeds

Manchester

ENGLAND

Birmingham

WALES

Cardiff • Bristol

Thames London

English Channel

FRANCE

0   50   100 Miles

0   50   100 Kilometers

Political Development

Why study the British political system? There are a number of answers to this understandable question. Britain has the oldest operating political system in the world; some of its governmental institutions have been in continuous existence for nearly a thousand years. Symbolically this is illustrated by the memorials to many notable figures in public and cultural life in Westminster Abbey, the building of which was begun in the eleventh century. No one needs to be reminded of the intellectual and literary influence of Britain's writers, such as Chaucer, Shakespeare, Milton, Austen, Dickens, Shaw, Woolf, and Auden, and its philosophers, such as Hobbes, Locke, Hume, Mill, Bentham, and Russell. Its political influence, both directly and indirectly, has been equally important.

Through its former control of about one-quarter of the world's population on every continent, Britain has directly influenced many countries, including the United States. From Britain, the United States has absorbed a similar idea of the rule of law and a concern for personal freedoms. There are similar political institutions, such as a single-member-constituency electoral system for the lower house, a two-chamber legislature, a two-major-party system, a cabinet, and a civil service based on merit. Oscar Wilde once said that Britain and the United States were two countries separated by a common language. Certainly there are great differences in the way that political power is exer-

cised and institutions function in the two countries. Nevertheless, it was appropriate that the British memorial to President John F. Kennedy be placed at Runnymede, where King John was tamed by the feudal barons into signing the Magna Carta in 1215.

Today the British Empire, on which the sun never set, no longer exists. But most of the countries once ruled by Britain belong to the 52-member Commonwealth with its population of over 950 million. Though not a political power in itself, the Commonwealth is a unique organization and the largest multiracial association in the world.

Indirectly, Britain has influenced other countries by its political ideals and values and by some of its political practices, such as a meaningful parliament which could control the excesses of executive power, an officially recognized loyal opposition, political moderation and tolerance, and a process of change by gradual and peaceful means.

The British system is also instructive for those interested in modernization and political development. Britain was the world's first industrialized country, a process which began at the end of the eighteenth century. For Karl Marx, Britain was the model of the capitalist system in the middle of the nineteenth century. The proportion of the working population employed in factories and manufacturing rose while that in agriculture declined. With the re-

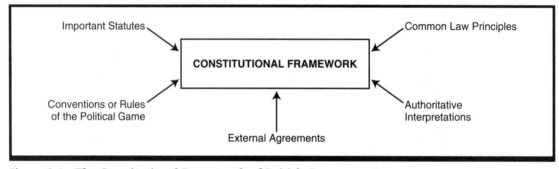

Figure 2.1   The Constitutional Framework of British Government

No. 10 Downing Street, the residence and office of the Prime Minister, is located in a small street off Whitehall about half a mile from Parliament. The only other houses in the street are occupied by the Chancellor of the Exchequer and by the office of the government chief whip.

peal of the Corn Laws in 1846, allowing the entry of cheap food, and the adoption of free-trade principles, Britain lived by exporting its manufactured goods and by importing food and raw materials. As a result, the country has been very concerned with problems of foreign trade and international exchange. London became the financial center of the world in banking, insurance, and shipping: the British currency, the pound sterling, became the medium for much of the world's trade.

A century ago Britain was the workshop of the world, producing two-thirds of the world's coal, half of its iron, over half of its steel, half of its cotton goods, and almost all of its machine tools. Britain's exports of capital goods—machines and technology—led to industrialization in other major countries, which soon became competitors and began to supplant Britain technologically and industrially. Yet with the industrial exports had also gone other exports such as ideas, institutions, and ways of life. Britain

Whitehall, the street at one end of which is Parliament, symbolically represents the departments of government and civil service though only a few ministries are now located on the street. In the forefront is the Cenotaph, which commemorates soldiers killed in the two world wars.

Buckingham Palace, the residence in London of the monarch. It is the largest house in Britain, containing over 600 rooms.

The High Court, which hears most important cases of common law, equity, divorce, and custody, and hears appeals from lower courts in certain instances in civil and criminal cases.

was the foremost example of the process of modernization and industrialization without a revolution from either above or below.

But Britain has also paid a heavy price for having the first mature industrial system and for being dependent on international trade. Its capital equipment became outmoded, and its relative economic position in the world weakened as other countries advanced industrially. Its dependence on imports of food and raw materials made it vulnerable to outside forces.

In the modern age, Britain has become a postindustrial society with a mixed economy and a significant social welfare system, in which private enterprise coexists with a public sector and public expenditure now amounts to about 40 percent of the gross national product. In the 1980s Britain was acutely troubled by problems such as inflation, less-than-full employment, and comparatively slow economic growth, which have plagued other advanced nations to differing degrees.

POLITICAL DEVELOPMENT

The British system illustrates the gradual evolution from internal chaos and divisions, which resulted in the Wars of the Roses between rival

contenders for the throne in the fifteenth century and the Civil War between the king and Parliament and the peaceful "Glorious Revolution" in the seventeenth century, to a stable unitary system with a long process of development of political structures, institutions, and behavior.

Britain exemplifies political change from a strong monarchy with an important aristocratic class to a political democracy. A constitutional monarch reigns over a country in which the parliamentary cabinet system and political parties are the dominant political organizations representing the different political expressions of the power of the people. With the gradual expansion of rights and privileges and the removal of civil and religious disabilities, all can legally participate in politics without discrimination (see Table 2.1).

But all political systems retain certain traditional practices and institutions that seem to run counter to the logic of political development. In Britain these would include anomalies such as the continued existence of the House of Lords, now composed of over 1,200 members, most of them hereditary peers; the rebuilding of the destroyed House of Commons after World War II so that it physically resembles the old chamber and can seat only half of its members; and the uses of eighteenth-century wigs by the Speaker of the House of Commons and by the judges and barristers in the High Courts of Law. Indeed, it is ironic that the leading political figure, the prime minister, was long paid for holding an office, First Lord of the Treasury, which no longer has a function, but was not paid for being prime minister, the functions of which are nowhere legally or precisely defined.

There is no end to political development in Britain. In recent years the British system has been responding to social and cultural changes as well as to economic difficulties and political problems. Innovations such as the referendum on the European Community in 1975, the proposal for devolution of power to Scotland and Wales in 1978, and the restoration of direct rule in Northern Ireland since 1972 have been just some of the responses. The Labour Party exercised power between 1974 and 1979 even though it was supported by less than a majority in the House of Commons. New parties of the political center, such as the Social Democrats, were started and ended in the 1980s. The nationalist parties in Wales and particularly in Scotland obtained greater support from the electorates in the two countries, though the support has fluctuated. The Greens, a group and party reflecting the growing concern about environmental issues, emerged in the 1980s. The Greens got 15 percent of the vote in the 1989 European Parliament elections, but only 1.3 percent in the 1992 British election. Britain has been trying to find a new role in international affairs after its days of imperial glory and since becoming a member of the European Community in 1973. In public policy, British governments have tried to overcome the difficulties of slow economic growth, trade union power, and poor management by attempts at voluntary price and income controls and then by removal of those controls.

BRITAIN AS A MODEL IN POLITICS

For the student of politics, Britain has long been useful as an example in the comparison of dif-

Table 2.1 REMOVAL OF POLITICAL AND CIVIL DISABILITIES

1656	Jews allowed back into the country
1689	Toleration Act—members of all religious orders except Catholics and Unitarians permitted freedom of worship
1774	Residency qualifications for members of Parliament declared unnecessary
1778	Some restrictions against Roman Catholic worship removed
1779	Dissenters relieved from subscribing to some of the 39 Articles
1807	Slave trade abolished
1828	Dissenters allowed to become members of Parliament
1829	Catholics permitted to become members of both Houses of Parliament
1858	Jews permitted to become members of both Houses of Parliament
	Property qualification for members of Parliament ended
1871	University religious tests abolished
1872	Secret ballot instituted
1888	Atheists allowed to become members of Parliament
1918	Women over 30 obtain the vote
1928	Women over 21 obtain the vote

ferent systems. Britain with its constitutional and civilian government, essentially two-party system, and representative democracy has been instructive for this purpose.

Britain has adhered for three centuries to the subordination of the military to political power, and the military has been loyal to governments of all political complexions. Not since Oliver Cromwell's government (1653–1658) has Britain had a military dictator or been seriously threatened by fear of a military coup. Britain had also been an example of an essentially two-party system as distinct from regimes with one dominant party, a number of parties, or none at all. In Britain, as in the United States, only two parties have, in effect, been strong enough to share the bulk, though a declining proportion since the 1960s, of the electoral vote and exert political control while alternating in the exercise of executive power.

Britain is a constitutional democracy. All citizens, individually and through organizations, can participate and attempt to influence political decisions. For the most part this is done indirectly through the electoral system, by which the representatives of the people are sent to the House of Commons, the powerful chamber of Parliament, the supreme legal power in the country. The representative system based on the majority principle, by which a plurality is sufficient to win, is also based on the permitted existence of political minorities, which have the right to try to become the majority in their turn, and on basic freedoms of speech, meeting, and the press which allow political commentary of all kinds.

Britain is one of few countries which do not have a single formal document regarded as a constitution to define the political system and state the rights and duties of citizens. Unlike most other systems, all changes of a constitutional nature take place without any special legal provision for them; nor is there a supreme or constitutional court to decide on the constitutionality of legislation passed by Parliament. But Britain is the classical example of a system that is "constitutional" in the sense of adherence to rules and to accepted ways of political behavior as contrasted with countries that are nonconstitutional, or arbitrary, in their political practices.

The British constitutional framework results from the following different components (see Figure 2.1).

1. A number of legislative statutes and documents of outstanding importance have provided the foundations of a considerable number of political institutions. These include the Magna Carta, 1215; the Petition of Right, 1628; the Bill of Rights, 1689; the Habeas Corpus Act, 1679; the Act of Settlement, 1701; the Acts of Union with Scotland in 1707 and with Ireland in 1801; the Franchise Acts of 1832, 1867, 1884, 1918, 1928, 1948, 1958, 1963, and 1969; the Parliament Acts, 1911 and 1949; the Crown Proceedings Act, 1947; the Ministers of the Crown Act, 1937; the Nationalization Acts between 1947 and 1950; the European Communities Act, 1972; the British Nationality Act, 1981; the European Communities (Amendment) Act, 1986. They differ from other statutes, not in a technical sense, but only in their political importance.

2. Certain principles have been established by common law, which is comprised of the decisions of judges and the courts in individual cases. Personal liberties of speech, press, and assembly are to a considerable degree the result of judicial decisions over the last two centuries.

The most important principle is the rule of law, which implies the certainty of legal rules rather than arbitrary judgments in determining the rights of individuals and in examining the behavior of authorities. There is no punishment unless a breach of the law has been established in a court of law. False imprisonment is prevented by a writ of habeas corpus, by which an individual obtains an explanation of the reason for detainment. The rule of law also implies that everyone, includes all officials, is subject to the law. No one can plead the orders of a superior official in defense of illegal actions or can claim the right to be tried in a special court under a different code for official actions.

In recent years some, such as the group Charter 88, have argued for a more formal bill of rights provided by a written code as in the United States. This demand has grown largely as a result of two of Britain's external agreements. Britain ratified the European Convention of Human Rights in 1951 and has thus been subject to grievances taken before the European Commission on Human Rights, which has decided against Britain on over 30 occasions. The British government must therefore decide whether to alter domestic law if it does not agree with the European convention. Furthermore, British membership in the European Union, the laws of which may take precedence over British law, has allowed judges to decide on conflicts between the two sets of law.

Yet, though the British judiciary since the 1970s occasionally ruled against the interpretation by ministers of the extent of their powers, it still cannot rule on the validity of statutes passed by Parliament. Britain does not have a court like the United States Supreme Court that can declare legislation unconstitutional. However, the British courts in recent years have reviewed some actions of government ministers and administrative officials to see if they have exceeded the powers allowed them by parliamentary statute and encroached on rights of individuals. The courts have sometimes declared such actions *ultra vires* (beyond legal power).

3. Certain books written by constitutional experts are regarded as so authoritative that some of their views on constitutional issues are commonly accepted. They include such works as Walter Bagehot's *The English Constitution*, A. V. Dicey's *Introduction to the Study of the Law of the Constitution*, and Erskine May's *Parliamentary Practice*.

4. Numerous political rules and practices, known collectively as conventions, are observed by all participating in the system. Though they have never been passed in any formal or legal manner, they are usually observed as completely as any laws. Occasionally, however, there may be differences about the exact meaning of a convention. Among the most important of these conventions are the following:

a. The real heads of the government are the prime minister and the cabinet.

b. The government is formed from the party that can control a majority in the House of Commons.

c. Cabinet ministers will normally be chosen from the two Houses of Parliament, and the prime minister will come from the House of Commons.

d. The cabinet will operate on the basis of collective responsibility to ensure political unity.

e. The government will resign or ask for a dissolution of Parliament if defeated in the House of Commons on a motion of no confidence.

f. The monarch will ultimately accept the wishes of his or her government.

g. Only the government can propose votes on grants of money in the House of Commons.

h. Those affected by a proposed action will normally be consulted by the government before a final decision is made.

Without these conventions, regular and orderly government in its present form could not function. They create harmony between the executive and legislative branches of the government through various understandings about the workings of the parliamentary cabinet system. The conventions ensure that government is ultimately responsible to the will of the people because an election decides which party is to form the government and thus who is to be prime minister. In a society such as the British, in which traditional institutions have survived changing political circumstances, as the monarchy has done in a political democracy, conventions allow institutions to adjust to political reality.

Conventions are observed not because it is illegal to disregard them, but because they enable the political system to work in accordance with the agreed fundamental principles on which consensus exists.

THE IMPORTANCE OF CONSENSUS AND ITS LIMITS

Britain until very recently has been a model of political stability and consensus. This consensus on the nature of the regime and on the method of change has been the outcome of two factors: (1) "the quiet and orderly habits of the people,"[1] and its generally nonviolent behavior in comparison with other European countries, and (2) the avoidance of any serious political disruption, except in Ireland, arising from religious differences. British politics has depended on all participants abiding by "the rules of the political game" or understandings. These rules include the pragmatic working and adaptation by gradual change of political institutions and organizations; tolerance of different political positions; the belief that government should govern, and have adequate powers; agreement on procedural matters, the validity of political dissent and of trade union organization, through which the working class has a stake in the system; the view that the people should be consulted about political action, through their representatives and groups to which they belong; and moderation in political behavior.

All parties accept the essence of the British political system: a stable democracy which provides for the exercise of strong power by the government, but which also allows substantial personal freedoms and rights. There has been an alternation of political power between the parties in a system characterized by a limited constitutional monarchy, a bicameral parliament, the supremacy of parliament, the linking of the executive and the legislature through the members of the government sitting in parliament, the responsibility of the government to parliament and indirectly to the people and on an independent nuclear deterrent.

All accepted the existence of a welfare state, the need for full employment and adequate incomes, free collective bargaining, a mixed economy with both private and state enterprises, and a foreign policy based on membership in the Western alliance.

However, that consensus on substantive issues has been qualified in two ways. Alternation of Labour and Conservative governments in the 1970s led to reversal of policies, sometimes called "adversary politics," in a number of areas including rent control, old age pensions, and comprehensive schools. Even more significant, Conservative governments under Margaret Thatcher and John Major since 1979 reduced and sold off a considerable part of the public sector in their efforts to obtain a more efficient and competitive economy, low inflation, and a more self-reliant society, and tried to reduce the influence of trade unions and curtail the spending of local authorities.

POLITICAL STABILITY

The last revolution was in 1688 when the struggle between the King and Parliament led to the overthrow of the monarch. The principle was established that Parliament, not the King, had supreme power. The monarch could not suspend laws, levy taxes without parliamentary consent or maintain a standing army in peacetime.[2] How is this remarkable political stability to be explained? There are various explanations of why the British people accepted the political institutions and those classes which controlled them. Some of them are analyzed in the following paragraphs.

Political Culture

The acceptance by the population of political authority, on the one hand, and the existence of individual rights, on the other, has resulted in political moderation. The balance among the British people between limited political activity and general acquiescence in what government does has led to an attachment to the political system and to agreement on the rules of political behavior. Britain has been regarded as the model of a democratic political culture in which there is regular competition for the control of government (the existence of which is dependent on the electoral will of the people). Training in this civic culture takes place in many social institutions—for example, the family, peer group, school, and workplace—as well as in the political system itself.

Deference of the People

Since Bagehot introduced the idea in the nineteenth century,[3] some have stressed the deference of the population, including a significant part of the working class, to the social elite or members of the upper social classes, the well-born or the wealthy, who because of their social position are regarded as the natural or uniquely qualified political leaders by a people that accepts traditional values and authority. In practice, the Conservative Party came to be regarded by many as the embodiment of the natural ruling class or as particularly gifted to govern. But whatever the significance of the deference of people in the past, the fact that the Conservative Party, though it governed from 1979 to 1996, did not win four of the nine elections since 1964 has suggested that deference is less important today and not the sole explanation of the political stability.

Pattern of Authority

Some analysts suggest that there is a correlation between the pattern of authority in government and administration and that in parties, interest groups, and nonofficial organizations and institutions. In Britain the pattern is strong leadership, which is efficient and can make itself obeyed but which is limited by substantive and procedural restraints. There is minimal direct participation by the vast majority of the population. Voters choose between alternatives presented by party leaders. The parties themselves are not only disciplined but also dominated by the leadership.

Traditional values uphold leadership and authority in politics and society. They permeate the elite institutions such as the monarchy, the established Church, the "public" schools, Oxford and Cambridge, the military and administrative hierarchy, and the senior civil service.

The Conservative Party has controlled the government for 70 of the 100 years since 1895.

Relative Deprivation

One hypothesis suggests that the feeling of people that they are deprived economically or socially—and their consequent political behavior—depends on which other people or group they compare themselves with rather than on real social conditions. The British working class has usually

not taken the nonmanual privileged classes as a comparative reference group.[4] Therefore, the working class's feeling of deprivation has not been as strong as objective inequalities might have led them to believe. This, in turn, has produced a less disruptive and less revolutionary political attitude than in other major countries.

Effect of Geography

Perhaps the most important single factor explaining British stability and the continuity of social and political life is that Britain is an island. Since 1066 the existing political institutions have not been disrupted by invasion. This happy fact permitted the creation of stable borders, a luxury not enjoyed by other European countries that were forced into wars to create or maintain national unity. Moreover, this island power developed both a navy (until 1939 the largest in the world) for its protection, as well as a shipping fleet that became the basis for its commercial expansion, capital accumulation, and the conquest of an empire, which at its height consisted of over 15 million square miles of territory on every continent of the world.

THE UNIFIED SYSTEM

The process of unification of the country took more than five centuries. The United Kingdom is now composed of four national units on two main islands and surrounding small islands. England constitutes 52 percent, Wales 9 percent, Scotland 33 percent, and Northern Ireland 6 percent of the total area. Northern Ireland, or Ulster, constitutes 16 percent of the area of the second island, the rest of which is occupied by the Republic of Ireland (see Table 2.2).

The British population is a heterogeneous mixture of people: Celts, Romans, Scots, Picts, Angles, Jutes, Danes, Norsemen, Normans, East Europeans, West Indians, and Asians. With the recent large increase in nonwhite immigrants, who constitute 6 percent of the total population, Britain is now a multiracial society. But the prospect of much greater immigration from the Caribbean and Asian Commonwealth countries such as India, Pakistan, and Bangladesh, led to

Table 2.2   THE UNITED KINGDOM

	Area (100 square miles)	Population (million)
England	50.3	47.8
Scotland	30.4	5.1
Wales	8.0	2.9
Northern Ireland	5.4	1.6
Total	94.1	57.4

Table 2.3 RACE AND SEX IN BRITAIN

Immigration and Nationality	
1948	British Nationality Act: Commonwealth citizens able to enter Britain
1962	Commonwealth Immigration Act: restricted entry for overseas British subjects
1971	Immigration Act: entry restricted to those with at least one British grandparent, or who were naturalized, or who had lived in Britain for five years
1981	Nationality Act: British citizenship restricted to those already legally in Britain, or who had one British parent and registered abroad

Civil Rights	
1965	Racial discrimination in housing and jobs outlawed
1968	Racial discrimination in provision of goods and services outlawed
1970	Women to get same pay as men for similar work
1975	Discrimination on grounds of sex forbidden; Equal Opportunities Commission set up
1976	Criminal offense to incite racial hatred; Race Relations Board to assist conciliation among races; Commission for Racial Equality set up to investigate complaints of racial discrimination

limitations on that immigration by statutes in 1962, 1968, and 1971, which were passed after there had been a certain amount of opposition in the country.

Though English is the standard language (the form spoken in the southeast is the most prestigious norm), other languages are also spoken. About 20 percent of the Welsh population speaks Welsh, a form of British Celtic which is of equal validity with English in the administration of justice and the conduct of government business in Wales. Some 2 percent of the population of Scotland, mainly in the Highlands and western coastal regions, speak Gaelic, and about 2 percent in Northern Ireland speak the Irish form of Gaelic. The newer Asian communities speak a variety of languages.

A NEW PLURALISTIC SYSTEM?

Although Britain is a pluralistic society in ethnic origin, language, religion, and race, the differences have rarely caused political problems affecting the unity and centralization of the system. But in recent years the issue of race and the emergence of nationalist sentiment have upset the stability of the political order.

The presence of the new nonwhite communities, with their different languages, religions,

life-styles, and tendency to remain in certain inner-city areas, has caused friction and riots and led to statutes such as the 1976 Race Relations Act, which makes discrimination unlawful on grounds of color, race, or ethnic and national origins in employment, housing, education, and provision of goods and services (see Table 2.3). Some extreme, members of the Islamic community called for the recognition by the state of Islamic laws on marriage, divorce, and inheritance.

The areas of Scotland, Wales, and Northern Ireland are ruled by departments of the central government in London. The centralized, unitary political system has been troubled in the last decades by the rise of nationalist sentiment in Scotland and Wales, and the constitutional framework has been disturbed by political problems in Northern Ireland.

In Northern Ireland the minority Catholic population, numbering about 600,000, has long objected to discrimination against it in political rights, employment, and housing by the Protestant majority of about 1 million. The Catholic civil rights campaign in 1969 resulted in greater tension between the two separate communities and an increasing level of violence, which led the British government to send army units to maintain order (see Feature 2.1). Though concessions were made on civil rights, no agreement could be reached on Catholic political demands. As a result of the continuing violence and the terrorist activity by the Irish Republican Army (IRA), the powers of the Northern Irish government and Parliament were suspended, and direct rule by the British government began in March 1972. Attempts to restore devolution of power from London to Northern Ireland have so far failed, though Britain in 1978 shifted the responsibility for security back to the local police and a part-time civilian corps, both largely Protestant.

An assembly elected in Northern Ireland in 1982 charged with making proposals for devolution failed and was dissolved. By a 1985 agreement with Britain, the republic of Ireland was given a consultative role about the future of Ulster. Attempts in 1991 to foster talks among Britain, the main constitutional parties in Northern Ireland, and the Irish government on home rule for Ulster failed. In December 1993 the British and Irish prime ministers agreed on the Downing Street Declaration for general principles for peace talks on Northern Ireland. These include agreement of the people in both the north and the south (Ireland). Since then the leaders of the different parties in Ulster have met with the British government to discuss the peace process.

In Scotland, after the Act of Union of 1707, the continuation of separate educational, legal and religious institutions, and a local government system provided the country with a distinctive historical and cultural identity. But not until recently has there been a revival of the political nationalism that was strong in the eighteenth century. Economically, industrial production and commerce in Scotland has been tied to the rest of the British economy, with which it trades two-thirds of its imports and exports.

Politically, Scotland now sends 72 members to the House of Commons, which is 11 percent of the total members even though Scotland represents only 9.5 percent of Britain's electorate. The British system responded to Scottish concerns in 1927 by the establishment in London of the position of Secretary of State for Scotland, now a cabinet minister, who has responsibility for both the formulation and execution of a wide range of policies. Central administration is implemented by the Scottish Office, a group of

---

Feature 2.1 The Irish Problem

1690	Battle of the Boyne—Catholic King James II beaten by Protestant King William III of Orange Siege of Derry
1795	Battle of the Diamond—the two religions clash over land ownership in Armagh Orange Society formed
1886	Gladstone introduces Home Rule bill which fails
1893	Second Home Rule bill leads to violence
1912	Protestants sign Ulster Covenant to resist home rule
1916	Easter rebellion in Dublin against Britain
1920	Ireland becomes independent, but six northern counties form Northern Ireland or Ulster
1937	Ireland becomes Eire
1968	Riots in Londonderry over Catholic civil rights
1969	Police ban most marches British troops in streets of Northern Ireland
1972	Britain suspends Northern Ireland Parliament and assumes direct rule
1985	Anglo-Irish agreement on search for a peaceful solution
1993	In December the British and Irish prime ministers agreed on the Downing Street Declaration for general principles for peace talks on Northern Ireland, which include agreement of the people in both the north and the south (Ireland)

Scottish departments in Edinburgh, the capital of Scotland. In general, Scottish affairs are discussed in parliamentary legislative committees only by those 72 members of Parliament (MPs) from Scottish constituencies and by the Scottish Grand Committee.

The argument that Scotland's problems, especially those of ailing heavy industry and shipbuilding, were due to neglect or exploitation by London, the increased emphasis on national pride, and the discovery of large oil reserves in the North Sea off the Scottish coast stimulated the Scottish National Party (SNP) to become the proponent of self-government in the 1960s. In 1966 the SNP obtained 5 percent of the Scottish vote in the general election and 4 percent in local elections. In the October 1974 election, it won 11 seats and came second in 42 of the other constituencies. The SNP was supported by people of all social classes and geographic regions of the country, though most leaders came from middle-class backgrounds. However, it declined in recent elections, getting only three seats with 14 percent of the poll in 1987, and three seats with 21.5 percent of the poll in 1992.

In the sixteenth century, Wales was united with England and became part of the English system of administration. Since then, nationalist expression has been more literary and cultural than political. But for some years there have been demands for administrative arrangements similar to those of Scotland. Only in 1957 was a full-time Minister of State for Welsh Affairs appointed. In 1964 a Welsh Office was set up in Cardiff, the Welsh capital, and a Secretary of State for Wales with a seat in the British cabinet was appointed. In Parliament, to which Wales now sends 38 MPs, there is a Welsh Grand Committee, on which the Welsh MPs sit to discuss Welsh affairs in general, as well as all legislation pertaining to Wales. The Welsh nationalist party, Plaid Cymru, gained three seats and 7 percent of the votes in Wales in 1987, and four seats in 1992.

In 1969 a Royal Commission on the Constitution—the Kilbrandon Commission—was appointed to examine the problem of Scotland and Wales. Reporting in 1973, the commission rejected both the division of the United Kingdom into independent states (separatism) and the creation of states sharing sovereignty with Parliament (federalism). It recommended the devolution of political and administrative powers from London for both countries. The British Parliament in 1978 passed two statutes that would establish elected assemblies with responsibility for a wide range of internal affairs in Scotland and Wales.

Both statutes were submitted to referendums in March 1979 with the stipulation that they would only take effect if at least 40 percent of the electorate, as well as a simple majority, approved. The voters in Wales rejected the statute by nearly 4 to 1. Scottish voters approved their statute by 51.6 percent of the voters but only 32.5 percent of the total electorate. Both statutes were therefore repealed in June 1979. Devolution has not yet been implemented, though many in Scotland and Wales still favor it. Scots in particular want greater control over their affairs and their own elected assembly with real power.

POLITICAL PROBLEMS

Britain is now confronted by a number of complex political problems. The relationship of the four countries within the United Kingdom remains undecided. The impact of membership in the European Union on British sovereignty and on the rights and duties of citizens is uncertain. The growing numbers of nonwhite immigrants has led to greater racial tension. There are now six parliamentary constituencies in which nonwhites are a majority, and ten others in which they are prominent.

Over the last few years the British system has been troubled by difficult economic, social, and constitutional issues. The weakness of the currency was shown when Britain withdrew from the Exchange Rate Mechanism of the European Union in 1992. The downturns in the economic cycle helped increase ethnic tensions which led to urban riots, mostly of blacks, in 1981 and 1985. The monarchy has come under sharp criticism with questioning of the finances and cost of the Queen and her household and concern about the continuing drama of the failure of the marriage of the heir to the throne, Prince Charles, and Princess Diana. The question arises of whether a divorced Charles could become King, and therefore head of the Church of England.

Among the various problems facing Britain today some are high on the political agenda. One is a certain dissatisfaction with some aspects of the political system and of the unwritten constitution. Proposals have been made for change of the electoral system, reform or abolition of the House of Lords, regional autonomy, especially to Scotland and Wales, and peace in Northern Ireland. Above all, some call for a bill of rights, on U.S. lines, to provide better protection for basic British freedoms.

A second problem is the increased centralization in government with the reduction of powers of local authorities, the abolition in 1986 of the Greater London Council and five metropolitan councils, and more central intervention in decisions about universities, police authorities, and health service regions.

A third issue is the strong difference of opinion about the development and powers of the European Union and on the extent to which its laws and regulations may limit the sovereignty of Britain.

THE NATURE OF BRITISH SOCIETY

Political systems inevitably reflect economic, social, and cultural forces in the country, though there is no inevitable or automatic link among them. The British system has reflected, among other forces, a prosperous industrialized economy; sharp differences between social classes; the aristocratic values such as obedience, fair play, and sportsmanship that lasted into the present era; the ideal of the gentleman; a working-class subculture; and religious differences.

Certain significant characteristics of contemporary British society will be discussed in the following sections.

A Postindustrial Society

Britain is now a postindustrial society in which there has been a shift from the production of goods to a service economy, with a very prominent professional and technical class and with a sophisticated technology (see Feature 2.2). Occupationally, services now account for 70 percent of the work force of the country, industry for 24 percent, and agriculture for 1.2 percent.

There has been a dramatic increase in the service sector in the last two decades. Services now account for about 62 percent of the gross domestic product, manufacturing for about 30 percent, construction for 6 percent, and agriculture, fishing, and mining for about 1.4 percent.

The public sector grew at a faster rate than the private sector until the late 1970s, after which private employment increased relative to public jobs. Of the total 27.7 million in the current work force, 17.5 million (71 percent) are employed in the private sector, 2.3 million (9 percent) in central government, 3 million (12 percent) in local government, and 750,000 (3 percent) in public corporations. The number of self-employed rose from 1.9 million in 1979 to 3.1 million in 1989, about 12 percent of the work force.

About 10.2 million belong to the 309 trade unions; of these, 6.9 million in 67 unions are affiliated with the Trades Union Congress (TUC).[5] Union membership has declined 25 percent since 1979, especially among manual workers and particularly in southeast England. This decline can be attributed to the replacement of old industries, a base for strong unionization, by high-technology firms; the increase of the self-employed to 3.1 million; and the privatization which reduced the numbers working in the public sector, a union stronghold. By 1992, only 38 percent of British workers were unionists.

Women, now 40 percent of the labor force, are also less unionized than men. With their consciousness raised by the women's liberation movement, women have been more eager to obtain a job than remain in the home. Women in Britain now tend to marry younger, have children later, bear fewer children, and stay in a job at least until their first child is born. Increasingly they return to full- or part-time work after having children. The higher divorce rate has reinforced the trend for women to work.

Women have been protected by law in a number of ways. The 1970 Equal Pay Act states that women are entitled to the same pay as men when performing similar work. The 1975 Sex Discrimination Act makes sexual discrimination unlawful in employment, education, occupational training, and provisions of housing, goods, facilities, and services. With regard to both statutes, the Equal Opportunities Commission exists to promote equal opportunities for women.

Feature 2.2   Profile of Britain 1996

Population	57.8 million
	Ethnic minorities are 5.5 percent (9 percent of children), 1.5 million Hindus; .5 million West Indians
	Households with a married or cohabiting couple and dependent children have fallen to 24 percent; average size of families is 2.4 (Asian families' size over 4); single parents are 22 percent of total; increasing rate of divorce; life expectancy is 74 for men and 79 for women
Social Life	16 million homes are owner-occupied (in 1971, 10 million)
	Food takes one-ninth of family budget (in 1971, one-fifth)
	99 percent have TV, 96 percent have color TV; 90 percent have a telephone; 88 percent have a washing machine; 73 percent have videos; 62 percent have a microwave; 38 percent have cars; 1.4 million are in higher education
Economic Life	Real disposal income average is £215 ($345) a week, one-quarter more than in 1979; income differentials have widened; welfare system is a third of government spending; increase in number of people claiming income support; 80 percent of health cost is paid by state, which is 7 percent of GDP

There has been a steady rise in the general standard of living and in the consumption of goods, especially of housing, cars, better-quality food and drink, and recreation, and more credit borrowing. At the beginning of the twentieth century only 1 in 10 families owned their own home; in 1952 the proportion was less than 1 in 3; and by 1988, 66 percent of the 21 million homes in Britain were owner-occupied. In spite of occupational changes, Britain is still a highly urban as well as densely populated country. About 60 percent of the population lives in cities of over 50,000 people, though only 28 percent of the population of Wales does so, and only one-fifth of the total population lives in rural communities. In recent years there has been an increase in the population of the suburbs and a decline in those in the inner-city areas.

A Class Society

Britain has remained a divided, though changing, society in which people of different occupations, income levels, and education have different lifestyles, modes of dress, speech patterns and accents, favorite games, ways of leisure,

and mortality rates due to different standards of health. It has been dominated by an elite, albeit an open elite into which the successful could enter, that has occupied the key positions in the financial world, the professions, government administration, and the Conservative Party. The principles of the elite have been moderation, fair play, loyalty, and its ideal of the gentleman and the cultivated amateur.

A class theory of politics would argue that class is the major factor influencing voting behavior and that the political parties are representative of the different social classes. In Britain this would mean that the working class would vote for the Labour Party, and the middle and upper classes, for the Conservative Party. But this broad generalization is only partly true. About one-third of the working class does not vote Labour, while one-fifth of the middle class does. Nor are the leaders and members of the parties recruited from one class. The programs of the parties do not reflect the interest of one class, as all of them have tried to broaden their appeal.

Britain is still a country with great inequality in the distribution of wealth. About 25 percent of total personal wealth is owned by 1 percent of the adult population and about 61 percent by 10 percent. In 1914 the bottom 90 percent of the population owned 8 percent of all personal wealth; by 1974 they owned 37 percent. The top tenth got 30 percent of pretax income in 1987, compared with the 22 percent obtained by the bottom 50 percent. Britain remains a society in which class differences, due to these inequalities in wealth and income, are strongly felt, and where barriers to social and economic mobility still exist. Yet dramatic changes in the last few years have reduced the old class consciousness, with the shrinkage of the manual working class and with the striking increase in shareholders to 11 million in 1991, compared with 3 million in 1979. This has resulted from three factors: the sale of public enterprises (privatization), employee share schemes, and personal equity plans making it more attractive for small savers to invest.

A Dominant but Pluralistic Religious Society

Britain is also a pluralistic society in its religious diversity after centuries of discrimination (see Table 2.4). There is now no religious disqualification for public office. (The only exception is the monarch, who must be a member of the established Church of England.)

Protestant Though few people go to any church on a regular basis, Protestantism is still the dominant religion, with the Anglican Church nominally accounting for 65 percent of the English and 45 percent of the Welsh population.

Table 2.4 CHURCH MEMBERSHIP IN THE UNITED KINGDOM (MILLIONS)

	1970	1980	1992
Trinitarian Churches			
Anglican	2.55	2.18	1.81
Presbyterian	1.81	1.51	1.24
Methodist	0.69	0.54	0.46
Baptist	0.30	0.24	0.23
Other Free Churches	0.53	0.52	0.66
Roman Catholic	2.71	2.34	2.04
Orthodox	0.19	0.20	0.28
Total	8.78	7.53	6.72
Non-Trinitarian Churches			
Mormons	0.09	0.11	0.15
Jehovah's Witnesses	0.06	0.08	0.13
Spiritualists	0.05	0.05	0.04
Other Non-Trinitarian	0.08	0.11	0.14
Total	0.28	0.35	0.46
Other Religions			
Muslims	0.25	0.31	0.52
Sikhs	0.08	0.15	0.27
Hindus	0.05	0.12	0.14
Jews	0.35	0.30	0.29
Others	0.05	0.05	0.08
Total	0.78	0.93	1.30

The free or nonconformist churches account for 20 percent of the population in England and 45 percent in Wales.

The Church of England is the established church (the concept of "establishment" derives from this fact) and the monarch is its Supreme Head. The chief dignitaries of the Church—the two archbishops of Canterbury and York, the 43 bishops, and the deans—are formally appointed by the monarch, who accepts the recommendation of the prime minister, who is advised by ecclesiastical representatives. Politically, 26 of the higher clergy sit as members of the House of Lords, but no clergy of the Church of England can sit in the House of Commons. The Church is a large landowner and has considerable possessions in industrial shares and property; however, though many of the senior figures in the Church have come from elite backgrounds, the Church does not speak with a monolithic voice in political, social, and economic affairs. The present Archbishop of Canterbury, George Carey, comes from a working-class background. The monarch is also head of the Presbyterian Church of Scotland, which has been the established Church since 1707.

The free or nonconformist Protestant churches, strong in the west of England and in Wales, have historically been critical of or opposed to the establishment. In general, there has been a correlation between areas of religious nonconformity and those of political dissent, associated first with the Liberal Party and later with the Labour Party. The largest of the free churches are the Methodist Church, with about a half million adult members and the Baptist Church with 230,000 members.

Catholicism   There are some 4.24 million adherents to Roman Catholicism. The religion is strongest in Northern Ireland, where it accounts for about 40 percent of the population, and in northwest England. Though some old aristocratic families are Catholic, as are some prominent converts and members of the upper class, most Catholics are members of the working class and the majority stem from Irish immigrants. Catholicism has not been the politically divisive issue that it has been in many other political systems, but the Labour Party has sometimes nominated Catholic candidates in heavily Catholic constituencies.

Other Religions   The Jewish community dates from 1656, after being expelled from Britain in 1290. In the twentieth century it was increased by immigration from Eastern Europe after pogroms and anti-Semitic outbreaks and from Germany during the Nazi regime in the 1930s. It now consists of about 300,000 people. As a result of the recent immigration of Asians, there is now a considerable number of non-Christian adherents, primarily Muslims, of whom there are now over 1.5 million, Buddhists, Hindus, and Sikhs. Most live in large urban areas.

Since World War I, religion has not been a divisive political issue, except in Northern Ireland. In general, the correspondence between a particular religion and a particular party has remained—the Anglican Church with Conservatives, the Catholics with Labour and the nonconformists with the Liberals and Labour—but the ties are much less strong, especially among Anglicans, than in previous generations. In the late 1980s, a small Islamic fundamentalist movement emerged, demanding separate status and insisting on Islamic law.

A Welfare State

The British welfare system developed to deal with problems of poverty and unemployment; to provide for the aged, the sick, and the infirm; and to maintain minimum living standards. The main elements of the current welfare system are the national health service, personal social services, and social security, which now account for about 40 percent of total public expenditure.

The national health service provides almost free treatment for all who want to use it and allows free choice of medical practitioners and hospitals. Personal social services include services for the elderly, the physically disabled and mentally ill, home care, social clubs, and day care for children under age 5. Social security exists to provide a basic standard of living for people in need through nonemployment benefits, retirement pensions, sickness benefit and invalidity pensions, child benefits, benefits to widows, and death grants.

A Mixed Economy

Britain was the first capitalist country in the world when, in the eighteenth and nineteenth centuries, the ownership and control of industry was in private hands. Today it is more appropriate to regard the economy as a mixture of private enterprise and various public controls.

Most manufacturing enterprises are privately owned except for the steel, aeroengine, and (since 1977) most of the aircraft and shipbuilding industries. Few, since 1945, argued a laissez-faire position and a minimal role for public control over the economy. Although only the left wing of the Labour Party believes in the state ownership of the means of production, distribution, and exchange, most people in the different political parties accepted a substantial role for the state, the largest employer in the country. Since 1979 public policy, under the Thatcher and Major governments, has emphasized the reduction of the state sector, the sale of public enterprises to private ownership, and a freer market economy.[6]

THE SOCIALIZATION PROCESS

Education and Class

Class distinctions have long been a prominent feature of British society. Though classes have been defined in different ways—the easiest way is to talk of the upper class, the upper middle, the lower middle, and the lower class—they differ in accent and language used, dress, style of life, nature of schooling, and occupations.

The educational system has reflected and helped to perpetuate the class structure. In 1944 the system was reorganized and students were streamed into separate modern secondary, technical, and grammar schools. Most students ended their education between 14 and 16 years of age to become manual workers. The occupational pattern and the working-class status of these youngsters who had left school was in most cases set for life. Those who left school at age 18 entered white-collar or minor managerial jobs and became part of the lower middle, some-

times middle, class. Only those who had further education beyond 18 years of age were likely to enter the professions or become managers and executives, the middle-class occupations.

In the 1970s comprehensive schools, which like high schools in the United States provide a wide range of education and educate students of different backgrounds and abilities together, replaced many of the selective secondary and grammar schools to help end the class stratification of educational streaming based on passing of examinations at an early age. During the 1980s, Conservative governments removed many of these comprehensive schools from local government control to enable them to become more selective again. Whether schools are comprehensive, as in the United States, and local government controlled, or selective and self-governing, varies on whether the Labour or Conservative Party, respectively, is in power.

Outside the state system are parochial schools, independent grammar schools stressing academic achievement (many have impressive reputations), and the 260 "public" schools, which are expensive and socially significant. The most prominent of the public schools—such as Eton, Harrow, Winchester, and Rugby—are prestigious institutions, consciously training young men for leadership positions in politics and society by discipline, building of character, and inculcation of traditional values. They have been a unique means of recruiting members of elite groups, constituting an "old boy" network in prominent positions. Though they represent only 4 percent of the British student population, graduates of the public schools, like those of the older universities, have occupied a highly disproportionate number of positions in the cabinet, the House of Commons, the senior civil service, the upper ranks of the armed forces, the High Courts, and the Church of England, as well as in major banking and financial institutions. Perhaps more surprisingly, public school graduates also accounted for 42 percent of the Labour Cabinet in 1966–1970 and 18 percent of Labour MPs in 1978. About 75 percent of Conservative MPs in the House of Commons elected in 1987 attended a public school. Between 1900 and 1985 old Etonians alone accounted for almost one-fourth of government ministers and top ambassadors. It is interesting in light of this that none of the last five prime ministers, including three conservatives, attended a public school.

Traditionally, higher education has been dominated by Oxford and Cambridge, which have provided the political and social elite. In the last two decades, there has been a considerable expansion of higher education for both social and educational reasons. The full-time student body has increased to over 844,000, about 20 percent of the 18-year-old population. There are now 46 universities attended by about 270,000 students. Another 250,000 take courses on a wide range of topics at the 30 polytechnics in England and Wales or attend other colleges providing further education in Britain. The most prestigious of the universities remain Oxford, with its 39 individual colleges, and Cambridge, with 29. Graduates of "Oxbridge" still constitute a high proportion of the elite groups in the country, including the Cabinet and the House of Commons. Nevertheless, the Conservative government in 1991 called for abolishing the distinction between universities and polytechnics, which have increased in importance in recent years, thus removing barriers between academic and vocational education.

A CHANGING BRITAIN

Britain is confronted by social problems, of which the challenge to authority is one of the most difficult. Although these matters are difficult to measure statistically, most observers would agree that there has been a decline in discipline in the family, especially with the higher divorce rate, and in the school, and that there is less respect for authority in general.

Britain has long been a free and—despite unnecessary secrecy in government—open society. It has also generally been a peaceful society in which the police went unarmed. A sign of increased social problems has been the considerable rise in crime. The increasing violence and the terrorist acts, perpetrated mostly by the IRA in British cities, have meant that some of the police now carry weapons, though the majority still go unarmed. But it has been the economic problem that has been of most concern to British politicians.

Britain is still a significant industrial and economic power. It is the fifth largest trading nation, exporting nearly 9 percent of total ex-

ports of manufactured goods by the industrial countries of the world. These exports constitute about one-half of all British exports. Britain still accounts for nearly one-third of all international banking business. About 10 percent of "invisible" trade in the world (banking, insurance, shipping, tourism, and income from overseas investment) is handled by Britain.

As Britain became industrialized, it also became a larger importer of foods and raw materials; today its imports also include a growing proportion of semimanufactured and manufactured goods. For almost 200 years the value of British imports of goods was usually larger than the value of exports. The deficit on this balance of "visible" trade was overcome in the total balance of payments by a surplus on invisible trade, the receipts from which are about one-third of total receipts. But in recent years, as the deficit in visible trade increased partly due to the rise in raw materials prices, the dramatic rise in oil prices, the large contribution to the budget of the European Union, the lower exchange rate of sterling, foreign competition, and the loss of many Commonwealth markets to other industrialized countries, the earnings on invisible trade were often not enough to overcome the deficit.

Discovery of oil in the North Sea helped change the picture. Britain is currently the world's fourth largest producer of oil, which now provides some 10 percent of total exports. Between 1979 and 1986, Britain had two deficits and six surpluses in its balance of payments. Since 1986, there have been only deficits.

The economic problems of recent years have preoccupied British politics. Britain has suffered the disadvantages, as well as having gotten the rewards, of being the first mature industrial nation in the world and of now having old capital equipment. Its older industries— coal, textiles, and shipbuilding—have contracted, and productivity per worker remained low compared with that of other advanced nations. It suffered from having exported capital abroad rather than using it internally and for being dependent on the international economy, which has made Britain vulnerable to external factors. The persistent balance of payments problem discouraged sustained investment and limited the rate of growth. Britain's economic and political problems were aggravated in the 1970s by the very high inflation rate, which in 1975 rose to over 26 percent, and by exchange rate difficulties. The unemployment rate rose to 13 percent in 1983; by 1996 it had fallen to 8 percent or 2.25 million people, a lower level than that of most European countries.

The postwar British performance in production, trade, and growth disappointed its political leaders. In the 1950s Britain was one of the ten richest countries in the world. From the mid–1960s to the mid–1970s, the economy grew by only 2.7 percent per year. In 1976 Britain ranked twenty-fourth in per capita gross national product, which was about half that of the United States.

There have been differing explanations for the low level of productivity per worker and the relatively slow economic growth. Some criticize the overmanning of jobs and the restrictive practices and obstructions of the powerful trade unions, which they see as more interested in job security than in increases in production, as well as the immobility of the labor force. Other critics stress inadequate management that is slow to introduce innovations, insufficient research and development, low levels of replacement of capital goods, reluctance to adapt production to new needs, and poor sales drive. The ethos of the social system and the ideal of the cultivated amateur and gentleman have been blamed for the failure to attract well-educated people as industrial managers and for the view of industrial activity as distasteful. Britain's desire to remain an important world power has meant large expenditure on overseas bases, large military forces, and considerable expenditure on nuclear research and development and on expensive delivery vehicles in the attempt to become a nuclear power.

Government policies have been criticized for many reasons: the disincentive of high tax rates, the lack of effective economic planning, the slowness in retraining unemployed workers, the concentration on prestigious and wasteful items such as supersonic aircraft rather than on more profitable industries likely to grow, and the inability to control inflation. Though there is validity in all of these criticisms, much of the British economic problem has been caused by external factors: the inevitable growth of other countries, many of which are industrializing rapidly and some of which are technologically mature; the rising cost of imports of food and raw materials; the loss of protected markets for exports to the former colonies; the sacrifices made by Britain in the two world wars, which seriously depleted British capital and led to the sale of overseas investments; and large external debts.

All British governments tried to solve the economic problem by increasing productivity, growth, and exports; by reducing the rate of inflation; and by maintaining confidence in the British pound. In the decade after 1979 the Thatcher government encouraged growth by cutting taxes, controlling the money supply for a time, approving only those wage settlements connected with increases in productivity, and stressing the value of competition. The economy has grown faster, inflation fell, and strikes declined, while trade unionism was weakened. But the share of manufacturing in the economy has declined, and deficits have occurred in some years.

KEY TERMS

Anglican church
Bill of Rights
class
consensus
constitutional democracy
conventions
deference
devolution
Magna Carta
majority principle
mixed economy
Northern Ireland (Ulster)
Oxbridge
pluralistic society
postindustrial society
privatization
public school
referendum
Reform Acts
representative system
rule of law
sovereignty
United Kingdom
welfare state

FURTHER READINGS

Bagehot, Walter. *The English Constitution* (Ithaca, NY: Cornell University Press, 1966).

Barker, Rodney. *Political Legitimacy and the State* (Oxford: Clarendon Press, 1990).

Beetham, David. *The Legitimation of Power* (London: Macmillan, 1991).

Crick, Bernard, ed. *National Identities* (Oxford: Blackwell, 1991).

Ewing, Keith, and C. A. Gearty. *Freedom under Thatcher: Civil Liberties in Modern Britain* (New York: Oxford University Press, 1990).

Gamble, Allen. *The Free Economy and the Strong State: The Politics of Thatcherism* (London: Macmillan, 1988).

Holme, Richard, and Michael Elliott, eds. *1688–1988: Time for a New Constitution* (New York: Oxford University Press, 1989).

Judge, David. *The Parliamentary State* (Newbury Park, CA: Sage, 1989).

Kearney, Hugh. *The British Isles: A History of Four Nations* (New York: Cambridge University Press, 1989).

Political Processes and Institutions

VOTING

The electoral system for the House of Commons is a simple one, comprising single-member constituencies, plurality decision or top-of-the-poll winner, and the principle of one person, one vote. Since the first Reform Act of 1832, which began the process of standardizing the qualifications for voting, the suffrage has gradually been extended to the whole citizenry over the age of 18. During the same period, factors such as the necessary ownership of property, double or triple voting based on ownership of a business or possession of an MA degree, residential qualification, feminine gender, and deliberately unequally sized constituencies have been eliminated (see Table 2.5).

Registration of voters is the responsibility of the local authorities, not of the individual, and an annual register of those eligible to vote in each constituency is issued every February. Since 1948, a postal vote has been possible for those who are incapable of voting in person, have moved from the constituency, or will be away on business. Middle-class voters are more likely to register for a postal vote than working-class voters, and the Conservative organization is better able to mobilize postal voters than other parties.

There are now 651 constituencies with boundaries that are a compromise between population and geographical size. In 1944, four boundary commissions—one each for England, Wales, Scotland, and Northern Ireland—were set up to ensure an equitable relationship between representation and population and to recommend, every five to seven years, alteration of constituency boundaries as population shifts. The changes in 1983 and 1992 increased

Table 2.5 EXTENSION OF THE FRANCHISE

Year	Main Group Enfranchised	Other Features
1832	Industrial middle class	Redistribution of seats from small boroughs to the counties and towns
		Registration of voters necessary
		Increased suffrage by 217,000
1867		Increased suffrage by 1 million
1872	Urban workers	Secret ballot
1883		Bribery and corrupt electoral practices become criminal offenses
1884	Agricultural workers	Increased suffrage by 2 million
1885		Equal-sized constituencies
1918	Women over age 30	Increased suffrage by 12.5 million
		Redistribution of seats
		Limit to two votes (places of residence and business or university)
1928	Women over age 21	Increased suffrage by 7 million
		Universal suffrage over age 21
1948		One person, one vote
		Abolition of university vote and seats
		Abolition of business vote
		Redistribution of seats
1969	Persons over age 18	Increased suffrage by 3 million

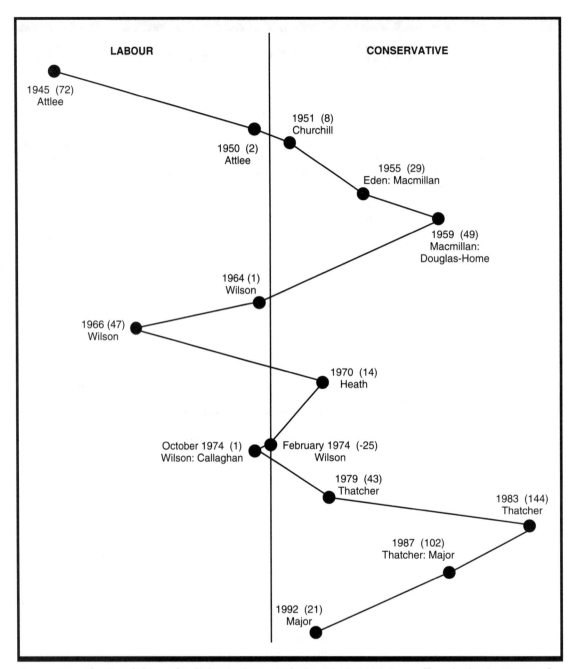

LABOUR   **CONSERVATIVE**

1945 (72)
Attlee

1951 (8)
Churchill

1950 (2)
Attlee

1955 (29)
Eden: Macmillan

1959 (49)
Macmillan:
Douglas-Home

1964 (1)
Wilson

1966 (47)
Wilson

1970 (14)
Heath

October 1974 (1)   February 1974 (-25)
Wilson: Callaghan   Wilson

1979 (43)
Thatcher

1983 (144)
Thatcher

1987 (102)
Thatcher: Major

1992 (21)
Major

Figure 2.2   The Pendulum of Politics in Great Britain, 1945–1991 (overall majority in House of Commons)

constituencies to 524 in England, 72 in Scotland, 38 in Wales, and 17 in Northern Ireland. Wales and Scotland are deliberately overrepresented as a concession to nationalist sentiment.

Election is by plurality, or the highest vote obtained. This method has the virtue of clarity and simplicity. Politically it has helped to sustain the system of two major parties in which the Conservative and Labour parties have shared the bulk of the electoral vote and seats in the House of Commons. These two parties alternated in political power for almost the same number of years between 1945 and 1979—the Conservatives remained in power from 1979 to 1996—while until 1983 the third party, the Liberal, had not obtained more than 14 seats (see Figure 2.2). But the plurality system has also produced serious inequities and distortions of the will of the people at both the level of the individual single-member constituency and the national level.

At the individual constituency level, seats may be won by a minority vote where there are more than two parties and the successful candidate polls fewer votes than those of all the other candidates. In February 1974 there were 408 seats (64.3 percent of the total) won by less than a majority. Between 1945 and 1979, 30 percent of all seats were won by a minority vote.

At the national level the opinion of the people may be distorted and political parties may not be truly represented in proportion to the votes they receive in the country, as is shown in Table 2.6.

There is no exact correlation between the votes obtained by a party in the country as a whole and the number of seats it wins in the House of Commons. Indeed, it may even happen, as in 1951 and February 1974, that the party with the smaller percentage of votes in the country may win more seats than the party with a larger percentage of votes. The Conservatives in 1992 won 52 percent of seats with only 42 percent of the vote.

A second problem is that a relatively small change in electoral opinion may produce a much larger proportional change in the distribution of seats between the parties. This disproportionate result is produced by changes in voting in the "marginal seats," those that are normally won by small numbers of votes. In 1979 there were 74 seats held by the Labour or Conservative parties by margins of less than 2,000 votes; 83 seats were won by majorities under 5 percent.

The main inequity in the system is that the Liberal Party, in spite of considerable support all over the country, has not won more than a few seats in the postwar period. Unlike a regional party such as the SNP or the Plaid Cymru, whose votes are concentrated in a small number of constituencies, the Liberal and, in 1983 and 1987, the Social Democratic vote was spread throughout the country. The Liberal Democrats only got 20 seats in 1992 with 17.8 percent of the vote. Minority parties are underrepresented in the House of Commons.

The present system is unfortunate for the Liberal Democrats and other minor parties in two other respects. The first is that its candidates often lost a large number of their deposits (304 in 1979); elections were therefore expensive for the party. The system has now changed. Deposits are lost if a candidate gets less than 5 percent of the constituency vote; in 1992, 897 candidates lost deposits of £500 each. The second is that Liberal Democrat electoral support is very fluid. Persons who might vote Liberal if they thought a party candidate were likely to win are reluctant to do so if they feel the candidate is likely to lose and the party as a whole will do badly. They might prefer to influence the outcome of the election by voting for a candidate of one of the two major parties. Not surprisingly, the Liberal Party and the former Social Democratic Party (SDP) advocated a change in the electoral system. But the two major parties are still unwilling to approve a change because they benefit from the present

Table 2.6   GENERAL ELECTIONS, 1974–1992

Election	Percentage of Votes Cast			Number of Seats Won			
	Con.	Lab.	Lib.	Con.	Lab.	Lib.	SDP
1974 (Feb.)	38.2	37.2	19.3	297	301	14	—
1974 (Oct.)	35.8	39.3	18.3	277	319	13	—
1979	43.9	36.9	13.8	339	269	11	—
1983	42.4	27.6	25.4[a]	397	209	17	6
1987	42.3	30.8	22.6[a]	376	229	17	5
1992[c]	41.8	34.4	17.8[b]	336	271	20[b]	

[a]Combined vote of the Liberal and Social Democratic (SDP) parties (Alliance)

[b]Liberal Democratic Party

[c]At the 1992 election, 3 blacks, 3 Asians, and 60 women were elected

Table 2.7   DISTRIBUTION OF SEATS IN THE HOUSE OF COMMONS, 1992 ELECTION, USING DIFFERENT ELECTORAL SYSTEMS

Con.	Lab.	Lib.	Dem.	Nationalists (Welsh and Scottish)	Others (Mainly Northern Ireland)
Present system	336	271	20	7	17
Proportional representation	274	222	118	14	23
Single transferable vote	282	239	93	19	18

system. This method has helped perpetuate the two-party system in the postwar period by normally producing a majority of seats for one of the two major parties, which is then able to form a government. Not since 1935 has one party obtained 50 percent of the total poll, but parties have had comfortable majorities in 10 of the 14 postwar elections. A different electoral system would result in a fairer distribution of seats in relation to the votes cast for the parties; but it would also lead to an increase in the number of parties represented in the House of Commons, make it difficult to obtain a majority, and therefore change the formation and functioning of government (see Table 2.7).

IS THE ELECTORAL SYSTEM WORKING?

The present electoral system has, therefore, been defended essentially on the grounds that it provides one of the two major parties with a comfortable majority in the House of Commons. The winning party can then form a strong gov-

ernment which is able to formulate a coherent policy that will be approved by Parliament. This has generally been true in the postwar period when the Conservative and Labour Parties have obtained the bulk of the electoral vote and one of them has obtained a majority of seats. The peak was reached in 1951, when their combined vote was 96.8 percent of the poll and 77 percent of the total electorate.

But from 1951 there was a steady drop in their electoral support, as well as a decline in the proportion of those voting in general. The decline in strength of the two major parties resulted in February 1974 in a minority government, with Labour getting 25 seats less than an absolute majority, and in October 1974 in an overall majority of only 1 seat. The two major parties got only 76 percent of the poll in 1992. In 1959, parties other than Conservative or Labour gained only 9 seats, 6 of which were Liberal, whereas in 1987 they gained 45 seats, of which 22 went to the Alliance, 6 to the nationalist parties, and 17 to Northern Ireland.

Table 2.8   PERCENT SHARE OF THE VOTE BY THE TWO MAJOR PARTIES, SELECTED ELECTIONS

Election	% Total Electorate	% Actual Vote	Seats Won Con.	Lab.	Total Seats
1945	64.6	88.1	213	393	640
1951	79.9	96.8	321	295	625
1966	68.1	89.8	253	363	630
1974 (Oct.)	54.6	75.0	277	319	635
1983	50.9	70.0	397	209	650
1992	58.8	76.3	336	271	651

The decline in recent electoral support for the two major parties is attributable to two main factors: the rise in nationalist sentiment and, perhaps temporarily, in Liberal-Social Democratic support, and the decrease in the strength of partisanship for the Conservative and Labour Parties.

The cumulative rise in Scottish nationalist strength has been rapid in recent elections: from 11.5 percent in 1970 to 30.4 percent of the vote in Scotland in October 1974 (see Table 2.8). Not only did the SNP win 11 seats in October 1974, but it also came in second in 42 other constituencies, taking votes from both major parties. The party slogan "It's Scotland's oil" appealed to those who believe that Scotland should control the North Sea oil revenues. By 1974 the SNP had become a broad-based party drawing support from all social classes, geographical regions, and age groups, and from former voters, especially younger people, from other parties. In Scotland it can be considered part of a three-party system, though its support declined in 1992 to 21.5 percent of the poll (see Table 2.9).

Table 2.9 Voting in Scotland and Wales, 1987 and 1992

	Scotland			
	1987		**1992**	
Party	Votes (%)	Seats (%)	Votes (%)	Seats (%)
SNP	14.0	3	21.5	3
Labour	42.4	50	39.0	49
Conservative	24.0	10	25.7	11
Liberal Democrat	19.2	9	13.1	9

	Wales			
	1987		**1992**	
Party	Votes (%)	Seats (%)	Votes (%)	Seats (%)
PC	7.3	3	8.8	4
Labour	45.1	24	49.5	27
Conservative	29.5	8	28.6	6
Liberal Democrat	17.9	3	12.4	1

In October 1974 the Welsh Plaid Cymru won three seats, with 10.8 percent of the Welsh vote, and came in second in six constituencies, but its strength was largely confined to the rural, Welsh-speaking part of the country. Influenced by literary figures, the party has been more concerned about the extinction of the Welsh culture and language than about broader political issues. The Welsh protest vote against the major parties—unlike the Scottish, which has increasingly gone to the nationalist party—has often gone to the Liberals. In 1992 it won four seats and 8.8 percent of the poll.

The Ulster Unionists, once automatically associated with the Conservative Party, are now more independent. Elections in Northern Ireland had little reference to the rest of the United Kingdom and were primarily concerned with political affairs in Ulster since 1974.

In spite of the fact that many electors have a partisan self-image or psychological commitment to one of the two major parties, there has been a drop in support for them. The Conservative vote fell in October 1974 to 36 percent, the lowest in its history. The Labour Party lost considerable support among those who should be its firmest adherents—the young, males, and working-class trade unionists. In 1979 the party got the votes of less than half of the working-class voters. But after 1983 it recovered a considerable part of the working-class vote.

Both parties have experienced a decline in membership, a weakening of party allegiance, and expressions of dissatisfaction with their leadership. The perception has grown that neither major party is coping well with issues, both national and international. This view is made stronger by the evidence of important differences within each of the parties on issues such as the European Union prices and incomes policy, and industrial relations.

Nevertheless, despite the decline in the major party vote of the electorate as a consequence of the rise of minor parties and the decline in partisanship, there has not been a similar decrease in the number of seats gained by the major parties. The working of the present electoral system still allowed Conservatives and Labour to obtain 93 percent of the seats while getting only 76 percent of the electoral vote in 1992, which was the fourth successive win for the Conservatives.

ELECTIONS

When are general elections held? The whole House of Commons is elected for a period of five years, but only one Parliament since 1945 has lasted the full allotted time. Most elections were called by the prime minister at a time thought best for the ruling party to win. Campaigns last less than a month, and in recent years, especially because of television coverage, have concentrated on the major party leaders.

By-elections in an individual constituency are held on the death or resignation of a member of Parliament (MP). The number of by-elections during the life of a Parliament thus depends on the duration of the Parliament and the age of MPs. During the 1987–1992 Parliament there were 23 by-elections in four years.

There are two interesting features of by-elections. The first is that the vote is always considerably lower than in the same constituency at general elections. The second is that the voters usually register a more antigovernment view than they did at the previous general election, thus decreasing the strength of the government party in the House of Commons. Between 1922 and 1979 the government party lost 126 seats and gained only 9 in by-elections. Between 1989 and 1991 Conservative candidates lost seven by-elections; by 1996, Conservatives had lost the last 15 seats they defended.

The Candidates

There are no primaries or nominating conventions in British politics. Primaries are virtually impossible in the British context because of the unpredictable timing of elections mentioned above.

By law a candidate for a constituency is simply nominated by ten registered electors of the area; until 1970 no party affiliation was officially attached to the name of the candidate. In fact, almost all candidates are sponsored by a political party. It has been rare for a nonparty candidate to run or for a candidate not associated with a major party to win.

Until World War II a varying number of constituencies were uncontested. Since 1951 all constituencies have been contested. In 1992 the number of women candidates increased to 568, of whom 60 were elected. The total number of candidates increased to 2,946.

Any person over age 21 can stand as a candidate with certain exceptions: those who are disqualified from voting; clergymen of the churches of England, Scotland, and Ireland, and of the Roman Catholic Church; and people holding certain offices, including judges, civil servants, members of the armed forces, police officers, and various public officials, except members of the government. Candidates need not reside in their constituencies.

One requirement is that each candidate must deposit £500 with the registrar, which is returned if the candidate gets over 5 percent of the total vote in a constituency.

Who Are the Candidates?

An implicit problem in representative democracies is that the candidates and the representatives elected are not a model of their constituents. The British system bears out this generalization. The percentage of male candidates is far greater than the percentage of men in the general population, and candidates are wealthier and better educated than the average constituent.

Among Conservative candidates it is noticeable that 57 percent attended a public school, 35 percent went to "Oxbridge" (Oxford or Cambridge), and 33 percent to some other university (see Table 2.10). What is perhaps more surprising in a party that gets most of its support from the working class is that 14 percent of the Labour candidates went to public school, 13 percent went to Oxbridge, and 45 percent to some other university.

In 1992 the two dominant occupations were business and the professions (see Table 2.11). Most Conservative professionals were lawyers, while most Labour professionals were teachers at some educational level. The Liberals also had a high proportion of teachers among its candidates. The Conservatives have become a less aristocratic group and Labour more professional.[7]

In all parties there have been a limited number of women candidates; in only three elections have there been more than 100. The

Table 2.10   EDUCATION OF CANDIDATES, 1992: TOTAL 2,946

	Conservative		Labour		Liberal	
	Candidates	Elected	Candidates	Elected	Candidates	Elected
Eton	43	34	2	2	5	—
All public schools	313	105	77	40	133	10
Oxford	107	83	51	28	44	4
Cambridge	91	68	25	16	33	2
All universities	428	245	370	166	372	15

highest number was the 568, or 14 percent of the total, who ran in 1992 (see Table 2.12).

The Nature of Voting

Though recent changes in voting behavior must be borne in mind, and despite the fluid political situation, certain general statements about voting in the post–World War II period can be made in the following paragraphs.

A High but Declining Poll   Voting is not compulsory, but the vote in general elections in the postwar period has always been over 72 percent of the electorate, though smaller at by-elections, and reached a peak of 83.9 percent in 1950. There was a steady, though irregular, decline until October 1974, when it dropped to 72.8 percent, before increasing to 75.5 percent in 1979 and then declining to 72.7 percent in 1983. In 1992 it increased to 77 percent.

The abstention rate is higher among younger people, new residents of a constituency, the unmarried or divorced, blacks, the unemployed, and private rather than council tenants. These groups are less involved in political parties, less interested in politics, and less exposed to political information in general. Demographic factors have reinforced an overall decline in political interest and the belief, perhaps temporary, that the outcome of elections is

Table 2.11   OCCUPATION OF CANDIDATES, 1992

Occupation	Conservative		Labour		Liberal	
	Candidates	Elected	Candidates	Elected	Candidates	Elected
Barrister	65	39	18	9	18	5
Solicitor	39	21	19	8	19	1
Doctor/dentist	10	4	7	2	13	—
University teacher	7	4	20	14	14	1
Polytechnic teacher	6	2	57	24	46	—
School teacher	32	16	111	38	106	3
Total professionals	238	131	303	115	315	12
Business	259	128	66	22	174	2
White collar	20	9	100	36	70	1
Politician	37	20	41	24	12	2
Publisher/journalist	37	28	27	13	22	3
Farmer	25	10	2	2	8	—
Skilled worker	4	3	70	43	15	—

Table 2.12   WOMEN CANDIDATES AND MPS, SELECTED ELECTIONS

Election	Candidates	Elected
1945	87	24
1950	126	21
1959	75	25
1970	97	26
1979	206	19
1983	276	23
1987	327	41
1992	568	60

| | Women Candidates and MPs | | | |
| | 1987 | | 1992 | |
	Candidates	MPs	Candidates	MPs
Conservative	46	17	59	20
Labour	92	21	138	37
Liberal Democrat	105	2	144	2
Others	84	1	227	1 (SNP)
Total	327	41	568	60

Source: Times Guide to the House of Commons, 1992 *The Times,* London.

not important. The decline in the poll may also be explained by the greater mobility of the population, the reduction of voting in safe seats in the inner cities, and abstentions by some potential Liberal supporters.

Class   There has been a strong correlation between class and party voting. The Conservatives normally get 90 percent of the upper-middle-class vote and between two-thirds and three-quarters of the middle-class vote. Labour gets some two-thirds of the working-class vote, while the Liberals and Social Democrats draw from all social classes. The middle class as a whole is more strongly Conservative than the working class is Labour (see Table 2.13). In a society where class consciousness has been as strong as in Britain, this relationship is understandable.

Yet, the link between class and party voting has never been complete. About one-third of the electorate does not vote according to this premise. In addition, extremist class parties

such as the Communist Party have always done rather poorly. But the most serious qualification of class-party voting has always been the working-class Conservative vote, which has amounted to about one-third of the total working-class vote. There are a number of possible explanations for this contradiction of class voting. Those who, though objectively part of the working class, see themselves as middle class and adopt middle-class values and ways of life are more likely to vote Conservative than those who think of themselves as working class. Members of the working class who have had more than the minimum secondary and further education are more likely to vote Conservative than those who have not. Workers in agricultural areas who have close contacts with their employers, who do not belong to unions, who are religious, who belong to local organizations and are integrated into the local community are more likely to vote Conservative than the average worker. Above all, there is an explanation, discussed in Chapter 1 in connection with political stability, based on the deference of part of the working class. It used to be argued that this group preferred a socially superior political leadership, which it believed to be a natural ruling group. But it is more likely that this group believes that the Conservative Party is more efficient than its rivals and that its wielding of power will ensure greater material benefits. Whatever the explanation, the Conservatives have done particularly well in the working class among older people, women (until 1979), those who own their own homes and those who own shares. The increase in home ownership—66 percent of voters now own homes—has meant greater Conservative support. About 44 percent in 1987 and 40 percent in 1992 of the home-owning working class voted Conservative compared with 32 percent voting Labour in 1987 and 41 percent in 1992. By contrast, about 57 percent of working-class tenants in public housing voted Labour in the same election. In the same way, a majority of first-time shareholders voted Conservative, and only 17 percent voted Labour, in 1987.

The evidence is mixed at present, but there appears to be less subjective class identification, a weakening of class alignment, especially by young voters, and less acceptance of the basic principles of a party by its supporters. In 1992 the Conservatives did less well than in the previous two elections with voters of the "new" working class, those who live in the south of England, are homeowners, work in the private sector, and are non-unionists.

Party Identification   The best guide to voting choice for most of the electorate has been identification with a party and psychological commitment to it. This allegiance has been the basis for response to party programs, for evaluation of the competence of party leaders, and for voting and political behavior in general. Among Labour and Conservative voters in 1974, 9 out of 10 thought of themselves as Labour or Conservative. In contrast, only half of the Liberal voters felt a similar identification with the party.

Why do people identify with a party? The strongest single influence has been the party preference of parents, especially if both parents voted the same way. Identification also results from other factors, including the supposed link between the party and a class, and the image of what policies and principles the party represents. For the Conservatives, the image has included such characteristics as capable leadership, skill in foreign policy, patriotism, and

Table 2.13   VOTING CATEGORIES, 1992 (PERCENT)

	Con.	Lab.	Lib.
Trade union member	31	46	19
Men	41	37	18
Women	44	34	18
Council tenant	24	55	15
18 to 24 years	35	39	19
55 and over	46	34	17
Unskilled working class	31	49	16
Skilled manual	39	40	17
Professional and managerial	56	19	22
White-collar workers	52	25	19
Owner/occupier	40	41	17
South of England	40	38	20
North of England	23	52	23

Feature 2.3 Party Identification and Class

Social class has been the main form of identity, and British voters have identified in general with the party they think represents the interests of their social class. In elections between 1945 and 1970, nearly two-thirds of all voters voted for their class-party. Since 1974, the percentage has declined, though class remains the single most important factor. On one hand the increase in public sector professions, whose members are more concerned with service than with wealth, meant more middle-class support for Labour. On the other hand, social factors (home ownership, mobility from north to south, and from inner cities to suburbs, decline in trade union membership) meant working-class support for non-Labour parties. Moreover, the working class has declined from 41 percent of all voters in 1979 to 34 percent in 1992. The new social cleavages have weakened, though not ended, class voting.

---

maintenance of the free enterprise system. For Labour it has been the pursuit of a more egalitarian society and concern for the underprivileged. Part of the dilemma of the Liberals is that their image is rather diffuse, devoid of specific policy content of general appeal.

In the early 1980s the Labour Party moved to the left and alienated some traditional supporters. In the 1990s it moved to more centrist positions, renounced extreme policies that lost votes, gave up unilateral disarmament, accepted the market economy, and agreed not to revoke privatization of enterprises.

In the recent past the party identification factor has given considerable stability and predictability to the voting pattern for the major parties. But in the 1970s and 1980s strength of party identification appears to have declined and the ties of voters to a particular party to have grown weaker (see Feature 2.3). Voters are less prone to vote for the party of their parents. The changes in the social structure discussed in Chapter 1, a general criticism of the performance of governments of both parties, and the presence of new issues that cut across party lines have contributed to this decline in party identification, the rise of the Social Democrats, and perhaps also to a certain cynicism about parties. In particular, part of the decline since 1970 in the Labour and Conservative vote and in the turnout at the poll has been attributed to two factors: (1) less party identification in the young and newly enfranchised part of the electorate, and (2) a decline in the number of those who define themselves as "very strong identifiers" with a party.[8]

Gender   Women constitute 52 percent of the electorate. Until recently, men have been more politically active than women, with a particularly low political interest among working-class women. Women voted Conservative to a greater degree than did men (see Table 2.14). In 9 of the last 12 elections a majority of women voted Conservative. But, since 1979, women have tended to vote less Conservative. In 1983, for the first time, the Conservatives got less support from women than from men, but in 1992 they got 15 percent more support from women than did Labour, for which a majority of men voted.

Race   Nonwhite immigrants have overwhelmingly voted Labour, partly because the vast ma-

Table 2.14 CONSERVATIVE VOTE BY GENDER, SELECTED ELECTIONS (PERCENT)

Year	Men	Women
1945	35	43
1955	47	55
1966	36	41
1979	45	48
1983	45	44
1992	37	43

Source: Anthony Seldon and Stuart Ball, eds., *Conservative Century,* (London: OUP, 1994).

jority are members of the working class. In 1992 only about 90 percent of blacks (Afro-Caribbeans) and 71 percent of Asians voted Labour. But the presence of a significant number of immigrants in a constituency and the nonwhite immigration issue may also produce the opposite effect on voting. In the 1970 election the Conservatives were believed to have gained about six seats as a result of their being perceived—largely owing to the speeches made by the then-prominent Conservative Enoch Powell—as the more restrictive major party on allowing immigration. Some voters—190,000, or 0.6 percent of the total—supported the anti-nonwhite-immigration National Front, which in 1979 ran 303 candidates, of whom all but one lost their deposits. The racial appeals of the National Front have drawn more support from working-class and poorly educated voters than from other groups, but its 13 candidates in 1992 all did poorly in the election. By contrast, in 1992, 23 ethnic minority candidates ran, and 6 won. It appears there is some resistance to an ethnic minority candidate by the voters.[9]

Religion   In contemporary times, religion has not been a politically divisive issue, except in Northern Ireland and, in the early part of the 1990s, among parts of the Islamic community. Because there is a link between class and membership in a particular religion, there are similar explanations for voting behavior as resulting from those two factors. In general, members of the Anglican Church vote more Conservative than do individuals of other religious denominations; members of the nonconformist churches are likely to support the Labour or Liberal Parties; and Catholics, largely working class, vote strongly Labour.

Age   Younger people tend to vote Labour in greater proportions than their elders, especially those between 50 and 64. But the youngest people also have the lowest rates of turnout. On the whole it is true that the Conservatives are supported more by older than younger voters; yet in the 1960s the early-middle-aged group was less Conservative than their juniors. This has been explained in one analysis by the argument that it is the conservation of those political tendencies that were established when young that

increases with age, not conservatism itself. Voting habits will therefore be influenced by those tendencies that were dominant when people first entered the electorate. Older people became adults when Labour was still a minor party and therefore have less allegiance to it than younger people. Some recent changes in the voting patterns of young and old have appeared in recent elections; in 1983 and in 1992, young voters supported the Conservatives more than Labour.

Regional Variations   For generations, certain areas have been strongholds of particular parties. Labour does well in south Wales, central Scotland, the industrial north of England, and in the inner cities. The Conservatives are strong in southern and eastern England, and in the suburbs and country areas, which have grown in population and economic prosperity. In 1987 Labour won only 3 of the 176 seats in southern England, excluding London. In this part of the country, average earnings are much higher than in the rest of the country. Recent elections reinforced Labour control over urban areas and Conservative control over rural areas. The Liberals and Social Democrats do best in the west of England, Wales, and the Scottish islands. Labour has a plurality in Wales and Scotland, though the latter was challenged by the SNP in October 1974. The Conservatives usually have a plurality in England and, until recently, in Northern Ireland. In the 1970s and 1980s, politics in Ulster were very fluid because of complex internal problems.

Occupation   Those employed in nationalized industries and public service organizations are more likely to vote Labour than those working in commercial organizations and the self-employed. People in both the working and middle class who have experienced unemployment are more likely than the average to vote Labour. Trade unionists vote Labour to a greater degree than do non-unionists. The strongest working-class support for Labour comes from predominantly working-class constituencies in large towns, industrial areas, and mining villages; union members; workers in large factories and offices with over 250 employees; those with working-class parents; those living in council

---

**Feature 2.4   Major Issues of Conservative
and Labour Parties, 1992 Election**

Conservative	Defense, Europe, inflation, law and order, taxation
Labour	Health, unemployment, education, homelessness

---

apartments; and those who have been unemployed for a period of time. However, the number of manual workers and of those working in large factories, and the number of council tenants all have been declining (see Feature 2.4).

Party and the Leader

Voting may depend on the images people have of the parties and their leaders and on perceptions of party positions on issues. The assumption that people were more likely to vote for a party than a leader may no longer be true in view of the prominence of the leaders on television and the time given to their speeches and personalities.

POLITICAL PARTIES

The British system has often been regarded as the classic example of a two-party system in which the Conservative and Labour Parties—national, large, cohesive, disciplined, ideological but generally moderate—have alternated as the government and the opposition. The Liberals have not won more than 20 seats since 1945. A considerable number of minor parties have existed and run candidates in national and local elections. But none, except the nationalists in recent years, has had much success. Extremist parties have fared poorly. On the left, the Communist Party, founded in 1920, has never gained more than two parliamentary seats and since 1950 has been unrepresented. On the right, the present National Front, a party opposing nonwhite immigration, has not been able to win a parliamentary seat. The Green Party emerged in 1985 out of an ecological group. In 1987 it received less than 1 percent of the vote, but in the 1989 election for the European Parliament it obtained 15 percent. In the 1992 election, its 258 candidates rarely got more than 1 percent of the vote.

A possible change to a multiparty system appeared with the formation of the Social Democratic Party (SDP) in 1981 by some prominent Labour politicians who were disturbed by militant leftism in their party and by organizational changes allowing more influence to extraparliamentary forces, extremists in some of the constituency parties and the trade unions. The SDP argued that it was committed to parliamentary democracy, rejected the idea of class war, favored controls on trade unions, approved a mixed economy, and supported British membership of both the European Community and NATO.

The SDP and the Liberals agreed to form an Alliance to support each other electorally. This did well at some by-elections and in local elections. But the Alliance was less successful nationally, though it won 23 seats and came second in 311 constituencies and got 25 percent of the poll in 1983, and it won 22 seats and came second in 260 constituencies and got 22 percent in 1987.

As a result of this disappointment, a majority in SDP agreed to merge with the Liberals and form a new party, the Social and Liberal Democrats (SLD), who were generally called Liberal Democrats in 1988. A minority of the old SDP remained as a small separate group, transforming itself in 1990 into the Campaign for Social Democracy. In the 1992 election the Liberal Democrats got 17.8 percent of the vote and 20 seats. The future of the political center and of the party system remains uncertain.

PARTY ORGANIZATIONS

Local and Regional

All the major parties have the parliamentary constituency as the basic unit of party organization. The Conservative and Liberal constituency associations are composed of individual members who subscribe to the party and who manage the local organizations, elect their own officers, select parliamentary and local government candidates, raise funds, engage in educational work, and conduct the electoral campaign in their area. However, the constituency Labour parties are composed not only of individual members but also of affiliated organizations, such as trade unions, cooperative societies and branches of the Cooperative Party, branches of Socialist societies and some professional organizations, and trade councils.

Total membership of all parties has declined in the last two decades. The Conservative Party has declined from about 3 million in the late 1950s to less than half a million members, the SLD now have about 60,000 members and the Labour Party has about 200,000 individual and 4 million affiliated members.

National Organization

Each party has a national organization that works through different committees, holds an annual conference in the autumn, and has a central headquarters to control the working of the party machinery and prepare publications.

The National Union of Conservative and Unionist Associations is a federation of constituency associations (see Figure 2.3). It is responsible for the organization and growth of these associations and acts as a link between the leader of the party and the associations. The Union is nominally governed by the Central Council, which meets once a year and which, in the postwar period, has chosen the officers of the Union. But because the Central Council is too large a body for effective action, the group that acts on its behalf and meets more frequently is the Executive Committee; this committee is composed of the party leader, chief officials, and representatives of the regional organizations.

The Conservatives hold an annual conference to discuss the reports of the Council and of the Executive Committee. It is understood that the conference is purely advisory; it is usually a platform for the main party leaders rather than a challenge to them. Nevertheless, the leaders recognize the importance of wide party support.

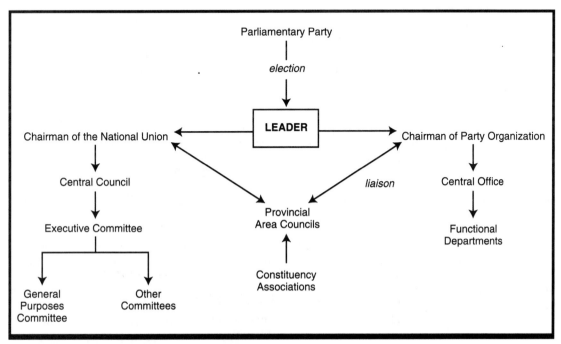

Figure 2.3   Organization of the Conservative Party

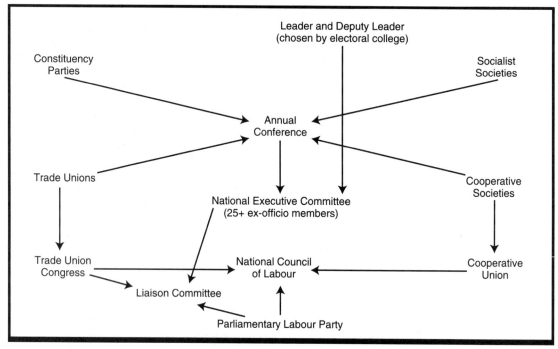

Figure 2.4 Organization of the Labour Party

Most of the resolutions are congratulatory of the leadership, which has never been beaten by a vote on any serious issue. The resolutions in any case are not binding on the party leadership. It is characteristic of the Conservative conference that it is usually more right-wing than the leadership.

The Conservative Central Office, the party headquarters, is concerned with the efficient organization of the party. It provides general guidance and technical assistance, helps the formulation of policy by supplying background material through its research department, and offers advice on electioneering. It is headed by a chairperson, appointed by the party leader, and officers who are responsible for the different departments concerned with specific functions.

The Central Office cannot coerce the constituency associations, which operate through local volunteer workers and obtain and spend their own funds. The local associations also, in the main, control the process of selection of parliamentary candidates, though the Central Office supplies a list of available candidates on request and may influence the final choice.

The Labour Party has the most complex organizational structure. It began as, and has remained, a federal body composed of four main groups (see Figure 2.4):

1. The more than 600 constituency associations, which now have about 200,000 members: They are responsible for their own organization and selection of parliamentary candidates. The number of activists is relatively small, and they are usually more left-wing than either the party leaders or their MPs. Most party members spend little or no time at party meetings or activities.

2. The 27 affiliated trade unions, which account for 4 million, or 95 percent, of the members: Not all unions are affiliated with the party—67 unions are now attached to the Trades Union Congress—and not all members of a union that is affiliated want to be members of the party. About one-third of the membership of the affiliated unions have "contracted out," or refused to have part of their union dues go to a political levy for the party. About three-quarters of the Labour Party's funds come from the unions.

The largest union affiliations are the Transport and General Workers (TGWU), the Amalgamated Union of Engineering Workers (AUEW), the General and Municipal Workers (GMWU), and the National Union of Public Employees (NUPE).

Since all organizations are represented at the annual conference in proportion to their membership, the four largest unions constituted a majority if they all voted the same way. But in 1995 the union vote was reduced to 50 percent of the whole conference.

A number of unions sponsor parliamentary candidates, most of whose election expenses they pay. Because their constituencies are usually safe seats, those candidates are much more likely to win than nonsponsored candidates. In 1992, of the 634 Labour candidates, the unions sponsored 173. Of these, 143 won, of whom 22 were women.

3. The cooperative organizations are linked to the Labour Party in the same way as the unions are: One cooperative society, the Royal Arsenal, has been affiliated since 1927 and another since 1979. There is a separate Cooperative Party, founded in 1917, but it is now in reality an adjunct of the Labour Party. Since 1922 all Cooperative Party parliamentary candidates have been endorsed by the Labour Party and have run as Labour and Cooperative.

4. A number of Socialist societies, small in size and composed largely of professionals or intellectuals: The most well known of these bodies is the Fabian Society, which was founded in 1884. The total membership of these societies and of the cooperative groups is about 54,000.

The nominal policy-making body in the Labour Party is the annual party conference, which debates resolutions, changes the constitution of the party, and elects the major administrative organ, the National Executive Committee (NEC). The conference is attended by representatives from the four different elements making up the party and by the chief officials of the party, MPs, and parliamentary candidates.

The NEC in 1996 consists of the leader of the party, the deputy leader, the treasurer, and 28 other members who are elected at the conference. Of these 25 people, 12 are chosen by the trade union delegates, 7 by those from the constituency parties, 4 by representatives of the

cooperative and Socialist societies, and 5 women by the whole conference.

The NEC is the administrative authority of the party and is the body responsible between annual conferences for deciding policy matters and enforcing the rules of the party. It controls the central organization, supervises the work of the party outside Parliament, decides disputes between members or associations, and manages the party funds. Together with the Parliamentary Labour Party (PLP), the NEC draws up the election manifesto based on conference proposals, but there is sometimes friction between them.

The NEC also plays a role in the selection of parliamentary candidates. Like the Conservative Central Office, it maintains a list of acceptable candidates that the local constituencies can request, but the final choice is made by the local parties.

The NEC can expel a member or disaffiliate an organization for activity contrary to party decisions. In the postwar period a number of organizations, described as Communist-front groups, were forbidden to members. Since the mid–1980s, a number of left-wing members, belonging to the Militant group, have been expelled or suspended for challenging or defying party policy.

THE PARTIES IN PARLIAMENT

The major Conservative organ in Parliament is the 1922 Committee, which is composed of the nongovernmental Conservative MPs and expresses their opinions to the leadership of the party. When the party is in power, its leaders, now members of the government, do not attend the committee's weekly meetings. After the discussion of policy issues or political problems, the chairperson of the committee expresses its views to the leadership.

The leader of the party is now chosen by the MPs. From 1881, after the death of Disraeli, until 1963 the Conservative leader "emerged" after a series of informal "soundings" of the views of different sections of the party. Of the 11 leaders in this period, 5 were of aristocratic descent and the others came from business or professional politics.

The Conservative leader is now elected by the MPs in the House of Commons and is then presented for confirmation to a meeting composed of the Conservative MPs and peers, prospective candidates, and members of the Executive Committee of the National Union. In 1965, Edward Heath was first elected in this way, and in 1975, after the voting rules were revised, he was replaced by Margaret Thatcher, the first woman to lead a major British party. Her leadership was challenged in 1990 when she failed to win the necessary absolute majority and lead over her opponent. She decided not to run in a second ballot, which was won by John Major. In July 1995 Prime Minister Major, wanting to end speculation about his leadership of the party, ran for reelection, beating his right-wing challenger by 218 to 89. He emerged as a stronger leader but one-third of Conservative MPs had not supported his candidacy.

The Parliamentary Labour Party (PLP) consists of Labour members in the House of Commons and those in the House of Lords. It is led, when the party is in opposition, by the Parliamentary Committee, or "shadow cabinet," which consists of the leader and deputy leader, 15 others elected by Labour MPs, and 1 elected representative of Labour peers. The leader and deputy leader of the PLP are the same people who have been elected as the leaders of the party by the electoral college. In this electoral college, the trade unions, the constituency parties, and the PLP each have one-third of the votes.

In recent years most of the members of the shadow cabinet have become cabinet ministers if the party gains power. This custom was reinforced by a party rule in 1981, which states that all 18 members of the shadow cabinet will be given cabinet positions if the party wins the next election. When the party is in power, a liaison committee links the government and other Labour MPs, who thus have the opportunity to influence the policies of the government. Groups of Labour MPs based on territory and subject matter have also been formed for that purpose.

PARTY LEADERSHIP

In all the parties the parliamentary leader has until recently been regarded as leader of the whole party. Unlike the formal process of demo-cratic decision making in the SLD and Labour Parties, the Conservative Party leader is responsible for deciding party policy and for the choice of the shadow cabinet, or consultative committee, when the party is in opposition. The leader controls the party headquarters and appoints the chief officials, who are responsible to him or her. The leader must retain both the allegiance of the Conservative back benchers and the support of the party in the country, and, above all, not split the party.

Paradoxically, the Labour Party has been more loyal to its leaders than have the Conservatives, in spite of the latter's stress on unity and loyalty. In the twentieth century the Conservatives have had 12 leaders, 7 of whom were overthrown by a party revolt, while an eighth was almost overthrown twice. During the same period Labour had eight leaders, one of whom (MacDonald) left his party, and another (Lansbury) resigned because of disagreements with party policy. All the others died in office or resigned voluntarily. The current leader, Tony Blair, who reflects a moderate liberal position, was elected in July 1994 (see Feature 2.5).

Until 1976 the Liberal leader was also elected by the MPs of the party. In that year the Liberals established a new procedure by which the leader was chosen by an electoral college composed of about 20,000 delegates from the constituencies. The new SLD party elects its leader by ballot of all members.

POWER WITHIN THE PARTIES

A complex relationship exists among the different sections of the parties, in which no one element has complete power over the others, and in which each section has some, if unequal, influence on decision making in the party. Differences over policy and personnel exist between the central party organizations and the constituency associations, especially the activists in them; between the organizations in the country and the parliamentary party; and between the leadership of the party, especially when it is in power, and the MPs of the party (see Table 2.15).

Important as the party organizations are, the real power in the formulation of policy has remained with the parliamentary elements of

Table 2.15 POWER IN THE POLITICAL PARTIES, 1996

	Con.	Lab.	Lib.
Leader	John Major, makes policy, controls party HQ, chooses shadow cabinet, chooses cabinet, approves election manifesto	Tony Blair, chooses cabinet	Paddy Ashdown, shares making policy, controls party HQ, approves election manifesto
Parliamentary Party	Elects leader	Shares in election of leader, chooses shadow cabinet	Shares in policy making, approves manifesto
Party conference	—	Makes policy	Makes policy
Party HQ executive	—	Makes policy, approves manifesto, controls party organization	Makes policy, controls party organization
Constituency associations	The constituency associations in all the parties choose or help choose parliamentary candidates		
Individual members			Elect leader

the parties. The Liberal and Conservative parliamentary parties, from which comes the prime minister and governmental leaders, existed before the mass organizations in the country were created. The dominance of the Conservative parliamentarians over the rest of the party is understandable in view of the fact that between 1886 and 1996 the Conservatives were in power for 78 years and the party leaders were also prime ministers and cabinet ministers.

Although the Labour Party is different from the others in having begun as a mass organization, by the 1920s the Parliamentary Labour Party had become the strongest element and the body that chose the political leaders. This has been partly due to the fact that the parliamentary leaders have generally been strongly supported in the past by the trade union leaders, who for the most part held similar political opinions.

Activists of the party, at both the national and local level, have rarely been able to challenge the parliamentary leadership successfully. The political reality is that the national electoral decision and the parliamentary representatives, not the party as a whole, determine who is to be prime minister. The party organizations have been able to influence and sometimes limit the activity for the parliamentary leadership, but they rarely formulate policy.

Skillful manipulation by political and union officials controlled the agenda and the debates

---

Feature 2.5 Tony Blair, Labour Leader

Blair, 43 years old in 1996, is a modernizer, pledged to a left-of-center policy not an extreme one, and has successfully persuaded the party to eliminate the controversial Clause IV of the party's constitution, which called for "common ownership of the means of production, distribution, and exchange." Like the conservative leader John Major, Blair is a pragmatic politician, calling for a society based on fairness, family, and patriotism.

This would be one nation, in which a sense of community can be achieved only by overcoming class. It would be cohesive at home, and strong in Europe. The global economy means that Britain should have an active economy that encourages savings and public investment, especially in education.

of the annual conference, and tended to exalt the parliamentary part of the Labour Party over the mass movement. In recent years the Labour conference has asserted itself and changed the organization of the party. In 1979, when the left wing of the party controlled a majority, resolutions were approved for all Labour MPs to be automatically subject to a reselection process by their constituency parties in order to remain as candidates for the next election and for the NEC to take, after appropriate consultation, the final decision on the contents of the general election manifesto. The other party conferences have also tried to play a more significant role. Even in the Conservative Party, the leader since 1966 has attended the whole conference rather than simply being present to speak at the end.

The constituency parties on a number of occasions have attempted, sometimes successfully, not to renominate MPs who differ politically from the activists controlling the local organization. Selection of candidates is now in the hands of the local organizations. Though the central offices keep a list of nationally approved candidates and can veto an undesirable local choice, they cannot force the local organization to accept a candidate, and only very rarely have they exercised a veto even when it involved an individual who had rebelled against party policy or leadership.

The internal struggle for power within the parties continues. This has recently been shown in a number of ways. All the parties have made the choice of the party leader open to wider participation: the Conservatives by election by the MPs; the Liberals by bringing the whole membership of the party into the process; and Labour by establishing an electoral college in which the trade unions and other affiliated organizations, the PLP, and the constituency parties would each have one-third of the vote. Within the Labour Party, the extreme left—Militant Tendency—has challenged the policies of the leadership, and ethnic minorities have demanded separate black sections.

INTEREST GROUPS

Interest groups have long existed in British politics and now play a significant role. They are usually differentiated from parties in that they do not hold or seek political office, though some groups sponsor parliamentary candidates. Interest group leaders now participate in consultative or even administrative functions and serve on government committees and advisory boards. In certain matters, they may even have a veto on government decisions.

There are numerous interest groups concerned with all aspects of life. For analytical purposes, a frequently used distinction is between sectional interest and promotional groups. Sectional interest groups defend and promote the interests of their members, whether individuals or enterprises. They include organizations concerned with the economic interests of labor, business, and agriculture, with social affairs such as automobile organizations, or with living arrangements such as tenants' groups. Promotional groups are concerned with a particular general cause, principle, or policy issue. They advocate a specific conception of the public interest. Examples of such groups are the Howard League for Penal Reform, the National Society for the Prevention of Cruelty to Children, and the Royal Society for the Prevention of Accidents. Recent years have seen the rise of a number of protest movements, of which the most vocal has been the Campaign for Nuclear Disarmament, and groups concerned with welfare and environmental issues, such as Greenpeace with nearly half a million supporters, and Friends of the Earth, which has a quarter million members. The most significant interest groups affecting the working of the political system are the business organizations and the trade unions.

Business

There are hundreds of business organizations concerned with a number of functions: providing common services, exchanging information, regulating trade practices, negotiating with trade unions on wages and conditions of work, and representing the business position to the government.

Most employers' groups are organized on an industry rather than the product basis. Some are local or deal with a part of or the whole of an industry. There are about 150 national employers' organizations, most of which belong to the Confederation of British Industry (CBI), formed in 1965 of a number of industrial groups. The CBI is the central body representing national business and industry. It acts as an advisory and consultative body for its members and presents their views publicly. Its representatives sit on many official bodies and advisory groups. The CBI has been called the voice of British business, but this is only partly true because of the widely varied interests of industrial and commercial organizations.

The CBI has had little consistent direct influence over government policy as a whole, though it has had an impact on some industrial and business issues. On the other hand, the important financial institutions—usually referred to as the City—have been politically important.

This importance results from two factors. First, the City is still the world's most significant financial and credit center, including the Bank of England and the central offices of many British banks, the largest number of foreign banks, the stock exchange, the largest gold market and international insurance markets, and international commodity markets. Second, many public issues have been connected with regulation of money, credit, price levels, and currency relationships and balance of payments, all of which need the expertise of the City. The leading persons in the City are usually closely connected with the Conservative Party in the same way that union leaders are with the Labour Party.

Trade Unions

Trade unions began with the Industrial Revolution, but not until the mid-nineteenth century did unions of skilled and semiskilled workers become well organized in their demands for higher wages and better working conditions. In the latter part of the century, unions of unskilled workers that pursued a more active industrial policy were formed. The attacks on the unions by court decisions led to the establishment of a political lobby, the Trades Union Congress (TUC), and later to the Labour Party.

The TUC is a loose confederation which does not direct individual unions and has little power over them, but acts on behalf of the whole union movement to achieve objectives that would be difficult for separate unions to obtain.

Since World War II, the TUC has sat on countless governmental committees, advisory bodies on economic issues, agricultural marketing boards, and consumer councils, and has given its views on questions of general economic and social policy. The leaders of the TUC have become members of numerous QUANGOs (Quasi Autonomous Non-Governmental Organizations).

The unions have been linked with the Labour Party since their decision to establish a pressure group in Parliament. The unions still provide the bulk of party membership and financing. Of the 67 unions in the TUC in 1996, 27 are affiliated with the party. About 60 percent of the members of these affiliated unions have paid the political levy which automatically makes them party members, though many do not realize they are doing so. They represent about 4 million members, or over 95 percent of the total party. The large manual and industrial unions form the basis of Labour's main union strength. They supply not only most of the annual funds of the party but also the extra money needed for campaigns. The unions constitute one-third of the electoral college which chooses the leader and deputy leader of the party. The unions also sponsor parliamentary candidates.

But the alliance between the unions and the party has been an uneasy one. There was considerable cooperation between 1945 and 1951, when there was a voluntary restraint on wage demands, largely because of the close personal relations between the government and union leaders. Again, under the Labour government of 1964–1970, the unions generally supported the government, including its income policy, until 1969, when an attempt was made to introduce legislative controls over unions. Similarly, in the Labour government of 1974–1979, the unions abided by the social contract and restraint in wage increases, until 1978–1979, when they defied the government's income policy that sought to limit wage increases to 5 percent per year.

The significant influence of the unions on policy—especially in 1974, when a series of strikes led the Conservative government to call an election which resulted in its defeat—brought calls for limits on their power; the Conservatives after their return to power in 1979 imposed such limits. The most important of these are ending the legal case for the closed shop; allowing employers the right not to recognize unions; union contributions to political parties have to be approved by secret vote of members; forbidding political strikes; forbidding mass picketing; strikes must be approved and union leaders must be elected by secret ballot. Working days lost through strikes have been substantially reduced. So has the membership of unions which dropped from 13.3 million in 1979 to 9 million in 1992. The power of unions in relation to government and to employers has greatly declined.[10]

Tactics of Interest Groups

Interest groups have used a variety of different techniques to influence decision making:

1. An occasional method is to organize a public campaign or demonstration. This was done in the 1950s by the Campaign for Nuclear Disarmament and the movement to abolish capital punishment. Most groups see this as neither desirable nor effective.

2. Groups are more likely to try to influence the government and civil service. They keep in contact with the administration in those departments concerned with their problems. This enables them to provide information and advice, try to affect policy planning, and be consulted on the implementation of policy. This interaction with government takes place on several levels:

a. Governments need the advice and information of expert groups. Car manufacturers will be consulted on safety regulations for vehicles. Those groups with special authority or reputation, such as the Howard League, are likely to be heard when they wish.

b. Policy may be decided in collaboration between government and interest groups. The annual farm price review results from bargaining between officials of the Agriculture Department and the National Farmers' Union (NFU). The latter decides what share of government support will go to specific types of farmers and regions. A close relationship, more like a partnership than merely one of consultation, exists between the NFU and the government.

c. The administration of policy may be dependent on cooperation of groups. For example, the National Health Service relies on the various branches of the medical profession. Administration may even be delegated to groups. The University Grants Committee, composed of university administrators, is to a large degree entrusted with the organization and financing of higher education. At the local government level the National Society for the Prevention of Cruelty to Children and the Women's Volunteer Service help implement welfare policy.

d. Groups participate in countless advisory committees or councils which make recommendations to ministers and officials. The bodies may be permanent or ad hoc organizations. Most are national bodies, but some are regional (economic planning councils) and local (national insurance advisory councils).

3. Groups seek to persuade MPs or try to have them act on their behalf. Groups other than the unions, such as the veterans' organization and the farmers after World War I, sponsored parliamentary candidates, but this is now rare. But MPs, who sometimes accept an honorarium from a group, speak at party meetings, introduce bills, or move amendments to other bills on behalf of groups. A number of junior ministers in the Conservative government of 1994 were obliged to resign for taking payments in return for asking questions in the House of Commons on behalf of a store owner.

4. A serious moral problem has arisen in recent years with the revelation that about one-third of back benchers hold paid outside consultancies and about three-quarters have some financial relationships with outside bodies connected to their work as MPs. A committee in 1995 recommended that payments from lobbyists be ended, though not from other businesses and associations.

In Britain, with the government's considerable intervention in and expenditure on economic and social affairs stemming from the welfare state and the mixed economy, the role of groups whose information and participation in the policy-making process is essential has increased. This greater role has led some analysts to argue that decisions are taken on the basis of cooperation among politicians, officials, and leaders of the interest groups, and that the functional representation of corporate interests is more significant than the representation of voters. Some even suggest that business organizations and trade unions in practice have been able to exercise a veto over public policy. Yet, in spite of the tripartite interaction and the strong influence of groups in executive actions, the role of government and the executive remains central in British politics.

THE EXECUTIVE

Over a century ago, Bagehot in *The English Government* distinguished between the dignified and efficient parts of the political system. Some

Queen Elizabeth II, who ascended the throne in 1952, at one of the ceremonial functions she performs as head of state.

institutions, such as the monarchy, were important for symbolic reasons, while others exercised real power.

The British executive can still be viewed in the same fashion. The head of the state is the monarch, who reigns but has virtually no political power and only limited influence. The real political power is centered in the prime minister and the cabinet, with the civil service assisting and influencing the exercise and administration of that power. The British system has been based on the existence or possibility of strong, effective government. Over the last three centuries, the executive power of the king was first restrained by Parliament and then transferred to ministers.

THE MONARCHY

The present monarch, Queen Elizabeth II, can trace her descent back to at least the ninth century. The powers formerly exercised by the monarch are now in the hands of various individuals and institutions. By a series of arrangements beginning in 1760, the monarchy turned over to the government the hereditary revenues derived from the Crown Lands and other sources and has received in return an annual grant (Civil List) to cover the salaries and expenses of the royal household.

The functions of government are now exercised by political ministers who are collectively and individually responsible to Parliament, but the monarch still participates in a formal way in some executive and legislative activities. The monarchy survived in Britain because the sovereign became a constitutional monarch, neither exercising the wide powers of the crown nor being responsible for their exercise. According to constitutional procedure, the sovereign always ultimately accepts the will of the government, although the monarch may make known his or her opinion and can attempt to influence the decision made.

The most important single political power of the sovereign is the choice of a prime minister. When there is a clearly recognized leader of a party that is able to control a majority in the House of Commons, the choice of the individual is obvious and immediate. But where one or both of these conditions are not present, a real choice may exist for the sovereign. Referring to the monarchy, it used to be said that "we must not let daylight in upon magic," but in this television age, the royal family has been more exposed to the public eye.

The monarch today still has a symbolic and ceremonial role to play in the system, but the monarchy has been divested of its former political power, though legally it still has the power to dissolve Parliament.

THE GOVERNMENT

The real power is exercised by the government, composed of the political ministers and junior ministers, of whom the most politically important are the prime minister and the cabinet (see Feature 2.6).

The government consists of about 100 members, all nominated by the prime minister and appointed by the monarch. It essentially consists of holders of administrative posts of a political character and the whips of the government party. It never meets as a whole to discuss policy or to take action. There is no fixed number of departments. These are established to deal with issues or to meet changing conditions or political and social crises. In the postwar period the number of major departments has been reduced and almost all of them are now in the present cabinet, usually 20 to 25.

Concessions to nationalist sentiment have been made by the transfer of certain social services in Scotland to the Scottish Departments and the consequent strengthening of Scottish administration in the 1950s, and by the establishment in the cabinet of the Welsh Office, which was given responsibility for many functions in 1964.

Ministers are individually responsible to Parliament for the work of their departments. They introduce legislative proposals, press the concerns of their department, and argue its case and requests for money in cabinet and interdepartmental committees. They discuss departmental issues with interest groups and others affected by or interested in those issues and speak in defense of the department in Parliament. It is their task to see that decisions and policies are correctly implemented by the civil servants in the department.

THE CABINET

The most significant members of the government constitute the cabinet, those ministers who are chosen by the prime minister to attend cabinet meetings and are made privy councillors. The cabinet has replaced the privy council as the chief source of executive power since the eighteenth century, but the latter still exists as an executive organ, largely giving formal effect to policy decisions made by the cabinet and making orders-in-council. A significant heritage from the past is the Judicial Committee of the Privy Council, which is the final court of appeal on certain legal issues arising in the colonies and in those independent countries of the Commonwealth that have decided to retain the arrangement.

The cabinet, which is not a legal body, is based on political understandings or conventions. Its members are normally the leading figures of the party controlling a majority in the House of Commons. The cabinet is the chief single body concerned with the initiation, control, and implementation of political policy and the most important decision-making body. It initiates most legislation and controls the legislative process. It is responsible for the coordination of governmental activity; all ministers must implement cabinet decisions insofar as their departments are affected.

For politicians, the cabinet is the top of the political ladder, except for the position of prime minister. It constitutes the core of the British political elite. A number of conventions underlie the existence and operation of cabinet government:

1. The cabinet is ultimately dependent on the support of the House of Commons which has come into existence as a result of the general election. A government that is defeated on a major issue or on a vote of censure or no confidence is expected to resign or to ask for a dissolution of Parliament. A government whose party has been clearly defeated at a general election will resign immediately.

2. Unlike the American cabinet, the members of which are drawn from a wide variety of sources and backgrounds, the British cabinet is

drawn, with rare exceptions, from members of the two Houses of Parliament. This fusion of executive and legislative functions in the hands of the same people is a striking denial of the concept of the separation of powers. This convention also means that the members of the cabinet are selected from a relatively small pool of available people. Moreover, in recent years most of the members of both Labour and Conservative cabinets have come from the shadow cabinets of the two parties.

3. Except in wartime or in a serious political or economic crisis, the entire cabinet will be members of the same political party if that party can control a majority in the Commons. In this way, political coherence and unity can be obtained. Britain is the only country in Western Europe that has not had a coalition government in the postwar period.

4. The monarch is excluded from the discussions of the cabinet, though he or she is kept informed of its conclusions by the prime minister, who is the acknowledged head of the cabinet. The advice offered by the cabinet, even on personal issues (as in 1936 on the marital plans of King Edward VIII, who was eventually obliged to abdicate), must be accepted by the monarch or a constitutional crisis will result.

5. All members take the oath of privy councillors and are bound to secrecy by this and the

---

Feature 2.6   Some Key Terms in British Politics

Backbencher—members of the House of Commons (MPs) who are not members of the government or leaders of the opposition; they sit on the back benches of the chamber

Cabinet—the most senior ministers in the government, usually about 20

Constituency—the geographical area, now 651, represented by an MP

Dissolution—the ending of the life of the House of Commons by royal proclamation on the advice of the prime minister (PM)

Government—the ministers, usually about 100, who form the political executive; most are in the House of Commons (HoC)

Great Britain—the countries of England, Scotland, and Wales

Hansard—the daily official report of the proceedings in Parliament

Law Lords (Lords of Appeal in Ordinary)—senior judges appointed to the House of Lords to hear appeals in civil and criminal cases

Money bill—legislation on spending and taxation introduced in HoC; it becomes law within one month

Opposition—second party in HoC with an officially paid leader and a "shadow cabinet"

Prime minister—head of the government and the cabinet (PM)

Public bill—proposed legislation on public policy, which affects everyone

Question time—one hour four times a week when ministers answer questions in HoC

Speaker—presiding officer of the HoC

10 Downing Street—home of the PM

United Kingdom—the countries of Great Britain and Northern Ireland

Usual channels—consultations between whips of different parties on parlimentary business

Whips—MPs who provide information to and from their party members and leaders and who discipline their party in HoC

Whitehall—term used for civil service and administration

Official Secrets Act. There is now a 30-year limitation on the publication of cabinet documents, and secrecy is generally preserved.

6. The members of the cabinet are collectively responsible for all decisions and actions, as well as individually responsible for the performance of the particular department or unit each may head. There is free and frank discussion of issues in the cabinet.

Members may and do disagree about the desirability of a policy, but they must support and implement policy decisions once they have been made. The British system is based on the premise that a government that is publicly divided on a given subject cannot govern.

The principle of collective responsibility means that all ministers must support and defend government policy and not speak or act against it. The principle applies now not only to cabinet ministers but also to all members of the government. If ministers continue to oppose or cannot accept a decision made on an important issue, the principle suggests that they should resign. Since 1945 there have been only 12 important resignations over policy issues, mostly over financial and economic matters. But the resignation in October 1990 of Sir Geoffrey Howe, a prominent cabinet minister, in protest against the prime minister's policies, led to the downfall of Mrs. Thatcher herself three weeks later. In recent years cabinets have sometimes remained divided, but without resignations. In addition, the development of the system of cabinet committees and the dominant role of the prime minister has meant that cabinet members tend to feel less personally committed to every decision.

Collective responsibility also implies that an attack on a minister in regard to important policy, as distinct from criticism of the administration of that minister's department, will be taken as an attack on the whole government unless it disclaims responsibility. If the latter is the case, strong criticism of a minister may lead to resignation, but not to a vote on the government as a whole.

This concept of collective responsibility and decision making is to be distinguished from the principle of ministerial responsibility, which means that individual ministers are responsible for all the work and actions of the government departments that they head. Though it is most improbable that ministers will be familiar with all

the work of the department, they must respond to parliamentary criticism of or inquiry about it.

Theoretically, if parliamentary criticism of a department or of a minister's performance or neglect of duties or competence is sufficiently great, the minister is obliged to resign. Resignation has also resulted from ministerial indiscretion, either inadvertent or more blatant, as in sexual escapades, improper behavior, or the use of indiscreet language. But there are many more examples of ministers not resigning in spite of considerable parliamentary criticism of their activity. Over the last century, there have been only about 25 resignations on the principle of ministerial responsibility. Since 1945, 4 have resigned because of personal scandals, 5 because of conduct in office, and 13 because of principle or policy.

Cabinet Membership

The number and members of the cabinet depend on the prime minister, whose decisions result partly from the administrative needs and governmental functions to be performed and partly from political necessity to accommodate the ambitions of colleagues, to have different ideological sections of the party and territorial parts of the country represented, and to include some individuals loyal to himself or herself. The cabinet, which realistically contains the political rivals and possible successors of the prime minister, is thus the result of administrative, political, and personal factors.

Except during the two world wars, when the size of the cabinet was reduced to 8 or 9, it has numbered between 18 and 23 ministers. Usually, the important departments will be included in the cabinet, though no one becomes a member simply because of his or her office. The minister of a department has been included in one cabinet but excluded from the next, depending on the priority given it by the different cabinets or on the political weight of the minister.

Although members of the cabinet are drawn from both Houses, certain ministers, especially those with financial responsibilities, will almost always be chosen from the Commons. Only occasionally will someone outside Parliament be appointed. The average tenure of a departmental office between 1964 and 1991 was under 2 1/2 years. Ministers are not experts and rarely have executive experience, as they have spent much of their lives in politics.

In reality, the choice of the prime minister is constrained by the existence of the shadow cabinet, the group of opposition party leaders who criticize the government and formulate alternative proposals. Though there is no compulsion, prime ministers in recent years have appointed most of the members of the shadow cabinet to the cabinet itself. In 1979, for example, 17 of the 21-member shadow cabinet became members of the 22-member Conservative cabinet. In 1974, Prime Minister Wilson appointed all 12 members of the Labour shadow cabinet to his cabinet. This is now mandatory in the Labour Party.

Procedure in the Cabinet

Cabinet meetings are called by the prime minister, usually once or twice a week. Members ask the cabinet secretariat to put items on the agenda and receive copies of it before each meeting. They are thus able to study the issues and to attend meetings with an informed opinion on them. Ministers who are not cabinet members are normally invited to attend when a subject affecting their department is on the agenda.

It has usually been assumed that the cabinet does not vote on issues, but that discussion takes place until a collective decision is reached when the prime minister sums up "the sense of the meeting." But some cabinet ministers have stated that voting did sometimes take place on substantive as well as procedural matters.

There are two other qualifications of the principle of collective decision making by the cabinet. First, in reality members do not always participate in discussion, especially as the range of subjects has increased. This is largely the result of the heavy burden of duties imposed on cabinet members, which includes the reading of official papers, attending and speaking in Parliament, supervising the work of their departments and giving directions to officials, attending official functions, maintaining contact with their parliamentary constituencies, and undertaking a round of speeches throughout the country, as well as attending cabinet meetings. Ministers tend to fight in cabinet for their departmental policies and budgets.

Second, not all issues are fully discussed by the cabinet as a whole. Various devices are used to reduce the burden on it. Decisions made by individual ministers have sometimes been accepted by the whole body. Agreement on issues has been reached by interdepartmental ministerial meetings or in private meetings between ministers, including the prime minister. Above all, cabinet committees, consisting of a small number of cabinet members, and occasionally nonmembers, have been established to relieve the burden on the cabinet as a whole and to speed up decision making now that there has been a great increase in governmental activity. Sometimes the real decisions are made by a small committee rather than by the cabinet as a whole. In crisis or wartime, a small cabinet of five or six members is usually set up to make major decisions. This was done during the 1990–1991 Gulf crisis and war.

The number and membership of cabinet committees were kept secret until 1992. There are about 25 standing and 130 ad hoc committees set up to discuss specific subjects or problems. Often the committee decision is allowed to stand, and thus the agenda of the cabinet as a whole can be reduced. The membership of the committees is usually paralleled by similar committees of civil servants.

THE PRIME MINISTER

The prime minister is the acknowledged head of the executive. Unlike the U.S. presidency, the office of the prime minister is largely based on conventions. Despite the office now being over 250 years old, there are still few statutes referring to it or to the functions to be performed. The prime minister was once regarded as *primus inter pares* (first among equals) in the cabinet, but this is an inadequate description for an individual who is preeminent in it and is the dominant political personality.

As already mentioned, legally the prime minister is chosen by the monarch, who selects the person capable of forming a government. The choice is obvious if one political party possesses or controls an absolute majority of seats in the House of Commons and if that party has an acknowledged leader. This was the case with the appointment of Harold Wilson in October

Table 2.16 THE RISE OF JOHN MAJOR (1943–)

1959	Left grammar school without diploma; worked as clerk and laborer
1965–79	Worked in a bank
1968–71	Conservative local councillor in London
1979	Elected MP at third attempt
1981–83	Parliamentary private secretary to ministers in Home Office
1983–85	Assistant to Conservative whip in House of Commons
1985	Junior minister in Ministry of Health
1986	Minister of state for Social Security and the Disabled
1987	Chief secretary to the Treasury
1989, July	Foreign Minister
1989, Oct.	Chancellor of the Exchequer
1990, Nov.	Elected party leader, and immediately became Prime Minister, the youngest in the twentieth century
1992, April	Led the Conservative Party to election victory
1995	Reelected party leader

1974 and Margaret Thatcher, the first woman to become prime minister, in 1979.

But there are other occasions when the monarch has a real choice between individuals. If the prime minister dies or resigns, the choice of a successor is not always obvious. The monarch had to choose between rival candidates in 1957 and 1963. If no party has an absolute majority in the Commons, as in February 1974, the monarch might have a choice between the leaders of the different parties. In those situations the monarch will not act without directly or indirectly consulting a number of political leaders.

A convention of the twentieth century has limited the monarch's choice to members of the House of Commons. Since 1923, when Baldwin rather than Lord Curzon was appointed, all prime ministers have been members of the lower chamber. When Lord Home was appointed in 1963, he immediately disclaimed his title, left the House of Lords, and won a seat in the Commons. This convention illustrates the predominance of the Commons over the Lords, the fact that governments can be defeated and forced to resign by vote of the Commons but not by the Lords, and the reality that the Labour Party is stronger in the lower than in the upper House.

Prime ministers differ in personality, energy, political interests, and administrative abil-

ities, but all are seasoned politicians with experience in Parliament and in the cabinet. All prime ministers have had considerable apprenticeships in Parliament before appointment. In the twentieth century as a whole, as in the postwar period, the prime minister's average tenure as an MP has been 28 years. Most of them have held a number of other cabinet positions. The average tenure in this century has been three different posts and eight years in the cabinet. Mrs. Thatcher had only one previous post and four years in cabinet, and John Major had only one year in a senior cabinet post before becoming prime minister.

In the twentieth century there have been 19 prime ministers. They have differed in social background: five came from the aristocracy, seven from the middle class, six from the lower middle class, and one from the working class. All the aristocrats and five of the seven middle-class prime ministers went to a public school, five of them went to Eton and two to Harrow. Twelve attended university at Oxford or Cambridge. It is distinctive that the last five, including Margaret Thatcher and John Major (see Table 2.16), came from the lower middle class, attended state (nonpublic) schools, and can be regarded as examples of the principle of meritocracy. John Major, like James Callaghan, Labour PM (1976–1979), is unusual in never having gone to a university.

Functions

The prime minister chooses and can dismiss members of the government. But, unlike the U.S. president, the prime minister's range of choice is restricted; rarely does he or she choose someone from outside Parliament and even more rarely from outside the government party. Many choices will be obvious because the leading members of the successful party, especially many of those who have been in the shadow cabinet, will be appointed; the most important of them may even be consulted by the prime minister in choosing the others. The prime minister must keep the confidence of senior colleagues. He or she can dismiss or demand the resignation of ministers, but may not always be able to get rid of those who have some independent political strength in the party or country.

The prime minister decides the size and composition of the cabinet. He or she forms a cabinet that is satisfactory from both a political and an administrative point of view. Thus, prime ministers will usually include not only people who reflect different elements or political opinions in the party but also some on whose loyalty they can rely or whose counsel they value.

The prime minister also establishes and appoints the members of cabinet committees. He or she sets up task forces, working parties, and ad hoc meetings as may seem necessary to deal with issues.

The prime minister calls cabinet meetings, takes the chair, determines the items of business, and controls the agenda, as well as also chairing some cabinet committees. In the task of summing up the sense of the meeting, the prime minister is allowed to interpret to some extent the decision reached. He or she is also the ultimate decider and spokesperson of cabinet policy, controlling the flow of information about the government.

The prime minister reports the conclusions of the cabinet and is the chief channel of political communication to the monarch. By convention, no minister can see the monarch without first informing the prime minister. Many of the prerogatives of the Crown, such as declarations of war and peace and dissolution of Parliament, are, in fact, exercised by the prime minister.

The prime minister acts as an arbiter and tries to resolve disputes between departments.

The degree of interest the prime minister today has in any particular department varies, but traditionally he or she is always in close touch with the Foreign Office.

The prime minister dispenses considerable patronage and has a power of appointment that includes not only the members of the government but also the senior members of the civil service, the chief members of the judiciary, military leaders, and the archbishops of the Church of England. Twice yearly an official Honors List bestows some title or honor on individuals chosen by the prime minister for some contribution to public life.

The prime minister controls the major appointments in the civil service, especially those of the permanent secretary to the Treasury and the secretary of the cabinet, who is the prime minister's chief adviser on problems concerning the machinery of government.

The prime minister is also the leader of his or her party within Parliament and in the country. In Parliament he or she answers questions twice a week in the House of Commons and speaks on important occasions and in debates.

The prime minister's task is to keep the party as united as possible; and his or her political survival depends on it. When the prime minister loses control of the party, as did Chamberlain in 1940, Eden in 1956–1957, and Thatcher in 1990, he or she is obliged to resign. But normally the prime minister can expect loyalty from his or her party, and he or she is aided in the maintenance of discipline by the whips, who since 1964 are paid and are regarded as part of the government team. Mrs. Thatcher served as prime minister for 11 years, the longest consecutive term in the twentieth century. In 1995 a deputy prime minister was appointed and given special duties in the cabinet. The title, however, does not imply a right to succeed the prime minister.

Is the Prime Minister a Quasi President?

There is universal agreement that the prime minister is the most important political figure in Britain. This has led some to regard the office as similar in the extent and degree of its power to that of the U.S. president. Some argue that the country is governed by the prime minister, who leads, coordinates, and maintains a series of ministers who are advised and supported by the civil service. Richard Crossman, himself a former cabinet minister, thought that prime ministerial government had replaced cabinet government as a result of the increased role of political parties, the influence of the cabinet secretariat, which is close to the prime minister, the control of the prime minister over major civil service appointments in the departments, and the influence of the mass media and television in particular, which normally focus attention on the leader.[11] In addition, the prime minister has more time for thinking about general policy issues or current problems than do the ministers at the head of particular departments who are responsible for a heavy administrative load.

Certainly it is true that the prime minister has sometimes taken the initiative in foreign affairs and in emergencies and has been personally responsible for political decisions, of which in recent years the Falklands war in 1982 to resist the seizure by Argentina of the Falkland Islands administered by Britain and the poll tax were the most striking.[12] In addition, until recently, the cabinet did not discuss the annual budget and was only informed about it a few days before the budget was introduced in the House of Commons. However, there are examples of the prime minister's views not prevailing in cabinet.

Although the powers of the prime minister are strong, they are qualified in certain respects:

The prime minister can retain power only as long as he or she retains control over the party, and over both the cabinet and Parliament. Unlike the U.S. president, he or she does not have a fixed term of office.

The range of the prime minister's choice of cabinet is very limited compared with that of the U.S. president; moreover, he or she is always aware of potential successors in the cabinet.

The prime minister relies more than the U.S. president on collective decision making. While he was prime minister, Harold Wilson thought the cabinet was supreme as the decision-making body. The relationship between the prime minister and the cabinet changes with the individuals and issues involved. Mrs. Thatcher often appeared to act in an authoritarian way. By contrast, John Major is a more tactful and less abra-

sive person who is also less charismatic. But the place of the cabinet remains central in policy making, and the prime minister cannot really be regarded as a presidential figure.

THE CIVIL SERVICE

The British civil service has long been admired for its competence, political impartiality, and dedication, and only in recent years have mounting criticisms led to structural changes in its organization. In the nineteenth century, the civil service was based on patronage and was sometimes corrupt and inefficient. The modern civil service is based on the 1854 Northcote-Trevelyan report, most of whose recommendations were implemented. The civil service became a single organization instead of a series of separate departmental staffs. Entry into the service was based on open competition, not on patronage. The successful candidate entered the service, rather than a particular department, and could be transferred from one department to another. All examinations were conducted by the Civil Service Commission, not the individual departments, and corresponded to both the level and academic content of those taken in the educational system at the same age of applicants. The exams were always general rather than specific.

The civil service is organized into departments according to subject matter. Almost all departments have their headquarters in London in or near Whitehall, and branch offices throughout the country. The civil service, based on the distinction between intellectual and routine work, was divided into three servicewide classes: administrative, executive, and clerical. Outside these classifications were the professional, scientific, and technical officials, as well as the manual and manipulative workers, mostly in the postal and telegraph systems.

Criticism of various aspects of civil service organization and behavior mounted in the 1960s, based largely on the elitist nature of the senior civil service, their limited experience, their lack of initiative, the lack of scientists in top administrative positions, narrowness of outlook, and poor methods of training. As a result, the Fulton Committee on the civil service was established. Reporting in 1968, the committee was critical of the civil service's stress on the gifted amateur and generalist who was expected to be able to deal with any subject matter. It was also critical of the division of the civil service into general classes, the inferior status of scientists, the relative lack of specialized experts, and the frequent movement of senior civil servants between departments.

Only some of the changes recommended were introduced. A Civil Service Department was established, taking over the management of the service from the Treasury Department. A Civil Service College was set up to give courses in management techniques to new entrants. The three-class organization was ended, and part of the service was restructured along classless, unified lines. In the currently reduced (562,000 by 1990) civil service, the largest unit is the administrative group, composed of the former three classes. An important change was a new grade, administrative trainee, made to strengthen middle management. The Civil Service Department was abolished by Mrs. Thatcher in 1981, but the prime minister remains in charge of the machinery of government. In 1988, she proposed a plan for semiautonomous agencies to manage services now administered by departments. By 1991, 50 such agencies had been set up, employing 200,000 civil servants. The general idea behind these agencies is to introduce a more entrepreneurial and competitive spirit into administration. Besides the executive agencies a large number of QUANGOs have been set up, run by noncivil servants appointed by a minister (see Feature 2.7).

A constant cause of criticism of the senior civil service—the 3,000 top positions in the home and foreign service—has been that its members come largely from the middle and upper class, with less than 5 percent coming from the working class, and that a high proportion of those in the elite group, the former administrative class, was educated at the public schools and at Oxford and Cambridge. About three-quarters of top officials come from "Oxbridge" and about half from the public schools. The proportions are even higher for entrants into the senior foreign civil service, of which about 10 percent were educated at Eton.

The Role of the Civil Service

The senior civil servants advise ministers on formulating policy and decision making. Their role is based on impartiality and anonymity. All governments, irrespective of political persuasion, have been served loyally by the nonpolitical civil servants.

The work of the civil service is anonymous because of the principle of ministerial responsibility; the minister alone is responsible to Parliament for the operation of his or her department, even though in practice the minister may not always be aware of what has been done. Civil servants are free to give unbiased and frank advice to ministers without having to defend their views. On some occasions, however, the anonymity is shattered when civil servants appear before parliamentary committees to answer questions about their department's accounts or administrative procedures and occasionally to give evidence to a tribunal of inquiry.

Feature 2.7 *QUANGOS* (Quasi Autonomous Non-Governmental Organizations) or Non-Departmental Public Bodies

- About 4,800 QUANGOS in 1996, spending some $58 billion, one-fifth of public spending
- Responsible for administration (e.g. Audit Commission, Medical Research Council, Forest Commission) or advice (e.g. Parole Board, Consumers Panel, Political Honors Scouting Committee)
- Mostly appointed by ministers; many businessmen are appointed
- Decentralize administration and bring in non–civil servants
- Not directly accountable to those who use public services

The obverse of anonymity has been the secrecy behind the making of decisions, both in form and content. The shielding of the civil service from the glare of partisan politics has also meant that it is restricted in its political activities. No member of the senior administrative group, above the clerical staff, can participate in national political activity; a member can take part in local politics only with departmental permission.

The determination of policy is the responsibility of ministers; the task of the civil service is to carry out that policy with energy and goodwill. The minister is a politician, not an expert on the issues of his or her department, and he or she must decide policy not only on its own merits, but in light of the government program as a whole and of what is politically rather than administratively possible at a certain point.

But the reality of ministerial–civil service relations is often different from the theory. Departmental policy may often result from past administrative experience and the cumulative decisions made by the civil servants while dealing with individual cases. Moreover, civil servants do not merely implement policy; they also play a role in policy making, advising on options for new policies. The long experience and great knowledge of the senior administrators may often lead them to take the initiative in suggesting new policies. Ministers are not experts in the affairs of their departments and have time to pay attention to only a relatively small number of those affairs.

Ministers may often accept the advice or acquiesce in the views of their civil servants. The role of the civil service has grown with the vast increase in government business, owing to the expanded activity of government in internal affairs; the time pressures on ministers; the influence of the cabinet secretariat; the growth of interdepartmental committees, which tend to settle problems at an early stage; and the creation of high-level civil service committees to parallel and give advice to cabinet committees.

But influential as the civil service may be, ministers are not its puppets, nor are civil servants "statesmen in disguise." Senior civil servants are mostly concerned with the administration of existing policies rather than policy planning, with immediate needs rather than long-term policy. The interaction between ministers and senior civil servants is complex, but the political ministers are still the dominant element in the policy-making process.

THE LEGISLATURE

Parliament—or strictly speaking the Queen-in-Parliament, since the monarch must assent to all legislation—is the supreme legislative body. It has the authority to pass, change, or repeal any law without being subject to restraint or veto by the courts of law or any other body; on the contrary, Parliament can reverse the decisions of the courts. No issues are outside the control of Parliament. It can pass retrospective legislation that legalizes past illegalities and punishes actions that were lawful when performed. By the 1911 Parliament Act, the term of Parliament is fixed at five years, though it can be dissolved at any time. But Parliament is able to prolong its own life as it did during both world wars. One Parliament cannot bind its successors.

In fact, Parliament uses self-restraint in the exercise of this legal supremacy. It is conscious of the common law tradition and of political conventions that foster moderation. The effective power of Parliament is limited in real ways. Parliament rarely passes legislation which is contrary to the views of the population or deprives individuals of rights. The principle of the mandate suggests that the electorate has given general approval of changes proposed by the electoral manifesto of the successful party. Though this does not mean that the electorate has approved of all proposals in the manifesto, it implies that a major change will only rarely be introduced in Parliament if it was not included in the party manifesto, except in a time of emergency or crisis.

Parliamentary action is also affected and influenced by the major interest groups in the country, which by convention are always consulted on legislation related to them. In the 1960s and 1970s some regarded the trade unions as having a virtual veto power on proposals concerning industrial relations and incomes policy. Perhaps most important of all,

Parliament is dominated by the government, which, as the majority party, generally controls the time, procedure, and actions of Parliament and is responsible for the initiation of all financial and most legislative proposals.

In the 1970s a new factor, British membership in the European Community (EC), now the European Union (EU), affected parliamentary supremacy. Britain is now pledged to adhere to the rules and decisions of the Community, which signifies some qualification of Parliament's legal supremacy. The European Court of Justice ruled in 1990 that British courts could suspend a statute that was incompatible with law of the European Community. The Court ruled in 1991 that parts of a British law breached the law of the EC and therefore had to be changed. Parliamentary supremacy has also been limited by the 1950 European Convention on Human Rights, by which Britain accepted the obligation to recognize certain fundamental rights.

Composition of Parliament

The two chambers of Parliament now at Westminister have existed for seven centuries. Though for some time the House of Commons has been the more significant political body, the House of Lords had an unlimited veto power over legislation until 1911. In that year the Parliament Act limited the veto of the Lords to two years over bills passed by the Commons in three successive sessions and abolished the veto over financial bills. In 1949 this delaying power of the Lords was reduced to one year.

House of Lords

The House of Lords today consists of about 1,200 members. Its heterogeneous composition still reflects the nature of its origin with the greater noblemen and higher clergy. The main categories are the following:

1. Some 760 hereditary peers (since 1958 including women) who inherit or have been appointed to the peerage and who pass on the titles to their heirs; since the Peerage Act of 1963 they can disclaim their titles for their lifetime.

2. About 360 life peers created under the Life Peerage Act of 1958; their title expires at their death.

3. Twelve Lords of Appeal in Ordinary (law lords), who are appointed to act as judges when the House of Lords acts as a court of law; they must have been barristers for at least 15 years and have held high judicial office for at least 2 years.

4. Twenty-six senior dignitaries of the Church of England; they are the archbishops of Canterbury and York, the Bishops of London, Durham, and Winchester, and 21 other bishops in their order of seniority as bishops.

Although the House of Lords still has the function of considering and approving all legislation, its powers have been significantly limited by the Parliament Acts of 1911 and 1949. The Lords can propose amendments to bills and can delay them by voting against them, but they have no power of absolute veto. Since 1949, a bill passed by the Commons in two successive sessions does not need the consent of the House of Lords. In 1991 the War Crimes Bill became law in this way after having been voted down twice by the House of Lords in 1990 and 1991. The House of Lords has no power over finances. It can still reject, however, delegated legislation, which requires the approval of both Houses. By convention, it will not vote against the principles of a government bill if the bill was featured in the governing party's electoral manifesto. The Lords in 1991 did defeat parts of a government bill on life sentences for murder that was not in the 1987 Conservative manifesto.

Formerly a body consisting almost entirely of hereditary peers, relatively few of whom attended its sittings, the Lords since 1958 has included life peers (men and women), who are more likely to participate in its activity. Whereas the average daily attendance in 1955 was 92, there are now 300 who attend.

The Lords are unpaid; however, since 1957, attending members receive a daily allowance for expenses and lodging. Because of the experience in public affairs and the intellectual caliber of many of the new life peers—as well as the presence of past and present cabinet ministers, other public servants, and former

Table 2.17   THE POWERS AND LIMITS OF PARLIAMENT

Powers

Provides road to political success and to becoming a minister

Main forum for discussion of grievances of constituents

Approves legislation and policy thus giving them greater legitimacy; debates legislation and motions

Allows representation and expression of different views of citizens on policy

Asks questions of ministers

Recent Activities

Greater independence of MPs in voting in 1970s and 1980s; governments defeated in some standing committees, and in 1986 on a bill

Departmental select committees set up in 1979 in House of Commons to investigate administration and recommend policy; House televised since 1989

More attention paid to constituents

Some committees discuss issues of European Union

Limits

Power of executive

Increasing impact of interest groups outside of Parliament

Increasing burden of work

Little impact on decisions of European Union

MPs—debate on important topics in the House of Lords may often be on a high level.

On the whole, the House of Lords has exercised its functions with discretion. Only four bills—the 1949 Parliament Act, two statutes passed in 1914, and the 1991 War Crimes Act—have become law under the provisions of the 1911 Parliament Act. The subordination of the Lords to the Commons and to the executive has been accepted in general, but proposed legislation has sometimes been delayed.

It is this power of delay and the Conservative majority in the House of Lords that have been the main reasons for criticism. In a democratic system like the British, it seems paradoxical for a nonelected body to delay the legislation passed by the elected lower chamber and to claim it is acting in the best interests of the country. Because of the automatic Conservative plurality in the House of Lords, a Labour government has more to fear in this regard than a

Conservative one. Because of the unrepresentative nature of the House of Lords, the Labour Party is still theoretically pledged to its abolition.

The House of Lords still performs a useful role as an organ of review in the revision of legislation, the initiation of noncontroversial legislation, the discussion of important topics, and the examination of delegated legislation—which all save the time of the Commons. It performs an important judicial function as the final Court of Appeal and Court of Criminal Appeal. By convention, only the law lords and the lord chancellor attend these sittings of the House as a court.

House of Commons

There are now 651 members (MPs) of the House of Commons elected from the territorial constituencies of the country. The number and distribution of the seats can be altered according to population changes after recommendations by the four boundary commissions. Currently, 524 represent English, 38 Welsh, 72 Scottish, and 17 Northern Ireland constituencies. Members are elected at a general election or at a by-election on the death or resignation of an MP.

There are no property, religious, sex, or education disqualifications. Any person over 21 can be elected, except members of the House of Lords, aliens, clergy of the established churches and the Catholic Church, felons, and holders of most official positions other than members of the government. Since 1963, an MP who has succeeded to the peerage can disclaim his title and remain in the Commons. MPs are paid less and have inadequate facilities compared with U.S. congressional members. Only in recent years have they obtained some secretarial assistance and office space. They now receive a salary of about £33,000 and another £25,000 for secretarial costs. Nevertheless, there is no shortage of candidates for the Commons. People are attracted to it for nonmaterial rewards, including public service, personal prestige, and the opportunity to exert influence on public affairs.

The glory of Parliament may have dimmed somewhat in recent years, but the Commons still plays a significant role in the political system. Parliament not only possesses legislative supremacy and authorizes all expenditure and taxation; the Commons is politically important because its party composition is the basis for the formation of governments. It enables the leaders of one political party to rule and those of the opposition party to be considered as a possible alternative government. It is the major political arena in which there is continuous interaction among the parties. Ministers explain and defend their policies in it against the attacks of the opposition.

If it is not the real determinant of policy or decisions, Parliament wields influence over the executive which makes concessions to it. For its members, Parliament is a forum for the raising of complaints and grievances on behalf of their constituents, for arguing political views of their own, and for subjecting the executive to criticism. It is also the main path to political distinction and to membership in the government (see Table 2.17).

Who Becomes an MP?

The members of the different parliamentary parties have become similar from the standpoint of social background and career. MPs have become increasingly professional in their background and lifestyle and, therefore, less characteristic of their constituents. This is especially true in the Parliamentary Labour Party, where the proportion of manual workers has fallen and that of professionals has increased since 1945. The average age of the PLP has fallen; recruiting younger MPs generally means less opportunity for working-class candidates, who tend to emerge later in life.

The Conservative MPs illustrate the postwar shift away from landowners, farmers, and people with an aristocratic background to businesspeople and industrial technocrats. A considerable number have been local councillors. Conservative MPs have rarely had working-class backgrounds.

The number of women MPs in the postwar period has remained approximately the same: about 5 percent until 1987 and 8 percent in 1992. In 1992, a record number of 60 women were elected. Women have always been underrepresented in the Commons, which has been a male-dominated "club." Parliament is thus a more middle-class, better-educated group of people than the average citizen, and it contains a disproportionately greater ratio of males to females than the general population.

There has also been a trend for MPs to remain longer in Parliament and thus to be regarded as professional politicians. The House of Commons has always been attractive to people in the professions, who in many cases combine their careers as lawyers, journalists, or businesspeople with afternoon and evening attendance in the House.

MPs and Political Parties

About 80 of the 651 members of the House of Commons are in the 1992 government. All MPs are members of political parties, and the arrangements in the Commons reflect the fact that its working is interrelated with the party system and the operation of government.

The only exception to the partisan nature of MPs is the Speaker (with three deputies), who is the chief officer of the House of Commons. Unlike the U.S. counterpart, the British Speaker is an impartial, nonpartisan figure who gives up party associations. The general rule is that the Speaker, who is elected at the beginning of a Parliament, will be reelected in subsequent Parliaments irrespective of which party controls a majority. For the first time a woman was elected in 1992.

The chamber is small and rectangular. It is a political arena in which the opposing parties physically face each other, as shown in Figure 2.5. The Speaker sits at one end of the chamber. The benches to his or her right are used by the government party, while the official opposition party and other parties not supporting the government sit on his or her left. The members of the government and the shadow cabinet sit on the front benches, with their supporters behind them on the back benches. The physical separation reflects the political differences between the two sides.

The smallness of the chamber, which seats only 350 MPs, together with the fact that MPs speak from their places rather than from a rostrum, has led to a more intimate style of speech than is often the case in other countries. By tradition, MPs do not read speeches or speak boisterously. They refer to colleagues in a dignified and polite way.

With rare exceptions the MPs are organized in parliamentary parties. The Parliamentary

The Speaker of the House of Commons, Betty Boothroyd, who was elected to the position in 1992 after being a deputy Speaker for five years. She is the first woman to become Speaker and won in the first contested election for the position since 1951.

policies, get concessions on government bills, and defeat the government. By convention, governments resign or request dissolution of Parliament if defeated on a major question, though since 1867 only five governments have resigned for this reason. In 1979 the opposition successfully moved a vote of no confidence for the first time since 1892. In Parliament, the opposition is continually addressing itself to the electorate as a whole with its eyes on the next election.

The opposition also cooperates with the government party in formulating the business of the Commons. It chooses the subjects for debate on a number of occasions, currently on the 16 days available to it. It is given time at the committee stage of bills to move amendments and time in the House of Commons itself for both opposition leaders and backbenchers to question ministers. The government even provides the time for the opposition to move motions of censure against it. Since 1937 there has been an official, paid leader of the opposition who is consulted by the prime minister on political arrangements; by convention, the shadow cabinet receives information from cabinet ministers relevant to the conduct of affairs. There is consultation between the two sides on some questions concerning foreign affairs and defense.

The opposition is represented on standing and select committees in proportion to its membership in the Commons. An accepted rule is that the chairpersons of some committees are members of the opposition.

Labour Party (PLP) is composed of Labour members of both Houses. The major organ of the Conservative Party in Parliament is the 1922 Committee, composed of all Conservative backbenchers.

The Opposition

The official opposition, the largest nongovernmental party in Parliament, is a vital part of the British system. Its leaders are seen inside and outside Parliament, as an alternative government. Its function is both to subject government to criticism and to seek to replace it, as well as to participate in the working of the system.

The opposition acts as a responsible group in criticism of the government. It proposes alternative policies and tries to change government

How Important Is the MP?

Important though MPs are, their prominence has declined for several reasons: the extension of the suffrage, the organization of constituency associations and the rise of disciplined political parties; the increase in the function and activity of government and the growth in power of the bureaucracy; and the nature of modern general elections, which are to a large degree about which party leader will become prime minister.

MPs are aware that the electorate is the ultimate political sovereign and that their reelection depends on their activity in Parliament. Attendance is not compulsory, and no financial loss is attached to nonattendance, but it is rare for MPs to neglect their parliamentary duties. MPs also frequently visit their constituencies, particularly on weekends, and hold "surgeries," at which they meet their constituents. They ask questions in the Commons and speak in debates on matters affecting their areas.

The crucial fact about MPs is that, with rare exceptions, they are members of parties that they are expected to support loyally and without which they could not have been elected. In the Commons, MPs are still subject to the persuasion, if not the discipline, of the whips and rarely engage in a conflict with the parliamentary leadership. Party cohesion exists partly because of agreement by party MPs on policy issues, partly because of ambition for promotion, especially among those of the government party, and partly because of the probable political isolation experienced by those consistently opposing party policy. The ultimate threat by a prime minister, faced by revolt within his party, is to dissolve Parliament, but

this is a theoretical rather than a real menace. Nevertheless, some revolts against the leaders, when the party is in power and in opposition, have occurred.

This recent greater assertiveness and independence of MPs can be attributed to a number of factors. MPs found that they were seldom denied readoption as candidates or ministerial promotion because of their rebellious actions. Defeats of the government—65 times between 1972 and 1979—did not mean resignation or the dissolution of Parliament, which will occur only on a motion of no confidence. The major parties have been internally divided on significant recent issues such as the European Union, devolution, and income policy. MPs have believed, correctly in a number of cases, that fear of defeat may make a government change its mind.

For some time the dominant body in the operation of the Commons has been the government, which controls the timetable, the allocation of time, and the procedure of the Commons and is responsible for the initiation of most legislation. During the years from 1939 to 1948,

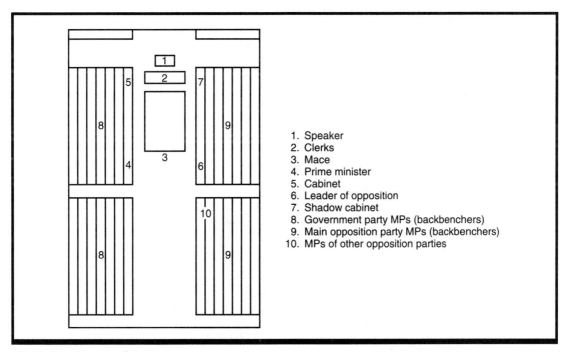

1. Speaker
2. Clerks
3. Mace
4. Prime minister
5. Cabinet
6. Leader of opposition
7. Shadow cabinet
8. Government party MPs (backbenchers)
9. Main opposition party MPs (backbenchers)
10. MPs of other opposition parties

Figure 2.5   House of Commons

backbenchers had no legislative initiative; they currently have 12 days to introduce bills as well as 10 days to move motions.

The great increase in the amount of legislation, and in its scope, variety, and technical nature, has meant both that few MPs are knowledgeable about much of the legislation and the wide range of problems with which it deals and that little time is available for the discussion of government legislation. Most amendments of that legislation are minor, and they are made or agreed to by the government. Of those amendments proposed by ministers, almost all are accepted by the Commons; of those proposed by backbenchers, few are successful.

In addition, many rules are now made by ministers in the form of delegated legislation. There are several reasons for this large development of ministerial power: the technical nature of the rules, the speed with which they can be made, the flexibility available to change them, and the opportunity of discretionary choice. Although some opportunity to discuss delegated legislation is available to MPs, there is little parliamentary scrutiny of it.

An Assenting Assembly

MPs participate in the work of the Commons in a variety of ways: through question time, participation in debates on legislation and on policy, membership on standing and select committees, and proposal of motions and initiation of some legislation.

In the parliamentary golden age of the mid-nineteenth century, the Commons regularly defeated governments without being dissolved. Since that period, few governments have been defeated and obliged to resign or have Parliament dissolved as a result of the actions of the House of Commons.

A number of criticisms can be made of the failings of contemporary parliaments. Parliamentary control over administration and finance is ineffective. Most MPs feel inadequately informed about administration. The real initiative in the legislative process and policy making is in the hands of the executive. Procedure in the Commons is still poorly organized and archaic. The majority political party

is the real strength underlying the operation of the political system. Nevertheless, recent experience has shown that MPs can exercise some control over governments. The assertiveness and dissent among MPs led to a surprising number of government defeats in the 1970s and 1980s.

JUDGES AND POLITICS

Unlike the United States, Britain does not have a system of judicial review, and courts cannot declare legislation void. As the legal sovereign, Parliament, not the courts, decides on the nature and extent of legislative power. The function of British judges is to apply the law to the particular cases before their courts rather than to decide on the desirability or correctness of the law itself. Some judges interpret the law in a way that upholds individual liberty or in accordance with social and personal justice. But most judges interpret statutes narrowly, holding that it is Parliament, not judicial interpretation, that should change a law that is unjust.

British judges have long had the reputation of being impartial and neutral. The judges' impartiality results partly from the common law tradition and judgment based on precedent and partly from the method of their appointment. Judges are not political appointees; few of them have been MPs, and even fewer have been partisans of a political party, as they come from the ranks of barristers with long and successful careers. In the legal profession, there are now about 5,500 barristers, of whom 750 are women, and over 40,000 solicitors (see Table 2.18).

Judges are independent of the other branches of government and their salaries are not open to discussion by Parliament. Since 1701, judges have been appointed on "good behavior," meaning until retirement, which since 1959 has been at age 75. They can only be dismissed by resolutions of both Houses, an event that has not yet occurred. They are scrupulous about a fair hearing in court and impartial application of the law.

The qualities of impartiality and neutrality are always present in cases concerning disputes between private individuals. But there are also other cases in which decisions of judges may affect a wider group of people, or in which they can exercise some discretion. These cases have recently included subjects such as immigration, industrial relations, race relations, police powers, and human rights. It is on questions of this kind that the generally conservative view of judges may be felt. Judges form one of the prominent elite groups of the country. Over 75 percent of senior judges were educated at public schools and at Oxford and Cambridge; over 80 percent come from upper-class or upper-middle-class backgrounds. A conservative position is to be expected from individuals who not only come from these social backgrounds but also have had a successful career and adhere to the tradition of the common law and precedent.

Judges have been reluctant to limit the scope of ministerial powers and have habitually upheld the exercise of the discretionary power of ministers (who can take action under a statute if they think it necessary). Judges have approved executive action, provided it was not out of bounds or exercised unfairly, unreasonably, or in bad faith.

But in the last three decades, some judges have tried to control ministerial administrative action and assert judicial discretion in cases on the scope of executive prerogative in war or on ministerial privilege, or if they decided that ministers had exceeded their legal powers and had encroached on individual rights.

The distinction between policy making by the politician and the application of law by the judges is not always easy to draw in practice. Judges, in reality, help to create criminal law by deciding what is criminal conduct. Judges have often been used by governments to chair tribunals of inquiry or Royal Commissions. In this role judges can influence public policy while maintaining their neutrality as judges.

Judges have a new function as a result of British membership in the European Union. This membership means that Britain is now bound by Common Market treaties and laws. The law of the European Union will be interpreted and applied by British courts, and if that law conflicts with parliamentary statute, courts may have to decide on its validity.

The increase in the scope of public activity has meant that the ordinary courts of law are inadequate to deal with many issues. To fulfill this function, administrative tribunals concerned with the justice or appropriateness of decisions have been established and judicial and quasi-judicial powers have been given to departments and administrative bodies. A series of administrative tribunals—the members of which are rarely lawyers—cover such issues as rent, immigration, pensions, family allowances, mental health, industrial injuries, and national health insurance.

The courts have played a historic role in restraining executive power to its legitimate function and in fostering the existence of individual

Table 2.18 BRITISH JUDGES, 1995

Position	Men	Women
Lords of Appeal in Ordinary (Law Lords)	12	—
Lords Justice of Appeal	31	1
High Court Judges	88	6
Circuit Judges	486	30
Recorders	853	53
Assistant Recorders	297	52
District Judges	273	29
Deputy District Judges	632	84

Source: The Times, April 10, 1995.

rights. In this age of strong public or governmental action, some have voiced concern that the common law may not be able to protect these rights and that a bill of rights along American lines should be passed. In fact, Britain has ratified the European Convention on Human Rights, and any British subject can now appeal to the European Courts on these matters. But individual rights in Britain have been, and remain, dependent not simply on legal safeguards imposed by judges, but also on traditions of civility, self-restraint, and tolerance.

KEY TERMS

backbencher
by-election
the City
civil list
civil service
collective responsibility
common law
Confederation of British Industry (CBI)
Conservative Party
constituency
Crown
legislation
frontbencher
House of Commons
House of Lords
individual responsibility
Labour Party
mandate
marginal seat
National Executive Committee (NEC)
opposition
Parliament Acts 1911 and 1949
Parliamentary Labour Party
party identification
permanent secretary
Plaid Cymru
prime minister
QUANGO
question hour
Scottish National Party (SNP)
Social Democratic Party (SDP)
standing committee
Trades Union Congress (TUC)

Treasury
vote of censure
vote of no confidence
Westminster
whip
Whitehall

FURTHER READINGS

Blackburn, Robert. *The Electoral System in Britain* (London: Macmillan, 1995).

Butler, David, and Martin Westlake. *British Politics and European Elections 1994* (New York: St. Martin's 1995).

Butler, David, and Dennis Kavanagh. *The British General Election of 1992* (New York: St. Martin's, 1992).

Conley, Frank. *General Elections Today,* 2nd ed. (New York: Manchester University Press, 1992).

Crewe, Ivor, et al. *The British Electorate 1963–87* (New York: Cambridge University Press, 1991).

Denver, D. T. *Elections and Voting Behavior in Britain* (New York: Allan, 1989).

Denver, David, and Gordon Hands, ed. *Issues and Controversies in British Voting Behavior* (New York: Harvester Wheatsheaf, 1992).

Hart, Jenifer. *Proportional Representation; Critics of the British Electoral System, 1820–1945* (New York: Oxford University Press, 1992).

Kavanagh, Dennis, ed. *Electoral Politics* (New York: Oxford University Press, 1992).

Miller, William, et al. *How Voters Change* (New York: Oxford University Press, 1990).

Norris, Pippa. *British By-Elections: The Volatile Electorate* (New York: Oxford University Press, 1990).

Richardson, Jeremy, ed. *Pressure Groups* (New York: Oxford University Press, 1993).

Seyd, Patrick. *The Rise and Fall of the Labour Left* (New York: St. Martin's, 1987).

THE EXECUTIVE AND JUDICIARY

Barber, James P. *The Prime Minister since 1945* (Cambridge: Blackwell, 1991).

Bogdanor, Vernon. *The Monarchy and the Constitution* (London: Oxford University Press, 1995).

Drewry, Gavin, and Tony Butcher. *The Civil Service Today*, 2nd ed. (Cambridge: Blackwell, 1993).

Hennessy, Peter. *Whitehall* (London: Secker and Warburg, 1989).

James, Simon. *British Cabinet Government* (New York: Routledge, 1992).

King, Anthony, ed. *The British Prime Minister* (Durham: Duke University, 1985).

Laver, Michael, and Kenneth Shepsie, eds. *Cabinet Ministers and Parliamentary Government* (New York: Cambridge University Press, 1994).

Marshall, Geoffrey. *Ministerial Responsibility* (New York: Oxford University Press, 1989).

Shell, Donald, and Richard Hodder-Williams. *Churchill to Major: The British Prime Ministership since 1945* (Armonk: Sharpe, 1995).

THE LEGISLATURE

Adonis, Andrew. *Parliament Today*, 2nd ed. (New York: Manchester University Press, 1993).

Bluth, Christopher, et al. *The Future of European Security* (Brookfield: Dartmouth, 1995).

Franklin, Mark, and Philip Norton, eds. *Parliamentary Questions* (Oxford: Clarendon Press, 1993).

Griffith, J. A. G., and Michael Ryle. *Parliament: Functions, Practice and Procedure* (London: Sweet and Maxwell, 1989).

Jogerst, Michael. *Reform in the House of Commons* (Lexington: University of Kentucky, 1993).

Norris, Pippa, and Joni Lovenduski. *Political Recruitment: Gender, Race and Class in the British Parliament* (New York: Cambridge University Press, 1995).

Norton, Philip. *Does Parliament Matter?* (New York: Harvester Wheatsheaf, 1993).

Norton, Philip, and David Wood. *Back from Westminster: British MPs and Their Constituents* (Lexington: University Press of Kentucky, 1993).

Rush, Michael, ed. Parliament and Pressure Politics (New York: Oxford University Press, 1990).

Shell, Donald. *The House of Lords,* 2nd ed. (New York: Harvester Wheatsheaf, 1992).

Public Policy

THE MIXED ECONOMY

Like other Western countries, Britain has a mixed economy. Part of it is owned and administered by public authorities; this public sector employs 5.5 million workers, including central and local government and public corporations. However, most of the economy is under private ownership and control. The private sector has increased since 1979 as the Conservative government cut the public sector and denationalized or "privatized" many enterprises.

Both Labour and Conservative governments intervened in economic affairs in the postwar period in differing degrees. This intervention stemmed partly from the desire to implement social principles such as the public ownership of resources, the welfare of citizens, and the reduction of unemployment, but also from the effort to solve economic problems by increasing production and trade. Governments therefore not only nationalized industries, but also promoted industrial development, supplied money and credits to both public and private enterprises, increased the level of investment, helped firms in trouble, proposed "targets" and planning agreements for industry and the restructuring of industry, and attempted to restrain wage increases.

The public sector today comprises three parts: central government, local government, and the nationalized industries.

Central government is responsible for all spending on Social Security benefits, health, defense, trade, industry, overseas payments and foreign aid, and central administration (see Table 2.19). It also partly finances housing, education, transport, and law and order programs.

Table 2.19 GENERAL GOVERNMENT EXPENDITURE BY FUNCTION

	Percentages				
	1981	1986	1991	1992	1993
Defense	10.8	11.7	10.2	9.6	8.9
Public order and safety	3.7	4.2	5.7	5.4	5.5
Education	12.2	11.9	12.9	12.6	12.4
Health	11.4	11.8	13.6	13.7	13.5
Social security	26.6	30.8	32.3	33.3	34.2
Housing and community amenities	6.1	5.0	3.8	4.0	4.0
Recreational and cultural affairs	1.3	1.5	1.7	1.5	1.4
Fuel and energy	0.3	−0.7	−1.3	−0.2	0.3
Agriculture, forestry, and fishing	1.4	1.3	1.2	1.2	1.4
Mining, mineral resources, manufacturing and construction	3.0	1.2	0.7	0.5	0.6
Transport and communication	3.6	2.3	2.9	2.5	2.5
General public services	3.9	3.9	5.0	5.0	4.6
Other economic affairs and services	2.5	2.5	1.9	1.8	1.8
Other expenditure	13.1	12.7	9.4	9.1	8.8
Total expenditure (billions)	117.1	162.3	228.4	254.2	272.8

Most of the expenditure is paid for by taxation (see Figure 2.6).

Local government now accounts for about one-quarter of total public spending. The largest item is education, followed by housing, transport, law and order, and social services. This expenditure is paid for by property taxes and by grants from the central government.

The nationalized industries in 1979 accounted for 10 percent of gross domestic product (GDP), employed almost 2 million (8 percent of the work force) and took 14 percent of fixed investment. The industries dominated areas such as coal, electricity, gas, broadcasting, public transport, communications, and iron and steel. Because they were producers of basic goods and services, as well as large consumers of raw materials, they significantly affected investment, employment, prices, and cost of living in the whole economy. By 1988, denationalization had reduced them to 6 percent of GDP, 750,000 workers, and 9 percent of investment.

THE DECLINE OF NATIONALIZED INDUSTRIES

The motives to nationalize industries were varied. They included public control over significant parts of the economic system; efficient organization and development of the economy; influencing the level of investment to achieve full employment; better industrial relations; preventing possible abuse of a monopoly situation; continuation of enterprises, even if unprofitable, to provide a social service or minimize unemployment; or assistance to failing firms. Added to these economic and social reasons was the ideology of the Labour Party, whose constitution (Clause IV) calls for "public ownership of the means of production, distribution and exchange."

The most prominent form of nationalization in the postwar period was the public corporation. Each nationalized enterprise is administered not by a government department but by the board of the corporation, which is free from

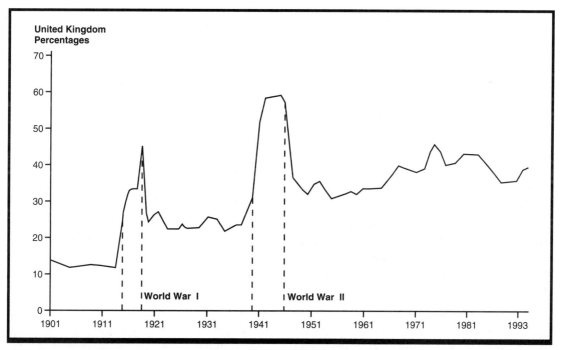

Figure 2.6   General Government Expenditure as a Percentage of GDP⁺

⁺ GDP adjusted to take account of change from rates to community charge. Data for 1919 are not available.
Source: Central Statistical Office.

political interference in its daily management and administration. The minister who appoints the boards does not have direct responsibility for the operation, but approves the general lines of capital development, research, and borrowing, and can give general directions.

In the main the nationalized industries, especially coal and railroads, suffered substantial deficits, and their overall performance was poor. In addition, two major issues lacked clarity: the objectives of nationalization and the relations between corporations and the ministers. Differences on the objectives are the result of mixed motives for nationalization. Should the enterprises be run primarily from the point of view of efficiency and along economic lines with balanced accounts, or should they be more concerned with low prices, convenience for customers (rail), and prevention of unemployment (coal mines), and thus act as a social service irrespective of deficits they may incur? Should they be used by the government to control parts of the economy and to help implement general economic, wage, and price policies? Should they help implement British technological inventions, or should they be regarded as possible experiments in workers' participation?

Some confusion also existed about the respective roles of ministers and the boards in decisions made by the corporations. Ministers have the general powers previously mentioned and particular powers over each industry. But ministers rarely gave directions in a formal way. Instead, to avoid political responsibility, they preferred to influence decisions by informal consultation or by "arm-twisting" or "persuading" the chairperson of the industry to do their bidding.

A major change took place with the privatization policy of the Thatcher government that consisted of selling off the assets and shares of nationalized industries to private owners. This policy also allowed some services previously administered by public authorities to be performed by private firms. Prime Minister Thatcher argued that privatization brought certain benefits: The industries would be more efficient and profitable in a more competitive market, away from interference of officials; their objectives would not be overridden by irrelevant

political, social, and economic factors, thereby increasing business confidence; the government would raise large amounts by sales; Britain would become a property-owning democracy (now 11 million shareholders). By 1991 about 60 percent of state industry had been privatized (see Table 2.20). The government claimed that output, profits, investment, and industrial relations in those enterprises had all improved.

The Conservative government also sought to promote competition by ending the monopoly of a number of enterprises, such as long distance buses and express delivery services, and of certain professional activity, such as some legal work.

ECONOMIC PLANNING

All postwar governments accepted the need for planning, which resulted from increased government activity and expenditure. They saw the need for creating nationalized industries and increasing productivity, economic growth, and exports. Governmental intervention took a variety of forms: financial aid and incentives to stimulate industrial investment; taxation changes and loans to strengthen development areas and transfer workers from services to manufacturing; physical controls to induce firms to move to less developed areas; subsidies to aid failing enterprises and controls on wages, prices, and foreign exchange. Bodies, such as the National Economic Development Council (NEDC) and the National Enterprise Board, were set up to assist the economy and to foster greater efficiency.

These governments sought, mainly through the annual budget, to maintain a high level of economic activity, and strove for full employment, economic growth, and a rising standard of living. They stressed expansion of demand rather than anti-inflationary measures, and relatively little attention was paid to restraint of money supply.

The Thatcher government broke with this approach. It sought, at first, to reduce inflation by restricting the money supply, hoping to increase output and employment. It tried to revitalize the private sector by lowering taxes and interest rates that would result from cuts in public expenditure and borrowing. It emphasized market forces by reducing the public sector, taming the trade unions, ending controls on prices and wages, and trying to curb the spending of local authorities. To do the last, and to attempt to make clear to citizens how much local authorities were spending, Thatcher imposed a poll tax on residents of an equal amount, to replace rates on property. This was seen by many as unfair, and was largely responsible for Conservative electoral defeats at by-elections in 1989 and 1990, and, to some extent, for her own downfall as party leader and prime minister in 1990. The poll tax was replaced by a new local tax, partly based on the value of residential property, in 1991–1992.

The government from 1979 on was particularly interested in limiting or controlling the power of the trade unions. Unions must now hold secret ballots for the election of union leaders, before a strike is called, and on their political funds. Limits have been set on picketing, secondary strike action, and closed shops. Union funds are now liable for damages in civil actions. Union membership declined substantially during the 1980s.

THE WELFARE STATE

Britain has long concerned itself with the poor. Before 1914, national insurance, old-age pensions, and unemployment insurance were adopted. But it was not until after World War II that the plans for a welfare state and for social improvement were implemented. The Beveridge Report in 1942 had proposed the extension of the process of insurance to provide adequate subsistence for all. Two years later Beveridge called for a system of full employment.

The Labour government of 1945–1950 introduced the basic elements of a welfare system which has been modified and extended during the ensuing 50 years. Three elements of this

Table 2.20   PRIVATIZATION, 1982–1993

Industry	Year	Employees
National Freight Company	1982	28,000
Britoil	1982	14,000
Associated British Ports (formerly British Transport Docks Board)	1983	—
Enterprise Oil (separated from British Gas Corporation)	1984	—
British Telecom	1984	250,000
British Shipbuilders	various dates from 1984	—
British Gas Corporation	1986	89,000
National Bus Co. Subsidiaries	1986–88	30,000
British Airways	1987	36,000
Royal Ordinance Factories	1987	17,000
British Airports Authority (BAA)	1987	7,000
British Steel	1988	53,000
Passenger Transport Executives	various dates from 1988	8,000
Regional Water Authorities and Water Authorities Association	1989	40,000
Girobank	1990	6,700
Area Electricity Boards and National Grid Company	1990	119,000
National Power and Powergen	1991	26,400
Scottish Power	1991	9,800
Northern Ireland Electricity Service	1993	5,000

Source: Based on "Employment in the Public and Private Sectors," *Economic Trends*, January 1994.

system have been particularly important: social security, the national health service, and personal social services. The last is the responsibility of local authorities and voluntary organizations, while the first two are the direct responsibility of central government.

Social Security

The social security system is a complex one with over 30 different benefits. The major postwar reform in this area has been the extension of national insurance to cover unemployment, sickness, maternity, retirement, industrial injuries, and death. A National Insurance Fund was established, to which insured persons and their employers contribute and from which they are paid when necessary. The contributions cover about 90 percent of the benefits paid, with the state paying the rest. The system is universal, applying to everyone, but individuals can have their own private insurance in addition to the national system.

Unemployment benefit is payable for one year in each case of unemployment. Sickness benefits of various kinds cover loss of earnings during absence from work. Maternity pay, normally for 18 weeks, is now usually paid by employers. A variety of different grants, depending on the individuals and relationships, are paid on death. The most significant of these grants go to widows who receive allowances for the first 26 weeks of widowhood, as well as other possible allowances.

Since 1946 pensions have been paid to men at age 65 and women at age 60; individuals may defer retirement for five years and qualify for a higher pension, however. Since 1959, the basic pension has been supplemented by an additional amount in return for larger contributions, an earning-related scheme. Pensions are also paid to disabled veterans. An injured worker receives benefits for a period depending on the disablement.

Family allowances have been given since 1945 to mothers who receive a sum for all children who are below the minimum school-leaving age or in full-time education (now up to the age of 19). In 1977, child benefits replaced family allowances and the income tax allowances, which have been phased out. Children also receive other benefits: medical examinations, free milk (which since 1971 has been limited to those under 7 years of age), and school meals. Benefits introduced in 1988 included income support for families whose income is under a certain level, a family credit for low-income working families with children, and aid for rent and local rates.

The cost of these services has been high. Social security accounts for about 9 percent and retirement pensions alone for 6 percent of GNP. If health and education are included, the social services account for over 23 percent of GNP and 47 percent of total public expenditure. But, in spite of the cost, for political reasons Conservative governments did not reduce the services and benefits. Indeed, expenditure increased under Thatcher and Major, partly because of the larger numbers of elderly and unemployed people and single-parent families.

The National Health Service

Introduced in 1946, the National Health Service (NHS) was one of the towering achievements of the Labour government. When the NHS was established, the state acquired all hospitals except teaching hospitals. Doctors could no longer sell their practices or set up practice in an area that already had too many doctors. But concessions included the right of doctors to private practice, maintenance of private paying beds in hospitals, the right of the patients to choose their doctor, and local rather than central administration of hospitals. Medical and dental services were free to all who used the service. Doctors in the service receive a basic salary plus a certain fee for each patient. Hospitals have been run by regional boards and committees. Over 90 percent of doctors decided to enter the service. Residents in Britain can choose to join the system, as over 90 percent have done. They have free choice of an NHS doctor, dentist, optician, and pharmacist and have access to specialists and hospital treatment through their doctor.

The creation of the NHS and the provision of free medicine resulted initially in higher costs than had been anticipated. Charges, covering only a small part of the cost, were therefore imposed for drug prescriptions, dental treatment, dentures, and spectacles. But over 80 percent of the cost is financed from the regular tax. The most costly item has been the hospitals, which now account for about three-fifths of the total cost; the teaching hospitals are particularly expensive. The NHS, employing 1 million people, including 30,000 doctors, now accounts for 10 percent of public expenditure and 6 percent of GDP. The NHS has faced some difficulties in recent years because of the demands on it. Problems have arisen over pay for medical personnel, industrial disputes, low morale, waiting lists in hospitals and for operations, a shortage of specialists, demands caused by the increasing proportion of older people, and the high cost of medical care and high-technology equipment. The cost of the NHS, which treats 30 million patients a year, rose 50 percent in real terms between 1979 and 1990. The government has therefore recently tried to shift emphasis from the treatment of illness to the promotion of health and the prevention of disease, and to decentralize the system by allowing some hospitals to administer their own budgets and to become self-governing trusts with their own boards of directors.

HAS BRITAIN FOUND ITS ROLE IN FOREIGN POLICY?

At the end of World War II, Britain was still one of the three major powers; its empire and Commonwealth contained one-quarter of the world's population. It remained the major European economic and military power until the mid–1950s. By 1952 Britain had manufactured atomic bombs, and in 1957 it exploded a thermonuclear bomb. It was the dominant power in the Middle East and the second most important power in the Far East, and had a "special relationship" with the United States.

But in the postwar period, Britain has become an important but middle-sized power. It declined economically, in both production and trade, as other nations developed industrially. British economic growth was lower than that of other major Western European countries. Britain increased its imports not only of raw materials but also of manufactured chemical and semimanufactured products. Britain never fully recaptured its export markets, over half of which had been lost as a result of World War II. Britain has been technologically inventive—for

example, television, radar, the jet engine, and the swing-line plane—but has been deficient in exploiting inventions.

The British Empire has been almost completely transformed into independent nations, most of them now members of the Commonwealth. Unable to produce missiles to launch its bombs, Britain became dependent on the United States, which supplied it with the Polaris missile. Britain could not sustain the burden of supporting other countries, such as Greece and Turkey, or of protecting Palestine, from which it withdrew in 1948. It began withdrawing its forces from other areas: the Suez Canal zone in 1956, Jordan in 1957, Iraq in 1958, the Persian Gulf in 1969, and Singapore in 1971. In 1997 the colony of Hong Kong will come under Chinese rule.

Britain's relative economic decline, as well as the demand for independence of its former colonies, affected its foreign policy. Both major parties agreed that Britain should be a nuclear power and for a time sought to maintain its bases east of Suez. Both Labour and Conservatives intervened to help keep the peace, to safeguard oil, tin, and rubber supply lines, and to protect other countries, such as Malaya from 1948 on, Kenya between 1952 and 1960, and Kenya and Tanganyika in 1964, as well as the Middle East. About 10 percent of the central government's expenditure was for defense.

Britain had to adjust its foreign policy to three developments: the decline in its special relationship with the United States, the end of the empire and the increase in the Commonwealth, and the creation of the European Community.

From Special Relationship to Ally

The close British-American relationship during World War II was transformed by postwar events, the first of which was the quick termination of the U.S. lend-lease program in 1945; this forced Britain to borrow heavily in the immediate postwar period. The strategic strength and economic might of the United States and its emergence as the dominant world power meant that Britain was an ally, not an equal partner. The relationship is now one of consultation and exchange of information and opinions on issues of common interest.

Britain is one of five countries in the world with a military nuclear capacity, and it intends to maintain that capacity. The core of its defense effort is now based on its membership in the North Atlantic Treaty Organization (NATO). Britain is committed to the deterrent strategy of NATO and to consultations of the Nuclear Planning Group within it. It contributes forces to all three elements of NATO's strategy: strategic nuclear, theater nuclear, and conventional armaments.

Britain's contribution to the first is its force of four nuclear submarines, each equipped with 16 Polaris A3 missiles armed with nuclear warheads with a range of 2,800 miles. This Polaris system is due to be phased out by the mid–1990s. To replace it, the government decided to buy the U.S. Trident submarine-launched missiles and to construct four new submarines to carry them. The submarines will be assigned to NATO, but will be under British control.

The Royal Navy, the strongest European navy in NATO, contributes its wide variety of ships—the third largest number of surface combat ships in the world—including an aircraft carrier, nuclear-powered submarines, and guided-missile destroyers to the alliance. In addition to its NATO assignments in the Atlantic and the North Sea, the navy sends task forces into the Indian Ocean, partly to help safeguard oil supplies.

Britain's main field army, the British Army of the Rhine (BAOR) is stationed in northern Germany. BAOR, recently reduced to 25,000 soldiers, has a full range of modern mobile weapons at its command, including tactical nuclear weapons, that can be dropped from aircraft or fired from artillery. It is supported by a tactical unit of the Royal Air Force (RAF). The RAF as a whole has some 500 combat aircraft at its disposal, including units in Britain that provide part of NATO's mobile force.

Out of the NATO area, Britain still stations troops or plays a role in a number of areas such as Hong Kong (until 1997), Cyprus, Gibraltar, the Falklands, and in the major oceans. Britain played a significant role in the Gulf War of 1991. With the end of the Warsaw Pact in 1991, Britain plans to make substantial cuts in all its armed forces. Its army will be reduced to a ceiling of about 116,000 troops.

From Empire to Commonwealth

Before World War II the British Commonwealth, as it was then called, consisted of Britain and six dominions, which (except for South Africa) were largely populated by individuals of British extraction, economically modernized and politically developed, with democratic systems and values (again except for South Africa) similar to the British. Preferential trading arrangements, adopted in Ottawa in 1932, were extended to all the dominions.

The rest of Britain's possessions throughout the world were colonies ruled by Britain. They began demanding independence soon after the end of the war, beginning in Asia and then throughout Africa and the rest of the world. Most nations on gaining independence have chosen to be members of the Commonwealth, which in 1996 numbers 52 countries with a population of 1.3 billion (see Table 2.21). Britain, however, is still responsible for 14 dependent territories around the world.

The Commonwealth, now consisting of diverse races, religions, and cultures, is a voluntary association with members all being equal in status. Some are republics which acknowledge the monarch as head of the Commonwealth, some are constitutional monarchies owing allegiance to the monarch, and four have their own monarchs. Some are political democracies in the British sense, but others have one-party systems or are under military control. Some are based on private ownership, while others regard themselves as Socialists. A few are wealthy, but most are poor countries with a low per capita income.

The Commonwealth is a loose association of independent nations, all once ruled by Britain, which have in no way chosen each other but are linked by accident. British law no longer extends to the Commonwealth. It does not reach collective decisions or take united political action. It is neither a trade bloc—although some economic privileges do exist—nor a military alliance, though its weapons, uniforms, and military training are similar to Britain's and there are combined exercises and joint research organizations. It has no center of sovereignty, no central law-making body or parliament, and no organ to speak for it; in 1965,

Table 2.21   INDEPENDENT COUNTRIES IN THE COMMONWEALTH (IN ORDER OF DATE OF INDEPENDENCE OR MEMBERSHIP)

1. United Kingdom		27. Swaziland	1968
2. Canada	1867	28. Republic of Nauru (special member)	1968
3. Commonwealth of Australia	1901	29. Tonga	1970
4. New Zealand	1907	30. Western Samoa	1970
5. India	1947	31. Bangladesh	1973
6. Sri Lanka	1948	32. Commonwealth of the Bahamas	1973
7. Ghana	1957	33. Grenada	1974
8. Malaysia	1957	34. Papua New Guinea	1975
9. Nigeria	1960	35. Seychelles	1976
10. Republic of Cyprus	1961	36. Solomon Islands	1978
11. Sierra Leone	1961	37. Tuvalu (special member)	1978
12. United Republic of Tanzania	1961	38. Dominica	1978
13. Jamaica	1962	39. St. Lucia	1979
14. Trinidad and Tobago	1962	40. Kiribati	1979
15. Uganda	1963	41. St. Vincent and the Grenadines (special member)	1979
16. Kenya	1963	42. Zimbabwe	1980
17. Malawi	1964	43. Vanuatu	1980
18. Republic of Malta	1964	44. Belize	1981
19. Zambia	1964	45. Antigua and Barbuda	1981
20. The Gambia	1965	46. Maldives	1982
21. Singapore	1965	47. St. Christopher and Nevis	1983
22. Guyana	1966	48. Brunei	1984
23. Botswana	1966	49. Pakistan	1989
24. Lesotho	1966	50. Namibia	1990
25. Barbados	1966	51. South Africa	1994
26. Mauritius	1968	52. Cameroon	1995

Note: The special status of Nauru, Tuvalu, and St. Vincent and the Grenadines provides for all the privileges of Commonwealth membership and attendance at all Commonwealth meetings with the exception of the meetings of Commonwealth heads of government. Eire left the Commonwealth in 1949, South Africa in 1961, and Pakistan in 1972. In 1965 Rhodesia unilaterally declared its independence, but in 1979 it again came under British administration and in 1980 became the independent republic of Zimbabwe. Fiji, which joined the Commonwealth in 1970, left it in 1987. Pakistan rejoined in 1989. South Africa rejoined in 1994. Nigeria was suspended in 1995.

a secretariat was established, but it does not make decisions that are binding on its members.

Tangible and intangible bonds have linked the Commonwealth. The latter result from the use of English by the professional classes, similar educational experiences, and common backgrounds in some cases. More tangible have been the regular meetings of heads of governments, political leaders, and professional people; collaborative functions in areas such as health, education, and agriculture; and representation of the members by High Commissioners in London. Some preferential trade arrangements still exist. Most of Britain's bilateral and much of its multilateral foreign aid has gone to the Commonwealth.

But Britain's ties with the Commonwealth have weakened. The very diversity of its members means that no common ethnic or cultural bonds exist. Controls have been imposed on nonwhite immigration into Britain. Britain can no longer offer military protection to the members. Few of them retain the Judicial Committee of the Privy Council in London as the final court of appeal from their own courts.

The Commonwealth is a useful bridge among races, areas of the world, and richer and poorer nations. But it has declined in economic value and political importance for Britain. This is especially true in the changing pattern of trade as Britain has turned to Europe, and the Commonwealth countries have begun manufacturing their own products. British exports to the Commonwealth decreased from 37.3 percent of the total in 1958 to 8.5 percent in 1987. In the same period, exports to the European Community increased from 13.9 to 42 percent, and imports from it rose from 9 to 52 percent. British trade has shifted from the Commonwealth to other industrial countries, especially those of Western Europe.

This may change because in the mid–1990s, 5 of the 10 fastest growing economies of the world are Commonwealth countries in the Asia-Pacific Rim. But the Commonwealth was not a real obstacle to closer economic and political relations with Western Europe.

Britain and Western Europe

In the immediate postwar period, Britain was not interested in joining in the proposals for greater European unity. Its status as one of the "Big Three" powers, its worldwide role, its Commonwealth, its special relationship with the United States, its higher standard of living and trade pattern, and its insular political tradition and fear of European entanglement—all led Britain to refuse to participate in the Economic Coal and Steel Community in 1951, the proposed European Defense Community in the 1950s, and in the formation of the European Economic Community (EEC) and European Atomic Energy Community (Euratom) in 1957.

Britain preferred to maintain a much looser free-trade area and organized the European Free Trade Association in 1959 as an alternative. But the speedy success of the EEC, popularly known as the Common Market, the rapid recovery of Western Europe after the war—at first assisted by U.S. economic aid—the realization of the importance of a large single market, and weakening relations with the United States and the Commonwealth led Britain to apply for membership in the European Community (EC). After being vetoed twice by France, in 1963 and 1967, Britain was accepted and joined the Community in January 1973.

When the Labour Party, split on the issue of the EC, formed the government in 1974, it decided to renegotiate the terms of Britain's membership and then put the issue to a vote by the people. A number of changes were made, including the system of financing the EC budget, the reduction in the cost of the common agricultural program, and better access for certain Commonwealth produce. As a result, the government, though still divided, recommended that Britain remain in the EC. The referendum, the first in British history, was approved by 67 percent of the vote in 1975.

Britain accepted the EC's agricultural policy, which means higher prices for food and the gradual reduction of Commonwealth trade preferences. In return, it hoped that the larger market and progressive removal of European tariff barriers would induce a faster rate of economic growth, a restructuring of the British economy, and greater economies of scale in production.

Membership in the EC did not immediately revive British industry, but trade with it increased and now accounts for about half of Britain's imports and exports. However, Britain in the late 1980s had a trade deficit with the EC.

Britain was also concerned about the size of its net contribution to the EC budget, as it contributed considerably more than it received in return. This inequity resulted from two facts: the EC largely raises its revenue from customs duties, farm levies, and value-added taxation (VAT), which is costly to Britain, which imports most of its food; most EC expenditure goes to farmers, thus benefiting countries with a larger farming population than Britain's. As a result of vigorous protest by Prime Minister Thatcher, Britain's contribution was reduced in the 1980s.

Britain is now subject to EU's law, which has direct effect in the country, as it accepts and gives the force of law to the rules, principles, and procedures of the EU, the new name of the EC. The Court of Justice of the European Union has ultimate authority to rule on interpretation of the law. In the institutions of the EU, now composed of 15 states, Britain has 2 of the members of the European Commission, the executive of the EU, and 87 of the 626 members of the enlarged European Parliament, which was directly elected for the first time in 1979.

For Britain some new political problems exist. The historic concept of the supremacy of Parliament is now qualified by the right of EU institutions to make rules applying to Britain without parliamentary consent and by the ability of the EU Court of Justice to rule on whether British law is compatible with European Union law as it did in 1990. Though there has not as yet been any serious constitutional clash between Britain and the EC institutions, problems remain now that there is a level of government above that of Britain and now that Britain is for the first time bound to some extent by the written constitution of the European Union. Britain welcomed the EU objective of a free internal market by 1992, and approved of a greater European role in world affairs, but it has been reluctant to become a member of the European Monetary System or to accept the idea of a European bank, let alone a United States of Europe, or to adopt the European Social Charter.

It did, however, join the exchange rate mechanism of the European Monetary System in October 1990, though it remained opposed to rapid moves to an economic and monetary union, and to a single European currency. It also still insists that any such union must be based on free markets and price stability. Equally, the Conservative governments under Thatcher and Major rejected the idea of a federal Europe, and have been concerned about any reduction of British sovereignty. Though the Conservatives agreed that some common European policies, such as a single market and a negotiating position on world trade, are necessary and that Europe should have a more coordinated foreign policy and a stronger voice in world affairs; they did not accept the view that all European cooperation must take place through the institutions of the European Union.

In the field of defense, this view has led Britain to suggest that the Western European Union (WEU) should be the bridge between NATO and transatlantic security and defense on one hand and common political and security policies of the EU on the other. In this way WEU could be the basis for a European defense identity, without NATO being undermined.

Politically, Britain under the Thatcher and Major governments has been opposed to an extension of majority voting in the EU, to wider powers being exercised by the Commission, or to the EU having larger taxing powers. It has called for the reform of the Common Agricultural Policy of the EC, which is costly for Britain, and for a single market that should be realized in all states, especially in the fields of financial services, transport, and public procurement. Britain has also been troubled by the diminution of its sovereignty, as in late 1991 when the Community threatened to take legal action to stop British Rail construction projects for environmental reasons.

CONCLUSION

Whether examined from an international, social, economic, or political point of view, the British system has changed in the postwar world. Internationally, Britain cannot be seen as a superpower, though it is still a significant world power with a capacity for independent action as was displayed in the 1982 Falklands war. It has drawn closer to Western Europe, which now accounts for half of British trade. Nevertheless, Britain still maintains a variety of important foreign ties, especially with the United States, with which it shares common political and democratic values as well as military and intelligence-gathering connections.

It is a leading member of NATO and the European Union, a permanent member of the Security Council of the United Nations, and one of the Group of Seven Economic Summit countries.

British troops are deployed or stationed in over 40 countries in the mid–1990s.

Britain is the world's sixth largest economy, though its share of world trade has fallen from 11.5 percent in the early postwar years to 4.9 percent in 1994. However, Britain has considerable investments overseas; it is the biggest foreign investor in the United States. Since about a quarter of the GDP comes from the overseas market, promoting trade is as important as diplomatic activity.

Socially, Britain is now a country with a mixture of peoples of different races and background, a less rigid class system, and, for most individuals, a more affluent lifestyle. Economically, Britain has experienced mixed success. It is currently a self-sufficient oil-producing country. In the mid–1980s, real GDP grew at a faster rate than in the United States, the inflation rate was low, and the trade unions, with a declining membership, in general were less militant. The Thatcher government stressed individual responsibility, encouraged economic initiative, sold off many nationalized industries, and dismantled state controls over the economy. At the same time, unemployment remained relatively high, and the proportion of total GDP spent by government did not diminish significantly.

Britain in the mid–1990s has witnessed an increasing centralization of public administration as the Conservative government under John Major reduced the autonomy of local councils, universities, police authorities, health regions, armed forces, and nationalized industry boards. The Conservatives did not reduce the size and scope of government which in 1995 still account for 43 percent of the GDP. Moreover, some new nationalized or quasi-nationalized bodies have been set up, such as the National Lottery, Child Support Agency, and the National Health Service Management Executive.

Britain has been regarded in the postwar world as a model of a successful and stable political system with two strong parties, which alternated in power, and with a general consensus that included approval of full employment, a welfare state, and free collective bargaining. That admired model has not, in recent years, fully corresponded to current reality. The Conservative Party was elected to power for the fourth successive time in 1992, and the electoral base on which the Labour Party depended for support appeared to be shrinking. Other parties, especially the nationalist parties and the Social Democratic and Liberal Parties at different elections, have registered considerable strength. In the major parties, ideological positions have been emphasized and, in the case of the Conservatives, implemented into legislation but have been less emphasized in the 1990s. Difficult issues, such as the Irish question, the inequality of women, racial discrimination, environmental problems, and the role of Britain externally, remain to be adequately resolved. It is clear that in the 1990s there will be no shortage of difficult problems on the British political agenda.

The need for constitutional and political changes has been raised. Britain is the only country in Western Europe which does not have a bill of rights providing constitutional protection for individual and group rights. In recent years, the government has extended police powers and suspended part of the working of criminal law. It has also in the 1980s and 1990s increased centralization in a number of policy areas, reduced powers of local authorities, and set up a considerable number of independent government agencies and QUANGOs whose political responsibility is unclear. This has led some to argue that Britain should have a formal bill of rights, decentralization of power to regional and local authorities, a fairer electoral system, and more parliamentary scrutiny of the executive.

On the other hand, Britain remains a stable democracy in no danger of military defeat, revolution, or political collapse. Defenders of the present system contend that it should continue to operate by tradition and convention, and that it already has a regional tier of government both for Scottish, Welsh, and Northern Ireland affairs and for regional offices of government departments. Difficult issues remain to be adequately resolved.

KEY TERMS

Commonwealth
devolution
economic planning
European Community (EC) (now European
    Union, EU)
European Free Trade Association (EFTA)
family allowances
mixed economy
National Health Service
nationalized industries
North Atlantic Treaty Organization (NATO)
Polaris missiles
privatization
social security
Western European Union (WEU)

FURTHER READINGS

Bartlett, Christopher J. *British Foreign Policy in the Twentieth Century* (Basingstoke: Macmillan, 1989).

Bulmer, Simon, et al., eds. *The United Kingdom and European Community Evaluated* (London: Pinter, 1992).

George, Stephen, ed. *Britain and the European Community: The Politics of Semi-Detachment* (New York: Oxford University Press, 1992).

Grant, Wyn. *Pressure Groups, Politics and Democracy in Britain* (New York: Allan, 1989).

Grant, Wyn. *Business and Politics in Britain*, 2nd ed. (London: Macmillan, 1993).

Grant, Wyn. *The Politics of Economic Policy* (New York: Harvester Wheatsheaf, 1993).

Hampton, William. *Local Government and Urban Politics* (New York: Longman, 1991).

Hills, John, ed. *The State of Welfare: The Welfare State in Britain Since 1974* (New York: Oxford University Press, 1990).

Jenkins, Simon. *Accountable to None: The Tory Nationalization of Britain* (London: Hamish Hamilton, 1995).

Kavanagh, Dennis. *Thatcherism and British Politics: The End of Consensus?* (New York: Oxford University Press, 1990).

Kellas, James. *The Politics of Nationalism and Ethnicity* (Basingstoke: Macmillan, 1991).

Kellas, James. *The Scottish Political System*, 4th ed. (New York: Cambridge University Press, 1989).

Louis, Wm. Roger, and Hedley Bull, eds. *The Special Relationship: Anglo-American Relations Since 1945* (New York: Oxford University Press, 1986).

Marsh, David. *The New Politics of British Trade Unionism: Union Power and the Thatcher Legacy* (Ithaca, NY: ILR Press, 1992).

Pierson, Christopher. *Beyond the Welfare State? The New Political Economy of Welfare* (Cambridge: Polity Press, 1991).

Sanders, David. *Losing an Empire, Finding a Role: British Foreign Policy since 1945* (Basingstoke: Macmillan 1990).

Smith, Michael, et al., eds. *British Foreign Policy: Tradition, Change and Transformation* (Boston: Allen and Unwin, 1988).

Timmins, Nicholas. *The Five Giants: A Biography of the Welfare State* (New York: Harper-Collins, 1995).

NOTES

1. G. M. Trevelyan, *Illustrated English Social History*, vol. 2 (New York: McKay, 1951), p. 89.
2. Peter Stearns, *World History: Patterns of Change and Continuity* (New York: Harper-Collins, 1995), p. 285.
3. Walter Bagehot, *The English Constitution* (Ithaca, NY: Cornell University Press, 1966).
4. W. G. Runciman, *Relative Deprivation and Social Justice* (Berkeley: University of California Press, 1966).
5. *Annual Report*, Trades Union Congress, 1995.
6. Peter Riddell, *The Thatcher Era and Its Legacy* (Cambridge: Blackwell, 1991).
7. David Butler and Dennis Kavanagh, *The British General Election of 1992* (New York: St. Martin's Press, 1992).
8. Frank Conley, *General Elections Today*, 2nd ed. (New York: Manchester University Press, 1994), p. 161; Ivor Crewe, "Voting and the

Electorate," in Patrick Dunleavy, *Developments in British Politics* (New York: St. Martin's Press, 1993), pp. 101–102.

9. Butler and Kavanagh, p. 338.

10. Sid Kessler and Fred Bayliss, *Contemporary British Industrial Relations*, 2nd ed. (London: Macmillan, 1995), p. 260.

11. Richard Crossman, "Introduction" to W. Bagehot, *The English Constitution*, pp. 51–53; Michael Foley, *The Rise of the British Presidency* (Manchester: Manchester University Press, 1993).

12. Desmond King, "Government Beyond Whitehall," in Dunleavy, p. 197.

The Government of France

Jean Blondel

Political Development

HISTORY AND SOCIETY: TRADITIONS AND CONTRADICTIONS IN FRENCH POLITICS

The Instability of French Politics through the 1960s

France refuses, almost doggedly, to fit the political framework of the rest of Western Europe and of the Atlantic world. On the one hand, the Fifth Republic, set up by Charles de Gaulle in 1958, has proved to be a stable regime, but on the other hand, as recently as 1958, the country seemed on the verge of political catastrophe, with generals in Algiers threatening a military invasion. The previous regime, the Fourth Republic, had ended after 13 years marked by great political instability. During the 150 years before that, France had had about 20 constitutions, of which only one—that of the Third Republic, inaugurated in 1870—lasted over 20 years. The First Republic was installed at the end of the eighteenth century and lasted 7 years (1792–1799); the Second was established in 1848 and lasted 3 years to 1851; the Fourth Republic was set up after World War II and lasted 12 years (1946–1958).

Indeed, both the Third and the Fourth Republics were characterized by much instability greater even than that of contemporary Italy. During those periods, governments rarely lasted more than half a year and almost never had any real authority. It may be that France has at last acquired real political stability in the Fifth Republic, but if so, this stability has been acquired at a price. France's political system is somewhat different from those of other Western countries and poses as yet unresolved problems about the respective position of president and government.

Social and Economic Development

Explanations for France's political instability are not easy to find. Economic performance does not provide the answer. France is one of the richest countries in the world. Its per capita GDP of $22,300 in 1992 was somewhat higher than that of the Netherlands ($20,590), a little lower that that of West Germany ($23,030), and markedly higher than that of Britain ($17,666). If, as political scientists believe, wealth and political stability are closely associated, France should be as stable as the Netherlands, and more stable than Britain or Ireland.

The distribution of wealth and the class structure do not provide clues either. Incomes and wealth are somewhat more unevenly distributed in France than in northern Europe, but the large majority of the population has sizable incomes, and a very substantial proportion are small property owners. Indeed, France has traditionally been a nation of "small" business-people—shopkeepers, artisans, and, above all, farmers. While in Latin America and the countries of southern Europe political unrest can be attributed to conflict over land reform, in France the land is owned by large numbers of small holders, making agricultural workers and sharecroppers a tiny minority.

The sources of French contemporary difficulties are, therefore, not the direct consequence of social and economic characteristics common to Latin or other countries which experience instability. Political unrest is more deeply embedded in the culture of the country, in its history, and in many of its structures, especially the administrative structures. Conflicts appear to arise in large part from a number of contradictions, which the French do not seem able to surmount. The result has been that the legitimacy of the regime has been relatively low; indeed, only recently has the political system been fully accepted by almost all the French citizens.

The Clash between Liberalism and Authoritarianism

Since the eighteenth century, perhaps the most obvious contradiction has been between traditional authoritarianism and liberal democracy. It has left its scars. The Revolution of 1789 introduced values of republicanism, liberalism, and egalitarianism which a substantial segment of the French population not only did not readily accept but at times combated by force. The first continental country to adopt constitutionalism and liberalism, France was also the first country to experience modern authoritarian rule (under the two Napoleons) at the beginning and in the middle of the nineteenth century. Because that experience was distasteful to so many, France escaped twentieth-century totalitarianism in peacetime. However, it succumbed once again to totalitarian rule under the impact of the German occupation between 1940 and 1944. Liberal democracy became truly legitimate only very recently indeed.

Nationalism and Internationalism

The French are internationally minded, but largely only to the extent that the world reflects and adopts their own values. Thus the Revolution of 1789 was the only time when the contradiction was resolved, since the imperialism of the French was then associated with the desire to spread an idealistic gospel. The armies of the Republic invaded Europe to defeat the "tyrants" and liberate the "people." This same idea existed 100 years later, as France made assimilation its colonial policy. By contrast, British colonial policy was based on the principle of noninterference with local traditions. Opposition to French colonial rule was misunderstood and often held to be wholly misguided as it did not recognize the blessings of France's "civilizing mission."

France's view of the outside world reveals a third contradiction: a belief in the greatness of the country which simply does not correspond to reality. Previously, when political power was based on the strength of armies and on cultural prestige, France did rather well. It was the most populous of European countries, and it had spread its language and civilization all over Europe; European aristocrats worshipped French culture, while French armies periodically fought and imposed their will. But the Industrial Revolution gradually changed the basis of power, and suddenly a small country like England could control the world by its exports of manufactured goods. France was caught unprepared. Although it had a rich tradition of public works (roads and urban planning), it entirely lacked one of industrial enterprise. To this day objects of French national pride are more likely to be grand projects of dubious commercial value, such as the Concorde, rather than successful ventures in light engineering or consumer goods.

Cultural pride helps to explain the peculiar relationship France had with the Soviet Union. In the late 1940s, the French Communist Party

Entrance to the Channel Tunnel between England and France, inaugurated in May 1994, initially for freight services and then for high-speed passenger trains.

Feature 3.1   French Culture and the French Language

In some ways, France remains outside the major social and cultural changes which have taken place in the second half of the twentieth century. The determined resistance to "Americanization" accounts in large part for the awkwardness with which French governments react to world developments. Many of the country's elites believe that French culture must be defended against all kinds of encroachments, particularly against the "invasion" of Anglicisms into the French language. The enduring belief that the French language is a flagship that helps to propagate French culture has prompted the French government to continually extol the "francophonie" (the supposed cultural realm defined by French-speaking peoples throughout the world). In the mid–1990s a law was even passed to attempt to protect the language. Such a policy helps to keep some weakening cultural ties from dissolving completely, particularly in Africa, but it isolates France from the rest of the world. Foreign language skills are still not seen as essential, and French citizens are even often officially told that they must use the French language while abroad.

---

had over 25 percent of the votes; only very slowly did it fall to under 10 percent four decades later. The French Communist Party was probably the most "Stalinist" of Western Communist parties, following quite faithfully the policy dictated by the Soviet Union in the pre-Gorbachev era. Communist Russia exercised attraction in part because France has always wanted to be "independent" of the United States and of the Western nations which have formed the Atlantic alliance. In reality, France's geographical position as well as its culture and history make it a part of Western Europe. As such, it can scarcely be "independent." In spite of this, its leaders periodically by various means endeavor to affirm this "independence."

Centralization and Decentralization

The Role of the Bureaucracy   The final fundamental contradiction in French government is the bureaucracy. Historically it has been both a major instrument of change and a major hindrance to development. Authorities had viewed the centralization of the French State as a necessity dictated by the fact that civil servants and technocrats had been the originators of industrial strength who often saw themselves as agents in the midst of a population which

was passive and often markedly antagonistic to their innovations. Further justifications were added. Government centralization meant a uniform structure: Who would want education to be less developed in some parts of the country than in others? Moreover, if the civil service did not intervene, so the argument went, localism would prevail and there would be much patronage and graft. A centralized bureaucracy was thus morally justified.

These contradictions remain, although they are less acute than in the past. The cultural prestige of France has dwindled, and many now know it. Many also know that industrial strength is the key to prosperity and world influence, as the growth of West Germany and Japan has shown. Yet, while there is awareness of these realities in some circles, old views about French "greatness" still linger on, as the utterances of many leaders, even in the 1990s, clearly demonstrate.

THE HISTORICAL PERSPECTIVE OF FRENCH POLITICS

France's political history has been highly complex. To unravel this jumble, one must begin with the great event of French history—the Revolution of 1789. With great drama, with a missionary and military zeal which threatened the *anciens régimes* of much of the rest of Europe, the French routed the monarchy, the aristocracy, and the privileged Roman Catholic Church in the name of liberty, equality, and the republican form of government. Yet the old order, though defeated, was not destroyed. Its defenders were able to revive the monarchy in the nineteenth century and delay for decades any final regulation of the Church's powers. Meanwhile, the antirepublican tradition resisted through time. After attempting to undermine all the republics from the First (1792) to the Fifth (1958), its supporters have taken until the last 40 years to reconcile themselves to the processes of popular sovereignty.

The Revolution of 1789

The defenders of the Revolution and Republic were not long in becoming divided over whether they should give priority to equality or to liberty. In the early revolutionary period, great effort was made to destroy the political privileges of the titled and aristocratic classes. The Declaration of the Rights of Man and the Citizen, adopted tumultuously in the revolutionary Assembly of 1789, detailed the expectations of French citizens to be given basic freedoms and to be granted justice on the basis of the law. The Declaration represented the momentary ascendancy of libertarians over egalitarians.

There were, however, strong undercurrents in the Revolution which were bent on leveling all economic and social distinctions between men. The dictatorship of the Jacobins, the "progressive" party of the time, was a move toward the use of the State as an instrument of vigorous social change. The efforts of the Jacobins failed, only to be replaced in 1799 by Napoleon's much more conservative (and stabilizing) regime. However, the Jacobins added to the matrix of French political development a powerful political strain.

Traditionalists and Liberals in the Nineteenth Century

For most of the nineteenth century the libertarians had only a shaky hold on France and the an-

tirevolutionaries returned in 1814–1815. As the returning monarch, Louis XVIII agreed to a considerable dose of liberalism which did not sit well with his brother and successor, Charles X. Charles's reactionary attempts ended in revolution in 1830, when the French put Louis-Philippe d'Orléans on the throne. The new Orleans monarchy started as a parliamentary regime, but ended once again in revolution, after having made too many efforts to manipulate Parliament instead of concentrating on the new political aspirations of the French. The Revolution of 1848 (which swept all over continental Europe as well) put an end to the liberal monarchy in France and, indeed, to the monarchy altogether.

The Napoleonic Tradition

The most curious intermixture of political strands flowing from the French Revolution was the imperial tradition, into which Napoleon Bonaparte (1799–1814) stumbled, which his nephew Louis Napoleon perfected in the Second Empire (1852–1870), and which some contemporary commentators felt was reincarnated in the Fifth Republic of General de Gaulle (see Table 3.1). Claiming that they were embodying the "general will" of the nation as expressed in the plebiscites which chose them, the Bonapartes could thus pretend that they were the descendants of the revolutionary assemblies.

The imperial tradition, despite some trappings borrowed from the Revolution, was in fact both politically antiliberal and socially conservative. It was aimed essentially at maintaining the rights of the newly enfranchised bourgeoisie. Indeed, the Second Empire can be said to have been more progressive than the First Empire, as France then began to move from a predominantly agricultural economy and experienced her first great industrial boom.

Napoleon's primary achievement was to maintain and develop the bureaucracy inherited from the monarchy. Through him, France was given a well-functioning administration, codes of law, and a theory of the administrative process which were envied by many countries for several generations. Much of the Napoleonic bureaucracy is still in existence. Political battles

Table 3.1   CHRONOLOGY OF POLITICAL DEVELOPMENT IN FRANCE

To 1789	*Ancien régime* (dates of reign): Louis XIV, 1643–1715. Louis XV, 1715–1774. Louis XVI, 1774–1792.
1789–1792	Constitutional Monarchy. Constituent Assembly. Constitution of 1791. First legislative Assembly.
1792–1799	First Republic. Convention Constitution of 1793 (not applied). Directory Constitution of 1795.
1799–1804	Consulate. Napoleon, first consul. Constitutions of 1799 and 1802.
1804–1814 and 1815	First Empire. Napoleon I, emperor. Constitutions of 1804, 1814 (not applied), and 1815.
1814–1815 and 1815–1830	Restoration. Louis XVIII, 1814–1824. Charter of 1814 Charles X, 1824–1830.
1830–1848	Orleans monarchy. Louis-Philippe I, 1830–1848. Charter of 1830.
1848–1851	Second Republic. Napoleon Bonaparte (nephew of Napoleon I), president. Constitution of 1848.
1852–1870	Second Empire. Napoleon III, emperor. Constitutions of 1852 and 1870.
1870–1940	Third Republic. Constitution of 1875.
1940–1944	Vichy Regime. Pétain, "Head of State."
1945–1958	Fourth Republic. Constitution of 1946.
From 1958	Fifth Republic. Constitution of 1958. Charles de Gaulle, president, 1958–1969. Georges Pompidou, president, 1969–1974. Valery Giscard d'Estaing, president, 1974–1981. François Mitterrand, president, 1981–1988, reelected, 1988–1995. Jacques Chirac, president, elected 1995 (mandate expires 2002).

have been fought over governments and their policies, but not over the administrative instruments of governments.

Republicanism and Its Elements

Nineteenth-century French republicanism originally comprised only a few simple elements: the expression of the public will through a sovereign and directly elected assembly, a society free from the institutionalized influence of the Church, and distrust of executive authority as a threat to freedom against which the people had an obligation to rise when and if tyranny appeared imminent. Several times the people did take to the streets, making this form of civic violence take on an almost mythical value. It was used (rather symbolically) against the Germans leaving Paris in 1944, and again by students in the university district of Paris, the Latin Quarter, during the 1968 uprising.

The egalitarian strand of French republicanism never succeeded for long. The 1793–1794 "Reign of Terror" eventually led to Napoleon; the 1848 revolution led to the Second Empire; and when this regime fell after being defeated by Prussia in 1870, the Paris Commune seized power in the capital, but it was

smashed, ending in one of the bloodiest episodes of repression in French history.

Moderate republicanism became truly established after the Paris Commune. A national assembly composed mainly of monarchists drafted constitutional laws, hoping that a monarchical restoration could take place. The republic triumphed by default, and almost by accident, in 1875. The Constitution then grudgingly adopted lasted until 1940. It was destroyed by German arms after a series of attacks coming from both Right and Left and by the weakness and internal divisions of its supporters.

The Second World War and Its Consequences: The Vichy Regime, the Resistance, and the Fourth and Fifth Republics

Modern French history spans the Third (1875–1946), Fourth (1946–1958), and Fifth Republics (since 1958). It was interrupted between 1940 and 1944 by the "corporate state" of Pétain, whose authority derived from the German victory over France and not, despite the appearances of a legal transfer, from the will of the French people. In many ways, the Vichy regime (so called because the seat of government was transferred to Vichy, in central France, while northern France was occupied) symbolized the antirepublican element in French life.

While Nazi Germany occupied northern France and the collaborationist Vichy regime was in power, a Resistance movement began organizing against German occupation. The Resistance contained elements of all shades of French republicanism, from conservative nationalists to communists. Although General de Gaulle had created a government in exile long before, at the time of liberation in 1944, the Resistance remained the main political force in the country. The new constitution, adopted in 1946, established the Fourth Republic on the basis of traditional republican principles, but also on strong left-wing overtones inherited from the Resistance. But the Left was not strong enough to retain power and the Fourth Republic resembled the Third. It was characterized by a powerful popular assembly, a weak executive, and an administrative apparatus floating in an ambiguous limbo below the government.

The Weakness and Fall of the Fourth Republic Being weak and transient, the governments of the Fourth Republic were unable to solve France's major political problem: decolonization. Defeat in Indochina in 1954 severely undermined France's political system. A strong prime minister, Pierre Mendès-France, did manage to produce a settlement which effectively disengaged France from its Indochinese colonies, but he remained in power for only six months afterwards. By then, war had broken out in the French colony of Algeria between supporters of the status quo (mostly comprising of the million French settlers in Algeria) and those who demanded Algerian independence. Successive governments proved too weak to make any move in the direction of reform. Despite the presence of a million French conscripts to the other side of the Mediterranean, France lost the war. By May 1958, pushed by civilian extremists, commanders in Algiers ceased to recognize the authority of the Paris government and even landed a small military force in Corsica. Rumors of an impending army coup spread throughout France; these created a

climate of tension, plots, and counterplots. De Gaulle was recalled to office by a large majority of the Assembly on June 1, 1958, some hoping he could keep Algeria French, others thinking that he alone had the power to solve the problem. The Fifth Republic was born.

THE BACKGROUND OF THE SOCIAL ORDER

In the 1950s and 1960s, France leapt forward both socially and economically. Many consider the tragedy of modern France the inability of its politics to keep pace with socioeconomic change. At the same time aspects of the traditional social divisions remain visible in many parts of the country. The French population—long static at 40 million and now over 55 million—has peasant origins. France is geographically and even linguistically divided, and the class system (particularly the division between bourgeois and worker) has long dictated lifestyles. France is traditionally Roman Catholic, but it also was fiercely anticlerical in the nineteenth and early twentieth centuries. It was on such a social landscape that the kings first and Napoleon later built a centralized administrative machine and that the Republic imposed a centralized political culture.

Peasant Origins

France has historically been a peasant nation—indeed perhaps the only peasant nation with a substantial proportion of its population who worked as small holders instead of farm laborers. By the outbreak of World War II, as much as one-third of the population worked on plots inherited from their parents and to which they were passionately attached (see Table 3.2).

Though owners of the land, these farmers had a difficult life. Plots were small and often fragmented, because the civil code of Napoleon required that estates be divided equally among all the children. This led to low productivity and low incomes even in rich areas—a state of affairs which fostered pessimism among large numbers of farmers. This also led to a low birthrate, lower, before 1945, than in all other developed nations.

Table 3.2 OCCUPATIONS OF THE FRENCH POPULATION

	Percent of the Active Population			
	1954	**1962**	**1975**	**1990**
Farmers and farm laborers	26.5	24.0	9.4	4.5
Owners of businesses	12.0	10.0	7.8	7.9
Higher management and professions	3.0	4.0	6.7	11.7
Middle management	6.0	7.5	12.7	20.0
White-collar workers	16.0	17.0	22.3	26.5
Manual workers	33.5	35.0	37.6	29.4
Other (army, police, etc.)	3.0	2.5	3.5	—
	100.0	100.0	100.0	100.0
Total (millions)	19.3	20.1	21.7	22.3

Migrations from village to city were characteristic of Western Europe, yet the new city-dweller was less adversely affected by them than in other countries. Peasant origins remained very important, and residents of cities often took on attitudes more characteristic of rural than of urban communities. Preconceptions, fears, worries, and a rather negative and anarchistic individualism came to dominate much of the middle and lower-middle levels of French society—shopkeepers, artisans, mechanics, workers in commerce and in industry, and civil servants.

The peasant complex, as this orientation might be called, is a strong element in that much-discussed French characteristic—individualism. It appears in the negative way in which the French have traditionally reacted to voluntary groupings. They did not believe in them and supported them with great hesitation, thus demonstrating, in a self-fulfilling prophecy, that most groupings conferred few benefits. The respect for negative criticism, the fear of appearing naive, and the suspicion of all peoples and institutions had considerable drawbacks for the French economy. It rendered experimentation an object of ridicule and was indeed the very cause of the outside imposition of rules which the peasant community could not and would not establish.

Since World War II the characteristics of the farming community have altered markedly. The flight from the land took on such propor-tions in the late 1950s and 1960s that the weight of the peasantry in society diminished. From 1954 to 1975 the farming population fell by more than 50 percent, from 5.2 million to under 2 million; by 1990, the farming population had declined to a little over 1 million. Farmers who remained on the land acquired larger plots, and mechanization and the commercialization of farm products gave farmers a different outlook on their role in society. With only one person in twenty engaged in agriculture, and with farms becoming businesses, modern France no longer has a large body of citizens who alone can tilt the scales in elections and generally flavor the political culture. But attitudes die hard and memories are long, and the past political order still plays a substantial part in the political life of the present.

Regional Sectionalism and the Influence of Paris

The second characteristic of the traditional French social structure is sectionalism maintained partly by the size of the peasantry, but also by general historical and geographical characteristics. Mountains and plateaus separate the country into natural regions and isolate certain areas from the main communication axes. Brittany, the Southwest (sometimes known as Aquitaine), the Alpine area, and Provence (of which the southeastern tip on the Mediterranean has a very hilly interior, and is known to tourists as the Cote d'Azur) all constitute sharply differentiated regions. These regions are somewhat isolated from the more accessible northern and northeastern parts of the country, whose wide plains give them an easier agriculture, more industry, and more natural lines of communication. History has in large part been molded by these geographical constraints and local particularism has been widespread.

French sectionalism manifests itself in many ways. As everywhere, there are differences in accent, in turn often the product of the survival of local dialects, some of which, as in the south, have a Latin origin and are related to Italian (Provençal) or Spanish (Catalan), while others (Alsatian and Flemish) have Germanic roots and yet others (Breton and Basque) have little or nothing in common with the main European languages. But different forms of living are often also the consequences of different climates, which vary sharply as one moves from humid but temperate Brittany to the cold Massif Central or Alsace and to the pleasant, almost Californian, Mediterranean coast. The shape of local architecture make towns and villages in Alsace, Provence, or the Paris area so different that they seem to belong to different countries. But these variations are the symbols of other, more profound variations in modes of living, and the outdoor life in the clement south and southeast contrasts sharply with the indoor life of the tougher north and east.

These differences have naturally led the French to be attached to their *petite patrie*—to their home areas—while outsiders who come to an area find real human relationships slow to develop. Important consequences follow; for instance, for a long time, political candidates had little chance of being elected if they ran for office in areas where they had no local roots.

The peculiar position of Paris has to be considered in this context. The political, social, economic, and cultural preeminence of the capital is beyond doubt, but it is much resented. Paris is much larger than any other French city or metropolitan area. Eight million people live in Paris and its suburbs (the city proper has a population of only about 2 million), but the next three largest metropolitan areas—Marseilles, Lyons, and Lille—barely reach a million, while the fifth largest town, Toulouse, has about half a million. Provincial capitals are therefore not in a position to challenge the metropolis. Those who have "arrived" have to be in Paris; those who are not in Paris often feel they have not "arrived." The weight of Paris is felt even by those who do not wish to move to the capital.

Factors such as the car and television are minimizing sectionalism, also bringing Paris nearer to those in the provinces. The wider economic context of the European Union decreases the preeminence of Paris, but the capital remains a pole of attraction, as well as a drain on the better resources of the provinces, to a much greater extent than in other European countries.

Social Class

Class consciousness, the third main influence on French society, is a function of the cleavages which have torn the fabric of modern society, and also an outgrowth of the Industrial Revolution, which acquired full momentum in France only at the end of the nineteenth century. Social distinctions run sharp and deep, particularly in the large cities, although these have begun to decrease since the 1950s. The large size of the Communist vote is clearly a consequence of the bitterness which these conflicts have caused.

Social mobility occurs at about the same rate as in other developed societies. Moreover this development is not new. Through education in particular, large numbers of the sons and daughters of peasants, of lower middle-class employees, and even of manual workers have entered the middle class. Some educational channels have always long made social promotion possible, in particular through prestigious graduate schools, such as the *Ecole Polytechnique* and the *Ecole Normale Supérieure,* as well as numerous other schools or examinations leading to the middle ranks of the civil service or the armed forces. Thrifty working-class young people have often set up small businesses which they hope slowly to expand.

In France social class is based to a large extent on occupation, education, and income. Though there is in France a tradition of respect for the crafts (the skills of artisans are often extolled), the esteem for industrial manual work is low. Class tension as such has decreased somewhat, partly as a result of the "embourgeoisement" of many workers who have adopted a middle-class lifestyle, from cars to holidays abroad.

Class tensions may also have decreased in part because large-scale immigration has enabled the French to avoid working in the mines, the building trades, and certain sections of the engineering industry where they have been replaced by workers from Poland, Italy, Spain, and, since the 1950s, Portugal and North Africa. This situation may have helped the French avoid less pleasant forms of work, but it is at the root of the major ethnic tensions which have characterized contemporary France. Tension between the native French and North Africans have erupted in violence in many vast suburban high-rise housing projects where immigrants are often in the majority. While government policy is officially against all forms of discrimination, repressive measures, including forced repatriation, have occasionally been taken against immigrants. Terrorist incidents have occasionally provided authorities with grounds for surveillance and repression of the immigrant population. These measures have been taken in part to compete with and hopefully stop the development of a strong extreme-right movement which emerged in the 1980s, the National Front, which will be discussed later.

There has also been an increase in the proportion of women in higher-status positions, particularly in the civil service and the professions and more recently in business, though less so in politics, especially at the parliamentary level. This improvement has taken place despite the fact that there has been markedly less pressure from women's organizations than in Anglo-American countries. Nonetheless, France has not, any more than most industrial countries, ceased to be mainly male-dominated.

THE CHURCH

France is nominally a Catholic nation. One million Protestants (Calvinists in the south, Lutherans in Alsace) and less than half a million Jews are the only other sizable "indigenous" religious groups. The country's more than a million Muslims are drawn from among immigrants, mainly from North Africa, many of whom have settled perma-

nently. But this Catholic nation is profoundly anticlerical, in parts wholly de-Christianized, and still somewhat affected by the great political battles which led to the separation of Church and State in 1905. For the majority of French people, Roman Catholic practice is limited to social rites such as baptisms, marriages, and funerals. Weekly attendance at mass and general observance of religious prescriptions is limited to a rather small minority which is not uniformly spread throughout the nation. Brittany and Alsace are strong Catholic areas; the western part of the Massif Central and the southeast are antireligious or at best areligious. The historical origins of these variations are complex and are often related less to the priests than to the behavior of the local gentry before or during the Revolution of 1789.

As in most predominantly Roman Catholic countries of Western Europe, Church and social order are closely associated in France. Since the Church was close to the Right in the nineteenth century, the Left, both moderate and extremist, has always attacked it. The attempt to restore the monarchy in the 1870s was viewed partly as an effort of the Church. Anticlericalism therefore spread among supporters of the Republic. The climax was reached in the 1890s with the Dreyfus case, in which a Jewish military officer was accused and convicted of a dubious charge of treason. In spite of numerous signs that a judicial error had been committed, the case was reopened only after a long and bitter struggle between his defenders and his accusers (the Church, the military, and the conservatives). In 1905 and in response to the "Dreyfus Affair," Parliament passed a law separating Church and State. Priests (as well as Protestant ministers and Jewish rabbis) lost their status as civil servants, various religious orders were disbanded or had to leave the country (among them the Jesuits, who were "tolerated" again after 1918 only and not formally allowed in the country before World War II).

Many Roman Catholics became embittered against the Republic, but others began to realize that a change of attitude had to take place. The pronouncements of Pope Leo XIII helped in this respect, though his successor, Pius X, returned to more traditional ways and condemned a progressive Catholic movement, *Le Sillon,* created in 1894, thereby making it difficult for a strong Catholic or Christian Democratic party to develop in France. This was to occur only in the 1940s, too late to enable the party to have a permanent social base as the country was by then rather de-Christianized. On the other hand, progressive Catholics did play a large part in the development of some trade unions and of some other organizations, as we shall see in the next section.

The climate has changed since the 1950s, although some antipathy against the Roman Catholic Church still exists. While the status of the Catholics and of the Church has increased and the reconciliation between the two sides is not total, there are no longer the big battles of the early part of the century. Major skirmishes have centered on Church schools, to which State subsidies were granted in the 1950s; the last installment of this conflict occurred after the 1981 Socialist victory, when the government attempted to establish greater control over the schools. Vast demonstrations occurred—so large than the proposals had to be abandoned. There is thus still sensitivity with respect to Church questions, but the issue has ceased to be truly central.

THE ADMINISTRATIVE AND CULTURAL CENTRALIZATION OF MODERN FRANCE

Divisions run deep in France. Not all are due to the Revolution, as we have seen; many date back from an earlier period. They cut across each other and lead to a fragmentation of the basic social attitudes which accounts for much of the ideological and political sectionalism of the country.

The very number and complexity of the social divisions account for state centralization, both administrative and cultural. It is often thought that had not the French kings, and later the Empire, set up a strong administrative system, the country would not have survived. It is also often thought that had not the Republic introduced a uniform political culture cutting across geographical and social barriers, the Republic would not have survived. Administrative centralization was thus practiced by all regimes in order to defend themselves; not surprisingly, the strength of the impressive network of state agencies existing throughout the country has proved difficult to reduce.

The Republic did introduce a new political culture, mostly since the 1880s; this was spread by means of a centralized educational system, which was to be liberal, lay, and egalitarian; it was not totalitarian, as it aimed at developing critical faculties, but it was uniform. It was largely based on the frame of mind of the writers of the eighteenth-century French Enlightenment, particularly Voltaire, who for about half a century had waged a war against the power of the Church and of the State, which were viewed as opposed to rational thinking in order to reduce criticisms of the social order.

This critical frame of mind was probably instilled too quickly to too many, through the village schoolteacher, the *instituteur,* who was to become the "priest" of the Republic and whose opposition to the *curé* became a classic joke in French local politics at least up to World War II. This critical ideology clearly undermined the authority on which all States, even republican ones, have to be based; only the centralized administration was therefore able to maintain the State. This, of course, made France more difficult to govern, although one can understand why republican politicians thought it necessary to spread their somewhat negative ideology. By emphasizing the right to criticize, they created problems for their successors. The political system has been bedeviled in the twentieth century by the very success of the republicans of the 1880s and 1890s, who bequeathed their political culture to millions of their fellow citizens. But had the republicans not been so successful, France might not have been a republic for long.

Such is the background with which modern French governments have had to contend; not surprisingly, the various traditions reduced the margin of maneuver of ministers and governments. The centralizing tendencies are of course the most visible—and the most overwhelmingly strong—of these traditions. But the weight of traditions can be seen also in the very large part played by the public sector, in its various facets, on the French economy. Centralization brought about a spirit of "enlightened despotism" and of *dirigisme* which has prevailed in the political, administrative, and economic life of the country. France underwent major changes in the second half of the twentieth century, but the impact of the past lies close to the surface. It would be as foolish for observers to forget these traditions as it would be fatal for politicians to disregard them.

KEY TERMS

administrative centralization
Church vs. State
class consciousness
The Declaration of the Rights of Man and
     the Citizen
The Dreyfus Affair
Jacobins
Napoleon Bonaparte
regional sectionalism
republicanism
Revolution of 1848
Revolution of 1789/Revolutionary Assembly

FURTHER READINGS

Ardagh, J. *The New France* (Baltimore: Penguin Books, 1973).

Bodley, J. E. *France* (London: Macmillan, 1898).

Brogan, D. W. *The Development of Modern France* (London: Hamish Hamilton, 1940).

Ehrman, H. *Politics in France,* 3d ed. (Boston: Little, Brown, 1974).

Frears, J. R. *France in the Giscard Presidency* (London: Allen and Unwin, 1981).

De Gaulle, C. *Memoirs* (New York: Simon & Schuster, 1968–1972).

Hall, P. A., Hayward, J., and H. Machin, *Developments in French Politics* (London: Macmillan, 1990).

Hoffmann, S., Ross, G. and S. Malzacher, eds., *The Mitterrand Experiment* (Oxford: Polity Press, 1987).

Macridis, R. *French Politics in Transition* (Cambridge: Winthrop, 1975).

Pickles, D. *The Government and Politics of France,* 2 vol. (London: Methuen, 1973).

Stevens, A., *The Government and Politics of France* (London: Macmillan, 1992).

Williams, P. M. *Crisis and Compromise* (New York: McKay, 1964)

Williams, P. M. and M. Harrison, *Politics and Society in De Gaulle's Republic* (New York: Doubleday, 1973).

Wylie, L. *Village in the Vaucluse* (Cambridge: Harvard University Press, 1964).

Political Process and Institutions

The advent of the Fifth Republic in 1958 marked the emergence of modern politics in France, although, as we have already noted, elements of the past are still prominent. The constitution was changed, transforming the roles of president, government, and Parliament. At the same time, the strength and characteristics of groups and of parties were markedly affected, although these remain weaker and less well organized than those elsewhere in Western Europe.

INTEREST GROUPS

Interest groups have historically been frowned upon in France. The Revolution of 1789 fought the "corporate state" of the *ancien régime,* in which each trade was organized in closed craft networks that were entered only after long periods of apprenticeship, but which provided their members with monopoly privileges. In the name of liberty, the Revolution abolished these guilds and forbade individuals to coalesce to limit production or regulate the entry of others into a profession (with several important exceptions). Trade unions were barely tolerated 75 years after the Revolution and had to wait for another 25 years to be fully recognized. Political parties were undermined by the conception that politicians should have direct contacts with electors and remain free from the bureaucratic influence of headquarters and leaders. In the 1950s, a major change of attitude occurred, paradoxically as de Gaulle continued to attack groups and parties but needed a party to maintain his hold on the country.

While more pluralistic than at any time since 1789, present-day France still has fewer associations than other Western countries. The target of group attacks is often the State and the typical approach is still to ask the State to make the provisions or to force (for instance, by law) private employers to make concessions. The idea of partnership between economic actors is only slowly gaining ground.

Trade Unions

Workers' Unions The French trade union movement is very divided, largely for political reasons. Its membership is proportionately the smallest in Western Europe, indeed smaller than that in the United States, though participation is high in works councils mandated by law in firms of a certain size. The relatively late development of the union movement and political divisions account for these weaknesses.

The early history of French trade unions was difficult. Full recognition was achieved only in 1884. Very quickly, trade unions came to be controlled by militants who believed in direct action. By the turn of the century they displaced the more reformist or even Marxist elements of the leadership. These "syndicalists" were against employers and against all politicians. The *Confédération Générale du Travail* (CGT), created in 1895 as a federation of all major trade unions, did not look for piecemeal victories through Parliament. Rather, it sought one major push through the general strike. The union was never powerful enough to launch an effective general strike, and when war broke out in 1914, even trade unionists rushed to defend the "bourgeois" State.

After World War I, the majority of labor leaders adopted a more reformist stance, but the emergence of communism brought about a split in union leadership and introduced politics into the trade union movement. While the CGT followed the Socialist party, the more militant trade union leaders set up a Communist-led union, which was disbanded in 1936 in a "popular front" alliance. This move enabled Communists to gradually acquire influence in the newly reunited body and to dominate it in 1945. In 1947, when the CGT was openly used for political reasons in a wave of strikes launched by the Communists, the Socialists broke away and set up a new union, the CGT-*Force Ouvrière*.

Meanwhile, in 1918, a Catholic union, the *Confédération Française des Travailleurs Chrétiens* (CFTC), formed among white-collar employees and in strongly Christian parts of the country and slowly gathered followers in the whole of the country. By 1964 it was the second largest trade union in France and, to widen its appeal, changed its name to the *Confédération Française Démocratique du Travail* (CFDT), although a small segment of the union continued under the old name.

Today, there are three main trade union organizations catering to manual and white-collar workers. Yet the membership is small, a million or less in each union. This means that about 10 to 15 percent of the total work force is unionized, although there are substantial variations between occupational groups.

The Consequences of the Divisions among Workers' Unions Division has been detrimental to the interests of the workers, giving employers and governments the opportunity to play one union against the other, leading unions to make demagogic proposals in order not to be overtaken, and convincing many French workers that unionization is not necessary. There are exceptions to these divisions, admittedly. In printing, for instance, all the members belong to the CGT, and in many firms and offices one or at most two unions predominate. The CGT is strong mostly in the coal mines, on the docks, and in mechanical engineering (particularly around Paris); the CFDT's strength tends to be in light industry and among white-collar workers; and *Force Ouvrière* leads among textile workers in the north and among civil servants everywhere, though it is not, as is sometimes claimed, the main trade union among civil servants. Competition between two unions is common, however, and, at the national level, all three major unions take stands and are involved in consultations among themselves, with the government, and with employers.

The combination of the traditional weakness of unions and of legislative efforts to integrate union representatives into society led to a mixture of compulsory cooperation at the top and of semianarchistic and often ineffective outbursts at the bottom. Formally, unions are often involved in decision making. The social security system, for instance, is largely administered by unions; factory committees of union representatives (*comité d'entreprise*) are in charge of large sums of money devoted to leisure and cultural

activities; and union representatives serve on the boards of nationalized industries. Many government advisory committees, for instance, include trade union members. Yet because unions do not agree on a common stand and cannot promise financial help in case of strikes, they are often unable to press their demands at the level of individual companies. As a result, many workers continue to work when a strike is called. This has occurred despite the fact that the CFDT has called for a new approach to the relationship between workers and society. Instead of emphasizing the need for workers' organizations to prepare for an eventual onslaught on the State, as the CGT has traditionally tended to do, the CFDT aimed at developing cooperation. It thus played a large part in developing collective bargaining, which came about in France only at the end of the 1950s, although it was legalized in 1936. It was also the first union to place emphasis on the need to improve job conditions, in particular to reduce boredom and repetitiveness.

Yet these gains have not fundamentally altered old patterns of behavior. Unions are weak and workers are generally passive. Occasionally, however, there are somewhat anomic massive protest movements which start from the grass roots and extend to a large proportion of the work force. This was the case in 1968, the catalyst having been provided by the student movement. No action on such a grand scale occurred until late 1995, although, from time to time, especially among students, revolts seemed about to occur. Strikes had become rarer, in part perhaps because of the reforms of the Socialist government of the first half of the 1980s. The influence of the CGT has markedly declined, as was shown at elections for the Social Security Boards since the 1980s in particular. The entrenched class antagonism of the past seems to be giving way to more realism and greater moderation.

However, in December 1995 a large movement took place against a proposed governmental reform of pensions and social security. Strikes, in particular in the railways, urban public transport, and the post office were on a grand scale which resembled the 1968 outburst. The movement seemed to indicate that some of the old forms of discontent continued to exist, especially, in this case, as the government had tried to impose changes without consultation.

Other Unions   In theory, the three major trade union organizations cover all types of employees. But many white-collar workers, most lower and middle management (*cadres* is the French expression), the professions, and students have typically been organized in different unions. Sectional unions exist among professional people—doctors, dentists, and lawyers, for instance, who are typically self-employed. Special unions also exist for some other groups, such as school and university teachers. For a while, in the 1950s and early 1960s, students succeeded in creating one of the best and most active French trade unions, the *Union Nationale des Etudiants de France;* but the Algerian war and the events of 1968 led to a radicalization of the leadership which proved unacceptable to the mass of students. Finally, much of the employed middle class—the various levels of man-

agement in commerce and industry—are organized in a general union, the *Confédération Générale des Cadres* (CGC), which aims at maintaining the differentials which *cadres* have acquired in the growing French economy. Together with the three major workers' unions it participates in general government-union discussions, but clashes with workers' unions are frequent in view of basic ideological differences.

Business Organizations

Business organizations, too, are somewhat divided both because of the traditional influence of small business and because of the economic changes which have benefited large firms. Before 1945, industrial pressure on the government was frequent and tended to occur in secret and outside the framework of organizations. Change began to take place with the first French Socialist government, elected in 1936, which initiated general negotiations between

French public sector workers on strike.

government, unions, and business. This led to an overall agreement, the "Matignon Accord," which indirectly strengthened the role of business organizations and trade unions. Immediately after World War II the reconstituted *Conseil National du Patronat Français* (CNPF) started to operate in an unfriendly environment of strong antibusiness ideology. Employers seemed divided among themselves. Though the CNPF was a federation covering all types of firms, small and medium-sized enterprises were organized into a semi-independent confederation, the *Confédération Générale des Petites et Moyennes Entreprises* (CGPME), which because of the larger number and smaller incomes of its members and the prevailing cult of the *petit* in France was often more militant. Meanwhile, a section of the *patronat*, organized into a *Centre des Jeunes Patrons*, displayed a more progressive attitude and criticized their colleagues for their conservatism.

The division between the CNPF and the CGPME (later renamed CGPMI) has remained a feature of the contemporary French business scene. On the whole, the CNPF has cooperated with government, in part because governments have usually been of the Right or Center and in part because of many personal ties between leaders of large businesses and civil servants. Both business leaders and civil servants tend to go through the same elite schools or be members of the *grands corps,* as we shall see later. Big business has also been broadly sympathetic with the policy of growth and industrialization promoted by French governments since the 1950s, which still prevailed, albeit in a somewhat bruised manner, in the conditions of economic depression of the late 1970s and early 1980s. Relations have been relatively good even with Socialist governments of the 1980s, despite the large-scale nationalization program. State and business became engaged in a form of partnership.

The Defensive Attitudes of Small Business Small businesses, on the other hand, came to view with suspicion civil servants, who are anxious to rationalize the economy, and the public, who found cheaper goods in supermarkets and discount stores. They lost certain tax advantages granted to them earlier, when the cult of small business made good political capi-

tal. Discontent spread, not just through the CGPME but also through more radical organizations, two of which acquired for a time national political significance—the *Union de Défense des Commerçants et Artisans,* founded by Pierre Poujade in the mid-1950s and the *Comité d'Information et de Défense-Union Nationale des Artisans et des Travailleurs Indépendants* (CID-UNATI), founded by Leon Nicoud in the late 1960s. Both leaders favored direct action. Nicoud was jailed several times for being involved in operations against government buildings. The success of these organizations was short-lived, however, while the PME continued throughout the period to voice, in a more responsible manner, the basic grievances of shopkeepers and small-business owners. Some results were occasionally obtained, however, for instance with respect to restrictions on the development of large discount stores.

Outbursts of the "underdogs" of French business thus occurred in the Fifth Republic, but more sporadically than before 1958. The party system of the Fifth Republic has been better able to contain the activities of these groups. Yet the contrast between the "civilized" forms of pressure exercised by large businesses and the somewhat anomic and occasionally violent actions of small-business owners indicates that traditionalism continues to play a part in contemporary France.

Farmers' Organizations

Agriculture has evolved more rapidly than any other sector of French society. The flight to the cities and the development of mechanized farming have altered the conditions of farmers in every part of the country. Those who stayed have gained more room and some scope for expansion, but they have also been confronted with severe problems of capital and investment. Admittedly, the problems of the farming community differ according to geography. In the north and in the Paris area, wheat and beetroot growers have long constituted a farming aristocracy, with larger plots, more widespread mechanization, and higher incomes. In this area, industrial firms are often involved in agricultural production in a capitalist fashion. Elsewhere in France, small farms are the norm. Although they are sometimes efficient (particularly for fruit, grapes, and vegetables), they are generally inefficient because of their size.

The main pressure group of farmers is the *Fédération Nationale des Syndicats d'Exploitants Agricoles* (FNSEA). It emerged out of an abortive 1945 attempt to organize an all-embracing *Confédération Générale de l'Agriculture* (CGA), which would have included cooperatives as well as agricultural workers; but this comprehensive body proved unable to solve conflicts which arose among its various components. For most of the 1950s it was led by the larger northern farmers, but it was challenged as rapid changes took place in the structure of agriculture and its relation to the rest of the community. At first, the leadership was challenged only by protests of small farmers, which began to resemble those of shopkeepers, characterized by roadblocks and the dumping of unsold vegetables. Gradually, however, strong Catholic associations which stressed the long-term benefits of the industrialization of farms came to pose a greater challenge. The *Jeunesse Agricole Chrétienne* and the *Centre National des Jeunes Agriculteurs* succeeded in educating large sections of the farming community and in making them willing to participate in a major modernization process as well as to promote the spread of cooperative ideas in a sector of the population that was hitherto highly individualistic. Gradually these ideas were adopted by the FNSEA itself, as some of the Catholic leaders became leaders of the organization. The agricultural policy of the European Union also suggested that there were immense opportunities. Yet recurring complaints have been made by farmers' unions, in particular when new countries joined the European Union or over the relationship of the Union with the United States in connection with farm subsidies. On the whole, farmers' unions have succeeded in forcing French governments to support their cause on the international scene, indeed to an extent which seems out of proportion with the size of the farming population.

Other Groups

Since the mid–1960s, interest groups have come to play a regular part in the panorama of French political life, although the development remains somewhat patchy. Until the late 1950s, promotional groups had not been influential. For instance, while the nuclear disarmament campaign was reaching a climax in Britain, there was almost no equivalent in France, though the subject could have become controversial when de Gaulle embarked on a worldwide nuclear strategy. The first upsurge of group activity occurred at the time over Algeria and over the question of institutions, with clubs, primarily political in outlook, being in some ways the heirs of the salons of the eighteenth century.

The Relative Weakness of Promotional Groups

The Algerian war was instrumental in the development of protest organizations, as political parties seemed impotent and none of them, not even the Communist party, was able or willing to take a firm line against the war. The end of the Algerian war in 1962 made the protest organizations obsolete, but, gradually, new groups emerged. Consumer associations started to inquire into the quality of products, forms of marketing, and relative costs. Environmental societies have campaigned against the pollution of the seaside and the development of private beaches, attacked the takeover of vast areas of land for army camps, and opposed plans for highways and, more recently, plans for new lines for "very rapid" trains. Some groups are purely local and exclusively concerned with one issue; others are national and foster general aims. Occasionally, from the mid–1970s, antinuclear groups have also become vocal and often violent, while women's groups have begun to make themselves felt; but both types have remained relatively low-key.

In the late 1960s and early 1970s, there was an upsurge in the activity of regionalist groups. Long limited to the Bretons and (though less so) the Basques, regionalist ideas extended for a while to large parts of the country, particularly the southern half, where the *Mouvement Occitan* stated that the "colonization" of the country by the north and by Paris had to be ended. The strength of most of these movements declined, however, in part probably because the Socialist government of 1981–1986 introduced regionalist and decentralization measures. Only in Corsica and to an extent in the French Overseas Territo-

---

Feature 3.2   The Weakness of Protest Groups in France

Groups are unquestionably still much weaker in France than in other Western democracies. What was true in the nineteenth century continues to be true, despite some changes, at the end of the twentieth. It is not just that trade unions are weaker and more divided than elsewhere; it is that the groups which flourish in other countries do not emerge, or scarcely emerge, in the French context. The huge protests of antibomb groups in Britain had no counterparts in France, despite the fact that France has nuclear weapons. The limited reactions within France to the bombs exploded in the Pacific in the mid–1990s are a case in point. Moreover, there have also been relatively few demonstrations against nuclear power stations despite the fact that France has more nuclear power stations than other countries. Even feminist groups have been weak, and not because women have made more advances in France than elsewhere. The low level of associationalism in France was mentioned by Tocqueville in his *Democracy in America* in the 1830s, and remarkably, the same trend prevails even today. This characteristic is unquestionably among the most important aspects of French political culture.

---

ries (New Caledonia, in the Caribbean, and Tahiti) did radicalization occur to an extent. But even in Corsica, autonomist movements have been too divided to truly keep up the momentum. The only major terrorist activities which France has known since World War II have occurred during the Algerian war in the early 1960s and, in the late 1980s and mid–1990s, in the form of sporadic outbursts of bombing connected with Muslim, and in particular Algerian, opposition to French government policies.

Groups and the Political System

The Role of Consultation   The Fifth Republic began in 1958 with an anti-interest-group bias. Yet de Gaulle was soon confronted with large waves of protest on the part of veterans and of opponents of Church schools. The government took little notice of the huge demonstrations and won. De Gaulle seemed to have proved his point—that when the State is strong, it can withstand the pressure of groups. However, his policy of "benign neglect" led to an accumulation of grievances which finally exploded in May and June 1968. Since then, leaders of the Fifth Republic have been more cautious and have developed consultation as a means of addressing grievances.

The origins of consultation can be traced to the *ancien régime* and to the Napoleonic system.

Although it was initially limited to narrow sectors of the population, representation gradually increased. After World War I, consultation was institutionalized through an economic council mandated by the constitution in 1946. The council is composed of representatives of all sectors of the population, including consumers and intellectuals. It gives advice on bills and on the more important government regulations, and it debates economic and social plans. Together with the many representative bodies on which trade unionists are present (boards of nationalized industries, social security boards, and others) and with the associations of farmers (*Chambres d'Agriculture*) or of business leaders (*Chambres de Commerce*), the Economic and Social Council provides a broad formal basis to the consultative process.

Yet what had been lacking until recently has been not so much a formal machinery for consultation, but a will to discuss or a climate of consultation. Previously partnership existed only in one privileged sector, big business, where personal ties between leaders of industry and higher civil servants made informal discussions possible and indeed frequent. For small business, agriculture, employees, and consumers, no similar relations existed. Admittedly, the uncooperative and unrealistic attitudes of many trade unions and of many other groups can be blamed, but these uncooperative attitudes were also in part the product of an earlier lack of partnership.

A change occurred in the 1970s with Presidents Pompidou and Giscard d'Estaing. Pompidou's first prime minister, Jacques Chaban-Delmas, undertook to bring about a partnership between the various "live forces" (*forces vives*) of the nation. Then, in the 1980s, having accused the Gaullists and their associates of not giving enough scope for consultation, the Socialists who came to power in 1981 attempted to increase consultation; but the program of reforms which they undertook was so large in the fields of local and regional government, public enterprise, and workers' participation that the gov-

ernment was primarily anxious to act quickly. The return of the Right to power in the late 1980s and in 1993 did not lead to much change, if any, in the direction of greater consultation.

The role of interest groups has decidedly increased. The civil service can no longer implement its big projects without engaging in discussions with vocal groups. Yet, much still has to be done to reconcile the French with the basic need for and the real value of association. As few workers belong to unions, these are weak and their leaders often feel impotent. Much has still also to be done, despite recent changes, to bring government and civil service nearer to the nation. A centralizing spirit and centralized structures are major handicaps to a real partnership between groups and the State. Therein lies perhaps the major problem of French society, a problem which the 1981–1986 Socialist government began to tackle, but to which truly high priority has not been given, although lip service is periodically given to the need to find a solution.

THE PARTY SYSTEM

Ups and Downs in the Streamlining of Parties: Gaullists and Socialists

Before 1958, French political parties were weak, poorly organized, and undisciplined. This was largely due to the traditions which we examined earlier and in particular to the high degree of localism. With the advent of the Fifth Republic, the situation changed somewhat, but neither regularly nor indeed continuously. In a first period, roughly during the 1960s, the Gaullist party established itself as the dominant party. It won an unprecedented victory in 1968, when it gained a large majority of seats (though only 45 percent of the votes); but this was followed by a decline in the 1970s. The Gaullist party has scarcely polled above 20 percent in the 1980s, most of the votes lost going to groups of the center only loosely held together.

The election of 1981 changed the party configuration, in more ways than one. The French Socialist Party, for the first time in the history of the country, won an absolute majority of seats; it gained only 38 percent of the votes, admittedly, but this, too, was a first, as never before

General Charles de Gaulle (1890–1970) was the leader of the Free French movement in London during World War II, the head of government in 1944–1946, the last prime minister of the Fourth Republic in 1958, and president of France 1959–1969.

had it obtained the support of more than 25 percent of the electorate. For the first time since 1958, too, there had been a change in the party in power. The victory of the Socialists in 1981 was also remarkable in that it signaled the end of the Communist Party as a major force in French politics. That party declined first to 16 percent and subsequently to under 10 percent.

The 1986 parliamentary election brought about the return of the Right with a small majority, but the Socialist president, François Mitterrand, who was reelected in 1988, immediately dissolved Parliament. The Socialist Party was returned to power, though this time short of an absolute majority. It was to suffer a crushing defeat at the parliamentary election of 1993, in part as a result of a number of financial scandals. The Right confirmed its victory in the 1995 presidential election in which Gaullist Jacques Chirac won by a relatively small majority.

Thus the French party system remains fractionalized. Yet it has had periods—the 1960s and the 1980s and early 1990s—during which first the Gaullists and then the Socialists dominated the scene. Even in the 1970s and since 1993, when complex coalitions have controlled the government, these have remained more disciplined and cohesive than before 1958.

THE ELECTORAL SYSTEM

The streamlining of the party system was helped by the electoral system which (with the exception of the 1986 parliamentary election) has been in force since 1958. The system is known as the *scrutin d'arrondissement à deux tours,* a two-ballot system within single-member constituencies taking place on two successive Sundays. This type of electoral system had been in use during most of the Third Republic, but it was replaced in 1945 by proportional representation, traditionally advocated by the Left as being fairer. Proportional representation was indeed introduced by the Socialist majority in 1985 but the Conservative coalition which won in 1986 returned to the majority system. At the first ballot, only candidates receiving 50 percent or more of the votes cast in the constituency are elected. Between the first and the second ballot (at which the candidate who gets the most votes

is elected irrespective of result, but at which only candidates who obtained more than 10 percent of the votes on the first ballot may run), deals take place and candidates withdraw voluntarily, sometimes without further ado, sometimes in favor of other candidates better placed in the race.

The effect of the two-ballot system on the French party system has varied somewhat over time and is not entirely straightforward. In some cases, it has had the same apparent consequences as the British first-past-the-post system. It has made it possible for one party to be temporarily dominant, as in the case of the Gaullists between 1962 and 1973 and of the Socialists between 1981 and 1993 (except for the 1986–1988 period). But, at other times, the effect has been more to create two "blocks"—on the Right and on the Left—within which agreements are made between component parties. This type of agreement has become essential to the government of the Right. After the decline of the Gaullist Party in the mid–1970s, a coalition of loosely organized parties closely connected with president Giscard d'Estaing, the *Union pour la Démocratie Française* (UDF), consistently obtained between 20 and 25 percent of the votes in parliamentary elections. On the Left, Communists, smaller extreme-left or center-left parties, and occasionally new and rather weak parties, such as the ecologists, have been associated with the Socialist party. France thus remains a multiparty system with only some tendencies towards dominance. The effect of the electoral system consists thus perhaps more in bringing parties within two broad blocks than in forcing the mergers of parties or their disappearance.

The Right and Center

The Ups and Downs of the Gaullist Party

Unlike Britain, France never had a Conservative party, yet on at least two occasions, it seemed that the Gaullist party would be able to unite the large majority of the electors on the Right. The first time was in the late 1940s, when de Gaulle created the *Rassemblement du Peuple Français* (RPF), which was pointedly called a "rally" because its founder wanted to indicate that his organization was different from all other political movements. The RPF was for a time very successful. In the municipal elections of 1947, it swept most large towns, obtained nearly 40 percent of the votes cast and seemed to be a major challenge to the government of the Fourth Republic. Traditional parties of the center, however, proved to be resilient and gradually eroded Gaullist strength. In the 1951 General Election the Gaullists obtained only little over one-fifth of the votes cast; a year later they split, and by 1956 Gaullism as a movement had all but disappeared.

The resurgence of Gaullism was the direct consequence of de Gaulle's return to power in 1958 as a result of the inability of the Fourth Republic political leaders to deal with the Algerian problem. But this time the return of Gaullism seemed likely to be more than a passing phenomenon. The *Union pour la Nouvelle République* (UNR), as the Gaullist party then came to be named, obtained 25 percent of the votes in 1958 and 40 percent in 1962. These successes were repeated at the elections of 1967 and 1968 and, by then, the Gaullist party seemed fully established. It was the closest to a mass party on the Right that France ever had, even though the party itself did not have a very large membership (unlike the old RPF of the late 1940s)—50,000 members in the early 1960s and about three times this figure in the early 1970s. Membership drives occurred from time to time, but they seemed neither to be pushed hard nor to be really successful.

The policies of the first Gaullist party— that of the 1940s—were, on the whole, those of the authoritarian right. De Gaulle ostensibly favored ideas of collaboration between capital and labor and announced a profit-sharing scheme, but its details were not worked out in practice. What was more apparent was a nationalistic tone and a strong anti-Communist stance; the policies on colonial issues were somewhat ambiguous. The first Gaullist party allowed its militants to behave with brutality against opponents. Fighting often broke out and local Communist Party headquarters were occasionally burnt. The second Gaullist party, which emerged after 1958, acted more re- sponsibly and its policies were also more moderate.

In its heyday in the late 1960s, the Gaullist party seemed to have been able to attract the support of a large proportion of the electorate without having to build a massive organization. It had provided de Gaulle and his government with a solid majority, although it was no longer as monolithic as it was once accused of being. No longer authoritarian as the first Gaullist party had been, the UNR seemed to be based on a strong discipline which was naturally accepted; whips were not imposed in a ruthless fashion. In parliamentary debates, criticism may not have been voiced on major matters, but it was often expressed on less important questions. This was in part because there was a "community of feeling," or common approach, between de Gaulle and his supporters in Parliament and elsewhere. Some may have disagreed on tactics, but most Gaullists agreed on basic aims.

The Decline of the Gaullist Party   In part because of the large parliamentary majority which de Gaulle bequeathed to his successor, the dominance of the Gaullist party in French politics continued for a time after the de Gaulle's departure and death. But the beginnings of the decline can be traced to one of the first decisions of de Gaulle's successor, Pompidou, which was to appoint to the government a number of members of small fringe parties who had hitherto remained on the sidelines. Unlike Adenauer in West Germany in the 1950s, Pompidou did not attempt to force non-Gaullist parliamentarians of the Right and Center to choose between joining the Gaullist party or abandoning political life. Pompidou undermined his own party by relying increasingly on non-Gaullist politicians— in particular on Giscard d'Estaing—to counterbalance the strength of the Gaullists. The real blow to Gaullist supremacy was administered in 1974 by one of the younger leaders of the Gaullist party at the time, Jacques Chirac, who led a substantial group of Gaullist members of Parliament to support the candidacy of Giscard d'Estaing for the presidency against the official Gaullist candidate, Chaban-Delmas. Giscard won and the Gaullist party lost its dominant position. It lost the prime ministership in 1976, and the subsequent efforts of Chirac, who became Gaullist party leader, to strengthen the organization and to oppose the president whom he had so significantly helped to elect proved unsuccessful and even futile. The Gaullist party, which had by then been renamed *Rassemblement pour la République* (RPR), had ceased to embody the Fifth Republic. The electorate of the Right began to desert the party. By 1978, the Gaullist party obtained only a quarter of the votes cast, a proportion which did not change markedly during the 1980s and 1990s, despite Jacques Chirac's efforts. The Right was once more divided.

The Resilience of the Center

By the late 1970s, France seemed to be reverting to some of its traditional divisions on the Right. Almost alone among the large Western democracies, and, indeed, alone among Western democracies outside Scandinavia (where the Right is disciplined although not united), France has been characterized traditionally by an undisciplined and loosely organized Center and Right—which curiously seems to succeed in staying in power for very long periods.

This constant inability of the Right to be organized was accompanied by periodic efforts to streamline the many groups which belonged to it, the efforts of the Gaullists being only one in a long line of earlier endeavors. In the late 1930s, a new party, the *Parti Social Français,* seemed for a while poised to make considerable gains, but because of the Second World War, the 1940 election which would have provided the test never took place. In 1945, when prewar conservative groups had been badly shaken by the fact that many of their members had collaborated with the Vichy regime of 1940–1944, a Christian party, the *Mouvement Républicain Populaire* (MRP), obtained over a quarter of the votes. Its policies were not moderate enough to satisfy the conservative electorate, however, and its alliance with the Communists made it somewhat suspect. The emergence of the RPF caused the vote for the MRP to drop to about 10 percent. Yet, too, as we saw, the strength of the RPF was in turn quickly eroded. Finally, by 1956, the shopkeepers' party of Pierre Poujade

seemed to be on the verge of constituting a new catalyst, but its policies were too crude to attract the bulk of the Right and it gained only 12 percent of the votes and was soon swept away by the second Gaullist tide.

Neither organization nor ideology can provide the real explanation for the resilience or recurrence of groupings on the Center and Right. The explanation can be found only by considering the social base. Before World War II, and to a large extent in the 1950s as well, conservative and center groups were composed of prominent local politicians who had first established their influence at the municipal and county levels and had enough following to be elected to Parliament. These developments flourished in a context in which political behavior was highly sectional; they accounted for the fact that parties remained both organizationally weak and undisciplined in Parliament. The village and small-town basis of politics thus mirrored the rather static character of society.

The socioeconomic changes which followed World War II seemed likely to end the dominance of the traditional politicians, especially since the war record of many of them had been poor or downright inadmissible. The old Radical party, which had long ceased to be radical except in name, was discredited for having led France during the years which preceded the collapse of 1940. Yet, in the late 1940s and early 1950s, the same Radical party as well as other traditional groupings on the Center and Right made a surprisingly rapid comeback. Their leaders showed considerable skill and strength in opposing the first Gaullist party of the late 1940s; they became partners in government with Christian Democrats and Socialists, since those two parties alone could not command a parliamentary majority. They eventually provided most of the prime ministers of the last years of the Fourth Republic, only to show once more, in 1958, their inability to lead the country decisively in times of crisis.

The Two Major Center Groupings: The UDF and the CDS

The gradual return of small Center and Right parties to the fore in the 1970s after over a decade of Gaullist dominance illustrated the French political tradition, and the appeal of the "independent" Right and Center parties continued to be strong in spite of major economic and social changes. In order to compete with the Gaullists, these parties had to be better organized than they had been in the past. In the 1978 General Election, the small Center and Right parties federated under the label *Union pour la Démocratie Française* (UDF). But the various segments of the UDF have kept their identity, the two strongest elements being the Republican party founded by President Giscard and the *Centre démocratique et social* (CDS), which is the heir to the Christian party of the 1940s and 1950s. Overall, the UDF remains an uneasy coalition of somewhat autonomous chieftains joining forces to repulse a common enemy. It is not a true federation, let alone a single party.

From the 1978 General Election and throughout the 1980s and 1990s, the Right and Center have been divided into two major forces of about equal strength—the Gaullists and the non-Gaullists. Moreover, since the early 1980s, a challenge to the Gaullists and non-Gaullists has come from the extreme right, with the National Front led by Jean-Marie Le Pen, an ex-Poujadist deputy of 1956.

The National Front has somewhat fascist undertones. Its main plank–and source of success—has been an attack against immigrants, mainly those from North Africa. It gained substantial successes in particular in a number of suburban areas. The 10 percent of the votes it gained in the 1986 election grew to 14 percent in the 1988 presidential elections. Since then, support for the National Front has remained somewhat static, both at the parliamentary elections of 1988 and 1993 and at the 1995 presidential election. Support has clearly reached a plateau, below which it has not fallen, but above which it seems unable to grow, in part because its ideology is clearly unappealing to most electors and in part because of a number of internal divisions.

The Left

While the Right and Center were traditionally based on loose, personalized groupings, the Left has long been organized around several political parties. Before World War I, the Left consisted of the Socialists, who competed with the Radicals. After World War I, the Communist Party (CP) quickly gained votes, with 12 percent in 1932, 15 percent in 1936, and peaking at 28 percent in 1946. Though it lost votes when de Gaulle returned to power in 1958, it hovered around 20 percent for about two decades and was a force to be reckoned with, especially because of the decline of the Socialist party in the 1950s and 1960s. Only in 1981 did the CP's strength substantially diminish again, first to 15 percent and later to under 10 percent. The party has become marginalized as a result, and the Socialist Party has become the dominant party of the Left although it suffered a major defeat in 1993 when it obtained under 20 percent of the votes.

The Communist Party   The long hold of the CP on French politics had much puzzled observers, as France has been one of the few European countries (along with Italy, Finland, and Portugal) in which Communist strength has been large for more than a generation after World War II. Simple economic explanations are obviously not sufficient. The standard of living is as high in France as in other Western European countries—indeed higher than in some; and development in France was just as fast, at least until the mid–1970s. Those who in the late 1940s had hoped that an improvement of living conditions would be accompanied by a substantial decrease in Communist Party membership have been disappointed. The Communist vote eventually fell, but not at that time and not for economic reasons.

One has to go back to history to account for the resilience of the CP, a history marked in large part by the discredit of the Socialist Party and by that party's subsequent decline. The CP was born out of post–World War I discontent felt by many Socialists, whose party had firmly supported the war. The Resistance provided a second boost during World War II. Up to 1941, when the war was labeled bourgeois and imperialist by the Soviet Union, French Communists refused to participate in the defense of their country (their members of the Parliament were dismissed in 1940) and even supported the Germans in the early period. But after the Nazi invasion of the Soviet Union, the Communist Party took a leading part in the Resistance. It gained considerable prestige as a result (nicknaming itself the *parti des fusillés,* the party of the fired-on), successfully infiltrated the underground trade union organizations, and made inroads in parts of the countryside (particularly in those regions which the Resistance had freed from the Germans long before liberation). The party went into the government in 1944, probably hoping to remain in it for long periods, but in May 1947 the Communist ministers were dismissed. With the intensification of the Cold War, the Communist Party used trade union strength to harass the government (the strikes of November 1947 were among the most difficult episodes of postwar French politics). But the government won, and the Communist challenge became less effective. By the end of the Fourth Republic, in 1958, the Communist Party was a nuisance, not a menace. It could help any party to overthrow governments, but it could do little to achieve its own aims.

The CP thus occupied, from the 1950s at least, the comfortable position of being the only "real" defender of the workers against capitalism; yet it was at the same time (its supporters would say that this was precisely for that reason) a rigid, indeed monolithic organization. Its detractors criticized it for its complacency and its total lack of intellectual life, as much as for its internal dictatorial methods. Purges had taken place from time to time, enabling the secretary-general to remain at the helm of a large machine (potential successors were "shown" to be wrong or traitors to the party); but vitality was absent. While the Italian Communist Party gave signs of independence and vigor, its French counterpart remained Stalinist long after the death of the Soviet dictator, felt no official concern for the invasion of Hungary in 1956, and did not urge any liberalization; it simply repeated the theory of the impoverishment of the proletariat in capitalist regimes. This enabled the party to weather its defeat in 1958 without much trouble, but it did not make for a very rosy future.

In the 1960s, however, signs of liberalization seemed to emerge. In August 1968, for the first time in its history, the French CP dared to voice a criticism of the Soviet Union and (though in a somewhat lukewarm manner) attacked the occupation of Czechoslovakia, but it did not come back to the subject again until four years later. Even then, the CP voiced criticisms only to placate the Socialist party, with which it had just formed an electoral alliance. A few years later, after the 1978 defeat at the polls, the French Communist Party retreated once more into its characteristic position of faithful and loyal supporter of the "Socialist Motherland."

The Reasons for the Strength of the Communist Party
Why, then, has the French Communist Party been so strong electorally? What did Communist electors think when they voted for the party? One of the most potent attitudinal factors has been the ability of the Communist leadership to use to its advantage the disgruntlement of the working class as well as antigovernment feelings among sections of the peasantry and of the petty bourgeoisie. Regardless of the Soviet Union's transgressions, many manual workers felt that only by voting Communist could they protest against the government, the employers, and the bourgeois system in general. These feelings, on the other hand, can be linked to the antiestablishment and egalitarian tendencies of other sections of the community. They are naturally more marked in those parts of the country which are more opposed to Paris and to what it represents, such as the center of the country and the southeast (all along the Mediterranean coastline) than in the eastern and western regions. This accounts for the fact that the most individualistic of French people could conceive of the Communist vote as a natural mode of expression.

The tightly knit character of the party organization also accounts for its longevity. The Communist Party is the only French party which can be deemed to have ever created a "society," and a very disciplined and hierarchical one at that. Membership figures have been unreliable, but the party seems to have had about 300,000 to 400,000 paid-up members (about 8 to 10 percent of its voters) in the 1960s and 1970s—more than other parties had. For long periods in many cases, these members have been tied to the party through a network of cells (of a few members, mostly on the basis of residence, despite efforts of the party to create large numbers of factory cells), "sections," and county and national organizations. In theory, decisions have been made on the basis of "democratic centralism"; in practice, the views of the secretariat and of the executive committee have virtually always been adopted unanimously at congresses and opponents are quickly singled out and in most cases dismissed from the party.

Thus the Communist Party could be successful for a long period, with more officials and a more elaborate structure than other parties; but in the long run it suffered from bureaucratic tendencies. It started to decline in 1981 and continued to lose support in the mid–1980s but remained stable afterwards, despite the events which took place in the Soviet Union and Eastern Europe, which appeared to have had very little impact on the internal life of the French Communist Party. Substantial dissent began to take place in the 1980s, culminating with the fielding of an "unofficial" Communist candidate, alongside the official one, at the presidential election of 1988, but not at the 1995 election. Yet the top leadership has been able to remain in control. While the secretary-general elected in the 1990s is more ostensibly prepared to accept discussion, real behavior within the party has little changed.

In the wider context, it is difficult to measure the extent to which the working class has been helped as business and conservative governments have been induced to agree to concessions for fear of the CP increasing its strength; but the debit side of the balance sheet is apparent. The French Left has been torn; it has devoted much energy to discussing problems of ideology and of "line" in relation to the Communists. Left-wing governments of the 1940s and 1950s have been paralyzed, as in 1936; more frequently, the Left has been prevented from coming into being after World War II by the presence of the Communist Party, never perhaps as markedly as in 1978 after the CP decided that the "Common program of the Left," which it had drafted a few years earlier jointly with the Socialist Party, had become obsolete.

Here lies, perhaps, the reason why the French CP suffered its major setback of 1981. With the Socialist government of 1981–1986, it became apparent that the Left was able to act and form an effective government. From then on, the CP was no longer necessary—and it was abandoned by large numbers of its electors.

The Socialist Party   The victories won by the Socialist Party in 1981 and 1988 can be regarded almost as miraculous given what the party had been in the 1960s. Born in 1905, and for over half a century called the French Section of the (Second) Working Class International (SFIO), the Socialist Party originated from two groups created in the 1890s, one, humanitarian and liberal, the other, Marxist. Until 1914, the party practiced "noncollaboration" with bourgeois governments and seemed to be moving gradually toward a commanding position. At the 1914 General Election, the party had about 100 deputies, or one-sixth of the chamber. Jaurès, the great humanitarian leader of the party, tried with all his strength to rally the antiwar forces, but he was assassinated just before hostilities started, and French Socialists, as their German colleagues, were made to accept the *Union Sacrée;* some of its members joined the cabinet.

Earlier Setbacks of the Socialist Party   The Communist split of 1920 had little immediate effect on the Socialist organization, but it did hamper its electoral appeal; the party stagnated at the polls during the 1920s and 1930s, gaining votes on its right but losing about the same number on its left. At the 1936 General Election, the party emerged apparently as the great winner, having led to victory the Popular Front coalition, which included the Radicals on its right and the Communists on its left, as well as various socialist splinter groups. For the first time a Socialist, Léon Blum, was called to head the government, and for a few tense spring days the dream of the Socialist Party seemed to have become reality.

But the victory was in fact small (the Socialist Party obtained only one-quarter of the votes) and hollow. Expectations of manual workers had been raised so high by the election result that sit-down strikes soon became the norm in large factories. The Communists pushed for takeovers while the liberals were already backing out. Blum, a follower of Jaurès, a *grand bourgeois* who strongly believed in both equality and liberty, made a number of important reforms (the 40-hour work week, paid holidays, and collective bargaining), but he did not succeed in retaining the confidence of the workers nor, of course, in acquiring that of the employers. Financial difficulties grew, and the government, in difficulty with the upper house of Parliament, the Senate, resigned after a year in office. The Socialist Party then entered a long period of decline. It was divided over the Vichy regime in 1940, and while it took an important part in the Resistance, it was far behind the Communists. It was central to many coalitions of the Fourth Republic after World War II, but, perhaps as a result, its support dwindled, falling from 25 percent of the votes in 1945 to 15 percent in 1958. It entered the era of the Fifth Republic as a losing and demoralized party.

The Reorganization of the Socialist Party

From the mid–1960s, however, efforts were made to broaden the base of the party and to change its image. Hopes were entertained, in the first instance, around the creation of a federal organization which was expected to be substantially larger than the Communist Party. The Radicals and the Christian Democrats, as well as representatives of some of the political clubs, were to belong to the new grouping, sometimes viewed as a potentially large umbrella for the Left; but minor Socialist groups opposed the move, and the Christian Democrats, unsure of their conservative voters, rejected the proposal, while the old anti-Catholic reflex grew in the Socialist Party itself. A smaller and looser grouping comprising Socialists, Radicals, and some tiny organizations was to be a more modest but influential alternative. Its presidential candidate, Mitterrand, polled 45 percent of the votes in the presidential election of 1965, and it returned 121 members of Parliament in the 1967 General Election; but the old Socialist Party did not survive a crushing electoral defeat in 1968.

Mitterrand was to prove stubborn in his aim to unite and, indeed, lead the Left, however. Helped by the disarray caused by a further defeat of the Left at the polls at the presidential election of 1969, which followed de Gaulle's resignation, Mitterrand campaigned for the reconstruction of the Socialist Party—now known simply as the *Parti Socialiste*. Having become leader of the new party, he entered a series of negotiations with the Communist Party designed to expand the collaboration between the two organizations. The "Common Program of the Left" adopted in 1972 was markedly Socialist, but was nonetheless more moderate than the Communists would have wanted. The result was the first upsurge in Socialist votes in 30 years in the 1973 General Election.

The Socialist Party continued to increase its strength subsequently. At the 1974 presidential election, Mitterrand was once more defeated, but by a small margin. Hopes were increasingly entertained that economic difficulties and the natural unpopularity of a majority coalition in power for 20 years would result in a victory for the opposition. Divisions between Socialists and Communists appeared to have been buried, with the Socialist Party being the clear leader of the opposition. The "Common Program of the Left" was generally viewed as the natural alternative. Being the result of an agreement between Socialists and Communists at a time when the Communists were still the stronger partner, it had a truly radical flavor and included in particular large-scale nationalization proposals. In the municipal elections of 1977 the two opposition parties did particularly well—the Socialist candidates being especially successful.

In late 1977, however, the Communist Party decided to make strong demands for a redrafting of the Common Program; it made suggestions for major changes which were to sharpen the "radical" character of the program. Negotiations broke down; the Communist Party then endeavored to undermine the Socialist Party at the grass roots but failed. It did, however, undermine the credibility of the Left in general and therefore bore responsibility for its defeat at the 1978 General Election. The 1978 result was nevertheless the best result achieved by the Socialist party since 1945; for the first time since World War II it was the largest party in the country.

The breakdown of the Common Program led to a short period of stagnation, and divisions within the Socialist Party seemed even to point to a further victory for Giscard. Yet, during the winter of 1980–1981, the tables were turned rapidly. Mitterrand declared himself a candidate and rallied the whole Socialist Party behind him. The Communist Party fielded their secretary-general, Georges Marchais, whose popularity was low and personal record unappealing. The scandals and arrogance associated with Giscard, coupled with the ever deepening economic recession meant an upsurge in the fortunes of the Socialist Party, whose slogan ("*Une force tranquille*") and whose symbol (the rose) tuned out to be clear winners.

The Unprecedented Socialist Victory of 1981 and the Subsequent Decline of the Party

At the first ballot of the presidential elections of April–May 1981, Mitterrand was still 2 percent behind Giscard, but the Communists had lost 5 percent of the votes. On the second ballot, two weeks later, when only the top two candidates could stand, Mitterrand edged out as the winner with 52 percent of the votes. A large bandwagon effect then occurred. The National Assembly was dissolved and on June 21, 1981, for the first time in French history, the Socialist Party had an absolute majority of seats in Parliament; the Communist representation had been halved; the CP could be given four seats in government between 1981 and 1984 without danger.

Five years of stable government of the Left then followed—for the first time in French history. At first reforms took place rapidly and on a large scale; nationalizations, industrial reforms, and administrative decentralization were among the main changes. By 1983, however, economic difficulties led to a major rethinking, as France could not push for growth alone in a world in which retrenchment and "monetarism" were dominant. The Socialist government became moderate; this led the Communists to leave the government in 1984.

The Socialist Party lost votes at the subsequent General Election of 1986, but it remained the largest party with 32 percent of the votes. It had gained a reputation for moderation and statesmanship; it had shown greater unity than

the conservatives who, while pledged to rule together, as they did between 1986 and 1988, did display a high level of dissension. This may explain in part the second victory of Mitterrand at the 1988 presidential election and of the Socialist Party at the subsequent general election, although the party this time remained a few seats short of an absolute majority. The prime minister appointed by the president in 1988, Michel Rocard, practiced a policy of "openness" (*ouverture*) to the elements of the center parties and stressed sound management rather than ideological pronouncements. The head of the government remained popular in the country, though perhaps not among the party activists, throughout his three years in office. He was perhaps for this reason suddenly replaced by Madame Edith Cresson, who was to be the first woman French prime minister. Although this was regarded as a rather skilful move by Mitterrand, largely because the new incumbent was a woman, the result proved to be a failure. Madame Cresson was replaced a year later by a faithful supporter of Mitterrand, hitherto minister of finance, Pierre Beregovoy. By then, however, recovery was impossible. The party had become embroiled in a number of financial scandals which seemed to concern both the organization and a number of prominent personalities, both at national and local levels (though similar scandals also affected the parties of the Right and Center). Defeat at the 1993 parliamentary election was crushing, the Socialist Party receiving fewer votes than at any time since 1962, and the result was even worse at the European parliamentary elections which took place one year later. There has been some recovery since then, both at municipal elections—where the party gained control of a number of towns—and at the presidential election of 1995 when the candidate of the party, Lionel Jospin, an ex-minister of education who as subsequently to become secretary-general of the party, obtained 47 percent of the votes. Thus the true dominance of the Socialist Party lasted no more than a decade, but the party did remain the major party within the Left. The Communist Party did not profit from the defeat of the Socialist party in the 1990s; nor did the more moderate and typically very small "Left

Radical" party, except at the European election of 1994. To this extent at least, the panorama of French politics has been profoundly modified after the 1981 parliamentary election.

THE SPIRIT OF THE CONSTITUTION OF 1958

The Constitution of 1958 was introduced primarily to strengthen the executive. From 1870 to 1958, French governments had been weak and unstable, except for about a decade at the turn of the century, when the campaign against the Catholic Church gave cohesion to the majority and some real strength to the leader of the government. De Gaulle was convinced that chronic instability was one of the major causes of the decline of France; he felt that only by a change in the institutions could the man at the top be able to take a long-term view of the interests of the country. He thus based his cure on constitutional remedies; but the medicine was somewhat unorthodox.

De Gaulle and the Constitution of 1958

De Gaulle did not adhere to any of the constitutional models devised in the eighteenth and nineteenth centuries and broadly adopted in the major democracies. He wanted to ensure governmental stability and executive authority; he was not anxious—to say the least—to give representatives of the people effective means of supervising the executive, nor did he wish to devise an equilibrium between executive and legislature. Thus he proposed neither a revamped cabinet system nor a presidential system, but plumped for a hybrid system giving marked preponderance to the executive. Yet, as the cabinet system and the presidential system are the only two forms of constitutional arrangements (together with a streamlined party system) which seemed effective elsewhere in sustaining liberal democracy, the new French institutions were attacked from the start as being both authoritarian and impractical. Few expected that they would last beyond de Gaulle; indeed, though they were kept alive under the subsequent presidents, there are still some

doubts about the long-term future of the constitution, in that the hybrid character of the system appears to make it rather vulnerable.

This hybrid system divides executive authority into two sharply distinct segments. The president has the somewhat lofty and almost undefinable task of looking after the long-term interests of the nation; the government, headed by the prime minister, is in charge of the country's affairs. This raises two main problems. First, there is a large "gray area" of divided responsibility. Because the constitution does not define "sectors" for the president and the prime minister, clashes between the two are thus likely. Second, while the president appoints the prime minister, the prime minister needs the support of the legislature. There is, therefore, potential for conflict when the majority of Parliament differs from that of the president. This did not occur between 1958 and 1986, but it did between 1986 and 1988 and between 1993 and 1995, both times under Mitterrand. The "cohabitation," as it was called, was relatively painless in both cases, but the role of the president was clearly diminished.

PRESIDENT AND GOVERNMENT

The Formal Powers of the President

Formally at least, the powers of the president are relatively limited, as, in 1958, de Gaulle had to agree to compromises with the politicians of the time who feared full-scale presidentialism. Whether de Gaulle wanted a presidency on American lines was never clarified; he had in any case to settle for much less in the constitution.

Thus most of the powers of the president of the Republic, who is elected for seven years as previously, existed in the Third and Fourth Republics. There is nothing unusual, by French republican standards, in the following eight powers of the president:

1. Appointment of the prime minister and of the ministers on the proposal of the prime minister (without any formal power of dismissal of the prime minister).

2. Promulgation of laws voted by Parliament (the president may ask Parliament to recon-

sider a law within two weeks of its having been voted, but he has no power of veto).

3. Signature of regulations ("decrees"), but these must have been approved by the council of ministers.

4. Chairmanship of the council of ministers.

5. Chairmanship of the high councils of the armed forces.

6. The right to send messages to the National Assembly.

7. Ratification of treaties, after parliamentary approval.

8. The power of pardon.

As in other Western European countries, the fact that the Head of State signs regulations and ratifies treaties merely means that the seal of authority of the State is given to these decisions; but these decisions must be countersigned by the prime minister and/or, when appropriate, by some of the ministers. The rule of the countersignature is basic to the operation of the parliamentary system, as the government, not the Head of State, is held to be politically responsible. No particular significance must therefore be attributed to the fact that the president of the Fifth Republic signs decrees or ratifies treaties.

Feature 3.3 De Gaulle and Mitterrand

By far the two most important presidents of the Fifth Republic have been Charles de Gaulle, who founded the regime in 1958, and François Mitterrand, who reorganized the Left and gave it a new strength. Charles de Gaulle, born in 1890, had a military career during which he unsuccessfully attempted to give the French army a more modern outlook. Shocked by the defeat of June 1940, he rallied London and created the Free French Movement, which was to become the embryo of the government of liberated France in 1944. Having led this government until January 1946, he resigned in disgust at what he considered to be party domination of the regime. He founded his movement, which he called the Rally of the French People, in 1947, but remained in the wilderness of the opposition until 1958, when the events of Algeria gave him an opportunity to implement his ideas of a president-led as well as a more nationalistic form of government. Ten years later, in 1968, confronted by massive popular demonstrations, he sought to retake the initiative by proposing to the people in 1969 a reform of the constitution. He was defeated in a referendum, immediately resigned, and retired to his home in the East of France where he died one year later, in 1970.

François Mitterrand can be regarded as having done for the Left what de Gaulle did for the nation. Born in 1916, he started as a young parliamentarian and minister in the 1940s; at the time he belonged to a small party of the Center. He opposed de Gaulle from 1958 and moved gradually to the Left, being a strong challenger to the founder of the Fifth Republic at the election of 1965, when he obtained 45 percent of the votes. He was instrumental in giving the Socialist Party a new life in 1971 and boldly agreed to an alliance with the Communist Party in 1972, being determined to overtake that party, a policy which succeeded triumphantly at the presidential and parliamentary elections of 1981, when, for the first time, the French Socialist Party gained an absolute majority of seats in the National Assembly. He agreed to appoint a conservative government in 1986, after the Socialist Party had lost its majority, but was reelected president in 1988 for a further seven years. By the early 1990s, however, as de Gaulle's earlier, his popularity began to wane as his political flair, in both internal and foreign policies, seemed to desert him. In 1993, the Socialist Party suffered a crushing defeat. Mitterrand had to appoint, once more, a conservative government with which he "cohabited" during the last two years of his term which ended in 1995. He died in January 1996 after a long cancer illness which he bore with great courage. His death was viewed as the passing of an era.

François Mitterand (1916–1996), president of France in 1981–1995. He had been a government minister on many occasions in the Fourth Republic, became leader of the Socialist Party in 1971, and ran unsuccessfully for the presidency of the Fifth Republic in 1965 and 1974.

The Presidential Power of Dissolution

Alongside these eight traditional powers, four others are new in the Fifth Republic and constitute the extent of the *formal* innovation in the regime. These powers are the prerogative of the president alone. No countersignature is required, but these powers can be exercised at rare intervals or in emergencies only. Of these four powers, only one, the right of dissolution, has been really effective and has markedly helped to modify the conditions of political life. Before 1958, dissolution had been used rarely

(in fact not at all between 1877 and 1955, when Parliament dominated the scene); because of the ill-organized nature of the party system, the one dissolution which occurred, that of 1955, had no effect on political life. On the other hand, since 1958, dissolutions have been used to great effect in 1962, 1968, 1981, and 1988, in the context of a more streamlined party system; moreover, the threat of dissolution also plays a major part in helping to render governments more stable.

The President and Referendums

The other three new powers of the president have been used relatively rarely. One gives the president the power to decide that a constitutional amendment proposed by the government to Parliament need not be approved by referendum after it has been adopted by Parliament (which is the normal procedure). In this case, the proposal has to be approved by a joint meeting of the two chambers separately. This provision was used by de Gaulle in 1960 to loosen the links between France and her African ex-colonies, by Giscard in 1976 with respect to the duration of parliamentary sessions, by Chirac in 1995 to extend both the duration of parliamentary sessions and the scope of legislative referendums.

Article 11 of the Constitution gives the president the right to refer certain government bills to the electorate. Up to 1995, this exclusively concerned bills dealing with the organization of public authorities, those carrying approval of a (French) community agreement, or proposals to ratify treaties which, without being contrary to the constitution, would affect the functioning of the institutions. The 1995 constitutional amendment extended this right to bills dealing with social and economic matters.

De Gaulle liked referendums, as these enabled him to go directly to the people without having to bother about parties; he indeed used the technique in a highly dubious manner from a constitutional point of view. First, he introduced the practice of bypassing Parliament altogether, as if the referendum was an alternative and not merely a complement to the parliamentary approval of bills. The constitution was silent on this point, but the president's interpretation was, to say the least, highly "innovative."

Yet de Gaulle went further. According to the Constitution, constitutional amendments must be passed in identical terms by both chambers of Parliament. A referendum then takes place though the president has some power to avoid this referendum by sending the amendment to a joint meeting of the two chambers, in which case the amendment must be approved by a majority of at least three-fifths of the votes cast. It is therefore clearly unconstitutional for an amendment to be approved without a positive vote of Parliament. In 1962, however, de Gaulle proposed directly to the people an amendment stipulating that the election of the president would be by direct universal suffrage. This created considerable stir (including the fall of the government and the dissolution of the National Assembly), as the move was clearly unconstitutional. It was also the last time that the referendum led to an important reform. During the following seven years the procedure was not used at all; in 1969, de Gaulle did use it again, on regionalism, but he lost and left power. His successor, Pompidou, used it only once; Giscard did not use it at all; Mitterrand proposed to use it in 1984, but the constitutional change he sought was blocked by the upper chamber; it was used in 1988 to change the status of the Pacific island of New Caledonia (when only 33 percent voted) and in 1993 to ratify the Maastricht Treaty of the European Union (when the majority in favor was wafer-thin).

Emergency Powers

The fourth new power was given to the president by Article 16 of the Constitution. It concerns emergencies and was used only once, in 1961, following an attempted coup by four generals in Algiers. A heated conflict had arisen at the time of the drafting of the constitution, because the article allowed the president to assume full powers in some situations. De Gaulle wanted the power to enable the Head of State to take appropriate measures in cases of national catastrophes such as that of 1940; but opponents saw it as a means of installing a legal dictatorship. The experience was mixed, to say the least. Such an article does not by itself give authority to a president who does not already have it; moreover, Parliament is required to meet a somewhat ludicrous provision in the case of a national catastrophe.

As a matter of fact, the procedure proved cumbersome when it was put in use, in part because the scope of parliamentary action in the context of Article 16 was not defined. It was, in fact, a great relief for the government (more than for Parliament!) when at the end of the summer of 1961, Article 16 ceased to be operative, as those who had benefited most from the emergency powers were the farmers, whose lobby was able to make itself felt in the chamber.

The Popular Election of the President

Such are the powers of the president. The four new ones point to de Gaulle's main preoccupation, namely, that the president should be able to steer the ship of State. For this, as was already noted, authority was necessary. This is why de Gaulle forced a change with respect to the election of the president. He had had to accept in 1958 the setting up of a limited electoral college composed of about 80,000 delegates, mainly representatives of local authorities in which rural areas were overrepresented. By 1962, he had acquired the political strength to launch a referendum introducing the direct popular election of the president (with a two-ballot, or run-off, system, the second ballot taking place two weeks after the first between the top two candidates only). Opposition to the proposal was fierce, largely due to the fear of Bonapartism. As we alluded to, the only popularly elected president, Louis-Napoleon, made himself emperor after a coup d'etat in 1851.

The fear proved misplaced and out-of-date. The popular election of the president, however unconstitutional, as was noted, was approved by the people in 1962 by a majority of over 3 to 2 (61.7 percent voted yes). Three years later, in December 1965, the first popular election of the president led to a very active campaign. The direct election of the president remained popular ever since and the measure clearly enhanced the position of the president in relation to Parliament and government, as de Gaulle had hoped.

From then on, presidential elections have been the central event of French politics. It was indeed the presidential election which rendered alternance possible in 1981 when Mitterrand,

---

Feature 3.4 **The Popular Election of the President May Weaken Parties**

The election of the French president by universal suffrage contributed to an extent to the streamlining of French politics; but it may also have led to new divisions between neighboring parties and even within parties. One of the main reasons why the Right of the political spectrum is not united is that both the Gaullists and the Centrists (the UDF) have their presidential hopefuls. The Socialist Party has avoided major problems in the 1970s and 1980s because of the towering position of President Mitterrand. Difficulties began to arise in the party in the 1990s, as there were a number of presidential hopefuls. As a matter of fact, mechanisms of selection of candidates are still unclear. The idea of primaries has been made moot and it was to an extent applied in the Socialist Party, but not elsewhere. It was indeed rejected among the Gaullists, with the result that there were two candidates of the RPR in 1995 at the first ballot, Balladur and Chirac. The French Fifth Republic seems still unable to develop the kind of discipline which is required if politics is to proceed smoothly and responsibly.

---

the Socialist candidate, won. Thus contests have been heated; margins of victory have tended to be small; turnout has been high. Clearly, the Fifth Republic has succeeded in one respect: It had introduced a procedure which was very popular. The Left, which originally opposed it, abandoned its attacks and was, indeed, a marked beneficiary in 1981 and 1988. The president (of whatever party) has acquired an authority which he did not have in the past, enabling him to be the main actor in French political life.

THE GOVERNMENT

The influence of the president on the government stems from his authority alone, as the constitution clearly states that the government, headed by the prime minister, is in charge of the policy; this was rediscovered, *a contrario,* after the 1986 election and repeated in 1993, when President Mitterrand had to appoint a government composed of Gaullists and of members of the Center parties. According to Article 20: "The Government shall determine and direct the policy of the nation. It shall have at its disposal the administration and the armed forces." And Article 21 continues: "The Premier shall direct the operation of the Government. He shall be responsible for national defense. He shall ensure the execution of the laws." There is no ambiguity: Though the president of the Republic, according to customs dating back to the Third

Republic, chairs the council of ministers, the government as a whole, headed by the prime minister, is responsible for national policy.

The Role of the Prime Minister

As in many other countries, the position of the prime minister grew gradually in the course of the last century. The Constitution of 1875 did not formally recognize the premier, but in practice all governments had a head, then known as "president of the council of ministers" (rather illogically since the president of the Republic chaired the meetings of ministers). However, since French governments were often uneasy coalitions, premiers tended to be compromisers rather than leaders. The Constitution of 1946 sought to increase the authority of the premier by giving him specific powers. He alone was designated by the chamber; he alone appointed the rest of the cabinet. These provisions had no effect. There was little difference between a premier of the 1930s and of the 1950s. In the Constitution of 1958 the premier (now named prime minister for the first time) did retain some of these powers. He or she leads the government, has the power to implement the laws (*pouvoir réglementaire*), is responsible for national defense, and makes a number of important appointments. The constitution stresses the leadership role of the premier as much as is compatible with the position of the president of the Republic and with the collective character of the government.

The government remains legally a collective organ. Important measures of the government are taken in the council of ministers (as we noted, decrees are signed by the president after they have been approved by the council). The government as a whole is empowered to "determine and direct the policy of the nation." Collective decision making is also associated with collective responsibility through the mechanism of the vote of censure, which automatically results, if adopted, in the resignation of all the ministers. The conflict between prime ministerial leadership and collective decision making is as difficult to solve in France as it is elsewhere; but the matter is further complicated by the role of the president.

The Structure and Composition of the Government

Formal arrangements have not markedly modified the internal structure of French governments. Names of ministries change from time to time, but the structure has followed a gradual evolution since the Third Republic. Typically, a government has about 20 ministers (slightly fewer than in the last years of the Fourth Republic); it includes

about as many secretaries of state of lower status. A number of changes have markedly affected the decision-making processes and even the nature of the cabinet, however. Three of these changes in particular must be mentioned.

First, prime ministerial instability has sharply decreased. From 1958 to 1995, France has had only 14 prime ministers: Debré, Pompidou, and Couve de Murville under de Gaulle; Chaban-Delmas and Messmer under Pompidou; Chirac and Barre under Giscard; and Mauroy, Fabius, and Chirac under Mitterrand I; Rocard, Cresson, Bérgégovoy, and Balladur under Mitterrand II (see Table 3.3). Only two prime ministers of the Fourth Republic lasted over a year, and no prime minister since 1875 lasted continuously in office as long as Pompidou. Ministers, on the other hand, change fairly frequently—though rather less than under the Fourth Republic.

Second, there has been a marked influx of technicians in the government. De Gaulle first brought civil servants into the cabinet in 1958, in part on the grounds that the government should in some sense be (like himself?) above the daily turmoil of political life. The government should run the State, and de Gaulle conceived of politics as an activity divorced from

Table 3.3   PRESIDENTS AND PRIME MINISTERS IN THE FIFTH REPUBLIC

Presidents		Prime Ministers	
C. de Gaulle (reelected 1965 for 7 years; resigned 1969)	1958–1969	M. Debré	1959–1962
		G. Pompidou	1962–1968
		M. Couve de Murville	1968–1969
G. Pompidou (died in office)	1969–1974	J. Chaban-Delmas	1969–1972
		P. Messmer	1972–1974
V. Giscard d'Estaing	1974–1981	J. Chirac	1974–1976
		R. Barre	1976–1981
F. Mitterrand (reelected 1988 for seven years)	1981–1995	P. Mauroy	1981–1984
		L. Fabius	1984–1986
		J. Chirac	1986–1988
		M. Rocard	1988–1991
		Mme E.Cresson	1991–1992
		P. Bérégovoy	1992–1993
		E. Balladur	1993–1995
J. Chirac (elected 1995 for seven years)	1995–	A. Juppé	1995–

State policy making, a view which probably stems from the part played by the civil service in the running of modern France. Thus, Couve de Murville, successively foreign minister and prime minister, was from the career foreign service; Pompidou, a teacher and a banker, had never been in politics before 1962, except as a personal adviser to de Gaulle; Chirac was a personal adviser of Pompidou before entering politics as such. Since the early 1960s, cabinets have included between one-quarter and one-third of civil servants; but many of these subsequently became members of Parliament, as Pompidou or Chirac, while successive presidents continued to draw their prime ministers (Barre by Giscard) and ministers (Cheysson or Dumas by Mitterrand) from outside politics.

Third, in order to give the executive more independence, Article 23 of the Constitution, introduced at de Gaulle's specific request, stipulates that there shall be *incompatibility* between the function of minister and that of member of Parliament. This incompatibility rule also exists in some parliamentary democracies (the Netherlands and Norway), but it contravenes the general principle that the executive stems from the majority of the National Assembly and aims at leading it. What de Gaulle wanted was to detach ministers from the legislature, as ministerial crises often occurred in the past to help the personal careers of ambitious men. Though they can come and speak (but not vote) in Parliament, ministers no longer belong to the legislature and thus can be expected to take a loftier view of daily politics; they are also nearer to the president and more likely to follow his leadership. Yet the provision has been partly bypassed, as ex-ministers often seek to be reelected. This results in a cascade of by-elections at many ministerial reshuffles, as when Chirac became president in 1995. Yet the rule reduces somewhat the desire of parliamentarians to become ministers.

PRESIDENT, PRIME MINISTER, AND GOVERNMENT IN THE FIFTH REPUBLIC

Institutional changes have thus brought about a new framework and introduced hurdles which have helped the Fifth Republic to give France a stable political system; these institutional changes alone do not explain the whole story, however. In theory, as we saw, the government is collective; in practice, it is rather hierarchical, as, from the very start, de Gaulle did intervene in governmental life, and Pompidou, Giscard, Mitterrand, and Chirac followed his lead. The role of the president, always somewhat in question, has never been seriously challenged, even with the advent of what came to be known as "cohabitation." Let us examine developments somewhat more closely.

The Extent of Presidential Intervention

Until 1986, presidential intervention had gradually tended to increase. In the early period, de Gaulle's involvement was seemingly due to the special problem of the Algerian war and was held to be confined to some fields only. Reference was made to a presidential "sector" including foreign affairs, defense, Algeria, overseas France, and key institutional problems and of a prime ministerial and governmental "sector" comprising the rest and particularly economic and social matters.

These sectors never were recognized by de Gaulle as marking the limits of his area of intervention; yet they went beyond the letter and spirit of the constitution. But de Gaulle went further and intervened in many aspects of internal policy making, possibly because these might have had an impact on the political system. He had said in 1964:

> Clearly, it is the president alone who holds and delegates the authority of the State. But the very nature, extent, and duration of his task imply that he be not absorbed without remission or limit by political, parliamentary, economic, and administrative contingencies.

This meant a hierarchical distinction rather than sectors. The prime minister was left to deal with those contingencies which are "his lot, as complex and meritorious as it is essential."

Subsequent presidents came to view their role as one of steering important matters affecting the well-being of the nation, directly or by implication. Hence the many instances of direct action by the president in financial matters. De Gaulle decided in 1968 not to devalue the franc; less than a year later Pompidou reversed the decision. Many aspects of regional or cultural policy, economic development, or social security reform can be ascribed to the president's steering.

The Semi-presidential Character of the Fifth Republic

Yet the system is only half presidential in that, on many issues as well, the president remains an arbiter rather than an actor. On various important economic and social problems, especially under de Gaulle and Pompidou, prime ministers and individual ministers initiated policies with the president of the Republic being seemingly neutral. Giscard was also somewhat aloof, although his commitment to the policies of his second prime minister, Barre, was clearer than that of the two previous presidents had been to the policies of their prime ministers. In this respect, the role of the third president was greater, partly also because Giscard had more knowledge of and interest in economics and economic difficulties made solutions more pressing.

Mitterrand embarked on the same path, keeping some distance from the daily turmoil and letting the prime minister deal with the major economic and social problems resulting from the government's efforts to counter economic depression. But Mitterrand was also closely associated with government policy, and he decided on a major change of economic policy in 1983 from expansion to orthodoxy. His involvement in governmental policy was less apparent but nonetheless deep between 1988 and 1993.

Intervention on such a scale implied the development of a presidential staff. Indeed, in the early period, de Gaulle seemed to want to dismantle the Council of Ministers and to replace it by a number of committees chaired by the president; this was not to occur, but the president maintained a large personal staff of *chargés de mission* and *conseillers techniques* who have constituted a parallel organization to that of the prime minister. They cover most important fields of government action and are the sign of the president's interest in a given problem, though they are far less numerous than the members of the American presidential staff.

The "Cohabitation" Periods of 1986–1988 and 1993–1995

The 1986 General Election brought about for the first time an entirely new situation, one which had long been expected to occur, but did not materialize for a quarter of a century, namely the arrival of a parliamentary majority different from that of the president's party. Since the mid–1970s at least, the possibility of such an occurrence had been canvassed; what presidents would then do had remained the object of major speculation. Giscard had promised in 1978 that he would abide by the decision of the people if the Left were to win in Parliament. This did not happen and, in 1981, the newly elected president, Mitterrand, could dissolve the chamber and obtain a Socialist majority. But the 1986 election produced the converse result. With Gaullists and "Centrists" together having a small overall majority, Mitterrand was faced with the decision to abide—or not—by the results of the polls; a repeat of the same scenario occurred in 1993, with the difference that the parliamentary victory of the Right and Center was then overwhelming.

Mitterrand's reaction was quick in both cases. He appointed the prime minister from among the new parliamentary majority, Chirac, the leader of the Gaullist party, in 1986, and, on the advice of Chirac, Balladur in 1993. In such circumstances, the president's role became limited; a *modus vivendi*—the "cohabitation" idea—was adopted by prime minister and president. The president would accept what the new majority would propose, provided that it was within the limits of what might be called "fair" and "honest" government. Thus denationalization proposals or changes in the electoral system (in fact, the return to the two-ballot system) would be accepted by the president, on condition that parliamentary debates not be curtailed and the rights of citizens maintained. The arrangement functioned well in both cases, two elements playing a major part. First, the president retained the right of dissolution had there been conflicts with the prime minister—a threat which was real as the popularity of the new conservative government tended quickly to decline; second, as Chirac wished to be a presidential candidate in both 1988 and 1995 (he was indeed to be defeated by Mitterrand in the first case and win against Jospin in the second), neither the prime minister nor conservative politicians in general wanted to reduce the role and status of the presidency. Thus both in its more "presidential" phase and in its "dualist" phase in 1986–1988 and 1993–1995, the system of the Fifth Republic helped France achieve a level of political stability and of institutional legitimacy which it had not known before.

THE LEGISLATURE

In order to understand previous French instability, and in order also to grasp the *raison d'être* of many of the constitutional provisions which attempt to curb this instability by reducing what was considered (with much justification) to be the excesses of the *régime d'assemblée,* it remains necessary, even after several decades, to recall, before the installation of the Fifth Republic in 1958, how much of French political life swirled around the lobbies of the Palais Bourbon, the seat of the lower house of Parliament, known as the Chamber of Deputies during the Third Republic and renamed the National Assembly in 1946. The Chamber of Deputies came to symbolize the Republic and all its works; it finally became the focus of all criticism aimed at the shortcomings of French politics.

The Traditional Dominance of the French Parliament

Perhaps because it was the arena where the rights of man were first enunciated and defended, the National Assembly came to be in time the repository of republican legitimacy. Inevitably, however, confusion over rights and privileges developed; members became more and more parochial and tended to regard their function as the defense of advantages which had accrued to their district by circumstance, natural good fortune, or government action. From being protectors of civil liberties, the members of the National Assembly slowly became champions of vested and purely local interests, a not uncommon development in legislatures, particularly in the U.S. Congress, whose mores resemble in many ways those of the French Parliament before 1958.

The Consequential Traditional Weakness of the Government

In these circumstances, the mark of a promising premier was his ability to deflect or postpone the demands for the extension of special privileges which poured in on the government. Yet, to survive, a premier had to nurse along the majority coalition, pleading with his own ministers not to lead an attack against him, while compromising the integrity of his legislative program to maintain the cohesion of his cabinet. To compound difficulties, the premier had to submit the plans of his legislative action to the often hostile committees of the house, whose chairs were usually more anxious to further their own careers (perhaps by replacing the relevant minister) with brilliant critiques of the legislation under discussion than to contribute to the progress of public business. Here, too, parallels can be drawn with the committees of the U.S. Congress, though the French Parliament never resorted to public grilling through hearings. This behavior tended to be based on a supporting philosophy according to which, since the revolution, there were crucial enemies of republicanism, namely the Church, the bureaucracy, and the armed forces. A kind of rampant anarchism (*le citoyen contre les pouvoirs,* the citizen against the powers) justified the harassment of the government, this harassment being regarded as a republican virtue.

Yet the system, despite its faults, gave France a long period of liberal government, interrupted only by the collapse of the French army in 1940 and by major colonial wars in the 1950s. Admittedly, the Napoleonic bureaucracy did help and if the regime showed resilience, it never reformed itself. The personal stakes were too high; the life of parliamentarians was too often punctuated by the ritual of government crisis. Reform had to come from outside, as it did in 1958, and only because of de Gaulle did a substantial curtailment of the rights of Parliament take place.

General Principles of Parliamentary Organization in the Fifth Republic

The framers of the Constitution of 1958 introduced a number of devices designed to enhance the position of the government and to give Parliament the power to supervise, but not block, executive action. These devices come under five headings. First, some provisions aim at reducing harassment and at diminishing opportunities for conflict. Second, the scope of legislation is reduced and governmental prerogatives correspondingly increased. Third, opportunities for "guerrilla" warfare in Parliament are limited. Fourth, the operation of censure motions is severely restricted. Fifth, parliamentary activity is controlled by the Constitutional Council. To these devices must be added the power of dissolution given to the president of the Republic.

The Organization of Parliament   Parliament is composed of two chambers, the National Assembly and the Senate, the upper house having regained the title, but not all the powers, it had under the Third Republic, while the lower house kept the name given to it by the Constitution of 1946. The National Assembly is elected for five years (if not dissolved before) by direct universal suffrage. The Senate, sometimes nicknamed the "Grand Council of French Communes," is elected for nine years, one-third of its members retiring every three years, by a complex electoral college composed of representatives of local authorities, which favors rural areas—and the center-right parties. Senators are elected within *département* (county) districts on a two-ballot basis.

Since the constitutional reform of 1995, Parliament meets during nine months of the year, instead of during two sessions of three months each, in the autumn and the spring. The government can also call for special sessions, a procedure which was originally interpreted very restrictively but came to be used more often and indeed led to the 1995 reform extending sittings to nine months.

The speaker of the National Assembly is elected for the duration of the legislature, instead of once a year, as was the case before 1958, thus avoiding the repeated conflicts of the past. The speaker of the Senate is elected after each partial reelection of the Senate every three years. Both speakers are assisted by a *bureau* composed of vice presidents and secretaries drawn from the various parties. The speakers, who are drawn from among top politicians, are consulted by the president of the Republic, according to the constitution, in various circumstances (such as dissolution or the use of Article 16). They conceive of their role more as speakers of the U.S. House of Representatives do than as speakers of the British House of Commons; they attempt to influence the conduct of business by informally talking to members. Indeed, before 1958, these offices were stepping stones toward the presidency of the Republic as in Italy and were strongly contested.

Since 1958, the government plays a major part in the organization of parliamentary business. Previously the order of business was decided by a "Conference of Presidents," a body which plays a similar role to the Rules Committee of the House of Representatives (and indeed resembled it in its behavior before 1958) and which includes chairs of committees and of the parliamentary groups (the parties in the chamber). The government was only represented and had no vote. In the Fifth Republic, the government's power is based on Article 43 of the Constitution which states that "Government and Private Members' Bills shall, at the request of the Government or of the Assembly concerned, be sent for study to committees especially designated for this purpose," while Article 48 stipulates that "the discussion of the bills filed or agreed to by the Government shall have priority on the agenda of the Assemblies in the order set by the Government." Government bills are thus sent automatically to a committee and are then extracted from the committee and presented on the floor of the Assembly.

Scope of Legislation

Traditionally, as in other parliamentary systems, the French Parliament could legislate on any matter. Constitutions merely regulated the principles of organization of the public powers; there was no Supreme Court. Statutes (*lois*) were defined merely as texts adopted by Parliament, by contrast with decrees (regulations adopted by the whole government) and *arrêtés* (adopted by a minister or a local authority). These documents derived their legal power from each other; the government could not make decrees, and ministers or local authorities could not make *arrêtés* unless a *loi* had given them the authority to do so. Parliament could invade any field and correspondingly decrease the influence of the government, although Parliament often had little time to devote to major issues. It therefore also often delegated its statutory power to the government by means of *décrets-loi.*

Article 34 of the Constitution of 1958 attempted to provide a solution to the problem. Having stated that "all *lois* (statutes) shall be passed by Parliament," the article defines what the *lois* are by saying that "laws determine the rules" (*régles*) with respect to a list of matters as well as the "fundamental principles" with respect to others. The article then adds that its provisions "may be elaborated and completed by an organic law." Yet there are difficulties over these arrangements. While the list includes all the important matters with which one would expect a parliament to be concerned, the concept of *régle* is not precise in French law; nor is it clear what a "principle" is. Conflicts have arisen, the arbiter being the Constitutional Council. Finally, what "elaboration" and "completion" by an organic law means is also rather vague.

The drafters of the constitution tried to buttress the system by introducing two new distinctions among the statutes, those of "organic" laws and of "ordinances." Organic laws are passed by Parliament by a somewhat more stringent procedure and must be deemed to be constitutional by the Constitutional Council before being promulgated. On the other hand, when Parliament delegates its legislative powers to the government, the government's texts are known as ordinances, which have to be ratified by Parliament at the end of the delegation period. The procedure proved to be of value for governments anxious to pass controversial legislation rapidly, especially in 1986–1988, when the conservative majority was small: Mitterrand then used his presidential authority to ensure that the government did not overstep its rights.

This complex machinery has functioned surprisingly smoothly, although there have been occasional complaints by the opposition, both of the Left, before 1981, and of the Right, between 1981 and 1986 and between 1988 and 1993, and for the same reasons.

The Legislative Struggle

In a parliamentary system, the two main activities of a parliament consist in voting laws and in controlling the government; but the two are intertwined. Before 1958 it was indeed through the legislative struggle that the patience, wits, and skills of ministers were being tested, as governments needed laws to implement their program. Thus the question of the control of the executive over the legislative process had to be regulated if the government was to be stronger.

A bill debated in the French Parliament goes through the following sequence—not very different from that which bills go through in the U.S. Congress. After having been laid on the table of either chamber by a member of that chamber or by the government (with the exception of finance bills which must be presented first to the National Assembly), the bill is sent to a committee which then reports to the house (each house has a *rapporteur* from the committee which is in charge of presenting this report). The house discusses the bill first in general, then clause by clause, and votes on each clause. A final vote is then taken, at which point the bill goes to the other house, which follows the same procedure. If both houses agree on the same text, the bill is sent to the president for promulgation (he can ask for a second deliberation, but has no veto). If the houses disagree, the bill goes again to each house; if there is still disagreement, a joint committee comprising an equal number of members of each house is set up with a view to drafting a common text. Only if the government intervenes, as we shall see, is there a possibility of breaking the deadlock between the two chambers.

Committees before and since the Advent of the Fifth Republic

Before 1958, parliamentary committees were very powerful. Organized, as in the United States, on the basis of specialized subjects (finance, foreign affairs, etc.), the 20 or so committees of the pre–1958 parliaments had great opportunities to make trouble for the government. Their members (elected on the basis of proportional representation of the parliamentary groups) were specialists or more often had electoral reasons to be interested. Their chairs, elected every year (the seniority system never took root in France, though some officeholders did remain in office for long periods), were highly influential persons. They were natural leaders of any opposition in their field and were the real shadow ministers.

Committees made life difficult for governments because the procedure of the chambers gave them full responsibility in relation to bills. These, whether from the government or from private members, became in effect the committee's bills; their substance could be so altered that they became unrecognizable. The government, therefore, had to ensure that proposed changes were overturned after the bills came on the floor of the house, a process whose outcome was always uncertain.

These practices have become impossible since 1958. The number of permanent committees in each house has been reduced to six. It was hoped these would become so large that they would include more than experts, but, despite various rulings from the Constitutional Council, the government could not avoid the setting up of informal subcommittees. More importantly, committees can no longer substitute their bills for those of the government; Article 42 of the Constitution states that the discussion on the floor has to take place on the government's text.

The Power of the Government to Curb Debate

Harassment on the floor of the Assembly used to be continuous. For instance, amendments could previously be withheld to embarrass the government and its supporters at the last moment; this is now forbidden. There used to be no closure and no guillotine; now Article 44 allows the government to request the chamber to vote by a single vote (*vote bloque*) on the text under discussion. The procedure is harsh, but it is designed to block the practice of presenting hundreds of amendments which could not be reasonably dealt with but were aimed at stopping the progress of bills. As a result, government bills now clearly take precedence over others (see Table 3.4).

The government has two further sets of powers with respect to legislation. First, finance bills used to be much delayed before 1958; Parliament has now 70 days to discuss and decide on the budget. If the finance bill is not voted on by then, the government can promulgate it by ordinance, a stringent weapon which has not had, in fact, to be used.

Second, the government, and the government alone, can end a deadlock between the two chambers by asking for yet another reading by each chamber of the text adopted by the National

Table 3.4   ACTIVITIES OF THE NATIONAL ASSEMBLY

	Hours of Sitting (yearly)	Numbers of Bills Passed		
		Government Bills	Private Members'	Total Bills
1968	425	53	11	64
1971	632	92	26	118
1974	543	64	14	78
1977	609	144	35	179
1980	709	74	20	94
1981	789	54	3	57
1985	793	122	3	125
1989	835	85	17	102
1994	996	121	36	157

Assembly. If there is still disagreement between the two chambers, the National Assembly then votes once more, and this decision is final. Thus the Senate is not in a position to block *governmental* legislation. This provision was used frequently between 1981 and 1986, as much of the legislative program of the Socialist government—in particular, but not only, its nationalization program—was strongly opposed by the Senate.

The balance has clearly been tilted and, according to some, tilted too much in favor of the government, a view which is arguable in light of the behavior of Parliament in the past. The executive had to be strengthened. Since a variety of clever tricks were used by Parliament against the government, tough rules had to be introduced to prevent the recurrence of previous tactics.

The Vote of Censure

Only comparatively recently has the procedure of the vote of censure, in France and elsewhere, appeared to constitute a major problem. Traditionally, as in Britain, parliaments could censure governments at will. However, in France and some other countries where party discipline was weak and parties numerous, the result was governmental instability. Yet the problem is complex because censure and legislation are often linked. If the right to censure the government is curtailed but Parliament can nonetheless easily reject bills proposed by the government, and in particular reject or delay financial bills, the government will simply resign without having been censured. This was the case in the Third and Fourth Republics. Vote of censure and votes on legislation must, therefore, be linked.

This is what the 1958 Constitution does in a curious provision which stipulates that an absolute majority is needed to defeat the government, but that only those voting for the censure motion (that is, against the government) will record their votes, while government supporters simply do not vote at all. Abstainers are thus counted on the government side. Furthermore, if the government wants to see a bill through but encounters difficulties, it can "pledge its responsibility on the vote of (the) text." In this case, the bill passes without a vote unless a motion of censure is tabled; if the censure is not adopted (the procedure is the one just de-

scribed) the government is, of course, safe but the bill is adopted as well.

Thus the government has the upper hand; governments cannot be suddenly overthrown. Deputies have only two means of curbing the executive. They have the question, which was introduced in the Constitution of 1958, allegedly on the British model, but which has taken the form of short debates, not of a grilling, although its scope has been extended; there is no vote at the end of these debates. The other curb is the motion of censure. These are the Assembly's only means of supervision and control of the government; the rest of its activities are legislative and budgetary. The constitution may have gone too far; the governmental instability of the past suggested that a stringent medicine was needed, but the restrictions may be too strong. Indeed, gradually, some loosening has taken place from the Giscard presidency of the second half of the 1970s onwards. With more compact majorities, the government can be more ready to make concessions, while Parliament recognizes the need for self-discipline.

THE CONSTITUTIONAL COUNCIL AND EXECUTIVE-LEGISLATIVE RELATIONS

Another and indeed most important new development of the Fifth Republic is constituted by the part played by the Constitutional Council in controlling legislation. The Constitutional Council is composed of nine members appointed in equal numbers by the president of the Republic and the speakers of the two chambers (and includes the ex-presidents of the Republic). It was set up in 1958 principally as a means of ensuring that Parliament did not overstep its powers. It thus has to approve the standing orders of both houses (a matter which led to conflicts in the late 1950s); it has jurisdiction over referendums and national elections, both presidential and parliamentary, which it must officially declare and settle in cases of disputes.

Yet the main power of the council turned out to be different. As it was entitled to assess whether laws were in conformity with the Constitution, it became gradually a Supreme Court. Admittedly, it differs from the U.S. Supreme Court in that it can consider the validity of legislation only if the government or one of the houses asks for a ruling and does so in the period immediately following the approval of the bill by Parliament; but the impact has been strong. At first, it tended to side with the Gaullist government; gradually, it became more independent and started to rule that bills or parts of bills were not "in conformity with the Constitution." In 1982, for instance, it declared that, subject to a few minor amendments (which were subsequently introduced), the nationalization program of the government was in conformity with the Constitution; in 1986, it also adjudicated over the "privatization" legislation of the conservative coalition; in 1991, it stated that a law could not refer to a "Corsican people" as this would undermine the unity of the nation, but it added that special rules could be introduced for different areas, a major innovation in the context of centralized France; in 1993, it quashed parts of a law attempting to make the French language obligatory in many fields on the grounds that this went against the freedom of expression.

The New Equilibrium of Powers in the Fifth Republic

The Constitution of 1958 has thus profoundly changed the character of French political life. Parliament's power has been reduced—too much according to some; governmental instability is a thing of the past. For the best part of four decades, the system has been dominated by the president, whose authority was enhanced by the legacy of de Gaulle and by the mechanism of the popular election; this domination was put in question by the "cohabitation" periods, but the authority of the president remained high throughout even if the effective power of the Head of State diminished. Because of the popular election, the president continues to have authority; he can both ensure continuity in foreign policy and broadly supervise the workings of the executive.

Meanwhile, Parliament also changed in the course of the last three decades. Its social composition has been somewhat altered, although women remain markedly underrepresented and manual and white-collar workers are very few, while lawyers, members of the liberal professions, and teachers are numerous; but there are civil servants, managers, and even farmers in

Table 3.5	OCCUPATIONAL BACKGROUND OF FRENCH DEPUTIES, 1994 (PERCENTAGE)
Business proprietors	17.0
Professions	22.2
Lawyers	6.1
Teachers	18.6
Civil servants	17.9
Managers (private sector)	17.0
White collar	1.4
Manual workers	0.7
Other	1.7
None	3.5
Women	6.1
Total (number)	576.0

substantial numbers, agriculture and business being particularly represented in center and right-wing parties (see Table 3.5). This ensures that at least part of the "active strata" of the nation are in the legislature. In terms of powers, the pendulum swung originally too far against the Assembly, though not quite as far as critics and parliamentarians claimed. Gradually, the right of the legislature to discuss, supervise, and suggest has been recognized, while the government's right to lead has been fully accepted.

Indeed, the constitutional reform of 1995, which increased somewhat the role of Parliament by extending its sessions, is evidence that Parliament is regarded as having abandoned some of the irresponsible forms of behavior in which it engaged in previous regimes. Thus, by and through its institutions and the effects these institutions have had on the party system and on the behavior of the actors, the Fifth Republic can be said to have brought about a real and lasting transformation of French political life.

 EY TERMS

Algerian war
arrêtés
Chambres d'Agriculture/Chambres de Commerce
Jacques Chirac
Communist Party

Confédération Française Démocratique du Travail (CFDT)

Confédération Française des Travailleurs Chrétiens (CFTC)

Confédération Générale de l'Agriculture (CGA)

Confédération Générale des Cadres (CGC)

Confédération Générale des Petites et Moyennes Entreprises (CGPME)

Confédération Générale du Travail (CGT)

Conseil National du Patronat Français (CNPF)

Constitution of 1958

Council of Ministers

decrees

Valery Giscard d'Estaing

European Union (EU) (formerly European Economic Community, EEC)

Fédération Nationale des Syndicats d'Exploitants Agricoles (FNSEA)

Gaullist party (RPF, then UNR, then RPR)

interest groups

François Mitterrand

National Assembly/Senate

Parliament

Georges Pompidou

Régime d'Assemblée

Socialist Party

Union pour la Démocratie Française (UDF)

vote of censure

FURTHER READINGS

GROUPS

Ehrman, H., *Organized Business in France* (Princeton University Press, 1957).

Kesselman, M., ed. *The French Workers' Movement* (London: Allen & Unwin, 1984).

PARTIES

Anderson, M. *Conservative Politics in France* (London: Allen & Unwin, 1973).

Bell, D. S., and B. Criddle, *The French Socialist Party,* 2nd ed, (Oxford: Oxford University Press, 1988).

Charlot, J. *The Gaullist Phenomenon* (London: Allen & Unwin, 1971).

Converse, P., and R. Pierce, *Political Representation in France* (Cambridge, MA: Harvard University Press, 1986).

de Tarr, F. *The French Radical Party from Herriot to Mendès-France* (New York: Oxford University Press, 1961).

Frears, J. R. *Political Parties and Elections in the French Fifth Republic* (London: C. Hurst, 1977).

Irving, R. E. M. *Christian Democracy in France* (London: Allen & Unwin, 1973).

Kriegel, A. *The French Communists* (Chicago: University of Chicago Press, 1972).

Pennniman, H. R., ed. *France at the Polls* (Washington, DC: American Enterprise, 1975).

INSTITUTIONS

Leites, N. *On the Game of Politics in France* (Palo Alto: Stanford University Press, 1959).

Williams, P. M. *The French Parliament* (London: Allen & Unwin, 1967).

Public Policy

THE ORGANIZATION OF THE STATE

It is commonplace to contrast the traditional weakness of the French political institutions with the strength of the French bureaucracy. It is also commonplace to stress the virtues of this bureaucracy. There is indeed much evidence to support this praise. The French civil service helped the monarchs to build the unity of the nation, actively implemented laws, and intervened in the life of the provinces. It ensured the continuity of the State—indeed embodied in the State—throughout the various regimes.

The Civil Service and French Society

There is, however, another side to the picture, more commonly stressed in France than abroad. The strength of the bureaucracy had, and continues to have, the effect of stifling initiative, of breeding irresponsibility, and of slowing down moves toward participation and democracy. The bureaucracy's aim is to unify and develop, often against the wishes of the population. This "enlightened despotism" may have brought about change, but it led to paternalism. Local political and social elites were not encouraged to be entrepreneurial. This is being redressed, but many psychological barriers remain, two of which are particularly important—the belief in the need for uniformity and the overwhelming importance of rules and regulations. As a result, while citizens feel impotent and aggrieved, they also accept these bureaucratic canons. The role of the bureaucracy is thus far from being wholly positive.

The Idea of the State

The pervasive nature of the bureaucracy stems from the nature and role of the French State. As in many continental countries, the State is much more in France than a set of bodies designed to initiate and implement public policies; it is the legal embodiment of the nation. *It thus encom-passes all the public organizations and corporations,* both central and local. In the United States and in Britain many public bodies began, and some still are viewed, as groupings of like-minded persons wanting to run a service. Such an associational conception of public bodies has never prevailed in France, where public services are run in the context of a general organization of the State, which can coerce or compel, but also protect citizens, as local authorities and other public corporations are deemed to be better controlled in this way. In the French legal jargon, these are merely "decentralized" entities of the State. For the French, State and law go together because the organization of the State is the embodiment of the principles of the law, and no public authority, large or small, can operate outside this framework.

The Mission of the State and the Bureaucracy

Moreover, the French State is not only a legal entity; it is a legal entity with a purpose—the well-being of the citizens. From the seventeenth century, and even more so from the early nineteenth century, the tradition of the French State has been one of "social engineering." Born from the strong mark which the kings and later Napoleon wanted to make on the nation, an approach which can be described as *dirigisme,* French social engineering was given its intellectual stamp of acceptability by various writers, philosophers, and sociologists, and in particular by Saint-Simon and Auguste Comte in the early years of the nineteenth century. Society has to be molded; it is a machine, which can be perfected by appropriate means. In this the *Ecole Polytechnique* is a key element, and, characteristically, Saint-Simon and Comte were associated with teaching at that school. While Saint-Simonism faded out as a doctrine, its influence on attitudes was profound, indeed determining, during most of the nineteenth century (Napoleon III was a Saint-Simonian), particularly in those

Table 3.6 DISTRIBUTION OF CIVIL SERVICE POSTS, 1992 (PERCENTAGE)

Education	62.1
Economy and Finance	11.3
Interior	9.1
Equipment	6.0
Justice	3.2
All other	9.3
Total (number)	1,783,000.0

periods when economic development took place at a rapid rate.

French Traditional Centralization Among the consequences of this tradition, perhaps the most important is State centralization, which includes as its corollary the spreading of public agencies across the whole nation. Another consequence, perhaps not sufficiently stressed, is the greater concern for economic than for social well-being, as the happiness of men is viewed as dependent on the better organization of society for the *production* of goods and services; the approach is expansionist. Ideas are changing as the potential dangers of economic growth to the health of citizens and the protection of the environment become more widespread, but old ideas die hard.

THE CIVIL SERVICE AND ITS CHARACTERISTICS

This philosophy is implemented and even to a large extent initiated by a civil service which has high prestige and considerable competence and is widely dispersed throughout the nation, although some of the differences between France and other Western countries have decreased in this respect.

The strength of the French civil service comes in part from its size. Nearly 2 million men and women are employed by the central government (see Table 3.6). It comes also from the organization and the traditions of the service. First, the bureaucracy extends widely in the provinces in a pyramidal manner. Ministries are divided into a number of *Directions*

Générales and *Directions,* which have a large staff in Paris, but most of which also have offices (external services) in regions, *départements* (counties), and sometimes even small towns; these offices are supervised by a prefect on behalf of the government as well as by their hierarchical superiors in Paris.

The *Grands Corps*

Another element in the civil service tradition results from the existence of the *grands corps.* Indeed, until 1945, the service was not united. The *fonctionnaires* had some common rights (pensions for instance), but real unity was achieved only in 1946 by the general code for the civil service (*Statut de la fonction publique*). Before 1945, civil servants were appointed by the various ministries to fill certain jobs, and for the more technical or specialized jobs (not necessarily senior, but at least skilled), they were recruited on the basis of corps. These corps have been the basic cells of the service, with a spirit of their own (*esprit de corps*), marking them differently from other branches and divisions and with a desire to excel.

As these differences were prejudicial to the unity of the service and fostered inequality, postwar reforms tried to abolish the corps and replace them by general grades, but the post–World War II reforms of the civil service did not abolish the most prestigious of the corps, the *grands corps.* In the economic field (Inspectorate of Finance), the administrative judiciary (Council of State), the home and local government sector (Prefectoral Corps), and various technical branches (Corps of Mines, Corps of Roads and Bridges)—these bodies have for generations attracted bright aspiring civil servants. There was an attempt to link members of these corps to the rest of the service, but it failed. Thus the French civil service continues to be run, in most of the ministries, by members of the *grands corps.* Although they may each have barely a few hundred members, they dominate the civil service and give it its tone.

The *Grandes Écoles*

The domination of the *grands corps* occurs through the special training given in a few elite schools, the *grandes écoles,* whose members are recruited by tough competitive examinations and in which high quality training is given. There are many of them, some of which are old (School of Mines, for instance), while others are recent (School of Taxes). Two are particularly important—the *Ecole Polytechnique* and the *Ecole Nationale d'Administration* (ENA). The *Ecole Polytechnique* was set up in 1795 to provide officers for the artillery and engineering branches of the army; it now gives the nation its best technical administrators. The ENA was set up in 1945 as part of the effort to unify the civil service and prepare candidates for higher management jobs in all government departments (including the foreign service). Meanwhile, a school of similar status, the *Ecole Normale Supérieure,* trains the most brilliant of the future secondary school and university teachers. Competition for entry into these schools is fierce.

The ENA is a postgraduate school. Students have first a year of field training (usually in the provinces); this is followed by a year of study in the school itself, and a further training period (*stage*) (usually in a large firm) before the new civil servant chooses where to go (in fact, only top candidates can truly choose, as the others are left with less prestigious positions). The final examination, which leads to the posting, decides in particular whether students are to become members of a *grand corps;* typically, the first 20 of each class can do so, while the other hundred or so become *administrateurs civils* and never reach the very top posts of the civil service.

The Role of the *Grands Corps* in the Nation

Except for the diplomatic corps, which remains somewhat separate and whose members typically stay in the foreign service all their lives (the service still retains some of its older aristocratic flavor), members of the *grands corps* do not work in the same department for more than a few years. They typically tend to be "detached" (the official expression) to be posted over a wide range of public bodies (including nationalized corporations). Thus inspectors of finance do not merely serve in the Inspectorate, but are in charge of practically the whole of the Treasury and of numerous other divisions and branches in which financial or economic expertise is required. Thus graduates of the *Ecole Polytechnique* who have achieved particular excellence enter one of the two technical *grands corps,* the Corps of Mines and the Corps of Roads and Bridges, and are later detached to run, not merely the relevant divisions of ministries, but other government departments and various nationalized industries. This may mean technical excellence, but there is a cost. The

---

Feature 3.5   Education: Still Strongly Elitist

The emphasis in France is not on social policy, which does not have the same importance as economic policy, though social security is now as developed as elsewhere in Europe. The one element of social policy which is given high priority, however, is education, in part because it is traditionally regarded as a ladder for upward mobility and in part because of the massive student protests which take place periodically. The best-known are those of 1968, but these have been followed by further waves of protests, for instance, in the second half of the 1980s. The French education system, and in particular the French higher education system, has traditionally been elitist. The *grandes écoles* are regarded as providing their alumni with great careers; hence the tough competitive examinations set up to enter them. The rest of the higher education system tends to be a Cinderella. Universities are badly provided for and there is little contact between staff and students (of whom there are over 2 million). Centralization makes matters worse and in particular induces professors to want to reside in Paris (even if they have a post in the provinces). Despite some changes, no real reform has as yet taken place to render universities more autonomous and more responsible.

rigid distinction created between the very successful elements of the higher civil service and the others can lead to disillusionment and constitutes a waste of early training efforts.

Finally, the role of top civil servants does not stop at the civil service itself. The best students of the prestigious schools also provide large numbers of managers to the private sector. The situation is the converse of what occurs in the United States where private sector managers often join the federal service for a period. In France, the prestige of the training schools is such that their graduates transfer to business (an operation known as *pantouflage*). This gives the civil service, indirectly, a substantial influence on the whole of the economic life of the nation.

Civil Service Control

The quality of the *grands corps* accounts for much of the excellence of the service, but it also leads to conflicts among the various branches, each of which is primarily concerned with its own sector. Supervision and coordination can therefore be difficult and, not surprisingly, control plays a crucial—and often frustrating—part in the French public sector.

Control takes many forms. Some of these forms are internal to the civil service and date back in part to Napoleon. First, there are inspectorates, which are often weak, in part because the inspectors-general stayed in the service while most of their colleagues of the same age group found a more active and more lucrative life in private business. As a matter of fact, the main role of inspectors-general is now not so much to inspect but to inquire. They are often asked to examine long-term problems and thus act in a way similar to royal commissions in Britain or presidential commissions in the United States. A second type of control is provided by the administrative courts, headed by the Council of State. These courts started as internal organs of supervision on the model of inspectorates and, as inspectors do, still conduct some inquiries and have advisory functions (on bills and decrees the Council of State advises the government about legality, opportunity, and effectiveness); but they have become real courts and are at some distance from the "active" administrators.

Ministerial Staffs (Cabinets)   Internal controls seemed insufficient to liberal governments issued from Parliament and suspicious of administrators. Hence the development, around each minister, of a staff known as the "ministerial *cabinet.*" Members of the *cabinet* (to be sharply distinguished from the "cabinet," or government) are appointed by the minister. They help him or her to remain in touch with constituents and with Parliament. They prepare drafts of bills and of other reforms; they follow the implementation of policies; they inform their minister about what goes on in the department. They are thus both a protection against undue civil service independence and a brain trust for innovations.

The character of ministerial *cabinets* has changed somewhat in recent decades. These *cabinets* have come to include specialists drawn from the civil service itself, as ministers increasingly need technical advice. The staff of a minister of transport will thus include among others an engineer of roads and bridges, an inspector of finance (to examine costs), a member of the Council of State (to help draft legal documents). These are civil servants, usually young, loyal to their minister, of course, as their future career depends in part on the help which they give, but they are civil servants and part of their loyalty is to the civil service and especially to the corps to which they belong. As other civil servants, they are anxious to foster development rather than control other civil servants on behalf of constituents or politicians. *Cabinets* thus now provide only a limited check on the bureaucracy.

LOCAL GOVERNMENT

While the civil service and central government agencies were strong, local government was traditionally weak. It was shaped by Napoleon, who, rejecting the early decentralizing schemes of the Revolution, imposed an authoritarian plan. Local authorities were not only supervised but indeed run by agents of the central government. Liberalization slowly took place in the nineteenth century, in the 1830s and the 1880s in particular, but there never was a decisive break with the origins. A large amount of central government control was maintained in part for political reasons. Even liberals always felt that full devolution of power to local authorities was dangerous, since much of the opposition to the government was opposition to the regime as well. Local government has thus been caught in a vicious circle, as yet not entirely broken, despite some changes in structure and a modification in attitudes, especially since the 1950s when an entrepreneurial spirit began to prevail.

Département and *Commune*

The current structure of French local government dates from the Revolution of 1789, as modified by Napoleon. The French territory is divided into *départements,* of which there are now 96. This entirely artificial creation was designed to break the hold of the old provinces (such as Brittany or Provence). New counties were set up with names drawn from mountains or rivers (Jura, Var, and the like). The *départements* are in turn divided into communes—usually corresponding to the old parishes—of which there are about 37,000. This helped centralization and prevented real local autonomy from developing, despite the democratization of the appointment processes, as the average commune is too small to be effective and has to rely on the services of central government agents. Yet no significant reduction in the number of communes has ever taken place, in part because of local resistance, but in part also because the strength of the civil service is better maintained by the present structure. Since the 1960s there have only been a number of joint authorities (urban districts), linking towns to the suburban communes, and a Paris district, which has a similar purpose for the Paris area.

Communes maintain strong sentiments of local patriotism. Their representatives play a large part in French local life. Elected every six years by universal suffrage, municipal councilors in turn elect a mayor and a number of assistants (*adjoints*). Mayors have some of the authority of the State, while running the local authority. As the basic law of municipal government of 1884 states: "The mayor is in charge of the affairs of the commune." Mayors pass bylaws relating to police or health matters, register citizens, supervise the maintenance of roads, street lighting, street cleaning, and the like. Aspects of education and housing come directly or indirectly under their jurisdiction. Particularly in large cities, the mayor is a focal point especially because, in practice, mayors tend to stay in office for long, even very long periods—two or three terms of six years are common. The stability of communal government has always contrasted with the instability of national politics. Communal government is executive-centered; the municipal government is typically dominated by the mayor.

Decentralization Efforts Traditionally, mayors and municipal councils were tightly supervised by central government agents, especially those at the level of the county (*département*). This is in part because counties had, up to the 1980s, a peculiar organization, based on an osmosis between central government agents and locally elected councilors. Until 1982, the executive of the *département* was indeed the prefect, who both served Paris and the elected county council. This helped to perpetuate the dependence of local authorities on the central government and has in particular prevented *départements* from being true local authorities. A major step was therefore taken by the Socialist government of the 1980s. While prefects were retained as agents of the central government, *départements* came to be run by an elected representative, the president of the general council. Meanwhile, communes were given greater autonomy; they no longer need, on the whole, prior approval to undertake most activities.

Regionalism

Reform also took place higher up, through the setting up of regions. The 96 *départements* are too small, but change has been slow to come. First, regional councils composed of representatives of *départements,* communes, and economic and social groups were set up. This occurred for the Paris area in 1959, where a post of government-appointed delegate general was created; regional economic development councils were introduced elsewhere in France in 1964. Participation having been one of the main themes of the 1968 revolutionary outburst, a scheme for regionalization was presented to the

---

Feature 3.6 The French Media

France has not been truly well served by its media. For a long period after World War II, State radio and television were closely controlled by the government; a number of private radio stations located at the periphery of the country provided much needed fresh air to information. Improvements took place since the de Gaulle period, the three main channels having become independent networks; under President Mitterrand's Socialist governments, private television began to flourish. There is now more choice and genuine independence from the government, though the quality of the programs still leaves much to be desired.

Most of the press is regional and of indifferent quality. Not surprisingly, the best newspapers are Parisian, *Le Monde* being the outstanding example, though some of the competitors which were set up in the 1970s and 1980s have also endeavored to develop a modern form of journalism. Weeklies have moved in the direction of investigative stories and have uncovered problems and scandals. By and large, the media suffer from the classic French characteristics of nationalistic elitism. Culture is given great emphasis—with such ministers of culture as Andre Malraux under de Gaulle and Jack Lang under Mitterrand—but culture is regarded as being true if it is essentially French. As a result, the "Americanization" of the media is (officially at least, if not necessarily in reality) markedly frowned upon. It was a strong bone of contention in the discussions leading to the GATT agreement of 1995.

French people in 1969. It was limited in scope; being coupled with a reform of the Senate, it was rejected in the referendum and de Gaulle resigned as a result. In 1972, a regional reform was presented to Parliament for approval and passed. Members of the councils continued to be drawn from local authorities, while regional prefects were appointed alongside the regional presidents and councils; these administered a small portion of the matters hitherto handled centrally by the civil service. Finally, the Socialist government of the 1980s instituted regional elections; the councils in turn elect their executive. Independent political bodies thus exist in each region, though their powers and influence are still limited. Yet, despite the fact that these moves have been relatively slow and half-hearted, France is at last engaged in a process which may gradually dispose of many of the old habits of centralization.

ECONOMIC INTERVENTION AND PUBLIC ENTERPRISE

The weakness of French local government stems in large part from the widespread belief that France needs a strong civil service if it is to be a modern industrial and commercial nation and the inertia of the provinces is to be shaken. A parallel view has traditionally been adopted with respect to business. Hence the development of large public and semipublic undertakings often takes the form of mixed companies (*sociétés d'économie mixte*), while large-scale nationalizations took place in 1945–1946 after World War II and in 1982 after the Socialist victory. An attempt was also made to supervise business generally by means of economic plans. The tide then turned. A "privatization" program was launched by the 1986–1988 conservative government and an effort started to be undertaken to reduce the traditional role of the civil service in the economy (see Table 3.7).

The Plan

French economic development from the 1940s to the 1980s has often been associated with the activities of the *Commissariat général au Plan*, although its role is now almost nominal. It started under the leadership of Jean Monnet, a strong-willed ex-civil servant and ex-businessman who was to be crucial to the psychological success of the idea and was later, much in the same vein, to foster European unity. The Plan was to be flexible; it was to be run by a team, not by a hierarchical and bureaucratic organization. Its strength came from the intellectual authority of the experts belonging to it.

The character of the Plan changed over the years. It was first concerned with reconstruction and the development of basic industries; it then extended its purview to the whole economy, to regional development (it helped decentralization to an extent), and even to social policies. Meanwhile, after having been originally drawn exclusively by officials with little discussion, even in Parliament, large segments of the community later became involved through numerous committees. Employers, leaders of nationalized industries, and trade unionists were associated with the preparation of the Plan; there were also increasingly discussions in the Economic and Social Council, in the regional economic committees, and among the public at large. However, the idea could only suffer in a climate of greater liberalization and of free enterprise. With the advent of the Socialist government of 1981, its importance was revived somewhat, but, because of the imperative of economic retrenchment it never again had the importance

it once had. By the 1990s, it had effectively disappeared in all but name.

The Vast Size of the Public Sector

The downgrading of the Plan coincided with the first real attempt made by post–World War II French governments to reduce the size of the public sector, which up to 1986 was among the largest in Western Europe and had already been so before the large-scale nationalization measures of the 1981 government. From a base which included, before World War II, the post office, the railways, some shipping lines, and undertakings, such as potash mines in Alsace, electricity production in the Rhone Valley, and luxury china in Sèvres, the public sector expanded in 1945–1946 to include the coal mines, the major banks, insurance companies, gas, electricity, and much of aircraft manufacturing; Renault, the largest car manufacturer, was nationalized because the owner had collaborated with Nazi Germany during the Second World War; much of air and shipping transport also came under direct governmental control. There was a de facto monopoly of radio and television within France and the State acquired majority capital in several of the private radio stations which operated at the periphery of the country. A public news agency, *Agence France-Presse*, replaced the private prewar *Agence Havas*. As demand for oil increased (France has very little within its territory), the State created companies, typically as a major shareholder, which engaged in research, production, and distribution of oil and natural gas on a worldwide basis.

This was the situation before 1981. The Socialist government, following to the letter the party's pledge at the election, then carried through Parliament the nationalization of practically all the banks (including old, established private banks such as Rothschild) and of five major industrial groups in the chemical and electronic fields, while the major steel companies, already heavily subsidized by the State, were taken over.

These developments took a variety of legal forms which had been perfected since World War I. Originally State control was direct, as in the case of the post office. Later came the model of the *établissement publics* whose funds are public and where control is tight, but where a

Table 3.7   DISTRIBUTION OF BUDGETARY EXPENDITURE, 1989 (PERCENTAGE)

Economy and finance	45.9
Education (including universities)	16.7
Labor, health	9.3
Defense	7.4
Equipment and transport	7.0
Interior	3.9
Agriculture	2.9
Veterans	2.2
Foreign affairs	1.5
Industry and commerce	1.2
Justice	1.0
Culture, tourism	0.6
P.M. Office (including Planning Commissariat)	0.2
Overseas departments	0.1
Total budgetary expenditure	1,197,600 million francs

board takes decisions and contracts with third parties on behalf of the agency; the formula has often been adopted by local authorities as well. Then, to increase flexibility, companies and corporations were set up with the same structure, the same rights, and the same obligations as private firms. In the case of the large undertakings nationalized in 1945–1946 and in 1982, special legislative arrangements gave the corporations a somewhat different organization, with boards including representatives of the State, the users, and the employees, for instance; but in many other cases there was simply no difference between private and public firms, thus making it possible for State corporations to combine with private bodies to set up subsidiaries.

The Privatization Moves of the Late 1980s and 1990s

The development of the public sector reached a peak in the mid–1980s. In 1986, for the first time, a government came to power both committed to privatization and to abandoning the traditional practice of linking private and public bodies. For the first time, too, the Left no longer wished to modify the new equilibrium by again increasing the public sector when it returned to power in 1988. No new nationalization was even suggested. The French governments of the 1990s thus came to follow the same direction as other European governments; in line with European Union policy, they made moves toward more classical forms of private enterprise at the expense of both wholly public and mixed forms of companies, although the latter had been regarded as the way of the future for at least a generation.

FOREIGN POLICY

De Gaulle's Worldwide Policy

Foreign policy was the main interest of de Gaulle. Even the reform of institutions was in some sense provoked by the bias of the founder of Fifth Republic for foreign affairs, as he felt that the instability and impotence of previous regimes had been the cause both of defeat in 1940 and of the generally limited influence of the country in the world ever since. Yet although there were indeed external effects of

French internal political uncertainties, de Gaulle markedly underestimated the extent to which the country could any longer be a prime mover in the contemporary world. Thus his efforts at pushing for a strong and independent foreign policy ended in failure. Indeed, he himself may have realized that he could not go much beyond symbolic gestures, such as the effort to build closer links with the Soviet Union or to defend the rights of some countries or groups against Anglo-Saxon "imperialism" (as he tried to do in Quebec or Latin America). In practice, he did keep France within NATO (despite some changes) and within the European Community, despite a continuous emphasis on the fact that Europe should be a "Europe of Nations" and despite the fact that he unquestionably retarded the development of European unity.

Pompidou's Greater Realism

De Gaulle's departure from the scene meant a slow, indeed very slow, return to the recognition of France's international position, that of a medium-sized power, with some influence stemming from her cultural and economic ties with parts of Africa and, to a more limited extent, with Latin America; but she cannot have a direct effect on the course of events outside Western Europe where, on the contrary, she has a significant part to play, albeit as a partner and not as a leader. Thus Pompidou, de Gaulle's successor and heir, began to make some moves away from grand world involvement and toward the acceptance of the country's limited European role. His acceptance of British entry into the European Community was partly motivated by the hope that Britain, as France, would reduce the spread of "supranationalism." In this he was proved right, though the entry of Britain into the European Community (now Union) also meant that the Union was gradually including of all Western European nations.

The More Limited Ambitions of Giscard, Mitterrand, and Even Chirac

The third president of the Fifth Republic, Giscard d'Estaing, went further. His close working relationship with the German chancellor of the time, Helmut Schmidt, continued the rapprochement of de Gaulle with Adenauer a decade or more earlier, but with a different purpose. De Gaulle used Adenauer to assert his leadership over Europe; Giscard was more modest and recognized the economic superiority of Germany and was primarily concerned with economic association. A step was thus taken toward real collaboration and toward the abandonment of the (wholly unrealistic) idea that France could do more than partly influence the course of events in Western Europe, let alone in the rest of the world.

Mitterrand's role was markedly more positive. Not being associated, directly or indirectly, with de Gaulle and Gaullism, he was able to assert that France's position was in Europe and, in effect, in Europe only. Economic difficulties (and the consequential social problems of unemployment) made it impossible for Mitterrand to expect to move at a truly different pace from his European partners, as we saw; but his European conviction was also part of a general recognition that France was in Europe and that, if her commitment was wholehearted, she could play an key part in the European Community. Perhaps as a result, Mitterrand was able to appoint his ex-minister of finance, Jacques Delors, to the presidency of the European Commission from 1985, a post which he was to occupy for ten years in a very able manner. Mitterrand could thus exercise indirect influence on Community affairs. He was not a full federalist; nor did he completely abandon the idea that France should have a worldwide policy; but the greater realism of the first Socialist president that France has known was an important development. His successor, Jacques Chirac, has seemed torn between traditional Gaullism—in words—and realism—in deeds. He clearly took a Gaullist line on nuclear weapons, at least in a first phase, insisting that France should have a truly "independent" nuclear deterrent. He doggedly proceeded with a series of tests in the South Pacific that antagonized almost every country, not just in the Pacific but in Europe as well. Yet Chirac then stated that the tests conducted until January 1996 would be the last and that he would from then on act strongly to reduce the nuclear threat—not a line which de Gaulle would have easily adopted. He adopted also a similar, more realistic line in favor of

Europe; he had previously supported the Maastricht treaty of the European Union; once in office, he has appeared constrained to adopt a European orientation.

French governments display ambiguous attitudes with respect to foreign policy. Even those led by Gaullists have come to proclaim their belief in the European idea, but there is still a lingering desire to play a large part—an unrealistically large part—in worldwide developments, whether in the Middle East, Africa, or Latin America. The commitment to Europe is also somewhat ambiguous, in that French governments have more than occasionally been concerned to defend their economic interests to the hilt, as over the GATT negotiations of 1993–1994, while being rather slow at applying in practice the principles which they claim to support in theory. Such a mode of behavior is perhaps inevitable in a period of transition during which France, as the other Western European powers, has to recognize that her role in the world must diminish and that only through a common European policy can the voice of the whole area be of real moment. The dilemma between "going it alone" and further integration is one which has almost daily affected the actions of French governments over the last decades. It is likely to continue to affect them at least for a period.

CONCLUSION

In the 1950s and 1960s, the French economy was transformed dramatically; the colonial problems which destroyed one regime and brought another at times near the precipice were solved and forgotten; the international status of the country was high. Yet social tensions, which seemed to diminish for a while in the 1960s, reemerged dramatically in 1968. This reinforced the feeling of many among the French that the Fifth Republic remained provisional. Yet the departure of de Gaulle one year later, in 1969, did not shake the institutions, and the transition from de Gaulle to Pompidou was smooth. Nor was the regime shaken by the transition from Giscard to Mitterrand in 1981, despite the many predictions made earlier that "alternance" from Right to Left would be difficult, if not impossible; nor was it even shaken by "cohabitation" in two instances—a president

Jacques Chirac was elected president in 1995, the third time he ran for the position. Chirac has been mayor of Paris since 1977, is leader of the Gaullist Rally for the Republic (RPR), and was twice prime minister.

of the Left and a government of the Right and Center, despite further gloomy predictions that conflicts would be intense.

In 1981, a Socialist government embarked on a major reform program. This was possible only because of institutions which had been said to have been tailor-made for de Gaulle. In 1986, a conservative government undid many of these reforms, but the regime, then too, was flexible enough to make these movements possible, as were two further swings of the pendulum, first toward the Left in 1988, and second again toward the Right in 1993. The institutional ambiguity of the 1958 Constitution turned out to be a major asset of the Fifth Republic.

Cynics had claimed that de Gaulle wanted to have it both ways—namely, to be able to run the executive and yet have considerable control over the legislature, to have the elbow room of a U.S. president but the hold over the chamber of a British premier, and, in practical terms, to be immovable for seven years but be able to dissolve Parliament and appeal to the people. Others had claimed that de Gaulle was unable to understand and appreciate the importance of constitutional structures, a view which has some truth, though the attitudes of the first president of the Fifth Republic on this matter were complex. He seemed at the same time to consider that constitutional arrangements were matters for lawyers who can always find solutions if they are firmly led, and yet he had a simple, naive, almost religious, belief in the virtues of constitutional reform to redress the imperfections of a political system. His approach to political analysis was more institutional than behavioral, to adopt the widely used expression of modern political scientists.

Yet he made a change which, however ambiguous—or perhaps because it was ambiguous—allowed for a transition to occur and turned out to be adapted to French patterns of political behavior.

De Gaulle was often criticized because he preferred to introduce constitutional change to establishing a streamlined and responsible party system as Adenauer succeeded in achieving in West Germany. De Gaulle was indeed old-fashioned in this respect. He did not like parties, which he often referred to as "factions"; he saw them as divisive and as the cause of the ineffectiveness of French political life in the past. Yet, in practice, while concentrating on institutional change and endeavoring to reduce the role of parties, he did streamline the party system. He built a party on the Right, which his successors, Pompidou and Giscard d'Estaing, but not he, undermined; indirectly, too, he enabled Mitterrand to build his popular support and to restart the Socialist Party.

The election of 1981 constituted a historic event in more than one way; indeed, in the broadest political sense, more than Pompidou and Giscard, Mitterrand was the heir and the continuator of de Gaulle's approach. Mitterrand, as de Gaulle, defeated the Communist Party on coming to power; he, as de Gaulle, established a strong majority party, since the election of 1981 had the same political effect of streamlining and strengthening the party system as the election of 1962; Mitterrand, as de Gaulle, came to power with a mission, albeit a different one. De Gaulle's mission was to solve the Algerian crisis and, beyond this crisis, to bring France back to political and psychological sanity; Mitterrand's mission was to reconcile the French among themselves, to make them no longer fear to take on their own destiny at the grass roots, whether in the regions and the communes or in the firms.

Here the comparison stops. To achieve this tall order, Mitterrand needed to exorcise the twin specters of unemployment and inflation. He reduced the latter, but unemployment probably contributed to the first setback of his party in 1986 and unquestionably led to the major Socialist defeat of 1993. As a matter of fact, Mitterrand could not hope to succeed in his mission

without the collaboration of other Western European countries, of the United States, and of Japan. These nations practiced economic orthodoxy. Mitterrand had to accept the need for retrenchment and, with it the clipping of many of his ideals. Yet, while the French turned away from the Left in view of its relative failures, Mitterrand himself, and indeed the Socialist Party in general, gained a central position in French political life of respect and of acceptability which the party had not had before, as the good performance of Jospin at the 1995 presidential election showed, less than a year after what looked like a collapse at the 1994 European election. As a result, France has become a country in which pluralism and alternance became firmly established.

Observers around the world have tended to admire the British form of government but have been fascinated by the French political system. For a while, under the Fifth Republic, it was fashionable to say that a new French political system, streamlined and dull, had emerged. This was scarcely true at the time of the Algerian war, when virulence added unpleasantness to the political fights of the French; this has not become true with the end of the colonial wars. Since the 1970s, there has been a difficult search for a better equilibrium between the various forces in society, between Paris and the provinces, between employers and workers, as well as between the majority of the French and the many minority groups—immigrants, the young, and the deviants. No doubt the Socialist experiment of 1981 disappointed some and repelled others; but France also changed in the process in that the central bureaucracy or the elite groups are no longer able to maintain their traditional hold on the society.

By 1981 the Gaullist (and Giscardian) phase of the Fifth Republic seemed to have outlived its usefulness. By 1995, the Socialist party, too, seemed to have proved unable to give France the "new deal" which many wanted, while some among its political elite appeared to have succumbed to the lust for money as well as for power. It is to the lasting credit of de Gaulle that he made it possible for French citizens to bring about responsible changes in policies and changes in personnel, developments which had not been possible for many generations. It is to the credit of the French that they seized this opportunity, though, of course, many motivations, from unemployment to scandals, have played a substantial part. Thus France may gradually overcome its social problems while also overcoming the institutional difficulties from which it suffered for almost two centuries. Yet the path is narrow and tortuous; ingenuity and imagination will no more suffice than a competent bureaucracy. Patience and determination—not the qualities for which the French are best known—will have to be shown if the motto "Liberty, Equality, Fraternity" is to be brought, in full, closer to reality.

KEY TERMS

adjoints
bureaucracy
civil service control
Départements
Directions Générales/Directions
French civil service
Grandes Écoles
Grands Corps
mayors
ministerial *cabinets*
prefects
regions
social engineering

FURTHER READINGS

Bauchet, P. *Economic Planning: The French Experience* (London: Heinemann, 1963).

Cerny, P., and M. Schain, eds. *French Politics and Public Policy* (New York: Methuen, 1980).

Chapman, B. *Introduction to French Local Government* (London: Allen & Unwin, 1953).

Crozier, M. *The Bureaucratic Phenomenon* (London: Tavistock, 1964).

Crozier, M. *The Stalled Society* (New York: Viking, 1973).

Gregoire, R. *The French Civil Service* (Brussels: Institute of Administrative Science, 1964).

Machin, H., and V. Wright, eds., *Economic Policy and Policy-Making under the Mitterrand Presidency, 1981–1984* (London: F.Pinter, 1985).

Ridley, F., and J. Blondel. *Public Administration in France*, 2nd ed. (London: Routledge & Kegan Paul, 1968).

Suleiman, E. *Politics, Power, and Bureaucracy in France* (Princeton, Princeton University Press, 1974).

Suleiman, E. *Elites in French Society* (Princeton: Princeton University Press, 1978).

CHAPTER 4

The Government of Germany

Donald Kommers

Political Development

On October 3, 1990, after 45 years of painful separation, Germany was once again a united nation. After midnight on that day, East Germany ceased to exist. The territory formerly governed by the German Democratic Republic (GDR) and its hard-line Communist leaders was now an integral part of the Federal Republic of Germany (FRG). Accession was the magical term used. Under Article 23 of West Germany's Constitution, "other parts of Germany" outside the territory governed by the FRG could join or "accede to" the Federal Republic. Accession meant that these "other parts" of Germany joining the FRG would henceforth be subject to its Constitution, better known as the Basic Law or *Grundgesetz*. In this instance, accession took place under the terms of the German Unity Treaty signed by the FRG and the GDR. In signing the Treaty the GDR agreed to dissolve itself, to embrace the Basic Law, and to bring its entire social, political, and economic system into conformity with the legal order of the FRG.

Unification did not restore to Germany all the territory lost as a result of World War II. In 1945 the Soviet Union annexed northern East Prussia, including Königsberg, while all German territory east of the Oder and Neisse Rivers (East Prussia, Silesia, and part of Pomerania and Brandenburg) was placed under Polish administration. The Allies divided the rest of Germany and Berlin into four zones of occupation: a Soviet zone in the east and three zones in the west occupied by France, Britain, and the United States, respectively. The western zones, united in 1949 to form the Federal Republic of Germany, constituted only 60 percent of the territory of the German nation that existed between 1871 and 1937. The Saarland, annexed by France after World War II, was returned to the FRG in 1957 after its residents voted in favor of reunion. It too entered the Federal Republic by accession under Article 23, becoming the smallest of West Germany's territorial states. With the GDR's accession in 1990, Germany has recovered three-fourths of the territory contained within its 1937 borders.

The division of Germany after World War II recalls the tragic course of German history through the centuries. This history has been marred not only by territorial dismemberment but also by political discontinuity, which has manifested itself in recurrent patterns of revolution and reaction. It has left the German nation with a diverse and fragmented political legacy of democratic, authoritarian, and even totalitarian systems of government.

HISTORICAL BACKGROUND: MOLDING THE GERMAN NATION

The First Reich (800–1806)

Centuries after Britain and France had been unified under strong national monarchs, Germany was still a dizzying patchwork of sovereign powers—over 300 feudal states and some 1,300 smaller estates—each with its own political institutions, laws, and customs. No imperial institution was prestigious enough to unify these diversities, and no emperor was strong enough to merge them into a single national state. The shape of the Holy Roman Empire of the German Nation (the predominantly German parts of the Empire founded by Charlemagne and restored by Otto I—and quite rightly described as "neither holy, nor Roman, nor an empire") changed repeatedly over its thousand-year history, stretching in and out like an accordion—a process facilitated by the absence of natural frontiers on the northern plains of Europe—depending on the fortunes of war or the outcome of princely rivalries.

Religious and political division matched the severity of Germany's territorial fragmentation. The Reformation (1517–1555) polarized Germans religiously, creating a legacy of intolerance and hatred that lasted well into the nineteenth century. The Thirty Years' War (1618–1648) was equally devastating in long-range political impact. Reputed to be the most destructive war in the first millenium of German history, it decimated the population, wrecked agriculture and industry, and destroyed an emergent middle class that might have formed the nucleus of a nationalizing and moderating force in German politics. Yet, it restored power to the princes, reinvigorated feudalism, and set the stage for the nineteenth-century struggle between feudal and proletarian forces. Moreover, Protestant religious teaching and princely absolutism combined to emphasize the duty of obedience to the State, thus inhibiting popular participation in politics.[1]

Napoleon to Bismarck (1806–1871)

An invader laid the basis of German unity. Occupying Germany in 1806, Napoleon banished the ghost of the old Reich and forced hundreds of principalities into a confederation of some 30 states governed by a unified code of civil law. Like so much else in German history, this experience led to contradictory results. On the one hand, French rule stimulated the development of a liberal movement focused mainly in southwestern Germany and rooted in the eighteenth-century revival of classical humanism. On the other hand, it triggered an outburst of German nationalism built almost exclusively on antipathy toward the liberal reforms of the French Revolution—a reaction paralleled in the cultural domain by a literary backlash that glorified tradition over reason, heroism over compassion, and the folk community over cosmopolitanism.

France's defeat in 1815 led to the Congress of Vienna and the establishment of a new confederacy of 41 states that largely retained Napoleon's extensive remodeling of Germany. In its effort to strengthen Germany vis-à-vis France, the Congress ceded large possessions in the Rhineland and Westphalia to Prussia, a German state which by then had grown into a formidable power in central Europe. The Prussian-led conservative Hohenzollern monarchy and militaristic Junker caste were destined to finish, through "blood and iron," the work of national unification started by Napoleon. Economically, the Prussian-sponsored customs union (*Zollverein*), which resulted in the removal of most

trade barriers among the German states, was an important tool of national integration.

A watershed year in this period was 1848, when revolutions against monarchical regimes broke out all over Europe. German liberals had gathered enough strength to persuade several princes to go along with the election of a national assembly, which convened in Frankfurt am Main. Known as the Frankfurt Parliament it proceeded to create a united Germany under a new federal constitution containing an impressive bill of rights, an independent judiciary, and parliamentary institutions. By the following spring, however, this "revolution" had been put down as Germany reverted to its traditional pattern of authoritarian governance, increasingly under Prussian domination. In 1866, under the leadership of Otto von Bismarck, Prussia defeated Austria, its closest rival for hegemony in Germany. Austria's defeat led to the creation of the North German Confederation in 1867, also under Prussian domination. Five years later, after conquering France, Prussia proceeded to establish a truly national state in the form of a constitutional monarchy.

The Second Reich (1871–1918)

The constitutional order installed by Bismarck in 1871 was a semiauthoritarian system that (1) limited the franchise to the wealthier classes; (2) subordinated the popularly elected house of parliament (*Reichstag*) to the executive; (3) established a Prussian-dominated and nonelected upper parliamentary chamber (*Bundesrat*) composed largely of landed proprietors and members of reigning families; (4) divided executive authority between a chancellor and the emperor (*Kaiser*), with effective political power lodged in the latter; and (5) empowered the emperor (preeminently the king of Prussia) to appoint and dismiss the chancellor, dissolve the Reichstag, declare martial law, and serve as supreme commander of the armed forces. In the socioeconomic sphere, the imperial era was marked by (1) an economic revolution that transformed a backward and predominantly agrarian society into a powerful urban, industrialized nation; (2) the establishment of an alliance between agrarian and industrial interests in foreign policy; (3)

the colonization of overseas territories; (4) the adoption of a comprehensive program of state social legislation designed to purchase the loyalty and support of the working masses; and (5) an arms race with Britain and France, triggered in part by an increasingly chauvinistic nationalism, as many Germans, including intellectuals, dreamed of a larger and even more powerful global order under German hegemony.

Ralf Dahrendorf has characterized imperial Germany as an "industrial feudal society,"[2] meaning that industrialism failed to produce a modern polity as in Britain and France. Whereas modernization brought about liberal traditions of civic equality and political participation in Britain and France, Germany remained a preindustrial class society based on rank and status. The state bureaucracy, professional army, landed aristocracy, and patriarchical family remained the central pillars of the social structure. Human rights or other fundamental guarantees were conspicuously absent in the imperial constitution. Social conflict was put down either by repression or state paternalism, thus encouraging the political passivity of the German people, inducing them to seek the satisfactions of life by turning inward, toward themselves (internal freedom), and to the fostering of private values associated with friendship and family, rather than by turning outward toward the cultivation of public virtues.

The Weimar Republic (1919–1933)

Germany's defeat in World War I and the abdication of the monarch led to the establishment at Weimar of its first constitutional democracy since the short-lived National Assembly of 1848. The Constitution of 1919 continued the tradition of German federalism, guaranteed numerous social and political rights, and adopted a parliamentary system capped by the popular election of the president. It also contained structural features that contributed to the instability of the new polity: The president could dismiss the chancellor, dissolve the Reichstag (the powerful new lower chamber), control the armed forces, suspend constitutional rights, and exercise broad emergency powers; the system of proportional representation splintered the electorate, leading to a succession of weak governments; basic liberties were judicially unenforceable; and the ease with which the Constitution could be amended or suspended tended to trivialize it.

It is doubtful whether any constitution, however artfully drawn, could have contained the social and political chaos unleashed in postwar Germany. The disgrace of military defeat and the harsh terms of the Versailles Treaty—for example, the enforced reparations and the Allied occupation of the Rhineland—gave birth to yet another round of frenzied nationalism. Against the backdrop of an unchanged social structure, a large segment of Germany's elite also questioned the legitimacy of Weimar's republican institutions. At length, these institutions were easily manipulated for antidemocratic purposes in the face of social turmoil and economic collapse. Violence erupted in the streets as right-wing extremists, often fighting left-wing extremists, gathered strength and influence. The political unrest led to Hitler's installation as chancellor on January 30, 1933. Nazi success in the elections of March 5, 1933, following the February burning of the Reichstag, anchored his hold on power. The passage of the Enabling Act shortly thereafter, which granted the government dictatorial powers, ended the life of the Weimar Republic.

The Third Reich (1933–1945)

With Hitler's rise to power, constitutional government succumbed to National Socialist totalitarianism. Popular assemblies of the various states were abolished; political parties banned; autonomous groups and associations suppressed; dissent crushed; anti-Nazi political figures imprisoned, tortured, or murdered; and ordinary citizens deprived of liberty and property without due process of law. Having consolidated his power and in violation of the Versailles Treaty, Hitler proceeded to remilitarize the Rhineland and to build a war machine that by 1941 would sweep across Europe, threatening the security of the entire world.

Between 1933 and 1945, Hitler engineered what Lucy S. Dawidowicz called "the war against the Jews."[3] It started when the German dictatorship stepped up its campaign of anti-Semitic propaganda; it continued with decrees to boycott Jewish businesses, to remove Jews from the civil service and the professions, to divest them of their citizenship, to seize their property, and to forbid them from marrying non-Jews; it ended in the "night of the broken glass" (*Kristallnacht*) when gangs of storm troopers all over Germany assaulted Jews on the streets, invaded their homes, destroyed their shops, and set fire to their synagogues. The Holocaust followed as millions of Jews in Germany and Hitler's Europe, including women and children, were rounded up, herded into cattle cars, and sent to concentration camps designed for their extermination. Six million Jews died in these camps, almost completing Hitler's goal of ridding Europe of its Jewish population.

Although the German dictatorship met with the brave resistance of various religious and political groups—including several attempts on Hitler's life—it took the near total destruction of Germany from the outside to topple the Nazis from power. World War II (1939–1945) resulted in yet another enforced dismemberment and foreign occupation of the German nation, along with the elimination of Prussia as a separate territorial unit. Hitler had inadvertently facilitated the long trek back to political democracy. In a 12-year orgy of repression and violence the Nazis succeeded in destroying the old order, including many traditional institutions and values. Thus Hitler's "social revolution," combined with Germany's physical destruction, cleared the way for the rebuilding of a new society.

TOWARD A NEW FRAMEWORK OF GOVERNMENT

The Occupation (1945–1949)

In 1945 Germany lay smoldering in ruins. Its once powerful military machine was shattered, its industrial establishment heavily damaged, its urban centers demolished, its transportation and communication networks disrupted, its government at all levels in a state of collapse, and its people demoralized and starving. Politically, Germany's future seemed bleak. At the Yalta and Potsdam conferences the victorious powers had agreed (1) to eliminate every trace of Nazism and militarism in Germany, (2) to disarm the nation completely, (3) to punish those responsible for war crimes, (4) to force the payment of reparations to nations hurt by German

aggression, and (5) to prevent the re-emergence of industries capable of military production.

In each of their zones of occupation the Allies embarked upon programs of *denazification* and *democratization* as the first steps toward the reconstruction of a new political order. By 1947–1948, however, cooperation among the Allies had ceased. For France, Britain, and the United States, democratization meant parliamentary institutions, competitive elections, civil liberties, and a free enterprise economy; for the Soviet Union, it meant Communist Party rule and state ownership of the means of production. Furthermore, the Soviet Union had embarked upon a policy of conquest and one-party rule in Eastern Europe, creating satellite states organized in accordance with Marxist-Leninist principles out of the countries it had liberated from the Nazis.

The Cold War was gathering force with a vengeance, and Germany was its flash point. Unable to reach an agreement with the Soviet Union over the future of Germany, the three Western powers decided to combine their zones of occupation into a single economic unit. The Soviet Union responded with the Berlin blockade, but the famous airlift of 1948–1949 foiled the Soviet attempt to drive the Western powers out of Berlin.

Economic union in the western half of Germany was soon followed by political union. With the establishment of state and local governments and the licensing of political parties committed to democratic constitutionalism, the Allied military governors laid the groundwork for a new all–West German political system. A constituent assembly dominated by Christian and Social Democrats, elected in turn by the state legislatures, convened with Allied approval to write a new constitution. They called it the Basic Law (*Grundgesetz*), rather than the Constitution (*Verfassung*), to underscore the provisional character of the new polity pending national unification. This Basic Law, which created the Federal Republic of Germany, entered into force on May 23, 1949 after its ratification by the legislatures of more than two-thirds of the participating states (*Länder*).

The Soviet Union responded by founding the German Democratic Republic whose constitution entered into force on October 7, 1949. From that date until 1990, Germany remained a divided nation, and for most of these 40 years the FRG and GDR viewed each other with mistrust and hostility. The Berlin Wall stood out as the chief symbol of their mutual antagonism. Although some relaxation had taken place in the relations between the two German states in the wake of *Ostpolitik*,[4] tensions remained, and they seemed bound to persist so long as Europe itself remained divided militarily and politically between East and West.

The New Polity of the Basic Law

Although the Basic Law incorporates many of the values and structures of earlier constitutions in the democratic tradition, it broke radically with the past in three respects. First, while the Weimar Constitution could be amended by popular initiative or legislation, the Basic Law can be changed only by extraordinary majorities (two-thirds of all votes in the Bundestag and Bundesrat). Second, previous constitutions did not generally have the status of supreme law; many of their provisions served rather as political directives. The Basic Law, by contrast, is the supreme law of the land and is absolutely binding on all government officials and citizens. In earlier constitutions, individual rights could be restricted or abolished at the whim of the legislature; however, the Basic Law proclaims these rights immutable and establishes a powerful Federal Constitutional Court to enforce them.

In addition, the so-called eternity clause of the Basic Law (Article 79 [3]) prohibits any constitutional amendment that would erode the principle of federalism, the general right of the states or *Länder* to participate in legislation or the values laid down in Articles 1 and 20. These two articles express the constitution's core values. Article 1 provides the foundation of the bill of rights, declaring, "The dignity of man shall be inviolable. To respect and protect it shall be the duty of all state authority." Article 20 sets forth the guiding principles of the new constitutional order: popular sovereignty, representative government, federalism, separation of powers, the rule of law, and the principle of the social welfare state.

Equally significant is the Basic Law's commitment to internationalism, for Article 24 allows Germany to transfer sovereign powers to international organizations, whereas Article 25 provides that the "general rules of public international law shall be an integral part of the federal law." Finally, the framers of the Basic Law sought to stabilize the new polity by establishing a party democracy and combining it with a constitutional ban on political parties that would threaten to destroy or seriously undermine Germany's constitutional democracy.

Reunification

Forty years later, as noted at the outset of this section, the "impossible dream" happened. Owing to seismic changes in the geopolitics of Eastern Europe and the subsequent end to the Cold War, the Allied powers set the stage for Germany's reunification (see Section C for a description of these developments). Günter Grass's comment, taken from a speech the noted author delivered in 1970 (see Feature 4.1), recalls Eric Honecker's observation that reuniting East and West Germany would be like "mixing oil and water." Even former Chancellor Helmut Schmidt in 1988 was constrained to say that German unity could not be realized "in our lifetime." A year later, Schmidt witnessed the unpredictable and welcomed it, although Günter Grass lamented the event, describing it as the creation of a "super-Federal Republic," precisely the state he found impossible to envision in 1970.

SOCIETY AND ECONOMY

An understanding of contemporary German politics requires some attention to the profound social and economic changes that have occurred, first in the FRG since 1945 and then in the *Länder* that acceded to the FRG upon the dissolution of the GDR. While these five reconstituted *Länder* come with a vastly different political and socioeconomic formation from that of the western *Länder*, both societies are committed to the process of raising the standards of living and of production in the eastern area to parity with those enjoyed in the western area. German political leaders have indicated that they are determined to erase all vestiges of the former GDR's command economy and to replace it with the mixed economy of the advanced social welfare state—an ideal which the national governments have pursued, more often than not, since the days of Bismarck.

Economic Background

Within a single decade, West Germany emerged from the wreckage and devastation of World War II to count herself among the top industrial giants of the world. Marshall Plan aid in the amount of $4.5 billion; a preexisting industrial base available for the production of capital goods; a burgeoning export trade generated by the Korean crisis; a plentiful supply of foreign workers; and the discipline, skills, and sacrifices of the German people—all contributed to the West German economic revival.

The most important factors setting the FRG on its way to economic recovery were the currency reform of 1948 and the founding of a central bank that in time would become the main pillar of budgetary discipline and monetary stability. These were the initial building blocks of the FRG's celebrated "social market economy" (SME). Other features of the SME are competition and individual entrepreneurship, intervention by the state to ensure the realization of both, and social responsibility. Unlike in the United States, in Germany governmental regulation is not seen as a barrier to the flourishing of the market economy. Rather, the state is seen as both a protector of fair competition and a necessary agent in fostering social solidarity.

The FRG's economy percolated at an astoundingly rapid rate without any significant leveling off until the late 1960s. Motor vehicles, precision engineering, brewing, chemicals, pharmaceuticals, and heavy metal products were among Germany's strongest industries. Growth rates in the national economy in each of the four decades since 1950 were 7.96, 4.45, 2.74, and 2.21 percent, respectively,[5] placing the FRG fourth among the world's top industrial nations while transposing the country itself into a prosperous and mass-consumption society.

During these years, East Germany had experienced its own "economic miracle." By 1970, concentrating on heavy industry and mechanical engineering, the GDR ranked second, after the Soviet Union, in industrial production within the Communist bloc, outstripping all other Socialist countries in per capita national income. By the 1980s, however, under a totally state-owned economy, the GDR's increasingly outmoded industries could no longer compete in the new, "postindustrial" global market. The state itself was on the verge of bankruptcy, workers were becoming restless, and consumer goods were scarce and markedly inferior to West German products.

With reunification, finally, the FRG faced an economic challenge more formidable than the effort to revive West Germany after the war. East Germany's instantaneous integration into the FRG exposed serious weaknesses in the GDR's centrally planned economy. Its factories were unproductive and overstaffed, its technological base inferior, and its infrastructure in need of rebuilding from the ground up. The cost of reconstructing the old GDR's economy would

---

Feature 4.1   Incompatible Social Realities

There can be no unification of the GDR and the Federal Republic on West German terms; there can be no unification of the GDR and the Federal Republic on East German terms. What blocks such a unification—such a concentration of power—is not only the objections of our neighbors in Eastern and Western Europe, but also the fact that these two social systems are mutually exclusive. . . . In other words . . . we have to recognize not only the territorial and political division, but also the incompatibility of two existing German social realities.

Source: Günter Grass, *Two States—One Nation?*
Translated by Krishna Winston and A.S. Wensinger
(New York: Harcourt Brace, 1990), pp. 54–55.

Table 4.1   GROSS DOMESTIC PRODUCT: GERMANY'S RANKING AMONG SELECTED NATIONS, 1993

Nation	GDP (billion)	GDP per Capita ($)
USA	$6,260	$24,302
Japan	4,214	33,802
FRG	1,911	23,573
France	1,252	21,706
UK	941	16,279
Spain	479	12,227
Canada	546	19,001
Italy	991	17,371

Source: Facts About Germany (Frankfurt am Main: Societäts-Verlag, 1995), p. 221.

require enormous financial transfers, which would result in higher taxes for West Germans and increased deficit spending. By 1995, these transfers amounted to around 640 billion in Deutsche marks (DM), and billions more would be required to close the still-large gap in productivity and living standards between the old GDR and FRG.

The rapidity of the transformation in the old GDR resulted in scores of factory shutdowns. Some areas of the economy collapsed under the pressure of enormous competition from western Germany. The result was massive unemployment as industrial output fell by some 40 percent between 1990 and 1993. Although by 1995 over 14,000 East German industries and businesses had been privatized, productivity remained much lower than in the west. Still the future was far from bleak. Corporate-sector investment in plant and equipment has been far stronger in the eastern *Länder* than in the west and, as would be expected in the "underdeveloped" east, the construction industry has played a dominant role in the growth of an East German economy whose gross domestic product (GDP) expanded from 5.8 percent in 1993 to 8.5 percent in 1994; by contrast, the growth rates in West Germany for these years were –1.7 and 2.4 percent, respectively. Although East Germany's economy slowed to a growth rate of 5.6 percent in 1995, it was still way ahead of the 1.6 percent increase in the west. During these years, the growth rate in Germany as a whole bordered on 2 percent. By 1994, as Table 4.1

notes, Germany's gross domestic product reached a record $1,911 billion, ranking it third in the world, just behind the United States and Japan.

Territory and Population

In territorial size, reunited Germany is the fifth largest nation in Europe, up from tenth place. Bordered by nine countries ranging from Denmark in the north to Austria in the south and flanked by Poland and the Czech Republic in the east and France and the Benelux countries in the west—a 2,350 mile border—Germany takes up 137,787 square miles in the center of Europe. Geographically, Germany is the third largest nation in the European Union, behind France and Spain. But even if the Germany of today had the desire or the ability to return to its 1937 borders, it would nonetheless remain a medium-sized state on the global scale, although as an industrial power the FRG ranks third in the world.

The more important figures for contemporary Germany, both in Europe and the world, are those concerning her population. Before reunification, the FRG was the most populous state in Western Europe and second on the continent only to the USSR. The acquisition of some 16 million East Germans does not dramatically change this picture, although it augurs well for Germany's future economic potential. Along with expanding its borders and its population, the FRG has gained a new neighbor, Poland, and a new set of demographics. The overall population of nearly 81 million is now marginally younger, somewhat more East European in origin, and proportionately more Protestant.

The population figures in Table 4.2 contain a fascinating tale of human migration and dislocation. Between 1950 and 1989 the old FRG's population increased by 13 million, while the ex-GDR lost over 2 million of its inhabitants, nearly all of whom migrated or fled to West Germany. The indigenous birthrate had little to do with these statistics. In fact, West Germany had experienced a measurable decline in its native population since 1970. The rapid increase in population recorded after 1949 resulted mainly from the influx of 13 million German refugees and migrants from Poland, the Soviet Union, East Germany, and other eastern countries and the arrival of 2.5 million foreign workers who entered under the FRG's labor recruitment program in the 1960s. The *German* "immigrants"— not technically foreigners—consisted of Polish and Sudeten Germans expelled from their homes and property (*Vertriebene*), ethnic Germans from Eastern Europe resettling in the FRG (*Aussiedler*), and East Germans who abandoned their homes and careers in the GDR to resettle in the FRG (*Übersiedler*).

Since 1970, an additional 1.9 million *Aussiedler* entered Germany from Poland, Romania, and the former Soviet Union. (Some 1.8 million East Germans moved to the western *Länder* after the collapse of the Berlin Wall.) Finally, some 900,000 asylum seekers arrived in Germany from 1988 through 1991; the figure leaped to 430,191 in 1992 alone.[6]

By 1995, there were 6.88 million foreign residents in reunited Germany, nearly 50 per-cent of whom had lived there for ten years or more. The FRG's foreign nationalities, which make up 7.6 percent of the population, include 1.9 million Turks and 1.3 million persons from the former Yugoslavia. Italians, Greeks, Poles, Austrians, Romanians, Spaniards, Iranians, and Portuguese residents account for another 1.9 million residents, not to mention 300,000 British, American, and EU nationals and 360,000 persons of non-European origin. What is impressive about these figures is that they represent a rate of entry relative to the national population that is not only twice the rate of mass immigration to America in the 1920s but, apart from Israel, several times more than that of any other EU country today.

From Bonn to Berlin and in Between

Germany at last has a hub like London, Paris, or Rome and one around which the economic, cultural, and political life of the country is likely to swirl. Berlin is that hub, the new capital of united Germany. With a population of 3.5 million, it is Germany's largest city. A sprawling urban landscape scarred by 40 years of division— half the city lay in the West and half in the old Soviet zone—Berlin is experiencing an unprecedented building boom as it prepares for the presence of the national government, parliament, and numerous federal ministries expected to move from Bonn to the city by 1999. With its major universities, research institutes, cultural institutions, technical industries, and ongoing improvements in transportation, including its incorporation into Germany's high-speed intercity railroad network, Berlin is

Table 4.2   POPULATION OF GERMANY (MILLIONS)

Year	Old FRG	Ex-GDR	Germany
1950	49.9	18.4	68.3
1960	55.4	17.2	72.6
1970	60.1	17.1	77.2
1980	61.5	16.7	78.2
1993	65.5	15.6	81.1

Source: Statistisches Jahrbuch für die Bundesrepublik Deutschland 1995, p. 46.

Feature 4.2   Berlin

Berlin in 1995 is yet another world. Straddling the old border is what must easily be the largest construction site in the world. An entire new government quarter is going up around the old Reichstag . . . East Berlin, or at any rate much of it, is booming. Everywhere are the paraphernalia of reconstruction and renovation. A decade or so from now this will be one of the most monumental capitals of Europe (a dubious international asset for Germany, I would think). The old Stalinist-style buildings stand empty, awaiting demolition and revamping. Here and there, in Berlin Mitte, one comes on a few places still intact from the more remote past—Prussian, sober, Protestant—as around the Opera and the Cathedral. But on the whole it is as if the Kurfuerstendamm had exploded to incorporate the entire city with its showy prosperity and neo-European with-it-ness.

Peter L. Berger, "Berlin Again and Again," *First Things*, January 1996, p. 15.

---

poised to become the gateway between East and West if not "the de facto metropolis of the new free Central Europe."[7]

Apart from Berlin, the economic and political life of the country is centered in a number of conurbations in the Rhine-Ruhr (Essen, Dortmund, Cologne, and Düsseldorf), Rhine-Main (Frankfurt), and Rhine-Neckar (Mannheim) regions; in the business-industrial concentrations around the cities of Stuttgart, Hamburg, Hanover, and Munich; and now in the east around Dresden, Leipzig, and Chemnitz. Fourteen cities boast a population of more than 500,000. The new east German *Länder*, however, are less urbanized than those in the west. Of 19 cities with more than 300,000 inhabitants, three (Leipzig, Dresden, and Halle) are in the ex-GDR. Thirty-five percent of the former FRG's population live in cities with more than 100,000 inhabitants, but only 10.2 percent of former GDR residents live in such areas. In Germany as a whole, 10 percent of the population lives in predominately rural areas—that is, with fewer than 150 inhabitants per square kilometer—although these areas constitute over 60 percent of the national territory. Twenty-eight and 62 percent of the population live in intermediate and concentrated areas, respectively.

Economic and Social Stratification

Germany's occupational structure shows a nation gradually transforming itself from an industrial into a postindustrial society. As Table

---

Table 4.3   EMPLOYMENT STRUCTURE BY ECONOMIC SECTOR (PERCENT OF TOTAL)

Sector	Old FRG			Ex-GDR			Germany
	1950	1970	1993	1950	1970	1993	1995
Agriculture and forestry	24.6	8.8	3.3	27.9	12.8	4.2	3.5
Productive enterprises	42.7	48.7	39.1	43.9	49.1	37.1	38.8
Commerce, transport, and communication	14.3	17.7	18.0	15.7	18.3	18.4	18.1
Other trades and services	18.4	24.8	39.6	12.5	19.8	39.8	39.6
Total	100.0	100.0	100.0	100.0	100.0	100.0	100.0

Source: Ein Vergleich: Bundesrepublik Deutschland-Deutsche Demokratische Republik (Bonn: Bundesminister für innendeutsche Beziehungen, 1973), p. 28 and *Statisches Jahrbuch für die Bundesrepublik Deutschland 1995*, p. 110.

4.3 indicates, the services and trades sector of the economy has grown the fastest in both western and eastern Germany, overtaking industry. Most jobs created in West Germany were connected with banking, insurance, education, the health professions, and the civil service. The social transformation suggested by the tabular data has given way to a rising middle class composed of salaried employees associated with the worlds of finance, commerce, and innumerable trades. These salaried employees, along with 2.5 million public servants and 3.2 million self-employed persons constitute 61.7 percent of the German work force. No longer is the holding of property the decisive factor in class distinction, but rather the nature of a person's job and the prestige and income that go with it are what determine status.

The traditional crafts are another declining sector of an increasingly technological society. Tailors, shoemakers, painters, typesetters, and carpenters have seen their numbers dwindle in the face of a far greater demand for the services of building cleaners, automobile mechanics, TV technicians, plumbers, electricians, and hairdressers—underscoring the widespread availability of discretionary income among most occupational groups, including common laborers. The craft trades still remain an important part of the economy. In 1994, there were 668,000 craft firms headed by a master craftsman. The crafts employ 15 percent of the work force, train 37 percent of apprentices, and account for 9 percent of the FRG's economic output.

While Table 4.3 shows substantial differences in the developing economies of the FRG and GDR between 1950 and 1970, it conceals other realities. The dominance of manufacturing industries in the eastern *Länder*, combined with central planning and the lack of competition, inhibited the emergence of a modern diversified economy as well as the development of new technologies. In addition, 94.7 percent of all persons employed in the GDR in 1988 worked for state-owned enterprises. The figure was 99.9 percent in industry, 92.3 percent in construction, and 98.5 percent in agriculture and forestry. Only the traditional crafts (excluding construction) remained largely privatized.

Since unification, however, all crafts, trades, and professions have been privatized. More important, they have seen their numbers increase dramatically. Craft firms in the ex-GDR increased from 82,000 to 146,000 by 1994 and claimed a work force of 1.2 million persons. In the professions there were four times as many doctors and dentists by 1994 than before unity. The number of private lawyers has more than doubled and tax advisors have shot up from 350 to 2,800. Other professions experienced similar increases. Their number, together with the proliferation of the service trades, promises to accelerate the arrival of the postindustrial age in the eastern *Länder*.

Another major sign of postindustrialism in the old FRG is the increasing replacement of industrial employment by automation and the substitution of moving machines with electronic and communications technology, resulting in the emergence of a large technocratic and managerial elite. Jobs in highly skilled professional and technical areas are increasing at a much faster rate than unskilled or semiskilled jobs. In the 1970s the number of engineers, computer technicians, economists, teachers, accountants, lawyers, and social workers in the FRG almost doubled, while university admissions in the natural and social sciences nearly tripled. By 1985 the professional-technical-managerial class contained 6.2 million persons, representing 23.4 percent of the total work force.

The socioeconomic changes described here have affected the nature of political cleavage in the FRG. While the society may reveal residues of a traditional class structure, FRG politics in recent decades has not been determined by old class divisions. The ascendancy of a new professional, technical, and managerial class supported by a vast army of white-collar employees performing highly specified roles in the social economy has blunted the class feeling of earlier generations. The old class structure has entirely disappeared in the eastern *Länder*, and the political pressure from this part of Germany is likely to be in the direction of greater egalitarianism.

Security and Equality

The portrait of German society sketched up to now is one of general affluence and economic opportunity, particularly in preunification Germany. If industrial wages, home ownership, and possession of consumer goods are considered, then income and property are widely distributed in the western *Länder*. Even as the *social* market economy tries to provide minimum levels of decency for all, the social *market* economy tolerates large disparities in income and economic power. As Figure 4.1 indicates, a significant gap separated the lowest and highest paid persons in 1994. The bell-shaped curve of the ex-GDR shows much less disparity among income levels than in the west. Figure 4.1 also underscores the different levels of prosperity in the east and west. Noticeable, too, is the much larger income gap between the sexes in the old FRG. The higher the income category, the greater the inequality, whereas in the east the inequality is far less at all income levels.

What Figure 4.1 fails to show are unemployment levels. Unemployment reached a postwar preunification high of 10.2 percent of the work force in 1983, tarnishing the image of the FRG's well-run social market economy. Even in 1990, with the economy running at full capacity, unemployment persisted at around 6 percent of the work force, indicating serious structural problems in Germany's export-intensive industries. The unification-induced slump in employment drove this figure up to 9.2 percent in the early 1990s, representing 8.7 percent of unemployment in the old *Länder* and as much as 25 percent in the new. By 1996, unemployment in Germany as a whole was on the verge of reaching a postwar high of 4 million or 10 percent of the total work force, a figure still lower than the rate of unemployment in France (11.5 percent) and Italy (10.5 percent) and significantly higher than the United States (5.7 percent) and Japan (3.1 percent).[8]

For eastern Germany, unemployment was especially painful. Emphasizing equality over liberty, ex-GDR leaders had constructed a socialist state where the right to work was guaranteed and where there was little disparity in income among persons employed in various sectors of the economy. Finally, social welfare was universal in the old GDR, but the system lacked the efficiency and quality of social welfare planning in the FRG. In 1988, the year before the GDR's collapse, pensions and medical care accounted for 47.4 and 43.6 percent of the system's social expenditures respectively. The average old age pension in the GDR covered about 45 percent of net wages as opposed to about 50 percent in the FRG,[9] but again the latter was of far greater value. The child-care system and leave policy for child-bearing women, however, were more generous in the east.

The FRG's social security system remains one of the most comprehensive in the world. The national pension system alone covers nearly all private sector employees, accounting for 30 percent of the social budget in 1991. Still, based as it is on an income strategy tied to lifetime earnings, its redistributive effect is limited. Elderly persons, especially widows on pensions, are the hardest hit, in part because of a discriminatory policy which allows such persons only 60 percent of the pension to which a living husband would have been entitled. Pensioners are the least well off. In the mid–1970s approximately 35 percent of pensioners over 65 lived on or below the poverty line and in grossly inadequate housing.[10] Although Germany may not have as large an underclass of destitute persons as some other Western nations, the pockets of poverty that do exist are a continuing challenge to the nation's social conscience. (See Section C for additional details on German social policy.)

Women, Law, and Society

The West German Constitution guarantees equal rights to men and women. In reality, women have not shared equally in the opportunities offered by the social economy. Germany's legacy of male supremacy has been extremely difficult to overcome (even in the reputedly more egalitarian eastern *Länder*), especially in the domain of family affairs, where tradition and law have for generations confined women to hearth, children, and the guardianship of their husbands. Although the tradition persists, the legal structure of gender discrimination has been gradually torn down, thanks in part to the Federal Constitutional Court. Laws favoring the patriarchal family have been invalidated, the last remnant of which fell in 1992 when the court struck down a provision requiring married persons to adopt a single family surname

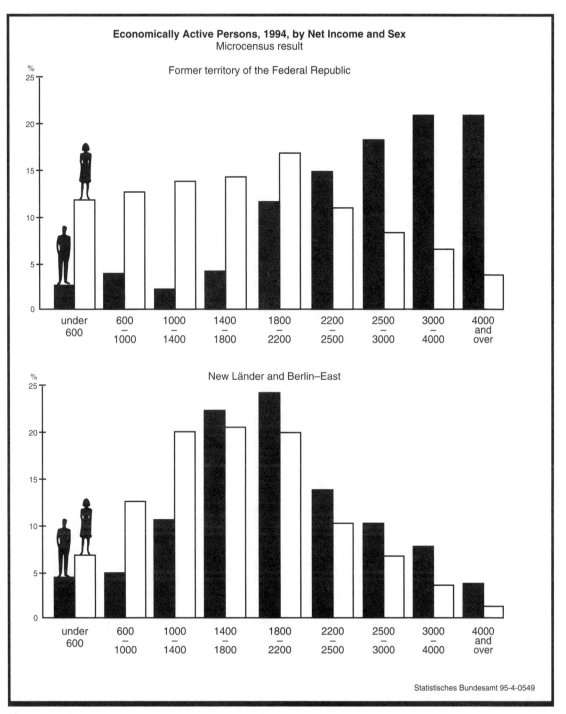

Economically Active Persons, 1994, by Net Income and Sex
Microcensus result

Former territory of the Federal Republic

New Länder and Berlin–East

Statistisches Bundesamt 95-4-0549

Figure 4.1

and, in the event of spousal disagreement, the surname of the husband. Already in 1977 a new family code had provided for no-fault divorce, spousal support arrangements keyed to economic status rather than gender, and an equal division of property.

Opportunities for women outside the home can be measured by comparing their participation rates in the work force, their earnings, and the kinds of jobs they perform to those of men. In 1989 women in the FRG constituted 38.9 percent of the work force, whereas in the GDR it was about 50 percent. (Ninety percent of East German adult women were employed in 1989.) In the GDR's system of state-mandated liberation, however, women were expected to lead a dual life of homemaker and working person. Its labor intensive economy and low productivity also helped to drive women into the working world. But as in the west they did most of the household work as well.

Social policy in the GDR was designed to make a dual career possible for women. For example, child care facilities were everywhere and free of charge; maternity leave with pay (at 75 to 90 percent of wages) was available for up to 26 weeks; and working parents could count on at least 40 days per year of paid time to care for their sick children. These generous benefits were not available in the east after reunification. In addition, as businesses remodelled and factories modernized, huge numbers of women were forced to withdraw from the labor market. In 1993, they constituted nearly 65 percent of the unemployed in the old GDR. Deprived of child care facilities and other social benefits for working parents, single women with children were among the hardest hit, while women over 50 who had lost their jobs had little hope of reemployment.[11]

As for earning power, women lagged substantially behind men in the western *Länder*, owing both to wage rate discrimination and to the lack of promotional opportunities associated with less stable and skilled jobs. Moreover, the disparity showed little improvement between 1983 and 1993, and in some categories of employment the gap had actually widened.

For example, the average gross monthly salary of female white-collar employees in these years was DM 2541 and DM 3670 respectively, as opposed to more favorable male salaries of DM 4153 and DM 5987. Available household income revealed a similar gap. In 1993, the average income of a female-headed household was 63 percent of that available to a male-headed household.[12] These differences in earnings and disposable income can be attributed in part to the limited number of hours women were able to work because of their child-care and household duties.

Finally, as Table 4.4 shows, women are found in every occupation in Germany but gender-based job segregation remains solidly anchored. The overall representation of women is extremely high in low to mid-level occupational categories. Textiles, retail sales, social services, and health care are almost wholly feminized. The old GDR had a better record of female participation in several professional categories than west Germany. In fact, by 1985 more women than men were being admitted as students of medicine, mathematics, and economics. With reunification, however, the overall figures, except for public school teachers, show significant disparities. Segregation in the job market is often ascribed to employee recruitment mechanisms that, although not always overtly discriminatory, tend to channel women into traditional female roles.

In 1980 the West German Parliament sought to remedy these inequalities by imposing certain duties on private employers. The European Community Adaptation Act, as it was called, incorporated EC nondiscriminatory directives into domestic law. The act requires equal pay for equal work; bars gender discrimination in hiring, promotion, and dismissal; eliminates job descriptions based on sex; shifts the burden of proving nondiscrimination to the employer; and requires the latter to display prominently copies of equal rights legislation in the workplace. (These provisions were extended to public employers in 1994.) The Adaptation Act has not been vigorously enforced, however—owing in part to the lack of enforcement agencies—and the success rate of individual victims who have initiated actions against their employers under these provisions has been low.[13]

Perhaps the most important recent victory for women on the employment front is the *Nocturnal Employment* case of 1992. In this landmark decision, the Federal Constitutional Court invalidated as unconstitutional a federal statute that barred women from working at night. Invoking Article 3 (2) of the Basic Law, which declares that "men and women shall have equal rights," the court flatly rejected the gender stereotyping that produced the night-shift ban. *Nocturnal Employment* was decided against the backdrop of a national debate over affirmative action. By now, women were organizing in defense of their interests and the political parties were beginning to pay attention. Efforts were being made to demand more than antidiscriminatory legislation and the dismantling of legal classifications based on sex. In 1994, after years of lobbying for such an amendment, the needed two-thirds parliamentary majority added this sentence to Article 3 (2) of the Basic Law: "The state shall seek to ensure equal treatment of men and women by removing existing disadvantages [between them]."

Following the rise of the Green Party in the 1980s, affirmative action on behalf of women was most visible in the world of politics. By highlighting feminist issues and by requiring that 50 percent of all their party posts and parliamentary seats be held by women, the Greens

Table 4.4   FEMALE OCCUPATIONAL REPRESENTATION (PERCENT)

Selected Occupations	1989		1994
	FRG	GDR	Germany
Engineers	4.7	—	9.6
Architects	8.5	—	21.3
Scientists	12.7	—	16.5
Lawyers	16.7	39.7	25.3
Judges	17.6	50.0	22.9
Public prosecutors	17.6	28.3	25.8
University professors	5.2	—	—
Public school teachers	48.3	78.7	53.3
Public servants	31.9	64.2	24.2
Physicians	27.8	53.4	39.8
Social welfare workers	80.0	91.6	85.1
Health care workers	85.4	83.0	86.4
Top managers	16.7	—	21.3
Accountants and tax advisors	—	—	33.3
Sales clerks	62.0	—	81.5
Machine fitters	—	—	12.3
Textile workers	—	—	90.5

Source: These percentages were calculated from data found in *Statistisches Jahrbuch der deutschen Demokratischen Republik 1990* (Berlin: Rudolf Haufe Verlag, 1990), p. 448; *Statistisches Jahrbuch 1991 für das Vereinte Deutschland* (Stuttgart: Metzler-Poeschel Verlag, 1991), *Statistisches Jahrbuch 1992 für die Bundesrepublik Deutschland* (Stuttgart: Metzler-Poeschel Verlag, 1992), p. 119; and *Statistisches Jahrbuch 1995 für die Bundesrepublik Deutschland* (Stuttgart: Metzler-Poeschel Verlag, 1995), p. 113.

effectively became a "woman's party." The Greens drew their electoral support disproportionately from women under 40 years of age. Other parties soon got the message. They grew more sensitive to women's issues, made an effort to expand their female membership, and placed increasing numbers of women on their ballots. In 1994, 176 women were elected to the Bundestag, representing 26 percent of its membership, the most ever. In the two major parties, the SPD and the CDU-CSU, women accounted for 48.3 and 23.3 of their respective representatives.[14]

Finally, whereas women remained underrepresented in the judiciary as a whole, they occupied no fewer than 5 of 16 seats on the Federal Constitutional Court in 1995, also a new high. Moreover, with her election in 1994, Jutta Limbach became the first woman president or "chief justice" of the Federal Constitutional Court, Germany's highest tribunal. Evelyn Haas was chosen as an associate justice in the same year. Her appointment was significant because she was the first woman nominated to the high court by Christian Democrats. Still another woman was among the candidates for election to the high court in 1996. Only the future will tell whether these advances in the nation's highest judicial and legislative arenas will carry over into other areas of law and society.

Other Minorities

While grievances based on sex have been the object of the law's special solicitude, those based on ethnicity have been allowed to fester. Large-scale immigration in the postwar era has transformed the FRG's racially homogeneous society into a nation of ethnic minorities. Most of the older immigrants—that is, the postwar expellees (mainly ethnic Germans)—have been almost wholly integrated into the dominant culture. The new immigrants consist mainly of foreign workers recruited by industry on a massive scale during the 1960s. These workers and their families—mainly Turks, Yugoslavs, Greeks, and Italians—number 5,037,072 or 6.4 percent of reunited Germany's total population. (They make up 7.7

percent of the population in the western *Länder*.) Despite governmental incentives that encouraged nearly a million of these guestworkers (*Gastarbeiter*), as they are called, to return to their homelands during the mid–1970s recession, higher wages and the promise of a better life prompted most of them to remain in the FRG.

For these guestworkers and their families, the FRG has been anything but a "melting pot." Their experience is not unlike that of black or Hispanic Americans in the United States. Occupying low-status jobs that Germans do not want, they live in culturally isolated urban ghettos marked by substandard housing.[15] Even though millions of guestworkers speak German fluently, send their German-born children to German schools, pay taxes, and have no plans to leave Germany, they are denied the right to vote and find that citizenship is extremely difficult to secure in a nation that still defines itself largely in ethnocultural terms.

Recent waves of *Aussiedler* have also experienced difficulties in adjusting to German life and society. These ethnic Germans are economically disadvantaged, come from culturally diverse backgrounds, and often have little or no knowledge of the German language. As noted in the section on population, hundreds of thousands of persons seeking asylum in West Germany have been added to this multicultural mix, triggering not only acts of violence and terrorism against these "foreign elements," but also an explosive national debate over what to do about the increasing numbers of persons seeking freedom and opportunity in Germany. One recent solution has been intergovernmental agreements providing for the deportation of asylum seekers to their country of origin or other deals encouraging their return (see Feature 4.3). By 1992, after extreme right-wing parties entered two state parliaments on their antiforeigner platforms, pressure was building to limit the right of asylum and to adopt an American-style system of quotas on immigration to Germany. (For a discussion of immigration and citizenship policy, see Section C.)

CULTURE: SOCIAL AND CIVIC

Education and the Media

Reunited Germany boasts high levels of literacy, cultural and educational diversity, and opportunities for personal development and leisure. As in Berlin, so too in the country at large, parks, sport clubs, museums, public libraries, theaters, choral societies, art galleries, opera houses, and multimillion member book clubs abound in the country at large. There is a high consumption rate of media output; book and magazine readership is one of the highest worldwide. In 1993, some 2,000 book publishers released 67,206 titles, second only to the United States. In contrast to the United States, however, most theatrical groups, orchestras, and opera houses are government-subsidized. In united Germany, for example, there are 121 subsidized opera houses, and one could easily predict in this nation of opera lovers a swift end to any government or to the political career of any politician who would have the temerity to advocate an end to these government subsidies.

The wealth of cultural opportunities in the western *Länder* builds on their efficient and diverse educational system. A common four-year primary system splits at the secondary level into three tracks: the five-year continuation of primary school (*Hauptschule*), the six-year intermediate school (*Realschule*), and the nine-year senior grammar school (*Gymnasium*); the former two emphasize preparation for later vocational and technical jobs, respectively; the lat-

ter, university preparation. Originally based in the classics, the *Gymnasium* offers a tough modern curriculum of arts, languages, mathematics, and science, leading to the famous school-leaving certificate, the *Abitur*. This tripartite system of secondary education has been sharply criticized for its tendency to perpetuate social and class differences. Yet the system produces the most highly trained and credentialed population in Europe. Almost all non-farm youth outside the universities are in vocational or technical schools of one kind or another. Fifty-nine percent of all German youth are in school until the age of 18, as opposed to 24 percent in England and 41 percent in France, while 44 percent are licensed to practice a trade or craft as opposed to 20 percent in England, 10 percent in Italy, and 6 percent in Spain.[16]

With the accession of the eastern *Länder* into the Federal Republic, Communist ideological control has ended in the schools and universities (as have the jobs of Communist ideologues in law, the humanities, and social sciences) and the *Länder* themselves, as in the west, have taken charge. Religious instruction has been reintroduced, western language education expanded, and the humanities and social sciences reconstituted on their own basis. Independent schools have reopened and the *Abitur* restored to its pride of place. Reunification might have provided the opportunity to reorganize the entire system of German education on a more equalitarian basis. To the dismay of most eastern German educators and many western crit-

---

Feature 4.3 Meltdown of the Melting Pot

In April 1995, the German government signed an agreement with Vietnam that guaranteed $140 million of development aid if Vietnam would take back 40,000 Vietnam citizens who had not yet received legal asylum in Germany. The first four deportees arrived in Vietnam on October 18, and the Vietnamese government promised they would be treated in a "humanitarian manner." But human rights groups and Vietnamese groups in Germany expressed concern that some of the deportees, many of whom had been long-time residents of Germany, might face persecution if returned to Vietnam.

Source: Human Rights Watch: World Report 1996
(New York: Human Rights Watch, 1995), pp. 219–220.

ics, this opportunity was lost in the rush to reconstruct the old GDR system on the West German model.

Religion and the Churches

The relatively equal numbers of Catholics and Protestants in the earlier FRG has been tilted in favor of the Evangelical Lutheran Church with the accession of the five new *Länder*. Thus, on the eve of reunification, the old FRG counted official religious affiliation among its permanent residents (German and foreign) as roughly 26 million Roman Catholics, 25.75 million Protestants (both Evangelical Lutheran and "Free Church"), 50,000 Jews, 1.5 million Muslims, 1 million members of other religions, and 4 million with no religious affiliation. Figures from the ex-GDR are more difficult to present, both because of the reluctance of the Communist regime to admit any significant religious aspiration in a would-be atheist state and the concomitant reluctance of its citizens to make a declaration of official affiliation that would automatically reduce them to second-class status at work and in school and bar them from the upper reaches of all professions. Nonetheless, it is clear that what religious activity there was between 1945 and 1989 remained overwhelmingly Protestant: Catholic figures, which remained free of direct government intervention, showed the six bishoprics within the five eastern *Länder* as ministering to only 5 percent of the local population, approximately 800,000 out of 16,000,000 people.

The denominational strife that once buffeted Germany has virtually disappeared as new forms of political and social cooperation have evolved out of the common struggle of the major churches against the Nazi regime. Even in the purely religious sphere, the major denominations have been trying to reconcile their differences. An ecumenical high point was the November 1980 meeting of Pope John Paul II with German Protestant leaders in Osnabrück, the site of the signing of the Treaty of Westphalia in 1648, which confirmed the sectarian division of the German lands.

It is difficult to assess the role of religion in contemporary Germany. Figures in the old FRG showed a long-term decline in official affiliation.

Thus, between 1950 and 1989, the proportion of Catholics decreased slightly from 44.3 to 42.9 percent, while that of Protestants dropped from 51.5 to 42.2 percent. An Allensbach Opinion Research Institute poll conducted in West Germany on the eve of the breaching of the Berlin Wall suggested that this secularization affected not only practice but basic belief.

However, the rates of basic religious identification do remain high, both in paying the church tax and in choosing a marital partner from one's own confession. The 1989 figures for marrying within one's faith in the old FRG showed 68.7 percent for Catholics, 63.0 percent for Protestants, and 32.5 percent for Jews. The social impact of the churches likewise remains high. They operate and maintain hospitals, facilities for the handicapped, nursing homes, schools, and large charitable organizations such as the Protestant Diaconal Works and the Catholic Caritas Association.

Organized as corporate bodies under public law—a constitutional status carried over from the Weimar period—the organized churches are entitled to state financial support. All wage earners on the official rolls of the main denominations are subject to a church tax equal to about 8 percent of their net tax. A wage earner can escape the tax by formally resigning his or her church membership—433,724 (279,971 Protestants and 153,753 Catholics) did so in 1994. Collected by state revenue officers, these taxes amount to several billion dollars a year and are distributed to the major denominations in amounts proportionate to their total membership. The funds help to pay for ecclesiastical salaries, construction and maintenance costs, the churches' far-flung social welfare functions, and their immense overseas charitable programs.

This *modus vivendi* between church and state is not without its critics, both secular and religious. The most radical secular critics fear excessive church influence on politics and would divorce religion altogether from the nation's public life. The most radical religious critics see the contemporary church as the captive of the liberal state, having compromised its spiritual mission by adopting middle-class values and copying the latter's bureaucratic forms of organization. They would have the church call society to account for its injustices and hypocrisies, and in the name of faith ally itself with the poor of Germany and the world. Most Germans who have thought about these matters situate themselves between these extremes. Finally, even though formal religious observance in Germany is down, the biennial Catholic and Protestant national "church day" conferences remain well attended and the influence of each denomination within its own worldwide communion remains strong.

Political Attitudes and Participation

West Germans were characterized in the first 20 years of the Federal Republic as voting in high numbers but with little feeling. Opinion polls showed that the older age groups retained some sympathy for monarchy or dictatorship and that most voters were prouder of their economic system than of its political corollary. By the 1980s this had changed. The FRG was a proven success and an increasing percentage of the electorate had grown up in it and come to identify with its procedures and institutions. On the other hand, national pride remained well below the average for European Community member states. Reunification in 1990 thus posed two issues: Would the East Germans follow the pattern of quick adaptation to democratic practices and slow internalization of democratic feelings? In the meantime, if unforeseen economic difficulties arose, would West German civic culture now prove to be well enough rooted to weather the storm?

One measure of political democracy is the level of participation in elections. The turn-out rate for federal elections in the FRG began at 78.5 percent in 1949, exceeded 90 percent by the 1970s, and fell to a record low of 77.8 percent in the first all-German election of December 2, 1990. It rose again to 79.1 percent in 1994. This is a respectable rate for an industrial democracy—and consistently higher than for U.S. presidential elections. As Section B shows, the results of these elections have given the FRG a highly competitive and relatively stable party system. The 1994 national election, however, revealed a more volatile electorate and established the Party of Democratic Socialism (PDS) as a force to be reckoned with in German politics.

The measure of the health of a civic culture, however, extends beyond formal electoral and institutional arrangements. Since the late 1960s, the FRG has witnessed massive demonstrations against the war in Vietnam, development of nuclear power, restrictions on university admissions, missiles stationed on German soil, assaults on foreign residents, and airport construction plans that threaten deforestation. These *Bürgerinitiativen* (citizens' initiatives) have also championed forms of direct democracy (e.g., referenda). Some commentators have asked whether this species of "politics of protest" bespeaks a widening gap between formal democratic institutions and actual grassroots democratic sentiments. Some would respond that these protests represent a vital outlet for minority sentiments that is politically acceptable; others, that they represent an internalization and therefore a triumph of democratic values; and still others would note that both the Christian Democratic Union (CDU) and the Social Democratic Party (SPD) have successfully remodeled their local party electoral activities on these same *Bürgerinitiativen*.

The participatory character of the FRG's civic culture seems reasonably related to changes that have taken place in family, school, and society under the impact of advanced industrialization and its accompanying patterns of social stratification—changes likely to be enhanced by the incorporation of the ex-GDR's social democracy into the FRG. The entrance of housewives into the labor market, the separation of family and workplace, increased social mobility and income, and the enormous expansion of communications have loosened up old authoritarian structures such as the male-dominated family and the traditional school curriculum. As agents of political socialization, family and school appear increasingly to promote values more consistent than in the past with the regime's formal values of human dignity, mutual respect and cooperation, and the pragmatic adjustment of social conflict. Generational change has also been an important source of political socialization. By the 1980 election the postwar generation constituted 48.8 percent of the population and 25.5 percent of adult voters. Levels of political interest and participation have been found to increase significantly with the length of residence and accumu-

Supporters of the former Communist Party, the Party of Democratic Socialism (PDS) at the German election in October 1994. The PDS got 4.4 percent of the vote, thus falling below the 5 percent threshold. But it obtained 30 seats in the Bundestag because it won four directly elected seats in East Berlin.

lated experience under the democracy of the FRG.

Politics and Literature: A Footnote

When unified in 1871, Germany had a humanist tradition characterized by the genius of Goethe and Schiller, renaissance men of letters and civic leadership. Yet the predominant cultural expression of the Wilhelmine and Weimar years was one of flight from political affairs into an "inner freedom" or strictly private culture. Persons already in authority were left to conduct public affairs, to define the aims and limits of state power, and to suggest, albeit broadly, the proper form and content of culture.

The works of Hermann Hesse (1877–1962), such as the novel *Siddhartha* (1922; still a U.S. collegiate favorite), continued the age-old inquiry into the Germanic conflict between Nature and Spirit but did so in the relatively new form of stressing the need for personal, rather than communal or authoritarian, responsibility in selecting values. With Thomas Mann (1875–1955), this need was cast against the backdrop of the violent currents sweeping Germanic society: the degeneration of the great nineteenth-century mercantile order in *Buddenbrooks* (1901), the quest for regeneration and personal understanding through flight from society and its conventions in *The Magic Mountain* (1924), and the descent of artistic creativity itself into the demonic in *Doctor Faustus* (1947). More than anyone else, Mann gave expression to the struggle between the power and the subtle pessimism of *Germanism*.

During the life of the Federal Republic, the works of Günter Grass such as *The Tin Drum* (1963) were especially noteworthy for their inquiry into how German culture had fallen into National Socialism and also what should be retrieved and replanted from the ashes it left in 1945; Grass opposed German reunification until the very end, claiming that Germany lacked a sense of responsibility before history and might have served as a beacon for spiritual renewal and the deflation of purely national aspirations.[17] The work of Heinrich Böll (1917–1985), was also popular. His work, *The Clown* (1963), portrayed a sense of the intrinsic worth and redemptive possibilities in life. And now a postunification literature has begun to appear as authors such as Martin Walser (*Die Verteidigung der Kindheit*, 1991) and Helga Königsdorf (*Im Schatten des Regenbogen*, 1993) seek to describe and reflect on the painful changes and disorientation that many East Germans have experienced since the collapse of the Berlin Wall.

Thus, where humanism temporarily failed, history—and perhaps now reunification—may have retrieved the situation. In the wake of two world wars, Germans have abandoned the turn to "inner freedom" and its concomitant neglect of public cultural and civic responsibilities. They have acknowledged Hesse's point that responsibility is personal and that it becomes communal in its effect. The Germans continue to question their values and to extend the breadth and depth of their pluralist democracy.

CONCLUSION

This section has traced Germany's development from a feudal society into a modernized postindustrial state and the merger by accession of the eastern *Länder* into the FRG. The FRG's economy, even before the merger, was among the richest in the world, and its social system, notwithstanding pockets of poverty, measurable and increasing discrimination against ethnic minorities and, most daunting of all, the massive reconstruction and clean up of the east, is marked by extremely high levels of economic security and welfare benefits. The political system created under the 1949 Basic Law, together with its liberal values, is, of course, a congenial framework for the development of a social market economy; both its durability in the west and its general acceptance in the east augur well for the future.

Religious divisions are no longer readily apparent in either sector of the reunited country; traditional class and economic divisions also have given way to the rise in the west of an overwhelmingly predominant new middle class of white-collar employees and professionals generated by ever-expanding service industries and technological enterprises; western business managers, industrial trainers, and university professors hope to replicate their success in the east. Although youth and intellectuals reproach the society for sinking into materialism, there is no evidence to suggest that western Germans are willing to forego what the economy has wrought; on the contrary, their challenge will be to redistribute their wealth so as to rescue and then revive the east. Germany has put its political and religious divisions behind it; now it resolves to do the same socially and economically.

KEY TERMS

Abitur
Basic Law
Bürgerinitiativen
church tax
Deutsche Mark
guestworkers
Länder
North German Confederation
Parliamentary Council
social market economy
Treaty of Versailles
Treuhandanstalt
Weimar Republic

FURTHER READINGS

HISTORY AND PEOPLE

Ardagh, John. *Germany and the Germans* (London: Penguin Books, 1991).

Barraclough, Geoffrey. *The Origins of Modern Germany* (New York: Capricorn Books, 1963).

Craig, Gordon. *The Germans* (New York: Putnam, 1982).

Elias, Norbert, *The Germans*, translated by Eric Dunning and Stephen Mennell (New York: Columbia University Press, 1996).

Koch, H. W. *A Constitutional History of Germany in the Nineteenth and Twentieth Centuries* (London and New York: Longman, 1984).

Pachter, Henry M. *Modern Germany: A Social, Cultural, and Political History* (Boulder, CO: Westview Press, 1978).

Pinson, Koppel S. *Modern Germany*, 2nd ed. (New York: Macmillan, 1966).

Stern, Fritz. *The Politics of Cultural Despair* (Berkeley: University of California Press, 1961).

THIRD REICH

Bracher, Karl Dietrich. *The German Dictatorship* (New York: Praeger, 1970).

Burleigh, Michael, and Wolfgang Wippermann. *The Racial State: Germany 1933–1945* (Cambridge: Cambridge University Press, 1991).

Dawidowicz, Lucy S. *The War Against the Jews* (New York: Holt, Rinehart and Winston, 1975).

Gallagher, Hugh G. *By Trust Betrayed* (New York: Henry Holt, 1990).

Müller, Ingo. *Hitler's Justice* (Cambridge, MA: Harvard University Press, 1991).

Snyder, Louis L., ed. *Hitler's Third Reich: A Documentary History* (Chicago: Nelson-Hall, 1981).

FEDERAL REPUBLIC

Bork, Dennis L., and David R. Gress. *A History of West Germany*, Vols. 1 and 2 (Oxford: Basil Blackwell, 1989).

Conradt, David P. *The German Polity*, 6th ed. (New York: Longman, 1996).

"Germany in Transition" (Symposium Issue). *Daedalus* (winter, 1994).

Jones, Larry E. *German Liberalism and the Dissolution of the Weimar Party System, 1918–1933* (Chapel Hill and London: The University of North Carolina Press, 1988).

Junker, Detlev, et al. eds. *Cornerstone of Democracy: The West Germany Grundgesetz, 1949–1989.* (Washington, DC: German Historical Institute, Occasional Paper No. 13, 1995).

McGhee, George. *At the Creation of a New Germany.* (New Haven and London: Yale University Press, 1989).

Merritt, Richard L. *Democracy Imposed: U.S. Occupation Policy and the German Public, 1945–1949* (New Haven: Yale University Press, 1995).

Rist, Ray C. *Guestworkers in Germany: The Prospects for Pluralism* (New York and London: Praeger, 1978).

Roskamp, Karl W. *Capital Formation in West Germany* (Detroit: Wayne State University Press, 1965).

Smith, Eric Owen. *The German Economy* (London: Routledge, 1994).

Spotts, Frederic. *The Churches and Politics in Germany* (Middletown, CT: Wesleyan University Press, 1973).

GERMAN REUNIFICATION

Grass, Günter. *Two States—One Nation?* translated by Krishna Winston and A.S. Wensinger (New York: Harcourt Brace, 1990).

Hancock, Donald M., and Helga A. Welsh, eds. *German Unification: Process and Outcomes* (Boulder, CO: Westview Press, 1994).

James, Harold, and Marla Stone, eds. *When the Wall Came Down* (New York and London: Routledge, 1992).

McAdams, James A. *Germany Divided* (Princeton, NJ: Princeton University Press, 1993).

Merkl, Peter M. *German Unification in the European Context* (University Park: The Pennsylvania State University Press, 1993).

Quint, Peter. *The Constitutional Law of German Unification* (Princeton, NJ: Princeton University Press, 1996).

Wallach, Peter H. G. and Ronald A. Francisco *United Germany* (Westport, CT: Praeger Publishers, 1992)

B.

Political Processes and Institutions

POLITICAL PARTIES

The FRG was long described as having a two and one-half party system. Social and political circumstances had combined to produce a competitive party system in the FRG that was marked by persisting political loyalties. In the first national election, held in 1949, the three most popular parties—the Christian Democratic Union (CDU) and its Bavarian affiliate, the Christian Social Union (CSU); the Social Democratic Party (SPD); and the Free Democratic Party (FDP)—captured 72.1 percent of the total votes. By the 1970s and well into the 1980s, these same parties commanded the support of virtually the entire West German electorate.

In 1987, two years before unification, the three parties still managed to win 90.4 percent of the vote, a drop from their total of 98.0 percent in 1980. In 1983, however, a fourth party, the Greens, entered parliament for the first time since 1949. The postunification elections of 1990 and 1994 resulted in the entry of a fifth party—the ex-GDR's old Socialist Unity Party (SED) now recast as the Party of Democratic Socialism (PDS)—into the national parliament. Reunification had altered German politics, at least for the time being. The established parties would now surely begin to devise strategies to recapture the allegiance of voters attracted by the upstart parties. Then too the presence of new parties in the national legislature would almost surely complicate the creation and maintenance of a stable governing coalition.

By 1994, observers wondered whether the Greens would replace the FDP as the balance wheel and "kingmaker" in the Bundestag. Yet the three traditional parties still managed to receive 84.8 percent of all votes cast, which was one sign of the remarkable continuity of German politics. This continuity—and stability—has often been traced to the Federal Election Act's 5 percent clause. Enacted early on to avoid fragmenting the electorate, the Act grants parliamentary representation only to those parties securing 5 percent or more of the votes cast in a national election or at least three single-member district seats. The 5 percent rule has kept numerous splinter parties out of parliament over the years, thus avoiding the coalitional instability that might otherwise have arisen. This bit of institutional engineering seemed to show that given the right set of circumstances, election rules could effectively channel political activity in predetermined directions.

Christian Democrats

The CDU (*Christlich Demokratische Union*) was founded in 1945 by old Center Party Catholics together with liberal and conservative Protestants who had been members of other pre–1933 political parties. These groups came together to reconstruct the political order on Christian principles and to present a united front against the Left. Although it originally lacked an ideologically coherent political program, the CDU nevertheless evolved, under the brilliant leadership of Chancellor Konrad Adenauer (ex-mayor of Cologne and Germany's wiliest politician since Bismarck) into a broadly based "catch-all" party more pragmatic than Christian and commanding the support of nearly half the German electorate. It represented nearly every major occupational and class grouping in the country and completely dominated West German politics during the FRG's first two decades (see Table 4.5).

The party's leadership after Adenauer, however, was not nearly as capable, contributing to declining membership and the loss of power. In the 1970s, the CDU launched a major membership drive, leading once again to a larger—and much more diverse—membership. Not coincidentally, the 1980s saw the party's return to power under the leadership of Helmut Kohl, a man in whom few had much confidence, yet who rallied his party to a stunning victory in 1983 and has since shown great leadership ability, particularly in spearheading the drive for German reunification—a feat that led to his reelection in 1990 as the first freely chosen chancellor of *all* the German people since 1932.

Table 4.5   BUNDESTAG SEATS OCCUPIED BY THE CDU-CSU AND SPD, 1949–1994

Year	CDU-CSU (percent)	Seats	SPD (percent)	Seats	Total BT Seats
1949	31.0	139	29.2	131	402
1953	45.2	243	28.8	151	487
1957	50.2	270	31.8	169	497
1961	45.3	242	36.2	190	499
1965	47.6	245	39.8	202	496
1969	46.1	242	42.7	224	496
1972	44.9	225	45.8	230	496
1976	48.6	243	42.6	214	496
1980	44.5	226	42.9	218	497
1983	48.8	244	38.2	193	498
1987	44.3	223	37.0	186	497
1990	43.8	313	33.5	239	662
1994	41.5	294	36.4	252	672

Sources: Peter Schindler, *Datenbuch zur Geschichte der Deutschen Bundestages 1949 bis 1982*, 4th ed. (Baden-Baden: Nomos Verlag, 1984), pp. 34–48; *Statistisches Jahrbuch 1991 für das Vereinte Deutschland*, p. 101; and *Statistisches Jahrbuch für die Bundesrepublik Deutschland 1995.*

The CDU's diverse policies have reflected its different constituent groups. Christian social pressures within the party (reflecting its roots) have supported progressive policies such as government-sponsored savings programs and subsidized housing. Yet the party's increasingly prominent business, industrial, and middle-class constituencies have also encouraged it to support policies favoring free-market economics. In recent years, the party has favored tax and spending cuts as well as government deregulation as a means of boosting an economy overburdened by the cost of unification. Outside the economic realm, the party has generally emphasized traditional moral values with a heavy accent on law and order. Internally, the CDU often defends the FRG's federal structure against the centralizing influences of the national government; in foreign policy, it has been an ardent supporter of the Atlantic Alliance, European Union, and the German-French axis as the key European political and economic integration.

Social Democrats

The SPD (*Sozialdemokratische Partei Deutschlands*), one of the largest mass-membership parties in Europe, traces its roots back to the General Workingman's Association founded in 1863 by the brilliant young radical Ferdinand Lassalle. The first party to organize the working masses on a large scale, the SPD of Imperial Germany won the votes of the emerging industrial proletariat and moved on from that popular base to share power in 7 of the Weimar Republic's 21 governing coalitions. When the party reorganized after World War II, it failed to expand its influence much beyond the industrial working class. It remained for almost a decade a staunchly left-wing party, openly embracing socialism. In 1959, however, with the passage of the famed *Godesberg Platform*, it embraced the social market economy and Adenauer's foreign policy, seeking to shed its Marxist image and transform itself from a narrow ideological party into a broadly based, pragmatic people's party.

The strategy worked: The party diversified its membership by attracting more white-collar, middle-class members, and by 1966 had wide enough support to become part of a governing coalition with the CDU-CSU, after which the SPD went on to elect the chancellor in four consecutive national elections. During the 1980s, however, spurred by internal disputes over foreign affairs and by growing disagreement with Western (especially American) defense policy, the SPD lurched abruptly to the left. Perceived by voters as faction-ridden, impractical, and unfit to govern, it languished electorally. In 1989, the SPD blundered into opposing the immediate reunification of Germany, allowing Chancellor Kohl to seize the initiative and ride to yet another victory in 1990 on the CDU's speeding "unity now" train.

During the early 1990s, the SPD went through another series of leadership changes. The left-leaning Oscar Lafontaine, minister-president of Saarland, stepped down as party chairman after the SPD's election defeat in 1990. The party then turned to Björn Engholm, the pipe-smoking and laid-back centrist minister-president of Schleswig-Holstein, until his sudden demise in 1993 following his admission of having given false testimony in a *Land* election scandal. Rudolf Scharping, minister-president of Rhineland-Palatinate, succeeded Engholm as party chairman. Young, intelligent, and bearded, he projected a professorial image and, given the state of public opinion polls, looked like a sure bet to emerge as chancellor in 1994. However, Kohl's reputation as an effective leader appeared to play a significant role in another CDU-CSU-FDP victory, albeit by a single vote in the German parliament. Finally, in need of more dynamic and aggressive leadership in the face of rising unemployment and other economic problems arising out of reunification, the SPD turned once again, in 1995, to Lafontaine, expecting him to unify the party and produce the magic that would lead to victory in 1998.

Free Democrats

The FDP (*Freie Demokratische Partei*), founded in 1945, is the modern counterpart of the older German liberal parties. Although considerably smaller than the CDU or SPD, the FDP is the third party to have played a consistently influential role in postwar German politics. It is the only minor party to have survived the 5 percent clause in all federal elections, and it has determined the governing coalition in 9 out of 13 such elections. Until 1966 it was allied with the CDU, then from 1969 to 1982 with the SPD, and recently with the CDU again. Drawing its support primarily from business people, professionals, and the secular

middle classes, the FDP is a traditional liberal party which stands for free enterprise and individual self-determination in all areas of social life. It has quarreled with the CDU over foreign policy and with the SPD over spending and social programs, and it has often taken strong, independent stands on issues such as education reform, abortion, and church taxes. Because it has often controlled the fate of governing coalitions, the FDP's impact on German politics has been considerable, and it has used its leverage to gain important government positions—on two occasions even capturing the federal presidency.

Splinter Parties

In addition to these three parties, Germany has seen the regular rise and fall of numerous splinter parties. The most successful of these parties have been the National Democratic Party (*Nationaldemokratische Partei Deutschlands*) and the Republicans (*Republikaner*), both far-right parties identified most conspicuously with their campaigns to rid Germany of its large foreign population. By exploiting the fears of the most vulnerable sectors of the electorate, especially in times of economic downturn, these parties have managed to surmount the 5 percent clause and gain entry into various *Land* parliaments, but these successes have been short-lived. Many splinter parties have turned out to be localized "movements" with programmatically untenable platforms, and collectively they have rarely won more than 1 percent of the national vote.

The Greens

Representing a loose alliance of ecological, antinuclear, and peace groups, the Greens emerged on the German scene in the early 1980s. This group, a left libertarian party committed to nonviolent methods of protest and change, rejected politics as usual and envisioned nothing less than the total transformation of society. Popular with young voters, feminists, and middle-class environmentalists, the Greens entered the national parliament for the first time in 1983 with 5.6 percent of the vote. Blustery and often disdainful of formal rules of procedure, the Greens prided themselves on being an "anti-party" party, declared "war" on the "bourgeois-democ-

---

Feature 4.4   The PDS Builds Its Nest

In their hearts [many older persons] clung to [socialist] values that in their heads they thought to be superannuated. It is precisely this gap between heart and head upon which the PDS has been able to build its nest. That is, the party appeals neither purely to easterners' nostalgia for the past nor to their rational self-interest in the redistribution conflicts of unification. Instead, it reflects their ambivalence about the past and present. . . . The PDS has succeeded in positioning itself as the defender of this eastern desire to maintain biographical continuity without threatening to disrupt seriously the on-going integration process.

Source: Lawrence H. McFalls, "Political Culture: Partisan Strategies, and the PDS: Prospects for an East German Party," *German Politics and Society*, vol. 13 (1995) p. 55.

---

ratic state," and sought to revitalize grassroots democracy by insisting that their parliamentary representatives rotate in office and by pledging themselves to following the orders of their local constituencies.

After the 1987 election, when they won 8.3 percent of the vote, the Greens began to lose their appeal as well as their representation in some *Land* legislatures. With the defeat of their confrontational fundamentalist wing after an internal party battle, the Greens transformed themselves into a more pragmatic party now willing to cooperate with other parties in achieving their aims. Having failed to clear the 5 percent hurdle in 1990, the Greens merged with Alliance 90, an East German party consisting largely of those citizens rights groups that helped to topple the old GDR's Communist government. Winning 7.3 percent of the votes in 1994, the Alliance 90-Greens, as the party now called itself, entered parliament with 49 seats, but nearly all of its popular votes came from the western *Länder*. Its postindustrial emphasis on environmental and "lifestyle" issues had little appeal for eastern Germans worried about unemployment and other material concerns.

Party of Democratic Socialism

The PDS is the successor to East Germany's old Socialist Unity Party (SED). With the impending demolition of the GDR in 1989, the party's membership dropped from 800,000 to 320,000 in 1990, and to 130,000 in 1994. Discredited by its control of the former Communist govern-

ment, the party changed its name and campaigned for a reformed socialism with a human face. In 1994, the PDS won proportional representation (30 seats) in the national parliament by winning four single-member districts, all in East Berlin. (The PDS failed to win 5 percent of the national vote.)

Even though the PDS's leaders and members are mainly old SED comrades, the party was able to attract voters from a much wider segment of the electorate. There was no surprise in learning that the ex-GDR's old managerial and professional elite—reunification's losers—supported the PDS (see Feature 4.4). But the party also won the support of thousands of other easterners who were angered by the "arrogance" of their western "colonizers" and by the rapidity with which they were "destroying" values, such as solidarity and egalitarianism which were long associated with the tradition of democratic socialism.

Party Organization

The major parties are formally organized at the federal, *Land*, and precinct levels. The CDU bears the imprint of the FRG's federalized structure, with organizational power residing in the party's 13 *Land* associations. Like the American Republican and Democratic Parties, the CDU is a loosely structured party held together by a coalition of interests with a common goal of winning elections. The SPD, on the other hand, is a mass-organized party under a centralized leadership that is served by a large and disciplined core of full-time professionals who are in charge of various district parties (*Bezirksparteien*). The relative power and autonomy of the party district associations have permitted the development of strong regional leaders whose views the national leadership cannot ignore with impunity.

The highest formal authority in each party is the national party convention held every two years—although the FDP meets annually—consisting of delegates elected mainly by *Land*, district, and county associations. The convention sets the general outlines of policy, votes on organizational matters, and elects a national executive committee consisting of the party chairperson, several deputy chairpersons, secretary-general, treasurer, and other elected members. At the national level, the SPD's organizational chart also includes a large party council, consisting of *Land* and local party leaders, and a nine-member presidium to supervise the work of the party executive committee.

The Basic Law (Article 21) recognizes a privileged role for the political parties in the inculcation and articulation of democratic values. This role has been reaffirmed by the Political Parties Act of 1967. Apart from provisions on the disclosure of finances, the act largely codifies existing party practices and procedures, many of them prescribed in decisions of the Federal Constitutional Court. To safeguard internal party democracy the act provides, *inter alia*, for (1) the right of all members to vote for party convention delegates; (2) the right of such delegates to vote on party guidelines and programs; (3) a secret ballot for the election of party officers, who must be elected every two

years; (4) a reasonable balance of *ex officio* and elected members on the party executive committee; and (5) a written arbitration procedure for the resolution of intraparty disputes.

Party Finance

The parties derive their funds from several sources including public subsidies, private donations, receipts from party events and publications, and contributions from party members and members of parliament. As Table 4.6 shows, the parties draw their funds from their strongest constituencies: The SPD relies mainly on membership dues, whereas the CSU and the FDP rely heavily on donations from corporations and other private groups. Private contributions filled the party's coffers during the Adenauer years, but as a result of the CDU's membership drive in the 1970s, when it first experienced financial difficulties, it began to catch up with the SPD in dues-paying members.

The state began to reimburse the parties for their election campaign costs in 1959. By 1990, their election campaign costs exceeded DM 400 million, representing approximately 5 DM ($3.13) for each second ballot vote cast, an amount divided among the parties proportionate to each party's total vote. (See discussion of the electoral system below.) In a series of decisions, the Federal Constitutional Court has handed down rulings to ensure that the funding provisions treat all parties fairly. In 1968, the court ruled that any party receiving as little as 0.5 percent of the vote is constitutionally entitled to state support at the rate, per voter, established by federal law. The original purpose behind

Table 4.6 PARTY FINANCES, 1980–1984 (DM MILLION)

Party	Total Income	Public Subsidies	Donations	Membership
SPD	343	137	37	129
CDU	321	140	71	85
CSU	91	35	36	16
FDP	83	44	23	11
Greens	60	20	11	11
PDS	—	28	1	30

Source: Das Parlament, March 20, 1992, p. 11.

state funding was to help the parties compete on a more equal basis and to liberate them from the excessive influence of interest groups. Yet in the late 1970s, as the cost of political campaigning skyrocketed, numerous illegal campaign finance practices dominated the news. In 1983, the Bundestag enacted a legislative reform package to put a stop to practices that deliberately circumvent the law (*Umwegfinanzierung*).[18]

Finally, unable any longer to distinguish adequately between legitimate campaign costs and other party expenditures, a Constitutional Court judgment of April 9, 1992, declared major parts of the existing party finance law unconstitutional and ordered the German parliament to enact a new law by the end of the year. Initiated by the Greens, the case was decided against the backdrop of declining party membership and the increasing public perception that the parties were more interested in shoring up their own power than in caring for the public interest. To encourage the parties to revitalize their ossified structures, increase their membership, and raise more funds on a voluntary basis, the court ruled that state subsidies and reimbursements may not constitutionally exceed the amount of funds the parties raise by themselves.

INTEREST ASSOCIATIONS

German constitutional theory regards political parties as the chief agencies of political representation, providing the vital link between state and society that facilitates effective majority rule. In reality, public policy results from the complex interplay of political parties and private interests who seek special favors from the government. Hundreds of national associations, ranging from recreational and fraternal to economic and professional groups, maintain offices and highly skilled professional staffs in the capital on a year-round basis. Bonn is the site of most lobbying activity because of the central importance of federal executive agencies in making public policy.

Contact between interest group representatives and public officials in the FRG is much more direct and formal than in some other advanced democracies, which is partly a vestige of the German corporatist tradition. (Corporate representation is still the norm in the upper house of Bavaria's bicameral legislature.) Major social and economic interests are represented on ministerial advisory councils, agency consultative committees, regional planning councils, public broadcasting stations, and the parliamentary study groups of the political parties. Additionally, federal ministerial officials meet on a regular basis behind closed doors with the top representatives of industry, banking, agriculture, and labor for the purpose of coordinating national economic policy. (The quasi-official compulsory-membership trade and professional associations empowered to regulate occupational standards and practices are still other examples of direct interest group influence on public policy.)

The link between organized interests and the political parties is equally firm. Far more than in the United States, these interests are actually represented by their functionaries in the national and the parliamentary parties (*Fraktionen*). Representatives of business, religious, agricultural, and refugee organizations have been conspicuous among CDU-CSU members of parliament, whereas trade union officials are to be found in SPD leadership positions at all levels of party organization. Members of parliament associated with trade unions, business associations, and other organized interests actually dominate the membership of parliamentary committees such as labor, social policy, food, agriculture, and forestry.[19]

This complex web of public and private interlocking directorates prompted Peter Katzenstein to characterize the FRG as a "semi-sovereign state."[20] The FRG is semi-sovereign because the State shares its sovereignty with private centers of power and influence. In this view, popular elections do not empower the victors to change policy in strict accordance with an electoral mandate. Politics by consensus is the norm in Germany, a norm promoted by the regular practice of formalized cooperation between a decentralized government and highly centralized private interest associations. Thus "incrementalism rather than large-scale policy change typifies West German politics,"[21] a reality that helps to explain the stability of the FRG's political system as well as the frustration felt by citizens who feel the system is insulated and biased against change.

Citizen Initiatives (*Bürgerinitiativen*)

The sudden appearance of numerous urban and rural protest groups in the 1970s was one sign of the citizens' frustration with the political process. Tens of thousands of German citizens have staged protest rallies involving quality of life issues such as nuclear power plant construction, urban renewal, air and water pollution, land-use regulations, new highway construction, and the cost of inner-city transportation. Their grassroots activism—protest marches, letter-writing campaigns, petition gathering, sit-ins, home-drafted newsletters, and other forms of spontaneous action—expresses the disenchantment of many citizens with the unresponsiveness of political parties, private corporations, and official bureaucracies. Their efforts have been most effective at the local level, resulting in the rollback of some public transportation prices, delays in the building of some nuclear power plants, and the postponement of official decisions to cut new highways through certain residential and open areas. Both the CDU and the SPD have responded to these successes and to the disenchantment that fueled them; they have done so by making the *Bürgerinitiativen* models for their local party interelection activities.

Major Interest Aggregations

Business The three largest business associations in the FRG are the German Federation of Industry (BDI), the Federation of German Employers (BDA), and the German Chamber of Trade and Commerce (DIHT). By the late 1980s, approximately 90 percent of employers belonged to such associations, a far higher percentage than that of employees in trade unions. The German Federation of Industry, which is dominated by a few large firms, embraces 23 major industrial associations. Its financial resources, expertise, high-powered staff, and close links to the federal ministries make it one of the most effective lobbies in Bonn. The Federation of German Employers, whose economic experts engage in collective-bargaining negotiations on behalf of nearly 90 percent of all private firms in the FRG, consists of 44 trade associations and 13 *Länder* organizations representing some 740 regional associations. The DIHT, speaking for 81 chambers of commerce, is concerned with the legal and promotional interests of organized business. Collectively, these groups have been heavy contributors to the CDU-CSU, though the BDI's leaders have also donated funds to the FDP, a strategy calculated to secure a measure of access to Bonn's ruling circles under SPD-FDP coalition governments.

Labor West German workers are organized into four major unions: the German Salaried Employees Union (DAG), the German Federation of Civil Servants (DBB), the Christian Trade Union Federation of Germany (CGB), and the German Trade Union Federation (DGB). These four unions represent 46 percent of the FRG's organized labor force. They are not strictly blue-collar organizations. The DGB, the largest of the unions, consists of 17 affiliated unions with a total membership of 7.5 million persons, only 70 percent of whom are blue-collar workers. Higher civil servants (794,000), middle-level white-collar employees (473,000), and many Catholic workers (245,000) are represented in the DBB, DAG, and CGB, respectively.

The unions serve their members with an extensive infrastructure of educational, social, and political activity, and keep them and the general public informed through a massive communication network that includes some 50 periodicals with a monthly circulation of 13 million.[22] The unions are also heavily represented in parliament. In the ninth Bundestag, 69.4 percent of SPD and 30.6 percent of CDU-CSU delegates had formal interest group ties to trade unions or other employee organizations.[23] Nonetheless, membership levels have fluctuated. For instance, between 1982 and 1990 the CGB grew from 297,000 members to 309,000 members, while between 1980 and 1990 the DBB dropped from 821,000 to 799,000.

The entry of East Germany's work force into the western unions has not been smooth. As eastern workers demand wage settlements on a par with western levels, western employers become more disinclined to invest in the less productive and all too often antiquated eastern plants. Likewise, where western unions exercise "a sense of proportion in the national interest" by taking modest raises, such as the 6 percent settlement accepted by the civil service union leaders in the spring of 1991, the grassroots membership complains that it is being made to pay for the problems in the east. Calls for western union members to make direct contributions to their eastern fellow members have been particularly poorly received. Hence, the goal of achieving equality in eastern and western living standards is not susceptible to quick or easy attainment.

Churches   The Basic Law forbids the establishment of a state church. Its preamble, however, reminds the German people of "their responsibility before God." In addition, the Basic Law defines religious communities as "corporate bodies under public law," in which capacity they are entitled to levy taxes and enter into agreements with the state. While the state is constitutionally bound to remain neutral in religious matters, the neutrality that governs church-state relations in Germany is one that leans toward accommodation rather than strict separation. The prevailing view of this relationship acknowledges the important role of religion in the nation's public life. The relationship is governed by *Länder* concordats and church covenants, and they cover matters such as religious instruction in the public schools, observance of religious holidays, establishment of confessional schools, and appointment of chairs in theology at state universities.

The Evangelical Church in Germany (EKD) is an alliance of 24 largely independent Lutheran, Reformed, and United Churches. Their 29.9 million members include some 5 million eastern Germans. Its top legislative organ, the Synod, takes positions on various social, cultural, and educational issues, in which respect it often cooperates with the Roman Catholic Church. The Catholic Church consists of 27 dioceses, seven of which are archdioceses. Its 28 million members include 800,000 eastern Germans. The Conference of Catholic Bishops, which like its Evangelical counterpart has a secretariat in Bonn, is the church's top policy-making organ. It functions independently of the Central Committee of German Catholics, an influential lay organization consisting of more than 100 Catholic associations. Other religious organizations include the Protestant Methodist Church, the Old Catholic Church, and the Central Council of Jews. These congregations are relatively small. The Jewish community, for example, consists of around 50,000 members, a far cry from the 530,000 Jews who lived and worked in Germany prior to the Holocaust.

The two major confessions continue to be influential in selected areas of public policy. Both religious establishments—Catholic and Evangelical—are represented on the governing boards of various public agencies, including those of the major public broadcasting stations. The churches are also critical players on the field of social welfare. They spend billions of dollars operating hundreds of kindergartens, hospitals, hospices, old-age homes, and homes for the handicapped, all of them activities that enjoy broad public support. In addition, the churches have a history of involvement in hotly contested political issues such as nuclear missile deployment, compulsory military service, and abortion. The Evangelical Church can even be credited with spearheading the West German peace movement as well as East Germany's peaceful revolution. What the churches seem unable to do today—certainly far less than in the earlier years of the Federal Republic—is to deliver votes in national election campaigns.

ELECTORAL POLITICS

The Electoral System

The German electoral system combines single-member districts with proportional representation. Each voter receives two ballots: The first is cast for a specific candidate running in a district, the second for a party list. The second ballot includes the names of those candidates nominated by their respective parties, and they are chosen in the order in which they appear on the list. The number of parliamentary seats allocated to a party is determined by second-ballot votes, that is, by its total share of the nationwide vote. Under this system, which the *Länder* also use, party list candidates would be added to the single-member district winners until the total number of seats equals the percentage of its nationwide, second-ballot vote.

The functioning of the system can be illustrated by the election results of 1983. In winning 48.8 percent of second-ballot votes, the CDU-CSU also captured 180 districts; the figures for the SPD were 38.2 percent and 68 districts; and for the FDP and the Greens they were 7.0 and 5.6 percent, respectively, and no districts. These results meant that Christian Democrats were entitled to 244 Bundestag seats. Thus, under the formula, the CDU-CSU was awarded 64 list seats which, when added to its district seats, totaled 244 or 48.8 percent of all second-ballot votes. The SPD, having won 68 district seats, was awarded an additional 125 list seats, totaling 193, whereas the FDP received 34 and the Greens 27 list seats, representing their respective shares of the national (second-ballot) vote. It is possible, however, for a party to win more district seats than it would normally be entitled to by its second-ballot vote. When this happens, such "overhang" seats are retained, thus increasing the total number of parliamentary seats by that much.

The voting system can also be skewed by the 5 percent clause, which often results in "wasted" votes. In 1990, for example, the western Greens won 4.7 percent of the votes in the old FRG, just missing the 5 percent requirement. Under "pure" proportional representation, the Greens would have been entitled to 23 seats in the Bundestag but, having failed to win 5 percent of the vote, they received none. The

CDU-CSU's ten-seat majority after the 1994 election was due entirely to its overhang seats. The SPD had four such seats. (In a subsequent judicial challenge, the Constitutional Court sustained the validity of these overhang seats.)

The 5 percent clause was not regarded as equitable, however, with respect to the first all-German election of December 1990. The Federal Constitutional Court ruled that political parties in the eastern Länder would be severely handicapped if the rule were to apply nationwide. For this particular election, therefore, as Table 4.7 indicates, the 5 percent rule applied separately to Germany's eastern and western regions. If seats in the Bundestag had been allocated on a nationwide basis, as is usually the case, neither the Greens (eastern or western) or the Party of Democratic Socialism (the old SED) would have achieved parliamentary representation. The two-constituency tabulation presented in Table 4.7 was a one-time exception to the 5 percent nationwide rule.

Finally, if a political party fails to get 5 percent of the national vote, it may still obtain proportional representation in the national parliament by winning at least three single-member districts. This happened in 1994; the PDS won 4.4 percent of the national vote—only 0.9 percent of these votes came from the western Länder—but won 4 constituency seats in East

Table 4.7   FEDERAL ELECTION RESULTS, 1990*

Party	Nationwide (percent)	Old FRG (percent)	Ex-GDR (percent)	Seats Won
CDU	36.7	35.0	43.4	262
SPD	33.5	35.9	23.6	239
FDP	11.0	10.6	13.4	79
CSU	7.1	9.1	—	51
Greens (West)	3.9	4.7	—	—
PDS	2.4	0.3	9.9	17
DSU	0.2	—	1.0	—
Greens (East)	1.2	—	5.9	8
Republicans	2.1	2.3	1.3	—

*The percentages do not include the election results in Berlin. The DSU (German Social Union) ran as the "sister" party of Bavaria's CSU. The Greens (East) were allied with Alliance 90.

Sources: Statistisches Jahrbuch 1991 für das Vereinte Deutschland, p. 101 and The Week in Germany (New York: The German Information Center, December 7, 1990).

Table 4.8 FEDERAL ELECTION RESULTS, 1994

Party	West (percent)	East (percent)	Total (percent)	Seats
CDU-CSU	42.2	38.5	41.5	294
SPD	37.6	31.9	36.4	252
FDP	7.7	4.0	6.9	47
Alliance-Greens	7.8	5.7	7.3	49
PDS	0.9	17.7	4.4	30
Republicans	2.0	1.4	1.9	—
Other parties	1.9	1.3	1.7	—
Total	100	100	100	672

Berlin, entitling the party to 30 seats in the thirteenth Bundestag (see Table 4.8).

Split-Ticket Voting

The German system gives voters the opportunity to split their tickets, a method by which coalition partners can help each other. In 1972, for example, the SPD openly encouraged its voters to cast their second ballot in favor of the FDP, while 60 percent of second-ballot FDP voters supported CDU and SPD candidates with their first ballot. Split-ticket voting was also prevalent in the 1987 election when many SPD voters, troubled by their party's military and ecological policies, cast their second ballot for the Greens, whereas many CDU voters cast their second ballot for the FDP. The FDP, in turn, appeared to convince voters that the best way to keep the CDU-CSU "honest" and on the right course was to ensure its presence in the new government. As Table 4.9 indicates, large numbers of German voters appear to be leery of

one-party government. No fewer than 40.1 percent of CDU-CSU voters and 41.7 percent of SPD voters thought that it would "not be good" for their respective parties to win an absolute majority of seats in the Bundestag. The corresponding percentages for the 1983 election were 27.1 and 29.5. These figures point to an increasing tendency on the part of German voters to split their ballots. The German preference for governing coalitions contrasts sharply with the attitudes of British voters who tend to associate responsible parliamentary government with unified party leadership backed by electoral majorities. This split-ticket voting is one indicator of the Americanization of FRG electoral behavior; another is the phenomenon of the "floating voter" who does not owe a deep and consistent attachment to any one party.

Candidate Selection

Political parties monopolize the candidate selection process. Candidates seeking district seats

Table 4.9 VOTERS PREFERRING ABSOLUTE MAJORITY FOR SPD OR CDU-CSU IN 1987 ELECTION (PERCENT)

Absolute Majority	CDU-CSU	SDP	FDP	Greens	Total
Good for SPD	0.0	57.7	1.0	14.3	22.2
Good for CSU/CSU	59.8	0.0	8.5	0.0	26.5
Not good	40.1	41.7	90.5	85.7	50.3

Source: Bundestagswahl 1987; Eine Analyse der Wahl zum 11. Deutschen Bundestag am 25, January 1987 (Mannheim: Forschungsgruppe Wahlen E.V., 1987), p. 48.

are nominated either directly by party members or by conventions of party delegates. (There is no system of primary elections as in the United States.) In the CDU and SPD parties, executive committees, elected in biennial congresses at the *Land* level, select candidates for the Bundestag. Naturally the party will seek to nominate the candidate with the broadest popular appeal. But invariably he or she is a well-known party loyalist with years of faithful service to the organization. "Independent" candidates who circumvent the party organization are rarely if ever nominated. Party control over *Land* list candidates is even tighter. These lists are determined by secret ballot in party conferences, but in truth delegates vote mainly to ratify lists already put together by district and *Land* party executive committees in cooperation with national party officials. These lists are usually headed by leading party officials to ensure their election to the Bundestag.

Campaign Styles and Techniques

West German elections have evolved into major media events and highly professionalized undertakings similar to American presidential campaigns. While both the CDU and the SPD continue to speak in terms of the traditional FRG mass party, the *Volkspartei* ("People's Party"), both have been highly Americanized and centralized in their campaigns, especially in the use of new communication technologies and new marketing approaches. (The German courts, however, put an end to U.S. -style direct phone canvassing as an illegal infringement of individual privacy.) Campaign advertisements fill newspapers and popular magazines, while election posters and richly colored lifestyle photographs of leading candidates dot the landscape. Lapel buttons, paper flags, T-shirts, imitation money, letter openers, and bumper stickers by the tens of thousands convey their partisan messages. In the 1980s, the art of selling candidates and creating political images reached new heights of sophistication and brilliance as public relations firms assumed a central role in mapping campaign strategy. As part of this strategy, each party seeks to establish a "brand image" with matching colors and catchy slogans. For example, the CDU-CSU, in empha-

sizing the "take charge" quality of its leader, Helmut Kohl, sought to personalize the 1994 campaign by turning the election into a referendum on his chancellorship. One influential campaign poster showed a huge and smiling Kohl under the caption "Politics Without a Beard," referring to the bearded SPD leader, Rudolf Scharping. The SPD countered with its issue-oriented emphasis on "Jobs, Jobs, Jobs" in the face of rising unemployment. The FDP, on the other hand, has cultivated itself as a "creative minority" by emphasizing its independence and portraying its leaders as persons of reason and common sense who are concerned about the problems of small businesspeople and the "besieged" middle class. The Greens, finally, have seen in their color a powerful symbol of their commitment to environmental preservation.[24]

GERMAN POLITICS IN TRANSITION

Federal Elections, 1949–1994: An Overview

The year 1969 marked the turning point of West German politics in the postwar era. Prior to that year, the CDU-CSU had won five successive national elections, most of them by wide margins over the SPD. Yet the clearest observable trend seen in Table 4.10 is the clockwork regularity of SPD gains between 1953 and 1972. The SPD's chance to enter a governing coalition occurred in 1966 when Ludwig Erhard, the CDU chancellor, resigned against a backdrop of discord within his own party and a widening rift between the CDU-CSU and its regular coalition partner, the FDP. There followed the three-year period (1966–1969) of the so-called Grand Coalition under the CDU's Kurt-Georg Kiesinger (chancellor) and the SPD's Willy Brandt (vice-chancellor). In 1969, when Social Democrats reached a new high of 42.7 percent of the popular vote, the FDP, with 5.8 percent of the vote, decided to join hands with Brandt in producing Bonn's first SPD-led government.

The new coalition ruled with a slim voting edge of 12 votes, which by 1972 had virtually disappeared in the wake of defections from Brandt's Eastern policy (*Ostpolitik*). Christian Democrats, smelling an opportunity to get back

Table 4.10   FEDERAL ELECTION RESULTS, 1949–1990 (PERCENTAGE OF VOTES CAST)

Year	Turnout	CDU-CSU	SPD	FDP	Greens	PDS	Others
1949	78.5	31.0	29.2	11.9	—	—	27.3
1953	86.0	45.2	28.8	9.5	—	—	16.5
1957	87.8	50.2	31.8	7.7	—	—	11.3
1961	87.7	45.3	36.2	12.8	—	—	6.6
1965	86.8	47.6	39.3	9.5	—	—	5.6
1969	86.7	46.1	42.7	5.8	—	—	4.9
1972	91.1	44.9	45.8	8.4	—	—	0.9
1976	90.7	48.6	42.6	7.9	—	—	0.9
1980	88.7	44.5	42.9	10.6	—	—	1.9
1983	89.1	48.8	38.2	7.0	5.6	—	6.0
1987	84.4	44.3	37.0	9.1	8.3	—	8.9
1990	77.8	43.8	33.5	11.0	5.1	2.4	4.0
1994	79.1	41.5	36.4	6.9	7.3	4.4	3.5

into office, moved for a vote of no confidence, the first time that the parliamentary opposition had tried to topple a ruling government between federal elections. On April 27, 1972, the coalition survived the CDU-CSU challenge by a razor-thin margin of two votes. On the very next day the Bundestag rejected Brandt's budget, plunging the government into still another crisis. The failure of the budget to win parliamentary approval came at a time of economic downturn and bitter wrangling in the cabinet over fiscal policy. Yet Brandt's personal popularity was at an all-time high, prompting him late in 1972, when the economic news was much brighter, to call for new elections in the hope of increasing his margin of parliamentary support. Accordingly, the chancellor invoked Article 68 and lost his vote of confidence, as planned, whereupon the federal president dissolved the Bundestag and scheduled new elections for November 19.

The 1972 federal election campaign—a bitterly fought contest—resulted in a solid victory for Brandt, marking the first time Social Democrats had exceeded the CDU-CSU in popular votes. Shortly thereafter, however, the party's fortunes declined again as the SPD suffered severe losses in several state and local elections, only to be followed by Brandt's resignation in May 1974. This set the stage, after Helmut Schmidt's takeover, for the 1976 election.[25]

In 1976 the CDU-CSU not only recovered its 1972 losses, but narrowly missed securing the majority that would have toppled the SPD-FDP coalition—a popular victory without power, as many editorial writers characterized the election. The CDU's revival was widely attributed to the expansion of its grassroots membership campaign in the early 1970s under its able general-secretary, Kurt Biedenkopf, and to a highly effective national advertising campaign. Yet many spectators saw the election as an issueless campaign, decided mainly by the styles and personalities of the leading candidates.[26]

The 1980 and 1983 elections were largely a replay of 1976. However, the fortunes of Helmut Schmidt's SPD-led government declined rapidly. The popular chancellor's days were numbered in the face of increasing opposition from the FDP over his economic policy and from his own party over his strong pro-American nuclear missile policy. On October 1, 1982, after the FDP had pulled out of its coalition with the SPD, switching its support to the CDU/CSU, parliament chose the CDU's leader, Helmut Kohl, as chancellor. The new chancellor pledged forthwith to call new elections in March. It turned out to be a banner year for Christian Democrats. Far ahead of the SPD in the polls, they obtained their highest percentage of the national vote since 1957 but fell just short of a majority. Again in 1987 the CDU-CSU-FDP coalition emerged victorious, this time against the challenge of Johannes Rau, the moderate SPD chancellor candidate. Although the Greens had been gaining strength on the left, often at the expense of the SPD, Rau promised the electorate that he would not consider a coalition with the Greens. But as the SPD organization itself moved steadily leftward to draw votes away from the Greens, many other voters, particularly the swing vote in German politics, supported the existing coalition led by Chancellor Kohl.

With the FRG's economy booming in the summer of 1989, the SPD under Oskar Lafontaine planned a 1990 campaign focusing on "a policy of ecological and social renewal of industrialized society." Intervening events in the GDR, however, conspired against the SPD. Massive antigovernment demonstrations led to the collapse of the communist regime and the breaching of the Berlin Wall as East Germans prepared for their first free election in nearly 60 years, an election widely interpreted as a prounification vote. Chancellor Kohl seized the opportunity at his doorstep. With the capable support of his FDP Foreign Minister, Hans-Dietrich Genscher, he obtained Allied support for negotiations with East Berlin and Moscow that would reunite the two German states on October 3, 1990 and thereby make Kohl the first chancellor of all Germany since the the war.

Kohl's extraordinary determination and enthusiasm overcame all obstacles and all cautionary notes, including those of the president of the Bundesbank as to the costs of reunification. Kohl's project was, of course, welcomed by tumultuous crowds wherever he went in the east. Meanwhile, the SPD was reduced to reacting to his initiatives and to warning in a Cassandra-like manner, of their possible unpleasant side effects. Its support was popularly perceived in the east as too little, too late; Kohl had the diplomatic power and the deutsche mark to offer; Lafontaine offered little more than his qualified consent.

As the election year 1994 approached, the SPD looked like a sure winner. Unemployment was reaching unprecedented highs, reunification was driving up the national debt, business leaders were dissatisfied with the government's economic policies, and the the FDP was in decline. From 1991 to 1993, the SPD was running substantially ahead of Christian Democrats in public opinion polls against the backdrop of talk of the SPD's readiness to enter a coalition with the Greens at the national level. In addition, the SPD had an attractive and articulate leader in Rudolf Scharping who appeared to have united, for the time being, a seriously fractured party. On the other hand, no postwar German chancellor had ever lost his job as a direct result of a general election, and the SPD was not about to underestimate Kohl's "genius" for political survival.

Superwahljahr 1994

The year 1994 was known as *Superwahljahr* (super election year). Ten elections took place between March 13 and October 16, 1994: the European parliament election, eight state (*Länder*) elections, and the Bundestag election. As Table 4.11 shows, 1994 was disastrous for the FDP. By falling below the required 5 percent of the votes, the FDP was swept out of the European Parliament and all the *Land* parliaments. The FDP survived at the federal level—thanks only to the willingness of Christian Democratic voters to support the party on their second ballot. The Greens, by now accepted as an "establishment" party, had supplanted the FDP as Germany's third largest party, although its strength was confined mainly to the western *Länder*. The PDS was clearly on the ascendancy in the eastern *Länder,* whereas the right-wing Republicans, who entered the European Parliament in 1990 with 7.1 percent of the vote, were reduced to relative insignificance in 1994.

The coalitional outcome of the 1994 election remained uncertain until election day. Kohl's popularity grew stronger in mid–1994 as the economy began to perk up, but polls showed the CDU-CSU-FDP ruling coalition falling just short of a majority amid speculation that an SPD-Green coalition might be in the offing for the first time and, barring that, perhaps even a

Table 4.11 *SUPERWAHLJAHR,* **1994** (PERCENT)

Election	CDU-CSU	SPD	FDP	Alliance-Greens	PDS	Republicans	Other
Lower Saxony	34.6	44.3	4.4	7.4	—	—	7.5
European Parliment	38.8	32.2	4.1	10.1	4.7	3.9	6.3
Saxony-Anhalt	34.4	34.0	3.6	5.1	19.9	—	3.1
Brandenburg	18.7	54.1	2.2	2.1	18.7	—	3.3
Saxony	58.1	16.6	1.7	4.1	16.5	—	3.0
Bavaria	52.8	30.1	2.8	6.1	—	3.9	4.3
Mecklenburg-Pomerania	37.7	29.5	3.8	3.7	22.7	—	2.6
Thuringia	42.6	29.6	3.2	4.5	16.6	—	3.5
Saarland	38.6	49.4	2.1	5.5	—	—	4.4
Bundestag	41.5	36.4	6.9	7.3	4.4	1.9	1.6

Source: German Politics (Special Issue on 1994 German Election), vol. 4 (August 1995): 160–164.

CDU-CSU-SPD grand coalition. The SPD hurt itself, however, by running on a platform of large-scale income distribution; the CDU-CSU's message of continuity and stability seemed a safer bet with most voters. In the end Kohl inched into the chancellorship by a single vote, but with the assistance of overhang seats the government coalition ended up with a majority of ten seats in the thirteenth Bundestag.

A Changing Electorate

In the two decades prior to the 1994 election the FRG's electorate had changed in significant ways. Voting patterns in the 1950s could be explained largely in terms of class and religion. By the 1970s these variables, although still important indicators of voting, were no longer sure predictors of how Germans would vote. In the 1970s, the SPD began to advance beyond its labor union support into urban Catholic, white-collar Protestant constituencies, just as the CDU was beginning to broaden its appeal in urban white-collar districts previously weak in CDU affiliation. On the whole, Catholicism and ruralism correlated positively with high CDU-CSU voting, whereas the SPD's success over the long term seemed to lie less with its working-class membership than with the broadening of its base in the middle class.[27]

As the data in Table 4.12 indicate, the most dramatic shift in postwar voting patterns has taken place as a consequence of the changing character of the German middle class. Traditional middle-class voters—property owners and farmers—have seen their numbers dwindle and replaced by a new middle class of civil servants and white-collar employees connected with the FRG's mushrooming service trades. Highly urbanized, younger, and less attached to traditional values, these voters seem more responsive to newer issues centering on environmental matters, educational reform, and alternative lifestyles than to older economic issues. In the 1980s, many of these voters—especially those in districts with high concentrations of students, salaried workers, and civil servants—cast their

Table 4.12 SOCIAL CLASS AND PARTY SUPPORT, **1987** (PERCENT)

Social Class	CDU-CSU	SPD	FDP	Greens
Working	39	53	2	6
New Middle	45	41	6	8
Old Middle	54	27	7	12

Source: Russell J. Dalton, *Citizen Politics in Western Democracies* (Chatham, NJ: Chatham House Publishers, 1988), p. 155.

votes in favor of the Greens, seriously cutting into traditional FDP strongholds. First-time voters and younger voters (18–44) cast their ballots disproportionately for the Greens.

Two Electorates

In the 1994 election, the entire German people reaffirmed their commitment to and acceptance of reunification. On that score, there was no possible way that the clock could be turned back. Electoral research, however, shows that social cleavages and voting patterns differed significantly in the east and west. In the western *Länder*, as Table 4.13 shows, the SPD retained the support of its working-class voters but in the eastern *Länder* lost this constituency in overwhelming numbers to the CDU. Moreover, the CDU won the support of workers—very few of whom had any attachment to religion. On the other hand, the left-wing parties—SPD, Alliance-Greens, and PDS—won the bulk (60.6 percent) of the middle-class vote. The PDS did extraordinarily well among pensioners and the old GDR upper class (i.e., members of the old socialist power structure). In need of emphasis is the role of religion in the voting of East and West Germans. As expected, Catholic and Protestants in the east voted overwhelmingly for the CDU, but 52 percent of CDU voters described themselves as nonreligious, underscoring the heavily secular orientation of eastern voters compared to the relatively high number of western voters who are more inclined to identify themselves as religious.

In short, as Dalton and Bürkin note in their analysis of the 1994 election returns, "the western electorate is fairly religious, as well as conservative on economic and social welfare issues; the eastern electorate is more secular and liberal on social issues, and displays the reversal of the traditional class-party relationship."[28] The two scholars suggest that these regional differences in party behavior "can create sharp intraparty tensions." How these tensions will be resolved or whether party voting in the east will begin to reflect western voting patterns remains to be seen. In any event, Dalton and Bürkin are probably correct in concluding that class cleavage and religion "will be further weakened in a unified German party system."[29]

POLICY-MAKING INSTITUTIONS

In this subsection we turn our attention to the FRG's major policy-making institutions, its federal system, and its scheme of separated and divided powers. Upon their accession to the FRG, the eastern *Länder* brought their governmental systems into conformity with the Basic Law.

Table 4.13   CLASS VOTING PATTERNS 1994 (PERCENT)

	GDU-CSU	SPD	FDP	Alliance-Greens	PDS	Other
West						
Worker	37.2	55.9	1.1	3.6	—	2.2
Self-employed	59.7	14.6	17.1	5.9	—	2.6
Salaried	38.6	39.4	8.0	12.7	—	1.4
Combined middle class	42.9	34.5	9.9	11.5	—	1.1
East						
Worker	51.5	34.1	2.5	1.8	9.8	0.3
Self-employed	39.1	26.6	9.4	7.8	17.2	0.0
Salaried	33.5	32.5	3.9	8.0	21.6	0.5
Combined middle class	34.3	31.6	4.6	8.0	21.0	0.4

Source: Russell J. Dalton and Wilhelm Bürkin, "The Two German Electorates: The Social Bases of the Vote," *German Politics and Society*, vol. 13 (1995) p. 84.

Roman Herzog, president of Germany since 1994. Herzog, a Protestant from Bavaria, had occupied ministerial positions in one of the *Länder,* Baden-Württemberg, and then became a member and later president of the Federal Constitutional Court in 1987.

Thus, unless otherwise indicated, the institutions, structures, and policy-making processes discussed here are applicable to all of Germany.

Germany's main legislative institutions are the popularly elected Bundestag (house of representatives) and the Bundesrat, the nonelected upper house, whose appointed delegates represent the *Länder* governments. The leading executive institutions are the chancellor and cabinet, collectively known as the federal government. The president, once a powerful head of state directly elected by the people, has been reduced in the FRG to a figurehead akin to the British monarch. One of the unique features of Germany's federal system is that the states are entrusted under the Constitution with the adminis-

tration of national law. This system, often dubbed *administrative federalism,* is a carryover from the past. Finally, empowered to enforce the provisions of the Basic Law, the judiciary, at the top of which is the Federal Constitutional Court, serves as a check on the activities of the other branches of government.

The Federal President

The federal president is the FRG's highest-ranking public official, but he functions mainly as a ceremonial head of state, a vestigial reminder of the once thriving presidency under the emperor. Symbolically, he remains important as a spokesman for the nation. Although the presidency is perceived as a nonpartisan office, its occupant is elected for a five-year term—under Article 54 of the Basic Law he may be reelected only once—by a federal convention composed of party representatives from national and state parliaments. The president is chosen as a result of bargaining between the coalition parties forming the majority in the convention. Yet the office has been filled by respected public officials widely recognized for their fair-mindedness and ability to communicate across party lines. Up to now, the office has served as a capstone to a successful career in politics.

On May 23, 1994, Roman Herzog, a Christian Democrat—and former president of the Federal Constitutional Court—became the FRG's seventh president. He was preceded by Theodore Heuss (FDP, 1949–1959), Heinrich Lübke (CDU; 1959–1969), Gustav Heinemann (SPD, 1969–1974), Walter Scheel (FDP, 1974–1979), Karl Carstens (CDU, 1979–1984), and Richard von Weizsäcker (CDU; 1984–1994). Until 1979, an incumbent president otherwise competent and prudent in the exercise of his authority could expect, if he wished, to be reelected to a second term. Some recent elections, however, have been largely an exercise in partisan politics. In 1979, the CDU forced the resignation of Walter Scheel as presidential candidate and elected its own candidate (Karl Carstens) by a slim majority of 26 votes. In 1994, there were three serious presidential candidates: Johannes Rau (SPD), Hildegard Hamm-

Brücher (FDP), and Herzog (CDU)—Chancellor Kohl's personal choice for the office. Herzog won on the third ballot when the FDP switched its vote to the CDU candidate, another indication that the governing CDU-CSU-FDP coalition would hold together later in the election year.

The president's powers include the appointment and dismissal of various public officials, including cabinet officials and military officers, and the pardoning of criminal offenders. His exercise of the pardoning power has occasionally caused a public uproar, as in 1989 when President Weizäcker pardoned two imprisoned terrorists—female members of the Red Army Faction—after they had served twelve years of their prison terms and showed that they were prepared to reenter society as responsible citizens. His most common official duty, apart from receiving and visiting foreign heads of state, is to promulgate, with his signature, all federal laws. It is disputed whether he can reject a statute on substantive constitutional grounds, although presidents have done so on at least five occasions. A president's refusal to sign a properly enacted bill could conceivably bring about a constitutional crisis resulting in demands for the president's resignation or his impeachment. If the president resigns, dies, or is impeached—or is otherwise unable to perform the duties of his office—the president of the Bundesrat, as the second highest official of the Federal Republic, assumes the powers of the presidency. In their absence from the country, presidents have often requested the Bundesrat's president to serve as acting president.

The Federal Government

The Chancellor The Basic Law puts the chancellor in firm control of the federal government. He alone is responsible to parliament, whereas his ministers—that is, the members of his cabinet—whom he may hire and fire, are responsible only to him. Constitutionally charged under Article 65 (see Feature 4.5) to lay down the guidelines for national policy, he is chosen by a majority of the Bundestag and is usually the leader of the largest party in the governing coalition. Parliament is not empowered to dismiss the chancellor at will, however, as it was

able to do in the Weimar Republic. Under the so-called constructive vote of no confidence, prescribed by Article 67 of the Basic Law, the Bundestag may dismiss a chancellor only when a majority of its members simultaneously elects his successor. The stabilizing effect of this provision has led many persons to label the FRG a "chancellor democracy."

The constructive vote of no confidence has succeeded only once, in 1982, when the Bundestag voted Helmut Schmidt out of office after the FDP's withdrawal from the coalition government. (In 1972, Willy Brandt survived a Christian Democratic challenge to his leadership, the only other occasion on which parliament invoked the procedure under Article 67.) A new alliance between the FDP and the CDU-CSU elected Helmut Kohl as chancellor by a vote of 256 to 235, the first time in the FRG's history that a government had been replaced without an election.

Article 68 allows the chancellor to initiate a vote of confidence and to authorize him, if he loses the vote, to request the president to dissolve parliament and call for new elections. Brandt used this procedure in 1972, and Kohl used it again in 1983. Both chancellors planned to lose in the expectation that new elections would increase their parliamentary majority and thus their hold on governmental power. In both instances the strategy worked, although some constitutional lawyers argued that these were cynical political moves designed to circumvent the intent and spirit of the Basic Law. They held that the Constitution permits the dissolution of parliament in advance of its regular expiration date only when the chancellor actually loses its confidence or is unable to govern with his current majority. To deliberately contrive a vote of no confidence for the purpose of holding new elections trivializes the Basic Law in their view by undermining the principle of regular elections.

The Chancellor's Office The most powerful instrument of executive leadership in the FGR is the chancellor's office. Originally a small secretariat serving the chancellor's personal needs, it has evolved into an agency of major political importance, even overshadowing the

---

Feature 4.5   Article 65 (Chancellor Government)

The Federal Chancellor shall determine, and be responsible for, the general policy guidelines. Within the limits set by these guidelines, each Federal Minister shall conduct the affairs of his department autonomously and on his own responsibility. The Federal Government shall decide on differences of opinion between Federal Ministers. The Federal Chancellor shall conduct the affairs of the Federal Government in accordance with rules of procedure adopted by it and approved by the Federal President.

---

cabinet. It contains departments corresponding to the various federal ministries as well as a planning bureau, created in 1969, to engage in long-range social and economic planning. Its staff of about 500 persons keeps the chancellor informed of domestic and foreign affairs, assists him or her in setting policy guidelines, coordinates policy making among the federal ministries, and monitors the implementation of cabinet decisions.

The chancellor's office is headed by a chief of staff, usually an experienced public official and close personal advisor. The chief of staff is a person of immense power in Bonn—his influence often exceeding that of federal ministers. Other chancellery advisors have obtained national prominence in their policy-making role. Such a person was Egon Bahr, the principal architect of Brandt's *Ostpolitik*. Finally, the chancellor is served by a press secretary, who in turn heads the Federal Press and Information Office (staffed by over 800 persons), which is also under the chancellor's direct control.

The Cabinet While prescribing a chancellor-led government, the Basic Law (Article 65) also envisions a high level of cabinet responsibility. In practice, however, the cabinet has not functioned as a true collegial body. First of all, the chancellor decides how much authority is to be accorded to each minister: Adenauer and Brandt, for example, virtually served as their own foreign ministers, as did Schmidt in certain areas of foreign policy. On the other hand, certain ministers achieve enormous prominence in their own right and occasionally overshadow the chancellor. Hans-Dietrich Genscher, the chief architect of German foreign policy in the 1980s,

was often thought to have been the dominant figure in foreign affairs under Chancellor Kohl.

Furthermore, cabinet members are not all equal in rank (see Table 4.14). For example, the minister of finance—probably the cabinet's most powerful official in the field of domestic policy—has a qualified veto over proposals af-

Helmut Kohl, chancellor of Germany since 1982, speaking to European parliamentarians in Strasbourg, France, in 1995.

fecting public finances. His objection to such proposals can be overridden only by the vote of the chancellor, with whom he is ordinarily closely affiliated, and a majority of the cabinet. The ministers of justice and interior also have special powers of review over cabinet proposals impinging upon their jurisdiction.

In creating the cabinet, a chancellor is constrained by the demands of coalition politics and the interests of groups allied to and rivalries within his party. Often he is required to negotiate at length over the nature and number of ministries to be awarded the minor party in his coalition government. The FDP, the perennial minor party in German coalition governments, has often threatened to withhold its votes for the chancellor (i.e., the head of the major party in the coalition) until it secures agreement on certain policy issues and is assured adequate representation in the cabinet. After the 1994 election, Chancellor Kohl had not only to ensure that the FDP was satisfied with its apportionment of cabinet posts; he was also required to achieve a measure of religious and geographic balance among the CDU's cabinet members, while including members from the eastern *Länder* and granting proportionate representation to Bavaria's CSU.

Parliamentary State Secretaries The office of parliamentary state secretary—to be distinguished from the permanent state secretaries of the various ministerial bureaucracies—was introduced in 1967. Parliamentary state secretaries are selected from among the more junior members of the Bundestag to help the ministries run their departments, defend their records in parliament, and maintain contact

Table 4.14 FEDERAL GOVERNMENT MINISTRIES, 1994

Cabinet Minister	Minister's Party
Minister of the Chancellery	CDU
Foreign Minister	FDP
Minister of the Interior	CDU
Minister of Justice	FDP
Minister of Finance	CSU
Minister of the Economy	FDP
Minister of Nutrition, Agriculture, and Forestry	CDU
Minister of Labor	CDU
Minister of Defense	CDU
Minister of Family, the Elderly, Women and Youth	CDU
Minister of Health	CSU
Minister of Transportation	CDU
Minister of the Environment, Protection of Nature and Reactor Safety	CDU
Minister of Postal Services and Telecommunications	CSU
Minister of Regional Planning and Urban Development	CDU
Minister of Education, Science, Research and Technology	CDU
Minister of Economic Cooperation and Development	CSU

Bundestag in Berlin.

with the public. A new element in the Schmidt cabinet was the high number of former parliamentary state secretaries who were elevated to cabinet posts. The office is now widely recognized as a training ground for cabinet service by all the major parties.

The Bundestag: Legislative Branch

The Bundestag (the parliament of the FRG) is the successor to the old imperial (1871–1918) and republican (1919–1933) Reichstag. In these earlier regimes the legislative branch was politically, and in some respects constitutionally, subordinate to the executive establishment, just as elected representatives played second fiddle to professional civil servants. In contrast, the Basic Law elevates parliament to first rank among the FRG's governing institutions. Though commentators agree that parliament has fallen short of the founders' vision of a vigorously self-confident body in control of the executive, they are also of the view that the Bundestag has evolved from the rather submissive body of the Adenauer era into an increasingly assertive and vi-

tal agency of the national policy-making process. Even in the event of a national emergency, which only it can declare, the Bundestag's authority remains largely intact, thus helping to ensure that ultimate power shall always reside in the hands of civilian leaders and the elected representatives of the people.

Power and Functions While playing a role similar to that of the U.S. Congress, the Bundestag is structurally a very different institution. First of all, it is "the parliament of a parliamentary system of government" in that "it [also] determine[s] the political composition and tenure in office of the government."[30] Second, and by the same token, the highest officials in the executive branch—that is, the chancellor and his ministers—are among the most important and influential members of the Bundestag. This symbiotic relationship between executive and legislative power is wholly incompatible with the U.S. notion of separation of powers. In the FRG, separation of powers is embodied largely in the role of the opposition within parliament. Its task is to call the government or ruling coalition—and thus the executive—to account in the crucible of parliamentary inquiry and debate.

Parliament checks the executive by its power to review the national budget, to pass upon all bills introduced by the government, to hold hearings and investigations, and to confront the chancellor and his ministers in the legislative question hour, a device borrowed from British parliamentary practice. The screening of proposed legislation absorbs most of the Bundestag's time. By far, the largest number of bills screened are initiated by the government. Of the 800 bills received by the twelfth Bundestag (1990–1994), 407 were government bills, 297 originated in the Bundestag itself, and 96 were sent over by the Bundesrat. The government managed to pass 77 percent of the bills it introduced, as compared with a 16 and 7 percent success rate, respectively, for the Bundestag and Bundesrat. As these statistics show, the federal government dominates the law-making process.

Fraktionen and Committees

The most important groups in the Bundestag are the parliamentary parties, or *Fraktionen*. In practice, they control the Bundestag's organization and decision-making machinery. Although constitutionally regarded as "representatives of the whole people, not bound to instructions [from any group]," deputies who plan on advancing their legislative careers will not lightly oppose the policy decisions of the party hierarchy, for party unity and discipline are strongly embedded in the parliamentary party system. Party discipline, however, is exercised in only a small number of cases. Most bills—over 85 percent—are the product of group negotiation in which representatives of the federal government, the Bundestag, and the Bundesrat participate, and they are passed unanimously.

Each *Fraktion* divides itself topically into working groups or councils, which parallel the Bundestag's committee structure and serve as instruments for crystallizing party policy and developing the expertise of deputies. Indeed, the deputy who does his homework in the party group to which he is assigned—showing leadership, skill, forensic ability, and mastery of sub-

ject matter—often winds up as an influential member of a corresponding legislative committee and eventually a parliamentary state secretary. The Bundestag also has a differentiated committee system, including standing, investigating, and special committees. Of these, the 23 standing committees are the most important. Comparable to the committees of the U.S. Congress, they and their numerous subcommittees are parliament's workhorses. In the Bundestag, however, committee chairs are shared by all the *Fraktionen* in proportion to their strength in the chamber as a whole and are allocated on the basis of expertise instead of seniority.

Members of Parliament   Typically, having studied law, political science, or economics, members of parliament often begin their careers in the youth branch of a political party, frequently assisting established politicians. Successfully fulfilling an apprenticeship in the party apparatus or, as is often the case, in a trade, farm, or labor organization closely linked to their party, they are then, in their late 30s, elected to parliament. They remain there for about 16 years, only to resign in their mid–50s to draw a comfortable pension and to enter the employment of an organized interest group. The careerism and security inherent in this system of political recruitment are not calculated to staff parliament with "movers and shakers," and often insulate deputies against new and evolving trends in society.

Not all groups are equally represented in parliament. In the twelfth Bundestag (1990–1994), members of the government, civil servants, party functionaries, and trade association officials made up 67.1 percent of the 662 members. Another 23.3 percent were self-employed businesspersons, farmers, and members of the various professions—8.9 percent of whom were lawyers and notary publics. Nearly two-thirds were university graduates. For most of the 1980s women represented about 15 percent of the membership, more than double the number elected in the 1970s. In the Bundestag elected in 1994, however, this figure jumped to 26 percent, the highest ever. (The PDS and the Greens had more women than men in their delegations.) Of the 176 women elected to the thirteenth Bundestag, 48.3 and 23.3 percent belonged, respectively, to the SPD and CDU-CSU.

The Law-Making Process Bills may be introduced by any member of the Bundestag or by the Bundesrat. As indicated earlier, however, the overwhelming majority of legislative bills originates with the federal government. A bill sponsored by the latter is first submitted to the Bundesrat, which is required to act on the bill within six weeks. If there are any changes, the Bundesrat must return the bill to the cabinet for its approval or disapproval. (Bills originating in the Bundesrat are submitted to the Bundestag by the cabinet after the latter has expressed its opinion on the bill.) The bill is then submitted to the Bundestag, where it is given a first reading. From there it is assigned to the proper committee. If it survives this stage, together with a second and third reading, it is transmitted to the Bundesrat. If the Bundesrat amends the bill, it may be sent to a joint conference committee for mediation. Any changes by the committee again require the Bundestag's approval of the entire bill. The Bundesrat, however, has a suspensive veto over ordinary legislation and an absolute veto over legislation involving the *Länder* (for a discussion of these vetoes see the discussion of the Bundesrat)—but any such veto can be overridden by the Bundestag. After final approval, a bill is countersigned by the chancellor or appropriate federal minister and then signed by the federal president, whereupon it is promulgated as law in the *Federal Law Gazette*.

The chancellor, federal and *Land* ministries, and representatives of organized interest groups are the major actors in the law-making process. They work closely with the *Fraktionen* in hammering out legislative policy, though, as earlier noted, committees play a critical role in filtering legislation for final passage. So successful are the committees in the performance of this role that few bills, once reported out of committee, are the subject of amendment or even debate from the floor. The intense plenary debates in 1979 on energy policy and in 1996 on cutting social benefits—debates stretching over several days—are exceptions to the customary practice of securing broad interparty agreement on most bills that become law.

Federalism and Bureaucracy

Like the United States, Germany divides power constitutionally between national and state governments. Federalism is in fact one of the unamendable principles of the Basic Law. The 16 *Länder* consist of 13 territorial states and the three city-states of Berlin, Bremen, and Hamburg. Each *Land*, like the national government, has its own constitution based on principles of republican and democratic government. Each has a parliamentary system. A minister-president—lord mayor in the city-states—responsible to a one-house popularly elected legislature is the head of government in the territorial states. Historically, however, German federalism differs from the U.S. brand. The crucial distinction is that in the United States both federal and state governments exercise a full range of separate legislative and administrative functions, whereas German federalism confers the bulk of legislative powers upon the national government, with the *Länder* being mainly responsible for the administration of both federal and state laws.

The boundaries of the *Länder* were drawn without much reference to their ancestral ties. Only Bavaria, Saxony, and Thuringia survived with their pre-1945 boundaries relatively intact. In 1952, however, the GDR abolished the *Länder* and replaced them with 14 administrative districts under the control of the central government. These *Länder* were reestablished in July 1990 as one of the conditions of reunification. The *Länder* now range in population from 680,000 in Bremen to 17.3 million in North-Rhine Westphalia, more than eastern Germany's entire population. They also differ vastly in territorial size: excluding the small city-states, they range from Saarland with 2,570 sq. km. to Bavaria with 70,554 sq. km. The largest and richest states, measured in terms of population and geography, are in the west. The eastern *Länder*, by contrast, are relatively smaller and much poorer.

This imbalance between the eastern and western *Länder* has revived proposals to redraw state lines for the purpose of creating larger and more integrated political and economic units. The Basic Law permits the restructuring of the *Länder* so long as the system as a whole remains federal in design. Under the terms of the Basic Law (Article 29), any federal law proposing a state boundary change must be approved by the Bundesrat, and subsequently ratified by referendum in the affected *Länder*. This procedure was first used in 1952 when the states of Baden, Württemberg, and Württemberg-Hohenzollern were consolidated into the single state of Baden-Württemberg. The next change is likely to be Berlin's incorporation into Brandenburg, a change that the all-German government is obligated to consider under the Unity Treaty.

One possible solution to the enormous disparity among the states in territory and population would be a merger based on the reorganized council of Germany's central bank (Bundesbank). Instead of giving each *Land* a vote on the Bundesbank Council, the system was changed in 1992 to accord representation to nine economically integrated regions that were defined by existing state boundaries but relatively balanced in population and territory. The nine regions consist of Schleswig-Holstein and Mecklenburg-Pomerania; Berlin and Brandenburg; Bremen, Lower Saxony, and Saxony-Anhalt; North Rhine-Westfalia; Hesse; Thuringia and Saxony; Rhineland-Palatinate and Saarland; Bavaria; and Baden-Württemberg. Any such fundamental change in *Land* boundaries, however, would almost surely lack the required popular support and face resistance by political and economic interests favored by the current system.

The Bundesrat

The Bundesrat, the mainstay of German federalism, was designed to safeguard the vital interests of the *Länder* (see Table 4.15). But it is not a second chamber like the U.S. Senate. First, its powers are not equal to those of the Bundestag; second, its 69 votes are cast by officials who serve at the pleasure of the *Länder* (see Table 4.15). Thus each *Land* delegation votes as a unit and in accordance with the instructions of its government. How a delegation—or the person appointed to represent the state—votes often depends on the party composition of the *Land* cabinet. Nearly all seats in the Bundesrat are occupied by *Land* minister-presidents or their delegates.

To accommodate the interests of the eastern *Länder*, the Unity Treaty also amended Article 51 of the Basic Law, changing the allocation of seats in the Bundesrat. As before, each state is entitled to at least three votes, but now states with a population of more than 2 million are entitled to four votes, those with more than 6 million receive five votes, and those with more than 7 million receive six votes. (In the past, the largest states had five votes.) This system favors the smaller states. The five largest states, with 64.4 percent of the population, have 28 votes in the Bundesrat; the remaining states, with 35.6 percent of the population, have 41 votes.

The Bundesrat's consent is required for all federal legislation affecting the administrative, financial, and territorial interests of the *Länder*. With respect to other legislation, it has a suspensive veto, as noted earlier. If the Bundesrat objects to a bill by a majority vote, the Bundestag may override by a majority vote; if the former is by two-thirds, the vote to override must also be two-thirds. Additionally, the Bundesrat is authorized to approve all federal action enforcing national law in the *Länder*, to participate in major legislative decisions taken during a national emergency, and to elect half of the members of the Federal Constitutional Court. This last prerogative is important, for the Bundesrat has a record of electing judges with strong federalist leanings, thus giving to the upper house an indirect influence in constitutional cases involving the interpretation of federal laws and ordinances.[31]

An Emerging Instrument of Opposition

In spite of its considerable powers, the Bundesrat during its first 20 years functioned largely

Table 4.15   THE BUNDESRAT, JANUARY 1, 1996

Land	Votes	Ruling Coalition	Population (million)	Percent
Baden-Württemberg	6	CDU-SPD	9.8	12.2%
Bavaria	6	CSU	11.4	14.2
Berlin	4	CDU-SPD	3.4	4.3
Brandenburg	4	SPD	2.6	3.3
Bremen	3	SPD-Greens	0.6	0.9
Hamburg	3	SPD-Statt Party	1.7	2.1
Hesse	5*	SPD-Greens	5.8	7.2
Mecklenburg-W. Pomerania	3	CDU-SPD	1.9	2.5
Lower Saxony	6	SPD	7.4	9.2
N. Rhine Westphalia	6	SPD	17.3	21.6
Rhineland-Palatinate	4	SPD	3.8	4.7
Saarland	3	SPD	1.1	1.3
Saxony	4	CDU	4.8	6.2
Saxony-Anhalt	4	SPD-Greens	2.9	3.7
Schleswig-Holstein	4	SPD	2.6	3.3
Thuringia	4	CDU-SPD	2.6	3.4

*Hesse received 5 votes in the Bundesrat in January of 1996 when its population exceeded 6 million.

in the shadow of the Bundestag, ratifying the latter's policies and those of Bonn's ruling party or coalition. Its leaders have tended to view the Bundesrat as a nonpartisan chamber concerned exclusively with the merits of proposed legislation, an image reinforced by the dominant role of bureaucratic officials in its proceedings.

Since 1969, however, the Bundesrat has risen in political importance and popular awareness. Until then the parties dominating the "lower" house also controlled the "upper" chamber. Owing to the distribution of power among the parties within the states, however, the Christian Democrats—the party out of power in Bonn—enjoyed a 21-to-20 voting edge in the Bundesrat between 1969 and 1975—an advantage that swelled to 11 votes by 1979—leading to sharp confrontations with the governing parties in the Bundestag.

In the 1990s, however, as Table 4.16 shows, the tables were turned. The ruling CDU-CSU-FDP coalition in the Bundestag confronted a Bundesrat overwhelmingly controlled by SPD-led coalitions in the *Länder*. Given that all financial legislation and nearly all legislation affecting the administration of federal law require the Bundesrat's consent, this house—contrary to the expectations of the Basic Law's founders—has evolved into a body virtually coequal with the Bundestag. In recent legislation periods, between 50 and 60 percent of all bills passed by the Bundestag required the Bundesrat's consent. The clash between the CDU-CSU-led government coalition was most evident in the twelfth Bundestag. No fewer than 85 government bills had to be taken up by the Mediation Committee, as opposed to 13 in the eleventh and 6 in the tenth Bundestag. Under these circumstances, important policy initiatives cannot be passed into law without considerable give-and-take by the two parliamentary bodies and by the major parties.

The Legal System and the Judiciary

Germany's Legal Tradition and the *Rechtsstaat*

The *Rechtsstaat* or "law state" is a key concept in the German legal order.[32] All just states are based on law, of course, but in its original form the German *Rechtsstaat* placed extraordinary emphasis upon legality. Germans viewed the state as a neutral entity entrusted with the resolution of public issues in accordance with objective standards of law, unsullied by the play of selfish interests or the machinations of political parties. The sovereign state—the axis of the law state—was the guarantor of freedom and equality, just as rights and obligations arose from membership in the state. Liberty did not precede law; rather, law defined it, and the judiciary, staffed by a professional class of impartial and apolitical civil servants loyal to the state, existed to enforce the law as written.

Under the Basic Law the *Rechtsstaat* remains a vital principle of German constitutionalism, but not in its earlier nineteenth-century sense. The *law state* would henceforth be limited by constitutionally guaranteed individual rights enforced by the judiciary, just as it would be moderated by the humanity implicit in the constitutional notion of *Sozialstaat* (freely translated, a *socially conscious state*). In legal theory the sovereign is no longer supreme. Article 20 reads: "All state authority emanates from the people," and further, "Legislation shall be subject to the constitutional order; the executive and the judiciary shall be bound by law *and justice*" (italics added). Finally, Article 20 contains this remarkable provision: "All Germans shall have the right to resist any person or persons seeking to abolish [the] constitutional order should no other remedy be possible."

The Court System

Germany has a uniform and integrated judicial system. All lower and intermediate courts of appeal are state courts, whereas all courts of final appeal are federal tribunals. Federal law specifies the structure of state courts, but their administration and staffing, including the training of judges, is under the control of the *Länder*. The trademarks of the German judiciary are collegiality and specialization. Except for courts of minor jurisdiction, all tribunals are multijudge courts. Most operate in panels of three. In addition to the regular courts, which handle ordinary civil and criminal cases, there are separate judicial hierarchies consisting of labor, administrative, social, finance, and constitutional courts. The federal courts, as shown in Table 4.17, cap these hierarchies.

Justice in the FRG is carried out by 20,150 judges (as of 1995), nearly 80 percent of whom serve on the regular courts of ordinary civil and criminal jurisdiction. Some 4,926 judges sit on the courts of specialized jurisdiction. The high federal courts, listed in Table 4.16, consist of 467 judges. Other legal professionals associated with the courts are some 4,000 public prosecutors. The 51,266—60,460 if notary publics are included—attorneys practicing law in 1995 are also regarded as officers of the courts, although their practice is by law limited to a certain level

Table 4.16   Courts of the Federation and the *Länder*, 1995

Jurisdiction	Courts of the Federation	Courts of the *Länder*
Constitutional	Federal Constitutional Court	13 constitutional courts
Ordinary	Federal Court of Justice	25 higher regional courts; 116 regional courts; 717 local courts
Labor	Federal Labor Court	19 higher labor courts; 124 labor courts
Administrative	Federal Administrative Court	16 higher administrative courts; 52 administrative courts
Social	Federal Social Court	16 higher social courts; 69 social courts
Finance	Federal Finance Court	19 finance courts

Source: Wolfgang Heyde, *Justice and the Law in the Federal Republic of Germany* (Heidelberg: C. F. Müller Juristischer Verlag, 1994), p. 9.

of the judiciary as well as to certain courts within a given geographical area.

The Judges   The training and professional standing of German judges varies from that of their peers in the United States and Britain. In the United States, for example, judgeships are usually awarded to lawyers in their middle years following successful private practice or experience in public office. In Germany, by contrast, lateral mobility of this kind is rare among legal professionals. After six years of study, which includes practical training in various administrative and judicial capacities, law graduates must make their choice of a legal career. Those deciding to become judges go through still another three-year probationary period. Upon the successful completion of this training they receive a judgeship with lifetime tenure and security. Judges can expect to ascend slowly in the hierarchy of the judicial establishment if they meet with the approval of the Land Justice Ministry—the *Länder* are in charge of the training, recruitment, and supervision of judges—and if they are lucky and know the right persons in Bonn, they may end their careers as judges of one of the high federal courts.

The civil service orientation of the judiciary tends to be reinforced by the narrow social base from which judges, particularly those appointed by the *Länder*, are recruited. Almost half are themselves the sons and daughters of parents who have spent their lives in the civil service. Federal judges tend to be more diversified in social background and occupational experience, largely because of the method by which they are selected. They are chosen by a committee of electors composed of 11 members of the Bundestag together with those *Land* and federal ministries whose authority is similar to the federal court to which a judge is to be named. This mechanism allows interest groups, political parties, state and federal agencies, and the public to participate in the selection process, producing a federal bench somewhat less characterized by professional inbreeding and political conservatism than the state judiciary.

The Federal Constitutional Court   The Federal Constitutional Court with its sweeping powers of judicial review is only as old as the Basic Law. To the surprise of many observers, this tribunal has developed into an institution of major policy-making importance in the FRG. Judicial review was a relatively new departure in German constitutional history. Postwar German leaders were of the opinion that, in the light of Germany's authoritarian and totalitarian past, traditional parliamentary and judicial institutions were insufficient to safeguard the new liberal democratic order. They created a national constitutional tribunal, as well as equivalents at the *Land* level, to supervise the judiciary's interpretation of constitutional norms, to enforce a consistent reading of the constitution on the other branches of government, to resolve conflicts between branches and levels of government, and to protect the basic liberties of German citizens. Thus the old positivist belief separating the realm of law from the realm of politics was abandoned, together with the idea that justice could automatically be achieved through the mechanical application of general laws duly enacted by the legislature.

Structurally, the Federal Constitutional Court is divided into two chambers, called senates, each of which is composed of eight justices chosen for single 12-year terms. Half of the justices are chosen by the Bundestag's 12-member Judicial Selection Committee and the other half by the Bundesrat. A two-thirds vote is required in both electoral organs. This method of selection, together with the requirement that the Bundestag and Bundesrat alternate in the selection of the Court's president and vice president, usually means that judicial appointments are the subject of intensive bargaining both among the parliamentary parties and, occasionally, between the Bundesrat and Bundestag. No one party has been strong enough to make appointments over the objections of the other parties. Thus the Court's membership has reflected fairly well the balance of forces in parliament as a whole.

Judicial Review in Operation   The Constitutional Court's jurisdiction includes 14 categories of disputes, nearly all of which the Basic Law itself prescribes. The Basic Law authorizes both judges and legislators, as well as state governments, to petition the Court directly. Judges may initiate a "concrete" judicial review proceeding by asking the Court to rule on a constitutional question arising out of a pending case if in their view the law under which a case has arisen is of doubtful validity under the Basic Law. On the other hand, a state government or one-third of the members of the Bundestag may initiate an "abstract" proceeding by petitioning the Court to review the constitutionality of a federal or a state statute. Cases on abstract review tend to draw the judges directly into the arena of political conflict, prompting its harshest critics to deplore what they perceive as the "judicialization" of politics.

Constitutional complaints account for about 95 percent—an average of 5,000 per year between 1990 and 1995—of all cases coming to the court and for about 55 percent of its published opinions. These cases relate to fundamental rights and freedoms guaranteed by the Basic Law. To encourage Germans to view the Constitution as the source of their rights and freedoms, the Basic Law (Article 93 [13]) authorizes ordinary citizens to file complaints with the Federal Constitutional Court in the event that their basic rights have been violated by the state. (Prior to 1969, this right was conferred by statute.) Such an action involves neither court costs nor even the participation of legal counsel, an ideal situation in which "Hans Everyman" can bring his woes to the attention of the country's highest tribunal.

The Constitutional Court's Impact   Public opinion polls continue to show the high regard German citizens have for the Constitutional Court. In this respect, it outranks all other institutions in the nation's public life, including the civil service and the churches. When the Court speaks, Germany's "attentive public" listens; what people hear is often an outspoken tribunal reminding them of their constitutional values, their political morality, and their ethical goals as a nation.

The Federal Constitutional Court's landmark cases include decisions (1) outlawing the neo-Nazi Socialist Reichs Party and the former Communist Party of Germany; (2) upholding a *Land* education statute over the federal government's objection that it violated an international treaty; (3) nullifying an attempt on the part of the federal government to establish a national television station; (4) invalidating a federal statute providing for the general public financ-ing of political parties; (5) declaring a liberal abortion law unconstitutional on the ground of its interference with the right to life; (6) creating a new right of informational self-determination (after striking down parts of a federal census statute); (7) striking down the display of the crucifix in public school classrooms; (8) nullifying a law prohibiting women from working night shifts; (9) banning the application of the 5 percent clause to all of Germany in the first all-German election in 1990; and (10) invalidating a law requiring a married couple to adopt the husband's surname.[33]

KEY TERMS

abstract judicial review
Bundesrat
chancellor democracy
citizen initiatives
constructive vote of no confidence
Council of Elders
Federal Law Gazette
Fraktion
Godesberg platform
Grand Coalition
Greens
iron chancellor
new middle class
overhang votes
parliamentary state secretary
PDS
Realos
Rechtsstaat
Republicans
second ballot
semisovereign state
vertical equalization

FURTHER READINGS

Baker, Kendall, Russell J. Dalton, and Kai Hildebrand. *Germany Transformed: Political Culture and the New Politics* (Cambridge, MA: Harvard University Press, 1981).

Blair, Philip M. *Federalism and Judicial Review in West Germany* (Oxford: Clarendon Press, 1981).

Braunthal, Gerard. *The German Social Democrats since 1969*, 2nd ed. (Boulder, CO: Westview Press, 1994).

Burkett, Tony. *Parties and Elections in West Germany* (New York: St. Martin's Press, 1975).

Carr, Jonathan. *Election Year 1994: Continuity and Change in the German Political Parties* (Washington, DC: American Institute for Contemporary German Studies, 1994).

Cerny, Karl H. *Germany at the Polls: The Bundestag Elections of the 1980s* (Durham, NC: Duke University Press, 1990).

Clemens, Clay. *Reluctant Realists: The Christian Democrats and West German Ostpolitik* (Durham, NC: Duke University Press, 1989).

Dalton, Russell J. *Germans Divided: The 1994 Bundestagswahl and the Evolution of the German Party System* (Oxford and New York: Berg Publishers, 1996).

Dalton, Russell J., and Andrei S. Markovits, "Bundestagswahl 1994: The Culmination of the Superwahljahr," *German Politics and Society* (Special Issue), vol. 13 (spring 1995).

Doering, Herbert, and Gordon Smith. *Party Government and Political Culture in Western Germany* (New York: St. Martin's Press, 1982).

Dyson, Kenneth H. F. *Party, State and Bureaucracy in Western Germany* (Beverly Hills, CA: Sage Publications, 1977).

Foster, Nigel. *German Law and Legal System* (London: Blackstone Press Limited, 1993).

Gunlicks, Arthur. *Local Government in the German Federal System* (Durham, NC: Duke University Press, 1986).

Heyde, Wolfgang. *Justice and Law in the Federal Republic of Germany* (Heidelberg: C. F. Müller Juristischer Verlag, 1994).

Jesse, Eckhard. *Elections: The Federal Republic of Germany* (Oxford: Berg Publishers, 1990).

Johnson, Nevil. *State and Government in the Federal Republic of Germany*, 2nd ed. (Oxford and New York: Pergamon, 1983).

Kelly, Petra. *Fighting for Hope* (London: The Hogarth Press, 1984).

Kennedy, Ellen. *The Bundesbank* (New York: Council on Foreign Relations Press, 1991).

Kommers, Donald P. The *Federal Constitutional Court* (Washington, DC: American Institute for Contemporary German Studies, 1994).

Langguth, Gerd. *The Green Factor in West German Politics* (Boulder, CO: Westview Press, 1986).

Loewenberg, Gerhard. *Parliament in the German Political System* (Ithaca, NY: Cornell University Press, 1966).

Mayntz, Renate, and Fritz Scharpf. *Policy-making in the German Federal System* (Chapel Hill: University of North Carolina Press, 1963).

Merkl, Peter H., ed. *The Federal Republic of Germany at Forty-Five* (New York: New York University Press, 1995).

Padgett, Stephen, and Tony Burkett. *Political Parties and Elections in West Germany* (New York: St. Martin's Press, 1986).

Roberts, Geoffrey K., "Superwahljahr: The German Elections in 1994" (Special Issue), *German Politics*, vol. 4 (August 1995).

Smith, Gordon, Gordon Patterson, and Peter Merkl, eds. *Developments in West Germany Politics* (London: Macmillan Education, 1989).

Spath, Franz. *The Federal Presidency* (Washington, DC: American Institute for Contemporary German Studies, 1996).

Thaysen, Uwe. *The Bundesrat, the Länder and German Federalism* (Washington, DC: American Institute for Contemporary Germany Studies, 1994).

Thaysen, Uwe, et al. *The U.S. Congress and the German Bundestag* (Boulder, CO: Westview Press, 1990).

Public Policy

CIVIL LIBERTIES: AN ORDERING OF CONSTITUTIONAL VALUES

The first part of the Basic Law (Articles 1 to 19) is a charter of fundamental rights and an affirmation of human personhood. It is rooted in the natural law thesis that certain liberties of the individual are antecedent to organized society and beyond the reach of governmental power.

As interpreted by the Federal Constitutional Court, the Basic Law has established a value-oriented order based on human dignity. Article 1 is no idle declaration. As the Basic Law's "highest legal value," the concept of human dignity has been employed by the Constitutional Court as an independent standard of value by which to measure the legitimacy of state actions as well as the uses of individual liberty.

Feature 4.6   Basic Law: Selected Basic Rights

ARTICLE 1

1. The dignity of man shall be inviolable. To respect and protect it shall be the duty of all state authority.
2. The German people therefore acknowledge inviolable and inalienable human rights as the basis of every community, of peace and of justice in the world.

ARTICLE 2

1. Everyone shall have the right to the free development of his personality insofar as he does not violate the rights of others or offend against the constitutional order or the moral code.
2. Everyone shall have the right to life and to the inviolability of his person. The liberty of the individual shall be inviolable. These rights may be encroached upon pursuant to a law.

ARTICLE 3

1. All persons shall be equal before the law.
2. Men and women shall have equal rights. The state shall seek to ensure equal treatment of men and women and to remove existing disadvantages.
3. No one may be prejudiced or favored because of his sex, parentage, race, language, homeland and origin, faith, or religious or political opinions. Persons may not be discriminated against because of their disability.

ARTICLE 5

1. Everyone shall have the right freely to express and disseminate his opinion by speech, writing, and pictures and freely to inform himself from generally accessible sources. . . . There shall be no censorship.
2. These rights are limited by the provisions of the general laws, the provisions of law for the protection of youth, and by the right to inviolability of personal honor.

Apart from the freedoms guaranteed by Articles 1, 2, 3, and 5 (see Feature 4.5), the Basic Law's fundamental rights include the freedoms of religion (Article 4), assembly (Article 8), association (Article 9), privacy (Articles 10 and 13), and movement (Article 11), together with the right to property (Article 14), the right to choose a trade or occupation (Article 12), and the right to refuse military service for reasons of conscience (Article 12a). (Additionally, criminal defendants are accorded most of the rights and privileges normally associated with the Anglo-American notion of due process of law.) The primacy of these rights in the FRG's constitutional order is underscored by Article 19, paragraph 2, which states that "in no case may the essential content of a basic right be encroached upon."

These rights, however, have been proclaimed with an important German twist—that is, they are to be exercised responsibly and used to foster the growth of human dignity within the framework of the political and moral order ordained by the Basic Law. Article 2 is a paradigm of the German approach to basic rights. While individual liberty and personal autonomy are jealously guarded values of the legal order, they are also constrained by the equally important values of political order and social morality. Thus, the right to develop one's personality is limited by the moral code, just as the right to freedom of speech is limited by the inviolability of personal honor. As the Federal Constitutional Court noted in the Privacy of Communications Case: "The concept of man in the Basic Law is not that of an isolated, sovereign individual: rather, the Basic Law has decided in favor of a relationship between individual and community in the sense of a person's dependence on and commitment to the community, without infringing upon a person's individual value."[34]

With regard to the polity as a whole, the Basic Law creates what the Federal Constitutional Court refers to repeatedly as a "militant democracy." This means that certain forms of speech and behavior described as anticonstitutional—activities that would probably be protected under prevailing U.S. constitutional doctrine—may be legally punished. The Basic Law itself predicates political freedom on the acceptance of certain principles of political obligation.

Freedom of association, for instance, is guaranteed, but associations "the purposes or activities of which . . . are directed against the constitutional order" are prohibited (Article 9). Similarly, political parties "whose aims . . . seek to impair or abolish the free democratic basic order" may be declared unconstitutional (Article 21). These provisions spring from the abiding conviction of the Federal Republic's founders, who drafted the Basic Law in the aftermath of Weimar's collapse and Hitler's totalitarianism, that a democracy is not an unarmed society, and that it has the right to dissolve organizations and prohibit activities aimed at the destruction of republican government so long as the rule of law is thereby preserved.

ASYLUM AND CITIZENSHIP

A portrait of the FRG's civil liberties record, like that of other advanced constitutional democracies, would reveal much light and some shadows. The shadows include recent attacks on asylum seekers and foreign residents by youthful gangs and other acts of aggressive nationalism. Western observers have applauded the government for cracking down on the most xenophobic of these groups, but they find little evidence of any strong national commitment to absorbing the FRG's immigrant population into the mainstream of society. As examples of this lack of commitment, they point to German policies on asylum and citizenship.

Until 1993, Article 16 (2) of the Basic Law granted the right of asylum to all persons persecuted on political grounds, a powerful expression of the FRG's constitutional morality in the light of Germany's Nazi past. The policy behind Article 16 (2) was extremely generous. Any person arriving on German soil who claimed asylum on the ground of a well-founded fear of political persecution could have that claim adjudicated, during which time the claimant would be entitled to free housing and other benefits under German law.

In the early 1990s, however, following the influx of over a million asylum seekers, parliament introduced a constitutional amendment to limit the right of asylum. The ensuing debate took place as extreme right-wing parties won seats in a number of *Land* parliaments by pandering to popular antiforeign sentiments. Mainstream politicians, however, were also concerned about the heavy strain that asylum seekers were placing on the nation's welfare system and the presumed threat to the security of job-seeking Germans in the face of rising unemployment. In the end, parliament reincorporated the right to asylum into the first paragraph of a new Article 16a, but added several qualifying paragraphs that some critics thought would seriously vitiate that right.

According to the new article, which parliament ratified in June of 1993, aliens may not claim a right to asylum if parliament has designated their country of origin as safe from political persecution (Article 16a [3]). In addition, aliens may not claim a right to asylum if they come to Germany overland from a member state of the European Union or from a third country statutorily defined as politically safe (Article 16a [2]). If such persons fail initially to seek asylum in the safe country through which they pass en route to Germany—by land or by air—they forfeit their right to apply for asylum in Germany and thus can be summarily turned back at the border or at an international airport. Finally, aliens claiming asylum from a country of origin that has been declared safe will not have their asylum claims heard unless they can overcome by direct evidence the legislative presumption that they will not suffer political persecution or inhumane treatment upon their return.

Article 16a and its implementing statutes had their intended effect, reducing asylum applications to a fraction of their previous number. However, unsuccessful asylum seekers from Ghana, Iran, Iraq, and Togo challenged the constitutionality of the new policy's most controversial features—i.e., parliament's definition of safe countries of origin, the "third state rule," and the possibility of instant deportation at German airports. In a 234-page opinion handed down on May 14, 1996, the Court sustained the validity of each of these practices, claiming that they did not violate the Basic Law's guarantee of political asylum in that the petitioners were afforded the opportunity for asylum in secure third countries.

The asylum controversy of the 1990s was part of a larger debate over immigration and citizenship policy. The influx of refugees and the presence of millions of permanent foreign residents and their families, many of whom had lived and worked in Germany for decades, triggered demands to make it easier for resident aliens to acquire citizenship. Under the Nationality Act of 1913, which remains the law today, citizenship is based on the principle of *jus sanguinis* (i.e., by right of blood or descent rather than by *jus soli* or place of birth). Because of this policy, it is easier for a non-German speaking ethnic German from Eastern Europe to acquire German citizenship than it is for a third-generation resident alien who is fluent in the language and thoroughly privy to German ways but whose ancestors came from Turkey.

In reality, the FRG is a country of immigrants. At 8.5 percent of the population, it has more foreign residents than any other European nation. In some large cities, foreign residents exceed one-fourth of the total population. Yet these residents are not permitted to vote or run for public office, they experience discrimination in housing and education, and they are subject to deportation on specified legal grounds. Despite the de facto presence of a large immigrant population and the long-term need for such residents in light of the low native birthrate,[35] the FRG continues to understand itself in ethnocultural terms, one reason for Germany's low rate of naturalization.

Numerous proposals have been advanced to reform the citizenship and naturalization laws. They range from policies that would base citizenship on place of birth, facilitate naturalization, permit dual citizenship, grant full political rights to resident aliens, and encourage the development of a multicultural society all the way over to policies of retrenchment that would deny the legitimacy of immigration, reinforce the ethnic basis of citizenship, and reaffirm the importance of social and cultural homogeneity. SPD- and CDU-led governments at both national and state levels have taken a centrist position, with the SPD generally advocating a policy of integrating ethnic minorities into the FRG's social and economic system, whereas the CDU has tended to encourage the return of recent minorities to their countries of origin while offering citizenship to long-term residents on proof of full cultural assimilation.

The current law is closer to the position of the ruling CDU-CSU-FDP coalition. Legislation enacted in 1991 permitted naturalization after ten years of residence in the FRG, but only on condition of full assimilation into German society and renunciation of dual citizenship. Even then, admission to citizenship could be denied at the discretion of administrative officials unconvinced that naturalization would be in the state's best interest. In 1993, additional amendments to the Nationality Act narrowed the discretion of state officials and granted certain categories of immigrants a right to become naturalized citizens. But these reforms are unlikely to increase the rate of naturalization substantially in the light of strong resistance both to multiculturalism and dual citizenship.

PUBLIC ADMINISTRATION: DECENTRALIZED FEDERALISM

There are five levels of public administration in Germany, organized mainly on a spatial or territorial basis.[36] The first of course is the national level. But here, (except for those few functions administered directly by the national government), the various ministries are engaged mainly in formulating general policy. Under Article 65 of the Basic Law, each federal minister is in complete control of his or her department, though it must be run within the limits of the chancellor's policy guidelines. The command hierarchy includes the federal minister, the parliamentary state secretary (the ministry's chief spokesperson in the Bundestag), and the permanent state secretary—a career civil servant who, along with aides, plays a significant rule in the policy-making process. Finally, undersecretaries head the major departments of each ministry, which in turn are divided into sections, offices, or bureaus.

The ministries work out their programs in accordance with the general policy guidelines and political predispositions of their top executives. Yet the ministries do not shape policy by issuing central directives from on high any more than they shape it from the bottom up on the basis of purely professional considerations. The planning units of the various ministries weave their program recommendations out of clientele demands, the expertise of bureaucrats, and the political orientation of top executives. In general, policy planning is more of an interactive process, following what Mayntz and Scharpf call a "dialogue model" of policymaking,[37] involving a good deal of discussion and bargaining within and among bureaucracies.

Land governments are the next level of administration. In addition to administering federal law as a matter of their own concern, they enact laws in certain areas within the framework of national policy guidelines and in areas of their exclusive jurisdiction. Public policies at the *Land* level are carried out by *Land* ministries, various functional *Land* agencies, and several self-governing corporations. The last three levels of administration are the administrative district, counties and county-free independent cities, and municipalities. The administrative district (*Regierungsbezirk*), found in the six larger *Länder*, "is a general purpose regional *Land* institution of administration."[38] The county, at the lowest level of *Land* administration, carries out functions delegated to it by state governments. Finally, municipalities or associations of local governments, whose independence is also guaranteed by the Basic Law, are responsible, within the framework of *Land* law, for the provision of local public services.

SOCIAL AND ECONOMIC POLICY

Fiscal Policy

The fiscal articles of the Basic Law (Articles 104a through Article 115l) mandate a system of revenue sharing among the federation, *Länder*, and local governments, the administration of which requires close cooperation among levels of government. Total tax revenue in 1993 amounted to DM 748.8 billion, of which federal and state shares were each 42.5 percent and that of municipalities 15 percent. The federal government derives its tax revenues mainly from corporate and personal income taxes, the value added tax, the turnover tax on imports, and selected excise taxes. (It has exclusive rights to taxes on mineral oils, tobacco, insurance, and hard liquor.) The main source of *Land* revenue is from taxes on property, automobiles, beer, and inheritance, whereas local governments depend primarily on real estate and business taxes. In addition, *Land* and local governments draw a portion of their tax revenue from income, turnover, and value added taxes.

The goal of German fiscal policy is to bring about a "unity of living standards" in the various *Länder* and throughout the FRG. This is the reason for the detailed revenue-sharing provisions of the Basic Law. Income, corporate, and turnover taxes are among the tax receipts shared between levels of government. Federal and state governments have an equal claim to these funds after local governments have received their share. In addition, federal and state governments are constitutionally bound to help each other financially. Under so-called vertical equalization procedures, the federal government redistributes a given proportion of its revenues to the poorer states, just as equivalent horizontal procedures require the wealthier states to share a portion of their revenues with poorer *Länder*. The exact sharing arrangements are set forth in law and subject to review by the Federal Constitutional Court.

The new eastern *Länder* did not participate in the revenue-sharing scheme until 1995. The Unity Treaty exempted the new *Länder* from the fiscal provisions of the Basic Law for five years, during which time it was hoped that their deficient economies and substandard social structures could be repaired. In the interim, federation and *Länder* agreed to establish an off-budget plan known as the "German Unity Fund." Under this plan, billions of DM were transferred annually to the eastern *Länder*, 80 percent of which was raised in capital markets and the rest supplied from the federal budget.

General Economic Policy

The FRG is noted for its *Sozialmarktwirtschaft* or "social market economy" (SME), a system of free enterprise guided and supported by the strong hand of government and undergirded by a comprehensive scheme of social welfare. In this way, Germany has managed to avoid the extremes of a pure laissez-faire economy and centralized state control (see Feature 4.7).

German federalism has made its own distinctive contribution to the growth of the SME. As Christopher Allen notes, *Land* governments encouraged banks to adjust "their investment and loan policies to improve the competitive position of key industries in various regions" and to "invest heavily in vocational education to provide the skills so necessary for high quality manufactured goods" capable of competing in world markets.[39] *Land* governments also worked closely with business and organized labor, not only to encourage the development of a modern, competitive economy, but also to shape the framework of cooperation among trade unions, corporations, banks, and educational institutions, a process of coordination matched at the national level by such major policy initiatives as the Economic Stabilization Act of 1967 and the Codetermination Act of 1975.

The Codetermination Act The issue of codetermination offers an excellent example of

---

Feature 4.7 **The Social Market Economy**

An outgrowth of German neoliberal and Catholic social thought, the social market economy is predicated on the belief that a free market is compatible with a socially conscious state. It seeks to combine the principles of personal freedom and social responsibility in a unified political economy. The production of goods and services, according to the theory, is to be left to free choice in an open market, but the marketplace is to function within a social framework created by law. This framework includes general public policies designed to enhance competition, ensure honest trade practices, and protect consumers. It is also government's duty in neoliberal economic theory to stabilize the economy as a whole and to care for the needs of persons not served by the market.

the usual pattern of politics and policy in post-war Germany, one that encourages bargaining and mutual partisan adjustment among state agencies, private groups, and political parties, particularly those in the governing coalition. Here the main actors in the process of consultation were interests representing labor and management within and outside the political parties. Codetermination has roots far back in German history. Already in the 1840s workers were demanding a voice in shaping the conditions of their labor. Their influence was gradually solidified and augmented through a series of acts in the late 1800s and the first few decades of the 1900s, so that by 1922 employees were legally entitled to at least one representative on factory management boards. The progress of workers' rights received a brief setback under the Nazi regime, but following the war all the German *Länder* reestablished work councils—employee groups designed to offer proposals to management—and gave them varying degrees of influence in determining company policies relating to production and operating methods.

Current codetermination policy is based on the Works Constitution Act of 1952 and its successor, the Works Constitution Act of 1972. The 1952 act established one-third employee representation on the management boards of all private industries employing between 500 and 2,000 workers (a principle that was later extended to the public sector), and its 1972 replacement authorized every factory or business with more than five employees to elect a work council to bargain with plant managers over issues not dealt with in collective bargaining agreements.

Finally, in 1976, after four more years of struggle and compromise among various parliamentary groups, an overwhelming majority of the Bundestag passed the Codetermination Act, underscoring the consensus achieved during several years of negotiation. This act extended the principle of numerical parity, requiring equal representation of workers on company supervisory boards, to include all enterprises with more than 2,000 employees, affecting about 7 million workers in more than 500 firms. It did this by providing for 12- to 20-member supervisory boards, depending on the size of the plant, with an equal number of shareholders and rep-

resentatives from the work force, the latter to include delegations elected separately by blue-collar, white-collar, and managerial staff.

Although the unions were not entirely pleased with the allocation of seats on the boards or with the provision that allows the chairperson—usually a shareholder—to break a tie vote, it nevertheless gave them a significant foothold in the industrial decision-making process. Not long after the act's passage, it was challenged in the Federal Constitutional Court on grounds that it violated the rights to property, association, and entrepreneurial freedom (Articles 14, 9, and 12 of the Basic Law). But the Court cautiously upheld the act, suggesting that codetermination is a legitimate application of the constitutional ideal of a "social federal state" (Article 20) based on law, and codetermination remains official German policy.

The example of codetermination illustrates the institutionalized process of bargaining among various interests that create policy in the FRG, a process requiring extensive cooperation, consultation, and compromise. This filtering process through the FRG's decentralized political system means that a large degree of consensus is necessary before any real movement in public policy can be achieved. This is why policy change in the FRG has been aptly described as *incremental* rather than *large-scale*, even in the face of major shifts in electoral politics.

Economic Stabilization Act   Until the mid–1960s, German economic policy contained a strong antiplanning bias. With the adoption of the Economic Stabilization Act, however, long-term fiscal planning became a vital element of the FRG's economy. Influenced in part by Keynesian economic theory, the act authorized the federal government (1) to coordinate the budgetary policies of state and national governments, (2) to change, temporarily, rates of taxation on personal and corporate incomes without prior parliamentary approval, (3) to stimulate the economy during periods of recession by public expenditures up to specified amounts, and (4) to harmonize general fiscal policy with monetary policy.

Here, too, as with codetermination, an enormous amount of cooperation is required within and among various governmental and nongovernmental bodies to make the Stabilization Act work. A Fiscal Planning Commission (FPC) consisting of federal and state representatives, as well as representatives from the Federal Bank (Bundesbank), business, and the political parties, was formed to coordinate budgetary policy between the national government and the *Länder*. Over the years, the FPC has contributed to the development of fiscal policy by drawing up draft budgets for national and state governments, by laying down guidelines for rates of economic growth, by devising plans for coordinating tax policy with cuts in expenditures, and by making sure that federal and state policies complement rather than contradict each other.[40]

Social Welfare Policy

In 1993 Germany spent nearly 35 percent of its GNP on social services—among the highest in Western Europe. Social policy expenditures of all governmental levels amounted to approximately 47 percent of total governmental expenditures. As Figure 4.2 shows, the FRG's social welfare system draws upon a long tradition of state-supported social policies. The current system includes generous programs of health insurance, unemployment compensation, industrial accident insurance, retirement pensions, housing benefits, and youth welfare programs (see Feature 4.8). Old-age pensions, the largest of these programs—they accounted for 30 percent of the social budget in 1990—are financed by contributions from the insured and their employers. Adjusted to inflation and other economic indicators, social security payments have increased nearly every year since 1957. (By 1990 recipients who had contributed to the system for 35 years were entitled to pensions close to 75 percent of their pre-retirement income.) The system of benefits also includes relief payments for the needy, child benefit allowances, rent subsidies for old-age pensioners, vocational rehabilitation services, nursing care for the aged, and special reparations for former prisoners of war and persons who suffered losses under Nazism because of their race, religion, or political beliefs.

After unification, the FRG's social policy, like other economic programs, was extended to the new Eastern *Länder*. Social benefits, however, particularly unemployment pay and retire-

ment pensions, were adjusted to eastern economic standards and would not reach Western levels until the East achieved economic parity with the West. Even so, these benefits resulted in significant increases in pensions for East Germans who were also given the option of retiring at 57 years of age at 75 percent of their former gross pay. West Germany would bear most of the social costs for health and welfare, although some advantages associated with the GDR's old system, such as the 20 weeks of paid leave women were entitled to after giving birth, were phased out. The costs of these programs were met in part by large transfers of public funds from the federal and state governments.

Summary

As noted earlier, social welfare policy in postwar Germany has been the product of consensus politics. The CDU, SPD, business organizations, and labor unions can all take some credit for Germany's comprehensive and generous system of social insurance and welfare benefits. The system represents not only a longstanding accord between these groups but also a social compact between the generations. In 1996, however, the CDU-CSU-FDP coalition proposed substantial cuts in corporate taxes and social spending, including plans to raise the retirement age for both men and women, in order to spur economic growth, facilitate job creation, and reduce a public debt aggravated by the high costs of reunification. In response, union leaders organized a massive protest demonstration in Bonn; they attacked the "savings package" as an assault on the social market economy and as a threat to the time-honored consensus between labor, management, and government. For its part the SPD, in alliance with labor, intensified its opposition to these measures in the hope of forcing the government into compromises that would maintain current social policies and restore "social peace" as well.

Even if the governing coalition succeeds in passing its "savings package" into law, the FRG's social economy will continue to be less centralized than the French or the British and notably more sensitive socially than the American. Government ownership of industry and intervention in the market determination of goods

Sphere of Social Policy	1881–1918	1918–1933	1933–1945	1949–1993
Employee Protection	1891: Employee Protection Act 1901: Child Protection Act	1918: Regulation of Industrial Employees' Working Hours 1927: Maternity Leave Act	1935: Maternity Benefit Act 1938: Youth Protection Act	1951: Employment Protection Act 1952: Maternity Protection Act 1960: Act to Protect Employed Young Persons 1963: Federal Holidays Act 1971: Pupils', Students', and Kindergarten Children's Accident Insurance
Social Insurance	1883: Employees' Health Insurance Act 1884: Accident Insurance Act 1889: Invalidity and Retirement Insurance Act 1911: National Insurance Regulations	1923: National Miner's Guild Act 1927: Unemployment Insurance and Employment Exchange Act	1938: Act for Retirement Provision in German Handicraft Trades	1957: Act to Reform Retirement Pensions 1957: Retirement Provisions in Agriculture 1965–1968: Retirement Pension Reform 1972: Health Insurance in Agriculture 1972: Retirement Pension Reform 1982: Health Insurance Reform 1984: Early Retirement Act 1984: Hospital Reform Act 1992: Retirement Pension Reform 1993: Health Service Reform
Labour Market Policy		1918: Collective Bargaining Regulation 1920: Establishment of a National Office for Employment Exchanges (Regulations) 1922: Employment Exchange Act 1923: Regulation of Arbitration System	1933: Employment Trustees' Act 1934: Act to Regulate National Employment 1934: Act to Control the Deployment of the Labour Force	1949: Collective Bargaining Act 1952: Establishment of Minimum Working Conditions Act 1969: Employment Promotion Act 1985–1986: Work Promotion Act
Establishment and Company Constitution Policy	1916: Auxiliary Service Act	1920: Works Council Act 1922: Representation of Works Councillors Executive Boards Act		1951: Codetermination (Coal, Iron, and Steel) Act 1952: Company Constitution Act 1955: Personnel Representation (Public Service) Act 1972: Company Constitution Act 1976: Codetermination Act
Social Welfare and Social Assistance		1922: Youth Welfare Act 1924: Principles of Public Welfare Activities		1961: Federal Social Assistance Act 1961: Youth Welfare Act 1974: Disabled Persons Act
Family Policy			1935: Regulations to Provide Child Benefits to Large Families	1954: Child Benefits Act 1979: Maternity Leave 1985–1986: Child Rearing Assistance 1991: Maternity Leave
Housing Policy				1950: House Building Act 1952: House Building Incentives Act 1964–1965: Rent Rebate Act
Wealth-Formation Policy				1959: Savings Incentives Act 1961: Act to Promote Asset Creation
Vocational Training Policy				1969: Vocational Training Act 1971: Federal Vocational and Education Promotion Act 1981: Vocational Training Promotion Act

Figure 4.2   Schematic Expression of Basic Social Policy Acts

Source: Eric Owen Smith, *The German Economy* (London and New York: Routledge, 1994), p. 199.

and services are still other features of the social market economy, although in the 1990s the government has begun to divest itself of ownership in areas such as transportation and postal services. In addition, the federal government owns stock in nearly 500 companies, but here too it has proceeded to denationalize some of them. On the other hand, several state governments have subsidized certain industries either for the purpose of reviving them or to keep them from moving their plants to other states or countries.

FOREIGN POLICY AND THE ROAD TO UNITY

The "German Problem" and *Ostpolitik*

One aspect of the "German problem" was the simple yet age-old one of how to define Germany. This problem remained at the center of East-West conflict for two decades following World War II. It was a problem involving the FRG's relationship to the German Democratic Republic (GDR) and Eastern Europe. West German rearmament within the North Atlantic Treaty Organization (NATO), coupled with the refusal under a succession of Christian Democratic governments to recognize the Oder-Neisse

line as a permanent boundary between Poland and Germany, was viewed by the Soviet Union as a dangerous threat to peace in Central Europe. The city of Berlin represented still another component of the German problem. Cleft by concrete and barbed wire and later by the infamous wall, the city had become the most poignant living symbol of German separation and East-West confrontation.

There clearly could be no resolution of the German problem without a relaxation of tension in Central Europe. Moscow was the key to any such resolution. It is significant that both Adenauer and Brandt journeyed to the Soviet Union—the former in 1955, the latter in 1970—in search of "normalized" relations between Bonn and Moscow. For Adenauer, however, normalization meant the reestablishment of diplomatic relations with the Soviet Union, which he accomplished, and the reunification of Germany, which he failed to achieve. In his Moscow talks, he spoke of the "abnormality" of Germany's division, leaving his Soviet hosts with the message that "there can be no real security in Europe without the restoration of German unity." A decade and a half later, with Germany still divided, Willy Brandt appeared before a Soviet television audience, redefining *normalization*. He announced that "it is now time to reconstitute our relationship to the

---

Feature 4.8 Germany's Social Code

1. Purposes of the Social Code [*Sozialgesetzbuch*]

(1) The provisions of the Social Code are intended to provide for social benefits, including social and educational assistance, with the object of making social justice and social security a reality. Its aim is to contribute to ensuring an existence worthy of human beings; providing equal opportunities for the free development of the personality, especially for young persons; protecting and encouraging the family; enabling persons to derive a livelihood through freely chosen activity; and averting or compensating for special burdens in life, *inter alia*, by helping persons to help themselves.

(2) The provisions of the Social Code are also intended to contribute to ensuring that the social services and institutions required to achieve the purposes specified in subsection (1) are available at the proper time and on the proper scale.

Source: Social Code (*Sozialgesetzbuch*), The Federal Minister of Labor and Social Affairs (Translation by International Labor Organization) Bonn, 1981; BGBl., I, 1975, 3015.

East upon the basis of the unrestricted, reciprocal renunciation of force, proceeding from the existing political situation in Europe."

Brandt's Eastern policy (*Ostpolitik*) was designed to achieve this result. The cornerstone of the new policy was the Soviet–West German treaty on the renunciation of the use of force, signed in Moscow in August 1970. The Warsaw Treaty, signed in November of the same year, rounded out the foundation of detente. Essentially, these treaties recognized existing boundaries in Europe, including the Oder-Neisse line separating the GDR and Poland. Another stone in Brandt's rising edifice of detente was the 1971 Quadripartite Agreement on Berlin. In fact, Brandt conditioned Bonn's ratification of the Moscow and Warsaw treaties upon progress toward settlement of the Berlin question. Pledging to settle all their disputes by peaceful means, the four powers reaffirmed their individual and joint responsibility for Berlin. While the Soviet Union acknowledged the special ties between West Berlin and the FRG, the Western Allies deferred to the Soviet contention that West Berlin was not "a constituent part of the Federal Republic and not to be governed by it."

The capstone of detente was the Basic Treaty between East and West Germany, signed in December 1972. The FRG and GDR both agreed to develop normal relations with each other on the basis of equal rights. The concept of "two German states in one nation," which the FRG urged on the GDR, was conspicuously left out of the treaty. Instead, the right of both German states to "territorial integrity" and "self-determination" was affirmed, along with an agreement "to refrain from the threat or use of force." In addition, the two states agreed that "neither . . . can represent the other in the international spheres or act on its behalf." In supplementary protocols both states also agreed to settle their frontier problems, to improve trade relations, and to cooperate in scientific, technological, medical, cultural, athletic, and environmental fields.

Gorbachev and *Glasnost*

The advent of Gorbachev in the Soviet Union and the associated policies of *glasnost* (openness) and *perestroika* (reform) placed East-West relations in a new light and encouraged many Germans to think once again about the prospects of eventual reunification. GDR leaders, however, remained adamant in their view of the Basic Treaty as a step toward a fully sovereign and independent GDR—an interpretation the FRG had never accepted. Unlike Poland and Hungary and the Soviet Union itself, the GDR refused to move toward democracy or free markets. The hard-liners in charge of the regime—most of them old men—brooked no opposition to the socialist system of their creation. By 1989, however, as thousands of young GDR citizens fled to the FRG by way of Hungary in search of freedom and employment, GDR leaders seemed to be standing alone, isolated in their own backyard. They accused Hungary of violating various legal treaties and denounced the FGR for encouraging the exodus, but these charges were seen for what they were: feeble attempts to hide the fragility of a regime deeply in trouble in the face of a "new order" emerging in Eastern Europe.

The GDR was impaled on the horns of an excruciating dilemma. It could either loosen up the regime and allow the free movement of its people in and out of the country or continue on its present course. The first option would lead to greater contact between East and West Germans and intensify the desire for reunification. The second option—keeping a tight grip on its people—would lead to another crisis of legitimacy and to the continued flight of its most productive citizens. With the collapse of the hard-line Communist regime in October 1989 a hastily reassembled government under younger and more pragmatic leadership chose the first option. In the following weeks, events unfolded with dizzying speed, surprising and confounding even close observers of German affairs (see Feature 4.9). By the end of the year the Communist Party had disavowed its leading role, promised to hold free elections in the months ahead, and exposed the corruption of its long-time leaders as an increasingly angry and outspoken citizenry demanded their prosecution. In the meantime, the Brandenburg Gate flew open, GDR citizens waved FRG flags in the streets, and East and West German leaders began to talk about a new relationship against the backdrop of Chancellor Helmut

Kohl's controversial ten-point plan for German reunification.

The Progress and Politics of German Unity

The story of German unity is a fascinating tale. On the one hand, the story seems to show that the forces of history, once unleashed, cannot be stopped. On the other hand, unity would not have come about without the cooperation of the Allied powers, especially the United States and the Soviet Union, and the intense negotiations between the GDR and FRG. Although the FRG held most of the trump cards in these negotiations, the GDR managed to extract significant promises from the FRG, including some changes in the Basic Law. The negotiations between the GDR and FRG, and those between Britain, France, the Soviet Union, and the United States, did not proceed on separate tracks. They were conducted—in coordinated simultaneous fashion—over many months; hence, the common reference to the *two-plus-four* talks. This mix of international and domestic politics, with its interplay of constitutional law and public policy, made the new Germany possible.

Several months earlier, Chancellor Kohl had proposed a ten-point plan for Germany's eventual union (see Feature 4.10). He had envisioned the development of a *contractual community* in which the two Germanys would establish confederative structures leading first to social, monetary, and economic union and eventually, perhaps in a few years, to political union. Events, however, overtook him as well as those East German reform groups who pre-ferred the building of a humane socialism in the GDR over reunification. The "bloodless coup" occurred on March 18, 1990, when East Germans voted in their first free election since Hitler was named chancellor in 1933. Unity *now* was their unmistakable message. Fired up, and with Chancellor Kohl at the controls, the "unity train" roared toward its destination. One possible route to reunification was the election and formation of a new all-German government under the terms of a new constitution ratified by all Germans. Instead, East Germany agreed to become part of the existing FRG under the simple procedure of accession laid down in Article 23 of the Basic Law.

Four landmarks paved the way to reunification. These are the State Treaty on Monetary, Economic, and Social Union (May 18, 1990), the All-German Election Treaty (August 3, 1990), the Unity Treaty (August 31, 1990), and the Treaty on the Final Settlement with Respect to Germany (September 12, 1990). The GDR and the FRG negotiated the first three treaties, but often in consultation with the Allies; the last was the product mainly of the two-plus-four negotiations.

The State Treaty   The State Treaty united the social, economic, and monetary systems of East and West.[41] It effectively extended the FRG's social market economy eastward, installing in all of Germany an economy based on private ownership, competition, and the free movement of goods and services. As of July 2, 1990, the West German deutche mark became the official currency of the GDR. Under the terms of the Treaty, "[w]ages, salaries, grants,

---

Feature 4.9   An Indivisible Nation

On the night of October 2–3, 1990, East and West Germans came together on the great lawn before the Reichstag (the *Platz der Republik*) to celebrate their reunification. Many of them flew the black-red-gold flag of the FRG, which had been the tricolor of the two previous German democracies as well (1848 and 1918). Germany was felt to be reclaiming the best elements of its common past. At the same time, a good number of European Community flags were also in evidence, with the circle of 12 gold stars on a field of blue, seeming to reflect the often-stated aim of the two societies to work together henceforth—not for a "German Europe" but for a "European Germany."

Feature 4.10   The Path to German Unity

1989

July–September	GDR citizens flee to the FRG by way of Hungary.
October 9	100,000 persons demonstrate in Leipzig to the chant, "We are the people."
October 18	Honecker is removed as head of the GDR.
November 7	GDR government resigns after 1 million persons demonstrate in Berlin.
November 9	Berlin Wall is breached.
November 28	Chancellor Kohl announces a ten-point program for unity.
December 1	GDR Constitution amended to end the SED's monopoly of power.

1990

March 18	First free election in GDR. Overwhelming victory for parties allied with the CDU.
April 12	GDR legislature elects first democratic government. Lothar de Maiziere elected prime minister.
May 18	State Treaty on Monetary, Economic, and Social Union.
July 22	GDR legislature reestablishes its five constituent states.
August 3	All-German Election Treaty signed.
August 31	Unity Treaty signed.
September 12	Two Plus Four Treaty signed.
October 3	Day of German unity. GDR ceases to exist.
October 4	First all-German legislature meets in the Berlin Reichstag building.
October 24	Five eastern states elect new parliaments.
December 2	First all-German Bundestag elections.

---

pensions, rents and leases as well as other recurring payments shall be converted at a rate of one [east German] to one [west German mark]." All other claims and assets were to be converted at a rate of two to one. One effect of the currency union was to increase the importance of Germany's central bank, already renowned for its control over monetary policy in the FRG.[42] The bank would now take responsibility for all of Germany and sorely test its capacity to fight inflation in the face of price rises that were surely to occur from the transfer of billions of deutche marks into the east.

The State Treaty covered other areas such as intra-German and foreign trade, agriculture, environmental protection, social and health insurance, pension plans, budgetary planning, revenue administration, and tax policy. For each of these areas, the treaty required the GDR to adopt laws consistent with policies prevailing in the FRG. In some instances, however, transitional arrangements were worked out to ease the pain of the legal and structural changes that the GDR would have to make. One of these temporary arrangements was the establishment of an arbitration tribunal to resolve GDR-FRG disputes arising under the treaty in the event that they could not be settled by negotiation.

The All-German Election Treaty The GDR election of March 18, 1990, set the stage for the all-German election of December 2, 1990. The March election resulted in an impressive victory for the CDU-led Alliance for Germany and thus for German unity. The new People's chamber went on to create a grand coalition consisting of the Alliance for Germany, the SPD, and the Federation of Free Democrats under the leadership of Lothar de Maiziere (CDU). It was this coalition that negotiated the unity treaties with Bonn's CDU-FDP coalition government, one of which was the All-German Election Treaty. The GDR, which had a system of pure proportional representation, objected to the FRG's 5 percent clause, expecting that it would keep smaller parties out of a new all-German parliament. Negotiations led to an agreement that would retain the 5 percent clause for all of Germany, but provided for an arrangement that would permit smaller parties and groups in the GDR to field candidates in alliance with other, larger parties in the west. This plan, however, favored some small parties at the expense of others. In response to petitions by the PDS, Greens, and the far-right Republicans, the Federal Constitutional Court held that the election agreement discriminated against these parties, and it went on to recommend that for this first all-German election the 5 percent clause should be adopted separately in both East and West. An amended election law followed this recommendation. (See Section B for a discussion of the first all-German election.)

The Unity Treaty The Unity Treaty—a massive document consisting of 433 printed pages—was the historic agreement that provided for the GDR's accession to the FRG and the application of the Basic Law to all of Germany. Its 45 articles, annexes, and special provisions touched almost every aspect of German public policy. The treaty's "Special Provisions on the Conversion to Federal Law" appeared in 19 chapters that dealt with the laws, procedures, and institutions subject to the jurisdiction of the various federal ministries. While extending FRG law immediately to numerous policy areas in the eastern *Länder*, these special provisions also contained transitional and interim measures that sought to accommodate the special interests of or conditions in the ex-GDR.

Constitutional Amendments The Unity Treaty amended several provisions of the Basic Law. First, the preamble was amended to delete all references to the goal of reunification, for "Germans in [the sixteen *Länder*] have [now] achieved the unity and freedom of Germany in free self-determination." This new language effectively froze Germany's present borders, making it legally impossible for Germany to lay claim to other territories lost as a result of World War II. Second, and to the same end, the treaty repealed Article 23—the very provision under which the GDR acceded to the FRG. In short, no "other parts of Germany" were left to be incorporated into the FRG by accession. Third, the treaty added the following italicized words to Article 146: "This Basic Law, *which is valid for the entire German people following the achievement of the unity and freedom of Germany*, shall cease to be in force on the day on which a constitution adopted by a free decision of the German people comes into force." Fourth, Article 135a was amended to relieve the FRG of certain liabilities incurred by the GDR or its legal entities. Finally, the treaty changed the number of votes allocated to the states in the Bundesrat under the terms of Article 51.

In addition to these amendments, the Unity Treaty inserted a new article—Article 143—into the Basic Law. The new article allowed the all-German government to deal flexibly with issues that might otherwise have slowed down or even stopped the unity train. Abortion, property rights, and intergovernmental relations were among these issues. The eastern *Länder*, for example, were unable to abide by the revenue-sharing provisions of the Basic Law or other obligations growing out of its scheme of federal-state relations. Allowing the East to deviate from these provisions was a practical necessity, and there appeared to be no constitutional objection to this particular deviation clause.

Abortion The deviation clause of Article 143 (1), however, was another matter. Its incorporation into the Unity Treaty represented a compromise between East and West over abortion. In 1975, the Federal Constitutional Court struck down West Germany's liberalized abortion law, holding that it violated the right to life within the meaning of Article 2 (1) of the Basic Law as well as the principle of human dignity that the state is duty-bound "to respect and protect" under Article 1 (1).[43] In so ruling, the Court obligated the state to make abortion a crime at all stages of pregnancy subject to exceptions specified by law. The GDR, on the other hand, permitted abortion on demand within the first three months of pregnancy. The effect of Article 143 was to allow East and West Germany to follow their respective policies on abortion. The FRG conceded this much to the GDR. But the treaty also required the Bundestag to enact an all-German policy on abortion by the end of 1992 "to ensure better protection of unborn life and provide a better solution in conformity with the Constitution of conflict situations faced by pregnant women" (Article 31 [4]). This was the GDR's concession to the West.

These concessions, however, raised a difficult constitutional issue, for Article 143 bans deviations from the Basic Law in violation of Articles 19 (2) and 79 (3): The first flatly prohibits any encroachment on a basic right; the second bars any amendment to the Basic Law contravening principles laid down in Articles 1 (protecting "human dignity") and 20 (enshrining the rule of law). The constitutional issue was whether the deviation clause encroached upon the principle of human dignity with respect to abortion. In addition, may a treaty suspend the application of a Constitutional Court ruling authoritatively defining the meaning of this principle? These questions remained unanswered in 1991 as the Bundestag heatedly debated a number of abortion reform proposals. In the end, a compromise law was passed that decriminalized abortions performed during the first trimester of pregnancy, although in a subsequent ruling the Federal Constitutional Court required women contemplating abortions to submit to strong pro-life counseling before making their final decision.

Property   The deviation clause of Article 143 (1) was also designed to deal with the problem of property rights. On June 15, 1990, the GDR and FRG governments signed a Joint Declaration on the Settlement of Open Property Issues. This agreement provided that all property taken by the GDR's Communist government between 1949 and 1989, including expropriated businesses and property placed under state administration, was to be returned to their rightful owners. Compensation would be paid in the event that property could not be returned. The

treaty contained one exception to this policy of restitution: Expropriated property would not be returned to their former owners if needed for investment purposes—a rule applied mainly to factories and large businesses—if innocently acquired by third parties, or if incapable of being returned in its original form. In each case, however, compensation would be forthcoming.

The most controversial of the Unity Treaty's property-settlement provisions was the exclusion from restitution of property expropriated by the Soviet Union in eastern Germany between 1945 and 1949. The Soviet Union had seized all land holdings over 250 acres and distributed most of them to small farmers. Prime Minister de Maiziere refused to undo these takings. For one thing, any return of these millions of acres to their former owners would have caused enormous social unrest in the east. For another, the Soviet Union insisted on the exclusion. Yet the right to property, the rule of law, and equality under law are core values of the Basic Law. Accordingly, former owners of land in the east, invoking these values, challenged the 1945–1949 exclusion in the Constitutional Court. In this instance, however, the achievement of unity—one of the Basic Law's highest values—outbalanced the right to property in the form of its restoration. Furthermore, said the Court, the 1945–1949 takings occurred before the Basic Law entered into force.

Other Treaty Provisions   The Unity Treaty provided for the creation of a special trust agency (*Treuhandanstalt*) charged with privatizing East German businesses and industries, and revised the constitutional formula for intergovernmental revenue sharing. In addition, all property and assets owned by the GDR, including the special funds of its railway and postal systems, would become the property of the FRG. Several provisions dealt with the status or continuing validity of GDR treaties, court decisions, and administrative rulings, most of which were to remain in effect unless incompatible with the Basic Law or federal law. GDR school certificates, university degrees, and titles were to retain their validity, although only in the eastern *Länder*, whereas judges and civil servants would be required to submit to recredentialing procedures. The treaty also required the former GDR to adopt EEC regulations, to maintain the church tax, and to decentralize cultural, educational, and athletic institutions. The German government would also be responsible for "rehabilitati[ng the] victims of the iniquitous SED regime" obliging it to sponsor "appropriate arrangements for compensation" (Article 17). In this connection, and at the insistence of the GDR, the 6 million files of the disbanded state security policy (*Stasi*) were to remain in the ex-GDR until an all-German parliament could enact a law regarding their storage and access. GDR officials were interested in keeping control of the files and allowing public access to them. The FRG, on the other hand, wanted them moved west and kept under the control of federal security police.

The Two Plus Four Treaty After seven months of negotiation, the four wartime Allies and the two Germanys signed the treaty that finally closed the books on the Second World War.[44] The Allied powers relinquished all their occupation rights and restored full sovereignty to a united Germany. Under the treaty, the new Germany (1) accepted its present boundaries and guaranteed the border with Poland; (2) renounced aggressive warfare as well as the production and use of biological, chemical, and nuclear weapons; and (3) agreed to reduce its armed forces (ground, air, and naval forces) to 370,000, to allow Soviet troops to remain in the ex-GDR until 1995, and to finance their return to the Soviet Union. Germany also agreed to ban any NATO presence in the East while Soviet troops remained there. A major Soviet concession was to allow the FRG to choose its military alliance.

Finally, in a supplementary letter to the Allied foreign ministers, Foreign Minister Hans-Dietrich Genscher and Prime Minister Lothar de Maiziere noted that Germany would abide by the June 15, 1990 Joint Resolution excluding property expropriated between 1945 and 1949 from the general terms of the Unity Treaty. They also pledged on behalf of Germany to preserve monuments to war victims erected on German soil and to maintain war graves. The two German leaders also declared that in united Germany "the free democratic basic order will be protected by the Constitution. It provides the basis," they continued, "for ensuring that parties which, by reason of their aims or the behav-

ior of their adherents, seek to impair or abolish the free democratic basic order as well as associations which are directed against the constitutional order or the concept of international understanding can be prohibited." This language was taken directly from Article 21 of the Basic Law, which authorizes the Federal Constitutional Court to pronounce antidemocratic parties unconstitutional. Thus reunited Germany would also be a "fighting democracy."

Post-Unification Foreign Policy

The novelist Günter Grass opposed unification because, as he put it, "we Germans would become, once again, something to be feared" and "our neighbors would draw away from us with distrust," for a "reunited Germany would be a colossus loaded with complexes, standing in its own way and in the way of European integration."[45] The FRG's political leaders, however, proceeded forthwith to reassure their eastern neighbors that Germany would honor all treaties respecting its present boundaries and obligations to the European Union. This reassurance was reinforced in March of 1991 by the Treaty Between the Federal Republic of Germany and the Union of Soviet Socialist Republics on Good Neighborliness, Partnership and Cooperation. In this treaty the two countries pledged to "respect each other's sovereign equality, territorial integrity and political independence." Most important, they declared their unqualified adherence to "the territorial integrity of all States in Europe within their present frontiers" and "that they have no territorial claims whatsoever against any State and will not raise any in the future."

The FRG has adhered to these principles even in the face of the Warsaw Pact's dissolution, the breakup of the Soviet Union, and the collapse of Communism in Eastern Europe. With the approval of the old Soviet Union, reunited Germany was able to remain a member of NATO's military alliance. In addition to its continued adherence to NATO, the central pillars of German foreign policy support the further growth of European unity, an enlarged role for the United Nations in protecting human rights around the world, the further integration of the European and North American

---

Feature 4.11 **Foreign Policy**

Together with the Americans, we will promote closer cooperation among NATO, the EU, the WEU and the OSCE to tighten Europe's network of cooperative security. No new divisions must emerge in Europe, and there must be no relapses into the conflicts of old. It is therefore crucial to make Russia a part of this security architecture. Russia must have a special security relationship with NATO as well as a close political and economic partnership with the European Union. Within the OSCE, we must strive for the highest possible cooperation. The ghastly war in former Yugoslavia is still the acid test for the new, post-Cold War, multilateral security policy. Neither the United Nations nor the European Union has been able to stop the fighting, but when we think of the enormous casualties during the first year we realize that the presence of the "blue helmet" forces has indeed saved many lives. Germany is making a significant contribution—politically through its efforts in the Bosnia Contact Group, through humanitarian aid, and now through the employment of its armed forces as well.

Source: "German Foreign Policy Five Years After Unification"
by Klause Kinkel, Germany's Foreign Minister, Bonn, October 3, 1995.

---

economies, arms control and the indefinite extension of the Nuclear Non-Proliferation Treaty, and the FRG's solidarity with other nations committed to resolving the ecological and economic problems caused by an increasingly globalized industrial economy (see Feature 4.11).

In recognition of its increased power and influence in the world since reunification, Germany seeks to strengthen its voice and vote in the United Nations by becoming a permanent member of the Security Council. The FRG also plans to use its enhanced power to take the lead in building a new security order for Europe that will protect Russian interests while expanding NATO eastward to include Poland, Hungary, and the Czech Republic. The leadership Germany is beginning to exert on this and related issues does not imply the absence of tensions with Russia and the United States. For example, Russian leaders have warned that the eastward expansion of NATO could lead to a replay of the old East-West conflict between Russia and the Atlantic Alliance. The United States, on the other hand, experienced considerable frustration with Germany's initial refusal—albeit on constitutional grounds—to deploy its military forces abroad in support of UN peacekeeping operations, not to mention disagreements between the two countries over the utility and

propriety of sanctions against countries such as Iran, Iraq, and Cuba. Germany absorbed additional criticism in other Western circles for allegedly contributing to the Yugoslavian debacle by its "premature" recognition of the independence of Croatia and Slovenia.

Yet Germany sees itself as a bridge between East and West, one designed especially to encourage the democratization of Russian and Eastern Europe. Thus, while Germany supports the eastward expansion of NATO, it has not insisted on accelerating this process for fear of aiding anti-Western factions within Russia and tilting the country into nondemocratic directions. At the same time, through a series of bilateral talks, Germany seeks to resolve remaining problems with its eastern neighbors, particularly with Poland and the Czech Republic over compensation for the victims of Nazism and the confiscation of German property in these countries immediately after the war. Germany will seek to resolve these problems peacefully just as it strives to create what FRG leaders are fond of calling a "European Germany."

CONCLUSION

The portrait of Germany sketched in this chapter is of a polity that up to now has worked and one that has brought about a high measure of stability and prosperity. The FRG also appears to have come of age politically. Its people are committed to democratic values, its party system is open and competitive, and its policy-making institutions are responsive to public opinion. Only time will tell whether the transition to democracy will be as smooth in the eastern *Länder*.

The FRG is a decentralized state marked by a system of administrative federalism, a fragmented bureaucracy, autonomous federal ministries, and a powerful Bundesrat capable of blocking parliamentary action. These institutions, like the political parties and parliament itself, are closely linked to various social and economic groups in the private sector, producing a politics largely of compromise and consensus, notwithstanding the conflict in the 1990s, over budgetary policy. The Federal Constitutional Court, another independent center of power, watches over this system, keeping the major organs of government within their proper spheres of competence while helping to protect individual rights and liberties. Finally, having regained full sovereignty under the Two-Plus-Four Treaty of 1990, and increasingly confident of its power to influence events in Europe and the world, Germany can be expected to define its own foreign policy, preferably in harmony with American interests but against them if necessary, but indubitably within the framework of the Atlantic Alliance and an expanding European Union.

Key Terms

Article 16a
Article 143
codetermination
decentralized federalism
Economic Stabilization Act
German Unity Fund
Lothar de Maiziere
militant democracy
Ostpolitik
Socialist Unity Party (SED)
Treuhandanstalt
Two-Plus-Four Treaty
works council

Further Readings

Ash, Timothy Garton. *In Europe's Name: Germany and the Divided Continent* (New York: Random House, 1993).

Böckenförde, Ernst-Wolfgang. *State, Society and Liberty,* translated by J. A. Underwood (Oxford: Berg Publishers, 1991).

Braunthal, Gerard. *Political Loyalty and Public Service in Germany* (Amherst: Massachusetts University Press, 1990).

Bulmer, Simon, ed. *The Changing Agenda of West German Public Policy* (Brookfield, VT: Gower Publishing, 1989).

Hancock, Donald M., and Helga A. Welsh eds. *German Unification: Process and Outcomes* (Boulder, CO: Westview Press, 1994).

Hanrieder, Wolfram P. *Germany, America, Europe: Forty Years of German Foreign Policy* (New Haven: Yale University Press, 1989).

Katzenstein, Peter J., ed. *Industry and Politics in West Germany* (Ithaca, NY:Cornell University Press, 1989).

Kommers, Donald P. *The Constitutional Jurisprudence of the Federal Republic of Germany*, 2nd ed. (Durham, NC: Duke University Press, 1996).

Markovits, Inga. *Imperfect Justice* (Oxford: Clarendon Press, 1995).

Schweitzer, C. C., et al., eds. *Politics and Government in Germany, 1944–1994* (Oxford: Berghahn Books, 1995).

Smith, Eric Owen. *The German Economy* (London and New York: Routlege, 1994).

Swenson, Peter. *Fair Shares, Unions, Pay, and Politics in Sweden and West Germany* (Ithaca, NY: Cornell University Press, 1989).

Notes

1. This and the following historical subsections rely heavily on Geoffrey Barraclough, *The Origins of Modern Germany* (New York: Capricorn Books, 1963); Koppel S. Pinson, *Modern Germany*, 2nd ed. (New York: Macmillan, 1966); and H. W. Koch, *A Constitutional History of*

Germany in Nineteenth and Twentieth Centuries (London and New York: Longmann, 1984).

2. Ralf Dahrendorf, *Society and Democracy in Germany* (Garden City, NY: Doubleday, 1967), p. 62.

3. See Lucy S. Dawidowicz. *The War Against the Jews* (New York: Holt, Rinehart and Winston, 1975). See also David S. Wyman, *The Abandonment of the Jews* (New York: Pantheon Books, 1984).

4. *Ostpolitik*, which means Eastern policy, is the term used to describe the efforts of West Germany, especially its Chancellor Willy Brandt, to normalize relations with the eastern countries. The high point of these efforts, which took place between 1970 and 1973, was the Basic Treaty between the Federal Republic of Germany and the German Democratic Republic.

5. Eric Owen Smith, *The German Economy* (London and New York: Routledge, 1994), p. 9.

6. "Political Asylum Seekers," *Week in Germany*, January 15, 1993, p. 2.

7. John Ardagh, *Germany and the Germans* (London: Penguin Books, 1991), p. 63.

8. *The OECD Observer* (August–September, 1995), p. 49.

9. Günter Thumann, "The System of Public Finance in the German Democratic Republic," in Leslie Lipschitz and Donough McDonald, *German Unification: Economic Issues* (Washington, DC: International Monetary Fund, December 1990), p. 159.

10. For a discussion of the West German social welfare system see Wolfgang Zapf, "Development, Structure, and Prospects of the German Social State," in Richard Rose and Rei Shiratori, *The Welfare State: East and West* (New York: Oxford University Press, 1986), pp. 126–155.

11. On the other hand, precisely because the right and duty to work in the GDR was state-decreed, "many [East German women] appear[ed] to link self-realization to a life in which homemaking is a preferred option, and employment limited or not necessary at all." See Sabine Hübner, "Women at the Turning Point: The Socio-Economic Situation and Prospects of Women in the Former German Democratic Republic," *Politics and Society in Germany, Austria, and Switzerland*, vol. 3 (1991) p. 26. For other sources on the plight of East German women after reunification, see Marilyn Rueschemeyer, "Women in the Politics of Eastern Germany" in M. Rueschemeyer et al. (eds.), *Women in the Politics of Postcommunist Eastern Europe* (Armonk, NY. M. E. Sharpe, 1994) pp. 87–116 and

Friederike Maier, "The Labor Market for Women and Employment Perspectives in the Aftermath of German Unification," *Cambridge Journal of Economics* 17 (1993) p. 267–280.

12. "Zur Einkommenslage der westdeutschen Arbeitnehmerinnen," *Wochenbericht* 61 (Berlin: Deutscher Institut für Wirtschaftsordnung, 21 September 1994) pp. 655 and 659.

13. For a discussion of the effects of the European Community Adaptation Act, see Josephine Shaw, "Recent Developments in the Field of Labor Market Equality: Sex Discrimination Law in the Federal Republic of Germany," *Comparative Labor Law Journal*, vol. 13 (1991) p. 27–41.

14. Eva Kolinsky, "Women and the 1994 Federal Election" in Russell Dalton (ed.), *Germans Divided: 1994 Bundestagswahl and the Evolution of the German Party System* (Oxford: Berg, 1996), pp. 265–290.

15. See Ray C. Rist, "Migration and Marginality: Guestworkers in Germany and France," *Daedalus*, 108 (spring 1979) pp. 95–108.

16. *European Marketing Data and Statistics 1995*, 30th ed. (London: Euromonitor International, 1995), p. 411.

17. Günter Grass, *One State—One Nation?* Translated by Krishna Winston and A.S. Wensinger (New York: Harcourt Brace, 1990), pp. 12–14.

18. This section on party financing relies heavily on Arthur B. Gunlicks, "Campaigns and Party Finance in the West German 'Party State,' " *The Review of Politics*, 50 (winter 1988), pp. 30–48.

19. Gerhard Loewenberg, *Parliament in the German Political System* (Ithaca, NY: Cornell University Press, 1964), pp. 197–198.

20. See Peter J. Katzenstein, *Policy and Politics in West Germany* (Philadelphia: Temple University Press, 1987), p. 10.

21. Ibid., p. 362.

22. Richard J. Willey, "Trade Unions and Political Parties in the Federal Republic of Germany," *Industrial and Labor Relations Review*, 28 (1974) p. 46.

23. Russell J. Dalton, *Politics: West Germany* (Boston: Scott Foresman, 1989), p. 236.

24. For an excellent study of changing campaign styles in Germany, see Susan Edith Scarrow, *Organizing for Victory: Political Party Members and Party Organizing Strategies in Great Britain and West Germany, 1945–1989* (Ph.D. Dissertation, Yale University, 1991), Chs. 5 and 10.

25. For a detailed discussion of the 1972 campaign see Arnold J. Heidenheimer and Donald P. Kommers, *The Governments of Germany*, 4th ed. (New York: Thomas Y. Crowell, 1975), Ch. 5.

26. A fine treatment of the 1976 election is Karl H. Cerny, ed. *Germany at the Polls* (Washington, DC: American Enterprise Institute, 1978).

27. Good treatments of the 1969, 1972, and 1976 federal elections are "The West German Elections of 1969," *Comparative Politics*, 1 (July 1970); David P. Conradt and Dwight Lambert, "Party System, Social Structure, and Competitive Politics in West Germany: An Ecological Analysis of the 1972 Federal Election," *Comparative Politics*, 7 (October 1974); and Cerny, *Germany at the Polls.*

28. Russell J. Dalton and Wilhelm Bürkin, "The Two German Electorates: The Social Bases of the Vote in 1990 and 1994," *German Politics and Society*, vol. 13 (1995) p. 92.

29. Ibid., p. 94.

30. Winfried Steffani, "Parties (Parliamentary Groups) and Committees in the *Bundestag*" in Uwe Thaysen et al., *The U.S. Congress and the German Bundestag* (Boulder, CO: Westview Press, 1990), p. 273.

31. See Donald P. Kommers, *Judicial Politics in West Germany* (Beverly Hills, CA: Sage, 1976), pp. 128–144.

32. This subsection on law and the courts draws heavily from Donald P. Kommers, *The Constitutional Jurisprudence of the Federal Republic of Germany*, 2nd ed. (Durham, NC: Duke University Press, 1996).

33. Ibid.

34. Walter F. Murphy and Joseph Tanenhaus, *Comparative Constitutional Law* (New York: St. Martin's Press, 1977), p. 660.

35. See Rainer Münz and Ralf E. Urich, "Depopulation After Unification? Population Prospects for East Germany, 1990–2010," *German Politics and Society*, vol. 13 (1995) p. 1–48.

36. Arthur B. Gundlicks, "Administrative Centralization in the Making and Remaking of Modern Germany," *Review of Politics*, 46 (1984) pp. 336–340.

37. Ibid., p. 100.

38. Gunlicks, p. 336.

39. "Corporation and Regional Economic Policies in the Federal Republic of Germany: The 'Meso' Politics of Industrial Adjustment," *Publius*, 19 (1989) pp. 156–157.

40. See Eric Owen Smith, *The German Economy* (London and New York: Routledge, 1994), pp. 61–62.

41. Treaty Between the Federal Republic of Germany and the German Democratic Republic Establishing a Monetary, Economic and Social Union (New York: German Information Center, 1990 [official translation]).

42. For an excellent study of the role of the Bundesbank in the FRG's political system, see Ellen Kennedy, *The Bundesbank* (New York: Council on Foreign Relations Press, 1991).

43. For a full translation of this decision see Robert E. Jonas and John D. Gorby, "Translation of the German Federal Constitutional Court Decision," *John Marshall Journal of Practice and Procedure*, 9 (1976) pp. 605–684.

44. The Treaty on the Final Settlement With Respect to Germany (New York: German Information Center, 1990 [official translation]).

45. *Two States—One Nation?*, translated by Krishna Winston and A. S. Wensigner (New York: Harcourt Brace, 1990), p. 13.

CHAPTER 5

The Government of Japan

Theodore McNelly

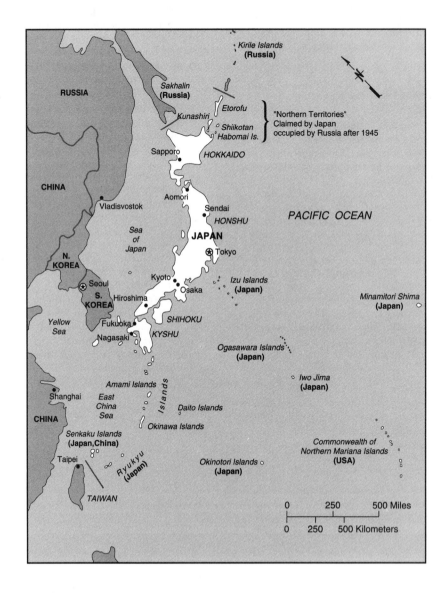

Political Development

In terms of area, Japan is a middle-sized country like Great Britain, France, and Germany, but its population (about 125 million in 1995) is roughly twice that of any of those nations. Today Japan's gross national product (GNP) is the world's second largest, and the GNP per capita is one of the world's highest. The quality of life, however, suffers from overcrowding and long commutes, since one-fourth of the population is jammed into Tokyo and its immediate surroundings.

The Japanese are keenly aware that their country lacks the natural resources necessary for modern industry, the most obvious being iron ore, coal, and oil; these must all be imported and paid for by exports. If the present global trading system were to break down or if Japan were excluded from it, its now prosperous economy could be threatened with imminent collapse.

THE LAND AND THE PEOPLE

Japan is an island nation. Although its total land area is slightly less than that of California, its four main islands and outlying smaller islands are dispersed over a huge area of the western Pacific Ocean. As the crow flies, the distance from the northern tip of Hokkaido to the southernmost of the Ryukyu Islands (just east of Taiwan) is about 1800 miles. Japanese territory extends as far south as Okinotori Shima, between the Philippines and the Commonwealth of the Northern Mariana Islands (a U.S. possession), and as far east as Minamitori Shima (Marcus Island), midway between Wake Island (U.S.) and Japan's Izu Islands. The strategic importance of Japan's outlying possessions is substantial, because responsibility for their defense is increasingly being assumed by Japan's controversial Maritime Self-Defense Force.

Japan's four principal islands are, from north to south, Hokkaido, Honshu, Shikoku, and Kyushu. They are located in the north temperate zone. Hokkaido and northern Honshu are notable for their cold winters and heavy snows, and much of Japan suffers from heavy rains in the spring and smoldering summers. Earthquakes are common, and have sometimes resulted in major disasters, as in the case of the Kanto (Tokyo-Yokohama) quake in 1923 and Kobe earthquake in 1995. The Kobe disaster, in which over 5000 people were killed, has impelled the government to insist on more rigorous standards for the construction of buildings and elevated highways.

Kyushu is separated from Korea, on the Asian mainland, by 100 miles of high seas. Throughout history this location has helped Japan protect itself against foreign invasion. Although at times foreign influence has been intense, the Japanese have largely developed their culture and institutions in isolation. Therefore, many Japanese cultural characteristics, such as language, architecture, and traditional food and clothing, are very different even from those of the closest neighbors.

Yet modern Japan has much in common with other developed countries: science and industry, nearly universal literacy, a high material standard of living, a large investment in education at all levels, and a fondness for television and automobiles. A western tourist in Tokyo would find that city—with its noise, tall buildings, and traffic jams—disappointingly similar to big cities anywhere in the world. The principal exotic feature would be the Chinese characters on the fronts of stores. The spoken Japanese language is fundamentally different from Chinese, but the Japanese use Chinese characters to write their language. Although English is a required subject in Japanese schools, the percentage of Japanese who can speak it fluently is very small.

Ancient Chinese descriptions of Japan written in the third and fifth centuries A.D. suggest that it was originally inhabited by warlike, nature-worshipping tribespeople. Archeological and anthropological evidence indicates that the land was originally inhabited by Ainu, a caucasoid race of which only a few thousand still exist in Hokkaido. Later, in prehistoric times, mongoloid peoples evidently migrated from northern Asia, and some migrants apparently came from the South Seas.

By the sixth century A.D., one tribal clan and its allies had consolidated their rule over other tribes and established their chief as the "emperor," Jimmu. The new imperial clan propagated the myth that the first emperor, Jimmu, was the grandchild of the sun-goddess, Amaterasu, who had commanded her descendants to rule the land. The sacred sword, jewel, and mirror, all of legendary origin, constitute the imperial regalia and are treasured by the imperial court as evidence of the antiquity and legitimacy of the dynasty.

CHINESE INFLUENCE

The coming of Buddhism and Confucianism from Korean kingdoms (with which Japan's rulers had political relations for a time) and China in the sixth century exacerbated existing clan rivalries as different groups sought either to sponsor the new ideas or to rally around traditional religious beliefs and ideologies. In order to distinguish the traditional nature worship from Buddhism, the old beliefs came to be referred as *Shinto,* or "way of the gods." Gradually, as often seems to be the case in Japan, these foreign ideas gained widespread acceptance, but they were adapted to the needs of the Japanese. For example, the Buddhist pantheon came to be superimposed on the gods of the traditional Shinto faith. One emperor is said to have dreamed that the Hindu deity Vairocana appeared in the form of a bright sun and declared itself to be none other than Amaterasu, the emperor's ancestress.

Late in the sixth century, Crown Prince Shotoku distinguished himself as a scholar of Confucianism. Acting as regent, in 604 he proclaimed his famous "Seventeen-Article Constitution," which was actually a collection of Confucian precepts calling for harmony, obedience, diligence, and honesty in the conduct of administration. Confucian ideology provided a convenient rationale for the establishment of a centralized bureaucratic monarchy in place of quasi-feudal rule by clan chieftains. Emperor Kotoku's Edict of Reform of 646, largely inspired by the ideology of the Seventeen-Article Constitution, formally abolished hereditary

guilds, set up a system of imperially appointed governors to rule the provinces, reformed the distribution of land among the people, and set up a system of taxation, usually in the form of rice, that would be paid to the central government. The centralizers cited the Chinese doctrine: "Under the heavens there is no land which is not the king's land. Among the holders of land there is none who is not the king's vassal."

The Taiho Code of 702, compiled by scholars of Chinese law, established a central administrative structure in imitation of the government of Tang China. The old custom of the Japanese court had been to maintain no fixed residence but to move from one place to another. In 710, following the Chinese example, a permanent Japanese capital city with straight streets and Chinese-style buildings was established in Nara. A university was set up where the sons of the nobility could learn the teachings of Confucius. A few years later, apparently to escape the overweening influence of the Buddhist clergy, the capital was moved to Kyoto, which remained the emperor's capital until 1868.

FEUDALISM

Although the imperial court in Kyoto was evidently committed to the ideal of a centralized, bureaucratic monarchy, the Confucian notion of government by merit tended to be ignored in favor of hereditary rule. The Chinese theory that a wicked imperial dynasty could be overthrown was not adopted by the Japanese, who did not accept the idea that their divinely descended monarch could be anything other than virtuous. The Fujiwara family of hereditary court nobles, who—like the emperor—traced their descent from mythological deities, dominated the court and usually provided imperial consorts, regents, and civil dictators (*kanpaku*). The latter carried on the actual administration of state affairs.

The imperial court and capital soon became the center of intrigues and plots within and among the imperial family, the Fujiwara nobility, and rival Buddhist monasteries. From time to time successive emperors, yielding to political or physical pressures, made large grants of tax-exempt land to presumably deserving members of the imperial family, Fujiwara bureaucrats, Buddhist monasteries, and Shinto shrines. As less and less land provided revenue for the central government, the imperial court gradually became impoverished. Great tax-exempt manors grew into hereditary feudal baronies with their own armies. Unable to finance its own military forces and to maintain order in the provinces and even in the capital, the imperial government became dependent on the barons in order to enforce its rule.

In 1192, the emperor appointed the most powerful feudal baron, Minamoto Yoritomo, as "Barbarian-Subduing Generalissimo," or *shogun,* a title which became hereditary in the Minamoto family. (Throughout this chapter, the family name precedes the given name of Japanese individuals, as is customary in Japan.) Minamoto Yoritomo, Japan's military ruler, established his own capital at Kamakura in eastern Japan, hundreds of miles from Kyoto. From 1192 until 1868, Japan was ruled not by the emperor or his court but by the military government (*bakufu*) of the successive shoguns. While the emperor, powerless and isolated in Kyoto, sometimes lived in poverty, the military government presided over a full-fledged feudal system. Within the hierarchy of lords and vassals, the code chivalrous of the *samurai* (the ruling caste of hereditary warriors) emphasized loyalty to one's overlord and military discipline. Aided by this discipline, the Kamakura *bakufu* defeated the Mongols, who twice tried to invade Japan by sea in the thirteenth century. The defenders of the nation were reputedly aided by the prayers of Buddhist and Shinto priests and great storms, the "winds of the Gods" (*kamikaze*), giving rise to the tradition that Japan enjoyed supernatural protection and was invincible.

The Tokugawa Regime

Warfare among local feudal lords raged across the land in the sixteenth century, when the country was nominally under the control of the Ashikaga dynasty of shoguns. Finally in 1603, after decades of civil war, Tokugawa Ieyasu, using political guile as well as military strategy, brought the country under his rule. Tokugawa Ieyasu, the first of the Tokugawa dynasty of shoguns, had remarkable political skills. After subduing or making alliances with the other feudal lords (*daimyo*), he established a regime

that endured over two and a half centuries. He set up his capital in a swampy town called Edo, in eastern Japan. He required his defeated rivals to support the construction of a huge system of moats around his palace, redistributed their fiefs in such a way that his former enemies were kept separated from one another, and required them to live alternately in Edo and in their fiefs. When the feudal lords left Edo they had to leave their families behind as hostages. When they returned to Edo they were forbidden to bring weapons with them.

In order to prevent a possible conquest of the country by the European powers, Christianity was forbidden. In 1636 all Japanese ships without exception were forbidden to leave Japan. Only the Dutch (who were confined to an island in Nagasaki harbor and who agreed not to propagate the teachings of Christ) and the Chinese were permitted to trade with the Japanese. The long period of peace enforced by the shoguns combined with the growing use of money as a means of exchange (which replaced rice) encouraged the rise of a large merchant class. By 1772 Edo's population reached 1 million, making it the world's largest city at that time. The isolationist policy helped to prevent the conquest of Japan by European imperial powers.

THE IMPERIAL RESTORATION

These changes in the economy during the Tokugawa period wrought hardship on many of the samurai and peasants, whose income was in the form of rice and who became indebted to rice brokers and merchants. At the same time samurai scholars fostered the study of "national literature," which was based on Shinto legends that emphasized the divine origin of the state and of the imperial dynasty. Some nationalist scholars contended that the shoguns had usurped the emperor's authority and that the emperor should be restored to his rightful position.

In 1853, during this period of internal division, Commodore Matthew Calbraith Perry came to Japan with a message from the American president demanding that the country open its door to foreign trade. The American fleet steadfastly refused to leave Japanese waters despite military threats, placing shogun Tokugawa Iesada in a grave predicament. The nationalists and the shogun's feudal rivals demanded that the shogun "expel the barbarian and revere the emperor."

The shogun simply did not have the military and naval resources or the political support needed to resist American demands and had no choice but to make a treaty with the Americans. This provoked the shogun's enemies to intensify their demands that he abdicate. Efforts to work out a compromise of joint rule between the emperor and the shogun failed. Finally shogun Tokugawa Keiki agreed to a restoration of the emperor, with the understanding that the shogun would be a principal councilor to the throne. When it became clear that the western daimyo, who leagued against him, were determined to exclude him from the new regime, some of the shogun's followers rebelled. A full-scale civil war was averted when the shogun agreed to abdicate, and the imperial regime was restored.

In 1868, the youthful Emperor Meiji established his capital at Edo, took over the shogun's palace and moats, and renamed the city Tokyo, or Eastern Capital. At first, there was much confusion about what the new group of ruling clans wanted. Some of the architects of the restoration would have been happy to leave things as they had been under the Tokugawa shoguns but with themselves as the effective rulers. Others felt that the times called for sweeping economic, political, and military changes. After considerable debate and outbreaks of violence (especially by samurai who were unhappy about the inadequacy of the pensions promised them by the new regime), the advocates of change won out. The feudal system was formally abolished with the return of the land and population from the daimyo to the emperor. The daimyo and the samurai were pensioned off, and their privileged status was abolished. The outcast *eta* (a caste of "untouchables" engaged in hereditary occupations related to the slaughtering of animals, such as the making of leather and leather goods) were declared emancipated, and everyone became equally a subject of the emperor.

During the Meiji period (1868–1911), the Western powers forced the Japanese to sign "unequal treaties" that prevented Japan from trying foreigners in Japanese courts and from freely setting tariffs on foreign imports. To facilitate negotiations to end the unequal treaties and reassert Japan's independence, the Japanese modernized their legal system using European models.

The Imperial Constitution

During the struggle for power, some samurai leaders had demanded that a representative assembly be established. In 1889, after several false starts, a new constitution was promulgated. The principal author of the Imperial Constitution (usually referred to as the Meiji Constitution) was Count Ito Hirobumi, a leader of the Choshu clan, who hailed the new Japanese constitution as the "Emperor's gift to the Japanese people." Ito had studied constitutions in Europe, and had been greatly impressed by the basic law of Prussia, which provided for a powerful executive branch. The autocratic ideology of the Imperial Constitution was explicitly declared in Article 1: "The Empire of Japan shall be reigned over and governed by a line of Emperors unbroken for ages eternal." The theory and interpretation of the document were further clarified in Ito's *Commentary on the Constitution of Japan.* Although the text of the Constitution was never altered until the entire document was replaced in 1947, the actual operation of the government, as we shall see, underwent significant changes during the 58 years that the Meiji Constitution was in existence.

Japan's new leaders (samurai who had brought about the imperial restoration) were determined to make Japan a rich and powerful country and wanted to ensure that their influence in Tokyo would not be hobbled by the newly established Imperial Diet (Parliament). The Diet consisted of an aristocratic House of Peers and a House of Representatives composed of members chosen by a small electorate of high-paying taxpayers, but its powers were limited by the Constitution. The Diet was powerless to control the executive branch using the power of the purse: If the two houses failed to approve the budget proposed by the government, the government could simply enforce the budget of the preceding year. Prime ministers were appointed by the emperor on the recommendation of the *Genro,* or Elder Statesmen, a powerful group of former samurai not mentioned in the Constitution. Until 1918, all prime ministers were appointed from either the samurai class or, in one instance, from the hereditary court nobility. The emperor had "supreme command of the army and navy." This provision largely removed the military from the control of the prime minister and the Diet. The prestige and power of the executive and the military were vastly enhanced during the victorious wars with China (1894–1895) and Russia (1904–1905). These wars resulted in Japan's acquiring Taiwan, Southern Sakhalin, and a foothold in Manchuria. Korea was forcefully annexed in 1910.

TAISHO DEMOCRACY

Political parties emerged in the 1880s, organized by disgruntled samurai who felt that they were being excluded from the Meiji power structure. Their influence in the Diet had to be recognized by the oligarchy. In 1918, a year of widespread rice riots, the emperor and the Genro for the first time chose a commoner, Hara Takeshi, the leader of the Seiyukai (Constitutional) Party, to serve as prime minister. With the establishment of party government in 1918 and the agitation for democratic rights after the First World War, party leaders began to talk of the coming of "normal parliamentary government," in which the leader of the majority party (or majority coalition) in the House of Representatives would serve as prime minister. The movement favoring universal manhood suffrage became irresistible. In 1925, the Diet passed the universal manhood suffrage law, which made the lower house a more democratic body. Some intellectuals and party leaders had hoped that Japan would become a parliamentary democracy like England, but the Diet enacted a peace preservation law that made illegal any attack on the principle of the emperor's sovereignty. The trend towards parliamentary government came to be known as Taisho democracy, referring to the reign of the Taisho emperor (1912–1925). Had it not been for the world depression in the 1930s, which had devastating consequences in Japan, democracy might have become more firmly established in that country.

THE RISE OF MILITARISM

Junior officers in the army, largely drawn from the impoverished peasantry, tended to blame capitalists and the politicians, believed to be controlled by the capitalists, for the plight of the people, who were suffering from the depression. Advocating a "Showa Restoration," or restoration of direct imperial rule, they aspired to a more equitable social order. In the 1930s several military coups d'etat were attempted and leading cabinet ministers were assassinated. Prime ministers lived in fear for their lives. To strengthen control over rebellious junior officers and to appease the militarists, with increasing frequency, the Genro chose military men to serve as prime ministers and the representation of the political parties in the cabinets was reduced. The ministers of war and navy (who had to be generals or admirals according to an imperial ordinance) would threaten to refuse service in a cabinet or proposed cabinet whose chief or whose policies did not please them. Thus the military exercised an effective veto over the policies and personnel of the government.

The civilian government in Tokyo was even unable to restrain the Kwantung Army (the Japanese forces stationed in Japan's basehold on the southern tip of Manchuria, China) from carrying out its own policy. In 1931, Japanese troops seized all of Manchuria and later established a puppet state (Manchukuo) headed by the former emperor of China ("Henry" Pu Yi), who collaborated with the Japanese in order to gain wealth and prestige. Under international condemnation, Japan resigned from the League of Nations, and in 1937 a full-scale war broke out between China and Japan. Japanese forces captured Nanking, the Chinese capital, and brutalized and murdered tens of thousands of civilians. In 1940, Japan allied itself with Germany and Italy to deter American and Soviet opposition, and the three Axis powers announced their intention to establish "New Orders" in Europe and Asia.

War broke out in Europe in 1939, and on December 7, 1941 ("a date that will live in infamy," President Roosevelt called it), Japanese carrier-based aircraft made a surprise attack on Pearl Harbor in an attempt to prevent American interference with Japan's invasions of the Dutch East Indies, Malaya, and the Philippines. The Japanese attack devastated the American navy and aroused the wrath of the American people, who regarded the attack as unprovoked. Within a few months, Japan conquered the Philippine Islands and the British and Dutch possessions in Southeast Asia.

The Japanese drive was halted in the sea battle with the Americans at Midway Island in June 1942, and the Japanese were thrown on the defensive. By the spring of 1945, the Americans had captured island bases close enough to mainland Japan to launch frightful air attacks on Japanese cities. In August, after two cities had been destroyed by American atomic bombs and the Soviet Union (with which Japan had a neutrality treaty) had declared war on Japan, the Japanese government accepted the terms set forth by the Allies in the Potsdam Declaration of July 26, 1945.

THE ALLIED OCCUPATION

The main purpose of the Allied occupations of previous Axis countries was to ensure that those nations never again threaten the security of peace-loving countries. Because of the common belief that people, as distinguished from leaders, are peace loving, it was thought that democratic regimes were less inclined to be warlike than autocratic governments. Thus, in addition to completely disarming Germany and Japan, the Allies set about establishing democratic institutions in the defeated countries. Moreover, it was widely thought that fundamental economic and social reforms were essential to provide a lasting basis for democratic political institutions. There was continuing controversy about the need, extent, and precise character of the social reforms that would have to be carried out. The unconditional surrender of the defeated states meant that there was virtually no limit to the authority of the occupying powers to intervene in the internal affairs of Germany and Japan.

The occupations of Germany and Japan differed in two essential respects: (1) Unlike Germany, which was administered in four zones, one for each Allied power, all of Japan (except Okinawa and Japan's former possessions, Korea and Taiwan) was placed under the unified control of the Supreme Commander for the Allied Powers (SCAP), General Douglas MacArthur, who had been appointed by President Truman with the concurrence of Joseph Stalin. The policies of the United States were in effect controlling, and the other Allies represented in the Far Eastern Commission could do little more than give their advice or complain about measures already taken by MacArthur's staff. (2) In Germany, where no national German government existed following the surrender, the Allied authorities directly enacted legislation. In Japan, the emperor and imperial government remained in place, and SCAP issued directives to the Japanese government, which was required to enact laws or issue ordinances to carry out the Allies' (essentially American) policies. Thus the policies of Allied military government in Japan were uniform for the whole country and were administered indirectly.

Democratization

From the beginning, critics in the United States and the Allied countries complained that the emperor should have been arrested and either tried as a war criminal, or made to abdicate, or both, and that the Japanese government, composed of reactionaries, could not be trusted to carry out the sweeping reforms required by the Allies. However, the system worked with a minimum of friction between the Allied (overwhelmingly American) forces and the Japanese, and, as we shall see, substantial democratic reform was accomplished in Japan. By contrast, the occupation of Germany was the focus of continual bitter controversy within and among the Allied countries, and at the time of the Berlin blockade (1948–1949), there were fears that war might break out between the Soviet Union and the Western powers. While Germany became the center of the Cold War confrontation, Japan seemed to represent the epitome of tranquillity, and MacArthur enjoyed wide praise for the smoothness of his operation.

The policies of the Allied occupation of Japan were largely based on the Potsdam Declaration of July 26, 1945. It stated that Japanese military and naval forces were to be disarmed and repatriated, Taiwan was to be reverted to Chinese rule, and Korea had to be liberated from Japanese control. In addition to trials set up among the East Asian countries for the punishment of Japanese violations of the laws of war, an International Military Tribunal for the Far East ("Tokyo War Crimes Trial") was established for the trial of class A war criminals, those accused of crimes against peace (planning and carrying out aggressive war) and crimes against humanity, following the precedents of the Nuremberg trial. Officeholders or office seekers who had been military or naval officers or holders of positions in the Imperial Rule Assistance Association (a totalitarian organization) or in other militaristic or ultranationalistic organizations were declared ineligible for public office. This "purge," the administration of which was entrusted to the Japanese government, was intended to clear the way for new leadership in Japan.

Under SCAP guidance, a sweeping land reform was carried out which made virtually every peasant a landowner. Partly as a result, Japanese farmers became politically very conservative because they suspected that Communists might try to deprive them of their land. The government broke up the great family-controlled business and financial combines (*zaibatsu*) and sold their stock publicly, encouraged the unionization of labor, and, for the first

General Douglas MacArthur, Supreme Commander for the Allied Powers in East Asia, with Emperor Hirohito of Japan at the American embassy in Tokyo in September 1945.

time, gave women the right to vote. Freedom of speech and of the press was granted.

THE DEMOCRATIC CONSTITUTION

In MacArthur's view, the occupation's most notable accomplishment was the establishment of a thoroughly democratic constitution. The general first raised the issue of constitutional revision in 1945, but Prime Minister Shidehara publicly stated that it was unnecessary to amend the Meiji Constitution, which, he said, had failed because it had been abused by the militarists. In his view, all that was needed to democratize the country was the enactment of the appropriate legislation. But as it became increasingly clear that the Allied Powers would require drastic reforms, private groups and individuals, as well as the government, began to propose a variety of democratic constitutional amendments.

By February 1946, the Shidehara cabinet was still unable to produce a sufficiently democratic constitution. General MacArthur's Government Section secretly drew up a model constitution which they presented to the cabinet for its guidance. The Shidehara cabinet, faced with the possibilities that the Far Eastern Commission might insist on abolishing the monarchy, that the Allies might try the emperor as a war criminal, or that MacArthur might submit the draft constitution directly to the Japanese people for their decision, accepted the American proposal as the basis for a new constitution.

The cabinet's constitutional revision bill was submitted to the Diet as an "imperial project" in accordance with Article 73 of the Imperial Constitution concerning constitutional amendment. The imperial project was passed by overwhelming majorities in both houses of the Imperial Diet, approved by the Privy Council, and on November 3, 1946, promulgated by the emperor. The new "Constitution of Japan" became effective on May 3, 1947.

Japan's new Constitution proclaimed the sovereignty of the people, guaranteed basic human rights, and renounced war and the maintenance of military forces. The emperor was declared to be "the symbol of the State and of the unity of the people," and would have no "powers related to government." The House of Peers, the Privy Council, and all titles of nobility (save those of the imperial family) were abolished. A parliamentary-cabinet system of democratic government (in which the cabinet was responsible to the lower house of the Diet) was set up. The new upper house, whose members would have six-year terms, would be popularly elected but would be less powerful than the lower house. The constitutionality of legislation and governmental acts would be subject to judicial review. Sexual and racial discrimination were forbidden.

The new Constitution represented such a radical departure from the previously published conservative (some said "reactionary") views of the Japanese cabinet that the document was obviously the product of urging from occupation officers. Nonetheless, after several decades during which public schools taught the provisions of the new Constitution, it gained widespread popular acceptance. The antiwar provision enjoyed popularity from the very beginning, and women, students, intellectuals, journalists, laborers, indeed, just about everyone, became attached to their new constitutional rights.

Many Japanese conservatives, however, have been unhappy with the document. They hold that the no-arms clause, if strictly interpreted, makes it difficult or impossible to defend the country. The emperor, they say, should be made "head of the state" and be more respected. The family should enjoy more constitutional protection. The Constitution, they assert, overemphasizes people's rights and neglects to set forth their duties. When the occupation ended, there appeared a spate of articles and books exposing real and purported facts about the occupation that had hitherto been suppressed by SCAP censors. The conservatives began to insist that the Constitution had been forcibly "imposed" on Japan and that an independent Japan should have an "autonomous" constitution.

Popular Acceptance of the Democratic Constitution

In 1954, the conservative-dominated Diet created a Commission on the Constitution that would examine the origins and operation of the document and make possible recommendations for its amendment. By the mid–1960s when the commission made its report, however, the conservatives were still unable to win the two-thirds majorities needed in both houses of the Diet to amend the Constitution. Although several prime ministers publicly declared their support of constitutional amendment as a matter of principle, they made no serious effort bring it about, given the extremely controversial nature of the issue. In the meantime, the government, citing a controversial interpretation to be described later in this chapter, has been able to strengthen the Self-Defense Forces without amending the Constitution, thus reducing the urgency of the issue. It must be said that there has been widespread unhappiness in Japan and abroad with the manner in which the government had gradually rearmed the country in apparent violation of the disarmament clause of the Constitution and with the reluctance of the Supreme Court to deal forthrightly with this issue.

The democratic Constitution is now 50 years old. Despite the conservative drive to amend it, not a word of it has been altered. Much controversy has surrounded its interpretation and a number of famous constitutional debates have been heard by Japan's Supreme Court. On the whole, however, the document is popular and its principles have been adopted as accepted components of the political culture.

THE RETURN OF INDEPENDENCE

After the new Constitution went into effect in 1947, MacArthur felt the occupation's only remaining task was to revive the Japanese economy. The time was drawing near for the Allies to sign a formal peace treaty with Japan. As the Cold War worsened, however, American policymakers became reluctant to withdraw their military forces from Japan given the growing Communist threat in China and North Korea. American policymakers devised a plan whereby the Allied occupation would formally end, Japan's sovereignty would be restored, and the Japanese government would invite the United States to station forces in Japan. The Soviet Union, however, would not consent to this arrangement. Such a treaty would favor the United States over the Soviet Union and compromise the neutrality of Japan. War broke out in Korea in 1950, and the American negotiators pushed ahead with their proposals in Japan, finally prompting the Japanese government to agree. Japanese socialists and pacifists strongly opposed the "one-sided" peace, asserting that it would alienate Japan's powerful neighbors, the Soviet Union and Communist China, and could drag Japan into a U.S.-Soviet war. The Japanese government asserted that a treaty acceptable to both superpowers was not a possibility. If Japan wished to end the occupation and regain its independence promptly, the best thing to do was to sign the treaty with the non-Communist powers.

The Japanese Peace Treaty was formally signed in San Francisco on September 8, 1951, to become effective on April 26, 1952. The Soviet Union sent a delegation to the conference but it refused to sign the treaty, the details of which had been worked out before the conference was convened. Neither the Nationalist nor the Communist government of China was represented. On the same day that the peace treaty was signed, Japan and the United States signed a mutual security treaty, which provided for the stationing of American forces in Japan. Urged by the United States, the Japanese government negotiated a peace treaty with the Nationalist government of China, based on Taiwan. In April 1952, Japan's independence as a sovereign state was restored and SCAP headquarters in downtown Tokyo was closed, but American forces remained in Japan under the terms of the security treaty.

The peace settlement alienated Japan from both the Soviet Union and Communist China and in effect made Japan an ally of the United States. The Japanese sought to negotiate a peace treaty with the Soviet Union but were unable to do so because of disagreements over the Japanese claims to northern islands under Soviet military occupation. In 1956, the two countries issued a "joint peace declaration" formally ending the state of war between them. The territorial dispute continued unabated and 50 years after the end of the fighting there was still no formal peace treaty between Japan and Russia.

THE EMPEROR SYSTEM TODAY

According to the 1889 Imperial Constitution, Japan was to "be reigned over and governed by a line of Emperors unbroken for ages eternal." The emperor was "sacred and inviolable." He was "the head of the Empire, combining in Himself the rights of sovereignty."

In the 1930s, militarists exploited the emperor's authority and prestige to mobilize public support for their empire-building efforts in Asia. After World War II, hoping to prevent the revival of Japanese militarism and imperialism, many people in the Allied countries strongly urged that both the system of emperor worship and the imperial throne be abolished once and for all. The incumbent emperor, they believed, should be tried as a war criminal. MacArthur feared that the indictment of the emperor would provoke a popular uprising in Japan and that the people's resentment of the occupiers would make it virtually impossible to educate them in the ways of democracy and peace. So the emperor was not tried, and the imperial throne was preserved.

On New Year's Day, 1946, the emperor issued a rescript in which he renounced the notion that he was divine. This statement pleased General MacArthur and was apparently an important factor in the rehabilitation of the imperial institution. Under the postwar democratic Constitution, the emperor was deprived of all powers related to government, and war and the maintenance of armed forces were banned. The postwar emperor would be a powerless and harmless symbol.

Hirohito

In January 1989, Emperor Hirohito died at the age of 87. He had served as prince regent for five years during the mental illness of his father and in 1926 ascended to the imperial throne. He served as emperor for 20 years under the Imperial Constitution and for over 40 years under the democratic Constitution. He survived several assassination attempts and lived through two world wars and seven years of occupation by foreign military forces. Few of the world's statesmen had so closely witnessed or

Emperor Akihito and Empress Michiko on January 9, 1989, when he pledged to uphold the democratic constitution of Japan. His father, Hirohito, had died two days earlier.

participated in so many great events. With the accession of Emperor Akihito to the throne in 1989, the Showa era ended and the Heisei (Peace Attained) era began. The new emperor pledged to uphold the Constitution and to strive for world peace.

The Imperial Family

The imperial reign name rather than the western calendar is often used in designating years. For example, 1996 is frequently referred to as "Heisei 8," the eighth year of the reign of the present emperor. When an emperor dies, his reign name is used to designate him, so that Emperor Hirohito is now called the Showa Emperor. Progressive critics say that the use of reign names unduly exalts the emperor.

The imperial family, whose popularity was enhanced by the marriage of the present em-

peror (then the crown prince) to a beautiful and intelligent commoner in 1959, is constantly in the news. Prince Naruhito, the older of the present emperor's two sons, is the crown prince. The crown prince, like his uncle, Prince Mikasa, is a serious historian and has given lectures on Japanese history. In 1993 he married Owada Masako, a graduate of Harvard University, who had studied law at Tokyo University and passed the examination to join the diplomatic service. (Her father was a career diplomat.) Only males may inherit the throne.

A Modern Monarchy

In Japan, under the democratic Constitution, the emperor "appoints" as prime minister the individual chosen by the Diet and "appoints" as chief judge of the Supreme Court the person chosen by the cabinet. The emperor presides over the openings of Diet sessions and his seal is necessary for important state documents.

In 1966, the Diet enacted a law that revived the annual celebration of the founding of the state by the mythical first emperor (presumably in 660 B.C.). Called "National Foundation Day" (*Kenkoku Kinen no Hi*), this is one of 13 national holidays. This move and other conservative attempts to enhance the status of the imperial throne have been fervently resisted by progressives and pacifists in Japan and viewed with concern by foreign observers.

In 1988, the mayor of Nagasaki publicly blamed Emperor Hirohito for having needlessly prolonged World War II. This statement was made during the emperor's prolonged fatal illness and provoked a nationwide controversy. A year later, a rightist shot and gravely wounded the mayor in front of the city hall. The would-be assassin was tried and sentenced to 12 years of penal servitude. When the mayor ran for reelection in 1991, he was denied the support of the Liberal Democratic Party, but was reelected by a narrow margin. (In 1995, he was defeated in a bid for reelection.)

Many progressive Japanese were especially disturbed by the reactionary implications of the Shinto ceremonies connected with the funeral of the Showa emperor and the formal accession to the throne by Akihito. At the same time, imperial court circles tend to be cautious about doing anything that would make the throne a focus of controversy.

HISTORY AND THE POLITICAL PROCESS IN JAPAN

How is Japan's political history relevant to what is happening in Japan today? As we have seen, the occupation of Japan had as one of its principal aims the democratization of that country's political and social institutions. The ideals of peace and democracy have been subscribed to by an overwhelming majority in Japan. The quality of Japanese politics may be measured against the democratic ideals of the immediate postwar era and the provisions of the democratic Constitution. The sources of some contemporary political phenomena may be sought in the history of the country as well as in its present-day social system.

In 1987 Prime Minister Nakasone talked of "closing the books on the postwar [period]." The statement seemed to imply a repudiation of the postwar reforms. Nakasone formally visited the Yasukuni Shrine where Japan's war dead are deified. For some years, the Ministry of Education has been using its authority to review textbooks so that Japan's aggressions against China and Korea are glossed over. Official visits to Yasukuni and the textbook issue have provoked protests from China, Korea, and others of Japan's erstwhile victims as well as from religious groups, intellectuals, and others in Japan. Since 1985, several Japanese cabinet ministers have been forced to resign because of tactless statements justifying Japan's militaristic record.

In the United States, too, controversy has surrounded the issue of Japanese guilt in World War II. In 1995, the fiftieth anniversary of the end of the war, the Smithsonian Institution set up an exhibit of the *Enola Gay,* the B–29 airplane that had dropped the atomic bomb on Hiroshima. The original plan called for the display of heart-rending photographs and relics of the destruction of Hiroshima and its inhabitants, but protests that the museum was portraying Japan as a war victim rather than as an aggressor forced the museum to forego a display of the materials. Wartime atrocities by the Japanese—the Bataan Death March, the Nanking Massacre, maltreatment of prisoners of war, and the exploitation of "comfort women" and forced laborers—were recalled in the American media. Heated controversies arose in both Japan and the United States concerning Japanese aggression, the morality of the use of the atomic bombs, the purported obligation on one side or the other to apologize, and freedom of historical inquiry. Fifty years after the Japanese surrender, the memory of Japan's war record still complicates relations with its neighbors and trading partners. Japanese intellectuals and politicians continue to debate the meaning of the prewar and wartime policies of their nation and the constitutionality of the Self-Defense Forces or their dispatch as United Nations peacekeepers.

MINORITIES

In Hokkaido, Japan's northernmost main island, there remain several thousand Ainu, a caucasoid people whose ancestors lived in Japan before the arrival of the mongoloids. Some make their livelihood by making and selling souvenirs depicting their picturesque culture to tourists.

In the Ryukyu Islands reside well over 1 million Okinawans, who until two generations ago were as likely to speak Okinawan as they were to speak Japanese. Since coming under Japanese rule over a century ago, many have intermarried with the Japanese, and while Okinawa was under American military government from 1945 to 1972, they sought the return of their land to Japanese rule. At the same time, some Okinawans seek to preserve their distinctive language, art, and music from being submerged completely by Japanese culture. The majority of American military bases in Japan are located in Okinawa, and suffering from crimes committed by American servicemen and the noise and danger of American military aircraft, Okinawans have been eager to reduce the American presence.

In addition to Okinawans and Ainu, there are two other substantial minorities. There are over 650,000 Koreans whose families have lived in Japan for several generations. Many are descendants of Koreans brought to Japan during World War II for forced labor. They are not

Japanese nationals and insist on the right to Korean-language schools and complain of discrimination, such as having to be fingerprinted (as are other aliens) by Japanese authorities.

There are also about 2 million *burakumin* (literally, "village people"), who are the descendants of *eta*. Communities of *burakumin* may be found concentrated in certain areas of large cities, and their occupations and diet as well as other cultural characteristics may distinguish them from majority Japanese. Racially, *burakumin* are indistinguishable from majority Japanese, but employers and the families of potential marriage partners try hard to avoid people with *buraku* ancestries. Discrimination against this minority is illegal, and the Burakumin Liberation League regularly makes political or judicial issues of apparent cases of flagrant discrimination.

All told, fewer than 2 percent of Japan's population may be considered "minority." Except for the importation of 2 or 3 million Korean laborers into Japan during World War II, there has been no substantial immigration to the Japanese islands in recorded history. As a result, the Japanese have a strong consciousness and pride in their racial distinctiveness and homogeneity. Japan, as contrasted with India, the United States, and a number of other countries, is blessed with the relative absence of ethnic strife. Japanese society is not pluralistic nor does it seriously aspire to be. The Japanese government does not encourage immigration in spite of labor shortages. In the past few years, the lure of good jobs in Japan has attracted legal and illegal immigrants from other parts of Asia as well as Brazilians and Peruvians of Japanese ancestry. Given the fact that the Japanese islands are already overcrowded and that Japan has historically had no experience with an ethnically diverse population, the relative closing of Japan to immigrants is understandable.

RELIGION

Over the centuries various religious sects have been introduced to the point that Japan has sometimes been referred to as a "museum of religions." Opinions differ as to how religious the Japanese people really are, and some experts cite the ready tendency of the population to ac-cept new religions or sects as evidence of the shallowness of religious convictions. It is, however, true that for many Japanese, religion is an important force in their lives.

The various religious organizations in Japan report a combined membership of over 220 million. Because this is almost twice the total population, it is evident that many people are adherents of two or more religious persuasions: 108 million Japanese are said to be Shintoist, 89 million are reportedly Buddhist, 1.5 million are Christians, and 11 million belong to other organizations. Most people are married in Shinto ceremonies and are buried according to Buddhist rites. Before the enactment of the postwar democratic Constitution, the national government subsidized the indigenous Shinto religion, which asserted the divine origin of the Japanese nation and the divinity of the imperial dynasty. Christianity became widespread, especially in Kyushu during the early seventeenth century, but because of suspicions arising from its foreign origin it was forbidden by the Tokugawa shoguns and its followers were mercilessly persecuted. Although Christians are a small minority in Japan, there are many well-attended Christian colleges in the country, and Christians probably exercise greater influence in the society than their small numbers might suggest. Christians are especially prominent in the peace movement and in the advocacy of other progressive causes.

Because the new Constitution forbade the state from subsidizing religious organizations, Shinto organizations that had received state subsidies (called "state Shinto"), including the Yasukuni shrine, had to become self-supporting. At the same time there emerged numerous "new religions," which were often sects of Buddhism, that paid special attention to psychological and economic insecurities. The most conspicuous perhaps was the Soka Gakkai, a layman's educational and social organization that had been founded in the 1930s in affiliation with the old Nichiren Shoshu sect of Buddhism. In the 1960s this organization sponsored the organization of the Komeito, a political party that soon became the third largest political representation in the Japanese Diet, as we shall note later in this chapter.

The relation of the state to religious organizations became a very delicate issue in 1995, when members of the Aum Shinrikyo sect, led by a domineering guru, were accused of involvement in the placement of sarin gas, a chemical weapon, in several subways in central Tokyo. Twelve passengers were killed and hundreds were hospitalized. Police made mass investigations of Aum establishments in scattered parts of Japan, and discovered that the sect's members were manufacturing and using hallucinogenic drugs as well as sarin. They had begun experimenting with and making other chemical weapons and firearms. They were implicated in the kidnapping and murders and attempted murders of defectors from the sect and their relatives, and of individuals engaged in exposing Aum activities. The Aum sect came to be feared as a terrorist organization, and the public began to demand that the government cancel the sect's official designation as a religious organization.

KEY TERMS

Ainu
Amaterasu
Aum Shinrikyo
burakumin
Edo
Fujiwara
Hirohito
Japanese Peace Treaty
Okinawa
purge
Supreme Commander for the Allied Powers (SCAP)
Shinto
shogun

Feature 5.1 **Women in Japanese Politics**

Women were given the right to vote by General MacArthur in 1946, a right confirmed by the democratic Constitution adopted later that year. In the 1946 General Election, 39 women were elected to the House of Representatives, which had a total of 464 members. Never since have women candidates for the lower house done so well.

In the 1989 upper house election, which the JSP under the leadership of a woman, Doi Takako, won by a landslide, 22 women were elected. When to these were added the members whose seats had not been at stake, the number of women councilors came to 33, or 13.1 percent of all of membership. Recently, the House of Representatives elected Doi as its speaker.

The women candidates who emerged in the 1989 campaign were popularly dubbed "madonnas." They were very sensitive to education, consumer issues, pacifist and environmental issues, and had

Doi Takako

been especially aroused by the imposition of the consumption tax. After the upper house election in 1995, there were 12 women (2.4 percent of the membership) in the House of Representatives and 39 (15.5 percent of the membership) in the House of Councilors. Ten of the 38 Socialist councilors were women, and 4 of the 14 Communist councilors were women.

Taisho democracy
Tokugawa
zaibatsu

FURTHER READINGS

Field, Norma. *In the Realm of the Dying Emperor* (New York: Pantheon, 1991).

Framing the Japanese Constitution: Primary Sources in English, 1944–1949 (Bethesda, MD: University Publications of America, 1989). This is a massive collection of documents on microfilm.

Fujimura-Fanselow, Kumiko, and Atsuko Kameda, eds. *Japanese Women: New Feminist Perspectives on the Past, Present, and Future* (New York: Feminist Press at CUNY, 1995).

Gordon, Andrew, ed. *Postwar Japan as History* (Berkeley: University of California Press, 1993).

Hane, Mikiso. *Japan: A Historical Survey* (New York: Scribners, 1972).

Hardacre, Helen. *Shinto and the State, 1868–1989* (Princeton: Princeton University Press, 1989).

Ienaga, Saburo. *Pacific War, 1931–1945: A Critical Perspective on Japan's Role in World War II* (New York: Pantheon, 1979).

Inoue, Kyoko. *MacArthur's Democratic Constitution: A Linguistic and Cultural Study of Its Making* (Chicago: University of Chicago Press, 1991).

Ishii, Ryosuke. *A History of Political Institutions in Japan* (Tokyo: University of Tokyo Press, 1980).

Ito, Hirobumi. *Commentaries on the Constitution of the Empire of Japan.* Translated by Ito Miyoji (Tokyo: Insetsu Kyoku, 1889).

Japan: An Illustrated Encyclopedia, 2 vols. (Tokyo: Kodansha, 1993).

Kades, Charles A. "The American Role in Revising Japan's Imperial Constitution," *Political Science Quarterly,* summer, 1989, pp. 215–248.

Kataoka, Tetsuya. *The Price of a Constitution: The Origin of Japan's Postwar Politics* (New York: Crane Russak, 1991).

Kawai, Kazuo. *Japan's American Interlude.* (Chicago: University of Chicago Press, 1960).

Large, Stephen S., *Emperor Hirohito and Showa Japan: A Political Biography* (London: Routledge, 1992).

Maki, John M., trans. and ed. *Japan's Commission on the Constitution: The Final Report* (Seattle: University of Washington Press, 1980).

Nakamura, Masanori. *The Japanese Monarchy: Ambassador Joseph Grew and the Making of the "Symbol Emperor System," 1931–1991.* Translated by Herbert P. Bix, Jonathan Baker-Yates, and Derek Bowen (Armonk, NY: M.E. Sharpe, 1992).

Newman, Robert P. *Truman and the Hiroshima Cult* (East Lansing: Michigan State University Press, 1995).

Nishi, Toshio. *Unconditional Democracy: Education and Politics in Occupied Japan, 1945–1952* (Stanford: Stanford University Press, 1982).

Pharr, Susan J. *Political Women in Japan* (Berkeley: University of California Press, 1990).

Reischauer, Edwin O. *The Japanese Today: Change and Continuity* (Cambridge University Press, 1988).

Sugihara, Seishiro. *Japanese Perspectives on Pearl Harbor.* Translated by Theodore McNelly (Hong Kong: Asian Research Service, 1995).

Supreme Commander for the Allied Powers, Government Section. *The Political Reorientation of Japan,* 2 vols. (Washington, DC: US Government Printing Office, n.d.).

Takeuchi, Tatsuji. *War and Diplomacy in the Japanese Empire* (Garden City, N.Y.: Doubleday, Doran, 1935).

Ward, Robert E., and Yoshikazu Sakamoto, eds. *Democratizing Japan: The Allied Occupation* (Honolulu: University of Hawaii Press, 1987).

Ward, Robert E., and Frank Joseph Shulman, eds. *The Allied Occupation of Japan, 1945–1952: An Annotated Bibliography of Western Language Materials* (Chicago: American Library Association, 1974).

Wray, Harry, and Hilary Conroy. *Japan Examined: Perspectives on Modern Japanese History* (Honolulu: University of Hawaii Press, 1983).

Political Processes and Institutions

THE EMERGENCE OF POLITICAL PARTIES

Political parties arose in Japan among samurai who felt excluded from the Meiji regime in the 1880s. By organizing and agitating, they sought to pressure the government into establishing an assembly, and the government did so when it promulgated the Imperial Constitution in 1889. That Constitution, however, left the executive dominant over the legislative branch, the Diet.

In 1898, the samurai leaders of the two principal political parties joined forces to form the Constitutional Party (Seiyukai). The new party's strength in the House of Representatives was sufficient to pressure the Genro to appoint one of its leaders, Okuma, as prime minister. In 1900 Prime Minister Ito, in order to organize a working coalition in the House of Representatives, accepted the leadership of the Seiyukai Party. Thus political parties proved their usefulness in organizing lower house elections and in mobilizing support in the lower house for the passage of the government's legislation. In 1918, with the appointment of Hara, a commoner and leader of the Seiyukai, as prime minister, it appeared that the power of the samurai oligarchy was greatly weakened and that political parties might come into their own as a dominant factor in politics.

The rise of militarism in the 1930s checked the ascendance of political parties, and beginning in 1932, most of the prime ministers were either generals or admirals. In 1940, the major parties voted to dissolve themselves, and a quasi-totalitarian state, led by the Imperial Rule Assistance Association (IRAA), came into being. At the end of the war, the IRAA was abolished and the prewar political parties were revived with the strong encouragement of MacArthur's headquarters. Indeed, the Americans hoped that the promise of "normal constitutional government," advocated by the political parties in the 1920s, would be realized.

POLITICAL PARTIES IN MODERN JAPAN

Political parties seem to be a necessity in modern states, whether they be democratic or totalitarian. Parties initiate and advocate government programs, sponsor candidates who will work for the adoption of these programs, raise money and campaign for their candidates, and provide blocs of votes in the legislature for enactment of their programs (or defeat of their rivals' programs). In a parliamentary-cabinet system of democracy, the leader of the party or coalition of parties that controls a majority in the parliament normally serves as the prime minister.

From 1945 to 1955, Japan had a multiparty system. In 1955 the two wings of the Socialist Party reunited, and the two conservative parties combined to form the Liberal Democratic Party (LDP), thus inaugurating an essentially two-party arrangement that became known as "the 1955 system." However, the Socialist Party was never able to capture a majority in the lower house, so that there was no rotation in office of prime minister between the two major parties. Thus from 1955 until 1993, the "dominant party system" prevailed in Japan. That is to say, until 1993 only one political party consistently controlled majorities in the House of Representatives and held the prime ministership. For 38 years, without exception the prime ministers and nearly all their cabinet ministers were members of the Liberal Democratic Party. The other political parties were unable to muster enough votes among the electorate to elect majorities in the lower house of the Diet.

Because an acquaintance with Japan's unusual electoral systems is essential to an understanding of party politics in that country, we shall now look at how elections there are conducted.

THE ELECTORAL SYSTEM FOR THE LOWER HOUSE

We shall first discuss the electoral system for Japan's House of Representatives (the lower house), which is more powerful than the House of Councilors (the upper house).

The term of the members of the House of Representatives is four years, but normally the house is dissolved before the four years have elapsed, so that general elections are normally held once every two or three years.

The Constitution provides that the qualifications of both the voters and the members of the Diet shall be determined by law, but there can be no discrimination because of race, creed, sex, social status, family origin, education, property, or income. The law provides that to vote one must be a mentally competent, currently unincarcerated Japanese national 20 years of age or older.

Before the reform of 1994, the electoral system for the House of Representatives was different from that of any other major national legislative assembly. At the time of the 1986 and 1990 elections, there were 130 electoral districts as determined by law. The 130 districts altogether sent 512 members to the House of Representatives: 1 district elected six members, 43 districts each elected five members, 39 districts each elected four members, 42 districts each elected three members, 4 districts each elected two members, and 1 district elected one member.

Each voter was permitted to vote for only one candidate. The candidates receiving the most votes were declared elected. Thus, in a five-member district, each voter selected only one candidate and the five candidates receiving the most votes were declared the winners and would represent the district. This arrangement made it possible for a minority party to win a seat in the district, and it reduced the possibility that a plurality party would win all the seats in a district. (In a single-member-district [SMD] system, with which the British and Americans are familiar, the plurality party wins the single seat for the district and the other parties are left with nothing to show for their pains.) The Japanese called their setup the "medium-sized district system" and it is known to political scientists as the single nontransferable vote (SNTV) system.

Table 5.1 shows the results of lower house elections since 1957.

The SNTV system worked best for the LDP and the Social Democratic Party of Japan (SDPJ); they generally received more seats than their respective proportions of the vote would justify under proportional representation (PR). The system worked badly for the small parties, which won fewer seats than their proportion of the votes would justify under PR. Another problem was the failure of the government to redistribute seats when some districts lost population and others gained population. The LDP majority in the Diet was reluctant to reduce the representation of rural areas which had been loyally electing conservative candidates. Several years ago, the Japanese Supreme Court declared unconstitutional the apportionment plan then in force, and a new distribution of seats was used for the 1986 election. As things turned out, the reapportionment did no appreciable damage to the LDP, which won a landslide victory in that election.

Mechanical factors tended to emphasize the individual candidate over the party; the ballot did not carry either the names of the candidates or the parties, forcing the voter to write his or her favorite candidate's name on the ballot.

ELECTORAL STRATEGIES

A problem with the SNTV is that if a party endorsed too many candidates in a district, the votes of the party's supporters will be spread too thin among too many candidates, and none (or fewer than would otherwise be the case) would get enough votes to win a seat. Because the LDP usually endorsed several candidates in each district, conservative voters had to choose among the LDP candidates. The pressure in the party to sponsor too many candidates was great. In recent years, the LDP managed to severely restrict the number of its endorsements to assure the optimal result, usually endorsing two or more candidates in each district.

Rarely did the SDPJ have enough supporters to elect more than one Socialist candidate in a district, so it usually endorsed only one candidate. The Communists also endorsed only one candidate per district. In most districts, the Communists usually failed to win a single seat, so many Communist votes were "wasted." (If the Communists had refrained from sponsoring Communist candidates in the hopeless districts, at least their supporters could have voted for candidates of other progressive parties; but the Communist strategy in recent years has been to oppose the other progressive parties as much as they opposed the conservatives.) The Democratic Socialist Party (DSP) and Komeito each normally endorsed one candidate only in those districts where a fair chance of success existed. The DSP, Komeito, and SDPJ occasionally made electoral alliances, by which they agreed to support one another's candidates in some electoral districts, thus making the most effective use of progressive votes.

The nature of the electoral system often made it possible to determine the outcome of the election in advance—in broad outline. For example, in the 1990 General Election only the LDP endorsed more than 257 candidates, the number necessary to have the possibility of winning a majority (257) of the 512 seats in the lower house. Even if every one of the 148 Socialist candidates had won seats, they still would not have captured a majority of the seats in the chamber. The same could be said of the other parties. Thus, even before the election was held, everyone knew that none of the opposition parties could possibly win a majority of seats. Because only the LDP had a mathematical potential to win a majority of seats, the LDP was the only party that would be able to establish a one-party cabinet, whereas a cabinet made up of the other parties probably would be an unpredictable and unstable combination. Voters desiring political stability would have been inclined to vote conservative in order to produce a single-party cabinet with the stable majority in

Table 5.1   HOUSE OF REPRESENTATIVES ELECTIONS

Party	1958	1960	1963	1967	1969	1972	1976	1979	1980	1983	1986	1990	1993
Liberal Democratic Party	287	296	283	277	288	271	249	248	284	250	300	275	223
New Liberal Club							17	4	12	8	6		
Renewal Party													55
Japan New Party													35
New Party Sakigake													13
Democratic Socialist Party		17	23	30	31	19	29	35	32	38	26	14	15
Social Democratic Federation								2	3	3	4	4	4
Komeito				25	47	29	55	57	33	58	56	45	51
Social Democratic Party of Japan	166	145	144	140	90	118	123	107	107	112	85	136	70
Japan Communist Party	1	3	5	5	14	38	17	39	29	26	26	16	15
Minor parties	1	1				2						1	
Independents	12	5	12	9	16	14	21	19	11	16	9	21	30
Totals	467	467	467	486	486	491	511	511	511	511	512	512	511

Table 5.2   PROPORTIONAL REPRESENTATION REGIONS

Region	Number of Seats
Hokkaido	9
Tohoku (northern Honshu)	16
Kita Kanto (northern Tokyo plain)	21
Minami Kanto (southern Tokyo plain)	23
Tokyo	19
Hokuriku-Shinetsu (central Japan Sea coast)	13
Tokai (Pacific coast southwest of Tokyo)	23
Kinki (Kyoto-Osaka-Kobe area)	33
Chugoku (western Honshu)	13
Shikoku	7
Kyushu	23
Total	200

the House of Representatives necessary to govern effectively.

ELECTORAL REFORM FOR THE LOWER HOUSE

The tendency of American political scientists is to analyze elections in terms of a triad of variables: candidate, issue, and party. A fourth factor, a constant usually taken for granted and therefore not often mentioned in American analyses, is the electoral system. The Japanese party system, indeed any party system, would function very differently if the electoral system was changed. The Japanese SNTV electoral system was criticized on a number of grounds: (1) It favored large parties over small parties, (2) The size of the electoral districts was too large, which increased the cost of campaigning, (3) LDP candidates found themselves competing against one another for conservative votes, which increased the total cost of conservative campaigns. (It was rare that any other party sponsored more than one candidate in a district.) The high cost of campaigning required politicians to raise large amounts of money, which was a source of corruption. (4) The districts were not promptly reapportioned to take into account changes in the distribution of the population. Thus districts with small populations might have more seats in the lower house than was merited while districts with large populations were underrepresented.

Because of these complaints, every few years, serious proposals were advanced to correct these problems. However, reform proposals provoked opposition as any given proposal was apt to favor certain parties, factions, or individuals over other parties, factions, or individuals.

In the 1980s and 1990s the Liberal Democratic Party especially, but most of the other parties to some degree, were so embarrassed by widely publicized political scandals that political reform became a leading issue. Proposed legislation especially concentrated on the reform of political financing and on the electoral system. Prime Ministers Kaifu and Miyazawa were unable to secure the adoption of reform legislation. In 1993, when the reformer Hosokawa became prime minister of a coalition cabinet that excluded the LDP, the Diet enacted a new electoral law and a reapportionment law for the lower house.

The radical new laws established the total number of seats at 500, with 300 seats to be filled by voting in 300 single-member districts (SMDs), and 200 seats to be filled by proportional representation (PR) in 11 regions, in which the system of party lists would be used.

The 300 SMDs were created by dividing up each of the 47 prefectures (Japan's major political subdivisions) into electoral districts. This was comparable to the system used in the U.S. House of Representatives, according to which each of the states is divided into SMDs.

In order to fill the 200 seats to be elected by proportional representation, Japan was divided into 11 regions. The islands of Hokkaido, Kyushu, and Shikoku were each designated a region for PR. Honshu was divided into eight regions (see Table 5.2) roughly arranged from north to south and the number of seats to be filled by proportional representation in each region.

Each voter would cast two votes. One vote would indicate the candidate that the voter preferred to represent the voter's single-member district. The other vote would indicate the party list the voter preferred. (Each party would propose a list of its candidates for seats representing the relevant region.) After an election, the candidates winning pluralities in the 300 SMDs would be declared elected. The 200 PR seats would be assigned to the political parties in proportion to the votes received by their party lists. For example, after the votes for a regional party list are counted and a certain party is awarded four seats, the top four individuals named on that party's list are declared elected. (In Japan, there would be no intimate link between the SMD system and the PR system such as exists between the two systems used in the election of the German Bundestag.)

A law was enacted to reform the system of campaign financing that, among other things, would limit corporate donations to individual politicians, provide public funds to parties for campaigning, and strengthen enforcement of the rules.

Expected Advantages of the Electoral Reforms

The use of single-member districts was expected to encourage the development of a two-party system because small parties would have little chance to win the pluralities necessary to win seats and would ultimately wither away. With two large parties of about equal strength, there would be alternation in office, that is, the cabinet would be alternately controled by the two parties. The prospect of having to assume responsibility for government of the country would discourage politicians from demagogically advocating impractical policies for the sole purpose of gaining electoral advantage. The single-member districts would end the practice of LDP candidates competing with one another for votes in the same district. Thus campaigning would be cheaper for the LDP and there would be less temptation to engage in corruption. There would be less pork-barrel politicking, and the influence of *koenkai* (organizations that support individual politicians) would be reduced. There would be more emphasis on winning elections on the basis of issues and parties. The central party leadership would be strengthened, as the composition of the party lists would be under their supervision.

UPPER HOUSE ELECTIONS

The House of Councilors consists of 252 members, 100 of whom are elected using a system of proportional representation and 152 of whom

represent electoral districts. The six-year terms of the members are staggered so that elections are held every three years to fill one-half of the seats.

At each election, 50 seats (of the 126 seats at stake) have to be filled by proportional representation. Each political party proposes a list of candidates and each voter indicates the list that he or she prefers. For proportional representation the country is not divided into districts or regions, but, instead, the party lists provide for representation of the nation at large. In 1995, the New Frontier Party, whose list won 30.75 percent of the votes, was awarded 18 of the 50 seats. The top 18 candidates on the New Frontier Party's list were then awarded the seats. Largely because some of the minor parties did not win sufficient votes to be assigned any seats at all, their votes were "wasted," and the larger political parties were assigned a larger proportion of the seats than the proportion of their votes would otherwise have entitled them to. That is why the New Frontier Party was able to win 36 percent of the seats with only 30.75 percent of the votes. This system was first used in Japan in the 1983 election and remains controversial. (In previous elections, the relevant 50 seats had been filled by SNTV, using the country at large as a single district. Each voter chose one candidate and the 50 candidates winning the most votes won the seats.)

A principal objection to the list system of PR is that candidates at the top of the lists of the major parties are virtually assured election whether they campaign or not, whereas those at the bottom of the list have almost no chance. Voters are not given a voice in choosing the candidates for a party's list. The lists are composed by party bosses who tend to favor old-guard party regulars who have the support of their faction leaders.

Also, at each election 76 seats are filled by using the 47 prefectures as electoral districts. At each election each district is entitled to send to Tokyo from one to four councilors depending on the size of the district. The SNTV is used. Each voter chooses one candidate, and the candidates winning the most votes in each district are declared elected. (For an example of an election, see Table 5.3.)

The 1995 upper house election was notable in two respects. First, the percentage of qualified voters who voted, 44.52 percent, was the

Table 5.3   HOUSE OF COUNCILORS ELECTION RESULTS—July 23, 1995

Party	Elected in Districts in 1995	Elected by Proportional Representation in 1995	Seats not at Stake; Carried Over	Total Seats Held After 1995 Election
Liberal Democratic Party	34	15	61	110
Social Democratic Party of Japan	7	9	22	38
New Party Sakigake	1	2		3
New Frontier Party	22	18	16	56
Komeito			11	11
Japan Communist Party	3	5	6	14
Democratic Reform League (Minkairen)	2			2
Peace-Citizens	1		1	2
Ni-in Club	0	1	1	2
Sports-Peace Party	0		1	1
Other groups	0		1	1
Independents	6		6	12
Totals	76	50	126	252

lowest ever in any national election in Japan since World War II. The low turnout was usually attributed by most to voter apathy. The enthusiasm for political reform that had led to the defeat of the LDP and the formation of the Hosokawa cabinet had given way to disillusionment after Hosokawa resigned as the result of a scandal, Hata was unable to establish a stable coalition cabinet of the reform parties, and the SDPJ and LDP compromised their long-held political ideals when they formed the Murayama government. Second, the New Frontier Party replaced the SDPJ as the second largest political party in the House of Councilors, inspiring some analysts to conclude that if a lower house election were held at that time, the NFP would win a majority in that house. Table 5.4 shows upper house election results since 1955.

The electoral systems for the two houses of the Diet seem complicated when they have to be described to non-Japanese. For the voters, however, elections are simple. The rules of the game have a lot to do with who wins and who loses, so that politicians are much preoccupied with purported improvements in the system. In Japan, as elsewhere, abstract theories of justice do not always prevail over the realities of political power.

THE LIBERAL DEMOCRATIC PARTY

The Liberal Democratic Party (LDP) was formed in 1955, largely in response to the reunification of the Socialist Party earlier that same year. The big businesses that had been financing the two rival conservative parties, the Liberal and the Democratic, were concerned that these two parties would waste their funds fighting with each other and fail to protect business from the establishment of a socialist government committed to the nationalization of privately owned companies. Some critics say that the faction-ridden Liberal Democratic Party is misnamed—that it is neither liberal nor democratic nor a party. LDP politicians and their supporters are commonly referred to as "conservatives."

The Liberal Democrats stand for private enterprise, protection of the interests of farmers, close economic and strategic ties with the United States, and the maintenance and strengthening of Self-Defense Forces. The top leaders of the party usually are either former bureaucrats or professional politicians. Only a tiny percentage are lawyers by profession.

Factions in the LDP

The LDP is essentially a coalition of the party's factions in the two houses of the Diet. Some LDP factions alone have more seats in the Diet than do some of the other political parties. These factions are groups of politicians working together to raise money and gain political power, and rarely do they stand for a particular policy distinct from the policies of the party as a whole. Each faction has a leader, ordinarily one of the faction's most senior members in terms of number of times elected to the House of Representatives. No faction is headed by a woman, possibly because few, if any, women have been able to acquire the necessary seniority. An important qualification for faction leader is the ability to raise funds for the faction. Table 5.5 gives a no-

Table 5.4 HOUSE OF COUNCILORS ELECTIONS

Party	1956	1959	1962	1965	1968	1971	1974	1977	1980	1983	1986	1989	1992	1995
Liberal Democratic Party	61	71	69	71	69	63	62	63	69	68	72	36	68	46
New Liberal Club								3	0	2				
Japan New Party													4	
Democratic Socialist Party			4	3	7	6	5	6	5	6	5	3	4	
Komeito			9	11	13	10	14	12	12	14	10	10	14	
Social Democratic Party of Japan	49	38	37	36	28	39	28	27	22	22	20	46	22	16
Social Democratic Federation								1	1					
Ryokufukai	5	6												
Ni-in Club													1	1
Sports-Peace Party													2	0
Minor Parties	1	1	4				1	2	2	4	3	16	2	0
Independents	9	10	3	3	5	2	7	5	8	3	6	10	5	9
Japan Communist Party	2	1	3	3	4	6	13	7	7	7	9	5	6	8
New Frontier Party														40
New Party Sakigake														2
Peace Party														1
Minkairen (People's Reform League)														2
Totals	127	127	129	127	126	126	130	126	126	126	125	126	127	126

Table 5.5   FACTIONS IN THE LIBERAL DEMOCRATIC PARTY, AS OF DECEMBER 1993

Faction	Representatives	Councilors	Total
Mitsuzuka	53	18	71
Miyazawa	54	14	68
Obuchi	31	33	64
Watanabe	46	17	63
Komoto	21	6	27
Neutral or unaffiliated	15	11	26

Source: Asahi Nenkan, 1994, p. 136.

tion of the size of the factions after the critical 1993 election for the lower house.

Virtually every LDP Diet member belongs to a faction. A politician will affiliate with a faction (1) to use the faction's influence in obtaining sponsorship of the party in an election (sponsorship by the party means that one gets money and publicity from the party headqarters in a campaign), (2) to receive campaign funds from the faction leader, and (3) to get the faction leader's support for nomination to a position as cabinet minister or parliamentary vice minister. The faction leader may hope that his faction and the leaders of several other factions will support him one day for the coveted post of president of the LDP. From 1955 to 1993, the Diet would elect as prime minister whoever happened to be the LDP president. After a faction leader retires or dies, the faction normally continues in existence and under the leadership of another senior faction member.

For years the factions have borne the brunt of much criticism. On the face of it they seem undemocratic and feudalistic. Political idealism seems to be completely absent in the factions, which are only out for power and money for their members. Every few years, some party leader proclaims that the factions have been abolished, or that a leader's own faction has been abolished, but within a few weeks, newspapers report meetings of the faction members. Factional rivalries have occasionally threatened to tear the LDP apart, but at election time the LDP leaders have usually been able to bring the party together to make a solid stand against the opposition parties.

Until the Socialist landslide in the 1989 upper house election, the LDP never failed to win a majority, or at least a plurality, of seats in every election to the upper or lower house of the Diet. In this sense, Japanese politics were boring, because one always knew in advance that the conservatives would win. Two unpredictable factors were the size of the LDP victory and the size of the victories or losses of each of the LDP factions. The relative strengths of the factions are of vital importance in the intraparty fights for the party presidency, seats in the cabinet, and other benefits for the party members. Thus, after each election, the newspapers report the new factional strengths.

Every two years, the LDP members of the Diet elect their party's president. Because from 1955 to 1993, whoever was the LDP president was normally destined to become the next prime minister, the rivalry for the party presidency was very intense. In the past, various procedures have been used to choose the president. Since no single faction leader has enough followers of his or her own to become elected, a leader must make alliances and deals with the leaders of other factions. In the course of the intrigues and maneuvers among the faction leaders, substantial sums of money may secretly change hands and promises may be made that are not always kept. The system is open to corruption and chicanery, and, since the stakes are money and power for individual politicians rather than the public good, the LDP's internecine conflicts, frequently discussed in the newspapers, often provoke public disgust.

In the 1995 election for LDP president, each party branch and each Liberal Democratic member of the Diet could vote. In that contest, the youthful Hashimoto Ryutaro, who was serving as minister of international trade and industry in the Murayama coalition cabinet, won and succeeded Foreign Minister Kono as the new LDP president. In 1996 the Diet chose Hashimoto for the prime ministership. The newspapers carried summary biographies of the new cabinet ministers including the factional affiliations of the LDP ministers.

Scandals

A survey made by the National Diet Library found that in Japan four times more money is spent on politics than in any other country. Partly because of the lower house electoral system, in which candidates from the LDP competed with one another for votes in the general election, enormous amounts of money had to be raised by politicians in order to finance successful campaigns.

In 1976 many prominent Japanese politicians, bureaucrats, and businessmen were caught up in a massive scandal in which the Lockheed Company of the United States paid generous bribes and kickbacks in Japan and other countries to bring about the purchase of civilian and military aircraft manufactured by the company. Most conspicuous in Japan was former prime minister Tanaka, who was sentenced to hard labor in 1983. He continued his political activities while he appealed his case to higher courts, and until his stroke in 1985 was the most powerful man in Japanese politics. (He retired from politics in 1990 and died three years later.)

In 1988, it was revealed that many politicians and bureaucrats had received from the Recruit Company, a large information-industry firm, shares of stock in a subsidiary of the company before the stock was placed for public sale. Later, the recipients sold their shares for large profits. Prime Minister Takeshita (leader of the former Tanaka faction) and three members of his cabinet resigned because of their involvement. As most of the principal leaders of the LDP were implicated, it was almost impossible to find a suitable successor to Takeshita. Finally, Foreign Minister Uno Sosuke was offered the LDP presidency, although he was not a faction leader. (He

was a member of the Nakasone faction.) On June 2, 1989, he became prime minister.

Almost immediately, Uno's past affair with a talkative former geisha (a professional female entertainer) was exposed in the press. The sex scandal, added to the unpopular new sales tax, helped bring about a Socialist landslide in the 1989 upper house election. Uno resigned the party presidency and was succeeded by Kaifu Toshiki (Komoto faction). Kaifu became prime minister on August 9, 1989.

As part of a political reform package Kaifu proposed a new electoral system that was bitterly opposed not only by the opposition parties but by some LDP politicians as well. The leaders of the major factions who had been compromised in the Recruit affair now decided that it was time to reenter the race for the party presidency, and they contrived to defeat Kaifu's proposals. Although Kaifu was more popular with the public than his powerful rivals, he felt that he had no choice but to renounce any effort to win a second term as party president and with it the prime ministership.

Kaifu's successor, Miyazawa, had held cabinet positions of foreign minister, finance minister, and deputy prime minister. He had acquired a reputation both as a diplomat and economist, and as a fluent speaker of English he was expected to conduct Japan's relations with the United States effectively.

Former Prime Minister Takeshita had succeeded Tanaka as leader of the former Tanaka faction, but was compromised in connection with the Recruit scandal. Kanemaru Shin succeeded as the faction's leader, but while deputy prime minister in the Miyazawa cabinet, he was arrested and later found guilty of tax evasion and illegally receiving large sums of money from the the Sagawa Kyubin trucking company.

After their electoral defeat in 1993, the Liberal Democrats lost control of the cabinet. However in 1994, they emerged as by far the best-represented party in the coalition cabinet led by the Socialist, Murayama. In August 1995 the LDP elected Hashimoto Ryutaro as its president, and in 1996 Hashimoto succeeded Murayama as prime minister in a coalition government that included the SDPJ and the Sakigake.

Hashimoto Ryutaro

THE NEW FRONTIER PARTY

In 1992, much of the Tanaka-Takeshita faction under the leadership of Ozawa Ichiro seceded from the Liberal Democratic Party to form the Japan Renewal Party. In the 1993 election, the LDP lost its majority in the lower house. In June 1993, the House of Representatives passed a resolution of no confidence in the Miyazawa cabinet. With Ozawa's blessing, an eight-party coalition government, which excluded the LDP and included the Social Democratic Party of Japan (SDPJ), was established under the premiership of Hosokawa Morihiro. The coalition ended the "1955 system" of dominant party politics.

Hosokawa, the leader of the recently organized Japan New Party, was a grandson of Prince Konoe Fumimaro, who had led three cabinets before World War II. Hosokawa and most of his fellow party members had never before served in the Diet. Hosokawa's candid, unpolitician-like manner made him popular among the public, which had tired of the self-seeking and corruption

endemic among traditional politicians. Hosokawa promised political reforms and it seemed that a new day had arrived in Japanese politics.

Hosokawa presided over the passage of a sweeping electoral reform bill, but announced controversial proposals for tax reforms without first adequately discussing them with other politicians, and the Socialists seceded from his coalition. A financial scandal in which Hosokawa had been involved several decades previously came to light, and he resigned from office.

In April 1994 Hata Tsutomu of the Japan Renewal Party succeeded as prime minister and organized a coalition cabinet. It excluded the LDP. The SDPJ, claiming that other coalition parties were intriguing against it, withdrew its support almost from the beginning. Thus the Hata administration could count on the support of only a minority of the members of the lower house. After only two months in office, Hata, threatened by a vote of no confidence, resigned.

In 1994, the Renewal Party, the Komeito, the Japan New Party, the Democratic Socialist Party, the Liberal Reform League, some prominent Liberal Democrats, and several minor groups merged to form the New Frontier Party. As of July 25, 1995, the New Frontier Party held 56 seats in the upper house and 169 seats in the lower house. It had the second largest number of seats of any party in each of the houses of the Diet, replacing the Socialists as the number two party. Former Prime Minister Kaifu served as the party's president, and its secretary-general was Ozawa Ichiro. Japan appeared to have what was close to a two-party system, with the LDP as the dominant party in the coalition cabinet and with the New Frontier Party the dominant party in opposition.

In December 1995 a new party president was elected—anyone paying a ¥1000 ($10.00) fee could vote. Ozawa, with 1,120,012 votes, defeated former Prime Minister Hata (566,998 votes) to become the new party president. If the New Frontier Party should win the next lower house election, its president (now Ozawa) would probably become the prime minister.

THE SOCIAL DEMOCRATIC PARTY OF JAPAN

The Japan Socialist Party (JSP) won a plurality of the seats in the lower house in the 1947 election. As a result, the JSP and the conservatively inclined Democratic Party formed a coalition government under the leadership of Katayama Tetsu, the JSP leader. The coalition cabinet, however, could not survive the defection of left-wing Socialists who differed with Katayama over the budget. The successor coalition cabinet included Socialists but was led by the Democrat Ashida Hitoshi. In 1948 the Ashida cabinet was forced to resign because of a major scandal, and Mr. Yoshida formed a conservative cabinet and remained prime minister until 1954. From 1948 to 1994 no Socialists served in the cabinet. The lack of governmental experience was a substantial handicap to the image of the Socialists among the voters, who place a premium on competence. In 1950, the JSP split into rival left and right wings because of a dispute over the peace treaty.

When the left and right factions of the JSP reunited in 1955, it appeared that the party had a new lease on life. Most of the party's support came from labor unions and Marxist intellectuals. However, Japan's economic recovery, touched off by the Korean War boom in the early 1950s, deprived the Socialist ideology of its earlier appeal. The Socialists, however, were able to capitalize on the public suspicions of conservative efforts to amend the Constitution and the unpopularity of the new security treaty negotiated by Prime Minister Kishi with the United States in 1959. Massive street demonstrations and factional rivalries in the LDP forced Kishi's resignation. Although the LDP won the subsequent general election, the Socialists hoped that they would soon become the governing party. Instead, the economic boom of the 1960s made the LDP virtually invincible, and with the secession of Nishio's right-wing Socialists, the emergence of the Komeito, and the revival of the Communists, the JSP was faced with rivals for the leadership of the opposition camp.

The JSP, from its very beginning, was torn by internal strife. An uncompromising doctrinaire left wing refused to accommodate itself to pragmatic realities, and, when moderates seceded from the party, the left became even less inclined to compromise. Unlike the Socialist parties of Western Europe, which strongly supported NATO, the JSP long opposed the alignment with the United States, and instead seemed to show a preference for the USSR, Communist China, and North Korea. When the Sino-Soviet dispute broke out in the 1960s, some of the JSP members praised the Chinese and blamed the Soviet Union. The external influences on the party tended to discredit it. When the JSP leadership perennially proposed a coalition of leftist parties, it was faced with the adamant refusal of the Communists to collaborate with the Democratic Socialists and with the latter's refusal to work with the Communists.

In the 1970s as the security treaty with the United States and the existence of the Self-Defense Forces became more widely accepted, the Socialists were no longer able to capitalize so successfully on these issues. Their advocacy of "unarmed neutrality" seemed increasingly irrelevant and had to be deemphasized to make electoral alliances with other opposition parties.

After its 1986 electoral debacle, the JSP, in an uncharacteristically imaginative stroke, elected Doi Takako, a female pacifist law professor, as its leader. Making the unpopular new sales tax its principal issue, the JSP won a landslide victory in the 1989 upper house election. Doi announced plans to moderate JSP stands on the security treaty and defense in order to pave the way for a JSP-led coalition cabinet. However, in the 1990 lower house election, the poor showing of the JSP's potential coalition partners (DSP and Komeito) and their alienation from the JSP made a JSP-led coalition cabinet an impossibility. The party formally moderated its opposition to the Self-Defense forces and changed its English (but not its Japanese) name to Social Democratic Party of Japan (SDPJ). Doi resigned as chair of the party, while tensions continued among the pacifist, leftist, and moderate factions.

The 1993 lower house election was catastrophic for the JSP, when it won only 70 seats, its fewest seats in any election since 1949. So-

Murayama Tomiichi, leader of the Social Democratic Party of Japan, and prime minister from June 1994 to January 1996. He was the first Socialist prime minister since 1948, and was succeeded in 1996 by Ryutaro Hashimoto, leader of the Liberal Democratic Party.

cialists, however, served in the Hosokawa cabinet, which was formed in 1993.

Murayama's Coalition Cabinet

The following year, after denying their support to the Hata cabinet, the Socialists now found themselves in the opposition together with the LDP. This prompted an event that had been hitherto considered a fantastic impossibility in Japanese politics: The Socialists and the LDP, which had staunchly advocated opposing ideologies and contrasting foreign policies, joined forces in June 1994, to form a coalition government. Murayama Tomiichi, an SDPJ leader,

became prime minister of a cabinet that included 13 members of the LDP, 6 Socialists, and 2 members of the New Party Sakigake. (The New Party Sakigake, or Sakigake for short, was made up largely of LDP members who had defected from the LDP before the 1993 General Election.) Thus the LDP held a majority of the cabinet posts, and Kono Yohei, then the president of the LDP, served concurrently as deputy prime minister and foreign minister.

When he assumed the premiership of a coalition government in 1994, the Socialist leader Murayama publicly proclaimed that the Self-Defense Forces were constitutional and the security treaty with the United States should be maintained, thus repudiating the most salient policy positions held by the Socialists for decades. The majority of the ministers in the cabinet were LDP members, and the Socialist Party had lost much of distinctive identity.

The Socialists' disastrous showing in the 1995 upper house election resulted in their decline to the number three position in that house, with only 38 seats. The SDPJ had lost its position as one of the two major parties to the New Frontier Party. Socialist leaders had already been openly discussing the replacement of the SDPJ by a new political organization. At a meeting with labor leaders in August 1995, Murayama said that the proposed new party should be based on high ideals such as had characterized the SDPJ. He said that the Socialists should be proud of their record and be credited with having prevented the runaway rearmament of Japan and Japan's involvement in the Vietnam War. Murayama resigned as prime minister in January 1996 and was replaced by Hashimoto of the LDP.

Probably a basic reason for the precipitous decline of the SDPJ is that the dissolution of the Soviet Union and the end of the Cold War largely deprived it of the issues of neutralism and disarmament that had earned it support among much of the middle class in Japan. At the same time, the decline of the influence of labor unions deprived the Socialists of much of their traditional support.

THE DEMOCRATIC SOCIALISTS

In 1960, some of the Socialists of the right wing quit the JSP in protest against its ties with the JCP, its use of street demonstrations that sometimes became violent in opposition to the U.S.-Japan Security Treaty, and its apparently pro-Soviet, anti-American posture. The seceding group formed the Democratic Socialist Party (DSP).

In 1989, the dissolution of the Domei labor union federation and the absorption of its members into the newly established Rengo labor union federation deprived the DSP of critical support. The loss of nearly half of its seats (from 26 to 14) in the 1990 election raised serious questions about the party's viability. In 1994 the DSP merged with other parties to form the New Frontier Party.

THE COMMUNISTS

The Japan Communist Party (JCP) had a very troubled and usually illegal existence before World War II. At the end of the war, occupation officials obtained the release from jail of the Communist leaders, including Tokuda Kyuichi, the prewar party leader. Nosaka Sanzo, who had taught communist doctrine to Japanese prisoners of war in Yenan, returned from China. The Communists, who had been the prime targets of the discredited Japanese militarists and ultranationalists, were regarded by the Left as martyrs and heroes after the war, but they soon made themselves unpopular by demanding an end to the emperor system.

At the beginning of the Allied occupation, the Communists proclaimed many of the same goals championed by the occupation officers, such as the breakup of the monopolies and land reform. For a while they advocated the formation of a democratic front and aspired to join a coalition cabinet made up of the progressive and moderate parties. Communists won positions of leadership in labor unions and in 1947 called for a general strike. When MacArthur ordered that the strike be called off, the Communist leaders lost much of their prestige in the labor movement.

Communist Eclipse

In 1950, the Cominform (the Soviet-run organization that directed the policies of Communist parties worldwide) published a devastating criticism of the opportunism of the JCP, and the party became involved in instigating serious riots and sabotage. This provoked MacArthur's headquarters to ban the leaders of the JCP from political activity. The party lost most of its popularity and all of its seats in the Diet. In the 1960s, even as it was embroiled in internal controversies over the Sino-Soviet dispute, the JCP attempted with some success to modify its image. During student uprisings of the late 1960s, the JCP occasionally assumed the role of moderator between the most radical students and the university authorities. Because of the JCP's opportunism and willingness to compromise matters of principle, the student radicals were alienated from the Communists.

The JCP has softened its revolutionary rhetoric and adopted issues that immediately concern the voters, such as the environment, railroad fares, and education. Following the 1995 House of Councilors election, there were 14 Communist councilors including 4 women, and 15 representatives including 2 women. Because the electoral system, discussed earlier in this chapter, has operated to the disadvantage of the JCP, the Communists have made a big issue of it. Increasingly the JCP assumed an image of bourgeois respectability and has asserted its independence from outside control by criticizing the Soviet occupation of Japan's northern territories and the bloody suppression of the student democracy movement in China in 1989. Largely because of revenue from their publications, the JCP is Japan's second richest party and during electoral campaigns its loudspeaker trucks are a very common sight and sound.

THE KOMEITO

At the close of World War II, many Japanese were without food or shelter, unemployment was widespread, and people sought refuge in religion. Among the "new religions" that emerged at this time was the *Soka Gakkai,* or Value-Creating Society. (The Soka Gakkai is not to be confused with the New Party Sakigake, previously mentioned in this chapter.) The Soka Gakkai is a lay educational organization founded before the war as an auxiliary to the old Nichiren Shoshu sect of Buddhism. The Soka Gakkai, in addition to emphasizing traditional forms of chanting and scripture study, practices faith healing and stresses a wide variety of social and cultural activities. Evangelism is the duty of all the members, and high-pressure methods are used to recruit converts. The Soka Gakkai has become a global organization and has branches in many countries, including centers in major U.S. cities. (In the United States it is known as Nichiren Shoshu in America.)

The Soka Gakkai has claimed that faith in its doctrines has brought material prosperity to many believers. The worldly concerns of the Soka Gakkai have involved it in politics. In the 1960s it formed the *Komeito,* or Clean Government Party. This party would be unlike either the LDP or the JSP. It would not represent capitalistic interests nor would it propagate socialism. The formal ties between the Komeito and the Soka Gakkai were officially severed in the 1970s, but in the public mind the Komeito remains closely associated with the Soka Gakkai. Because of the rapid growth of the Komeito in the 1960s, some observers feared that it might become a mass-based authoritarian party that might use its influence to impose its religious beliefs on the rest of the society. In recent years, the party has focused its attention on peace, the environment, and other conventional issues, and it occasionally has made electoral alliances with the Socialists.

The Komeito has normally sponsored candidates only in districts where there is a high probability of victory. As a result, its ratio between number of seats won to number of votes has been the highest among the parties. Where it did not sponsor a candidate, the candidates of other parties were most tactful in their treatment of the Soka Gakkai and Komeito. Until 1995, the Komeito was the third largest party in terms of seats held in both the upper and lower houses of the Diet, and it played a leading role in the opposition. In 1995, the Komeito candidates ran for seats in the House of Councilors as members of the New Frontier Party. It remains to be seen how the former Komeito and Soka Gakkai will fare as participants in the fortunes of the New Frontier Party.

THE DIET

The Japanese call their parliament *kokkai,* which literally means "national assembly," but the English word *Diet* is usually used to render *kokkai.* The Japanese Diet, created in 1889, is the oldest parliament in Asia. Today's House of Representatives represents a continuation of the prewar lower house. But today's House of Councilors (the upper house), is a democratic institution, very different from the prewar House of Peers, an aristocratic body.

While the postwar democratic Constitution was being drafted, MacArthur's staff pointed out that Japan did not have a federal system and therefore did not need an upper house (such as the United States Senate) to represent the constituent states. The Japanese believed that a second chamber was needed to act as a check on the popularly elected chamber. They wanted an upper house based on functional (or vocational) representation. The Americans held that functional representation would violate the Constitution, which provided that qualifications of both Diet members and electors could not involve discrimination because of "race, creed, sex, social status, family origin, education, property, or income." As enacted, the democratic Constitution provided for a House of Councilors but failed to indicate the nature of its composition. Later, a law was passed prescribing the electoral system described earlier in this chapter. The six-year staggered terms of the members of the House of Councilors and the relevant electoral laws were expected to make that body more conservative than the lower house.

From the beginning, the function of the House of Councilors, the product of a compromise, was an enigma. If the House of Representatives was a truly democratic body that accurately represented the people's will, there was no need—from a strictly democratic point of view—for a second chamber, which at best would only confirm the will of the democratic lower chamber and at worst would obstruct the democratic will.

The Legislative Process

To become law, a bill must be debated in both chambers of the Diet. If the House of Councilors does not pass a bill within 60 days after its approval by the House of Representatives, the bill is considered to have been rejected by the councilors. The councilors' veto may be overridden in the lower house by a two-thirds vote. If the councilors refuse to pass the budget or to approve a treaty, and their difference with the House of Representatives is not resolved in a joint committee, the will of the House of Representatives prevails. The amendment of the Constitution requires approval of two-thirds of the entire membership of each house and ratification by a majority of the voters. No party, not even the LDP, has ever captured the majorities in both houses of the Diet necessary to amend the Constitution, and it is very conceivable that

the House of Councilors could veto a proposed amendment.

Most bills originate in a ministry of the government, which is sensitive to the demands of big business, agriculture, and the (usually) conservative voters that put it in office. After the ministry has approved the bill, it must be approved by the cabinet. It may be discussed with the relevant study group in the LDP's Policy Research Council, it is circulated among various concerned ministries, and is considered by the full Policy Research Council. After the cabinet's approval of a bill, arrangements must then be made to put the bill on the Diet's agenda.

In each house, bills are referred to the appropriate standing (permanent) committees. Each committee specializes in a particular subject matter as in the United States. Thus there are lower house standing committees on foreign affairs, education, agriculture and fisheries, justice, etc. In addition there are special committees working on particular issues. Many important bills are debated in the lower house budget

The Diet building, which houses Japan's two parliamentary chambers in the heart of Tokyo. Photo courtesy Myra McNelly.

committee, whose proceedings are sometimes televised. In past decades, because the LDP usually commanded a majority in every committee, and often held the chair of every committee, committee approval was assured. If the bill was sufficiently repugnant to the sensibilities of the opposition, the opposition may use obstructive tactics in either the committee or the plenary session, or both, to prevent a vote from being taken. The use of obstructive measures is not purely the function of emotional outrage; by using boycotts and filibusters, the opposition may sometimes extract concessions from the government. Delaying tactics may prevent a bill from coming to a vote before a Diet session is closed. Faced with enough opposition, which may include massive street demonstrations, the government might even give up trying to enact its bill. (This happened in 1959, when the government tried to enact its police duties bill.)

Unlike the lower house, the upper house is not subject to dissolution, so that the members may serve out their full terms. With longer terms of office and with the system of staggering terms, the composition of the upper house is much more stable than that of the lower house. This stability is enhanced by the fact that incumbents in both houses stand a very strong chance of being reelected. The incumbency principle is aggravated by the tendency of sons or sons-in-law of retiring Diet members to stand for election with a very strong prospect for success. A retiring member's *koenkai* is often inherited by a family member.

THE CABINET

Under the Meiji Constitution, executive powers were dispersed among the *Genro,* the Privy Council, the cabinet, and the military Supreme Command. When needed, the residual power of the sovereign emperor to issue ordinances could be employed. Although executive authority overwhelmed the power of the weak Imperial Diet, the authority of the cabinet, which was not even mentioned as such in the Imperial Constitution, was subject to constant challenge from the Genro, the Privy Council, and the military. Under the postwar Constitution, these rivals of the cabinet no longer exist,

and "Executive power shall be vested in the Cabinet."

Responsible Government

"Responsible government," insisted upon by the Allied Powers, required that the executive be answerable directly to the people or answerable to an assembly elected by the people. Either a congressional-presidential system after the American model or a parliamentary-cabinet system after the British model would have been acceptable to the Allied Powers, but given the existence of a monarch and the precedent of Taisho democracy, the British model was much more compatible with Japanese tradition. At the time of the drafting of the postwar Constitution, Japan had a multiparty system. It was apparently anticipated that the cabinet, unsupported by a stable majority, would be subservient to the Diet, which was declared to be the "highest organ of state power."

The first business of the Diet after a general election for the lower house is to designate the prime minister from among the Diet members. An election is held in each house, and if the two houses are unable to agree on a single individual even after deliberation by a joint committee of the two houses, the decision of the House of Representatives prevails. The Constitution requires the emperor to "appoint the Prime Minister as designated by the Diet."

The prime minister occupies a position in Japanese politics that is fundamentally different from that of the president of the United States. The American president is elected by the people (via the electoral college) and therefore may claim a popular mandate for his program. His link with the voters is virtually direct. The prime minister, on the other hand, is not directly chosen by the people but rather by the Diet, which serves as an electoral college for this purpose. From 1955 to 1993 because of the LDP's control of the House of Representatives, the president of that party was invariably chosen for the prime ministership by the Diet. Personal popularity or oration skills were not necessary in order to become prime minister. (Of course if the prime minister is thoroughly unacceptable to the pub-

Feature 5.2 Parliamentary Democracy According to the Japanese Constitution

Article 1. The Emperor shall be the symbol of the State and of the unity of the people, deriving his position from the will of the people with whom resides sovereign power.

Article 3. The advice and approval of the Cabinet shall be required for all acts of the Emperor in matters of state, and the Cabinet shall be responsible therefor.

Article 6. The Emperor shall appoint the Prime Minister as designated by the Diet.

The Emperor shall appoint the Chief Judge of the Supreme Court as designated by the Cabinet.

Article 41. The Diet shall be the highest organ of state power, and shall be the sole law-making organ of the State.

Article 65. Executive power shall be vested in the Cabinet.

Article 67. The Prime Minister shall be designated from among the members of the Diet by a resolution of the Diet. This designation shall precede all other business.

If the House of Representatives and the House of Councilors disagree and if no agreement can be reached even through a joint committee of both Houses, provided for by law, or the House of Councilors fails to make designation within ten (10) days, exclusive of the period of recess, after the House of Representatives has made designation, the decision of the House of Representatives shall be the decision of the Diet.

Article 69. If the House of Representatives passes a non-confidence resolution, or rejects a confidence resolution, the Cabinet shall resign en masse, unless the House of Representatives is dissolved within ten (10) days.

Article 70. When there is a vacancy in the post of Prime Minister, or upon the first convocation of the Diet after a general election members of the House of Representatives, the Cabinet shall resign en masse.

Article 71. In the cases mentioned in the two preceding Articles, the Cabinet shall continue its functions until the time when a new Prime Minister is appointed.

Article 81. The Supreme Court is the court of last resort with power to determine the constitutionality of any law, order, regulation or official act.

---

lic, the public may choose to punish his party at the next election.)

In the 50 years since the end of the World War II, Japan has had 23 different prime ministers, while during the same period, the United States has had only ten presidents. The prime minister's average tenure of office was slightly over two years as compared to the American chief executives' five years. Between 1955 and 1993, two formal events were crucial in determining the prime minister's official longevity: elections for the presidency of the LDP, which

normally occured every two years, and lower house elections (which must occur at least once every four years if not oftener), after which the Diet designates the prime minister to be appointed by the emperor. Thus the tenure of a prime minister may include successive formal appointments to the office by the emperor. The relatively short tenures of the Japanese heads of government may be explained by bitter interfactional rivalry in the LDP, the short term of office of LDP presidents, and ill health. Since 1945, prime ministers who have served the longest

Table 5.6   JAPAN'S PRIME MINISTERS, 1945–1995

April 7, 1945	Admiral Suzuki
	(August 15, 1945, Japan time, World War II ended.)
August 17, 1945	Prince Higashikuni
October 9, 1945	Shidehara (Progressive)
May 22, 1946	Yoshida (Liberal)
	(May 3, 1947, new Constitution became effective.)
May 24, 1947	Katayama (Socialist)
March 10, 1948	Ashida (Democrat)
October 19, 1948	Yoshida (Democratic Liberal)
December 10, 1954	Hatoyama (Democrat)
	(The political system from 1955 to 1993 was characterized by LDP predominance in both houses of the Diet and an LDP monopoly of the premiership—"the 1955 system.")
December 23, 1956	Ishibashi
February 25, 1957	Kishi
July 19, 1960	Ikeda
November 9, 1964	Sato
July 7, 1972	Tanaka
December 9, 1974	Miki
December 24, 1976	Fukuda
December 7, 1978	Ohira
July 17, 1980	Suzuki
November 27, 1982	Nakasone
November 6, 1987	Takeshita
June 2, 1989	Uno
August 9, 1989	Kaifu
November 5, 1991	Miyazawa
	(In 1993, the "1955 system," during which all of the prime ministers were LDP members, ended.)
August 9, 1993	Hosokawa (Japan New Party)
April 28, 1994	Hata (Japan Renewal Party)
June 30, 1994	Murayama (SDPJ)
January 11, 1996	Hashimoto (LDP)

periods in office have been Sato, Yoshida, and Nakasone, in that order. These leaders managed to maintain their influence over their own and rival factions in order to prolong their hold on the office, and thus may be regarded as effective, if not always popular, leaders. Table 5.6 lists the prime ministers since 1945.

Cabinet Members

The Constitution requires that all cabinet ministers be civilians and that the prime minister choose a majority of his cabinet ministers from among the members of the Diet. In practice, cabinet members are selected primarily on the basis of political expediency. Most cabinet members are from the lower house, but a few may be members of the upper house, or not be members of the Diet at all. Occasionally, a woman is appointed as a cabinet minister. The prime minister and his advisors try (but do not always succeed) to allocate cabinet posts to members of the different parties or factions of parties in such a way as to assure maximum stability. Diet members strive to become cabinet ministers because the title is one that confers prestige on them for the rest of their lives. It is one of the duties of a faction leader to get as many cabinet posts for his followers as is possible. The most prestigious posts are the ministries of finance and of foreign affairs. These are often stepping stones to the prime ministership.

After the 1995 upper house election, in which the Socialists did badly, there were demands for an early lower house election. Instead, Murayama reorganized his cabinet to reflect the party and factional basis of his coalition. When Murayama resigned in 1996, Hashimoto Ryutaro of the LDP was elected prime minister. His coalition cabinet included 12 LDP members, 6 members of the SDPJ, 2 members of the Sakigake, and 1 nonparty individual, a woman.

The cabinet lasts only as long as it is acceptable to the lower house of the Diet. If the House of Representatives votes no confidence in the cabinet, the cabinet must within ten days either (1) resign, in which case a new prime minister must be designated by the Diet or (2) ask the emperor to dissolve the house, in which case elections are held for the lower house. In practice, it was usually unlikely that the members of the majority party, the LDP, would allow a no confidence resolution to pass and possibly force an election which might imperil their seats. (But this did happen in 1980 and again in 1993 when some LDP members temporarily deserted their prime minister after a no confidence resolution was proposed.) A prime minister and his cabinet may resign without waiting for a no-confidence vote if it appears that they are no longer supported by a majority in the lower house.

Dissolutions

The constitutional term of office for members of the House of Representatives is four years, but the cabinet normally does not like to wait that long and prefers to hold general elections when it is politically advantageous for the ruling party. Only once, in 1976, have the lower house members been able to serve out their full four years.

The Constitution does not provide for the dissolution of the House of Councilors. At the same time, the House of Councilors does not have the authority to vote no confidence in the cabinet.

In 1980 and 1986, the government scheduled the lower house elections to coincide with the triennial elections of the upper house. Thus the ruling party was able to make the most politically profitable use of the issues that worked in its favor, citing these issues in the upper house campaign as well as in the lower house campaign. In both of these "double elections" the LDP won resounding landslide victories.

THE BUREAUCRACY

The Confucian tradition exhalts the role of bureaucrats, and bureaucrats regulate much of Japan's economy by "administrative guidance." In pre–World War II Japan, bureaucrats selected through competitive examinations were regarded as servants of the revered emperor and enjoyed more power and prestige than did the elected politicians. Although the democratic Constitution has enhanced the authority of elected officials, the power of the bureaucracy in Japan remains overwhelming. The short terms of office of the cabinet ministers make them unusually dependent on the bureaucrats for advice in matters of policy. After retiring at a fairly young age, many high-level bureaucrats go into politics (especially in the LDP) or "descend from heaven" to good positions in private business or public corporations that are subject to government regulation. Most of Japan's postwar prime ministers are former career bureaucrats. Thus the bureaucratic approach permeates much of society.

THE COURTS AND JUDICIAL REVIEW

There are several levels of courts: the Supreme Court, 8 high courts, 50 district courts, 50 family courts, and 448 summary courts. All of the courts pertain to the national government. Supreme Court judges are appointed by the cabinet and are subject to the approval of the people at the time of the next general election and every ten years thereafter. No judge has ever been turned down as a result of the popular vote. The chief judge of the Supreme Court is

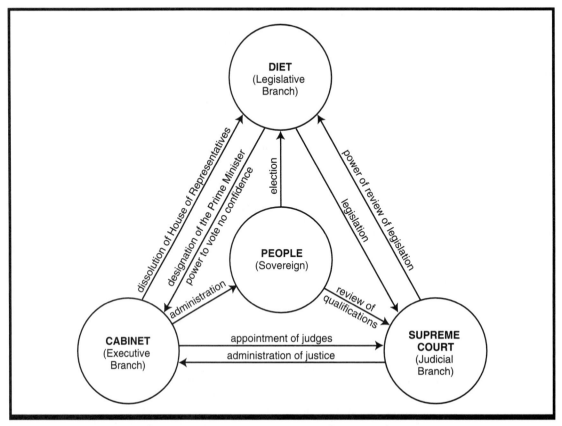

Figure 5.1   Separation of Powers and Checks and Balances in the Japanese Constitution

Adapted from Kawamata Noboru, *Shakai no Kenkyū* (The Study of Society) (Tokyo: Obunsha, 1960), p. 70.

"designated" by the cabinet and "appointed" by the emperor. The imperial appointment presumably places the chief judge on a plane of equality with the prime minister.

Japan's prewar legal system under the Meiji Constitution was heavily influenced by the French and German models, which represented the European civil law tradition. Under Japan's postwar Constitution, it is fair to say that while the legal principles introduced by the occupation are clearly evident, old attitudes still exist among the senior members of the judiciary, who are predominantly conservative.

Under the 1948 Code of Criminal Procedure the former inquisitorial procedure was replaced by the adversary procedure, believed to be more favorable to the interest of defendants. The right of trial by jury, such as prescribed in the Bill of

Rights of the U.S. Constitution, does not exist in Japan. Judges make decisions without the assistance of juries of laymen. The Japanese Supreme Court has held that capital punishment is not unconstitutional. In the years 1993 through 1995, 15 convicted criminals were hanged in Japan.

A notable power of the courts in Japan is their authority to review the constitutionality of governmental acts and of legislation. In Japan, as in America, it has become customary for the political opposition to challenge the constitutionality of legislation they especially dislike, so that the courts may serve political purposes. Although the Constitution explicitly grants the power of judicial review, the courts have been rather reluctant to strike down legislation, partly out of deference to tradition and to the Diet, which according to the Constitution is "the highest organ of state power," and partly because of concern about the political consequences of a highly controversial decision.

Article 9

The most controversial clause of the Constitution, Article 9, which renounces war and the maintenance of military forces, has been the focus of much judicial attention. In 1959 in the Sunakawa case, a district court declared that the security treaty with the United States was unconstitutional, because it provided for the maintenance of military forces. If this decision had been allowed to stand, American forces in Japan would have had to go home. The Supreme Court, however, promptly overruled the district court, indicating that the treaty was not *clearly* unconstitutional and that a political question was involved.

In the Naganuma Nike missile case, a district court declared that the laws creating the Self-Defense Force and the Defense Agency violated Article 9. A high court and finally the Supreme Court ruled in 1982 that the original plaintiffs lacked standing to sue. The Supreme Court left undecided the question of the constitutionality of the Self-Defense Force, and to this day there is no definitive ruling on this issue.

For some years it was feared that the failure of the Supreme Court to come directly to grips with the interpretation of Article 9 would result in the ultimate disappearance of the review authority. But since 1970 the Supreme Court has found some statutes unconstitutional.

LOCAL GOVERNMENT

The political relationship of the national government and the provincial and local governments, as we have seen, has historically been a contended issue in Japanese politics. The establishment of feudalism in the twelfth century represented a victory over the Chinese theory of absolute centralized monarchy, and in 1868, the imperial restoration revived the power of the imperial capital.

Before World War II, the imperial government in Tokyo seemed all powerful. Prefectural governors were appointees of the Home Ministry, which controlled the national police. The Education Ministry controlled the country's system of public schools and universities. The prefectural governments were more like American county governments than like autonomous state governments. Like those of France and England, Japan's governmental system was unitary rather than federal.

Japan's relatively modest area (about the size of Montana) and the religious, linguistic, and cultural homogeneity of its population seem to argue against the need to establish a federal system. The postwar Constitution did not create federalism or a panoply of "state's rights" in Japan, but it did provide that prefectural governors and other local officials, including mayors and assemblymen, be elected. Prefectural governments do not have constitutions of their own (as American states do), but exercise powers delegated to them by the national government, and the laws they enact may not contradict laws passed by the national Diet.

Japan is divided into 47 prefectures, including one metropolitan prefecture (Tokyo), two urban prefectures (Kyoto and Osaka), and Hokkaido prefecture, which includes Hokkaido Island. Most Japanese live in or near the great urban complexes such as the Tokyo-Yokohama area, the Osaka-Kyoto-Kobe area, and the Kitakyushu and Fukuoka area. The urban buildup has largely wiped out the agricultural areas that separated many of the cities and towns from one another. In the 1950s and 1960s, many cities, towns, and villages were legally merged, thus greatly reducing the number of local government entities.

The main concerns of prefectural and local governments are education, roads, sewage, garbage collection, police, and protection of the ecology. The public continuously complains about the inadequate management of these concerns, yet local governments often do not have adequate financial resources to run them effectively. The dependence of the local governments on the national government for financial aid severely limits the scope of local authority.

In the 1970s a number of the mayors and governors of leading cities and prefectures were "progressives" (usually Socialists), supported by progressive assemblies. By earning recognition as a local elective official, a progressive politician might aspire to a seat in the national Diet. Local government thus seemed to provide a base for the expansion of progressive power, which ultimately sought to take control of the national government. In the 1980s, as the result of losing critical local elections, the progressives lost their grip on principal local governments, and the LDP landslides in the elections for the national Diet dampened their optimism. In 1995, apparently out of disgust with the political parties, the voters of both Tokyo and Osaka prefectures elected as their governors nonpartisan TV personalities who had served a number of terms in the House of Councilors.

KEY TERMS

Doi Takako
factions
Hashimoto Ryutaro
Heisei
"highest organ of state power"
House of Representatives
judicial review
Komeito
Liberal Democratic Party (LDP)
Lockheed scandal
New Frontier Party
no-confidence resolution
Ozawa Ichiro
party dominant system
prefecture
proportional representation (PR)
Social Democratic Party of Japan (SDPJ)
Soka Gakkai
SNTV
Tanaka Kakuei
unitary government

FURTHER READINGS

Bayley, David H. *Forces of Order: Policing Modern Japan* (Berkeley: University of California Press, 1991).

Baerwald, Hans H. *Party Politics in Japan* (Boston: Allen and Unwin, 1986).

Beer, Lawrence W. *Freedom of Expression in Japan: A Study of Comparative Politics, Law, and Society* (New York: Kodansha International, 1984).

Curtis, Gerald. *Election Campaigning: Japanese Style* (New York: Columbia University Press, 1971).

Curtis, Gerald. *The Japanese Way of Politics* (New York: Columbia University Press, 1988).

Flanagan, Scott C., Shinsaku Kohei, Ichiro Miyake, Bradley M. Richardson, and Joji Watanuki. *The Japanese Voter* (New Haven: Yale University Press, 1991).

Hayao, Kenji, *The Japanese Prime Minister and Public Policy* (Pittsburgh: University of Pittsburgh Press, 1993).

Hrebenar, Ronald J. *The Japanese Party System: From One Party Rule to Coalition Government* (Boulder, CO: Westview Press, 1986).

Ishida, Takeshi, and Ellis S. Krauss, eds. *Democracy in Japan* (Pittsburgh: University of Pittsburgh Press, 1989).

Itoh, Hiroshi, and Lawrence Ward Beer, eds. *The Constitutional Case Law in Japan: Selected Supreme Court Decisions, 1961–1970* (Seattle: University of Washington Press, 1978).

Johnson, Chalmers. *Japan: Who Governs? The Rise of the Developmental State* (New York: Norton, 1995).

Kishima, Takako. *Political Life in Japan: Democracy in a Reversible World* (Princeton: Princeton University Press, 1991).

Koh, B. C. *Japan's Administrative Elite* (Berkeley: University of California Press, 1991).

Luney, Percy R., Jr., ed. *The Constitution of Japan: The Fifth Decade* (an issue of *Law and Contemporary Problems,* Vol. 53, Nos. 1 and 2 [Winter + spring, 1990], published by School of Law, Duke University).

McCormack, Gowan, and Yoshio Sugimoto, eds. *Democracy in Contemporary Japan* (Armonk, NY: M. E. Sharpe, 1986).

Maki, John M., ed. *Court and Constitution in Japan: Selected Supreme Court Decisions, 1948–60* (Seattle: University of Washington Press, 1964).

Okimoto, Daniel I., and Thomas P. Rohlen, eds. *Inside the Japanese System: Readings on Contemporary Society and Political Economy* (Stanford: Stanford University Press, 1988).

Pharr, Susan. *Losing Face: Status Politics in Japan* (Berkeley: University of California Press, 1990).

Reed, Stephen R. *Japanese Prefectures and Policymaking* (Pittsburgh: University of Pittsburgh Press, 1986).

Scalapino, Robert A. *The Japanese Communist Movement, 1920–1966* (Berkeley: University of California Press, 1962).

Steiner, Kurt, Ellis S. Krauss, and Scott C. Flanagan, eds. *Political Opposition and Local Politics in Japan* (Princeton: Princeton University Press, 1980).

Tanaka, Hideo, ed. *The Japanese Legal System: Introductory Case Studies and Materials* (Tokyo: Tokyo University Press, 1976).

Thayer, Nathaniel. *How the Conservatives Rule Japan* (Princeton: Princeton University Press, 1969).

Upham, Frank K. *Law and Social Change in Postwar Japan* (Cambridge, MA: Harvard University Press, 1987).

Weinstein, Martin E. *The Human Face of Japan's Leadership: Twelve Portraits* (New York: Praeger, 1989).

Public Policy

At the end of World War II, Japanese industry had been thoroughly devastated. In 1992, Japan's gross domestic product (GDP), amounting to $2.47 trillion, was the second largest in the world. What accounts for Japan's "economic miracle"?

THE ECONOMIC MIRACLE

At the end of World War II, the Allied powers did not regard the reconstruction of the Japanese economy as their responsibility. They believed that the Japanese were themselves to blame for the war that had brought disaster to their country and should be made to learn from the experience. Moreover, industries that would facilitate Japanese rearmament (such as the manufacture of aircraft) should be banned, it was held.

This tough policy, however, proved impractical. In 1946 when there were severe food shortages in the cities and Communist agitators were capitalizing on the food crisis, General MacArthur imported food from America. If only to relieve the American taxpayer of the burden of feeding Japan, the Japanese economy would have to be rehabilitated. The United States opposed the policy of extracting reparations from Japan, as it was believed that the Americans would be indirectly footing the bill. The American occupiers belatedly began to foster the economic revival of Japan. Poor in natural resources and overpopulated, Japan would have to "trade or die." As the labor unions fostered by Allied policies increasingly fell under the domination of Communists, MacArthur took action to check their influence. Notably, he ordered that the general strike scheduled for February 1, 1947, be called off, causing its leftist leaders to lose face. The labor relations law was modified to forbid strikes by government employees. The honeymoon between the political left and MacArthur's headquarters began to come to an end. In 1948, the program of breaking up Japan's family monopolies, the *zaibatsu,* was halted in midstream.

The Korean War Boom

By 1950 neither the policies of the Japanese government nor of the SCAP had been able to rescue Japan from unemployment, inflation, and every kind of shortage. When war broke out in Korea in June of that year, the American military hired Japanese firms to repair damaged equipment and manufacture uniforms, blankets, trucks, and other war materiel. "The Korean War boom" nudged the Japanese economy off dead center, and soon prewar levels of production were achieved. From 1950 to 1973, the average annual growth rate of Japan's GNP was over 10 percent, possibly the highest sustained rate of increase that the world has ever seen.

The Japanese no longer had to maintain a costly military establishment, and—unlike the British, French, and Dutch—they were not encumbered with rebellious colonies; it thus became easier to raise funds for economic reconstruction. Most of the money needed for rebuilding Japanese enterprises was obtained as loans from banks, rather than from the sale of shares.

Characteristically, the Japanese are remarkable for the very high percentage of their income that they save. In the 1950s Japanese and American entrepreneurs set up "joint ventures" in Japan, which facilitated the introduction of advanced American technology. Later the Japanese, rather than attempt to duplicate in their laboratories what had already been discovered elsewhere, purchased the most recent American technology. In the 1970s, the Japanese became the world's leaders in the application of modern technology to industrial production. The Japanese pioneered the development of fully automated assembly lines and now leads the world in the use and manufacture of robots.

Over the decades, Japanese businesses have gradually changed the mix of their manufacturers. From textiles they moved to transistor radios and cameras. They then went to steel, ships, and automobiles. The Japanese lead the world in the manufacture and export of automobiles, musical instruments, photocopiers, cameras, and VCRs. By the mid–1980s, the production of supercomputers seemed to be one of the increasingly rare technological areas where Japan had not caught up with or surpassed the United States. With vast amounts of currency from exports and savings, Japanese banks became the leaders in global finance, making Japan the world's leading donor of development assistance to third world countries.

Costs of the Miracle

Japanese economic leadership has come at a cost. Pollution of the atmosphere and destruction of greenery by Japanese factories became leading political issues in Japan in the 1970s. The country's trading partners continually complain of unfair trading practices and of Japan's refusal to import from, as well as to export to, foreign countries. Many Americans blamed widespread plant closings and unemployment in America's Northeast and Midwest—the "rust belt"—on Japanese trading policies. The Japanese were charged with "dumping," that is, the sale of goods abroad at a price higher than the price at home, or the sale of goods at a price lower than the cost of production, often in order to drive competitors out of business. Demands for sanctions against dumping, for protective tariffs, and for the opening of the Japanese markets have become major political issues in the United States.

THE GLOBALIZATION OF THE ECONOMY

Japan is afflicted with many of the same economic and social problems that plague the other postindustrial countries in Europe and in North America. Constant modernization of production processes requires that new jobs or retraining be provided to those who become unemployed

because of technological advances. South Korea, Taiwan, Hong Kong, and Singapore are becoming "Little Japans" by manufacturing and exporting many goods, including automobiles, TV sets, and computers, that compete with Japanese exports. In a decade or so, Japan may be faced with serious competition from industries in China, India, and Brazil, which have large populations and substantial natural resources. Because of the high cost of labor and land in Japan, Japanese entrepreneurs, like their American counterparts, are increasingly seeking overseas sites for their plants. The dramatic appreciation of the yen in relation to the dollar has accelerated Japanese acquisition or construction of manufacturing plants in the United States.

The world's economy is rapidly ceasing to be divided along national frontiers and has become globalized. Japanese firms are becoming increasingly multinational as the structure of the Japanese economy is undergoing rapid change. These changes are imposing great stress not only on the Japanese people but also on the people of the world who do business with them. For example, Japan's trade imbalances and the appreciation of the yen may require that the Japanese—who are money rich but whose actual standard of living is modest—save and produce less but consume more. In the past ten years, the average Japanese household has been saving over 15 percent of its disposable income, as compared with American families, who save only 3 or 4 percent. The expansion of the Japanese market that would accompany an increase in Japanese consumption might reduce Japan's reliance on exports and increase imports.

The Quality of Japanese Products

It seems unlikely, however, that there are any quick fixes for the trade imbalance between Japan and its principal trading partner, the United States. Before World War II, "Made in Japan" was a synonym for shoddy quality, but since 1960 Japanese products have earned a reputation for being the best. Although for a time Japanese goods enjoyed a price advantage over American products, increases in labor costs in Japan and the appreciation of the yen have made them less price-competitive. However, consumers are often willing to pay considerably more for a quality product.

Although Japan's population is only half that of the United States, its colleges and universities train an equal number of engineers. Japanese manufacturers are not content merely to produce goods of superior quality. Their market research is excellent and they are willing to sacrifice profits in order to enhance and preserve their market share. As competitors are driven out of the market, they find it difficult or impossible even to remain in business.

GOVERNMENT INTERVENTION IN THE ECONOMY

In the Meiji era (1868–1912), the imperial government fostered the establishment of modern industries in Japan, often using funds borrowed from abroad and employing Europeans as advisers. Once the industries were brought to a profitable basis, they were sold to private companies. Thus, it was the government, not private entrepreneurs, who launched the industrial revolution in Japan. While England was preoccupied with World War I, the Japanese took over a large share of the British market in Asia and became a leading manufacturer and exporter of light industrial goods. The Japanese navy, the world's third largest, fostered the production of advanced communications and optical equipment.

After World War II, the nationally regulated banking system directed funds to companies for the construction of new factories, replacing those destroyed by the war. Thus Japan's postwar industrial plants were more up to date and efficient than those of other countries.

Although Japan is often said to be a capitalist country with a free-market economy, there seems to be no ideological commitment to the notion that government should not involve itself in the economy. Quite the contrary, the government is expected to and is ready to intervene not only to correct economic imbalances but also to take the lead in directing national economic change.

The Ministry of International Trade and Industry (MITI), has played a conspicuous role in fostering the development of Japanese industry and foreign trade since the 1960s. Government bureaucrats, who enjoy substantial prestige, are often longtime school friends of business and political leaders. It is not necessary for the Diet to continually pass new laws to facilitate government's involvement in the economy. *Administrative guidance* is the term usually used to denote the great influence of the bureaucracy on business activity. Businesses are aware that the bureaucracy has at its disposal effective, albeit informal, rewards and punishments to ensure conformity to government policies.

In recent years, members of the Diet have become increasingly involved in policy making. Groups of legislators belonging to Diet committees who are experts in the policies of particular government agencies are noticeably influencing policy. Known as *zoku* (literally, tribes), they act as lobbies at the highest level of government. The growing influence of the *zoku* suggest that the democratically elected Diet and the political parties are increasing their influence in relation to the bureaucracy.

Privatization

Japan has long had a very extensive system of railroads. Much of their revenue comes from passenger traffic, as commuters in Japan's great metropolitan centers depend on them to get to work. Until the 1980s most, but by no means all, of the railroads were owned and operated by the national government. The *shinkansen* trains (known among foreigners as "bullet trains") were introduced by the Japan National Railways beginning in the 1960s. They became world famous for their speed and convenience, linking most of the major cities and running at 10- and 15-minute intervals. In their frequency of operation, they resemble a city subway system but operate much faster and on a national scale. The bureaucratic structure and politicized national railroad workers union, however, seem to have acted as dampers on efficiency and the system ran up enormous deficits. In 1987, the Japan National Railways was divided into privately owned and operated regional segments which immediately improved services and stopped operating in the red.

The Nippon Telegraph and Telephone Public Corporation was privatized in 1985. Although the government may be strongly inclined to involve itself in the economy, it is no longer committed to the principle of directly owning and managing enterprises.

THE JAPANESE ECONOMY TODAY

The holding companies of the prewar *zaibatsu* were partly broken up during the Allied occupation. However, many of the businesses formerly controlled by the family-owned holding companies are still affiliated in various ways and now are often referred to as *keiretsu* (economic groups). The names of some of the prewar *zaibatsu* (Mitsubishi, Mitsui, Yasuda, Sumitomo) may still be found attached to leading Japanese companies. There are, for example, the Mitsubishi Bank, Mitsubishi Chemical Industries, Mitsubishi Electric Corporation, Mitsubishi Heavy Industries, Mitsubishi Mining and Cement Company, Mitsubishi Motor Corporation, Mitsubishi Paper Mills, Mitsubishi Steel Manufacturing Company, and Mitsubishi Trust and Banking Corporation (not to be confused with the Mitsubishi Bank), to mention only some of the Mitsubishi affiliated companies.

Most major Japanese corporations are connected with one or another *keiretsu*. The name of a company may not necessarily indicate what its affiliations are. The directorships of the affiliated companies often interlock, and companies often own stock in affiliated companies. The varied enterprises (including banks) making up a *keiretsu* often prefer to do business with one another rather than with outsiders, without regard to cheaper prices or rates tendered by the outsiders. Sensitive to the hazards of cutthroat competition and economic instability and the need to compete in global markets, the Japanese government has not always been zealous to engage in trustbusting. Foreigners often find the system very difficult to penetrate.

Banks (many with *keiretsu* affiliations) play a leading role in the growth of Japanese business. Interest rates in Japan have long been lower than elsewhere and the Japanese are great savers, so that companies are able to obtain money cheaply for the improvement and expansion of their facilities, or sometimes for stock or land speculation. In the late 1980s, the price of stock and of land had been driven to unprecedented heights, and these were used as collateral to obtain loans for more speculation.

The Collapse of the "Bubble Economy"

In December 1989, the Nikkei stock market average reached its all-time high, ¥38,916. It then began to drop precipitously at first, reaching several false bottoms until it reached a low in June 1995 of ¥14,485. Thus within five years, Japanese stocks had lost half of their value. There was a similar collapse in land prices. The phenomenon was referred to as the collapse of "the bubble economy." Obviously, individual investors and land owners were hard hit by these events, but the effects went far beyond individual distress. Much of the stock and land had been bought with money borrowed from banks and housing loan companies, stock and land being used as collateral. When the value of these largely disappeared, and the borrowers were unable to repay their loans, the financial institutions found that the collateral was no longer adequate. The banks themselves owned shares of stock and land which had lost much of its value. Loans that the banks had made were in too many cases "nonperforming." (Interest was not being paid on them). In August 1995 depositors began runs on several leading financial institutions, demanding the return of their deposits. The Ministry of Finance and the Bank of Japan became involved in the takeover of weak banks by stronger ones. The government promised that depositors could be sure of the safety of their deposits, and it began to look as if the government itself would have to bail out troubled institutions with government funds.

Financial scandals were exposed when individuals and institutions that had borrowed money in violation of legal requirements failed to repay their loans. The borrowers may have planned to repay the money when their investments increased in value—as they usually had in the past—but the collapse of the bubble economy sent them to prison or bankrupted them and was disastrous to the lenders.

In 1995, the sudden dramatic rise in the value of yen in relation to other currencies, most notably the American dollar, raised the price of Japanese goods in the international market. Sales of Japanese automobiles abroad declined while American and European automobiles became more competitively priced, and the Japanese automobile industry contracted. In order to maintain their international competitiveness, Japanese manufacturers had to lower their labor costs. Because of the high cost of labor in Japan, Japanese factories are being increasingly automated, and Japanese firms have been setting up factories abroad.

Business associations such as the *Keidanren* (Federation of Business Organizations), *Keizai Doyukai* (Committee for Economic Development), and *Nikkeiren* (Japanese Federation of Employers Associations) effectively lobby both the Liberal Democratic Party and the bureaucracy on behalf of their interests. Japan's financial leaders, usually referred to as *zaikai,* are the nation's economic elite. The LDP and its factions get most of their funds from Japanese business. It is often said that Japan is run by a triumvirate of big business, the LDP, and the bureaucracy. But small business and agriculture are often able to use their electoral clout with the LDP to extract benefits from the state.

The Pro-Business Climate

There is a national consensus in Japan that government, business, and labor must all collaborate in order to seize and hold shares of the global market for Japanese goods. The patriotic solidarity among Japanese in their national endeavor to compete effectively with other countries has led some observers to refer to the country as "Japan, Inc." By contrast, the adversarial relationships among business, labor, and government that prevail in the United States put Americans at war with one another and no doubt weaken America's position as a competitor in world markets.

After World War II, although Japan had lagged behind the other leading industrial states in the development of welfare programs, such programs were vastly expanded in the 1970s, and Japan became a welfare state. Before the collapse of the bubble economy, there was a severe labor shortage and unemployment even during slumps did not exceed 2.5 percent. However, in 1995 new college graduates, especially women, had difficulty finding jobs.

There is no underclass of hereditary welfare recipients in Japan as there is in the United States. The LDP stresses the importance of a prosperous capitalist system in order to finance welfare programs and social security. With one of the world's most modern medical and hospital systems and with nationalized health insurance, the Japanese now have the longest average life span among the nations of the world.

As people live longer, a great strain is imposed on pension systems and the medical and hospital costs for the elderly rise. In the traditional farm villages common in prewar times, grandparents lived with their children and grandchildren, but in the modern urban environment, the expensive apartments are barely large enough to accommodate two generations, and separate living quarters must be provided for the elderly with or without some measure of government subsidy. A principal issue in contemporary Japanese politics as in the other industrialized countries has been the question of how the needs of the growing numbers of elderly will be met.

The budget of the national government is heavily strained by the cost of education, welfare, agricultural subsidies, and the like. In the 1980s and 1990s, administrative reorganization (to reduce the size and cost of government) and tax reform became hot political issues.

THE JAPANESE ECONOMY IN GLOBAL PERSPECTIVE

In the immediate postwar years, when industrial production was virtually at a standstill and unemployment and inflation were rampant, socialist ideologies were especially popular among intellectuals (many had been Marxist before the war) and labor leaders. When the Left and Right Socialists reunited in 1955, there seemed to be a possibility that Socialists might soon gain control of the Diet and carry out a socialist revolution in Japan. The dramatic expansion of the capitalist economy in the 1960s, however, brought unprecedented prosperity to virtually every sector of the population and prevented radical ideologies from attracting a popular following. By the 1970s the overwhelming majority of Japanese considered themselves members of the "middle class" and few seem to take socialist doctrine seriously today.

Dependence on Global Trade

The nation's enormous economy is, as every Japanese is keenly aware, extraordinarily dependent on world trade. Resource-poor Japan relies on other countries for iron ore and other essential raw materials. Japan has been trying to reduce its dependence on the Middle East for petroleum, but in 1986 petroleum supplied 56.8 percent of its energy, and most of this oil had to pass through the Strait of Hormuz (in the Persian Gulf). Economic self-sufficiency is not an option for Japan. The global trading system established largely under American leadership after World War II is based on the concept of free trade. The theory was that the free movement of goods across national frontiers is essential for global prosperity and world peace. Japan, a powerful competitor, has prospered under this system. A global war or, more likely than that, the erection of national or regional barriers against Japanese goods would be disastrous for Japan. "Comprehensive security" and "resource diplomacy," concepts favored by Japanologists, emphasize Japan's dependence on global trade.

As Japan emerged as a leading international trader in the 1960s, its trading partners began to complain about the destruction of their own industries by Japanese competition. Indeed, by the 1990s, most of Japan's trading partners suffered from trade deficits with Japan. For decades, the United States has complained that Japan enjoyed the right to sell its products in vast quantities to America but refused to buy from America. Actually, Japan is the world's leading importer of American agricultural goods and has accepted "voluntary" limits on auto exports to the United States, but the imbalance has remained huge.

In 1990 the United States began negotiating with Japan concerning a structural impediments initiative (SII). The archaic distribution system in Japan, consisting of multiple layers of middlemen and many small-scale retailers,

seemed closed to foreign imports. The small-business lobby in Japan had brought about the enactment of legislation seriously restricting the establishment of large discount stores that might distribute inexpensive imports. The SII negotiations were successful in obtaining Japanese agreement to modify the large-scale retailers law.

At the same time, the Japanese Agriculture Ministry and the LDP leadership has insisted that no foreign rice be imported by Japan: Japan should preserve self-sufficiency in rice, closing this market completely to foreign, especially American, producers. The Japanese were paying several times the going international price for rice, and Japanese rice production could be destroyed by imports of this food. There was much talk of the almost mystical relation between rice farming and the essence of Japanese culture, and about the need to be self-sufficient in food from the standpoint of national security. In 1994 when Japan's rice crop was hurt by bad weather, foreigners were permitted to sell rice to Japan, and the taboo against foreign rice now appears to be weakening.

While the Liberal Democrats pride themselves on their ability to manage relations with America, Japan's principal trading partner, LDP politicians are keenly aware of their traditional dependence on small-business owners and farmers for their electoral support. The *zoku* Diet members who watch after the interests of these businessmen and farmers are among the most important fundraisers for the party and exert corresponding clout in the Diet. While the Liberal Democratic cabinets may strongly favor trade liberalization, they are faced with the problem of resistance in party ranks and voter defections.

Some Japanese writers pointed out that a liberalization of imports would greatly reduce prices for the Japanese people and enhance their living standards, but the consumer movement in Japan has thus far shown itself no match for producers' lobbies. Many Japanese resent the idea that they must reorganize their society or distinctive culture—purely internal matters—in order to accommodate the demands of foreigners. At best it may take a number of years to bring about the kind of structural changes in the Japanese economy necessary to correct the trade imbalances that distress the country's trading partners. Japanese leaders are becoming increasingly aware that unless some changes are made, barriers may be erected against Japanese goods and the trading system hitherto so profitable for the Japanese may be closed to them.

EDUCATION

Japan's leaders have long been keenly conscious of the importance of education in the development of their country's economic strength. During the Meiji period, the imperial government established a system of public education to indoctrinate the population in patriotism and to train a literate work force. By 1940, Japan had one of the world's highest literacy rates. The Allied occupation sought to democratize the content of education and reduce the role of the national government in its administration. Elected school boards and parent-teacher organizations were established. (Later, when members of the leftist National Teachers Union were being elected to the school boards, these institutions were made appointive.) The term of compulsory education was increased from six years to nine. Although the schools are locally administered, national standards must be maintained. About half of the cost of public education is borne by the national government and expenditures per pupil are essentially equal nationwide.

The Japanese regard their schools as the key to individual and national economic success. Although some foreign observers seem to regard the Japanese educational system as a model to be emulated, the Japanese are keenly aware of its shortcomings. Because entrance to a prestigious university is necessary to entrance into the best careers, parents are determined that from kindergarten on their children will pass the competitive examinations allowing them to move upward from one reputable school to the next. The first nine years of education are compulsory, and no tuition is charged for admission to public schools. After the ninth grade, nearly every child attends high school, although it is legally not required, and tuition is charged by public as well as private institutions.

In recent decades, bullying among school children has become a national issue. Children who are in some way different from the others are especially apt to be the targets of harassment or ostracism. Persecuted children, often with the connivance of their parents, sometimes feign illness in order to avoid attending school. Sometimes children have killed themselves, leaving behind pathetic suicide notes describing their suffering. There were 14 such deaths in 1995. The Education Ministry and local school officials have been making well-publicized efforts to deal with this major problem.

School meets on alternate Saturday mornings as well as all day Monday through Friday, and summer vacation lasts only one month. Homework assignments begin in first grade, and helping the child with his or her schoolwork is a principal duty of every parent. To prepare for examinations to enter a good high school or a university, about half of the children attend *juku,* privately operated schools, after regular school hours. The examination system tends to stress rote memory of information rather than creative thinking. It generates great stress on both children and parents, and the "examination hell" is generally believed to interfere with the wholesome physical and moral development of children. Just as there have been efforts to reduce the working week for adults, there have been recent attempts to eliminate Saturday morning classes for children, an idea resisted by some parents. There is general agreement that the examination system must be radically reformed or replaced with something else, but there is no consensus as to which specific changes should be made.

Higher Education

In Japan, about one-third of all college-aged young people attend college. The most prestigious is the University of Tokyo ("Todai"), followed by the other former "imperial universities," most notably Kyoto. There is at least one national university in each prefecture, and some prefectures and municipalities support their own public universities. The most famous private universities are Keio and Waseda, in Tokyo, together with a number of reputable private institutions established before World War II. Many private universities were established during the 1960s when the national government encouraged their proliferation with substantial subsidies.

The academic demands on undergraduates in Japan are modest, and there is a tendency for the students to spend much of their time trying to enjoy life and to recover from the rigors of the examination system that got them into university. In the 1960s, Japanese universities, like those of other leading industrial nations, were seriously disrupted by mass student demonstrations. Students nowadays are apt to be politically conservative. One-third to one-half of all top positions in the government bureaucracy and in big business are occupied by products of Todai, and graduation from a leading university is regarded as a sine qua non for success in life.

FOREIGN POLICY

Alignment with the United States

As indicated earlier, when Japan made a peace treaty with the United States and other non-Communist countries in 1951, it also entered into a mutual security treaty with the United States, which permitted American forces to remain at bases in Japan. Since then, the debate over Japan's foreign policy has revolved largely around the two poles of unarmed neutrality on the one hand and rearmament and the American alignment on the other.

Japan's position as America's "junior partner" in a world divided by the Cold War largely determined Japan's orientation toward the rest of the world. In 1960, the U.S.-Japan Security Treaty was replaced by a "revised security treaty" more favorable to Japan, although there was widespread opposition to it in Japan. Demonstrations opposed to the new treaty and to President Eisenhower's scheduled visit to Japan resulted in the death of a coed (regarded as a martyr by activists), the "postponement" (in effect the cancellation) of Eisenhower's visit, and the resignation of Prime Minister Kishi. Japan remained loyal to its commitments to the United States and did not recognize Communist China until after Nixon made his famous trip to China in 1972.

Continuously since the end of the occupation in 1952, American military, naval, and air forces have been stationed in Japan. They have served as a deterrent against invasion or attack

---

Feature 5.3 "Automatic Approval" of Treaties

Where treaties are concerned, if the decision of the upper house differs from that of the lower and no agreement can be reached in a joint committee of the two houses, the decision of the lower house becomes that of the Diet. Or if the upper house fails to take action in 30 days after receiving the treaty from the lower house, the decision of the lower house becomes that of the Diet. The joint committee option has been neglected in recent decades, so the government may simply wait for the 30-day period to elapse. The procedure is known as "automatic approval" of a treaty. Thirteen treaties have been approved automatically, without action by the upper house. Thus, unlike the U.S. Senate, the Japanese upper house cannot veto treaties.

Perhaps the most dramatic case of the automatic approval of a treaty occurred in 1960. The new U.S.-Japan security treaty had been approved at a riotous session of the House of Representatives that the Socialists refused to attend. The House of Councilors failed to deliberate on the treaty because of the boycott of that chamber by the Socialists. On June 18, 1960, the date of the expected automatic approval of the treaty, thousands of demonstrators surrounded the Diet building protesting against the treaty and the manner of its passage in the lower house. But the parades, speeches, shouts, and placards of the multitude were of no avail against the inexorable ticking of the clock, and the treaty was officially deemed approved by the Diet at the stroke of midnight.

and in that sense have advanced the cause of Japan's security. American air bases in Japan were used during the Korean War to launch raids against North Korea, provoking fears that the Communist powers might make retaliatory air attacks on the Japanese bases, which are uncomfortably close to Japanese cities.

It would be virtually impossible to defend Japan's great cities from air attack, especially from nearby Russian, Chinese, or North Korean aircraft or missiles, and a war against a major country to defend Japan would likely be suicidal. Japan is covered by the American "nuclear umbrella," which implies that any nuclear attack on Japan would be met by retaliation by the United States. Thus the presence of Japanese and American forces in Japan is primarily designed to *deter* a possible attack against Japan. After the American withdrawal from Vietnam, there were nagging doubts—reinforced by President Carter's talk of withdrawing American forces from Korea—that the United States would have the will or the perseverance to defend Japan if the need arose.

The end of the Cold War in 1990 has seemed to reduce the importance of Japan's strategic affiliation with America. During the 1991 war in the Persian Gulf, American requests for Japanese military and financial assistance provoked a revival of the peace movement in Japan. The JSP especially asserted that such involvement would violate the pacifist provision of the Japanese Constitution. After prolonged and largely public negotiations between the United States and Japan, Japan contributed some $11 billion as its share in the costs of the war against Iraq. However, both foreigners and Japanese ridiculed Japan's "checkbook diplomacy" and advocated a larger role for Japan's military forces in the world.

About 47,000 American military men are stationed in bases in Japan. The total cost of maintaining these American troops—$2.7 billion—is paid by Japan. Most of the Americans are stationed in Okinawa, where American bases cover one-fifth of that prefecture's territory. The rape of a school girl by three American enlisted men in Okinawa in 1995 precipitated a reconsideration of the status of forces agreement between the United States and Japan. The governor of Okinawa called for the removal of American bases from his prefecture and the national government began negotiations concerning the scaling down or transfer of American bases from Okinawa to other places in Japan.

Some of Japan's neighbors as well as many Japanese approve of the American troop presence in Japan because that presence is a disincentive to Japanese rearmament. So long as the Americans remain in Japan in force, there would seem to be less likelihood that Japan would again become a military power and a threat to her neighbors.

RELATIONS WITH THE SOVIET UNION

After the conclusion of the Hitler-Stalin nonaggression treaty of 1939 it was widely believed that the Soviet Union might join the Axis powers (Germany, Italy, and Japan). In April 1941, Japan entered into a Neutrality Treaty with the Soviets. Two months later, Japan's ally, Germany, invaded Russia, but Japan and the Soviet Union did not go to war, nor did the outbreak of war between Japan and the United States result in hostilities between Japan and the Soviet Union. However, in the spring of 1945, the Soviets told the Japanese that they would not renew the neutrality treaty, which would expire in 1946.

After the war in Europe had ended, the Japanese tried to enhance their relations with the Soviets and to induce Stalin to mediate a peace between Japan and the Allied powers. Stalin replied to this request on August 8 (two days after the atomic bombing of Hiroshima), with the announcement that on the next day the Soviet-Union would be at war with Japan. The treacherous attitude of the Soviet Union toward its commitment in the Soviet-Japanese Neutrality Treaty was regarded by Japanese diplomats as outrageous. After the war, hundreds of thousands of Japanese prisoners of war were detained for several years in the Soviet Union, many as laborers, and indoctrinated with Leninism-Stalinism. In 1956 the Soviet Union and Japan issued a joint peace declaration, but because of the dispute over the "Northern Territories," to be discussed later, the two countries have thus far failed to conclude a peace treaty for the conclusion of World War II.

The argument for unarmed neutrality after the dreadful war were very compelling to the Japanese. But the Soviet record of almost unrelieved hostility toward Japan provoked anti-Soviet suspicions and a popular reluctance to scuttle the tie with America. In any event, once the alignment with America had been in place for several years, a Japanese withdrawal from it would seem to appear pro-Soviet and anti-American rather than neutral. But more than appearances were involved. The U.S.-Japan Security Treaty has long been a key factor in the balance of power in the Far East. The abandonment of the treaty might invite new problems in the Korean peninsula, the disputed Northern Territories, or elsewhere. Conceivably the ending of the security treaty would stimulate Japanese rearmament, with a corresponding rise in tensions in East Asia.

After the United States had returned Okinawa to Japanese administration in 1972, the pressure in Japan for the return of certain northern islands occupied by the Soviet Union intensified. Although in the Japanese Peace Treaty with the non-Communist countries, Japan gave up its claims to Karafuto (Southern Sakhalin) and to the Kurile Islands, the Japanese insist that the islands of Habomai, Shikotan, Kunashiri, and Etorofu (from which the attack on Pearl Harbor was launched) do not pertain to the Kuriles and are rightfully Japanese. These islands had served as important fishing bases and as homes for several generations of Japanese. These Northern Territories are part of a chain of islands extending from Hokkaido to the Kamchatka Peninsula and limit the access from Siberia to the Pacific Ocean. They are now highly fortified by the Soviets.

The buildup of the Soviet fleet and air force in the Western Pacific in the 1980s and spy scandals involving Soviet agents and Japan Self-Defense Force personnel deepened Japanese distrust of the Soviet Union. Relations were not improved when in 1983 the Soviet air force shot down a Korean airliner that had wandered over Soviet territory (near the disputed islands), with the loss of 269 passengers including 28 Japanese.

From time to time, the Soviet government hinted that a negotiable solution might be found for the Northern Territories dispute. A complication was the presence of thousands of Soviet citizens in the disputed territory, who may have reservations about coming under Japanese rule or emigrating. The dissolution of the Soviet Union in 1991 and the apparent end of the Cold War inspired some hope that the Russia would be more responsive to Japan's desires in the near future. Visits by Japanese to the Northern Territories have been permitted, and trade relations have developed between these territories and Hokkaido. However, apparently fearful that the return of the disputed areas to Japan would encourage secessionist tendencies in other Russian possessions, the Russian government has recently taken a hard line on this issue.

RELATIONS WITH THE TWO CHINAS

In the 1960s and 1970s, the security tie with the United States involved Japan in the American political and economic boycott of Communist China. However, Japan, with a policy of "separation of politics and economics" engaged in limited trade with Communist China through unofficial channels and informal cultural contacts. Beijing encouraged these unofficial contacts with its policy of "people's diplomacy," which eschewed normal diplomatic channels. The Japanese official boycott of the Beijing government ended in 1972 with Prime Minister Tanaka's visit to Communist China and the establishment of formal diplomatic relations between his country and the People's Republic of China (PRC).

After prolonged and difficult negotiations, a Sino-Japanese peace treaty was finally signed in 1978. It contained an "antihegemony" clause, insisted upon by the Chinese, which was regarded as provocative by the Soviet Union. China had been complaining of the Soviet military buildup on China's border, the invasion of pro-Chinese Kampuchea by Vietnam (a Soviet ally), and the Soviet invasion of Afghanistan. When the Carter administration recognized Communist China the following year, there was speculation that a U.S.-China-Japan alliance aimed against the Soviet Union was in the making.

Before Japan's rapprochement with Communist China, Japanese progressive intellectuals harbored romantic notions about the high ideals of the Communist revolution in China while many businessmen fondly expected a boom in exports to the PRC when trade restrictions were lifted. These attitudes were encouraged by a sense of guilt for Japan's past aggressions against China, the concept of cultural indebtedness to China, the idea that China's radicalism was an understandable response to America's hostility, the notion that, as Asians, the Japanese could understand the Chinese better than the Americans could, and the view that American Cold War diplomacy was to blame for the alienation between Japan and China.

After 1972, when the PRC was officially opened for visits by the Japanese people, the excesses of Mao's cultural revolution and the trial of the "gang of four" in China disillusioned Japanese intellectuals. At the same time, China's poverty and backwardness seriously obstructed the growth of trade with that country. In 1989 the ruthless suppression of the prodemocracy demonstrators in Tiananmen Square (Beijing), shocked the Japanese and reminded them of the blessings of their own democratic system. There has been, however, a substantial infusion of Japanese capital and tourists into China.

In 1995, China resumed nuclear testing in spite of Japanese protests. In 1996, the Beijing regime carried out missile tests and military exercises in the vicinity of Taiwan. When President Clinton and Prime Minister Hashimoto announced plans for closer military cooperation between America and Japan, Chinese commentators accused them of conspiring to enforce a containment policy against China. At the same time, China's economy was expanding at a phenomenal rate. China, with an area more than 25 times that of Japan, has enormous quantities of natural resources and her population is 9 1/2 times that of Japan. Thus the Japanese are becoming increasingly conscious of possible strategic and economic threats from China.

Taiwan

Taiwan had been a part of the Japanese Empire from 1895 until Japan's defeat in 1945, when it reverted to Chinese rule. After its defeat by the Communists in 1949, the Nationalist Government of China moved its capital to Taipei, in Taiwan. When Japan officially recognized the Beijing regime in 1972, it simultaneously withdrew its formal recognition of the government of the Republic of China (ROC) in Taiwan. Quasi-official relations, however, continue between Japan and the ROC, and the economic ties between the two countries are very important for both of them. Taiwan is Japan's third largest customer, while mainland China ranks as the sixth. At the same time, Taiwan is the seventh largest exporter of goods to Japan, while mainland China ranks as the second largest exporter to Japan. In Japan, as in the United States, political conservatives and some commercial interests have been unhappy with the treatment that has been meted out to the ROC by their government. The continuing close relationship between Japan and Taiwan has been a continuous source of irritation and complaint by the Beijing government.

THE TWO KOREAS

Japan's relations with Korea are still poisoned by the memory of Japanese colonialism. The events leading to the annexation of the Korean kingdom in 1910 and the cruelty with which Japanese authorities suppressed the national independence movement are still fresh in the minds of Korean patriots. Although the country gained its independence in 1945 with Japan's defeat, it was immediately divided between U.S. and Soviet occupation zones, in South and North Korea, respectively. When American and Soviet troops withdrew from Korea, they left behind anti-Communist and pro-Communist governments in their former zones, and the Korean War broke out in 1950.

The Japanese were fearful that their own country might be engulfed in the war, but when it ended in 1953, the Japanese economy had been invigorated by the Korean War boom. American policy discouraged the Japanese government from establishing relations with Communist North Korea. The fact that both South Korea and Japan have security treaties with the United States did not seem to mitigate the distrust between the Japanese and the Koreans. In 1965, 20 years after the attainment of Korean independence, South Korea (the Republic of Korea, ROK) and Japan negotiated an agreement that normalized relations the two countries. Although there was agreement that Japan should grant economic assistance to Korea (and it did), the Koreans made their claim on the basis of their right to reparations, a moral assertion that the Japanese were reluctant to concur with. The treaty was bitterly attacked by neutralists and leftists in Japan on the ground that it was aimed against the Communist states in Asia, especially North Korea and Communist China, and would further alienate Japan from her Asian neighbors and involve Japan in American anti-Communist adventures.

Bad feelings between Japan and South Korea are perpetuated by reports of discrimination against the Korean minority in Japan, the apparent revival of Japanese nationalism, and the tendency of Japanese government to maintain informal relations with North Korea. The South Koreans feel that they bear a disproportionate share of the burden for the defense of the Free World in the Far East and that the Japanese should recognize this. Trade friction has risen between the two countries, as the Koreans accuse the Japanese of refusing to buy from Korea while Korea is importing large amounts of Japanese goods. At the same time Korean automobiles, steel, ships, TVs, VCRs, and computers, compete with Japanese products on the world market.

With the end of the Cold War, Japan became involved in efforts to assist with Korean reunification and the reduction of tensions in Northeast Asia. Japan, like the United States, has been deeply concerned about the development of North Korea's nuclear capability, which could threaten Japan's security. In April 1996, large numbers of heavily armed North Korean troops on separate occasions entered the demilitarized zone between the two Koreas. In response, South Korea placed its forces on high alert. If war breaks out in Korea as it did in 1950, the American forces there would immediately become involved, with the possibility of entangling Japan, where the United States maintains major air and naval bases.

THE UNITED NATIONS

Although the Japanese had very mixed feelings about the United Nations involvement in the Korean War (in which Japan-based American forces were participating), after that war was over and Japan had regained its independence, Japan was able to become a member of the UN in 1956. Japanese participation in the UN has enjoyed almost unanimous support in Japan. The UN provided a vehicle for Japanese participation in world affairs outside of the confining framework of the U.S.-Japan Security Treaty. Membership in the global organization appealed to the neutralist and pacifist tendencies of the political left in Japan as well as to the internationalist tendencies of the right.

Largely because of constitutional restraints, only since the passage of the International Peace Cooperation Law in 1992 has Japan contributed to UN peacekeeping operations. On the other hand, Japan's economic contributions have been very substantial. In 1986, Japan's contribution to the UN budget exceeded that of the Soviet Union, so that Japan became the second largest contributor, after the United States. In 1994 over 12 percent of the UN budget was covered by the Japanese contribution. The United Nations University (primarily a research institution) has its headquarters in Tokyo. In a speech at the UN in 1994, Foreign Minister Kono Yohei not only affirmed Japanese interest in disarmament, nuclear nonproliferation, and human rights but also called for a permanent seat in the Security Council for Japan. If Japan obtained such a seat, it would be the only permanent member without nuclear weapons. Of course, the debate over a permanent seat for Japan would provoke protests from Japan's World War II victims and perhaps more importantly raise the issue of permanent seats for other important countries, most notably India.

NATIONAL DEFENSE

"Realists" tend to evaluate Japan's defense policies in terms of the global distribution of power and Japan's diplomatic and strategic position. Many Japanese, however, tend to begin their discussion of Japan's defense in terms of Article

9, the "pacifist clause," of their postwar Constitution, which they dub the "Peace Constitution."

Article 9 of the Japanese Constitution reads:

> Aspiring sincerely to an international peace based on justice and order, the Japanese people forever renounce war as a sovereign right of the nation and the threat or use of force as a means of settling international disputes.
>
> In order to accomplish the aim of the preceding paragraph, land, sea, and air forces, as well as other war potential, will never be maintained. The right of the belligerency of the state will not be recognized.

(The actual text of the Constitution is cited here because it is often misquoted.)

When the Constitution was adopted in 1946, it was generally believed that Article 9 prohibited *defensive* as well as offensive wars and banned *defensive* as well as offensive arms. Most constitutional scholars insist on this strict interpretation, but the Japanese public has over time come to accept the existence of the Self-Defense Forces (SDF) as legitimate. However they interpret its technicalities, the majority of the Japanese people approve of and support the no-war no-arms clause of their Constitution. They do not want to repeat the horrors of the 1930s and 1940s and view Article 9 as a formidable obstacle to militarism and war.

THE SELF-DEFENSE FORCES

In 1950, shortly after the outbreak of war in Korea, General MacArthur directed the prime minister to create a 75,000-member "National Police Reserve," evidently to help maintain internal security in Japan while the American occupation forces were fighting in Korea. The Police Reserve was shortly renamed the Security Force. In 1954, the Land, Maritime, and Air Self-Defense Forces (incorporating the former Security Force) and the Defense Agency were brought into being by acts of the Diet.

In 1995, there were 180,000 persons and 1,160 tanks in the Land SDF; there were 46,085 persons and 164 ships in the Maritime SDF, and there were 47,556 persons and 446 airplanes in the Air SDF.[1] In terms of size, Japan's Self-Defense Forces are very modest as compared with the military establishments of its Asian neighbors. But Japan's defense budget is among the world's largest even though it may account for only less than 1 percent of the gross national product. In addition, about 47,000 American military men are stationed in Japanese territory.

The Japanese government has said that the Self-Defense Forces did not constitute "war potential" prohibited by the Constitution because they were not capable of fighting a modern war. In more recent years, the government has been saying that the defense of Japan is not forbidden by the Constitution and that although offensive weapons and the dispatch of the SDF overseas are banned, the minimum force needed for Japan's defense is permissible. During the national debate over Japan's participation in the UN military actions against Iraq in 1991, the public looked more favorably than before on sending SDF personnel overseas provided their purpose was to enforce UN-sponsored peacekeeping operations and they were not involved in combat. Japan's Supreme Court has avoided ruling directly on the constitutionality of the Self-Defense Forces and has thus avoided saying that they are unconstitutional.

The prime minister has supreme control over the SDF and is advised by the National Defense Council, which includes the director of the Defense Agency (a cabinet minister), the foreign and finance ministers, and the director of the Economic Planning Agency. Because the prime minister is a civilian and is responsible to the Diet, this system, according government sources, assures civilian control.

In 1970, Japan signed (and in 1976 ratified) the Nuclear Nonproliferation Treaty, committing the country not to make or acquire nuclear weapons. Japan maintains the three principles that the nation will (1) not produce nuclear weapons, (2) not acquire them, and (3) not allow their introduction into Japanese territory. There have been reports over several decades that American vessels visiting Japanese ports carry nuclear weapons in contravention of the three principles. The United States government refuses as a general principle to confirm or deny the presence anywhere of its nuclear weapons. The Japanese government has not tried to publicly embarrass the United States by insisting on an unequivocal denial of the presence of American nuclear weapons on Japanese territory, since Japan is shielded by the American nuclear umbrella.

Military Technology

Japan manufactures fighter planes under American licenses. In the 1980s the point was reached where the American military began to ask for Japanese technology. In 1991 a prominent Japanese politician asserted that America's sensational victory over Iraq would not have been possible without Japanese technology.

If Japan develops its own fighter planes and other weapons systems, it may feel the need to export them to help defray development costs. The export of military technology and of weapons has become an extremely controversial issue in Japan, involving as it does very delicate diplomatic and economic questions as well as the spirit of the "Peace Constitution." Japan's rules for the export of military technology are: (1) not to Communist countries, (2) not to countries where the UN prohibits exports, and (3) not to countries involved in international conflicts (except the United States). In 1991, the Japanese proposed that the United Nations oversee a program for making public all international weapons sales.

The Mission of the Self-Defense Forces

The Japanese government's position has been that the SDF may fight only in the defense of Japan. They may possess only defensive weapons and its personnel may not be sent overseas into combat. These and related questions were thoroughly aired during the debate over the dispatch of SDF personnel to the Gulf War in 1991. The SDF is often mobilized to deal with earthquakes (such as the Kobe earthquake in 1995) and other natural disasters, and in the minds of many Japanese such humanitarian projects represent their most appropriate use.

The mission of the SDF in the event of an invasion of Japan would be to fight for up to two weeks while the United States came to Japan's rescue. Japan would provide America with intelligence and protect shipping lanes. Because a modern war in Japan would be calamitous, it is hoped that the American commitment to defend Japan together with Japan's defensive capability would constitute a credible deterrent against a potential aggressor.

With the breakup of the Soviet Union and the end of the Cold War, the possibility of a Soviet attack on Japan seems remote. The issue in 1991 was the nature and extent of Japan's participation in the UN-sponsored liberation of Kuwait. After bitter and confusing debate, in addition to sending humanitarian aid and making a very substantial financial contribution to the anti-Iraq coalition ($11 billion), the Japanese sent a mine sweeping mission to the Persian Gulf—after the fighting had ended.

Only rarely—and after much debate—has the cost of Japan's military establishment exceeded 1 percent of Japan's gross national product. However in 1995, notwithstanding the costs of the peacekeeping operations, the Defense Agency recommended a 5 percent reduction in the Defense Forces budget as well as substantial reductions in their personnel.

Meeting President Clinton in Tokyo in 1996, Prime Minister Hashimoto agreed on closer logistical and intelligence cooperation between American and Japanese forces and a larger role for Japan in maintaining peace and security in Asia. Later, apparently responding to criticism that Japan's new policy might allow the United States to drag Japan into a war, Hashimoto announced that his government continues to hold that the Constitution forbids Japan from entering collective self-defense arrangements.

Two questions remain unanswered: (1) In the defense of Japan's interests and international responsibilities, can economic prowess serve as a substitute for military might? (2) Will Japan, an economic superpower, become a military superpower?

KEY TERMS

administrative guidance
antihegemony clause
Article 9
dumping
Japan, Inc.
juku
keiretsu
MITI
nontariff barriers
Northern Territories
Okinawa
structural impediments initiative (SSI)
Todai
U.S.-Japan Security Treaty

FURTHER READING

Allinson, Gary D., and Yasunori Sone. *Political Dynamics in Contemporary Japan* (Ithaca: Cornell University Press, 1993).

Calder, Kent E. *Crisis and Compensation: Public Policy and Political Stability in Japan, 1949–1986* (Princeton: Princeton University Press, 1988).

Campbell, John. *Contemporary Japanese Budget Politics* (Berkeley: University of California Press, 1979).

Cowhey, Peter F., and Mathew D. McCubbins, eds. *Structure and Policy in Japan and the United States* (New York: Cambridge University Press, 1995).

Dore, Ronald. *Taking Japan Seriously: A Confucian Perspective on Leading Economic Issues* (Stanford: Stanford University Press, 1986).

Farrell, William R. *Blood and Rage: The Story of the Japanese Red Army* (Lexington, MA: D. C. Heath, 1990).

Harries, Meirion, and Susie Harries. *Sheathing the Sword: The Demilitarization of Postwar Japan* (New York: Macmillan, 1987).

Ishida, Takeshi, and Ellis S. Krauss, eds. *Democracy in Japan* (Pittsburgh: University of Pittsburgh Press, 1989).

Lincoln, Edward J. *Japan's Unequal Trade* (Washington, DC: Brookings Institution, 1990).

McKean, Margaret A. *Environmental Protest and Citizen Politics in Japan* (Berkeley: University of California Press, 1981).

Morley, James W., ed. *Security Interdependence in the Asia Pacific Region* (Lexington, MA: D. C. Heath, 1986).

Okimoto, Daniel I., and Thomas P. Rohlen, eds. *Inside the Japanese System: Readings on Contemporary Society and Political Economy* (Stanford: Stanford University Press, 1988).

Packard, George R., III. *Protest in Tokyo: The Security Treaty Crisis of 1960* (Princeton: Princeton University Press, 1966).

Pempel, T. J. *Policy and Politics in Japan: Creative Conservatism* (Philadelphia: Temple University Press, 1982).

Prestowitz, Clyde V., Jr. *Trading Places: How We Allowed Japan to Take the Lead* (New York: Basic Books, 1988).

Schoppa, Leonard James. *Education Reform in Japan: A Case of Immobilist Politics* (New York: Routledge, 1991).

Tabb, William K. *The Postwar Japanese System: Cultural Economy and Economic Transition* (New York: Oxford University Press, 1995).

Van Wolferen, Karel. *The Enigma of Japanese Power; People and Politics in a Stateless Nation* (New York: Knopf, 1989).

Vogel, Ezra. *Japan as Number One; Lessons for America* (Cambridge, MA: Harvard University Press, 1979).

Welfield, John. *An Empire in Eclipse: Japan in the Postwar American Alliance System* (London: Athlone Press, 1988).

NOTES

1. *Gendai yogo no kiso chishiki* (Tokyo: Jiyu Kokuminsha, 1996) pp. 693–694. Figures show authorized personnel strengths.

A Changing Europe
Michael Curtis

The European Community,
Now the European Union

The diverse proposals since World War II for some kind of union of Western European countries reflect the complexity and richness of European history and politics. Europe is not a given entity with a single past or tradition. Eastern and Western Europe are both heirs to Roman and Christian traditions, but the Byzantine Empire, Orthodox religion, and Islamic Arabs have made Europe more than a predominantly Romanic and Germanic group of peoples.

After the fourteenth century, the word "Europe," until then rarely used, tended to be identified with "Christendom." But, in fact, there was never a single political organization for the whole of Christendom or a medieval international order, and Latin and Greek were not really universal languages. In the sixteenth century, the influence of the humanists and of the new cartography, which emphasized political authority in territorial areas rather than ecclesiastical rule, began to challenge Europe's identification with Christendom.

European culture cannot be simply defined or described by a single formula. Rationalism, individualism, the devotion to economic activity, industrialism, and the preoccupation with ideals of democracy, communism, fascism, and socialism have all contributed to the pattern of European behavior. Political concepts such as the rule of law and constitutional government, social concerns such as care for the handicapped and the distressed, personal qualities of tolerance and a reliance on persuasion rather than coercion, and shared cultural values exemplify those characteristics still confined largely to European nations or their direct descendants.

The movement for European integration has a long lineage, going back to the Greeks and continuing in various ways throughout history and up to the present. Although the motives have always been complex, the essential reasons have remained largely the same: the preservation of peace, the need for a common

defense, the ambition to act as a stronger power bloc, the conservation of a common European culture, the wish to create greater material well-being, and the easing of restrictions on trade.

The present movement to some form of European union has been influenced not only by these same motives, but also by significant external factors. The role of the United States as common friend, supplier of material aid in the immediate postwar years, defensive protector of the West, and now economic competitor, has given an Atlantic dimension to the European story. The fear of Soviet expansion and the threat of Communism to western democracies after 1945 led Western Europe, in association with the United States, to common defense and security arrangements.

The new Europe has been impelled by both positive and negative factors. Europe needed to recover from the devastation and depletion of material resources caused by World War II, and economic growth and social improvements would be advanced by European cooperation. The small, separate European markets compared poorly with the size and economic strength of the United States, as individual countries were politically weaker than before the war, less significant internationally, and obliged to end their colonial empires.

Political factors also spurred the moves toward a more united Europe. Many thought that, after two world wars in one generation, it was imperative to prevent the possibility of further intra-European conflict, especially between Germany and France. (The German problem seemed incapable of solution except within the framework of a larger community.) The economic and military dependence of Western Europe on the United States created a desire for protection against a possible American recession, and inspired awe of American strength. Europe recognized that it was no longer the political center of the world, that apart from Britain it did not possess nuclear weapons, and that it would be difficult for it to play an independent political role or act as a third force in world politics. In addition, there was a strong fear of expanding Soviet imperialism, which had reached to Berlin and Prague and had substantial ideological support in the West, where one-third of the Italian electorate and one-quarter of the French had voted Communist.

The interrelation of political, economic, and military factors explains the large spectrum of alternative proposals concerning the new Europe and the various institutions that have been constructed. Politically, the proposals ranged from regular meetings of heads of governments, to regional and functional conferences on specific problems, to a confederal and finally a federal political system. Economic alternatives ran from a tariff and customs community to a full economic union. Possibilities for integration also existed in military alliances among individual sovereign states, collective alliances with common leadership, and integrated defense forces.

A UNITED STATES OF EUROPE?

These European proposals also took account of differing attitudes toward the United States. Some favored an Atlantic alliance, partnership, or community with the United States, whereas others called for an independent Western European political entity, economically sound and militarily strong, capable of acting as a third force without ties to the United States or anyone else.

At the core of the different views toward European integration have been attitudes toward the continued existence of sovereign nation-states. The European nation-state has been a constructive force in the creation of political unity, cultural homogeneity, patriotic feeling, and personal identity. But the destructive twentieth-century wars, partly resulting from militant nationalism, led Europeans to question whether the sovereign nation-state could provide the basis for a peaceful Europe. Some still argue that only the nation-state can be responsible for its own protection and welfare, and that nations should be associated only in some framework of intergovernmental cooperation, with unanimity as the procedure for decision making. This view that sovereign power should largely remain with nation-states was reflected

in the policies of Charles de Gaulle and Margaret Thatcher. Others hold that limited cooperation of this kind, while useful, is inadequate for solving problems of peace, order, and economic well-being in modern life. They argue that the solutions will come not from the nation-states but from some form of European integration or unity, or a United States of Europe.

The movement toward European integration was created by intellectuals and political elites rather than by mass demand. The postwar attempt to influence the citizen body and make European integration a popular movement, in fact, hardly lasted after 1949 and the institution of the Council of Europe. All other European organizations have been formulated and organized by elite political groups or key political actors whose dedication to Europe is strong and whose idealism has been tempered by political reality. But even if the integration idea does not enflame millions as communism and nationalism have done, it nonetheless attracts increasing support by the success of these European organizations (see Feature 6.1).

The impetus to European integration began simultaneously in the political, economic, and military fields. In September 1946, Winston Churchill, then leader of the opposition in Britain, talked of "recreating the European family, or as much of it as we can" by building "a kind of United States of Europe." Representatives of a number of organizations aiming at such a result met in The Hague in May 1948 and agreed on the establishment of an assembly of representatives of European parliaments, a European charter of human rights, a European court, an economic union, and the inclusion of Germany into a European community.

During this time the United States, for a number of political and economic reasons, took a historic initiative. In June 1947, Secretary of State George Marshall, in a commencement speech at Harvard, proposed American aid for a Europe still suffering from physical destruction, economic dislocation, and lack of productivity, and suggested "a joint recovery program based on self-help and mutual cooperation." Moscow forced Poland and Czechoslovakia to withdraw their requests to be included among the Marshall Plan recipients, and none of the Eastern

---

Feature 6.1   Europe: A Brief Guide

ACP Countries—70 African, Caribbean, and Pacific region countries associated with the European Union through the Lomé Agreements

Council of Europe—founded 1949, located in Strasbourg, now has 39 democratic European states including Russia

Euratom—founded in 1965 for common European research on nuclear energy

European Research and Coordinating Agency—founded in 1985 for greater cooperation in research and technology; participants are the EU and EFTA countries and Turkey

Eurocorps—a military unit organized by France and Germany for joint military security, which will be open to other countries

ECU—the European Currency Unit, based on the exchange rates of the EU member currencies, is part of the EMS

EMS—set up in 1979, provides a common exchange rate mechanism, of stable but flexible exchange rates

EEA—the European Economic Area came into effect January 1, 1994; includes the 15 EU states and EFTA except Switzerland and provides for free movement of goods, capital, services, and labor across national borders

EFTA—the European Free Trade Association, located in Geneva, now has four members

Europol—the European police authority, located in The Hague, supervises activities against organized crime and the narcotics trade

European Social Fund—the EU unit to finance common social policy, including help and training for unemployed youth, adults, and migrant workers

Subsidiary Principle—the principle that issues should be dealt with by higher levels of government only if they cannot be handled at a lower level

WEU—Western European Union, founded in 1954, is a European defense organization, linked to NATO; it now includes ten members and three associate members

---

European countries, then under Soviet control, accepted the Anglo-French invitation in July of 1947 to join an organization of European economic recovery. The Iron Curtain had effectively divided Europe. In April 1948, after 16 Western European governments agreed that cooperation would continue even after Marshall Plan aid had ended, the Organization for European Economic Cooperation (OEEC) was established, and a series of bilateral agreements was concluded between the United States and OEEC countries.

Western Europe, meanwhile, was concerning itself with its military defense. In March 1947, the Treaty of Dunkirk was signed by France and Great Britain for mutual protection against any renewed aggression by Germany. As a result of changing international relationships, this pact was extended to include the

Benelux countries—Belgium, the Netherlands, and Luxembourg—in the Brussels Treaty Organization (BTO) set up in March 1948. The BTO was set up under Article 51 of the United Nations Charter as a regional organization able to undertake individual or collective self-defense if an armed attack occurred. The Organization was a 50-year alliance based primarily on the principle of collective defense; members agreed to take steps in the event of renewed German aggression and pledged automatic mutual military assistance. The BTO was intended not as a supranational organization, but as an intergovernmental one in which the chief policy organ was the Consultative Council of the five foreign ministers.

The Communist capture of power in Prague raised the possibility of the whole of Western

Europe being at the mercy of the Russian forces. With the advent of the Berlin blockade in April 1948, it rapidly became apparent that the BTO was not strong enough to resist the Communist threat. Already in March 1946 Winston Churchill, in a speech at Fulton, Missouri, talked of an "iron curtain" in Europe and called for a military alliance between the United States and the Commonwealth. In April 1948 the Canadian Foreign Minister, Louis St. Laurent, suggested an Atlantic defense system. After the Vandenberg Resolution in the U.S. Senate, which ended the historic American policy of no entangling alliances, the Truman Administration went ahead with negotiations throughout the summer of 1948. On April 4, 1949, the North Atlantic Treaty Organization (NATO), with twelve members—Belgium, Britain, Canada, Denmark, France, Iceland, Italy, Luxembourg, the Netherlands, Norway, Portugal, and the United States—was established.

From the beginning of the discussion on the new Europe, differences existed between the "federalist" and the "functionalist" point of view about the nature of a European political institution. The federalists believed that the best way to encourage collaboration among European nations and deal with the problem of sovereignty was to set up a constitutional convention and a European constitution. The functionalists argued that vested interests, multilingual nations, and diverse customs and traditions prevented such a radical step, and that any new organization must be based on the power of the states. At the same time, however, they recognized the need to subordinate the separate national interests to the common welfare.

The issue was decided with the establishment of the Council of Europe in August 1949. In the debate on the nature of the Council the federalists, who argued for an elected bicameral legislature and an executive federal council responsible to the legislature were defeated. The Council has remained an intergovernmental organization.

EUROPEAN COAL AND STEEL COMMUNITY

The first step to a European community came in May of 1950 with a proposal for a common mar-

ket for coal and steel. The proposal was made by French Foreign Minister Robert Schuman, on the suggestion of Jean Monnet, the French public servant often regarded as the inspiration of the European movement. From an economic standpoint, the plan could lead to joint Franco-German control over the Ruhr and assure the French a coke supply, and could end the struggle between the two countries over the Saar's coal and steel. It would also increase the internal market needed for economic expansion. But above all, the motivations were political. National antagonisms could be transcended, and the reconciliation of the two old enemies could lead to a closer European political association. The plan could thus be the first concrete step toward the goal of European unity. For Germany, the plan meant the removal of Allied controls over the German economy; for German Chancellor Konrad Adenauer, the Rhinelander, it meant the realization of an idea of friendship he had proposed 30 years earlier.

The plan was greeted enthusiastically in some European countries, but Britain refused to participate. After a year of negotiations, the governments of six countries—France, Germany, Italy, Belgium, the Netherlands, and Luxembourg—signed the Treaty of Paris in April 1951, and in July 1952 the European Coal and Steel Community (ECSC) came into existence, the first European body in which any institution had supranational powers. The six nations set up the ECSC High Authority, a unique institution to which member governments transferred part of their sovereign powers in the area of coal and steel. ECSC had a Council of Ministers, an Assembly (to be renamed a Parliament) and a Court of Justice, and could act directly on the citizens and businesses of the member states. ECSC achieved quick success with the increase of coal and steel trade among the six countries by 129 percent in the first five years.

Monnet regarded the ECSC as the first of several concrete achievements which would be the building blocks of the new Europe in military, political, and economic matters. Even before ECSC came into operation, another proposal was put forward for a European army, and in May 1952 a treaty for a European Defense Community (EDC) was signed by the six

ECSC nations. The EDC would be supranational with common institutions, common armed forces, and a common budget. The six countries also began discussing proposals for an even more ambitious European Political Community (EPC) which would include a European Executive Council, a council of ministers, a court, a bilateral assembly, and an economic and social council. But when the French Parliament refused to ratify the EDC treaty in August 1954, both plans failed.

At this point Anthony Eden, Foreign Minister of Britain—which had refused to participate in EDC or to put its forces under supranational control—proposed that the BTO be enlarged to include Germany and Italy in a new organization, the Western European Union. Britain pledged to keep some forces on the European mainland, and Germany would be admitted to NATO and supply troops to it. But with the defeat of EDC and EPC, the European integration process had been temporarily checked. Defense policy for the moment would remain a national responsibility. The advocates of European unification then decided that the best policy was to pursue economic integration.

THE ECONOMIC COMMUNITY

The proposed EPC had included provisions for a common market with free movement of goods, capital, and persons. Two organizations already existed to facilitate trade. On the international level, the General Agreement on Trade and Tariffs (GATT), concerned with reduction of tariffs and quantitative restrictions on goods and setting up a common set of trade rules, was signed by 23 nations in October 1947. A narrower agreement in 1944 by Belgium, the Netherlands, and Luxembourg created a customs union (Benelux), which actually came into operation in 1948. Benelux abolished tariff barriers among the three countries and imposed a common tariff on imports from nonmember countries.

In May 1955 the Benelux countries, aided by Monnet and others, proposed a wider common market and other steps toward integration. These proposals for organizations to deal with a common market and customs union, and with atomic energy, were discussed by the six ECSC

countries, with Britain again refusing to participate. In March 1957 the Treaties of Rome were signed (see Feature 6.2), and on January 1, 1958 the European Economic Community (EEC) and the European Atomic Energy Community (Euratom) came into existence. The EEC would merge separate national markets into a single large market that would ensure the free movement of goods, people, capital, and services, and would draw up a wide range of common economic and social policies. Euratom was designed to further the use of nuclear energy for peaceful purposes. In 1965, the three executive bodies of ECSC, EEC, and Euratom were merged into the European Community (EC). (For a list of organizations and their member nations, see Table 6.1.)

THE SIX BECOME FIFTEEN

Attempts in 1957–1958 to create a wider free trade area to include the six ECSC nations and other European countries failed. Instead, Britain, wanting an organization with no common external tariff or objective for economic or political unification, led the move toward the establishment in November 1959 of the European Free Trade Association (EFTA). This body, consisting of Austria, Great Britain, Denmark, Norway, Portugal, Sweden, and Switzerland, was to be concerned with liberalization of trade, not with political objectives.

Within two years, however, Britain changed its mind because of the obvious success of the EEC and applied for membership in July 1961. After being rebuffed twice, Britain became a member of the European Community on January 1, 1973, together with Denmark and Ireland. The government of Norway had also agreed to join, but the Parliament refused ratification after the Norwegian electorate voted against accession. Greece joined the EC in 1981, and Spain and Portugal in 1986.

In 1992 the EC consisted of 12 members. Other countries—Turkey, Malta, Cyprus, and several Eastern European countries—have applied for membership. The five *Länder* of the German Democratic Republic (East Germany) joined the EC as part of united Germany in 1990. In 1995, Austria, Finland, and Sweden were admitted to the newly named EU, which now stretches from the Mediterranean to the Arctic Circle (see Table 6.2). Enlargement of the EC means that it will become more diverse economically, geographically, and culturally.

The EU countries vary widely in population, from Germany with 81 million to Luxembourg with 400,000, and in GNP (see Table 6.3). Some states, Britain and the Netherlands in particular, are more enthusiastic about free trade than others, such as France and Spain. Most states benefit from the EU budget, but four states pay more than they receive in return.

A UNIQUE ENTITY

The EU is not a federal political system, but it is considerably more than an intergovernmental agreement or commercial arrangement. Its objective is integration, not merely cooperation among states. The Single European Act (SEA), which was signed in 1986 and became

Table 6.1 EUROPEAN AND REGIONAL ORGANIZATIONS

Country	EU	Council of Europe*	NATO	OECD	EFTA	WEU	EEA
Belgium	X	X	X	X		X	X
Denmark	X	X	X	X			X
Germany	X	X	X	X		X	X
Greece	X	X	X	X		X	X
Spain	X	X	X	X		X	X
France	X	X	X	X		X	X
Ireland	X	X		X			X
Italy	X	X	X	X		X	X
Luxembourg	X	X	X	X		X	X
The Netherlands	X	X	X	X		X	X
Portugal	X	X	X	X		X	X
United Kingdom	X	X	X	X		X	X
Austria	X	X		X			X
Cyprus		X					
Iceland		X	X	X	X		X
Liechtenstein		X			X		
Malta		X					
Norway		X	X	X	X		X
San Marino		X					
Sweden	X	X		X			X
Switzerland		X		X	X		
Turkey		X	X	X			
Finland	X	X		X			X
United States			X	X			
Canada			X	X			
Japan				X			
Australia				X			
New Zealand				X			
Mexico				X			

*Council has 39 members

Feature 6.2   Key Events in European Integration

1947	Treaty of Dunkirk linked Britain and France
	Secretary George Marshall proposed joint recovery program for Europe
	General Agreement on Trade and Tariffs (GATT) ratified
1948	Benelux began to operate
	Organization for European Economic Cooperation (OEEC) formed
	Brussels Treaty Organization set up
1949	North Atlantic Treaty Organization (NATO) formed
	Council of Europe established
1950	Robert Schuman proposed that coal and steel be put under a common European authority
1952	European Coal and Steel Community (ECSC) formed
1954	European Defense Community (EDC) defeated
	Western European Union (WEU) formed
1958	European Economic Community (EEC) and European Atomic Energy Community (Euratom) established
1960	European Free Trade Association (EFTA) formed
	Organization for Economic Cooperation and Development (OECD) replaced OEEC
1962	Common Agricultural Policy (CAP) adopted
1963	Yaoundé Convention between EEC and 18 African states
1967	Merger of Commissions of ECSC, EEC, and Euratom in European Community (EC)
1968	EEC customs union completed
1973	Great Britain, Denmark, and Ireland joined EC
1974	European Council met for first time
1975	Lomé Convention between EC and 46 African, Caribbean, and Pacific states
1979	Direct election of European Parliament
	European Monetary System (EMS) became operative to achieve exchange rate stability
1981	Greece joined EC
1986	Portugal and Spain joined EC
	Single European Act signed, became operative in 1987, amended the EC treaties and proposed a European single market by 1992
1989	EC countries endorsed a plan for European Monetary Union
	EC coordinated Western assistance to Poland and Hungary
1990	Five *Länder* of former East Germany joined EC as part of united Germany
	Two intergovernmental conferences, on economic and monetary union, and on political union, opened
1991	Europe Agreements with Poland, Hungary, and Czechoslovakia, to include political dialogue and free trade area
1992	European Economic Area (EC and EFTA) proposed
	Maastricht Treaty on European union signed
1993	Single market enters into effect
	Maastricht Treaty on the European Union (EU)
1994	EEA comes into force
1995	Austria, Finland, and Sweden join EU

Table 6.2   THE EU COMPARED WITH THE UNITED STATES

	EU (15)	U.S.
Area (1000 sq. miles)	1,249.0	3,732.4
Population (millions)	370.5	258.3
Population (density/sq. mile)	296.6	69.2
GDP (billions)	$7,293.8	$6,638.2

operative in 1987, speaks of transforming relations among the states "into a European Union." The EU is a unique society, and its institutional structure and procedural rules do not fit easily into any of the categories of political systems discussed in the introduction of this book.

The Community became the European Union in November 1993 based on three pillars: the three Communities which now include the creation of the Economic and Monetary Union, the formulation of a common foreign and security policy, and action on common problems of justice and internal affairs.

The EU does not operate on the basis of a clear separation of powers. It is founded on international treaties (of Paris, Rome and Maastricht) among sovereign nations, not on a constitution (see Features 6.3 and 6.4). Yet it is more than an international organization because it has power in certain fields to enact laws and regulations that are directly binding and applicable to citizens of the member states, and to adjudicate cases in certain topics in its court. The voting arrangements by ministers, allowing some decisions to be made by simple or weighted majority rather than by unanimity, means qualification of national sovereignty, as does the obligation of members to take specific common actions and decide on common policies. The legislative power of states is limited by their commitment to achieve coordination of economic and monetary policy and harmonization of social legislation. The Community method is to seek communally devised solutions rather than individual or bilateral state action.

In recent years, the EU has said that it operates on the basis of "subsidiarity." This term, drawn from Catholic socioeconomic doctrine, means that the EU is granted jurisdiction and is responsible only for those policies that cannot be handled adequately at the state, national, regional, or local level.

Budget

The European communities have been financed in different ways. The ECSC is financed by a levy on the value of coal and steel production paid directly to the EU. The EEC and Euratom were originally financed by differing amounts from the member states, but in 1970 the EC decided to raise its own resources for additional

Table 6.3   1994 TRADE: EU COMPARED WITH THE UNITED STATES

		EU (12) ($ billions)			
		Imports		Exports	
	Total	Percent of Total	Total	Percent of Total
World	640.3	19.0	639.1	19.2
U. S.	110.5	17.3	112.8	17.6

		U.S. Trade ($ billions)			
		Imports		Exports	
	Total	Percent of Total	Total	Percent of Total
World	689.0	20.0	512.3	15.4
EU	114.9	16.7	102.8	20.6

revenue. Its income now comes from a number of sources (see Figure 6.1): levies on imports of agricultural produce, customs duties on other imports from non-EC countries, a small part of the Value-Added Tax (VAT) collected in member states, and a proportion of the GNP of the states.

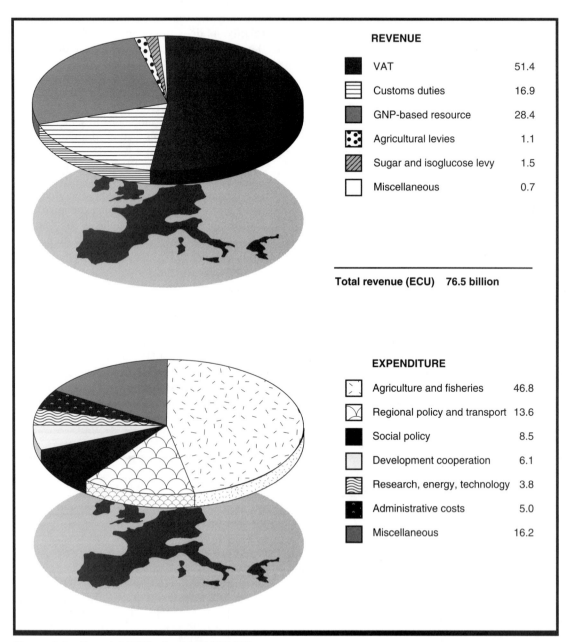

REVENUE

■	VAT	51.4
▤	Customs duties	16.9
▩	GNP-based resource	28.4
▦	Agricultural levies	1.1
▨	Sugar and isoglucose levy	1.5
□	Miscellaneous	0.7

Total revenue (ECU)   76.5 billion

EXPENDITURE

	Agriculture and fisheries	46.8
	Regional policy and transport	13.6
	Social policy	8.5
	Development cooperation	6.1
	Research, energy, technology	3.8
	Administrative costs	5.0
	Miscellaneous	16.2

Figure 6.1   General EU Budget in 1995 (%)

Feature 6.3   The European Communities and Union

There are three European communities governed by separate treaties: the European Coal and Steel Community (ECSC), by the Treaty of Paris, 1951; and the European Economic Community (EEC) and the European Atomic Energy Community (Euratom), by the Treaties of Rome, 1957. The term "European Communities" was used in legal documents to refer to the three bodies, but the generally accepted term was "European Community" (EC). According to the 1993 Maastricht Treaty the term "European Union" (EU) is now used, and the name of the previous EEC is now EC.

Feature 6.4   Law in the European Community and Union

The foundation of the European Union rests on the Treaty of Paris, signed in 1951, and the Treaties of Rome, signed in 1957, amended by the Single European Act of 1986, and the Treaty on European Union signed in 1992. The European Economic Community (EEC) provides a framework, to which legislation and policies have been added, calling for a customs union, ending cartels and monopolies in the EEC, guaranteeing free movement of people, services, and capital, and a common policy for agriculture and transport. The treaty has been amended by the Single European Act, signed in 1986. The treaty was amplified by case law resulting from determinations made on the basis of the treaty, and by regulations, directives, decisions, recommendations, and opinions.

European Parliament

THE INSTITUTIONS OF THE COMMUNITY

As in the original ECSC, there are four major institutions in the EC: the Commission, the Council of Ministers, the European Parliament, and the Court of Justice. Other bodies, such as the European Council, the Committee of Permanent Representatives (Coreper), the Economic and Social Committee, and the Court of Auditors, also play roles of different kinds.

European Commission

The central institution is the Commission, which is both an executive and a civil service of the EU as well as the body that prepares and formulates policy proposals and legislation for approval. It is responsible for administering the Community and for ensuring that decisions are carried out. It has authority to bring legal action against persons, companies, or states that have violated EU rules. The Commission is the guardian of the Community treaties, seeing that the treaties and rules are correctly applied and properly implemented. In addition, its task is to defend the interests of the Community (see Table 6.4).

There are now 20 commissioners—two each from Britain, France, Germany, Italy, and Spain, and one each from the other ten countries—who are nominated by their governments and approved by agreement of the 15 states for a renewable five-year term. The European Parliament approves the Commission as a whole but has not yet been given the power to approve

Table 6.4 THE COMMISSION OF THE EUROPEAN COMMUNITIES

President
1
Vice-Presidents
2
Members
17
20 Members appointed by common accord of the governments of the Member States for a term of five years

Members			**Members**	
1	Belgium		Italy	2
1	Denmark		Luxembourg	1
2	France		The Netherlands	1
2	Germany		Portugal	1
1	Greece		Spain	2
1	Ireland		United Kingdom	2
1	Austria		Finland	1
1	Sweden			

Responsibilities			
Proposing	**Monitoring**	**Administering**	**Representing**
measures for the further development of Community policy	observance and proper application of Community law	and implementing Community legislation	the Community in international organizations

individual nominations. The president is chosen from among the commissioners. All commissioners are expected to act in the interest of the EU rather than in defense of national interests, although they have not always followed this rule. The Commission acts in collegiate fashion with decisions made by majority, not unanimity. Each commissioner is assigned a specific policy area or areas of main responsibility, and each has a "cabinet" or small staff of aides. The Commission as a whole has a staff, based mainly in Brussels, of about 13,000 people, a third of whom are employed in translation and interpretation services.

The Commission's chief role as initiator is to propose new policies and regulations to the Council of Ministers; decisions under the first pillar can only be taken on the basis of these proposals, which are agreed on by the Commission as a whole at its weekly meetings. The Council of Ministers can accept or reject these proposals, or it can modify them by a unanimous vote. The Commission has often amended its own proposals to meet criticism by the Council, but the Single European Act and the Maastricht Treaty have strengthened the position of the Commission in many areas. The Council will be able to make more decisions by majority vote rather than by unanimity, and the Commission always tries to find a consensus.

The Commission also is also charged by the Council to negotiate on behalf of the EC in some areas: competition policy, farming, trade policy, and customs duties. It does not have power over fiscal or monetary policies or over central banking, though it has been trying to extend its general authority. Since 1993 it shares in initiatives in foreign policy.

The Council of Ministers

The main forum for decision making is the Council of Ministers. The Council consists of representatives of the 15 states and must approve proposals of the Commission before they can be implemented. The Council, unlike the Commission, is not a fixed group of people. Its membership changes according to the subject being discussed, such as finance, agriculture, transportation, or the environment; the ministers responsible for these activities in the states will make up the Council. But most often the Council consists of ministers responsible for foreign policy who meet once a month (see Table 6.5).

The Council differs from international organizations that require unanimity to make decisions. The logic of European integration was that the Council would increasingly decide by majority vote. This was stalled by the Luxem-

Members of the Commission of the European Union meeting in Brussels.

Table 6.5   THE COUNCIL OF MINISTERS

	Representatives of the Governments of the Member States 15	
	Permanent Representatives Committee (Coreper)	

LEGISLATION

Weighting of votes		Weighting of votes	
10	France	Greece	5
10	Germany	The Netherlands	5
10	Italy	Belgium	5
4	Sweden	Austria	4
10	United Kingdom	Denmark	3
8	Spain	Ireland	3
5	Portugal	Finland	3
		Luxembourg	2

Qualified majority:
62 votes out of 87

bourg Compromise of 1966, a concession to the nationalism of President de Gaulle, which said that the other governments would not overrule a member state that opposed proposals it held to be contrary to its national interest. This veto power by a state has rarely been used since 1966, because the Council has generally acted by consensus. The Single European Act, which took effect in 1987, provides for greater use of majority voting in the Council, though unanimity is still needed for certain matters such as taxation, company law, agreements with non-Community countries, workers' rights, free movement of people, and admission of a new state.

In other matters, ministers, who are helped by working groups of national officials, can decide by majority vote. The Council has 87 votes that are weighted. Of the total, 62 votes are needed for a "qualified majority" to approve proposals. Coalitions of 26 or more votes can therefore still block decisions.

An essential part of the decision-making process has been the Committee of Permanent Representatives (Coreper)—the representatives of the member states who hold ambassadorial rank—which meets weekly to prepare meetings of the Council of Ministers. Coreper has played a significant role in coordinating the attitudes of the states with the proposals of the Commission. Most of those proposals go to Coreper before going to the Council, and decisions on some issues have been reached by the states at the Coreper level.

Other Executive Bodies

Although they have no formal status and were not created by the Treaties of Paris or Rome, two other significant bodies have been acknowledged by the Single European Act. One is the European Council (not to be confused with the Council of Ministers), which consists of the 15 heads of state or government assisted by their foreign ministers and the president of the Commission. This Council meets at least once under each Council Presidency, primarily to discuss foreign policy, defense, and important economic subjects. Since 1993 the European Council is an official body of the EU.

The second body is European Political Co-operation (EPC), which began in 1970 and is now acknowledged in the Single European Act, and is now part of the EU institutional arrangements. EPC is a forum in which the 15 foreign ministers meet regularly to discuss coordination of foreign policy and the political and economic aspects of security. Assisted since 1981 by a small secretariat in Brussels, EPC has coordinated the policy of the 15 countries at several meetings of the United Nations and on a number of international issues, beginning with the 1980 Venice Declaration on the Middle East.

The EPC, like the Council of Ministers and the European Council, is chaired by one of the states every six months. The overlap between the different executive groups, which are all trying to coordinate the opinions of the national foreign ministries, has sometimes made it difficult to differentiate the working of the EPC from that of the Council. The Single European Act recognized the EPC and suggested it would play an even more important role in the future, a development which may help to resolve the question of who makes foreign policy in the EU. It could also decide whether nonmember states such as the United States should deal with officials from the Commission, the Council, or the individual 15 countries, a problem that is complicated by the fact that a different country assumes the presidency of the Council and the EPC every six months.

THE EUROPEAN PARLIAMENT

The Parliament, renamed from the Assembly established under ECSC, is composed of 626 members (now directly elected in the 15 states for a five-year term) in approximate proportion to the size of the different populations (see Figure 6.2). The Parliament meets one week in each month in plenary sessions in Strasbourg, France, but its committees meet in Brussels and its secretariat of 3,600 meets in Luxembourg. Its members come from over 60 political parties and almost always come together in political groups—nine in 1992—not in national blocs. They can use any of the 11 official languages of the EU.

The Parliament has been useful as an arena for the discussion of EU matters and as a representative of over 360 million people. But its powers go beyond giving its opinion on draft directives, proposals, and regulations coming from the Commission. The latter may decide to amend its proposals as a result of that opinion. The Parliament has power to dismiss the Commission on a vote of censure by a two-thirds majority, but this has never been done. It also must approve or reject the budget which is prepared with its help by the Commission for decision by the Council of Ministers; it has amended or rejected the draft budget on three occasions.

The new headquarters of the European Union.

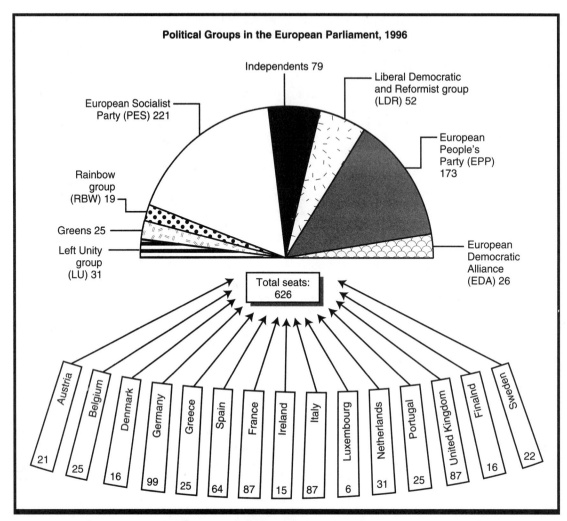

Figure 6.2   The European Parliament: 626 Members

Since 1975 the Parliament has helped the Commission draw up the budget, and can make amendments in limited areas. The Parliament has no formal powers of control over the Council. But it is now consulted before governments nominate the president of the Commission, and approve the Commission as a body.

The Single European Act has increased the Parliament's legislative role, allowing it to accept, reject, or amend some legislative proposals. The act has also given it power to ratify new international agreements and even veto some agreements concluded by the Council and the admission of new members to the EU. In the complicated process of decision making, the Commission can accept or reject any amendment asked for by the Parliament, and the Council of Ministers can overturn the result only by unanimity (see Figure 6.3). Parliament is now allowed to question or dismiss members of the Commission and to question the Council.

THE COURT OF JUSTICE

The Court of Justice, located in Luxembourg, consists of 15 judges—one from each state and the president of the Court—appointed for six years. By the Single European Act, a junior court of First Instance was set up in 1988 to assist the Court. The European Court of Justice (ECJ) differs from two other bodies: the International Court of Justice in The Hague (the World Court), and the European Court of Human Rights, which was established by the Council of Europe in Strasbourg. Member states of the EU must accept the final decisions and judgments of the ECJ but have no legal obligation to accept those of the other two courts, which are not part of the EU (see Table 6.6).

The essential functions of the ECJ are to ensure that EU law is properly applied and to resolve disputes over that law. It works by unanimity and thus, unlike the U.S. Supreme Court, no public dissent is registered. All member states are obliged to accept its rulings and its powers which are stated in the Treaties of Paris

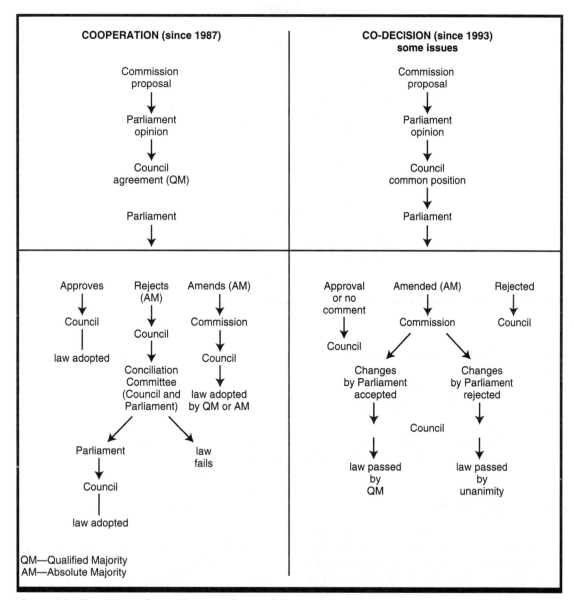

Figure 6.3   Two Procedures: Cooperation and Co-Decision

Table 6.6   THE EUROPEAN COURT OF JUSTICE

Governments of the
Member States appoint
the 15 judges
and 9 Advocates-General
by common accord for
a term of six years

Court of Justice

Full court of 15 judges
2 chambers with 5 judges
4 chambers with 3 judges

Types of Proceeding

Actions for failure to fulfill obligations under the Treaties (Commission vs. Member State)	Actions on grounds of failure to act (against Council or Commission)	References from national courts for preliminary rulings to clarify the meaning and scope of Community law
Actions by one Member State against another		Claims for damages against the Community

Court of First Instance

15 judges

Staff cases
Actions in the field of competition law
Actions under anti-dumping law
Actions under the ECSC Treaty

and Rome. The states have accepted that EU law is now also national law in their countries, that EU law prevails over national law if there is a conflict between them, and that the ECJ's decisions overrule those of national courts. The ECJ has by now laid down a body of Community law that applies to the EU institutions, states, and citizens. Its decisions are not subject to appeal. Up to 1995 the ECJ has made over 3,800 judgments

OTHER AGENCIES

The Economic and Social Committee consists of 222 persons representing employers, workers, and various interests such as consumer groups and professional associations. It meets once a month in Brussels to give its opinion on policies

and legislative proposals in certain fields. It has the right to be consulted, but has no right of amendment.

The Court of Auditors, based in Luxembourg, consists of 15 members appointed by the Council of Ministers. It supervises expenditure, checking all EU revenue and spending, and has investigated cases of mismanagement and fraud.

The Committee of the Regions, established in 1993, comprises 222 members, representing local and regional authorities, and is consulted before decisions affecting regional interests are adopted.

The European Investment Bank provides loans in many economic sectors to help less-developed regions of the EU, to modernize enterprises, and to create employment.

Feature 6.5   The Common Market

The Common Market has ended all internal customs duties and has replaced the individual national tariffs on imports from outside the European Community by one set of tariffs, the Common External Tariff. Goods entering the EC can then circulate within the EC without any further tariffs.

THE COMMON MARKET

The original objectives of the EC stated in the Treaties of Rome were the development of economic activities, a balanced expansion, greater stability, a higher standard of living, and closer relations between the member states. The members were therefore supposed to establish a common market and to try for similar economic policies.

The first step was a customs union among the original six countries, which meant removing tariffs on internal trade and imposing a common external tariff against nonmember countries (see Feature 6.5). By 1968 the union had been completed but other barriers to trade continued, preventing the establishment of a real common market. In the late 1980s the EC proposed new measures to eliminate barriers to free trade and movement. These included ending customs checks and border controls within the EC, harmonization of technical standards, mutual acceptance of professional qualifications and diplomas, a Community market for financial services such as banking and insurance, and approximate taxation rates. The Single European Act, with its important amendments to the Community treaties, has facilitated the implementation of most of these measures to complete the internal market (see Feature 6.6).

The essential objective of the SEA is the creation of a common market in which goods, services, people, and capital can move without obstacles such as frontier delays, fiscal barriers (including Value-Added Tax [VAT] rates and excise taxes), or technical obstructions such as national health and safety regulations. Tariffs and direct trade barriers have been ended since the mid–1960s. The new plan is to end all indirect barriers that hinder commerce or prevent competition and to allow a citizen of the 15 countries to be able to practice a trade or profession in any of the other countries.

The Maastrict Treaty on European Union

After the SEA, the heads of governments of the then–12 members of the EC agreed on a treaty on European Union at Maastricht in 1991. The

---

Feature 6.6   Single European Act, Signed in 1986, Operative in 1987

Amend the Treaties of Rome
Qualify majority voting in Council of Ministers on certain subjects
Cooperation procedure to give Parliament more input into legislative process
Timetables set up
Implement a complete common market by 1992
Formal recognition of European Political Cooperation

treaty was signed in February 1992 but ratification was delayed because of a lack of enthusiasm in some of the member states, especially Denmark, France, and Britain. Concessions were made to Britain, which did not accept the Social Charter of the Treaty that will deal with employment, working conditions, social security, and minimum wages.

The Maastrict Treaty came into force on November 1, 1993, creating the European Union (EU). The EU is not founded on a constitution but on international treaties. It is more than an international organization because it can enact rules that directly bind all citizens of the countries in the EU that have relinquished part of their national sovereignty to the EU institutions. The treaty provides the basis for a European citizenship; citizens of a EU state can vote and be a candidate for office in any EU country in which they reside.

The EU is not intended to become a unitary state. The treaty makes clear that decision making is based on the principle of subsidiary, by which the EU will deal only with those matters that cannot be better dealt with by the states at the national level.

More Power to the EU   The institutions of the EU were given more power in a number of areas. These include consumer protection, visas, health, transport networks, telecommunications, industrial policy, education, culture, research and development, social policy, and justice and home affairs. Majority decisions will increasingly replace the need for unanimity.

The Parliament   By the 1987 SEA the power of the European Parliament was increased by the cooperation procedure, which enabled it to reject or alter the decision of the Council of Ministers. The Maastricht Treaty gave Parliament more power by the co-decision process in which Parliament and the Council join. Parliament now has a limited right of initiative and enactment, approves EU international agreements, can set up·a committee of inquiry, and in the future can approve the Commission.

The Three Pillars   The EU now rests on three pillars (see Feature 6.7).

European Monetary Union   By 1999 a single European currency is supposed to replace the currencies of the member states, which will give up part of their sovereignty over monetary policy and public finances. A European central bank will be responsible for management of the monetary policies of the states. Since 1979 the European Monetary System (EMS) has attempted to coordinate economic policies and to stabilize the currencies of the EC countries. The exchange rate mechanism of the EMS obliges member states to limit fluctuations in the value of their currency to small amounts. Central banks of the states ensure that these limits are kept by raising or lowering interest rates, buying and selling currencies, and adjusting fiscal policies. The EMS uses the European currency unit (ECU) to fix central rates for the member states (see Features 6.8 and 6.9). The EMS has helped to keep inflation and interest rates low and rates of investment high.

Foreign Policy   A common foreign and security policy (CFSP) will be decided by the member states by unanimity and intergovernmental cooperation. In certain areas, such as control of arms exports, decisions can be made by qualified majority. The treaty recognizes European Political Cooperation and the future role of the Western European Union (WEU).

Justice and Home Affairs   Policies on these subjects are to be decided on an intergovernmental level. They include immigration, asylum, drug trafficking, and other international crimes. The Maastricht Treaty provides for a central police office (Europol).

Common Agricultural Policy

In 1950 Robert Schuman said that "Europe will not be made all at once or according to a single general plan. It will be built through concrete achievements, which first create a de facto solidarity." Among the most significant achievements has been the Common Agricultural Policy (CAP).

The objectives of the CAP are to maintain food supplies at stable and reasonable prices, to improve agricultural productivity, and to ensure a fair standard of living for farmers. The CAP

Feature 6.7 European Union

THE MAASTRICHT TREATY: THREE PILLARS

EUROPEAN COMMUNITY

Treaty of Rome amended by the Single European Act
  Democratization of the institutions
  Citizenship
  New powers
  Enhanced powers
  Economic and monetary union: single currency
  European Central Bank
  single monetary policy
  economic policy coordination

COMMON FOREIGN AND SECURITY POLICY

Common foreign policy: systematic cooperation, joint positions and actions
Common defense policy based on the Western European Union (WEU)

JUSTICE AND HOME AFFAIRS

Enhanced cooperation: asylum policy; rules governing the crossing of the external borders of the
Member States; immigration policy; combating drug addiction; combating international fraud; customs, police, and judicial cooperation on crime and terrorism

Note: The Maastricht Treaty officially changed the name of the previous EEC into EC.
This EC includes the new chapter on EMU.

---

initially accounted for about 90 percent and now accounts for about 60 percent of total EU expenditure and covers about 90 percent of farm output in the 15 countries. A number of goals underlie the CAP: price guarantees for farmers, common prices for agricultural commodities, variable import levies to raise import prices to the EU level, and subsidies to EU farmers to enable them to export and sell at world prices, which are generally below the internal EU market.

The CAP has been successful and important for the farming community, now a much smaller part of the employed than 30 years ago, but it

---

Feature 6.8 The ECU

The ECU is a "basket" of specified amounts of each EU currency which are determined by reference to the economy of member states. The value of the ECU depends on the current market rate of each currency. The ECU is also the accounting unit of the EU and plays a role in international payments and in lending and borrowing. However, the single European currency which will replace national currencies will be called the Euro.

Feature 6.9 How the Monetary System Works

The European Monetary System was started in 1979 to foster currency stability and promote policies to reduce inflation. The currencies of the European Union countries, except Britain, are linked in trading bands. When an individual currency reaches the top or the bottom of its range, the country's central bank must take steps to keep it within the trading band. The bank can buy or sell the currency or can move interest rates up or down. If these actions are not successful, the currency must be revalued.

has also been severely criticized on several grounds. It is expensive, and some argue that it takes too large a part of the EU budget. The Community spent about $37 billion in 1991 in state subsidies to farmers. Prices of agricultural commodities are higher than world market prices. The high prices stimulated production, resulting in surpluses that were very costly to store. These "wine-lakes" and "butter mountains" distorted competition and depressed world prices. Many outside countries, especially the United States, have accused the CAP of being protectionist by preventing or reducing imports. They have called in particular for the elimination of EU subsidies which encourage excessive and inefficient production.

In the mid-1980s, the EC reduced financial support for agricultural products in surplus, and price cuts were made in 1988. Further reforms of the high-cost CAP came in 1992 with sharp price cuts to restrict overproduction and the break of the links between price support and production. A system of price guarantees is now combined with direct payments to farmers.

EXTERNAL RELATIONS

The EU is the world's largest trading unit, accounting for about 20 percent of world trade (see Figure 6.4). (The United States accounts for 15 percent and Japan 9 percent of world trade.)

It therefore plays a significant role in GATT and its tariff negotiations. In the Uruguay Round of multinational negotiations, the European Commission was the bargaining agent for the EU. The Commission, on behalf of the EU, negotiates all external trade arrangements, which are then formally accepted by the Council of Ministers by majority vote.

Complex Relations

The EU has diplomatic relations with over 140 countries, varied trade agreements with countries throughout the world, and association agreements with Turkey, Malta, and Cyprus (see Table 6.8). Two of these external links are particularly interesting. One is the relationship between the EU and the European Free Trade Association (EFTA), which now includes four countries with a combined population of 12 million. Both the EU and EFTA have abolished customs duties and restrictions on trade in manufactured goods in a free trade area, and in 1991 the two bodies agreed on the creation of a European Economic Area (EEA). This involves a single market with free movement of goods, services, people, and capital, but without EFTA having any vote on EU laws.

A second important link is with the countries of the third world. Since the Yaoundé Convention of 1963, the EU has extended special preferential trading arrangements to the ex-colonies of EU countries. The EU is now linked to 70 African, Caribbean, and Pacific (ACP) countries through a series of Lomé Conven-

Feature 6.10
Central and Eastern Europe: One Clasification

Central Europe: Poland, Czech Republic, Slovakia, Hungary, Slovenia

Eastern Europe: Russian Federation, Ukraine, Romania, Bulgaria

tions, the latest of which was renewed in 1989 for a ten-year period. The ACP countries are freed from customs duties on almost all their exports to the EU and also receive financial aid from the EU.

In addition to EFTA, the third world Lomé Conventions, and the association agreements, the EU has concluded cooperation arrangements with many other countries, including Eastern and Southern Mediterranean nations, which have been given duty-free access for their industrial exports and agricultural trade and have received financial grants and loans. The EU has also entered into a Euro-Arab dialogue, discussing agricultural, trade, and technical matters with Arab countries.

Since the decline of communism and the end of Soviet control in Eastern Europe, the EU has become involved in the affairs of the Eastern Europe in a number of ways. It coordinated the 1989 PHARE program in which 24 countries sent aid to Poland, Hungary, and other Central and Eastern European countries. It entered into bilateral trade agreements with each of the Eastern countries and assisted in their environ-

mental problems. This has meant allowing these states a degree of free trade with the EU, granting them aid and loans, and providing for a number of joint projects. The EU does not regard these states as politically or economically ready for EU membership or association.

THE COMMUNITY'S FUTURE

The three communities have as official objectives the creation of "an organized and vital Europe," laying "the foundations of an ever closer union among the peoples of Europe," and combining together to "contribute to the prosperity of the peoples." The EU has already become an important part of European politics. Many decisions have been made that affect the states and their citizens in important ways (see Table 6.9).

At this point the nature of the EU has not been clearly defined. It is still a confederation of independent states that have pooled some powers and some aspects of sovereignty in economic matters, but that retain their authority to deal internally with law and order, foreign policy, and defense. The EU, however, can act in

Table 6.7   EU 15: 1993

	Population (millions)	Unemployment Rate Percent	Employment Percent Work Force			Sectors Percent of GDP		
			Agriculture	Industry	Services	Agriculture	Industry	Services
EU 15	369							
Belgium	10	9.4	2.9	30.9	66	1	31	66
Denmark	5	10.3	5.2	27.4	67	3	27	67
Germany	80	7.2	3.7	39.1	57	1	39	57
Greece	10	7.7	21.9	25.4	52	17	25	52
Spain	39	21.8	10.1	32.7	57	3	32	57
France	57	10.8	5.9	29.6	64	3	29	64
Ireland	3	18.4	13.8	28.9	57	7	28	57
Italy	57	11.1	7.9	33.2	59	3	33	63
Luxembourg	3	2.6	3.1	29.6	67	1	35	62
Netherlands	15	8.8	3.9	25.2	70	4	30	65
Austria	7	3.6	7.1	35.6	57	3	43	52
Portugal	9	5.1	11.5	32.6	56	6	39	54
Finland	5	17.9	8.6	27.8	63	6	38	55
Sweden	8	8.1	3.2	26.6	70	3	40	56
Britain	58	10.4	2.2	30.2	67	1	34	64

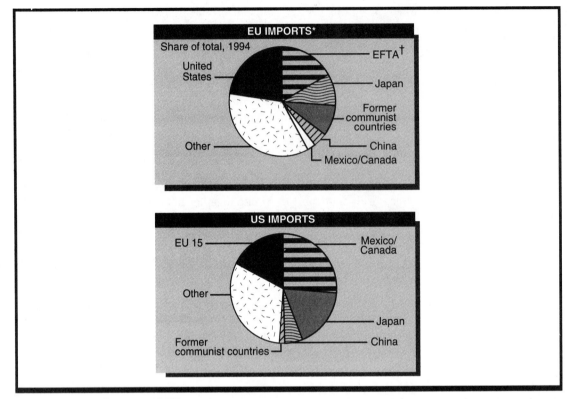

Figure 6.4   Trade: EU and US

some areas, including trade, agriculture, competition, transport, research and technology, environment, and education. Strong differences exist between those calling for more supranational government and more EU impact on citizens and those who think that active cooperation between sovereign states is the best way to build a successful European community, and would be content with little more than an intergovernmental body.

Differences on two other matters are of great concern to the United States. The first is the dispute about the Community's subsidies on agricultural exports and the degree of European protectionism. The United States claims that these subsidies are unfair and that they distort markets in the rest of the world. The second issue is that of defense. Some in the Community believe that there should be a strong European pillar in NATO on which Europe could rely for its defense. Others argue that Europe should be

responsible for its own security and defense, and suggest that the Western European Union would be the best organization for this purpose. France and Germany proposed in 1991 a joint military brigade that would be the basis for a European corps.

Table 6.8   EU Trade Agreements

Customs Union: Turkey, Malta, Cyprus

Free trade: European Economic Area

Association: Central and Eastern Europe

Preferential: Lomé Convention and agreements with Mediterranean countries

Special arrangements: some developing countries

Nonpreferential: a number of countries

Partnership and cooperation: Russia (1994)

There are also important disagreements over questions such as the relative merits of free trade and protectionism; a complete market economy or one with the state intervening to a considerable degree; the extent of welfare systems and of social rights; the enlargement of the Community to embrace new members, in particular Central and Eastern European states; and the problem of democratic control over the work of the Community institutions. Resolution of these questions will not come easily to a group of states that have had such a long and complex history, and that now must reformulate their attitudes toward the former Soviet Union and Central and Eastern Europe and toward policies on many issues, such as arms control, nuclear proliferation, the Middle East, the United Nations, and the United States. The political dimension of the EU is still to be decided.

KEY TERMS

Benelux
Brussels Treaty Organization
Committee of Permanent Representatives (Coreper)
Community Method
Common Market
Council of Europe
European Atomic Energy Community (Euratom)

European Coal and Steel Community (ECSC)
European Community (EC)
European Currency Unit (ECU)
European Economic Area
European Free Trade Association (EFTA)
European Parliament
General Agreement on Trade and Tariffs (GATT)
Maastricht Treaty
North Atlantic Treaty Organization (NATO)
Organization for Economic Cooperation and Development (OECD)
Single European Act
Treaty of Paris
Treaties of Rome
Western European Union (WEU)

FURTHER READINGS

Archer, Clive, and Fiona Butler. *The European Community: Structure and Process* (New York: St. Martin's, 1992).

Brown, L. Neville, and Francis Jacobs. *The Court of Justice of the European Communities* (London: Sweet and Maxwell, 1989).

Duchêne, François. *Jean Monnet: The First Statesman of Interdependence* (New York: Norton, 1994).

Duff, Andrew, et al., eds. *Maastricht and Beyond: Building the European Union* (New York: Routledge, 1994).

Table 6.9   MAASTRICHT TREATIES ON EUROPEAN UNION AND ECONOMIC AND MONETARY UNION, SIGNED FEBRUARY 1992

Chief features of the treaties: EC will now be known as the EU

1. Single currency by 1999, but optional for Britain and Denmark, and transition to an Economic and Monetary Union with a central bank
2. Eventual European defense, but in collaboration with NATO
3. Common foreign policy and security making, and implementation by majority vote
4. Some more legislative power given to the European Parliament with a veto on some items
5. Common citizenship of European Union: citizens can vote and be candidates in all the countries
6. More majority voting in the Council of Ministers
7. European Social Community accepted by all states except Britain
8. Fund set up to help poorer EC countries in transport and environment
9. Cooperation on justice and home affairs, immigration, drugs and terrorism

George, Stephen. *Politics and Policy in the European Community,* 2nd ed. (New York: Oxford University Press, 1991).

Greenwood, Justin, et al. *Organized Interests and the European Community* (Newbury Park, CA: Sage, 1992)

Harrop, Jeffrey. *The Political Economy of Integration in the European Community,* 2nd ed. (Brookfield: Elgar, 1992).

Jacobs, Francis, et al. *The European Parliament* (Detroit: Gale, 1992).

Lodge, Juliet, ed. *The European Community and the Challenge of the Future,* 2nd ed. (New York: St. Martin's, 1993).

Mazey, Sonia and Jeremy Richardson. *Lobbying in the European Community* (New York: Oxford University Press, 1993).

Nelson, Brent F., and Alexander Stubb, eds. *The European Union* (Boulder, CO: Reinner, 1994).

Pinder, John. *European Community: The Building of a Nation* (New York: Oxford University Press, 1991).

Serfaty, Simon. *Taking Europe Seriously* (New York: St. Martin's, 1992).

Urwin, Derek W. *The Community of Europe: A History of European Integration since 1945,* 2nd ed. (New York: Longman, 1995).

Wallace, William, ed. *The Dynamics of European Integration* (New York: Pinter, 1990).

Wallace, William. *Regional Integration: The West European Experience* (Washington: The Brookings Institute, 1995).

B.

Political Change in Central and Eastern Europe

For over 40 years following World War II, Europe was divided into two blocs: a Democratic West, becoming more prosperous, and a Communist East, relatively poor with political systems modeled on that of the Soviet Union. The latter nations were ruled by a Communist Party (the only legal party), a large secret police, a Marxist ideology, central planning and direction of the economy, strict censorship, control of information, and restrictions on travel. They were also dominated by the Soviet Union itself and were members of Comecon and the Warsaw Pact.

At the end of the 1980s the changes in Central and Eastern European systems were rapid and dramatic, and have transformed the European continent. Much of this was due not only to their own economic, social, and political problems, but also to the people of the Soviet Union and their differences over the proposals of Soviet leader Mikhail Gorbachev for *perestroika,* or restructuring. The Central and Eastern Europeans were aware of the decline of Communism as a force, of the lack of support for Communist Party leadership, and of the fact that the Soviet Union under Gorbachev would no longer intervene in their internal affairs or use force to prevent change.

Eastern Europe also appreciated that the Communist decline and the policy of *perestroika,* calling for economic and political reforms, was leading to moderation of the Cold War between the Soviet Union and the United States. The tension in the postwar period between the two countries was partly an ideological struggle between a liberal democracy with a market economy and a Communist system with a centrally planned economy, and partly a conflict over influence and competing interests in a world dominated by two superpowers. The tension was lessened in the 1980s with a growing mood of political cooperation with the West.

Internal dissension within the Central and Eastern European system came to a head in

1989 (see Features 6.10 and 6.11). Movements for an end to Communist rule and for change to a more prosperous and productive economy began in Poland and Hungary and rapidly spread to Czechoslovakia, East Germany, Bulgaria, and to a lesser extent, Romania. This revolution, almost entirely peaceful, was most dramatic in East Germany, the German Democratic Republic. On November 9, 1989 the Berlin Wall, a symbol of the Cold War dividing East and West, came down; in December 1989 and March 1990 two Communist governments collapsed; and in October 1990 the GDR was united with the Federal Republic of Germany.

The former Communist systems are in different phases of transition to some other form of political system. The dramatic changes can be analyzed in the following way (see Table 6.10 on page 310).

ALBANIA

The Socialist People's Republic of Albania set up in 1946 has not been overturned as have those in the other Eastern European countries. Although the government embarked on limited reforms in 1989, power in 1992 was still held by the Communist Party of Labor, the only legal party, which won the election held in March 1991.

BULGARIA

The People's Republic of Bulgaria set up in 1946 was close politically and economically to the Soviet Union, which accounted for 75 percent of its trade. However, in 1989 the Communists took the lead in political change by removing Todor Zhivkov, leader since 1954, who opposed Gorbachev-style reforms. The Communists renounced the leading role of the party—which was renamed the Socialist Party—and organized a free election. At this parliamentary election in 1990, the Commu-

Feature 6.11 The End of the Communist Systems

1989	April:	Poland	Solidarity became legal again, some political reforms en-acted.
	May:	Hungary	fences along Austrian border dismantled; East Germans began crossing that border.
	June:	Poland	Overwhelming victory by Solidarity in parliamentary elections; General Jaruzelski elected president (July).
	August:	Poland	Tadeusz Mazowiecki of Solidarity became first non-Communist prime minister.
	September:	Hungary	Restrictions ended on East Germans entering the country and escaping to West Germany via Austria.
		Poland	Solidarity dominated new government coalition.
	October:	Hungary	Communists changed name to Socialist Party; agreement on multiparty system.
		East Germany	Mass exodus and demonstrations led to downfall of Communist leader Erich Honecker.
	November:	East Germany	Travel restrictions abolished; Berlin Wall opened; new coalition includes many non-Communists.
		Bulgaria	Communist leader Todor Zhivkov ousted.
		Czechoslovakia	Street demonstrations lead to downfall of Communist leader Milos Jakes; talks with Civic Forum; end of "Leading role" of Communist Party.
	December:	East Germany	"Leading role" of Communists (Socialist Unity Party) ended.
		Czechoslovakia	New coalition government with non-Communist majority; Vaclav Havel elected President; Alexander Dubcek became speaker of Parliament.
		Bulgaria	Communists renounce "leading role," and call for free elections.
		Romania	Massacre of demonstrators in Timisoara led to downfall and execution of Communist leader Nicolae Ceausescu; National Salvation Front took power.
1990			Boris Yeltsin elected president of the Russian Republic; Mikhail Gorbachev ends monopoly of power of Communist Party in Soviet Union.
			Lech Walesa elected president of Poland
	October:		Federal Republic of Germany and German Democratic Republic reunited
1991			Eleven former Soviet republics form Commonwealth of Independent States; Gorbachev resigns; Soviet Union is dissolved

nists won 47 percent of the votes and a majority of the seats, partly because opposition groups were poorly organized. Bulgaria was the first Eastern European country in which a reformed Communist Party won power in a free election. Its constitution of 1990 proclaims Bulgaria as a parliamentary form of government with a directly elected president.

Feature 6.12 **Life and Death of the Communist Pact**

1955	May 14	Warsaw Treaty signed by Albania, Bulgaria, Hungary, East Germany, Poland, Romania, Soviet Union, and Czechoslovakia.
1956		Hungarian withdrawal canceled by Soviet invasion.
1961		Berlin Wall crisis.
		Albania pulls out after split with Moscow.
1968		Pact forces invade Czechoslovakia.
1969		Command structure changed after Romanian complaints of inequality.
1973		Pact begins 16 years of fruitless negotiations with NATO on mutual and balanced force reductions in central Europe.
1975		Pact renewed for another 10 years.
1985		Renewed for a further 20 years.
1988		Gorbachev announces he will withdraw 50,000 Soviet troops from Eastern Europe.
1989		Pact and NATO open CFE talks.
	June	Poland elections.
	July	Pact summit acknowledges right of each member to its own political line.
	November–	
	December	Berlin Wall falls; Communist governments collapse in East Germany, Czechoslovakia, and Romania.
1990	February–	
	March	Czechoslovakia and Hungary agree on complete withdrawal of Soviet forces.
	June 7	Pact summit turns alliance into "treaty of sovereign and equal states built upon democratic principles."
	June 26	Hungary withdraws.
	September 24	East Germany withdraws.
		Moscow agrees its 370,000 troops in East Germany will return home by 1994.
	November 19	Pact and NATO sign CFE (Conventional Forces in Europe) treaty and declare they no longer regard each other as enemies.
1991	January 16	Czechoslovak Parliament asks government to negotiate abolition of Pact.
	February 1	Bulgaria says it will quit Pact.
	February 12	Soviet Union agrees to dismantle Pact's military structures.
	February 25	Military cooperation scrapped.
	March 31	Soviet commanders surrender powers.
	June 18	Czechoslovakia says Pact to be wound up.
	June 19 and 27	Last Soviet troops leave Hungary and Czechoslovakia.
	July 1	Pact dissolved.

CZECHOSLOVAKIA

Czechoslovakia, which had the most significant pre–World War II democratic tradition, came under Communist control in 1948. Attempts to liberalize the regime by the Communist leader Alexander Dubcek in the "Prague Spring" of 1968 were brutally suppressed by the Soviet Union and most Warsaw Pact countries. In 1989 street demonstrations calling for political change

Table 6.10 PROFILE OF CENTRAL AND EASTERN EUROPE

	Area (1,000 sq. km)	Population (million)	GDP per Capita, 1993	GDP (million) 1993
Poland	312	38.5	$5,010	$85,853
Czech Republic	79	10.3	7,700	31,613
Slovakia	49	5.4	6,450	11,076
Hungary	93	10.3	6,260	38,099
Slovenia	20	2.0	6,540	85,665
Bulgaria	111	8.4	1,330	10,369
Romania	238	22.7	1,130	25,969

led to the resignation of the Communist leader and most of his colleagues. Opposition activists formed the Civic Forum consisting of 12 groups, including Charter 77, a human rights group set up after the 1968 repression. The most prominent figure was Vaclav Havel, a distinguished writer and human rights activist whose plays were banned and who had been imprisoned for five years. A new government with a non-Communist majority was formed. In December 1989, Havel was elected unanimously as interim president when all other candidates withdrew, and was reelected for two years in July 1990. Dubcek was chosen as the parliamentary speaker. Free multiparty elections in June 1990 led to victory for the groups that led the 1989 protests. Economic reforms were introduced in 1991. Most price controls were removed, the currency was made convertible, privatization was begun, and the economy was opened to foreign investors.

The two parts of Czechoslovakia split in 1993 with the formation of two separate republics. Vaclav Havel was elected president of the new Czech republic, and moderate parties won the elections for the new Chamber of Deputies. In the new republic of Slovakia authority is vested in the 150-member National Council, which is directly elected and which elects the president by secret ballot.

The Czech Republic remains the only Central European country not to have elected former Communists to power, largely because of the organizational skills and policies of Vaclav Kraus, the prime minister, who built a strong party and promoted the free-market economy.

HUNGARY

The People's Republic of Hungary proclaimed in 1949 became the Hungarian Republic in October 1989. Hungary was the Eastern European country most anxious to transform itself economically, especially after the brutal suppression by the Soviet Union of an attempted uprising in 1956. In that period Hungary was a unique laboratory for economic experimentation in the Communist world. As a result of reform efforts in the Communist Socialist Workers Party, the name of the party was changed to the Socialist Party; the party gave up its leading role in October 1989 and began discussions with opposition groups. In 1990, elections were held for a single-chamber parliament in which Democratic Forum, a center-right group with 25 percent of the votes, and Free Democrats, a center-liberal group with 21 percent of the votes, emerged as the leading parties, with the reformed Communists getting 11 percent and the unreformed Communists 4 percent of the votes. A coalition government was formed led by the Democratic Forum. However, in 1994, the Social Democrats, the renamed former Communists, won an overall majority in the National Assembly. They pledged they would maintain the market economy, which is due to be privatized by 1998.

POLAND

The People's Republic of Poland set up in 1947 was replaced in December 1989 by the Polish Republic. Some political concessions had been made in 1980 by the Communist regime after shipyard and other strikes and the organization of a free trade union (Solidarity) led by Lech Walesa, a shipyard electrician in Gdansk. Those concessions were halted with the imposition of martial law. Growing difficulties and more strikes in late 1988 led Communist leaders to discuss economic and social problems with Solidarity and Walesa, who was awarded the Nobel Peace Prize in 1983. In 1989, Solidarity was again legalized and the Catholic Church was more officially recognized. In the parliamentary election in June, Solidarity won an overwhelming victory. In the Senate it won 99 out of 100 seats; in the lower house, where it was only allowed to contest 35 percent of the seats, it won all 161 allowed. General Jaruzelski, elected president in July, invited Solidarity into a coalition government. This, the first non-Communist government in postwar Eastern Europe, was headed as prime minister by Tadeusz Mazowiecki of Solidarity. Two major political groups emerged: the Center Alliance and the Civic Movement for Democratic Action. In December 1989 Walesa, backed by almost all political and social organizations and by the Catholic Church, won the presidential election in a second ballot by 74 percent of the vote. But the parliamentary election in October 1991 produced a deeply fragmented chamber, with 29 different parties gaining seats.

Walesa's policies caused a splintering of the liberal anti-Communist forces, the alliance of workers, intellectuals, and the Church. As a result, parties formed by former Communists gained control of the legislature in 1993. In his five years as president (1991–1995), Walesa had to deal with three parliaments and six prime ministers, and vetoed bills passed by the Communist majority. His continuing warfare with his governments delayed the process of privatization. Walesa ran for reelection as president in 1995. But the man whose anti-Communist Solidarity movement helped bring down the Soviet Union and who changed the history of Poland was narrowly defeated. Both the presidency and the parliament are now controlled by former Communists.

ROMANIA

The People's Republic of Romania set up in 1947 was replaced by the Republic of Romania in De-

cember 1989. Change occurred in 1989 partly as a result of spontaneous anti-Communist and pro-Western protests of the people, and partly by the action of some parts of the Communist Party and the security police who were critical of the corruption, the economic mismanagement, and the brutal rule of Communist leader Nicolae Ceausescu. After the violent suppression and killing of several hundred demonstrators in Timisoara by the police, protesters took over Communist Party headquarters and later executed Ceausescu, who had fled. A number of violently anti-Communist political groups emerged, but the new National Salvation Front, containing many past and present Communists, remained the dominant party. At the May 1990 parliamentary election, the Front got 66 percent of the vote. A month later, demonstrations by students and workers in Bucharest were repressed with considerable force by coal miners specially brought in to restore order.

A new constitution was approved in 1991 with political power located in a directly elected president who appoints a prime minister and a cabinet accountable to the legislature.

YUGOSLAVIA

In 1945 the Federal People's Republic of Yugoslavia was proclaimed following an election that the Communists won. The Communist Party voted in 1990 to give up its monopoly of power in favor of a multiparty system. Later that year the Republic of Slovenia voted for independence from Yugoslavia, as did Croatia and Macedonia in 1991. With the independence proclaimed by Bosnia and Herzegovina in 1992, the federation came to an end and the two remaining republics, Montenegro and Serbia, proclaimed themselves the Yugoslav Republic.

UNEVEN CHANGE

The changes in Eastern Europe have been uneven. Three countries—Poland, Hungary, and Czechoslovakia—appeared committed to democratic regimes and liberalized economies. But Communist elements retained some power in Romania and Bulgaria, and they hold considerable power in Albania. Yugoslavia is a separate case, with its federal system disintegrating because of civil war between rival ethnic and national republics and groups. But apart from Albania, the totalitarian systems and monopolies of power by the Communist Party have ended.

After renouncing their Communist systems and after the collapse of the Warsaw Pact and the Comecon trading bloc, the Central and Eastern European countries formed new political parties and wrote new or adapted their existing constitutions. The countries all have parliaments, reflecting free elections and a multiparty system, free markets, mixed economies that are part state-owned and part privatized, and a civil society not controlled by the state.

Yet discontent with persisting poor economic conditions, a fall in the standard of living in some countries, inefficient bureaucracy, the extent of corruption, and ethnic tensions led to a weakening of democratic forces and of the coalitions that brought down the Communist systems. As a result, the countries have experienced the resurgence of strength by former or old-style Communists who rebuilt their organizations and sometimes appeared as nationalists. They have done well in elections in most of the countries and retained a prominent place in government in the other nations.

The Eastern European states have been taking varied roads, and at different speeds, in search of pluralistic democratic systems, protection of political and human rights, and economies more oriented to the market and private ownership than to management by state-owned enterprises, price controls, and central planning. In this period of transition these states have experienced problems of economic hardship, inflation, high taxes, and unemployment. Many of the states also face complex internal problems because of the presence of ethnic minorities in their territories, territorial disputes with their neighbors, and mutually hostile national movements.

CENTRAL AND EASTERN EUROPE AND THE SOVIET UNION

Relations with the Soviet Union changed as it relinquished its hold on Eastern Europe. The countries now make their own external economic and military decisions and their own security arrangements. In January 1949 Stalin created the Council for Mutual Economic Assistance (Comecon), consisting of ten states, to coordinate the economies of Eastern Europe and other Soviet bloc countries such as Cuba and Vietnam. It was always dominated by the Soviet Union, the largest member, but began disintegrating in the late 1980s as some European members sought to make bilateral trade and investment arrangements with the EC. In 1991 it was agreed that it should be ended.

Similarly, the Warsaw Pact, founded in 1955 by the Soviet Union and seven Eastern European countries to counter the inclusion of the Federal Republic of Germany into NATO, was dissolved in March 1991, when all its military arrangements and structures were ended. The Pact, which was superimposed on a number of bilateral agreements on military matters among the states, was always an instrument of Soviet power. The Soviet Union used the Pact to suppress demands for liberty in Hungary in 1956 and Czechoslovakia in 1968, and to coerce local leaders to impose martial law in Poland in 1981.

In October 1989, the Warsaw Pact countries renounced the Brezhnev doctrine, formulated by the former Soviet leader, which stated that the Soviet Union had the right to intervene militarily in other Pact countries if Socialist systems were in danger of being overturned. Instead, they adopted the "Sinatra doctrine": each state would do things its own way. The military part of the Pact came to an end when it was clear that the Soviet Union was no longer able or willing to be concerned about the other six members. These states are now responsible for their own security. They also called for the removal of Soviet troops from their countries.

CENTRAL AND EASTERN AND WESTERN EUROPE

In the less threatening atmosphere of Europe today, a larger role may be played by the Conference on Security and Cooperation in Europe (CSCE), a summit meeting of leaders from Eastern and Western Europe, the United States, and Canada, which originated in the Helsinki Final Act of 1975. CSCE addresses itself to questions of European security, economic, scientific and technological cooperation, and to humanitarian principles. Now consisting of 35 countries including the United States, Canada, and all of Europe, CSCE is an important forum for wider political and military dialogue among the leaders of these countries. It has welcomed the end of confrontation and division in Europe and the new era of democracy and peace. In November 1990, CSCE adopted a "Charter of Paris for a New Europe," in which the then 34 states committed themselves to human rights, minority rights, self-determination, democracy, and economic freedom. At the same time the states signed an agreement on conventional armed forces in Europe, imposing a ceiling on non-nuclear weapons of East and West. Whether CSCE will evolve into a closer relationship and a solid framework for cooperation among the countries will depend on the evolution of the Eastern European states and the various republics of the former Soviet Union.

KEY TERMS

Civic Forum
Comecon
Conference on Security and Cooperation in Europe (CSCE)

Democratic Forum
Lech Walesa
National Salvation Front
perestroika
Solidarity
Warsaw Pact

FURTHER READINGS

Brown, James F. *Hopes and Shadows: Eastern Europe after Communism* (Durham, NC: Duke University Press, 1994).

Brown, James F. *Surge to Freedom: The End of Communist Rule in Eastern Europe* (Durham, NC: Duke University Press, 1991).

Lederer, Ivo, ed. *Western Approaches to Eastern Europe* (New York: Council on Foreign Relations, 1992).

Pridham, Geoffrey, et. al., eds. *Building Democracy? The International Dimension of Democratization in Eastern Europe* (London: Leicester University Press, 1994).

Pridham, Geoffrey and T. Vanhanen. *Democratization in Eastern Europe* (New York: Routledge, 1994).

Roskin, Michael. *The Rebirth of East Europe* (Englewood Cliffs: Prentice-Hall, 1991).

PART 2

Communist and Post-Communist Systems

The Government of the Russian Federation

Roger E. Kanet and John S. Reshetar Jr.

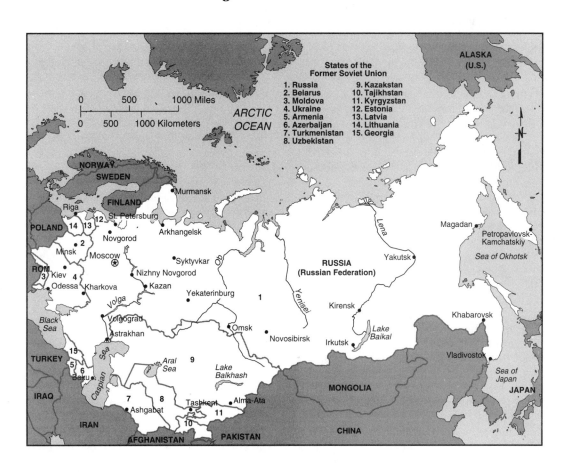

States of the Former Soviet Union

1. Russia
2. Belarus
3. Moldova
4. Ukraine
5. Armenia
6. Azerbaijan
7. Turkmenistan
8. Uzbekistan
9. Kazakstan
10. Tajikhstan
11. Kyrgyzstan
12. Estonia
13. Latvia
14. Lithuania
15. Georgia

Political Development

In the parliamentary elections of December 17, 1995, less than four years after the collapse of the Soviet Union, the widely proclaimed demise of the Communist Party of the Soviet Union, and the euphoric proclamations about the rise of Russian democracy, Communists and their allies won more than one-third of the seats in the 450-seat Russian Parliament, or Duma. The ill-named extreme nationalist Liberal Democratic Party of Vladimir Zhirinovsky emerged from the elections as the second most powerful political force with 50 seats. Parties and political leaders committed to the continuation of democratic reforms and to strengthening a market economy fared especially poorly, in part because of their refusal to cooperate with one another. For example, only two of the democratic reform parties—Yabloko headed by former economics minister Grigorii Yavlinsky and the party Our Home Is Russia of Prime Minister Viktor Chernomyrdin—were among the top four vote-getters; however, together they gained less than 18 percent of the party-list vote. In a very close presidential race Boris Yeltsin emerged from the first round of the elections on June 16, 1996 with 35 percent of the votes, approximately 3 percent more than his primary challenger, Gennadi Zyuganov of the Communist Party of the Russian Federation. Yeltsin moved immediately to strengthen his position for the runoff election that was held on July 3, 1996, by allying with General (ret.) Aleksandr Lebed, who had come in a surprisingly strong third in the first round, with almost 15 percent of the vote. Lebed, who had run on a platform that emphasized rooting out corruption and crime from Russia and reassuring Russia's place as a world power, took over the leadership of the National Security Council, a power body that advises the president on both domestic and foreign security issues and exercises great influence in these areas. In response to Lebed's conditions for support, several hard-line leaders of the Russian security apparatus who had earlier opposed Lebed were sacked—including Defense Minister Grachev

(and seven generals with close ties to him), the chief of presidential security service Maj. Gen. Korzhakov, and the head of the federal Security Service (the successor of the KGB) Maj. Gen. Barsukov. In the runoff election Yeltsin won a strong victory with 53.7 percent of the vote to Zyuganov's 40.4 percent, with 4.86 percent against both candidates.

The Communist Party of the Russian Federation, unlike the reform Communists who have been elected to power in Hungary, Lithuania, and Poland, represent in many respects a more direct continuation of the old Soviet party. During the election campaign, Communist Party leader Gennadi Zyuganov espoused most of the policies of the pre–1985 party—depending on the nature of the audience to which he was speaking. He and other Communists called variously for an end to indiscriminate privatization, a reinstitution of the social services that collapsed after 1991, the renationalization of many of the privately formed companies, the elimination of the crime that has swept across Russia, a reassertion of Russia's role as a great power, and the reextension of Russian control over the lost territories of the former Soviet Union. Communist strength proved to be highest among those sectors of Russian society that have suffered the greatest dislocation as a result of the economic, political, and social upheavals of the past decade—elderly pensioners, growing numbers of unemployed industrial workers, the population of the countryside, the millions who lost perks associated with their membership in the ruling Communist Party, and those fed up with growing criminality and the role of Russian organized crime. Moreover, Russians were appalled by the collapse of the Soviet state, the loss of superpower status for Russia, and the reputed discrimination against 25 million ethnic Russians who, in December 1991, found themselves minorities in the 14 new countries that emerged outside the borders of the Russian Federation and who were attracted to the nationalist rhetoric of Zyuganov and his Communist Party.

The return of the Communists to a major role in Russian politics occurred after a decade of economic and political change that verged on the chaotic. All this happened in a country which earlier had been seen by most analysts as one of the two world superpowers that was likely to continue to "muddle through," although it might have some serious internal problems. President Mikhail Gorbachev's efforts to reform the Soviet Union had very mixed results. Although he succeeded in dismantling most of the structures of an authoritarian state, he failed to introduce meaningful economic reform and was completely unprepared to deal with the ethnically based pressures against continued control by the central government—a development that occurred among Russians, as well as among the people of the Baltic republics and elsewhere. The end result of Gorbachev's failed efforts at reforming the Soviet Union was its collapse in December 1991.

Although Russian President Boris Yeltsin made much progress in creating the foundations for a market economy and a participatory political system, he also failed as of mid-1996 to resolve the problems of economic decline, growing corruption and criminality, and political chaos. What was made evident by the elections of December 1995 was the fact that only a minority of the general population continued to support economic market reforms, while the majority in many social groups supported a return to policies and goals from the past. It is among this large segment of the population that Zyuganov's Communists, as well as Zhirinovsky's extreme nationalists, find their political support—among Russians for whom the events of the decade after 1985 represented an unmitigated personal and collective disaster. Evidence of popular attitudes can be gained from a survey conducted by the All-Russian Public Opinion Research Center in April 1996. Forty-two percent of the random sample of 1,600 people polled favored a planned economy, while only a third preferred a market economy. Forty-one percent thought that a Soviet-style political system was best for Russia, while only 27 percent favored Western-style democracy. President Yeltsin well understood the public mood, as his shift away from reform policies and his removal of the last committed reformers from his cabinet in early 1996 indicated.

In the following pages we will attempt to trace the very complex, almost tortuous, road by which Russia reached its current economic and political impasse. For Russia, and for Russians, the past hundred years represented, in many respects, a lost century. The problems that faced the tsarist government at the beginning of the century—economic backwardness, ethnic conflict, and authoritarian political structures and attitudes, among others—remain central to the political landscape in the new Russia at the end of the century. The experiment in social engineering that was the Soviet Union did little to solve those problems. Moreover, the policies of the Soviet state—for example in the environmental arena and in relations among ethnic communities—actually exacerbated the situation, while wasting huge amounts of social and material resources.

THE POLITICAL SETTING

During the fall of 1991 the political structures that for seven decades had made the Soviet Union a highly centralized and authoritarian state and a global superpower crumbled in the face of the failed effort to reform the system and the growing nationalist sentiment in Russia and elsewhere throughout the huge expanse of Soviet territory. The Soviet political system that had represented revolutionary change and utopian promise in the second decade of the twentieth century found itself in a profound crisis, as it entered the last decade of the century. The failure of centralized economic planning and state ownership to meet the challenges of rapidly expanding external competition and rising international demands and expectations resulted in negative economic growth, empty store shelves, growing inflation, strikes, rising unemployment, and a declining standard of living. After more than four years of even increased political and economic turmoil, the Russian Federation, the largest and most important of the 15 states to emerge on the territory of the former Soviet Union, was still searching for its future. The Communist Party dictatorship had been replaced by multiparty political competition; but the foundations for a democratic society remained fragile, and many of the key political figures were publicly committed to reestablishing authoritarian political structures. Much of the economy that in the past was state-owned and centrally planned had been privatized; but criminal elements referred to as "mafia," usually in cooperation with government officials whose roots are in the old *nomenklatura* system of party and state officials, controlled much of the economy. Moreover, growing pressures existed to expand the role of the government in the economy, in particular in subsidizing economic enterprises that had not proven to be competitive in the new market environment. Thus, despite the dramatic changes that occurred in the former Soviet Union, Russia and most of the other successor states had yet to establish stable and effective political and economic structures by mid-1996. Moreover, the legacies of the Communist past remained very influential in setting the agenda and determining the ways in which politics emerged at the end of the twentieth century. Thus, we will begin our examination of Russian government and politics with a review of the Russian and Soviet past, emphasizing those aspects likely to influence political developments in the "new" Russia.

In February 1986, General Secretary of the Communist Party of the Soviet Union (CPSU), Mikhail S. Gorbachev used the Twenty-seventh Party Congress to characterize the rule of his immediate predecessors as a period of stagnation and corruption. He warned then that "it is impossible to retreat and there is nowhere to retreat" and that "history has not given us much time."[1] Subsequently, in July 1991, Gorbachev noted that in the 1980s the country had been in a "state of depression" and "the previous theoretical and practical model of socialism [had] . . . proven to be insolvent." He lamented the fact that "old and new ailments of society were not exposed, let alone treated, but were suppressed, which further aggravated the situation and in the end led to severe crisis."[2] This proved to be a crisis of political leadership and economic policy, social and ethnic conflict, and "spiritual" and moral degeneration. After six years of ineffective efforts at reform, Gorbachev's Soviet government found itself in disarray, overwhelmed by events and demands as the non-Russian republics and the Russian Republic itself asserted their lack of

confidence in the political center and the growing desire for sovereignty. During 1991 the very name of the Soviet Union (or, Union of Soviet Socialist Republics) became a matter of dispute, as its disunity became increasingly evident. Although often mistakenly referred to as a "nation," the Soviet Union was actually a collection of nations and peoples, a multinational empire comprising more than a hundred officially recognized ethnic and linguistic communities. The Soviet crisis thus represented an extraordinary combination of the collapse of a political system and the disintegration of an empire. In fact, the disappearance of the Soviet Union initiated in the 15 major constituent units a process of "triple transition" characterized by the need (1) to establish new states, in almost all cases where none had ever existed before, with accepted borders and supportive populations among multiethnic societies; (2) to create democratic and representative political institutions and values in place of the authoritarian structures and values of the Soviet and pre-Soviet past; and (3) to lay the foundations for competitive market economies where a centralized command economy had dominated. In varying degrees the challenges of this simultaneous triple transition faced all the former Communist states that emerged in Central and Eastern Europe and Eurasia. Everywhere the task is indeed daunting.

The Soviet political order had evolved from its beginnings in military defeat, revolutionary war, and utopianism into a cruel totalitarian dictatorship under Stalin, and subsequently into an oligarchy of aged and ineffective leaders. It had its origins in the Russian Revolution of 1917—one of the most significant events of the twentieth century—and emerged on the ruins of the Russian Empire, which failed to survive the dislocations and crises created by World War I. The Russian Revolution began in February 1917 with the abdication of Tsar Nicholas II and the collapse of the monarchy. Administrative breakdown, war weariness, and an inability to supply the army and feed the population of the capital precipitated the empire's collapse. A weak and indecisive Provisional Government of liberals and moderate Socialists headed by Alexander Kerensky, attempted to continue Russia's participation in the war on the side of the Allies (Great Britain, France, Italy, and the United States), meanwhile putting off needed internal reforms until a new constitution could be written and a legitimate government elected. As the war grew more unpopular and the army disintegrated, the Provisional Government was unable to defend itself from the growing discontent and the threat of a seizure of power.

The threat of a takeover of the Russian capital of Petrograd (formerly St. Petersburg, later Leningrad, and now again St. Petersburg), came from the most extreme Russian Marxists, known as the Bolsheviks, under the leadership of Vladimir Ilyich Ulianov, better known as V.I. Lenin. The Bolsheviks succeeded in gaining control of the soviets (or councils) of workers, peasants, and soldiers' deputies in Petrograd and Moscow. The soviets, which were revolutionary organs that arose spontaneously at the very beginning of the Revolution, were only haphazardly representative and not popularly elected. Initially they were controlled by such non-Bolshevik parties as the agrarian Socialist Revolutionaries and the more moderate Marxists known as the Mensheviks. Although the Russian word *sovet* means "council," the takeover of the soviets in the principal cities by Lenin's Bolsheviks gave the word a distinct political meaning associated with Communist rule and a new type of system based on the dictatorship of a single party.

Lenin succeeded in seizing power from the Provisional Government because it was never fully in command. From the very beginning of the Revolution, it had to share power with the Petrograd soviet, which by the summer of 1917 came under the domination of Lenin's associate Leon Trotsky. The Provisional Government also lacked the intelligence-gathering ability and the security police of the previous imperial regime. It could not rely on the army, because the troops stationed in the capital were not loyal and had come under the influence of Bolshevik agitators. In addition, Lenin's supporters were tightly disciplined and organized. Lenin had the support of the so-called workers' red guard—a paramilitary force that could be armed and sent into the streets to intimidate those who opposed the Bolsheviks. Thus, Lenin's takeover of the Russian capital on November 7, 1917 (October 23 by the Julian calendar still in use in Russia at the

time), was a relatively easy undertaking, but years of bloody civil conflict followed. In a very literal sense the Soviet system was spawned by war (World War I) and also succeeded in establishing itself by means of war (civil war).

Initially Lenin gained control of only the central portion of European Russia. He established a Russian Socialist Federated Soviet Republic in July 1918, but was confronted with several centers of resistance. Russians who opposed the establishment of a Communist regime, including part of the tsarist military, waged a civil war that Lenin eventually won in 1920–1921 because of the fatigue brought on by Russia's demoralization and the absence of any unified military command or political center among the forces opposed to the Bolsheviks. Lenin had the advantage of having a divided opposition that could not develop an attractive and sufficiently powerful alternative to Bolshevik rule. Political moderates had little chance to succeed in a time of turmoil and simple propaganda slogans, while Lenin's principal Russian opponents were political conservatives or reactionaries who sought to restore the old order.

The more numerous non-Russian peoples who had been subjected to Russian rule within the empire seized the opportunity presented by Russia's collapse and proclaimed their independence in 1917–1918. The Finns, Ukrainians, Georgians, Armenians, Poles, Estonians, Latvians, Lithuanians, and others established independent states. Lenin was ultimately able to establish Soviet (and Russian) rule over most of the non-Russian peoples, and the form and name of the Russian state was changed. In December 1922 the Union of Soviet Socialist Republics was formed as a federation, at least in theory, consisting of separate Soviet republics for the major nationality groups.

The Imperial Legacy

Lenin's Bolshevik Party and the Soviet political system that it created became the successors to the tsarist Russian Empire, although ironically Lenin had dedicated his political life to the overthrow of that empire and its monarchy. The monarchy was not overthrown, but collapsed in March 1917 (February on the old Russian calendar) with the abdication of the tsar, a lack of leadership, and a breakdown of the military and administrative systems which touched off bread riots and disorder in the capital. Eight months later the overthrow of the Provisional Government gave Lenin the opportunity to extend Soviet rule from the center of the former empire. But he faced the same problem that the Russian autocrats had faced: how to rule a huge ethnically diverse empire from a single distant center. Although the Bolsheviks rejected many traditional Russian values and introduced significant changes in the Russian way of life, in the end they came to represent Russian domination of the USSR. Thus, many Russians who might have had doubts about the nature of Soviet rule came to accept it as the heir to the Russian Empire and as the only available means of preserving Russia's claim to greatness and satisfying its yearning to rule over neighboring peoples—issues seemingly of as great importance in the new Russia of the 1990s as they were after the Bolshevik Revolution, given their importance in the current political debates in Russia.

THE GEOGRAPHIC SETTING

Tsarist Russia and the former Soviet Union could clam to be, in terms of area, the largest country under a single political regime. It covered one-sixth of the earth's landmass and extended a distance of more than 6,000 miles over 150 degrees of longitude and 11 time zones. Even after the dissolution of the Soviet Union, the Russian Federation, with an area of 6.6 million square miles, continues to rank as the largest country in the world physically, with almost twice the territory of either the United States or China.

Most of this vast land mass has an intemperate continental climate because it is remote from the oceans that would have a moderating effect, warming the land in winter and cooling it off in the summer, and is exposed to the frigid climate of the Arctic. Temperature extremes vary greatly—parts of Siberia have a range of 150°F. Much of the land has limited rainfall, receiving less than 20 inches of precipitation annually.

The land is reasonably well endowed with natural resources, including petroleum, natural gas, and all important minerals, and can be largely self-sufficient. However, transportation costs are often high when oil, coal, natural gas, and raw materials are distant from users. There is heavy reliance on railways that are slow and poorly maintained, and no modern highway system exists, even in the more densely populated regions of European Russia. Moreover, permafrost, which covers two-thirds of Siberia makes the construction and maintenance of buildings, railroads, and pipelines extremely expensive and difficult.

The area of the former Soviet Union has not been entirely self-sufficient in agriculture and has had to import grain. This has been partially the result of natural conditions such as the limited rainfall and the short growing season, especially in the northern latitudes. Despite the vast size of the country, the amount of land suitable for agriculture is limited. This has resulted in the costly cultivation of marginal lands and reliance on extensive agriculture, bringing more land under cultivation rather than developing intensive agriculture which would increase crop yields. It has also meant high reliance on irrigation and chemicals, which are both costly and damaging to the environment. Low crop yields have also resulted from the absence of an effective, modern agricultural infrastructure and the administrative inefficiencies inherent in the collectivized and state-farm systems of the former Soviet Union. The failure to reform the agricultural sector since the collapse of the Soviet system in 1991 resulted in even further declines in agricultural production. The 1995 harvest was the worst since 1963. Grain output, for example, dropped to 63 million metric tons, down from 81 million tons in 1994 and 117 million in 1990.

Thus, in geographical terms the Soviet Union possessed both advantages and disadvantages. Its sheer size provided it with a measure of invulnerability, although the region has historically remained open to invaders over the steppe route from the east (the Mongols and Tatars) and the west (Poland, Sweden, France, and Germany). The Russian Federation, which shares most of the former USSR's advantages and disadvantages, claims the world's longest coastline, and yet much of the region faces icebound Arctic waters and the North Pacific. Ice-free ports on the Baltic and Black Seas, many of which are no longer a part of Russian territory, have historically been vulnerable to closure by the countries that control access to them. Such apparent disadvantages have been compensated for in other ways. An excellent year-round ice-free port at Murmansk on the Barents Sea in far northern European Russia provides naval forces and commercial shipping with ready access to the Atlantic Ocean and world sea lanes, and ports on the northern Pacific Ocean can be kept open during the winter with icebreakers.

Although not landlocked, both the Russian Empire and the USSR have historically sought to penetrate such neighboring lands as Poland, the Balkan countries, Turkey, Iran, Afghanistan, Mongolia, China (including Manchuria), and Korea in a bid to gain strategic advantage—including enhanced access to open seas. Some see in current efforts of the Russian Federation to reassert influence in its new neighbors of the so-called "near abroad"—the Central Asian countries, the Baltics, the Transcaucasian states, Belarus, Moldova, and Ukraine—a continuation of this effort to control neighboring states and gain strategic benefits.[3]

NATIONS AND SOCIAL CLASSES

The Soviet Union possessed the world's third largest population, exceeded in size only by those of China and India, while the Russian Federation ranks sixth in world population (following also the United States, Indonesia, and Brazil). Although the population of Russia is slightly less than 150 million, compared with the 285 million of the former Soviet Union, this population is not homogeneous and must be viewed in terms of its ethnic and social composition. The principal nationalities (see Table 7.1) in both the former USSR and the present Russian Federation represent highly diverse peoples with distinctive ethnic, linguistic, religious, and cultural qualities. Although the Russians constituted approximately one-half of the population of the USSR, their relative weight declined from 58.4 percent in 1939 to 50.8 percent in 1989. They now comprise about 82 percent of the population of the Russian Federation.

The eastern Slavic population consists of Russians, Ukrainians, and Belarusians and together comprised about 75 percent of the total population of the former Soviet Union. The Ukrainians, who were the second most numerous Slavic people in the Soviet Union, trace their origins to the Kievan Rus' of the ninth to thirteenth centuries. Subsequently they were part of the medieval Lithuanian states which united with Poland in 1569. The eastern Ukrainians, who rebelled against Polish rule in 1648, established an independent state that soon came under the influence and then control of Moscow—after making a fatal decision to turn to the Muscovite tsar for military aid in 1654. The Belarusians, who differ from Russians, did not come under Russian rule until the end of the eighteenth century. Only small numbers of Ukrainians and Belarusians remain within the borders of the Russian Federation—less than 4 percent of the total population.

The various Turkic peoples constituted approximately 17 percent of the Soviet population and make up somewhat less than 10 percent of the population of the Russian Federation. They are related to the Osmanli Turks of Turkey and extend from Sakha (Yakutia) in northeastern Siberia across Central Asia to Azerbaijan. Their subjugation by the Russians began in the sixteenth century (in the cases of the Kazan and Volga Tatars) and was not completed until the 1890s in Turkmenistan. The largest groups of Turkic peoples—the Uzbeks, Kazaks, Turkmens, Kyrgyz, and Azerbaijanis—now enjoy nominally independent states, although significant numbers of Kazaks and Azerbaijani also live in Russia. The Turkic peoples also include numerous smaller groups which are part of the population of the Russian Federation itself. The Volga Tatars live along the middle section and east of the river of that name, and the Siberian Tatars in the Tobolsk area of western Siberia. The Crimean Tatars came to the Crimea in the thirteenth century, but were forcibly resettled during World War II; their return to their homeland, now officially a part of Ukraine, was long delayed. Other Turkic peoples include the Bashkirs, Chuvash, Kara-Kalpaks, Tuvans, Karachai, and Balkar located variously in southern Siberia and the northern

Table 7.1 Population and Principal Nationalities of the Russian Federation and the Other CIS States

Nation	Population	Percentage
Russian Federation		
Population	147,022,000	
By nationality		
Russian	119,866,000	81.5
Tatar	5,522,000	3.8
Ukrainian	4,363,000	3.0
Chuvash	1,774,000	1.2
Bashkort	1,345,000	0.9
Belarusian	1,206,000	0.8
Mordvinian	1,073,000	0.7
Chechen	899,000	0.6
German	842,000	0.6
Udmurt	715,000	0.5
Mari	644,000	0.4
Kazakh	636,000	0.4
Avar	544,000	0.4
Jewish	537,000	0.4
Armenian	532,000	0.4
Buryat	417,000	0.3
Ossetian	402,000	0.3
Kabard	386,000	0.3
Yakut	380,000	0.3
Dargin	353,000	0.2
Komi	336,000	0.2
Azerbaijani	336,000	0.2
Kumyk	277,000	0.2
Lezghin	257,000	0.2
Ingush	215,000	0.1
Tuvinian	206,000	0.1
Moldovan	173,000	0.1
Kalmyk	166,000	0.1
Gypsy	153,000	0.1
Karachai	150,000	0.1
Komi-Permiak	147,000	0.1
Karelian	125,000	0.1
Adygei	123,000	0.1
Korean	107,000	0.1
Lak	106,000	0.1
Polish	95,000	0.1
Other	1,614,000	1.1
Armenia		
Population	3,305,000	
By nationality		
Armenian	3,084,000	93.3
Russian	52,000	1.6
Other	169,000	5.1
Azerbaijan		
Population	7,021,000	
By nationality		
Azerbaijani	5,805,000	82.7
Russian	392,000	5.6
Armenian	391,000*	5.6
Other	433,000	6.2
Belarus		
Population	10,152,000	
By nationality		
Belarusian	7,905,000	77.9
Russian	1,342,000	13.2
Other	905,000	8.9
Georgia		
Population	5,401,000	
By nationality		
Georgian	3,787,000	70.1
Armenian	437,000	8.1
Russian	341,000	6.3
Other	836,000	15.5
Kazakstan		
Population	16,464,000	
By nationality		
Kazak	6,535,000	39.7
Russian	6,228,000	37.8
Other	3,701,000	22.5
Kyrgyzstan		
Population	4,258,000	
By nationality		
Kyrgyz	2,230,000	52.4
Russian	917,000	21.5
Other	1,111,000	26.1
Moldova		
Population	4,335,000	
By nationality		
Moldovan	2,795,000	64.5
Ukrainian	600,000	13.8
Russian	562,000	13.0
Other	378,000	17.4
Tajikistan		
Population	5,093,000	
By nationality		
Tajik	3,172,000	62.3
Uzbek	1,198,000	23.5
Russian	388,000**	7.6**
Other	335,000**	6.6**
Turkmenistan		
Population	3,523,000	
By nationality		
Turkmen	2,537,000	72.0
Russian	334,000	9.5
Uzbek	317,000	9.0
Other	355,000	10.1
Ukraine		
Population	51,471,000	
By nationality		
Ukrainian	37,419,000	72.7
Russian	11,356,000	22.1
Other	2,696,000	5.2
Uzbekistan		
Population	19,810,000	
By nationality		
Uzbek	14,142,000	71.4
Russian	1,653,000	8.3
Other	4,015,000	20.3

*These figures do not reflect the exodus of most Armenians, except about 150,000 in Nagorno-Karabakh, from Azerbaijan since the outbreak of hostilities in Nagorno-Karabakh.

**These figures do not reflect the exodus of much of the European population during the civil war that began in 1992.

Sources: These statistics come from Stephen K. Batalden and Sandra L. Batalden, *The Newly Independent States of Eurasia: Handbook of Former Soviet Republics* (Phoenix, AZ: Oryx Press, 1993). The Bataldens draw upon the official Soviet census of 1989 and a variety of more recent statistical estimates.

Caucasus region. Inhabiting a rugged mountainous country along the Afghan frontier, the Tajiks are linguistically an Iranian people and are also Muslims.

As a result of several centuries of Russian rule over Armenia, Georgia, and the Baltic states, substantial numbers of individuals from these ethnic communities, especially the Transcaucasians, can also be found scattered across the Russian Federation. The Armenians represent an old culture that flourished long before the Russians emerged as a people. Armenia was also the first Christian state and has a unique national church. The Georgians, neighbors of the Armenians, have a very distinctive language and accepted Christianity in the fourth century. These two peoples came under Russian rule early in the nineteenth century as a result of pressure from their Muslim neighbors and Russian penetration of the area south of the Caucasus Mountains.

A Russian ethnic minority.

The Baltic peoples belong neither to the Slavic nor the Germanic worlds, but constitute separate ethnic entities that came under Russian rule in the eighteenth century. They include the Estonians and Latvians, who are Lutherans, and the Lithuanians, who are Roman Catholics. Although the Baltic states obtained their independence after World War I during the Russian Revolution, they were forcibly annexed by the Soviet Union in 1940 and again in 1944. They played a key role in the disintegration of the Soviet state and seceded from the USSR and regained their independence in September 1991, immediately following the abortive coup attempt against the government of Mikhail Gorbachev. Other non-Slavic peoples of the former Soviet Union included the Moldovans, who are actually Romanians of the region of Bessarabia conquered by Russia in 1812 and returned to Romania from 1918 to World War II, after which the Soviet Union reannexed the region.

Among the nationalities that had no union-level Soviet republic were the Jews, Germans, and Poles. The Jewish population came under Russian rule in the late eighteenth-century annexations of Polish-ruled territories. Although one-half of the world's Jewish population lived in the Russian Empire prior to World War I, subsequent events, such as the Holocaust—the mass execution of Jews and others in Nazi-occupied Europe including Ukraine, Russia, and Belorussia (now Belarus)—repressive practices on the part of Soviet authorities, and emigration caused their number to diminish to the level of 1.3 million according to the 1989 census. Germans in the former Soviet Union are largely descendants of colonists invited by the Russian government to settle there in the eighteenth century; their Volga German Autonomous Republic was liquidated and its population deported to Central Asia in 1941. Since 1985 substantial numbers of ethnic Germans have left for Germany. Among the other peoples who have been under extensive demographic pressure from the Russians are the Finno-Ugric peoples, including the Mordvinians, the Udmurt, the Mari, the Karelians, and the Komi.

Among the most serious problems facing the Russian government of President Boris

Yeltsin was the explosion of ethnically based nationalism among a number of the minority peoples of Russia. Although the most serious and visible example occurred in the Republic of Chechnya, where, despite more than eighteen months of warfare and the use by Russian troops of their full military arsenal against the Chechen rebels, Russian military forces had failed as of mid-1996 to eradicate military resistance to continued Russian rule over this small Muslim people in the Caucasus. Elsewhere across Russia some ethnically based constituent republics of the Federation—for example, Tatarstan along the Volga River and Buryatia north of Mongolia—have declared their autonomy or "independence" from Moscow and resisted the imposition of full central authority. Throughout most of the 18 other ethnically based republics within the Russian Federation, nationalist movements have emerged that make various claims for greater autonomy. Overall, however, the Russian government seems to have succeeded—for the time being at least—in assuaging the most radical demands of the non-Russian peoples of the Federation by a combination of granting to them substantial autonomy, while simultaneously demonstrating in Chechnya the costs of refusing to cooperate with Moscow. However, the long-term viability of Russia's control over its subject peoples remains in doubt.

Although the Soviet Union claimed to be building a "classless Communist society"—according to the 1977 Constitution—social strata recognized officially included the "working class, the collectivized peasantry, and the people's intelligentsia." Social classes can be distinguished in terms of income levels, status, and prestige, and by the degree of their influence in society. Yet, Soviet rulers, for ideological reasons, sought to minimize social differences. Thus, "workers" were said to constitute 58.8 percent of the population in 1989, collective farmers 11.8 percent, and "salaried" persons 29.3 percent. The self-employed and others were a mere 0.2 percent of the population. Such broad categories blur real social distinction, since each contains numerous subgroups.

Official Soviet social categories also omitted the political class—an elite usually referred to as the *nomenklatura* that consisted of the leading *cadres* (officials) of the ruling Communist Party, as well as government ministers and high-level bureaucrats, economic managers, leading diplomats, military figures, and KGB personnel. This ruling class enjoyed superior housing, country homes, chauffeur-driven automobiles, servants, vacations and foreign travel, and access to special "closed stores" that sold scarce and imported items at discount prices or for "certificate rubles" worth much more than ordinary rubles. There were also fringe benefits such as medical care in exclusive clinics and hospitals that were far superior to those serving ordinary Soviet citizens.[4] Leonid Brezhnev as general secretary of the Communist Party could acquire a large private collection of expensive foreign automobiles. The elite could accumulate considerable wealth, often by corrupt means, and give their children academic diplomas and arrange prestigious and well-paid positions for them. One of the unfortunate characteristics of post-Communist Russia is the fact that a new elite is emerging, often from among the very membership of the old Soviet *nomenklatura,* that controls an ever-growing percentage of economic resources which it uses to "buy" political influence and flaunt its economic success.

In the 1980s the term *mafia* gained currency in the Soviet Union and was used in several senses. It applied to CPSU officials and to members who held key positions in nonparty organizations and participated in networks based on mutual advantage and self-enrichment. *Mafia* also referred to those engaged in large-scale black market activity. With the emergence of individual and private (nominally cooperative) enterprise resulting from changes in economic policy in the Gorbachev period, another type of mafia appeared—racketeers engaged in extortion and theft at the expense of successful legitimate businesses. The expansion of organized crime and of its influence on society continued unabated during the first four years of the new Russian Federation. In 1995, for example, reported murders rose to 32,000, up from 15,500 five years earlier.

Soviet society came to be characterized by significant inequalities of income, education, and educational opportunity—despite official claims to the contrary. Yet the intelligentsia—which included professional, scientific, scholarly, educational, artistic, and literary persons—represented great differences in rewards. Thus, physicians, two-thirds of whom were women, were poorly paid. Many Soviet citizens, including unskilled workers and pensioners, fell below the poverty level by the early 1990s. At the same time there emerged a new class of "ruble millionaires" as a result of increased corruption, severe goods shortages, and a developing market. By the mid–1990s over half of the population found itself below the official poverty level, as inflation eroded the buying power of all those on government incomes, such as teachers, government employees, and retirees.

The Soviet population was long characterized by a disparity in the sex ratio. Women significantly outnumbered men as a result of famine, the bloody Stalinist purges, and World War II, apart from longevity differences. There were 17.6 million more women than men in 1979 and 15.7 million more in 1990—at a time when the effects of events in the 1930s and 1940s were beginning to lose their impact. The USSR experienced a steadily declining birth rate that was especially evident in Russia and in Ukraine. The natural increase declined from 17.8 (per thousand population) in 1960 to 7.6 in 1989, with current estimates indicating that deaths outnumbered live births in the mid–1990s. However, the rate of population increases in the Muslim areas of the former Soviet Union have been four to eight times greater than among the European population groups.

One of the great ironies of the post-Communist period across Central and Eastern Europe and the former USSR concerns the position of women. While governmental coercion has been greatly reduced and political systems have become much more open, the economic and political situation of women has deteriorated. First of all, the impact of economic depression has hit women harder than men. They are likely to be the first to be laid off from work, and two-thirds of all officially registered employed workers are women; even more than in the Communist period they continue to find it difficult to achieve senior positions of leadership within the economy. Although they comprise 47 percent of the work force, 48 percent in the state sector, they make up only 25 percent in the dynamic new private sector. An indication of the official place of women's issues in the new Russia is the response of Russian Labor Minister Melikian to questions about tackling the problem of unemployment among women: "Why should we employ women when men are out of work? It is better that men work and women take care of children and do housework. I don't think women should work when men are doing nothing."[5]

In the political sphere, the position of women has also declined dramatically. In the Soviet Union prior to the initiation of political reforms, women usually made up 30–35 percent of those in leadership positions in the Communist Party and in governmental bodies at the regional, republic, and federal levels excluding the very top CPSU organs and the Council of Ministers. Women were also visible in upper-level positions in governmental ministries, even though the equality of women in the Soviet system was often more apparent than it was real. In the Supreme Soviet, elected with substantially more openness in 1989, however, only 5.4 percent of the deputies were women (57 of 1,063). In the first two elections to the newly created Duma in 1993 and 1995, the number of women who emerged victorious was well below 10 percent. Although women continue to dominate in numbers of employees in such governmental ministries as Finance and Public Health, very few are in leading positions.

In an attempt to ensure that issues of special importance to women—such as escalating violence against women (15,000 were murdered by their husbands or lovers in 1994), drastic declines in the quality of health care and in the availability of affordable childcare, skyrocketing unemployment, and related issues—a political party called Women of Russia was created to focus especially on these issues. The party generated only 4.6 percent of the popular vote in the parliamentary elections of December 1995 and elected only three candidates. Public opinion polls in Russia indicated that even a high percentage of women do not support the idea of women in positions of political leadership.

Summarizing the political situation of women in Russia, sociologist Galena G. Sillaste has emphasized the fact that political reforms and democratization in the former Soviet Union and Russia have resulted in a situation which has provided on the one hand, broad political rights and freedoms for women in Russia and a real (not verbal and formal) abolition of sexual discrimination in all spheres of social life, and on the other hand, the deliberate expulsion of women from politics, power, and participation in political decision making and responsibility for the implementation of decisions.[6]

RUSSIAN POLITICAL VALUES AND SOVIET POLITICAL CULTURE

In the midst of society-wide transitions that appear chaotic and unpredictable, the Russian population is being asked to change its expectations of government and of the broader political environment. Just as political forces in Russia are required to contend with the difficulties of the triple transition from old methods of political, economic, and social orientation and organization, the population at large finds itself facing changes of monumental proportions that challenge the belief system, or political culture, that dominated the Soviet past. A political culture reflects the ideals, beliefs, and values that a people hold in common. It defines a people's attitudes toward authority, relations between rulers and ruled, and the degree of trust accorded rulers and what they are permitted or not permitted to do. The degree of loyalty that a political system elicits will depend on the extent to which it is in accord with the dominant political culture.

However, certain reservations must be kept in mind. There are various subcultures (regional, social, ethnic, religious) that may be in conflict with the dominant political culture. St. Petersburg traditionally has represented somewhat different values from those accepted in Moscow. The numerous non-Russian nationalities have not necessarily shared the values and preferences of the Russians. Also culture represents learned behavior; it is acquired, being transmitted from generation to generation, and is not biological or based on racial attributes. As learned behavior, cultural patterns and values can be changed over time; the degree and speed of such change will depend upon circumstances and on a willingness to reappraise and modify existing values.

No people or political system can escape its past. Each people possesses a political tradition and fund of experience that influence its institutions, practices, values, and norms of political conduct. The Russian political experience reflects certain unique traits, issues, and problems that can be characterized as syndromes. The question under debate among analysts of contemporary Russian politics is the degree to which Russians are attracted to and supportive of authoritarian political institutions and leaders. Many believe that Russians lack most of the values that are essential for the effective functioning of political democracy—a sense of political efficacy, a willingness to compromise with those with different views, and so on. They note that the Communist successes in the elections of December 1995 and the tone of the political rhetoric and directives emerging from the political leadership belie the democratic institutions that have been created in Russia. They raise serious questions concerning the interaction of new and old methods of political behavior. However, other analysts present the view that Russia has long possessed an alternative political culture that derived from community-based activism and that Soviet totalitarianism did not represent continuity in Russian political traditions.[7] Prospects for the growth and acceptance by the Russian population of the underlying attitudes and values associated with democracy are favorable, they maintain.

Although the answers to the argument concerning existing political culture in Russia are not self-evident, what is clear is the fact that, for a stable democratic system to emerge in Russia, the peoples of Russia must accept and internalize the assumptions about politics and government that are necessary for a functioning democracy—assumptions that diverge significantly from the Russian autocratic tradition that was, in the words of noted historian Robert V.

Daniels, "reincarnated in Stalinism and perpetuated in Brezhnevism."[8]

KEY RUSSIAN SYNDROMES

Closely associated with Russian political culture and central to an understanding of the patterns of political organization and behavior that have characterized Russia in the past are several persistent traits or key syndromes: (1) centralized power and absolutist rule; (2) truth seeking; (3) resistance, sectarianism, and anarchic tendencies; (4) alienation of the intelligentsia; (5) Russia's identity and its appropriation of foreign ways; and (6) pretense and mendacity. Let's look at each one in more detail.

Centralized Power and Absolutist Rule

Centralized power and absolutist rule comprise one of Russia's most persistent traits.[9] The Russian political tradition emerged from the Muscovite state, which developed an autocratic order originally headed by princes, one of whom, Ivan IV ("the Terrible"), adopted the title of tsar, a Russian version of *caesar*. The Muscovite state and its rulers gained an advantage over neighboring principalities by collaborating with the Mongol-Tatar conquerors who had subjugated much of Eastern Europe in 1240. By serving as collectors of tribute and by being outwardly servile, the Muscovite princes succeeded in establishing a power base that enabled them to subjugate their neighbors, including Finnish peoples living to the east and north of Moscow. Muscovite princes learned much from the Mongols and Tatars regarding taxation, intelligence gathering, military organization, census taking, and the importance of the postal system and communications.[10] Mongol rule gradually weakened, but it lasted nearly two and a half centuries until 1480.

The rulers of Muscovy were also influenced by the autocratic political system of the Eastern Roman (Byzantine) Empire, in which Orthodox Christianity was the state religion and the emperors posed as defenders of religious doctrine. Muscovy received Christianity from the early Rus', but Byzantium taught the Russians that the West (Rome) was "heretical" and not to be trusted. Orthodox Christianity also meant that Muscovy would develop in cultural isolation from the West. After Constantinople fell to the Turks in 1453, Muscovite rulers could depict themselves in the sixteenth century as the "Third Rome." As the successor of the first two Romes, both of which had fallen, and the only Orthodox Christian state free from Ottoman Turkish and Muslim domination, Muscovy allegedly was specially chosen. This sense of exclusiveness and self-satisfaction helped to motivate Muscovite expansionism and the urge to acquire an empire.

Russian political development was fated to adopt an autocratic pattern when Muscovy annexed the principality of Novgorod in 1478. Novgorod had been the most prominent Russian polity for three centuries prior to the emergence of Muscovy. It was an important commercial center, but it also had a unique political order. Novgorod developed as a republic with nonhereditary princes and with other elected officials. A popular assembly met in the marketplace, but actual power was exercised by a limited number of local magnates. If Novgorod had prevailed instead of Muscovy, Russian political culture might not have developed in the autocratic pattern of absolutist rulers, but would probably have assumed a republican form.

Absolutist rule in Muscovy was also made possible or even necessary by the steady territorial expansion of the Muscovite state. Muscovy is first referred to in the chronicles in 1147. By the fifteenth century it covered 15,000 square miles, but in the course of the subsequent four centuries it expanded approximately 570 times to an area of 8.5 million square miles by the end of the nineteenth century. The Muscovite state was renamed the Russian Empire in 1721 by Peter I ("the Great"). Empire building meant the subjugation of other peoples. The Volga Tatars were conquered in 1552, and within a century Siberia, with its alien peoples, was acquired. Eastern Ukraine came under Muscovite influence in 1654 as a result of a treaty of alliance against Poland between the Ukrainian Cossack state and the Muscovite tsar—the terms of which were then systematically violated by the Russians. The Baltic peoples (Estonians, Latvians, and Lithuanians) were annexed during the eighteenth century, as were the Belarusians, more than half the Poles, and the Crimean Tatars, along with the central and western Ukrainians. During the nineteenth century the Russian Empire annexed the Caucasus, Georgia, Armenia, Azerbaijan, Finland, and Turkestan (Central Asia). The end of the nineteenth century saw the empire seeking gains at the expense of a weakened China, in Manchuria especially, and in Korea—an effort that was thwarted as a result of Russia's military defeat at the hands of Japan in 1905.

Russian territorial expansionism, pursued on an unparalleled scale, could hardly have been accomplished without an autocratic political order. The fact that the Russian emperors ruled large numbers of alien subjects—the Russians were a minority of 43 percent in their own empire at the turn of the twentieth century—guaranteed the perpetuation of autocratic rule. The last emperor, Nicholas II, remained an autocrat even after the 1905 Revolution, when he was compelled to agree to the establishment of a weak legislative body, the Imperial Duma.

The idea of service to the ruler who personified the state was well established in the Russian political experience. Strong monarchs such as Ivan IV were able to keep the nobles (boyars) subordinate by making land ownership of estates dependent upon service to the state and unconditional obedience to the tsar. When the monarchs were weak personalities, the autocracy functioned through the bureaucracy, whose officials were just as arbitrary and demanding as the absolute monarch.

It is not surprising that the heavy weight of Russian autocratic rule doomed the brief experiment with democracy under the Provisional Government in 1917. Russians had failed to develop any effective restraints on autocratic power, and it was relatively easy for Lenin and his Bolsheviks to adapt the Russian tradition of centralism and absolutist rule to their own purposes. The Communist ruling class claimed the right to rule on the basis of its professed monopoly of philosophical truth, wisdom, justice, and moral good. The Communist Party assumed

the role of a collective counterpart or successor to the Russian tsars and emperors, who in their claim to total power ruled on the basis of divine right. The Russian autocrats were said to be responsible to God and to their own conscience, whereas the Communist rulers claimed to be responsible only to "history" as understood in the Communist philosophy.

In the brief period that has passed since the collapse of the Communist system in 1991, it has been evident that the roots of authoritarian political culture run deep in the Russian population. In the face of growing social and economic problems in post-Soviet Russia, a majority of the population has voiced its preference for strong and stable political leadership. As was noted at the outset of this chapter, most of the important emerging political parties are committed to reestablishing strong central authority in Russia.

Truth Seeking

Truth seeking and the claim to possess truth have characterized the Russian understanding of political values. In Russia political power has traditionally been wedded to ideology based on total solutions, sweeping assertions, absolute values, and the notion of official truth. The claim to possess truth and to be pursuing maximal goals in its name promoted a brand of unyielding politics that tended to reject moderation and compromise.[11] It also favored the adoption of "devil" theories of politics emphasizing enemies and "dark" and "impure" forces seeking to destroy Russia—behavior that has reemerged in Russia to explain the purported role of Western intelligence organizations and corporations in the collapse of the Soviet Union and the emergence of the problems facing Russia.[12] In imperial Russia the truth was embodied in the official Russian Orthodox Church, and it served as a major source of support for the autocratic political order, with the emperor serving as guardian of the faith.

The official "truth" of the Soviet political system—Marxism-Leninism—represented different values from those of the tsarist regime; however, the notion of official truth remained a basic attribute of both regimes. The Russian philosopher Nikolai Berdyaev contended that the Russians are an "apocalyptic people" concerned with ultimate ends and total solutions and with the prophetic element in life.[13] If this is the case, it is easier to understand why Marxism-Leninism could be accepted as the ideological basis of the Soviet system. Marxism-Leninism offered predictions in the guise of social science and depicted the ultimate triumph of good, as represented by the Communist Party, over evil. Social justice would supposedly triumph, and the Russians would serve as interpreters and guardians of the doctrine and could claim to be carrying out the will of history. Marxism-Leninism and its vision of the future could claim to have universal application and to be internationalist in outlook. It had wider appeal abroad than the official truth of the Russian Empire and served to rationalize Russian imperial ambitions and expansionism in the Soviet period. Many of the tenets of the doctrine continue to attract widespread support, as the showing of the Cummunist Party in parliamentary and presidential elections have shown.

One of the problems facing reformers as they attempt to generate support for democratic and free-market ideals relates to the immensity of the economic and social problems facing Russia and the lack of familiarity of most Russians with the values associated with democracy. It is easier for the Communists to find support for their simplistic, nationalistic, egalitarian, and redistributive slogans.

Resistance, Sectarianism, and Anarchy

Resistance, sectarianism, and anarchic tendencies have represented a reaction by the Russians to the harsh absolute rule of political centralism. There is much evidence to indicate that Russians have not submitted totally or unquestioningly to their rulers. Historically there has been a wide and deep gulf separating the rulers and the ruled. Authority has been distrusted and resisted when circumstances have permitted. The *veche* (popular assembly) in the pluralistic eastern Slavic society of Rus' in the pre-Mongol period opposed princes, especially in Kiev and

Novgorod. Russia witnessed the great peasant revolts of Ivan Bolotnikov and Stenka Razin in the seventeenth century and Emelian Pugachev in the eighteenth century—although Bolotnikov claimed to act in the name of the tsar and both Razin and Pugachev claimed to be true tsars come to reclaim their thrones from usurpers; none presented himself as a challenger to the existing order.[14] In the nineteenth century the fierceness of Russian revolt prompted the greatest of Russia's poets, Aleksandr Pushkin, to characterize it as "senseless and ruthless." The twentieth century saw the burning of the manor houses and the murder of estate owners and the bursting forth of peasant wrath during the revolutionary upheavals of 1917.

Russian resistance is also evident in a rich tradition of religious sectarianism that flourished despite the existence of an official Russian Orthodox state church. The seventeenth century saw a great schism between the official church and the Old Ritualists (Old Believers), who refused to accept a revision of religious practices. Subsequently a variety of exotic sects emerged, including the *Dukhobory* (Spirit Fighters), who refused to accept political authority, perform military service, or pay taxes. In the Soviet period various Protestant sects made their appearance in opposition to the regime's official atheism and to the subordination of the Russian Orthodox Patriarchate to the Soviet rulers.

Russian interest in anarchism prompted Berdyaev to observe that anarchism was largely a Russian creation and that the Russians do not really like the state, but either meekly submit to it or rebel against it as circumstances dictate or permit.[15] It is significant that such prominent Russians as Mikhail Bakunin, the novelist Leo Tolstoy, and Prince Peter Kropotkin contributed to the theory of anarchism. Bakunin's anarchism was violent and atheistic, based on "creative" destruction; Tolstoy's was nonviolent and religious; and Kropotkin's anarchic communism was based on mutual aid in place of the wage system. If Russians have had an inclination toward anarchism and resisting the state, as Berdyaev contends, the existence of harsh and repressive authoritarian systems in Russia becomes more understandable. The fear of anarchy may explain why Soviet rulers insisted on "moral political unity," and some current Russian leaders call for a return to strong central authority.

Alienation of the Intelligentsia

Alienation of the intelligentsia was a problem for both the tsarist imperial and Soviet Russian regimes. The term *intelligentsia* is one of the few Russian words to be adopted into foreign languages. It originally referred to the nineteenth-century "men of ideas" who criticized contemporary conditions on the basis of abstract ideas. In rejecting prevailing values, the intelligentsia became alienated from the Russian state, church, nation, and way of life, and instead often embraced foreign ideas, including Marxism. The Soviet rulers created a large intelligentsia of specialists, but alienation persisted among political dissidents and persons who sought to emigrate.[16] It is ironic that Svetlana Alliluyeva, the only daughter of the late Soviet dictator Joseph Stalin, defected in 1967, rejecting the Soviet system and its values and renouncing her membership in the Communist Party, as well as her Soviet citizenship.[17] The effort of Mikhail Gorbachev to co-opt the intelligentsia by allowing it greater freedom of expression was designed to obtain its support for his reforms and deal with its alienation.

Russia's Identity

Russia's identity and its appropriation of foreign ways have also contributed to its reliance on a severe and demanding political order. Russians have persistently debated the question of Russia's relationship to Europe and Asia, what Russia is, and whether or not it has some special historic mission to fulfill. The problem of Russia's identity was complicated by its efforts to subjugate and assimilate neighboring peoples and by the scale of its borrowing and appropriation of foreign technology beginning with he reign of Peter I. The Russian elite has contained many non-Russians or assimilated elements. Peter I recruited Baltic Germans to carry out his reforms and hired foreigners to develop a Russian navy. Many Russian explorers in the eighteenth and nineteenth centuries were actually

Germans. The Russian ruling dynasty, known as the House of Romanov, became ethnically German after 1762 during the reign of Catherine II, a German princess, and her ill-fated husband, Peter III. Italians constructed much of the Kremlin, and Italians and other foreigners erected most of the imposing structures of the new capital of St. Petersburg. The Muscovite state, in its expansion and transformation into the multinational Russian Empire, developed an imperial consciousness prior to the emergence of a Russian national consciousness and thus created a persistent identity problem that is still evident today in the debates about the very nature of Russia and its orientation toward both Europe and Asia. As the noted philosopher Aleksandr Tsipko has argued, "without Kiev there can be no Russia in the old, *real,* sense of the word."[18]

Russia's heavy reliance on borrowing is reflected in the presence of large numbers of English, French, and German loan words in the Russian language as common nouns for household objects. All languages contain foreign loan words, but the degree of their presence in the Russian languages is vivid testimony to the Russian ability to borrow and appropriate. Yet this practice and the Russian effort to dominate and assimilate non-Russian peoples have resulted in the need for an imposed identity—such as the notion of a "Soviet people" or the recent revival of the distinction between *Russkie* (ethnic Russians) as opposed to *Rossiiskie* (inhabitants of Russia)—and have posed the related threats of "contamination" and fragmentation. Russia's unity has been complex and synthetic, and its rulers have traditionally resorted to extreme measures in attempting to preserve it—as illustrated currently by the policies of President Yeltsin in Chechnya.

Pretense and Mendacity

Pretense and mendacity have been employed to justify and maintain the political order and society. Fedor Dostoevsky, in an essay entitled "Something on Lying" (1873) published in his *Diary of a Writer,* posed the unusual question: "Why does everyone among us [in Russia] lie and without exception?" The writer contended that lying was engaged in "out of hospitality" and for effect, noting that the truth is "for us too boring and prosaic, insufficiently poetic, too commonplace."[19] The reliance on pretense, deception, and self-deception was evident in the claims of Soviet political leaders, who for decades maintained that Soviet society was "superior" and that its political system under a party dictatorship was "democratic." The Soviet Union, based on coercion and territorial aggrandizement, was said to be "voluntary." Concealment was evident in such matters as the denial of the famines of 1932–1933 and 1947, official statistics on Soviet fatalities in World War II, the size of the Soviet military budget, the declining life expectancy of males, fatalities resulting from the Chernobyl nuclear catastrophe, the claim that there were budget surpluses when there were actually large deficits, and the inflated official exchange rate for the ruble in the absence of convertibility.

The revelations made by Nikita Khrushchev in his campaign against Stalin's dictatorship and by Gorbachev regarding his predecessors served to confirm the role of mendacity and pretense in Soviet politics. The Communist Party's reliance on resolutions and proclamations reflected a preference for verbal "solutions" and claims, with assertions being equated with achievement but actually reflecting problem avoidance. Aleksandr Yakovlev, who as an adviser to Gorbachev investigated the party's crimes and rehabilitated large numbers of victims, told the Twenty-eighth Party Congress, "Over the course of seventy years we have too frequently permitted ourselves to ignore everything that was not to our liking. Even today . . . we sometimes continue to deceive ourselves and play the hypocrite."[20] Ample evidence exists in post-Soviet Russia to indicate that this attribute of Russian political culture still flourishes; official treatment of the effort to regain control over Chechnya militarily is a clear example of the effort to avoid full disclosure and even to deceive.

PSYCHOCULTURAL THEORIES

Theories of the Russian character, which have been used to explain Russian and Soviet politi-
cal behavior, have been based on various hypotheses and on a limited amount of clinical psychological evidence. Some observers have noted contradictions in the Russian character evidenced in "mood swings" and in sudden shifts in attitude and behavior—as from activity to passivity, from euphoria to melancholy, or from friendship to hostility. The philosopher Berdyaev saw the Russian character as a "combination of opposites" including such contradictory traits as individualism and collectivism, nationalism and universalism, God-seeking and militant atheism, humility and impudence, and slavery and rebellion.[21] Similarly, Russians have been both attracted to and repelled by the West.

Other observers have noted the presence of guilt, hostility, and fear in Russians. Preoccupation with enemies (internal and external) and "dark forces" has played an important role in Russian life. The Soviet media readily denounced such "enemies" as capitalists, fascists, Trotskyites, Maoists, imperialists, neocolonialists, bourgeois nationalists, monopolists, revisionists, and dogmatists. In much the same way, current nationalists, including key figures in the Russian Orthodox Church, have emphasized the corrupting role of Western influence in Russia, the direct role of Western intelligence agencies in the downfall of Soviet power, and the current problems of Russia. Such allegations are indicative of the Russian tendency to blame their ills and failings on foreigners. Moreover, guilt feelings persisted in the Soviet practice of "criticism and self-criticism" and in the inability of Soviet citizens to fulfill all the demands made upon them by the authorities (including the numerous obligations incorporated into the 1977 Soviet Constitution).[22]

LENINISM—THE RUSSIAN VERSION OF MARXISM

Although Marxism-Leninism as an official state doctrine meant to explain social reality and provide a blueprint for the future lost its preeminent position with the collapse of the Soviet Union in 1991, for more than 70 years it had inspired much Soviet organization and behavior and served as the political language of communication. For many it continues to serve these functions. The core of Soviet ideology was the

Marxian critique of capitalism and the call for violent revolution by workers to replace capitalism with a stateless and classless society. Based on the writings of the German philosopher, historian, and social scientist Karl Marx, Marxism provided a doctrine that claimed to explain all of history and human behavior and to be "scientific" as well. Russian intellectuals under Lenin's leadership appropriated Marxism and modified it to suit Russian needs. Thus, the Soviet Union acquired an official ideology that can be said to have replaced the Russian Empire's state religion of Orthodox Christianity.

Marxism-Leninism as an ideology is a system of thought, a "world outlook" that attempts to explain or rationalize all of reality. It is a method of political analysis that offers a plan of action and a vision of the future. It acquired some of the characteristics of a sectarian or quasi-religious movement despite its claim to be scientific and its advocacy of militant atheism. It promised humanity a form of secular salvation and claimed to be the sole source of truth and ultimate knowledge. It required converts to master the Marxist-Leninist "scriptural" writings, as understood in their current interpretation, and to accept Communist Party discipline. In insisting upon ideological orthodoxy, party leaders employed the practice of condemning deviationist movements, which were the Communist counterpart of religious heresies. Leninists even made Lenin's embalmed body in the Red Square mausoleum an object of veneration comparable to a religious relic.[23]

Tenets of Leninism

Although Lenin reinterpreted and developed the thought of Karl Marx (1828–1895), Leninism reflected the basic tenets of Marxism and its view of capitalism. Marxism provided a Communist analysis of capitalism rather than a clear blueprint for a Communist society. In the Communist version of capitalism and of precapitalist societies (feudalism and slaveholding societies), the class struggle is seen as the principal motive force. History evolves as the result of a dialectical conflict, which emphasizes the interdependence of all phenomena and objects, the centrality and irreconcilability of conflict in human

existence, and the ultimate victory of Communist society social structures in human society.

Marxism has assumed different forms in various countries. Marx and Engels provided a general appraisal of the capitalism of their time, but they did not offer any specific advice concerning the political form that the Communist revolution would assume. Leninism provided not merely a Russian version of Marxism, but also a means by which Marxists could establish a Communist political order. The vehicle for this purpose was the party of professional revolutionaries established by Lenin. As early as 1902, in his booklet *What Is to Be Done?* Lenin advocated the formation of a unique type of elite political party composed of a limited number of dedicated, disciplined, tested, and trained professional Communists. The party was to be the vanguard of the working class and of the industrial proletariat. In practice, Lenin substituted his Communist (Bolshevik) Party for the working class because he distrusted the "spontaneity" of the masses. He established a new type of highly centralized party that was trained in conspiratorial methods and capable of acting unquestioningly under the leadership's direction.

Priority of the political struggle was a basic tenet of Leninism, largely because its founder warned against the "dangers" of having the workers settle for mere economic benefits and reform through trade unions and strikes. Leninism was also to give meaning to the term "dictatorship of the proletariat." The notion of the dictatorship of any ruling class is basic to Marxism-Leninism, whether it is the slaveholding class, the feudal lords, or bourgeois interests. In Marxism-Leninism, the economic order determines the political order, and each ruling class is said to use the instrument of the state and its laws to oppress and exploit. Although Marx had used the term "revolutionary dictatorship of the proletariat" in his writings (in his *Critique of the Gotha Program*), it was left to Lenin to establish the first one-party dictatorship in the name of the industrial working class. The dictatorship of the proletariat was really to be the dictatorship of Lenin's Bolsheviks for the purpose of completing the revolution by crushing the bourgeoisie and establishing socialism. Lenin could promise the "withering away" of the state in 1917 (in *State and Revolution*), but his successor, Stalin, would boast in June 1930 that the Soviet dictatorship of the proletariat was "the strongest and most powerful of all state authorities." He justified the Soviet dictatorship in dialectical terms "for the purpose of preparing the conditions *for* the withering away of state authority."[24]

Leninism was also characterized by tactical flexibility, which accepted the notion of temporary retreat for the purpose of future gains—as in the conclusion of a peace treaty with the Central Powers in 1918 at any price and the granting of concessions to small-scale capitalism associated with the New Economic Program of 1921 as a means of reviving the war-damaged economy.

Lenin's theory of imperialism was developed hastily in 1916 from the writings of others in an effort to explain why World War I had occurred and why most Socialists were supporting their countries' war efforts. In *Imperialism, the Highest Stage of Capitalism,* Lenin argued that a new type of "finance capital" (as opposed to industrial capital) had arisen as a result of the merger and concentration of banking and industry. It exported capital abroad because of domestic stagnation, in order to benefit from abundant raw materials and cheap labor. Capital was said to be exported because of the domestic stagnation that resulted from the growth of monopolies, declining profits, and shrinking markets at home. The export of capital led to colonialism, and the competition for colonies and redivision of the spoils were said to lead to military alliances and wars.

Lenin's theory of imperialism was based on very limited historical evidence and did not fully explain the phenomenon of war. However, Lenin used it to attempt to explain why proletarian revolutions were not occurring in the most industrially developed countries, as they were supposed to occur according to the teachings of Marx and Engels. According to Lenin, the increased profits from colonialism made it possible for the capitalist ruling class to "buy off" important parts of the working class with high wages and other concessions, thereby creating "privileged sections" that became bourgeois in

outlook (a "labor aristocracy"), and postponing or even preventing proletarian revolution led by Communists. He concluded that Communist-led revolutions were more likely to occur in economically underdeveloped countries with no industrial proletariat.

Leninism was subsequently modified by Lenin's successors—but always in the name of Leninism. For more than seven decades, Marxism-Leninism was the official ideology of the Soviet Union, and dialectical materialism was the officially recognized philosophy. Marx and Engels were acknowledged in the Soviet Union, but their many statements critical of imperial Russia were suppressed by the Soviet rulers.

RELEVANCE OF MARXISM-LENINISM

From the very beginning there were those who raised many questions concerning the validity of Marxism-Leninism. Because it reduced all of human history to several stages and based them on the a materialistic theory of history, Marxism-Leninism is seen as oversimplifying and neglecting the importance of nonmaterial factors such as sex, nationalism, and religion in human behavior. Critics also pointed out that, while claiming to be a science, Marxism-Leninism has also served to make moral judgments and to declare one social class evil and another the source of virtue. Moreover, as many critics have noted, virtually all of the predictions of Marxism-Leninism have been inaccurate; for example, neither the industrial proletariat nor the middle class has become impoverished and nationalism did not disappear.

Yet, for Soviet rulers Marxism-Leninism was more than a philosophy or theory, since it served to justify and legitimize their system of rule. For seven decades Soviet leaders sang the praises of their ideology, as Gorbachev did at the Twenty-seventh Party Congress in 1986:

> Marxism-Leninism is the greatest revolutionary world view. It has substantiated the most humane objective that

humankind has ever set for itself—the creation of a just social system on earth. It points the way to the scientific study of the development of society as a single, law-governed process in all of its vast many-sidedness and contradictoriness, and it teaches [us] to understand correctly the nature and interaction of economic and political forces, to select the correct directions, forms and methods of struggle, and to feel self-confident at the decisive turning points in history.[25]

So long as the Soviet system appeared to function successfully, the adherents of Marxism-Leninism could claim that their ideology was correct. They could also find confirmation of it in the competition for markets between capitalist countries, in the growth of corporate mergers and "monopolies," strike activity, bankruptcies, business failures, inflation, and unemployment in capitalist countries.

The ideology was the source of much Soviet political practice. The Communist Party used it to justify its claim to a monopoly of political power and its role as the chosen instrument of "history" and the source of official truth. It also justified by means of the concept of "socialist internationalism" Soviet domination over other Communist states and parties. Ideological requirements dictated many Soviet government policies: the nationalization of all land, state ownership of the economy, collectivization of agriculture, forced industrialization, the refusal to permit even small private business enterprises based on hired labor (as distinct from cooperatives), and the global confrontation with the United States and other capitalist countries. The teaching of "scientific atheism" as an obligatory subject in Soviet schools was based on Marxism-Leninism. Ideology prompted the Communist Party to dictate standards in literature and in the arts and to influence the writing of historians and social scientists. In the past ideological tenets even dictated acceptable findings in the natural sciences. Censorship was justified by the Marxist-Leninist view that ideas are important and have consequences.

LENINISM IN RETREAT

Although Mikhail Gorbachev, as party leader, continued to profess belief in Marxism-Leninism, he ceased quoting from Lenin's writings because they provided no prescriptions for the Soviet malaise and were incompatible with the market economy that Gorbachev claimed to be establishing. Marxism-Leninism, which for decades had suffered from increasing irrelevance to sociopolitical and economic reality in the USSR, came under attack in the intense discussion prompted by Gorbachev's reformist policies. The acknowledgment by Gorbachev of widespread failure on the part of his predecessors contributed further to discrediting the ideology.

Statues of Lenin, regarded as the symbol of the totalitarian dictatorship, were removed by democratically elected non-Communist officials, initially in the Baltic states, Georgia, and western Ukraine, but subsequently elsewhere. In some jurisdictions statues of Lenin were guarded by the police and military in a futile effort to defend an old and exhausted ideology that was incapable of providing solutions to the problems that it had created. Indeed, in an effort to solicit poplar support, Communist leaders abandoned the blatant propagation of militant atheism as state policy, and sought to co-opt religious leaders and appear with them in public. The numerous paid professional propagators of Communist ideology in the Soviet educational establishment sought to "requalify" themselves and retain their positions as specialists in the "theory and history of culture."

Marxism-Leninism had been able to claim credibility only so long as the Soviet leadership was able to demonstrate some degree of competence in problem solving and claim that the ideology had a certain relationship to reality. As the Soviet economy deteriorated and the society became more fragmented, the claims made for the ideology proved to be vacuous and irrelevant. The abandonment of Marxism-Leninism by the East European countries in 1989 and also by Angola, Ethiopia, Nicaragua, South Yemen, and other states also served to discredit it.

Russians who desired to perpetuate the empire and the rule over other peoples had found Marxism-Leninism a convenient artifice for "justifying" their dominance and claiming to be adherents of "internationalism." However, the inadequacies of the ideology made it necessary for Gorbachev in 1991 to undertake another revision of the 1986 revised Communist Party program "to include in our arsenal of ideas all of the wealth of the fatherland and world Socialist and democratic thought."[26] But the swift pace of events nullified this effort. Russians, in their claim to an empire, have lacked a suitable replacement for Marxism-Leninism, although Russian security concerns and the welfare of the ethnic Russians living outside the Russian Federation have been used as a justification for reestablishing the linkages broken in 1991.

Gennadi Zyuganov and other Communists have succeeded in selecting and modifying portions of the old dogma that seem to apply to the current problems of Russia and implied calls for reinstituting some of the old imperial order. Most importantly, they have married elements of the old ideology to Russian nationalism. While neither the democrats nor the radical nationalists have developed a message that gives hope to the demoralized population of Russia, Zyuganov and the new Communist Party emphasize both a new Russian patriotism and a call for social equity. They are not clear on the issue whether the state should renationalize those parts of the economy that have been privatized. Rather, they argue for guarantees of income and living standard and a more equitable distribution of income in Russia. Yet, in advocating social guarantees, they also cynically advocate subsidies from an empty state treasury.

Marxism-Leninism did not die in 1991, as so many in Russia and the West declared. Rather, it continues to have a strong hold on a substantial portion of the population and even tends to shape the way that its opponents conceptualize reality.

EY TERMS

Bolsheviks
cadres

Communist Party of the Soviet Union (CPSU)
intelligentsia
mafia
Marxism-Leninism
Muscovite state
nomenklatura
Novgorod
political culture
Russian Empire
soviet (*sovet*)
"triple transition"

FURTHER READINGS

Anderson, Thornton. *Russian Political Thought: An Introduction* (Ithaca, NY: Cornell University Press, 1967).

Brown, Archie, and Jack Gray, eds. *Political Culture and Political Change in Communist States* (New York: Holmes and Meier, 1979).

Carrère d'Encausse, Hélène. *The End of the Soviet Empire: The Triumph of the Nations* (New York: Basic Books, 1993).

Conquest, Robert. *The Great Terror: A Reassessment* (New York: Oxford University Press, 1990).

DeGeorge, Richard T. *Patterns of Soviet Thought: The Origins and Development of Dialectical and Historical Materialism* (Ann Arbor: University of Michigan Press, 1970).

Daniels, Robert V. *Is Russia Reformable? Change and Resistance from Stalin to Gorbachev* (Boulder, CO: Westview Press, 1988).

Dmytryshyn, Basil. *USSR: A Concise History*, 4th ed. (New York: Charles Scribner's Sons, 1984).

Gregory, Paul R., and Robert C. Stuart. *Soviet and Post-Soviet Economic Structure and Performance* (New York: HarperCollins, 1994).

Hewett, Ed A. *Reforming the Soviet Economy: Equality versus Efficiency* (Washington, DC: The Brookings Institution, 1988).

Hunczak, Taras, ed. *Russian Imperialism: From Ivan the Great to the Revolution* (New Brunswick, NJ: Rutgers University Press, 1974).

Goldman, Marshall I. *Gorbachev's Challenge: Economic Reform in the Age of High Technology* (New York: Norton, 1987).

Kaiser, Robert J. *The Geography of Nationalism in Russia and the USSR* (Princeton, NJ: Princeton University Press, 1994).

Lewin, Moshe. *Russia, USSR, Russia: The Drive and Drift of a Superstate* (New York: The New Press, 1995).

Meyer, Alfred G. *Leninism* (Cambridge: Harvard University Press, 1957: reprint, Boulder, CO: Westview Press, 1986).

Millar, James R., ed. *Politics, Work, and Daily Life in the USSR: A Survey of Former Soviet Citizens* (New York: Cambridge University Press, 1987).

Nahaylo, Bohdan, and Victor Swoboda. *Soviet Disunion: A History of the Nationalities Problem in the USSR* (London: Hamish Hamilton, 1990).

Nove, Alec. *The Soviet Economic System,* 3rd ed. (Winchester, MA: Allen and Unwin, 1986).

Pipes, Richard. *The Formation of the Soviet Union: Communism and Nationalism, 1917–1923,* rev. ed. (Cambridge, MA: Harvard University Press, 1964).

Pipes, Richard. *Russia under the Old Regime* (New York: Charles Scribner's Sons, 1974).

Riasanovsky, Nicholas V. *A History of Russia,* 5th ed. (New York: Oxford University Press, 1993).

Rumer, Boris. *Soviet Central Asia: "A Tragic Experiment"* (Winchester, MA: Unwin Hyman, 1989).

Rywkin, Michael. *Moscow's Muslim Challenge,* 2nd ed. (Armonk, NY: M. E. Sharpe, 1990).

Shatz, Marshall S. *Soviet Dissent in Historical Perspective* (New York: Cambridge University Press, 1980).

Treadgold, Donald, ed. *Twentieth-Century Russia,* 7th ed. (Boulder, CO: Westview Press, 1989).

Tucker, Robert C., ed. *Political Culture and Leadership in Soviet Russia* (New York: Norton, 1987).

White, Stephen. *Political Culture and Soviet Politics.* (London: Macmillan, 1979).

Political Processes and Institutions

The Communist Party of the Soviet Union (CPSU) enjoyed a legal monopoly of political power from the establishment of the Soviet political system in 1917–1918 until it formally relinquished that monopoly in 1990. In the aftermath of the unsuccessful coup of August 19–21, 1991, by several top political leaders and part of the military and the security police, the CPSU experienced a precipitous collapse with the resignation of Mikhail Gorbachev as its general secretary, his dissolution of the Central Committee on August 24, the suspension of all party activity, and the confiscation by the governments of most of the republics of its real property and other resources. For over seven decades the CPSU had shaped the institutions and political practices of the Soviet system. It also brought it to its deplorable condition in the 1980s and to its final collapse.

The transformation from an absolutist dictatorial party to a beleaguered political dinosaur, stubbornly seeking to retain its leading role while steadily losing credibility, can be understood in terms of the CPSU's development and its methods of operation. It had emerged from the small Bolshevik wing of the All-Russian Social Democratic Labor Party (RSDLP), founded by Vladimir Ilyich Lenin. While in exile in 1898 for his involvement in establishing the party, Lenin developed a plan for organizing it more effectively, and after completing his sentence in 1900 he joined several émigrés in Western Europe in establishing a revolutionary newspaper, *Iskra* (The Spark).

Lenin planned to have the newspaper published abroad and smuggled into Russia for the purpose of developing a leadership that could be used to recruit members for his conspiratorial underground party of tested, dedicated, and disciplined professional revolutionaries. At the second RSDLP Congress, held in Brussels and London in 1903, a momentous division developed between Lenin's Bolsheviks and the more moderate Mensheviks. The division centered on such issues as the size of the party, membership requirements, and centralism in its organization. Lenin favored a smaller party and a more rigid definition of membership qualifications and demanded complete centralism and denial of local autonomy. Contrary to the Jewish Marxists in the party, he opposed the notion of a party organized along ethnic lines and consisting of separate nationality groups.

Other issues that later divided the Bolsheviks and Mensheviks included disagreement about retaining an illegal underground organization after the 1905 Revolution. While Lenin favored the use of both legal and illegal means to achieve revolutionary goals, the Mensheviks advocated greater reliance on legal and open forms of activity. In general, the Mensheviks were willing to let the bourgeois revolution and the development of capitalism in the Russian Empire run its course, whereas Lenin was very impatient and wished to accelerate the revolutionary process. To a large extent the disagreement between the two factions was over methods and tactics rather than goals.

All efforts to heal the widening gulf between the Bolsheviks and Mensheviks failed. Lenin maintained his separate Bolshevik organization and factional treasury and heaped scorn on the Mensheviks, his fellow Marxists, denouncing them as "Liquidators" (for wanting to liquidate the underground party organization) and opportunists. The break became complete in January 1912 when Lenin held a conference of his followers (with only 14 voting delegates) in Prague. He formed a new central committee, declared his conference to be the "supreme party body," and designated himself leader of the "RSDLP (of Bolsheviks)."

However, Bolshevism was not a fully united faction, since Lenin had disagreements with his closest followers. These disagreements persisted even after the establishment of the Soviet regime and throughout the first ten years after the Revolution. Lenin was opposed by leftist Bolsheviks on the issue of concluding a peace treaty with the Central Powers in March 1918; the leftists wanted to conduct a revolutionary war, even though Russia lacked an effective army and was likely to be overpowered by German troops. Others opposed Lenin's decision to hire bourgeois specialists, especially tsarist military officers, and to create a standing army. The Democratic Centralist Opposition criticized the development of a party bureaucracy and the appointment (rather than election) of party officials. The Workers' Opposition was dissatisfied about the influx of nonproletarian elements into the party—which in their view had ceased to be a workers' organization. In May 1921 at the Tenth Party Congress, Lenin took measures to outlaw all such oppositionist groups by adopting a formal ban on factions. This action, which failed to eliminate factions, was followed by a purging of the party membership that resulted in the expulsion of 170,000 members, most of whom were seen as careerists.

PARTY LEADERSHIP

The Communist Party of the Soviet Union had remarkably few leaders when compared with European democratic countries or the United States. During more than 70 years only seven men held the top leadership position. Lenin was unique as the party's founder; he never held the position of first (or general) secretary that would become the top political position in the USSR, but each of his successors headed the Secretariat. Originally the Secretariat was regarded as a service organization charged with keeping the party's records, but Stalin converted it into a powerful vehicle for his personal dictatorship, and it eventually became the principal means for achieving ultimate power in the Soviet political system. Joseph Stalin became general secretary in 1922 and, after Lenin's death two years later, ruled until his own death in 1953. He used the Secretariat and the Central Committee administrative apparatus to reward followers and punish opponents. Lenin, during his final illness, called for Stalin's removal from the post in January 1923, but his "Testament" was suppressed in the Soviet Union for more than 30 years.

Lenin established the Soviet security police, originally known as the *Cheka* and eventually as the KGB, in late 1917 to deal with opponents to his regime both inside and outside the country.

Stalin would expand and use this instrument as one of the pillars of his cruel and bloody dictatorship.[27] Lenin also provided Stalin with the organizational means of disposing of political opponents by outlawing factions and conducting purges of the party's membership. Nonetheless, Stalin had to wage a fierce power struggle from 1923 until 1927, first against Leon Trotsky, then against the Left Opposition headed by Grigorii Zinoviev and Lev Kamenev, and finally against the Right Opposition led by Nikolai Bukharin. Stalin first allied with the Right of Nikolai Bukharin and others which favored greater economic concessions to the peasantry, a slower rate of industrialization, and a continuation of the moderate New Economic Program (NEP), introduced by Lenin in 1921. After ousting Trotsky and the Left, Stalin adopted their program of centralization of the economy and rapid forced industrialization and defeated his erstwhile allies of the Right. He thus proved to be a master at dissimulation and at creating a party apparatus that became his personal political machine.

Stalin's name is correctly associated with full-blown totalitarian rule in the Soviet Union and the attempt to have the Soviet state equate itself with the totality of society and with control over all aspects of life. He employed terror and blood purges on a massive scale, established a huge network of forced-labor camps in which millions perished, and embarked on a program of forced industrialization and collectivization of agriculture which, in turn, resulted in famine and additional millions of deaths.[28] The justification for this totalitarianism was social discipline so that the process of socialist development could be speeded up. Rapid economic growth was based on deprivation and forced savings and on the lives of tens of millions of Soviet citizens.

Besides living in great fear and personal insecurity, Stalin's subjects were required to praise his wisdom and "genius." He proclaimed the establishment of socialism in the Soviet Union in 1936 and made himself the supreme authority in ideological matters. Under Stalin the central party institutions ultimately declined in importance and were replaced by his personal secretariat and the secret police. In addition to being repressive, Stalin's rule was so-cially conservative in making divorce extraordi-narily difficult and in banning abortions while coming to terms with the Russian Orthodox Church during World War II, and favoring Russ-ian nationalism at the expense of the non-Russ-ian nationalities.

During the 30 years that he ruled the Soviet Union, Stalin presided over a profound socioeco-nomic transformation of the country. He elimi-nated whatever capitalism remained when he took power; he pushed industrialization and ur-banization, led the country through the devasta-tions of World War II against Nazi Germany (when more than an estimated 20 million Soviet citizens perished), and created a massive military machine after World War II with which to chal-lenge the United States for global dominance.

Stalin's death in March 1953 ended his ruthless and arbitrary dictatorship. Following the arrest and execution of Lavrenti Beria who had headed Stalin's repressive secret police and a period of collective leadership of several se-nior party officials, a power struggle ensued in which Nikita S. Khrushchev, who had replaced Stalin as first secretary, also became the head of government. In February 1956, at the Twenti-eth Party Congress, Khrushchev, himself a long-time lieutenant of Stalin, launched an attack on Stalin's system of rule in a "secret speech" de-livered at a dramatic late-night session, in which the dead dictator was depicted as an evil psychopath. The criticism of Stalinism (which Khrushchev called the "cult of personality") was accompanied by a fresh political style, with Khrushchev traveling about the country, offer-ing impromptu statements and advice, and per-mitting some relaxation of the rigid censorship. Khrushchev also revived the various central bodies of the party, including the Congress and the Central Committee. After the execution of Beria and his principal aides, instead of physi-cally eliminating political rivals, Khrushchev had them forcibly retired with a pension paid for by their silence. Khrushchev attempted a variety of reforms affecting economic policy and administrative reorganization. He virtually eliminated the reliance on indiscriminate mass terror and initiated an increase in popular in-volvement in government, although the basic

dictatorial and coercive nature of the system re-mained, as his reivigorated attacks on religion indicated. He also oversaw the emergence of the Soviet Union as a world power, by emphasizing the development of a blue-water navy, strength-ening the Soviet nuclear missile arsenal, and ex-panding Soviet political, military, and economic commitments to many of the newly independent states of the third world. Unlike Stalin, he trav-eled abroad extensively. Khrushchev's domestic and foreign politics, his efforts to replace party officials, and his political style resulted in con-siderable instability and opposition and led to his abrupt ouster on October 14, 1964, by his associates, most of whom he had elevated to high office.

The plotters who removed Khrushchev in a palace coup formed a collective leadership with Leonid I. Brezhnev, Khrushchev's former protégé, as first secretary of the party. The new oligarchy repealed Khrushchev's major administrative and economic reforms and crit-icized him and his policies. As part of the ef-fort to emphasize discipline and ideological or-thodoxy both inside and outside the party, it substantially toned down his anti-Stalin cam-paign and partially rehabilitated Stalin's reign, and raised a monument over the dictator's grave (Khrushchev had removed Stalin's em-balmed body from Lenin's Red Square mau-soleum in October 1961). Khrushchev was treated as an "unperson" by his former associ-ates and lieutenants. His numerous published speeches were withdrawn from circulation, and he was even denied a state funeral and burial near the Kremlin Wall when he died in September 1971.

Brezhnev assumed Stalin's title of general, rather than first, secretary of the party in 1976, although he could not acquire Stalin's powers. Brezhnev reaffirmed political centralism by restoring a large number of central government ministries, but he did not become head of gov-ernment, as Khrushchev had. The general sec-retary did become chief of state, largely a cere-monial position, in June 1977 and also had a new constitution adopted in that year. As party leader, Brezhnev sought a consensus in the So-viet oligarchy and tried to obtain prior approval for his actions, thus avoiding Khrushchev's method of publicly advocating highly controversial policies prior to any high-level discussion. As a result of the search for consensus, decision making under Brezhnev became slower and more cumbersome, and needed reforms were neglected.

In the international sphere, Brezhnev continued the expansion of the Soviet role and, by the mid–1970s, the USSR reached the maximum extent of both its military power vis-à-vis the West and its involvement in the developing world. The later years of Brezhnev's rule, called "the period of stagnation" by Gorbachev, witnessed a considerable downturn of economic growth and a deterioration of living conditions for most Soviet citizens. The refusal to move away from the Stalinist approach to economic management meant continued inefficiency in the use of the natural and human resources of the country.

Brezhnev died in November 1982. However, the oligarchy of aged party officials who still dominated the Soviet political system was unwilling to face the realities of the problems facing the country or to turn to the next generation of potential leaders. Rather, two aging and ill leaders followed in succession before the selection in March 1985 of Mikhail Gorbachev as first secretary of the party. Yuri Andropov, a party official who for 15 years had headed the security police (KGB), replaced Brezhnev. In addition to his experience in the security police, Andropov had served as Soviet ambassador to Hungary (where he oversaw the suppression of the Hungarian rebellion in 1956) and as a CPSU secretariat official responsible for relations with East European Communist parties from 1957 to 1967. As KGB chief, he had intensified both overt and covert Soviet foreign intelligence operations and employed repressive measures against political dissidents at home. As would befit a security police chief, Andropov attempted to deal with flagging economic production and growing social problems by emphasizing discipline and order and by launching an anticorruption campaign within the party and governmental apparatus. Andropov's brief tenure of only 15 months as general secretary ended with his death in February 1984, after he had disappeared from public view for nearly six months because of illness.

Konstantin Chernenko, at the age of 72, succeeded Andropov. His election probably resulted in part from the inability of two rivals, Mikhail Gorbachev and Grigori Romanov, to obtain sufficient support. His election was the last collective act of the gerontocratic "old guard," and it provided a respite for officials threatened by Andropov's anticorruption campaign. Chernenko's poor health limited his tenure to 13 months—a period used to advantage by his successor, Mikhail Sergeyevich Gorbachev.

The election of Mikhail Gorbachev as general secretary on March 11, 1985, represented an important leadership change. Relatively young at age 54, Gorbachev would initiate needed reforms. He had become a party member while a student at the age of 21. From 1955 (when he graduated from the Moscow State University's faculty of law) until 1978, his career was confined entirely to his native Stavropol Territory (*krai*), north of the Caucasus Mountains. He first served in the local Communist youth organization and in 1963 assumed the first of several posts in the territory's Communist Party organization. In 1970 at the age of 39 he became the first secretary of the Stavropol Party Committee, a post that entitled him to Central Committee membership. Unlike his predecessors, Gorbachev had no experience in any of the non-Russian republics—a distinct disadvantage in dealing with troubling nationality issues that would later test his leadership abilities. He also had limited experience in Moscow, having served there for less than seven years before becoming general secretary. As a Secretariat member he acquired full membership in the Politburo in 1980.

Gorbachev proved to be an articulate, shrewd, and reasonably sophisticated leader. In his career he also benefited from some fortunate circumstances, including friendship with Andropov, also a native of Stavropol. Although he had significant abilities, Gorbachev obtained the post of general secretary almost by default. He had the advantage of being able to remove his two principal rivals, Central Committee Secretary Grigori Romanov and Moscow Secretary Viktor Grishin. Romanov was a weak contender because of various indiscretions, lack of polish, and inexperience and ineffectiveness in foreign policy. Grishin, who had arranged Chernenko's election as general secretary was vulnerable because of his age and corruption in the large Moscow party organization that he headed.

Gorbachev also had the advantage of organizing and presiding over the Twenty-seventh Party Congress in February 1986, asserting his leadership there and in summit meetings with President Ronald Reagan in Geneva, Reykjavik, Washington, and Moscow. His vigorous but controversial reform efforts prompted him to publish a book *Perestroika: New Thinking for Our Country and the World* (Harper & Row, 1987). Designed to appeal to foreign readers, the book was also available to the Soviet public. Although less candid than some of the speeches on which the book drew, the work reflected his determination to make the Soviet system more effective. Yet, Gorbachev's leadership style, policies, and reorganizational efforts also elicited uncertainty, skepticism, and resistance among critics who were alarmed by rapid change. The need for change and "new thinking" meant that the Sovet system confronted very serious difficulties. Gorbachev issued a revised version of the 1961 Party Program (a response to the many extravagant claims and unfulfilled promises made by Khrushchev), and enhanced his powers in October 1988 by assuming the chairmanship of the Supreme Soviet and then by establishing for himself the presidency of the USSR.

THE FAILED MODEL

The Soviet political and governmental system was based on the Leninist-Stalinist model that, according to the conventional wisdom of many observers, would be able to perpetuate itself. Its principal components were the mass membership CPSU and its auxiliary, the Leninist League of Communist Youth (*Komsomol*), which was to serve the party as a ready recruiting and training ground for young members. The CPSU apparatus (staffed by generalists, usually with specialized technical training and a narrow educational experience) operated through republic, province (*oblast'*), district (*raion*), and city party committees. The more than 3,000 district party committees were directed by 122 province party committees and, in turn, supervised the more than 440,000 primary party organizations

(p.p.o.) that were charged with carrying out party directives in factories, collective and state farms, educational institutions, government ministries, military units, embassies abroad, and housing developments.

The p.p.o. was charged with attempting to promote productivity, reduce waste, and meet output quotas. It also organized campaigns and mass meetings to mobilize public opinion in accordance with party directives and provided information for superior party bodies, serving as their eyes and ears. It enlisted new members, supervised their training, and expelled members (with the approval of the district or city party committee to which it was subordinate).

Advancement was based on a partisan patronage system known as the *nomenklatura,* representing the lists of positions in all institutions and enterprises that could be filled only with the approval of the responsible CPSU (territorial) committee—each at its own level—from lists of approved prospective candidates. Promotion under this system generally depended more upon compliance and acceptability to party officials than on the competence of candidates. Acquaintance, connections, and "political correctness" in expressing verbal support for party positions tended to determine advancement. Party dominance was also based on the administrative-command economy that established and enforced economic priorities and utilized scarcities to reward the faithful and bind them to the system.

The Partocracy

The Soviet political system was aptly termed a "partocracy"—a system of rule by and in the interests of a single political party that Lenin had immodestly deemed to be "the intelligence, honor, and conscience of our epoch."[29] The partocracy functioned either through an individual dictator, like Lenin or Stalin, or by means of an oligarchy (a collective dictatorship) consisting of a small group of men who comprised the Politburo and Secretariat of the CPSU Central Committee.

The Central Committee, as the parent body, was elected by the Party Congress held every five years. The Central Committee was authorized "to direct all party activities and local party bodies" in the lengthy intervals between party congresses but would usually meet only twice a year because of its large size. In its place the Politburo (political bureau or "executive committee") served as the Soviet Union's supreme policy-making body; it held weekly meetings and usually consisted of 11 or 12 voting members and half as many (nonvoting) candidate members. The chief oligarch in this body was the CPSU general secretary, who was elected by the Central Committee. He headed its Secretariat, a collective body that varied in size and was responsible for the functioning of the various administrative departments of the CPSU apparatus. These departments were concerned with the various sectors of the Soviet economy and with personnel matters, as well as the supervision of science, education and culture, the media, the security police, the courts, prosecuting agencies and the legal profession, foreign policy, and relations with foreign Communist parties. In effect, the departments of the Secretariat oversaw and regularly meddled in the activities of the parallel and larger governmental bureaucracy. The Secretariat also administered the party's central fund, controlled its press organs and journals, and was responsible for placing personnel in both party and governmental positions.

The CPSU had its own central bureaucracy with headquarters in the center of Moscow. The entire CPSU administrative apparatus had approximately 250,000 full-time officials and employees of 4,625 territorial party committees at various levels. Prior to 1991 it also had the full-time services, at no cost, of secretaries and officials of 52,000 larger p.p.o.'s. These officials remained on the payrolls of enterprises, but did no productive work, instead distributing Communist propaganda among the workers, holding endless meetings, and often interfering with management or colluding with it in various forms of corruption.

The Reckoning

According to conventional wisdom, the partocracy would attract the "best people" and its longevity would be assured by the self-perpetuating oligarchy. Marxism-Leninism would provide answers and solutions to its problems. The

massive Soviet governmental and economic bureaucracy, backed by the security police and the military, would muddle through by means of sheer weight and omnipresence. However, the agonizing and seemingly endless "moment of truth" that Gorbachev was compelled to initiate in 1985–1986 was a consequence of profound systemic failure.

In endeavoring to explain what "went wrong," we can note that Marxism-Leninism promoted closed minds and a form of rote learning that, combined with Russian self-satisfaction and complacency, produced a very debilitating condition. Under the superannuated Brezhnev oligarchy, many Soviet citizens could be deceived into believing that the Soviet Union was an advanced society representing "developed socialism" with a viable and advanced economic system. Information that did not fit this image— such as rising infant mortality rates and rampant environmental pollution—was simply purged from the public record. Under Gorbachev the elaborate, costly, and self-deluding notion that the Soviet leadership had been capable of solving problems could not be sustained. Indeed the CPSU was, for the most part, not attracting the best people but was actually attracting and rewarding some of the worst types: self-seekers, careerists, opportunists, and sycophants who could be counted on to sustain the exercise in mass pretense. This was a long-standing problem noted earlier by Nikita Khrushchev, who said that the CPSU had "many people without principle, lickspittle functionaries and petty careerists [who] seek to get much more out of our society than they put into it."[30] Thus, the CPSU rewarded mediocre hangers-on and apparently had no place for honest persons of intellect with questioning and inquiring minds. As a result, it paid a high price in the end.

GORBACHEV: REFORMER IN SPITE OF HIMSELF

A fundamental contradiction in the reform process was the fact that *perestroika* was undertaken in defense of Marxist-Leninist socialism in its Russian version that had brought the Soviet empire to economic, political, and moral bankruptcy. Gorbachev was convinced that the system itself was still viable and hoped to save its essentials, especially the dominant role of the party and the planned economy, by opening up the system to controlled democratization and limited marketization. In almost any other country, a political party that had brought about such deplorable conditions would have resigned in disgrace, but the CPSU arrogantly entrusted itself with the task of remedying all of the folly that had resulted from its own ideology, leadership, and policies.

This unenviable and even impossible task fell to Mikhail Gorbachev, who as CPSU general secretary developed a tripartite approach to reform based on *perestroika* (economic restructuring), *glasnost'* (openness), and "democratization." *Perestroika* was depicted as an effort to loosen the dead hand of the state's economic bureaucracy by giving plant managers greater authority regarding wages and hiring, placing greater reliance on sales and profits, and requiring self-financing (elimination of subsidies and interest-free investment capital) and economic accountability. Gorbachev sought to reduce (but not eliminate) centralism, especially as it impinged upon details of management and resulted in what was condemned as "petty tutelage." He permitted various producer cooperatives, as well as self-employment in the small-scale manufacturing and services sectors. Private housing was encouraged, while social leveling in the form of consumption and wage egalitarianism was condemned. Joint economic ventures with foreign investors were authorized. Thus, the aim of *perestroika* was to make Soviet socialism less inefficient and somewhat competitive.

The *glasnost'* component of Gorbachev's reform effort was intended to promote discussion of economic problems and to develop support for *perestroika*—a sort of alliance between reformers at the top of the political system and the masses of Soviet citizens against the opposition to change of the ingrained bureaucrats. Yet, in admitting the corruption, mendacity, and failures of the Brezhnev era, Gorbachev could not confine the discussion to economic issues. Decades of repression, intolerance, and the "white [blank] spots" of historical censorship had created a tidal wave of frustration, resentment, and anger that led to demands that all the ugly carbuncles and cancers on the Soviet body politic be confronted and revealed.

Gorbachev's "democratization" was initially more tactical in nature, since it definitely did not involve abandonment of the CPSU's political monopoly. The plan was to have party secretaries and even plant managers elected in an effort to introduce some accountability into the bureaucracy, get rid of the most odious Communist officials, and restore some modicum of public confidence. Gorbachev also sought to involve more non-Communists and women in the work of the local soviets (government councils). As with *glasnost'*, there could not be just a little democratization. Demands were made for religious freedom, for legalization of opposition parties, and for sovereignty and independence for the union republics.

In fact, Gorbachev's reform program contained yet another important element: namely, a dramatic restructuring of the foreign and security policy of the Soviet Union. Gorbachev noted the tremendous costs and the counterproductiveness of the arms race, as well as of the competition with the West for political, economic, and military influence in the third world. He pointed to the commitment of ever-increasing amounts of resources to the arms race and to supporting unpopular Communist regimes in Eastern Europe and self-proclaimed Marxist allies throughout the developing world that had debilitated the Soviet economy. Breaking with the traditional Soviet view of class conflict as the sole basis of Soviet foreign policy, he argued for "new thinking" in foreign and security policy based on the fact that all peoples share certain overriding interests that take precedence over class. The result was a major reorientation of Soviet foreign policy between 1986 and 1989, including major initiatives in relations with the West and pathbreaking agreements on arms reductions, the withdrawal of Soviet troops from Eastern Europe, and the acceptance in 1989 of the anti-Communist revolutions throughout the region. The Soviet Union even supported the military operations of the United States and its Western allies in 1991 that drove the troops of its erstwhile ally Iraq from occupied Kuwait. These initiatives contributed substantially to the liberation of the Communist states of Eastern Europe from Soviet dominance and to ending the global confrontation between the Soviet Union and the United States. They also resulted in the opening up of political and economic contacts between the Soviet Union and the West.

Contradictions in the Reform Process

Gorbachev's reform program developed in four major phases.[31] During 1985 and 1986, as Gorbachev outlined the breadth of the problems facing the Soviet Union, he tried to rely on traditional Soviet methods of stimulating the economy—greater investments in key sectors of the economy and, picking up on the earlier efforts of Yuri Andropov, an emphasis on labor and social discipline. The second phase of reform, from the January 1987 plenary meeting of the Central Committee to the Nineteenth Party Conference in late June 1988, was characterized by a movement away from mere reform from the top to greater democratic involvement and the focus on *glasnost'* and "democratization." Rather than strengthening the system or helping to resolve the serious problems, the revelations about the past actually undercut even more the legitimacy of the system as a whole.

After the party conference, a third stage of reform set in that included the development and actual implementation of programs of reform. Plans were developed to create a one-party democracy based on single-party parliamentarianism, and the establishment of a state governed by law. In the political sphere the elections of March 1989 for a restructured parliament were marked by a relative openness that resulted in the defeat of many Communist Party officials and the election of some democrats. Plans were discussed for radical restructuring of the economy. However, it became increasingly evident that Gorbachev and the CPSU were losing control of the reform process. On February 4, 1990, influenced by the collapse of the Communist systems in Eastern Europe during the final months of the prior year, an estimated half million people marched in Moscow in support of a multiparty political system. A few days later a Central Committee plenum agreed to eliminate the constitutional monopoly that was guaranteed to the Communist Party. "Thus an era of one-party rule that had in effect begun in October 1917 with the Bolshevik seizure of power came to an end."[32]

The fourth and final stage of *perestroika* stretched from March 1990 until the abortive coup of August 1991. The period was characterized by growing conflict over economic policy and escalating political and nationalist demands across the entire policy spectrum. Gorbachev, whose commitment to reform had shown signs of flagging since the very beginning and whose "new thinking" was often negated by "old thinking," began to move away from reform as he faced growing opposition during the course of 1990 and 1991. During this period, reformers, most conspicuously Boris Yeltsin, emerged in the Russian Republic to demand sovereignty and to challenge the decaying Soviet system. On December 20, 1990, Foreign Minister Eduard Shevardnadze, Gorbachev's closest political ally who along with Gorbachev had been instrumental in revamping Soviet foreign policy, announced his resignation on the floor of Parliament. He accused Gorbachev of having abandoned his own reform program and of allying himself with the very individuals committed to seizing power and reinstating the policies of the past.[33]

Probably the most sinister side of Gorbachev, and one that contributed to his undoing, was his strange relationship to and reliance on the KGB. His role as the protégé of KGB chief Yuri Andropov was consummated with KGB sponsorship of him as CPSU general secretary.[34] For Gorbachev, the KGB was above all criticism; he simply ignored the numerous crimes perpetrated by its agents and maintained its privileged status, and promoted its chiefs Viktor Chebrikov and Vladimir Kryuchkov to full membership in the Politburo. He made it clear that the KGB was the mainstay of his regime, along with OMON—the interior ministry's special deployment forces under the command of Boris Pugo, a KGB general whom Gorbachev appointed to head the ministry.[35]

Gorbachev countenanced the use of armed force against civilians in Tbilisi (Georgia) in April 1989, in Baku (Azerbaijan) in January 1990, and in Vilnius (Lithuania) and Riga (Latvia) in January 1991, with considerable loss of life. *Glasnost'* and "democratization" did not eliminate KGB disinformation and calumny against opposition leaders and groups such as Boris Yeltsin, the democratic Ukrainian *Rukh* organization, and Lithuania's nationalist movement, *Sajudis*. Police brutality was employed against peaceful demonstrators, and police provocation and violence were used against democratically elected deputies.[36]

GORBACHEV'S ERRORS AND FAILURES

The six and a half years of Gorbachev's leadership left a profound impression on all the republics of the USSR and offered great opportunities for change. Yet, his popularity plummeted from 80 percent approval for his program of reforms in 1988 to 10 percent in 1990 and about 3 percent in December 1991 at the time that the Soviet Union was dissolved.[37] In part this was related to the series of errors that prevented him from fully utilizing these opportunities. These errors and failures had their source in Gorbachev's initial error: his gross underestimation of the seriousness of the malaise plaguing the Soviet system and what would be required to deal with it.[38] The very concept of "restructuring" implied that a mere reordering or rearrangement of Soviet management and administration and some concessions to small-scale entrepreneurship in the service sector would suffice to unbind the "flywheel" of the Soviet economy.[39] However, if the Soviet structure was fundamentally unsound and its structural integrity was in question, no amount of "restructuring" would suffice. In effect, Gorbachev wasted the first two years of his tenure as party leader before he initiated real reforms and, even then, he failed to develop a coherent program of economic reform or to curb the political forces committed to maintaining the old system—as indicated by the attempted overthrow of Gorbachev in August 1991 by a conspiracy of reactionary forces representing the military, the security police, and the central government bureaucracy whom he himself had put into office.

A second error was Gorbachev's failure to establish clear priorities. Although he called for the need to "accelerate" the economy, in 1988 Gorbachev shifted positions and undertook political, rather than economic, reform measures that rapidly undermined the political structures of the Soviet state, destroyed whatever authority

the system retained among the people, and opened up a Pandora's box of demands. Had he been able, as were his political counterparts in China, to concentrate on improving production of agricultural goods and of certain everyday household commodities—sectors of the economy in which improvements would have been readily evident—he would have been able to claim some credit as an economic reformer, at least in the short term.[40] After establishing as part of his political reforms an ineffective presidential system, Gorbachev shifted to a new priority: the preservation of the deteriorating union-empire. In the face of opposition from the republics that was possible because of the opening up of the political system, he made an ill-advised attempt to force the signing of a "new union treaty." This move precipitated the August 1991 coup, as the forces of reaction concluded that he had made too many concessions to the republics and weakened the power of the political center. Each of Gorbachev's priorities, then, was dissipated and led to diametrically opposite results from those that he had intended.

Gorbachev's third error was in his lack of appreciation of the utter failure of the CPSU's nationalities policies and for the seriousness of the non-Russian peoples' grievances against Moscow's centralist rule. Speaking in 1987, for example, he declared, "We have settled the nationalities question" and proclaimed the USSR's nationality policy "one of the greatest triumphs of the October Revolution."[41] As a Russian Communist official whose entire career was limited to Russia, Gorbachev was ill-prepared to deal with these crucial issues. His stubborn refusal to understand the republics' demands for sovereignty and independence cast him in the reactionary role of guardian of an anachronistic empire, even as it was disintegrating. Indeed, his efforts to impose a new union treaty in 1991 directly contributed to his downfall and to the final dissolution of the Soviet imperial system.

Gorbachev's fourth failure resulted from his indecisiveness and his attempt to placate hardline Communists, neo-Stalinists, and other reactionary forces. Gorbachev's reform-minded economic advisers came and went as through a revolving door, while he first embraced and then rejected new economic reform proposals put forth every few months. He attempted in vain to reconcile irreconcilable reform plans in the name of "market socialism." He could not adopt the "shock therapy" of rapidly introduced market conditions in April 1990 that he had publicly advocated. This accelerated his loss of credibility, ironically at a time when he was acquiring greater "presidential powers." Gorbachev's temporizing and his unwillingness to remove from party political leadership positions those, such as Yegor Ligachev, who strongly opposed the economic and political reforms to which he was supposedly committed, contributed to his declining authority. As it was, the record of economic performance under Gorbachev was dismal, as GNP declined 10 percent in 1990 and 14 percent the next year. Budget deficits soared from 25 billion rubles in 1985 to 200 billion rubles five years later. Shortages, black market expansion, inflation, increased criminality, growing poverty—these were the fruits of Gorbachev's attempts at economic reform.[42]

A fifth failure was Gorbachev's inability to abandon Marxism-Leninism and his ideological illusions regarding the CPSU. While conceding that "deformations" had occurred in the party and its policies, he remained committed to "more socialism" and to an "improved socialism."[43] Despite a pragmatic bent and a certain appreciation of realities, Gorbachev expressed this continued commitment as late as 1991: "I adhere to the Communist idea, and with this I will leave for the other world."[44] Even on his return from house arrest after the August 1991 coup, Gorbachev's immediate response was to assign to the Communist Party the task of regenerating the reform. Not until the extent of party officials' complicity in the coup and the loss of credibility of the party were clear to him, did Gorbachev abandon his hope that the party would be the engine of reform in the USSR. Gorbachev's commitment to the party and to Marxism-Leninism created a mental block that diluted every serious reform effort. Gorbachev remained bound by the CPSU and served as its head for too long, thus failing to develop the strength of his presidency which had the potential of providing him with a power base independent of the Communist Party and the political forces that were resistant to change.

Gorbachev's excessive reliance on verbal pronouncements, legal decrees, and Communist Party resolutions comprised his sixth error. His prolix and rambling style were often evident at press conferences and in speeches, and he tended to treat verbal pronouncements as a substitute for decision and to equate the written word with action. The end result was a lengthy period in which effective action was not taken, despite the evidence of dramatic deterioration, as in the economy.

A seventh failure was both political and moral in nature and resulted from Gorbachev's association with the KGB and its long-time chief, Andropov, and its sponsorship of the rise to power of both men. Gorbachev failed to condemn explicitly the horrendous crimes perpetrated by the security police and did not bring responsible officers to justice. *Glasnost'* did not extend to the heinous activities of the KGB or its predecessor organizations—except for the publicity given some of them by part of the media and by branches of *Pamyat'* (Memory), a public, non-Communist nationalist organization. Gorbachev's poor judgment in casting his lot with the organs of repression in the fall of 1990 and betraying his reform-minded supporters became evident in the abortive military and police putsch of August 19–21, 1991, when he experienced the humiliation of house arrest.

A related error was Gorbachev's refusal to obtain a mandate based on popular election. His election as a member of the Soviet Parliament in 1989 was as a representative of the CPSU Central Committee, and proved to be a handicap. A mandate that Gorbachev could have obtained in 1988 or 1989 as a popularly elected president could have provided decisive support for a coherent program of radical reform—if he had developed such a program.

SUCCESS IN FAILURE

Gorbachev's critics pointed out that he presided over a deteriorating economy in which ordinary citizens were driven to engage in "speculation" (reselling of goods at a higher price); standing in line in front of stores became a form of "employment" as purchasers of goods in short supply could sell them at a profit. Boris Yeltsin and others accused him of pursuing contradictory policies and half-measures. However, Gorbachev did have success in terms of the long-range impact of his actions, whether they were intended or not. He was a qualitatively different Soviet leader from his predecessors and the first to acknowledge the symptoms of decay and degeneration. He could be criticized for treating symptoms rather than causes, but his admissions and policies had a profound effect on both Soviet ideology and policy. In fact, Gorbachev may have been more successful as a debunker of the Soviet system than as its reformer. He failed to preserve the system and made possible (often unintentionally) the many profound changes that led to its demise.

The reduced fear, especially among the youth, created a different political climate. It even resulted in the ouster of the prime minister of Ukraine, Vitali Masol, in October 1990 by hunger-striking students who demanded fulfillment of the July 16, 1990, Ukrainian declaration of sovereignty.[45] Gorbachev introduced a substantial degree of freedom of speech and press, which resulted in an outpouring of frustrations, grievances, and suppressed information and historical evidence. Yet, many complained that free speech had little effect on the KGB and police provocations or on local Communist Party bosses who were reluctant to change their old ways. Although independent newspapers emerged, they often had difficulty obtaining newsprint and access to printing facilities. Despite the difficulties, however, the ferment of opinion and the questioning of old ways had a long-term salutary effect.

Soviet citizens were permitted to travel abroad, although usually with hard-currency restrictions, as part of Gorbachev's effort to make the Soviet Union a more normal or "civilized" country. Various taboos were abandoned; this included a truce in the Soviet war against political émigrés and especially against the politically active Ukrainian diaspora. The costly and only partially effective jamming of foreign radio broadcasts was suspended, including that against Radio Liberty, in November 1988. In addition, foreign tourists were permitted greater freedom of movement.

The holding of republic elections in March 1990 gave citizens a degree of choice between Communists and democrats despite certain electoral irregularities and intimidation, especially in rural areas. This resulted in the election of anti-Communist governments in the Baltic states and in western Ukraine and Georgia. Democratic oppositions emerged in various legislative councils (soviets) and parliaments. Former political prisoners, who had been arrested and imprisoned for being unappreciated forerunners of *glasnost'* and democratization, were elected as parliamentary deputies in Ukraine.

The political dissidents were vindicated when Gorbachev acknowledged the need for "pluralism" and the right to establish unofficial "informal" organizations not controlled by the Communist Party or the KGB. The recognition of a multiparty system in July 1990 (which had been stubbornly opposed by Gorbachev in 1989) placed the CPSU increasingly on the defensive.[46] Yet the partocracy sought to delay change by requiring (and obstructing) the official registration of political parties and organizations by the Ministry of Justice.

The acknowledgment of "pluralism" made it necessary to recognize freedom of religion and to reduce the dependence of the Russian Orthodox Church (Moscow Patriarchate) on the Soviet government and its use by the KGB.[47] In 1989 the Ukrainian Greek Catholic (Uniate) Church emerged from more than four decades of underground existence, and conducted mass demonstrations demanding that it be legalized and regain control of its church properties. Gorbachev's visit to the Vatican in 1989 resulted in a promise of religious freedom and the recognition of all religious bodies. The Ukrainian Autocephalous Orthodox Church, which had also been banned by Stalin, reemerged in the same year demanding legal recognition, as its clergy and parishes rejected the Moscow Patriarchate; in 1990 it established its own Patriarchate of Kiev and All Ukraine. Since 1989 significant friction has emerged among the three Ukrainian churches—that portion which has remained loyal to the Moscow Patriarchate and the revitalized Greek Catholic and the Ukrainian Autocephalous churches—as they have jousted for control of parishes and church property.

These developments and reforms constituted the most substantial and pervasive legacy of Gorbachev's efforts. Yet, while Gorbachev basked in his image abroad as a reformer—influenced, no doubt, by the central role that he played in bring to an end the global arms race and superpower confrontation with the United States—his ability to control the course of domestic events diminished. His declining popularity at home was a consequence of his failure to consummate radical economic and political reforms as well as reform of the legal system.

GORBACHEV'S LEADERSHIP

Gorbachev as Governmental Leader

Gorbachev, as Communist Party chief, avoided any direct role in the Soviet government until he became chairman of the USSR Supreme Soviet in October 1988. He then introduced an unusual presidential system that culminated in the new office of President of the USSR established in March 1990. The new presidency was created by a simple amendment to the Soviet Constitution of 1977, the fourth Soviet constitution.

As a would-be political reformer, Gorbachev established an unusual and unwieldy legislative structure. In place of the bicameral Supreme Soviet that had been created by Stalin in 1937 but had exercised extraordinarily little political authority, Gorbachev established a large Congress of People's Deputies of 2,250 members elected for five-year terms. The Congress, in turn, was to elect the two chambers of the Supreme Soviet, the Soviet of the Union and the Soviet of Nationalities, each with 271 members. In contrast to the Supreme Soviet of 1937–1989, which met for only about one week of the entire year to approve policies already decided upon within the Communist Party hierarchy, the new legislative bodies were to hold both spring and autumn sessions of several months' duration. The new Supreme Soviet elected the USSR Supreme Court and appointed the Procurator General, the highest legal officer of the government. It also formed the Defense Council and could order mobilization and declare war. However, the Supreme Soviet was subordinate and accountable to the Congress of Deputies.

Gorbachev's legislative creation proved to be cumbersome, and much of its membership was of such a character as to cause the new parliament to lose legitimacy. Fewer than half (1,101) of the deputies were popularly elected in contested elections; 399 were elected without opposition in accordance with the Stalinist-Brezhnevist practice of single-candidate elections. The electoral results could hardly be democratic when 87 percent of the deputies were CPSU members (party membership never exceeded 6.8 percent of the population and was declining dramatically in response to political revelations and the growing irrelevance of the party) and 5.9 percent of the deputies were *Komsomol* members.[48] Such disproportion reflected Gorbachev's massive blindspot regarding the CPSU and its "leading role" as the "political vanguard." Thus the overwhelming mass of the population that was not Communist was, in effect, accorded 7.1 percent of the seats in the Congress. The 353 women deputies (15.6 percent) represented Gorbachev's pledge to give women an enhanced role in public life. The Congress also included 82 active-duty military officers.

Despite the heavy concentration of members of the *nomenklatura* in the Congress, clear divisions did appear: a pro-reform Interregional Group, clearly defined nationality and republic groups, economic interests, and the backward-looking, anti-reform *Soyuz* (Union) group of hard-line Communists and military officers. In March 1990 the Congress elected Gorbachev to a five-year presidential term, with 41 percent of the deputies opposed to his election. On the surface this was a "strong" presidency with extensive decree-issuing and emergency powers. Gorbachev wanted his presidency to serve as a counterweight to the CPSU Politburo, but instead found that his broad—even quasi-dictatorial—powers were not sufficient either to solve the economic problems or to curb the rebellious republics and prevent the disintegration of the union-empire. In fact, over the course of the next 17 months until the August 1991 coup, *Soyuz* and other conservative groups mounted a relentless attack on Gorbachev. They regularly berated him and Foreign Minister Shevardnadze for their failures in foreign policy and came close to charging them with treason—in particular, for having abandoned traditional

Communist foreign policy dogma, for having "lost" Eastern Europe, for initiating "unilateral disarmament" of the country in arms control agreements signed with the United States, for abandoning long-term Soviet allies, as in the Gulf war against Iraq, and for permitting the erosion of the Soviet state itself. By 1991, as Gorbachev moved to resolve the growing conflicts between the federal government and the republics, the reactionaries moved to more drastic measures, culminating in the abortive coup, to reverse developments.

As the principal Soviet executive and head of state, Gorbachev was unable to gain adequate control over the central government. Although he often presided over parliamentary sessions and wagged his finger at critics, he failed to dismantle the centralized bureaucracy that obstructed his reform efforts in the economic ministries and in the military-industrial complex. He also lost any ability to control the activities of republic parliaments and *oblast'* and city governing councils. He was ineffective in attempting to abrogate laws and acts of republic authorities, and he found himself in the unusual position of issuing "legal" pronouncements regarding the alleged "unconstitutionality" of various acts of democratically elected republic and *oblast'* authorities, while at the same time being unable to prevent or rescind them.

By late 1990 Gorbachev found himself the target of attacks from both the conservatives and the democratic reformers. In response to the former, Gorbachev had since 1989 increasing stepped back from his support for radical reform. Rather than supporting the pro-reform elements in his government, he removed many of them and appointed to top positions—as prime minister, vice president, and minister of internal affairs, for example—the very reactionaries who in summer 1991 would attempt to topple him from power. Thus, the reformers gave up on Gorbachev and turned to Boris Yeltsin, who by 1990 had replaced Gorbachev as the champion and symbol of reform in the Soviet Union.

The Rise of Boris Yeltsin

The contradictory nature of Soviet reform was reflected in the tense relationship between Gorbachev and his nemesis and rescuer in 1991,

Boris Nikolaevich Yeltsin. These two Communist officials clashed because of profound differences in personality and temperament, in their perceptions of events, and in the policies that they advocated. The early careers of these two leaders were very different, despite a common peasant background. While Gorbachev entered Communist Party work as a bureaucrat at age 24, Yeltsin pursued a successful career as a construction engineer after completing his studies in civil engineering at the Urals Polytechnic Institute in 1955, becoming the head of a large housing construction firm in Sverdlovsk (now renamed Yekaterinburg). He did not join the CPSU until 1961 (at age 30) and did not enter party work as an official until 1968. He became a Central Committee member in 1981, ten years after Gorbachev. As a native of western Siberia, Yeltsin was far closer to the Russian heartland than Gorbachev, who came from the Russian periphery.

In 1986, after heading the party organization in the province of Sverdlovsk and establishing a reputation as a pragmatic, innovative, and honest manager, Yeltsin was named head of the Communist Party organization in Moscow, and was thus chosen to deal with the rampant corruption and economic woes of the municipal administration. When Yeltsin attacked these problems directly and forcefully, he encountered much opposition from entrenched venal interests. He purged almost the entire Communist Party and city bureaucracy in Moscow and arrested the most corrupt retail managers. Yeltsin faulted Gorbachev for the slow pace of his reform efforts and criticized conservative Politburo member Yegor Ligachev for obstructing reform. He did not endear himself at the Twenty-seventh Party Congress in 1986 when he attacked the "social injustice" of the benefits and material advantages that separated the party privileged from the Soviet public.[49]

In order to appease the corrupt but ideologically orthodox in Moscow and rid himself of an outspoken critic, Gorbachev supported the conservative Ligachev and removed Yeltsin from his Moscow city post and as candidate member of the Politburo in November 1987. Yeltsin accepted a junior ministerial post and appeared to be just another minor loser in the game of Soviet hardball politics. When he requested that the Nineteenth CPSU Conference "rehabilitate" him in July 1988 (while he was alive, rather than posthumously, as was usually the case in party practice), he was once again humiliated, as Gorbachev rejected his request. But Yeltsin achieved a dramatic comeback in August 1991 when, in a remarkable turn of events, Gorbachev was forced into the role of a hapless supplicant, depending upon Yeltsin to rescue him from house arrest and from the conspirators who sought to depose him. Yeltsin had been able to acquire support as an outspoken populist while Gorbachev and the KGB sought to discredit him. Yeltsin's growing political strength during 1989–1991 derived from his advocacy of radical reform at the very time when Gorbachev maneuvered and meandered in his search for an unattainable "consensus." Yeltsin also acquired popularity as a defender of the interests of ethnic Russia and of the Russian Republic against the union-center represented by Gorbachev, who stubbornly continued to advocate and personify a thoroughly compromised and ineffective centralism. Yeltsin's reputation for forthrightness won him favor among those who perceived Gorbachev as guileful and evasive.

Despite opposition from Gorbachev, Yeltsin was elected from Moscow to the USSR Congress of People's Deputies and played a key role in the developing parliamentary opposition. In March 1990 Yeltsin was also elected with 90 percent of the vote in a contest with Gorbachev's candidate to represent the city of Moscow in the new Russian Parliament; two months later he was elected its chairman. In June 1990 he demonstrably withdrew from the CPSU at the Twenty-eighth Party Congress before a national television audience.

Yeltsin called for Gorbachev's resignation in February 1991 after the attacks by Soviet troops on civilians in the Baltic republics, but he subsequently sought an accommodation with the USSR president on an ill-fated plan to reform and rescue the divided union. When Gorbachev sought to ban a pro-Yeltsin demonstration in March 1991 (to counter Communist efforts to unseat Yeltsin in the Russian Parliament) he was successfully defied, and the mass demonstration took place despite the presence of troops in the capital.[50]

When the Russian Republic opted for a popularly elected president, Gorbachev again sought covertly to prevent Yeltsin's election. However, Yeltsin easily won 57 percent of the vote against five opponents in June 1991 and became the first popularly elected president in the history of Russia. As president, Yeltsin began to express the long-repressed grievances of Russians against the union-center. Already on November 19, 1990, in Kiev he had signed a treaty with the government of Ukraine that acknowledged the sovereignty of both Ukraine and Russia and recognized their existing borders.

Yeltsin insisted that the Russian Republic have its own KGB free of union control and its own defense ministry and military forces; he claimed the republic's right to control all its natural resources, which the union-center had used for its own purposes while flagrantly neglecting the republic's domestic needs.[51] Yeltsin called for an end to Soviet aid to Cuba, and exacted a ban on Communist Party organizations in the workplace and their control of patronage, promotions, and various benefits. Earlier, in January 1991, when the Kremlin sought to employ violence against the seceding Baltic states, Yeltsin had directed an appeal to Soviet troops in Lithuania (delivered while he was in Estonia) warning them not to be used by the forces of reaction and not serve as "a pawn in a dirty game, a grain of sand in the Kremlin's building of an imperial sand-castle." He appealed to the troops not to believe the political officers and not to betray their own generation, warning that "dictatorship is arriving, and it is you who is bringing it, sitting with a submachine gun in a tank!"[52]

THE AUGUST 1991 COUP

The coup that sought to unseat Gorbachev and turn back the calendar was organized by a cabal representing the KGB (Vladimir Kryuchkov), the military (Marshal Yazov), the interior ministry or MVD (Boris Pugo), and the military-industrial complex. It included the premier, Valentin Pavlov, and had as its spokesman Vice President Genadi Yanayev, whom Gorbachev had insisted be elected to that post after he was initially rejected by the Congress of Deputies. The gang of eight constituted a self-proclaimed State Committee for the State of Emergency in the USSR. It claimed mendaciously that Gorbachev was unable to exercise the duties of the presidency for unspecified reasons of "health" and announced that Yanayev would serve as acting president. It soon became clear that Gorbachev was being held under house arrest in his Crimean vacation retreat at Foros, near Yalta, and was cut off from all means of domestic communication and had to obtain news of events from foreign radio broadcasts.

The putsch extended far beyond the self-proclaimed junta; it included numerous higher military officers and was supported by many CPSU apparatus officials at the republic and oblast levels. The coup, a futile attempt to prevent the breakup of the empire, was precipitated by Gorbachev's plan to return to Moscow for the signing of the "new union treaty" on August 20 that had been worked out in spring with nine of the constituent republics of the Soviet Union. The putsch leaders claimed that Gorbachev's reform policies had reached a dead end, but promised to pursue a "consistent policy of reform." In a vague and confusing statement the plotters condemned the turmoil and the "extremist forces" that allegedly sought to destroy the Soviet Union. They objected to the "war of laws" between the republics and the Union's president and the "destruction of the unified machinery of the national economy which has taken decades to evolve." The plotters contended that "the country has become ungovernable" and condemned the alleged use of power as "a means of unprincipled self assertion" with the aim of establishing "an unbridled personal dictatorship"–although they did not specify whether this was the "sin" of Yeltsin or Gorbachev.[53] Although it promised to act against "the octopus of crime and scandalous immorality" as well as the "propagation of sex and violence" and the "tyranny of those who plunder the people's property," the junta had no specific program for rescuing either the economy or the empire. Its offer to conduct a public debate on Gorbachev's "new union treaty" reflected its misplaced suspicion of that instrument.

The coup of August 19–21, 1991, proved to be poorly planned and the plotters ill-prepared. They apparently assumed that the removal of Gorbachev would be as easy as the 1964 ouster of Khrushchev, which was accomplished by hauling him before a Central Committee that was insistent

on his removal. The junta contended themselves with a televised press conference that revealed to viewers a motley assortment of undistinguished and unattractive bureaucratic types. Interior Minister Pugo sat beside the principal spokesman, acting president Yanayev, whose hands shook visibly as he attempted to cope with the barbed and ironic questions of correspondents.

The junta sent tanks and armored personnel carriers into the streets of Moscow and issued orders to all military forces and CPSU organizations in a vain effort to intimidate the opposition. But they miscalculated in relying on the divided and dispirited military establishment and in not obtaining the support of the elite Alpha force of the KGB. They also failed to obtain the acquiescence of Gorbachev or to arrest or assassinate Boris Yeltsin, who quickly moved to lead the widespread opposition to the coup. Although they were able to control the major media, they could not control foreign radio broadcasts, the independent press, and recently developed nongovernmental information networks. In the end, the plotters experienced a failure of nerve.

Yeltsin defied the plotters and took refuge in the government house of the Russian Republic—the White House—with aides and armed guards, as tens of thousands of supporters surrounded the building day and night and erected barricades for its defense. Military, KGB, and interior ministry forces loyal to Yeltsin refused to move against the government house and instead took up its defense. The plotters failed to cut off Yeltsin's communications and utilities, and he was able to communicate with world leaders and to project an image of the defender of constitutional government.

The plotters failed largely because of their inability to rely on the military, their ineptitude and questionable reputations, and their failure to inspire public confidence in the unanticipated confrontation with the popularly elected Russian president, Boris Yeltsin. The plot unraveled within 72 hours (despite the failure of Yeltsin's call for a general strike), and a shaken but not entirely chastened Gorbachev was able to return to Moscow to denounce the coup. Interior Minister Pugo committed suicide, and the other plotters were arrested. Gorbachev's military adviser, the old-line Marshal Akhromeyev, also committed suicide.

An intriguing question prompted by the coup was that of Gorbachev's unwitting complicity in it. Had he been less self-assured and more perceptive, he would have heeded the various warnings and ominous events that should have alerted him to the danger of a coup. Foreign Minister Eduard Shevardnadze had warned of the threat of dictatorship when he resigned in December 1990. In June 1991, in an attempted "constitutional coup," Premier Pavlov had sought unsuccessfully to have the Supreme Soviet grant him some of Gorbachev's presidential powers, and KGB chief Kryuchkov, Defense Minister Yazov, and Interior Minister Pugo had expressed profound dissatisfaction with political and economic developments in a closed session of the Supreme Soviet.[54]

Gorbachev cannot be viewed as an innocent victim of the coup. He appointed and promoted all of the plotters and had to know their political positions. It can be argued that Gorbachev implicitly encouraged the plotters by his shift toward their position in the autumn of 1990, relying on coercive methods, police provocations, and intimidation. Gorbachev permitted Kryuchkov, Pugo, and the military a free hand in the Baltic states and reimposed media control and news blackouts. Thus Gorbachev, in casting his lot earlier with the KGB, the military, and the interior ministry, apparently led the plotters to believe that he relied upon them, condoned their methods, and would be prepared to join them when presented with a *fait accompli.*

In a sense, Gorbachev was an unwitting or silent accessory to the plotters, if not an actual "co-conspirator." He demonstrated poor judgment in selecting, promoting, and relying upon the plotters. He handpicked men of middling abilities and questionable character, possibly because he felt more compatible with them than with the various aides and advisers of superior intellect whom he had alienated. Several of his closest staff cooperated with the plotters. Gorbachev became a victim of his own guile and equivocation as well as his ego, his excessive self-confidence, and his carelessness. Some have speculated that Gorbachev cynically sought to utilize the very real threat from the anti-reform hard-line Communists as a means of extracting economic and financial aid from the West and

Japan. In possibly seeking to use this threat as an undesirable alternative to his own leadership, Gorbachev became its victim.

THE FINAL DAYS

The outcome of the failed coup was the very opposite of the plotters' intentions. It greatly accelerated the dissolution of the Soviet Union and once again demonstrated the endemic incompetence, mismanagement, and potentially dangerous nature of the center and of the CPSU. Yet the coup proved to be a remarkable turning point for Russia and the republics, paid for with the lives of three young men who died on the barricades in Moscow. It was very literally a coup d'etat in which part of the Communist state—indeed, some of the very highest officials who presumably enjoyed the unquestioned confidence of the USSR president—struck a fatal blow at the entire fabric of the Soviet polity. It also created a vacuum in the center which gave Russia and the other republics a freedom of action they had not enjoyed since 1917–1918.

The coup and the resistance to it were essentially Russian phenomena; the plotters were all ethnic Russians (except for Boris Pugo, a Russified Latvian) and the immediate decisive resistance to the coup was largely Russian. The coup represented a conflict between Moscow and the Kremlin, between Russia and the Union. Boris Yeltsin emerged from the coup as the de facto political leader of the country and the leading force committed to destroying the old political order, while Gorbachev returned to Moscow in a greatly weakened and isolated position. Initially, Gorbachev did not comprehend the profound changes caused by the failure of the coup. Indeed, the coup demonstrated the irrelevance of the CPSU as a constructive factor in the political system.

Yeltsin, as the leader of Russia, issued various decrees appointing new military commanders for Moscow and Leningrad (St. Petersburg) and placing troops of the army, KGB, and interior ministry in the Russian Republic under the jurisdiction of his office. The Russian Republic assumed ownership of all economic enterprises and properties on its territory, and Yeltsin restored the imperial Russian tricolor as the republic's flag, abandoning the red banner and the hammer and sickle, (although he later reinstated the red flag with star but minus the hammer and sickle as a co-equal national—or imperial?—flag) and suspended all activities of the Russian Communist Party. Yeltsin insisted that Gorbachev approve all decisions taken by the Parliament and president of the Russian Republic during the coup, and Gorbachev had no choice but to give his assent.

The lack of support for Gorbachev within the central party apparatus during the coup prompted him to dissolve the Central Committee and the central party organization on August 24. Similar bans were imposed throughout the former USSR. However, several republic Communist parties sought to change their names and continue in existence, many party leaders at the *oblast'* level, who were locked out of their party offices, continued to hold local or regional governmental posts and issue orders in an attempt to retain their powers and privileges. The USSR Supreme Soviet, by a vote of 283 to 29 with 52 abstentions, suspended all CPSU activities on August 29, 1991.

Gorbachev's "new union treaty" could not be signed as a result of the coup, and the USSR president was compelled to witness the adoption of declarations of national independence by nearly all of the former union republics. The process that had begun with Lithuania's abrogation of the Communist monopoly of power on December 7, 1989, and its declaration of independence and secession from the USSR on March 11, 1990, was largely consummated when Ukraine proclaimed its independence on August 24, 1991. But Russia, though insisting on its sovereignty, proclaimed on June 12, 1990, was reluctant to secede from the defunct Union.

The Baltic republics, where the drive for secession and independence had begun, made clear throughout 1991 that they were not interested in a revamped union treaty or a restructured Soviet Union and had not participated in the discussions concerning a new union treaty. Estonia and Latvia declared their full independence during the August coup; and after the coup all three Baltic

states, with support from the West, demanded their full separation from the USSR. On September 6, 1991, the Kremlin granted full independence to the three states. Almost immediately separatists in the other republics speeded up their efforts at independence. By mid-October Ukraine announced that popular demands for greater sovereignty precluded its signing the union treaty that had been negotiated in the spring.

With the collapse of the coup and the union treaty proposal, Gorbachev was compelled to employ other tactics in his tattered strategy of imperial revival. His dissolution of the USSR cabinet of ministers because of its support for the coup meant that there was no longer a central union government. The Congress of People's Deputies was convened early in September 1991 in an effort to preserve some semblance of a political center. Yeltsin told the Congress that "the collapse of the empire is final, but the republics have got to take its place."[55] The Congress balked at legislating itself out of existence but agreed to a new "transitional" center. The compromise, enacted at the insistence of Gorbachev and ten republic leaders, created a new interim executive body, the State Council, consisting of republic representatives and Gorbachev as chairman.

The supposed "transitional" arrangement, was actually a "terminal" arrangement. Republics that had proclaimed their independence were suspicious of possible collusion between Gorbachev and Yeltsin and were apprehensive that the Russian Republic would usurp or seek to restore the role of the collapsed center. When the restructured Supreme Soviet met, four republics (Ukraine, Azerbaijan, Georgia, and Moldova) refused to participate. In a referendum held on December 1, 1991, more than 90 percent of voters in Ukraine approved secession from the Soviet Union and the establishment of an independent country. By this time Boris Yeltsin had come to the conclusion that further efforts to hold the Soviet Union together were fruitless. Moreover, he had also decided that Russia could be more successful alone in implementing effective economic reform.

On December 8, 1991, the presidents of the three Slavic republics of the Soviet Union—Russia, Belarus, and Ukraine—which together contained 73 percent of the Soviet population and 80 percent of its territory, met in Minsk, the capital of Belarus, to announce their secession from the Soviet Union and create a new Commonwealth of Independent States (CIS).[56] Ignoring Gorbachev's criticisms of their actions, the three presidents submitted their agreement to their respective parliaments for ratification; on December 10, 1991, the Commonwealth officially came into existence. Ten days later the five Central Asian republics joined the CIS after gaining assurances that they would be treated as fully equal members, and on December 22, three more republics (Armenia, Azerbaijan, and Moldova) joined, leaving only Georgia, which was preoccupied with a bloody civil war, outside the new Commonwealth. On December 20, the Russian Federation took formal jurisdiction over virtually all of the governmental bodies and resources of the Soviet state. On December 25, Gorbachev informed a national television audience of his resignation as president and the formal demise of the Union. The next day the Supreme Soviet passed a resolution acknowledging the dissolution of the Soviet state. A little more than 74 years after Lenin and the Bolsheviks seized power in Petrograd and began laying the foundations for a new social, political, and economic order, that order crashed to an ignominious end.

The August 1991 coup proved to be the denouement of Gorbachev's singular achievement: the introduction of significant democratic conditions and the partial dismantling and weakening of the centralized bureaucratic structures of the empire's metropol-center. Prior to this, the entire Soviet political system had been based on a triadic structure consisting of the following principal components: the CPSU oligarchy and its administrative apparatus that determined basic policy and conducted propaganda on its behalf, the governmental bureaucracy that managed the state-owned economy, and the organs of repression—military, police, and internal security organs (the MVD and the KGB).

Gorbachev's reform efforts challenged and weakened an exhausted power structure but did not develop a viable substitute and the new personnel needed to give such an alternative life and substance. The ultimate source of this enormous failure must be sought in the policies pursued by the CPSU leadership for decades and the methods that it chose to employ.

BUILDING THE RUSSIAN FEDERATION

Over the first four years of the existence as an independent state of the Russian Federation the media have presented an expansive picture of drug dealers and mafia hit men, corrupt businessmen, destitute pensioners, an embittered and impoverished intelligentsia— all providing a plausible explanation of the growth of support for extremists of the Right (such as Vladimir Zhirinovsky) and the return of the Communist Party as the leading force in Russian politics. The euphoria of the early 1990s, when Russian and foreign observers alike assumed that the collapse of the authoritarian and centralized structures of the Soviet state would usher in a period of stable participatory government and expanding economic welfare, has given way to the realities of creating new social, political, and economic structures in Russia and in the other successor states of the USSR. Russia and the other post-Soviet states[57] are engaged, in fact, in a complex process that analysts have called a "triple transition." They are attempting simultaneously to create new states and national identities, to establish new political institutions based on the rule of law, and to build the foundations for effective and productive market economies. In many respects the demands associated with one of these three areas—for instance, expanding political participation—may conflict with the prerequisites for success in another—such as the unemployment that may result from introducing market mechanisms into the economy.

Russia is not alone in attempting to deal with the multiple demands of sociopolitical and economic modernization. In fact, at least in the political sphere it is part of what Samuel P. Huntington has referred to as the "third wave" of democratization.[58] Between 1972 and the mid–1990s the number of countries in which authoritarian political systems have been overthrown and efforts initiated to establish democratic political systems more than doubled, from 44 to 107. Countries in Southern Europe, Latin America, East Asia, Africa, and most recently the former Communist states of East-Central Europe and Eurasia have joined the list of mature and fledgling democratic states. However, most of them have found the process of transition from authoritarian to stable democratic rule a long and difficult one. Most of the countries currently making the transition to democracy are doing so in the context of established geographic borders, a relatively homogeneous population, and an economy that even during the period of authoritarian rule operated on the basis of market principles. For the post-Communist states, however, the situation is much more complex.[59] The negative legacies of the past are especially strong and deeply rooted throughout much of the post-Communist world. The political values essential for a functioning democracy are weak among both the population and the political elites; hostilities across ethnic communities create special problems for political transition and state building; moreover, many of the infrastructural prerequisites for market economics are absent. Thus, the process of transition in the post-Communist states, including the Russian Federation, has proven to be especially difficult and problematic.

Nation Building in the Russian Federation and the CIS

For the most, part, neither Russia nor as the other CIS states have existed historically within the current boundaries of the Russian Federation or those of the other new states. In fact, tsarist Russia emerged over the course of several centuries as a result of imperial conquest and expansion into territories populated by a diverse mixture of peoples. At the end of the tsarist period ethnic Russians comprised a minority of 43 percent in their own empire.

Territorial and population losses after World War I brought the figure to 58 percent in 1939; additional territorial changes after World War II and demographic developments over the next 50 years reduced the percentage of ethnic Russians in the Soviet Union to only slightly more than 50 percent in 1989. Moreover, the boundaries which emerged as the *de jure* limits of the post-Soviet states were based on purely administrative determinations of the Stalinist period and have little to do with the historical borders of earlier states or with the ethnic composition of the new states. For example, the Crimea, populated largely by ethnic Russians and a part of the Russian Republic, was given to Ukraine by Khrushchev in 1954 during the celebrations of the tercentenary of the Pereyaslavl Treaty that brought much of Ukraine under Russian rule. The portion of eastern Moldova whose Russian and Ukrainian plurality have de facto seceded from Moldova since 1992, was transferred from Ukraine to the new Soviet Republic of Moldavia by Stalin after World War II.

Besides the fact that existing territories and populations of the post-Soviet states have for the most part not existed historically as independent political units, there are several other, primarily psychological, factors that influence the process of nation and state building in Russia. A significant portion of Russians, including members of the political elite, find it difficult to accept the existence of Russia without its former non-Russian territories and are, in fact, committed to reestablish the old empire in some form. As former Vice President Aleksandr Rutskoi put it, "the historical consciousness of the Russians will not allow anybody to equate mechanically the borders of Russia with those of the Russian Federation and to take away what constituted the glorious pages of Russian history."[60]

Two serious issues emerge that relate directly to the view of what constitutes Russia and Russians. First, there is the issue of the millions of ethnic Russians who remain in the countries of the "near abroad" (the other post-Soviet states) and the impact that this has had on Russian relations with those states. For the most part their presence results from the policies of Stalin and his successors to bring Russians into areas depopulated by the famine and purges of the 1930s (e.g., in Ukraine), the "Virgin Lands" program of the 1950s in Kazakstan, and the overall commitment to ensuring Moscow's control over non-Russian populations. Russian leaders, including former Foreign Minister Andrei Kozyrev and President Yeltsin, have made clear that they view the well-being of these populations as a central concern of the Russian state. They point to real and alleged discrimination against Russians in the countries of the "near abroad" as a justification for greater Russian influence in these countries—and even for reintegrating the independent post-Soviet states into a new Russian-led political entity. One must distinguish between ethnic Russians who are indeed natives of the new states and those who were in effect recent colonists. The Soviet policy of demographic inundation of indigenous populations, as in Estonia and Latvia, was accompanied by discriminatory language policies of various kinds that favored Russian speakers. Hence, it is not surprising that tensions exist in the post-Soviet environment. What is surprising is that greater tension does not exist. Moreover, there is ample evidence that indicates that various political figures in Russia seek to provoke ethno-linguistic hostilities in the "near abroad" as a pretext for intimidation and destabilization, if not subversion and intervention.

The second issue regards the place of non-Russian minorities in the Russian Federation and the possible impact of ethnic hostility and separatist tendencies on the political processes and institutions being developed. The most serious of Russia's problems in this regard are to be found in the Caucasus, where numerous ethnic groups have long coexisted, although divided by language, religion, and a history of feuding with one another and opposing domination by the Russians. During the Soviet period these antagonisms were kept under control primarily by coercive measures. With the collapse of Soviet power, however, conflicts broke out between the Christian Ossetians and the Muslim Ingush (who, in turn, had refused to secede from Russia along with the

Chechens, a fellow-Muslim people, with whom they had shared the Chechen-Ingushetia autonomous republic until 1992). In late 1992 President Yeltsin sent Russian troops into the region to separate the warring sides. However, this was but a prelude to a much more serious threat to Russian authority in the region. President Dzhokhar Dudayev, a former general in the Soviet Air Force and leader of the secessionist independent state of Ichkeriya, declared that the presence of Russian troops in the region violated the territorial integrity of Chechnya. After an additional year of confrontation and fruitless negotiations, President Yeltsin decided to put down the Chechen secession by military force. In December 1994 thousands of Russian troops, backed by tanks, heavy artillery and aircraft, attacked Dudayev's forces. Only after months of brutal battle, during which the Russians killed thousands of civilians and destroyed the cities and villages of Chechnya, did the Russians declare victory—prematurely, as it turned out. As of summer 1996 Chechen guerrillas continued to challenge the Russian presence and had mounted several attacks into Russia proper where they seized hostages in the attempt to force a Russian withdrawal from their homeland. The Russian response has continued to rely on brute force and the total destruction of Chechen opposition, including the massive bombardment in January 1996 of Chechen guerrillas and their hostages holed up in a village outside Chechnya. President Yeltsin has been widely criticized at home—except by the extreme nationalist Zhirinovsky—and abroad for his policies in Chechnya. As part of his election campaign and to counter widespread opposition to the war throughout Russia he moved to establish a cease-fire and negotiated settlement by early June 1996. That cease-fire broke down immediately after the election.

The challenges to Russian control over Chechnya, and the Caucasus more generally, were but one part of a much broader problem faced by President Yeltsin as he attempted to create the constitutional foundations for the new Russia. Other ethnically based republics scattered across Russia, including especially

Tatarstan, also declared their sovereignty soon after the collapse of the Soviet Union. The Tatars, a Turkic Muslim people living about 500 miles east of Moscow on the Volga River, voted overwhelmingly in March 1992 in favor of complete independence from Moscow. As the Chechens, they refused to hold nationally scheduled elections on their territory, claimed control over their national resources, and refused to send tax payments to the federal government in Moscow. Similar developments have occurred elsewhere across Russia, as in Buryatia, north of Mongolia, and in the Republic of Sakha (Yakutia) comprising most of the gold- and mineral-rich northeastern portions of Siberia. It is especially interesting to note that in none of these three republics does the titular nationality comprise a majority (49 percent Tatars; 24 percent Buryats; 33 percent Yakuts). In these and other cases ethnic Russians have supported the call for sovereignty, which they view largely in terms of greater economic and political independence from the heavy administrative hand of Moscow (see Table 7.2).

With the major exception of Chechnya, however, the Yeltsin government seems to have resolved the most significant issues dividing the central government in Moscow and the 21 ethnic republics of the Federation, at least for the time being. This represents a major achievement in state building and was accomplished by a combination of the forceful example of Yeltsin's coercive policy in Chechnya and the simultaneous granting of substantial amounts of autonomy to the republics. The constitution approved in a national referendum in December 1993 and agreements negotiated between Moscow and various republics have helped create a degree of stability in relations between the federal government and the constituent units of the Federation. For example, although Russian tax laws apply in the 59 nonautonomous Russian provinces and territories and approximately 60 percent of local tax revenues from these provinces flow to Moscow, the governments of the autonomous republics negotiate with Moscow the amount of taxes to be paid to the center—usually at rates 80 percent lower than that for the provinces. One result of this permissive approach, however, has been the fact that legisla-

tion of the republics—and the other provinces—increasingly conflicts with the federal constitution. For example, the Republic of Tuva, along the northwestern border of Mongolia, outlaws private land ownership, although the Russian constitution permits it. Legislation in 75 of Russia's constituent provinces (including the 21 republics and one autonomous *oblast*) is reportedly at odds with the federal constitution.[61] Thus, the constitutional issues have not been worked out fully, and the relationships between the central government and the republics are evidence of the larger and more general problem of weak governmental institutions and a continued lack of established rules for conducting the business of government.[62] Although the demands for independence of the republics have been muted, in part because of the flexibility of the policies of President Yeltsin, efforts by a future more nationalistic government to reimpose strong central control might well encourage renewed separatist tendencies that will challenge the nation- and state-building requirements of the Russian Federation.

In many respects the problems of state and nation building are even greater in most of the other Soviet successor states. For example, Ukraine, Moldova, and Kazakstan all have substantial Russian minorities, most of whom are geographically concentrated, who represent a real or potential threat to national unity (very real in the case of Moldova, where the central government lost control of Transdniester to Russian secessionists soon after independence, and in Ukraine, where the Russian majority of Crimea has called for reunion with Russia).[63] The ongoing war between Armenia and Azerbaijan over control of Nagorno-Karabakh and the devastating civil wars in Georgia are evidence of the seriousness of the problem of creating political loyalties to the new states of the CIS among their diverse populations.

Democratization and Political Institution Building

Besides the problems associated with nation and state building in Russia and the CIS, there are also those related to the creation of a stable representative or democratic political system. The

Table 7.2 Ethno-Territorial Units of the Russian Federation, Including the Share of Titular Nationality and Russians in the Population

Unit	Total Population	Percent of Titular Nationality	Percent of Russians
Republics			
Adygei	432,046	22.1	68.0
Altai	190,831	31.0	60.4
Bashkortostan	3,943,113	21.9	39.3
Buryatia	1,038,252	24.0	69.9
Checheno-Ingushetia	1,270,429*		
Chechens		57.8	23.1
Ingush		12.9	
Chuvashia	1,338,023	67.8	26.7
Dagestam	1,802,188	80.2	9.2
Kabardino-Balkaria	753,531		
Kabardians		48.2	31.9
Balkars		9.4	
Kalmkia	322,579	45.4	37.7
Karachai-Cherkessia	415,970		
Karachais		31.2	42.4
Cherkess		9.7	
Karelia	790,150	10.0	73.6
Kharkassiay	566,861	11.1	79.5
Komi	1,250,847	23.3	57.7
Mari-El	749,332	43.3	47.5
Mordvinia	963,504	32.5	60.8
North Ossetia	632,428	53.0	29.9
Sakha (Yakhutia)	1,094,065	33.4	50.3
Tatarstan	3,641,742	48.5	43.3
Tuva	308,557	64.3	32.0
Udmurtia	1,605,663	30.9	58.9
Autonomous Oblast			
Jewish AO			
Autonomous Okrugs**			

Aga Buryat (Chita oblast)	Koriak (Kamchatka oblast)
Chukchi (Magadan oblast)	Nenets (Arkhangelsk oblast)
Evenki (Krasnoyarsk oblast)	Taimyr (Krasnoyarsk oblast)
Khanty-Mansi (Tyumen oblast)	Ust' Orda Buryat (Irkutsk oblast)
Komi-Permiak (Perm oblast)	Yamalo-Nenets (Tyumen oblast)

*Separate data for the two republics of Chechnya and Ingushetia, which separated officially in 1992, are not available.

**Autonomous okrugs are under the administrative jurisciction of provinces (*oblasti*) that are not territorially defined; the names of these provinces are given in parentheses.

Source: Elizabeth Teague, "Center-Periphery Relations in the Russian Federation," in Roman Szporluk, ed., *National Identity and Ethnicity in Russia and the New States of Eurasia* (Armonk, NY: M. E. Sharpe, 1994), pp. 21–57.

Russian Federation has established a complex political system that, although it includes a strong presidency, also establishes the separation of powers. Therefore, presidential-parliamentary (executive-legislative) relations have been at the very center of Russian politics. The first two years of Russian independence witnessed a move toward parliamentary democracy in Russia with a parliament that increasingly attempted to exert its authority in the legislative process relative to the power of the executive. The result was a growing confrontation between President Yeltsin (and his reform-minded government) and a parliament, elected in March 1990 prior to the collapse of the Communist system, that represented the old bureaucratic interests and opposed the dismantling of state enterprises. The conservative forces aligned against Yeltsin also charged him with being too supportive of the West and with undermining the strategic security interests of Russia. They opposed the rapid and widespread introduction of economic reforms that included privatization of state industries. Many of them were strong nationalists for whom the collapse of the Soviet empire and the emergence of independent states on the territory of the former USSR were unacceptable.

By 1993 various factions or groupings had emerged within the Russian Supreme Soviet and Congress based on political and ideological differences concerning the breadth and timing of economic reforms. Increasingly the factions attempted to exercise some control over their members, much as occurs in Western parliamentary systems. These factions, in turn, were joining in much broader coalitions. Three broad coalitions emerged: the democratic Left, representing about 225 members (with Democratic Russia the most important party) who usually fully supported Yeltsin's economic reforms and his foreign policy oriented toward emphasizing ties with the democratic West; an ideological center of about 200 members (headed by the Civic Union) who opposed some of the specifics of the reforms and called for greater attention to relations with the other post-Soviet states; and a bloc of right and left extremists of about 375 members (including both Communists and extreme nationalists) who opposed almost all aspects of Yeltsin's domestic and foreign policy agenda.

President Yeltsin himself contributed to the opposition that he faced in Parliament by ignoring the legislature's views concerning some of his initiatives and by ruling by presidential degree when he could not get parliamentary support. His authoritarian approach to rule meant that he often acted contrary to the existing Russian constitution which gave limited authority to the president. An indication of the style of Yeltsin's leadership can be seen in the fact that, although Russia has a much smaller population and controls less territory than the former Soviet Union, the Russian government is in fact larger than its Soviet predecessor was in 1991. For example, a presidential apparatus headed by Sergei Filatov until late 1995 and modeled after the Central Committee apparatus of the old CPSU evolved in order to permit Yeltsin to get around the state bureaucracy which was still dominated by former Soviet bureaucrats. One especially important element of the new presidential bureaucracy has been the National Security Council, which has played a key role in both domestic and foreign security policy. Immediately after the first round of the presidential elections in June 1996, President Yeltsin appointed General (ret.) Aleksandr Lebed—who ran a strong third to Yeltsin and Zyuganov—to head the Council, in return for the latter's support against Zyuganov in the July runoff. In the aftermath of Yeltsin's reelection the openly nationalistic Lebed and the more pragmatic Prime Minister Chernomyrdin, who represent two very different political styles and policy orientations, jockeyed for position and influence in Yeltsin's new government.

The large multistory White House, the home of the Russian Parliament until its partial destruction by Yeltsin's troops in October 1993, has been filled with members of the presidential staff. In the words of one American analyst, "The problem of the presidency is that it is now beginning to take on many of the characteristics of the entrenched bureaucracy that it was designed to supersede."[64]

By the end of 1992 Yeltsin faced increasing defection from among his past supporters and allies and growing confrontation with Parliament. For example, his hand-picked Vice President Aleksandr Rutskoi broke with him on various issues related to economic reform and foreign policy. Ruslan Khasbulatov, whom Yeltsin selected

Siege outside Russian Parliament, October 4, 1993.

to replace himself as speaker of the Russian Parliament when he was elected president, became a focal point of opposition to Yeltsin and his policies. The central issue that divided the Russian political elite concerned the type of government that would be established by the new Russian constitution. While Yeltsin insisted that the new Russian government must be based on a strong presidency, along the lines of that of the Fifth Republic in France, a majority in Parliament favored a parliamentary system of government in which the legislature would play the major role.

By early 1993 a stalemate ensued, with the president and Parliament pushing for the approval of very different drafts of a new constitution. Moreover, the president insisted that, until such time as a new constitution was enacted, he had the right and obligation based on his popular election to rule by decree in order to ensure the country's well-being. In April 1993 Yeltsin called a referendum in which Russian voters were given the choice to indicate who should rule the country: Yeltsin or Parliament. After a bitter three-week electoral campaign, 59 percent of those voting (representing only 39 percent of registered voters) indicated that they had confidence in Yeltsin's leadership.

Despite the referendum, the constitutional crisis continued throughout the summer, since

the Constitutional Court whose members had been appointed by Yeltsin had made a ruling prior to the referendum that it would require a majority of all registered voters to force Parliament to disband and call new elections. Although 64 percent of those voting called for early parliamentary elections, they comprised only 43 percent of registered voters; thus, their preferences were not deemed legally binding. The confrontation continued throughout the summer, with the pro-Yeltsin members of the Congress and the Supreme Soviet boycotting all sessions. Finally, on September 21, 1993, President Boris Yeltsin ordered the dissolution of both the Supreme Soviet and the Congress of Peoples' Deputies—an act that the Constitutional Court declared illegal. Simultaneously he suspended the existing constitution and scheduled elections for a new parliamentary body, the State Duma, and a referendum on his version of a new constitution.

Led by Vice President Rutskoi and Speaker Khasbulatov, 400 Congress deputies (289 less than a quorum) met in Parliament and voted to impeach President Yeltsin and replace him with Rutskoi; they then barricaded the White House, or parliament building, against a feared attack by Yeltsin—an attack complete with tanks shelling the White House that did come on October 4, 1993, by Russian paratroopers and elite militia units loyal to Yeltsin that was witnessed worldwide on television. During that ten-day interval the rump Parliament called on the armed forces to oppose Yeltsin and support Parliament. In effect, the leaders in the White House set up a competing government and called for an overthrow of President Yeltsin's government.

On October 3, "President" Rutskoi harangued supporters in the streets outside Parliament who had just overwhelmed militia units that tried to stop them with nightsticks, tear gas, and rubber bullets. That evening the crowd responded to his call to seize the office of the Mayor of Moscow and the state television and radio. The next morning troops loyal to Yeltsin launched a counteroffensive against the parliament building. By late afternoon Rutskoi, Khasbulatov, and their supporters surrendered. The "Battle of Moscow" had resulted in 150 deaths, 1,000 wounded, and 2,000 jailed and in the defeat of those opposing Yeltsin.

It is ironic that little more than two years earlier Boris Yeltsin—along with political allies who included Rutskoi and Khasbulatov—had achieved political prominence in Russia by opposing, at this very same location, the forces committed to reversing the changes underway in the Soviet Union. In the intervening two years, Yeltsin had managed to alienate these men, and others, in part because of his authoritarian approach to political leadership. However, political and ideological differences, as well as aspirations for political leadership among many politicians, contributed to the split. One of the important results of the confrontation was the enhanced role of the military, including Defense Minister Grachev, in Yeltsin's government. Immediately after the first round of presidential elections in June 1996, however, Grachev was sacked in response to General Lebed's demands for supporting Yeltsin.

For the next two months after the storming of the White House, Yeltsin ruled with a heavy hand, banning radical opposition groups and parties and removing the members of the Constitutional Court and provincial political leaders who had opposed his dissolution of Parliament. Yeltsin himself attempted to stay above the politics associated with the election campaign for a new parliament scheduled for December 12. He did not associate himself with any of the political parties maneuvering for position prior to the

elections in the attempt to present himself as the president of all of Russia who was above party politics. As the elections drew near, scores of parties and factions competed for positions on the ballot. Eventually more than 2,000 candidates registered to run for the new Federal Assembly. Of these more than 1,500 competed for the 225 single-mandate seats that would comprise half the membership of the lower house, or State Duma (the remaining 225 Duma seats would be distributed proportionately to those parties or election blocs that received at least 5 percent of the national vote). The remaining 500 candidates were competing for the 178 seats in the Federation Council, the upper chamber of the Federal Assembly.

Thirteen parties and blocs ended up winning the 5 percent of the national vote required to be represented on the party lists. Four of these represented the reformist wing of the political spectrum and were associated with major political figures: Russia's Choice of Yegor Gaidar, Yeltsin's first prime minister; the Russian Party of Unity of Yeltsin's advisor Sergei Shakhrai; the Movement for Democratic Reforms headed by the reformist mayors of St. Petersburg (Anatoly Sobchak) and Moscow (Gavriil Popov) along with Aleksandr Yakovlev who had been an important force for reform under Gorbachev; and Yabloko (meaning "apple" in Russian), the party that took its name from letters in the surnames of its three founders—Grigory Yavlinsky, one of Yeltsin's many former economic advisors; Yury Boldyrev, another former Yeltsin appointee, and Vladimir Lukin, a career diplomat who had served as Russia's first ambassador in Washington. The key issues dividing these three parties were the personalities of their leaders, more than major differences of political perspective, as well as the long-standing tendency among Russians, even those whose views are similar, to emphasize the importance of ideological differences over areas of agreement. This appears to be a engrained aspect of Russian political culture that historically has made agreement or compromise on political matters very difficult, even among individuals or groups whose positions are close together.

The political center for parliamentary elections was represented by six parties and blocs, the most important of which was Civic Union, the party of former Vice President Rutskoi who

Voting in Russia.

had been imprisoned after Yeltsin's attack on the White House in early October. The extremes of the political spectrum were held on the Left by the relegalized Russian Communist Party, and the Agrarian Party and on the Right by Vladimir Zhirinovsky's radical nationalist Liberal Democratic Party. In the 1991 elections for the presidency of Russia, Zhirinovsky had received 6 million votes and placed third behind Boris Yeltsin.

The results of the the parliamentary election of December 1993 represented a serious political defeat for the reformers and, in effect, for President Yeltsin, even though he had not voiced his support for any of the parties that competed in the elections. Although Russia's Choice did emerge with the largest number of seats in the Duma (96 combined single-member and party-list seats of the total 450 seats), the other reform parties together won only 68 additional seats. The real winners in the December 1993 election were Zhirinovsky's extreme nationalist Liberal Democrats, who received almost 23 percent of the popular vote and 59 seats on the party lists, and the anti-reform Russian Communist and Agrarian Parties, which together won an additional 53 seats on the party lists. Since the three parties that opposed most of the reforms that had been introduced by the Yeltsin government also won 70 single-member seats, they controlled 182 of the 450 seats in the Duma and represented the largest single group of delegates.

The elections of December 1993, therefore, did nothing to resolve the problems of executive-legislative relations in Russia that had resulted in confrontation between President Yeltsin and Parliament. In fact, very early in its existence and over the strong protests of President Yeltsin, the new parliament provided a general amnesty to those arrested and imprisoned on criminal charges for their roles in the violence of October 1993, including both Aleksandr Rutskoi and Ruslan Khasbulatov. The Parliament also released from prison and dropped all charges against the plotters involved in the August 1991 attempt to overthrow Soviet President Gorbachev.

The most unexpected result of the 1993 parliamentary elections was the emergence of radical nationalist Vladimir Zhirinovsky as a major political force in Russian politics. Zhirinovsky had campaigned on a platform that opposed the economic reforms, emphasized law and order, and advocated an assertive and nationalistic foreign policy. The support for Zhirinovsky, as well as that for the Communist and Agrarian Parties of the Left, indicated the widespread alienation of large portions of the Russian population that resulted from the collapse of the Soviet Union and the resulting deterioration of economic conditions throughout the country. Two years later, again confounding the political pundits, Zhirinovsky's nationalists would hold onto a larger percentage of the vote than had been expected (with the third largest number of total seats of any party). At the same time, the Communists would emerge as the dominant political force in the second State Duma.

Already in 1991 in his first campaign for the Russian presidency, Zhirinovsky voiced support for extreme measures in foreign policy. Over the next five years he regularly made the most outlandish nationalist claims for Russia and racist attacks on others, including calling for the use of force to reconquer for Russia the territory of the former Soviet Union and threatening the devastation of those countries that opposed Russian "interests."[65]

Although the election of December 1993 did not resolve the problem of confrontation between the legislature and President Yeltsin, compromises often were worked out. In fact, throughout the next two years political forces within the legislature were fairly equally divided between those who in general supported the policies of the president and those who opposed them. Moreover, given the evidence of public support for parties that opposed the central elements of the early domestic and foreign policy orientation of Yeltsin's government, his policies in several areas shifted, especially in foreign policy. While still claiming to be committed to a policy of cooperation with the West and treatment of the countries of the "near abroad" as sovereign equals, Russia became visibly more assertive on issues as wide-ranging as behavior toward the former republics, policy in former Yugoslavia, arms sales to countries viewed as international "pariahs" by the West, and the entry into full NATO membership of the countries of Central Europe.

Since the general confrontation between President Yeltsin and the parliament continued to dominate Russian politics, the run-up to the parliamentary elections of December 1995 were filled with charges and countercharges among the major political figures, as well as widespread speculation about the growing strength of anti-reform political forces in Russia. However, the election process itself was much more open, fair and clean, according to virtually all Russian and foreign observers, than the election two years earlier. This time the Duma was elected for a full four-year term; no political parties were prevented from running candidates, and a total of 42 parties and movements participated in the political race. Sixty-five percent of registered voters turned out for the election, a full 15 percent more than had voted in 1993. The new Duma included 157 members who has served in the former Duma. The number of women declined from 58 members to 46, thus continuing the very visible trend since the Gorbachev reforms of the reduced presence and role of women in positions of political importance in Russia (see Table 7.3).

The results of the election represented a major defeat for democratic and reform forces and for President Yeltsin. Anti-reform parties of the Left (the various Communist parities and the Agrarian Party with almost one-third of the party-list vote and 188 seats in the 450-seat Duma) and of the Right (Zhirinovsky's Liberal Democrats and other nationalist groups with more that 15 percent of the party-list vote and 56 seats in the Duma) controlled a majority in the Duma. Democratic parties fared especially poorly; Yabloko, for example, drew only 7 percent of the popular vote and a total of 45 seats. Former Prime Minister Yegor Gaidar's reformist Russia's Choice did not manage to make the 5 percent threshold to win party-list seats, although it did elect nine delegates in single-seat races. Prime Minister Chernomyrdin's centrist party, Our Home Is Russia, won slightly less than 10 percent of the popular vote and emerged with 54 seats in the Duma. Overall the results of the election indicated even more clearly than those of 1993 that the Russian population, especially in areas outside the major metropolitan areas of Moscow and St. Petersburg that the positive results of market reforms have yet to reach, do not trust the government's program of reforms which they associate with the dramatic collapse of the Russian economy and of their standard of living. They are tired of escalating crime and corruption that have taken over much of Russian society.

The impact of the election results on the Russian government and its policies was evident early in 1996 as President Yeltsin removed from his government the last officials and advisors committed to significant economic reform. New government subsidies were allocated for government-owned industries, major wage concessions were made to striking coal miners, and additional financial commitments were announced for the beleagured Russian defense industries.

Table 7.3   MEMBERSHIP IN THE STATE DUMA, RESULTS OF THE ELECTIONS OF DECEMBER 1995

Party	Leader	Percent of Vote on Party Lists	Party-list Seats	Single-Member Seats	Total Seats 1995	Total Seats 1993
1. *Communist Parties*						
Communist Party of Russian Federation	G. Zyuganov	22.31	100	58	158	45
Agrarian Party of Russia	M. Lapshin	3.78	0	20	20	55
Power to the People	N. Ryzhkov	2.10	0	9	9	NA
Communists-Working Russia	V. Tyul'kin	4.52	0	1	1	0
2. *National-Patriotic Parties*						
Liberal Democratic Party of Russia	V. Zhirinovsky	11.06	50	1	51	64
Congress of Russian Communities	Yu. Skokov	4.29	0	5	5	NA
3. *Democratic Parties*						
Yabloko	G. Yavlinsky	6.93	31	14	45	25
Russia's Democratic Choice/ United Dem.	Y. Gaidar	3.90	0	9	9	55
4. *Statist Parties*						
Our Home Is Russia	V. Chernomyrdin	9.89	44	10	54	NA
Women of Russia	A. Fedulova	4.60	0	3	3	23
Party of Workers' Self-Management	S. Fedorov	4.01	0	1	1	NA
5. *Others*						
Independents		—	—	77	77	} 183
Minor, regional parties		—	—	17	17	
Total		77.39	225	225	450	450

Source: ITAR-TASS, December 22, 1995.

These shifts in policy—which follow a pattern of movement away from reform that was evident ever since 1993—when considered in the context of the much more assertative foreign policy rhetoric of new Foreign Minister Yevgeny Primakov,[66] indicate a dramatic shift in policies of Yeltsin's government. During the electoral campaign President Yeltsin continued to make budgetary commitments that were viewed as potentially inflationary and to make various promises about reasserting Russia's role in world affairs.

Given the new distribution of political power in the Duma, it was to be expected that control over the key committees would be lost by the democrats and centrists who chaired these important bodies. On January 17, 1996, Gennadi Seleznev, former editor of *Pravda,*

deputy speaker in the prior Duma, and a key figure in the Communist Party of Russia, was elected speaker of the Duma, with 231 votes (5 more than the required 226). His support came from his own party, the Agrarian Party, Power to the People-Communists, and some Liberal Democrats. Seleznev announced that his first priority would be to review and act on more than 500 pieces of legislation left over from the previous Duma. According to media reports of January 28, 1996, Communists head 9 of the 28 parliamentary committees (including those concerned with legislation, economic policy, security and veterans' affairs). The Agrarian Party and Power to the People chair two and three committees, respectively. Zhirinovsky's Liberal Democrats head four committees, as do members of the centrist party Our Home Is Russia and the democratic Yabloko.

The comeback of the Communists, who were banned in 1991 after the failed coup attempt and declared dead by many analysts, can be explained in part by the success of Gennadi Zyuganov and others in the party to take up the call of Russian nationalism, while also supporting the interests of the ordinary Russian whose entire existence has been disrupted by events of the past decade. The image of the new Communist Party is one that mixes elements of traditional Marxism with Great Russian nationalism. Zyuganov and his party have responded more effectively than either the democrats or the radical nationalists to provide the Russian people, disillusioned and demoralized by the collapse of their imperial state and of much of the social net that had undergirded their personal existence, with hope for the future. Only the Communists, Zyuganov has argued, can prevent the breakup of the Russian Federation or the dominance of crime and corruption in Russian society. The results of the 1995 parliamentary elections indicate that millions of Russians have found this message attractive.

In early 1996 Zyuganov announced his candidacy for the presidential elections of June 1996. Most of the other parties of the Left announced their willingness to support his candidacy. On February 14, despite the opposition of Yegor Gaidar and other reformers and public opinion polls that indicated that his support among Russian voters remained below 10 percent, President Yeltsin announced from his home city of Yekaterinburg that he would run for reelection.[67] With the takeover of the Duma by political forces opposed to a continuation of the reform policies of the prior four years, led by the Communists, the election of Zyuganov would result in a reversal of many of the political and economic developments of the past decade. Duma speaker Seleznev, for example, noted the Communist Party's commitment to eliminating the presidency and the Duma and reestablishing a Soviet-style governmental system with a Council of Ministers accountable to a reinstated Supreme Soviet.

The presidential election campaign of spring 1996 presented two quite different perspectives on the future direction that Russia should take. For example, in mid-May Gennadi Zyuganov outlined the main points of an economic program committed to a centrally-managed economy. Although some forms of private ownership would be permitted, the state would own a controlling share in various sectors of the economy, including energy, transport, military industry, education, and science. Zyuganov's program envisaged strong state intervention to stimulate investment, control prices, and protect domestic producers. Zyuganov also called for forms of censorship to protect Russian culture and morals. Yeltsin, on the other hand, committed himself to a continuation of the reforms that had characterized the prior four and a half years, although he seldom spoke of privatization and, as part of his electoral campaign, made a vast array of expensive commitments that threatened to undermine economic stabilization and contradicted commitments made to the International Monetary Fund. Only in the foreign policy area, where Russian policy had already become much more assertive than it was in the first year of independence, were the differences in policy minimal.

In some respects Russia has made substantial progress in establishing the bases for a functioning democratic system. The constitution approved in December 1993 provides the framework for a political system and for the legal transfer of political power that has functioned. The fact is that, despite serious political differences among political parties and between the executive and the legislature, legislation has been passed, and political compromises have been reached. What is less positive, however, is the fact that there is little evidence to lead one to conclude that democratic values have taken root among the majority of the Russian population, including the political elites. Of crucial importance for the future of democracy in Russia will be President Yeltsin's commitment to constitutional procedures and the outcome of the political struggle between Prime Minister Chernomyrdin and Security Council head Lebed.

Political developments elsewhere throughout the Commonwealth of Independent States generally have been even less positive in most countries than those in Russia from the perspective of establishing functioning democratic systems. Many of the countries have very weak national governments that have found it virtually impossible to govern. Civil war, sectionalism, and virtual anarchy have characterized large portions of Georgia, Moldova, and Tajikistan, for example. Across Central Asia presidential dictatorships of the Right and the Left have emerged as the predominant form of government. In a referendum in Kyrgystan in February 1996, for example, with voting figures akin to those of the Soviet past, more than 90 percent of the population voted with over 95 percent favoring expanded powers for President Askar Akaev. In Tajikistan the old Communist *nomenklatura* rules the country and is carrying out, with Russian assistance, a relentless struggle against its political and religious enemies. Uzbekistan under President Islam Karimov and increasingly Nursultan Nazarbayev's Kazakstan are ruled by presidential decree. In the Transcaucas continuing warfare and ethinic strife make any semblance of political stabilization and democratization a virtual impossibility.

Only in the three western states—Belarus, Ukraine, and Moldova—can one begin to speak of the foundations for stable participatory political systems. Even here, however, prospects for long-term stability and for the resolution of serious underlying problems remain problematic. Throughout the region, the two central political questions of importance concern the relationship with Russia and the degree to which effective independence can be maintained and the creation of productive economies from the residue of the old Soviet system can proceed. Moreover, in Belarus President Lukashenka has resorted increasingly to police brutality against peaceful demonstrators and the arrest of journalists and members of parliament (in violation of the right of immunity).

Toward a Market Economy

The third major task facing Russia and the other post-Communist states—after state and nation building and the establishment of democratic institutions—has been the creation of the institutions needed for a productive market economy. It is important to recall that prior to the Gorbachev reforms—and, in fact, in most respects at the time of the implosion of the Soviet Union—Russia lacked most of the prerequisites for a market economy. Central planning, price controls, the absence of a real banking system, the lack of a sense of entrepreneurship were but a few of the characteristics of the old economic system that impeded the emergence of a market economy. Moreover, the efforts at reform, both under Mikhail Gorbachev and Boris Yeltsin, resulted in precipitous declines in production in both the industrial and the agricultural sectors. By 1995 estimated gross national product for the Russian Federation had fallen to less than 53 percent of the figure for 1989 and industrial output was only 47 percent as high as six years earlier—although production data for 1995 indicate that the depression may have bottomed out. Indeed, production in certain areas, such as the iron and steel and chemical and petrochemical industries, actually rose for the first time since the collapse of the Soviet Union.[68] Yet, overall, the economic situation in the country has been in disastrous decline with the standard of living falling an additional 12 percent during the first nine months of 1995 (see Table 7.4).[69]

Despite the disastrous collapse in Russian production, there are those who view President Yeltsin's economic reform program as "Russia's Success Story," to cite the title of a recent article by Anders Åslund, a noted Swedish economist and former economic advisor to the Russian government. The gist of his argument is the following:

> The Western caricature of Russia as a destitute country on the verge of either collapse or falling into the hands of fascists could not be more wrong. Naturally, things are far from perfect, but no one thought communism would go away without costs. In a new openness all problems are discussed in the Russian media, and often exaggerated. But few in the West write about Russia's successes, like the end of shortages and the risk of famine. Moreover, the true disaster of other former Soviet republics is often confused with Russia's. Of course major problems such as crime and inflation remain in Russia, but even monthly inflation fell to five percent in June [1994].[70]

Åslund and others support their argument by noting that much of the supposed depression of the Russian economy is not real. Under Communism overreporting of production was notorious; under the current capitalist system underreporting to avoid taxes is even more prevalent. Åslund maintains that the consumption of electricity is probably a better indicator of actual industrial production that the output statistics. Here one finds decreases one-third to one-half those of production statistics. The central problems of the emerging capitalist economy in Russia, according to Åslund, result from the rise of organized crime and its growing role in controlling an ever increasing portion of the economy and the unfettered domination of the workers by management in the workplace. He concludes that Yeltsin and Prime Minister Viktor Chernomyrdin, to whom he gives much of the credit for the success, have created the foundations for a functioning free-market economy. The issue is not the impending collapse of Russia, but rather the direction that it will take in the future.

Other analysts—mainly those who emphasize the negative impact of the changes on the lives of individual Russians—paint a very different picture of the results of the economic restructuring that has occurred in Russia since independence. They note that the costs of the "shock therapy" approach to economic reform introduced by President Yeltsin were extraordinarily disruptive and contributed to severe dislocations in the economy. Shock therapy refers to a set of short-run policies that were designed to create a free and open economic market and to achieve macroeconomic stability. As the first part of this program, Yeltsin deregulated prices on most consumer goods on January 2, 1992. Producers could set whatever price they pleased on their goods, with distributors adding an additional 25 percent. As a result, prices soon quadrupled on foodstuffs. However, the reformers expected that the increased prices would encourage all producers to bring their products to market, thereby eliminating shortages and thus reducing prices once again. The expectation was that after an initial period of inflation, supply would catch up with demand. However, this did not occur, for in many areas of the economy—including large segments of the consumer sector—monopolies that did not respond effectively to factors of supply and demand dominated production or distribution.

A second important aspect of the shock therapy was the attempt to stabilize the Russian ruble and to make it fully convertible on international financial markets—the latter in response to the demand of the International Monetary Fund as a precondition for financial assistance. By the standards of free-market economies, the Communist monetary system was exceptionally stable. Prices

Table 7.4   KEY ECONOMIC TRENDS IN RUSSIA, 1990–1995

	Real Index, 1989 = 100						Year-to-Year Change in Percent					
	1990	1991	1992	1993	1994	1995*	1990	1991	1992	1993	1994	1995**
GNP	98.0	89.2	72.2	63.6	54.0	52.6	−2.0	−9.0	−19.0	−12.0	−15.0	−4.0
Gross Industrial Output	99.9	91.9	74.6	63.6	50.3	47.3	−0.1	−8.0	−18.8	−14.8	−20.9	−3.0
Gross Agricultural Output	96.4	92.1	83.3	80.2	73.0	72.0	−3.6	−4.5	−9.5	−3.8	−9.0	−8.0
Gross Investment in Fixed Capital	100.1	84.6	50.8	44.7	32.6	31.0	0.1	−15.5	−40.0	−12.0	−27.0	−13.0

*Forecast

**Percent data for 1995 come from Interfax/CIS Statistical Committee Statistical Report 4–5/199; *Delovoi mir,* January 17, 1996, pp. 3–5.

Source: *Russian Economic Monitor, PlanEcon Report: Developments in the Economies of Eastern Europe and the Former USSR,* vol. 10, nos. 7–8 (1995), p. 5.

and currency exchange rates were fixed by decree and often did not change officially for decades. Inflation was allegedly eliminated, which facilitated long-term planning. In fact, this was but an illusion. The Russian ruble itself was a mysterious entity that had no monetary value outside the Soviet Union and had multiple rates of exchange for convertible world currencies. Initially the Russian Central Bank, under the direction of Viktor Gerashchenko, continued to provide enormous credits to enterprises that otherwise would have gone bankrupt, thereby contributing significantly to the hyperinflation that Russia suffered in 1992 and 1993. Only after July 1993 did President Yeltsin and Prime Minister Chernomyrdin bring the Central Bank under government control. The tight money policy of the next two years contributed to bringing inflation down and stabilizing the value of the Russian ruble. The attempt to deal with this issue required major government budget cuts, especially in the military sector where earlier cuts had reduced military spending from about 25 percent of GNP in the USSR to less than 5 percent. Despite these efforts, the Russian government until 1995 consistently ran budget deficits in the neighborhood of 9–10 percent per year of GNP, thereby contributing to the explosive inflation that characterized the economy through 1994.

A third major aspect of the radical economic reforms introduced in Russia in early 1992 was privatization of Russia's state-owned industries. Privatization of the consumer service sector of the economy proceeded relatively smoothly. It has been quite a different matter with the large industrial enterprises, most of which are still not privatized. The privatization of these large industrial complexes brought with it a whole series of potentially explosive social and political problems. First, the fact that most industrial enterprises in the former USSR were not really competitive and did not incorporate contemporary technology into their production meant that they would not be competitive in a market economy. The privatization of large industrial enterprises, therefore, would likely bring with it widespread unemployment for workers considered redundant. A related matter concerned housing and social services, much of which in the former Soviet Union was provided by employers. As enterprises were privatized, or as state enterprises lost portions of their government subsidy, responsibility for housing and for other social services devolved on local governments ill-prepared to deal with them.

One group in Russia that has benefited greatly from the substantial privatization that has occurred is the former Soviet *nomenklatura*. The liberalization of state control over the prices of commodities and consumer goods, as well as the legalization of domestic and foreign trade, opened up substantial opportunities for the so-called "new Russians"—Russia's new entrepreneurial class which includes a disproportionately large percentage of former state and party officials. It was these officials who commanded the expertise and were positioned to take advantage of the new opportunities open to them.[71]

Reform of the agricultural sector of the Russian economy has lagged far behind that in the service and industrial sectors. In fact, it is in agriculture that the strongest resistance to change can be found in Russia, and it is in rural Russia that the Communist and Agrarian Parties of the left find major support. The Russian government has lacked a coherent plan for agriculture and what efforts were make to privatize land holdings and develop effective market mechanisms have proven to be counterproductive. In part, this results in the continued dominance of the old Soviet *nomenklatura* at the district level in Russia. The government's tight money policy and the high cost of credit and production has actually resulted in a drop of agricultural production and of food processing.

The victory of the Communist Party in the December 1995 elections and the strong showing of their ideological allies, the Agrarian Party, is likely to result in increases in subsidies for agriculture. However, as has been very evident since the late 1980s, the Russian countryside is politically weak and not likely to exert major influence on government policy. This means that the prospects for real reform in the countryside remain very low.[72]

A fourth element of the reform program put into place by Yeltsin's government, one closely related to monetary reform, was the creation of a modern banking system.[73] Although banks existed in the former Soviet Union, their primary function was to distribute governmental subsidies to enterprises. They did not play the role, as they do in market economies, of taking risks by supporting entrepreneurial projects. They played no role in decision making about the directions that the economy would take. After Russian independence a whole new system of banking emerged in Russia—not without serious problems of corruption and an unhealthy role of organized crime—that is essential to the emergence of a functioning market economy.

Possibly the most serious problem that has resulted as a side effect from the economic reforms has been the emergence of organized crime, or so-called mafia groups, across Russia. The objective is control of the lucrative private economic activity that, in many areas of Russia, is flourishing. Among their major targets are the private banks that have mushroomed in Russia in an environment with very few and very inadequate regulatory controls. These have provided great opportunities for sophisticated swindling and scams. Smuggling, protection rackets, and extortion are other widespread forms of economic crime. Much of the new criminal class finds its roots in unemployed or underpaid members of the former Soviet security forces. They also have close ties to supposedly "legitimate" businessmen and politicians. Moreover, they are not loath to execute or assassinate bankers, politicians, and journalists

who either resist their activities or report on them. Governmental bodies at the federal, provincial, and local level have devoted major resources to combating organized crime; however, according to one Russian analyst, "the wave of organized crime continues to sweep across Russia. . . . There is ample evidence to support the MVD's [Ministry of Internal Affairs] recent declaration that 70 percent of the country is ruled by the mafia."[74]

Although many serious problems have been associated with the efforts of Russian reformers to create a market economy, they have made significant progress in laying the foundations for such an economy. During the first four years of the new Russian state, the "economy was effectively demilitarized, decentralized, demonopolized, privatized, monetarized and reoriented toward the people's needs," in the words of one analyst.[75] For example, one American economist lists Russia tenth out of 25 post-Communist states on an index of "radicality" of economic reforms—ahead of all other post-Soviet countries except the three Baltic states.[76] Economic data for 1995 also indicate that the depression may have bottomed out. Even though production did fall for the sixth straight year, the losses were far less than those experienced in the previous three years. When one

The stock market in Russia.

takes into account the fact that production in the private sector is significantly underreported, the economy most likely equaled production for 1994. Inflation dropped from a monthly rate of 18 percent in January to 4 percent in December, and 2.2 percent in April 1996 in part the result of a drop in the government budget deficit from 11 percent of GNP in 1994 to only 5 percent in 1995. Another related accomplishment was the fact that the ruble stabilized against Western currencies. This, in turn, meant that "imported inflation"—that is, rising prices of imported goods resulting from a decline in the value of the ruble—virtually ceased, thereby reducing the difficulties of the Central Bank in fighting inflation. Other important positive developments related to reduced inflation and stability of the ruble have been Russian firms' ability to expand exports—Russia had a $23 billion surplus in its foreign trade in 1995, based on exports of $64 billion and imports of $41 billion—and the beginning of a return to Russia of capital that had earlier fled abroad. The positive trend in trade continued into 1996. Agriculture suffered a disastrous year, with grain production 22 percent below that of 1994 and total production down 8 percent.

According to government and private analysts, 1996 should see the beginning of economic recovery in Russia with industrial production up 2–4 percent.[77] The situation in agriculture, however, will depend upon both the weather and the ability of the government to introduce the structural changes required to stimulate agricultural production. These estimates could be confounded, however, by political developments—for example, a shift in the priorities of Russian economic policy by increasing government subsidies to noncompetitive enterprises. Other factors that currently hamper Russia's economic development include (1) the failure to date to implement the full set of legal reforms necessary to guarantee predictability, validity and enforcement of contracts, property rights, and the like; (2) the major differences across regions in the implementation of economic reforms and the "take off" of the economy; (3) the growing social cleavages across Russian society and the political pressure that these cleavages exert on government policy; (4)

the limited amount of capital available for investment; and (5) the ineptitude of the governmental apparatus.

In general the economic situation in the other post-Soviet states—except in the Baltics where developments have been unexpectedly positive—is bleaker than that in Russia. Most of the other countries have suffered severely because of the break-up of the single economic space that characterized the USSR, created to tie regional economies together and ensure Moscow's control. Their access to needed raw materials and energy, as well as their access to markets, has been disrupted. Moreover, the focus of government policy throughout most of the CIS has been on issues of internal security or ways to assure independence from Russia rather than on economic reform. Not until 1995, for example, did the government of Ukraine begin to look seriously at the question of economic reform, although economic trends in 1995 were generally quite positive. The depression suffered by all the post-Soviet states has been even more severe throughout the other CIS states than it is in the Russian Federation.

Toward the Future

Russia has made much progress in the triple requirements of state building, democratization, and marketization—although most other post-Soviet states outside the Baltics have seen little success in one or more of the areas. However, much more remains to be done if the successes of the first four years are not to founder and be lost. With the major exception of Chechnya, the most serious challenges to Russian authority in the ethnically based republics have been resolved. However, the issue of federal relations with both the republics and the provinces remains serious, with control over local resources high on the priority list of the subnational units and Moscow's ability to impose and collect taxes in question.

Significant progress has also been made in Russia in creating the institutions associated with democracy. However, it is in this area that Russia has the most yet to accomplish. First, there is the appeal among many in the Russian political elite—including President Yeltsin himself—for authoritarian approaches to solving problems. Moreover, the costs of change have fallen disproportionately on various groups in Russian society. Although significant strides have been made in rehabilitating the Russian economy, the benefits are not falling equally to all groups. Those displaced by the changes or for whom the presumed security of the Communist past remains an overriding concern—including especially the elderly, industrial workers, and the rural population—blame Yeltsin and the reformers for their depressed plight. They, as well as those dismayed by the decline in Russia's world status and the loss of the old empire and by the pervasive influence of organized crime, are attracted to the supposedly easy solutions offered by the Communists of Gennadi Zyuganov or the nationalists led by Vladimir Zhirinovsky. It is ironic that the very democratic institutions that have been put in place in Russia are being used by those committed to reestablishing a more authoritarian system that would return to many of the policies of the past.

Another indication of the weakness of democracy in Russia—and a problem that was highlighted during the presidential election campaign—relates to government ownership of much of the mass media and of printing plants and of the continued existence of partial censorship. Many Western commentators noted, for example, the virtually total domination of President Yeltsin in media coverage in the weeks running up to the election. For example, while he and his program were daily given prominence on television and in the press, the content of Zyuganov's speeches was ignored in favor of images of anti-communist protestors at his rallies.

Finally, despite many serious problems that remain in the Russian economy, substantial progress was made in a very short period of time in dismantling the old command economy and creating a functioning market economy. What remains to be done is to deal with issues related to income distribution and the collapse of the social network, to corruption and the role of criminal elements in the economy, and to the depressed status of rural areas and many provincial cities. The key question is whether the Russian people still have the patience to wait for the solution to these problems within the context of a democratic political system and a market economy.

KEY TERMS

"Battle of Moscow"
Bolsheviks
Central Committee
Cheka
Commonwealth of Independent States (CIS)
CPSU (Communist Party of the Soviet Union)
"cult of personality"
"democratization"
General Secretary
glasnost'
KGB (Committee for State Security)
Komsomol
Mensheviks
nation building
nomenklatura
oblast'
oligarchy
partocracy
perestroika
Politburo
p.p.o. (primary party organization)
Secretariat
"shock therapy"
State Duma
Supreme Soviet
totalitarian rule
"triple transition"
Workers' Opposition

FURTHER READINGS

Adelman, Jonathan R. *Torrents of Spring: Soviet and Post-Soviet Politics* (New York: McGraw-Hill, 1995).

Armstrong, John A. *The Politics of Totalitarianism* (New York: Random House, 1961).

Barner-Barry, Carol, and Cynthia A. Hody. *The Politics of Change: The Transformation of the Former Soviet Union* (New York: St. Martin's Press, 1995).

Breslauer, George W. *Khrushchev and Brezhnev as Leaders: Building Authority in Soviet Politics.* (London and Boston: Allen and Unwin, 1982).

Conquest, Robert. *Power and Policy in the USSR* (New York: St. Martin's Press, 1961).

Carrère d'Encausse, Hélène. *Confiscated Power: How Soviet Russia Really Works* (New York: Harper & Row, 1982).

Daniels, Robert V. *The End of the Communist Revolution* (London and New York: Routledge, 1993).

Dawisha, Karen, and Bruce Parrott, series eds. *The International Politics of Eurasia* (Armonk, NY, and London: M. E. Sharpe, 1994–1996. A ten-volume series with the following eight titles already published:

The Legacy of History in Russia and the New States of Eurasia, ed. by S. Frederick Starr, vol. 1 (1994).

National Identity and Ethnicity in Russia and the New States of Eurasia, ed. by Roman Szporluk, vol. 2 (1994).

The Politics of Religion in Russia and the New States of Eurasia, ed. by Michael Bourdeaux, vol. 3 (1994).

The Making of Foreign Policy in Russia and the New States of Eurasia, ed. by Adeed Dawisha and Karen Dawisha, vol. 4 (1995).

State Building and Military Power in Russia and the New States of Eurasia, ed. by Bruce Parrott, vol. 5 (1995).

The Nuclear Challenge in Russia and the New States of Eurasia, ed. by George Quester, vol. 6 (1995).

Political Culture and Civil Society in Russia and the New States of Eurasia, ed. by Vladimir Tismaneanu, vol. 7 (1995).

Economic Transition in Russia and the New States of Eurasia, ed. by Bartlomiej Kaminski, vol. 8 (1995).

Fainsod, Merle. *How Russia Is Ruled,* rev. ed. (Cambridge, MA: Harvard University Press, 1967).

Hough, Jerry F., and Merle Fainsod. *How the Soviet Union Is Governed* (Cambridge, MA: Harvard University Press, 1979).

Knight, Amy W. *The KGB: Police and Politics in the Soviet Union* (Boston: Unwin Hyman, 1988).

Knight, Amy W. *Spies Without Cloaks: The KGB's Successors* (Princeton: Princeton University Press, 1996).

Laqueur, Walter. *The Dream That Failed: Reflections on the Soviet Union* (New York and Oxford: Oxford University Press, 1994).

Löwendardt, John. *The Reincarnation of Russia: Struggling with the Legacy of Communism, 1990–1994* (Durham, NC: Duke University Press, 1995).

McCauley, Martin, ed. *Khrushchev and Khrushchevism* (Bloomington: Indiana University Press, 1988).

McNeal, Robert H. *Stalin: Man and Ruler* (New York: New York University Press, 1988).

Powell, David E. *Antireligious Propaganda in the Soviet Union* (Cambridge, MA: M.I.T. Press, 1975).

Ramet, Sabrina P. [a.k.a. Pedro]. *Cross and Commissar: The Politics of Religion in Eastern Europe and the Soviet Union* (Bloomington: Indiana University Press, 1987).

Roeder, Philip G. *Red Sunset: The Failure of Soviet Politics* (Princeton, NJ: Princeton University Press, 1993).

Sakwa, Richard. *Russian Politics and Society* (London and New York: Routledge, 1993).

Schapiro, Leonard. *The Communist Part of the Soviet Union,* rev. ed. (New York: Random House, 1971).

Jonathan, Steele. *Eternal Russia: Yeltsin, Gorbachev, and the Mirage of Democracy* (Cambridge, MA: Harvard University Press, 1994).

Ulam, Adam B. *The Bolsheviks: The Intellectual and Political History of the Triumph of Communism in Russia* (New York: Macmillan, 1965).

Ulam, Adam B. *Stalin: The Man and His Era* (New York: Viking Press, 1973).

White, Stephen. *After Gorbachev,* 4th ed. (Cambridge and New York: Cambridge University Press, 1994).

Public Policy

The Soviet Union acquired the status of a superpower not only by being on the victorious side in World War II, but also as a consequence of deliberate policies pursued by its leadership after 1945. These policies, as well as the Soviet (Marxist-Leninist) view of international relations, served to maximize Soviet power and caused many countries to be suspicious or fearful of Soviet intentions. The Soviet Union's human and material resources were mobilized and its military capabilities rapidly developed so that it could acquire nuclear parity or even superiority. The Soviet rulers were unashamedly power-oriented, and the 1977 Soviet Constitution (Article 62) obligated all citizens to strengthen the "might and authority" of the Soviet State.

The policies and actions of other countries also contributed to the Soviet Union's emergence as a great power. The Soviet Union was sought as an ally by the French and Czechs in 1934; negotiations with the British in 1939 eventually broke down at the time when the Soviet Union was faced with the possibility of a two-front war—in Asia where they were already fighting Japanese troops based in the Japanese province of Manchukuo (occupied Manchuria) and also in Europe against Nazi Germany. Eventually Stalin concluded a "nonaggression" pact with Nazi Germany in August 1939 and two weeks after Germany had invaded Poland joined in the military campaign that led to the destruction of the Polish state and had precipitated World War II. The Nazi-Soviet Pact enabled the USSR to annex western Ukraine and western Belorussia (Belarus), as well as Estonia, Latvia, Lithuania, and the region of Bessarabia (which had been part of Romania between 1918 and 1940)—territories with a non-Russian population of more than 22 million. Hitler's invasion of the Soviet Union in June 1941 involved Stalin's regime in World War II, despite efforts to remain neutral.

The war was very costly to the Soviet Union (resulting in more than 20 million deaths) and initially involved a year and a half of military retreat. It was won, but not solely because of Soviet patriotism, Russian nationalism, or belief in Marxism-Leninism. The Soviet victory was also the result of other factors, including brutal German occupation policies that provided no attractive alternative to Stalin's rule, and, in part, to $12 billion of U.S. Lend-Lease aid made available unconditionally to Stalin's dictatorship by the Roosevelt administration. In addition, the USSR was spared having to fight a war on two fronts in Europe and in the Far East in 1941–1945 thanks to the decision of the Japanese militarists to attack the United States at Pearl Harbor and to seize Southeast Asia, Indonesia, and the Philippines in 1941–1942, instead of attacking Siberia at the time that Soviet forces were retreating in the West.

The total defeat of Germany and Japan in 1945 and the weakened condition of France and Italy added to the Soviet Union's advantage and resulted in a U.S.-Soviet bipolarity in place of the prewar multipolar international situation. The U.S. policy of demanding Germany's unconditional surrender resulted in the postwar Soviet military presence in Central Europe.[78] The failure of Britain and the United States to prevent the establishment of Communist regimes in eight East European countries and in North Korea (largely as a result of Soviet military occupation) led to the emergence of a Soviet bloc under Moscow's leadership. The wartime United Nations military alliance that defeated Nazi Germany and Japan deteriorated quickly, as Stalin launched an intensive campaign to end the U.S. atomic weapons monopoly; the Soviets succeeded in detonating an atomic bomb in 1949 and acquired the hydrogen bomb in 1953. In the 1960s and 1970s Soviet military power was deployed in Cuba, Angola, Ethiopia, Vietnam, South Yemen, and Afghanistan. The Soviet Union's lead in the acquisition of the heaviest intercontinental ballistic missiles, the largest nuclear warheads, a limited antimissile defense capability, a hunter-killer satellite, the largest submarine fleet in naval history, and the first mobile intercontinental ballistic missiles, did not prove the success or even the viability of the Soviet system. In fact, as Gorbachev was later to admit, the arms race resulted in a profligate waste of scarce resources in the Soviet Union and contributed significantly to the economic crisis that he inherited in 1985.

THE SOVIET VIEW OF INTERNATIONAL RELATIONS

Soviet rulers viewed and understood international politics largely in terms of Marxism-Leninism, although traditional Russian expansionism and a sense of a special Russian role in history (Russian messianism) also affected the Soviet view of foreign countries. Marxism-Leninism emphasized conflict and the class struggle as the motive force in historical development. Class warfare was extended into the realm of international relations, and a certain level of tension and conflict was regarded as a normal condition in relations between states; however, tension was to be kept within limits in order to avoid high-risk military confrontations or "adventurist" undertakings. By the 1970s, after the U.S. military defeat in Vietnam and the emergence of a growing number of countries in the developing world that proclaimed the establishment of Marxist-Leninist regimes, the Brezhnev leadership was especially confident about the future. As late as 1986 the CPSU Program declared, "The dialectics of development are such that the very same means which capitalism puts to use with the aim of strengthening its positions inevitably lead to an aggravation of all its deep-seated contradictions. Imperialism is parasitical, decaying and moribund capitalism; it marks the eve of the socialist revolution."[79]

In the Soviet view of international politics, at least until the late 1980s, quantitative changes were seen as leading to qualitative change that favored the Soviet Union. International developments were depicted and analyzed in terms of the "correlation of forces" concept, which reflected the relations between the great powers—actually, the strategic balance. Foremost among the Soviet Union's objectives was the enhancement of its strategic power and its ability to influence the actions of other states and play a prominent, if not dominant, role in the world.

Soviet foreign policy makers sought to prevent the formation of coalitions that could be directed against the Soviet Union and result in its isolation. Moscow attempted to divide its "capitalist" opponents by driving wedges between them and disrupting alliances, such as NATO, established to deter the possible threat of Soviet aggression. The Soviet Union always attempted to isolate the state that it regarded as its principal enemy: Great Britain was cast in this role in the 1920s, Nazi Germany in the 1930s, and the United States after World War II.

The Soviet Union also sought to retain some degree of primacy in the Communist world. This claim was first asserted in 1919 when Lenin founded the Communist International (Comintern). Although this organization was dissolved in 1943, the CPSU continued its practice of interfering in the affairs of foreign Communist parties and governments. The USSR intervened militarily in Hungary (in 1956), in Czechoslovakia (in 1968), in Afghanistan (in 1979–1989), and threatened to intervene in Poland (in 1991) in order to overthrow Communist leaders and install or keep in power others deemed more loyal to Moscow. The CPSU rejected the Yugoslav Communist attitude that approved of polycentrism (the existence of several centers of Communism), but had to acquiesce in the fragmentation of the international Communist movement while claiming a special role as the world's first socialist state.

The accumulation of serious, even debilitating, domestic problems and a costly arms race may have been the factors that prompted Gorbachev at the Twenty-seventh Party Congress in 1986 to present a far more sobering picture of world affairs than that proclaimed by his predecessors:

> The present-day world is complex, diverse, dynamic, permeated with contending tendencies, [and] full of contradictions. It is a world of very complex alternatives, anxieties and hopes. Never before has our earthly home been subjected to such political and physical overloads. Never has man exacted so much tribute from nature, and never has he proved to be so vulnerable to the might that he himself has created.[80]

This was a harbinger of Gorbachev's "new thinking" which led to a general reappraisal of Soviet foreign policy and had profound consequences for both that policy and for the world at large.

THE STRATEGIC RETREAT: FROM SUPERPOWER TO SUPPLICANT

When Gorbachev assumed the Soviet leadership in 1985, he eased out of office the foreign minister, Andrei Gromyko, who had served in that post for 18 years. He appointed an outsider, Eduard Shevardnadze, former head of the Communist Party of Georgia, for the purpose of undertaking a thorough reorganization of the foreign ministry and a reorientation of foreign policy.

As Gorbachev probed into the morass of the Soviet Union's internal and foreign affairs, he apparently concluded that the empire's foreign commitments greatly exceeded its capabilities. He sought to end the "isolation of Socialist countries from the common stream of world civilization."[81] He undoubtedly understood that the assertive and aggressive policies of his predecessors had set the Soviet Union apart as an abnormal entity that lacked respect in the international community and fell further behind the technologically advanced world—and, in some areas, behind the industrializing states of East Asia. Central to the reassessment in Soviet foreign policy (termed "new thinking" by Gorbachev) was the recognition that the domestic economic and political reforms necessary to rejuvenate the Soviet state simply did not permit continued profligacy in Soviet foreign policy. Rather, a cutback in commitments abroad and the redirection of resources to domestic needs, as well as improved relations with the West and a less threatening international environment, were essential for the success of Gorbachev's domestic reform program.

The Reagan administration's decision to pursue an antiballistic missile defense (Strategic Defense Initiative) posed the fundamental question of whether the Soviet Union could afford to compete in this new stage in the arms race. In the 1970s the USSR had unwisely deployed the intermediate-range SS–20 missile in Europe and had mistakenly thought that this would not elicit an effective response from NATO. When it did, the Kremlin was forced to rethink its entire missile deployment strategy and much more.

This led to the December 1987 and July 1991 agreements between Washington and Moscow which significantly reduced intermediate and strategic missiles.

Gorbachev's foreign policy also included abandonment of the so-called Brezhnev Doctrine, under which the Soviet Union engaged in armed intervention in foreign countries to prevent the overthrow of Communist rule. The doctrine failed its most crucial test in Afghanistan, from which the Kremlin had to withdraw its forces in 1989 when the cost of occupation became too prohibitive. In 1986–1987 Gorbachev had attempted to crush the Afghan resistance by means of a punitive aerial offensive directed against the civilian population. This offensive failed because of the antiaircraft missiles provided to the resistance by Western and Muslim countries, but it did not prevent Gorbachev from being awarded the Nobel Peace Prize in 1990.[82]

The Soviet failure in Afghanistan demonstrated its vulnerability and fueled resistance to Communist rule in Eastern Europe. In 1989, when semicompetitive elections in Poland forced by domestic opposition resulted in the emergence of a government dominated by the Solidarity trade union movement, the Soviets accepted the results. When thousands of East Germans sought refuge in the West via Hungary and Czechoslovakia, where officials proved to be indifferent or tolerant of the exodus, and more still demonstrated for democracy in East German cities, Gorbachev advised the East German authorities that Soviet troops would not come to their support. The Soviet leadership was thus confronted with widespread resistance in several Eastern European countries. If Gorbachev had invoked the Brezhnev Doctrine, he would have faced a disruption in relations with the West which could have led to an economic embargo and general condemnation, and he would have destroyed his image as a reformer. Rather, Gorbachev had to acquiesce in the dissolution of the German Democratic Republic, demolition of the Berlin Wall, and the unification of Germany. He agreed to the withdrawal, in stages, of Soviet troops from Germany. Moreover, the pullout of Soviet troops from Czechoslovakia and Hungary in 1990–1991 presaged the dissolution on March 31, 1991, of the Warsaw Pact, the Soviet Union's Eastern European military alliance. All of this was done while the Soviet Union accepted the continued existence of NATO as a defensive alliance and the extension of NATO into eastern Germany after unification.

The Council for Mutual Economic Assistance (CMEA or Comecon), Moscow's organization for controlling the Eastern European economies for four decades, also unraveled, as the Soviets were forced to cut those countries loose because of increasing difficulties in their own economy. CMEA had been based on unrealistic planned pricing which made it impossible to determine real costs. It also lacked viable terms of trade because of the inconvertibility (and uncertain value) of the ruble, resulting in a reliance on barter arrangements.[83] Another aspect of the dramatic reorientation of Soviet foreign policy was the establishment of diplomatic relations between Moscow and the Vatican in March 1990.

The decision to retreat from the external Soviet empire in Eastern and Central Europe—despite objections from some in the military—was not accompanied by a comparable willingness to give up the internal empire that consisted of the 14 non-Russian republics and the many ethnically based regions of the Russian Federation. This intransigence on the part of Gorbachev and his cohorts could only prolong the agony that would confront the Soviet Union as it sought to cope with its insoluble domestic problems.

FOREIGN AND DOMESTIC POLICIES

Soviet foreign and domestic policies were always closely related. Ambitious and costly foreign policies influenced domestic policies, and domestic conditions necessitated changes in foreign policy. Initially, in order to save the Soviet regime and his dictatorship in 1918, Lenin had to accept a very unequal peace treaty with the Central Powers. Following years of war that greatly damaged the economy, he had to improve relations with some of the capitalist countries, especially Germany, to promote economic recovery. The Soviet Union joined the League of Nations in 1934 at a time when Stalin was engaged in costly industrialization and increasingly concerned about German expansion. Several years later, when the Soviet Union needed to avoid or postpone a war for which it was not prepared (as a result of the purging of the military and domestic dislocations), Stalin signed a pact with Nazi Germany.

Although the Soviet Union was a victor in World War II, the wartime alliance was replaced by the Cold War; Stalin closed the country to foreigners and lowered the "iron curtain" to conceal the country's weakness and extensive wartime losses and to ensure control over the population. When domestic conditions improved, the iron curtain was partly lifted in the mid–1950s. The detente of the 1970s was prompted, in part, by the need to import foreign technology and obtain financial credits. In the 1980s Gorbachev advocated a "dialog" and reaffirmed the "peaceful coexistence of states with different social systems" because of the deplorable state of the Soviet economy. The Soviet need for more butter instead of more guns required a degree of international stability and a reduction of tensions.

The crisis that confronted the Soviet leadership in the late 1980s was, to a considerable extent, a consequence of its costly foreign policy and excessive preoccupation with military power. Such priorities resulted in the development of a "command economy" with all *basic* economic policy decisions made by political authorities and central economic planners. Wages and prices, capital investment, and consumption levels were centrally determined rather than left to market conditions. Nevertheless, consumer resistance developed as buyers refused to purchase goods of inferior quality. The "second economy" (termed by Gorbachev the "shadow economy") produced more expensive goods of better quality but with materials obtained in questionable ways through illegal diversions, embezzlement, and barter. The command economy reflected a fear and distrust of market forces associated with capitalism, whether they represented consumer choices, the money market competing for available investment capital, or the supply market that provided the raw materials and components needed by industry. Such an economy could produce (and waste) large quantities of steel, coal, petroleum, and cement. It enabled the Soviet Union to engage in space exploration and to undertake costly large-scale projects, such as the heavily subsidized Baikal-Amur Mainline (BAM), a new rail line 3,200 kilometers long, linking central and eastern Siberia along a route north of the Trans-Siberian Railroad farther removed from the Chinese frontier. It enabled the Soviet Union to acquire a large modern merchant fleet and to develop several cities within the Arctic Circle.

However, the imbalances, the system of administratively fixed prices that did not reflect real costs, and the heavy subsidization of rents, food, public transportation, and other items led to a grossly distorted economy. In the absence of a money market (with capital investments often based on grants), capital was frequently wasted and not put to work quickly. Gorbachev criticized "laughable interest rates" that made efficient use of investment capital impossible and that resulted in the absence of a financial credit system.[84] Construction projects chronically lagged. A prominent factory director told the Nineteenth CPSU Conference: "With us it is regarded as normal to take 15 to 20 years to build a factory—and no one shoots himself, no one goes insane."[85] Wages rose ahead of productivity, and workers were paid to produce goods of inferior quality ("for the warehouse") that consumers refused to buy. Savings bank deposits grew at a rapid rate from a total of 18.7 billion rubles in 1965 to 337.8 billion rubles in 1989. This economic factor reflected an oversupply of money in relation to goods and services available. It also testified to a large pent-up demand, inflationary pressures, and the ability of Soviet citizens to obtain additional income. Gorbachev revealed that in the 1971–1985 period the ratio between the growth in the money supply and the increase in consumer goods was 3.1 to 2.0.[86]

Soviet leaders had claimed for years that the governmental budget had annual surpluses. This claim proved false, and Gorbachev informed the Central Committee that revenues were only able to cover expenditures by several extraordinary means. These included the sale on the world market of petroleum and other energy and material resources and the appropriation or transfer of funds belonging to enterprises and organizations (probably including tapping the reserves of the state insurance monopoly of the Ministry of Finance). The budget deficit was also dealt with by increasing the highly profitable production and sale of vodka and other spirits. Gorbachev revealed that the turnover (excise) tax revenues from the sale of alcohol during the Eleventh Five-Year Plan were 169 billion rubles.[87] He summarized the unsatisfactory financial condition of the Soviet Union when he told the Nineteenth CPSU Conference: "Over a period of many years expenditures of the state budget grew more rapidly than revenues. The budget deficit exerts pressure on the market, undermines the stability of the ruble and monetary circulation, [and] gives rise to inflationary processes."[88]

The priorities of the Soviet oligarchy resulted in serious dislocations in such areas as housing, public health and medical care, and ecology. In 1961, the CPSU Program promised that by 1980 every Soviet family would have its own apartment or dwelling. In 1986 the revised CPSU Program promised that by the year 2000 every Soviet family would have its own apartment or house. But, in 1988 Gorbachev stated that more than 35 million new apartments and dwellings were needed to fulfill the goal.[89]

In the area of public health, Minister of Public Health Dr. Yevgenii Chazov revealed to the Nineteenth CPSU Conference that for years leading Soviet officials had acknowledged the "bitter truth" of inadequate expenditures for health care, and yet had stated that there were higher priorities. Dr. Chazov revealed that as a result, in terms of the portion of gross domestic product devoted to public health, the USSR ranked in the middle of the seventh decile among 126 countries. In infant mortality it ranked fiftieth in the world—after Mauritius and Barbados—and in average life expectancy it ranked thirty-second. Dr. Chazov noted that a hospital for handicapped war veterans in Moscow was under construction for 11 years. He complained of the shortage of pharmaceuticals. He pointed out that "as a result of poor water supply and a low sanitary-hygienic level in many dairies and meat-packing enterprises . . . annually in the country 1.7 million persons suffer from severe gastro-intestinal ailments."[90] Dr. Chazov resigned from the ministry because Gorbachev would not provide the resources needed to improve the health care system.

Under *perestroika* serious ecological problems were finally acknowledged, including soil depletion and loss of humus content, cutting of forests without reforestation, and air pollution in 102 cities—often exceeding safe levels by ten times. Major rivers were badly polluted and the damming of the Volga and Dnieper (Dnipro) Rivers to form large reservoirs had deleterious ecological consequences. It was reported that the principal polluters of air, soil, and water were the enterprises of seven central economic ministries.[91] Such costly ecological disasters resulted from unsound planning and false priorities, as well as the Soviet leadership's neglect of domestic problems.

Seven decades of Communist rule exacted a horrendous toll in material, ecological, and human terms, and contributed to the degradation of Soviet society. The problems were exacerbated by the older population's willingness to accept an economy based on rationing, low wages, dependency, and artificial egalitarianism; any wealth was suspect unless it was acquired under Communist Party auspices. These conditions promoted cynicism, the stifling of initiative, and the decline of the work ethic and self-reliance.

If the Soviet system quite literally self-destructed, it was for a variety of reasons. State ownership of the economy had spawned a wasteful and inefficient central government bureaucracy staffed by surly, self-aggrandizing, and only marginally competent officials. The system provided tragic examples of what happens when the center imposes its power-driven priorities at the expense of republics and cities (see Feature 7.1). The metropole's priorities ignored the development of the infrastructure and resulted in inadequate and crumbling utilities systems in the largest cities. In St. Petersburg— a city with a population of more than 4 million—the water system became a disgraceful source of infectious disease and toxicity.

Vast sums were expended on excessive military programs, and space technology was given priority (largely for military purposes) at the expense of civilian needs. The security police organs expanded beyond real needs, and their employees were overpaid in comparison with other occupations. The extension of financial credits to a variety of third world and Communist countries left the Soviet Union an unsatisfied creditor as recipients such as Cuba, North Korea, and Vietnam expressed ingratitude. Ironically, Lenin's denunciation of the capitalist "bureaucratic-military institutions which subordinate everything to themselves and suppress everything" was actually applicable to the Soviet bureaucracy and the military and security establishments.[92]

THE PRICE OF EMPIRE

The peoples of the Soviet Union bore the enormous costs of an assertive foreign policy. Maintaining the empire involved spending more than 25 percent of the Soviet gross domestic product for military purposes. It meant reliance on conscription and the rejection of conscientious objection. Non-Russian conscripts were frequently abused while in military service, and homicide and suicide rates among them were excessively high. Service in the Soviet army was reduced from three to two years in 1967, and service in the navy was reduced from four to three years. At that time, compulsory military training with weapons practice for both sexes was introduced into the secondary schools.

Empire meant neglect of domestic problems. Its very size in territorial terms created large bureaucratic establishments that declined in competence and effectiveness. In addition to costly military forces, it required large police establishments to keep subject peoples intimidated and to impose internal order and an apparent unity. The attempt to govern diverse peoples from a single center (which was also the center of the dominant nationality—the internal hegemon) bred resentment and resistance. The imperial system was costly and wasteful because of its swollen bureaucracy and apparatus of coercion, and because of its efforts to retain conquests and great-power status. Bigness led to the sacrifice of quality for quantity and to numerous forms of corruption and venality. The former Moscow city party committee's first secretary, Boris Yeltsin, observed at the Nineteenth CSPU Conference that "the decay is evidently deeper than some have assumed, and I know, on the basis of Moscow, that a mafia definitely exists." He also noted that there were "millionaire bribetakers" among CPSU officials at the republic and *oblast'* levels who were not being punished by the Committee of Party Control.[93]

The unity of the imperial system, for all of its apparent power, had a synthetic quality and was unstable because it attempted to embrace too many and too much. Because of its size and heterogeneous nature, it was difficult to identify with the imperial system. Yet vast sums were squandered on grandiose public monuments and displays of military might in an attempt to sustain the myth of omnipotence and invincibility.

Feature 7.1   The Decline of Empire

The decline of several great continental empires has been a twentieth-century phenomenon. The collapse of the Austro-Hungarian, Ottoman, and Russian empires after World War I was as remarkable and consequential as the collapse of the USSR. Attempts to reform and preserve empires have failed because of their essentially anomalous nature, and many were not acknowledged to be aberrational until the process of implosion was evident. Major characteristics of imperial decline include the following:

1. Widespread corruption, including theft and embezzlement; officials at all levels expect bribes for performing their duties.
2. The imperial bureaucracy not only proves incapable of initiating reforms, but actually obstructs and sabotages such efforts and seeks to preserve its privileges, opting for stagnation rather than innovation.
3. The military may suffer outright defeat or retreat and have serious morale problems, especially if it must rely on unwilling and unreliable conscripts from subject nationalities. In addition it often faces the dilemma of whether to serve as an instrument of repression against its own people.
4. Imperial rule proves to be excessively costly and ultimately exhausts revenue sources. Military power and economic bankruptcy provide an incongruous combination when the empire becomes dependent on foreign capital and technology.
5. Imperial decline is accompanied, and to a degree concealed, by hubris—the arrogance, overweening pride, insolence, and self-deception on the part of the ethnic hegemon that the early Greeks recognized as preceding decline and fall. Hubris reflects the corrupting and perverse nature of imperial rule as the ethnic hegemon demonstrates loss of a sense of reality.
6. The quality of the empire's political leadership is crucial as its efforts at modernization, reform, and empire preservation fail.
7. The final stage in the collapse of empire is a failure of nerve and a crisis of confidence, as it finally becomes evident that the attempted solutions for crises and defeats are ineffective.

The Russians, as the dominant and core nationality, paid a high price for empire. In denying non-Russian subject peoples the right of self-determination, Russians greatly limited their own freedom by having to sustain an authoritarian system designed to preserve the imperial patrimony and hold restive subject peoples within its grip. By creating and sustaining the synthetic entity known as the USSR, Russians experienced (and imposed upon themselves) a diminution or loss of original identity. Because of the multinational nature of the USSR, the adjective "Russian" was often supplanted by "Soviet" and even by the strange adjective "fatherland" (for example, with reference to machine building, medicine, and music). Russians were thus unable to acquire and develop genuine nationhood as part of the USSR. In professing a contrived "internationalism," Russia submerged itself in the union-empire.[94] It is ironic that the Russian Republic in effect surrendered its membership in the United Nations to the union-empire, while Ukraine and Belarus, as charter members of the United Nations, actually acquired greater international and legal recognition than Russia.

The Russians paid a high price if, as Aleksandr Solzhenitsyn contends, the Russian "national way of life" and "national character" were disappearing and if Russian nationhood was being destroyed "without pity" by Soviet leaders who claimed to be of Russian nationality. Despite greater use of the Russian language, Solzhenitsyn argued that in its Soviet version it became "a sullied and bastardized form of the Russian language."[95] If so, this was a part of the price of empire as the Russian language ceased to be the possession of Russia and was corrupted by non-Russians and Russians alike.

An additional price of empire was the inundation of the metropole and imperial capital by subject peoples and alien elements. In the process the dominant Russians increasingly alienated the subject peoples. Fear of fragmentation of the empire promoted suspiciousness of "subversion" and obsession with security. It also engendered arrogance and blindness, as Russians failed to understand the national ideals and aspirations of subject peoples. Solzhenitsyn, in his essay "Repentance and Self-Limitation in the Life of Nations," counseled his people to withdraw and engage in self-examination and divest themselves of the burdens of empire.[96] He also warned the Soviet leaders that "the aims of a great empire and the moral health of the people are incompatible" and that empire inflicts spiritual harm.[97]

BUILDING THE NEW RUSSIA

The Soviet empire collapsed as a result of political and economic breakdown, as well as moral failure. The August 1991 coup was followed by the collapse of the ruble in late 1991 as a result of enormous government deficits. Proposals to "save" the nearly worthless ruble with foreign aid and an international hard currency "stabilization fund" simply demonstrated the pathetic plight of the Soviet economy. For years Soviet officials had to rely on hard currencies to calculate foreign trade transactions, since the convertibility of the ruble, like Communism itself, remained an unattainable goal. Convertibility must be based not only on an economy's productive capacity but on the willingness of foreign citizens, businesses, and governments to hold a country's currency and be able to use it for purchases and investments.

The collapse of the ruble was preceded by a secret depletion of the Soviet gold reserve and hard-currency stocks. It was alleged that CPSU officials had converted their vast ruble holdings into gold and hard currencies and had made deposits in European banks. The deaths of two of the highest CPSU administrative officials by suicide or homicide tended to confirm the worst suspicions regarding such transactions.[98] In Moscow rubles were being printed around the clock to finance the deficits of Gorbachev's shadowy "Union government." The grievances of the non-Russian peoples had been systematically ignored

by Moscow as a matter of course. Uzbekistan had been converted into a gigantic cotton plantation for the Russian textile industry, with Moscow setting the price of cotton. The irrigation required for cotton cultivation effectively dried up the Aral Sea to less than half its former size, with attendant loss of soil, and the careless use of pesticides created catastrophic health problems. In Ukraine the metropole-center constructed 22 nuclear power plants without the consent of the people; it also constructed gas and oil pipelines across Ukrainian territory without obtaining permission or paying any fees. In both cases electricity and fuel were exported to neighboring countries and the revenues were appropriated by Moscow. The horrendous aftermath of the Chernobyl catastrophe serves as a constant reminder of the costs of tolerating arbitrary rule from an external center.

Ukraine adopted an incremental approach in extricating itself from the toils of the Soviet Union. The process was spearheaded by the Ukrainian Parliament, the Supreme Rada, elected in March 1990. The Communist majority became divided, and on many issues its members sided with the democratic bloc, which held nearly one-third of the seats. Following the proclamation of Ukraine's sovereignty on July 16, 1990, a number of measures were adopted. Ukrainian laws were declared to have primacy over Soviet laws, and Ukraine declared its neutrality and its commitment to being a nuclear-free country. The Rada's Presidium and the Ukrainian ambassador to the United Nations condemned Moscow's use of force against Lithuania in January 1991. Ukraine reduced its financial payments to the union by 80 percent in 1991, established its own National Bank of Ukraine, and concluded bilateral agreements with other republics. Following the August 1991 coup, Ukraine established its own defense ministry and commenced formation of its own armed forces and national guard. It reorganized the KGB in Ukraine, renaming it the National Security Service (SNB). It also took steps to introduce its own currency.

The death knell of the Soviet Union was sounded by the Ukrainian referendum of December 1, 1991, which approved the August 24, 1991, declaration of Ukraine's independence by a 90.32 percent majority. Leonid M. Kravchuk was also elected president of Ukraine by a 61 percent majority against five other candidates.

President Kravchuk, armed with a clear mandate, asserted that Ukraine would not join any new union. In Moscow Yeltsin stated that, if Ukraine rejected Gorbachev's union, Russia would also refuse to join.

However, Yeltsin was apparently reluctant to have Russia formally declare its independence from the USSR as the other republics had done. Kravchuk seized the initiative by proposing the formal dissolution of the union and the formation, instead, of a Commonwealth of Independent States (CIS) that would not replace the defunct union but would serve as a consultative and coordinating forum for the former Soviet republics. The Soviet Union was dissolved by a declaratory act of the three remaining signatories of the December 1922 treaty that formally established the USSR. The heads of state of Belarus, Russia, and Ukraine met at a government estate in the Belovezha Forest Reserve near Brest, Belarus, and in Minsk on December 7–8, 1991, and declared that "the U.S.S.R. as a subject of international law and as a geopolitical reality ceases its existence."[99] The act and the formation of the CIS were approved by the parliaments of the three countries. The commonwealth decision was a means of removing Gorbachev and eliminating his presidency in the disappearing government of a disintegrated empire. It also negated Moscow's claim to be the imperial metropole. Gorbachev's presidency came to a belated end on December 25, 1991, with his resignation. The red flag with its hammer and sickle was lowered over the Kremlin and replaced with the Russian tricolor.

The CIS was established to facilitate cooperation among its members in the fields of foreign policy, economic relations, the environment, and immigration policy, and in combating organized crime. Coordinating bodies of the CIS were to be located in the Belarus capital of Minsk. Yeltsin and Kravchuk asserted that the CIS was not a state and its bodies would not constitute a government.

The Commonwealth, which was joined almost immediately by all the other former Soviet republics except Georgia and the Baltic states, began in difficulties and distrust. Yeltsin's decision to administer "shock therapy" to Russia's economy by "freeing" prices on January 2, 1992, meant that the other member states had no choice but to comply, as their lower prices would have resulted in massive outflows of food and goods to Russian purchasers. Yeltsin's higher prices provided little impetus for the development of a market economy in Russia in the absence of widespread privatization and competition, as the state enterprises remained the principal suppliers and maintained a sellers' market. However, the price increases did reduce the Russian government's budget deficits.

During the first four and a half years of its existence, the foreign policy of the Russian Federation, toward both the countries of the CIS (or "near abroad" as Russians term the region) and the world beyond, has shifted appreciably. Almost immediately after President Yeltsin and Foreign Minister Kozyrev proclaimed a policy that emphasized Russia's full integration into the Western-dominated international community, voices arose in Russia that condemned them for abandoning the interests of the Russian state and pursuing policies determined in Washington.

For millions of Soviet people who proudly regarded the USSR as their own state and homeland, its disappearance was seen as a disaster. But for imperial-minded Russians, it was also a national catastrophe that caused a deep psychological trauma. Russian grievances over the collapse of the USSR were further intensified by the highly publicized stories (both true and false) of violations of human rights of those ethnic Russians who found themselves outside the boundaries of the Russian Federation after the Soviet disintegration. Various constraints on acquiring citizenship imposed by local authorities, alleged language discrimination, the loss of former privileges, and other explosive issues concerning the rights of the Russians in the "near abroad" substantially radicalized the political process within Russia itself, thus providing a fertile soil for the growth of nationalist sentiments.[100]

Despite official disclaimers that Russia has no desire to reestablish its dominance over the newly emerging states, Russian leaders have generally not adjusted to the new reality in which they are expected to negotiate as equals with independent political elites in Kiev and Almaty, rather than merely issue instructions, as would have occurred in the past. This is part of a much larger psychological problem of redefining Russia's statehood and establishing a new concept of Russian identity. In the atmosphere of growing nationalism, it is not surprising that even former

Russian Foreign Minister Andrei Kozyrev, who was noted in the West for his liberal, antinationalist orientation, began to refer to former Soviet republics as comprising a de facto Russian dominion: "There is never a vacuum—if we refuse to live up to our geopolitical role, someone else will try and clean up the mess in our home."[101]

The nationalist shift in Russian foreign policy, however, manifested itself not only in more assertive statements. The rhetorical toughness was supplemented by the actual expansion of Russia's influence in the "near abroad." Thus, after 1993 several important developments occurred in security relations between the Russian Federation and other Soviet successor states, in part within the context of CIS institutions. Agreements with both Georgia and Armenia—extracted by Russia only after covert Russian military intervention in local conflicts helped to undermine the stability of these governments—have resulted in the continued presence of Russian troops in the Caucasus and the establishment of joint border guard units to protect the borders of both countries.[102] Relations with Ukraine have involved periodic confrontations over issues such as the disposal of Ukraine's nuclear arsenal, the disposition of the Soviet Black Sea Fleet, and Russian claims to Crimea, administratively part of Ukraine for four decades, but with a majority Russian population. Nationalists in both Moscow and Kiev (Kyiv) have made resolution of these problems difficult,[103] although the influence of nationalists in Moscow has been much greater than that of Ukrainian nationalists. Moreover, acceptance of Russian demands for dual citizenship and declaring Sevastopol (in Crimea) would serve to negate Ukrainian sovereignty.

In Central Asia the Russians have been active in coordinating security-related activities with the countries of the region. De facto Russia continues to view the borders of CIS members in the south as Russia's borders and has committed the military personnel to defend them. In Azerbaijan the Russians were reportedly involved in the overthrow of the elected president in early 1993, in his replacement with an old Kremlin hand, Heydar Aliev, and in late 1994 in efforts to undermine the latter when he refused to abrogate a deal with Western oil companies for the exploitation of Caspian Sea oil.[104]

Besides a more assertive stance with respect to the "near abroad," Russian foreign policy has also shifted on a number of other issues. On the matter of the civil war in former Yugoslavia, for example, the Russians consistently supported Serbia and the Bosnian Serbs against Western pressures. Although they initially voted for economic sanctions, they soon began calling for their reduction or elimination. They raised the issue of possible sanctions against Croatia and strongly opposed any international intervention against Serbia. As part of an effort to have Iraq and Libya pay large outstanding debts to Russia, the Russians have improved relations with the two countries and have worked to have international sanctions modified or lifted.

In early 1996 the most critical issue in which the nationalist tilt of Russian foreign policy was most conspicuously felt concerned prospective full membership of Central European states (i.e., Hungary, Poland, Slovakia and the Czech Republic) in NATO. Although initially accepting the possibility of NATO's enlargement, Yeltsin's policy towards NATO changed dramatically by 1994 under the influence of conservative and nationalist political actors at home. Indeed, many Russians still see NATO through a historic lens of suspicion and consider the alliance's activities as directed against their country. As a result, Moscow's leaders have made a strong effort to impede the process of NATO's expansion. Thus, for example, Foreign Minister Andrei Kozyrev announced in November 1994 that "Russia may give up [its participation in] NATO's Partnership for Peace Program if that bloc is enlarged," and that he "might forego submitting Russia's presentation document" [on its cooperation with NATO under the Partnership] if the next NATO council meeting adopted "a bloc enlargement calendar."[105]

Overall the progressive "toughening" of Yeltsin's foreign policy, as well as the results of the 1995 Russian parliamentary elections indicating the victory of conservative and nationalist forces, demonstrate that the severity of Russia's problems at home, aggravated by the country's international misfortunes, have been driving Russia to behave more assertively abroad. Nostalgia for the old empire has grown among many Russians disillusioned by the harsh reality of the reforms. Although Andrei

Kozyrev, one of the most consistent advocates of a Western orientation in Russian policy, repeatedly denied any shift in his policies, it became increasingly clear—even prior to the appointment of Yevgeny Primakov as his successor in early 1996—that Moscow was much more eager to respond to the nationalist mood of the Russian public than to the preferences of the international community.[106] Statements by both Communist leader Gennadi Zyuganov and new Foreign Minister Primakov about reestablishing the great-power status of Russia, including the "voluntary" reintegration of the CIS states under Russian tutelage, and Russia's failure to remove its troops from Moldovan territory, despite agreements with the Moldovan government and the conditions for its admission to membership in the Council of Europe, raise serious concerns about the future orientation of Russian foreign policy.

Closely related to developments in Russia's foreign policy have been military issues, some of which have served as a source of tension in relations with other Soviet successor states. Ukraine had made it clear from the beginning that it would organize its own armed forces, and it was joined by Azerbaijan and Moldova. Belarus and Uzbekistan expressed reservations concerning a common CIS military force. Yeltsin and the Russian-dominated military command in Moscow wanted to have the divided services of the former union recognized as the armed forces of the CIS, but under the old ethnic Russian command. Ukraine and other states saw this as a scheme to maintain what they regarded as occupation forces in their territories. In March 1992, Yeltsin announced that Russia would establish its own defense ministry—as Ukraine had done on October 22, 1991.

The nuclear weapons on the territories of Russia, Ukraine, Belarus, and Kazakstan added to the disagreement, since there was skepticism regarding Russia's ability and willingness to destroy nuclear weapons transferred to it by the other countries. President Kravchuk of Ukraine insisted that Russia not be given exclusive control of nuclear weapons but that they be under joint control of the four states. The issues concerning nuclear weapons were eventually worked out with the assistance of the United States, and the nuclear weapons of Belarus and Kazakstan have

been transported to Russia for destruction, as have most of those on Ukrainian territory.

Military relations among the CIS member states have continued to move in the direction of integration, based on the 1992 Collective Security Treaty. During 1995, for example, two summits of CIS heads of state agreed to a joint air defense system. Although agreement does not exist among all CIS members for joint border protection, the Russians continue to push the matter. In fact, they have signed bilateral agreements with several other CIS states that provide for the stationing of Russian troops in those states.[107] What emerges from the information available on CIS military relations is a Russian commitment to reestablish its military superiority across the geographic space of most of the former Soviet Union.

Another area of special significance of the military in the new Russia concerns military reform and emerging civil-military relations in the Russian Federation. In 1992 a new military force of the Russian Federation was established to replace the Unified Armed Forces of the Commonwealth of Independent States which, in turn, had replaced the Soviet military.[108] Almost immediately then recently appointed Defense Minister General Pavel Grachev, outlined plans for a comprehensive reform of the military. Over the next two to three years he planned to cut the size of armed forces without reducing its military readiness, to transform the military to meet the new geopolitical realities, and to increase its standing in Russian society. Four years later it was evident that none of these goals had been accomplished. Although substantial troop reductions and cuts in technical supply occurred in 1992 and 1993, they occurred in a way that did not maintain military readiness. Moreover, since the plans assumed a growing economy, actual expenditures were far out of line with budgets—by 300 percent during 1992–1993.

Overall, the process of reintegration of the states of the CIS has moved forward sporadically—pushed by Russia's use of various forms of military and economic coercion to force its partners into expanded cooperation, but countered by the general refusal of many of the member countries to implement agreements that had been reached. Russia has used a range of weapons from covert support for secessionist movements to overt economic blackmail to reassert a dominant position within the CIS under the guise of multilateral cooperation. The decision of the Russian State Duma in March 1996 to denounce the December 1991 dissolution of the Soviet Union gave clear evidence of the long-term objective of important political forces in Moscow.[109] Ukraine, on the other hand, has insisted on policies within the CIS that emphasize the full sovereignty of the member countries and rely on bilateral rather than multilateral agreements.

The decision to deploy troops in Chechnya to put down the de facto secession by former President Dudayev and the Chechen government demonstrated the degree to which Russian military preparedness had declined. Not only was the Russian Army unable to enforce peace after more than a year and a half of fighting, many of its troops proved to be inadequately trained and it was forced to rely on mercenaries (*kontraktniki,* "contract soldiers"), many of whom became notorious for looting.

In the increasingly nationalist and anti-reform environment in Moscow, the response to the inability of the military to reform itself and to the demands associated with "peacekeeping" operations in the "near abroad" and enforcement activities in Chechnya has been an increase in the defense budget for 1996 by $1.5 billion.[110] The military, along with the security and intelligence organs that have succeeded the old KGB, continues to warn of the dangers of too close contacts with the West and of the efforts of the West to undermine the ability of Russia to emerge once again as a world power. The inheritors of the legacy of the KGB have emerged virtually intact from developments of the past decade. Espionage remains a central component of Russia's internal and external policy. During the first four and a half years of the "new Russia" a whole list of European countries arrested or expelled Russian espionage agents on their territory.[111] Moreover, the paranoia of the Soviet security and intelligence communities about external threats appears to have been passed on to their successors in Russia, who now play an expanded role in the politics of a more nationalistic and assertive Russia.

We turn now to a brief discussion of other areas of policy concern for the new Russia. At the base of virtually all other issues is the question of

the economy and of government policies introduced to stimulate economic growth. We have already examined the general outlines of the reform policies of 1992–1994 and their impacts—both positive and negative—on the Russian economy. We have noted, as well, the intense unpopularity of many of the economic policies introduced by President Yeltsin that has been used most effectively by the Communists and other anti-reform groups to build a strong political base in Russian politics, to gain control over the parliament in the December 1995 elections, and to position themselves in the unsuccessful presidential election campaign in summer 1996. During 1995 and early 1996 Yeltsin backed off from some of the earlier reforms, and his cabinet no longer included individuals committed to economic reform. As the presidential election campaign heated up in spring 1996 Yeltsin made numerous commitments that could only undercut the process of economic reform—including extending subsidies to state enterprises, granting inflationary wage increases to government employees, and promising expanded expenditures of state funds in numerous areas of the economy.

The most relevant question, as Russia enters a period in which the Communists will exert strong influence in policy, concerns the degree to which the reforms which established the foundations for a market economy will be left in place. To what extent will government policy remain committed to privatizing large industrial enterprises which employ thousands of Russian citizens—or to permitting them to collapse rather that expanding governmental subsidies? Other policy realms of direct relevance for the economic future of Russia include the establishment of a legal system—still not fully in place—that will protect private ownership for both Russian citizens and foreigners and maintain a free flow of capital across Russia's borders and facilitate and encourage foreign investment and trade. Political developments in Russia since 1994 have brought into question the degree to which the Russian leadership will remain committed to policies appropriate for a market economy. An important element here is the long-term paternalistic approach to employees that has prevented the closure of factories and the laying-off of large numbers of workers. In early 1996 Yeltsin's government announced an expansion of the list of enterprises that would not be eligible for privatization (141 companies in aviation, shipping, communications, metallurgy, timber and grain production, and machine building) and proclaimed the introduction of protectionist measures in the foreign trade area.

Directly relevant to the economic concerns that face Russia are environmental and health problems. One of the worst legacies of the Communist past throughout Central Europe and Eurasia is the ecological and environmental devastation left behind by politico-economic systems that for decades were committed to expanded industrial and agricultural production at virtually any cost. The result has been a level of environmental degradation unmatched anyplace on earth. In Poland, for example, rivers from which the drinking water of major cities is drawn are so polluted that they do not meet the minimum standards for industrial water use in Western Europe. Much of northern Ukraine and more than 20 percent of all Belarusian territory has been made uninhabitable for the foreseeable future by the Chernobyl nuclear disaster. A substantial portion of the territory of Uzbekistan east of the Aral Sea has been turned into a toxic wasteland as a result of extensive irrigation that prevents 90 percent of water from reaching the Aral and has resulted in the exposure of more than 11,000 square miles of seabed covered with salts and other chemicals largely from the runoff of agricultural chemicals. In regions immediately adjacent to the Aral, infant mortality rates reached twice the Soviet average, maternal mortality rates tripled between 1984 and 1989, and 80 percent of all pregnant women were found to suffer from anemia.[112]

These represent but a handful of anecdotes concerning the devastation inherited by the Russian Federation and the other Soviet successor states. As Murray Feshbach and many other specialists have demonstrated, Russia is a giant country awash with nuclear materials, whose northern seas are threatened by radiation pollution, whose Siberian forests lose millions of acres a year to fire, pollution, and overcutting, and whose people face serious dangers from polluted water and contaminated food. Yet, the government has barely recognized the pervasiveness of the problem and, because of the economic disaster in which it finds itself, is financially unprepared even to begin tackling the problems of control and cleanup. Russian factories continue to pollute; nuclear power plants as dangerous as those at Chernobyl continue to operate throughout the territory of the former Soviet Union (with 15 operating in Ukraine alone); and the billions of dollars required to clean up the waters and air of Russia are simply unavailable. Just as important, given the immediacy of problems of economic decline, ethnic conflict, and related matters, environmental concerns are not high on the agenda of government priorities.

Closely related to the ecological devastation of much of the territory of the Russian Federation and the other post-Soviet states is the horrendous state of the health of the population and the precipitous decline in health care. In the final days of the Soviet Union the situation of the health care system was already in dire straits. The USSR devoted an inadequate and declining percentage of its GNP to health. Moreover, the government, which controlled the entire health care system, had refused to make the investments that would have permitted it to keep up with technological developments in health care that were occurring elsewhere. Moreover, basic medical supplies—from medicines to thermometers and needles—were in disastrously short supply.[113]

Male life expectancy dropped almost annually until in 1990 it had reached 63.8 years. Three years later it was at 58.9 years (57.9 in the countryside). Poor diet, alcoholism, cigarettes, and air and water pollution were among the major causes of this decline. But, since the collapse of the former Soviet Union an increase in unnatural deaths (murder and suicide, for example) was the primary source of the decline in life expectancy. Infant mortality rates in Russia are also the highest in the industrial world, up from 17.4 per thousand live births in 1990 to 19.9 per thousand in 1993 (although some experts estimate that the figure is more like 30 per thousand, three times that of the United States). Maternal mortality rates are also up significantly—to 63.5 per 10,000 live births in 1994—and a full 75 percent of Russian women experience complications during pregnancy. Only 45 percent of Russian births qualify as normal by Western medical standards.[114]

Throughout Russia deaths are outpacing births by more than two to one—7.6 births and

17.5 deaths per thousand in 1994 as compared with 10.5 births and 12.8 deaths four years earlier. Major diseases, long thought to be under control, have reemerged at epidemic levels throughout the country. The factors underlying these developments are many and complex. However, environmental, economic and social disintegration are at the root of the problem. The recent drop in the birth rate is directly related to the economic collapse and the bleak prospects for the future for most Russian citizens. The rising death rate results from growing alcoholism in a country in which this was already a serious problem, increased stress that has resulted in a suicide rate three times that of the United States, a collapse of the already inadequate health care system, and widespread environmental contamination. Presumably economic improvements will help to stabilize the demographic situation in Russia. However, the public health crisis, including the impact of the high levels of deadly pollution, are problems that the Russian government will find it difficult to overcome.

An area of public policy of special importance as an indicator of the degree of commitment of the Russian government to democratization concerns human rights. Russia does not have a strong tradition of the observance of human rights. Although the Bolsheviks who came to power in Russia in 1917 expressed high ideals in this area and the Soviet constitution included the protection of citizens' rights and although the Soviet government was always a strong advocate of international human rights agreements, actual practice fell far short of minimum world standards in protecting civil and human rights. Millions of Soviet citizens died in the terror campaigns initiated by Stalin. Even after the reforms introduced under Khrushchev in the 1950s, Soviet citizens were still subject to widespread abuses of their human rights. Political dissidents were harshly treated. Many were imprisoned on trumped up charges; others were declared mentally unstable and sent to psychiatric hospitals.

This approach to human rights must be understood within the context of the view of Soviet authorities that the collectivity was more important than the individuals who comprised it. In the Marxist-Leninist view, individuals were not endowed from birth with "inalienable rights." Rather, the individual gained meaning and, therefore, rights, only through membership in the larger community. The state took precedence over the individual, and individuals gained their rights through the state. As we have seen, this situation changed significantly during the Gorbachev reform period, when a whole series of guarantees were put into place that provided greater protections against the state for citizens of the Soviet Union.

After four and a half years of an independent Russia there are those who are concerned about the commitment of the government to strengthening human rights in the country. In fact, in early 1996, after issuing a very critical report on the state of human rights in the Russian Federation which noted "a visible retreat from democratic achievements," a majority of the members of the Presidential Commission for Human Rights resigned their positions. Subsequently President Yeltsin abolished the commission. The Commission had been headed by human rights champion Sergei Kovalev who regularly criticized the government for the behavior of Russian troops in Chechnya. Already in late 1995 the Commission's importance had been downgraded, presumably in response to its continued assertions that Yeltsin and his government were no longer committed to democratic reforms.

The last report of the Commission, as well as reports by the New York–based Human Rights Watch and the U.S. Department of State, raise concerns about the declining commitment to human and civil rights of Russian citizens. The Kovalev Commission referred to the increasing militarization of society (with special reference to Chechnya), the growing tendency to resolve internal conflicts by force, and the rise in racial discrimination and intolerance.[115] In addition, evidence has mounted that indicates that democratic activists have been prosecuted for political reasons and that government agencies have moved to try to silence some of the criticism by the media. Although it appears that most of the cases refer to the actions of individual officials, there is growing concern about a government that looks the other way. The growth of Communist influence in Russian politics enhances these fears.

TOWARD THE FUTURE

The decade beginning with the selection of Mikhail Gorbachev as leader of the CPSU in 1985 brought with it revolutionary changes in the Soviet Union and its successor states. With the failure of Gorbachev's efforts to reform the Soviet system and the implosion of the Soviet state, the Russian leadership faced the daunting task of creating a new state, new political institutions based on democratic principles, and a market economy. Over the next four and a half years President Yeltsin and his supporters succeeded in establishing the foundations for a new society. A constitution was in place that provided the ground rules for a presidential republic, but one in which for the first time in Russian history the power of the executive was balanced by representatives of popular interests. Moreover, after serious initial challenges to Moscow and despite the ongoing catastrophe in Chechnya, the relationship between the political center and the regions that comprise the Russian Federation has been stabilized. The political battles being fought in Russia are contested in elections and through the ballot box. In the economic realm, the basic foundations for a functioning market economy have been put into place and, after a long period of drastic economic decline, indicators for the future are positive—for the first time since before the collapse of the former USSR.

However, besides these basically positive indications of Russian success in the "triple transition" of state building, democratization, and marketization, there exist many important negative indicators. The constitutional arrangements that define relations between the federal government and its constituent parts remain fragile. Moreover, the horrors of the war in Chechnya indicate the continuing willingness of the political center to use virtually any means to accomplish its objectives. The rise of right-wing, nationalist, political groups and the reemergence of the Communists—both groups committed to reversing many of the political and economic reforms of the past decade—indicate the degree to which the values that comprise Russian political culture remain rooted in the past. Many Russians long for the stability of the authoritarian past and fear the uncertainties of a democratic and market-oriented present and future. More-over, the periodic and widespread discussion of the possibility of a coup is also cause for concern. This is especially relevant in a country which has experienced two coup attempts since 1991 and which suffered a (failed) coup in 1957 and a successful one seven years later. The current political instability in the country raises serious questions about the possibility of a seizure of power by groups who oppose the course of political development and are able to command support from adequate portions of the military and other organs of state coercion.

In the economic area, although positive indicators exist about future growth in the Russian economy, the disasters associated with the market reforms of the first four years of the Russian Federation have undermined support for the reforms, and recent indicators of poor economic performance raise new dangers. As a result, President Yeltsin has already been forced to retreat from the policies of 1992–1994 in response to political pressures expressed most clearly in the parliamentary elections of December 1995.

Russia in summer 1996 stood at an important historical crossroads. Although it dismantled virtually all of the instruments of state repression and authoritarian control over society and over the economy by 1992, strong pressures emerged over the next four years to reinstate some of those controls and to return to many of the policies that had characterized the Soviet Union. In response to these pressures, President Yeltsin has already modified both foreign and domestic policy. In many respects Russia is a "schizophrenic" polity and society. The country has two names, *Russian Federation* and *Russia (Rossiia)*. Yeltsin has given it a second, imperial flag, to complement the Russian tricolor. A *rossiiskoye* (Russian in the sense of the existing multiethnic society) state and government is attempting to function as a *russkoye* (in the sense of ethnic Russian) sate and government. Yet it is not clear when and how a *russkii* (ethnic Russian) is a *rossiianin* (citizen of the multiethnic Russian Federation). Russia has a declining population, but its leadership sends thousands of young men, including teenagers, to be killed in Chechnya in a war that Yeltsin admits was a mistake.

The outcome of the presidential elections of June-July 1996 was important for the future of Russia, since President Yeltsin has recommitted himself and his government to economic and political reform. As we have noted in discussing the election platforms of the two major candidates, President Yeltsin and Communist Party leader Zyuganov, the programs that the two presented for the future of Russia differed dramatically. However, some analysts—both in Russia and outside—have argued that, in reality, the differences between the two are not likely to be as dramatic as one might expect.[116] On the one hand, President Yeltsin has already responded to the conservative mood of the country by cutting back quite significantly on various aspects of political and economic reform. On the other, the fact that capitalism has already taken root in Russia— with more than 60 percent of GNP generated in the private sector—and that the reforms of the past five years have irrevocably changed Russia would limit the ability of Zyuganov or any other Russian president to return to the Soviet past. Given the poor state of President Yeltsin's health and the likelihood that Zyuganov and the left will remain an effective political force in Russia for the foreseeable future, this issue will remain an important one.

President Yeltsin's appointment as his chief of staff of Anatolyi Chubais, an unabashed reformer who earlier masterminded both the Russian privatization program and the president's reelection campaign, is evidence that his second term will witness a return to market reforms. However, whether or not Russia will emerge successfully from the disruptions of the past decade will depend primarily on the ability of the political elite, including the president, to move beyond the political struggle of the day to develop genuine wisdom in creating a functioning democracy with a market economy. As one noted U.S. analyst of Russian affairs has noted:

> We must not forget that the fire is not out. Russians must do more to control the flames of authoritarianism and totalitarianism before we can rest assured that Russia is joining the community of democratic, market-oriented nations. This does not mean that the elections have been a useless exercise. On the whole, they have advanced the process of Russian democratization; as did, by the way, the December parliamentary

elections in spite of a rather different outcome. These recent elections demonstrate a heroic commitment to decency on the part of the Russian people not always evident among their leaders. This is not a time for basking in glory. It is the time for serious hard work, the work of governing. There is little evidence to date that President Yeltsin has either the interest or the capacity to govern.[117]

KEY TERMS

Brezhnev Doctrine
Comintern
Commonwealth of Independent States (CIS)
Council for Mutual Economic Assistance (CMEA)
correlation of forces
hubris
imperial system
Lend-Lease
"new thinking"
Warsaw Pact

FURTHER READINGS

Allworth, Edward, ed. *Ethnic Russia in the USSR: The Dilemma of Dominance* (New York: Pergamon Press, 1980).

Bremmer, Ian, and Ray Taras, eds. *Nations and Politics in the Soviet Successor States* (Cambridge and New York: Cambridge University Press, 1993).

Brzezinski, Zbigniew. *The Grand Failure, The Birth and Death of Communism in the Twentieth Century* (New York: Scribner, 1989).

Colton, Timothy, and Thane Gustafson. *Soldiers and the Soviet State* (Princeton, NJ: Princeton University Press, 1990).

Conquest, Robert, ed. *The Last Empire: Nationality and the Soviet Future* (Stanford, CA: Hoover Institution Press, 1986).

Dibb, Paul. *The Soviet Union: The Incomplete Superpower* (Champaign: University of Illinois Press, 1986).

Dunlop, John B. *The Rise of Russia and the Fall of the Soviet Empire* (Princeton, NJ: Princeton University Press, 1993).

Feshbach, Murray, and Alfred Friendly Jr. *Ecocide in the USSR: Health and Nature Under Siege* (New York: Basic Books, 1992).

Garthoff, Raymond L. *Détente and Confrontation: American-Soviet Relations from Nixon to Reagan,* rev. ed. (Washington: The Brookings Institution, 1994).

Jones, Anthony, Walter D. Connor, and David E. Powell, eds. *Soviet Social Problems* (Boulder, CO, and Oxford: Westview Press, 1991).

Kanet, Roger E., and Alexander V. Kozhemiakin, eds. *The Foreign Policy of the Russian Federation* (Houndmills, UK: Macmillan, 1997).

Kaufman, Richard F., and John P. Hardt, eds. *The Former Soviet Union in Transition.* Joint Economic Committee, Congress of the United States (Armonk, NY-London: M. E. Sharpe, 1993).

Kolodziej, Edward A., and Roger E. Kanet, eds. *The Limits of Soviet Power in the Developing World: Thermidor in the Revolutionary Struggle* (Houndmills, UK: Macmillan; Baltimore: Johns Hopkins University Press, 1989).

Marples, David R. *The Social Impact of the Chernobyl Disaster* (New York: St. Martin's Press, 1988).

Matlock, Jack F. *Autopsy on an Empire: The American Ambassador's Account of the Collapse of the Soviet Union* (New York: Random House, 1995).

Matthews, Mervyn. *Poverty in the Soviet Union* (New York: Cambridge University Press, 1987).

Motyl, Alexander J. *Dilemmas of Independence: Ukraine After Totalitarianism* (New York: Council on Foreign Relations Press, 1993).

Nogee, Joseph L., and Robert H. Donaldson. *Soviet Foreign Policy Since World War II,* 4th ed. (New York: Macmillan, 1992).

Rowen, Henry S., Charles Wolf Jr., and Jeanne Zlotnick, eds. *Defense Conversion, Economic Reform, and the Outlook for the Russian and Ukrainian Economies* (New York: St. Martin's Press, A RAND Study, 1994).

Rubinstein, Alvin Z. *Soviet Foreign Policy Since World War II: Imperial and Global,* 4th ed. (New York: HarperCollins, 1992).

Saikal, Amin, and William Maley, eds. *Russia in Search of Its Future* (Cambridge and New York: Cambridge University Press, 1994).

Shearman, Peter, ed. *Russian Foreign Policy Since 1990* (Boulder, CO: Westview Press, 1995).

Shlapentokh, Vladimir, Munir Sendich, and Emil Payin, eds. *The New Russian Diaspora: Russian Minorities in the Former Soviet Republics* (Armonk, NY, and London: M. E. Sharpe, 1994).

Ulam, Adam B. *Expansion and Coexistence: The History of Soviet Foreign Policy, 1917–1973,* 2nd ed. (New York: Praeger, 1974).

Waller, J. Michael. *Secret Empire: The KGB in Russia Today* (Boulder, CO: Westview Press, 1994).

Wesson, Robert G. *The Russian Dilemma,* rev. ed. (New York: Praeger. 1986).

Yergin, Daniel, and Thane Gustafson. *Russia 2010 and What It Means for the World* (New York: Vintage Books, 1995).

Notes

1. *Pravda,* January 28, 1987.

2. *Isvestiya,* July 26, 1991.

3. These issues are discussed in Mark R. Beissinger, "The Persisting Ambiguity of Empire?" *Post-Soviet Affairs,* vol. 11, no. 2 (1995), pp. 149–185.

4. See Mervyn Matthews, *Privilege in the Soviet Union: A Study of Elite Life-Style Under Communism* (London: Allen and Unwin, 1978). See, also, Michael Voslensky, *Nomenklatura: The Soviet Ruling Class* (Garden City, NY: Doubleday, 1984).

5. Cited in Anatasiya Posadskaya, "Demokratiya minus zhenshchina—ne demokratiya," *Ogonëk,* no. 398 (1993), pp. 8–9. See also, Mary I. Dakin, "Women and Employment Policy in Contemporary Russia," *Demokratizatsiya: The Journal of Post-Soviet Democratization,* vol. 3, no. 3 (1995), pp. 252–261.

6. G. G. Sillaste, "Sotsiogendernye otnosheniya v period sotsial'noi transformatsii Rossii," *Sotsiologicheskie issledovaniya,* no. 3 (1994), pp. 15–22.

7. For the more positive view of Russian political culture, see Nicolai N. Petro, *The Rebirth of Russian Democracy: An Interpretation of Political Culture* (Cambridge, MA: Harvard University Press, 1995).

8. Robert V. Daniels, *Is Russia Reformable? Change and Resistance from Stalin to Gorbachev* (Boulder, CO, and London: Westview Press, 1988), p. 48.

9. A perceptive effort to compare traditional patterns of Russian political behavior with those of

the Soviet Union can be found in Edward L. Keenan, "Moscovite Political Folkways," *The Russian Review,* vol. 15, no. 2 (1986), pp. 115–181. Richard Pipes's *Russia Under the Old Regime* (New York: Charles Scribner's Sons, 1974) provides extensive evidence of the continuity of the character of the Russian state from medieval to modern times.

10. For a discussion of the Mongol-Tatar impact on Muscovy and the Russians, see Charles J. Halperin, *Russia and the Golden Horde* (Bloomington: Indiana University Press, 1985).

11. This point can be illustrated with the complaint of Gorbachev that "we do not yet have enough ethic of debate" and that some writers "tend to settle old scores with others or tag offensive labels on them." Mikhail Gorbachev, *Perestroika and New Thinking for Our Country and the Whole World* (New York: Harper & Row, 1987), p. 74.

12. A rather bizarre recent example is the charge that the dramatic increase in chicken imports to Russia (from a base of zero to $81 million in 1993 and $500 million two years later, an estimated 70 percent of all chicken in the market) is part of a Western plan to destroy Russian chicken production and capture the entire market. See Michelle Gordon, "U.S. Chickens in Russian Pots," *The New York Times,* January 18, 1996, pp. C1, C5.

13. See Nicolas Berdyaev, *The Russian Idea* (London: Geoffrey Bles, 1947), Ch. 9.

14. See Paul Avrich, *Russian Rebels, 1600–1800* (New York: Schocken Books, 1972).

15. Berdyaev, *The Russian Idea,* pp. 142–144.

16. See Adam B. Ulam, *Russia's Failed Revolutions: From the Decembrists to the Dissidents* (New York: Basic Books, 1981).

17. See Svetlana Alliluyeva, *Only One Year* (New York: Harper & Row, 1969).

18. Aleksandr Tsipko in *Komsomotskaya pravda,* January 14, 1992.

19. "Nechto o vran'ye," in Fedor M. Dostoevsky, *Polnoe sobranie sochinenii* (St. Petersburg: izd. A. F. Marska, 1895), vol. 9, pp. 320–322 and 330. Dostoevsky noted that lying was largely a male phenomenon in Russia and that women were "more serious" and less likely to engage in it. See also Ronald Hingley, *The Russian Mind* (New York: Charles Scribner's Sons, 1977), pp. 90–104.

20. *Pravda,* July 4, 1990, p. 3.

21. Berdyaev, *The Russian Idea,* p. 3.

22. These behavioral traits have been attributed originally to the traditional Russian patriarchal family, which is said to have bred tension between fathers and sons and to have produced a male personality type that was both domineering and servile in accordance with circumstance. For a discussion of various theories of the Russian character, see John S. Reshetar Jr., *The Soviet Polity: Government and Politics in the USSR,* 3rd ed. (New York: Harper & Row, 1989), pp. 33–44.

23. On Marxism-Leninism, see Alfred G. Meyer, *Leninism* (Cambridge: Harvard University Press, 1957; Boulder, CO: Westview Press, 1986, reprint). On the political usefulness of Lenin, see Nina Tumarkin, *Lenin Lives: The Lenin Cult in Soviet Russia* (Cambridge: Harvard University Press, 1983).

24. I. V. Stalin, *Sochineniya,* vol. 12, pp. 369–370 (Moscow: Gosudarstvennoe izdatelstvo, 1949).

25. *Pravda,* February 23, 1986. Gorbachev's views on the importance of Marxism-Leninism permeate the argument presented in his book *Perestroika.*

26. *Izvestiya,* July 26, 1991, p. 2.

27. See Lennard D. Gerson, *The Secret Police in Lenin's Russia* (Philadelphia: Temple University Press, 1976); and George Leggett, *The Cheka: Lenin's Political Police* (Oxford: Clarendon Press, 1981).

28. See Robert Conquest, *The Great Terror: A Reassessment* (New York: Oxford University Press, 1990). Information available since the collapse of the Soviet state indicates that no fewer than 20 million people died in the Soviet Union between the 1917 Revolution and the 1960s as a result of state terror.

29. V. I. Lenin. *Polnoe sobranie sochinenii,* 5th ed. (Moscow Gospolitizdat, 1962), vol. 34, p. 93.

30. Nikita Khrushchev, *Khrushchev Remembers* (Boston: Little, Brown, 1970), pp. 17, 57, 182.

31. This periodization of *perestroika* draws upon the discussion of Richard Sakwa, *Russian Politics and Society* (London and New York: Routledge, 1993), pp. 1–10.

32. Ibid, p. 4.

33. Excepts of his speech can be found in *New York Times,* December 21, 1990.

34. See Christopher Andrew and Oleg Gordievsky, *The KGB: The Inside Story of Its Foreign Operations from Lenin to Gorbachev* (New York: HarperCollins, 1990), Ch. 14.

35. The OMON (*otdely militsii osobogo naz-nacheniiy*) militia units for special assignment were also known as the "black berets" and played a key role in the repressive operations of 1990–1991. See, for example, Jonathan Steele, *Eternal Russia: Yeltsin, Gorbachev, and the Mirage of Democracy* (Cambridge, MA: Harvard University Press, 1996), pp. 193–201.

36. The most flagrant case was that involving the Ukrainian parliamentary deputy Dr. Stepan Khara, who was victimized in a police provocation in November 1990 and not released until after the August 1991 coup. See *The Ukrainian Weekly*, November 18 and 25, 1990; December 2 and 16, 1990; April 14 and 21, 1991, and subsequent issues.

37. See Stephen White, *Gorbachev and After* (Cambridge and New York: Cambridge University Press, 1992), Ch. 7; and Stephen White. *After Gorbachev* (Cambridge and New York: Cambridge University Press, 1993), pp. 242–255.

38. Gorbachev himself admitted that the leadership had underestimated the problems and had committed "miscalculations and errors" in undertaking *perestroika*. *Izvestiya*, February 6, 1990, p. 1.

39. In a visit to Vladivostok in 1986 he appealed for increased labor "discipline, responsibility, responsibility, creativity, productivity" as the means of "unbinding our Soviet flywheel." *Pravda*, July 27, 1986, p. 1.

40. For a comparison of the experiences of the Soviet Union/Russia and China in the reform area that emphasizes the overall benefits of the Chinese approach, see Peter Nolan, *China's Rise, Russia's Fall: Politics, Economics and Planning in the Transition from Stalinism* (New York: St. Martin's Press, 1995).

41. Cited in Hélène Carrère d'Encause, *The End of the Soviet Empire* (New York: Harper and Row, 1993) which provides an excellent overview of the ineptitude of Soviet nationalities policy. Gorbachev's and the Party's Russian "blind spots" on nationalities were evident in the Central Committee's platform adopted in September 1989. It called for the "international solidarity of the Soviet peoples," a "strong Union and strong republics," the "development of internationalist processes of mutual interaction of cultures," and "legal consolidation of the Russian language as the common state language." *Izvestiya*, September 24, 1989.

42. See Jonathan R. Adelman, *Torrents of Spring: Soviet and Post-Soviet Politics* (New York: McGraw-Hill, 1995), p. 232. See, also, Peter J. Boettke, *Why Perestroika Failed: The Politics and Economics of Socialist Transformation* (London and New York: Routledge, 1993).

43. M.S. Gorbachev, *Perestroika i novoe nyshlenie, dlia nashei strany i dlia vesgo miru* (Moscow: Politizdat, 1987), pp. 32–33.

44. Cited by Serge Schmemann, *New York Times*, February 28, 1991.

45. *New York Times*, October 18, 1990.

46. For Gorbachev's opposition to a multiparty system see his article in *Pravda*, November 26, 1989.

47. For evidence on the Russian Orthodox Church's dependence on Communist authorities and the role of the KGB in infiltrating the clergy, see the open letter to Gorbachev signed by three priests and three deacons (dated December 15, 1988), in *Glasnost* (U.S. edition), January–March 1990, pp. 25–27.

48. See *Pravda*, May 26, 1990.

49. *Pravda*, February 27, 1986, p. 3. For a discussion of Yeltsin's role as head of the Communist party organization in Moscow see Timothy J. Colton, *Moscow: Governing the Socialist Metropolis* (Cambridge and London: The Belknap Press of Harvard University Press, 1995), pp. 572–583.

50. *New York Times*, March 26 and March 29, 1991.

51. *New York Times*, May 17, 1990, report by Bill Keller on convoking the Russian parliament.

52. "Don't Shoot," *Moscow News*, no. 4, January 27–February 3, 1991, p. 5.

53. "Obrashchenie k sovetskomu narodu," *Izvestiya*, no. 197, August 20, 1991. Another issue of *Izvestiya*, no. 198 of the same date, was published by opponents of the coup as the regular evening edition and did not carry the plotters' appeal.

54. Serge Schmemann, "Soviet Hard-Liners Keep Up the Attack," *New York Times*, June 25, 1991.

55. See excerpts of his speech in *New York Times*, September 4, 1991.

56. For the text of the initial Minsk agreement and that of the Central Asian republics see *Diplomaticheskii Vestnik*, no. 1 (January 15, 1992), pp. 3–10.

57. "Post-Soviet states" or "Soviet successor states" refers to all 15 of the states that emerged from the former Soviet Union, including the Baltic states of Estonia, Latvia, and Lithuania. CIS, or Commonwealth of Independent States, refers to Russia and the other 11 Soviet successor states that have attempted to create political, security, and economic linkages among themselves: Belarus, Ukraine, Moldova, Armenia, Georgia, Azerbaijan, Kazakstan, Kyrgyzstan, Turkmenistan, Uzbekistan, and Tajikistan.

58. Samuel P. Huntington, *The Third Wave: Democratization in the Late Twentieth Century* (Norman: University of Oklahoma Press, 1992).

59. For a discussion of the special problems of democratization in post-Communist states see Valerie Bunce, "Comparing East and South," *Jour-*

nal of Democracy, vol. 6, no. 3 (1995), pp. 87–100.

60. *Pravda*, February 30, 1993.

61. According to then Head of the Presidential Administration Sergei Filatov. Interfax, December 27, 1995.

62. John W. Slocum, *Disintegration and Consolidation: National Separatism and the Evolution of Center-Periphery Relations in the Russian Federation*, Occasional Paper 19 (Ithaca, NY: Cornell University Peace Studies Program, 1995).

63. It is not clear that the majority of Russians there actually desire reunion with Russia. It appears that one strong motive is the desire to obtain better terms from Kiev (Kyiv). In fact, accepting Moscow's rule would interfere with the plans of certain groups within the very diverse "Russian" population which consists of an assortment of carpetbaggers, retired *nomenklatura* types (include KGB, MVD, and military retirees) and people of questionable repute (i.e., those associated with various forms of corruption). It is also important to recognize that a quarter million Crimean Tatars (roughly half the number brutally exiled by Stalin during World War II as a security threat) have returned to Crimea. Generally they fear Russia and wish to remain in Ukraine.

64. See Eugene Huskey, "Weak Russian State Expanding Exponentially," *Meeting Report*, Kennan Institute for Advanced Russian Studies, vol. 12, no. 18 (1995).

65. Speaking during a visit to Russia of radical French nationalist Jean Marie Le Pen, Zhirinovsky threatened that Polish entry into NATO would result in there being "no Poland and no NATO." During the same visit he said that, if NATO expanded into Central Europe, thereby provoking a third world war, he would not "cross swords" with Le Pen. Rather they would respectively send Chechens and France's black population to fight on Romanian territory. See *OMRI Daily Digest*, no. 31 (February 13, 1996), citing Polish media of February 12–13, and Romanian media of February 10, 1996. In *Vladimir Zhirinovskiy: An Assessment of a Russian Ultra-Nationalist* (Washington: Institute for National Strategic Studies, National Defense University, 1994), author James W. Morrison provides a comprehensive overview of Zhirinovsky's positions on domestic and foreign policy issues.

66. The former foreign minister, Andrei Kozyrev, resigned after his election to the Duma; under Russian law, Duma members may not serve simultaneously in government positions. Ever since 1992 Kozyrev was condemned by Russian nationalists for the foreign policy that he pursued, although by 1994 and 1995 he and President Yeltsin had refocused much of Russian foreign policy away from its earlier emphasis on cooperation with the West.

67. Evidence of the disarray in which the reformers found themselves only a few months before scheduled presidential elections can be found in Gaidar's opposition to Yeltsin's campaign and his refusing to support Grigory Yavlinsky's candidacy. At this point the reformers remained divided and unable to identify a single candidate. See *OMRI Daily Digest*, February 14, 1996. During the presidential election campaign much discussion was given to the possibility of fraud, with both Zyuganov and Zhirinovsky charging that President Yeltsin was likely to use his power position to rig the vote. In fact, some evidence emerged after the December 1995 parliamentary elections that the dominant position at the local government of communist officials facilitated falsification in favor of the Communist Party. See Kronid Ljubarskij, "Waren die Dumawahlen im Dezember 1995 'free and fair'?" *Aktuelle Analysen*, Bundesinstitut für ostwissenschaftliche und internationale Studien, no. 28, May 28, 1996.

68. The Russian gross domestic product declined an additional 4 percent in 1995, with industrial production down 3 percent. Several industrial areas, however, showed growth—iron and steel, up 9 percent; chemicals and petrochemicals, up 8 percent; and non-ferrous metals up 2 percent. *OMRI Daily Digest*, January 2, 1996 and January 19, 1995.

69. *ITAR TASS,* October 5, 1995.

70. Anders Åslund, "Russia's Success Story," *Foreign Affairs*, vol. 73, no. 5 (1994), p. 58. Åslund develops his arguments more fully in his book *How Russia Became a Market Economy* (Washington, DC: The Brookings Institution, 1995). For a similar positive assessment see Brigitte Granville, *The Success of Russian Economic Reforms* (London: The Royal Institute of International Affairs; distributed by The Brookings Institution, Washington, 1995).

71. Studies done by sociologist Olga Kryshtanovska indicate that 61 percent of the new business elite in Russia come from the old Soviet *nomenklatura*, while 75 percent of the political elite come from the old bureaucracy. *Izvestiya*, January 10, 1996. For information on favoritism in the privatization of Russian industry see Alessandra Stanley, "Russian Scandal Threatens Future of Privatization," *New York Times*, January 26, 1996.

72. See Stephen K. Wegren, "Rural Politics and Agrarian Reform in Russia," *Problems of Post-Communism*, vol. 43, no. 1 (1995), pp. 23–34.

73. For discussions of the Russian monetary and banking system, see the contributions to Anders Åslund, ed., *Economic Transformation in Russia* (New York: St. Martin's Press, 1994).

74. Aleksandr Zhilin, "Russian Organized Crime—A Growth Industry," *Prism: A Bi-Weekly on the Post-Soviet States*, vol. 1, no. 26 (December 22, 1995).

75. Dmitry Mikheyev, "The Transformation of the Economic System," in *Russia Transformed*, (Indianapolis, IN: Hudson Institute, 1996).

76. Richard W. Judy, "Nations in Transition: Relative Progress in Economic Transformation," Hudson Institute, June 17, 1995, unpublished paper. Russia ranks similarly on the Heritage Foundation's *1996 Index of Economic Reform*, by Bryan T. Johnson and Thomas P. Sheehy (Washington, DC: The Heritage Foundation 1996), front tables.

77. Economic data for the first half of 1996 were less positive than expected. During the first half of the year gross domestic product dropped by 5 percent compared with the same period in 1995. Industrial output fell 4 percent, agricultural output 7 percent, and the volume of investment by 14 percent. See *Finansovye Izvestiya,* August 6, 1996.

78. Charles E. Bohlen, U.S. ambassador to the Soviet Union (1953–1957), contended that President Franklin D. Roosevelt's "greatest single mistake . . . was his insistence on the doctrine of unconditional surrender which . . . probably lengthened the war by convincing the Germans they should fight on . . . ," thus providing the Soviets with the opportunity to move their troops into the middle of Europe. Charles E. Bohlen, *Witness to History, 1929–1969* (New York: Norton, 1973), p. 212.

79. *The Programme of the Communist Party of the Soviet Union. A New Edition* (Moscow: Novosti, 1986), p. 18.

80. *Pravda,* February 26, 1986.

81. *Izvestiya,* February 6, 1990.

82. Soviet foreign minister Shevardnadze conceded in October 1989 that Soviet intervention in Afghanistan had been a mistake and that "we had set ourselves against all of humanity, violated norms of behavior, ignored universal human values." He revealed that the crucial decision had not been discussed in the Politburo, but was "made behind the back of the party and people." He also conceded that the Soviet leadership had lied regarding the Krasnoyarsk radar facility in claiming that this structure ("the size of an Egyptian pyramid") was for "space research" and not a violation of the 1972 Anti-Ballistic Missile Treaty. *New York Times,* October 25, 1989.

83. See Jan Winiecki, *The Distorted World of Soviet-Type Economies* (Pittsburgh: University of Pittsburgh Press, 1988).

84. *Izvestiya,* February 6, 1990, p. 2.

85. *Izvestiya,* July 1, 1987.

86. *Pravda,* June 26, 1987.

87. See Vladimir G. Treml, *Alcohol in the USSR: A Statistical Study* (Durham, NC: Duke University Press, 1982).

88. *Izvestiya,* June 29, 1988.

89. Ibid.

90. *Izvestiya,* June 30, 1988.

91. *Izvestiya,* July 2, 1988, as reported by Fedor Morgun, chairman of the U.S.S.R. State Committee for Preservation of the Environment. The most comprehensive assessment of the environmental degradation of the Soviet Union can be found in Murray Feshbach and Alfred Friendly, Jr., *Ecocide in the USSR: Health and Nature Under Siege* (New York: Basic Books, 1992).

92. In Chapter 3, Section 1 of *State and Revolution.* See also, Robert C. Tucker, ed. *The Lenin Anthology* (New York: Norton, 1975), p. 337.

93. *Izvestiya,* July 2, 1988.

94. See John B. Dunlop, *The Rise of Russia and the Fall of the Soviet Empire* (Princeton, NJ: Princeton University Press, 1993).

95. Aleksandr Solzhenitsyn, *The Mortal Danger: How Misconceptions About Russia Imperil America,* 2nd ed. (New York: Harper & Row, 1981), pp. 28 and 109.

96. Aleksandr Solzhenitsyn, ed. *From Under the Rubble* (Boston: Little, Brown, 1975).

97. Aleksandr Solzhenitsyn, *Letter to the Soviet Leaders* (New York: Harper & Row, 1974), p. 41.

98. Laurie Hays, "Soviets Tackle Mystery of Party's Hoard," *Wall Street Journal,* October 15, 1991, p. A–13.

99. *Izvestiya,* December 9, 1991, p. 1.

100. An estimated 3.5 million of the original 25 million Russians who found themselves in the "near abroad" in December 1991 returned to Russia by the end of 1995. According to the Federal Migration Service, in spring 1996 there were some 9 million forced migrants on the territory of the former Soviet Union. Forced migration totaled more than one-third of the 3 million people who have moved to Russia since 1993. More than 70 percent of the migrants have come from Central Asia, especially Uzbekistan and Kazakstan, and two-thirds of the arrivals have been ethnic Russians. ITAR TASS, May 23,

1996; reported in *Omri Daily Digest*, May 27, 1996.

101. Quoted in Leonid Bershidsky, "Georgia Peace Force Riles Duma," *The Moscow Times* (June 18, 1994), p. 3.

102. Bess Brown, "Armenians and Georgians to Serve in Russian Border Troops," *RFER/RL Daily Report*, no. 52 (March 16, 1994). It has been noted that these agreements were reached only after the Russians had exerted economic, political and security pressure on the partner states. Note that, under growing Russian pressure, Georgia did join the CIS and Azerbaijan, which had withdrawn at the height of the war with Armenia, also rejoined.

103. The newly elected Communist-dominated Duma passed a resolution on February 14, 1996 preventing the Russian government from relocating ships or transferring coastal infrastructure of the Black Sea Fleet. *Monitor*, February 16, 1996.

104. On the importance of Caspian Sea oil in Russian policy see David Nissman, "Ethnopolitics and Pipeline Security," *Prism*, October 6, 1995, and Rossen Vassilev, "The Politics of Caspian Oil," *Prism*, January 12, 1996.

105. *RFE/RL Daily Report* (December 1, 1994). Russia's furious public opinion campaign against NATO's enlargement and its threats to retaliate should NATO expansion go forward has raised serious concerns in Central Europe.

106. Volodymyr Zviglyanich, "Primakov and the Ambitions of a Great Power," *Prism*, January 26, 1996.

107. Russia has bilateral treaties with Armenia, Georgia, Kyrgyzstan, and Tajikistan. Similar treaties are under discussion with Belarus and Kazakstan. *Rossiyskie Vesti*, May 11, 1995; translated in *FBIS-SOV*–95–091, pp. 21–22. At the CIS summit on May 26, 1995 Ukraine, Moldova, Azerbaijan and Uzbekistan did not sign a document concerning the border issue. *Krasnaya zvezda*, May 30, 1995.

108. See Stanislav Lunev, "The Myth of Reform in the Russian Army," *Prism*, December 22, 1995.

109. Evidence of the centrality of the commitment to recreating the old Union in Russian politics can be seen in the fact that the Russian Council on Foreign and Defense Policy, headed by Sergei Karaganov, Deputy Director of the Europe Institute of the Russian Academy of Sciences, released in June 1996 a draft document entitled "Will the [Soviet] Union Revive by 2005?" The Council, whose past publications have provided the basis for official Russian foreign policy, emphasizes the centrality of Ukraine in the revival of the "Union." Increasing Ukraine's economic dependence on Russia is the key to Russia's policy. See Volodymyr Zviglyanich, "Russia Discusses Plans to Restore the Soviet Union by 2005," *Prism*, vol. 2, no. 4 (June 14, 1996).

110. *Monitor*, February 2, 1996.

111. For assessments of the major role of the successors of the KGB, see J. Michael Waller, "The KGB Legacy in Russia," *Problems of Post-Communism*, vol. 42, no. 6 (1995), pp. 3–10; and James Sherr, "The New Russian Intelligence Empire," *Problems of Post-Communism*, vol. 42, no. 6 (1995) pp. 11–17.

112. Feshbach and Friendly, *Ecocide in the USSR*, pp. 74–75. Murray Feshbach has long been among the most knowledgeable of specialists on the Soviet environment. His book represents a terrible indictment of a system that destroyed much of the environment of a substantial portion of the globe.

113. See Mark G. Field, "Soviet Health Problems and the Convergence Hypothesis," in Anthony Jones, Walter D. Connor, and David E. Powell, eds., *Soviet Social Problems* (Boulder, CO: Westview Press, 1991), pp. 78–93; and Feshbach and Friendly, *Ecocide in the USSR, passim*. See, also, Aleksandr Nemtsov, "When People Drink, It's Society that Gets the Hangover," *Rossiiskiye vesti*, December 2, 1995, pp. 12–13; translated in *The Current Digest of the Post-Soviet Press*, vol. 47, no. 49 (1995), pp. 12–14.

114. Toni Nelson, "Russia's Population Sinks," *World Watch*, (January/February 1996), pp. 22–23.

115. Reported in *Monitor*, February 7, 1996. On June 12, 1996 Amnesty International sent an open letter to all the candidates in the presidential election deploring the continuation of human rights abuses in the country. See *Omri Daily Report*, June 13, 1996.

116. This argument was developed most clearly by Nikolai Troitsky, "The 'Commie Patriot': A Finde Siecle Political Hybrid," *Prism*, vol. 2, no. 12 (June 14, 1996). Troitsky argues that Zyuganov is motivated primarily by the desire for personal political power. He has developed two constituencies, the old Communist Party and Russian patriots/nationalists. A Zyuganov government would not be staffed, Troitsky maintains, by Communist ideologues, but by a ministers representing a broad range of views and political tendencies.

117. Blair A. Ruble, "Russia's Election: What Does it Mean?" Statement presented to The Commission on Security and Cooperation in Europe, U.S. House of Representatives, Washington, D.C., July 10, 1996. Available in electronic form on http://www.cdi.org.

CHAPTER 8

The Government of China

Joseph Fewsmith

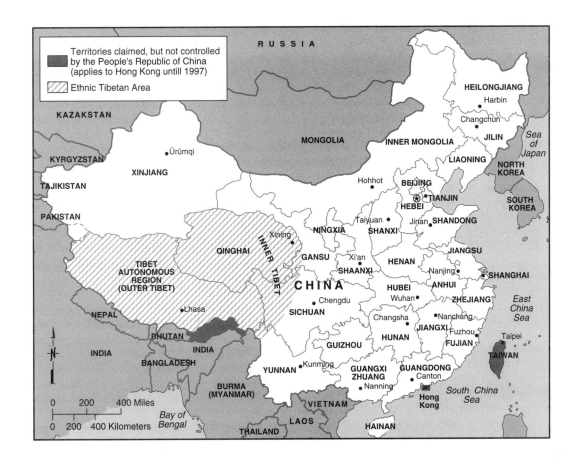

Political Development

China, the world's most populous nation, is also the oldest continuous civilization in the world. Moreover, it is historically the most self-conscious society in the world, and the legacy of its history and civilization continue to play an important role, consciously and unconsciously, in the way that China is governed. When Mao Zedong, the leader of the Communist revolution, sought guidance on governing his nation, he turned not to the works of Marx and Lenin, whose philosophy he espoused, but to China's dynastic histories to better understand the way in which China's emperors had ruled the nation.[1] He did so even as he excoriated China's imperial past as feudal.

The legacies of imperial China are many. Here we can outline some basic features that have resonated clearly in the contemporary period. First, China for two millenia has had a tradition of unified rule under a strong ruler, even if that tradition has often been honored only in the breech as domestic turmoil or foreign conquest engulfed China. This tradition stretches back at least to the first emperor of the Qin Dynasty (Qinshi Huangdi), who unified China in 221 B.C. A ruthless ruler, the emperor ended feudalism in China, starting China on a path remarkably different from that of Europe or Japan. The legacy of this crushing of local autonomy has been a powerful belief that China can be unified only under strong, central rule; the idea of federalism, although now advocated by some intellectuals, is alien to China's political tradition.

Second, this system of centralized rule was complemented and implemented by the most developed bureaucratic structure in the premodern world. China may have invented bureaucracy, but imperial China could hardly be considered a bureaucratic society. On the contrary, it was a rather lightly administered society (which does not mean that the government could not suppress rebellion by military force if necessary). Throughout the late imperial period, China's bureaucracy remained nearly constant

in size, at around 20,000 officials. This meant a ratio of 1 official for every 11,000 people in 1650 and only 1 for every 20,000 people in 1850.[2]

Third, the bureaucracy was staffed by officials trained in the Confucian tradition. The ideas of Confucius (551–479 B.C.) identified moral conduct as the core concern of governance. Thus, although the Chinese created perhaps the most rational bureaucratic structure of the premodern world, it did not generate a notion of rule by law. The stress in Confucianism was on the cultivation of "gentlemen" (*junzi*) who would know intuitively what correct behavior demanded in any given situation; laws were seen as inimicable to the development of such moral knowledge. This tradition left a legacy of "rule by men" (rather than law), but it also created a sense of duty among intellectuals that they must serve as the conscience of society, as well as its natural rulers.

Officials were recruited into the bureaucracy through an examination system that tested the candidate's knowledge of the Confucian classics. The Confucian classics included the instructions of Confucius, some of his followers, and other texts that Confucians took as illustrating important moral principles. The examination system itself consisted of three major levels, and candidates reaching the highest level were appointed to the most prestigious positions in the land. Thus the notion of a bureaucracy staffed by people well indoctrinated in a particular world view stretches back millenia.

Finally, bureaucratic officials were drawn from the so-called scholar-gentry class. The term "scholar-gentry" is a somewhat awkward importation of the British concept of "gentry" to the Chinese scene. But whereas British gentry were beneficiaries of landed titles, China's scholar-gentry attained their social status through a combination of wealth and scholarship. A successful farmer could send his sons to school in the hopes that one might succeed in the examination system, thus conferring status and opportunities to acquire greater wealth on the family. There were always many more aspirants to official positions than the bureaucracy could employ, so the majority of China's "scholar-gentry" stayed in their local areas, sometimes serving as secretaries for officials who came to rule that area and more often becoming the pillars of local society. Such people had a vested interest in maintaining the institutions of Confucian learning that underpinned their own standing in the community and legitimated their aspirations for themselves and their offspring.

Thus Confucianism was deeply embedded in both China's social structure and its political institutions. It is this combination that explains why Chinese society could remain stable while governed by such a small bureaucracy. It also explains why dynasties could come and go without fundamentally disrupting the social order.

China's imperial legacy leaves a clear, if sometimes indirect, imprint on contemporary China. More immediate as shapers of contemporary China's political institutions and behavior have been the decline of imperial China and the history of the national and social revolutions of the nineteenth and twentieth centuries. It is to that history that we now turn our attention.

Table 8.1   MAJOR PERIODS IN CHINESE HISTORY

Zhou Dynasty	B.C.	1122–255
Qin Dynasty	B.C.	255–206
Han Dynasty	B.C.	206–221 A.D.
Period of disunion		221–589
Tang Dynasty		618–907
Song Dynasty		951–1280
Yuan (Mongol) Dynasty		1280–1368
Ming Dynasty		1368–1644
Qing (Manchu) Dynasty		1644–1911
Republic of China		1912–1949
People's Republic of China		1949–

THE DECLINE OF IMPERIAL CHINA

By the mid-nineteenth century, China was suffering from population pressures and the resulting decline in social order on the one hand and from a weakening of imperial vigor caused in part by efforts to suppress domestic rebellion on the other hand. A long period of peace following the establishment of the Qing (Manchu) dynasty in 1644 and the spread of new foods such as yams allowed China to experience a population explosion unique in the premodern world. The population nearly doubled from 125 million in 1650 to 225 million in 1750, then nearly doubled again, increasing over the next century to 410 million in 1850.[3] This growth in China's population meant that ever larger numbers of people were cultivating increasingly marginal land, with the result that more people were vulnerable to the vagaries of nature, and the prospect of starvation, than ever before.

A series of rebellions starting in the late eighteenth century gradually drained the central treasury and the vigor of the dynasty. By the middle of the nineteenth century, when the largest rebellion in human history—the Taiping Rebellion—broke out, the central government no longer had the fiscal strength and military organization to effectively meet the challenge. As the armies of the Taiping rebels swept northward from their origin in southwest China, the Qing allowed a number of provincial officials to organize armies in their home localities. Although this effort to raise local armies eventually succeeded in suppressing the Taiping Rebellion, it also brought about a localization and militarization of Chinese society that would eventually undermine the foundations of China's last dynasty and lead to warlordism in the 1910s and 1920s.[4]

The Taiping Rebellion not only reflected domestic pressures but also the coming of the West. Many peasants were driven to join the rebellion by the deflation of copper currency that was caused, at least in part, by the export of silver to the West in exchange for opium. At the time, China had a bimetalic currency system, copper for small transactions and silver for large. Peasants generally earned copper when they sold their crops, but they had to pay the tax collector in silver. As silver rose in value, the effective tax burden on peasants increased, driving many to the point of rebellion. Western influence was also present in the ideology of the Taipings. The leader of the rebellion, Hong Xiuquan, had come into contact with Christian tracts and had become convinced (following a nervous breakdown) that he was the younger brother of Jesus Christ. The ideology of the Taiping Rebellion was a combination of erzatz Christianity and native Chinese traditions. Despite its strange origins, it presaged many trends that would later be present in the Communist movement. In particular, the Taipings called for communal ownership of land and an equalization of wealth. In this sense, the Taiping Rebellion really marks the beginning of an enormous social revolution that swept over China from the mid-nineteenth century to at least the mid-twentieth century.

The coming of the West was apparent in one other way. As the Taipings looked like they might genuinely threaten the existence of the dynasty, a Western-led and -financed "Ever-Victorious Army" was organized to help defeat the Taipings. The Qing may have eventually succeeded in defeating the Taipings, but the Ever Victorious Army nevertheless played a significant role.

Thus, by the time the Taiping Rebellion was ultimately suppressed in 1864, China's final dynasty and the Confucian society on which it was based were slowly disintegrating. Challenged from below, the dynasty responded by devolving authority to an increasingly active, and organized, society. Confronted by the intrusion of the West, the dynasty responded by adopting half-hearted Westernization. Unlike in Japan, no new elite emerged to reform the state, so Westernization efforts could only be sporadic, supported by a handful of reform-minded officials and declining when those officials moved or were removed. Neither emulated nor effectively challenged, the Western presence slowly chipped away at the efficacy of Confucian institutions and beliefs that had been the core of the Chinese system for 2,000 years.

The Self-Strengthening Movement

The decline of the Qing, however, turned out to be a lengthy process. Beginning in about 1860 a remarkable group of men in Beijing and in the provinces made an effort to breath new life into the dynasty. They tried, on the one hand, to restore the vigor of Confucianism, while, on the other hand, borrowing selectively from the West. This period, known as the self-strengthening movement, lasted nearly a quarter of a century until the Sino-Japanese War of 1894–1895 ended the hope of gradual transition.[5]

The self-strengthening period is important not only because it began a process of introducing Western technology and ideas, first in the military field and then gradually in industry and other areas, but also because it reflected a desire to integrate Chinese culture and Western learning selectively. The approach was expressed by the well-known scholar-official Zhang Zhidong as "Chinese learning as the essence, Western learning for practical use." This sense that Chinese culture, as it was then understood, could remain fundamental to the system while Western technology could be grafted selectively onto it has been a theme that has repeated itself throughout modern Chinese history, including in the reform period introduced by Deng Xiaoping starting in 1978. It has never worked well; the technology that was being introduced carried with it cultural values that could not be isolated from Chinese culture.

Nevertheless, the self-strengthening impulse remains strong in part because it has proven more successful in modernizing China than two other forces: cosmopolitanism and nativism. Cosmopolitan impulses, which grew strong in the early twentieth century, has sought to integrate China into the world by a wholesale adoption of foreign ideas. But cosmopolitanism has always run aground on nationalism, the most powerful force in modern Chinese politics. In contrast, the nativist tradition has tried to reject Westernization. Nativism has frequently merged with nationalism to produce radical movements. It was this combination that the Communist movement tapped so effectively in its rise to power, and it remains a potent force in China today.

Toward Social and National Revolution

The decline and fall of the Qing dynasty opened up a range of political questions and historical trends that continue to reverberate to the present day. As noted above, China had traditionally been ruled by a combination of monarchy and Confucian-based bureaucracy. Even the institution of the monarch (emperor) was tied to the Confucian value system through the notion of the "mandate of heaven." Thus, according to the ideology, the monarch did not rule simply because of blood, but also because he embodied virtue and earned the right to rule by winning heaven's favor. When the monarchy fell in China, it took with it the values and institutions that had upheld imperial rule. The fall of the monarchy meant the corresponding fall of Confucian-based knowledge and associated institutions. Therefore, any new system that would come into being would not have to simply transform old ideologies into modern ideologies but to legitimize political rule on the basis of a new ideology.

The fall of the Qing also ushered in a social revolution that would ultimately span the next half century. Efforts to overthrow the Qing were led by people who had been marginal in the old social order. Typical of these was Sun Yat-sen, China's first professional revolutionary and the leader of the Revolution of 1911 that ended the Qing dynasty. Sun was born into a middle-peasant family in the southeastern province of Guangdong. When he was still a boy, he followed his elder brother to Hawaii, where he acquired a command of English and a familiarity with a range of Western ideas, including Christianity. As someone who had not followed the traditional path of immersing himself in the Confucian classics in the hopes of passing the examination system but instead went abroad for a foreign education, Sun was of a different social class and background than his contemporaries in officialdom. The success of the Revolution of 1911 thus heralded the rise of a new type of political leader.

This combination of the decline of the old order and revolution by a new class of people reflected the fact that in China, the national revolution (state building) and social revolution would proceed hand in hand. State building in China would not be a top-down process as it was in Japan.

Mass Nationalism

If events of the late nineteenth and early twentieth centuries determined that China's efforts to modernize were going to be far more wrenching than those of its neighbor to the east, the eventual success of the Communist revolution was brought about by two other factors. First was the rise of mass nationalism. The impact of nationalism on Chinese politics might be dated from 1895 when Japan defeated China in a short but decisive war that destroyed China's nascent navy and brought its self-strengthening efforts to a close. A radical scholar by the name of Kang Youwei, then in Beijing to take the highest level of the imperial examination, led 800 of his fellow examinees in signing a petition demanding that the Qing government reject the peace treaty (which the Qing signed) and undertake fundamental reform. This initial nationalist movement, modest as it was, suggested the link between nationalist passion and the demand for radical political action on the one hand and foreshadowed the rise of far more powerful mass nationalism on the other.

The rise of mass nationalism in China can be dated from the May Fourth Movement of 1919. The cause of this movement was the decision of the Versailles Conference to turn over German concessions in the eastern Chinese province of Shandong to Japan (which claimed them because of a secret agreement it had signed with the warlord government in Beijing during World War I). When news of this agreement reached Beijing, students took to the streets demanding that the Chinese delegation refuse to sign the peace treaty. When government troops arrested some of the students involved, the movement spread throughout China. Moreover, in a sign of China's rapidly changing society, the movement quickly drew support from merchants and workers as well as intellectuals. Political participation would never be confined to a small elite again.

Protest demonstration in Beijing in spring 1989.

The May Fourth Movement boosted an intellectual revolution in China that was radically critiquing China's Confucian past, thus ushering in a period of new thought. At the same time, the May Fourth Movement ushered in a demand for political action. On the one hand, the May Fourth Movement led to the reinvigoration of the Chinese Nationalist Party (Guomindang, GMD), while, on the other hand, it led to the founding of the Chinese Communist Party (CCP) in 1921.

The Nationalist and Communist Revolutions

Under the auspices of the Communist International (Comintern), the GMD and the CCP joined together in a united front. The GMD was the larger, older, and better-known party, while the CCP brought in a core of highly dedicated young

activists—as well as foreign aid from the Soviet Union. In 1926, the GMD led a Northern Expedition from its base in the southeastern city of Guangzhou (Canton) to defeat the warlords and reunify the country under its rule. The Northern Expedition progressed remarkably rapidly toward the middle of China, but then paused when it reached the east coast metropolis of Shanghai.

For nearly two years after the 1925 death of Sun Yat-sen, who had led the GMD and forged the alliance with the CCP, tensions had built up between the GMD and the CCP and within the GMD itself. In 1927 the military commander of the Northern Expedition, Chiang Kai-shek, decided the time was right for him to take overall leadership of the movement. He did so by launching a bloody purge of the Communists, an action that ultimately claimed thousands of lives. Chiang was successful in establishing his own leadership over the GMD (although he was repeatedly challenged in the ensuing years) and in reunifying China, at least nominally, under the control of the GMD. Communist leaders who survived the purge of 1927 had little choice but to adopt a radically different strategy.

Rural Revolution

After several ill-fated efforts to launch urban insurrections and military uprisings, Mao Zedong and a handful of other party leaders headed for the mountainous areas of the south central province of Jiangxi. In the mountains of Jiangxi, Mao and his followers slowly worked out a different model of revolution. Instead of basing themselves on the urban working class, Mao and his followers exploited rural discontent to develop a powerful and remarkably well-disciplined guerrilla movement. The development of this path of rural revolution, however, did not come easily. In 1934, surrounded by a well-organized assault on their base area by the Nationalist army, the CCP was forced to retreat from the area. Breaking out of their encirclement in October 1935, the CCP headed southwest on what turned into an epic military retreat that ultimately would carry them 8,000 miles to the isolated and impoverished areas of northwestern China. Militarily this "Long March," as it came to be called, was a disaster. Overall, the party lost some 90 percent of its strength.

Nevertheless, the Long March did two things for the CCP. First, it took on mythological proportions as the tale of the march was told and retold, thus creating an image of CCP members as being of heroic stature and their movement as invincible. Second, the battle toughened veterans who survived the Long March became the core of the CCP in the years ahead. All the major leaders of the CCP, including Mao Zedong, Liu Shaoqi, Zhou Enlai, and Deng Xiaoping participated in the Long March. Even in 1996, as Deng Xiaoping hovers near death, the hand of this Long March generation is still felt in party councils.

In the course of this revolutionary history, which spanned 22 years from the retreat into Jiangxi in 1927 to ultimate victory in 1949, the party evolved a number of military and political tactics which became deeply imprinted in the party's behavior in the years after it came to power. This collection of experience is often summed up by the term "Mao Zedong Thought."

Mao Zedong Thought

Mao Zedong was a complex and contradictory man who ultimately towered over his age and left a legacy that will take the Chinese political system and people generations to digest and come to grips with. He was a man who insisted on investigation and research but repeatedly ignored reality to impose his own utopian visions, a man of great intellect and education who despised intellectuals as a class, and a man who led a peasant revolution only to oversee the deaths of millions of peasants in his ill-fated effort to bring crash industrialization to China.

In the revolutionary period when Mao and the movement he led were still confined to their rural base areas, Mao continuously stressed the need to combine theory and practice. Mao was not, initially at least, a sophisticated Marxist theoretician. On the contrary, Mao came to Marxism as a man already committed to revolution; in Marxism he found confirmation and reaffirmation of his own natural inclinations.

For instance, his famous 1926 "Report on the Peasant Revolution in Hunan" is most noted for its absence of Marxist vocabulary. What gave the essay its power was Mao's conviction that he had found in those peasant uprisings a powerful current that could carry the revolution to victory. Indeed, it was not until Mao reached Yanan in 1935 that he had any time to study Marxism-Leninism on a systematic basis. Even then his close associates could not get him to read more sophisticated Marxist writings. Mao preferred the Communist Manifesto, the meaning of which he summed up as "Class struggle! Class struggle! Class Struggle!"[6]

Mao was vulnerable to criticism from the more sophisticated Marxists in the party, many of whom had studied in Moscow. They criticized Mao as an unsophisticated leader who would never be capable of doing more than leading a peasant uprising. In response, Mao heaped scorn on his critics, accusing them of not understanding the realities of China. Mao asserted that all understanding arose from practice, and accused his opponents of being "lazybones."[7]

For Mao, the critical thing was to be able to combine the "universal truth" of Marxism-Leninism with the concrete reality of China. Mao asserted, in fact, that Marxism-Leninism did not exist as an abstract entity but could only exist in concrete manifestations. That is to say, there was only Russian Marxism or Chinese Marxism, not abstract Marxism. This idea of rooting the abstract formulations of Marxism-Leninism in the specific reality of China was part of a process known as the Sinification of Marxism; it was, in short, a process in which the language of Marxism was translated into the idiom of Chinese reality.

The ideas of practice and the Sinification of Marxism were closely connected with that of the mass line. Because knowledge derived from practice and because Marxism had to be made comprehensible in terms of Chinese reality, peasants could only be mobilized if cadres took the message of the revolution to the grass roots and made it comprehensible to the peasants. This was not an easy process, and the ideal was often violated in practice. Nevertheless, the mass mobilizational tactics of the CCP during the revolutionary war required an integration of

Mao Zedong (1893–1976) reviewing a rally of over a million Red Guards composed of students and school children, during the Cultural Revolution. Mao, Chairman of the Communist Party from 1935 until his death, established the People's Republic of China in 1949 and became chairman of the CCP.

party policy with reality. This meant a process of getting cadres to understand local realities and trying to integrate the concerns of peasants with party policy. The mass line, in Mao's words, was a matter of "from the masses, to the masses." That is, the party would take the scattered concerns of the peasants and try to integrate them with party policy so that when policy was implemented at the local level it could be accepted by the peasants.

Another idea that proved vital to the CCP's success was that of the united front. The idea of the united front was to try to bring together the majority of people in a common cause and thereby isolate those who were in opposition. In order to win the support of people who were not Marxists, it was necessary for the party to play down its most radical ideas and stress ideals that it had in common with the majority of Chinese—such as nationalism during the Sino-Japanese war of 1937–1945.

These four ideas—practice, the Sinification of Marxism, the mass line, and the united front—acted as a restraining mechanism on the party's more radical tendencies. In the face of hostile forces—the GMD on the one hand and the Japanese on the other—the CCP had no choice but to act in a prudent manner and thereby attract as much support as it could. In such a wartime atmosphere, there was an im-

mediate and obvious test of policy—whether the party gained support and won battles or whether it lost support and suffered defeat. Such an environment forced the party to pay great attention to the realities of China.

Indeed, one can view the radicalization of the CCP in the years between its victory in 1949 and the end of the Cultural Revolution in 1976 as the result in part of the removal of a hostile environment and hence of the factors that had led the party to adhere to a prudential course during the revolutionary years. In other words, the victory of the CCP in 1949 was overwhelming, indeed too much so. As the party consolidated power in the early 1950s, it destroyed and silenced all opposition. As a result, there was no countervailing force to check the radical tendencies of the party.

Among the most damaging of Chairman Mao's thoughts was his lifelong belief in the intrinsic value of struggle. Mao's faith in struggle served him and the party well in wartime, but very poorly in peacetime. Yet Mao was convinced that "contradictions" lay everywhere and that resolving them through struggle would have a purifying effect on the party. In fact, it had a debilitating effect. Accompanying Mao's belief in struggle was his faith in mass mobilization. Again, organizing and mobilizing people was very effective during the revolutionary struggle, but it proved to be a very poor way of building a modern economy. To these notions of struggle and mass mobilization, one can add that of will. As a person, Mao repeatedly demonstrated a will that carried him to the top of the CCP and the CCP to victory against great odds. Mao seemed convinced that with sufficient will China could achieve any goal. Combined with revolutionary romantic notions about building a classless society, Mao's faith in will, struggle, and mass mobilization would prove disastrous to China's modernization.

Consolidation and Radicalization

The end of China's civil war concluded a period of over 30 years in which the country had been more or less continuously divided and at war. The sense of stability and unity gave the CCP something that its Soviet counterparts never experienced, namely widespread support and popularity. There was a hope and a belief that the CCP would be China's salvation. This period of domestic stability also brought a resuscitation of China's agriculture and industry. Despite the widespread damage to China's infrastructure, by 1953 China had restored both agricultural and industrial production to prewar highs.[8] This rapid revival of the economy also rebounded to the party's favor, giving hope that it could indeed lead the country to prosperity.

Part of the new government's success in providing stability and restoring production was due to its ability to penetrate society and establish its power within every corner of society. This process was accomplished first through land reform and then through the socialization of the urban and rural economies. In the course of land reform, the CCP systematically destroyed the old social structure in the countryside. Landlords, social elites, those who had supported the GMD or, during the war, the Japanese, were systematically identified, criticized, and frequently eliminated physically. A new elite of activists was created, one whose basis of power was due entirely to their support of the CCP.

Through its penetration of local society, the CCP was able to establish unprecedented political authority and to mobilize resources on behalf of the state. The new government established an economic system that systematically distorted prices in a way that would funnel resources to the state. This was remarkably effective. In the pre-Communist period, economists estimate that the GMD was able to extract only about 4 percent of national income. By the mid–1950s the Chinese Communist government was able to extract some 30 percent of national income. That is approximately the same rate that the Soviet Union was able to extract in the mid–1930s, but China in 1950 had a per capita income of only one-fourth that of the Soviet Union in 1928.[9] Such figures testify to the degree of political power possessed by the new state and its ability to use that power on behalf of the state.

In the 1950s, the CCP used that power to support the First Five-Year Plan. This plan, which was heavily supported with aid from the Soviet Union, was extremely successful in terms of creating industrial production. Industrial production grew at an average annual rate of 18 percent.[10]

Nevertheless, by the end of the First Five-Year Plan, problems were mounting in the Chinese economy. Although industry had expanded rapidly, agriculture had lagged behind. Food grain is estimated to have grown 3.7 percent per annum during the First Five-Year Plan period, but that rate fell short of the demands created by rapid industrialization and urbanization. Moreover, there is evidence that the government had simply extracted too many resources from the Chinese economy, leaving the countryside bereft of inputs. It was also obvious that the centralization of economic authority in the First Five-Year Plan had created many inefficiencies as a newly created bureaucratic system grappled with problems that were simply beyond its capabilities.

In short, as China summed up the results of its First Five-Year Plan, it was apparent that China could not continue to follow the Soviet model. Something would have to give. Either the rate of economic growth would have to slow in order to allow agriculture to develop, or new ways of managing the economy would have to be found.

Political Factors

Rethinking China's course of development was also heavily influenced by political factors. In

1956, Khruschev shocked the Communist world by harshly denouncing Stalin as a person who had created a personality cult and condemned millions to their deaths. This speech, which caught the Chinese leadership completely off guard, had profound ramifications for China. "Mao Zedong Thought" had been written into the Chinese constitution as the fundamental guideline of the party, and a cult of personality had grown up around Mao (though not on the same scale as around Stalin or as would later develop around Mao). At the CCP's Eighth Party Congress in 1956, the party deleted the reference to Mao Zedong Thought from the party constitution, and Mao stepped back from day-to-day management of the system, allowing more managerial powers to flow to Liu Shaoqi and Deng Xiaoping. This opened up questions about Mao's role in the system, and wittingly or unwittingly opened a gap between the person of Mao on the one hand, and the bureaucratic organization of the party on the other.

At the same time, the rigidities of political control in the 1950s had given rise to many complaints of abuses of power and corruption. Contrary to the desires of his party colleagues, Mao decided to address these problems by opening up the door to public criticism of the party. Accordingly, in February 1957, Mao delivered a speech called, "On the Correct Handling of Contradictions Among the People," which argued that "non-antagonistic contradictions" could be handled through a public airing of complaints. This speech and subsequent urgings by the party leadership ushered in a period known as the "Hundred Flowers" movement (after the slogan "Let a hundred schools of thought contend, let a hundred flowers bloom").

The Hundred Flowers campaign soon brought forth a torrent of criticism that shocked the party leadership, and apparently embarrassed Mao since he had urged such a campaign against the advice of his colleagues. Mao had apparently felt confident that he and the party enjoyed overwhelming public support; after all, their accomplishments seemed evident. But people in general, and intellectuals in particular, chafed at the political controls that had been imposed and suggested opening up the political system, even allowing other political parties to compete with the CCP. Embarrassed and angered by this outpouring of criticism (and the organization of some demonstrations), Mao moved quickly to reverse himself. In June 1957, the party launched an "anti rightist" campaign against those who had spoken out. In the ensuing campaign, organizations were told to ferret out 5 percent of their members as "rightists," so even units that felt they could find no rightists still turned over 5 percent of their members as rightists. Altogether, at least 500,000 people were named as rightists; many of them would not have their labels reversed until the end of the Maoist era two decades later.

In other words, by the late 1950s both economic trends and political events were combining in ways to launch China on a path that was distinctively different from the Soviet model and far more radical. The result was the Great Leap Forward, one of the greatest economic and human policy failures in the history of the world.

The Great Leap Forward

Although the Great Leap Forward (GLF) was an unprecedented disaster, at least some aspects of it made sense. The GLF called for a decentralization of the economy and an expansion of local authority at the expense of China's central bureaucracies. This kernel of economic rationality (which has ripened in the post-Mao reforms) was distorted by other policies, which led the GLF to disaster. First, economic decentralization was accompanied by a belief in local autarky. Under the assumption that central planning had failed to effectively coordinate the economic activities of the nation, radicals urged that each locality develop local self-sufficiency. This led to a great deal of duplicative construction and a loss of economic efficiency through a diminution of interregional trade. Second, accompanying this decentralization was an undercutting of the central bureaucracies. No doubt critics were right that the central bureaucracies were stifling growth and local initiative through overcentralization and bureaucratic rigidity, but their efforts led China to the other extreme in which the central bureaucracies lost most of their coordinative functions. In other words, instead of paring the central bureaucracies to a size and function that they could reasonably expect to fulfill, the GLF destroyed their oversight function and left no constraints on the economic irrationalities that would follow.

It was, however, the radicalization of the political atmosphere that gave the GLF its character. In the wake of the antirightist movement, no one dared speak out against the policies. On the contrary, the atmosphere was such that the political demands of the center were inflated as they went down the hierarchy, with cadres at each level trying to prove their devotion to Mao and socialism by overfulfilling their quotas.

In short, the GLF was the apotheosis of the mobilizing techniques developed by the CCP during the revolutionary period and the early years of the People's Republic of China (PRC). Unchecked by either opposition forces or the normal bureaucratic checks that would have happened had there not been an antirightist campaign and a radicalization of the political atmosphere, the GLF threw tremendous human resources into enormously wasteful projects.

The campaign to develop backyard furnaces came to symbolize the wastefulness of the GLF. Determined to surpass England and catch up with the United States in steel production, Chinese leaders called for the creation of thousands of small-scale iron smelters. By late 1958, there were several hundred thousand small blast furnaces scattered throughout the country. Into these furnaces went every bit of scrap steel that peasants could locate—sometimes including their own cooking implements.

The result was wasteful in the extreme. The quality of the iron produced was so poor that most of it had to be discarded. In other words, in many instances perfectly good iron and steel products had been dumped into the blast furnaces only to produce useless lumps of iron. Moreover, forests were destroyed in this ill-fated effort to industrialize, causing an ecological disaster from which China has yet to recover.

If the economic effects of the GLF were bad, the human results were disastrous. The backyard furnaces, for instance, were erected at the time of the fall harvest, and some 20 percent of the rural labor force was diverted to build and maintain them. Moreover, in their zeal to bring about the "transition to communism," most localities built common dining halls. There people ate as much as they wanted, and pretty soon food supplies were depleted.[11] Because localities had sold excessive amounts of grain to the state to cover up the lies they told about their production "successes," there were no grain reserves. Particularly after 1959, when the political atmosphere was further radicalized by a challenge to Mao's policies, people began to starve in large numbers. By the time the GLF finally ended in late 1961, at least 20 million people had died.

The Cultural Revolution

The GLF marked a critical turning point that has affected all subsequent development of the CCP. Given the disaster of Mao's policies, he had no choice but to turn to others, indeed to those whose counsel he had rejected when he had launched the GLF, to restore the economy. Mao, however, would not, and perhaps could not, admit that he had been wrong in launching the GLF. The result was a period of policy oscillation in which party moderates implemented policies designed to rationalize the economy, while Mao continued to emphasize the socialist and egalitarian values that he had championed during the GLF.

Finally, Mao became convinced that others were creating a bureaucratic society inimicable to his vision of a revolutionary society. Accordingly, Mao launched the country on one last nightmare, the Cultural Revolution. In 1966, Mao mobilized the youth of the country, who were formed quickly into Red Guard units. Under the banner of opposing the "four olds" (old customs, old habits, old culture, and old thinking), Red Guards ransacked people's homes, confiscating or destroying anything deemed "feudal" in nature (including old books, paintings and ceramics), persecuting individuals deemed "bourgeois" or "rightist," and denouncing party leaders who were accused of opposing Chairman Mao. This phase of the Cultural Revolution, which cost thousands their lives, lasted about two years before Mao intervened to restore order. Millions of former Red Guards were sent to the countryside, where they were told to learn from the peasants. Disbanding the Red Guards, however, did not end the Cultural Revolution, for instead of admitting defeat and restoring the party, Mao called on the military to restore order throughout the country.

In the end, the Cultural Revolution dragged on for ten years until Mao himself finally died in September 1976. The human suffering caused by the Cultural Revolution was staggering, the waste appalling. Finally, a month after Mao died, veteran party and military leaders moved to arrest Mao's wife, Jiang Qing, and her cohorts, who collectively became known as the "Gang of Four."

As Deng Xiaoping later put it, China had wasted 20 years.

China Under Reform

The death of Mao and the arrest of the Gang of Four did not immediately bring a change to China's economic and political policies. Hua Guofeng, a 56-year-old vice premier, succeeded Mao as chairman of the party. He had been chosen by Mao as a compromise candidate who might maintain the balance between radical leftist and moderate forces that Mao had established in his last years. Hua, however, did not have the seniority within the party or the leadership abilities to maintain the top job for long. Soon, veteran party members purged during the Cultural Revolution demanded to be restored to their jobs, and many old revolutionaries still in power (known as "survivors") supported their efforts. The leader of this veteran cadre group was Deng Xiaoping.

In 1977, Deng Xiaoping was restored to his position as a vice premier, but he was not content with a second-tier position. Deng deeply felt the loss of time and believed that China must act quickly to develop its economy or it would never achieve its century-old dream of attaining "wealth and power." He also believed that China could not modernize its economy if it continued to adhere to the ideological dogmas espoused during the Cultural Revolution. In 1978, Deng supported a nationwide discussion on the theme of "practice is the sole criterion of truth."

The campaign harkened back to the theme of "practice" that had served the party so well during the revolution, arguing that policies could not be determined a priori to be socialist but rather had to be tested in practice.

The campaign on practice as the sole criterion of truth radically changed China's political atmosphere. Intellectuals, excoriated as the "stinking ninth category" during the Cultural Revolution, were restored to their positions and considered to be part of the working class. Deng Xiaoping spoke to the 1978 National Congress of Science and Technology and declared science and technology to be the "primary forces of production." More movingly, he declared himself willing to serve as the "logistics" officer for their research.

In December 1978 the party convened the Third Plenary Session of the Eleventh Central Committee. In the resulting communiqué, the party declared that large-scale class struggle was over and that the focus of the party's work would shift to economic modernization. The "four modernizations" of industry, agriculture, science and technology, and national defense were to be given top priority. A number of veteran party leaders were restored to high-level positions. Hua Guofeng was allowed to stay on as chairman until 1981, but the era of reform had clearly begun.

Some of the specific policies adopted under reform will be discussed in the next section. Here, it is important to point out that reform covered the whole range of state-society relations as well as foreign policy. Not only was the content of the CCP's ideology changed from Mao's romantic revolutionary notions of building a socialist state to Deng's far more pragmatic ideas of "building socialism with Chinese characteristics," but the role of ideology within the polity changed dramatically. Mao sought to modernize China through the mobilizing lever of ideology; Deng sought economic growth by reducing ideology to a set of prescriptions intended to uphold the authority of the party. This much more limited notion of ideology, both reflected and promoted a depoliticization of society. In the Maoist period, especially during the height of the Cultural Revolution, the most private of thoughts and acts were considered to be politically relevant. With the inauguration of the Dengist period, the state largely withdrew from society, allowing a "zone of privacy" to develop around individuals. Although there have been periodic attempts to prevent the growth of this zone of privacy, it has nevertheless continued to be enlarged throughout the Dengist period. The public expression of political ideas remains restricted, but the definition of what constitutes a political idea has constantly shrunk. Into the space vacated by the state has blossomed a vibrant popular culture that does not challenge the authority of the state but does restrict the impact of state ideology.[12]

Opening up to the outside world has reinforced this retreat of the state and diminution of the role of ideology. With the inauguration of reform, serious ideas and frivolous notions alike flooded into China, and were sometimes being taken with the same degree of seriousness. Although Western notions including such weighty concepts as democracy and human rights and less serious thoughts as expressed in Hollywood movies have poured into China, popular culture has been more influenced by Taiwan and Hong Kong, Chinese cultural areas that have developed strong and vibrant film and entertainment industries. The impact of outside ideas has often been decried, but it is clearly unstoppable.

There is no question that the reform and development of the economy as well as the opening up of Chinese society have generated forces that challenge the political status quo. The usual cliché that China has engaged in economic reform but not political reform contains both truth and exaggeration. In fact, the breakdown of the commune system in the countryside, the development of an economy beyond Beijing's direct control, the development of law and the role of China's legislative organ, the National People's Congress (see Section B), and the greater role of experts in policy formation all suggest that China's political system has evolved a great deal. It is nevertheless true that all power continues to reside in the CCP and that direct expression of contrary political opinions is not tolerated.

The tensions between an emerging society and a still-closed political system burst into international view in the spring of 1989 as thousands, then over a million Beijing residents, took to the streets to demand a more open political system. After six weeks of confrontation, and occasional movements toward conciliation, the protests were crushed by the military at the cost of some 700 lives. The images of tanks and armored personnel carriers moving into the center of Beijing, guns blazing, remains firmly planted in the minds of millions. It also obscures a complex reality. Indeed, controversy over the tactics of student leaders and the associated debate over how political change in China is best achieved has recently come to wider public attention with the release of two films.[13]

The suppression of the 1989 protests appeared for a while to mark the end of reform, as the reform-minded General Secretary Zhao

Deng Xiaoping, 93 years old in 1996, has done more than any other Chinese leader to secure China's dream of wealth and power.

Ziyang and other officials were purged from office and as intellectuals and others were subjected to investigation. As the immediate crisis passed, however, pressures for reform grew once again. As described in more detail in the next section, Deng Xiaoping in January 1992 traveled to the controversial Shenzhen Special Economic Zone (SEZ) to once again praise reform and opening up. Deng's trip effectively jump-started a new wave of reform and a new period of high economic growth. In October 1992, the party reaffirmed its commitment to economic reform by adopting the most liberal document in its history. Brushing off conservative objections, the document called for developing a "socialist market economy"—the first unambiguous statement that the goal of reform was a market economy.

With power passing to a new generation of leaders, there remain many uncertainties about China's political evolution. For all the difficulties of the reform period, including the tragedy of Tiananmen, China has been more successful in engineering an economic takeoff than any other socialist country. Indeed, China appears on the cusp of attaining its century-old goal of "wealth and power," and it is that success which legitimizes the government's claim to power, not Marxism-Leninism. That change only underscores the evolution the CCP has undergone from its founding to the present time.

KEY TERMS

cadre
Chiang Kai-shek
Chinese Communist Party (CCP)
Confucius
cosmopolitanism
Cultural Revolution (1966–1976)
Deng Xiaoping
four modernizations
Gang of Four
Great Leap Forward (1958–1961)
Guomindang (GMD, Chinese Nationalist Party)
Hundred Flowers Movement (1957)
Liu Shaoqi
Long March

mandate of heaven
Mao Zedong
mass line
May Fourth Movement (1919)
nativism
Northern Expedition (1926–1928)
practice
self-strengthening movement
Sinification of Marxism
Sino-Japanese War (1894–1895)
Sun Yat-sen
Taiping Rebellion (1850–1864)
united front

FURTHER READINGS

Barnett, A. Doak. *Cadres, Bureaucracy, and Political Power in Communist China* (New York: Columbia University Press, 1967).

Belden, Jack. *China Shakes the World* (New York: Monthly Review Press, 1949).

Bianco, Lucien. *Origins of the Chinese Revolution: 1915–1949* (Stanford: Stanford University Press, 1971).

Chang, Jung. *Wild Swans: Three Daughters of China* (New York: Simon and Shuster, 1991).

Chow, Ts'e-tung. *The May Fourth Movement: Intellectual Revolution in Modern China* (Cambridge: Harvard University Press, 1969).

Ch'u, Tung-tsu. *Local Government in China under the Ch'ing* (Stanford: Stanford University Press, 1969).

Eastman, Lloyd. *The Abortive Revolution: China under Nationalist Rule, 1927–1937* (Cambridge: Harvard University Press, 1974).

Fewsmith, Joseph. *Party, State, and Local Elites in Republican China* (Honoloulu: University of Hawaii Press, 1985).

Ho, Ping-ti. *Studies on the Population of China, 1368–1953* (Cambridge: Harvard University Press, 1959).

Hsiao, Kung-Chuan. *Rural China: Imperial Control in the Nineteenth Century* (Seattle: University of Washington Press, 1960).

Johnson, Chalmers. *Peasant Nationalism and Communist Power: The Emergence of Revolutionary China, 1937–1945* (Stanford: Stanford University Press, 1961).

Kirby, William. *Germany and Republican China* (Stanford: Stanford University Press, 1987).

Kuhn, Philip A. *Rebellion and Its Enemies in Late Imperial China* (Cambridge: Harvard University Press, 1970).

Li, Zhisui, with Anne Thurston. *The Private Life of Chairman Mao* (New York: Random House, 1994).

Lieberthal, Kenneth. *Governing China: From Revolution Through Reform* (New York: W.W. Norton, 1995).

Schram, Stuart R. *The Political Thought of Mao Tse-tung* (Middlesex, CT: Penguin, 1963).

Selden, Mark. *The Yenan Way in Revolutionary China* (Cambridge: Harvard University Press, 1971).

Spence, Jonathan D. *The Search for Modern China* (New York: Norton, 1990).

Spence, Jonathan D. *The Gate of Heavenly Peace* (New York: Penguin, 1981).

Schwartz, Benjamin. *Chinese Communism and the Rise of Mao* (Cambridge: Harvard University Press, 1951).

Shiffrin, Harold. *Sun Yat-sen and the Origins of the Chinese Revolution* (Berkeley: University of California Press, 1968).

Thomson, James C. *While China Faced West: American Reformers in Nationalist China, 1928–1937* (Cambridge: Harvard University Press, 1969).

Watt, John R. *The Chinese Magistrate in Late Imperial China* (New York: Columbia University Press, 1972).

Wright, Mary C. *The Last Stand of Chinese Conservatism: The T'ung-chih Restoration, 1862–1874,* rev. ed. (Stanford: Stanford University Press, 1966).

Political Processes and Institutions

From the overview of China's political development presented in the previous section, we turn here to the basic institutions and processes through which China is governed. Because China is ruled by the CCP we start with the party. We consider first how its historical legacy affects its behavior, and then look at the formal structure of the party. Then we turn to the organization of the state and to China's legislative body, the National People's Congress. In order to understand how these institutions function, we look at the implementation of reform, which began in the late 1970s. Finally, we look at the social tensions generated by reform.

THE PARTY

Historical Legacy

At the core of the Chinese political system lies the Chinese Communist Party. As suggested in Section A, the CCP arose in reaction to a number of interlocking crises facing China in the early and mid-twentieth century: the breakdown of political authority, the humiliations suffered at the hands of foreigners, the failure of Confucianism to provide an effective ideological framework, and the growing belief that social revolution was a necessary component of any effective response to these problems. Moreover, in its revolutionary period, the CCP suffered repeated setbacks, some of which almost destroyed the party altogether. This background left important legacies in the organization and functioning of the CCP.

First and foremost, the CCP inherited the mantle of nationalism. Born of the May Fourth Movement, the CCP was one (and ultimately the most successful) expression of the nationalist feelings that were felt deeply by the population. In this sense, Marxism-Leninism provided Chinese nationalists with a template for action, a belief that in adopting certain intellectual and organizational orientations they could realize their broader nationalist objectives. This sense of nationalism has pervaded the CCP throughout its existence, permitted it to survive such incredible policy failures as the Great Leap Forward and the Cultural Revolution, and it has been the anchor on which the party has based its continued existence following the failure of Communism in the former Soviet Union and Eastern Europe.

Second, the party developed organizational techniques that continue to affect the life of every Chinese even today though some of these techniques are beginning to loose their hold. Chief among these was the division of society into *danwei* ("units"). Under the *danwei* system, all Chinese are attached to specific bureaucratic, industrial, or agricultural organizations. Such organizations encompass every aspect of an individual's life. In the cities, housing is owned and assigned by specific units, and medical care and other social benefits are allocated by units. Employment was for life, and it was very difficult to move from one unit to another. In recent years, this system has begun to break down as the economy diversifies and there is greater labor mobility, but it nevertheless remains an important part of Chinese life. In the countryside, prior to the inauguration of the reforms, peasants were bound tightly to the land through the commune system and migration was not permitted. In recent years, peasants have been allowed to travel and migrate (though generally not to change their legal residence), which has brought about new problems (discussed below). The *danwei* system was enforced by the household registration (*hukou*) and dossier systems. Every Chinese was assigned a household registration that assigned him or her to a specific physical location, and until recently it was very difficult to move from one area to another. More important, a dossier was maintained on each Chinese citizen. In the dossier were included such things as the person's family background (thus making class background an inherited characteristic), his or her educational and employment history, as well as a complete record of one's political thought and activities. This latter part can include accusations against the individual that the individual does not even know exist.

The combination of the *danwei, hukou,* and dossier system allowed the state to impose very tight control over the population. In recent years, these controls have begun to break down as the opening up of the economy has necessitated allowing greater internal population movement and migration and as the decline of political criteria have made the dossiers less threatening. Nevertheless, these features continue to exist, particularly in the cities, and provide the means by which the state can tighten control over individuals when it seeks to do so. At higher levels of the state and party bureaucracies, the dossier system allows the Organization Department of the CCP to exercise tight control over the advancement of individuals.

Third, the party developed in strong reaction to the social and political disintegration of the earlier period. Its mission was to unify China. Internally, although a legacy of personal relations was inherited from the past, a strong norm against factionalism, in the sense of a group of people working together in an organized fashion to achieve a common aim, developed within the party. The corollary of this norm against faction, ironically, has been the belief that it is possible and necessary for one viewpoint ("line") to win complete victory against all others.[14]

Organizationally, this legacy has found expression in one person dominating, and in some sense transcending, the party. This feature of the party dates from at least 1943 when the party appointed three people, including Mao Zedong, to the Secretariat, but authorized Mao to make decisions on his own if he disagreed with the others.[15] In a well-known speech, Deng Xiaoping referred to the leader of the party as the "core," an evocative image that conjures up an image of a leader whose position is based on a combination of formal and informal authority.

This outline of some of the features of the CCP suggests that to understand its functioning and role in Chinese society, it is necessary to have an understanding of it in historical, ideological, formal, and informal terms. Having dealt with the party's historical development, we turn here to its formal organization.

Organization

The CCP, as befits a party that developed as a clandestine organization struggling to overturn the social and political order, is hierarchical in structure (see Figure 8.1). At the top of the system is the supreme leader (in Deng's phrase, the "core"). In the later revolutionary period and the first 28 years of the People's Republic of China, this was Mao Zedong, who held the title Chairman. The 1982 party constitution, adopted after Mao's death, abolished the position of chairman in order to prevent another person from so completely dominating the political system. In the reform period, the top party position has been that of general secretary, but real power has been retained in the hands of Deng Xiaoping and other party elders. Hu Yaobang was general secretary from 1980 to 1987, when he was ousted and replaced by Zhao Ziyang. After the Tiananmen incident in 1989, Zhao was ousted and Jiang Zemin took over as general secretary. It remains to be seen whether Jiang can consolidate power to match his title. This difference between office and the reality of power points to an important gap between formal and informal power, which will be discussed later.

The supreme leader generally serves on the Politburo Standing Committee (PSC). The PSC is usually composed of around seven people, generally but not always men, who make up the inner circle of political power. The actual power of the PSC as a policy-making body varies over time. In the early reform period (until 1987), Deng Xiaoping served on the PSC, but generally did not rule through it (Deng insisted on being the third

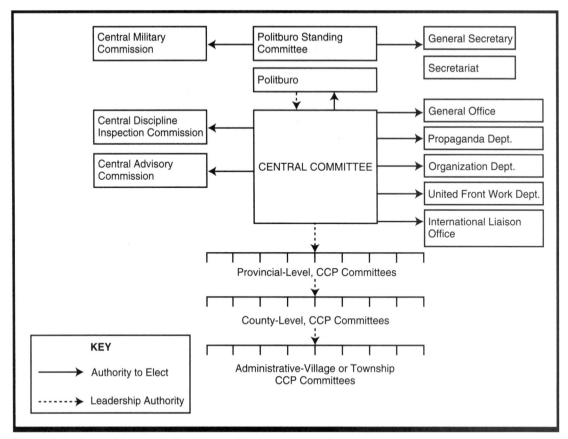

Figure 8.1   Organization of the Chinese Communist Party

Source: Adapted from *Policy Conflicts in Post-Mao China,* ed., John P. Barns and Stanley Rosen (M. E. Sharpe, 1986), pp. 360–361.

ranked member, after Hu Yaobang and Zhao Ziyang). In fact, to circumvent the PSC and the broader Politburo, which was dominated by a number of superannuated and conservative party elders, much authority was shifted de facto to the CCP Secretariat (see below). Since 1987 power has generally shifted back to the PSC, though as the Tiananmen crackdown vividly demonstrated, the power of elder cadres could eclipse the formal policy-making process. In recent years, power has begun to pass to a younger generation (headed by General Secretary Jiang Zemin and Premier Li Peng), and it appears that the PSC has become more powerful.

Each member of the Politburo Standing Committee is in charge of a particular func-

tional responsibility. For instance, the highest-ranking member of the PSC is in charge of overall party affairs, giving him the most powerful and far-reaching brief of all the leaders. The second or third ranking member of the PSC generally serves concurrently as Premier of the State Council (to be discussed later) and generally has overall responsibility for management of the economy (although this portfolio can be subdivided in a variety of ways). Another leader will be in charge of legal affairs, a broad area of responsibility that includes internal security. Yet other leaders will take charge of such areas as propaganda and organization.

This division of labor among the highest-ranking officials in the country reflects the organization of the Chinese polity into various *xitong,* or systems. A prominent student of these systems has identified six distinct systems: Party Affairs, Organization and Personnel, Propaganda and Education, Political and Legal Affairs, Finance and Economics, and the Military. Each of these systems combines several bureaucratic organizations that run from the top of the system to the bottom. In other words, almost everyone in China belongs to one *danwei* or another, and almost every *danwei* is encompassed in one of these various *xitong.*[16]

The PSC is elected by the membership of the whole Politburo. The Politburo, generally composed of around 20 people, ratifies decisions made by the PSC. On less critical issues, individual members of the Politburo will have responsibility for a particular issue area and will report on that issue to the whole membership, which then makes a decision.

The Politburo is selected by the Central Committee, a body composed of approximately 200 people, which is elected by a party congress. Party congresses are sup-

posed to meet every five years, but in the pre-reform era they were held only irregularly. For instance, the Seventh Party Congress was held in 1945 as the party prepared for its final push on power, but the Eighth Party Congress was not held until eleven years later in 1956. The Ninth Party Congress then was not held until 1969—three years after the start of the Cultural Revolution and after Mao's main adversaries in the party had been purged and denounced publicly. After Mao's death, however, party congresses have been held on a regular basis, starting in 1977.

Delegates to a party congress are supposed to represent lower levels of the party organization and number around 4,000–5,000. After the party congress is over and a new Central Committee is selected, the delegates to the party congress no longer play any political role (they may or may not be selected to attend the next party congress). In between party congresses, the Central Committee will meet periodically in plenary session (hence the term *plenum*). In the reform period, such plenums

Politburo standing committee after the Fourteenth Party Congress elected it in 1992. From left to right are: Jiang Zemin, Li Peng, Qiao Shi, Li Ruihuan, Zhu Rongji, Liu Huaqing, and Hu Jintao.

have generally been held once a year, though in recent years there have sometimes been two or more plenums a year. The first plenary session of a newly selected Central Committee is normally held immediately following the end of a party congress and is for the sole purpose of selecting the party leadership, particularly the members of the Politburo, the PSC, and the Secretariat. Central Committees are numbered according to which party congress selected them (there have now been 14 party congresses since the party began in 1921), and plenary sessions of the Central Committee are numbered during the tenure of that Central Committee. Thus, for example, the plenum that inaugurated the reform period in December 1978 was the Third Plenary Session of the Eleventh Central Committee.

Although in formal terms, the party is organized from the bottom up, with lower-level party organizations selecting delegates to higher-level meetings to select the party's leadership, in reality the selection of delegates from lower levels is heavily influenced by the opinions of higher-level bodies. Moreover, for most of the party's history, delegates to party congresses have had no choice in candidates for Central Committee, just as the members of the Central Committee have had no choice in who they select for the Politburo. Such sensitive personnel decisions have always been heavily influenced, if not absolutely controlled, by the highest-level leaders. Beginning in 1987, there has been some loosening up of this system. There are now more candidates for the Central Committee than there are seats on the Central Committee, so some people fail to be elected. In at least two instances, candidates widely reported to be slated to take a position on the Politburo have failed to be elected to the Central Committee, thus ending their chances of taking a position on the party's top policy-making body. Although very limited, this "inner-party democracy" has begun to have an impact on the way the party works.

The influence of higher levels of the party over lower levels of the party derives largely from the practice of democratic centralism. In theory, democratic centralism means that all party decisions can be dis-

cussed fully by lower-level party members before a decision is made, but that once a decision is made all party members must carry it out without dissent. Thus there is supposed to be a combination of "democratic" decision making and centralized implementation. In practice, the system has never worked in this fashion. Higher-level party members, particularly the party secretary at any given level, monopolize decision making, so that the decision-making process is centralized and top-down.

There are also several important organizations that nominally are under the Central Committee but, in fact, are run by the central party leadership. Most important is the Secretariat. The primary purpose of the Secretariat is to oversee the implementation of Politburo decisions. It plays an important role in drafting documents and overseeing the propaganda that promotes central policies. As noted above, in the 1980s it took on an even more important role by becoming deeply involved in policy making itself.

In addition, there is the Propaganda Department, which directly oversees publication of articles supporting the party and makes sure that publications not under direct control of the central party organization nevertheless do not deviate from the party line. There is also an Organization Department that vets all appointments to senior positions. The United Front Work Department has the difficult task of trying to persuade nonparty intellectuals of the correctness of the party's policy. It attempts to do this through the Chinese People's Political Consultative Conference (CPPCC), an organ that includes many prominent nonparty intellectuals and meets annually in conjunction with the NPC to listen to reports by government officials. The International Liaison Office is not as important as it used to be, for its function is to develop relations with foreign political parties, particularly socialist and communist parties. Finally, there is the General Office that overseas and coordinates the work of the central party, particularly that of the general secretary. It is also in charge of the security of China's top leadership.

In order to enforce control within the party there is also a Central Discipline Inspection Commission (CDIC), the main function of which is to root out violators of party discipline, primarily those involved in corruption, but it has also been used at times to rein in reformers. Finally, between 1982 and 1992 there was a Central Advisory Commission (CAC), which served as a vehicle for easing veteran party cadres into retirement. Members of the CAC had to retire from their other party and state positions, but they were allowed to retain important privileges, including access to important party documents and, in the case of Standing Committee members, the right to attend Politburo meetings. Although formally retired, members of the CAC played an important role from time to time, including in the dismissal of General Secretary Hu Yaobang in January 1987 and in the decision to use military force to suppress the Tiananmen demonstrations in 1989.

Central Military Commission

Standing in a category of its own is the Chinese military, the People's Liberation Army (PLA). From its origins in the mountains of the Jiangxi base area, the PLA has always been the party's army. All military commanders and many of the troops are party members, and a system of political commissars, serving along side professional military commanders, ensure the loyalty of the army. Control over the military has always been one of the keys to CCP rule, and personal leadership of the military has always been essential to attain the position of supreme leader. Mao Zedong was a co-founder of the PLA and one of its chief strategists during the revolutionary period; Deng Xiaoping was a political commissar in one of the five field armies in the same period. Both have maintained tight control over the PLA.

This control is maintained through the Central Military Commission (CMC), an organ that reports directly to the Politburo. Mao was head of the CMC until his death. After a brief interregnum in which Hua Guofeng served as head of the CMC, Deng Xiaoping took over. Deng continued to retain this position two years after he retired formally from the Politburo in 1987 (a change that necessitated a rewriting of the constitution). After Deng retired as head of the CMC in 1989, Jiang Zemin was named to this position. Nevertheless, there is every reason to believe that Deng has retained effective control over the CMC through his close associates on that body. Indeed, one of the critical questions in the succession to a new leadership is whether Jiang will be able to gain effective control over the CMC.

Local Party Organizations

The organization of the party described above is generally replicated at lower levels of the system, albeit somewhat less elaborately. Each of China's 30 provinces is headed by a party committee, which has a standing committee and party secretary. Members of the standing committee have a division of labor much like their counterparts at the central level. There are also provincial-level propaganda, organization, and other departments as well as a provincial-level discipline inspection commission.

Below the province, there are party organizations in each county (there are over 2,000 counties in China) or, in cities, in each district. Below the county there is the administrative village or township, where the party structure is replicated. In the Maoist period, this was the commune level. Below the administrative village or township, there is a party organization at the village level. The party has expressed repeated concern in recent years that at this level the party organization is moribund or, in some cases, taken over by local leaders who have no loyalty to higher-level party organizations.

THE STATE

The state apparatus in China can be thought of as consisting of two main parts, the administrative side and the legislative side. According to the Chinese constitution, the highest organ of state power is the National People's Congress (NPC), however, the NPC has never played a role anywhere comparable to its constitutionally stated authority. In recent years, however, the NPC has begun to play a more prominent role in the Chinese political system, and its role is discussed below. It is appropriate to discuss first the administrative side of the state—the State Council and its subordinate ministries—because they have been and continue to be the most important organs overseeing the management of the country.

State Council, Ministries and Commissions

The State Council is presided over by the premier, who is formally elected by the NPC upon the recommendation of the CCP Central Committee, a recommendation that has never been rejected (though in recent years there have been votes cast in opposition). In the Maoist period, the premier was Zhou Enlai; today it is Li Peng. Normally, the premier is the second or third ranked person on the PSC. Under the premier are several vice premiers (currently numbering four), who have a specific division of work (normally industry, agriculture, finance and banking, and foreign policy).

The primary role of the State Council is to oversee the work of the various ministries and commissions that administer the country. Most of these ministries and commissions, which currently number 45, oversee the economy, but other important areas of concern include foreign affairs, education, and science and technology. Each of these bureaucracies is headed by a person who holds at least ministerial rank. In the case of the most powerful commissions, the head might be a person who concurrently serves as a vice premier as well as on the Politburo or even its Standing Committee.

Historically, this organization of the state mirrored the organizational structure developed in the Soviet Union, and its primary purpose was to administer the planned economy. The planned economy in China, as in the Soviet Union, was based on the idea that the state could and should mobilize re-

sources from throughout the society for investment in areas deemed to be in the long-term interest of the country. This mobilization of resources was largely accomplished through a highly distorted price system that drew resources to a relatively small number of large state-owned enterprises, which then delivered profits and taxes to the state. This distorted price system, in other words, largely substituted for a tax system, and collecting taxes is perennially one of the most difficult tasks in developing countries.

The center of this planned economy was the State Planning Commission, a body first established in 1952 with the advice and help of planners from the Soviet Union. The purpose of the State Planning Commission is to oversee the development of the country through the drawing up of annual and five-year plans. These plans are supposed to set targets and allocate resources for reaching those targets.[17]

Implementation of the plans then falls to the various ministries overseeing the economy, such as the Ministry of Metallurgy, the Ministry of Petroleum, and so forth. These ministries oversee some industries directly and others indirectly. Indirect supervision is carried out by provincial-level bureaus that correspond to the ministries in the central government.

Vertical and Horizontal Control

This distinction between direct and indirect supervision brings up one of the most difficult problems that has plagued the Chinese economy and administration throughout the history of the PRC. The problem is basically that China is too large, its economy too diverse, and the resources of the state too few to effectively administer the whole economy from Beijing. This problem points to one of the basic differences between China and the former Soviet Union. In the Soviet Union, planners did in fact oversee the entire economy; in the 1970s as many as 60,000 commodities were allocated by the central government. In China, the central plan has never covered more than about 600 commodities, and has rarely had effective control over more than about 200. Even for items covered by the plan, the central government did not exercise full control. For instance, 25 percent of finished steel was allocated by local authorities.[18]

In other words, even at the height of planning in China, much of the economy was decentralized and run by provincial or sub-provincial units. This necessary dichotomy between a relatively small number of products and industries being supervised by the central government and a much larger number of products and industries being managed by local governments has led to a constant debate on how much control should be located at which level. In Chinese, this is expressed as a contradiction between *tiao* (vertical control) and *kuai* (horizontal control). Tight vertical control gives central planners greater control over the distribution and allocation of products throughout the society, allowing them to better allocate materials to fulfill centrally mandated plans. But it is highly inefficient. It can literally mean that one plant, in need of a product produced by a different plant across the street, must nevertheless apply to the central ministry for the product to be allocated—and then it is likely to be allocated from another plant far away.

Thus, centralization makes coordination at the local level extremely difficult, and therein lies the rationale for decentralization. By allowing localities to exercise greater control, better coordination can be achieved in local areas. That process, however, tends to undermine central plans, thereby provoking a recentralization of the economy. A common expression reflected this cycle: "Enterprises die as soon as they are controlled, there is chaos as soon as they are released, as soon as they are released they are controlled again, and as soon as they are controlled they die again." This debate over centralization and decentralization first found powerful expression in the Great Leap Forward when China moved radically away from the Soviet model to try to explore a path of local mobilization. When this failed, the economy was recentralized, only to be subject to another round of decentralization during the Cultural Revolution.

One of the most difficult tasks in the reform period has been to try to break this cycle.

Party Control of the State

As in the Soviet model, the party and state hierarchies are parallel to each other in China. The party maintains control over the state through two mechanisms. First there is a *nomenklatura* system in which the party appoints people to the most important bureaucratic (and industrial) jobs in the country.[19] Second, there are party groups (*dangzu*) at different levels in the state bureaucracy. For instance, in the typical ministry, the minister is usually the party secretary of the ministry's party group. Regardless of the formal rankings of different officials, it is this party group that sets policy for the ministry. It is also the party group's responsibility to carry out broader party policy, though frequently bureaucratic interests makes the formulation and implementation of coherent policy difficult.

The National People's Congress

Although formally part of the state apparatus, the NPC is a distinct part of the system and therefore deserves separate discussion. Like national party congresses, the NPC is supposed to be elected every five years, a schedule that has been adhered to in the reform period, though not before. Delegates to the NPC are elected from geographical and functional organizations (such as industry and the military). Though most delegates are members of the CCP, they do not have to be. Indeed, one of the functions of the NPC is to bring party and nonparty people together in a so-called united front in order to promote party policy among nonparty people.

Although the state constitution of the PRC calls the NPC the highest organ of state power, it has never played such a powerful role. The selection of delegates is highly influenced by party preferences, and the NPC itself has never wielded a truly independent role. The NPC meets in full session once a year, usually in March. Its primary function is to listen to and ratify various government reports. These normally include the Government Work Report, which is presented by the premier, the budget report presented by the minister of finance, and a social and economic development plan presented by the head of the State Planning Commission. In between annual meetings of the NPC, a Standing Committee meets at regular intervals. In recent years, Standing Committee meetings have been held approximately every two months. The task of the Standing Committee, like that of the full NPC, is to consider legislation and "supervise" the government. The NPC Standing Committee is generally headed by a member of the Politburo; prior to the Cultural Revolution and since 1993 it has been headed by a member of the PSC (currently the head is Qiao Shi, the third ranked member of the PSC).

Although frequently referred to in the Western press as a "rubber stamp" legislature, the NPC in recent years has taken on an increasing role as a sounding board as well as a body of opinion that has to be taken into account. In the reform period, as the regime has increasingly emphasized the development of the economy, the pace of legislation has been stepped up and the role of the legislature has accordingly become more important. Sometimes its role has been to hinder reform. That was notably the case in the 1980s when China was considering its first legislation on bankruptcy. Under the guidance of conservative party elder Peng Zhen, the NPC repeatedly delayed and diluted the legislation, though it finally had to yield. In the 1990s, particularly following Deng Xiaoping's landmark trip to Shenzhen, the NPC has become very active in shaping economic legislation. Increasingly a more sophisticated committee structure and greater expertise has allowed the NPC to play an independent role in shaping such legislation.

The NPC has also played a "safety valve" role of registering dissatisfaction with government policies. Policies and leaders are routinely subjected to skeptical questioning by delegates, although much of these interventions are done in separate discussion meetings that are not open to public scrutiny. Throughout the reform period, the NPC has routinely amended the Government Work Report. Although many of these amendments are minor in nature, some of them are clearly substantive.

This does not mean that China is on the verge of becoming a parliamentary democracy, but it does suggest that the NPC can increasingly play a role in reflecting public opinion.

The Emergence of Economic Reform

As discussed in Section A the Cultural Revolution left China politically, economically, socially, and spiritually exhausted. If there was any one impulse that dominated society at the time it was a desire to return to normal, to stop the ceaseless political campaigns that destroyed families and lives. Reform responded to this societal desire. It also responded to another, but parallel, desire, namely the widely felt belief that China had wasted two decades of time. In the 20 years since Mao had launched the Great Leap Forward, Japan had emerged as a major world economic power. Following very much in the path of Japan were the "four small dragons" of South Korea, Taiwan, Singapore, and Hong Kong. All were achieving the prosperity that China had long hoped for. It was apparent that despite the frenetic efforts of the Chinese people, the gap between China and the outside world was widening—and widening quickly.

In launching its reforms, China had many advantages not enjoyed by the Soviet Union or Eastern Europe. First and foremost, China had not destroyed its party elite as Stalin had. Indeed, many party leaders, including state president Liu Shaoqi, had died or been driven to their deaths during the Cultural Revolution. But most had survived. Moreover, the Cultural Revolution had had a sobering effect on them. It allowed them to see just how far out of control an overemphasis on ideology could go. It also gave them a taste of the party dictatorship that they themselves had inflicted on others. For some, the Cultural Revolution provided a time to come into contact with ordinary Chinese citizens for the first time in years. For instance, Deng Xiaoping worked in a tractor factory in Nanchang, the capital of Jiangxi province, and the experience appears to have given him at least some sense of the feelings of ordinary Chinese. In short, there was a heartfelt desire on the part of the party veterans who returned to power following the Cultural Revolution to return to the goals that had motivated them in their youth: the desire for China to become "wealthy and powerful."

Moreover, as party veterans returned to power they had something of a party program on which to build—the Eighth Party Congress program of 1956. That congress had laid out the basic theme of turning away from class struggle to concentrate on economic development that was subsequently adopted to much greater effect at the Third Plenary Session of the Eleventh Central Committee in December 1978. This background provided returning veterans with something of a consensus on policy and direction.

Although the decisions of the Eighth Party Congress had not lasted long before Mao launched the country onto the disastrous course of the Great Leap Forward, there were many policy legacies from the 1950s and 1960s (when China was recovering from the GLF) that could be built on in the reform era. One was in agriculture. At various times in the 1950s and early 1960s when the party had retreated temporarily from its efforts to implement collective agriculture, the peasants in many areas had turned to various forms of contracting land from the local collective. In other words, instead of restoring private ownership, which was forbidden, they had adopted a type of tenant farming with the local collective acting as the "landlord." This type of household responsibility system, as it would become known in the reform era, was particularly widespread in 1960–1961 in the wake of the Great Leap famine.

Another policy legacy of the 1950s and 1960s was the effort to promote various forms of accountability in industry. Intellectuals and industrial bureaucrats had long struggled with ideas about reforming industrial relations within the framework of socialism. For instance, the famous economist Sun Yefang had advocated increasing enterprise decision-making authority and giving the so-called "law of value" a greater role in the management of the economy. These were ideas for which Sun was condemned to seven years in jail during the Cultural Revolution, but he emerged from jail in 1977 with his ideas intact—and many new converts.

In short, there was a history of ideas and policy experimentation that predated reform by many years. Without this repository of ideas and experience, it is unlikely that reform could have been undertaken so quickly or succeeded so well.

Another "advantage" that China had in the late 1970s, though few central bureaucrats would have considered it as such at the time, was the decentralization of the economy. During the Cultural Revolution, much authority over economic activity had been decentralized to local governments. That meant that when veteran cadres, purged during the Cultural Revolution, returned to office and began to focus on restoring production, they had to try to recentralize economic authority in Beijing. But they could only do so to a certain extent. Local governments which had acquired authority over economic activities, and invested local economic resources in them, were not willing to yield easily.

One area in which this test of strength between local and central authorities became apparent was in the reform of the tax system. Desiring to step up investment in industry, the central government needed greater tax revenues. However, a simple demand to remit greater revenues to the center would have only encountered local resistance. Central authorities tackled this problem by means of a compromise. In 1980, a tax reform was instituted that provided localities with a financial incentive for increasing revenues by allowing them to re-

Table 8.2   CHINA'S ECONOMIC DEVELOPMENT UNDER REFORM

	GNP (in billion yuan)	Per Capita Income (in yuan)		Township and Village Enterprises (no. of employees) (in millions)	Foreign Trade (in billion U.S. dollars)
		Rural	Urban		
1978	362.4	138	615	28.3	20.6
1980	451.8	178	762	29.9	38.1
1985	899.5	347	1148	69.8	69.6
1990	1854.5	571	2140	92.6	115.4
1993	3447.7	855	3371	123.5	195.7
1994	4447.7	1087	4538	120.2	236.7

Source: *Zhongguo tongji nianjian* (China statistical yearbook), 1995 (Beijing: China Statistical Publishing House, 1995).

tain for local purposes a portion of the new taxes raised. This revenue system, which was subsequently extended to some sectors of industry as well, gave localities an incentive to develop new sources of revenues, particularly in those areas where they would be permitted to retain the receipts.

This was one of the main reasons why industries in China's rural areas, known as township and village enterprises (TVEs), took off. Although there was some basis for such industries in the pre-reform period, it was the new financial arrangements (along with the new emphasis on developing the economy) that stimulated local interest in developing industry. The TVE sector has been one of the great success stories of China's reform period, and one that distinguishes China's path of reform from that of other socialist countries. In 1978, there were approximately 28 million people employed in TVEs, which produced only 9 percent of China's total industrial output. Moreover, such industries were extremely backward in terms of technology and concentrated in such heavy industries as iron and steel, cement, farm implements, and so forth. By the mid–1990s, the situation had completely changed. In 1992, for the first time, TVEs produced more than 50 percent of China's industrial output. They employed approximately 120 million workers and accounted for some 20 percent

of China's exports. Although many TVEs remained technologically unsophisticated, others were producing advanced electronic products and precision instruments.

Rural Reform

China's reform began with the rural sector. This was more a matter of happenstance than design. The area in which rural reform advanced earliest and most quickly was the province of Anhui in central-east China. Anhui was a pioneer in rural reform in part because it had suffered more perhaps than any other province during the Great Leap Forward and had implemented the household responsibility system (although under a different name) more widely than any other province following the GLF. In 1977, Wan Li, a close associate of Deng Xiaoping, was appointed the leading party official in the province, and he quickly came to support agricultural reform in the province. Bottom-up initiative was as important as top-down support in the inauguration and spread of rural reform. A severe drought in 1978 provided an incentive, and a rationale, for adopting new forms of organization. Peasants in several areas demanded to contract their own land, and in one famous instance, 18 families signed a secret pledge to engage in household production (which was still illegal) and to support the families of anyone (particularly local cadres) who was arrested as a result of their actions.

The household responsibility system soon proved a great success in Anhui and elsewhere. The reform of agriculture went against everything that Mao Zedong had tried to accomplish in over two decades of rural collectivization and, therefore, encountered stiff resistance from many quarters. Nevertheless, the demonstrable success of the system, as well as the support of officials committed to reform; eventually overcame all opposition. In 1983, the household responsibility system was universalized throughout China, and communes began to be officially dissolved. The Maoist era had clearly come to an end.

The household responsibility system was successful in promoting the development of agriculture. Grain production increased by a third, from 305 million metric tons in 1978 to 407 million metric tons in 1984.

Rural reform was not only successful in resolving a food crisis that had beset China for three decades, it also had a number of other effects that not only changed rural life but also the visage of China as a whole. First, the increased rural incomes that came from increased grain output as well as the cultivation of other crops and the restoration of sideline production permitted peasants to purchase more goods, thus stimulating the growth of industry (this was particularly true of building materials as peasants began to build new homes throughout the country). Second, agricultural efficiency increased greatly, thus freeing millions of people from agricultural labor and allowing them to enter the growing TVE sector (which further supported the growth of rural incomes). Third, the breakdown of communes and the emancipation of rural labor quickly fed the growth of new circulation channels as peasants began traveling both locally and nationally to buy and sell goods. This activity brought new concepts of commerce even as it undermined the old, inefficient state channels of commerce. Finally, the success of the early rural reforms and the breakup of the communes changed the way state related to society in the countryside and provided an important

success for reform, thus fueling the demand for reform in other parts of the economy.

Industrial Reform

Industrial reform began almost as early as rural reform, but it progressed more slowly. It developed slowly for a number of reasons. First, given the decentralization policies followed during the Cultural Revolution, there was at least as much of an impulse to recentralize and strengthen the State Planning Commission's control over the economy as there was to reform. Second, industrial reform is intrinsically more difficult because of the interrelatedness of the urban economy. Unlike the rural reforms in which different areas could undertake reforms without adversely affecting other areas, a reform in one industry could have an effect on the supply of materials or the purchasing of products from another industry as well as on revenues delivered to the state. Thus, there was a tendency to retreat from any reform that proved disrupting—and most did. Third, unlike the rural economy, the industrial economy was managed by a huge bureaucratic apparatus composed of the ministries and commissions outlined previously. This meant that a great deal of bureaucratic coordination, and bureaucratic obstruction, was involved in any effort to reform.

However, there were also great incentives to reform industry. There was widespread recognition among economists, who were then being restored to positions of influence, that China's industries were highly inefficient and in need of reform. In particular, most economists accepted the notion (which had been sharply criticized during the Cultural Revolution) that enterprises needed to have incentives in order to increase efficiency. Apart from pressures from economists and policymakers to reform industry, there were also pressures from enterprises themselves as well as from some of the bureaucracies in charge of industries. Such bureaucracies recognized the difficulties the enterprises under their control were facing and hoped to alleviate some of their problems so that production would increase.

Thus, at the beginning of the reform period, there were pressures both in favor of reform and against reform, and these pressures led industrial reform to progress in fits and starts. In general, the period from 1979, when industrial reform got under way, to 1984 was a period in which initial reform efforts were followed by retreat. There were, however, two features of this period that merit particular attention. The first was that initial reform efforts created a foundation for reform on which later efforts could be based. Second, ironically, during the retreat from reform (1980–1982), cutbacks in government expenditures forced many industries to try to stimulate demand for their products by developing and marketing new products. Thus, reform advanced precisely in a period when the efforts of central planners were trying to tighten control over the economic system.

In 1984, spurred on by the success of the rural reform and better than expected conditions in industry, the CCP adopted a major reform document entitled, "Decision on the Reform of the Economic Structure." This document, along with efforts to create new institutions to support reform, inaugurated a new era of reform in which market forces advanced significantly.

The key reform, though few thought of it as such at the time, was the adoption of a so-called dual-track price system. Everyone realized that price reform was essential to the whole reform effort, but policymakers could not agree on how to go about it. The compromise was to allow above-quota production to be marketed by enterprises at prices higher than the state-set price. This immediately created an incentive to increase production so that a greater percentage of output could be marketed at the higher price. Economists have argued that this arrangement provided an incentive for enterprises to orient their behavior increasingly toward the market because their marginal increase in revenues would be derived from the market. In other words, products produced under the plan acted as a large tax, while enterprises were able to earn increasing amounts of income from sales on the market.

The other factor that came into play at this time was the TVE sector discussed previously. It was precisely at the time of the "Decision on Economic Structural Reform," 1984, that the TVE sector really took off. Since TVEs had never been included in the plan in the first place, their behavior from the beginning was determined by the market. They purchased their raw materials on the market and sold their produce on the market. When market demand changed, their product mix changed.

Moreover, by the mid- and late 1980s, the rise of the TVE sector was great enough to erode the profits of large state-owned enterprises. Under the planned economy, large state-owned enterprises had enjoyed monopoly profits. As new enterprises entered the market and as other enterprises reformed and began to compete with state-owned enterprises, the profit margins of the latter began to decline. This decline then put fiscal pressure on the state, which derived most of its revenues from large state-owned enterprises. One result of such pressures was that state-owned enterprises began to undertake reforms and become more efficient and market-oriented. It has often been pointed out that many of China's state-owned enterprises run deficits. This is true, but it is also true that many state-owned enterprises have become more efficient. It is just that in comparison with the nonstate sector, they have not reformed at sufficient speed, so their importance in the overall economy has continued to decline.

The result of the rise of the TVE sector and the relative decline of the state-owned sector has meant that the plan has become much less important in China. By the mid–1990s the market determined the prices of almost all consumer goods and most industrial goods. In short, China's economy "grew out of the plan."[20]

The Politics of Economic Reform

The process of economic reform in a socialist state is intrinsically difficult. This difficulty is in part because of the economic changes required. Prices must be reformed, markets must develop, ownership relations must be changed, and macroeconomic structures must be reformed. Even under the best of circumstances, this is a daunting list of changes. Frequently a change in one area causes difficulty in another area. Smooth reform of the economic system is probably impossible; the best one can hope for is to contain difficulties within certain parameters.

In addition to the intrinsic economic problems involved in reform, there are inevitable political difficulties. In part, these difficulties derive from different visions of the goal of reform. In the case of China, there were sharp disagreements about whether the goal of reform was to restore, with appropriate improvements, the old planned economy that had prevailed before and after the Great Leap Forward or whether that model of the economy was inherently flawed and should be fundamentally changed. In other words, there were those who at the beginning of the reform period thought that the basic problem in the Chinese system was Maoism; that if the political movements and radical policies promoted by Mao in the Great Leap Forward and Cultural Revolution were done away with, the system could be made to function. Others saw the problems as far deeper, believing that the basic patterns of a socialist economy had to be changed. Accordingly, they were willing to countenance more far-reaching changes than the former group.

Disagreements about how much reform was appropriate were not limited to the economic realm but had implications for party organization, propaganda, ideology, and even political structures. In short, reform was not just about changing economic arrangements but about changing the whole range of state-society relations. Such changes went to the core of what Marxism-Leninism was about and thus raised highly emotional questions about the type of society that should be created. And such questions are highly political.

In general, "conservatives" wanted to restore and preserve the basic parameters of the socialist system as they understood it. Led by economic policy specialist and party elder Chen Yun, these conservatives were in-

deed part of the reform coalition that came to power in 1978, but they had a much more limited notion of reform than their more radical counterparts. Chen Yun's slogan was "planned economy as primary, market economy as supplementary." He had believed this in 1956 when he had first raised the issue of expanding the role of markets, and he believed it in 1980 when he sought to limit the role of markets. But while Chen Yun had remained constant, the center of gravity of the political spectrum had shifted greatly. In the 1950s and 1960s, he was considered a "rightist" for his willingness to countenance market measures; by the 1980s he was considered a conservative or a "leftist" for his unwillingness to countenance a greater role for markets.

Deng Xiaoping, the paramount leader from 1978 onward, was willing to contemplate much more far-reaching measures to reform the economy and even the political system than was Chen. Although there is evidence to suggest that Chen Yun as well as Deng Xiaoping supported the early rural reforms, Deng was far more willing than Chen to countenance far-reaching change in the countryside. For instance, in late 1981, Chen expressed concern that the rural reforms were undermining state planning vis-à-vis the countryside, but Deng continued to support the deepening of rural reforms. This support included such things as the hiring of labor by private and quasi-private enterprises that grew up in the countryside, permitting peasants to engage in long-distance transport (which challenged the state monopoly over circulation), and, in 1983, the dissolution of communes. Deng was also far more supportive of the emerging TVE sector than was Chen, who feared that it would erode the position of state-owned enterprises.

Opening to the Outside World

Perhaps the most important area of disagreement between Chen Yun and Deng Xiaoping revolved around the issue of opening China to the outside world, both politically and diplomatically. On the political level, it was Deng who saw ties with the United States as an essential support for China's reforms. Chen, on the other hand, never met with Western leaders throughout the reform period, though he did meet with the Russian economic planner Ivan Arkipov in late 1984 thereby expressing indirect criticism of Deng's close ties with the West. Similarly, it was Deng who insisted on opening the Special Economic Zones (SEZ) that were created in Shenzhen (opposite Hong Kong) and three other locations. Deng also wanted to open an SEZ in Shanghai but yielded to Chen's objections to doing so. Years later, Deng expressed regret, calling the failure to open an SEZ in Shanghai one of his greatest mistakes.

Indeed, the decision to open up China and forge economic and political links with the outside world proved to be perhaps the single most important element of Deng's reforms. As important as the other reforms were, they could not have spurred either the degree of marketization or the rapid rate of economic growth in the absence of the international market and the access to technology, capital, and managerial know-how of foreign areas. In 1978, China's foreign trade amounted to only $20.6 billion; a decade later it had reached $80.5 billion, and by the end of 1995 it had reached $280 billion. China had become a major trader in the world economy, the tenth largest trader in fact.

Much of China's success in opening up to the outside was due to Hong Kong and Taiwan. By the time China was ready to open up, Hong Kong had developed to the point where its labor costs were rising and it had to find new paths to continue its economic growth. The opening of China provided the perfect complement to Hong Kong's managerial talent, financial resources, and marketing expertise. Before long, Hong Kong manufacturers began setting up joint ventures in neighboring Guangdong province and in the Shenzhen SEZ to tap the rich labor resources of the mainland. The products could then be sold on the international market, frequently in the United States. Already by the late 1980s, Hong Kong enterprises employed more workers in manufacturing jobs in Guangdong than in Hong Kong.[21]

As tensions began to ease across the Taiwan Straits during the 1980s and as labor costs in Taiwan began to increase, Taiwanese entrepreneurs began to emulate their Hong Kong counterparts. Just as Hong Kong entrepreneurs relied on their knowledge of the Cantonese dialect to develop business ties in Guangdong, so Taiwan merchants gravitated toward Fujian province, the province from which many Taiwanese migrated to Taiwan and where the dialect spoken is the same as that of the majority of Taiwanese. Over the years, investment in China from Hong Kong and Taiwan has developed steadily, now totaling over $40 billion from the former and another $10 billion or more from the latter.

China's reliance on overseas Chinese for investment and to develop its export industries has expanded in recent years to include Chinese residents throughout Southeast Asia and North America. Cumulative investment from the Southeast Asian countries now amounts to around $8 billion. The growth of this "greater Chinese economic circle," as it is sometimes called, has not created an exclusive Chinese trade bloc but rather served to integrate the Chinese economy into the world economy. By 1994, China's foreign trade as a percentage of its total GNP, after making appropriate adjustments, was probably in the range of 13 percent, suggesting a fairly high degree of openness for such a large and still developing country.[22]

Political and Social Tensions

Viewed in comparative perspective, China's transition from a planned economy to a market-oriented economy has been one of the smoothest in the world. Despite several oscillations between high growth and retrenchment and several periods of relatively high inflation (reaching 30 percent in 1988), China's development has been smoother and more successful than that of most rapidly modernizing nations.

Nevertheless, such rapid changes have generated considerable economic, social, and political tensions in China. These tensions have derived from the very different expectations of reform held by different leaders within the party, from conflicts of interests as reform produced economic "winners" and "losers," and from the rapid change in state-society relations and the maturation of a new generation of youth who had little memory of the Maoist period.

One way to understand why the reform process has generated such tension within Chinese society is to look at the impact of the rapid growth of the TVE sector. As noted before, the growth of TVEs is one of the great success stories of Chinese economic reform, contributing both to China's economic development and to the marketization of the economy. Their growth nevertheless proved controversial. One reason is because the growth of the TVE sector has reduced the profitability of state-owned enterprises, which has, in turn, created fiscal difficulties for the central government. Central revenues as a percentage of GNP had fallen from 31.2 percent in 1978 to 22 percent in 1987 to only 16.2 percent in 1993. At the same time, central government revenues as a percentage of all government revenues had fallen from about 60 percent at the beginning of the reform era to 33 percent in 1993. These figures reflect both the diminished role of the central government in the overall economy and the gradual shift of economic power from the capital to the provinces. The relative decline in central government revenues was reflected in continuous deficits, which in turn contributed to inflation, as well as in the declining ability of the central government to exercise macroeconomic control.

In the minds of conservatives, these trends were ominous and directly attributable to reform. Reform in their minds was undermining the role of state-owned enterprises in the economy and thus eroding the ability of the government to exercise both economic and political control. The increasing financial strength of the localities, and their increasing willingness to evade or reject controls on their behavior, led many to believe that it was necessary to recentralize authority in Beijing.

At the core of these concerns was not simply the technical matter of revenue and macroeconomic control but the political and ideological question of what type of system was being built. As noted above, the gulf between conservatives and reformers widened after 1984 as reformers tried to solve one problem after another by continuing to deepen reform while conservatives believed that each such effort led the country farther away from socialism.

This dispute over economic matters was exacerbated by ideological conflict. From the beginning of the Dengist period, conservatives had tried to maintain a rein on the reform process by stressing orthodox socialist values. Reformers, intent on creating a political and social atmosphere that would allow ever greater experimentation, were just as intent on breaking through one ideological barrier after another. As noted in Section A, the reform era was launched with a major effort to open up the ideological atmosphere and thus break free of the ideological shackles of the Maoist era. The discussion on "practice is the sole criterion of truth" broke through Maoist dogma by subjecting every program to the fundamental question: Does it work? This was a major break with the Maoist practice of asking: Is it socialist? It thus provided intellectuals with a much broader area of inquiry and protected reforms such as those in agriculture from ideological counterattack.

Loosening ideological restrictions, however, could and did lead to the expression of opinion that went well beyond party orthodoxy, thus raising the ire of more conservative party members. In March 1979, trying to rein in the tendencies that he himself had unleashed, Deng Xiaoping gave a major speech entitled "Uphold the Four Cardinal Principles," in which he said that the party must uphold Marxism-Leninism-Mao Zedong Thought, the leadership of the Chinese Communist Party, the socialist road, and the dictatorship of the proletariat (later amended to "people's democratic dictatorship").

This pattern of opening up and then restricting the ideological atmosphere was repeated many times in the Dengist period. One major effort to curtail expression of unorthodox ideological opinion was the campaign against "spiritual pollution" in 1983, which reflected deep divisions of opinion within the party and foreshadowed even more serious confrontations in the future.[23]

Such divisions within the party were greatly exacerbated by the changing relationship between state and society and by the emergence of a new generation that had little memory of the Maoist period and great hopes for more personal freedom. Despite periodic efforts to clamp down on the expression of opinion, the dominant trend in the 1980s was toward an ever-expanding expression of ideas. As the state became less involved in people's day-to-day lives and as economic reform took hold, the relevance of the old ideas of Marxism-Leninism faded rapidly and were soon in disrepute in many sectors of society. Efforts to reimpose more orthodox patterns of thought, such as during the campaign against spiritual pollution, evoked an ever greater sense of repulsion among the people, particularly intellectuals and college students. At the same time that official ideology became less relevant to the lives of most people, many of the bureaucratic rigidities of the old system remained. Bureaucrats came to be resented for their constant but largely inefficient and ineffective interference in people's lives. They were also increasingly resented for their corruption. Economic reform, particularly the dual-track price system, had opened up enormous opportunities for corruption and many state bureaucrats could not resist the opportunity of using their power to line their own pockets.

Popular resentments became visible in China's public life in the fall of 1985 when many students took to the streets to protest Japan's supposed "economic invasion" of China in the 1980s. Triggered by official commemorations of nationalistic demonstrations half a century earlier, such student activism suggested a newfound willingness to take to the streets in protest.

The following year, beginning in December 1986, students in Hefei, Anhui, took to the streets to protest the disqualification of candidates who had been nominated for the local people's congress by the students. The demonstrations soon spread to Shanghai where over 50,000 students protested the heavy hand of government.

These demonstrations had major repercussions within the party. General Secretary Hu Yaobang was hesitant to crack down on students, believing that a more conciliatory approach would produce better results over the long run. Conservative party leaders, long angered by Hu's relative liberalism, called for his dismissal. Deng Xiaoping, who appears to have had increasing doubts about the leadership abilities of his chosen successor in the preceding months and years, decided to take the lead in calling for a new crackdown on "bourgeois liberalization," a term that eludes strict definition but that implies thought, often influenced by the West, that opposes party control of various spheres of life. On January 13, 1987, Hu Yaobang was officially removed as general secretary, and a far-reaching campaign against bourgeois liberalization made an example of three intellectuals who were purged from the party and criticized repeatedly in the press. The virulence of the 1987 campaign against bourgeois liberalization reflected deepening divisions within the party, suggesting that Deng's long-standing efforts to hold conservatives and reformers together in an uneasy coalition were coming undone.

Deng, however, was not prepared to give up his efforts to reform the economy. As soon as Hu Yaobang was ousted, Deng named Zhao Ziyang, who had served as premier since 1980 and had been largely responsible for the implementation of economic reform, to replace Hu. Zhao had developed a reputation as a reformer who, like Deng, preferred to concentrate on economic reform rather than ideological liberalization. With the support of Deng, Zhao moved rapidly to bring the campaign against bourgeois liberalization under control and thereby create an atmosphere for further economic reform. However, Zhao also believed that economic reform could only proceed with a certain degree of political reform. Zhao's goal was not the implementation of a Western-style liberal democracy but rather a separation of party and state. It was his goal to end party interference in the day-to-day management of the economy while still allowing the party to maintain political control and to set the major policies that the state was to follow. This effort came to fruition in the fall of 1987 when the Thirteenth Party Congress adopted a far-reaching document that called for further liberalization of the economy and the removal of party groups from certain state organizations.

Tiananmen

The tensions and political conflict evident in 1986–1987 soon reprised themselves in a far more dramatic and serious fashion in 1988–1989. Zhao Ziyang seems to have underestimated the seriousness of the political crisis of 1987 and overestimated his ability to control events. Zhao, long frustrated by Hu Yaobang's repeated interference in the economy, had supported Hu's ouster as general secretary. But Hu's ouster weakened the position of reformers overall. With Hu gone, Zhao became the sole target of conservatives' criticism. As conservatives would soon demonstrate, they were not opposed to bourgeois liberalization alone but to economic reform itself. As they sometimes stated openly, they believed that it was economic reform that bred bourgeois liberalization. What they wanted was a major effort to recentralize the economy and strengthen planning. Now, only Zhao (and his patron Deng) stood in their way.

Conservatives did not have to wait long to strike. In the spring of 1988, with inflationary pressures heating up, Deng Xiaoping made an enormous error. Apparently frustrated at the slow pace of reform and the criticism of conservatives, Deng called for an effort to carry out comprehensive price reform. This was interpreted by many people as a signal that prices would soon be going up, so they immediately set out to protect the value of their money by purchasing consumer durables (such as washing machines and television sets). This spending spree added enormously to inflationary pressures and the rate of inflation shot up to around 50 percent in August 1988. With the economy spiraling out of control, conservatives were able to scapegoat Zhao. A variety of administrative measures were put into place to control inflation, and Zhao's authority over economic affairs was ended. Conservatives called for Zhao's ouster, and Zhao clung to power only by the good graces of Deng Xiaoping.

The party was thus deeply divided and the distribution of power among top leaders highly uncertain as China entered 1989. The decade of reform had also brought about major tensions between state and society, which soon became visible to the whole world. Many intellectuals worried that the pace of reform was slowing; they contrasted the relative failure of China to bring about political reform with the policy of *glasnost* (opening) being pursued by Gorbachev in the Soviet Union. Students reflected a similar frustration with the pace of reform, untempered by an appreciation of how far and how fast China had gone. Memories of the Cultural Revolution were dim for people who had been perhaps seven or eight years old when the reforms got underway; what they saw was not the progress but the obstacles in the way of faster reform. Students, influenced by the pop culture of Taiwan, Hong Kong, and the West, yearned for more freedom and self-expression. They resented the dull commentaries that appeared in the official press and the petty interference in their lives by low-level bureaucrats. Perhaps most of all they resented the corruption that they saw growing up around them. Finally, workers and those on fixed incomes had seen their standards of living eroded by the rate of inflation. Everywhere citizens had complaints about corruption. The atmosphere was highly combustible.

The match that set off the firestorm was the death of Hu Yaobang. Hu, who had been permitted to stay on the Politburo in an inactive role following his dismissal as general secretary, was apparently attempting to make a political comeback. In the midst of a heated argument during a Politburo meeting, Hu was struck by a heart attack. Efforts to save him failed and he died on April 15, 1989.

The timing could not have been worse. Students had already been organizing for a commemoration of the seventieth anniversary of the May Fourth Movement, so they had the rudiments of an organization already set up. On the morning of April 16, students headed to Tiananmen Square in the center of Beijing, to pay tribute to the fallen reformer. Much as people had headed to Tiananmen Square 13 years previously to pay their respects to Zhou Enlai, so students began to leave wreaths and poems in honor of Hu Yaobang.

The situation took a turn for the worse when on April 26, the party's newspaper, the *People's Daily,* ran an editorial which labeled the student movement as causing "turmoil" and as "anti-socialist." A major crackdown appeared to be in the offing. The following day, however, large numbers of students marched toward police and finally broke through police lines. Moderates within the party had prevailed in heated internal debates the night before over the use of violence. As students proceeded toward Tiananmen Square they were joined by thousands of Beijing residents. Students decided to occupy the square and continue their protest.

A major effort was made on May 4 by Zhao Ziyang. In a speech delivered to the Asian Development Bank, which was meeting in Beijing that day, Zhao described the motives of the students as patriotic. That was as far as Zhao could go, and he had bent party rules to go that far. Students, however, wanted an explicit retraction of the April 26 editorial. Their desire was perhaps natural. If they left the square without an explicit change in party policy, then they would have been highly vulnerable to arrest after public order was restored. More serious was that the student movement had developed a logic of its own in which more moderate leaders were denounced and ousted by more radical leaders.

The situation deteriorated further on May 13 when student leaders, fearing that the movement was losing momentum, started a hunger strike. The strike evoked sympathy from all over Beijing. Workers began to show up on the square in ever greater numbers, and small vendors and others began contributing sums of money to the stu-

dents. The sounds of ambulance sirens were heard throughout the city.

Soviet leader Gorbachev arrived in Beijing on May 15 to signify the normalization of Sino-Soviet relations after nearly three decades of hostility. China's leadership was deeply embarrassed and angered that they could not hold as planned a welcoming ceremony for Gorbachev in Tiananmen Square. The day after Gorbachev left China, the State Council declared martial law. Zhao Ziyang, unwilling to go along with the decision, was removed from power.

As the situation headed toward a violent resolution, moderates tried desperately to mediate. The situation, however, had gone on too long with both sides too deeply entrenched to permit compromise. The outspoken journalist Dai Qing tried to persuade student leaders to leave the square only to be contemptuously dismissed by student leaders. Her efforts were not appreciated by hardliners within the party either. After the Tiananmen crackdown, Dai was sentenced to a year in jail for trying to prevent a tragedy. It was symbolic of how the middle had dropped out of Chinese politics.

The crackdown finally came on the night of June 3–4. Under orders to take and clear the square by dawn, the PLA shot its way into the center of Beijing. Most of the violence was not in the square itself—students there being allowed to leave peacefully after prolonged negotiations—but in the approaches to the square. The toll may never be known, but it was clearly heavy. Perhaps 700 people died that night.

The Post-Tiananmen Era

It was frequently assumed that Tiananmen would bring about either the downfall of the CCP or the end of reform. In fact, neither happened. This is not to say that the period following Tiananmen was not one of crisis. On the contrary, Tiananmen touched off one of the deepest crises in the party's history. The continued presence of the aging patriarch, however, eventually ameliorated the crisis and indeed set off a new round of even more far-reaching reform.

Deng's presence was critical to the post-Tiananmen political situation because even though his prestige within the party declined significantly following Tiananmen, no one else was able to challenge his position as the core of the party and thus he was eventually able to dominate the political agenda once again. Even at his weakest, in the weeks and months following Tiananmen, Deng's views were decisive on critical issues. In particular, Deng was able to deny the fruits of victory to the conservatives who had led such a determined campaign to oust Zhao Ziyang. Indeed, four days before the crackdown, Deng called in Premier Li Peng and Politburo Standing Committee member Yao Yilin, both conservative leaders who might reasonably expect to succeed Zhao as general secretary of the party, and told them almost contemptuously, "The people see reality. If we put up a front so that people feel that it is an ossified leadership, a conservative leadership, or if the people believe that it is a mediocre leadership that cannot reflect the future of China, then there will be constant trouble and there will never be a peaceful day." Accordingly, Deng informed them that Jiang Zemin, then the mayor of Shanghai, would be named general secretary. Thus, even as his long-standing efforts to carry out reform seemed to be destroyed by Tiananmen and the purge of Zhao, Deng set about building a new coalition, carefully balancing divergent forces within the party.

Despite this and other efforts, it would take Deng a full three years to restore reform to its former prominence. In January 1992, Deng went on a well-publicized tour of the Shenzhen SEZ, where he harshly criticized conservatives within the party, called for deepening reform, and urged Guangdong province to catch up with the "four small dragons" within 20 years. The following fall, the Fourteenth Party Congress ratified a document that went further than any before in party history. It called for the creation of a "socialist market economy," thus firmly identifying the party with a market economy.

Deng's trip to the south and the subsequent decision of the Fourteenth Party Congress inaugurated another period of high-speed growth in China, one that caught the attention of economists and businesspeople the world over (see Feature 8.1). In 1992 China's economy grew by 11 percent, and then grew 12.9 percent in 1993, 12 percent in 1994, and 10.2 percent in 1995. For a large economy the size of China's to sustain such growth rates was unprecedented. At the same time, China was drawing in vast sums of foreign capital—over $33 billion in 1993—and expanding exports. By 1995, China's foreign trade amounted to $280 billion and China ranked as the tenth largest trading nation in the world.

Party and State in an Era of Reform

This overview of some of the major trends and developments in the course of reform suggests some of the ways in which the party and state hierarchies, outlined at the beginning of this section, have interacted, clashed, and been affected by reform. Overall, it is apparent that reform has eroded the position of both the party and state. Party ideology exercises very little positive influence among the people; indeed, in recent years the party has turned increasingly to nationalism as a legitimizing ideology. Similarly the growth of the TVE sector has diminished, though by no means abolished, the importance of the state and the state-owned economy in China.

Although generalizations are hazardous, it seems broadly true that opposition to reform was particularly concentrated in the state bureaucracy (particularly those organs whose *raison d'être* is to protect and nurture the planned economy), in those parts of the party whose function is to uphold ideological orthodoxy and discipline (particularly the Propaganda Department and the CDIC), and in the military (which suffered budgetary cutbacks and a decline in prestige within Chinese society). This pattern of opposition suggests some of the reasons why reform was generally promoted by decentralization, the growth of the TVE sector, opening up to the outside world, and a soft pedaling of ideology.

Another feature of reform was efforts to separate party and state. The basic reasons

---

Feature 8.1 How Wealthy Is China?

In 1993 the International Monetary Fund (IMF) issued a report that substantially increased the estimated size of China's economy, setting off both increased business interest in this new "economic giant" and fears of the role an economically and perhaps militarily powerful China would play in Asia and the world. The IMF undertook to estimate the size of the Chinese economy on the basis of purchasing power parity, a way of trying to compare economies by calculating the cost of a comparable basket of goods. This method is used when distortions in the exchange rate make the usual method of comparing economies by simply converting their gross national product (GNP) into U.S. dollars ineffective. The conclusion of the IMF study was that China's economy was nearly four times larger than previously believed. The IMF study has provoked other agencies and scholars to undertake a number of efforts to calibrate the size of China's economy. Nicholas Lardy, in his *China in the World Economy,* calculates that China's per capita income in 1990 was probably around $1,000, almost three times the official figure of $370 (figured according to the exchange rate), but still more modest than the IMF figures. A per capita income of $1,000 would mean that China's GNP in 1990 was about $1.25 trillion—that about three-quarters that of Japan and about one-fifth that of the United States. When thinking about China's economic size, it is important to remember the vast differences in income between the relatively prosperous east coast and the poor areas in the interior. There are an estimated 80 million people still living in dire poverty in China.

---

for doing so were twofold. First, direct party control of the state obscured lines of authority and undermined professionalism. It was difficult to develop a professional civil service if the chief criteria for promotion was loyalty to the party rather than competence in one's job. At the same time, party interference in state bureaucracies promoted an overconcentration of power that undermined efforts to reforms. Second, by involving the party in every decision, the party inevitably incurred the wrath of everyone unhappy with whatever decision emerged. By distancing the party from day-to-day management of the society, reformers hoped to make it so that not every complaint against every bureaucrat was *ipso facto* a complaint about the party.

However, efforts to separate party from state ultimately failed because the party was unwilling to risk the loss of control that it would entail. Thus, immediately after the Tiananmen crack down, Zhao Ziyang's efforts to remove party groups from state ministries were reversed. The example of Gorbachev, whose efforts to shift power to the state in the Soviet Union undermined the role of the CPSU, certainly served as a negative lesson for China.

Our overview of the reform process also suggests that despite the extremely elaborate structure of both party and state, the political process at the top is largely uninstitutionalized. This was dramatically underscored by the decision-making process during the 1989 Tiananmen crisis. The important decisions were made by eight party elders, none of whom served on the Politburo Standing Committee (two of them, including Deng Xiaoping, were on the CMC, suggesting the power of that organ). This lack of institutionalization remains perhaps the greatest challenge to reform, and it certainly affects current efforts to transfer power to a new generation of leaders, which will be discussed in the following section.

 EY TERMS

---

bourgeois liberalization
Chinese People's Political Consultative Conference

Central Advisory Commission (CAC)
Central Discipline Inspection Commission (CDIC)
Central Military Commission (CMC)
Chen Yun
danwei (units)
dangzu (party groups)
democratic centralism
dual-track price system
hukou (household registration)
Hu Yaobang
Jiang Zemin
Li Peng
National People's Congress (NPC)
People's Liberation Army (PLA)
Politburo
Politburo Standing Committee (PSC)
Secretariat
State Planning Commission
township and village enterprises (TVEs)
xitong (systems)
Zhao Ziyang
Zhou Enlai

Further Readings

Bachman, David M. *Chen Yun and the Chinese Political System* (Berkely and Los Angeles: University of California Press, 1985).

Baum, Richard. *Burying Mao: Chinese Politics in the Age of Deng Xiaoping* (Princeton, NJ: Princeton University Press, 1994).

Burns, John P. *The Chinese Communist Party Nomenklatura System: A Documentary Study of Party Control of Leadership Selection* (Armonk, NY: M. E. Sharpe, 1989).

Chan, Anita, Richard Madsen, and Jonathan Unger. *Chen Village: The Recent History of a Peasant Community in Mao's China* (Berkeley and Los Angeles: University of California Press, 1984).

Fewsmith, Joseph. *Dilemmas of Reform in China: Political Conflict and Economic Debate* (Armonk, NY: M. E. Sharpe, 1994).

Friedman, Edward, Paul G. Pickowicz, and Mark Selden. *Chinese Village, Socialist State* (New Haven: Yale University Press, 1991).

Goldman, Merle. *China's Intellectuals: Advise and Dissent* (Cambridge: Harvard University Press, 1981).

Goldman, Merle. *Sowing the Seeds of Democracy in China* (Cambridge: Harvard University Press, 1994).

Hamrin, Carol Lee. *China and the Challenge of the Future* (Boulder, CO: Westview Press 1990).

Harding, Harry. *Organizing China: The Problem of Bureaucracy, 1949–1976* (Stanford: Stanford University Press, 1981).

Harding, Harry. *China's Second Revolution: Reform After Mao* (Washington, DC: Brookings Institution, 1987).

Jacobson, Harold K., and Michel Oksenberg. *China's Participation in the IMF, the World Bank, and GATT: Toward a Global Economic Order* (Ann Arbor: University of Michigan Press, 1990).

Lardy, Nicholas. *China in the World Economy* (Washington, DC: Institute for International Development, 1994).

Lee, Hong Yung. *From Revolutionary Cadres to Technocrats in Socialist China* (Berkeley and Los Angeles: University of California Press, 1991).

Lieberthal, Kenneth, and Michel Oksenberg. *Policy Making in China: Leaders Structures, and Process* (Princeton, NJ: Princeton University Press, 1988).

Link, Perry. *Evening Chats in Beijing: Probing China's Predicament* (New York: Norton, 1992).

Manion, Melanie. *Retirement of Revolutionaries in China: Public Policies, Social Norms, Private Interests* (Princeton, NJ: Princeton University Press, 1993).

Nathan, Andrew J. *Chinese Democracy* (New York: Alfred A. Knopf, 1985).

Naughton, Barry. *Growing Out of the Plan: Chinese Economic Reform, 1978–1993* (Cambridge: Cambridge University Press, 1995).

Oi, Jean. *Rural China Takes Off: Incentives for Reform* (Forthcoming, University of California Press).

Riskin, Carl. *China's Political Economy: The Quest for Development Since 1949* (Oxford: Oxford University Press, 1987).

Rosenbaum, Arthur Lewis, ed. *State and Society in China* (Boulder, CO: Westview Press, 1992).

Seymour, James D. *The Fifth Modernization: China's Human Rights Movement, 1978–1979* (Stanfordville, NY: Human Rights Publishing Group, 1980).

Thurston, Anne F. *Enemies of the People* (Cambridge: Harvard University Press, 1988).

Tsou, Tang. *The Cultural Revolution and Post-Mao Reforms: A Historical Perspective* (Chicago: University of Chicago Press, 1988).

Vogel, Ezra. *One Step Ahead in China: Guangdong under Reform* (Cambridge: Harvard University Press, 1989).

Wassertrom, Jeffrey, and Elizabeth Perry, eds. *Popular Protest and Political Culture in Modern China* (Boulder, CO: Westview Press, 1992).

Womack, Brantly, ed. *Contemporary Chinese Politics in Historical Perspective* (Cambridge: Cambridge University Press, 1990).

Public Policy

The previous section has outlined the basic political institutions of the PRC, the content of reform, and the conflicts—both intraparty and between state and society—that arose in the course of implementing reform. The task of this section is to look at the decision-making process and some of the public policy issues that China faces as it moves toward the twenty-first century. Finally, it will conclude with a brief look at the succession issue.

THE DECISION-MAKING PROCESS

The description of the political process over the course of reform described in Section B suggests that informal politics and the struggle for power play at least as important a role in China's decision-making process as the formal institutions. Nevertheless, formal institutions do play an important role, for bureaucracies are rarely without resources and they frequently represent important interests in the society and state. So it is best to think of decision making in China as involving both informal and formal processes, the particular mix of which depends greatly on the type of decision being made. In order to understand this process, it is perhaps best to start with the informal political structure and then look at the formal structure.

The highest formal decision-making body in China, as we have noted, is the Politburo Standing Committee (PSC). Although being a member of the PSC confers great power on the incumbent, supreme power is based on a combination of formal and informal power. Particularly in the case of Mao, but also to a certain extent with Deng, power is also derived from (and is reflected in) the ability to set the party's ideological course. In a system pledged to upholding Mao Zedong Thought, Mao had an indisputable edge over any potential adver-

sary. Although Deng's theory of "building socialism with Chinese characteristics" is hardly a coherent philosophy or clear-cut vision of the future, it has nevertheless provided him with an important advantage over his rivals. The supreme leader cannot be displaced without a direct assault on his ideological system and hence an open and divisive struggle for power. This has only been accomplished successfully once in the history of the PRC, when Deng Xiaoping wrested power from Mao's designated successor, the relatively junior and ineffective Hua Guofeng.

Supreme power, then, is intensely personal and uninstitutionalized, even when power is maintained in part through the control of formal institutions. The ideological dimension of power suggests the importance of a political "line" or policy orientation in the maintenance of power. This does not imply that the supreme leader cannot reverse directions when it is politically expedient, but it does suggest that a sustained critique on the policies of the supreme leader is indeed a threat to his power. Thus, policy disputes quickly become struggles for power. In the history of the CCP, there have been repeated struggles for power, and they are always viewed by participants as a "struggle to win all" by destroying the opposition as an effective political force.[24]

This analysis of the components of power suggests that policy decisions can frequently have ramifications for power at the top of the system, so the formal policy-making process is frequently short-circuited as the highest-level leaders weigh in with policy initiatives or responses aimed at shoring up their own authority or parrying the thrust of an opponent. To take the example discussed in the previous section of Deng Xiaoping's decision to advocate comprehensive price reform in 1988, the evidence strongly suggests that the proposal emanated from Deng's own office, without preparation or vetting by any bureaucratic apparatus, and had a stronger political than economic rationale. Such decisions, and there are many of them, suggest a level of policy making that is not institutionalized—and this level has had major ramifications on Chinese politics.

If we widen our focus somewhat, we find that generally there is a group of about 25 to 35 people at the top of the system who are highly influential in the policy-making process.[25] This group of people include those occupying the highest formal positions in the political system but also a number of people who are influential because of their longevity in the party and personal relations with one or more of the highest leaders. In the Dengist period, this small group of party elites has certainly included the leaders of the Central Advisory Commission, people who were officially retired from formal office, as well as other party elders. The role of such party elders varied across time and issue arena. Frequently they had a little role in the policy-making process, but on important issues they could weigh in with decisive impact. For instance, when Hu Yaobang came under severe criticism for his allegedly lax handling of the December 1986 student demonstrations, such party elders took the lead in calling for his ouster.

Generally speaking, the role of the top 25 to 35 people is less dramatic but nevertheless important. For instance, such people—because of their geographical origins, professional ties, or even personal interest—will frequently promote a cause or issue that they care about. Indeed, it is difficult to get the top of the system to deal with an issue seriously unless someone in this top 25 to 35 people is willing to promote it at the highest level of the regime.

Across the panoply of potential issues, most are too routine to engage the attention of one of the top 25 to 35 people. Even when such people do become involved, policy responses must nevertheless be implemented through the bureaucracy. China's bureaucracy is, as previously suggested, enormous. It is also widely distributed over a vast array of issues, and, as in all political systems, different bureaucracies become wedded to their own interests. Since most public policy decisions require the agreement of more than one bureaucracy to be implemented, coordinating actions among different bureaucracies can be a time-consuming and difficult process. Indeed, the various commissions and leading groups of the State Council are set up as supraministerial organs to be able to force various bureaucracies to comply with central decisions.

China's bureaucracy also stretches from the top of the system to the bottom, but lower-level bureaucratic organizations are primarily responsible to their local-level leadership (province, county, or township) even if they are also supervised by ministries in Beijing. In other words, it is often a difficult and complex process to get a local bureaucracy to implement a decision made in Beijing. Despite China's Leninist system, central bureaucracies are rarely successful in commanding lower-level bureaucracies to carry out a central decision. Particularly in any decision involving the commitment of resources, lower-level bureaucracies are in a good position to bargain with their higher-level counterparts in order to secure financial and other benefits.

The dispersion of authority among China's bureaucratic units and the constant bargaining that takes place among central-level bureaucracies and between the center and localities has caused different observers to label China a "fragmented authoritarian system" or a "bargaining society."[26] Such labels convey a sense of the complexity of China's decision-making process, but as the authors of such terms themselves recognize, the amount of bargaining varies tremendously across issue area. Economic issues, which by their nature distribute resources and involve the interests of different bureaucracies and localities, are subject to almost endless bargaining. Other issues, such as population control, on which there is a strong national consensus and a firm policy direction from Beijing, are much less subject to bargaining.[27]

Looking over China's policy-making process as a whole, it seems apparent that there are different parts that operate according to different rules, depending on the issue and level. China's bureaucracy is in many ways highly institutionalized; China's political system is not. One issue might disappear into China's vast bureaucracy never to be seen again, while another issue might be raised at the highest levels of the system without any vetting by the relevant bureaucracies. Neither approach makes for optimal decision making.

STATE CAPACITY

One major issue that China must deal with over the coming years is that of state capacity. As pointed out previously, most of China's economic reforms involved devolving authority and giving financial incentives to enterprises and localities. Beijing was willing to grant such incentives both because it had little choice given the realities of the post–Cultural Revolution situation and because it recognized that incentives were necessary to promote economic growth. The tax reform system of 1980 and its subsequent transmutations gave localities incentives to promote local industry in order to cultivate new sources of revenue—which could be retained in whole or in part by the locality. Indeed, such incentives played a critical role in China's economic takeoff. As one political scientist put it, the economy took off because China "got the taxes wrong."[28]

Over time, however, such incentives allowed localities to develop greater fiscal independence from Beijing. Revenues retained by some bureaucracies or in the localities, known as "extra-budgetary revenues" because they were not subject to Beijing's direct control, grew very quickly over the course of reform. Whereas such revenues accounted for only Rmb 34.7 billion in 1978, they increased more than tenfold to Rmb 385 billion in 1992. Put another way, extrabudgetary funds rose from only 31 percent of budgetary revenues in 1978 to 98 percent in 1992.[29]

Such figures suggest that localities in China, particularly those along the more industrialized east and southeast seaboard, have become increasingly independent economically from Beijing. Indeed, many localities have pursued "beggar thy neighbor" policies by erecting tariff or other barriers around the province or county to keep out competitive products and to protect local industry. This phenomenon has led some to speak of China's economy as a "feudal-lord economy" (*zhuhou jingji*) in which local leaders pursue local self-sufficiency, often in defiance of central regulations. This decentralization of the Chinese economy does not presage the breakup of China as some have speculated, but it does suggest that Beijing is less able to enforce its decisions at the local level and perhaps even to exercise sufficient control to maintain macroeconomic balance, an essential function of the modern state. In short, the capacity of China's state is being undermined at a time when the economy is developing rapidly and ever greater demands will be placed on it. Building institutions and enhancing state capacity (in the sense of being able to govern society in a regularized manner, not in the sense of having a strong military or secret police forces) are among the greatest challenges China faces in the late 1990s.

PUBLIC POLICY CHALLENGES

In the late 1990s and the first part of the next century, China faces a number of daunting public policy challenges. These challenges include controlling corruption, building effective tools to manage the macroeconomy, defusing a variety of social problems, protecting human rights and intellectual property rights, ensuring a stable and growing food supply and protecting the environment. In short, China faces major public policy challenges at a time when the political system itself is undergoing fundamental changes. How successfully China handles these problems will determine the role the country plays in the world in the twenty-first century.

Many public policy problems, such as corruption, cannot be distinguished from reform of the political system itself. Corruption is rooted in inefficiencies in China's legal and market systems and in the ability of public officials to use power for private ends. The dual-track price system, in which some prices were controlled by the state while others were allowed to fluctuate according to market demand, created enormous temptation for state officials to use their control over the allocation of materials to sell some of them at higher, market prices. Sometimes officials used the extra income earned to benefit their units, but just as commonly such income was siphoned off for private benefit. Corruption appears to have grown as inflation eroded the worth of official salaries, as the growth of the economy and market forces made the boundary between state goods and private commodities less clear, and as standards of public morality declined. The latter is particularly difficult to define, much less measure, but in the late 1980s and early 1990s there appears to have been a palpable decline in a belief in the common good and hence in the willingness to serve that greater good; a sense that "everyone is doing it" seems to have taken over, making many officials feel that it is all right, if not down right good, to feather their own nests.

Although corruption was a major problem in the late 1980s—indeed the Tiananmen protests were largely fueled by public outrage at such corruption—a new and much larger wave of corruption appears to have commenced in the early 1990s. This new wave of corruption was stimulated in part by the rapid growth of the economy and in part by new reforms that expanded the formation of joint-stock enterprises and opened up real estate markets. Although such reforms are a necessary part of economic reform, they provide tremendous opportunities to those with power or inside information to make windfall profits. Frequently, in the name of economic reform, shares in an enterprise would

be sold at a favorable price to relatives of an enterprise manager, who could then sell the securities at a high price. In 1993, it was reported that at least Rmb 57 billion had been diverted through interbank loans from the interior regions, where it was supposed to have been used to purchase grain from peasants, to the coastal regions, where it was invested in speculative real estate ventures.[30]

Such rampant corruption has created a nouveau riche class in the major urban areas. Frequently the sons and daughters of high officials, such people can be seen spending enormous sums on luxurious meals or in the designer shops that have sprung up in Beijing and elsewhere. Conspicuous consumption has come to China.

At the same time that some people have benefited enormously, legally or illegally, from the economic reforms and the opportunities they have provided, others find their livelihoods threatened. In the cities, those most under threat are those on fixed or nearly fixed incomes, usually retirees, who see their income eroded by inflation (which has been running around 20 percent per year in recent years). Also under potential threat are the millions of urban workers who are threatened with dismissal if state-owned enterprises take the steps that they must to be competitive in the market. Since the beginning of the PRC, state workers have enjoyed lifelong employment, a literally cradle-to-grave welfare system. Because a major goal of state enterprises was to provide jobs for urban workers, such enterprises are greatly overstaffed—at least 20 percent of the work force in state-owned enterprises is considered redundant. This has been a powerful obstacle in the way of economic reform. Massive layoffs would clearly result in public disturbances, as suggested by stories in the press of laid-off workers beating up and sometimes murdering factory managers. A worker-led protest would dwarf the political threat posed by the spring 1989 protests.

Another major source of social tension lies in the regional inequality that has developed over the reform period. During the Maoist period, great resources were expended on developing industries in the interior of China. Indeed, this effort to develop the interior region, which was guided primarily by national security concerns over the vulnerability of the coast to foreign attack, starved the more developed coastal region for funds and thus retarded China's overall economic development.

With reform, however, priorities changed. The opening up of the country, the development of the TVE sector, and efforts to renovate and update aged machinery stimulated development in the east and southeast of China while interior regions began to lag behind. The rising rural incomes, brought about by the agricultural reforms of the late 1970s and early 1980s, prevented regional differences from developing quickly. By the mid–1980s, however, as grain output began to stagnate and as the TVE sector (which is primarily located along the eastern seaboard) began to take off, the differences quickly widened.

Areas that depend primarily on agriculture for their livelihoods (that is, areas in which sideline production and TVEs are not well developed) have seen incomes stagnate or even fall. Such areas are very sensitive to the arbitrary exactions assessed periodically by rural officials and to arbitrary policy changes that cost peasants money. In 1993, there was a major disturbance in one such area in eastern Sichuan province. The disturbance centered around a peasant who had campaigned for the local people's congress by demanding that financial exactions on peasants not exceed the 5 percent allowed by official policy (in practice, such exactions frequently reached 30 percent of income). When he received the highest number of votes, local authorities, in an apparent effort to prevent him from taking his seat, attempted to arrest him on a charge of failing to pay taxes. When police vans arrived to arrest the leader, some 10,000 peasants gathered and soon burned the vans and beat the cadres.[31]

The incident in Sichuan, which simmered for months, was not an isolated incident. Over a hundred similar, though apparently smaller scale, incidents affected 11 provinces in 1993, prompting new policies

from the central government. As one prominent official put it, "If there are problems in the villages, no one in the present regime can hold on to power."[32] The resources of the central government, however, are limited in dealing with such rural discontent. Rural unemployment or underemployment is estimated to be at least 100 million and is probably closer to 150 million people. With that number of people unemployed, many of them young, the potential for continued rural violence is quite great.

Not all such unemployed peasants remain in the countryside. In recent years, particularly since controls on population movements have broken down, millions of peasants have migrated to the cities in search of employment. Frequently they migrate seasonally, looking for construction and other jobs in the cities during the off season, and then returning to the countryside to help at harvest time. This influx of peasants into the cities has created new problems. Urban residents complain that they are a drain on urban resources and that they bring crime and a general deterioration in the urban standard of life. Such crime is not limited to the urban areas. Railroads passing through certain areas are a particular target of some apparently well organized criminal gangs. As Han Zhubin, the minister of railroads, once noted, "robbers and thieves rose in swarms" along certain sections of the rail system. "One or two villages or towns," he said, "even regard 'robbing trains of their cargoes and facilities' as a means to get rich."[33]

These bureaucratic and social problems, which reflect both the success China has had in breaking down the old Maoist system and the difficulty that it has had in creating a new system, are compounded by other difficulties, ranging from feeding its population to protecting the environment to human rights.

NATURAL RESOURCES AND THE ENVIRONMENT

China is a large country with seemingly plentiful natural resources, but when such resources are recalculated on a per capita basis it turns out that China's natural resource endowment is generally modest. For instance, China has 9.54 million square kilometers of land, but only 14.6 percent of that is arable. Put another way, China must support 22 percent of the world's population on only 7 percent of the world's arable land. Only 8.6 percent of China's land area is forested, giving it only 0.11 hectare per capita of forest land. That means that China ranks approximately 120 out of 150 nations in afforestation.[34]

In terms of fresh water, China receives about 6 trillion cubic meters of precipitation a year, with an annual runoff of about 2.6 trillion cubic meters. In per capita terms, this is only 2,600 cubic meters a year, about one-fifth of the world average. Worse, most of China's water supply is concentrated in the south, away from major population centers in the north, including the capital, Beijing. This has led to excessive efforts to tap underground water supplies in the north, frequently depleting underground aquifers.[35]

Such figures highlight some of the consequences of China's large population, a population that currently grows by about 14 million people per year. China's population, as noted in the first section, has historically been large, and by the middle of the nineteenth century China's population was pushing against the limits of what its land could support, given the prevailing technology. As China's population grew, it began expanding into ever more marginal land, felling trees and terracing fields as it went. Thus, the felling of China's primal forest areas began well before the establishment of the PRC.

The policies pursued in the Maoist period, however, greatly exacerbated population-resource pressures, causing great environmental damage. As forests have shrunk and population grown, China's rural population (80 percent of the total) has increasingly relied on the use of stalks, straw, and whatever firewood is available for their domestic fuel. Annual consumption of such material is estimated to be over 500 million tons. This deprives the soil of large quantities of nutrients that would otherwise be returned to it, thus depleting the soil's organic content.[36]

The distorted price structure adopted during the Maoist period also led to a great waste of energy. China is one of the least efficient users of energy in the world, being four times less efficient than Japan and more than twice as inefficient as India.[37] In addition, because there was no market for land, industrial enterprises frequently expanded onto valuable agricultural land whenever local leaders decided to do so. Thus, much valuable arable land was lost.

Reform has begun to straighten out China's price structure (although land and energy prices have been among the last to be adjusted to near market values), but the headlong rush for industrialization has created new stresses on the environment. The rapid growth of the TVE sector has been accompanied by tremendous pollution as environmental safeguards have been largely ignored. Rivers and streams have become badly polluted.

Food

During the Maoist period, China's food supply barely kept pace with its population growth. In the early Dengist period, the rural reforms brought relief from the constant fear of food shortages as harvests rose by one-third in only six years. In 1984, China produced 407 million metric tons of grain, or about 800 jin (1 jin = 1.1 pound) of grain per capita, a historic record. Since then, however, grain production has increased more slowly, and per capita grain production remains somewhat below the record of 1984.

China's increased prosperity, however, is placing new demands on China's grain supply. As urban residents have become wealthier in the 1980s and 1990s, they have demanded more meat in their diet, and now their example is being emulated by rural residents. If rural diets (about 11 kilograms of pork a year) were only to increase to the level of meat consumption presently prevailing in the urban areas (about 18.5 kilograms of pork per year), the production of feed grain would have to increase by at least 50 percent. Another pressure on the grain supply has been the increased demand for alcoholic beverages, particularly beer. This means planting greater acreage to barley.[38]

China's population trends and continuing industrialization will also place continuing strains on China's ability to feed itself. China's population will rise to at least 1.4 billion by 2010 and 1.5 billion by 2020. Every year approximately half a million hectares is taken out of agricultural production for use in industry, entertainment, transportation, and housing. This will mean the loss of 10–15 million hectares of farmland by the year 2020—enough to feed 125 million people at current yields.[39]

These trends do not mean mass starvation within a generation, but they do mean that China must begin now to improve its management of agriculture, through such things as better pricing, better inputs, and better environmental protection. So far, China has not adopted such strategies, as the decision to alleviate water shortages in the north by diverting huge amounts of water from the south suggests.[40]

Energy and Environment

One resource with which China is well endowed is coal. China has coal resources are approximately 80 percent of those of the former Soviet Union and nearly double those of the United States. This means that for the foreseeable future, China will continue to rely on coal for approximately 75 percent of its energy needs. Moreover, as China develops economically and per capita consumption goes up, its energy needs will inevitably increase. Even if China's energy efficiency improves, its use of fossil fuel, primarily coal, will continue to increase.

One result of this situation is that by early in the twenty-first century, China will become the largest emiter of carbon dioxide in the world. By 2020, it is predicted that China will produce approximately one-fifth of the world's carbon dioxide, as compared to 17 percent for the United States.[41] This will generate a difficult ethical dilemma for world control of the environment. As the wealthy nations in the world become more conscious of the negative effects of environmental pollution and more concerned about the greenhouse effect, they will almost inevitably put pressure on China and other developing countries to reduce their environmental pollution. But even if China's per capita energy consumption were to increase by 50 percent, its energy utilization would only be one-sixth of the average of the world's rich nations.[42] In other words, those who consume by far the greatest amount of energy are very likely to pressure those whose energy use is considerably less to spend scarce resources cleaning up the environment and reducing energy consumption, and the response of China and other developing nations is likely to be quite negative.

ETHNIC CONFLICT AND HUMAN RIGHTS

A very different sort of public policy issue that China faces revolves around the issues of ethnic relations and human rights, issues which overlap to a significant degree. Altogether there are 55 different ethnic minorities in China making up about 6 percent of China's total population. Although the size of this minority population is relatively small by the standards of most nations, China's minorities are concentrated in strategically sensitive parts of the country that do not have large concentrations of Han Chinese, the dominant ethnic group. These areas are primarily in the southwestern and western parts of the country and include the provinces of Yunnan, Guizhou, Xizang (Tibet), Sichuan, Qinghai, Xinjiang, and Ningxia. In recent years, the Tibetan situation has attracted a lot of international attention, and the spiritual leader of Tibet, the Dalai Lama who has been in exile since 1959, received the Nobel Prize for peace in 1989. Although Tibetans resent the rule of the Han Chinese, no nation has ever challenged the Chinese claim to rule Tibet, a recognition that dates back at least to the Anglo-Chinese Convention of 1906 and the Anglo-Russian Treaty of 1907. The vital security role played by the Tibetan highlands suggests that no Chinese government is likely to surrender control over the area.

Although the Tibetan issue has received the most attention in the West, other minority groups, particularly the Muslim populations of the northwest region, have long resisted Chinese rule, just as China has long claimed to rule the area. The northwest region (the province of Xinjiang) is a very sensitive area for China, containing as it does both rich mineral resources and important defense installations. China has been careful to maintain good relations with the newly independent republics of Central Asia as well as with such Middle East nations as Iran at least in part to dissuade such nations from stirring up trouble in China's northwest. Nevertheless, those Muslim populations have never been reconciled to Han rule, and there have been protests and riots from time to time. Incidents that are seen as inciting violence have been dealt with harshly.

Human rights have become a very emotional issue in recent years, particularly since the Tiananmen crackdown and the end of the Cold War. Definitions of human rights differ greatly as do assessments of both general trends in China and approaches to improving conditions. China remains highly unwilling to allow direct expressions of political dissent, and the penal system remains extremely harsh by world standards. Nevertheless, most people agree that China's human rights record has improved greatly since the Maoist era. There is far greater scope for the expression of opinion and the zone of privacy around individual behavior has grown constantly. The growth and diversification of the economy mean that individuals have more opportunities to get ahead, and are not so dependent on the state for everything. That in and of itself limits the ability of the state to exact compliance. In short, China has made much progress over the past 15 years, and that should not be forgotten, but it still has a long way to go.

Gender

Traditionally, Confucian culture emphasized the subordination of women to men, and despite much progress, such attitudes die hard.

In the Maoist period, there were efforts to improve the lot of women, including the Marriage Law of 1950 (which emphasized the voluntary nature of marriage and made divorce easier) and the large-scale employment of women in industry and agriculture. Mao declared that "women hold up half the sky," and women took up positions in the Central Committee and even Politburo. The reality, however, differed from the rhetoric, and closer examination reveals that women continued to suffer discrimination of various sorts throughout the Maoist period. Nevertheless, it must be admitted that a lot of progress was made in recognizing the equality of women.

In many ways, the reform period has been difficult on women. Although women have gained from the reforms, just as men have, they have not gained as much. Frequently, when peasants migrate from the countryside to the cities in search of better jobs, it is the man who goes and the woman who stays behind to tend the fields. In the urban areas, women generally do not get as good jobs as men or paid as well. Enterprises that are looking to reduce employment frequently lay off female workers.

One of the areas in which traditional patriarchal tendencies have been most noticeable has been in the area of population control. The policy of permitting only one child raised the prospect not only that a lineage would die out (since women marry outside the family) but also that there would be no one to support the parents as they aged (traditionally the son's responsibility). This combination of traditional attitudes and economic concerns forced the state to allow greater flexibility, frequently allowing couples to try for a second child if the first is a girl. Nevertheless, there are periodically efforts to strengthen the one-child policy and rarely is a third birth permitted. There is thus a strong preference for boy babies, and the introduction of sonogram technology into the countryside has facilitated sex identification and reinforced the tendency to terminate pregnancies of female embryos. This has opened up a major gap between the number of males and females born, a gap that is bound to have adverse social consequences in the future.

SUCCESSION AND LEGITIMACY

Building institutions and enhancing state capacity will not be easy in the current political atmosphere. When Deng Xiaoping dies, power will indeed fall to a younger generation, one that is currently led by Jiang Zemin (general secretary) and Li Peng (premier). This new generation differs in many respects from its revolutionary elders. The most obvious difference is simply the lack of revolutionary legitimacy of the new leadership. This will be the first generation of leaders in PRC history not to have established their leadership credentials through their action in China's revolutionary struggle. In some ways this is good. This generation carries neither the ideological baggage nor the history of intraparty conflict that their elders carry. If they can establish their authority, they may be less ideological and less conflictual than their elders. But establishing their authority will not be easy. They not only lack legitimacy in the eyes of society, they lack it in the eyes of their colleagues. There is, for instance, no particular reason why leaders of similar age and experience, not to mention those who are older, will defer to people like Jiang Zemin and Li Peng. Moreover, as the above analysis suggests, leaders like Jiang Zemin and Li Peng will not be able to count on institutional authority to bolster their leadership. This new generation of leaders will thus pay a price for the most unfortunate legacy of the Mao and Deng eras, namely, the failure to build sound and credible institutions.

This is also a generation typified by its technical and bureaucratic backgrounds. Much of this successor generation has trained as engineers. Jiang Zemin spent most of his career in electrical engineering, and Li Peng spent his in the hydroelectric power industry. Moreover, such people as Jiang Zemin and Li Peng spent most of their careers climbing specialized bureaucratic systems step by step.

These career paths underscore other major differences between this successor generation and their revolutionary elders. People of Deng Xiaoping's generation were largely political generalists. There were very few who did not participate in a whole range of military, political, organizational, and ideological affairs. The revolutionary elders were also supremely self-confident people. They were people who had engaged in one of history's great revolutionary struggles, "overturning heaven and earth" in their quest to create a new order. Both Mao and Deng had the confidence bred of their revolutionary lives to launch bold experiments, believing that whatever happened they would be able to maintain control. In contrast, the leaders of the third generation are products of that new order. They are people who have risen, usually slowly and step-by-step through a system that allows little imagination and creativity and demands great obedience and respect to higher ups and elders. They give little indication of being bold and innovative people.

Where this pattern of career specialization will hurt these new leaders the most is in their relations with the military. Since the fall of the Qing dynasty in 1911, civilian political control has always been combined with control over the military forces. This was true of Yuan Shikai, Chiang Kai-shek, Mao Zedong, and Deng Xiaoping. Is China ready to forge a new and more institutionalized relationship between the civilian and military hierarchies? Perhaps. But such an institutionalized relationship will not come about unless the civilian leadership is successful in managing the basic domestic and international problems facing the country. And in tackling such problems, they may not always have the support of the military. Corruption is one major issue where the military may not be willing to support leadership efforts; foreign policy is another.

This suggests that China is entering a period in which the political situation is likely to be extremely fluid. Opinion among observers of China is very diverse, with some arguing that the regime will collapse relatively quickly and others maintaining that it will continue to exist for the foreseeable future. If the current regime does indeed survive into the next century, it seems highly likely that the leaders currently taking over from Deng Xiaoping and his cohort will pass relatively quickly from the scene. They are likely to be replaced by younger, bolder people. Whether such people will move to open the system up or will, on the contrary, emphasize nationalism and control remains to be seen.

CHINA AND THE WORLD

Over the last decade and a half, China has indeed begun to emerge as an important world power. Although its interests and influence are concentrated in the Asia-Pacific region, the size of its economy, its role as a permanent member of the UN Security Council, and the potential global consequences of its actions on a range of issues from environmental pollution to arms proliferation make China an important actor in the international community. Whether it manages its own domestic problems and becomes successfully integrated into the world community is of more than marginal interest to the rest of the world.

China's relationship with the international community remains problematic because of a number of issues, including economic, security, and human rights. Assuming that China's economy continues to develop, China will clearly be a new power in the international arena. Indeed, it is already one of the largest economies in the world. At the official exchange rate, China's GNP is approximately $500 billion, about one-twelfth that of the United States. But if one accepts even the most modest effort to recalculate China's GNP in terms of purchasing price parity, then it is apparent that China's GNP is more in the range of $1.25 trillion, or about three-quarters the size of Japan's economy.[43] The size of China's economy in and of itself has made a number of issues more difficult than they otherwise would have been. For instance, China is not yet a member of the World Trade Organization (WTO), the successor organization to the General Agreement on Trade and Tariffs (GATT). There are many issues that have complicated the negotiations surrounding China's entry, but it seems clear that the fact that China is a large economy casts a shadow over the entire negotiation process. China already runs a trade surplus of over $30 billion annually with the United

States, and the fear is that this trade surplus could grow quickly to unmanageable proportions if China were granted the more favorable trade treatment of the WTO. Similarly, intellectual property rights have become a major irritant in Sino-U.S. trade relations. China's violation of intellectual property rights is probably no worse than those of most other developing nations, including states admitted to the WTO, but the fact that China's economy is so big looms large in discussions of such violations.

The size of China's economy has also aroused concerns about China's military potential and policies. China's military is rather backward in comparison with those of advanced nations, but it has embarked on a military modernization program that could substantially improve its ability to enforce its claim over a number of disputed territories. Part of the problem is one of perception. When China's military planners examine their own capabilities and look at the number of potential problems that could occur on their very long land and sea borders, they see a very real need to modernize. China's neighbors, in contrast, look at China's modernization efforts and wonder what threat China perceives. It becomes easy to assume that China is pursuing policies that could pose a threat to their interests.

Just as China's economy and foreign trade have not yet been integrated into the existing international trade regimes, there are few multilateral forums for discussing security issues in the Asia-Pacific region and enhancing mutual understanding. China remains wary of divulging much information about its military, leaving outsiders free to speculate about the size of its budget, its capabilities, and its intentions. There is thus a tendency on the part of other nations in the region to reinforce their own military capabilities.

Suspicions are fueled by the existence of important territorial disputes. The most important of these is over the status of Taiwan (see Feature 8.2). Following the Chinese Civil War, the Nationalist troops fled the mainland to Taiwan in 1949. With the outbreak of the Korean War in 1950, the United States interposed forces to prevent a PRC attack on Taiwan. Even after the United States established

Feature 8.2 Tension in the Taiwan Straits

In the summer and fall of 1995 and the spring of 1996, the PRC mounted a series of military exercises in the Taiwan Straits that were designed to convince the people and authorities of Taiwan (as well as those of other nations) that efforts to secure international recognition could bring full-scale military assault. These tensions have resulted from several factors. When the United States decided to extend diplomatic recognition to the PRC in 1979, Taiwan began to exist as a largely unrecognized but nevertheless independent political unit. This anomalous status prevailed for many years, but as the government on Taiwan moved toward democratization in the late 1980s, cries for independence or some sort of international recognition as a "political entity" began to grow louder. The president of Taiwan, Lee Teng-hui, launched a vigorous effort to secure greater status for Taiwan, including a return to the United Nations, though in what capacity was left unstated. In June 1995, the Clinton administration, in a change of long-standing policy, granted a visa to Lee Teng-hui for a "private" visit to the United States so that he could return to his alma mater, Cornell University. Because the United States is widely viewed by both the PRC and Taiwan as the key to any change in Taiwan's international status, this change in policy provoked an angry response from the PRC, which saw it as the latest and most significant in a series of moves that could lead to the permanent separation of Taiwan from the mainland. The PRC has vowed never to let that happen and seems prepared to use military force to make sure that it does not.

diplomatic relations with China in 1979 and ended its long-standing mutual security treaty with Taiwan, there was no resolution to the question of the status of Taiwan. In recent years, as Taiwan has democratized, there have been increasing calls for declaring the country a separate, independent nation. Such calls are vigorously opposed by the PRC, which continues to view Taiwan as a part of China. The potential for military conflict over this issue was demonstrated in 1995 when the United States, reversing long-standing policy, granted a visa for Lee Teng-hui, the president of Taiwan, to make a "private" visit to the country. The PRC responded with several large-scale military exercises, including firing missiles into the waters off Taiwan.

The other dispute that has garnered a great deal of international attention has been that over the Spratley Islands in the South China Sea. China has long claimed sovereignty over the islands—most of which are reefs that are covered with water at high tide—but anxieties were heightened in 1992 when the PRC wrote its claim into law. Various of the islands are claimed by Vietnam, Indonesia, Brunei, Malaysia, the Philippines, and Taiwan, and

there have been repeated conflicts, particularly with Vietnam, over the issue. Although no nation has been willing to escalate tension over this issue, it clearly remains a concern to many nations in the area, including Japan, whose ships regularly traverse the South China Sea to bring oil from the Middle East.

Other territorial disputes are outstanding with India, Vietnam, Japan, and Russia. Although none of these seem likely to fuel direct conflict, they do increase uncertainty in the region and make the absence of multilateral security forums regrettable.

The economic and security issues outlined here have been part of a complex and not very smooth relationship with the United States. Particularly since the Tiananmen incident in 1989, there have been sharp calls in the United States to press China on a range of issues, including human rights, the status of Tibet, intellectual property rights, security issues, and environmental pollution. Of these, the human rights issue has been the focus of the greatest amount of attention. After President Clinton was inaugurated, the United States attempted to pressure China by linking China's human rights behavior to the trade benefits granted China under Most Favored Nation status (which does not, contrary to the sound of the term, grant special privileges; the term merely indicates the normal rules of the game by which international trade is conducted). This effort was not successful, and the United States was forced to drop such linkage in 1994.

Regardless of the merits of human rights and other issues, it is clear that such demands have created a backlash within China. Today, many Chinese regard the United States as pursuing a strategy designed to hold China down and keep it weak rather than to integrate it into the international system. This perception underscores the fact that the status of China's international relations can affect the evolution of China's domestic politics, which will, in turn, affect its international relations. There is, in short, a danger of misguided policy bringing about a more truculent, more aggressive China and thus completing a self-fulfilling prophecy.

Key Terms

extrabudgetary revenues
"feudal-lord economy"
General Agreement on Trade and Tariffs (GATT)
Lee Teng-hui
Most Favored Nation
purchasing price parity
Spratley Islands
World Trade Organization (WTO)

Further Readings

Harding, Harry. *The Fragile Relationship: The United States and China Since 1972* (Washington, DC: Brookings Institution, 1993).

Harris, Lillian Craig. "Xinjiang, *Central Asia,* and the Implications for China's Policy in the Islamic World," *China Quarterly, 133* (March 1993): pp. 111–29.

Lampton, David M. "Chinese Politics: The Bargaining Treadmill," *Issues and Studies, 23,* no. 3 (March 1987): pp. 11–41.

Lampton, David M. ed. *The Politics of Policy Implementation* (Berkeley and Los Angeles: University of California Press, 1987).

Lardy, Nicholas R. *China and the World Economy* (Washington, DC: Institute for International Economics, 1994).

Lieberthal, Kenneth, and David M. Lampton, eds. *Bureaucracy, Politics, and Decision-Making in Post-Mao China* (Berkeley and Los Angeles: University of California Press, 1992).

Qu, Geping, and Woyen Lee, eds. *Managing the Environment in China* (Dublin: Tycooly International, 1994).

Ross, Lester. *Environmental Policy in China* (Blommington: Indiana University Press, 1988).

Smil, Vaclav. *China's Environmental Crisis* (Armonk, NY: M.E. Sharpe, 1993).

Walder, Andrew. *Communist Neo-Traditionalism: Work and Authority in Chinese Industry* (Berkeley and Los Angeles: University of California Press, 1986).

Waldron, Arthur. *The Great Wall of China: From History to Myth* (New York: Columbia University Press, 1989).

Wolf, Margery and Roxanne Witke, eds. *Women in Chinese Society* (Stanford: Stanford University Press, 1975).

Notes

1. Li Zhisui, with Anne Thurston, *The Private Life of Chairman Mao* (New York: Random House, 1994).
2. John R. Watt, *The Chinese Magistrate in Late Imperial China* (New York: Columbia University Press, 1972).
3. Ho Ping-ti, *Studies on the Population of China* (Cambridge: Harvard University Press, 1959).
4. Philip Kuhn, *Rebellion and Its Enemies in Late Imperial China* (Cambridge: Harvard University Press, 1970).
5. Mary C. Wright, *The Last Stand of Chinese Conservatism: The T'ung-chih Restoration, 1862–1874,* rev. ed. (Stanford: Stanford University Press, 1966).
6. Stuart Schram, ed., *Mao's Road to Power: Revolutionary Writings, 1912–1949, Vol. 1: The Pre-Marxist Period, 1912–1920,* (Armonk, NY: M. E. Sharpe, 1992) p. xvii.

7. Mao Zedong, "On Practice," in *The Selected Works of Mao Tse-dong* (Peking: Foreign Language Press, 1966), vol. 1.

8. Nicholas Lardy, "Economic Recovery and The 1st Five-Year Plan," Roderick MacFarquhar and John K. Fairbank, eds., *The Cambridge History of China*, vol. 14, The People's Republic, Part I: The Emergence of Revolutionary China, 1949–1965, pp. 144–184.

9. Ibid.

10. Carl Riskin, *China's Political Economy: The Quest for Development Since 1949* (Oxford: Oxford University Press, 1987), p. 57.

11. Dali Yang, *Catastrophe and Reform in China: State, Rural Society, and Institutional Change Since the Great Leap Famine* (Stanford: Stanford University Press, 1996).

12. A wonderful account of popular culture today is given by Jianying Zha in *China Pop* (New York: The New Press, 1995).

13. *The Gate of Heavenly Peace* directed and produced by Carma Hinton and Richard Gordon and *Moving the Mountain* directed by Michael Apted and produced by Trudie Styler.

14. Tang Tsou, "Chinese Politics at the Top: Factionalism or Informal Politics? Balance-of-Power Politics or a Game to Win All?" *The China Journal, 34* (July 1995): pp. 95–156.

15. Stuart Schram, *Mao's Road to Power, Revolutionary Writing, 1912–1949*, Vol. 1, *The Pre-Marxist Period, 1912–1920* (Armonk, NY: M. E. Sharpe, 1992), p. xix.

16. Kenneth Lieberthal, *Governing China: From Revolution Through Reform* (New York, W. W. Norton, 1995), pp. 194–208.

17. Wang Lixin and Joseph Fewsmith, "The State Planning Commission: Bulwark of the Planned Economy," in Carol Lee Hamrin and Suisheng Zhao, ed., *Decision-Making in Deng's China; Perspectives from Insiders* (Armonk, NY: M. E. Sharpe, 1995), pp. 51–65.

18. Barry Naughton, *Growing Out of the Plan Chinese Economic Reform, 1978–1993,* (Cambridge: Cambridge University Press, 1995), pp. 41–42.

19. John P. Burns, *The Chinese Communist Nomenklatura System: A Documentary Study of Party Control of Leadership Selection* (Armonk, NY: M. E. Sharpe, 1989).

20. Naughton, *Growing Out of the Plan.*

21. Ezra Vogel, *One Step Ahead in China: Guangdong under Reform* (Cambridge: Harvard University Press, 1991).

22. Nicholas Lardy, *China in the World Economy* (Washington, DC: Institute for International Economics, 1994), p. 39.

23. Thomas Gold, "'Just in Time!' China Battles Spiritual Pollution on the Eve of 1984," *Asian Survey, 24,* no. 9 (September 1984): pp. 942–62.

24. Tang Tsou, "Chinese Politics at the Top: Factionalism or Informal Politics? Balance-of-Power Politics or a Game to Win All?" in *The China Journal, 34* (July 1995): pp. 95–156.

25. Kenneth Lieberthal and Michel Oksenberg, *Policy Making in China: Leaders, Structures, and Processes* (Princeton, NJ: Princeton University Press, 1998).

26. Kenneth Lieberthal, "Introduction," in Kenneth Lieberthal and David M. Lampton, eds., *Bureaucracy, Politics, and Decision-Making in Post-Mao China* (Berkeley and Los Angeles: University of California Press, 1992); and David M. Lampton, "Chinese Politics: The Bargaining Treadmill," *Issues and Studies, 23,* no. 3 (March 1987): pp. 11–41.

27. Lieberthal and Lampton, eds., *Bureaucracy, Politics, and Decision-Making in Post-Mao China.*

28. Jean Oi, *Rural China Takes Off: Incentives for Industrialization* (Forthcoming, University of California Press).

29. Jae Ho Chung, "Central-Provincial Relations," in Lo Chi Kin, Suzanne Pepper, and Tsui Kai Yuen, eds., *China Review, 1995* (Hong Kong: The Chinese University Press, 1995), Ch 3.

30. "Central Authorities Urge Banks to Draw Bank Loans and Stop Promoting the Bubble Economy," *Ta kung pao,* July 1, 1993, p. 2, trans. Foreign Broadcast Information Service, *China Daily Report* (henceforth, FBIS-Chi), July 1, 1993, pp. 31–32.

31. Chou Wen-tao, "A Look at the Agricultural Crisis Through Popular Rebellion Caused by Officials' Tyranny,'" *Hsin Pao,* April 20, 1993, p. 22, trans. FBIS-Chi, April 29, 1993, pp. 10–12; and Chung Tzu-ming, "The CPC Takes Serious Precautions Against Possible Disturbances During the National People's Congress," *Ming Pao,* March 9, 1993, p. 2, trans. FBIS-Chi, March 9, 1993, pp. 12–13.

32. *South China Morning Post,* March 22, 1993, p. 8.

33. "Railroad Minister Han Zhubin on Reform and Comprehensive Improvement in Security of Railroad Transportation in China," *Liaowang,* no 12 (March 22, 1993), overseas edition, pp. 8–9, trans. FBIS-CHI, April 6, 1993, pp. 20–22.

34. Vaclav Smil, "China's Standing in the Developing World," *Current History,* September 1987, pp. 245–248, 271.

35. Ibid., and Vaclav Smil, *China's Environmental Crisis* (Armonk, NY: M. E. Sharpe, 1993), pp. 38–52.

36. Qu Geping and Woyen Lee, eds., *Managing the Environment in China* (Dublin: Tycooly International, 1994).

37. Vaclav Smil, "China's Standing in the Developing World," pp. 245–248, 271.

38. Smil, *China's Environmental Crisis,* pp. 83–84.

39. Vaclav Smil, "Who Will Feed China?" *The China Quarterly,* no. 143 (September 1995): pp. 801–813.

40. Ibid., p. 810.

41. Smil, *China's Environmental Crisis,* p. 134.

42. Ibid., p. 136.

43. Lardy, *China and the World Economy* p. 18.

PART 3

Third World Countries

CHAPTER 9

The Government of India

Bernard E. Brown

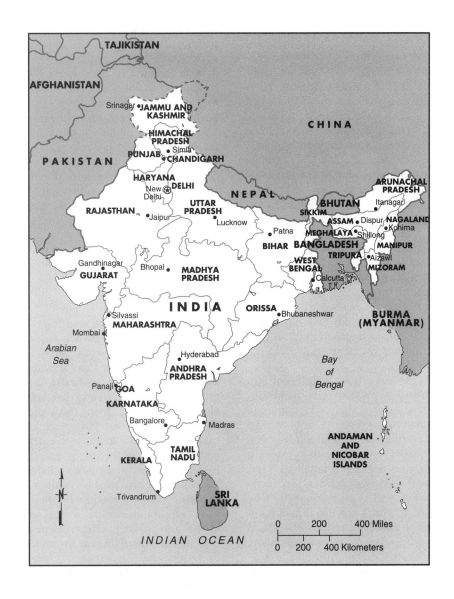

Political Development

For some in the West India summons up images from Rudyard Kipling—colorful bazaars, fabled palaces and temples, worshipers bathing in the waters of the sacred Ganges, snake charmers, cows wandering through streets, elephants as a means of transport, and red-coated English officers maintaining European customs in a completely alien land. Part of India's continuing fascination for outsiders is that aspects of the world described by Kipling may still be found. But alongside and more and more displacing the traditional culture are elements of a modern, industrial society. India now ranks among the ten largest industrial powers in the world, producing and exporting a wide range of products, including locomotives, diesel engines, and jet aircraft. In 1980, India entered the space age by becoming the sixth nation to launch a rocket and communication satellites. It is a major participant in research on telecommunications, space exploration, and nuclear energy. As of 1990 seven nuclear power reactors were in operation. Agricultural production has increased dramatically, spurred by a large research structure in universities and government. Life expectancy has gone up since independence from 32 to over 59 years, reflecting improvements in medical science and hospital care.

The contrast between the omnipresent bullock cart and the nuclear power plant makes India a compelling subject of study. The politics of modernization are spread out on a large canvas: the historical culture and society; the forces that penetrate and shatter that traditional synthesis; the dynamic tension between traditional and modern groups; the kinds of policies that facilitate modernization; and the problems thereby created. Students of politics are also drawn naturally to Indian affairs because they are concerned with power; and by virtue of its vast population, geographical location, industrial plants, and military strength, India is among the leading actors on the world stage.

The differences between Indian and European society are brought out in Table 1.2 of the introduction to this volume. The following ob-

servations may be drawn from this table: (1) Compared to European democracies, India is markedly poorer; the per capita income of Indians is about 3 percent of that of Western Europeans. (2) India remains an overwhelmingly agricultural country, with 63 percent of its population engaged in agriculture. By comparison, in the industrial societies of Western Europe only 2 to 7 percent of the people are still engaged in agriculture, and of course, the agricultural sectors of modern economies are far more productive than in preindustrial economies. (3) In cultural life and social structure, India is closer to the classic model of traditional societies—having a much lower literacy rate, a less developed educational system, and a lower life expectancy. To put it simply, India may boast of the same institutions that exist in Western Europe—parliament, prime minister, cabinet, president, supreme court, political parties, and the like—but these institutions serve and are responsible to a society that is still in the early stages of economic development.

Most political observers have assumed that there is a correlation between both education and high per capita income and democracy. Two reasons are suggested for this correlation: (1) Parliamentary democracy is based on competition among political parties and their leaders, with the electorate deciding among them after considering all arguments. If the governors are to be ultimately responsible to the people, there must be a widespread belief that the people are capable of making informed and rational choices. Such a political process presumably requires a high degree of literacy and of general education. (2) The delicate compromises worked out among interest groups and political parties in democracies reflect a social agreement on how the national income is to be divided. An expanding economy should make it easier to satisfy all claimants.

However, the correlation between democracy and both education and prosperity is not undisputable, as proven by the case of Germany. In the late nineteenth and early twentieth centuries, Germany was in the forefront of the industrial and scientific revolutions—as advanced in literacy, education, and national wealth as Great Britain or France—and yet did not establish a parliamentary democracy until after World War I. Following the collapse of the Weimar Republic, this same "advanced" European nation produced a Fascist regime. Clearly a high level of scientific and economic development is an insufficient condition for the emergence of democracy. The case of India is equally critical. Here is a society that after World War II was far less developed than those of Western Europe. Yet India—almost alone among the nations of the third world—created a parliamentary democracy that has endured. No one interested in the theory of democracy can ignore the case of India.

As was pointed out in the introduction to this volume, the terms "traditional" and "modern" are generally used to help explain economic, social, and political differences. The typology of Max Weber (see Chapter 1) implies that transition between traditional and modern (or bureaucratic) systems is often facilitated by the rise of a charismatic political leader. We shall now survey the Indian experience of modernization, using roughly the Weberian categories of traditional, transitional, and modern. First, India will be considered as a traditional society (before the arrival of the British), then as a transitional society (under British rule), and finally as a modernizing society (since independence).

TRADITIONAL SOCIETY IN INDIA

When the British first arrived in India in the seventeenth century, they found a vast, sprawling congeries of peoples whose historical unity went back five millennia. Recent archaeological discoveries indicate that great cities developed in the Indus Valley from 4000 to 2500 B.C. that had a level of civilization equal to or exceeding that of Egypt, Mesopotamia, and China during the same era. Some elements of the Indus culture somehow managed to survive the catastrophe that brought about the destruction of this civilization, and later reappeared in Hinduism. Beginning at about 1500 B.C. the northern and central plains of India were invaded by waves of nomadic Indo-Aryans. The light-skinned Aryans gradually pushed the native Dravidian people, generally dark-skinned, farther and farther south. A fusion of culture took place, out of which emerged the Hindu way of life. It was during this time that the caste system developed, probably in order to maintain an appropriate distance between Aryan invaders and the native inhabitants. Our knowledge of this period comes largely from the epic literature of the ancient Vedas (religious hymns handed down by word of mouth) and the later Gita (a long poem on war and duty).

The early Hindu society resulting from the Aryan-Dravidian synthesis proved durable and resilient. Successive invaders, including the Greeks under Alexander the Great, were either ignored or absorbed into the national life. A serious challenge was posed, however, by Muslim incursions beginning about 1000 A.D. For 700 years the Muslims, with their militant ideology, were a formidable force. They succeeded in governing most of the country under the Mogul dynasty, founded in 1526 by a Turkish descendant of Genghis Khan. Some of the Mogul emperors, particularly Akbar, were men of considerable skill and talent. But by 1700 A.D. the Mogul empire was in an advanced state of decay. The stage was set for a new period—that of European or, more specifically, British domination.

The economy, social structure, ideology, culture, and politics of India in the seventeenth and eighteenth centuries, at the time of the British invasion and conquest, constituted in every respect a model of the traditional type of society. The masses of India lived in some 700,000 villages, each a virtually self-sufficient, self-governing entity with its own class and caste divisions. A few towns or cities developed as centers of royal authority, trade, or pilgrimage, but the overwhelming majority of the people lived in the villages. Royal authority might be concentrated in the hands of some mighty personage in Delhi or Lahore, but his power was barely felt in the villages except through the intermediary of the inevitable tax collector. In general, a committee of elders, or *Panchayat,* was responsible for order and justice within the village. Minor matters of a personal nature were usually settled by caste councils, whereas more serious crimes, such as cattle stealing and murder, went before the elders. Invaders, revolutions, monarchs, and empires came and went, but the Indian village endured because of its self-sufficiency. In the face of a hostile army the villagers would arm and defend themselves; if attacked by superior force they fled, only to return later and take up cultivation again. The astonishing stability of this village system enabled the inhabitants of the Indus Valley to till their land and maintain their culture through 5,000 years of turmoil and troubles.

The dominant activity was agriculture, although some handicraft industries developed, along with the manufacture of cloth, under the Moguls. Finished products of cotton and silk and handcrafted silver objects were exported to Europe, and a small merchant class came into being. Yet these activities probably did not involve more than 2 or 3 percent of the population, nor were the merchant and trader accorded much respect in Indian society, which was led by Brahmins (the priests) and noblemen. Indian farmers produced barely enough for subsistence, husbanding the rain water that fell during the four months of monsoon. In the event of drought, reduction of fertility, or desolation caused by invaders, famine was practically unavoidable. The lack of a more advanced technology made it difficult to expand the country's resources to feed a rapidly growing population, let alone improve its lot.

As in all traditional societies, Indian economic and social institutions were pervaded by family values. Individuals did not own the land; rather, the village families enjoyed rights of occupation as a consequence of clearing and cultivating their tracts. In the event that a family died out, all rights concerning their land reverted to the village. The male played the dominant role, and the household consisted of all his sons, grandsons, and their womenfolk, except insofar as the women married and entered other households or the sons left the village to strike out on their own. The villagers, in a sense, constituted one large or "joint" family, with the committee of elders playing a paternal role.

An element of cardinal importance in traditional Indian society was Hindu ideology. Hinduism developed mainly during the period of fusion between Aryan and Dravidian cultures, but some of its elements can be traced as far back as the Indus Valley civilization. Like any traditional ideology, it affects and regulates all aspects of human behavior. It is more than a theology; it is

a way of life, a code that determines how people shall live, eat, marry, cultivate land, share produce, and raise children. Much of the morality that informs Hindu ideology may be found in the Vedas and the Gita, and in the religious prose of the Upanishads (the main source of information on the formative period of Hinduism).

The central concept in Hindu ideology has been that of salvation, which is considered a release or deliverance of the soul from the endless cycle of birth and death. Life is miserable and evil. Material things are an illusion. The object of religion is to permit the individual to free himself of evil and illusion and to merge with the Absolute, or the World Soul. Until release is obtained, the soul is condemned to wander about the earth incarnated in one body after another—the kind of body depending upon the soul's record in its previous existence. There are many varieties of Hindu beliefs, some stressing the importance of ritual and others emphasizing the gods, such as Brahma, Vishnu, and Shiva (representing, respectively, creation, preservation, and destruction). But the theme is constant: Life is a mystery; nature is to be accepted, not mastered; earthly existence is inherently evil; the true destiny of man is to escape from the melancholy cycle of birth and death through ultimate deliverance. Hinduism provided a scheme of thought that made life a little more tolerable in a society where the average individual could expect to live about 20 years, where famine was regular and catastrophic, and where hunger and unadulterated misery were the everyday lot of the great mass of people. But the striking drawback of Hindu thought, as of most traditional ideology, was that it offered little incentive to improve material conditions, to master and transform nature, to make more bearable the fate of men on earth. Hindu society was able to endure as a consequence of its stability and the widespread acceptance of its values, but it was not able to keep up with the rest of the world in technological development.

A distinctive feature of Hinduism as a way of life is the division of its Indian followers into over 3,000 castes and subcastes, each with its own rules for eating, marriage, and general behavior. The institution probably derives from the efforts of learned Aryans to preserve their racial purity and culture from contamination by the Dravidians. In terms of the theory of birth, rebirth, and incarnation of the soul, caste marks the progression from a lowly to a higher state and, presumably, to total liberation from the cycle. There are four main classes or orders in the caste system, each containing numerous separate castes. In order of nobility or grace these groups are the Brahmins (the learned or priestly class); Kshatriyas (the warriors and rulers); Vaisyas (the traders and merchants); and Sudras (the serfs). In the past, certain wild tribes and people who performed menial tasks were considered outside this general scheme of things—even below the Sudras—and were called untouchables, or outcastes. (Over half a million people make their living, for example, by emptying latrines and chamber pots.) There were about 60 million of these unfortunate people in 1950, when untouchability was abolished by the new constitution, and their number has more than doubled since. Members of the scheduled castes—as they are officially designated—continue to suffer social discrimination in spite of the special legislation designed to protect them. They now amount to some 135 million people, or about 16 percent of the population. Sudras, known as "backward castes," make up about 25 percent of the population, and receive some privileges separate from those given to the scheduled castes.

The caste system doubtless served a useful social purpose in a land subject to ceaseless invasion. Numerous races at different levels of development settled in India, and the caste system permitted each group to preserve its identity and yet somehow coexist with the others. Within a caste, no matter how lowly its general status, members found themselves accepted and helped. During periods of foreign occupation, there was a natural tendency for the Hindus to defend themselves passively by withdrawing more and more deeply into their separate world of ritual and *dharma* (sacred law or duty that often involves minute regulations concerning food and relations among the castes). They were thus able to maintain their Hindu way of life against the foreigner. But the price paid for survival of the culture was high, as popular energies were devoted to theology and *dharma* rather than to the development of science and technology and the improvement of economic and social conditions. The caste system also created deep divisions within the society, and greatly reduced the effectiveness of central institutions in achieving national objectives in an increasingly competitive world.

THE IMPACT OF BRITISH RULE

By 1700, the Mogul power in India had virtually disintegrated. No native chiefs or groups at that time were capable of conquering or unifying the nation. The political vacuum was filled at first by European trading companies and then by the European nations themselves. After a period of economic and military rivalry among Britain, Portugal, France, and Holland, the British emerged as the paramount power in India. Their dominance, registered by the decisive victory of Robert Clive and his Indian allies over an Indian army aided by the French at Plassey in 1757, was recognized by France in the Treaty of Paris of 1763. The British steadily extended their power into the interior, defeating one native ruler after another, sometimes permitting an Indian prince to retain his throne, sometimes assuming direct control themselves. The Mahrattas, the Gurkhas, the Sikhs, and the Burmese were all crushed in battle. By 1840 the whole Indian subcontinent was in British hands, with the exception of a few small enclaves retained by France and Portugal.

Thus, the inhabitants of a small island off the coast of Europe were able to extend their rule over a vast subcontinent in the other hemisphere of the globe, teeming with several hundred million people, and maintain their power there for almost two centuries. British supremacy was achieved by an amazingly small number of men. During the entire nineteenth century, the British ruled India with about 500 administrators and 65,000 troops. The disparity in numbers—at the most 100,000 Britons ruling 200 or 300 million Indians—reflected the difference between these nations in military potential and economic power. The British had complete control of the sea, an immense superiority in military equipment and tactics, and above all, surplus wealth that could be used to recruit and pay large numbers of Indian troops. They also created a far more efficient administrative system than had existed previously. Divisions between the Muslims and Hindus and among the princely states also enabled the British to play one region or community against another—sometimes deliberately adding fuel to the fire of ethnic and religious rivalries—and to succeed eventually in subduing them all. Their successes were made possible in part by their advanced technology, which produced the necessary wealth, ships, and firearms.

India had managed to absorb all of its previous conquerors with the single notable exception of the Muslims. But even at the height of Muslim rule, the Hindu way of life in the villages was hardly affected by events at the imperial court, except insofar as hostile armies might march through the countryside. British rule, however, profoundly transformed India—economically, socially, and culturally. In the course of the century and a half leading up to independence in 1947, India had changed more than during the preceding five millennia. Large portions of Indian society had been wrenched out of the traditional mold, and an irreversible process of modernization had begun.

Some of the earliest British social reforms dealt with the custom of *suttee* (the burning of widows on the funeral pyres of their husbands), the institution of *thagi* (organized robbery and murder), and slavery. Gradually a system of English law was established that profoundly affected relations among the castes. But perhaps the most important of the early British measures were the creation of a new educational system and the introduction of English as a kind of national language. (Fifteen major languages and more than 800 dialects are spoken by the people of India.) The Indians were brought into contact with English literature and law and the whole new universe of Western science and technology. In the British scheme, as it was conceived originally, the educated Indians were to form a huge intermediary class between the governing elite and the masses and thus constitute a bulwark of the regime. In fact, this Indian middle class deliberately created by the British eventually led the movement to overthrow British rule. But in any case, English education became an abiding source of Western influence in India, upsetting old ideas, introducing modern knowledge, and helping to form a distinct new social class.

British rule also stimulated economic growth. A network of railroads covered the nation by the end of the nineteenth century, and for the first time in 5,000 years the life of the village masses began to stir and change. The railroads opened regions to one another and India to the world.

The mobility of the population was vastly increased; transport of agricultural products made it possible to avert or at least deal with famine; capital flowed into the country; and a few industries, including coal, iron, jute, and cotton, began to develop. The postal system and the telegraph likewise provided part of the framework for a more modern economy. Population drifted into the urban centers of Calcutta, Bombay, and Delhi. By 1940, there were 58 cities with more than 100,000 inhabitants, and there was a total urban population of over 16 million. Thus, although India remained overwhelmingly rural, urbanization had become a significant social phenomenon. In foreign commerce, by 1940 India ranked sixth in the world and had the eighth most important industrial economy, employing over 2 million workers in large-scale industry. Nevertheless, agriculture was still the direct occupation of over 70 percent of the population, and 90 percent of the population continued to live in villages.

These changes—political, administrative, social, and cultural—shook Indian society to its roots. How did the Indians react to the challenge thrown down by the West? Perhaps the first, instinctive reaction was to exalt traditional values and seek refuge in a revival of orthodoxy. Some Indians, however, sought to adapt the values of Indian life to the new conditions. Still others, members of the educated elite, became completely Anglicized and lost touch with their ancient traditions. All these movements eventually merged into a nationwide drive for independence.

One of the early strongholds of religious orthodoxy was, curiously enough, the Indian troops in the pay of the British. These troops were mercenaries and had great pride in their military prowess, but no identification with the British regime as such. Their discipline took the form of a fanatic devotion to religious ritual. When British administrators began to reform Indian society, however, the reliability of the native troops was subjected to great strain. All the irritations and frustrations of the traditional groups burst into the open in the Sepoy Mutiny of 1857. Its immediate cause was the introduction of the new Enfield rifle, the cartridges of which were smeared with animal fat—said by outraged Hindus and offended Muslims to come from the cow, sacred to the one group, or the unclean pig, abhorred by the other. Native troops refused to accept the new cartridges, killed their officers, and seized control of large areas of the country. It took a year of bitter fighting to restore order, and the British thereafter were far more cautious in enacting reform measures. Other manifestations of the retreat into orthodoxy were the denunciation of everything European and the glorification of traditional Hindu or Muslim values and society. Among the new middle classes and intellectuals the view became widespread that the West was materialistic, inhuman, and crass, while the East was spiritual and humane.

But a number of keen Indian observers realized that traditional India could not resist the new invaders and that the only way to preserve the old values was by reform and purification. Most notable of the early Indian reformers was Ram Mohan Roy, who discerned in the Upanishads a central theme of reason with which practices like *suttee,* polygamy, and infanticide were declared incompatible; that is, Roy urged social reforms for Hindu reasons, not Western reasons. He contended that the role of the West was to supplement, not to supplant, the values of the East. Roy gave Indian intellectuals a new measure of self-respect and pride. Religious and theosophical movements mushroomed, all advocating a return to the essential values of Hinduism or Islam purged of irrational customs.

The various groups within Indian society were initially divided over the questions of Hindu orthodoxy, reform, and the extent of imitation of the West. But they were united in their desire for self-government. In shattering traditional Indian society, the British had let loose the forces that inevitably would turn against them. Members of the new Indian middle and professional classes were humiliated by social slights and discrimination, and angered by policies that favored British over Indian economic interests. Resentment evolved into defiance.

At first, the demand for dignity and self-government took the form of requests that more Indians be recruited into the civil service. The Indian National Congress, founded in 1885, was essentially a middle-class reformist organization during its early years. At annual meetings it respectfully petitioned for increased Indian representation in the civil service and legislatures, all the while affirming loyalty to the British Empire. The negative British response to these entreaties strengthened the hand of militants who turned against the empire, calling instead for self-rule (*swaraj*). In 1906 the Congress officially endorsed the goal of *swaraj,* and many "extremists" urged a resort to violence in order to achieve that goal. Nationalism in India remained largely a middle-class movement until the emergence of Mohandas Gandhi as its undisputed leader around 1920. Gandhi's contribution was to reach out to and arouse the great masses of the people. He understood the Indian mind and with a sure instinct always formulated political demands in a manner the people easily understood. Under his leadership the Congress was reorganized as a mass party extending across the entire nation and reaching down into the villages. Gandhi built up national pride by exalting native Indian languages and religious values, and by defending the spirituality of Indian village life in contrast to the materialism of Western civilization.

The technique Gandhi developed for advancing the cause of independence represented a masterly compromise between the policies of the liberal reformers, who wanted simply to register protests and sign petitions, and those of the extremists, who sought to oust the British by force and violence. Gandhi's supreme achievement was to involve the masses in the struggle against British rule while avoiding a direct challenge to British arms—that is, to keep the protest nonviolent. Although his preference for nonviolence was couched in religious and ethical terms, it probably did not escape Gandhi's attention that British superiority in military technology made a successful uprising an exceedingly doubtful prospect.

His technique of political action was far from passive, however, and indeed the term "nonviolence" is not an accurate translation of *Satyagraha*—a combination of two Sanskrit words meaning "truth-force." Elements of his doctrine were derived from Hindu practices; however, they also fitted quite nicely the particular needs of the Indian nationalists. The object was to win over the enemy by sympathy, patience, and suffering—by "putting one's whole soul" against the evil-doer.[1] The essence of the technique was noncooperation. Under British rule in this century, 400 million Indians were governed by about 1,000 British civil servants and 50,000 British troops. It would have been utterly impossible for the British to deliver the mail, run the railroads, police the streets, suppress crime, educate the children, or administer the economy without the cooperation of Indian civil servants, troops, teachers, nurses, and so on. Hence in political terms Gandhi's insight was correct: Foreign rule could maintain itself against violence but would founder if the Indian people simply refused to cooperate.

Gandhi's first call for nonviolent noncooperation, immediately after World War I, led to large-scale rioting which was stopped by the Mahatma himself. During World War II the British were increasingly reliant on Indian cooperation and thus vulnerable to the threat of noncooperation. Indian support for the war effort came to depend on a British commitment to independence—which was conveyed as early as 1942 by a special emissary of the British government, Sir Stafford Cripps, though at that time the discord between Muslims and Hindus made it impossible to work out an agreement. To understand the reasons for partition of the subcontinent between India and Pakistan, and the subsequent conflicts between the two nations, it is necessary to dwell upon the circumstances under which the British terminated their rule.

TOWARD INDEPENDENCE

The proposal by Sir Stafford Cripps, on behalf of the British cabinet, was to create a dominion of India with the power to choose independence at any time. Under his proposal, the British were to be responsible for India's defense for the remainder of the war, but otherwise the Indians were to govern themselves. Plebiscites were to be held in certain princely states and in Muslim areas to determine what role these regions would have in the future dominion. It was specifically provided that any province could choose not to enter the new Indian Union and instead create its own independent government. In his discussions with representatives of the Muslim League and the Congress, as well as associations of untouchables, Sikhs, and Anglo-Indians, Cripps came up against the bitter divisions that were to plague relations among all these groups in the future.

Congress rejected the Cripps proposal out of hand, demanding instead immediate creation of an independent national government; it

termed the principle of nonaccession for provinces a blow to Indian unity. The Muslim League also rejected the Cripps proposal, but because nonaccession did not go far enough. The League insisted on a partition of India into two zones, stating that it would be unfair to Muslims if they were under any constraint at all to negotiate their status within, or their exit out of, an Indian Union. The leader of the Muslim League, Mohammed Ali Jinnah, declared soon after the outbreak of war that the Muslims were a nation, not a minority within a Hindu nation. Said Jinnah, "We are a nation of a hundred million, and what is more we are a nation with our own distinctive culture and civilization, language and literature, art and architecture, . . . customs and calendar, history and tradition, aptitudes and ambitions. In short we have our own distinctive outlook on life and of life."[2]

To further complicate matters, the untouchables (or depressed classes) expressed the fear that the Cripps proposal would place them at the mercy of Hindu militants, and the Sikhs of the Punjab vowed that they would never permit themselves to be separated from the Indian motherland by the secession of Muslim provinces. After the failure of the Cripps mission, political debate in India became even more rancorous, ruling out any possibility that the British could extricate themselves gracefully from the subcontinent. Gandhi came to the conclusion that Japan was on the way to winning the war in Asia; the best course for India, he decided, was to invite the Allied forces to leave and then negotiate peace with Japan. As an ultimate weapon, he proposed using nonviolence if the Japanese insisted on invading and occupying India—a tactic that inspired little confidence among those familiar with the ruthless behavior of Japan's victorious army elsewhere. Under Gandhi's prodding, the Congress adopted a "Quit India" resolution; when the British thereupon arrested Gandhi, Jawaharlal Nehru, and other Congress leaders, the Indians responded with widespread civil disobedience.

The Muslim League and Jinnah spurned the Quit India movement, supported the Allied war effort, and insisted at every turn on the need for a separate Muslim state. As Jinnah put it in a speech in 1941: "It is as clear as daylight that we are not a minority. We are a nation. And a nation must have territory. . . . A nation does not live in the air. It lives on the land, it must govern land, and it must have a territorial state and that is what you want to get."[3]

After the war, the new Labour government in Britain discovered, to its shock, that the Indian problem could not be resolved simply by proclaiming independence. Elections held for the central and provincial legislatures immediately after the war revealed a dangerous polarization of communal groups. The Muslim League won almost all the seats in Muslim areas, and the Congress almost all the seats in Hindu areas; and the League and the Congress became increasingly irreconcilable. Jinnah vowed after these elections that the Congress flag would fly in the North "only over the dead bodies of Muslims."[4] The statement was prophetic. Independence for India was to be achieved only at the price of one of the greatest bloodbaths of modern times.

Physically unable to reinstitute imperial rule and politically unwilling to do so in any case, the British Labour government was intent upon granting independence to the squabbling groups somehow, and as rapidly as possible. In March 1946, Prime Minister Clement Attlee dispatched a cabinet mission to India with the task of finding a constitutional solution. Immediately the cabinet mission was confronted with the incompatible demands of the Muslims, who wanted the British to divide India and then quit, and the Hindus, who wanted the British to quit and leave it up to the Indians (and their Hindu majority, of course) to decide on a division. Unable to secure agreement, the cabinet mission made its own proposals. Pointing out that partition would leave huge minorities in each new nation and was therefore unworkable, the mission recommended that India not be divided, but that predominantly Muslim and Hindu areas should enjoy extensive autonomy within a very complex political structure with weak central power. A constituent assembly was to be elected, with representation from all areas, to assume responsibility for government and draft a constitution. The Muslim League and the Congress party both agreed, reluctantly and all the while laying down stringent conditions, to participate in the elections to this constituent assembly; in these elections, once again the League swept almost all seats in Muslim provinces and the Congress almost all seats in Hindu provinces.

Amid much confusion the League and the Congress continued to stake out incompatible political claims; Jinnah called for a "Direct Action Day" to protest "Hindu treachery." That day—August 16, 1946—saw one of the most murderous communal uprisings of the twentieth century: Almost 5,000 people killed in Calcutta alone, many more thousands hurt, and 150,000 people in flight; at least another 7,000 people were killed in the following months as communal rioting spread from Calcutta to nearby regions.

In despair, Clement Attlee announced in February 1947 that the British government intended to transfer power to Indian hands no later than June 1948, urging Indians to settle their differences before then. He sent Lord Louis Mountbatten to India as the new viceroy, with the mission of finding a way out. After fruitless consultation with League and Congress party leaders, Mountbatten concluded that there was no alternative to partition; with misgivings, the Congress party finally accepted the principle of partition. But now began a race against the clock—a thoroughly scrambled government of India had to be dissected, separated, and reconstituted over a territory in which most Muslims and Hindus were concentrated in separate areas but mixed together in some. In July 1947 the British Parliament finally passed the India Independence Bill, providing that power should be transferred to the two new nations on August 15, 1947. That day in New Delhi, Lord Mountbatten became governor-general of India and Nehru prime minister; the previous day, in Karachi, Jinnah took office as governor-general, and Liaquat Ali Khan as prime minister.

Both new states were immediately confronted with enormous problems. At the moment of independence, Pakistan consisted of two geographically separated areas. West Pakistan had some 34 million people living in a dry climate, while East Pakistan had 46 million people living in a wet, tropical climate—in an area only one-fifth as large as the western province. The peoples of West and East Pakistan spoke different languages and reflected wholly different cultural traditions. On top of the exceedingly difficult political and administrative problem of coordinating these two geographically separated areas there was a formidable challenge. Only three-quarters of the population of the new state was Muslim—that is, some 20 million Hindus were now ruled by their traditional Muslim rivals. Conversely, at least 40 million Muslims found themselves in the new state of India, subject to the rule of over 300 million Hindus.

The question immediately posed was, what would be the fate of 20 million Hindus at the hands of 60 million Muslims in Pakistan and of the 40 million Muslims confronted by 300 million Hindus in India? Would toleration and good sense prevail? Unfortunately, communal hatreds exploded immediately after independence. Violence was especially widespread and murderous in the Punjab, where whole villages were decimated and their inhabitants slaughtered or dispersed. Hundreds of thousands and then millions of terrified Muslims and Hindus fled for their lives—toward the sanctuary of either Pakistan for the former or India for the latter. But as those millions moved across hostile territory, they were fair game for thieves and killers. Almost 12 million people (slightly more Muslims than Hindus) fled from one state to the other—almost entirely to and from the Punjab. The situation remained relatively quiet in Bengal and East Pakistan. As many as 1 million people were killed in this holocaust.

In this climate of mutual hatred and killing, a territorial dispute pushed the new states of Pakistan and India into hostilities. The Muslim ruler of one princely state, Junagadh, disregarded the wishes of the overwhelmingly Hindu population and acceded to Pakistan. After the population rebelled, the ruler took refuge in Pakistan and Indian troops occupied the state. A similar situation existed in Hyderabad, a princely state in the middle of India where a small Muslim elite ruled over a largely Hindu population. India refused to accept the Nizam of Hyderabad's demand for independence, and took control of foreign affairs and defense as a first step toward complete annexation. The sticking point was Kashmir, where this time 80 percent of the population was Muslim, ruled over by a small Sikh and Hindu minority. When rioting broke out in Kashmir, New Delhi declared that the area would be taken over by India to restore order and hold a plebiscite on the state's future. An uprising by Muslims, supported by neighboring tribesmen, was countered by the Hindu ruler's own troops; to quell the re-

volt, New Delhi dispatched Indian troops to join the fighting. At the height of the tension created by communal rioting and armed conflict in Kashmir, the apostle of nonviolence and tolerance, Mahatma Gandhi, was struck down by an ultramilitant Hindu assassin. In announcing the news, Nehru declared, "The light has gone out of our lives and there is darkness everywhere."[5] The first year of independence was a terrible ordeal for all the inhabitants of the subcontinent, Muslims and Hindus alike.

An enormous task confronted Jawaharlal Nehru and the Congress Party as they set about creating order out of chaos. Consider briefly the dimensions of that task in August 1947. First, they had to provide for the safety of Muslims on Indian territory (of whom perhaps half a million were killed in a few months), assist and protect the millions of Muslims fleeing to Pakistan, and receive and care for the millions of Hindus who in turn were escaping to India. Second, they had to create a viable constitutional system out of the crazy quilt of princely states and provinces. In 1947 there were some 600 princely states, containing one-fourth of the population of India. Somehow this incoherent mass of governmental units had to be restructured, and something had to be done about the pretensions of Hyderabad to autonomy if not independence. Eventually Hyderabad was forcibly occupied by the Indian army.

The new political system had to be designed for a society far more heterogeneous than any in Europe. Although Great Britain, France, and Germany contain minorities (linguistic, religious, ethnic, and so on), each country has only one dominant, official language. The dimensions of the language problem in India are staggering (see Table 9.1). About 38 percent of the population speaks Hindi, and another 10 percent either Urdu or Punjabi (which are similar to Hindi), whereas Telegu, Bengali, Marathi, and Tamil are each spoken by 7 to 8 percent of the population and Gujarati, Malayalam, Kannada, and Oriya each by 3 to 5 percent. In all there are some 800 languages or dialects in India, of which over 60 are non-Indian languages. Most of these linguistic groups are fairly small, but about 100 of these languages or dialects are spoken by more than 100,000 people each.

The Constitution provided that Hindi would become the official language of India after a transition period of 15 years. When that provision took effect in 1965, widespread rioting was triggered in the south. The government then amended the Official Languages Act to permit the continued use of English as an alternative language. In practice, instruction in schools is mainly in regional languages. Drawing the lines of states to take into account linguistic patterns, while maintaining national unity, is a formidable and delicate task.

In other respects, at the time of independence India presented a social profile typical of any Asian developing country: an extremely low per capita income; an overwhelming mass of the people engaged in subsistence agriculture and mired in poverty; an average life expectancy of about 32 years; and a literacy rate of only 16 percent. However, by 1947 India also had created at least the rudiments of an industrial base, especially in textiles, with an earnest start in chemicals, iron and steel, and engineering. Through the educational system, opportunities were afforded for the training of an economic, scientific, and political elite.

The independent India that emerged in 1947 was thus vastly different from the nation first ruled by the British almost two centuries earlier. In spite of Gandhi's idealization of village life and Hinduism (perhaps necessary for political purposes), the economy and social structure had undergone profound transformations. Industries and cities had sprung up among India's 700,000 villages, and a new middle class had come into existence. Independence did not mean restoration of the society that had existed in 1757; it was rather the signal for a new departure (see Table 9.2).

Political energies in India now had to be redirected. Instead of overthrowing authority, the problem was to create it; instead of glorifying the village and denouncing material goods, the goal now was rapid industrialization; instead of opposing power, the need now was to rally popular support behind the government. The construction of a national authority was undertaken by the Constituent Assembly (chosen indirectly by provincial legislators), which first met in December 1946. A constitution was promulgated in November 1949 and took effect formally on January 26, 1950 (the date now celebrated annually as Republic Day). The political institutions outlined by the Constitution are inspired directly by the British parliamentary system. The Indian president, House of the People (Lok Sabha), Council of States (Rajya Sabha), Council of Ministers, cabinet, and prime minister were intended to be the counterparts, respectively, of the British monarch, House of Commons, House of Lords, ministry, cabinet, and prime minister. The major departure from the British model is the provision for a federal system dividing power between the central government and the states. The main powers, however, are held by the center, so that India has many of the characteristics of a unitary system.

Democratic institutions were created by the Constituent Assembly; then the structure had to be given its democratic content through the electoral process, with the full participation of competing political parties. The first national elections were held over a period of four months in the winter of 1951–1952. The largest electorate in the world was mobilized in order to

Table 9.1   MAJOR LANGUAGES OF INDIA

	Millions	Percentage
Indo-Aryan Languages		
Hindi	354.2	36.2
Bengali	69.1	7.6
Marathi	66.5	7.3
Gujarati	44.5	4.9
Oriya	30.7	3.4
Punjabi	24.9	2.7
Assamese	15.0	1.6
Dravidian Languages		
Telegu	72.7	8.0
Tamil	60.0	6.6
Kannada	36.0	4.0
Malayalam	34.8	3.8
Other		
Urdu	47.4	5.2
English (mother tongue)	0.3	0.1
English (lingua franca)	30.0	3.3

Source: World Data, *1995 Britannica Book of the Year,* p. 780. Percentages calculated on basis of a total population of 914 million.

Table 9.2   Chronology of Important Events in India

1500 B.C.	Invasion of Indus Valley by Vedic Aryans.
327–325 B.C.	Incursion into Northwest India by Alexander the Great.
300–600 A.D.	Golden age of Hindu culture under Gupta dynasty.
1192	Establishment of first Muslim kingdom, the Delhi Sultanate.
1510	Portuguese conquer Goa.
1526	Babur founds a Mogul empire, later consolidated by Akbar.
1612–1690	British East India Company establishes trading stations at Surat, Bombay, and Calcutta.
1757	Victory of Robert Clive over the Nawab of Bengal at Plassey. Beginning of British Empire in India.
1857	Sepoy Rebellion (or Mutiny), leading to abolition of East India Company and establishment of Crown rule through a Viceroy.
1877	Queen Victoria crowned Empress of India.
1885	Creation of the Indian National Congress.
1919	First nonviolent resistance campaign organized by Mohandas Gandhi.
1942	Sir Stafford Cripps offers a British commitment to independence.
1947	British Parliament passes India Independence Bill. Power is transferred to India and Pakistan. Assassination of Mohandas Gandhi (January 1948) by a Hindu militant.
1949	Promulgation of the Constitution of India.
1950	Constitution goes into effect on January 26 (Republic Day).

choose its first elected government under the new constitution.

KEY TERMS

Brahmins
caste system
Gandhi, Mohandas
Hindus
Lok Sabha
Muslims
Nehru, Jawaharlal
Rajya Sabha
Satyagraha
Sikhs
untouchables

FURTHER READINGS

Brecher, M. *Nehru: A Political Biography* (New York: Oxford University Press, 1961).

Brown, J. M. *Modern India: The Origins of an Asian Democracy* (New York: Oxford University Press, 1984).

Brown, J. M. *Gandhi: Prisoner of Hope* (New Haven: Yale University Press, 1989).

Crossette, B. *India: Facing the Twenty-First Century* (Bloomington, IN: Indiana University Press, 1993).

Lamb, B. P. *India, A World in Transition,* 4th ed. (New York: Praeger, 1975).

Moore, R. J. *Escape from Empire: The Attlee Government and the Indian Problem* (Oxford: Clarendon Press, 1983).

Nanda, B. R. *Mahatma Gandhi: A Biography* (New York: Oxford University Press, 1981).

Nehru, J. *The Discovery of India* (Garden City, NY: Doubleday, 1959).

Sarker, Sumit. *Modern India, 1885–1947* (London: Macmillan, 1983).

Wallbank, T. W. *A Short History of India and Pakistan* (New York: Mentor, 1958).

Wolpert, S. *A New History of India,* 4th ed. (New York: Oxford University Press, 1993).

Political Processes and Institutions

In India, as in the other parliamentary democracies treated in this volume, the people express their interests and convey them to government through a network of professional associations (or interest groups) and through political parties. In organizing themselves for elections, the Indians have adopted an electoral procedure very similar to that of the British. But the context in which groups and parties function in India is radically different from that in Great Britain. A segment of the Indian community, inspired mainly by orthodox Hindu values, repudiates the secular state and views its institutions with suspicion if not contempt. Another element in the community identifies itself with the Communist movement, many of whose leaders in the past denounced "bourgeois" democracy and sought to forward revolutionary goals (all the while being drawn into electoral politics that reduces ideological fervor). Thus, the consensus about political institutions and values on which the British system is based does not exist in India, or in most other developing nations.

Furthermore, the cleavages and contrasts in Indian society are far deeper and more intense than in Great Britain or any other industrial society. A relatively small though rapidly growing elite, Western in education and taste, is set off sharply from a largely illiterate mass attached to a traditional way of life. The gaps tend to be greater all along the line: between the rich and the poor, between urban life and village life, and between language groups and religious groups. There is also a stronger tradition of violence and impulse to resort to violence, in spite of Gandhi and perhaps because of the effort required to overthrow British rule. Above all, India is still largely a traditional society which has only started on its way to modernization, with all the social, economic, cultural, and political characteristics of such a society.

The evolution of the Indian party system was profoundly affected by the struggle for self-rule. Given the prestige of the Congress Party as leader of the national independence movement, a competitive party system could hardly have been expected to emerge immediately. As the Congress brought about unification of Indian society, inevitably economic, social, and communal groups began to affirm their identities and express their concerns. A process of interaction between party and society, characteristic of all democratic nations, was underway. The dominant party mobilized and developed the economy and society; and the diverse groups in turn made demands that led to the transformation of the ruling party and of the party system as a whole. Under democratic conditions, no one party can reconcile all interests. The coming of a multiparty system was a natural development, even though Congress remains the single most important party. We shall now review the changing role of interest groups and the movement from a one-party dominant to a multiparty system.

INTEREST GROUPS

There are trade unions, agricultural groups, business associations, and numerous professional societies in India, as in any democracy. But most Indians continue to gain a livelihood in the traditional sectors of the economy; for example, of the 222 million Indians in the work force as of the census of 1981, 93 million were classified as cultivators, and 56 million as agricultural laborers. On the other hand, 7.4 million were engaged in manufacturing, 11 million in social, community, and personal services, 1.5 million in construction, 3.5 million in transport and communication, and the rest in other services.

From this rough social profile, it is evident that the highly organized interest groups of business and labor so characteristic of Western democracies cannot draw upon similarly massive social forces in India. Nonetheless, workers and businesspeople, as well as peasants, have organized in order to promote their interests. In structure, Indian interest groups resemble more the French than the British or German, inasmuch as working class and peasant groups are divided along political and ideological lines. The Indian National Trade Union Congress (INTUC) is a creation of the Congress Party; the Bharatiya Mazdoor Sanga (BMS) is linked to the Bharatiya Janata Party; and the All-India Trade Union Congress (AITUC) is affiliated with the Communist Party of India. Similarly, each of these parties has created peasant groups and student associations.

Trade unions together have a claimed membership of some 10 million, which is a small percentage of the total work force of 222 million. Ten million unionized workers, nevertheless, could play an important role in the political process if they were disciplined, united, well organized, and well led. But such is not the case. Few union members pay dues regularly, and inadequate financing makes it difficult for unions to recruit, train, and pay competent leaders from within their own ranks. Leadership positions therefore tend to be assumed by intellectuals and politicians who are primarily interested in using the unions for personal or political ends rather than creating efficient structures through which the interests of workers might be defended.

Hence unions are not properly organized for the task of collective bargaining with employers; militancy takes the form of short, sometimes violent strikes. Because each union is either the creation of or is affiliated with a political party, most demands for higher wages and improved working conditions are conveyed directly to the government. When the Congress Party has been in power, it has been in the government's interest to make INTUC a "transmission belt" of its own economic plan, putting pressure on the workers to accept discipline in order to contribute to economic growth and higher productivity. Similarly, it is important for the Communist Party to utilize AITUC for its own political purposes—either to embarrass, subvert, or cooperate with the government, depending upon the Communist Party's relations with the Congress Party. Indian labor unions vigorously opposed the privatization program introduced by the Rao government in 1992, as well as moves to close down inefficient state-owned enterprises. Unions wish to protect jobs of their members, even though economic expansion in the long run will lead to more employment.

Business groups in India are organized for political purposes mainly through a great number of local associations and chambers of commerce, which are linked together loosely in national federations. The most important of these business groups is the Federation of Indian Chambers of Commerce and Industry, whose members include some 40,000 enterprises. Unlike the trade unions, the federation is not affiliated directly with any political party, but the business community as a whole tends to offer financial and other support to the more conservative wings of the Congress and opposition parties. The business community in India labors under several severe handicaps in its attempts to influence public opinion and the government. First, there is historic distrust of and disdain for commercial and business activity, characteristic of any traditional society. Aristocratic Brahmins have always looked down upon businesspeople as particularly unworthy, interested only in profits and accumulation of material objects (as opposed to more noble and uplifting spiritual activity). The lower classes and castes have generally believed that they are exploited by businesspeople and resent their opulent lifestyle. In addition, the founding fathers of modern India adopted socialism as an official policy and were openly contemptuous of the business or capitalist class.

Some business leaders created or supported a Forum for Free Enterprise, later affiliated with the Swatantra Party in an attempt to shape a more favorable public attitude toward the private sector and market economy. Business groups also regularly protest against expansion of the bureaucracy and of the nationalized sector. But the business associations tend to devote most of their efforts to consulting with administrative agencies and trying to stay out of the public limelight. Lobbying is not a well-developed institutional practice. Individual business leaders, however, contribute large sums to political parties, thereby ensuring access to the state. In the mid–1970s the climate of opinion became somewhat more favorable to business. Under Rajiv Gandhi, V. P. Singh, and Narasimha Rao there has been greater recognition of the need for entrepreneurial ability and professional management.

By far the largest single occupational group in India are the peasants, as is natural in any developing nation. But the peasant organizations of India are a far cry from comparable groups in Great Britain, France, and Germany. They have practically no structure and are little more than "outreach" agencies created by the major political parties to mobilize electoral support. The weakness of peasant groups and the absence of professional leadership among them reflects the lack of education and income of the peasants themselves. Both wings of the Communist Party have made a major effort to exploit peasant unrest, especially among landless agricultural workers and poor Muslims. The All-India Kisan Sabha, an adjunct of the Communist Party of India, has had considerable success in West Bengal; the more extreme Communist Party of India (Marxist) has been even more adroit in appealing to the landless and poor peasants. In some areas, Naxalite revolutionaries (almost entirely middle-class intellectuals) have managed to gain peasant support for their program of violent insurrection.

An unusual feature of Indian politics is the proliferation of community associations that defend and further the interests of a caste or of a linguistic or religious group. Among the most important are the associations of Sikhs (the Akali Dal), Dravidians, Nagas, and assorted linguistic groups. These community associations have succeeded in bringing about a redrawing of state boundaries in order to accommodate linguistic groups and are sometimes powerful forces in regional politics. In principle, the secular political parties have sought to avoid creating any associations that would strengthen the caste system; but they are frequently compelled to acknowledge the popularity and power of the existing community associations.

In short, the Indian interest groups are rarely as well organized, well led, well financed, or effective as their European counterparts. Although the Indian interest groups offer some opportunity for political action, more often than not they serve the purposes of political parties rather than of their members. The functions of the interest groups have thus been largely absorbed by the major actors within the political system—the political parties.

VOTING

Popular interest and participation in elections are unusually high in India. Turnout in the first two general elections was over 45 percent of the eligible voters. Since 1967 between 56 and 63 percent of eligible voters went to the polls, though in 1991 turnout declined to about 53 percent. The level of participation is all the more remarkable considering that almost half of the Indian electorate, according to official statistics, is illiterate; and it may be assumed that many of those classified technically as literate are not able to read campaign literature with ease. Candidates must therefore reach the overwhelming majority of their supporters directly—through personal canvassing and mass meetings—or by radio; they cannot rely on the press. In order to permit illiterates to choose among candidates, the ballot lists not only the names of the candidates in each constituency but also the symbols of their parties (or, in the case of nonparty candidates, personal symbols). Voters then secretly mark one of the symbols with a rubber stamp, fold the ballot, and drop it in a box. Most observers agree that the system works reasonably well.

The electoral procedure is otherwise quite simple and straightforward, inspired largely by British practice. The size of the Lok Sabha (House of the People) is now fixed at 542, so that each member represents approximately 1.5 million people. The country is divided up into single-member districts; the candidate who wins the largest number of votes wins the seat. Some districts are reserved for members of the scheduled castes (outcastes or untouchables) or tribals. Candidates are required to file nomination papers and also put up a deposit, which is returned if the candidate garners over one-sixth of the vote. Campaign finances are scrutinized by the Election Commission, but many contributions and expenditures go unreported.

The percentage of women voting in elections has increased dramatically, going from perhaps only one-half the rate for men in 1952 to two-thirds in 1962, to three-fourths in 1967, and to about the same rate today. Women are also participating in greater numbers as candidates for office. Congress generally reserves a small number of nominations for women to make sure that there is some representation of, and appeal to, female voters. In 1989 there were 198 women candidates for the Lok Sabha (up from 173 in 1984), but only 27 were elected (down from 43 in 1984); 36 women were elected in 1991. A number of women have been ministers, most notably Prime Minister Indira Gandhi.

ELECTION RESULTS AND PARTY SYSTEM

The single-member district system always works to the advantage of large parties. In the first five general elections (1952, 1957, 1962, 1967, and 1971) that advantage was enjoyed by the Congress Party—associated in the popular mind with the national independence struggle through the person of its leader, Jawaharlal Nehru. Its opponents were scattered among a number of smaller parties, representing conservatives, Socialists, Communists, orthodox Hindus, and ethnic and linguistic groups. In the first five general elections the Congress Party won a clear majority of the seats in Parliament, but it was not at any time a majority in the country as a whole. Its popular vote ranged from a high of 48 percent in 1957 to a low of 41 percent in 1967. The Janata Party, which won 55 percent of the seats in the Lok Sabha in 1977, was also a minority party (with only 43 percent of the popular vote). In the election of January 1980, Indira Gandhi's Congress Party won almost 70 percent of the seats with only 42 percent of the total vote. Under Rajiv, the same party swept a record 79 percent of the seats in 1984 with just under 50 percent of the vote. The rise of the Bharatiya Janata Party (BJP)—now the major opposition formation—has further splintered the party system. Congress scored 39.5 percent of the vote in 1989, but the opposition parties were fairly united; Congress won only 197 seats (out of 543) and was blocked from power. In 1991 the split between the Janata Dal and the BJP enabled Congress, with only 37.3 percent of the vote, to gain 225 seats, so that it could form a government with external support.

In the first 30 years of independence, the Congress Party dominated the political arena and furnished the prime ministers of the nation, an era interrupted in the election of 1977 when a coalition of opposition forces, coming together as the Janata Party, succeeded in ousting the Congress Party and Indira Gandhi from power. The victory of the Janata Party followed upon, and was a reaction against, the imposition of emergency rule by Prime Minister Gandhi in June 1975. The 19 months of emergency rule that followed were a watershed in the political evolution of India.

Emergency rule was proclaimed following a decision by the Allahabad High Court in June 1975 that Indira Gandhi had violated several provisions of the electoral law during the preceding campaign. The prime minister headed off opposition demands that she resign by declaring an emergency. When a portion of the Congress Party defected, Mrs. Gandhi succeeded in securing the support of the Communist Party of India, thereby maintaining her majority in Parliament. The government silenced the opposition by imposing press censorship, banning political demonstrations, and jailing critics. When Mrs. Gandhi decided to permit elections to take place in 1977, it was generally expected that the Congress Party would go on to an easy victory because the rate of inflation had been reduced and other economic gains were registered. But the opposition leaders came out of their prison cells, exploited deep popular dissatisfaction with censorship and other authoritarian features of the emergency, coordinated efforts through the newly formed Janata Party, and won an astounding victory.

The contrast between the pre- and postemergency party systems was striking. In 1971 the Congress Party won 43.7 percent of the popular vote but 67.7 percent of the seats in the Lok Sabha, because it could exploit divisions within the opposition. The 1977 election was contested by only four "All-India" parties: the Congress Party; the Janata Party—a coalition of the former opposition groups, united in their hostility to Indira Gandhi and emergency rule; the Communist Party of India, which supported the emergency; and the (Marxist) Communist Party of India, which opposed the emergency. This time the Janata Party, with about 43 percent of the popular vote, was able to benefit from the winner-take-all electoral system as the Congress Party went down to about 35 percent of the vote.

One of the leaders of the Janata Party, 81-year-old Morarji Desai, became prime minister. However, the contradictions within the Janata soon came to the fore, and the government began to drift. There was a sudden increase in inflation, communal violence, labor and student unrest, and—ominously—strikes by the police. Personality rivalries within the Janata led to unbearable tensions only a year after its landslide electoral triumph.

It was hardly possible for the public to follow the fortunes of the Janata Party, so confused and rapid were the expulsions and defections. In the summer of 1979 the Janata Party fell apart. Morarji Desai, anticipating a no-confidence vote, resigned as prime minister. After a week of parliamentary maneuvering, President Sanjiva Reddy asked Charan Singh (now head of a Janata splinter Party) to form a government. Singh had the support of his own party, anti-Gandhi Congress members, and Socialists. But the new government, opposed by Janata and unable to negotiate a working alliance with Indira Gandhi, lacked a majority in the Lok Sabha, and Charan Singh resigned after only three weeks in office.

Rather than ask Janata leaders to make another try at forming a government, President Reddy two days later dissolved Parliament and called for new elections, with Singh staying on as head of a caretaker government. The election was a resounding victory for Congress (I)—pro–Indira Gandhi—and Mrs. Gandhi, who won 351 out of the 525 seats at stake (elections having been cancelled in 17 districts because of violence). The squabbling Janata and Lok Dal went down to separate and ignominious defeats, reduced respectively to 31 and 41 seats.

The party system apparently had reverted to normal: A dominant Congress Party, approaching one-half the popular vote, could win a comfortable majority of seats because of the inability of a deeply divided opposition to act in concert.

Only a few months after taking office, Mrs. Gandhi's 33-year-old son and obvious successor, Sanjay, was killed senselessly in the crash of a stunt plane he was flying. Shortly thereafter Mrs. Gandhi prevailed upon her elder son, Rajiv, to enter into politics and take on responsibility for reorganizing the Congress Party. Her government was being buffeted by charges of corruption and an increasingly unmanageable situation in the Punjab, where militant Sikhs were demanding autonomy. On October 31, 1984, two Sikh members of Indira Gandhi's personal bodyguard assassinated her, triggering a wave of violence in New Delhi.

India was in a state of shock. Rajiv Gandhi, designated immediately as the new prime minister by President Zail Singh, benefited from an outpouring of popular sympathy and support. He called for parliamentary elections in December 1984 (about the time they were due in any case). The result was a great personal victory for Rajiv, and a new lease on life for Congress (I). Out of 508 seats at stake in the Lok Sabha (elections were postponed in Assam and the Punjab because of continuing violence), Congress won 401 seats, more than in any previous election, with almost 50 percent of the vote.

The 1984 election seemed to mark a return of the Indian party system to its historically dominant model: a Congress Party able to govern, despite its lack of a popular majority, because of the fragmentation of the opposition. But the party system continued to evolve. Rajiv Gandhi's government was rocked by charges (and evidence) of corruption, by mounting communal violence sparked by unrest in the Punjab, and by a surge of Hindu fundamentalism. In the election of November 1989, a reconstituted Janata Dal under the leadership of V. P. Singh won 17.8 percent of the popular votes and 143 seats, compared with 39.5 percent of the popular vote and 197 seats for Congress (I). Although Congress (I) had the largest block of seats, it could not command a working majority. President Venkataraman asked V. P. Singh to form a government after receiving assurance of "outside" support for Singh from the BJP (the militant Hindu party), which had won 85 seats, and the Left Front (mainly Communist parties) with 51 seats.

V. P. Singh's government lasted barely one year. It foundered on its internal contradictions—liberals versus Socialists, Communists, and Populists; secular forces versus Hindu militants and fundamentalists; and lower castes and outcastes versus higher castes. The BJP withdrew its support in November 1990 because the government ordered the arrest of its leader (who was demonstrating in favor of the building of a Hindu shrine on the site of a mosque), and the government fell. President Venkataraman asked Chandra Shekhar, leader of an anti-Singh faction within the Janata Dal, to form a government, which was supported "from the outside" by Congress (I) and allied parties. This government, India's least representative, lasted only four months. After a relatively minor dispute between Shekhar and Rajiv over police surveillance of political activities, Congress (I) boycotted Parliament. Both the prime minister and Rajiv recommended new elections in order to resolve the impasse, and the president then dissolved Parliament.

THE HORROR AND DRAMA OF THE 1991 ELECTION

As India prepared for its tenth general election, Congress (I) was still the dominant party and its leader, Rajiv Gandhi, the center of public attention. The opposition was neither united nor fragmented. Instead, it had evolved as two well-organized, mutually hostile parties—the Janata Dal, still led by V. P. Singh, and the Bharatiya Janata Party, whose best-known leader and potential prime minister was Lal Kishan Advani. India's party system entered into a new phase, that of tripolarity, modified by the existence of some locally dominant regional parties (the Communist parties in West Bengal, the Telugu Desam in Andrha Pradesh, and the AIADMK in Tamil Nadu). Of the three leading parties that squared off in 1991, the Congress (I) was present almost everywhere; the BJP was its leading opponent in the "cowbelt" of northern India, and the Janata Dal its main adversary in Uttar Pradesh, Bihar, and Orissa. Thus, in every state there was usually a two-way contest, but nationwide there were three major parties.

The distinctive feature of this modified three-party system is that only the Congress (I) has sufficient popular strength to gain or come close to a majority. Neither the Janata Dal nor the BJP, former members of the same National Front coalition, could possibly govern by themselves. They could only come to power if they rejoined forces—unlikely in view of their incompatible programs—or if one received the outside support of Congress (I).

The voting was scheduled to take place over three days (May 20, 23, and 26) in order to permit security forces to move from region to region. The day after the first round of voting, Ra-

jiv Gandhi made a campaign appearance in Sriperumbudur, a town in Tamil Nadu, near Madras. Horror once again struck the heart of India as Rajiv was assassinated by a bomb, which also killed over a dozen other people, including the terrorist carrying the concealed device. This was the culminating act of violence in an election that had already left over 100 killed during the campaign and another 50 on the first day of balloting. Rajiv's assassination was carried out by a Tamil nationalist suicide squad, seeking revenge for the Indian army's attack against Tamil rebels in Sri Lanka.

Voting was postponed to allow for burial of Rajiv and a respite from campaigning, then resumed on June 12 and 15. Violence continued unabated, and an additional 200 people were killed. Elections were postponed in the Punjab (later cancelled), and cancelled in the state of Jammu and Kashmir.

When the votes were counted, Congress (I) did better than expected, winning 37.3 percent of the vote and clearly outpolling its two major rivals. A wave of sympathy benefited the party after Rajiv's assassination. In the first round of voting on May 20 there had been a swing away from Congress of almost 6 percent; in the second round, in June, there was a swing in favor of some 2 percent. With fewer votes than in 1989, Congress (I) won 28 additional seats—because the major opposition force was now split into two separate parties. The big surprise was the increase in popular vote by the BJP, which almost doubled its share, going from 11.4 to 19.9 percent. The Janata Dal went down dramatically to 10.8 percent of the vote, compared to 17.8 percent in 1989. The results of the 1989 and 1991 elections for the three major parties are shown in Table 9.3.

The two Communist parties, now firmly entrenched in West Bengal, won 45 seats in 1989 and 48 seats in 1991 (the CPI 12 and 13 seats, the CPI(M) 33 and 35 seats, respectively), maintaining their popular vote of about 2 to 3 percent for the CPI and 6 percent for the CPI(M). In addition, the AIDMK, an ally of Congress, won 11 seats in 1991; the Shiv Sena, an ally of the BJP, won 4 seats; the Telegu Desam, a member of the National Front (led by Janata) gained 13 seats; and

Table 9.3 MAJOR PARTY ELECTION RESULTS

	1989		1991	
	Percentage of Popular Votes	Seats	Percentage of Popular Votes	Seats
Congress (I)	39.5	197	37.3	225
BJP	11.4	85	19.9	119
Janata Dal	17.8	143	10.8	55

Note: BJP-Bharatiya Janata Party. From *India Today,* July 15, 1991, pp. 40–55.

small revolutionary parties, members of the Left Front, took 6 seats.

Out of the 503 members of the Lok Sabha elected in May–June 1991 (the other seats remained vacant because of postponed or cancelled elections), the Congress (I) had swept 225. With the support of the AIDMK and other small parties, Congress (I) could count on a grand total of 244 members—about a dozen short of an absolute or working majority. Some members of the Janata Dal were tempted to join in a coalition with Congress, but V. P. Singh held firm for remaining in opposition. The leaders of the major opposition parties—National Front and Left Front—announced that they would make no attempt to topple a Congress government, but would rather seek to work out a "consensual" approach on specific issues. The political class was exhausted by the campaign and its ensuing violence; no one was ready for new elections.

Let us now take a closer look at the major parties—Congress, Janata, Bharatiya Janata, the Communist parties, and regional parties—that contested the 1991 elections.

THE CONGRESS PARTY

Founded in 1885, the Congress Party was the spearhead of the national independence movement, sharing in the glory and triumph of Indian nationalism. It was supported during the preindependence period by a broad coalition of interests, including the rising intellectual elite and business class, and enjoyed genuine popularity. Under Nehru's leadership, the Congress Party after independence pursued a policy of "democratic socialism" in the domestic arena and of nonalignment in foreign affairs. A key element of the party's democratic socialism has been reliance upon a series of national five-year plans, so that economic development and capital investment will proceed in a rational or, at any rate, deliberate manner. Despite the verbal emphasis on socialism, a planned economy, and nationalization of key sectors of the economy (especially the banks), after 30 years of Congress rule a large private sector continued to exist and even flourish. The Congress is also a party of social reform, seeking to eliminate patterns of caste discrimination and increasing opportunities for self-advancement by the disadvantaged. As a mildly left-of-center party, the Congress was able to retain broad support from peasants, workers, and members of the lower castes without alienating the business class as a whole. Given the deep divisions among the opposition parties—Socialist, conservative, Communist, and orthodox Hindu—the Congress appeared during the postindependence period to be the only party capable of governing.

In 1969, internal divisions and factionalism became a characteristic of the Congress Party as well as of the opposition; it was the beginning of the end of the first period of Congress domination. The split within the Congress Party began as a dispute between Prime Minister Indira Gandhi and the established party leaders over a candidate for the presidency. Mrs. Gandhi and the leadership supported different candidates. The leadership (known popularly as "the Syndicate") denounced Mrs. Gandhi for breaking party discipline; in turn, Mrs. Gandhi called a special meeting of the All-India Congress Committee, which vindicated her own position. Each group then expelled the other, with the courts finally deciding that neither faction had the right to use the symbol of the former Congress Party. The break was clean and complete; the Syndicate called itself the Congress (O)—for organizational or opposition, while the Gandhi faction called itself Congress (R)—for ruling. Defection of the Congress (O) members of the Lok Sabha left Mrs. Gandhi short of an absolute majority. She was compelled to seek allies, mainly the Communist Party of India. Mrs. Gandhi turned sharply to the left, advocating nationalization of banks and—a popular measure—elimination of allowances to former rulers of the princely states.

In the fifth general election in 1971 Congress (R) scored a clear victory over Congress (O), winning 352 seats in Lok Sabha compared to only 16 seats for the Syndicate. But the popularity of Congress (R) was fleeting, reflecting largely national pride in the performance of the Indian army in "liberating" Bangladesh and defeating the historic enemy, Pakistan. Mrs. Gandhi's political position became tenuous in the early 1970s, owing to runaway inflation, inability to avert a famine, and increasing cooperation among the opposition parties. The defeat of Congress (R) in 1977 was followed by another split between the faithful supporters of Indira Gandhi and those in the party who now condemned her authoritarian policies during the emergency. Mrs. Gandhi then created a new party, Congress (I)—for Indira—which went on to victory in 1980 while the anti-Gandhi Congress won only 13 seats.

The very name of the new party signaled the predominance of its powerful leader. Decisions were made at the top by Indira Gandhi and her immediate advisers. Mrs. Gandhi relied increasingly on her younger son, Sanjay, who had created a mass Youth Congress and played a key role in selecting candidates and organizing the 1980 election campaign. In recognition of Sanjay's power, and to designate him as the intended successor, he was appointed general secretary of Congress (I).

Mrs. Gandhi suffered a political as well as personal loss when Sanjay was killed in June 1980. Her other son, Rajiv, then started a political career. In a by-election he won the Lok Sabha

seat left vacant by his brother's death, and was appointed as one of the secretaries of Congress (I). When supporters of Sanjay found themselves out of favor, political and family intrigues crisscrossed. Sanjay's young widow, Maneka, attended and spoke at a convention of Sanjay's followers in defiance of her mother-in-law's wishes. After being ordered out of the prime minister's house, Maneka continued her political activities, inveighing against the corruption of her mother-in-law's party and government. She helped found a rival political party, the National Sanjay Organization, and eventually joined with Janata.

The assassination of Indira Gandhi in October 1984 left the party without a head. The party's executive committee immediately nominated Rajiv as prime minister, and its decision was accepted by the president. Rajiv took control of Congress (I), tried to soothe the nation, dissolved Parliament, and led his party to an unprecedented victory. Considering himself a spokesman for a new generation, Rajiv sought to introduce a more pragmatic style in Indian politics, emphasizing the importance of modern management techniques and results. He declared war on corruption, demanding instead professional devotion to the public interest. Rajiv vowed also to free business of bothersome government regulations, which would eliminate the need or temptation to bribe officials.

The anticorruption campaign was led by the finance minister, Vishwanath Pratap Singh, a poet and painter who was a loyal follower of Rajiv. V. P. Singh took his mandate seriously. To make tax reductions acceptable to the public, he insisted on vigorous enforcement of existing rules. Frequent raids by revenue agents at the homes and offices of India's richest families aroused both wonder and hostility. One major concern was the ability of wealthy Indians to smuggle money out of the country and into foreign bank accounts. Without informing the prime minister, V. P. Singh hired an American private detective agency, the Fairfax Group, to conduct an investigation. Among those targeted were powerful business leaders with close connections to Congress (I), including personal friends of Rajiv.

In January 1987, at a time of heightened tension with Pakistan, V. P. Singh was moved from finance to defense; this change also had the effect of stopping those controversial investigations. But as defense minister, Singh continued his anticorruption drive with renewed vigor. He discovered evidence that a large bribe (some $25 million) had been paid in 1981 by a German arms manufacturer in order to secure a contract to build two submarines. Singh's by-now numerous enemies accused him of revealing information that might weaken India's defense; allegations were also aired that the Fairfax Group was linked to the CIA, and that the anticorruption drive was an attempt by an unnamed foreign power (by implication, the United States) to destabilize Indian democracy. V. P. Singh was forced to resign.

Immediately thereafter the government was rocked by another kickback story. A Swedish radio station announced that a bribe had been paid by the Bofors arms manufacturer to sell artillery to the Indian army. When the Swedish government confirmed the report, Rajiv responded lamely by creating a committee to investigate the affair. Congress (I) was losing momentum as the elections of November 1989 approached. Rajiv's bold new initiatives, announced with much fanfare at the beginning of his term, were not always followed up. He was accused by critics within the party of suppressing dissent and weakening state and local party structures. After his defeat in 1989, Rajiv bided his time, awaiting the collapse of the Janata Dal government under the weight of its own contradictions. In the 1991 campaign he seemed confident of regaining power, if only because the split of the National Front into two rival independent parties—Janata Dal and BJP—condemned both to minority status. Rajiv spoke of the need for vision, promised a more assertive Indian role in South Asia and the world, and defended Nehru's legacy of secularism. But his economic policy remained hesitant; he called for more deregulation of the economy and reduction of government expenditures, but also pledged to roll back prices on essential goods and build housing for the poor (requiring regulation of the economy and an increase in expenditures).

Immediately after Rajiv's assassination, the 70-year-old Narasimha Rao was elected hastily as the provisional leader. (Rajiv's widow, Sonia, firmly refused to be considered for the post.) After Congress won a near majority of the seats, Rao was challenged by the powerful party boss in Bombay, Sharad Pawar. The younger Pawar eventually stepped aside, and on June 20 the party's members in Parliament unanimously chose Rao as leader; he was asked by President Venkataraman to form a government. For the first time since independence, no member of the Nehru-Gandhi dynasty was at the helm or in the wings of the Congress Party.

Rao, reputedly in poor health and considered a transitional figure at the outset, demonstrated remarkable ability to negotiate with the opposition, asserting himself as leader of both Congress and the government. He acted forcefully in adopting a program of economic reforms that moved India away from its historic commitment to democratic socialism (characterized by bureaucratization, stagnation, and corruption as well as good intentions) and to-

Narasimha Rao, leader of the Congress Party and the Prime Minister of India from 1991 to 1996. He was chosen to head the party after the assassination of Rajiv Gandhi.

wards a market economy. Although communal conflict erupted again when militant Hindus attacked the mosque at Ayodha in December 1992, Rao persuaded activists on both sides to agree to let the courts handle the issue. Violence in the Punjab was brought under control, but continued to flare up in Kashmir. Opposition parties were able to exploit inevitable popular discontent with the economic reforms, winning a string of victories in state legislative elections across India. Through it all, Rao maintained his composure, fended off challenges by rivals within Congress, surmounted one crisis after another, and presided over his government for a full term. With the approach of elections anticipated for the spring of 1996, Congress was faced with the need to find dynamic new leaders, and to redefine itself as a party.

THE JANATA PARTY

Although the Janata (or People's) Party was only founded in 1977, shortly after the sixth general election, most of its component members long had an independent existence, particularly the Socialist Party (itself a merger of parties dating from 1947 and later), the Jana Sangh (founded in 1951), and the Swatantra (founded in 1959). Diversity was at once the strength and the vulnerable point of the Janata. What kind of program could possibly unite advocates of socialism and defenders of free enterprise, proponents of secularism and orthodox Hindus? The Janata Party was able to promulgate a credible program in 1977 that—at least for the period of the electoral campaign—satisfied all its constituent groups. Most important was the common opposition to emergency rule and a determination to undo Mrs. Gandhi's authoritarian measures (limitations on the judiciary, suspension of civil rights, press censorship, and forcible sterilization). The Janata program was critical of planning and called for self-reliance (satisfying the Swatantra and Jana Sangh), but also promised to alleviate poverty and redistribute wealth (thereby pleasing the Socialists). There was also an emphasis on development of small industry and agriculture, which was more in line with Mahatma Gandhi's legacy.

In all, six major groups made up the Janata Party in 1977. The most important was the Con-

gress (O), from whose ranks came Morarji Desai, the new prime minister, and 6 of the 20 members of his cabinet. Another splinter group from the former Congress was the Congress for Democracy, whose founder was one of Mrs. Gandhi's ministers right up to the announcement of the election. When Jagjivan Ram resigned, formed the Congress for Democracy, and joined forces with the Janata, he brought with him the precious political and moral strength (and votes) of millions of outcastes, of whom he was the most influential spokesman. Jagjivan Ram succeeded Desai as leader of the Janata in 1979.

The other four member groups of Janata had a prior existence as independent parties. The Swatantra is basically a conservative party, sympathetic to free enterprise (though some members reject Western materialism altogether) and favoring closer relations with the West. The Jana Sangh was dedicated to preservation of the Hindu way of life, focusing mainly on defense of the Hindi language (in opposition to English), hostility toward Pakistan, and legislation protecting religious practices of the Hindu majority (such as the ban on slaughter of cattle). The Jana Sangh polled a respectable 9 percent of the vote in 1967, but went down a bit in 1971. It had special appeal in those areas of northern India with a large population of Hindu refugees from Pakistan.

The Socialists included two closely linked groups: the Praja Socialist Party and the Samyukta Socialist Party. The Praja Socialists had previously supported the Congress Party when it pursued Socialist policies; the Samyukta Socialists were more militantly opposed to the Congress Party and took the lead in forming anti-Congress electoral alliances even with Swatantra and the Jana Sangh. Finally, the Bharatiya Kranti Dal was a centrist, regional party in Uttar Pradesh that had considerable success in appealing to the middle class and wealthier farmers.

The Janata's fragile unity collapsed when the party assumed the responsibilities of office. Personality rivalries reflected the internal contradictions of the Janata coalition. Some leaders wanted to press forward toward rapid economic development; others considered modernity the ultimate expression of spiritual corruption and sought instead to favor home industries and agriculture. One group wished to assimilate the science and technology of the West; another group rejected Western materialism and resolved instead to revive and fortify Hindu culture. Some defended the outcastes, poor, and oppressed; others spoke out for wealthy business leaders and farmers. Opposition to the emergency rule turned out to be an inadequate program for a governing party. After its rout in January 1980, the Janata Party split—and then split again—reducing itself within a few months to little more than a legal fiction.

Each fragment of the former Janata campaigned separately in 1984, and all went down separately to crushing defeat. The party name was continued by the rump that remained after the others had defected. After pondering their loss, opposition leaders rallied and began to cooperate. Dissatisfaction increased with the government's handling of ethnic conflict in the Punjab and Assam. Rajiv's credibility as a crusader against corruption also suffered from the foreign "kickbacks" scandals. The opposition got a big boost when Rajiv's former finance and defense minister, V. P. Singh, created a new party, the Jan Morkha (People's Platform). In June 1988, V. P. Singh won handily in a by-election for a parliamentary seat in the city of Allahabad (Uttar Pradesh).

In August 1988, four opposition parties—Jan Morkha, Janata, Lok Dal, and Congress (S)—decided to fuse, calling themselves first the Samajwadi Janata Dal (Popular Socialist Party) and later simply the Janata Dal (People's Party). This party in turn took the lead in forming, along with some powerful regional parties (including Telegu Desam and Dravida Munnetra Kazhagam), a National Front. With V. P. Singh as general secretary and Rama Rao (chief minister of Andhra Pradesh and a former movie star) as chairman, the National Front went on to win the 1989 election.

V. P. Singh formed a Janata Dal government, with the support of the BJP and the Communist parties. But the prime minister had to perform an impossible balancing act. Committed to a secular and pragmatic program, V. P. Singh favored liberalization of the economy, opposed concessions to religious militants, and also sought to advance the interests of the lower castes and the outcastes. He thereby aroused the opposition of key elements in the coalition

on whose support his government depended. Communists and small farmers were suspicious of liberalization and privatization; militant Hindus resented Singh's defense of secularism and of the rights of Muslims; and members of the higher castes were outraged by his affirmative action policy.

By the summer of 1990, Singh's government was on the ropes. The deputy prime minister and minister of agriculture, Devi Lal, publicly criticized the prime minister for being "weak." He also was upset by charges that his son had engaged in electoral fraud. Lal was promptly dismissed, and joined forces with a long-time Singh opponent, Chandra Shekhar, to head up a strong dissident faction within the Janata Dal. In October, communal violence exploded over the issue of building a Hindu shrine on the site of a Muslim temple in Ayodhya. L. K. Advani, leader of the BJP, decided to place himself at the head of a religious pilgrimage to Ayodhya, which resulted in violence and fierce fighting between Hindus and Muslims. When Singh ordered the arrest of Advani, along with several hundred thousand demonstrators, the BJP withdrew its "outside" support for the government. Singh could no longer command a working majority. Rather than order new elections, the president summoned a special session of Parliament. Just before that session, the Janata Dal split apart. Lal and Shekhar created a new Janata Dal (Socialist). V. P. Singh entered the debate in Parliament having suffered the defection of some 60 members of his own party, and faced the opposition of both Congress (I) and the BJP. He lost a vote of confidence by an overwhelming margin: 346 to 142, with 8 abstentions.

When Shekhar's minority government collapsed after only four months, V. P. Singh rallied the remnants of Janata Dal around his call for a social revolution. Himself the descendant of a princely family and a high-caste Rajput, Singh argued that India could only enter the modern world through transformation of the caste system, which he wanted to bring about not by violence but by affirmative action in hiring for government jobs. "Our independence will remain hollow," declaimed Singh, "if the power and authority of the state is not deployed in the pursuit of equity." Considering that perhaps three-fourths of Indian society is made up of members of the lower and scheduled castes, Singh's arguments would appear to be both sensible and politically astute. But his attack on the caste system provoked a reaction by higher-caste Hindus, who were supported by large numbers of the very people Singh wished to liberate. The major beneficiary of the call for caste system reform turned out to be the party of Hindu identity, the Bharatiya Janata Party, whose emergence as the second political formation of India was the striking feature of the 1991 election.

THE BHARATIYA JANATA PARTY (BJP)

The meteoric rise of the BJP—going from 11.4 to about 20 percent of the vote between 1989 and 1991—has called into question India's status as a secular society. The BJP has moderate and militant wings. Hinduism by its nature is an all-encompassing and nondogmatic religion. The militant Hindu sects, especially the Shiv Sena, are more anti-Muslim than fundamentalist; but their hostility toward "special privileges" for Muslims, when pushed to an extreme, is expressed through devotion to Hindu ritual or culture. During the 1991 campaign, the leader of the Shiv Sena, Bal Thackeray, hailed the Hindu terrorist who had assassinated Mohandas Gandhi because "he saved the country from a second partition." A fiery female tribune of the "Hindu Awakening," Uma Bharti, saw the issue before the voters in simple terms: "whether this country belongs to Rama or to Babur!" (Rama is the incarnation of the Hindu deity, Vishnu; Babur is the founder of the Mogul Empire in India.)

The moderate leaders of the BJP—in particular the parliamentarian Lal Kishan Advani, and former foreign minister and amateur poet, Atal Behari Vajpayee—deny that the BJP is a religious party. But they believe it is important to assert the Hindu identity of India and, as Vajpayee has put it, "to take note of the changing Hindu psyche." A principal support of the BJP, perhaps surprisingly, is the upwardly mobile middle class, including successful small shopkeepers and artisans seeking to improve their social status through emulation of the behavior of higher castes. The BJP moderates are in favor of deregulation of the economy, privatization, and an infusion of foreign capital—all of which appeals to the progressive middle class. Another attractive feature of the BJP is that it seems to present a healthy or "clean" alternative—rooted in religion—to the perceived corruption of mainstream parties. The BJP's devoted volunteers present a sharp contrast to the hired toughs and rented crowds associated in the public mind with some of its competitors.

The episode that most clearly defined the character of the BJP was the pilgrimage it sponsored to the town of Ayodhya, the presumed birthplace of the Hindu deity Rama, the mythical character who is the central figure of the Ramayana. According to Hindu militants, a mosque (the Babri Masjid) was built on the precise spot where Rama was born. The shrine to Rama they have in mind can be constructed only if the mosque is destroyed or moved; and they have a long list of other mosques destined for a similar fate. L. K. Advani, usually thought of as a moderate, launched a Rath Yatra (march of Rama's chariot), making its way through the solidly Hindu areas of North India to the town of Ayodhya. Mounted on a chariot made up to look like that of Rama, Advani was surrounded by men dressed as the monkeys of Hanuman's army. (Hanuman was the head of an army of monkeys who helped Rama rescue his wife, Sita, from the clutches of the demon, Ravana.) The Rath Yatra, portrayed as a means of reuniting Hindus and making them proud of their culture, led to communal rioting between Hindus and Muslims wherever it went. Advani had organized it in response to V. P. Singh's proposal to reserve almost one-half of government jobs for the lower castes, which the BJP denounced as an attack on the integrity of Hindu society and a recipe for civil war.

One of Rao's first acts as prime minister was to hold talks with BJP leaders in order to avert a showdown; but no agreement was reached. At the prime minister's request, the Supreme Court issued an order prohibiting damage to the mosque or building of a temple. No measures were taken to protect the site, even though Hindu fundamentalist organizations and the BJP called upon militants to begin building a temple at 12:26 P.M. on December 6. At the appointed time the mosque was attacked and reduced to rubble, triggering six days of communal violence, particularly against Muslims in BJP-dominated Bombay, with a death toll of over 200. Several thousand people were arrested or placed in preventive detention. The Rao government was shaken, but did not fall. Rao dismissed the state government of Uttar Pradesh, banned five communal organizations (three Hindu and two Muslim), later dismissed three more BJP-led state governments, and cracked down on an attempt by the BJP in February 1993 to stage a mass demonstration in New Delhi. In October 1994, after deliberating for two years, the Supreme Court authorized the government to acquire the existing land subject to clearing of title. It also found the former BJP chief minister of Uttar Pradesh in contempt of

Table 9.4   MAJOR RELIGIONS IN INDIA

	Millions	Percentage
Hindu	734	80.3
Muslim	100	11.0
Christian	22	2.4
Sikh	18	2.0
Buddhist	6	0.7
Jain	5	0.5
Other	29	3.1

Source: World Data, *1995 Britannica Book of the Year,* pp. 628, 784.

court, requiring one day's symbolic imprisonment. The Rao government defused the conflict at Ayodha, at least temporarily, by making use of the courts, and the BJP apparently was willing to go along. But the issue had already served the purpose of firing up Hindu militancy, enabling the BJP to win victories in elections for state governments and to solidify its position as a national force.

Reaffirmation of Hindu identity, according to BJP leaders, will cleanse and strengthen Indian society. But it also leads to increased demands for autonomy and even separation by Muslims and other ethnic minorities, adding to the already formidable strains on the political system. Table 9.4 shows India's various major religious groups.

THE COMMUNIST PARTIES OF INDIA

The Communist movement of India is split between an orthodox party—the CPI; a rival party originally sympathetic to the Chinese—the CPI (M), for Marxist; and several militant and even terrorist groups inspired by Trotskyism, Maoism, and peasant violence—mainly the CPI (M-L), for Marxist-Leninist, and the Naxalites. The Communist movement has deep roots in Indian society and considerable success in appealing to intellectuals, workers, and poor and landless peasants. Since the election of 1952 the combined Communist vote has averaged about 10 percent of the total, falling slightly in 1977 to a

The sixteenth-century mosque at Ayodha was destroyed by Hindu extremists in December 1992. They were incited by the BJP and other political groups.

little over 7 percent, returning to almost 10 percent in 1980, dipping again to 8.6 percent in 1984, and remaining steady since.

The Communist Party of India (CPI), founded in 1928, was always closely linked to the Soviet Union. The CPI cooperated with the Congress Party during the struggle for independence in the 1930s, but relations between the two parties became strained with the outbreak of World War II. After the German invasion of the Soviet Union in 1941, the CPI and the Congress went separate ways: the Communists supported the war effort and the nationalists opted for noncooperation. Immediately after independence the CPI pursued a militant policy of organizing the workers for revolution, but Communist tactics were moderated as relations between India and the Soviet Union improved. In the 1950s, the CPI endorsed aspects of Nehru's foreign policy and pledged to achieve socialism by peaceful means.

However, the revolutionary elements in the party were restive. Pro-Chinese leftists withdrew from the secretariat in 1962; two years later they broke away completely and formed the Communist Party of India (Marxist). The CPI (M) hailed the Chinese as opposed to the Soviet model of communism, and sought to use elections as a means of mobilizing workers and peasants for revolutionary action. In 1969 another fission took place. The extreme left created the Communist Party of India (Marxist-Leninist), committed to a Maoist tactic of immediate armed struggle and terrorism. Indian Maoists called themselves "Naxalites" in honor of the tenant peasants of Naxalbari (a hill town in West Bengal), who were then forcibly seizing and occupying their land.

After the secession of the Marxists, the policy of the orthodox CPI remained the pursuit of its objectives through the electoral process, seeking alliances with all progressive forces. It collaborated with Indira Gandhi and her Congress (R) in 1969, providing the government the margin of support needed to stay in power. The Congress subsequently refrained from running candidates in about one-third of the districts where the CPI had a reasonable chance of winning. Cooperation with the Congress paid off for the CPI in 1971, enabling it to win 23 seats; but in 1977 the tactic backfired and the CPI was reduced to under 3 percent of the popular vote, retaining only 7 seats in the Lok Sabha. In 1980 the CPI did not collaborate with Indira Gandhi's Congress (I) but still managed to win 11 seats. It went down to 6 seats with 2.6 percent of the vote in 1984, and up to 13 seats with 2.5 percent in 1991.

Far from supporting Indira Gandhi during the emergency, the CPI (M) cooperated with the Janata, winning 4.3 percent of the vote in the 1977 election and 22 seats in the Lok Sabha—thus forging ahead of the orthodox party. The Marxists gradually toned down and finally abandoned Maoist policies. In 1980 they upped their vote to 6.1 percent, winning 35 seats. In 1984 they retained 22 seats with 6 percent of the vote, going up to 33 seats in 1989 and 35 seats in 1991, and seemed to be on the road to integration within the parliamentary system. The two Communist parties remained distinct, however. The CPI continued to acclaim the international leadership role of the Soviet Union, denouncing both Maoism and Eurocommunism. The CPI (M) refused to align itself with the Soviet Union, but became increasingly critical of China. Both Communist parties were critical of Gorbachev's reforms, rejoiced when hardliners arrested Gorbachev in August 1991, and lamented the triumph of Yeltsin.

Despite the crisis of communism elsewhere in the world, both Indian Communist parties have maintained their strength, mainly because of their grip on local governments. The CPI (M) has been the ruling party in West Bengal (which includes Calcutta) since 1977, and has taken turns at governing in two other states (Kerala and Tritura). The Communist parties are functioning more and more like Social Democratic parties—accepting a mixed economy and devoting their energies to defense of their constituents, rather than making a revolution. Both Communist parties announced after the 1991 election that they would not vote to bring down the Congress government formed by Narasimha Rao. After fighting against the liberalization policies instituted by the Rao government, the CPI (M)–led government of West Bengal in September 1994 formally adopted the cause of economic reform, throwing itself with fervor into a campaign to attract foreign capital and promote free enterprise. CPI (M) Chief Minister Jyoti Basu traveled to the United States in order to urge bankers and corporate executives to invest in West Bengal. India's Communist parties thus seem to be adopting the Chinese tactic of encouraging expansion of the private sector while retaining political control whenever possible.

REGIONAL PARTIES

In addition to the All-India parties just described, there are several locally important regional parties, especially in the Punjab, West Bengal, and Tamil Nadu. These parties focus on ethnic, religious, or linguistic identity and occasionally enter into alliance with national parties for mutually profitable reasons. Many regional parties disappear once immediate demands are met, but a few have become firmly established.

Here is a rundown of the regional parties that have fared well in recent elections:

1. The Dravida Munnetra Kazhagam (DMK) and its rival secessionist All-India Anna DMK (AIADMK) both agitate in favor of the Tamil language and greater autonomy for Tamil Nadu. The popular film star, M. G. Ramachandran, broke away from the DMK in 1972, and founded the AIADMK to protest policies of the party after the death of its creator, C. N. Annaduri ("Anna"). The AIADMK was allied with the Congress in 1984, while M. Karunanidhi, head of the DMK, joined the National Front in 1988. After the death of M. G. Ramachandran in 1987, the AIADMK was rent by factionalism but remained allied to the Congress.

2. The Telegu Desam, created by film star T. N. Rama Rao in 1982, urges a stronger role for states. It has continued to ally itself with Janata.

3. The National Conference has long been the ruling party of Jammu and Kashmir. In 1984 the new leader, Farooq Abdullah, was removed as chief minister by the governor, and the National Conference split into pro- and anti-Congress factions.

4. The Akali Dal—defender of the Sikh faith—is a major force in the Punjab, usually winning about 25 percent of the vote in that region. The Akali Dal has generally allied itself with opponents of the Congress, including Janata, the Communists, and the BJP.

The Indian party system is hardly distinctive because of the number of major parties or because of the importance of the Communist movements. After all, there are four major parties in France, and the Communist party is even stronger in France than in India. But there is a distinct "style" of politics in a country in which over two-thirds of the electorate is illiterate, the per capita income is just over $200 a year, and most people are still attached to traditional culture. That is, the Indian parties reflect not only the "modern" conflict among advocates of capitalism, liberalism, socialism, and communism, but also the still lively clash between a preindustrial and in many instances primitive society and the rapidly evolving, highly sophisticated industrial and scientific society. The conflict between secular forces and ethnic and religious movements has intensified with the rise of the BJP. Crosscutting currents of the primitive, traditional, and modern merge into a "mix" potentially more explosive than in the parliamentary democracy of any Western society.

1996 ELECTION UPDATE

The eleventh general election since independence was held over three days (April 27, May 2, and May 7) in 1996. Indian voters had to decide whether to continue or modify the economic liberalization reforms of the Rao government, and whether to preserve or change the secular nature of the state. The three major parties entered the campaign under the cloud of an ever widening corruption scandal. In January 1996 the Central Bureau of Investigation (a federal agency) brought bribery charges against three Congress ministers, the leader of the BJP (L. K. Advani), and several important figures in the Janata Dal Party.

The election was a severe setback for the Congress, which lost about one-fourth of its popular support (going from 37 percent of the vote in 1991 to about 28 percent in 1996) and almost half of its seats in Parliament (down from 225 to 136). Although the BJP stagnated at about 20 percent of the vote, it was the major beneficiary of the Congress's decline. It won 186 seats (up from 119), the largest bloc in Parliament. BJP strength is concentrated in large northern states, enabling it to take many seats that had previously gone to the Congress. A coalition of center and left parties, including the Janata Dal and the two Communist parties, won some 20 percent of the vote and 111 seats; and regional parties, garnering perhaps 25 percent of the vote, won 101 seats. No single party or alliance came close to the majority needed to form a government. The election results for 1996 (not including 15 districts where the count was delayed, 6 seats in Muslim-majority Jammu and Kashmir where voting was postponed, and 2 seats reserved for Anglo-Indians) are shown in Table 9.5.

Given the division of Parliament into four uneven parts, the following scenarios were possible: (1) A government under the leadership of the NF/LF, with either Janata Dal or the CP (M) contributing the prime minister, supported from

Table 9.5   1996 ELECTIONS

	Percentage of Popular Vote	Seats
Congress (I)	28	136
BJP-Allies	20	186
NF/LF-Allies	20	111
Regional parties, others	25	101

Breakdown of seats within blocs

BJP-Allies: Bharatiya Janata Party, 160; Shiv Sena, 15; Samata Party, 8; HVP, 3.

National Front/Left Front-Allies: Janata Dal, 43; Communist Party of India (Marxist), 32; Samajwari Party, 17; Communist Party of India, 11; RSP, 5; AIFB, 3.

Regional, Others: Tamil Maanila Congress, 20; Dravida Munetra Kazhagam, 17; Telegu Desam Party, 16; Bahujan Samaj Party, 11; Independents, 9; Akali Dal, 8; Asom Gana Parishad, 5; Indira Congress (T), 4; Others, 11.

Note: Above figures are unofficial. From *The Times of India*, May 14, 1996, p. 1.

the outside by Congress and some regional parties; (2) A government headed by the BJP with support from some regional parties, tolerated by Congress; or (3), probably after the failure of one or both of the above combinations, a government headed by the Congress and supported or tolerated by the NF/LF and some regional parties. Immediately after the election, it appeared that the NF/LF would form a government headed by Janata Dal or the CP (M), supported from the outside by Congress and regional parties. But the most prestigious Janata Dal chief, former prime minister V. P. Singh, under treatment for cancer, refused to take the post of prime minister. The Front then turned to Jyoti Basu, Communist chief minister of West Bengal state; but the Central Committee of the CP(M) declined to head or even join a government it could not control. The coalition then switched to a regional leader, H. D. Deve Gowda, a centrist member of the Janata Dal and chief minister of the state of Karnataka. President Shankar Dayal Sharma, impatient with the irresolute leadership of the NF/LF, instead appointed BJP leader Atal Bihari Vajpayee as prime minister. Although he presented a moderate program, Vajpayee failed to attract any outside support. He resigned after only 13 days in office, just before a confidence vote in Parliament that the BJP government was bound to lose. President Sharma then consulted with Narasimha Rao, still leader of the second largest group in Parliament. Rao declined to try to form a government, but promised that Congress would support a minority NF/LF government. The President thereupon appointed H. D. Deve Gowda as prime minister. As these lines were written it appeared certain that the new government, whose member parties controlled 192 seats and had the backing of Congress with its 136 seats, would easily win a confidence vote in Parliament.

Perhaps the most striking feature of the 1996 elections was the heightened political activity of the lower castes and ethnic groups. They want greater representation in government and more benefits, throwing their support increasingly to regional, local, and ethnic parties. Given the divisions within the NF/LF (renamed the United Front after the elections), and the isolation of the BJP, most observers expected a repeat of the experience that followed defeat of the Congress in the elections of 1977 and 1989: a period of instability and factionalism, due to the tendency of the anti-Congress coalition to self-destruct, followed by early elections. Fragile and shifting alliances will give greater weight to the demands of regional parties, which are pressing for a shift of power away from the center and toward the governments of the states. The Indian party system now seems to have entered into a new phase, characterized by coalition politics at the center and growing diversity among increasingly powerful states.

POLITICAL INSTITUTIONS AND POLICY MAKING

The political institutions through which Indians govern themselves were created by the 1949 Constitution of India—the product of almost three years' deliberation by the Constituent Assembly (whose members were originally elected by provincial legislatures). One reason for the long delay in promulgating the Constitution is that the Assembly also functioned as the Provisional Parliament immediately following independence, and therefore members had to conduct the business of the nation at the same time that they were drafting a basic law. The leaders of the Congress party—especially Nehru, Rajenda Prasad, Sardar Vallabhbhai Patel, and M. A. K. Azad (a Muslim)—dominated debates and presided over the drafting of the document.

THE CONSTITUTION OF INDIA

The new Constitution went into effect on January 26, 1950. It incorporates much of the Government of India Act of 1935, adding considerable detail on civil liberties and the federal system. With its 395 articles and 8 schedules, the Constitution of India holds the distinction of being one of the longest in the world. The Indians essentially adopted the British parliamentary system, but modified it to suit their own circumstances. They could hardly replicate an English Constitution that had evolved over several centuries and is expressed in unique medieval and early modern statutes and docu-

ments such as the Magna Carta (1215), the Bill of Rights (1689), and the Act of Settlement (1701). Instead, they followed the practice of all other democratic governments in the world by enacting a basic law. The preamble of the Indian Constitution reflects the philosophy of the movement for national liberation and is reminiscent as well of the Declaration of Independence and preamble to the Constitution of the United States.

> WE, THE PEOPLE OF INDIA, having solemnly resolved to constitute India into a SOVEREIGN, DEMOCRATIC REPUBLIC and to secure to all its citizens:
> JUSTICE, social, economic and political;
> LIBERTY of thought, expression, belief, faith and worship;
> EQUALITY of status and opportunity; and to promote among them all
> FRATERNITY assuring the dignity of the individual and the unity of the Nation;
> IN OUR CONSTITUENT ASSEMBLY . . . DO HEREBY ADOPT, ENACT AND GIVE TO OURSELVES THIS CONSTITUTION

The basic commitment of the Constituent Assembly was to a parliamentary system (that is, a cabinet responsible to the lower house); a republic (hence, an elected president would play the role of head of state); a federation with a strong center (striking a balance between national authority and provincial assemblies); and a secular system (not a state divided between Hindus and Muslims). Republican institutions and commonwealth membership were made compatible when India agreed to recognize the British monarch as the symbol of free association and as such the head of the Commonwealth, without otherwise acknowledging any allegiance to the Crown.

One respect in which the Indians departed from British practice and reflected American tradition was in guaranteeing civil liberties (called Fundamental Rights) and making them enforceable through courts. The rights thus protected under the Constitution make up an impressive catalog: equality, "freedom," freedom of religion, and the right to property, as well as some not specifically set forth in the American Bill of Rights—for example, freedom from exploitation, and cultural and educational rights. Especially important in Indian society are the abolition of untouchability, guarantees of equal opportunity in public employment, and prohibition of discrimination on grounds of religion, race, caste, or sex.

Balancing off the declaration of fundamental rights of citizens against the state are the "directive principles" that set forth the duty of the state toward the citizens. The Constitution enjoins the state to promote the welfare of the people by creating social, economic, and political justice. These principles are difficult to carry out because all political parties proclaim the promotion of the public welfare as their goal—but disagree on how to go about doing it. Similarly, abolition of untouchability and guarantees of full employment do not depend exclusively on constitutional provisions. Such measures become effective only under appropriate political, economic, and social conditions.

The Constitution of India goes further than most similar documents in stipulating that freedoms may be suspended or abrogated during an emergency. Part XVIII (Emergency Provisions) of the Constitution specifically gives the president the power to suspend the right to freedom in a national emergency, though the president may act only on the advice of the prime minister. After the Chinese incursion in 1962 a national emergency was declared—and lasted officially for six years. During this emergency, Parliament passed a Defense of India Act (modeled on the Defense of the Realm Acts in Britain), which empowered the government to detain any person it suspected on reasonable grounds to be "of hostile origin" or to be "likely to act" in a manner harmful to Indian defense, state security, maintenance of public order, India's relations with foreign states, or the efficient conduct of military operations.

The balance between individual rights and national unity or law and order swings decidedly toward the latter in an emergency. After the emergency relating to the conflict with China was finally lifted, Parliament passed an Unlawful Activities Prevention Act which continued many of the restrictions of the previous period. The power of the executive to override individual rights was further strengthened by the Maintenance of Internal Security Act of 1971. The most spectacular use of emergency power since the founding of the Indian Republic was the emergency rule invoked by Mrs. Indira Gandhi in 1975–1977.

After the decision of the Allahabad High Court in June 1975 that Mrs. Gandhi had violated the electoral law, the opposition parties began a mass campaign of civil disobedience to force the prime minister to resign. One of India's most colorful political leaders, Jaya Prakash Narayan, pointedly urged the army and police to refuse to obey "unjust orders." The prime minister thereupon advised the president to proclaim, by virtue of the power vested in him by Article 352 of the Constitution, that "a grave emergency exists whereby the security of India is threatened by internal disturbance." During the one year and nine months of the emergency, some 110,000 people all told were arrested and imprisoned without trial. Newspapers were forbidden to publish reports affecting India's relations with foreign countries, denigrating the office of the prime minister, causing disaffection among members of the armed forces or government employees, or bringing the government into hatred or contempt. These regulations were strictly enforced. The government also banned several militant Hindu organizations and the CPI (M).

Through the amending process the Constitution was changed so drastically that it became virtually a different system of government. Amendments can be added to the Constitution by a majority vote of both houses with at least two-thirds of the members of each house present and voting; in addition, amendments relating to the political institutions must be ratified by the legislatures of a majority of the states. Three amendments (the 39th, 40th, and 41st) were passed in rapid succession by Parliament and ratified soon after the emergency was declared. These amendments provided that the president's reasons for proclaiming an emergency could not be challenged in any court; also that all matters relating to the election of the president, vice president, speaker of the Lok Sabha, or the prime minister should be referred to a new authority to be created by Parliament and not be judged by the regular courts; that this authority not be questioned by any court; and that all pending proceedings against the president, vice president, speaker, and prime minister were null and void.

In addition, a Maintenance of Internal Security (Amendment) Bill was passed in 1976. It provided that the grounds on which a person had been detained should not be disclosed to the detainee or any other person. President Ahmed ordered the suspension for the period of the emergency of any person's right to apply to the courts for enforcement of Article 19 of the Constitution—that is, the rights to freedom of speech and expression and to peaceable assembly. The Supreme Court also held that the government could suspend habeas corpus. One justice declared that the public safety was the highest law in time of crisis.

The most sweeping change of all was instituted by the Constitution (42nd Amendment) Bill, known as A42. This amendment was passed by Parliament on November 11, 1976 (by a vote of 366 to 4 in the Lok Sabha and 191 to 0 in the Rajya Sabha); it was ratified by the legislatures of more than half the states within a month, received the assent of President Ahmed on December 18, 1976, and took effect a few weeks later. A42 amended 37 articles, repealed 4, and introduced 13 new articles. Among the most important provisions were the following:

1. *Preamble:* India was now described as a "sovereign socialist secular democratic republic."

2. *Fundamental rights:* No law giving effect to the "directive principles" might be declared unconstitutional on the ground that it infringed on the fundamental rights guaranteed by the Constitution. No law prohibiting antinational activities should be nullified on grounds of violating individual liberties. Antinational activities were broadly defined to embrace advocacy of secession; threatening the sovereignty or integrity of India or "the security of the state or the unity of the nation"; overthrowing the government by force; creating internal disruptions; and fomenting communal and caste hatred.

3. *Fundamental duties:* A new article was inserted into the Constitution, stating that every citizen has the duty to abide by the Constitution, cherish the ideals of the national struggle for freedom, defend the country, promote social harmony, and strive toward excellence.

4. *The executive:* The article stating that the Council of Ministers would "aid and advise the President in the exercise of his functions" was amended to read that the Council of Ministers would aid and advise the President, "who shall, in the exercise of his functions, act in accordance with such advice."

5. *Amendments:* It was stated that no amendment to the Constitution can be called into question "in any court on any ground."

Most of the provisions of A42 were reversed by two constitutional amendments adopted under the Desai government in 1977. Specifically, the provision empowering Parliament to legislate against antinational activity was repealed; and the president was given the right to ask the Council of Ministers to reconsider its decisions. Restrictions were also imposed on the use of emergency powers. A proclamation of emergency can now be issued only when the security of India is threatened by external aggression or armed rebellion. Internal disturbances not amounting to armed rebellion are an insufficient ground. The Council of Ministers must forward its request for an emergency to the president in writing; the proclamation must be approved by Parliament within a month by a two-thirds majority, can remain in force for only six months, and can be extended only after another vote by a two-thirds majority. Even though the main structures of the 1949 Constitution were restored, the emergency is a reminder of the fragility of civil liberties in India.

THE PRESIDENT AND VICE PRESIDENT

The Constitution vests the executive power in a president, who is elected for a five-year term by an electoral college consisting of members of Parliament and state legislative assemblies. The voting procedure is complex in order to maintain

Dayal Sharma became the ninth president of India in July 1992.

a rough parity among the states based on population, with electors casting a preferential ballot. The vice president is elected for a five-year term by both houses of Parliament in a joint session. As in the United States, the vice president presides over the upper house of Parliament (the Rajya Sabha). The vice president's main function, of course, is to take the place of the president in case of death or incapacity; in that event a presidential election must be held within six months.

In theory, the president is given vast powers under the Constitution. The president may dissolve Parliament, declare an emergency in a state, and rule that state by decree. The president may refuse to assent to a bill, although the veto may be overridden if the bill is repassed by both houses. Also, the president is commander-in-chief of the armed forces and appoints state governors and Supreme Court justices. It was understood by the framers of the Constitution that the president would act only on the advice of the prime minister, and this understanding has been respected in practice. The vast powers of the president have in fact devolved upon the prime minister. Perhaps the most important function of the president, consequently, is to appoint the prime minister. So far the president has had little discretion, because the leader of the majority party in the Lok Sabha is the only person who would have the confidence of Parliament. In

1979, however, the disintegration of the governing Janata Party created a power vacuum that was partly filled by President Sanjiva Reddy.

The formal powers of the office give the president considerable influence within the political system, especially during periods of party instability. The president is entitled to be informed and consulted by the prime minister, has recently been accorded the power to ask the Council of Ministers to reconsider a decision, and must sign all legislation. The president is also the major symbol of national unity; hence the election of a president has always been a matter of great concern to the political parties and arouses the interest of the public. When President Reddy resigned in 1980, the candidate of the Congress Party, Zail Singh, won election for the unfilled term easily, receiving almost three-fourths of the votes of the electoral college. He was a political ally of Prime Minister Indira Gandhi, and the first Sikh to hold that office. President Singh, however, did not get along well with Gandhi's successor, Rajiv, complaining bitterly that he was continually bypassed. The president and the prime minister began to feud, attacking each other in public. Singh chose not to run for reelection. In July 1987 R. Venkataraman, candidate of Rajiv and Congress (I), was elected with over 70 percent of the vote. He did not even bother to campaign. Because no single party received a majority in the elections of 1989 and 1991, President Venkataraman played a larger than usual role in the political process—particularly in deciding who should be invited to form governments and under what circumstances. In 1992 the Congress Party nominated Vice President Shankar Dayal Sharma for the presidency; he was supported by the Left Front. Janata Dal backed a Christian tribal, George G. Swell, in order to give someone from lower castes a chance. Curiously, the BJP went along with Swell as a way of broadening its appeal. Sharma won the presidency with 65 percent of the votes in the electoral college. For a list of India's presidents since 1950, see Table 9.6.

THE PARLIAMENT

There are two chambers of Parliament: the lower house, Lok Sabha (House of the People), which

Table 9.6 PRESIDENTS OF INDIA

President	Election
Rajendra Prasad	1950
Rajendra Prasad	1952
Rajendra Prasad	1957
Dr. S. Radhakrishnan	1962
Dr. Zakir Hussain	1967 (died 1969)
V. V. Giri	1969
Fakhruddin Ali Ahmed	1974 (died 1977)
Neelam Sanjiva Reddy	1977
Zail Singh	1980
R. Venkataraman	1987
Shankar Dayal Sharma	1992

now has 542 members, and an upper house, Rajya Sabha (Council of States), whose membership is limited to 250. The president appoints 12 members to the Rajya Sabha as representatives of the arts and professions, and all the other members are elected by the state legislatures; hence the upper house serves as a direct link between the state and national governments.

The Lok Sabha members are elected on the basis of single-member constituencies. Its normal term is five years, although it may be dissolved at any time by the president (on advice of the prime minister). According to the Constitution, the Lok Sabha must meet at least twice a year, with no more than six months between sessions. Most members speak in either English or Hindi but may use other languages if they wish. As in the British House of Commons, the Speaker is elected from among the members and is supposed to be nonpartisan once in office. Unlike the House of Commons, the Lok Sabha has a system of standing committees that covers the whole range of government operations—including a Rules Committee and others that oversee the budget, exercise of delegated power, and general performance of the ministries. In recent years, up to half of the members of each new Parliament have never before served in that body. Inexperience and lack of office space and staff have contributed to the relative weakness of Parliament in its dealings with the cabinet and the civil service.

Legislative procedure in the Indian Parliament is similar to that in the British Parliament—though the Rajya Sabha has a more important role than the House of Lords. Legislation is drafted and introduced by the government; a severely limited amount of time is reserved each week for bills presented by private members (those who are not members of ministries). As in Britain, there are three readings. The first reading is of the title only and with no debate. The Speaker then assigns the bill to a select (or ad hoc) committee, made up with the advice of party leaders, just to consider that bill. The second reading is based on the report of the select committee; it is at this stage that debate and voting on each clause take place. The third reading is merely on the formal motion that the bill be passed. Money bills can only be introduced in the Lok Sabha; other legislation can originate in either house, although in practice most bills are presented first in the Lok Sabha.

If the two houses do not agree, the bill may be sent back and forth until all differences have been resolved. If there is still no agreement, the president may call a joint session of Parliament, where the matter is settled by a majority vote, thus giving the more numerous Lok Sabha members the upper hand. Joint sessions are rarely necessary, however. If the Rajya Sabha rejects a money bill, it can be enacted into law simply by having the Lok Sabha repass it.

Another feature of Indian legislative procedure based directly on British practice is the question period, which begins each daily session of Parliament. Members are permitted to ask questions of ministers concerning most matters of public policy; replies are generally of interest to the press. Members may ask follow-up questions that test the minister's ability to think under pressure. Occasionally, ministers have been forced to resign because of incompetence or scandal brought out during the question period.

The central notion in parliamentary government is that the cabinet is responsible to Parliament and must resign when it loses the confidence of that body. The Lok Sabha possesses one important weapon in its relations with the cabinet: Any 50 members may introduce a motion of censure; if it carries, the cabinet must resign. The cabinet is not responsible to the Rajya Sabha, which has no power to censure the government. The opposition in the Lok Sabha has been so fragmented in the past that motions of censure were rare because no single opposition party had as many as 50 members. As in Britain, it is expected that the governing party will "manage" the deliberations of Parliament and in so doing will be supported by its members. Parliament plays an important role, not so much as policymaker, but as the forum in which declarations of government policy are made and government and opposition engage in structured debate.

THE PRIME MINISTER AND COUNCIL OF MINISTERS

The effective executive in India—the prime minister, Council of Ministers, and cabinet—is based squarely on the British model. Exactly the same distinctions are made in India as in Britain among all three groups; they have the same relationship to Parliament, but the dominance of the executive over Parliament is perhaps even greater in India. The prime minister is chosen by the president; but in general the president has no choice. He or she must nominate the leader of the majority party in the Lok Sabha—otherwise the government would not have the confidence of that body.

The prime minister chooses ministers, who are then officially appointed by the president. Ministers must be members of Parliament; nonmembers may be appointed if within six months they become members of Parliament through a by-election. The Council of Ministers is collectively responsible to Parliament for all decisions of the government; as in Britain, however, this collective responsibility does not mean that each minister is fully aware of decisions made by colleagues, for the good reason that the Council of Ministers never meets as a collective entity. The ministry is a large group that includes heads and deputy heads of all the departments. By tradition, the most important ministers (usually from 12 to 18 in number) are invited by the prime minister to join the cabinet, which is not mentioned in the Constitution. The cabinet meets regularly once a week and is responsible for formulation and coordination of all government policy. By invitation, other min-

isters or experts can attend cabinet sessions for discussion of matters in which they have special interest or expertise.

Even the cabinet is too unwieldy for policy making, so all prime ministers have created specialized committees consisting of a few ministers responsible for a specific area or problem. The prime minister, who usually chairs these committees, is in a position to dominate their deliberations. Nehru formed an emergency committee of the cabinet with six members as the equivalent of the "inner cabinet" in Britain; it virtually replaced the larger cabinet as a decision-making body for important policy. Since then each prime minister has continued the practice of consulting regularly with some sort of inner cabinet.

As in Britain, a special agency of the civil service is assigned to the prime minister and cabinet to furnish secretarial and administrative assistance in preparing agendas, recording decisions, following up on implementation, and coordinating the various special committees of the cabinet. The central secretariat, headed by a cabinet secretary, thus provides an indispensable element of professionalism and continuity in cabinet deliberations. In view of the secretariat's reputation for irreproachable professionalism, it came as a shock when it was revealed in 1985 that one of its trusted and most important members had long been a spy in the service of a foreign power.

The prime minister is the "buckle that binds" the president, Council of Ministers, cabinet, and Parliament. The dominance of the prime minister within the system was especially evident during the tenure of the first occupant of the office, Jawaharlal Nehru. As leader of the national independence movement and the Congress Party, Nehru was the towering figure of Indian politics in the years following independence. Many feared that his departure would usher in a period of chaos, but no succession struggle took place immediately after Nehru's death in May 1964. The Congress Party unanimously chose one of Nehru's close collaborators, Lal Bahadur Shastri, as prime minister. Shastri did not possess the charismatic qualities of his predecessor but proved to be a reasonably effective leader. When he died suddenly in January 1966, the Congress Party turned to Nehru's daughter, Indira Gandhi (no relation to

An Indian dynasty. Prime minister Jawaharlal Nehru, together with his daughter and future prime minister, Indira Gandhi, and her two sons Sanjay and Rajiv (who became prime minister after his mother's assassination in 1984). This photo was taken in 1956 during Nehru's state visit to West Germany. Chancellor Konrad Adenauer is directly behind Nehru.

Mohandas Gandhi), a former president of the party. Thereafter she was at the center of the political stage, except for the period between the defeat of the Congress Party in 1977 and its triumphant comeback in 1980. The two prime ministers who served from 1977 to 1979—Morarji Desai and Charan Singh—were forceful personalities but were not able to fashion a solid majority. Indira Gandhi's elder son, Rajiv, continued the tradition of leadership by a member of the Nehru family after his mother's assassination. The successors to Rajiv—V. P. Singh (1989–1990) and Chandra Shekhar (1990–1991)—were at the mercy of their outside supporters and could not fully wield their power. Narasimha Rao came close to a working majority after the election of 1991, but still depended on outside support from other parties to carry

out his program. He proved to be surprisingly adept at negotiating with opposition leaders in order to arrive at consensual policies. The office of the prime minister has remained the major source of policy making and the chief political prize sought by all contenders. For a list of India's prime ministers since independence, see Table 9.7.

THE SUPREME COURT

The Constitution creates a Supreme Court, consisting of a chief justice and 25 associates, appointed by the president after consultation with sitting members of the court and of state courts. The Indian Supreme Court, unlike its British counterpart, may declare an act of Parliament unconstitutional. It is relatively easy, however,

Table 9.7   PRIME MINISTERS OF INDIA

Jawaharlal Nehru	1947–1964	Congress
Lal Bahadur Shastri	1964–1966	Congress
Indira Gandhi	1966–1977	Congress
Morarji Desai	1977–1979	Janata
Charan Singh	1979–1980	Janata
Indira Gandhi	1980–1984	Congress
Rajiv Gandhi	1984–1989	Congress
V. P. Singh	1989–1990	Janata
Chandra Shekhar	1990–1991	Janata (Socialist)
Narasimha Rao	1991–1996	Congress
Aral Bihari Vajpayee	May 15–28, 1996	BJP
H. D. Deve Gowda	May 28, 1996–	Janata

for Parliament to reverse decisions by the Supreme Court through the amending process. Several court decisions invalidating land reform legislation were overridden.

During the 1975–1977 emergency, the Supreme Court pointedly sided with the government, damaging its reputation as a judicial guardian of civil liberties. In 1976 the Forty-second Amendment prohibited the Supreme Court from reviewing changes introduced by constitutional amendment. But in 1980 the Court reaffirmed its power to safeguard the "basic structure" of the Constitution, even in amendments. The modern judiciary has gained widespread acceptance in India. But the experience during the emergency raises serious questions about the ability of the Supreme Court to withstand strong political pressures. For a summary of the structure of Indian government, see Feature 9.1.

THE BUREAUCRACY

Indians have long believed that their political system is more effective than those of other developing countries because of the bureaucratic structures inherited from the British; the belief may be at least partly correct. After independence, the old Indian civil service of the British period was refashioned as the Indian Administrative Services (IAS). The membership of the IAS is only about 4,000 people—a minuscule fraction of the

13 million civil servants in India—but they are the "steel frame" of the whole edifice.

Recruitment into the IAS (approximately 140 annually) and into a few central services of individual ministries, such as the foreign service, is supervised by a Union Public Service Commission. As in Great Britain, an attempt is made through examinations and interviews to select young people of exceptional intelligence and talent, who are then given special training and form a policy-making stratum within the huge civil service establishment. One advantage of this system is to guarantee the competence of the higher civil service. However, the middle and lower levels of the civil service are generally far below the standard set by the top stratum.

In sum, the Indians have gradually adapted British-style institutions to their own circumstances. These institutions have become familiar to all Indians and are increasingly considered an appropriate mechanism for resolving political conflicts and working out compromises. The greatest crisis of the democratic system probably was the emergency; had it endured, the character of the Constitution as originally conceived would have been altered. But the Indian public brought the emergency to an end, and its verdict was accepted by Mrs. Gandhi and her supporters. Some observers have expressed concern that the personalization of power under both Indira and Rajiv Gandhi has led to an "erosion of institutions"—

Feature 9.1 **Structure of Government In India**

The chart below shows the channels of political responsibility within the government of India. The voters directly elect the Lok Sabha and the state legislatures; the state legislatures select the members of the upper chamber, the Rajya Sabha (except for 12 members selected by the president, not indicated on the chart). The president is elected by an electoral college, consisting of elected members of both houses of Parliament and of the legislatures in all the states, with the vote weighted on the basis of population. The president selects a prime minister, who is normally the leader of the majority party in the Lok Sabha, or enjoys the support of a majority. The prime minister selects the ministers. The president, after consulting with existing judges of the Supreme Court and of high courts of the states, appoints the judges of the Supreme Court.

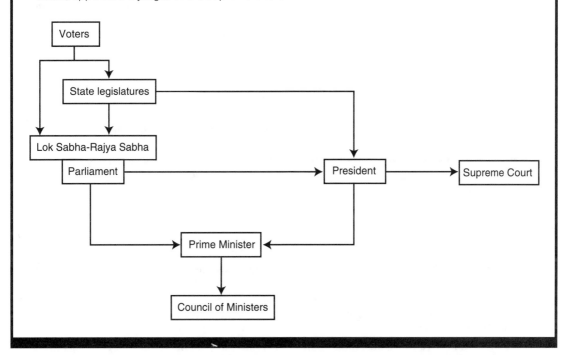

including the Congress Party as well as Parliament and state governments. Atul Kohli has attributed institutional decay to "the destructive and self-serving acts of leaders who find institutions a constraint on personal power," as well as to mounting social pressures.[6] Without strong institutions as intermediaries between state and society, he contends, policy making has become arbitrary and ineffective.

Certainly we should not underestimate the difficulty of maintaining viable democratic government in any third world society. Yet the Constitution held firm in the first 40 years of its existence and acquired genuine legitimacy. Every year that passes increases the chances that the system will be able to meet critical new challenges in the future, despite the heterogeneity of Indian society and the intensity of its political divisions.

 EY TERMS

Advani, L. K.
Bharatiya Janata Party (BJP)

Communist Party of India—CPI
Communist Party of India (Marxist)—CPI (M)
Congress Party
Congress (I)
Council of Ministers
emergency rule
Gandhi, Indira
Gandhi, Rajiv
Indian Administrative Services
Janata Party
Lok Sabha
Naxalites
President
President's rule
Prime Minister
Rajya Sabha
Rao, Narasimha
Singh, V. P.
Supreme Court

FURTHER READINGS

Brass, P. R. *The Politics of India Since Independence* (Cambridge: Cambridge University Press, 1990).

Das, B. C. *The President of India* (New Delhi: S. Chand, 1977).

Graham, B. *Hindu Nationalism and Indian Politics* (Cambridge: Cambridge University Press, 1990).

Gould, H., and S. Ganguly, eds. *India Votes: The Quest for Consensus, 1989 and 1991* (Boulder, CO: Westview Press, 1993.

Hardgrave, R. L., and S. A. Kochanek. *India: Government and Politics in a Developing Nation,* 5th ed. (New York: Harcourt Brace College Publishers, 1993).

Hart, H. C., ed. *Indira Gandhi's India: A Political System Reappraised* (Boulder, CO: Westview Press, 1976).

Kochanek, S. A. *The Congress Party of India* (Princeton: Princeton University Press, 1968).

Kochanek, S. A. *Business and Politics in India* (Berkeley: University of California Press, 1974).

Kohli, Atul. *Democracy and Discontent: India's Growing Crisis of Governability* (New York: Cambridge University Press, 1990).

Kohli, Atul, ed. *India's Democracy: An Analysis of Changing State-Society Relations* (Princeton: Princeton University Press, 1990).

Kothari, Rajni. *Politics and the People: In Search of a Humane India,* 2 vols. (New Delhi: Ajanta, 1989).

Pylee, M. V. *Constitutional Government in India,* 4th ed. (Bombay: Asia Publishing House, 1984).

Sankdher, M. M., ed. *Framework of Indian Politics* (New Delhi: Gitanjali Publishing House, 1984).

Seervai, H. M. *Constitutional Law of India: A Critical Commentary,* 4th ed., 2 vols. (Bombay: Tripathi, 1990, 1991).

Sen Gupta, B. *Communism in Indian Politics* (New York: Columbia University Press, 1972).

Sen Gupta, B. *Rajiv Gandhi: A Political Study* (New Delhi: Konarak Publishers, 1989).

Venkateswaran, R. J. *Cabinet Government in India* (London: Allen and Unwin, 1967).

Weiner, M. *India at the Polls, 1980: A Study of the Parliamentary Elections* (Washington, DC: American Enterprise Institute, 1983).

Weiner, M. *The Indian Paradox: Essays in Indian Politics* (New Delhi: Sage, 1989).

C.

Public Policy

Political institutions are not ends in themselves; they are designed to formulate policy. The ultimate test of a political system is its effectiveness in permitting a people to attain collective goals. The leaders of the independence movement in India were determined to modernize their nation and conquer poverty through democratic means. An appraisal of the political system they created, then, calls for a review of the effort by Indians to fashion a modern state, society, and economy.

MODERNIZATION:
A BALANCE SHEET

In the first decade after independence was won in 1947, Indians succeeded beyond the expectations of most observers in endowing themselves with a rational and workable structure. Their Constitution was drafted, promulgated, and implemented. The key position within this structure was occupied by a charismatic leader who had led the struggle of national independence, a struggle which was shared by a political party that stood ready to shoulder the burden and responsibility of power. Buttressing the system was a civil service of considerable competence, inherited from the days of British rule.

Almost immediately those bothersome remnants of feudalism, the princes, were cast aside, and the vast territory of the subcontinent was at last integrated under one authority. Almost 600 territorial units were consolidated into 27 states. Further reorganization took place in 1956 when the government of India created 14 states out of the earlier 27, mainly along linguistic lines. Agitation by linguistic groups in Bombay, the Punjab, and Nagaland subsequently resulted in the creation of more states, and there are now 25 states and 7 union territories in the Indian Union. By and large the delicate technical task of reconstructing the polity along linguistic lines was fairly well done, but ethnic tensions continue to plague the nation. In 1948,

Nehru expressed the fear that basing regional units on language would let loose the forces of "disruption and disintegration." In some measure his somber prediction came true. Strong regional parties have come to power or assumed important positions in key states—notably the CPI(M) in West Bengal, the DMK and AIADMK in Tamil Nadu, the Telegu Desam in Andrha, and the Akali Dal in the Punjab. Demands for state autonomy have often been accompanied by violent demonstrations, calling forth counterdemonstrations and police action that further embitter feelings. A particularly difficult problem developed in Assam in the 1970s, when the influx of Bengali refugees from Bangladesh was viewed by Assamese as a threat to the integrity of tribal cultures. A state election in 1983, boycotted by most Assamese voters to protest the participation of Bengali immigrants, led to rioting in which several thousand people were killed. Tribal unrest, punctuated by armed uprisings, has continued in the Northeast. The United Liberation Front of Assam killed almost 100 people in the last months of 1991 alone, including a number of Congress (I) politicians.

An even more serious challenge to national unity came in the 1980s from the Sikh population of the Punjab. The Sikh religion, which emerged in the fifteenth century, was an attempt to reconcile Islam and Hinduism. A series of gurus (or "teachers")—equivalent in Sikhism to Islam's Muhammad and Judaism's Moses—fashioned a monotheistic creed, holding that all religions are fundamentally alike; the gurus opposed idolatry, priesthood, and the caste system. Persecuted by Mogul emperors, Sikhs became bitter enemies of Muslims, despite their many religious similarities, and created a warrior society to defend themselves. After combating the British in the early nineteenth century, Sikhs served in large numbers in the British army in India, and subsequently in the Indian army. In 1947, Sikhs joined with militant Hindus in fighting Muslims. Since then, however, they have sought to maintain their distinctive identity in opposition to Hindus.

In 1966 the Akali Dal—or Sikh political party—attained its major demand for the creation of a Punjabi language state with a Sikh majority. But conflict persisted regarding the status of the capital city, Chandigarh (on the border between the Punjab and Haryana), and control of river waters. The Akali began to demand autonomy for the Punjab; Sant Jarnail Singh Bhindranwale (leader of a religious institution) galvanized many Sikh militants, who later formed an insurgent movement. However, Sikhs constitute a bare majority of the population in the Punjab, which was ruled by Sikh Congress leaders, except for the brief period of an Akali-Janata coalition from 1977 to 1980. The movement in favor of Sikh revival and independence gathered strength, especially among young people. Sikh militants resorted to acts of terrorism (shooting Hindus at random, for example); and the central government declared an emergency, imposing president's rule. But this only inflamed Sikh extremists, who stepped up agitation and acts of violence. The deadly cycle of terrorism and police repression continued, and hundreds of people were killed in the first months of 1983 alone.

Bhindranwale directed activities from his headquarters in Amritsar's Golden Temple. The Indian army finally moved in, triggering a three-day battle in which almost 1,000 people were killed, including Bhindranwale himself and over 80 Indian soldiers. Dozens of Sikh religious institutions were raided by the Indian army in their search for extremists. Several thousand Sikh soldiers mutinied, in some cases setting off armed confrontations with the regular army, and there was a surge of support among Sikhs for an independent Khalistan. On October 31, 1984, the horror reached a climax when Indira Gandhi was struck down by two Sikh members of her personal bodyguard. Mobs in the capital went on a rampage, killing almost 3,000 Sikhs.

After calling for an end to the violence, Rajiv Gandhi sought a political solution. Assuming that the Akali Dal had been seeking participation in power rather than autonomy, much less independence, he gambled on state elections permitting the Sikh party to win and govern. But the political concessions may have come too late. In May 1987 the central government imposed president's rule on the Punjab once again, on the ground that the Akali Dal ministry had permitted terrorists and advocates of independence to take over. V. P. Singh vowed to heal ethnic and regional conflicts without giving in to separatism—no easy task. He visited the Punjab twice, and met a number of Sikh demands (for example, promising action against those accused of killing Sikhs in the aftermath of Indira's assassination). Chandra Shekhar also took part in talks with an Akali Dal leader. But violence continued unabated. Sikh militants went on robbing banks, killing Hindus at random, and assassinating politicians. On the final day of balloting in 1991 Sikhs attacked a train in the Punjab, killing 68 Hindu passengers. The elections were rescheduled, finally taking place in February 1992. But the threat of violence by Sikh militants kept voter turnout down to about 22 percent of the electorate; most of those who voted were Hindus, giving Congress (I) 12 of the 13 seats at stake. Violence in the Punjhab subsided, but the ethnic problem was far from being resolved.

Ethnic conflict also flared in Jammu and Kashmir, the only state with a Muslim majority. India and Pakistan had gone to war over Kashmir at the time of partition, when its Hindu ruler acceded to the Indian Union over the opposition of the Muslim population. Many Muslims in Kashmir remained receptive to cultural and political influences from Pakistan, and a special effort was needed to secure their participation in Indian parties and government. In 1987 Rajiv compelled the National Conference to enter into a coalition with Congress (I), then used police extensively to win the state elections. Local opinion was inflamed by this open intervention from the central government, and an armed rebellion broke out which continued after Rajiv's defeat in 1989. The government, led by the National Conference, was dismissed in January 1990. Virtual martial law took effect in early 1991, and elections were cancelled. The BJP decided to unfurl an Indian flag in Srinigar, capital of Kashmir, to celebrate Republic Day on January 26, 1992. Their caravan was blocked by Kashmiri rebels, who also bombed police headquarters in Srinigar. The BJP delegation was flown into Srinigar at night in order to raise the flag, and then departed in haste. It is probable that Kashmir can now be kept within the Indian Union only by force. The effort required to maintain a proper and workable balance between national unity and state autonomy is taxing the governing ability of the political class.

Remaking the map of India has gone hand in hand with an attempt to reorganize Indian society. The Constitution abolished untouchability and asserted the equality of women. This amounted in practice to a declaration of intent, because the status of 60 million untouchables and of women could not be changed overnight. Nonetheless, an act of Parliament unified marriage laws for the entire nation, permitting marriages between members of different castes and providing for divorce. The Untouchability Offences Act of 1955 made it illegal and punishable to discriminate against members of the untouchable class. But here, too, the enforceability of a statute was limited. More important are other developments that have the effect of undermining the traditional caste system. The design of new industrial towns does not take caste differences into account. The growing urbanization and industrialization of the nation are creating new patterns of life that weaken the millennia-old social structures. In addition, the Community Development Program is a positive force in furthering social change.

Despite undeniable progress in the past 40 years, caste remains a central fact of Indian life. Outcastes are still the victims of discrimination, beatings, and even killings if they enter high-caste neighborhoods, use Brahmin temples, or violate any of the numerous rituals consigning them to inferior status. In the 1991 election V. P. Singh made reform of the caste system a major campaign issue. Indian democracy cannot advance, nor can modernization be achieved, he argued, so long as three-fourths of the population (outcastes and Sudras) are kept down. His specific remedy—reserving almost half of government jobs for the lower castes—provoked a virulent reaction by higher-caste Hindus. The

backlash helped the militant Hindu BJP to virtually double its vote and become the second party of India in 1991. The Rao government in October 1991 decided to add 10 percent of central government jobs to those reserved for Muslims, Christians, and the poor. Reservation of government positions, as well as seats in the Lok Sabha and state legislatures, continues as public policy, even though controversial and subject to court challenge.

As part of the Community Development Program, the Indian government has revived a tradition of village rule by elders that had existed before the advent of the British—the *Panchayat* (or "council of five"). Mohandas Gandhi praised the *Panchayats* as agencies of local democracy, but his plea to reinstitute them was turned down by the Constituent Assembly. In 1958 the government asked each state to create a system of *Panchayati Raj* as a way of involving village residents in democratic decision making; most areas in India are now covered. Basically, each village elects a council of about a dozen members; the heads of these councils within a large area, together with other members, form a second-level group; and the heads of all the councils within a district, along with elected legislators in that district and others, constitute the highest-level group. The *Panchayati Raj* have brought about impressive popular participation in local political life; but instead of the consensus dreamed of by Gandhi, local elections reflect national party conflict. Nor have the *Panchayats* assumed increasing responsibility for economic development and planning, as originally hoped. A proposal by Rajiv to deepen and broaden the system of local government was defeated in Parliament. Decentralization has not been achieved through the *Panchayats,* and remains a major item on the political agenda.

It is in the economic domain that the heritage from the past has weighed most heavily. Modernization of the social structure is ultimately possible only with simultaneous modernization of the economy—each process being indispensable to the other. The great leader of the national independence movement, however, was unalterably opposed to industrialization. Gandhi once said,

India's salvation consists in unlearning what she has learned during the last fifty years. The railways, telegraphs, hospitals, lawyers, doctors and suchlike have all to go; and the so-called upper classes have to learn consciously, religiously, and deliberately the simple peasant life. . . . Every time I get into a railway car or use a motor bus I know that I am doing violence to my sense of what is right.[7]

This attitude may have been sound political tactics during the period when British rulers, in the eyes of the nationalists, were exploiting the Indian economy. It also represented a concession to Hindu culture, which seeks salvation in liberation from earthly existence, not in improvement thereof. After independence, however, Gandhi's successors had to face the problem of India's mass poverty. Some continued to exalt the virtues of village life and of a poor but spiritual existence, but the leadership of the Congress Party, particularly the group around Prime Minister Nehru, broke completely with the Gandhian tradition. They set about deliberately to create a modern economy through a series of five-year plans. A noted Indian journalist observed, in this connection: "Posterity will probably rate Gandhi as one of history's magnificent failures."[8] A five-year plan in India covers a multitude of activities, both governmental and private. A planning commission in Delhi establishes certain targets and goals, measures progress, and calls attention to shortcomings. The process is relatively relaxed, involving little discipline over the economy. The goal is to launch India into a "take-off" period so that the economy will gain momentum and expand on all fronts.

The First Plan (1951–1956) emphasized expansion of agricultural production and public works. Considerable progress was made in agriculture through irrigation projects, reform of landholding, and construction of fertilizer plants. The Community Development Program and the National Extension Services introduced cooperative techniques in the villages. Throughout this period, agricultural and industrial production and per capita income rose. The Second Plan (1956–1960) was only a partial success. Some progress was made in creating the infrastructure

of a modern economy; by 1959 industrial production had increased by more than 50 percent over 1951. Among the bright spots was striking growth in such industries as iron ore and steel (63 percent increase), chemicals (114 percent), and machine tools (324 percent). The productivity of labor in some steel mills and locomotive works approached European standards. Modern forms of business enterprise began to spread in the private sector, displacing the older artisans and speculator-capitalists. But agricultural production faltered during this period, and severe food shortages materialized in some parts of the country. The overall rate of increase in the gross national product slowed down.

The Third Plan (1961–1965) reestablished a priority for agriculture, but the results were again disappointing. Land reforms were planned but not implemented, and agriculture stagnated. In 1964 and 1965 poor harvests caused hoarding, looting of granaries, and widespread hunger riots. In 1965, the United States shipped one-sixth of its total wheat crop to India as an emergency measure in order to alleviate hardship. Defense spending after the military clashes with China in 1962 and Pakistan in 1965 diverted badly needed funds and foreign exchange away from capital investment and economic development.

Since then, the plans have been primarily attempts to set goals that will stimulate national effort, and have not served as realistic guides to economic development. The Fourth Plan (1966–1971) placed renewed emphasis on agriculture and industry, but inflation and the cost of supporting millions of refugees from Bangladesh made it impossible to realize goals. The Fifth Plan (1974–1979), which was not even approved until 1976, also called for substantial increases in agricultural and industrial production, along with redistribution of income in order to bridge the gap between rich and poor.

During the emergency, the government sought above all to reinforce social discipline, now identified as the key element in making possible genuine increases in productivity. When the Janata Party came to power in 1977, Prime Minister Desai called into question the previous grandiose schemes for rapid industrialization, advocating instead reliance on village and cottage industries. The Congress Party after returning to office also emphasized the need for self-sufficiency and for making slower but steadier economic progress. The Sixth Plan (1980–1985) and Seventh Plan (1985–1990), adopted under Rajiv, both concentrated on antipoverty programs. The Eighth Plan (1990–1995) continued the emphasis on social services.

The five-year plans originally reflected Nehru's belief that the Soviet model of centralized planning offered the best hope for rapid industrialization and social justice. He distrusted capitalism, equating it with speculation, greed, and economic stagnation. Indian business leaders resisted Nehru's brand of socialism, demanding instead encouragement of private enterprise. Their spokesperson within the Congress Party was the powerful S. V. Patel. The conflict between socialism and capitalism, which is fought out in Europe generally by separate political parties, took place in India within the Congress Party. By the mid–1950s a compromise was reached. A mixed economy would exist in which the state would have direct control of some key sectors (armaments, nuclear energy, railroads), and the exclusive right to start new ventures in such sectors as iron and steel, shipbuilding, aircraft production, and telecommunications; the state would closely regulate most other key industries but would otherwise recognize and protect a large private sector; and—a concession to the heritage of Mohandas Gandhi—village industry would also be encouraged.

But within this mixed economy, where would the line be drawn between public and private? Under Nehru, the emphasis was on state control and Socialist values. But in the mid–1960s, there was growing dissatisfaction with the Nehru model and a widespread desire to better serve consumer interests. The Swatantra Party, expressing the views of business, attacked the very concept of central planning and demanded the relaxation of government controls. Reflecting changes in public opinion, some measures to liberalize the economy were adopted by Nehru's successor, Lal Bahadur Shastri (1964–1966), and continued by Mrs. Gandhi.

In 1969 a split took place between Indira Gandhi and her more traditional rivals within the Congress. Mrs. Gandhi then swung to the left, sought allies among Socialists and Communists, and revived the Socialist policies of her father. Her government nationalized banks and insurance companies, the coal industry, textile mills, railroad car manufacture, and iron and steel production. Government control over the private sector was extended and strengthened. But the results of this sudden swing toward state ownership and control were disappointing: inflation, shortages and black markets, corruption and bribery, and economic stagnation. Mrs. Gandhi changed direction, loosening some controls. During emergency rule from 1975 to 1977, economic liberalization was given a boost by Sanjay Gandhi, who criticized the bureaucracy and lauded private enterprise.

After her return to office in 1980, Mrs. Gandhi resumed a policy of gradual deregulation of the economy. Her successor and son, Rajiv, determined to cut down the size of the public sector. The challenge was formidable. To take one example, the nationalized Steel Authority of India employed 250,000 people in producing 8 million tons of steel a year, at double the international price. In South Korea, the private Pohang steelworks produced 9 million tons of steel with 14,000 workers. Air India, to take another example, employed 17,000 people in 1987 to run 20 aircraft while racking up a loss of $40 million. In contrast, Singapore Airlines (admittedly an exceptionally efficient enterprise) ran twice as many aircraft with half as many workers, and at a profit. Rajiv became the apostle of professional management and deregulation—all the while proclaiming his devotion to the goal of social justice.

The trend toward liberalization of the economy continued under V. P. Singh, but his short-lived government was too enmeshed in controversy over ethnic violence and secularism to bring about much economic reform. His successor, Chandra Shekhar, pledged to stop liberalization, contending that the ills of India were caused by multinationals. But as the head of a caretaker government, he was in no position to take an independent line. When Congress (I) returned to power in June 1991, several factors heavily favored a liberal rather than a socialist approach to economic development. India requested a loan from the International Monetary

Fund to meet a severe shortage of foreign exchange; and the IMF strongly recommended expansion of the private sector. Also, the collapse of communism in Europe, the decision of the Chinese Communist regime to encourage private enterprise, and the crisis of social democracy in Western industrial societies had brought about a change in political culture. It was now widely accepted that complex economies could not be managed from one central point; the emphasis became decentralization, flexibility, and deregulation. In its first months in office the Rao government adopted sweeping measures to attract foreign investment and abolish many licensing requirements. Finance Minister Manmohan Singh declared that 90 of India's 244 huge state-owned enterprises are "patently unviable" and should be shut down. These 90 enterprises have about 800,000 employees, and cost the taxpayers $750 million annually in subsidies. Economic restructuring, in India as in Eastern Europe, causes difficulties for a large part of the population. Trade unions and left-wing parties organized public demonstrations, some turning violent, to protest the move toward a market economy. L. K. Advani, leader of the BJP, agreed that the reforms would have long-term advantages, but warned that the disadvantages had to be "bearable." Some within the Congress were wary of a policy that they saw as a betrayal of Mohandas Gandhi's goals of village industry and planning for human development.

Monumental and probably irreversible changes have taken place in the Indian economy, even though reforms slowed appreciably with the approach of elections scheduled for 1996. India's foreign reserves, down to almost nothing in June 1991, amounted to $20 billion four years later. The Bombay stock exchange boomed, as foreigners invested heavily in the Indian market. The Indian government gave virtually automatic approval to foreign companies creating joint ventures, and the massive, intricate system of controls and permits was at least partly dismantled. By 1994 industrial production increased by 8 percent annually, exports by 15 percent annually, and total foreign investments by $6 billion. American companies invested $700 million in 1994 alone, more than either Western Europe or Japan. Entry policy

(opening the economy to entry of foreign capital) was quite successful, though also stirring nationalist reactions. In 1995 Maharashtra state cancelled a contract with Enron, an American energy company, to build the largest power plant in India; and Kentucky Fried Chicken outlets were closed down on grounds that their products would cause cancer in Indian stomachs. Legal proceedings afforded the American companies some protection, but the warning lights went on.

Less progress was made in exit policy (getting the state out of unprofitable business). The government was able to sell equity in several profitable state-owned companies (in steel, petroleum, and machine tools primarily), raising about $1 billion. But no one will buy into companies producing at a loss; and organized labor, supported by opposition parties, energetically opposes closing or downsizing of these firms. A National Renewal Fund, created to help workers laid off in unprofitable state-owned firms, has been a costly drain on the budget. One extreme example is the Hindustan Fertilizer plant, which employs 1,550 workers. Since it was opened in 1986, this plant has produced nothing at all! One observer commented: "There is a canteen, a personnel department, and an accounts department. There are promotions, job changes, pay rises, audits, and in-house trade unions. Engineers, electricians, plumbers and painters maintain the equipment with a care that is almost surreal."[9]

In 1994 the cabinet vetoed the Finance Minister's plan to restructure state-owned textile firms running up huge losses. With elections looming, the prime minister and other ministers were unwilling to assume responsibility for layoffs. The Finance Minister himself admitted that large-scale privatization required broad public support, which could only materialize "after the election if there is a strong, powerful government at the Center." Beyond a certain point, he continued, "absolute cuts in expenditures may not be possible in a democracy. We cannot throw people into the pool of unemployed."[10] It has also proved politically impossible to cut food and fertilizer subsidies, which add enormously to the budget deficit. Yet, the momentum in favor of reforms is now so great that no major party openly favors a return to the bureaucratized, stagnant economy of the past. As the Indian middle and professional class, already among the world's largest, continues to grow, political pressures in favor of market-oriented economic development are bound to increase.

The Indian political class has come a long way from the heady days just after independence, when many Congress Party leaders hoped that socialism would create a highly productive, classless society with equal opportunity and a "good life" (as Nehru put it) for all. Modest improvement has been made in the standard of living of the masses. GNP in the first 40 years increased by about one-third, and agricultural production tripled. But unemployment has gone up, and most people continue to live in poverty. It is increasingly accepted that there is no easy way to industrialize an overwhelmingly traditional society, that social discipline is an essential ingredient in any policy of modernization, and that economic progress often produces heightened social strains and pressures.

MODERNIZATION AND DEMOCRACY

In any democracy, social and economic groups make claims upon the state; these claims constitute the raw material of the political process. Peasants, landlords, workers, managers, capitalists, merchants, and professionals, as well as ethnic, religious, and linguistic groups, press for satisfaction of their demands and participate in the process of working out compromises embodied in legislation. This continuing "crisis of participation" is a difficult challenge to political leaders even in long-established and prosperous democracies. When political systems are "overloaded" with claims and counterclaims, they become ineffective and unstable.

The "load" on Indian democracy by any standard is enormous. A large part of the electorate is opposed to modernization as such because it threatens traditional religious beliefs; others are primarily concerned with promotion of their caste, linguistic, or regional interests; and still others call for the revolutionary transformation of society. Many Indians have wondered whether democracy is not a luxury for their nation—in any event, to be subordinated to other considerations. In a deeply divided society, democracy may permit so much criticism and obstruction that government can no longer function. This classic issue of democratic theory—the point at which the right of minorities to express themselves subverts the right of the majority to rule—was posed with special force by Prime Minister Gandhi during the emergency.

Mrs. Gandhi at first justified her policy of suppressing the opposition as necessary to assure the nation's security. "The actions of a few," she declared in a radio broadcast to the nation, "are undermining the rights of the vast majority." India's enemies were rejoicing, she warned, at the sight of a nation tearing itself apart. In the following months, Mrs. Gandhi presented a more fully developed explanation of her resort to coercive means in order to attain democratic ends. The real challenge facing India, she said, is not how to maintain the right of an opposition to oppose anything and everything, but how to eliminate poverty, backwardness, and social abuses. She declared in a radio and television broadcast on November 10, 1975: "We want to fight and eliminate the poverty in our country prevailing since time immemorial. We want to remove backwardness. We can do so only if there is stability in the nation. And stability is impossible to achieve if unity gets weakened. . . . That was the problem before us." What was needed, above all, were "simple measures" to stamp out social abuses and anarchy.

Democracy is desirable, Mrs. Gandhi assured the nation, on one condition—that opposition be constructive. "But no one could claim that in the name of democracy anyone could do what he pleased and that such license was more important than India's progress, more important than the good of the Indian people." What was to be done? "There is only one magic which can remove poverty, and that is hard work sustained by clear vision, iron will, and the strictest discipline." To hammer home her point, Mrs. Gandhi frequently cited the problem of student agitation in universities. In a speech to the Rajya Sabha on July 22, 1975, for example, she recounted the tale of a train forced to stop over 30 times by students playfully pulling the emergency cord. When the engineer removed the cord, the students beat him up, put out the fire in the engine's boiler, and immobilized the train. Yet, concluded Mrs. Gandhi, no one would say that this was a "wrong thing" done by the students; by constantly challenging all authority, she claimed, the opposition made this kind of anarchy inevitable.

Many Indians agreed that poverty could never be alleviated in a climate of permissiveness and indiscipline. On the other hand, there was widespread dissatisfaction with authoritarian rule during the emergency—in particular, the arrest of opposition leaders and censorship of the press. Ample opportunities were afforded to members of the ruling party to suppress legitimate criticism, make arbitrary decisions, and even profit personally from their expanded political power. Public prosecutors under the Desai government claimed that the prime minister's son, Sanjay Gandhi, took advantage of his position to forward his career and finances. Democracy without consensus and social discipline may be ineffective (as seemed to be shown when the Janata Party proved incapable of governing after its victory in 1977), but authoritarianism invites the abuse of power evident during the emergency. It is in India, perhaps more than any other nation, that the ability of democracies to cope with the problems of modernization in the third world is on trial.

FOREIGN AFFAIRS

From its preindependence period, India inherited Mohandas Gandhi's advocacy of nonviolence, and also the geopolitical concerns of the British Raj. These two principles or policies have proved incompatible. In order to secure its borders, head off potential threats to its security from neighbors and their allies, and assert its claim to be the dominant power of South Asia, India created and used powerful military forces and engaged in traditional diplomacy. The manufacture and underground explosion of an atom bomb in May 1974, making India the sixth nation to become a nuclear power, dramatically illustrated India's resolve to safeguard its interests by military means. There is also widespread agreement that keeping up with advances in military technology requires a solid industrial and scientific base. The drive to modernize the Indian economy and society is intimately linked to the overall objectives of Indian foreign policy. This is a far cry from the Gandhian vision of village economy, spirituality, and conversion of enemies by persuading them of the evil of their ways.

Independent India's first prime minister, Jawaharlal Nehru, formulated the major principle of Indian foreign policy, to which all of his successors subscribed—nonalignment. For Nehru nonalignment meant a refusal to become part of the military alliance structures of either superpower, but it did not mean isolation or withdrawal from the international scene. On the contrary, the independence of India would enable it to intervene even more forcefully on specific issues in the cause of world peace. By avoiding alliances with either the United States or the Soviet Union, Indian leaders explained, they retained freedom of maneuver to defend their own national interests. Also, any alliance inevitably would cause divisions within Indian public opinion, create political instability, and divert attention from the pressing problem of dealing with poverty at home. For some Indians, moreover, each superpower represented a perceived evil—either capitalism or oppressive communism—and India represented a "third way" in which concern for humanity and social justice is combined with freedom. Critics of Indian foreign policy may express skepticism concerning Indian aspirations to (or illusions about) a higher idealism, but the ideals are nonetheless constantly invoked.

Since independence, India has been engaged in three wars with Pakistan, one war with China, military action against the remnants of Portuguese rule in Goa, frequent military activity in restive frontier areas, and military intervention in Sri Lanka. The most pressing foreign policy problem confronting India in the aftermath of independence was its dispute with Pakistan over Kashmir; relations with Pakistan remained thereafter a constant preoccupation. In 1947 partition was accompanied by communal violence and the forced movement of millions of refugees. Kashmir, with a population 80 percent Muslim, was ruled by a Hindu maharajah. In the face of resistance by Muslims, aided by tribesmen from across the border in Pakistan, the Hindu ruler called upon India for protection, and war broke out between Pakistan and India in the winter of 1947. Both sides accepted a cease-fire arranged by the United Nations in June 1948, with about one-third of the area held by Pakistan. Negotiations chaired by the UN brought no agreement among the parties, and resistance to Indian rule by Muslims continued. In 1965 conflict flared up between India and Pakistan in the Punjab, though a cease-fire took hold a few months later. In August guerrillas from Pakistan joined Muslim rebels in Kashmir. Indian and Pakistani forces entered the fray, and Indian forces struck out towards Lahore, in Pakistan itself. China came out in support of Pakistan; and both parties accepted a call by the UN Security Council for a cease-fire. The leaders of Pakistan (President Ayub Khan) and India (Prime Minister Lal Shastri) agreed to attend a conference chaired by Soviet Prime Minister Kosygin in Tashkent in January 1966. Partly as a tribute to Shastri, who died during the conference, India agreed to pull its forces back. But Pakistan appeared to be the victim of aggression; it began receiving military aid from China, and to a lesser extent, the Soviet Union.

In 1971 a popular uprising took place in East Pakistan against a virtual military occupation imposed by West Pakistan leaders who refused to accept the legitimacy of an election there. Many Bengals were killed by the Pakistani military, and some 10 million refugees, most of them Hindus, sought sanctuary in India. The Indian government assisted the rebels, Pakistan retaliated, and a full-scale war erupted. In a lightning campaign Indian forces occupied the East Pakistan capital, Dhaka, forced the surrender of the Pakistan army in the East, and declared a unilateral cease-fire in the West. Three months later the Indian army withdrew, refugees began to return, and Bangladesh became an independent nation. The secession of Bangladesh virtually assured India of domi-

nance over Pakistan, whose hostility remained, however, a thorny problem. In 1984 India accused Pakistan of giving aid and succor to Sikh nationalists in the Punjab, and provocative military exercises were conducted by both countries. Clashes continued along the border in Kashmir, and India renewed its charges that Pakistan was behind the rebellion there. The leaders of both countries talked ominously of war, which cannot be ruled out as a possibility in the future.

War with China in 1962, ending in a rout of Indian forces, came as a shock to India. Nehru had been eager to secure the friendship of the Chinese, despite uneasiness over their occupation of Tibet. In 1954 India and China agreed on five principles, notably nonaggression and peaceful coexistence, as defining a mutually beneficial friendship. But growing revolt against Chinese rule in Tibet undermined this friendship. Even more disturbing were claims by China to about 40,000 square miles of Indian territory that it argued had never been within the authority of Great Britain to hand over. The Chinese were intent on securing lines of communication to Tibet, applying pressure also along the Northeast Frontier. India declared a state of emergency, and Chinese forces struck. After pushing back the Indian army, the Chinese announced a cease-fire, withdrew their forces in the Northeast, but retained control of roads to Tibet. In 1987 a threat of renewed hostilities was averted by diplomatic talks and a visit to China by Rajiv. But the quarrel over borders has not been settled, remaining a sticking point in relations between the world's two most populous nations.

India's continuing conflict with both Pakistan and China has been a fundamental determinant of its foreign policy. As the Chinese became embroiled with the Russians in a territorial as well as an ideological dispute, India was drawn closer to the Soviet Union. Russians and Indians saw in each other allies of a kind against a common foe—China. Similarly, India became less friendly to the United States as the Americans joined the Chinese in offering military and economic aid to Pakistan (which, in turn, was a valuable military asset in the Sino-

American confrontation with the Soviet Union). In 1971 India signed a treaty of peace, friendship, and cooperation with the Soviet Union that reflected also Indira Gandhi's growing collaboration with the Communist Party of India. The friendship treaty, it was argued by Indian leaders, did not represent a departure from nonalignment because no military alliance was involved. The "tilt" toward the Soviet Union did not prevent India from seeking and receiving massive aid from the United States to avert famine and help develop its economy. With the virtual elimination of Pakistan as a military threat, India became less sensitive over the U.S. program of aid to Pakistan, and relations between India and the United States improved markedly after the Janata Party's victory in 1977. The Russian invasion of Afghanistan in 1979 confronted Prime Minister Gandhi with an exceedingly delicate problem: how to prevent the United States from reinforcing and rearming Pakistan without at the same time endorsing Russian military intervention in an area of concern to India.

India was drawn into an ethnic conflict in Sri Lanka (formerly Ceylon) supposedly to protect the Tamil minority, but also to ensure that no foreign powers would exploit the situation and establish their influence in the region. Tamils, who make up one-fifth of the population of Sri Lanka, receive sympathetic support as well as material aid and arms from the Tamils of India, just across the strait. When the ethnic conflict worsened in 1987, Rajiv Gandhi took the lead in negotiating a peace agreement that in principle put an end to the turmoil. Nevertheless, some 50,000 Indian troops, dispatched to Sri Lanka to establish law and order, soon became involved in hostilities with the very Tamil militants whose interests they were originally supposed to safeguard. A suicide squad of Tamil terrorists (the Liberation Tigers) took revenge four years later by assassinating Rajiv.

In drawing up a balance sheet of independent India's foreign policy, the record of achievement is impressive. After a long period of stalemate, India emerged victorious from its historical rivalry with Pakistan and is now the dominant power in South Asia. However, India continues to accuse Pakistan of supporting Sikh nationalists in the Punjab and Muslim rebels in Kashmir, and is concerned that Pakistan is a wedge of American and Chinese influence in the region. The northern frontier is still vulnerable to Chinese pressure, and memories of India's defeat by the Chinese in 1962 still rankle. Until 1991 India adhered to its policy of nonalignment, avoiding alliances with either the United States or the Soviet Union, receiving economic and military aid from both, and reserving the right to disagree with both. In practice, India tended to be more free in its condemnation of the United States than of the Soviet Union (for example, defending Russia's intervention in Hungary in 1956).

Despite a continuing confrontation with its great neighbor to the north, it can be concluded that the Indian political class since independence has been fairly successful in defending the territorial integrity and basic interests of the nation. The ultimate test of a foreign policy is survival. Pakistan in its original form has failed that test; India—except for relatively minor incursions by the Chinese in the northern territories—has passed it. Given the deep social divisions and severe economic problems that existed when independence was proclaimed, foreign policy accomplishments attested to the vitality and effectiveness of the Indian political system.

With the growing crisis of communism in the 1980s, and the collapse of the Soviet Union after the failed coup of August 1991, a pillar of Indian foreign policy crumbled. Nonalignment can no longer have the same meaning in a world with one dominant superpower, and an ascendant Western economic model. When Iraq invaded Kuwait in 1990 the Indian government at first leaned toward Iraq, which had given India support on the Kashmir question and also was a major supplier of oil. After the Soviet Union gave its support to the United Nations, India went along with sanctions against Iraq. However, when the Chandra Shekhar government accorded permission to American air force planes to refuel, it was denounced by Rajiv for departing from the principle of nonalignment, and the government reversed course. The old reflex of backing any third world country against the West, and particularly against the United States, came to the fore. India seemed caught in a time warp during the attempted overthrow of Gorbachev by old-line Communists. Both Indian Communist parties applauded the coup, and the Indian government did not denounce it. Gorbachev's return and Yeltsin's triumph required a complete recasting of Indian policy towards Russia and the other successor states. Distrust of the United States, which for much of the intellectual class represents materialism and imperialism, runs deep. But the Rao government mounted a major effort to attract American capital, particularly in the form of joint ventures. Even the Communist-led government of West Bengal joined in the campaign to persuade Wall Street to invest in the Indian economy. Also, the almost 1 million Indians residing in the United States are beginning to serve as an important interactive channel between the two countries. With Russia no longer a counterbalance, India has a great incentive to improve relations with the industrial West, including the United States. But the heritage of Gandhian principles, Nehru's nonalignment policies, and solidarity with third world countries is weighty. A fundamental review of foreign policy is one of the major challenges facing Indian government in the post–Cold War era.

KEY TERMS

Akali Dal
Bhindranwale, Sant Jarnail Singh
The Emergency (1975–1977)
Five Year Plans
nonalignment
Panchayat
Punjab

FURTHER READINGS

Bardhan, P. *The Political Economy of Development in India* (Oxford: Basil Blackwell, 1984).

Bradnock, R. *India's Foreign Policy Since 1971* (New York: Council on Foreign Relations Press, 1990).

Frankel, F. *India's Political Economy, 1944–1977* (Princeton: Princeton University Press, 1978).

Frankel, F., and M. S. Rao, eds. *Dominance and State Power in India: Decline of a Social Order,* 2 vols. (New York: Oxford University Press, 1990).

Ganguly, S. *U.S. Policy Toward South Asia* (Boulder, CO: Westview Press, 1990).

Jalan, B., ed. *The Indian Economy: Problems and Prospects* (New Delhi: Viking/Penguin, 1992).

Kohli, Atul. *The State and Poverty in India: The Politics of Reform* (New York: Cambridge University Press, 1987).

Nadkarni, M. V., A. S. Seetharamu, and A. Abdul, eds. *India: The Emerging Challenges* (New Delhi: Sage, 1991).

Oldenburg, P., ed. *India Briefing: Staying the Course* (Armonk, NY: M. E. Sharpe, 1995).

Palmer, N. D. *The United States and India: The Dimensions of Influence* (New York: Praeger, 1984).

Rudolph, L. I., and S. H. Rudolph. *In Pursuit of Lakshmi: The Political Economy of the Indian State* (Chicago: University of Chicago Press, 1987).

Weiner, M. *Sons of the Soil: Migration and Ethnic Conflict in India* (Princeton: Princeton University Press, 1978).

Weiner, M. *The Child and the State in India* (Princeton: Princeton University Press, 1991).

Ziring, L., ed. *The Subcontinent in World Politics: India, Its Neighbors, and the Great Powers,* rev. ed. (New York: Praeger, 1982).

NOTES

1. From Gandhi's article, "The Doctrine of the Sword," written in 1920, cited in *Toward Freedom, The Autobiography of Jawaharlal Nehru* (Boston: Beacon Press, 1958), p. 82.
2. Cited in T. Walter Wallbank, *A Short History of India and Pakistan* (New York: Mentor, 1958), p. 196.
3. Ibid., p. 213.
4. Ibid., p. 217.
5. cf. Michael Brecher, *Nehru: A Political Biography* (New York: Oxford University Press, 1961), p. 149.
6. Atul Kohli, ed. *India's Democracy: An Analysis of Changing State-Society Relations* (Princeton: Princeton University Press, 1990), p. 309.

7. Cited in Wallbank, *A Short History,* p. 157.

8. Frank Moraes, *India Today* (New York: Macmillan, 1964), p. 89.

9. *The Financial Times,* London, June 6, 1994. Cited by Meghnad Desai, "Economic Reform: Shattered by Politics?" in Philip Oldenburg, ed., *India Briefing: Staying the Course* (Armonk, NY: M. E. Sharpe) p. 91. Desai added: "Like China, India may live with an inefficient public sector for a long time."

10. Interview with Finance Minister Manmohan Singh, *India Today,* October 15, 1995, pp. 28–29.

The Government of Mexico

Martin C. Needler

Political Development

Mexico is a distinctive country in many ways. When the astonished Spaniards first laid their eyes on the capital city, Tenochtitlán, at the beginning of the sixteenth century, they were looking at a city probably greater in population than any in Europe at the time. Counting methods vary depending on how much of the metropolitan region is included, but by some modes of reckoning Mexico City is today, with over 22 million people, again the largest city in the world.

The ancient Aztecs had one of the distinctive civilizations of the ancient world, and some of that distinctiveness is apparent today in the way of life of their descendants. To its Spanish conquerors, Mexico offered a deluge of products which have since made their way into the diets of people all over the world; today Mexico may be known abroad for its cuisine, its twentieth-century school of mural painting, or its considerable petroleum production. Politically, as we shall see, Mexico is significant in having pioneered the political system now found throughout Africa and Asia, that of the dominant single party, sometimes known as the hegemonic party or the "democratic single-party system."

Mexico City has all the ills of a metropolis in the third world—impossible traffic jams, overcrowded buses, slums, and pollution. It contains about one-quarter of the national population, currently estimated at 90 million. Although the metropolis is the country's preeminent city in commerce, culture, and communications, as well as in politics, five other Mexican cities have over 1 million inhabitants and about two-thirds of the national population is considered urban. But that also means that a third of the population continues to live in the country's villages, of which there are more than 50,000 distributed over the 761,000 square miles of the national territory.

The rural population is not spread evenly over the country, however. Much of Mexico is arid; perhaps 10 percent of the land surface receives rainfall adequate for unirrigated agriculture. Nevertheless, vast irrigation schemes have made possible the development of farming in these arid zones (especially in the Northern region of the country, which has emerged as a center for the export of fruit and vegetables to the United States), along with cattle raising, light industry, and tourism in the coastal resorts. Moving south, as the breadth of North America narrows toward the Central American isthmus, one encounters the mountainous, semiarid Center-North region, whose principal economic activity has always been mining; copper has overtaken silver as the leading product of this industry.

The Central region, focused on the national capital and the Federal District, has always had the densest concentration of population. In the rural areas there is dense settlement throughout the mountain valleys and the soils have been continuously worked for centuries, deteriorating in quality and providing no more than a bare subsistence for those who try to eke out a living on their tiny plots of land. A more productive agriculture is found in the Western region of the country, centering on the country's second largest city, Guadalajara. Its interconnected river valleys draining toward the Pacific provide rich soils and a long growing season. This rich area is a focus of Spanish colonial tradition and a stronghold of the Catholic Church. The Eastern region, on the coast of the Gulf of Mexico, resembles areas of the Caribbean; it has plantations growing tropical products such as rice and sugar cane, and in the past African slaves were brought to the region, which today has a large mulatto population.

What the Mexicans call the South, the mountains lying south and west of the capital city, is a region of small cultivators and only slowly growing population. Its principal state, Oaxaca, is the most Indian state of Mexico; it is only recently that a majority of the population of the state has come to use Spanish and not one of the Indian languages by preference. The Yucatán peninsula, the "Southeast," which juts out into the Caribbean, is also firmly Indian in culture, although the Indians there are Maya—akin to the people of Guatemala rather than those of central Mexico—and still hold to a distinctive way of life.

It should be noted that in Mexico, as in the rest of Latin America, "Indian" is a cultural rather than a physical or genetic category. Physically, most Mexicans are Indian or mixed Spanish and Indian, that is, *mestizo*. A person ceases to be an Indian by acculturating to dominant national norms and abandoning specifically Indian characteristics, such as going barefoot, sleeping in a hammock or on the floor, and especially speaking an Indian language rather than Spanish. Clearly, it is difficult to remain culturally Indian in a city, but many Mexicans in rural areas are in transition from one way of life to another, changing their style of dress, using Spanish predominantly, and modifying their diet to include bread and canned goods.

Interestingly, however, although the national culture and way of life are predominantly modern and European, with only an admixture of Indian elements, psychologically Mexicans identify with their Indian past and not with the Spanish conquerors. There are statues in Mexico of Moctezuma and Cuauhtémoc, the last Aztec emperors, but not one of Hernando Cortés, the Spaniard who conquered them. In fact, the tale of how heroic but doomed Indians were conquered by ignoble but technologically superior Spaniards has provided some interesting paradigms by which Mexicans understand their national history. As Mexican psychologist Jorge Carrión has put it, "The history of Mexico is full of stories which endure in it more because of their psychological value than because of the authenticity of their testimony."

HISTORICAL SUMMARY TO 1910

When most Mexicans think about the country's history, they see it as a pattern, repeated over and over. The pattern is that of heroic Mexicans trying to defend themselves against more powerful foreigners and being defeated, partly because of betrayal by some Mexicans who have sided with the foreigners. The conquest itself was made possible because Cortés had the assistance of some of the indigenous tribes and of

Pyramid of the Sun, Teotihuacan.

his mistress and interpreter, Malinche. The original movement for independence, led at the beginning of the nineteenth century by Father Miguel Hidalgo and Father José María Morelos, who were themselves defeated and killed by the Spaniards, was finally successful when the upper classes, afraid that their privileges would be taken away by a liberal Spanish government, joined the cause of independence. Their leadership, however, nullified the original populist impulse of the independence movement, and their military leader, Agustín Iturbide, proclaimed himself emperor.

During the chaotic period of revolts, rigged elections, and foreign interventions that constituted the first half century of Mexican independence, law and order broke down, the economy decayed, and the country's finances were looted. The United States, under President James K. Polk, took advantage of the situation to provoke a war in which U.S. troops occupied Mexico City. The war was concluded in 1848 by the Treaty of Guadalupe-Hidalgo, which led, together with the subsequent Gadsden Purchase, to the annexation by the United States of present-day Texas, New Mexico, Arizona, and California, approximately half of what had been the territorial area of Mexico.[1]

A few years later Napoleon III of France used the Mexicans' suspension of payments on their foreign debt as a pretext to send an army to Mexico whose real purpose was to create a French-dependent Mexican empire with Archduke Maximilian of Austria as Emperor. Maximilian and his bride, Carlotta, apparently believed in all innocence that the opportunistic reactionaries who came to his palace outside Trieste to offer him the crown represented the popular will of the people of Mexico.

In fact, they were simply looking for a way out of the anti-clerical and anti-elite program, known as La Reforma, being put into effect by a Liberal government under Benito Juárez. Juárez led the military resistance against Maximilian, who was finally executed after his May 1867 surrender. Juárez, regarded by Mexicans as their greatest president, only survived his triumph by five years, and his successor as president was overthrown in a successful revolt in 1876. The new caudillo—the dominant person-

alist leader—who took power and dominated the politics of Mexico for 35 years, was Porfirio Díaz. Díaz was to serve as president for all but one term of the period until he was overthrown in 1910. Díaz began in politics as a Liberal and follower of Juárez, but his regime reinterpreted the idea of progress embodied in Liberalism to mean social and economic development brought about by the encouragement of foreign investment, and the suppression of Mexico's Indian character. Díaz imposed a "law and order" that involved intimidating the lower classes, especially Indian peasants. He promoted economic development—railroad building, mining, communications, and power generation—on the basis of special concessions for foreign investors. Large estates were built up, sometimes in foreign hands, and traditional Liberal anti-clericalism was abandoned.

The Díaz regime was a great success, at least in the eyes of foreigners. But Díaz's fatal mistake was maintaining control with the same closed group that had come to power with him and leaving no openings for new middle- and upper-class elements. There were sectors of the population with legitimate grievances against the Díaz regime—Indians who were discriminated against, peasants who had lost their land to cronies of the president, workers in the new industries who were not allowed to organize and seek better conditions, business people whose competitors had better government connections. But just as a hydrogen bomb can only be set off by the explosion of an atom bomb that acts as its trigger, the great social movement that was the Mexican Revolution of 1910 needed a smaller revolution to get it going, the initial uprising against Díaz. This was an upper-class movement led by Francisco Madero, who came from a landholding family in the northern state of Coahuila.

Madero's original political goal had been limited to getting Díaz to open his regime to some new blood, but it was treated by Díaz as subversion, and Madero's movement became an open revolt. Taken by surprise by the support garnered by the uprising, Díaz resigned. An interim government held elections, which were won by Madero. However, Madero made the mistake of not being revolutionary enough, leaving in office the officials and generals who had served under Díaz; subsequently, some of them conspired with the ambassador of the Taft administration to overthrow Madero's government. Madero was removed, and then shot, by the military commander, General Victoriano Huerta, known for his brutality, corruption, and drunkenness. A revolution against the Huerta government was not long in coming. It did not have a single leader, however, and the division among the revolutionary forces led to fighting among them after Huerta was defeated and overthrown.

THE MEXICAN REVOLUTION: THE EARLY YEARS

The principal revolutionary forces were led by figures that have become legendary in Mexican history. Emiliano Zapata, from the state of Morelos, continued to fight, as he had since the Díaz administration, on behalf of small landholders whose land had been taken from them by force or fraud; he had opposed Madero once it became clear that Madero was not serious about land reform. In the northern border state of Chihuahua, an army was raised by Francisco "Pancho" Villa (Doroteo Arango). Villa was a former soldier in the federal army who had escaped from the military prison where he had been placed for disobeying orders. Vaguely populist in ideological terms, Villa attracted followers—including intellectuals who wrote his political material—by his colorful and forceful personality, but he repelled others by his cruelty and opportunism. Villa's historical reputation has never been secure, and only belatedly, and after much discussion, did the Mexican Congress agree to include him in the pantheon of Revolutionary heroes whose names are inscribed in its hall. Zapata, on the other hand, is regarded in Mexican history as a man of noble and unselfish ideals.

Venustiano Carranza was the leader closest, historically and politically, to Madero. As senator and acting governor of Madero's home state of Coahuila under Porfirio Díaz, Carranza's support of Madero was important in giving credibility and impetus to the original revolution. Moderate and quite unrevolutionary

---

Feature 10.1 The Position of Women in Mexico

In the political and social position of women, Mexico presents the picture of a traditional society only feebly beginning to modernize. This is not due directly to the strength of the Catholic church, since revolutionary governments were officially anti-clerical until recently and the promotion of family planning through birth control, despite Church opposition, has been national policy since President Echeverría. Women could not vote or run for office in national elections until 1953. Thereafter, women's organizations were formed within the PRI, but they were primarily self-promotional gimmicks for their leaders; females have constituted less than 10 percent of the membership of the national Congress and have had only token representation in the cabinet.

The contemporary feminist movement was stimulated by developments in the United States and has campaigned for legalized abortions and against rape and domestic violence. But the situation remains dismal. Abortions, though illegal, are common (estimated in 1987 at 2 million per year, with perhaps 10,000 fatalities). Even in Mexico City, estimates are that in 1990, when penalties increased from their previous trivial level, only 1 in 30 rapes was reported to the police; there seems to be no point, since only 1 in 20 rape complaints results in conviction and sentence. The Federal District has started to fund a few rape victims' counseling centers, but there are no shelters for battered women. Despite the extreme frequency of domestic violence, it has not been recognized as a problem for public policy.

Emiliano Zapata (1879–1919), Mexican revolutionary leader who advocated land reform and controlled part of Mexico, was killed by government troops in 1919.

in his aims, Carranza always regarded himself as the authentic heir to Madero and his logical successor. Carranza's claims were finally vindicated; he was recognized in October 1915 as de facto president by the United States and was formally elected constitutional president in March 1917 under terms of a new constitution.

This result was only achieved after much fighting, however. After the defeat of Huerta's forces, an interim national government representing all of the revolutionary factions was dominated by a coalition between Villa and Zapata. Carranza refused to accept the authority of this government; his armies, commanded by the best military strategist the revolution produced, Alvaro Obregón of the state of Sonora, defeated Villa's forces in a series of battles. Villa

finally made peace and was allowed to retire. He was later assassinated, presumably with Obregón's complicity, when he was preparing to resume political activity. Zapata—like all the leaders of the first phase of the Mexican Revolution—was also assassinated.

Carranza's election took place under the terms of the new revolutionary constitution. This document had been drafted by the radical majority of the constituent convention and represented a progressive social democratic perspective. Ownership of mineral resources was vested in the national government, not in the owner of the surface of the land; labor's rights to organize and strike were guaranteed; and religious bodies were forbidden to own property. Carranza himself ran a moderate administration, and the social provisions of the constitution were only implemented by the succeeding presidency of Obregón. For a list of Mexican presidents since 1917, see Table 10.1.

Obregón announced his presidential candidacy with criticisms of the moderation of the

Table 10.1   PRESIDENTS OF MEXICO, 1917–2000

Years in Office	Name
1917–1920	Venustiano Carranza
1920	Adolfo de la Huerta
1920–1924	Alvaro Obregón
1924–1928	Plutarco Elías Calles
1928–1930	Emilio Portes Gil
1930–1932	Pascual Ortiz Rubio
1932–1934	Abelardo Rodríguez
1934–1940	Lázaro Cárdenas
1940–1946	Manuel Avila Camacho
1946–1952	Miguel Alemán
1952–1958	Adolfo Ruiz Cortines
1958–1964	Adolfo López Mateos
1964–1970	Gustavo Díaz Ordaz
1970–1976	Luis Echeverría
1976–1982	José López Portillo
1982–1988	Miguel de la Madrid
1988–1994	Carlos Salinas de Gortari
1994–2000	Ernesto Zedillo

Carranza government, making it impossible for Carranza to support him. Given traditional Mexican political practices, under which the candidate favored by the incumbent administration always won the election, there was plausibility to Obregón's charge that Carranza was planning to rig the elections to impose his own choice of successor, and Obregón led a revolt. Against Obregón's instructions, Carranza—again, like the other major revolutionary figures—was assassinated. An interim government under Obregón's fellow-Sonoran, Adolfo de la Huerta, organized elections which were duly won by Obregón.

The administration of Alvaro Obregón (1920–1924) was especially significant. The revolt that made it possible was the last successful revolt in Mexican history, as Obregón himself foresaw. Of an unsuccessful revolt against his government in 1923, he wrote "a progressive evolution has been slowly taking place; . . . it is no longer possible to start a revolution in Mexico and immediately thereafter find popular support. . . . I feel strongly that this will be the last military rebellion in Mexico."[2] This was so in part because Obregón reorganized the guerrilla armies of the revolution—which had consisted of bands haphazardly recruited, trained, and organized, and owing loyalty to specific individuals—into a regular army based on discipline, hierarchy, and loyalty to the constitutional authorities. More important, he pursued policies that won broad popular support so that in a future crisis the great majority of the population would actively support the government, rather than remain passive bystanders or support armed insurrection. The Obregón administration took a clear position in favor of the efforts of labor unions to organize, establish a national trade union confederation, raise wages, and improve working conditions. Moreover, Obregón began to implement land reform legislation passed under Carranza, thus winning over the former supporters of Zapata.

The payoff came in the rebellion of 1923. Obregón chose as his successor General Plutarco Elías Calles, the third of the revolutionary leaders from Sonora. This was resented by the former interim president, de la Huerta, who thought the nomination should rightfully have

gone to him, and in the traditional fashion he began a revolt. The army, not yet thoroughly reorganized, split about evenly, but one of the major factors that tipped the balance of power in favor of Obregón was the participation on his side of volunteer battalions and irregular forces of workers and peasants. Something new had occurred in Mexican history: Workers and peasants fought on behalf of an incumbent government instead of against it.

The coalition that Obregón had put together degenerated somewhat under Calles. Although Calles started from a radical revolutionary position, this was soon modified by his growing conservatism and connivance in financial irregularities. A strong pro-labor position became in fact acquiescence in labor racketeering and allowing companies to buy their way out of labor difficulties. The threatened resumption by the Mexican state, under the terms of the new constitution, of mineral rights ceded to foreign oil companies was somehow negotiated through the good offices of the U.S. ambassador to allow companies active before 1917 to retain their oil concessions. Calles became disillusioned with the land reform program, coming to believe that land was more productive when privately owned than when collectively owned by Indian communities, which was the mode in which most of the expropriated land had been redistributed.

Calles, a former school teacher, nevertheless continued Obregón's program of expansion of the educational system and the building of schools. He also followed up the program of the professionalization of the military; purging of the officers who had supported de la Huerta's rebellion made it possible to reduce the size of the military budget, the officers corps, and the army as a whole. Moreover, Calles went further than Obregón in enforcing the anti-clerical provisions of the Constitution. Catholic resistance to the harsh measures taken by Calles included the suspension of religious services, and indeed a guerrilla war broke out against the government, centered in the devout Bajío region of western Mexico. The government conducted a ruthless counterinsurgency campaign against these "warriors of Christ the King" or *cristeros*, which was not called off until the end of Calles's term.

The country was in fact ready for a return to the more conciliatory and pro-agrarian policies of Obregón, and the former president indicated that he was ready to return for a new term. For this to happen, the Constitution had to be amended because it had enshrined the principle of no presidential reelection that had been the banner of Madero's revolution against Porfirio Díaz. Accordingly, Congress passed an amendment making the prohibition of reelection apply only to consecutive reelection.[3] Thus Obregón would be eligible for the term that began in 1928. Moreover, another amendment extended the presidential term from four to six years. Elections were held and the popular Obregón was reelected, although not before a revolt by three frustrated would-be candidates had been put down. The Cristero War, however, was to claim its last victim. A group of religious fanatics, under the mistaken impression that Obregón was responsible for the anti-clerical policies of Calles, organized the assassination of the president-elect, and Obregón joined the long line of revolutionary heroes brought to an untimely end.

At this point Calles rose to the occasion with an act of statesmanship. It was generally expected that he would use the pretext of Obregón's assassination to extend his own term; in fact, some disgruntled pro-agrarian supporters of Obregón went so far as to claim that Calles himself was behind the assassination. Calles, however, made clear that constitutional procedures, which called for the Congress to elect a provisional president until new popular elections could be organized, would be followed. Moreover, he took the assassination as a lesson that the political system of the Revolution should not have to depend on individual personalities, arguing that the time had come to place the regime on a more stable institutional footing by organizing a political party that would embody the aspirations of the revolution in permanent form. Up to that point, different leaders had organized ad hoc parties of their followers, while other parties represented major interest groups. Following the end of his term, accordingly, Calles organized the National Revolutionary Party, *Partido Nacional Revolucionario* (PNR), the precursor of the party that rules Mexico today.

For the provisional presidency, Congress elected Emilio Portes Gil, a young pro-agrarian former state governor acceptable to both Obregón and Calles supporters. The president elected to serve out Obregón's term was Pascual Ortiz Rubio, who turned out to be conservative, weak, and inconsistent. He referred all major decisions to Calles, who came to be regarded as Mexico's strong man and the real ruler of the country. Finally, the country's leading political figures refused to serve in Ortiz Rubio's cabinet, so he followed Calles's last piece of advice: He resigned. The remaining two years of the first six-year presidential term were filled by a moderate former general and associate of Calles, Abelardo Rodríguez, who had developed extensive business interests, especially in the North.

THE CARDENAS ERA

The first president to serve out the full six-year term (1934–1940) was General Lázaro Cárdenas, regarded by most Mexicans as the greatest president produced by the Revolution. He was also its most leftist president. Land reform proceeded at a pace that was probably the maximum technically feasible, and was no longer merely a question of restoring land wrongfully taken from Indian communities. Land could be expropriated from a landholder owning more than a certain amount and then assigned to any group of landless agricultural workers living in the vicinity. As with the Indian communities, however, ownership was vested in the group rather than in the individual, although—under an amendment to the law passed during the Calles administration—the right to farm specific plots of land could be inherited within a family. Under Cárdenas, however, some lands that were producing hemp (for rope) and cotton were set up as collective farms after expropriation, rather than being subdivided for individual family farming.

The Cárdenas administration was strongly pro-labor, promoting labor organization and consistently favoring workers in industrial disputes. The racketeering head of the principal labor federation, Luis Morones, who had been a major political figure under Calles but was cut off from government favor by Portes Gil, was now overshadowed as the dominant figure in organized labor by a leftist intellectual named Vicente Lombardo Toledano.

Although generally pragmatic on economic questions, Cárdenas inclined to nationalism and socialism and was responsible for setting up some state corporations. The railroads were nationalized, as was the oil industry, after an industrial dispute in which most of the foreign-owned oil companies had made themselves thoroughly unpleasant and unpopular. The oil nationalization in 1938 and the setting up of a state oil corporation, today called *Petróleos Mexicanos*, or PEMEX, is generally regarded as one of the high points in Mexican nationalism. After the expropriation, the foreign companies, which were vertically integrated—that is, they controlled the industry from exploration and development through processing and retailing—organized an international boycott of Mexican oil; the role of the state company was thus limited to supplying Mexico's own domestic needs.

Cárdenas also followed a left-wing line in foreign policy. He was president from 1934 to 1940, a highly emotional era in which the coming battle between democracy and the Fascist powers was taking shape. Cárdenas took a strong pro-Republican position in the Spanish Civil War and refused to recognize the Franco government at the war's conclusion. Mexico became the home of the Republican government-in-exile, and diplomatic relations with the government of Spain were not resumed until after Franco's death many years later.

Cárdenas also reorganized the ruling party to fit his leftist and nationalist principles. The party was renamed the Mexican Revolutionary Party, *Partido Revolucionario Mexicano* (PRM); it was reorganized explicitly as an alliance of classes, with separate "sectors" representing organized labor, collective peasant landholders, and progressive elements of the middle class. This last sector, called "popular," consisted primarily of unions of teachers and government white-collar workers, along with smaller associations of professionals, small private farmers, and small-business people. Cárdenas also included the armed forces as a full sector of the party, but this was not popular within the military itself, and the military sector was abolished

by Cárdenas's successor after two or three years of existence.

THE ERA OF "STABLE DEVELOPMENT"

The moderate Manuel Avila Camacho, who served from 1940 to 1946, was the last general to be elected president of Mexico. He continued the work of his predecessors in reducing the political role of the army. A staff officer rather than a heroic leader in battle, Avila Camacho was little known before his nomination for the presidency; in fact, some called him "the unknown soldier." In the presidential elections he was opposed by an extremely popular general, the highest-ranking officer on active duty before he resigned to enter politics, Juan Andreu Almazán. With support gathered from the interests alienated either by Calles or by Cárdenas—devout Catholics, business interests, disgruntled elements in the military, and even labor factions opposed to Lombardo Toledano—there seemed to be a chance that Almazán might get a majority of the vote. Unwilling to accept a victory for what looked like a coalition of the forces defeated by the revolution, Cárdenas agreed to the announcement of a fraudulent result. Apparently, Almazán won a majority in the Federal District, although not in the country at large, but in any case those were not the results announced.

Avila Camacho showed that the Mexican rule of no presidential reelection allows for the kind of flexibility that has enabled the system to survive; it is the tree that is able to bend with the wind that does not break. Another popular analogy has it that a presidential succession resembles a pendulum: Incoming presidents usually swing away from the unpopular or unviable policies of their predecessors, making concessions to the groups most dissatisfied with their predecessors' policies.

What this meant for the president who followed Cárdenas was a position of greater moderation. The pace of land reform was slowed down, and no other industries were nationalized. Avila Camacho did begin a social security system for workers, but its coverage is still limited to employees of government and larger modern firms and does not extend to all Mexican workers. Hostilities against the church were called off, and good relations were fostered with the United States. Mexico participated in its first war on the same side as the United States when an air squadron was sent to fight the Japanese in the Pacific. Arrangements were worked out for the *bracero* program, under which Mexican laborers were contracted to work in the United States for fixed periods. Lombardo Toledano was eased out of his leadership position in the CTM, the Mexican Confederation of Labor, and replaced by the more moderate Fidel Velázquez, still the secretary-general of the CTM over 50 years later.

Avila Camacho capped his policies of national reconciliation and government from the center of the political spectrum by again reorganizing the ruling party, this time renaming it the *Partido Revolucionario Institucional* (PRI), the Institutional Revolutionary Party, symbolizing the final coming to maturity of the revolution. Indeed, since Avila Camacho the country has been run by civilian presidents on the basis of centrist economic policies and a modus vivendi with the Church and with the United States. Stimulated first by the wartime lack of consumer goods to import, and then by the boom that followed World War II, the Mexican economy entered a long and sustained period of stable economic growth that ended only with the economic collapse that followed the fall in oil prices at the beginning of the 1980s.

The following president, Miguel Alemán (1946–1952), carried the pendulum further away from the Cárdenas years. Strongly pro-business, he presided over a threefold increase in Mexico's exports, a doubling of the value of agricultural production, and a 42 percent increase in industrial activity. At the same time, the state sector of the economy expanded and Mexico enjoyed a substantial increase in tourism. The increase in agricultural production resulted from the irrigation of vast expanses of dry land, especially in the North. This newly productive land was sold to private agribusiness interests, not distributed to landless peasants, who in any case live mostly in the center of the country. But the land reform program dwindled and some categories of large landholding were

made exempt from expropriation. These were golden years for private business interests, including the personal interests of the president and his associates. Lombardo Toledano quit the PRI in disgust and founded his own *Partido Popular*, later to become the *Partido Popular Socialista* (PPS) or Popular Socialist Party. It must be said that then, as in future years, Lombardo's tactics responded not only to Mexican realities but also to the international position being taken by Moscow-line Communists and fellow travelers, which at this time was to withdraw from wartime popular front coalitions.

If the three presidents—Carranza, Obregón, and Calles—who presided over the initial period under the new constitution were responsible for the establishment of the country's basic institutional framework, then the three presidents who were the first to serve six-year terms—Cárdenas, Avila Camacho, and Alemán—established policies that set the parameters for their successors. On the left, Cárdenas's policies favored labor and promoted land reform; in the center, Avila Camacho's policies advanced pacification, political reconciliation, and cooperation with the United States; and on the right Alemán's policies fostered economic growth through favoring export-oriented industry, agribusiness, and tourism. These policies provided the basic mix their successors have followed, with differences of emphasis, to be sure.

These differences in emphasis are what gave rise to the concept of a pendular swing between one president and the next. Sometimes, in fact, a candidate was chosen because his reputation made it politically plausible that he would move in the required direction.

This was the case with the president who succeeded Alemán, Adolfo Ruiz Cortines. Alemán was becoming notorious for enriching himself illegally, in those years of economic boom, and former president Cárdenas, who was still the most popular political figure in the country, made it clear that he would find unacceptable any continuation of the situation, either in the form of a constitutional amendment and the reelection of Alemán (which a presidential emissary suggested to him) or in the succession of one of Alemán's close associates. Ruiz Cortines, the candidate who was picked, had a reputation for honesty that went back to his early days in politics handling payrolls for revolutionary armies. His presidency was conservative and unimaginative, however, and he left office the oldest man to have served as Mexican president since Porfirio Díaz.

The succeeding president, Adolfo López Mateos, again provided a contrast with his predecessor. He was relatively young, and indeed was the first president to have been born after Madero first raised the standard of rebellion. He was politically on the left and had been secretary of labor in the cabinet. Tactically, a more left-wing orientation was called for; Fidel Castro's coming to power in Cuba aroused enthusiastic support in Mexico, and Lázaro Cárdenas had come out of retirement to head a movement supporting the Cuban revolution.

In the tradition of Cárdenas, López Mateos stepped up the pace of land distribution. Electricity generation and motion picture production were nationalized; significantly, however, López Mateos showed that his leftism was within the system and served to support it. His actions with respect to the labor movement showed that his service as secretary of labor had prepared him not merely to represent labor, but to manage the labor movement in the interest of the maintenance of the political system. A worker's profit-sharing program was legislated, but López Mateos showed no sympathy for unauthorized or politically motivated strikes and invoked the antisubversion laws to jail the leader of the railroad workers' union. Similarly, López Mateos continued Mexico's policy of being the only member of the Organization of American States to refuse, despite U.S. pressure, to break off diplomatic relations with Cuba, but he cooperated amicably with the United States in the resolution of various border problems. In addition, the electoral system was modified to guarantee the opposition parties a few seats in the Chamber of Deputies.

After López Mateos, the pendulum swung again. The unauthorized railroad strike and growing support for Fidel Castro suggested that law and order issues and the control of "political subversion" might be the key issues of the succeeding presidential term, so López Mateos chose his minister of governance, Gustavo Díaz

Ordaz, as his successor. Although the economy continued to grow, helped by Mexico's membership in the new Latin American free trade area, the Díaz Ordaz administration became a spectacular failure precisely with respect to the law and order issue. The late 1960s was the time of worldwide student protest movements sparked by the war in Vietnam. Díaz Ordaz was particularly nervous because Mexico would be hosting the Olympic Games in 1968; the focus of world attention would be on Mexico and political disruption would be a possibility. In this atmosphere, a trivial student dispute escalated until the government was facing huge demonstrations of students and sympathizers demanding political liberalization. In a stunning overreaction, participants in a massive demonstration taking place in a large public square in the Tlatelolco district were attacked by soldiers with tanks and automatic weapons, resulting in hundreds of deaths and universal repudiation of the Díaz Ordaz government.

After this incident the pendulum clearly needed to swing to the left, and the new nominee for the presidency was Luis Echeverría, a career administrator who had been born in the Federal District and had never been a candidate for elected office before. Echeverría attempted to model himself on Cárdenas and run a pro-labor, pro–land reform, leftist government. He particularly tried to reconcile students to the regime by appointing ambassadors and other high officials who were barely out of the university. Despite his good intentions, Echeverría's hyperactive leftism proved counterproductive and self-defeating. The president had to back down on neutralist and pro–third world foreign policy positions when these earned the disfavor of the United States and foreign tourists and investors. Speeches against foreign capitalism simply led to the flight of foreign investments, forcing Mexico to borrow heavily abroad and become more dependent on the world capitalist system. The resulting weakness of the peso forced its first devaluation in almost 25 years. The attempt to liberalize the regime met with opposition from entrenched party bosses and labor leaders, who organized gangs in universities that attacked the left-wing student groups thought to be the biggest agitators in favor of liberalization.

THE SYSTEM ENTERS PERMANENT CRISIS

For the next presidential term, the pendulum swung to José López Portillo, the moderate minister of finance and a well-regarded author of books on administrative law, and even of novels.

The increase in world oil prices forced by the Organization of Petroleum Exporting Countries (OPEC) made it worthwhile for Mexico to undertake the considerable costs of exploration in order to become an oil exporter. Exploration proved fabulously successful: Mexico surpassed Venezuela to become the world's fifth largest oil producer. Oil wealth gave Mexico the resources and self-confidence to follow a strong foreign policy independent of the United States; López Portillo backed Panama's efforts to renegotiate the Panama Canal Treaty and favored popular liberation movements in Central America. In the end, however, oil proved a curse as well as a blessing. Reckless spending of oil income provoked an inflation that hurt the poorer sectors of society; the flood of foreign exchange made it easy to import everything, and Mexico's own industries withered; and the temptations of easy money led to vast corruption, including that of the president himself. Meanwhile, consumer nations responded to higher oil prices by cutting back consumption, and prices began to drop. Instead of adjusting to the reduced levels of income, the López Portillo government assumed that the price drop was only temporary and maintained its high level of spending, then borrowed abroad to cover the difference. But the price drop continued, and Mexico's debts became astronomical before the government appreciated the seriousness of the situation. People with money read the signs correctly before López Portillo did, however; they converted their pesos to dollars and sent them out of the country before the government gave up defending the value of the peso. Eventually the peso was devalued, and Mexico witnessed runaway inflation that rapidly dropped the living standards of the poor.

In an attempt to recuperate politically what he had lost economically, López Portillo decreed the nationalization of the banking system. The subsequent burst of leftist and nationalist euphoria soon wore off, however, leaving Mexicans still burdened with unemployment, inflation, and debt. The feeling of despair that settled on the country was made complete in September 1985 when Mexico City was rocked by a devastating earthquake, which was not only disastrous in itself but also revealed that legal construction standards had not been followed. Poor construction was especially evident in government buildings, implying once again corruption and kickbacks. Under López Portillo's successor, various financial services the banks had provided, along with industrial interests they had controlled, were split off and privatized and eventually they were returned to private hands completely.

This successor was Miguel de la Madrid, whose nomination took control of the system by career bureaucrats one step further. Like his two immediate predecessors, de la Madrid had never held elective office before being nominated for the presidency. A technician in administration, programming, and budgeting, de la Madrid had a Harvard M.P.A. and had served as Minister of Programming and Budget in the López Portillo cabinet. Inheriting a collapsed economy, a demoralized population, and a regime that had forfeited much of the prestige of its earlier achievements, de la Madrid had little room for political maneuver. His government's weakness was demonstrated by its failure to follow up on pledges to fight corruption after initially managing to make examples of the notoriously corrupt head of PEMEX and the Mexico City police chief. Mexico's opposition to Ronald Reagan's counterrevolutionary policies in Central America died away, and the government cut back living standards even more in an attempt to reduce inflation and pay off the foreign debt. It seemed bitterly ironic that the bill for the spending spree of the oil-boom years was being paid by those Mexicans who had benefited least from it. Foreign exchange became scarce and Mexican wages became cheap in international terms, leading to steady growth in export industry, especially the in-bond assembly plants located in the northern border area. Inflation eased somewhat and oil consumption crept up once more in the industrialized societies of the world, thus providing some faint rays of hope for improvement in the economic situation.

The president who received credit for the subsequent economic improvement was Carlos Salinas de Gortari, who was elected in 1988. He was an example of the presidential nominee who could now be expected: a career administrator from the Federal District specializing in administrative and financial questions, with a foreign degree but without previous service in electoral office. Like his sponsor, de la Madrid, Salinas had an M.P.A. from Harvard but had carried the process a step further by earning a Ph.D. in political economy. Characteristically, again, he came from a family committed to the public sector; in fact, at the time of his nomination his father was serving as senator from the state of Nuevo León.

Concluding that there was no realistic alternative to a free-market strategy, in which his economic training in any case led him to believe, Salinas embarked on a radical reorientation of the Mexican economy, joining with the United States and Canada in a North American Free Trade Area, continuing de la Madrid's privatization of state enterprises, balancing the budget, and renegotiating foreign debt. Inflation was brought down to single digits, and the burden of debt service was reduced, while economic growth resumed. Moreover, budgetary savings and the income from the sale of state

Carlos Salinas, president 1988–1994.

enterprises was used to finance a poverty-reduction program, known as Solidarity, which followed the most advanced thinking on development by stressing bottom-up grassroots participation in the formulation and administration of projects, avoiding centralization and bureaucratic waste. Salinas apparently hoped that the Solidarity program would provide him with an alternative cadre of political organizers that would enable him to replace the entrenched national and regional political machines that formed the RPI.

But there were severe weaknesses in the Salinas formula. First, his economic policy rested on attracting a continuous flow of foreign investment in government bonds denominated in dollars, thus encouraging an overvaluation of the peso. Second, he tried to extend free-market principles to agriculture, which seemed to landless peasants to betray the agrarian principles of the revolution and caused disaster in coffee-producing areas when the withdrawal of government supports and guaranteed purchases coincided with a collapse in world market prices. Third, Salinas allowed opposition victories in gubernatorial elections, but only when opposition protests threatened a breakdown of public order, which had the effect of encouraging violent protests rather than leading to fair election procedures. Fourth, his government sold privatized state enterprises on very favorable terms to people with good political connections.

But it wasn't only the privatization program that created instant billionaires. The "war on drugs" certainly did not close down routes from Colombia to the United States, but it harassed them enough to make it worthwhile to develop connections through Mexico. Enormous drug-trafficking cartels grew, became wealthy, corrupted officials, and used violence with impunity. Drug money purchased and intimidated its way into the halls of power, and the business methods of drug dealers entered Mexican politics. Nineteen ninety-four was a terrible year for Mexico: Assassination claimed the lives of the presidential candidate of the PRI, Luis Donaldo Colosio; the party's newly appointed leader in Congress, José Luis Ruiz Massieu; and Cardinal Jaime Posadas. An armed rebellion of Indians

Ernesto Zedillo, president of Mexico since December 1994. He succeeded Carlos Salinas.

one of the leading candidates for the succession, as the heavyweights of the Salinas administration were. The leading candidates were Pedro Aspe, the Finance Minister; Colosio, the Minister of Social Welfare; and Manuel Camacho Solís, the governor of the federal district; and Colosio had been the original nominee. But when Colosio was assassinated, Camacho Solís had made himself impossible to nominate because of disloyal and sullen remarks he had made on being denied nomination himself; and Aspe was constitutionally inelgible, having served in the cabinet within the 12-month period prior to the presidential inauguration. Zedillo had fortuitously resigned from the cabinet at the same time as Colosio in order to manage Colosio's campaign, which also identified him with the assassinated popular leader and might have positioned him to become Colosio's successor. But his sudden elevation to the candidacy seemed to come six years too early.

Already in a weak position for these personal reasons, Zedillo inherited a party facing its strongest opposition yet. Cuauhtémoc Cárdenas, son of Lázaro, was a lackluster candidate for the leftist Democratic Revolutionary Party, but still retained the magic of his family name and was supported by the feeling that the PRD was closer to the values and ideals of the Revolution than the new-model PRI. But the National Action Party (PAN) fielded a dynamic orator and convincing debater in Diego Fernández, who outperformed the other major candidates, especially Cárdenas, in the first-ever televised presidential campaign debate in Mexico. And the assassination of Colosio suggested that powerful factions within the PRI were unhappy with the direction the party had taken. Colosio had been president of the PRI when it accepted the loss of the governorship of Baja California to the PAN, and it was in Baja California that the assassination took place. Colosio had also refused to invite a political figure with drug-dealing connections to a campaign function, suggesting that he would discontinue Salinas's tolerance of such connections.

Zedillo was weakened even further by an incompetently managed devaluation of the peso shortly after he assumed office. The peso sank like a stone, huge amounts of capital fled the country, and his finance minister was replaced

in the state of Chiapas, hurt by the crash in the coffee market and angered by the abandonment of land reform, raised the banner of Emiliano Zapata. When, shortly after Salinas left the presidency, his brother Raúl was arrested on suspicion of having ordered the killing of Ruiz Massieu, questions about Salinas's complicity or at least his cover-up of the murder were raised. Moreover, the investigation suggested that the Salinas family had enriched itself hugely at public expense. Carlos Salinas disappeared abroad and tried to keep his whereabouts secret.

Ironically, the arrest of Raúl Salinas was the good news for the president who took office at the end of 1994, Ernesto Zedillo, because it lent plausibility to his claim that he was determined to implant the rule of law and end impunity, no matter how politically powerful and well-connected the culprit. Zedillo's popularity needed all the help it could get. He had not been after less than a month in office. The resulting bailout by the U.S. government and international financial institutions meant another heavy burden of debt repayment, a year or more of crippling financial austerity at home, and the abandonment of any possibility of an independent foreign policy.

In his weakened political position, Zedillo had no alternative but to make a virtue out of necessity. Under pressure to resolve the question of culpability for the assassinations, he championed the implantation of the rule of law and the cleansing of the republic's corrupt police and judiciary systems, even appointing a member of the opposition PAN as Attorney General. Facing strengthened opposition parties able to protest effectively against rigged elections, he espoused a constitutional reform that would implant a system of fair and honest elec-

tions. Unable to control local party organizations, he announced support for a more authentic federalism that would devolve power from the center to the state governments. Perhaps political jujitsu, using his opponent's strength against him, would prove a viable political strategy, at least in the short term.

KEY TERMS

caudillo
mestizo
Partido Revolucionario Institucional (PRI)
the pendulum
Petróleos Mexicanos, or PEMEX
La Reforma
Sonora

B.

Political Processes and Institutions

Thus it appeared that President Zedillo had been chosen to preside over the final long-awaited transformation of the single-party system into one of genuine competition. Skeptics could argue, however, that there was a lot of life in the hegemonic-party model yet. After all, the opposition to the PRI was split between a major party to its right and one to its left, each of which had more in common with the PRI than it did with each other, and thus could not be expected to ally against it. And although they might be disgusted or exasperated with the PRI's highhandedness or corruption, more Mexicans sympathized with the centrist policies of the PRI than with those of its more extreme rivals. The PRI moreover retained the inertial force of several generations of identification with the party among voters, an organizational structure that extended to every hamlet of the republic, and a greater appeal to the powerful forces of opportunism and ambition. So the PRI might be expected to continue to win victories even under the most rigorously enforced standards of fair electoral competition.

But also, skeptics would point out, it was premature to expect the application of such standards. Opportunities will always exist for many of the techniques in which the PRI's "alchemists" had become expert: the electoral roll on which the names of known voters for opposition parties mysteriously fail to appear, the election-day breakdowns of public transportation in districts dominated by the opposition, the well-financed "illnesses" that suddenly inflict election observers of the opposition parties and prevent them from showing up at the polling places.

Perhaps circumstances will change so much that it will be increasingly difficult for PRI stalwarts to play these games. They will, however, doubtless continue to try to hang on to power by hook or by crook. Most importantly, state and local parties would try to do so even if the national party authorities should miraculously accept the new norms of honesty and

openness. The new situation faced by the party in the Zedillo era can thus be regarded as simply the latest version of the problem the party has had to confront for some time: that of maintaining a democratic façade while not abandoning the underlying authoritarian reality of the system.

As Mexico developed economically and socially, with a rise in general political sophistication and will to participate, sustained especially by a growth in the business and professional middle classes and the numbers of university students, the PRI's monopoly of power could be expected to erode; governments have handled the problem by yielding political space to the opposition, but always managing to maintain not only the substance of power but also the PRI's dominant position at the center of the political spectrum and some appearance of openness and democratic procedure.

During the 1920s and 1930s, the dissenting tendencies both inside and outside the ruling party had been genuine, lively, and intermittently violent. With the great pacification operation of Avila Camacho and the onset of the boom years of stable development, the regime's management of politics had become smooth and largely efficient. The opposition party to the right, the National Action Party, *Partido de Acción Nacional* (PAN), had at first been of the old vituperative type, vaguely threatening violence on occasion, but the small left and center-left parties had generally been well-behaved satellites of the PRI; their moderate opposition activities were genteel and regularly scripted beforehand, and their façade-strengthening merit was recognized with covert subsidies. During the 1970s the PAN was taken over by a more modern, more moderate leadership and began to win some local elections.

As opposition grew stronger and more autonomous, the regime's overall strategy became to build up the importance of the opposition to the right, which it then identified in its electoral

516

propaganda with the elements that had ruled Mexico before the revolution, thus enabling the PRI to campaign as the defender of revolutionary principles and obscure how far it had actually departed from those principles. Tame and subsidized microparties of the left and center-left were used to draw support away from uncontrollable opposition groups on the left, and their cooperation with the PRI after the elections served to validate the PRI's claim of being the authentic representative of the revolutionary tradition.

These political strategies were implemented by giving opposition parties seats in the Chamber of Deputies; originally this was done in a rather fraudulent manner, by disqualifying or withdrawing PRI candidates in selected seats to allow candidates of the cooperative minor parties on the left to win by default. López Mateos put this practice on a constitutional basis by introducing a proportional-representation feature into the electoral law, which gave the minor parties some representation in the Chamber in proportion to their total percentage of the national vote. This provision was amplified under successive presidents, so that 200 of the 500 seats in the Chamber are now awarded on a regional-list rather than an individual-district basis so as to give each party a share of the 500 total chamber seats more proportionate to its popular vote.

Opposition candidates regularly compete in presidential elections, and the regime was particularly disappointed when the PAN was unable to agree on a candidate and did not contest the presidential election of 1976. By the time of the presidential candidacy of Carlos Salinas, however, such tolerated and even encouraged opposition activities, which lent credibility to the system's democratic façade, had actually become threatening to continued national control by the PRI. Salinas's own victory in the presidential election had to be carefully managed so that his victory was convincing in two ways: His majority had to be large enough to make his mandate to rule seem clear, yet small enough to make it plausible that all of the opposition's votes had indeed been counted. The officially announced margin of his victory—50.36 percent—was not really convincing in either

way. Most people assumed Salinas had won less than a majority—perhaps less than a plurality—and the numbers had then been "adjusted" upward.[4] For Zedillo, the situation was even worse: He received slightly over 50 percent of the "valid" votes—that is, if blank and spoiled ballots are included, his total was under 50 percent. Clearly, the political status quo that had survived for half a century had entered its twilight years. (See Table 10.2 for the political affiliation of the current members of the Chamber of Deputies.)

THE ESTABLISHED SYSTEM

In the half century that has elapsed since the Cárdenas presidency, none of the country's leaders has acquired the historic proportions of Lázaro Cárdenas himself. Looking over this half-century as a whole, several tendencies can be discerned:

1. The outgoing president essentially picked the party's nominee as his successor, taking into account not only the skills of the different possible candidates but also their ability to carry on his own work and to handle problems that seemed to be emerging. However, each president, while representing continuity, was also concerned with distinguishing himself from his predecessor and making his own mark on history, with the result that change was as much a feature of the system as continuity.

Table 10.2 MEMBERSHIP OF THE CHAMBER OF DEPUTIES, 1994–1997

Party	Seats Won in Single-Member Districts	Seats Won by Proportional Representation	Total
PRI	277	23	300
PAN	18	101	119
PRD	5	66	71
PT	0	10	10
Total	300	200	500

Note: PRI = Institutional Revolutionary Party; PAN = National Action Party; PRD = Democratic Revolutionary Party; PT = Labor Party

Source: Communication from Professor Roderic Camp.

2. A politically stable system was achieved. Although revolts or military interventions in politics were talked of from time to time, governments have, in fact, served out their allotted terms with a regularity unmatched not only elsewhere in the third world but also, when the effects of World War II and its aftermath are considered, unmatched in most of Europe. On the whole, military men have been subordinated to civilians.

3. The system became institutionalized, as Calles wanted. The president was virtually an all-powerful figure until his successor was chosen. It is the formal office that conferred authority, not "charisma" or deeds of daring.

4. Although different presidential administrations varied in their policies, the variation took place within the generally accepted framework of a mixed economy that resembled the economies of Western Europe. There were some nationalized industries and a framework of government regulation, but most economic activity was in private hands. The Salinas administration—in keeping with world trends generally—moved the balance decisively in the "capitalist" direction with the dismantling of part of the state sector and the revision of trade laws to open Mexico to foreign products and capital.

5. Mexico experienced the social changes typical of developing countries. That is, mortality was reduced and life expectancy lengthened; illiteracy declined and the number enrolled in universities increased strikingly; a massive movement to cities shifted the balance so that a majority of the population became urban; rates of population growth at first increased dramatically, but started to level off as a result of urbanization and attitudinal changes (see Table 10.3).

6. The mix of economic policies arrived at by Mexican governments was particularly productive, and between 1940 and the early 1980s the country achieved a record of sustained economic growth whose duration was unmatched elsewhere in the world. This record was brought to an end by the collapse of oil prices in 1981, and was succeeded by an alternation between periods of decline and retrenchment, and readjustment and growth.

7. As the country developed economically and urbanized, its class structure changed. The

Table 10.3   CHANGE IN SOCIAL INDICATORS, 1970–1995

	1970–75	1990–95
Life expectancy (years at birth)	62.6	71.5
Crude birth rate (annual, per 1000)	43.2	27.0
Enrollment in higher education (% of age group)	5.8	13.2*
Urban population (% of total)	59.0	72.6*

*1990

Source: UN Economic Commission for Latin America, *Statistical Yearbook for Latin America and the Caribbean, 1994*, various pages.

benefits of economic growth went disproportionately to a new urban bourgeoisie, with a standard of living and pattern of consumption resembling those of the middle class in the United States. Alongside this new bourgeoisie in the modern sector of the urban economy are a growing lower middle class of sales clerks and office workers and an industrial working class holding down factory jobs. More significant and much more numerous, however, is the mushrooming urban underclass, the great number of people underemployed and self-employed in what has been called the "informal economy"— people who live in substandard housing; work in small establishments that evade the tax and minimum wage laws; peddle merchandise in the streets; and work as maids, shoeshine boys, or prostitutes. In this respect, Mexico presents a classic third world profile.

8. As educational standards rose and the social makeup of the population changed, and as the economy experienced new difficulties, political opposition grew and the ruling party was faced with difficult questions of what direction to take in order to contain opposition and retain its monopoly of power.

THE RULING GROUP

Today, Mexico is still more or less ruled by a "new class," similar to what Milovan Djilas described when writing of the bureaucratic elites that had arisen in Communist Eastern Europe.[5] This is a postrevolutionary ruling group of career administrators recruited primarily on the basis of merit, that is, by academic standing at the university. To some extent a hereditary element has developed, as public office has become a tradition in many leading families. Interestingly enough, the breeding ground for Mexico's national political leadership is the national university, the *Universidad Nacional Autónoma de México,* or UNAM. This has resulted in an almost complete segmentation of elite career patterns: the public sector elite trains in the national university just as members of the Roman Catholic church hierarchy train only in seminaries and military officers train only in service academies; the leadership of the private business sector is educated in the technological institutes and schools of business, which are also privately owned and managed. Prior to the Salinas administration, it was unheard of in Mexico for a political leader to be a graduate of a private institute of technology or school of business; a military academy background would be extremely rare, and a religious seminary out of the question.

This kind of leadership has developed only in the last 40 or 50 years. In the early days after the revolution, much of the political leadership emerged from the revolutionary army, in those days still an amateur political army and not the professionalized, academy-trained service it has since become. As the political system stabilized during the 1920s and 1930s, and as the fighting of the revolutionary era receded into memory, the military gradually withdrew from the political sphere. The ruling party had established its legitimacy, the political forces favoring the regime had become united, there was no power vacuum, and fighting was no longer a real possibility. The last military man to serve as president left office in 1946; the last military officer to hold a cabinet post not dealing with military affairs left office in 1970. As the generals and colonels retired from the political scene, their place was taken by the professional politicians, many of them lawyers, who had been active in organizing and operating the ruling party. Typically, they had come up through the ranks of state politics, sometimes in staff positions but often in elective posts.

With the final consolidation of the regime in its "institutional" phase, the central tasks of statecraft were no longer to foil uprisings or to weld a set of disparate regional politicians into a coherent national party, but became instead those of managing an expanding economy in the interest of maintaining economic growth; then the character of the country's leadership underwent another mutation, and the politicians yielded ground to the technocrats. The field has not been surrendered without a struggle, and one of the constant themes of recent political commentary, especially around the time when a new party candidate for the presidency has to be picked, has been the conflict between politicians and technocrats, or *políticos* and *técnicos.* This contest is always won by the technocrats, and Mexico has been presented with the extraordinary spectacle of a series of presidents, beginning in 1970 with Luis Echeverría, who never held elective office before being nominated for the presidency. In their careers, service in the higher reaches of the policy-making bureaucracy was relieved by occasional spells of teaching at the national university.

Until the inflations of the late 1980s and early 1990s shrank the value of the peso, service of this kind was generously compensated in salary, and additional stipends of various kinds. A tradition of laxity in the handling of public funds and an absence of effective policing of conflicts of interest have contributed to illegal and semi-illegal self-enrichment, especially in the lower reaches of the bureaucracy, but often touching the highest levels as well. During the easy-money years of the petroleum boom of the late 1970s and early 1980s, the defalcations of President José López Portillo were notorious. The anticorruption campaigns mounted with great fanfare by each new president typically peter out after a couple of spectacular symbolic arrests that often happen coincidentally to be of the president's political opponents.

TECHNIQUES OF CONTROL

The political system has several means of maintaining itself. Toward potential leadership elements in its own natural constituency, such as university students, the regime follows a strategy of co-optation. Toward the population as a whole, the regime strives to maintain its legitimacy by means of public relations, propaganda, and indoctrination. Toward the country's economic sectors and interest groups, the regime follows a strategy of reconciliation, attempting to spread around specific benefits to the extent that resources are available. To irreconcilable hard-core critics, exemplary punitive strategies are used as a last resort. We will now consider these strategies in more detail.

The leadership elements in the party's natural constituency are, in effect, the politicians and the technocrats we spoke of earlier. The technocratic leadership comes directly from the public universities, especially the national university in the capital city. The politicians emerge from local and state party organizations and from functional organizations affiliated with the PRI: labor unions, the peasants' syndicates (federated into the *Confederación Nacional Campesina*), neighborhood associations, and leagues of professionals. Co-optation occurs primarily through the concession of benefits that are personal in nature, that is, a job for the leader rather than a change in the legislation that will benefit the group he represents. Jobs are available for the politicians in the party itself and in elective government positions.

Disappointment of one's ambitions need only be temporary, because when the presidency changes hands every six years there is tremendous turnover as individuals are promoted, retire, or lose favor. University graduates generally go straight into federal bureaucratic jobs in some specialty; some professional graduates may set themselves up in private practice, with a sideline as consultant to a ministry or public corporation, or with a part-time teaching position at the university or one of its preparatory schools. A striking demonstration of this kind of co-optation was the appointment of young university graduates to government positions by incoming President Luis Echeverría while they were still in jail cells for having taken part in the 1968 Tlatelolco demonstration.

The politician and technocrat career tracks converge in the cabinet and subcabinet, in positions in public corporations and nationalized industries, and sometimes in state governorships, when the holder of a subcabinet or minor cabinet position may be assigned the governorship nomination by the central party authorities. This might occur for various reasons: The na-

tional government may not want to side with either of the local factions contending for the nomination, it may wish to remove from the national power center a figure proving awkward or inconvenient for some reason, or it may be acceding to an insider's desire to go home to his or her native state or change career direction. The co-optation of group representatives and regional political leaders includes an averted gaze with respect to money-making activities which may not be altogether legal. This is especially true for labor leaders, who are usually pressed not to push their constituents' demands too strongly in order not to accelerate inflation or raise the costs of nationalized industries and need to be bought off. It is also true of local and regional political bosses, many of whom build up powerful political machines that could be challenged only with a great deal of difficulty.

The legitimacy of the Mexican regime has two bases. First, the regime claims legitimacy as a constitutional democracy that functions in accordance with the norms generally accepted throughout the Western world: Elections are held, laws are passed by the legally constituted legislature, an opposition press functions, and so on. Today the regime's claim to legitimacy on these grounds is regarded with increasing skepticism. Although elections are taken very seriously and opposition parties win a share of the seats in the Chamber of Deputies and of municipal offices, it is generally believed that the regime loses only those elections it wants to lose or is forced to concede by popular pressure.

Second, the regime has claimed legitimacy as the heir to the great Mexican Revolution and the sacred values it embodied: nationalism, universal free public education, the restoration of the land to those who work it, and protection of the rights of the poor and humble—what is thought of in Mexico as a vindication of Indian Mexico, the true Mexican nation, against foreign interests and the selfish and opportunistic Mexicans who join with them in exploiting the country.

After all, the presidential succession has been continuous since Obregón himself. The party that rules today is the same one that distributed the land, built the schools, and nationalized the oil industry. In its liberation of the Indian and its defense of national interests, the regime has identified itself with the forces regarded generally in Mexico as the truly patriotic ones in the country's history. Of course, the government controls the content of education, specifying which approved history texts are to be used, so it is no wonder that school children in Mexico have been taught to identify patriotism and the country's major achievements with the tradition of which the ruling party claims to be the current incarnation. The party appreciates this source of strength; it is no accident that the party's colors are the same as those of the national flag. Moreover, the dominant television network, TELEVISA, although privately owned and conservative in political orientation, always presents government and PRI in a favorable light—as well it may, in view of its very advantageous tax situation.

Sophisticated Mexicans are skeptical of the party's claim to incarnate the values of the revolution. As a long-entrenched regime, the PRI government has spawned a distinctive class, or caste, with unrevolutionary privileges. Whether for reasons of sound economic policy, or because of pressure from "the north," its policies are favorable to business interests, including foreign interests, and acceptable to international bankers. Because of evasion of the law and corruption, the land reform has been compromised. Well-connected individuals, many of them former government and party officials, hold large estates in violation of the land reform laws.

In addition to positive methods of attracting support, the regime also resorts to intimidation and repression (see Feature 10.2) Agrarian dissidents and suspected urban subversives have been assassinated by army and police units. Several journalists have met with foul play. While such acts are committed by low-level government personnel or PRI partisans, presidents cannot necessarily be presumed to be innocent of direct or indirect complicity.

Normally, however, it is unnecessary to resort to such extreme measures. The discretion that is involved in the implementation of the laws is usually adequate to co-opt individuals and organizations or to penalize those who prove uncooperative. For example, until 1988 there was a government monopoly on the production and importation of newsprint, the paper used by newspapers, and the government sold it at prices considerably below the world market rates. A periodical might be punished by experiencing difficulties in its newsprint supplies, being then forced to buy paper at much higher prices on the free market; a favored publication might be supplied in excess of its needs and be able to sell the surplus at a profit. Mexico's joining the General Agreement on Tariffs and Trade (GATT) under Miguel de la Madrid, however, meant the end of the import monopoly, and thus of this technique of control.

Feature 10.2 **Abuse of Police Power in Mexico**

The international human rights organization, Amnesty International, has verified many reported cases of abuse of power by the various police forces in Mexico, including beatings, torture, and murder. Such reports, which previous governments often denied or swept under the rug, were taken seriously by the Salinas government, which at least ostensibly made the establishment of the rule of law part of its model for the modernized Mexico of the future. Because the mistreatment of prisoners occurs frequently in the attempt to extract confessions, the government introduced a law, passed by the Congress in August 1990, under which confessions are only valid if they are made in the presence of the suspect's lawyer or a judge. One year after the passage of the new law, however, the human rights organization Americas Watch concluded that it had had negligible effect in ending police brutality.

Campaigns have been mounted by each recent president to try to reduce corruption, including police corruption, without much success. President Miguel de la Madrid had the police chief of Mexico City, whose luxurious style of life was notorious, arrested and brought to trial; this seemed to have some deterrent effect on corruption for a limited time, but today extortion of bribes by the police is still routine.

Uncooperative businesses may experience labor difficulties. But repression falls most heavily on potentially radical elements of lower-status groups that are ostensibly the regime's own constituency—labor, peasants, and students—and it is against them that the most spectacular instances of repression have been directed.

The military is one of the basic supports of the regime. The major arena for political struggle during the early years after the revolution, the army was gradually depoliticized during the 1920s and 1930s. Nevertheless, its primary mission, which is the maintenance of internal order rather than border defense, has political implications, and presidents are always careful to give the military special treatment in pay increases and fringe benefits. Like civilian administrators, military officers are able to increase their incomes in ways not troubled by provisions against conflict of interest. In addition, retired military officers are in demand as candidates for lesser elective offices. Yet it is worthy of note that, despite relatively favorable budgetary treatment, the lack of a serious international defense assignment long made it possible to limit the size of the armed forces and to limit military expenditures to levels that, on a per capita basis, are still much lower than those common in Europe and elsewhere in Latin America. However, the onset of the Zapatista insurgency in 1994 gave the military arguments for a substantial budgetary increase which the weak Zedillo administration could not withstand, and military expenditures on new "counterinsurgency" functions started to rise in 1995.

INTEREST GROUPS

In classic Latin American fashion, economic interest groups are organized in an almost corporatist manner. Two organizations, the Confederation of Chambers of Industry, known as CONCAMIN, and the Confederation of Chambers of Commerce, or CONCANACO, group together local chambers of commerce or industry. Membership in one or the other organization is compulsory for manufacturing or commercial businesses, respectively, which have assets in excess of a rather low threshold. There are several other significant business associations, in which membership is voluntary: the Entrepre-

neurs' Coordinating Council, or CCE; the National Chamber of Manufacturing Industry, or CANACINTRA; and the Mexican Employers' Confederation, or COPARMEX. The CCE tries to speak for the private sector as a whole, which makes its voice very strong when the private sector is united on an issue. Many questions, however, create splits in the business community, which weakens the position of the CCE and throws into relief the views of the more homogeneous organizations, especially CANACINTRA and COPARMEX. CANACINTRA primarily represents manufacturers producing consumer goods, and thus has an interest in the expansion of the domestic market and tariff protection against competing imported goods. It is willing to accept a higher general level of wages and salaries, as this increases its customers' purchasing power. COPARMEX has in recent years taken an active political role in favor of free enterprise and against government control of the economy, which put it in tune with the revival of neoclassical economic thinking in the United States and Western Europe, and in 1988 the conservative opposition party, the PAN, nominated a former president of COPARMEX, Manuel Clouthier, as its presidential candidate.[6]

Most of Mexico's labor unions are affiliated with the ruling party through membership in confederations that belong to the party's "labor sector," although the government workers' and the teachers' unions are affiliated with the "popular" sector. Some unions, however, especially those with leftist political views, remain independent of the party. But whether unions belong to the PRI or not, labor organization is highly regulated, as is the case with most Latin American countries. In order to enjoy the protections of the country's labor code, unions must be registered with the Ministry of Labor, which can control them in various ways. For example, the law stipulates that a strike may only be called after certain procedures have been followed, such as a membership vote; only if the strike is declared legal are strikers eligible for benefits during the period of the strike. Moreover, if stipulated conciliation procedures have not reached a mutually satisfactory result, the government may settle the dispute by decree. The government, through the Ministry of Labor, thus has great discretion in handling labor cases. Nevertheless, at a time of economic distress any interruption in production through a strike is to be avoided, so labor retains some influence. In fact, labor leaders have often used their influence for their own personal advantage rather than that of the membership, so that the rank and file have not benefited as much as labor's potential bargaining power should have made possible. Nevertheless, for most of the twentieth century labor in Mexico apparently did better economically than labor in the rest of Latin America did by fighting against governments.

POLITICAL PARTIES

Even though the PRI was clearly the dominant party in the political system, the minor parties performed important functions. A former minister of governance, Jesús Reyes Héroles, once said, "Opposition is a form of support." He meant that by competing in elections the opposition parties signified their acceptance of the system as legitimate. In a sense, the dominant party had the best of both worlds. Unlike the single party in a dictatorship, it did not have to operate in a police regime that stamped out any sign of opposition, ruling by force over a sullen and resentful population. On the other hand, it did not run the risk, as it would in a completely competitive system, of losing office—with the attendant loss of jobs, contracts, and the whole structure of policy that embodied its values and aspirations. Thus, paradoxically, it used to encourage and subsidize opposition parties.

The major party on the right of the political spectrum is PAN, the National Action Party. Founded in 1939 as a party opposing the fundamental principles of the revolution, that is, pro-clerical and pro-business, its tactical line has fluctuated, but since the 1960s it has played the role of loyal opposition. It competes in elections, abides by the rules of the game, and has stated that it "accepts" the revolution. In religious policy, it would like the anti-clerical laws changed to remove provisions that the Church cannot hold property and cannot operate schools—provisions that are in any case ignored in practice. It would like the communal landholding units, or *ejidos* (discussed in Section C), broken up and converted into private landholdings. It supports various changes in the law in favor of private business, especially small-business interests. As an opposition party that has had success primarily at the municipal level, PAN criticizes electoral fraud and supports greater autonomy for local government. The party's vote increased fairly steadily, reaching a little over 17 percent in the 1988 elections, but then rose sharply in 1994 when its presidential candidate, Diego Fernández de Ceballos, made a strong favorable impression. Its support comes especially from religiously inclined members of the middle class. It is strongest in the Federal District and in the northern border states, where it has held some governorships.

The principal party on the left is now the PRD, the *Partido Revolucionario Democrático,* or Democratic Revolutionary Party, formed by Cuauhtémoc Cárdenas after the 1988 elections, using as his base the old Mexican Communist Party, which took a line independent of Moscow as far back as 1968, when it condemned the sending of Soviet troops into Czechoslovakia. The party is strongest in Michoacán, the home state of Cárdenas, in the southern states that are more heavily Indian, such as Oaxaca and Chiapas, and in the Federal District. Although initial enthusiasm for the presidential candidacy of Cárdenas gave the PRI a scare in 1988, his wooden performance as a campaigner in 1994 and his inability to formulate a clear position on international trade policy questions left the PRD clearly in third place. The party favors the traditional revolutionary positions now abandoned by the PRI leadership—agrarian reform, state ownership of industry, and subsidies for mass consumption.

The PRI is strongest among the less sophisticated elements of the population, the rural and urban masses that accept the image the party tries to project of itself as altruistic, the source of progress and material benefits, the embodiment of revolutionary ideals, and the bearer of legitimacy, democracy, and patriotism. As studies of early political socialization have shown, the child in the elementary grades conceives of political authority as caring and benign, and it is the segments with least education that accept the PRI, the regime, and the president on these terms.

As Mexico has developed a more literate, better educated urban society, however, the constituency for opposition parties has grown.

The PAN draws votes from the middle class in the private and business sectors, and the PRD draws from the intellectual and professional members of the middle class, together with some support from lower-class elements.

In the face of these changes, the PRI has modified its tactics. Until 1988 and the breakaway of Cárdenas, its line of policy was to treat the PAN as the principal opposition, identifying it with the forces that were defeated in the Revolution and implying that it had U.S. support. This reinforced the PRI's revolutionary and nationalist credentials and induced some people to vote for the PRI as the strongest bastion against counterrevolution and imperialism. However, after the rise of the PRD, and the decline of PRI strength in the Chamber of Deputies to below two-thirds of the membership, it became necessary to form an implicit alliance with the PAN in order to pass any of President Salinas's pro-capitalist economic reforms that required amendment of the constitution.

In fact, today the PRI fears PRD more than PAN. PAN has mostly attracted votes from those who are, for religious or historical reasons, not predisposed to vote for the PRI anyway, but the PRD seemed at its origin to have the potential of replacing the PRI altogether by taking away its core constituency.

Accordingly, the PRI draws on its traditional repertoire of political tactics, providing monetary and other incentives to co-opt sectoral leaders who might be drawn to the PRD, and encouraging minor left-wing parties that might cut into its vote. In Chiapas especially, hard-line elements within the local PRI representing landowner interests have assassinated PRD activists.

At the local level, the PRI shifts its position toward left or right depending on the nature of the challenge in a specific locality. Thus in the northern states, where business interests are strong, the PRI has nominated local business leaders as its candidates for mayoralties.

As opposition support among voters has grown, the regime has modified the electoral law several times to increase opposition representation in the federal legislature. This gives the opposition parties the illusion that they are gaining actual political power and gives them an incentive to play the electoral game instead of rejecting the existing political system.

VOTING AND ELECTIONS

The formal institutions of Mexican government are clearly based on those of the United States, but they have been modified in several respects. This is a system of separation of powers; the president is popularly elected separately from the two houses of the legislature, the Senate and the Chamber of Deputies. The Senate now has three members elected by each state and by the Federal District (in the U.S. Senate the District of Columbia is not represented).

Voting in Mexico is legally compulsory. This means that for various dealings with government agencies a voting credential, stamped to indicate that one has complied with his civic duty, is among the various papers and forms required legally, though the requirement is enforced only sporadically. Partly because it is compulsory, but also partly because there is a strong feeling—reinforced by government public relations campaigns—that voting is an important civic duty, electoral turnout is high, generally over 80 percent in presidential elections.

In a speech early in his campaign, Carlos Salinas acknowledged implicitly the existence of manipulation in previous elections, saying that the credibility of electoral democracy had suffered significant blows, "I want to win and I want also for people to believe in our victory, even if we suffer some defeats." In keeping with those sentiments, in the 1988 elections the PRI accepted the unprecedented loss of four senatorial seats and in 1991 the president went further and forced the resignation of the governors-elect of Guanajuato and San Luis Potosí after the PAN mounted popular protests against obviously rigged elections.

The lesson learned by this was not that elections could be fair, but that the outcome could be changed by massive and disruptive enough street violence. The PAN continued such protests and was successful on occasion, irrespective of the actual merits of its charge that the election was stolen. However, hard-liners within the PRI learned the same lesson. When President Zedillo, who was less hostile to the

PRD than Salinas, was about to recognize the victory of the PRD in the governorship election in Tabasco, street demonstrations and building occupations by the local PRI forced him to back down.

Years before opposition parties posed any kind of threat to the hegemony of the PRI, more progressive elements in the ruling party, believing that the maintenance of the system was better served by flexibility than by rigidity, convinced President Adolfo López Mateos to introduce legislation adding a proportional representation feature to the electoral law for the Chamber of Deputies, which gave opposition parties seats in the Chamber reflecting their percentage of the national vote. Today, electors vote twice in Chamber elections, once on each half of a divided ballot. On one side they vote for candidates in their individual districts, and on the other side they vote for a party to share seats in the proportional distribution.

When they were established, it seemed unlikely that the proportional provisions for opposition representation could ever get out of hand and threaten PRI control. The system was based on the premise of a single dominant party that wins a majority of the seats, with a minority of the seats earmarked as a concession to smaller parties, which remain in permanent opposition. What the changes in the electoral law signified was the PRI's intention to exercise its hegemony in subtler ways, requiring a more delicate touch. The democratic façade was to be given greater plausibility; the opposition was to be encouraged through its small victories, thus guiding dissidence into safe channels. However, changes have a way of outrunning the inten-

tions of those who introduced them, and that is what has happened in Mexico.

Federal elections in Mexico are on three- and six-year cycles. Deputies are elected every three years. Senators, like the president, have six-year terms that coincide with his.

CONSTITUTIONAL STRUCTURE AND NORMS

The Constitution of 1917 addresses itself to three substantive areas. It establishes the structure of national government, including the federal system and separation of powers; it provides for the defense of individual rights; and it establishes various principles and goals for public policy. Individual rights are guaranteed by the first 29 articles, which specify the rights and immunities of citizens with respect to government power of the states and localities as well as of the federal government.

The president is prohibited reelection. Members of Congress may be elected only after skipping terms—that is, consecutive reelection to the same office is not possible. Some members of the legislature have actually alternated for several periods between the Senate and the Chamber of Deputies. The "no reelection" rules were established in their present form through congressional amendment in the aftermath of the assassination of Obregón; the Constitution had previously been amended to allow Obregón to run for reelection. The prohibition of presidential reelection is one of the most significant features of the system. It avoids personal dictatorship and forces a policy review and change of direction every six years. It secures the loyalty

Table 10.4   Presidential Election Results, 1994

Party	Candidate	Percentage
PRI	Ernesto Zedillo	48.77
PAN	Diego Fernández	25.94
PRD	Cuauhtémoc Cárdenas	16.60
PT	Cecilia Soto	2.74
	Other candidates and blank and null votes	5.95

Source: Foreign Broadcast Information Service, *Daily Report,* August 29, 1994, p. 19.

of those whose immediate careers do not seem promising but who know they will shortly get another chance. The Revolution of 1910 broke out, after all, over the issue of the perennial reelection of Porfirio Díaz. The Bolivian Revolution, similar in many ways to the Mexican, finally came to grief when President Víctor Paz Estenssoro had the constitution amended to permit consecutive reelection. The "no reelection" rule allows for continuing renewal, adjustment, and hope.

Amendments to the Constitution must be approved by a two-thirds vote of the Congress meeting in joint session and must then be approved by a majority of the state legislatures. When the Congress is not in session, a commission, composed of 29 members drawn from both houses, may act on behalf of Congress on matters too urgent to be left over for the next session.

Partly because of constitutional disposition and partly because of legislation, the president has considerable legislative power of his own. Constitutionally, as head of the executive branch, he has authority to issue decrees regulating the manner in which legislation passed by Congress is to be enforced. In addition, Congress has voted him the power to issue decrees in other matters—for example, the authority to transfer funds among different budgetary categories and to incur expenses beyond the amounts appropriated by the original budget.

The judiciary in Mexico normally does not play a significant political role. Most of the time, the judiciary stays away from political questions. Of course, judges are appointed by the president, and, if the executive branch is interested in the outcome of a particular case, it can normally expect judges to be responsive to its wishes. However, there are cases on record in which a court has rendered decisions against the executive branch. This has occurred by means of the granting of a writ of *amparo,* a judicial order forbidding acts of administrative officers that violate a specific guaranteed right of an individual, or ordering an official to take an affirmative action called for by the exercise of such a right. *Amparo* has no exact equivalent in Anglo-Saxon common law; it combines features of the injunction with those of specific writs such as *habeas*

corpus or *mandamus.* One accustomed to the subtleties of politics in Mexico, however, may, be inclined to suspect that on some occasions when a court has ruled against the executive branch, its decision may, in fact, have been requested by the executive, attempting to get itself out of a situation that had been politically untenable or wishing to take a position for the record that contravened the results it hoped to achieve.

Below the Supreme Court are 6 circuit courts and 46 district courts in the federal system. The Federal District and the states have their own judiciaries.

STATE AND LOCAL GOVERNMENT

The state governments have their own distinctive constitutions; however, they all have elected governors and single-chamber legislatures, the number of members of which varies from state to state. Each state is on its own electoral cycle, and only one governor happens to be elected at the same time as the president. Hence, although it is the national party—in effect, the president—which decides who the candidates for governor will be, presidents inherit governors nominated by their predecessors, and it is only in their last two years of office, when they are already about to become lame ducks, that presidents have a complete set of governors of their own choice. Each state party has a convention to choose its candidate for governor, but until the Zedillo era always chose the candidate who had the president's approval. The governor of the Federal District has been an appointee of the president and a member of his cabinet but a 1996 all-party agreement provided that the position would be elective in the future.

There are 33 states and one Federal District. Because the national government is supreme over the states, politically if not always legally, commentators often refer to the Mexican federal system as fraudulent. That is not altogether the case. Because the federal government is engaged in a continuous balancing act, trying to proceed with its objectives while conciliating a variety of entrenched interests with a minimum of open dissension, a well-managed local political machine may normally run a state pretty much as it likes. On the average of once or twice in a presidential term, however, the behavior of a specific state governor may reach such publicly scandalous proportions—because of either monumental embezzlement of public funds, use of state power to promote private business interests, or the assassination of dissidents—that he is removed by the federal government. Impeachment by the state legislature is legally possible, but is a long, drawn-out operation that is likely to be unedifying. Normally governors simply resign under pressure from the president.

The basic unit of local government is the *municipio,* which resembles a North American township or consolidated city-county government. That is, it consists of a town plus the surrounding rural area. The *municipio* elects a mayor and council, who are not eligible for immediate reelection.

Opposition parties have been most successful at the municipal level. The PAN in particular has captured the mayoralties of several large northern cities, where a genuinely competitive political system exists. Politics at the local level is fairly fluid; an upcoming election will see new alignments and factional shifts, leading individuals crossing party lines, and parties trying to recruit prominent local editors or business leaders as candidates.

The funding of local government is very flexible. Municipalities receive subsidies from state governments but can also raise their own funds by charging fees for municipal services and licenses; for some purposes, federal funds are available. Some economic development expenditures are financed by partnerships between the municipality and the private sector.

Authorities at all three levels of Mexican government have concurrent jurisdiction in several subject areas. Coordination of their activities is effected by a federal delegate; there is normally one such delegate per federal ministry per state capital. State governments are financed partly by federal subsidies and partly by their own taxing powers; typical state taxes are those on property, sales, inheritance, and income.

The position of state governor (there are no lieutenant governors, just as there is no federal vice president) is an important one, not only ad-

ministratively but also politically. Conflicts frequently occur between local interests supporting a popular local candidate and a national party wanting to place its own candidate in the position. In the PRI the national party is normally successful in imposing its choice in such situations; its candidate is usually a nationally well-connected figure for whom the state governorship is an important stepping stone, perhaps between a subcabinet and a cabinet position. Such imposed candidates are often people who were born in the state but have made their careers entirely in the Federal District. Some aspirants for governor intend to carve out local empires for themselves and become rich and powerful on the local scene, but for most career politicians the major league is the president's cabinet, which is the pool from which future presidents are drawn.

Outside the cabinet departments are many independent agencies and public corporations, which seem to run their own affairs with a minimum of presidential supervision. In some cases, most notoriously in the case of the petroleum monopoly, PEMEX, the agency officials become involved in racketeering and embezzlement on a large scale.

Corruption has always been present in Mexican public administration. In the early years after the revolution, allowing graft was a deliberate policy of President Obregón to co-opt possible military rebels into the political system. "No one can withstand a cannonade of 200,000 pesos," he is reported to have said. Even though the danger of military insurrection has receded, corruption still plays a significant role in the political system. "Moralization" campaigns are waged periodically, especially after graft has become particularly notorious, as during the administrations of Miguel Alemán and José López Portillo. Sometimes a new governor of the Federal District will launch an anticorruption campaign. Some presidents may intend such campaigns seriously; for others, they are for show only. In either case, they don't get very far.

THE EVOLUTION OF PRESIDENTIAL TYPES

The characteristics of Mexican presidents, like the characteristics of the leadership group in general, have undergone striking modification over the years. The most noticeable differences are in family background, geographic origin, training, and career pattern.

As was noted before, the institutionalization of the revolution has brought about the development of a distinctive ruling group. The castelike features of this group have become especially apparent over time, and it is common to find people in political leadership positions who are the sons and grandsons of government officials and politicians in the dominant party. In fact, all three leading contenders for the PRI presidential nomination in 1988—Carlos Salinas, Manuel Bartlett, and Alfredo del Mazo— were the sons of important regime political figures, as was the leading opposition candidate, Cuauhtémoc Cárdenas.

Another symptom of the shrinking of the pool from which the ruling group is drawn is its dominant Mexico City flavor. In the early postrevolutionary years, Mexico was ruled by generals, who were usually from the provinces and usually from the North; the politicians who followed had made their careers in state and local politics. But the technocrats who rule today are overwhelmingly products of the capital.

The shift in academic training is also intriguing. The generals of the early revolutionary years, and their colleagues in government, frequently lacked higher education; the politicians who succeeded them were typically lawyers. In the technocratic era, there has been an increase in cabinet members trained in a technical specialty other than law, first in engineering or architecture, now in administration and fiscal management. This shift in skill and training among cabinet members was reflected, with a slight time lag, at the presidential level. From 1920 to 1946, all popularly elected presidents were generals (although two civilians, Adolfo de la Huerta and Emilio Portes Gil, served as provisional presidents). From 1946 to 1976, with the exception of Adolfo Ruiz Cortines, presidents were all lawyers by training; the four presidents since 1976 have been specialists in public administration and finance.

In terms of career immediately prior to the presidency, between 1920 and 1940 the incoming president had served as Secretary of War or Defense, except for the three presidents who

shared the term Obregón was unable to serve, from 1928 to 1934. With the exception of Adolfo López Mateos, who had been Minister of Labor, from 1946 to 1976 the position held by each candidate prior to his election had been Minister of Governance (*Secretario de Gobernación*). This department, among other things, is in charge of organizing elections and managing relations between federation and states, so it is the key ministry for handling political questions—just as the Ministry of War or Defense was the most important during the preceding era, when the possibility of an armed revolt was always present. José López Portillo, who served from 1976 to 1982, was selected while serving as Minister of Finance, and the three succeeding presidents had served as Minister of Programming and Budget, which only became a cabinet department during the López Portillo administration. Early in 1992, the Ministry of Programming and Budget was absorbed by the Ministry of Finance.

This shift in skills and career backgrounds clearly indicates the evolution of the character of the regime as the revolution has become institutionalized. We take the presidents in chronological sequence: Obregón, Calles, and Cárdenas were revolutionary generals, heroic leaders in war; Avila Camacho was a desk general, a military administrator. Alemán was a politician rather than a career administrator; Ruiz Cortines, López Mateos, and Díaz Ordaz combined bureaucratic careers with periods of elective office. Echeverría was a career administrator born in the Federal District who never held an elective office before the presidency. López Portillo, de la Madrid, and Salinas combined administrative with academic careers, teaching at the national university concurrently or intermittently while holding their administrative jobs. All three had gone abroad for advanced degrees after completing a first degree at UNAM—López Portillo to the London School of Economics, de la Madrid and Salinas to Harvard; Zedillo went to the University of Pennsylvania. The skills required evolved from combat to elective politics, to general administration, to fiscal management.

Each time a new president comes to office in Mexico, there is an extensive turnover in government jobs. The fact that the ruling party does not change does not make much difference in this, nor does the fact that the incoming president was picked by the outgoing one. Indeed, the fact that new presidents are picked by their predecessors seems to impose a psychological obligation on them to demonstrate that they are independent and not simply puppets. Moreover, they want to demonstrate that they will avoid the errors of their predecessors, and so ostentatious change in personnel and policy orientation is mixed in with the inevitable continuity from incumbent to incumbent.

In filling major positions in their administrations, new presidents usually choose notable figures who are popular with specific interests they want to conciliate—including the international banking community—and they retain or promote individuals of particular competence. They also surround themselves with people they have worked with during their careers, sometimes going back to their school days. This set of a politician's associates, colleagues, and cronies is called in Mexico a *camarilla*; they are people who think like he (or she) does, whom he can trust, who share similar backgrounds, and who have been loyal supporters. Carlos Salinas, for example, was a member of the *camarilla* of Miguel de la Madrid, their acquaintance going back to when Salinas was a student in a class taught by de la Madrid at the university. Luis Echeverría picked as his replacement José López Portillo, a lifelong friend since their days as students together.

THE PRESIDENT AND THE RULING PARTY

The keystone of the political system is the presidency. As in other presidential systems, the president is the dominant figure, prime mover, inspirer, motivator, and tone setter for all government activity. Of course, the president cannot do everything himself, but everything is done in his name and, on the whole, within the guidelines he has laid down and by the personnel he has selected. The president is also the leader of the dominant party, which is fairly well disciplined, so that normally a PRI member of one of the legislative bodies can be expected to vote with the party.

The president's power is wielded in various forms: the appointment of cabinet members, and the supervision of their work and that of the ministries they head; control of the party's nominations for the Senate, the Chamber of Deputies, and state governorships; control of the work of Congress and the passage of legislation; and the issuance of presidential decrees. These decrees are legally supposed to be limited to the matters within the president's own competence, as specified by the Constitution, or to provide for the implementation of legislation passed by Congress. Given the extent of legal presidential powers, there is generally no reason for the president to act illegally. However, on occasion the president exceeds his legal powers, and the situation is brought into conformance with the law only retroactively. For example, President López Portillo nationalized the banks by decree, a procedure that seemed to have no legal warrant. Legislation was then hastily prepared and passed by Congress subsequently to regularize the situation from a legal point of view.

The centralization of power in the president and ruling party belongs to the "institutional" era of the last half-century. In the 1920s, the president was the dominant *caudillo*, but there were other strong figures, regional bosses, and leaders of major interest groups. Pro-revolutionary forces were represented in several political parties, and competition among parties for legislative seats and governorships was lively and sometimes violent. This competition, although it was then competition for the nomination of the ruling party, continued after Calles founded the National Revolutionary Party in 1929, and some preexisting organizations continued their separate identities within the PNR. Cárdenas reorganized the affiliated groups into four sectors when he transformed the party into the PRM, or Mexican Revolutionary Party, in 1938.

Since Avila Camacho's term, toward the end of which the party's name was changed to the Institutional Revolutionary Party, the system has been consolidated and conflict reduced to a minimum. The presidential candidate who ran against Avila Camacho in 1940, General Juan Andreu Almazán, was the last to threaten a revolt. The electoral law, which had previously stipulated that the first citizens to arrive at a polling station to vote would be sworn in as electoral officials, and had thus led to battles between supporters of rival candidates over who was to be first in line when the polls opened, was changed to provide for a different method of choosing electoral officials. After 1940, genuine competition within the party over nominations was restricted mainly to local offices, with party headquarters in Mexico City deciding on the party's candidates for the federal congress and governorships. However, the political weakness of President Zedillo has led to a greater role being played by state party organizations in the choice of candidates.

Nominations for congressional seats and municipal presidencies (mayoralties) are traditionally supposed to go to that sector of the party—labor, agrarian, or popular—which is strongest in the district. In sectoral terms, it is the popular sector—which, after all, includes such political powerhouses as the bureaucrats' union, the neighborhood associations, and the lawyers' association—that garners the lion's share of congressional seats.

CHOOSING THE PRESIDENT

As already mentioned, the nomination of the presidential candidate is in the hands of the outgoing president. The president is supposed to consult over the nominations, although how much he consults and how much attention he pays to the advice he is given is up to him. Nevertheless, in keeping with the apparent democratization and gestures toward openness of recent years, an attempt has been made recently to make it appear as though a quasi-democratic method of choosing the ruling party's presidential nominee is being followed. A typical process of picking a president goes through nine stages:

1. By the two-thirds mark in the presidential term (that is, by two years from its end) the president has replaced any cabinet members who are not performing satisfactorily. The existing cabinet lineup is the group from which the nominee will be chosen. At this point, the president has probably decided who his successor will be but gives no indication for another year, because as soon as the identity of his suc-

cessor is known an incumbent becomes a "lame duck," and power begins to flow to the designated successor.

2. Twelve or 15 months before the election, the president may replace the party chair to make sure the person in this role is competent, sympathetic to his choice of successor, and able to handle any discontent that may arise.

3. About a year before the election the president gives the party chair a list of "precandidates" from among whom a nominee will be picked. The party chair releases this list to the press as representing the consensus of the party, and invites public discussion of the relative merits of each of the precandidates. This is largely a cosmetic exercise to give the impression of public consultation. It is possible, however, that a very strong adverse reaction or some especially derogatory information about the president's choice of successor might cause him to change his mind.

4. The actual candidate is unveiled (*destapado*) in October or November of the year preceding the election. The leader of one of the party's sectors announces that sector's choice; other sectors, party organizations, and individuals hasten to announce that the individual named is also their choice, and a general rush to get on the bandwagon occurs. Typically, the sector whose leader is picked by the president to make the announcement is the one likely to be unhappy with the choice, that is, which favored one of the other precandidates. Having that sector announce the choice first thus preempts the expression of any dissatisfaction. The last two presidents, Salinas and de la Madrid, were candidates particularly uncongenial to the labor sector, so labor was chosen to make the original announcement of support.

5. A party convention is held, which serves to ratify the choice already made by the president and to designate the presidential candidate officially.

6. The candidate then conducts a national campaign designed not so much to win votes as to familiarize the public with his name and features; to enable him (it has always been a "him") to make contact with local party leaders across the country, size them up, and learn of their concerns; and to create the im-

pression, through extensive media coverage, that his assuming the presidency is inevitable and right.

7. The election takes place on a Sunday during the first week of July; the percentage of voters turning out is regarded as a significant indicator of support for the system.

8. After the election the president-elect assembles a new cabinet team. Prominent figures not included in the cabinet are given positions in the nationalized segment of the economy or in autonomous agencies, such as the social security institute, or are designated ambassadors.

9. The inauguration of the new president takes place on December 1.

KEY TERMS

amparo
camarilla
Chamber of Deputies
Constitution of 1917
co-optation
Federal District
Ministry of Governance (*Gobernación*)
Ministry of Programming and Budget
municipio
the "new class"
Partido de Acción Nacional (PAN)
Partido Revolucionario Democrático (PRD)

Public Policy

AGRICULTURE AND LAND REFORM

Land reform policy has traditionally been regarded as the litmus test of the revolutionary character of Mexican governments. A government genuinely committed to alleviating the plight of the poorest Mexicans was one most wholeheartedly committed to land reform; conversely, a government that diminished the pace of reform, provided for limits, exceptions, or exemptions from the program, or placed maximum agricultural production ahead of social justice was a government that had betrayed revolutionary principles. Thus the government of Lázaro Cárdenas has been regarded as the most revolutionary for maximizing the rate of land distribution, and—until the presidency of Carlos Salinas—that of Miguel Alemán as the least revolutionary for promoting agribusiness rather than *ejido* communities. The leader of the early phase of the revolution who remains with most honor in Mexican history books is Emiliano Zapata, the agrarian leader from Morelos who never sold out, who never compromised, who never deviated from his goal of restoring land to those who worked it. So it was entirely logical that the Indians who rose in rebellion in the state of Chiapas on January 1, 1994, rejecting the drastic changes in the agrarian laws introduced by Salinas, should have called themselves Zapatistas.

Nevertheless, the drafters of the Constitution and of the statutes of the PNR, the earliest incarnation of the present ruling party, seem to have intended a mixed policy for agriculture. Such a policy would promote land reform for the benefit of Indian communities and poor landless subsistence farmers, but, bearing in mind the consumption needs of city populations and the country's requirements for foreign exchange, it would at the same time promote efficient production for the market. Thus a modern commercial sector would exist alongside a subsistence sector. In the early days, when land was relatively plentiful, this kind of mixed policy presented no difficulties.

The laws governing land reform have been modified over the years, but the basic premise had until 1991 remained that if a single landowner held land above a specific size, then the surplus could be expropriated by the state. This land was then given to what may have been an actual village, but was more likely to be a fictitious community, the members of which had to be adults whose primary economic activity was farming but who did not own land. The community, real or fictitious, which then became the owner of the land was called the *ejido*, and its members were known as *ejidatarios*. The land was then divided up among the *ejidatarios*, who farmed it as though they owned it outright—since the Calles administration, the right to farm a specific plot can be inherited—except that until the Salinas "reforms" of 1991–1992 the land could not be sold or mortgaged. In the event that it was abandoned or even improperly farmed by the *ejidatario*, the plot reverted to the *ejido*, whose elected management committee might then assign it to someone else.

The rule that the land could not be sold or mortgaged guaranteed that the *ejidatario* could not lose the land, and avoided reconcentration. In a situation of absolute private ownership, the vagaries of agricultural production often mean, in third world countries, that over time land steadily passes into the ownership of banks, moneylenders, or simply more efficient farmers, thus creating a situation in which a small landed elite coexists with a great number of landless laborers. The purpose of land reform, then, is (1) economic, because it ensures at least the means for subsistence to those engaged in agriculture; (2) moral and social, in the sense that landless laborers previously wholly dependent on the goodwill of landowners for whom they worked would now be independent and able to make their own decisions; and (3) political, because the peasants who had received land would become supporters of the government and agitation would not threaten government stability.

At present, almost 50 percent of the nation's land area planted in crops consists of *ejidos*, which enroll between 2 and 3 million members affiliated with the ruling party through their membership in the National Peasants' Federation, the *Confederación Nacional Campesina*. However, a greater number, probably over 4 million people, work in agriculture without owning land either privately or as members of *ejidos*.

In the early days, there seemed to be no contradiction between the goals of land reform and those of maximum economic production; Mexico was regarded as an underpopulated country with an unlimited supply of available land, adequate for all purposes. Population, however, has grown to the point where the supply of land available for distribution under the land reform program has been virtually exhausted—especially in the areas of central Mexico that contain the bulk of the population qualified and eager to receive land. New land has been brought into production by large irrigation projects, but primarily in the North of the country where desert land and usable water supplies have been available. This land made fertile by irrigation has been sold to larger-scale farmers able to invest in mechanization, who produce crops such as winter vegetables for export to the United States and thus provide the country with one of its major sources of foreign exchange.

In fact, wholesale violations of the land reform laws occurred. Large properties were exempted from expropriation by the simple device of subdividing them on paper, so that legally the situation was that of a series of properties owned by different individuals, perhaps members of the same family, each below the maximum amount allowed and thus safe from expropriation. Actually, all these properties were still owned by a single individual and continued to be farmed as a unit. Where land is expropriated, the law provides for compensation, but, in fact, compensation was given only in a few cases in which the former owner has had good political connections; otherwise, claims for compensation gather dust in the files. Until recently the law provided that *ejidal* property could not be rented, but that provision was generally violated and has now been repealed.

Controversy has been continuous in Mexico over the merits of the *ejido* system. Those further to the right in the political spectrum, who support private property on principle, have argued that the *ejidos* should be broken up so that the plots are held as absolute private property by the members, thereby enabling them to raise money by mortgaging properties, giving them incentives to improve the land, and in general bringing the benefits of capitalism to that sector of agriculture. Some left-wing critics, on the other hand, have argued that the *ejidos* should not only be held collectively, but should also be farmed collectively by large-scale mechanized methods, like a Soviet *kolkhoz*. All across the political scale criticisms have been made of how the *ejido* system works in practice, and *ejido* management committees are often guilty of abuse of power, extortion, and diversion of funds.

What merits do the various criticisms have? Arguments in favor of a Soviet-style collective farm management system seem ignorant of the actual drawbacks of Soviet collective farms, which are generally regarded as failures. Arguments that individual ownership would be more productive than *ejidos*, on the other hand, often make comparisons that ignore differences of scale, of land quality, and amount of capitalization of private as opposed to *ejidal* farms. It does seem to be true, however, that when these factors are held constant, privately owned land units, even very small ones on land of similar poor quality to that of most *ejidos*, do have somewhat higher productivity.

Attempts by pro-agrarian governments to make capital available to *ejidatarios* were not successful. The difficulty is that *ejidatarios* were not able to mortgage their land as security for payment of the loan, and the special banks set up to serve *ejidos* had the authority to write off a loan that was not repaid. The temptation was then very great for officials of such banks to loan the funds to their friends and relatives and take kickbacks when the loan was written off. There thus seems to be no foolproof way of trying to provide capital to the *ejidos*, even though there is no reason to expect that the bulk of such loans would not be repaid if they could be made.

In 1991 and 1992, as part of his program of "modernizing" the economy, President Salinas sponsored legislation making it possible for *ejidatarios* to sell their plots of land. He had clearly accepted the argument that outright private ownership would be more productive despite the risk of negative political effects arising from any resulting tendency to reconcentration of land. Salinas's speeches on the topic suggested that he believed the agrarian problem no longer had significant weight in Mexican politics, now that the country's urban population had passed 60 percent of the total and would reach 80 percent by the year 2000. Alleviating the plight of the poor now meant dealing with the problems of urban slums, not maintaining unproductive structures in the countryside. The Zapatista rebellion showed that he had made a political miscalculation, and Zedillo indicated that he would ease up on pressures to privatize *ejido* lands.

Traditionally, the government acted to stabilize the level of food prices through price controls and a commodities purchasing program. After minimal processing, foodstuffs and other articles of prime necessity are retailed by the government through a network of stores and mobile outlets operated as CONASUPO, the National Commission on Popular Subsistence.

Although Salinas originally raised the subsidized price of corn and beans, leading to an increased production that eliminated the politically embarrassing necessity of having to import those basic elements of the Mexican diet, the general tendency of his policy was to eliminate subsidies and fixed prices, for reasons of both free-market ideology and fiscal austerity. The problem of maintaining rural incomes would be met not by high fixed prices, but by direct payments to farmers, in a program called PROCAMPO, which opposition parties denounced–with good reason, since such payments seemed to be made in key states just prior to elections.

The drastic drop in coffee prices following the removal of price guarantees was clearly a catalyst in the Zapatista insurgency in Chiapas. Especially under Zedillo, however, food prices rose sharply, imposing very severe hardships on the poor.

GENERAL ECONOMIC POLICY

Like most governments in the modern world, the Mexican government attempts to fix the general parameters of economic activity: It tries to maintain the value of the national currency unit by fiscal and monetary means; it aims for sustained economic growth through planning and investment strategies; it attempts through welfare programs to mitigate the effect of inequality in income distribution; and it tries to maintain the autonomy of national decision-making processes by the regulation of foreign investment and international trade. Until the beginning of the 1970s, these objectives were achieved rather well. Except for a burst of inflation under Alemán, the peso remained fairly stable while, in one of the world's best economic performances, the economy grew fairly steadily at a high and sustained rate. Industry expanded on the basis of import substitution and production for the domestic market, protected by a system of tariffs and controls, while adequate amounts of foreign exchange were earned through agricultural exports and tourism. The rate of foreign investment, primarily from the United States, was high.

Although (with the exception of the crisis period during the 1980s) there were no restrictions on foreign exchange or on the repatriation of profits, there were controls on the types of activity in which foreigners could invest. Some industries were reserved for public enterprise, such as power generation, railroads, telephones and telegraphs, and petroleum. Between 1982 and 1990 banking was added to the list of industries from which foreign capital was excluded.

In addition, the general rule applied that individual firms had to have majority Mexican ownership; that is, foreign participation was limited to 49 percent of ownership in most economic areas, and 34 percent in areas thought to be politically sensitive, such as mining. In practice, there was a great deal of administrative discretion in how the rule was applied, and there were ways of evading its intent, if not its letter. As part of Echeverría's more nationalist and socialist program, legislation was passed regulating the payments that could be made to foreign entities for imported technology and the use of brand names, and limiting patent rights. Although this legislation caused grumbling on the part of foreign businesspeople, who regarded it simply as providing a framework for the extortion of bribes, it by no means prevented them from doing business in Mexico.

One of the areas of investment that particularly flourished was that of the so-called *maquiladoras*, the assembly plants built in a special customs zone along the border with the United States, in which materials could be imported free of duty if the finished product was then reexported. Essentially, this was a method of exporting Mexican labor without its having to cross national borders, and attracted European and Japanese investment as well as American. The decision of the Salinas administration to form a "free trade area" with the United States promised to extend this system to all of Mexico.

Even during the years of rapid growth, however, the number of jobs in the modern sector never kept up with population growth and migration to the cities; and Mexico faced the problems of unemployment and disguised unemployment—that is, the proliferation of self-created forms of economic activity such as guarding parked cars, shining shoes, and selling lottery tickets—so characteristic of third world countries, which produce very small incomes and add nothing to the nation's production.

Even before the boom and bust in petroleum that began in the middle 1970s, it was becoming clear that there were serious limitations to the country's strategy of development based on import substitution. Apart from the irrationalities, inefficiency, and excessive costs that such a policy entails, employment was not expanding fast enough to cope with the number of new job seekers each year, let alone absorb the backlog of unemployed.[78] The López Portillo administration tried to expand Mexico's exports by placing more emphasis on agriculture and the processing of Mexico's own raw materials, as well as promoting manufactured exports. This meant removing tariff protection and subsidies to internationalize Mexican manufacturing, a change of orientation which made it possible under de la Madrid for Mexico to join the General Agreement on Tariffs and Trade, the

international association of states promoting greater international trade by eliminating tariff barriers. Mexico had previously resisted U.S. pressure to join GATT, which in 1995 became the World Trade Organization.

With the oil boom, however, many of these policy problems were overtaken by events. The very rapid increase of petroleum production and export multiplied many times over the foreign exchange available, and thus led to an overvaluation of the peso. This made Mexican goods too expensive to export and foreign goods very cheap to import, which in turn led to a decline in Mexican manufacturing because everything the country needed could be imported more cheaply. Wealthy Mexicans took advantage of the relative cheapness of the dollar to buy property in the United States and build up dollar bank accounts. The size of the national government bureaucracy, and official corruption, increased greatly. When petroleum prices dropped later in López Portillo's term, the president gambled that the decline was only temporary and continued the same high levels of government spending with borrowed money. More capital left Mexico as it became clear to everyone except the president that a devaluation of the peso would have to come. Subsequent governments had very little freedom in managing the economy once the decision not to repudiate the foreign debt had been made.

The body blows to the economy represented by the decline in oil prices, the drop in the value of the peso, the need to pay huge amounts of interest on the new foreign debt, and the Mexico City earthquake of 1985, meant that the de la Madrid administration was one long period of austerity and reduced living standards for the poor. The Salinas administration was able to stage a recovery on the basis of the almost complete adoption of the norms of the international capitalist system and the abandonment of most traditional policies of protection, subsidy, and state ownership.

This new model depended for its success on an inflow of capital, foreign and repatriated Mexican, and the renegotiation of debt. To maintain the appearance of success, Salinas had built long-term structures on short-term capital while again allowing the peso to become overvalued. This hollow structure collapsed at the beginning of Zedillo's term, when a badly managed devaluation led to a massive flight from the peso and another even more drastic round of austerity and cruelly reduced living standards.

FOREIGN DEBT AND INCOME DISTRIBUTION

Mexican governments have felt that in order to maintain the credit necessary for continued international trade, it is not possible to contemplate repudiating the debt. Given orthodox economic assumptions, this has in recent years meant a policy of deflation, reduction in rates of economic activity, cutbacks in government spending, wage freezes, and the channeling of any surplus to foreign debt payment—a policy, in effect, of redistributing the income of poor and middle-class Mexicans to foreign bankers. One of the planks in the 1988 election platform of Cuauhtémoc Cárdenas was repudiation of the foreign debt, but Cárdenas never presented a consistent and credible economic policy, and he attracted fewer votes in 1994 than in 1988.

The capitalist system has a tendency to distribute income increasingly in the form of returns on capital—that is, as rent, profits, dividends, and interest—rather than in the form of wages and salaries. In other words, left to itself, the tendency of the capitalist system is to make the rich richer. To counterbalance this tendency, efforts can be made by labor unions in the form of wage demands or by government through a variety of tax and welfare measures that redistribute income to the less affluent members of society. Some programs of this character are permanent features of policy in Mexico, such as the system of distributing basic goods through government retail outlets. Some governments, however, have been especially notable for this "left-wing" character of their policies—that of Cárdenas, of course, and those of López Mateos and Echeverría. Among other measures, the government of López Mateos introduced legislation providing for companies over a certain size to distribute a percentage of their profits to their employees.

Given the parameters of the world economic system, however, it is extremely difficult to pursue left-wing policies successfully. Capital can go on strike just as much as labor. Within a week of the inaugural speech of López Mateos, in which he identified his government as on the left, $250 million in funds were transferred out of the country. Echeverría achieved the same results in more contradictory form. Attempting to reduce Mexico's foreign debt, he made anticapitalist remarks that resulted in capital flight and forced him, paradoxically, to borrow more money abroad.

In fact, the course of economic development in Mexico had left the country with a very unequal distribution of wealth and income even before the economic crisis that began in the early 1980s. The long period of stable economic growth created a small, comfortably well-off urban middle class and a small superrich elite; urban workers also benefited, but much less. Workers in agriculture and the "marginal" unemployed and underemployed people in the cities benefited little. The economic crises of the 1980s and 1990s hit particularly hard at those social elements least able to afford it, wiping out years of moderate economic improvement.

THE MEXICAN OIL INDUSTRY

Petroleum is a particularly sensitive subject in Mexico. The expropriation of foreign oil companies by Lázaro Cárdenas was a great symbolic act of national self-assertion, and the national oil company became a special object of patriotic pride. In fact, the symbolism goes back further than that; one of the policies of Porfirio Díaz that earned his government the charge that it was *entreguista*—that is, that it had sold out to foreigners—was allowing foreign companies to own subsurface minerals, contravening the traditional Hispanic doctrine that ownership of land meant only ownership of the surface, while rights to the products of the subsoil remained with the sovereign. It was thus the traditional Hispanic law on this point, abrogated by Díaz, that was restored by the Constitution of 1917. Under Díaz the oil companies operating in Mexico, like other mineral companies, were predominantly British; with the revolution, fa-

Feature 10.3 The North American Free Trade Area

Traditionally, Mexico's economic development was based on protection and import substitution. After the economic downturn of the 1980s, drastic remedies seemed to be needed. The international climate favored free-market ideas, and Mexico elected a president who believed in the promotion of free trade and close relations with the United States. As a result, a free trade area embracing Mexico, the United States, and Canada was established, though it has not yet been fully implemented.

With justice, some Mexicans feared a loss of political autonomy in return for what might prove a limited income gain.

A concern on the U.S. side was that a free trade agreement would result in the loss of jobs in the United States. But without the new system wouldn't they be equally as likely to move anyway to Thailand or Malaysia or China? Meanwhile, American consumers need lower prices, and Mexico needs all the jobs it can get.

Another objection to NAFTA as it was actually set up is more to the point: The agreement should have included effective guarantees that particularly polluting industries would not be able to relocate to Mexico to avoid U.S. environmental legislation, and that labor would have decent conditions of work and genuine rights to organize and bargain collectively. During the 1992 election campaign, President Bill Clinton conditioned his support for NAFTA on the stipulation of such guarantees, but in the end he settled for weak *pro forma* provisions without serious enforcement mechanisms.

But the more important effects of NAFTA are primarily psychological: Investors will be more likely to keep their money in Mexico because they feel more confident that the rules of the game won't be changed; and American workers will be deterred from asking for higher wages because they are afraid their jobs may go South if they do.

voritism to British companies ended, and American companies maneuvered themselves into a leading position.

The oil business has some characteristics that make it distinctive. The exploration phase requires large expenditures, which may all be lost if no oil is found. The production phase requires minimal expenditures but produces colossal revenues. Government concession to an oil company of a specific territory to operate in is necessary, but in the absence of competitive bidding for blocks of territory the award to one company or another is arbitrary. Once production has started, the revenues that are rolling in are a tempting target for government; the immobility of the production facilities means that the company is in effect a hostage to government demands.

The combination of these factors meant that oilmen in the early years were strongwilled, adventurer types who became hugely wealthy if successful. Their absolute dependence on essentially arbitrary government favor inevitably meant that they would try to reduce their risks through bribery, in one form or another, which meant that some politician would gain wealth for himself or his cause at the cost of the country's foregoing much larger amounts of wealth. It could hardly have been coincidental that the son of Porfirio Díaz served as a member of the board of directors of the major British oil company in Mexico, or that the U.S. Standard Oil Company contributed funds to the Madero revolution, after which the lawyer who represented Standard's interests in Mexico became Madero's attorney general. With one or two exceptions, the oil barons were too arrogant and cynical to know how to deal with a sincere revolutionary like Cárdenas, and their expropriation in 1938 owes much to their mishandling of relations with him. Their previous difficulties with a revolutionary government, that of Calles, had been satisfactorily re-solved, presumably by the usual methods.

After the expropriation, the companies or-ganized an international boycott of the pur-chase of Mexican oil, so that the state corpora-tion limited its role to supplying the domestic market from established producing wells. The world's growing need for petroleum was met from production in the Middle East, Venezuela, Romania, and the United States. With no com-petition, and with established sources of pro-duction in a guaranteed and growing domestic market, PEMEX became mismanaged, wasteful, and vastly corrupt. During the 1960s, PEMEX had three or four times as many employees, in terms of the size of its operations, as compara-ble companies elsewhere. Corporation execu-tives took kickbacks from suppliers, sometimes on quite unnecessary purchases; union leaders took kickbacks from the wages of people hired through their influence; both executives and union officials were part owners of favored sup-plying firms.

Until the early 1970s, domestic oil prices were deliberately kept low to encourage the de-velopment of the economy, even lower than re-tail prices in other countries, based as they then were on a wholesale price of $3 or $4 a barrel. In the early 1970s OPEC, the Organization of Pe-troleum Exporting Countries, was able to get its act together to limit oil supply and thus force world prices up—with the implicit prior ap-proval of U.S. Secretary of State Henry Kissinger, in a typical example of that myopic "statesman-ship" that inexplicably never deflated Kissinger's overblown reputation. Kissinger apparently be-lieved that this would enable the Shah of Iran, a U.S. protégé ironically soon to be overthrown, to buy vast numbers of weapons that would make him a bulwark of anti-Communist stability in the Middle East.

The rise in oil prices, which eventually ap-proached $40 a barrel before dropping back to under $10—since then they have usually fluctu-ated around $20—made it worthwhile for Mex-ico to incur the considerable expense involved in exploration. These efforts were fabulously successful, as they could hardly fail to be: It transpired that as much as 70 percent of the en-tire territory of Mexico consists of the sedimen-tary basins in which hydrocarbon deposits are found. Exploration of less than 10 percent of the national territory showed that Mexico had the potential to become a producer on the scale of Saudi Arabia.

OIL POLICY

Because of the sensitive character of petroleum from the point of view of national pride, various policies have been adopted to make sure that Mexico's oil remains in Mexican hands. PEMEX has developed the technical capabilities to han-dle most phases of the industry, except for some specialized tasks involved in offshore drilling. On occasion, PEMEX has even given technical assistance to foreign state oil corporations. Prior to the Salinas administration, the law pro-vided that all oil exploration and development on Mexican national territory was the responsi-bility of PEMEX; offshore drilling had to be con-ducted by Mexican companies. (In fact, how-ever, the so-called Mexican companies involved in offshore drilling were actually mere legal and financial shells for what were, in their technical aspects, essentially foreign operations. This arrangement provided lucrative possibilities for some Mexicans who served as "fronts" and pro-vided legal cover—many of them, curiously enough, relatives and associates of PEMEX ex-ecutives.) In keeping with its general economic policy line, the Salinas administration began to change the rules to allow some onshore devel-opment activity by foreign oil companies.

Logically, Mexican oil that is exported should find its principal market in the United States, which it can reach by pipeline. However, in defense of national autonomy, Mexican poli-cymakers were at first concerned to limit the dependence of the United States on Mexican oil supplies, fearing that such dependence would give the United States a major reason for inter-fering in Mexican affairs and even, in the event of an interruption of supply, for occupying the oilfields. Accordingly, policies were adopted un-der López Portillo to limit "any country" to no more than 50 percent of Mexico's oil exports, which should constitute no more than 20 per-cent of that country's oil imports. Given fluctuat-ing conditions of supply and demand in the world market, it has not been possible to keep consistently within these guidelines. Mexico has diversified its export markets fairly successfully, however, with purchasers in Japan, Western and Eastern Europe, and the Caribbean region.

FOREIGN POLICY

In its foreign policy, Mexico finds itself in a difficult and delicate position. Placed by fate next to the strongest country on earth, its economic well-being is heavily dependent on its relations with the United States. Yet because of its unhappy history, and because of the revolutionary principles that its government claims to represent, Mexico even more than other countries must assert its independence from its powerful northern neighbor. Approximately two-thirds of Mexico's exports go to the United States, and almost two-thirds of its imports come from the United States. Moreover, apart from oil, Mexico's largest foreign-exchange earner, by far, is tourism and border transactions, which are extremely sensitive to the quality of relations with the United States. Yet the United States is the country, let us remember, that has repeatedly intervened in Mexican affairs; its representative conspired in the overthrow of Francisco Madero; it waged aggressive war against Mexico and annexed half of Mexico's national territory.

Mexican governments thus find themselves under the dual necessity of maintaining good relations with the United States while making clear the distinctiveness of their values and objectives in foreign policy, and maintaining their independence of action. These contradictory elements form yet another of the three great ambiguities that have characterized Mexican politics: (1) From some angles of vision Mexico is a democracy, but from others it has an authoritarian regime; (2) its economic policies until recently seemed both capitalist and Socialist; and (3) in foreign policy matters, Mexico seems sometimes to be standing out against United States policies, proudly defending its autonomy and its revolutionary principles, whereas at others it seems to be meekly falling in line with U.S. dictates. Which tendency appears strongest depends partly on the relative strength of the two governments. When Mexico felt economically

strong during the oil boom, López Portillo staked out a policy clearly opposed to that of the United States with respect to Central America; in the waning days of the Reagan administration, de la Madrid also made his opposition to U.S. policies clear. But between those times, when Reagan was at his peak and the Mexican economy at its weakest, Mexican governments kept a low profile in Central American policy. Nevertheless, given Mexico's economic dependence on the United States, it is surprising how independent of American wishes Mexican foreign policy has sometimes been. Mexico refused to sign the "Declaration of Caracas," pushed through the Organization of American States (OAS) by U.S. pressure, which provided the ideological basis for the U.S.-backed exile invasion that helped to overthrow the leftist government of Guatemala in 1954. Mexico refused to go along with the other members of the OAS in breaking relations with Cuba, and declined to support the sending of an "Inter-American peace force" into the Dominican Republic in 1965. Mexico also resisted pressure from the Reagan administration to join in its crusade against the Sandinista government of Nicaragua, which resembled early postrevolutionary Mexican governments in many respects, and joined with other Latin American countries in trying to bring peace to Nicaragua; it made clear its sympathy with rebel forces in El Salvador, where the United States supported the conservative government side in a long-drawn-out civil war that neither side seemed capable of winning.

U.S. administrations have usually shown understanding for the Mexican government's need to demonstrate autonomy from the United States and have not gone to the most extreme lengths to secure Mexican adherence to purely symbolic measures, such as votes in OAS meetings. When U.S. governments have felt very strongly about specific questions, however, they have usually been able to secure Mexican compliance. For example, at one point President Nixon secured Mexican cooperation with U.S. drug policies by ordering a tightening of customs inspections at the border which, in effect, brought border traffic to a standstill.

In general, Mexican governments handle the conflicting requirements of national autonomy and pressure from the United States by resorting to the same calculated policies of deliberate ambiguity that they apply to domestic policy areas. Thus the Mexicans refused to break diplomatic relations with Cuba, but their secret services cooperated with the CIA in keeping track of travelers to and from Cuba through Mexico. Conversely, Mexico has respected U.S. wishes that it not join OPEC, but it has followed OPEC policies with respect to pricing without being a member.

There are a series of problems in Mexican-U.S. relations that grow out of the common border. Indeed, for some time the demarcation of the border was itself in doubt after the Rio Grande changed course. A final solution to that problem was reached during the late 1960s. The two countries have various cooperative mechanisms for attempting to solve other border problems, some of which have proved capable of solution, while others are perennial sources of difficulty. Some principal problems in recent years have been the division of the waters of the Colorado River, which both countries share; problems connected with Mexican migration to the United States; air pollution by industries on one side of the border which drifts across into the other country; the negative impact of U.S. food regulations on imports of vegetables from Mexico; the allocation of airline routes between the airlines of the two countries; fishing problems; and drug trafficking. From time to time, the U.S. government and U.S. public opinion fix on one of these issues and blow it up into a "crisis." For several of these issues, such as illegal immigration and drug trafficking, no satisfactory permanent solution appears possible, although intelligent joint management of policy may reduce the damage the situations create.

It is true that the long border, which is after all, as President López Portillo once said, the border between the first world and the third world, should give rise to a range of problems. It also gives rise to benefits and opportunities for both countries. The volume of tourism and retail sales to nationals of the other country is considerable on both sides; it constitutes a significant item in Mexico's balance of payments, about 25 percent of Mexico's total foreign income in an average year. At the same time, Mexicans contribute about one-fourth of all the income the United States derives from tourism.

Mexican immigrants, legal or not, contribute their labor to the U.S. economy and pay taxes greater than the value of public services they receive. At the same time, the money they bring back to Mexico from jobs in the United States is a significant source of capital for the founding of small businesses. In recent years, a significant and growing part of the Mexican economy has been the in-bond assembly plants, or *maquiladoras,* located in the border region.

CONCLUSION

Mexico has had one of the most stable political systems in the world. The constitutional succession has been unbroken since 1934; each president has served the full term for which he was elected and yielded his office to an elected successor. There are no more than a handful of other countries in the world about which a similar statement can be made. And yet this is a country that has been in a state of continual change. Mexico's population has increased enormously; it has gone from a predominantly rural to a predominantly urban society; a vast land reform program has been carried out; illiteracy has decreased almost to the vanishing point; the role of the military in politics has shrunk dramatically; and the role of opposition parties has grown.

Prediction in the social sciences increases in accuracy the fewer the number of variables in play and the more their effect can be fully grasped and measured. A great many factors will influence the future political evolution of Mexico; their interactions cannot be foreseen, nor their impact precisely assessed. The key question about Mexico's political future is the extent to which the ruling party can retain a dominant role and the extent to which changing circumstances will cause it to yield power, even the ultimate power of the presidency itself.

It is axiomatic that the PRI will try to remain in power. President Zedillo's show of sincere support for fairness and honesty in the conduct of elections was no more than could be expected from a politically weak president under pressure from a growing opposition. The party's apparent retreat from a hegemonic position is a strategic retreat that might be prolonged indefinitely without yielding the citadel. Yet the extraordinary events of 1994—the assassinations and the Zapatista rebellion—suggest the possibility that the situation may slip out of the grasp of the ruling elite.

Predictions are based on the experience of the past, and therefore tend to underestimate the likelihood of novel outcomes. But based on that experience—which shows the resilience and resourcefulness of the PRI's political managers, the party's capacity to co-opt dissidents, and its powerful will to remain in power—one should resist the temptation to expect anything other than that Mexico will retain its distinctive dominant single-party regime for the foreseeable future.

KEY TERMS

CONASUPO
disguised unemployment
ejido
maquiladora
North American Free Trade Area (NAFTA)
Organization of American States (OAS)
Organization of Petroleum Exporting
    Countries (OPEC)
PEMEX

FURTHER READING

Brand, Donald D. *Mexico: Land of Sunshine and Shadow* (Princeton: Van Nostrand, 1966).

Camp, Roderic A. *Entrepreneurs and Politics in Twentieth-Century Mexico* (New York: Oxford University Press, 1989)

Camp, Roderic A. *Generals in the Palacio* (New York: Oxford University Press, 1992)

Cline, Howard F. *The United States and Mexico* (Cambridge: Harvard University Press, 1953).

Gentleman, Judith. *Mexican Politics in Transition* (Boulder, CO: Westview Press, 1987).

Hellman, Judith Adler. *Mexico in Crisis*, 2nd ed. (New York: Holmes and Meier, 1988).

Levy, Daniel, and Gabriel Székely. *Mexico: Paradoxes of Stability and Change*, 2nd ed. (Boulder, CO: Westview Press, 1987).

Needler, Martin C. *Mexican Politics: The Containment of Conflict*, 3rd ed. (New York: Praeger, 1995).

Needler, Martin C. *Politics and Society in Mexico* (Albuquerque: University of New Mexico Press, 1971).

Paz, Octavio. *The Labyrinth of Solitude*, translated by Lysander Kemp (New York: Grove Press, 1961).

Paz, Octavio. *The Other Mexico: Critique of the Pyramid*, translated by Lysander Kemp (New York: Grove Press, 1972).

Philip, George. *The Presidency in Mexican Politics.* (New York: St. Martin's Press, 1992).

Rodríguez, Jaime, ed. *The Evolution of the Mexican Political System* (Wilmington, DE: SR Books, 1993).

NOTES

1. Texas (and, for a few days, California) had a period of existence as an independent republic before joining the United States. Mexico had been willing to tolerate the secession of Texas as an independent republic, but its refusal to accept the annexation of Texas to the United States was one of the causes of the war.
2. Obregón to Frank Bohn, February 12, 1924.
3. This was subsequently reamended so that anyone who has served as president can never be elected again.
4. According to a poll reported by the *Los Angeles Times* on August 20, 1989, 68 percent of Mexican respondents believed that Salinas had not actually won the election.
5. Milovan Djilas, *The New Class* (New York: Harcourt, Brace, 1957)
6. A good discussion of the organization can be found in Luis Felipe Bravo Mena, "COPARMEX and Mexican Politics," in Sylvia Maxfield and Ricardo Anzaldúa Montoya, *Government and Private Sector in Contemporary Mexico* (San Diego: Center for U.S.-Mexican Studies, University of California, 1987)
7. See Ruth Berins Collier, *The Contradictory Alliance: State-Labor Relations and Regime Change in Mexico*, International and Area Studies Research Series, #48 (Berkeley: University of California, 1992).
8. Even when the economy was doing well, only one-third of those entering the labor force each year found regular jobs in the "formal" sector of the economy, according to *The New York Times*, July 25, 1989.

CHAPTER 11

The Government of Nigeria
Stephen Wright

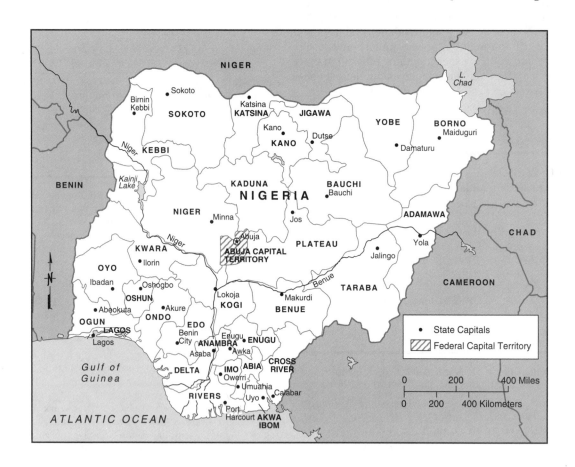

Political Development

Nigeria is Africa's most populous country and also one of its most unpredictable. Since its independence from British colonial rule on October 1, 1960, Nigeria has struggled to survive through numerous political crises, including a bitter civil war between 1967 and 1970. The country has been ruled by military governments for all but four years since 1966 (see Table 11.1). Three heads of state have been assassinated in office, and the country has witnessed numerous successful and attempted coups d'état. With such instability and rapid change, the development of the country's political process and institutions has been seriously affected; hence, the continuity and "rhythm" of government found in more developed countries is not present.

Nigeria's experience is somewhat typical within an African context. Most countries on the continent face severe economic and political challenges, and many remain ruled by authoritarian regimes despite the burst of democratization in Africa over the last six years.[1] The current transition program in Nigeria aims to return government to civilian control in October 1998, but past experience suggests this will not occur.

Despite the problems of governing and the prevalence of military regimes, Nigeria was until the late 1980s one of the more open African societies, where press freedom and civil liberties had generally been respected, though not always maintained. During the 1990s, military governments have become increasingly repressive and have tolerated little or no opposition to their rule.

Political intrigue has prevented an accurate census from being taken since independence, although the military government concluded a relatively uncontested one in 1993 (see Feature 11.1). This census calculated the population to be 88.5 million, down from the previously accepted estimate of 115 million. The population is expected to triple by 2030.

Electoral registers have always been inflated to promote illicit regional gains. A register drawn up in 1987 had 72 million electors; using this number the country's population was suggested to be 150 million, a figure disbelieved by

Table 11.1 NIGERIAN GOVERNMENTS, 1960–1996

Period	Head of State	Ethnicity	Type of Government	How Ended
1960–1966	Tafawa Balewa	Hausa-Fulani	Civilian	Attempted coup/ assassination
1966	Aguiyi-Ironsi	Ibo	Military	Coup/assassination
1966–1975	Gowon	Middle Belt	Military	Coup
1975–1976	Muhammed	Hausa-Fulani	Military	Attempted coup/ assassination
1976–1979	Obasanjo	Yoruba	Military	Elections
1979–1983	Shagari	Hausa-Fulani	Civilian	Coup
1984–1985	Buhari	Hausa-Fulani	Military	Coup
1985–1993	Babangida	Middle Belt	Military	Palace coup
(1993)	Abiola	Yoruba	Civilian	Election annulled
1993	Shonekan	Yoruba	Interim	Coup
1993–	Abacha	Hausa-Fulani	Military	

Feature 11.1 The 1991–1993 Census

The inability to count its population accurately indicates a relative immaturity in the Nigerian polity and provides difficulties in drawing up development plans to cater adequately for the people's needs. The fact that numbers influence both electoral district and revenue allocations has led to incessant intrigue, making accurate head counts impossible.

Since 1863, there have been 12 census attempts, but none has brought results to inspire confidence. Prior to the 1990s, two postindependence censuses had been attempted, with little success. The 1991–1993 census was undertaken in difficult circumstances, namely in the middle of a fierce electoral contest. Organization was a logistical nightmare. In order to minimize corrupt activities, millions of dollars were spent on computers and transport, and the country was divided into 250,000 enumeration areas, with close to 600,000 enumerators employed. Pre-census trials were undertaken in selected areas to smooth out administrative difficulties.

The census results were received in 1993 fairly calmly in contrast to those of the past. That should not necessarily indicate acceptance of the result. The total population was calculated at 88.5 million, considerably below expectation. For the first time ever, it was acknowledged that the southern population was larger than that of the North. The growth rate of 2.1 percent per year was low by African standards, casting doubt on the figures. Some northern states had incredulously grown by 100 percent since the last census. Few believe that this census has provided the true story of Nigeria's population.

---

everyone, including the government itself. A register used for the 1990 local government elections contained only 56 million names, but a register drawn up in late 1991 contained almost 65 million names. Whatever the precise figure, Nigeria accounts for approximately 15 percent of Africa's total population of 600 million, even though it is only one of some 50 states on the continent.

The political problems already mentioned reflect the strong undercurrent of diversity and division within contemporary Nigeria. The country is comprised of about 250 ethnic and linguistic groups, but the three largest groups have predominated: the Hausa-Fulani in the North, the Yoruba in the West (though geographically this is the southwest of the country), and the Ibo (or Igbo) in the East (geographically the southeast). Much of Nigeria's independent life has been dominated by the mutual suspicions and cut-and-thrust politics between (and sometimes within) these groups, who account for some 60 to 65 percent of the total population. The smaller groups, including the Nupe and Tiv clustered in the country's "Middle Belt" region, as well as the Edo, Ijaw, Kanuri, and

Ogoni, have increasingly striven to exert influence upon political life.

This complex picture of sociocultural cleavages and diversity is compounded by crucial religious differences within the country. While actual figures are again a source of controversy, most observers agree that the country can be divided roughly equally: The North is predominantly Muslim, and the South is predominantly Christian (although a number of traditional religions have also survived). The historical reasons for this division will be discussed later, but these religious differences, superimposed upon ethnic cleavages, have provided a most difficult issue for the Nigerian state to resolve.

It is important to point out that these ethnic tensions are not wholly a Nigerian creation or responsibility, because British colonial administrators deliberately sought to divide these various groups and mobilize them against each other. Moreover, the British model of parliamentary government inherited by Nigerians at independence soon proved to be a poor framework for local political conditions and only served to heighten competition and rivalry. Climatic, linguistic, and cultural differences were also responsible for sowing the seeds of discord that have weakened the country. Nigeria, then, developed not with any real internal logic, but as a "conglomerate" of ethnic and religious groups.

Unlike the British and American political systems, which have evolved gradually, the Nigerian system has made several significant readjustments in attempts to resolve the internal tensions and create a suitable style and structure of government. To some extent, Nigeria provides a case study to fulfill a political scientist's dream (or nightmare) because several distinct types of political structure have been utilized since independence. The First Republic (1960–1966) operated on a parliamentary system modeled after Britain's, whereas the Second Republic (1979–1983) adopted an American-style presidential constitution, complete with Senate and House of Representatives. The Third Republic, postponed since 1990, was also to have an American-style system. However, in 1995 the military government announced that the next civilian government scheduled to begin in 1998 would follow a hybrid French/Russian model of mixed presidential and parliamentary structures.

Military regimes have also varied considerably, from the crude, somewhat politically unaware rule of General J. Aguiyi-Ironsi (1966) to the benign, developmental approach of Yakubu Gowon (1966–1975), and from the crusading mood of Murtala Muhammed (1975–1976) to the harsh, repressive regimes of Muhammadu Buhari (1984–1985) and Sani Abacha (1993–). The other military heads of state, Olusegun Obasanjo (1976–1979) and Ibrahim Babangida (1985–1993), have been more "moderate" in policy style, although Babangida stifled numerous attempts at civilian government and became more repressive in the 1990s.

If the Nigerian panorama already appears to be complex, then it is further complicated by two fundamental factors. First, although the country is federal in structure, there has been a constant political struggle between federal and state centers. At independence, the three regional governments (North, West, and East) were powerful enough to disrupt the effectiveness of the federal government, contributing to the downfall of the First Republic in 1966. Sociopolitical cleavages and political necessity

forced a devolution of regional power to four regions in 1964, then to 12 states in 1967, 19 states in 1976, 21 states in 1987, and 30 states in 1991. The creation of yet more states is anticipated before 1998.

Second, the influence of the federal government over the states has been dramatically increased by its control of the country's oil wealth. During the 1970s, Nigerian oil production rapidly increased, making the country then the sixth largest producer in the world and Africa's preeminent member of the Organization of Petroleum Exporting Countries (OPEC). At the end of the decade, Nigeria was the wealthiest country in sub-Saharan Africa, with a strong voice on the world stage, but the subsequent oil glut, economic depression, and failure to diversify in the 1980s and 1990s caused serious political and economic problems for the country. In addition, this oil wealth was seized upon by military and civilian leaders, and greed and corruption became predominant features of Nigerian political life.

HISTORICAL INFLUENCES ON POLITICAL DEVELOPMENT

Nigeria in its contemporary geographical form was created only in the early part of the twentieth century, following the amalgamation of northern and southern colonial provinces for the convenience of British colonial administrators. The name "Nigeria" was, in fact, coined in Britain in 1897 in a letter to *The Times* of London; it was not decided upon by indigenes of the "new" country. The earlier historical development in western Africa concerns empires and competing kingdoms or principalities that no longer exist today, but whose former territories now comprise Nigeria as well as neighboring states such as Cameroon, Niger, and Benin. These kingdoms traded and competed with each other for many centuries prior to European colonization; they had reached advanced stages of technical, political, and cultural development—achievements overlooked in the arrogance and plunder of the colonial powers. The Benin empire, to take one case, was a classic example of a society developing from the twelfth century; its internal political system had pattern, legitimacy, and stability, while its bronze statues and sculptures are still widely recognized for their high artistic merit. The Oyo empire, which dates from the thirteenth century, has a similarly strong cultural history.

Cultural differences between these kingdoms were reinforced by geographical factors. In the southern areas, the tropical rain forest influenced the style of farming and living patterns and led to the development of what has been described as a "gun" society, a feature common after 1600 with the expansion of the slave trade in these areas. In the North, in contrast, the drier, open savanna lands led to the development of a "horse" society; the global slave system made less inroads here.[2]

For the last thousand years, Islam has influenced the northern savanna lands as trade by camel across the Sahara desert, to and from the Middle East and North Africa, made these people look inward toward the desert, in contrast to the southern kingdoms which looked outward toward the Atlantic Ocean. Islam has a much longer presence in Nigeria than has Christianity, and its influence in the North was reinforced and expanded in the early nineteenth century by the radical zeal of Usman Dan Fodio. Christianity first appeared with the Portuguese influence and missionaries along the coast some 300 or so years ago. Lagos (a Portuguese name) became a major port and later capital, and along with Calabar was used heavily in the slave trade, which was the dominant economic activity at that time. The British presence grew steadily through the nineteenth century, with Lagos annexed in 1861, and following the 1884 Berlin conference—which carved up Africa indiscriminately among the European powers—the British consolidated their grip on the disparate regions of what was to be the artificially created nation of Nigeria. At no time were the interests of "Nigerians" themselves considered.

British Colonial Rule

Although Nigerians were exposed to European and Middle Eastern influences for many centuries, the period of direct British colonial control lasted for less than 70 years. Nigerian resistance to British expansion was fierce, and the whole country did not come under British administration until the early 1900s. The British, like other colonizers elsewhere in Africa, had little idea of whom they had conquered or of the complexity of those societies. For some colonizers there was a sense of mission—the "white man's burden"—to improve the standard of living among Africans, but in reality the colonial period became more concerned with exploitation than development. The impact of colonialism on the economic and political fabric of the country was immense, and the repercussions have had serious implications for contemporary Nigeria.

Although slavery was officially outlawed, the British showed little hesitation in reorganizing the Nigerian economy to suit their own requirements. The three nascent regions became identified with individual cash crops: The North was dominated by groundnut (peanut) production, the West by cocoa, and the East by palm oil. Possessing distinct economic bases, the regions were further separated from each other by the policy referred to as "indirect rule." Although colonial administrators retained the controlling influence, this policy allowed chiefs and emirs to control local affairs within their own areas of jurisdiction. Distinct regional identities began to develop, with each looking inward for support and increasingly competing with the others for favors from the central colonial administration. Cultural differences were also reinforced in education, where southerners became deeply influenced and motivated by Western Christian, missionary, or "secular" education and values, while northern children (or the minority who received any formal education) were educated in a more traditional and "conservative" environment of Islam.[3] Prior to independence, this uneven educational pattern left many northerners feeling threatened that they would be unable to compete successfully for jobs with southerners, a valid fear which has still not been fully resolved, although quotas and federal initiatives (similar in some ways to "affirmative action" in the United States) have helped to restore the balance to some extent.

By 1946 three regions had been formally established by the colonial authorities, with commodity boards also at regional levels to purchase produce from within the region. Following World War II, nationalist agitation increased by building upon the prewar activity of groups such as Herbert Macauley's Nigerian National Democratic Party and the Nigerian Youth Movement. Such agitation became more successful as Britain's ability and willingness to maintain its colonial possession diminished. Nationalist movements formed nominally at the national level, but their activities were heavily influenced by regional and ethnic factors. Political parties established in the 1940s and 1950s were essentially monoethnic, and elections in the 1950s reinforced regional rather than national orientations. Politicians were forced to compete for control of the regional commodity boards because these held the key to finances and future political success.

A series of constitutional amendments during the 1940s and 1950s paved the way for independence. In 1946, the governor of Nigeria, Sir Arthur Richards, consolidated the process of regionalism by establishing three assemblies in the North, West, and East. In 1951, the MacPherson Constitution (named after another governor) allowed these regions to make their own laws and to elect their own representatives and ministers, and the three regions were given equal status in the central legislature. By 1954, problems had emerged that required a further readjustment of the political structure by the Lyttleton Constitution. Under this, a federal structure was organized dividing power between the federal government and the three regional governments. Direct elections were used to provide equal numbers of representatives for each region in the federal legislature. Regional orientations, however, were strengthened by giving taxation powers to each region, as well as by restricting administrators and bureaucrats to work only in their "region of origin."

This constitutional framework totally ignored the wishes of minority groups (approximately 40 percent of the population), a problem which was not addressed for more than a decade. The eastern and western regions gained self-government in 1957, but the North delayed this until 1959 in an attempt to buy more time to prepare for the competition and rivalry set to take place after independence was declared on October 1, 1960. At this time the North, which accounted for two-thirds of the territory of Nigeria and 40 to 45 percent of the population, had benefited from the alteration of electoral provisions from one that had seats shared equally among the three regions to one that awarded seats on the basis of population. The North managed to emerge at independence as the dominant partner within the federation, as well as have its own representative, Sir Alhaji Abubakar Tafawa Balewa, as prime minister.

THE FIRST REPUBLIC, 1960–1966

Nigeria emerged in October 1960 as a fragile amalgam of distrusting partners. Ethnic divisions accentuated during the colonial period were now magnified as groups vied with each other for patronage from and control over the federal center. Single political parties dominated the regional governments—the Northern People's Congress (NPC) in the North, composed essentially of Hausa-Fulani; the Action Group (AG) in the West, made up of Yoruba supporters; and the National Convention of Nigerian Citizens (NCNC) in the East, comprised almost exclusively of Ibo people.[4] Clashes over policy between federal and regional governments were exacerbated by divisions within the federal government itself, where the inherited parliamentary system promoted a confrontational attitude toward political debate. Minorities such as the Tiv, Nupe, Kanuri, and Ibibio could not get their voices heard. Within three or four years, the federal government had lost its control over the West, where political chaos became prevalent. Elections were rigged, thuggery and intimidation became widespread, and opposition leaders, notably the Yoruba spokesperson Chief Obafemi Awolowo, were imprisoned. The fragile political machinery of the country failed.

Against this political backdrop, other important developments were taking shape. The armed forces were becoming Africanized—at independence, only 10 percent of the officers were African, but by 1965 only 10 percent remained expatriate. Rapid promotion within the ranks had brought many southern, and specifically Ibo, officers to positions of leadership. These officers were predominantly trained in Britain, and were supposedly inculcated with the philosophy of nonintervention in politics. However, their skills of organization and discipline combined with their increasing concern over the political chaos in the country, helped to draw the military nearer to political involvement. The Ibo officer corps was also unhappy with what it considered to be northern domination of Nigeria, and the failure by Ibos to get a fair slice of the Nigerian pie.

These tensions came to a head on January 15, 1966, when the country's first military coup d'état took place, installing a government perceived by many to be Ibo-dominated and assassinating the North's two most powerful leaders, Tafawa Balewa and Sir Alhaji Ahmadu Bello, the Sardauna of Sokoto and premier of the North. In recent years, some scholars have interpreted the coup as having been nationalist in origin, striving to rid the country of ethnic (northern) domination. Evidence for this view is inconclusive, but there was no hesitation within northern Nigeria in perceiving this to be an outright assault upon its people. The collapse and overthrow of the First Republic led, within 15 months, to a bitter civil war and an unbroken 13 years of military rule.

MILITARY GOVERNMENT, 1966–1979

The seizure of power by the military on January 15–16, 1966, was an indication of the failure to provide stable government. The military, however, fared little better than the civilians, and the social fabric of the country rapidly deteriorated. The junior officers who perpetrated the coup proved to be badly organized, and so leadership reverted to the Army Chief of Staff, Maj. Gen. J. Aguiyi-Ironsi. Although he was already in a precarious position, his decision in May 1966 to abolish the regions in favor of a unitary system of government inflamed northern opinion and provided the grounds for a countercoup on July 29, 1966, in which Ibo officers were removed from power. Lt. Col. (later General) Yakubu Gowon, a 32-year-old, was chosen as a compromise candidate for leadership, both because he was from a minority ethnic group and because he was a Christian northerner.

Gowon attempted to defuse the tensions within the country by calling a Constitutional Conference in August–September 1966 to resolve regional differences. The North initially sought secession from the Republic, but in the end its leaders were persuaded against this, influenced by significant pressure from the United States and Britain. The East, however, came to favor secession, a desire strengthened by the massacre of many thousands of innocent Ibos in northern Nigeria during May and September–October 1966, causing millions to flee the North to the relative safety of the East. The East was also the center of the developing oil industry and thus had considerable economic potential; moreover, Ibos were renowned for their economic resourcefulness and expertise.

On May 26, 1967, Gowon attempted to preempt secession by splitting the regions into 12 states, but four days later the Eastern Region declared its independence as "Biafra," and the civil war, or the "war of national unity," was begun. The war claimed the lives of untold millions of Nigerians and proved to be the ultimate test of unity and loyalty for the nascent state. The complex problem of national integration was one faced by many African states, and so the war was watched closely by the rest of the continent. Only four African countries formally recognized Biafra, and many Western states would only provide humanitarian assistance to the secessionists. The rest of the Nigerian federation united against this challenge and, with large military assistance from the Soviet Union and other Eastern European countries, and after 1967 from Britain, finally crushed the rebellion in January 1970.[5]

Gowon, to his credit and Nigeria's benefit, was magnanimous in victory and sought the reconciliation of all the warring factions. Although Biafran soldiers were excluded from further military service, many officers were reintegrated into the Nigerian army, which had grown to over 250,000 troops by 1972—a significant social and political problem in itself. Economic reconstruction was facilitated by the rapid increase in oil production and revenues, which were themselves further boosted by the OPEC "revolution" of October 1973. Such was the confidence of the country by the mid-1970s that Nigeria cultivated its image as a continental leader, and the country appeared to be awash with oil money and large development projects. Across-the-board pay raises fueled inflation, but nobody seemed to worry. Indeed, the military leaders were at the front of the line helping themselves to Nigeria's wealth.

The vast corruption of the military leaders, the inefficiency and apparent lack of direction of development goals, the squandering of the oil wealth, and the failure to provide a program for return to civilian rule all helped to stir up divisions within the military, contributing to Gowon being overthrown by fellow officers on July 29, 1975, exactly nine years after he had come to power. Murtala Muhammed set out to tackle the worst excesses of corruption and fixed a timetable to return to civilian rule by October 1979. Murtala's radical and crusading zeal led to the dismissal of 10,000 government officials and 150 officers, and naturally upset many Nigerians who had gained illicitly from the previous regime. Murtala also threatened to trim the armed forces by 50 percent. Consequently, Murtala was assassinated on February 13, 1976 by disgruntled officers, many of whom were found to be from Gowon's home area.

Returning to Civilian Rule

Lt. Gen. Olusegun Obasanjo, the first head of state of Yoruba ethnicity, continued to implement the political transition program. A Constituent Assembly met in 1976 to draw up a new constitution and political framework for the country that would allow for potentially greater stability. Differences emerged between delegates, especially concerning the status of Shari'a, or Islamic, courts within the federation, but the Constitution when implemented in 1979 proved to be a balanced document, and it was generally welcomed by Nigerians.

Nigerians accepted that a federal system had to be maintained, and the discredited parliamentary system of the First Republic was replaced by an executive presidential system, balanced by a National Assembly of two federal houses, namely, the Senate and House of Representatives. Like their American counterparts, the Senate gave equal representation to the states of the federation (increased to 19 in 1976 following the report of the Irikefe Commission), and the lower House had its members distributed and elected on the basis of population. Government at the state level was to be under a governor and a single assembly. Following elections held in mid–1979, the Second Republic was born on October 1, 1979.

THE SECOND REPUBLIC, 1979–1983

Only five political parties had been allowed to register under guidelines for the 1979 elections, and of these the National Party of Nigeria (NPN) emerged as the dominant one. The new president, Alhaji Shehu Shagari, was elected on the NPN ticket, and the party was able to secure a majority in both houses of the National Assembly. At the state level the picture was more complex, as the smaller parties were able to gain control of nine state governments. Although the military had forced all five parties to be of "national" rather than "ethnic" origin, the election results confirmed fears that ethnicity had not been suppressed. The Unity Party of Nigeria (UPN) was backed predominantly by Yoruba supporters and won the states of the Southwest, whereas the Nigeria People's Party (NPP), closely linked to Ibo support, won the three states in the Southeast.

The NPN did succeed to some extent in cutting across ethnic barriers and striking bargains with southern elements, although it found it difficult to completely shed its image as the party representing northern interests. The electoral process was not as violent or combustible as it had been some 15 years earlier, but tensions grew in the early 1980s between a number of states and the federal government, and within a few states where the governor was not a member of the majority party. Pressure for the creation of more states rose dramatically as political elites around the country attempted to control their own futures. The power of patronage that the NPN possessed helped it to maintain its grip on the country, but opposition to the government grew substantially. Such antagonism was exacerbated by the chronic condition of the economy following the collapse in oil prices, as well as by the rampant and blatant corruption associated with the NPN.

Elections held in mid–1983 returned the NPN to office, but allegations of widespread ballot rigging cast serious doubts upon the results. Riots broke out in areas supported by opposition parties, particularly in the southwestern states, and the federal government appeared to be losing control and direction. Against this background, and with the fear of further bloodshed in the local government elections slated for

January 1984, the military intervened on New Year's Eve 1983 and started its second period in government.

MILITARY GOVERNMENT AND TRANSITION PROGRAMS, 1984–

Military government under Muhammadu Buhari proved to be a bitter experience for most Nigerians. Top civilian leaders, including the former president and vice president, were jailed, and tribunals were organized for those suspected of corrupt practices. A severe clampdown on press freedom was instituted and a "War Against Indiscipline" (WAI) started to instill better behavior and moral values in the population. Set within the acute economic hardship faced by most Nigerians—accentuated by falling oil revenues and deteriorating terms of trade—the initial euphoria that had greeted the overthrow of the civilians was soon displaced by a similar distaste for the military leaders. Such unease was felt within the military itself, and in August 1985 Buhari was removed by his colleagues in a "palace coup," and Gen. Ibrahim Babangida took over the reins of office.

Babangida's government relaxed some of the harsher policies of its predecessor and introduced radical economic measures in an attempt to alleviate the severe hardship faced by the majority. Although Babangida did not accept direct assistance from the International Monetary Fund (IMF), the policies implemented followed programs "suggested" by the IMF and enabled Nigeria to receive large World Bank loans. The most significant structural adjustments included an initial 60 percent devaluation of the national currency, the naira, the abolition of commodity boards, and the privatization of many inefficient government-owned corporations (or *parastatals*), the relaxation of import-export regulations and the gradual reduction of government subsidies. These were difficult and unpopular reforms that had marginal success.

On political reforms, Babangida (after surviving a coup attempt in December 1985) announced in January 1986 a plan to return the country to civilian rule by 1990. In July 1987 the complete program was detailed, with the transfer date pushed back to 1992. Significantly, the presidential system of government

was to be retained, but eventually only two government-created parties, the National Republican Convention (NRC) and the Social Democratic Party (SDP), were allowed to compete. All politicians and military personnel who served in federal or state governments or assemblies from 1960 to 1991 were initially barred from contesting for office in 1992 in an attempt to recruit a different political elite, though this ban was lifted in 1992.

Babangida postponed the presidential elections slated for 1992, claiming that northerners had been selected as candidates for both parties. A new transition timetable was drawn up for 1993, and after a tortuous process, new presidential candidates were nominated by their respective parties. The NRC had Bashir Othman Tofa, a Muslim northerner, as candidate, whereas the SDP nominated Bashoru Moshood Abiola, a Muslim Yoruba southerner and publishing tycoon.

The presidential election took place on June 12, 1993. The National Electoral Commission (NEC) announced that Abiola had received 58 percent of the vote, and won 19 of 30 states. Abiola's victory stunned the northern establishment, and on June 23, 1993, the military government annulled the election result, claiming various irregularities in polling—and being afraid of radical SDP elements probing into the financial affairs of the military leadership. Babangida, who had allegedly received financing from Abiola to launch his 1985 coup, was himself isolated within the military's inner circle and forced to relinquish office on August 27, 1993. An interim government was established under the nominal leadership of Ernest Shonekan, a prominent Yoruba businessman, and fresh presidential elections were promised for March 1994. These never occurred, as General Sani Abacha overthrew this government on November 17, 1993, abandoning the transition program and much of the structural adjustment.

During the second half of 1994, a Constitutional Conference was established to, yet again, consider the best political structure for the country. Tensions within Nigeria increased significantly. Abiola returned from exile in June 1994 to claim his presidency and was immediately jailed awaiting a treason trial, still not held by early 1996. In February 1995, more than 300 senior military and retired officers were rounded up, including former head of state Obasanjo, after allegations of a coup attempt by them. In October 1995, Abacha announced a program to return to civilian rule by October 1998. A new constitutional framework of "zoning" of top political offices was to facilitate ethnic/regional balance, as was a hybrid presidential and parliamentary framework of government. Abacha was criticized from within and outside the country for such a long drawn-out program, and few had any confidence that it would be adhered to.

SOCIETAL AGENDAS

It should be evident already that Nigeria is a volatile and unpredictable country. The fluidity of Nigeria's political structure, and the experimentation with different styles of government, is indicative of numerous social and political problems to which the country is striving to find solutions. Some of these issues are examined here.

Nation Building

Probably the most serious and difficult task facing the country since independence has been making people loyal to the concept of Nigeria, rather than allowing diverse ethnic sympathies to predominate over a national orientation. This task of nation building is common to African countries, where artificial state boundaries often force people of differing cultural backgrounds to live together. Since 1960, Nigeria has provided an arena for the struggle between ethnic identities and national identity as defined by the federal center, where the former has often won to the detriment of the common good.

Efforts by successive governments to control ethnicity have had some impact. "Federal character" is a term widely used in employment and political circles (and in the Constitution) to denote fair and equitable opportunities for all ethnic groups within the federation, so that discrimination is officially discouraged. Military recruitment also follows this guideline. Political parties can no longer legally be regionally or ethnically biased and must open offices in and recruit candidates from regions all over the federation. As we have seen, this did not prevent ethnic sentiment from surfacing in the Second

Republic, and it has become a critical factor in the politics of the 1990s. This is not only because of tensions generated by recivilianization, but especially because of the severe impact of structural adjustment policies in bringing deteriorating economic conditions to the majority, so heightening ethnic awareness and competition in the struggle to survive.[6]

The role within Nigeria of traditional rulers, chiefs, and emirs has declined as their powers have gradually diminished. The rapid changes taking place within the country mean that there is little continuity in government or precedent by which to act. The longest any civilian government has survived to develop such traditions is only six years (1960–1966).

The dynamics of growth and change have generated pressures from a variety of sources to increase the number of states in the federation from 3 to 30 (see Table 11.2). The creation of new states has alleviated some sociocultural tensions and allowed minority groups greater control over their affairs. New states have also produced jobs for underrepresented minority groups. Unfortunately, it has not automatically led to any more efficient control over resources or their use, and this multiplicity of government has become a major drain on the country's limited finances. These new states have also not provided more honest and capable leadership, and this has seriously hindered the development of a true national consciousness. Despite the creation of nine new states in August 1991, and the resulting confusion within the transition program, the Abacha government has intimated that more states will be created before 1998.

Religious Tolerance

Nigeria contains almost equal numbers of Christians and Muslims, who together account for 60–70 percent of the national population. Christianity provides the major religion of the South, with Protestants concentrated in the Southwest and Catholics in the Southeast. There are numerous sects and denominations which further divide Christians and make the religious scene more complex. Islam is the predominant religious force in the North, and Nigeria's Muslim pilgrims to Mecca in the 1980s formed the largest single group from any country. There

Table 11.2 Nigeria's Regions and States, 1963–1991

1963	1967	1976	1987	1991
Northern Region	Northwestern	Sokoto	Sokoto	Sokoto
				Kebbi
		Niger	Niger	Niger
	Northeastern	Borno	Borno	Borno
				Yobe
		Bauchi	Bauchi	Bauchi
		Gongola	Gongola	Adamawa
				Taraba
	North-Central	Kaduna	Kaduna	Kaduna
			Katsina	Katsina
	Benue-Plateau	Benue	Benue	Benue
		Plateau	Plateau	Plateau
	West-Central	Kwara	Kwara	Kwara
				Kogi
	Kano	Kano	Kano	Kano
				Jigawa
Eastern Region	East-Central	Anambra	Anambra	Enugu
				Anambra
		Imo	Imo	Imo
				Abia
	Southeastern	Cross River	Cross River	Cross River
			Akwa Ibom	Akwa Ibom
	Rivers	Rivers	Rivers	Rivers
Western Region	Western	Oyo	Oyo	Oyo
				Oshun
		Ogun	Ogun	Ogun
		Ondo	Ondo	Ondo
Midwestern Region	Midwestern	Bendel	Bendel	Edo
				Delta
Federal Capital Territory	Lagos	Lagos	Lagos	Lagos
			Abuja	Abuja

Note: The Federal Capital Territory was transferred from Lagos to Abuja under the 1979 Constitution.

Source: Adapted from Anthony Kirk-Greene and Douglas Rimmer, *Nigeria Since 1970. A Political and Economic Outline* (London: Hodder and Stoughton, 1981).

have been periods of extreme tension between Muslims and Christians, but general toleration has minimized the impact of differences on Nigerian political development. An example of such tolerance is to be seen in Yoruba families, where siblings often possess different religious affiliation. Religion has been used to reinforce divisions between competing political groups, but it has rarely been the sole or even fundamental issue of division. In this respect, Nigerian leaders have displayed both tolerance and maturity—or fear of the consequences to national unity should religious intolerance develop.

With the relative success in minimizing religious differences in the 1970s, it was surprising that intolerance increased in the 1980s and

1990s. This was partly influenced by the surge of Islamic fundamentalism. In December 1980, the first violent fundamentalist outbreak claimed at least 4,000 lives in the northern city of Kano, and continued outbreaks of fundamentalist agitation in other cities show the factionalism within Islam and challenges to the established order. The establishment was itself in disarray when the domestic leader of the Islamic faith, Sultan Abubakar III, died in 1988 after 50 years in office, and bitter rivalries emerged over the choice of his successor.

In 1987, violent clashes between Christians and Muslims flared up in northern Nigeria, with many lives lost and hundreds of churches burned to the ground. Similar riots in 1991 and May 1992 resulted in hundreds more dead and disrupted the transition process. Relations between communities had been sensitive after Nigeria joined the Organization of Islamic Conference (OIC) in 1986, as some Christians feared the creeping Islamicization of national affairs. Partly because of this debate, Nigeria's membership in the OIC was temporarily suspended in 1991. It is believed that religion is being deliberately used to inflame passions and destabilize the military government. Whatever the case, religion continues to be an issue in the transition period.

Economic Management and Social Class

Nigeria is a capitalist society. Drawing from colonial experiences, successive Nigerian governments have supported capitalist economic strategies, and have refused to countenance Socialist alternatives. Although there are minimum wage policies in force—raised to 250 naira ($30) per month in 1991—and health and education schemes provide some assistance for the needy, there are few constraints on the market economy. Initially at independence, British influence over the economy was paramount, but gradual indigenization and Africanization policies have placed more influence in Nigerian hands, although certainly only in the hands of an elite and still with very strong influence by multinational corporations (MNCs). These linkages with MNCs have enriched government representatives and businesspersons with privi-

leged access but have not really developed the administrative, technical and entrepreneurial skills of the average Nigerian. During the last 11 years, as part of structural adjustment of the economy, renewed emphasis has been placed on foreign investment and participation in enterprises, while the federal and state governments have sold off most *parastatals* to the domestic and foreign business elites.

This overtly capitalistic strategy has concentrated wealth in the hands of the few, and has consequently drawn widespread, though ineffectual, criticism. The universities provide the major source of radical opposition, with academics and students alike pushing for socialistic and egalitarian alternatives, but scant regard is paid to them. The Nigeria Labor Congress (NLC) has also been outspoken in support of workers' rights, but successive governments have ignored it or, worse still, detained its leaders and restructured the labor groups—only to restructure them again at a later date when they become outspoken. The Babangida government expressly refused to adopt socialism as the national ideology to be followed after 1992, but the government did not recommend any strategy, stating that it would "eventually evolve with time and political maturity."[7] In essence, successive elites have prevented a more egalitarian economic and development strategy from emerging (see Feature 11.2).

The prevailing economic structure of Nigeria provides other strains. Agriculture traditionally provided the backbone of economic wealth, but the oil boom led to the neglect of the agricultural sector. Investment was poured into expensive prestige projects, often industrial (and often with large "kickbacks" for business and government elites), and these did not bring much real benefit to the majority. For example, the Ajaokuta steel mill has been under construction at great cost over the last 15 years; many commentators think it will never open, or if it does, will never be economic. In contrast, the rural areas received little investment and were allowed to decay. In the early 1990s, the government desperately tried to rectify these policies, revitalize rural areas, and prevent the rural-urban population drift that has placed increasing strains on the urban areas. However, these policies recorded minimal success.

Feature 11.2 A Nigerian Development "Model"?

Nigeria's political and economic development since independence in 1960 provides a confusing picture to those unaccustomed to Africa. In the political arena, experimentation with a British parliamentary model between 1960 and 1966, an American presidential model from 1979 to 1983, and possibly a French/Russian hybrid model after 1998, highlights attempts to find a suitable pattern of government. Military governments, which have been in office for more than two-thirds of the postindependence era, have occurred because of failed civilian governments and, especially in the 1990s, a simple desire to retain power.

On the economic side, Nigeria has pursued a capitalist development model, officially scorning socialism. Over the last decade, successive governments have followed fairly closely economic programs laid down by the IMF and the World Bank. These programs, while bringing few short-term benefits, have contributed to extreme societal inequalities and hardship. Earlier efforts at economic indigenization have also been reversed, as Nigeria has been forced to open its companies to foreign ownership. Corruption, at high levels throughout postindependence, appears to have increased in the 1990s, with large amounts of money derived from the international drug trade supplementing more routine revenues from cross-border smuggling and trade. An internal government report, as one example, found $12 billion "lost" from official coffers during the Babangida administration.

Is there a Nigerian development model that has been followed? To a certain extent Nigeria's political and military elites have sketched out a "mixed economy" path of capitalism to follow. Unfortunately, corruption undermines the realization of the country's full economic potential and makes one conclude that the Nigerian model serves to benefit those in power, not the vast majority of citizens.

Nigeria remains a society of great inequalities—a factor which successive governments have failed to tackle. Class divisions are pronounced, but they have not been the basis of political action to date. Although there have been political parties in both Republics that claimed to provide for working class concerns and espoused class-conscious ideologies, none have been truly class-based, and they have all tended to rely upon residual ethnic support for their votes. Indeed, party leaders often have exploited ethnic sentiments in order to reduce the possibility that a true national working-class solidarity would develop.

The urbanized middle class, which was emerging strongly during the oil boom years of the late 1970s, was badly hit by austerity in the 1980s and has all but disappeared in the 1990s. The wealthy business and political elites, however, maintained their own privileged positions, and society has become more divided socially and economically. Class perspectives were vaguely worded into the two parties of the early

1990s but did not provide for class-based politics and elections. One of the big questions concerning any new civilian regime is whether the ideological orientation that has prevailed in Nigeria since independence will be altered. As money and the military tend to control Nigerian politics, a preliminary assessment would conclude that it will not.

Socialization

Socialization, the process by which people learn the values and beliefs of their society, is influenced by many factors within the Nigerian context. The newness of national identity contrasts with the pressures from long-standing traditions, while competing socialization processes take place to promote potentially mutually exclusive allegiances at ethnic and federal-national levels. The first language of most Nigerians is their own ethnic tongue, with English used as the only "national" language. Great emphasis in schools is placed on developing a national consciousness with loyalty pledges and instruction of national values, but this can run into conflict with learning experiences within the home or local community, where the belief that the state or federal apparatus has been discriminatory may prevail.

Military governments have attempted to instill greater self-discipline and national awareness among Nigerians, but with varied results. They have also stressed the need for greater honesty in society and have attempted to stamp out the corruption that plagues all levels of Nigerian life. Unfortunately, the armed forces themselves have been guilty of the very things they are attempting to erase in the civilian population, and so the values of society have been slow to change.

The status of women within the domestic power structure is also shaped by the traditions and norms of society. Generally, women suffer discrimination by males in access to positions of authority, as well as in opportunities for economic development. For example, Catherine Acholonu, vice president of the Association of Women in Politics and an aspiring female presidential candidate, was detained in 1993 by the military for several weeks to prevent her registering for the election. But the scale of this discrimination is not uniform across the country. In many southern areas, for example, women have controlled market enterprises for many years and have significant input into the economy; in the North, Islam tends to limit women's active participation in social and economic life because purdah tends to keep them confined to the home. Women were also denied the vote in northern states until 1979. Family planning, seemingly crucial in a country where women on average have six children each, tends to be given low priority by male administrators. In Islamic circles, many males are openly opposed to any form of family planning, charging it is a Christian conspiracy to hold down Islamic population growth.

Against the background of these and other agendas, Nigeria is struggling to develop a collective conscience and political processes and institutions that will be able to withstand the pressures that have plagued all Nigerian governments.

KEY TERMS

Biafra
civil war
colonialism
coup d'état
ethnicity
federal character
Hausa-Fulani
Ibo
Middle Belt
nation building
regionalism
religious tolerance
secession
socialization
Yoruba

FURTHER READINGS

Ake, Claude, ed. *Political Economy of Nigeria* (London: Longman, 1985).

Arnold, Guy. *Modern Nigeria* (London: Longman, 1977).

Balewa, B. A. T. *Governing Nigeria. History, Problems and Prospects* (Lagos and Oxford: Malthouse Press, 1994).

Dudley, B. J. *Instability and Political Order. Politics and Crisis in Nigeria* (Ibadan: Ibadan University Press, 1973).

Falola, Toyin, ed. *Britain and Nigeria. Exploitation or Development?* (London: Zed, 1987).

Graf, William D. *The Nigerian State. Political Economy, State Class and Political System in the Post-Colonial Era* (London: James Currey and Portsmouth: Heinemann, 1988).

Hatch, John. *Nigeria: A History* (London: Secker and Warburg, 1971).

Ihonvbere, Julius O. *Nigeria. The Politics of Adjustment and Democracy* (New Brunswick: Transaction, 1994).

Kirk-Greene, Anthony, and Douglas Rimmer. *Nigeria since 1970: A Political and Economic Outline* (London: Hodder and Stoughton, 1981).

Wright, Stephen. *Nigeria. Struggle for Stability and Status* (Boulder, CO: Westview Press, 1997)

Political Processes and Institutions

The political process in Nigeria is complex, and attempts to study and comprehend it are complicated by several factors. Accurate information concerning actors and decision making is often not present, so it can be difficult to isolate the forces at work. Severe problems such as ethnicity, religion, the civil war, economic inequalities and structural adjustment, and military coups d'état impinge directly upon the political process and have influenced its operation. There has been no direct or official continuity between political parties within the country; parties were banned in 1966 after the collapse of the First Republic, and new parties formed for the Second Republic in 1979. Likewise in 1983, these parties were proscribed, and two new parties were created for the Third Republic. These parties, in turn, were banned in 1993. Naturally, some of the leading political figures and policy bases have remained influential throughout, but these can only be understood on closer inspection.

To a considerable extent, the political process has been dominated by personalities rather than by parties or policies. Admittedly, vague promises and programs have been enunciated by parties, particularly on education, health, and the economy, but voters have been far more interested in who the leaders of each party are and, more crucially, what their ethnic identifications are. In many elections, ballot rigging has occurred on such a grand scale that it has been difficult to gauge real winners and losers. As a general rule, it has been assumed that each party cheats in roughly equal ratios to the others, so election results do provide a justifiable winner of sorts.

One issue to consider is whether long-term military control has had a positive or negative impact upon the political process, or whether military rule should be seen as an integral part of the process itself. Indeed, a favorite comment is that the Nigerian system contains only two parties, the civilians and the military, and that both are integral to the political process.

Since independence was gained in October 1960, Nigeria has also struggled to find a stable framework of political institutions through which to govern. The country has experimented with parliamentary (1960–1966), presidential (1979–1983), and military (1966–1979 and 1984–) structures of government, which have all operated within a federal system encompassing initially three regions and now 30 states. Many commentators, both in Nigeria and abroad, argue that it is not the political institutions themselves that have been at fault—particularly during the Second Republic—but the leaders.

Before turning to the political parties and institutions, we need to consider the composition of the civilian and military leadership groups.

CIVILIAN ELITE

Politicians around the world do not always have the best of reputations, but Nigerian politicians have been considered especially poor representatives and guardians of the state. The failure of the first two Republics (and certain military regimes also) can be blamed largely upon poor leadership, selfish interests, and gross corruption. Obviously not all Nigerian politicians can be so blamed, but citizens are rarely complimentary about the politicians who have represented them.

Such an unequivocal condemnation raises the question as to who these politicians are and how they get themselves elected. Most politicians are drawn from the wealthy business communities, professional groups, schools and universities, and government administration, and some hold religious or traditional positions of authority. Ethnic considerations have been of paramount importance in climbing the political ladder within any given party, and have proven to be more important than educational ability or qualifications. Ethnicity has been the major form of political mobilization to distribute benefits of development. The desire to assist people from one's own community provides a very strong impulse for Nigerians. Western values of impartiality and nepotism do not command much respect or are never properly implemented. It has been virtually impossible for politicians to be recruited—and certainly advance—without having the requisite ethnic identification, or at least promising to attract large numbers of his or her own ethnic constituency.

A major weakness of this elite has been the failure to apply a nationalist orientation to policy, with sectionalist or personal interest usually taking priority. In the First Republic, the ruling Northern People's Congress (NPC) was exclusively a mouthpiece of the Northern Region and the majority of federal spending inevitably went to that region. Its "successor," the National Party of Nigeria (NPN), attempted to be more national in outlook but still was biased toward northern states and sectarian interests. This inability of politicians to encompass a truly national orientation is a trait also found in many African states.

Perhaps the critical problem concerning the civilian elite is that its ethical and normative values have proved totally insubstantial. Civilians have unashamedly entered politics to make money. This has been called "extractive" politics, in which politicians merely seek their own personal gain rather than promote societal advancement. Frantz Fanon explicitly condemned such practices in African states, considering it just another form of exploitation under which the African masses have to suffer.[8] It may be unfair to paint all Nigerian politicians with such a broad brush, but they have tended to hold to stereotype. Respected scholars of Nigerian politics appear to be in agreement. Billy Dudley wrote:

> For the Nigerian political elite, politics involves not the conciliation of competing demands arising from an examination of the various alternatives entailed by any course of political action, but the extraction of resources which can be used to satisfy elite demands and to buy support.[9]

Terisa Turner and Gavin Williams shared a similar view that in Nigeria, "Politics thus comes to be the process of gaining control of public resources for the pursuit of private ends."[10]

The 1979 Constitution, the last to be used by a civilian government, laid down very clear guidelines against corruption, and politicians at least paid lip service to the need for probity in office. But the record of civilians between 1979 and 1983 was poor, with an estimated $5 to $7 billion embezzled, and arson resorted to in order to prevent official inquiries from finding evidence of such acts. By 1983, a number of important buildings had been burned, including two telecommunications centers in Lagos, as well as the Federal Ministry of Education and the Foreign Affairs Ministry.

MILITARY LEADERSHIP

Since 1966, the military has controlled the government for all but four years (1979–1983). The most important justification normally put forward by the military for its intrusion into politics (both in Nigeria and in Africa as a whole) is the failure by civilians to maintain the political structure and to act in accordance with societal norms.[11] The military itself has had numerous "millionaire generals" who have flaunted their wealth without hesitation or fear. This wealth was made possible by the rapid increase (and unaccountability) in national revenues accruing from oil. The overthrow of General Yakubu Gowon in 1975 was defended by his successors as necessary to stem this corruption, but they merely made it less conspicuous. Many believe that the outgoing military leadership in 1979 only handed over power to civilians when the latter agreed not to probe into the financial affairs of retiring officers. This seems to have been an issue during 1992–1993 also.

The armed forces do help to play a nation-building role, however, in the sense that recruitment and appointments are molded by considerations of federal character, and postings to various parts of Nigeria provide soldiers with greater awareness (and, it is hoped, empathy) of people with different social and cultural backgrounds. National rather than sectional interest is stressed through education and training, and officer recruitment is monitored for equality. Such a balance, however, is a goal rather than a reality, and imbalance has been a focus of bitter controversy in previous years.

At independence in 1960, only 10 percent of the officer corps of the Royal West Africa Frontier Force (RWAFF) was African, as British expatriate officers retained control. This was both for political reasons, because of the pro-Western and pro-British leanings of the federal government, and for practical reasons, in that very few Nigerians had been trained as officers. Africanization took place rapidly, so that by 1965 all but 10 percent of officers were Nigerian. This pace of promotion had obvious military significance; young officers rose in the ranks at great speed, leading to what has been termed "professional disorientation." But the political problems were equally severe because the appointments and promotions gave a disproportionate influence to officers from the Eastern Region.[12] The growing frustration with the northern bias of the ruling NPC, combined with the inability of Eastern Region politicians to influence the political process, provided these officers with a justification to use their military muscle to bring an end to the First Republic in 1966.

Few people foresaw such a military intervention, believing that British influence and military training would be sufficient to inspire a nonpolitical stance by military officers and to prevent their interference in the political process. But the political awareness of officers had been awakened in 1964, when they were asked by both antagonists to intervene in the constitutional crisis between the president and prime minister, even though this crisis was finally settled by the civilians themselves. The 1966 coup dramatically and irreversibly changed the nature of the political process, and set off a chain of events within the military that continues to trouble it. The civil war divided the military into two factions, and although the Biafran secession was defeated, only some officers of eastern origin were allowed to rejoin the federal armed forces. A shift in the profile of the military leadership took place in the 1970s, with "Middle Belt" officers from the smaller ethnic groups becoming more prominent.

The question whether military rule has a positive impact on the Nigerian political process is value-laden and ambiguous, and it is one that induces significant debate. Military force has been useful in suppressing political violence, but the military has not until recently used excessive force in the control of society. The military acted in apparent good faith in its attempts to draw up a constitutional program to return power to civilians in the Second Republic, although this was more questionable over the aborted Third Republic. Nevertheless, the military's intervention has not solved the problems inherent in the Nigerian polity, and the military has been unable to solve the deep-seated difficulties in the political system. The military has tended to favor the status quo, shoring up corrupt elites rather than working toward ridding the country of socioeconomic inequalities. Some have said, perhaps unfairly, that the failure of the Second Republic showed that 13 years of military rule did not affect or improve the political system, attitudes, or institutions, although the civilians must ultimately take the blame for failing to make the system work.[13]

The longer the military stays in office, the more disunity and divisions appear within its ranks. Some factions believe in the importance of military rule, whereas others support recivilianization. The military's training, discipline, and command structure do not really suit it for political office, and military governments have placed a heavy reliance upon co-opted civilians to administer the country. The option to share national leadership with civilians after 1992 was raised and rejected by the military, even though it did occur by default for a few months in 1993 during the Shonekan transition from Babangida to Abacha.

THE FIRST REPUBLIC, 1960–1966

Political Parties

The political parties of the First Republic all developed in preindependent Nigeria and thus began their operations within the context of colonial control. Although the first "protoparty" was formed in the 1920s, it was not until after World War II that parties really began to take the shape and form that made them active players in the political game.

As we have already seen, the regionalist philosophy of the colonial administrators served both to create and to reinforce divisions between groups within the country, and pushed political parties to seek support largely at an ethnic-regional level. Parties attempted to extend their influence outside their home bases, but this effort was not very successful, and where it was, success depended more upon forging alliances with minor parties representing smaller sectarian interests than upon actually breaking directly into another party's support base. By far the most dominant party of the era was the Northern People's Congress (NPC).

Northern People's Congress (NPC) The NPC, established in 1951, controlled the federal assembly in Lagos and had its deputy leader, Sir Alhaji Abubakar Tafawa Balewa, as federal premier. The party's leader, Sir Alhaji Ahmadu Bello, decided to remain as northern premier, indicating his preference as to which was the more powerful institution. The NPC dominated the Northern Region and made it a "closed" system because of the very tight association of personnel at legislative, executive, and judicial levels. The NPC was blatantly northern rather than national in outlook, and restricted membership of the party to people of northern origin. Its policies both at home and abroad reflected the Islamic conservatism of its leadership, promoting steady capitalist growth and no change in Nigeria's external orientation. This philosophy antagonized progressive and non-Islamic factions in the other regions.

The NPC maintained an electoral alliance from 1959 with the major party of the Eastern Region, the National Convention of Nigerian Citizens (NCNC). Rivalry in the South between the NCNC and Action Group over issues and alliances led to bitter electoral contests, the subsequent breakdown of law and order in the Western Region, and eventually to the military intervention of January 1966.

National Convention of Nigerian Citizens (NCNC) The NCNC, established in 1944, was the oldest party to operate in the First Republic, and centered itself upon the personality of Dr. Nnamdi Azikiwe, a leading nationalist in the independence struggle who became the first (ceremonial) president of Nigeria in 1963. At inde-

pendence, the party was almost exclusively based in the Eastern Region, relying largely upon Ibo support, and it was more progressive in its economic and social policies than the NPC. The NCNC's pressure and activism in the neighboring Western Region provoked many violent clashes. Frustration over its failure to make a greater impact on the Nigerian political process resulted following the 1966 coups in the NCNC becoming the primary caucus of the Biafran secessionary movement, although Azikiwe remained loyal to the federal camp.

Action Group (AG) The Action Group, established in 1948, was founded by and organized around the personality of Chief Obafemi Awolowo, a lawyer. The AG symbolized the cultural and political goals of the Yoruba, and the party's creation helped to formally dissolve a united nationalist movement. Its power center was the Western Region. Awolowo's belief was that the federation could only be kept together by the regions maintaining their own cultural identities and consulting as equal partners at the federal level. The AG strove hard to maintain control over its own region and to expand its influence beyond the West, but in both tasks it was less than successful.

The AG promoted "welfarism," but as the party moved toward adopting democratic socialism, splits appeared within its ranks. These divisions were deepened in 1962 when Awolowo gave up his position as premier of the West to become leader of the federal opposition in Lagos. His successor, Chief S. L. Akintola, was opposed by Awolowo but was able to hold sufficient support in the region to maintain his position. Differences within the Yoruba cultural entity, which have always been strong (and remained strong during the Second Republic and the 1990s transition), were exacerbated by these tensions, especially when Awolowo was imprisoned by the federal authorities for treason, a charge he always denied. By 1966, law and order in the West had all but disappeared.

Smaller Parties The NPC, NCNC, and AG represented, to some degree or other, the primary ethnic groups of Hausa-Fulani, Ibo, and Yoruba, respectively. The smaller groups in the country did not perceive their interests to be considered or promoted by these parties or within the regional governments, and so many of them formed their own parties to seek alliances and improve their negotiating position. One such party was the United Middle Belt Congress, which attempted to bring together groups within the country's central areas. Some of these parties held radical perspectives, particularly the Northern Elements Progressive Union (NEPU). NEPU was launched in 1951 under the leadership of Mallam Aminu Kano as a breakaway group and challenger to the NPC. Aminu Kano's radical challenge to the northern establishment continued until his death in 1983, but the effects of NEPU, like those of other smaller parties, were at best localized and at worst ineffectual. At elections in the First Republic, these smaller parties together never polled more than 15 percent of the vote.

Elections   The concern displayed by parties of the First Republic in manipulating the electoral process was partly inspired by negative perceptions of opponents. All parties were perceived as likely to exaggerate their voting support within their own region, and so each reinforced its own intention to do the same. Electoral registers and the census results from 1962 and 1963 were inflated for similar reasons; population was the factor determining seat allocations in the federal lower house (as well as federal revenue paid to the regions). This gave the North a built-in majority and added to the frustration of the other regions. With each party effectively controlling the electoral process in its own region, sweeping successes were usually recorded (except in the West for specific reasons), as opponents were unable to campaign and ballot boxes were stuffed with false votes. The result of this was that elections served to entrench parties within their own regions, increased sectarianism as a political force, prevented an accurate judgment on party policy, and caused increasing strain and tension in a country already fraught with problems. The elections, then, did not help to defuse tensions or redirect policy as they often do in Western democracies; instead, they helped to fuel a crisis.

The first ever popular, direct elections in Nigeria were held in 1959, a year prior to independence, and based on these results the government was established. The North received a greater allocation of seats than other regions on the basis of population, even though one-half of that population—the female population—was disfranchised by religious custom (and only received the vote in 1979). The NPC was able to win 134 of the 312 seats in the federal lower house, but within a year sufficient numbers had switched allegiances to the NPC so that the party, in an alliance with the NCNC, was able to control a majority.

For the 1964 General Elections, the NPC stood in coalition with Akintola's AG faction, the Nigerian National Democratic Party (NNDP), and together they took 200 seats, with the NPC taking 162 of those. The rump AG had joined in an alliance with the NCNC in the United Progressive Grand Alliance (UPGA), and together they accounted for some 100 seats. The level of violence and intimidation during this campaign led the UPGA to call a boycott of the elections, but this only occurred in the East, which held fresh elections in March 1965. The absence of what could be termed "electoral morality" was evident, and showed that, "for the political elite, power was an end in itself and not a means to the realization of some greater good for the community . . . and that any talk about the rules of the game must be irrelevant."[14]

INSTITUTIONS OF THE FIRST REPUBLIC

The parliamentary system of government which operated throughout the First Republic was a legacy of colonialism. The British government believed that what was good for Britain was good for its colonies. This proved not to be the case. We have already explained how, during the last decade of colonial rule, very strong regionalist tendencies developed, with a deep-seated distrust displayed by ethnic groups of each other. These factors were not conducive to the maintenance of political stability, nor did they foster respect for the institutions of government at independence.[15]

The President

To be accurate, Nigeria did not become a Republic until 1963, when Dr. Nnamdi Azikiwe became its first president after having served as leader of the Senate (until 1962) and as governor-general (in 1963). For the first three years after independence, Queen Elizabeth II (of England) technically remained the country's head of state, and she was represented in Nigeria by her governor-general.

Azikiwe became the country's first ceremonial president after independence, more out of recognition for his leadership of the nationalist movement than from any real political influence he possessed. He was the dominant spokesperson of the East, the Ibo people, and the National Convention of Nigerian Citizens (NCNC), which formed a coalition with the ruling Northern People's Congress (NPC). The NPC would certainly not have allowed Azikiwe to become president if that position had carried any real political clout. The president's role was almost purely ceremonial. Azikiwe was officially able to call on the largest party in the Federal House of Representatives to form a government, but he had no effective power to influence that process. In a major constitutional crisis during 1964, Azikiwe refused to accept the federal election results because of blatant malpractices that were detrimental to his own party, and thus would not call on the NPC leader, Sir Alhaji Abubakar Tafawa Balewa, to be premier. Azikiwe called on the army to support him, as did Tafawa Balewa, but in the end it was the president who was forced to back down.

In addition to these weaknesses, Azikiwe was not given authority to conduct foreign policy, even though he was nominally commander-in-chief of the armed forces. His authority also did not extend to influencing policy in federal or state houses, and he had little ability to prevent any of the conflicts afflicting the Western Region during the latter years of the First Republic.

The Prime Minister

Patterned closely on the British model, the position of prime minister, or premier, was the most important in the federal parliament, and was occupied throughout the First Republic by Tafawa Balewa. The premier, along with ministers selected by him, had ultimate responsibility for initiation and implementation of policy; the premier also used his strength within the federal lower house to ensure that policies were approved. Ultimately, the prime minister held responsibility for both domestic and international policy, including law and order and fiscal policy, but his failure to act decisively in the political problems of the West showed that he was not always willing, or able, to use these powers. It is also worth remembering that Tafawa Balewa was only the deputy leader of the NPC and that the real power broker, Ahmadu Bello, chose to remain as Northern premier.

The Federal House of Representatives

The House of Representatives was the central forum of political debate and was modeled very much upon the British House of Commons. The 312 seats were allocated on a population basis, which helped to give the NPC control, and the Action Group (AG) became the "official opposition." The parliamentary system requires a toleration of opposition groups, but this was not present. Awolowo was considered a threat to the government, and he and 20 colleagues were imprisoned in 1962 on a spurious charge of "treason."

The House held the responsibility for approving all major legislation in the federation. This duty specifically included the budget and other financial matters, as well as aspects of foreign policy. Strict party discipline, at least within the ruling NPC, made votes and victory a certainty for the government. Indeed, during the six years that the House was in existence, the government did not lose a single vote. As in the British system, policy decisions tended to be hammered out in private before being made public on the floor of the House. The presence of ministers and assistant ministers in the House also served to strengthen party unity. The significance of the House is perhaps lessened further when one realizes that it never met for more than 30 days in any one year.

The Federal Senate

The Senate was a nonelected body containing 48 chiefs and elders who were nominated in equal numbers by the federal and regional governments. This upper house had few if any powers of action or initiation but attempted to serve the symbolic purpose of bringing together traditional leaders into the modern political structure. It possessed the ability to delay fiscal bills for 30 days and other bills for six months, but was unable to overturn policy.

Regional Houses of Assembly

Each region—North, East, and West (and Midwest after 1964)—possessed its own single assembly with members elected in districts organized according to population. Only the West's assembly was not dominated by a single local party, and it was the scene of violent political controversy and turmoil. The regional government, each with its own premier nominated by the majority party, determined policy within its own jurisdiction, much like state governments do in the United States. These roles extended to areas such as education, the police, and economic planning and fiscal directives for that region. To this extent, they were powerful institutions within their own regions, and in the South this led to clashes with the NPC-dominated federal government over issues of policy implementation.

MILITARY GOVERNMENT, 1966–1979

The intervention of the military clearly had a serious impact upon the political process. Political parties were banned, elections became unnecessary, civilian elites were relegated to the sidelines, and the military ruled by decree. The military's claim to be both protector and cleanser of the political system was a dubious one, especially when the country was plunged into civil war in 1967 (see Feature 11.3). Following the war, however, the military did help to heal some of the wounds between the warring factions and can reasonably claim some responsibility for maintaining Nigeria as one country. In May 1973, General Gowon established the National Youth Service Corps (NYSC) in a further effort to promote integration and to assist with development schemes. Under this program,

new university graduates were asked to undertake a year's "national service" away from their home areas with the hope that this service would provide a greater national awareness and orientation. Unfortunately, the military leadership itself did not lead by example, and the military-technocratic alliance responsible for running the country accumulated personal wealth at the expense of other concerns.

Gowon had promised in 1970 that the country would revert to civilian rule in 1976. In 1974, however, this program was postponed without explanation or an alternative date offered. Dissatisfaction with Gowon's handling of affairs led to his overthrow in 1975 by a group of officers, who selected Murtala Muhammed as the head of state. Murtala began to act against corruption in society and laid down a timetable to return to civilian rule by 1979. Murtala also established a National Security Organization (NSO) to maintain a network of information and communication within the country, which unfortunately was unable to prevent Murtala's assassination in 1976.

The government of Lt. Gen. Olusegun Obasanjo, Murtala's successor, worked to create a constitution and political process that would tackle the disharmonies of the First Republic. A priority was to ensure that the former political parties were not recreated, and that the new parties would be national in organization, membership, and outlook. The military considered applications by 19 associations, but under its guidelines allowed only five parties to be registered and to contest the 1979 elections. None of these parties was truly Socialist, and this reflected the military's own political orientation. It was also assumed that the military would only disengage after passing power to a government that shared similar perceptions and interests. Although these five parties were superficially more nationalistic in composition and policy, many of the dominant personalities of the 1960s returned, and parties quickly became identified with the predecessors of the First Republic.

Institutions of Military Governments

Obviously, military rule is different from civilian rule: There is no attempt made to be "democratic," as decisions are issued by decree; there are no elections; there are no political parties; and there is expected to be less debate and criticism, as the military operates by command and obedience.[16]

When Maj. Gen. Aguiyi-Ironsi came to power after the coup d'état of January 1966, he established a Supreme Military Council (SMC) of top officers to be the main decision-making forum. In addition, he set up a Federal Executive Council (FEC), which included the top federal permanent secretaries and acted as the bureaucratic arm of the government. Ironsi's decision to scrap federalism and institute a unitary form of government sealed his fate and led to his overthrow in July 1966. The new head of state, General Yakubu Gowon, continued to use the existing institutions, but strengthened the SMC by having it ratify decisions made by the FEC. Gowon resuscitated the federal structure and broke up the four regions into 12 states in May 1967. In the early 1970s, following the civil war, Gowon broadened marginally the base of his government by enlisting civilians to take control of various ministries (though they were still under ultimate control by the military). This infusion of important skills—which the military lacked—did not detract from the negative aspects of Gowon's rule, and he was overthrown in 1975.

Murtala Muhammed (1975–1976) and Olusegun Obasanjo (1976–1979) refined the military institutions of government. Murtala established in 1975 a National Security Organization (NSO) to control opponents of the state, and Obasanjo had a significant impact on government by establishing a third institutional tier, the Council of State. The Council was composed of the military governors of all the states (19 after 1976) who were no longer able to sit on the SMC. This enabled a distinction to be drawn between state and federal governing bodies and was the pattern adopted by military governments after the demise of civilian rule in December 1983.

THE SECOND REPUBLIC, 1979–1983

Political Parties

To prevent regional identification, each party was required by law to have its headquarters in Lagos and an office in all the 19 states of the federation. This regulation ensured some form of national orientation, if not necessarily national support. Membership of the parties was open to all Nigerians and could not be restricted, as had been the case in the First Republic. Similarly, candidates could not be selected on any regionalist, ethnic, or religious grounds, and there had to be regular internal elections for leadership positions. The 1979

Feature 11.3 The Civil War

The civil war fought from 1967 to 1970 was one of the worst on the African continent. With more than a million people killed, and with many more homeless and destitute, the war severely tested the unity of the country. The Biafran aim had been to set up their own independent state in southeastern Nigeria, financed by oil revenues, and their claim received significant support within West Africa and from France. The federal side could not afford to let go of such an economically important area of the country, nor could it allow secession for fear of sparking claims by other dissatisfied ethnic groups.

The internationalization of the war, drawing in the superpowers and some European countries, was also a tragedy, but the end of the war brought an era of reconciliation that few thought possible. The painful memory of the war has probably prevented other secession attempts since, and it provides an incentive to find a viable system of government to bring the whole nation together. However, as the war recedes into history, there are fears that moves to break up the federation will increase.

Constitution provided all the necessary safe-guards and provisions for the maintenance of an equitable system, but political realities strained the system badly and prompted the military's return to government on December 31, 1983.

The ban on political activity was raised in September 1978, and the parties had nine months to prepare themselves for the elections. Parties received some funding from the government in an effort to minimize chances of corruption. The elections were monitored and controlled by the military government working through a Federal Electoral Commission (Fedeco), and, although protests were raised in some quarters, the results were generally accepted. In contrast, the elections held in 1983 were conducted under the control of the incumbent civilian administration, and were regarded by many as suspicious and influenced by electoral malpractices.

A fundamental difference in the political process in 1979 was the presence of a total of 19 states in the federation, as the large regional units of the First Republic had been subdivided in 1967 and 1976 to assist democracy and representativeness. The old Northern Region was now broken up into ten states, for example, and the other regions were also divided to give greater expression to minority groups.

National Party of Nigeria (NPN)   The NPN drew its strength and support from the states of the North, and bore some resemblance to the old NPC. Its leader, Alhaji Shehu Shagari from Sokoto state, became president of the Second Republic, and the party came to hold a majority in the Federal House of Representatives. The party was able to secure victory throughout the North, except in Borno and Kano states, and was able to build alliances in other areas of the country. This was most evident with the selection of the vice president, Dr. Alex Ekwueme, who was an Ibo from Anambra state in the Southeast, and the chairman of the party, Chief Akinloye, who was a Yoruba from the Southwest. The party instituted a system of "zoning" by which senior offices would be rotated among the various zones or clusters of states, thus allowing the party to maintain a national image

and balance. Some commentators have suggested that this was a ploy to allow a northern elite to rule under a national guise while never losing control over the party or the federation. Non-northerners wanted Shagari to step down after one term in office to rotate the presidency.

The NPN's program was bourgeois in promoting capitalist development, increasing foreign participation in the economy, and preserving the mixed economy developed under the military administration. Unfortunately for the NPN and the country as a whole, the massive oil revenues of the 1970s disappeared rapidly in the early 1980s as the global oil price fell and production and revenue targets were revised downward. Prestige development projects instigated by the NPN became white elephants, and disillusionment set in. Despite the downward economic spiral and the increased hardship faced by the majority, the party's representatives continued their conspicuous consumption of the nation's wealth.

Unity Party of Nigeria (UPN)   The UPN formed under the leadership of Obafemi Awolowo, who had kept the Action Group going as a "social" group during the military era, and was therefore assured of support from the majority of those living in the southwestern states of Ogun, Ondo, Oyo, and Lagos. Awolowo was the party's presidential candidate in 1979 and 1983, running Shagari very close in the 1979 election. The UPN's platform was more radical than that of the NPN, with free schooling, better healthcare facilities, and greater assistance for low-paid labor as its priorities. The party was able to capture the assemblies of the southwestern states, but it was unable in federal elections to make inroads into other parts of the country. Personality and political differences began to eat into UPN support as certain prominent leaders switched loyalty to the NPN, and history appeared to be repeating itself. The 1983 elections showed the NPN allegedly making substantial gains over the UPN, but widespread rioting drew attention to the dubious validity of the result.

Nigeria People's Party (NPP)   The NPP was originally formed by Alhaji Waziri Ibrahim, a wealthy businessman from the northeastern state of Borno. He attempted to pull together a national coalition, but divisions within the party soon made this impossible. Dr. Nnamdi Azikiwe originally stated his desire to remain outside of politics as the "father of the nation," but in December 1978 he agreed to join the NPP and became its presidential candidate, leaving Waziri to form a second party. Most of the NPP's support came from former NCNC members of the old Eastern Region.

The NPP's policies differed little from other parties; they promoted vague ideas of growth and economic development. The party made few inroads into other areas of the country, and gained little from its NPN-alliance, which was broken in mid–1981.

People's Redemption Party (PRP) The city of Kano has had a tradition of political radicalism, and the PRP's support was concentrated in that city and in neighboring Kaduna state. Formed under the leadership of Mallam ("teacher") Aminu Kano, the PRP had its roots back in NEPU. The party promoted a progressive platform, particularly on land rights, and thus offered a threat to privilege and established Islamic interests. The NPN eventually managed to draw the PRP into an alliance, and, following the death of Aminu Kano in 1983, factionalism weakened its vitality.

Great Nigeria People's Party (GNPP) The party was formed following the split in the NPP, and the "Great" was added to distinguish between the two. The GNPP was centered upon one man, Alhaji Waziri Ibrahim. Waziri was a former NPC minister in the First Republic who had then made his fortune as an arms supplier to the federal government during the civil war. Although the party was registered by the military in 1979, it had little support outside the Northeast.

Nigerian Advance Party (NAP) The NAP had attempted to become a registered party in 1979, but its application was rejected by the military because the party was not nationally organized. The association, under the leadership of Tunji Braithwaite, a Lagos lawyer, set out to establish its organization efficiently and was allowed to contest the 1983 elections as the sixth party.

The NAP offered a nonethnic, socialist platform, and its supporters were largely young professionals and students. Although its base was mostly in the Lagos area, it tried to elicit support all over Nigeria, with little success. By refusing to play on ethnic sentiment, the party foundered and was unable to win an election at any level or for any candidate.

The 1979 Elections

The elections in 1979 and 1983 were fought along the lines of the American and British models, with first-past-the-post, single-member constituencies. Both sets of elections were under the control of Fedeco, but the military's presence in 1979 made these elections fairer than those in 1983. Fedeco, established in 1977, was responsible the following year for drawing up electoral registers throughout Nigeria. These were hotly disputed, with fictitious names appearing, and many Nigerians found themselves disfranchised. The total number of registered voters was initially put at 47,433,757 in March 1978, but six months later additional registration pushed the figure above 48 million. This was considered to be very high, and in some areas contained 120 percent of those eligible to vote. This also partly explains the low turnout at the elections of, on average, 33 percent—that is, based on realistic numbers of eligible voters, this percentage was probably higher. Voting age in 1979 was lowered from 21 to 18 years, and women in northern states were allowed to vote for the first time.

Elections took place over five Saturdays in July and August. The first election was for the Senate, and subsequent elections were for the House of Representatives, state assemblies, and state governors. A two-week period was allowed before the election for president. With five election days to organize and control, the chances of problems increased, although teething troubles with the first election, such as insufficient ballot boxes or election officials, could most likely be corrected for later elections. This electoral system, unique in Africa, attempted to simplify the

Table 11.3 PRESIDENTIAL ELECTION RESULTS, 1979 AND 1983

Candidate	Party	Votes Cast	1979 (%)	1983 (%)
Alh, Shehu Shagari	NPN	5,688,857	33.8	47.5
Chief Obafemi Awolowo	UPN	4,916,651	29.2	31.1
Dr. Nnamdi Azikiwe	NPP	2,822,523	16.7	14.0
Mallam Aminu Kano	PRP	1,732,113	10.3	—
Alh, Hassan Yusuf	PRP	—	—	3.8
Alh, Waziri Ibrahim	GNPP	1,686,489	10.0	2.5
Mr. Tunji Braithwaite	NAP	—	—	1.1

process by asking the electorate to make one choice each week.

The ballot papers contained symbols of all the parties, and voters were expressly informed of which symbol to look for. These symbols included a key (to prosperity) for the PRP, a house and maize (for stability and food) for the NPN, a candle on a Nigeria map (to light the way) for the UPN, and a family for the NPP. Unfortunately, even ballot papers were open to fraud, and some appeared to have deliberate smudges over "opposition" symbols to make them unrecognizable.

The NPN emerged as the leading party in the elections, taking 38 percent of the votes for the Senate, 37 percent for the House of Representatives, and 36 percent for state assemblies. Shagari polled 5,688,857 votes in the presidential election, over half a million more than his closest rival, Obafemi Awolowo (see Table 11.3). Despite the appearance of these new parties and competing manifestos, voters still went with old allegiances: "ethnic, regional, religious, and personality-leadership parochialisms"[17] were maximized, and besides the presidential election, "in no election whatsoever did any of the parties present candidates who were not indigenous to the state in which such candidates were contesting."[18]

The results of the presidential election were challenged by Obafemi Awolowo, and the appeal went from an electoral tribunal to the Supreme Court. The Constitution called on the presidential victor to win the highest vote as well as score at least 25 percent of the vote in two-thirds of the states. The appeal centered upon the question of what was two-thirds of 19. Shagari and the NPN argued successfully that it was twelve and two-thirds states, so he only needed one-sixth of the vote in the thirteenth state. The military government clearly supported Shagari, and "Awo" was again left defeated.

The 1983 Elections

These were the first elections to be under full civilian control in almost 20 years. The election process cost an estimated $1 billion, and involved about 1 million officials. Fedeco drew up a new electoral register of 65.3 million voters, a staggering increase of 34 percent since 1978. Manipulation of these lists had been so great in some states that increases of 100 percent had been recorded. The NPN acted in its own interests by having the electoral timetable switched to place the presidential election first. The philosophy of this was simple: get Shagari reelected, and then gain from a bandwagon effect in the subsequent elections.

The NPN increased its majorities at all levels and took two-thirds control of the National Assembly. The loosely organized Progressive People's Alliance (UPN, NPP, and GNPP) made little or no advances in NPN territory, but the NPN appeared to make considerable gains across the South. Allegations of electoral abuse brought chaos to the Southwest, where many considered the NPN to have blatantly cheated. This frustration and protest, combined with poor governmental performance and gross corruption, persuaded the military to oust the politicians from power on December 31, 1983, just three months after Shagari had been sworn into office for his second term.

INSTITUTIONS OF THE SECOND REPUBLIC, 1979–1983

After four years of consultation and intense debate, Nigerians adopted a new set of institutions for the Second Republic, modeled on the American presidential system. These institutions and respective powers, combined with a redefinition of national values and mores, were enshrined in the 1979 Constitution, which, although suspended after 1983, continued to form the basis of constitutional life in Nigeria until the promulgation of the 1989 Constitution.

The 1979 Constitution

The 1979 Constitution appeared to be an excellent document but, unfortunately, its provisions were not fully respected by the politicians. The Constitution took three years to draw up. In October 1975, a Constitution Drafting Committee (CDC) was established by the military government to supply an initial draft that would provide viable institutions of government, consensual politics, and an end to violence and malpractices. This committee was composed mainly of academics, lawyers, and businesspersons (without a single female representative), and presented its draft in September 1976 for government consideration. A Constituent Assembly (CA) was indirectly elected by local government areas in August 1977, and the 203 members (including only one woman) began to deliberate on the draft in October 1977. These people were again mainly business and academic elites, but also included a number of old guard politicians. Following their deliberations, the military government announced a finalized version of the Constitution in October 1978. Although the government accepted virtually all of the CA's provisions, it decreed a total of 17 changes, including a decision not to allow quotas (ethnic or "federal") in armed forces' recruitment.

National integration and nation building were stressed as primary political objectives; these goals were to be promoted by encouraging "intermarriage among persons from different places of origin or of different religious, ethnic, or linguistic associations or ties," and by promoting "the formation of associations that cut across ethnic, linguistic, religious or other

sectional barriers." Most significantly, the aim was "that loyalty to the nation shall override sectional loyalties."[19] The Constitution also guaranteed freedom of speech, information, and association, and provided specific guidelines on the functions and duties of the respective political institutions of the Second Republic.

The President

Unlike in the First Republic, where the president was a ceremonial figure, the Constitution gave executive powers to the president, similar in range to those of the U.S. president. The president was directly elected by a popular vote throughout the whole country, and would hold office for a maximum of two four-year terms. No electoral college was provided; the president had to win not only the highest number of votes cast, but also one-quarter of the vote in at least two-thirds of the states. Failing that, a second election was to be held within a week with voting restricted to members of the National Assembly and State Houses of Assembly. This was not necessary in 1979 and 1983, because Shagari emerged as winner of the popular ballot.

The president, who had to be a citizen of at least 35 years of age, was officially Head of State, Chief Executive of the Federation, and Commander-in-Chief of the Armed Forces. The vice president, who was elected on the same party ticket as the president (although some had tried unsuccessfully to have the vice president be the runner-up in the presidential contest), was to succeed the president if the latter became incapacitated or died in office.

The president was able to select his or her own group of ministers, who were not to be members of the National Assembly. The president was responsible for initiating both national and international policies, and held a veto over the legislation passed by the National Assembly, although this veto could be overridden by a two-thirds vote of the Assembly. The process of impeachment against the president could be started by a petition signed by one-third of Senate members, but both a full investigation and final impeachment needed two-thirds support of both houses. This issue never arose in the short life of the Second Republic.

Shehu Shagari was the only president to serve under the 1979 Constitution. Shagari was an experienced politician and wealthy business leader, having initially founded the old Northern People's Congress in his home area in north-western Nigeria, and then going on to hold three federal ministerial positions between 1960 and 1965. His first cabinet in 1979 contained 42 members reflecting "federal character" (although with only two women), with 23 members from the North (ten states), 4 members from the East (two states), 8 from the West (four states), and 7 from the Middle Belt (three states). Any evenhandedness the NPN government had evaporated as it became dominated by selfish desires and policies and discredited by rampant corruption.

The National Assembly

The National Assembly comprised two houses of equal importance, the Senate and the House of Representatives. The Senate contained 95 members, with 5 representatives from each of the 19 states, irrespective of size or population. The House of Representatives was composed of 449 members whose electoral districts were based on areas of roughly equal population size. Both houses of the National Assembly were responsible for approving legislation before it could be passed on to Shagari for his signature. Each house had equal influence in this task, and each was able to initiate legislation. Senate ratification was necessary for presidential nominations to the Supreme Court, the National Defense Council, and the National Security Council. The Assembly also possessed important influence over the process of creating new states in the federation. Although there were calls for the creation of up to 50 new states, none was able to gain legal recognition in the short tenure of the Second Republic.

Despite the immense effort expended to establish the National Assembly, its operation left much to be desired. The NPN held a majority of seats in both houses through its alliance with the NPP (broken off in 1981), and after the 1983 elections the NPN held this majority by itself. It was never able to control a clear two-thirds majority necessary for constitutional amendments.

The failure to implement the Code of Conduct left many Senators and Representatives actively pursuing their business interests from within the Assembly.

State Governments

Each of the 19 states of the federation possessed a governor, deputy governor, and a single House of Assembly. Elections for each assembly were to be held during the same period as federal elections. The constitutional structure operated fairly smoothly in the majority of states, where the branches of government were dominated by a single political party, but serious divisions emerged in Kaduna state, where intense rivalries left an NPN assembly facing a PRP governor. After a series of clashes, the assembly forced through a politically inspired impeachment of the governor, in some ways adapting the presidential system of government to the rules and norms of the former parliamentary system.

RECENT MILITARY GOVERNMENTS, 1984–

The military's intervention in 1984 was initially well received by Nigerians who had suffered severe economic hardship under the Shagari government. The military could not offer a quick end to that, as chronic debt and deficit problems plagued the country, but promised a halt to the excessive corruption and abuse of power by the NPN. All political parties were proscribed by the military, the 1979 Constitution was suspended, and political activity in the country was banned.

The government of Muhammadu Buhari (1984–1985) used structures similar to the previous military era but allowed the NSO to run rampant, victimizing many innocent people. When General Ibrahim Babangida came to office in August 1985, he tried to distance himself from Buhari by reshaping the institutions, although some of these changes were cosmetic. He changed the name of the SMC to the Armed Forces Ruling Council (AFRC), but its 29 members (reduced to 19 members in February 1989) remained the central decision makers of the state. Babangida also reorganized the NSO in

June 1986 into three bodies: (1) the Defense Intelligence Agency, to oversee defense; (2) the National Intelligence Agency, for intelligence gathering overseas; and (3) the State Security Services, for internal monitoring. In addition, Babangida established two new institutions: the National Defense and Security Council (to provide public security), and the National Defense Council (to ensure territorial integrity).

By integrating a number of civilians into government, though rarely leading politicians, the AFRC gained valuable expertise and presented a "softer" image of its rule. Nevertheless, the absence of dialogue and the inability to force the AFRC to justify its policies make military governments unacceptable in the long term to most Nigerians.

The military introduced the War Against Indiscipline (WAI) in March 1984 in an attempt to improve national behavior and moral values with a "dose of military discipline." When this program did not have the desired effect, the government revamped WAI in July 1986 to become the National Orientation Movement (NOM). This, in turn, was superseded by the Mass Mobilization for Self-reliance and Economic Recovery (MAMSER) in 1987. All these programs stressed discipline, national consciousness, patriotism, and honesty, but the prevailing social and economic conditions in the country made these goals difficult to achieve, and the military's own example was a poor one.

Babangida's Transition Program

A government White Paper, issued on July 1, 1987, followed recommendations made by a National Political Bureau. The 17-person bureau (including one woman), under the chair of Prof. J. S. Cookey, had been established in January 1986 to consider the failures of previous systems and to make recommendations on a successful political framework for the country. Its final report was filed in March 1987, after receiving some 27,000 submissions.

Almost every type of political structure was reviewed over the year. Influential commentators favored the breakup of the federation into a confederation, while others recommended the "zoning" of the country into distinct political units so that each could provide the national leaders in rotation. The idea of joint leadership or "diarchy" of military and civilian elites received noticeable support, even though it had originally been mooted in 1972 by Dr. Nnamdi Azikiwe. This "mixed grill" government, however, did not gain majority support, nor did the idea of "triarchy," somehow bringing traditional leaders—such as chiefs, emirs, and so on—into the institutional framework.

The White Paper affirmed that the Third Republic was to inherit many of the institutional features of the Second Republic,[20] including an executive presidential system with a bicameral legislature. In deciding upon the retention of this framework, the military rejected the Cookey bureau's majority recommendation that there should be a unicameral legislature. It also rejected the proposal that 10 percent of the seats in the Assembly should be reserved for women and labor unionists. The military did decide, however, that elected representatives should receive small allowances, rather than salaries, to increase their national awareness and responsibilities. Another major difference with the new framework was that only two political parties were to be registered by the military (and "acceptable" to it). This novel feature aimed to dissipate ethnic differences by forcing new political alliances.

The military organized elections for local government areas in December 1987 as the first part of this timetable. Candidates were "nonpolitical" in that they had no attachment to any party or policy. A new electoral register was drawn up in November 1987, but as in previous years the figures appeared to be hopelessly exaggerated. The total of 72 million electors was 40 percent higher than the commission's own prediction.

The local government elections in December 1987 involved 13,000 candidates and proved chaotic in many areas. Results in some states were canceled and fresh elections held in March 1988. Other nonpolitical elections took place in May 1988 for members of the Constituent Assembly who were entrusted with the task of considering the Constitution, modifying it where necessary, and acting upon the recommendations of a Constitutional Review Commission, which had deliberated since September 1987. The assembly representatives were elected by the local government officers, but only one day's notice of the elections and candidates was given in order to minimize the chances of electoral malpractice. One-fifth of the 567 members of this assembly were government nominees, and their report was submitted to the government in April 1989.

The ban on political activity was raised on May 3, 1989 along with the promulgation of the new constitution. Within weeks, 49 associations were vying for official registration. With only two parties to be registered, these groups were forced into potential alliances and coalitions. The National Electoral Commission (NEC) was to monitor the rigorous registration procedures: a 50,000 naira registration fee, names and photographs of all members, and a detailed account of how the parties would tackle Nigeria's social, political, and economic problems. Only 13 associations managed to file applications prior to the July 1989 deadline, and after some deliberations the NEC sent a report to the president recommending the following associations: People's Solidarity Party, Nigerian National Congress, Peoples Front of Nigeria, Liberal Convention, Nigerian Labour Party, and the Republican Party of Nigeria.

Babangida's dislike of politicians was common knowledge, and he was quoted as saying that political parties were "natural grounds for the idle and illiterate who have over the years failed to qualify for any reputable profession."[21] It was also known that Babangida wanted to screen out radicals and those who threatened to expose the military's corruption. Nevertheless, most observers were surprised in October 1989 when Babangida refused to register any of the parties, claiming that they were residual ethnic parties from previous republics, and announced that the military would organize two new parties and prepare their manifestos. When these were released in December 1989, they followed identical frameworks, except that the Social Democratic Party (SDP) favored somewhat progressive policies, and the National Republican Convention (NRC) supported more conservative, laissez-faire programs. Despite some bitterness

about the controlled process, politicians quickly organized to occupy these artificial party shells. The transition program was modified to hold local government elections in December 1990, and gubernatorial elections in December 1991 (see Table 11.4), with national and presidential elections fixed for mid–1992.

The local government elections, held by open ballot (see Feature 11.4) in December 1990, were relatively peaceful but had a low turnout. The SDP fared marginally better than the NRC in the country as a whole, and managed to win healthy majorities in Kano, Kwara, Lagos, and Oyo states. The NRC, seen by many observers as the natural descendant of the NPC and NPN, won strongly in Akwa Ibom, Bauchi, and Sokoto states. Tensions rose in 1991 as each party strove to compromise on the allocation of senior positions among different ethnic constituencies. Both parties adopted "zoning" policies, but the bitter divisions within the parties were notable in the 1991 gubernatorial primaries, when fierce intraparty conflicts led the government to postpone the elections twice. Elections for governors and state assemblies were finally held in December 1991, and results showed a fairly even balance between the two parties.

The military's ability to control the transition period was questionable. Four attempts in three years to draw up an accurate voter register had brought four different figures. An abortive coup attempt in April 1990 unsettled the military leadership and showed deep divisions within the ranks.[22] The austerity and hardship under the structural adjustment program continued to "sap" the economy and promote bitterness and anguish among the populace, especially as stories of high-level corruption multiplied. Workers' strikes increased in intensity during 1991, and religious riots combined with political tensions to provide a volatile atmosphere. The creation of nine new states in August 1991 added further impetus to the political race to control the Third Republic and complicated the task of factional balancing.

National Assembly elections held in 1992 gave the SDP control of both federal houses and led to great anticipation for the presidential election slated for December 1992.[23] From a pool of 48 nominees, the parties selected their presidential candidates. The SDP picked Shehu Musa Yar'Adua, a former chief of military staff under Obasanjo, whereas the NRC selected Adamu Ciroma, formerly secretary-general of the NPN. The selection of two northerners alarmed many. Even the Sokoto northern establishment was concerned because neither candidate appeared to support its interests. Ba-

bangida announced his opposition to the candidates and the postponement of the election in November 1992, raising further doubts about his intentions. He had tried to strengthen his position within the military by giving everyone above the rank of captain a new car—at an estimated cost of 500 million naira. A transitional council, headed by Ernest Shonekan, was to

Table 11.4   GUBERNATORIAL AND STATE ASSEMBLY ELECTION RESULTS, DECEMBER 1991

States	Governors	Party	State Assemblies	
			NRC	SDP
Abia	C.O. Onu	NRC	25	9
Abamawa	Alh. Michika	NRC	18	14
Akwa Ibom	Obong Isemin	NRC	32	16
Anambra	Dr. C. Ezeife	SDP	14	18
Bauchi	Alh. Dahiru Muhammed	NRC	38	6
Benue	Rev. M. O. Adasu	SDP	14	22
Borno	Alh. Lawan	SDP	15	27
Cross River	Mr. David Ebri	NRC	13	15
Delta	Chief Alex Ibru	SDP	14	22
Edo	Chief Oyegun	SDP	10	17
Enugu	Mr. O. Nwodo	NRC	19	19
Imo	Chief E. Enwerem	NRC	27	15
Jigawa	Alh. Birninkudu	SDP	—	—
Kaduna	Dr. D. Tafida	NRC	20	16
Kano	Alh. Kabiru Gaya	NRC	68	33
Katsina	Alh S. Barde	NRC	18	30
Kebbi	Alh A. Musa	NRC	22	10
Kogi	Alh. A. Audu	NRC	22	10
Kwara	Alh. Lafiagi	SDP	2	22
Lagos	Sir M. Otedola	NRC	4	26
Niger	Alh. Inuwa	NRC	26	12
Ogun	Chief Osoba	SDP	1	29
Ondo	Mr. Olumilua	SDP	6	45
Oshun	Isiaka Adeleke	SDP	4	42
Oyo	Kolapo Ishola	SDP	13	37
Plateau	Tapgun Fidelis	SDP	11	35
Rivers	Rufus George	NRC	29	19
Sokoto	Alh. Abdulkareem	NRC	28	—
Taraba	No Election	—	—	—
Yobe	Alh. Abubakir Ibrahim	SDP	8	18

Source: West Africa, December 23, 1991–January 5, 1992.

Feature 11.4 Open Ballot Elections

Beginning in 1990, elections in Nigeria were often undertaken by open, rather than secret, ballot. This entailed voters arriving at the polling booth at a predetermined hour and lining up behind a picture of their candidate. In a public head count, tallies were recorded and then sent on to a central recording office. A similar electoral procedure has also been adopted in Kenya.

The open ballot has proved to be controversial, as one might expect, but a questionnaire undertaken by the National Electoral Commission (NEC) in 1991 found a substantial majority of voters to be in favor of it, largely because this system was less likely to be rigged. By voting out in public, everyone could see the result, unlike a secret ballot, where the very secrecy of it enabled people to falsify results.

The open ballot was able to work in many parts of Nigeria because of a strong (neutral) military presence. Local government elections held in March 1996 utilized the open ballot, and it is expected that other elections within the Abacha transition program will also do so. The system is unlikely to survive after 1998 when one party will control government and the police, and many believe that because of potential intimidation of voters, Nigeria will retain a secret ballot electoral system.

help nominally the military run the country until elections could be held and a new president installed in August 1993.

More than 200 candidates for the presidential elections were screened and approved by the military in January 1993. Campaigning began in April 1993, and the parties selected their presidential candidates. The NRC selected Bashir Othman Tofa, a former financial secretary of the NPN, with its vice-president being Dr. Sylvester Ugo, from the southeast. The SDP chose Moshood Abiola, a Yoruba Muslim, with its vice-president being Babangana Kingibe, a northerner. Tofa had the strong backing of the northern establishment and General Sani Abacha, chief of defense staff.

In the presidential election held on June 12, 1993, Abiola won a clear victory that broke the mold of traditional Nigerian politics. The NEC announced that he had won 8.4 million votes, or 58 percent of the total, and had taken 19 of 30 states, including the key northern states of Kano and Kaduna. Official figures showed that he had gained 97 percent of the military's votes. Despite Abiola's close ties to Babangida, the election results appeared to frighten the northern establishment and senior military officers. Brigadier Hailu Akilu, Head of National Intelligence Agencies and a powerful figure in the National Defense and Security Council (NDSC), was

quoted as saying, "Abiola will only become president over my dead body."[24] Abacha was also opposed to Abiola.

Babangida announced the annulment of the elections on June 23 and promised that new elections would take place shortly. In early August, these new elections were also canceled, and on August 27 Babangida was forced out of office.

Abacha and a New Transition Program

Babangida turned over power to a 32-member interim government, headed by Ernest Shonekan, but clearly serving only at the military's pleasure. Its mandate was to organize fresh presidential elections and hand over power by March 31, 1994. Shonekan's moderate approach, particularly in economic affairs, was welcomed in the West, but few saw him as holding real power. This was openly revealed on November 17, 1993, when General Sani Abacha appeared to preempt a junior officers coup and took power, overthrowing the interim government and imposing full military rule. Abacha had played a critical role in bringing Babangida to power a decade earlier, and had remained extremely influential within the military, being Babangida's right-hand man.

Abacha moved quickly to gain control. A Hausa from Kano, Abacha calmed the fears of the northern establishment by positioning northerners in many top positions, but aroused the anger of the majority of Nigerians favoring democracy. When Abiola, encouraged by the National Democratic Coalition (Nadeco), returned to the country in June 1994 to claim the presidency, Abacha detained him. Abacha also attempted to appease leading civilians by incorporating them into his government. During the second half of 1994, a two-month strike by oil workers supporting Abiola was beaten down by the military, and a constitutional conference went over the same old ground of considering a framework of government for the country. Issues of federalism and ethnicity were highly debated, but many observers thought the issues ought to be economic development and corruption. The conference called for a transition date of January 1, 1996, but the military forced that date to be withdrawn.

The military received the final report in May 1995 but was preoccupied with other issues. More than 300 officers, including retired generals Obasanjo and Yar'Adua, had been arrested in February 1995 for allegedly being involved in a coup attempt. There was less evidence of a coup than an attempt by the military to head off dissent by arresting elite officers. Many of those arrested received long-term sentences, including Obasanjo, sparking off international criticism. The invitation to Nigeria to host the 8th World Youth Soccer Championships was withdrawn, while TransAfrica, a major lobby for African causes within the United States, began strenuous opposition against Nigeria. Abacha continued to strengthen his power base by compulsorily retiring many senior officers early in 1996.

In October 1995, Abacha announced a new transition program aimed at transferring government to civilians by October 1998.[25] Whereas the constitutional conference had called for the country to be divided into three zones, Abacha announced that six zones would be created: North-East; North-West; Middle Belt; South-West; East-Central; and Southern Minority. Six high-ranking governmental positions would, in turn, be rotated through the zones. These positions were president, vice president, prime minister, deputy prime minister, senate president, and speaker of the house. No plan was given of how each zone would be demarcated, nor in which order the positions would be rotated.

Furthermore, the presidential system of the Second Republic was to be blended with a parliamentary structure, following along the lines of the French and Russian political structures. Abacha, with apparent seriousness, announced that this system would operate for a trial period of 30 years. In contrast, few observers were confident that it would even become operational in 1998. Many believed that the military would simply maintain its grip on power, so plunging the country further into chaos. This view remained prominent even after non-political local elections began the transition program in March 1996.

JUDICIARY AND LEGAL RIGHTS

Nigeria's legal system has been heavily influenced by norms, traditions, and practices inherited from Britain, but unlike Britain, Nigeria continues to have significant numbers of judicial executions. The country's legal practitioners have retained a relatively high profile and reputation in the country even through long periods of military rule. The judiciary gained credibility during the 1979 and 1983 elections when courts used their constitutional right to amend contested election results. The Nigerian Bar Association (NBA), established as long ago as 1886, attempted to maintain its independence from political pressures by boycotting military tribunals established after the 1983 coup d'état to try politicians suspected of corruption. During the 1980s, the AFRC had at times allowed the legal process to be maintained without excessive pressure. However, the widespread use of military tribunals has come under fire in the 1990s for providing poor means of defense for those on trial.

The Civil Liberties Organization (CLO), founded in 1987, along with other groups such as the Committee for the Defense of Human Rights and the National Association for Democratic Lawyers, have been hounded by the Babangida and Abacha governments. In a damning report published by the CLO in March 1991, the Babangida government was criticized for "executive lawlessness" in its disrespect for court orders, for imposing retroactive legislation, and for taking numerous illegal actions.[26] In mid–1995, the Abacha government preempted possible action in commemorating the second anniversary of Abiola's election "victory" by arresting about 50 key human rights campaigners. At the end of 1995, the quick trial and execution of nine Ogoni dissidents led to international condemnation of the judicial process and sanctions against Nigeria by the United States and European Union.

The 1979 and 1989 Constitutions provided legal structures at both state and federal levels. At the individual state level, three courts were established: a State High Court, a State Customary Court of Appeal, and a State Shari'a Court. A Federal Court of Appeal was inaugurated in 1979 to handle appeals from these three sets of courts. Pressure from Islamic groups to have a Federal Shari'a Court was unsuccessful, as only northern states instituted the State Shari'a Courts. Also at the federal level was a Federal High Court and a Federal Supreme Court. The Supreme Court was given the power of constitutional review and used it immediately in 1979 to consider the disputed presidential election result and to confirm, in a split ruling, Shehu Shagari as the victor. This power was also used in October 1981 when the Court declared the government's Revenue Act to be null and void, but overall it was not extensively used, although it was retained in the 1989 Constitution.

LOCAL GOVERNMENT

The structures and role of local governments have varied considerably since independence. During the First Republic, each region had its own system of local government. In the East and West, local governments were loosely organized and relatively weak, whereas in the North they remained strong and influential, particularly when used by emirs as their channel of rule. In the early 1970s, local government structures began to change as the western states instituted a council-manager system of administration and the northern states strove to weaken the powers of traditional rulers. In 1976, the military government introduced the Local Government Edicts, which forced all local governments in Nigeria to adopt similar structural and operating procedures. Decisions of all local governments were to be based on majority voting, and all governments were to be single-tiered, secular authorities. These changes helped to make local governments the natural third level of government in the country after the federal and state levels.

The trends of weakening the role of traditional rulers and increasing the efficiency of these local governments continued in the 1980s and 1990s. The number of local governments increased during the Second Republic, but the military after 1984 cut back the number to 301. The situation was dramatically altered in May 1989, when 148 new local government areas were created, bringing the total to 449. This action was taken to increase the responsiveness of local governments to the needs of the people. More areas were created in August 1991 after the creation of nine new states, bringing the total to 589. Although their powers are often undermined by state governments, local governments remain a primary level of participatory democracy, and it is only at the ward level that party membership was organized in the transition to the Third Republic. In 1978, 1988, 1990, and 1996 local government areas provided the initial elections and candidates as the first step to civilian rule.

INTEREST GROUPS

The distinction between interest groups and political parties is blurred in Nigeria, both because of the strong sectional interests, which parties have promoted, and because parties have been banned for more than two-thirds of the postindependence period. Most parties of the Second Republic developed from "social" organizations that were active prior to the raising of the ban on political activity. These groups generally comprised business leaders, high-ranking administrators, professionals, and former politicians. But these are by no means the only type of interest group, and it is useful to consider the most important ones here.

Business Groups

One of the most influential interest groups over the last decade has been the so-called Kaduna mafia. Kaduna is the former capital of the old Northern Region and remains an important locus of northern Islamic influence in the country. Members of this loosely organized group are prominent businesspeople, retired senior military officers, and others of equivalent stature. Nobody outside of the "mafia" really knows who belongs to this group, or whether it even exists, but it is a group about whom many have commented in recent years. These influential people are believed to have been inspirational in planning the December 1983 coup by giving backing to the coup leader, Muhammadu Buhari and by wanting to push aside Shehu Shagari, whose economic mismanagement (despite his "northernness") was damaging the infrastructure and business environment of the country. The "mafia" received a setback when General Babangida came to office in 1985, but it still casts a shadow over governmental affairs and has been considered instrumental in maintaining the Abacha regime in power.

There are, naturally, other groups of businesspeople, including retired senior military officers, throughout the country who have been able to influence state and federal policy. Given the lack of constraints on political leaders seeking economic fortunes while in office, the business community has had a considerable impact upon government by ensuring policies to suit their interests. Although not uncommon elsewhere, the open and blatant business group involvement in the political process has been, and will continue to be, of major significance.

A typical street market in southern Nigeria.

Labor Unions

In contrast to the successful interaction of business and political elites, the Nigeria Labor Congress (NLC) has had little success in influencing the policies of civilian or military governments or in promoting a more socialistic orientation in the country. Divisive internal battles within the labor movement caused the Obasanjo government to intervene and restructure the labor movement in 1978 into a total of 42 unions, all under the umbrella of the NLC. This has not prevented further internal squabbles. Membership declined considerably in the late 1980s and early 1990s because economic hardship led to unemployment and a growing desperation to cling to a job, whether unionized or not.

The NLC has aligned itself with radical political forces in the past but has been unsuccessful in attempting to make class issues the basis of political conflict, rather than ethnicity. The unions organized their only general strike in 1964, when 800,000 workers gained higher wages and the action by unions was considered a "strike against politicians" to protest the chaotic condition of the country. Strikes were made illegal by the military government after 1966, but numerous strikes nevertheless occurred in the 1970s. These strikes provided the stimulus for private and public salaries to rise by 30 percent after the Abedo Commission reported in 1971, and then helped provide even larger raises (up to 100 percent for the lowest paid) following the Udoji Commission in 1975.

Generally speaking, however, unions have not been a dominant force within society. As Douglas Rimmer concluded, labor "has been a fitfully active force, lacking sustained political influence and usually inexpert and ineffective in negotiation."[27] The NLC has vehemently protested the economic reforms implemented since 1986 but with little success. NLC leaders were arrested in June 1986, at the end of 1987, and in the middle of 1988, and Babangida and Abacha regarded the NLC with suspicion but with little concern. The NLC executive was dismissed by the government in February 1988, and a new structure was organized. The NLC actively supported the creation of a true Socialist party and the development of a Socialist ideology for the country, but was warned repeatedly by the military to stay out of any political affiliations.

When the presidential election result was canceled in 1993, there were massive strikes across the country, but these failed to change government policy, and workers were forced back to work.

The Media

The media in Nigeria was, until recently, one of the most active and independent in sub-Saharan Africa. The media has been outspoken since independence, despite periodic threats and intimidation by various governments. The media has not always been impartial, however, as many newspapers or state-controlled radio stations have favored a political party or regional interest, but there has remained a willingness to take firm positions on issues of national importance, particularly corruption.

Recent military governments have attempted to control the media's coverage of events. Babangida introduced Decree 19, under which it became an offense to comment "negatively" on the government's handling of the transition program, although discussion and positive suggestions were still acceptable. Despite active protests by the National Union of Journalists (which has been in existence since 1955), numerous jail sentences have been handed out over the last six years to journalists—and newspapers closed down—who have published articles embarrassing to the government. One prominent journalist, Dele Giwa, was assassinated in mysterious circumstances in November 1986. Giwa had written several scathing articles on government policy and fell victim to a parcel bomb which appeared to have arrived in a package carrying the government seal. There was intense speculation that the government's security forces were responsible, but no firm evidence was uncovered. Under the Abacha regime, action against journalists and newspapers has increased.

Book authors have also been major critics of Nigerian development, and their attacks have been much more difficult to contain. There are many excellent Nigerian authors helping to promote political development in this way, most notably Chinua Achebe and Wole Soyinka, the winner of the 1986 Nobel Prize for Literature. Soyinka is currently exiled abroad, committed to creating democracy in Nigeria.

Religious Groups

It is easier to comment that religious groups have an impact upon the political process than to pinpoint the groups involved and the policies influenced. During the First Republic, the Sultan of Sokoto and the Islamic establishment had obvious influence on policy through the sultan's brother, Alhaji Ahmadu Bello, the Sardauna of Sokoto, the Northern Premier, and the leader of the NPC. This influence was less evident in the Second Republic, but Shagari was from Sokoto state and had close connections to the sultan. An indication of the declining influence of the Islamic establishment has been noticed in recent years, particularly during the Babangida administration, when emissaries were dispatched to Lagos to pressure the military to modify policies.

The overall purpose of this lobbying pressure is to maintain the influence and cohesion of Islam, particularly in the North (and especially since the North is no longer a monolithic bloc), to keep the Shari'a system of courts and justice, and to attempt to maintain Nigeria's foreign policy on pro-Islamic-Arab lines. Nigeria's decision to become a member of the Organization of Islamic Conference (OIC) in 1986 was considered to be a concession by Babangida to the powerful northern lobby, both religious and business. At a more popular, domestic level, the Islamic League maintains the loyalty of many Muslims and is outspoken against any policy that threatens the status of Muslims. In recent years, pressure has been exerted over issues such as state creation, education, and family planning. Fundamentalism has been of obvious concern since 1980, with the challenge of its ideology and with the riots that have taken place, but its impact on policy has been minimal.

The Christian Association of Nigeria (CAN) helps to bring together the opinions of a diverse range of Christian churches and groups, and it exerts influence on their behalf. The CAN stands to protect Christian interests against what it considers to be aggressive and expansionist Islam. The organization is also working to maintain the secular disposition of the country and prevent the attachment of Nigeria to Islamic organizations overseas, such as the OIC and the Islamic Bank. During the early 1990s, the CAN was at its most active. The death of more than 500 people in religious riots in April and October 1991, and subsequent deaths in riots in May 1992, reminded everyone of the political potency of religion.

Universities

Universities provide the base for intellectual challenge to the status quo. By 1986, there had developed 17 federal universities, 6 state universities, and some 60 polytechnics and colleges in the country. The Academic Staff Union of Nigerian Universities (ASUU) has organized numerous actions in the past to attempt to influence a more radical appraisal of Nigerian development. Since 1993, university campuses have been closed for a total of 12 months, putting students more than a year behind in their programs. The students themselves have also been highly critical of government policy, notably structural adjustment and the increasing hardship faced by students on university campuses, and the military and paramilitary police have been involved in many campus clashes with students in the 1990s. For all these challenges, little political headway has really been gained, and the universities have been unable to link up with labor unions to make their views and actions more effective.

Declining financial assistance to higher education has led to deteriorating conditions and a falling standard of education on the campuses. Government harassment of academics combined with low salaries have also led to an exodus abroad of many Nigerian faculty. Full professors, on average, earn less than $100 a month.

Universities remain a critical center of action for democracy, and consequently will stay very closely monitored by the military over the coming months.

KEY TERMS

Action Group (AG)
Armed Forces Ruling Council (AFRC)
ceremonial president
civilian elite
Constituent Assembly
diarchy
electoral systems
executive president
extractive politics
Federal Electoral Commission (Fedeco)
federalism
Kaduna mafia
military elite
National Assembly
National Convention of Nigerian Citizens (NCNC)
National Party of Nigeria (NPN)
Nigeria Labor Congress (NLC)
Nigeria People's Party (NPP)
Northern People's Congress (NPC)
parliamentary and presidential systems
recivilianization
religious groups
Republics, the First, Second, and Third
sectarianism
Supreme Military Council (SMC)
triarchy
zoning

FURTHER READINGS

The Constitution of the Federal Republic of Nigeria, 1989 (Lagos: Federal Ministry of Information, 1989).

Diamond, Larry. Class, Ethnicity and Democracy in Nigeria. The Failure of the First Republic (Syracuse: Syracuse University Press, 1988).

Dudley, Billy. An Introduction to Nigerian Government and Politics (London: Macmillan, 1982).

Falola, Toyin, and Julius Ihonvbere. The Rise and Fall of Nigeria's Second Republic (London: Zed, 1985).

Joseph, Richard A. Democracy and Prebendal Politics in Nigeria (Cambridge: Cambridge University Press, 1987).

Kumo Suleiman, and Abubakar Aliyu, eds. Issues in the Nigerian Draft Constitution (Zaria: Baraka Press, 1978).

Odetola, Theophilius O. Military Politics in Nigeria: Economic Development and Political Stability (New Brunswick: Transaction, 1978).

Olorunsola, Victor A. Soldiers and Power: The Development Performance of the Nigerian Military Regime (Stanford: Hoover Institution Press, 1977).

Olowu, Dele, Kayode Soremekun, and Adebayo Williams (eds.), Governance and Democratisation in Nigeria (Ibadan: Spectrum Books, 1995).

Osaghae, Eghosa E. "Ethnic Minorities and Federalism in Nigeria," African Affairs, 90 (1991), pp. 237–258.

Oyediran, Oyeleye, ed. Nigerian Government and Politics under Military Rule 1966–1979 (London: Macmillan, 1979).

Oyediran, Oyeleye, ed. The Nigerian 1979 Elections (London: Macmillan, 1981).

Panter-Brick, Keith, ed. Soldiers and Oil: The Political Transformation of Nigeria (London: Frank Cass, 1978).

Post, K. W. J., and Michael Vickers. Structure and Conflict in Nigeria, 1960–1966 (London: Heinemann, 1973).

Public Policy

Nigeria's economy is dominated by oil. The export of this single commodity has consistently accounted for some 90 percent of the country's total foreign exchange earnings. Given oil's critical position in the economy, the commodity has also had a strong influence in shaping the country's foreign policy, especially during the oil boom years of the late 1970s, when Nigeria flexed its nascent muscles on the world stage. The relative demise of the oil market in the 1980s and 1990s has caused serious economic dislocation, and, when combined with gross mismanagement and corruption, has limited Nigeria's ability to strike a bolder profile in world politics. The failure to diversify economic output into high-tech, capital-intensive industry has stifled aspirations to move into the ranks of the Newly Industrializing Countries (NICs).

THE ECONOMY

The traditional pattern of agriculture prior to colonial occupation had been one of subsistence farming, but British intervention radically altered the nature of production. Cash-crop agriculture was developed, with crops grown not for domestic consumption but for export overseas. After the early part of this century, Nigeria's agriculture had been forged into the classic colonial, export-oriented structure, with groundnuts

Farm workers in Nigeria. Over 60 percent of workers are employed in agriculture.

produced in the North, cocoa in the Southwest, and palm oil in the Southeast. The British built a rail system to freight these commodities (and minerals) to the ports, but not to provide a means of passenger transportation. This rail framework is still used today, although it is in urgent need of repair and modernization.

At independence, these three commodities together contributed the majority of Nigeria's export earnings. The major trading partner was Britain, which retained a controlling hand in many sectors of the Nigerian economy. Minimal "horizontal" trade was developed with neighboring African states, which had also been geared to cash-crop production and "vertical" integration with the European colonial powers. During the First Republic, little in the way of structural economic change occurred. Political independence may well have been won, but Nigeria's economic profile remained unchanged; British involvement, investment, and areas of control were still being maintained. The impact of European and North American economic forces on the economy altered marginally in the 1970s, but many political economists argue that it remains of great significance today in Nigeria, especially with the privatization of state enterprises, the increasing emphasis on foreign investment, the problems of international debt, and the strong role of the IMF and World Bank.[28]

Oil Boom

Through geological good fortune, oil has been the single most important factor in Nigeria's economic development over the last 25 years, providing both positive and negative effects. Oil had been produced in the early 1960s, but the growth of the industry was hampered by the civil war. Once the war was over in 1970, oil production increased rapidly. From a level around the time of independence of 5,000 barrels a day (b/d), production had risen to 1.4 million b/d in 1970, and reached a peak of 2.3 million b/d in 1979. Throughout the 1970s, oil revenues increased by 30 percent a year, and in 1980 rose to $24.94 billion. By early 1989, production had fallen to 1.2 million b/d, and income was only $4.22 billion. The slight boom

during the Gulf crisis of 1990–1991 helped income, but prices and earnings had fallen again by the mid–1990s.

The government's expenditure levels had risen dramatically in the 1970s as a result of the financial bonanza. By 1980, the government was spending more money in one day than its predecessor in 1960 had spent in two months. The tremendous financial gains from oil led, in contrast, to rapid stagnation of other sectors. By the mid–1970s, the contribution to exports of the staple agricultural commodities of groundnuts, cocoa, and palm oil had fallen to zero. Oil ruled.

Nigeria joined the Organization of Petroleum Exporting Countries (OPEC) in 1971 to promote its economic (and political) objectives, and also established the Nigeria National Oil Corporation (NNOC) to monitor oil production. The NNOC was merged with the Ministry of Petroleum in 1977 to form the Nigeria National Petroleum Corporation (NNPC), which has controlled the oil sector to the present. The government introduced in 1972 an Indigenization Decree, which prohibited foreigners from certain economic sectors and limited participation to 40 percent in others. The major overseas oil corporations, such as Shell, Gulf, Mobil, and Texaco-Chevron were all limited to a 40 percent stake in the oil sector. Superficially, this appeared to shift economic control into Nigerian hands, but overseas interests remained extremely influential. In addition, leading Nigerian entrepreneurs—both inside and outside government—did not operate with the national interest at heart, and many simply set out to decimate national wealth. These "lootocrats," as they have been termed, operated within a system of "pirate capitalism" that effectively wasted a golden opportunity to provide real economic development for the country.[29]

Lavish prestige-enhancing projects were undertaken, such as the construction of a new federal capital at Abuja (on the model of Brasilia and Canberra). A worldwide black arts festival (FESTAC) was hosted in Lagos in 1977 at great expense, and it was held up as a symbol of Nigeria's growing status in the world. By the end of the 1970s, President Shagari was actively threatening to use the "oil weapon" against

Oil wells in the River Niger Delta. Oil has been the single most important factor in Nigeria's economic development.

Western countries to promote foreign policy goals. During this era, there was "skewed development" or "growth without development" in the country; money was often diverted to unnecessary projects, and pockets, while deserving schemes, primarily agricultural and infrastructural ones, suffered badly. Urban migration gathered pace while investment in rural areas dwindled. Overall, efforts to improve the living conditions of the majority of Nigerians were minimal. The opportunities offered by oil were squandered by successive governments, and when the oil glut emerged and prices collapsed in the early 1980s, the economy reeled.

Oil Bust: Rethinking Development Priorities

The rapid shrinkage of the economy in the 1980s and 1990s was a painful process to watch. In 1990, Nigeria's national earnings were only 20 percent of the 1980 figure. Industries, which had grown in the 1970s, were generally dependent upon imported spare parts, so they ground to a halt as supplies were cut. Nigeria found that its agricultural production had declined to such a level that the country could not feed itself. The rural areas, already depressed, suffered even greater hardship. Formerly in a position of handing out loans to African neighbors, Nigeria now had to look around for loans itself. As with the majority of third world states, Nigeria's debt situation became alarming, and in 1996 stood at $37 billion, with an impossible debt repayment schedule.

Development implies that there should be a reduction in both the absolute level of poverty and the economic inequalities between segments of the population. During the oil boom years, the government appeared to lose sight of this, as

Lagos, major port and former capital of Nigeria. Its population is now 3 million.

growth became synonymous with development. Some significant developments were recorded, most notably the provision of education in the country. At the primary school level (grades 1 through 6), the number of students increased from 2.9 million in 1960 to 11.5 million in 1980. But in the 1990s, with over 2 million students leaving school and hitting the already saturated job market annually, the underlying economic problems and weaknesses remain just as obvious.

Per capita income figures have declined in recent years, as have other economic indicators. These problems are accentuated by the rapid growth of the population at about 3 percent a year. Half of the population is below 16 years of age, and the average fertility rate is six children per female. The seriousness of this problem was such that in February 1988 a new national policy for population control was introduced. The plan hoped to introduce sex education in secondary schools and to lower the aver-

age number of children per mother from six to four. In the Islamic North, however, men generally have four wives, and this scheme could still enable wealthy men to have up to 16 children per family. In response to this, the policy emphasis in 1989 shifted to "one man: four children." But this plan faced considerable opposition from various groups, and from Nigerian men in general.

Perhaps one should not be overcritical and stress that the country had made some developmental gains in a number of sectors: the lowering of infant mortality levels; the improvement of health care and educational facilities; the raising of life expectancy figures; the improvement of transport infrastructure; all these and others were examples of beneficial development. Unfortunately, the country has struggled to maintain them in the austere conditions of structural adjustment, and with the continuing obscene corruption of the military government.

In 1991, Nigeria was ranked by the United Nations as the twenty-fourth poorest country in the world on the human development index, based on infant mortality, literacy levels, and real GDP per capita. By 1995, despite oil earnings of $210 billion since 1970, the country's per capita income of $320 was no higher than in the 1960s before oil was exported. As tables in the introductory chapter show, Nigeria is the poorest of all the countries compared in this volume.

A structural adjustment program (SAP) was implemented in 1985 to attempt to restructure and diversify the economy. This program included the privatization of many state-owned corporations—including the NNPC—as well as the massive devaluation of the naira (the naira fell in value from roughly 1 dollar to 10 cents) and the restructuring of the agricultural sector. Although these have proven to be marginally beneficial in an economic sense, their social impact on the population has been devastating. Inequality has deepened, as has general poverty and hardship, and environmental problems worsen (see Feature 11.5).

The IMF and World Bank, as well as numerous Western donors, have demanded the government's commitment to SAP, resulting in increasing bitterness among the Nigerian populace. The Shonekan "administration" during 1993 committed Nigeria firmly to IMF policies, but Abacha's first budget in January 1994 reversed structural adjustment, reverting back to fixed exchange rates and tight trade controls. IMF pressure led to a softening of these policies in the 1995 budget, but confusion over the government's economic and political policies left it isolated in international financial communities in 1996.

Revenue Allocation

Revenue allocation has been a divisive issue; it set states clashing against one another over their rights and needs and caused conflict between federal and state governments over respective allocations. The main issue at stake is how the income generated from economic production around the country is collected by the federal government and then how, and on what basis, it is redistributed to the states. During the 1950s, there were several changes in revenue allocations given by the colonial administration to the regions. Initially, the North pressed for allocations based on population size, the West on derivation of revenue, and the East on need. As their respective economic profiles changed, and as oil exploration grew in the East, the Western Region based its claims on uniformity, whereas the East began to favor derivation.

After independence the debate on revenue allocation intensified, but successive governments tended to favor derivation of income as a primary factor in assessing federal allocations.

Feature 11.5   The Environment

Concern for environmental damage has grown dramatically over recent years in the world as a whole, although little concrete action has been taken to date by industrialized powers. In Nigeria, the problems of merely making a living in a severely depressed economy leave little time for concern or money for action on the environment. The government, however, took some action in 1989 by setting up the Federal Environmental Protection Agency (FEPA). The greatest concerns in Nigeria focus upon pollution from oil spills, the storage of hazardous and toxic waste, the encroachment of the Sahara desert, and the rapid deforestation linked to rapid urbanization and overpopulation. Ironically for a global oil power, wood still remains the primary source of energy for most, and efforts at reforestation have not kept up with destruction of existing woodland.

Structural adjustment has put even greater strains on the government and has left less money available for a thorough conservation program. Consequently, with the Nigerian population expected to triple over the next 50 years, prospects are grim for the ecological balance of the country.

Feature 11.6 The Case of Ogoniland

The Ogoni people in southeastern Nigeria account for less than 1 percent of the country's population, but their land hosts some 70 percent of the country's oil fields. Even though much of the country's wealth emanates from Ogoniland, the Ogoni people have seen very little returned, and their standard of living remains poor. Unemployment is estimated at 85 percent, literacy at 10 percent, infant mortality at 40 per 1,000 children born; and chronic pollution has ruined much of the farming land.

During the 1990s, the Ogoni have challenged the federal government and oil companies, primarily Shell, to improve their living conditions and local environment, with action spearheaded by the Movement for the Survival of Ogoni People (MOSOP). MOSOP also called for a restructuring of Nigeria into a looser confederation of autonomous (ethnic) states, with each state having considerable control over revenue generated within it. By 1993, Shell, Agip and Elf were estimated to have lost $200 million as a result of protests, and these companies put pressure on the government to terminate the actions.

The military, directly threatened by these actions, acted ruthlessly in suppressing the Ogoni, and following a military tribunal late in 1995, nine Ogoni leaders, including the internationally renowned writer, Ken Saro-Wiwa, were hanged for allegedly inciting others to kill four pro-government Ogoni leaders. Prosecution witnesses admitted being bribed by the military, and those convicted were denied an appeal. Such highly questionable justice provoked outrage around the world; temporary expulsion from the Commonwealth and the freezing of aid and arms transfers by the EU and United States were among the actions taken. The Abacha regime was clearly stunned by the reaction, but hardened its siege mentality in 1996. Shell, though battered by hostile public opinion for its actions against the Ogoni, appeared likely to maintain strong investments in the Delta area, particularly in a future $3.6 billion liquefied natural gas project.

In 1970, a Distributable Pool was inaugurated. Using this pool, the federal government shared out payments to states, with half of the amount paid equally to all the states, and the other half paid on the basis of state population size. In 1975, this pool system was modified to receive 80 percent of revenue allocated to states, with the remaining 20 percent paid directly to the state of derivation. Income tax, now under federal control, was also paid back directly to the states. The civilian government of the Second Republic established the Okigbo Commission in 1980—the eighth such commission since 1946 to consider the allocation issue.

The new revenue act, initiated in 1982, decreased the influence of derivation (the NPN-controlled states were essentially nonproducers of oil) and stressed relative need and population size in allocations to states. The act consolidated the strength of the federal government, which kept 60 percent of all revenue generated nationally, with the remaining 30 percent and 10 percent allocated to states and local governments, respectively. Military governments since 1984 have maintained similar policies, although the Babangida administration changed these figures to 50 percent for the federal government, 35 percent to the states, and 15 percent to local governments, and at the same time allowed local governments more control over their spending. The clashes in Ogoniland[30] during the 1990s again focused attention on the issue of revenue allocation, and in October 1995 Abacha announced that 13 percent of revenue would be returned to areas of derivation (see Feature 11.6).

FOREIGN POLICY

Relations with African states, particularly in western and southern Africa, are considered to be priority areas of policy. Nigeria does have extensive diplomatic contacts with Western countries, however, and worked through these both to bring improved trade relations for itself and to pressure for change in South Africa. On the basis of its economic and demographic strength, Nigeria has always considered itself to be one of the leading countries in Africa, and its foreign policy has been geared to reflect this. Although there are numerous linkages with many African countries, particularly the neighboring countries in West Africa, the level of trade and general economic contacts with them remains low; relations can thus appear to lack a degree of depth and substance.

During the 1960s, the governing elite was content to play a quiet, conservative role in African and world affairs, and during the civil war (1967–1970) policy was geared toward securing a military victory against the secessionists. With the advent of the oil boom in the 1970s, Nigeria pursued an increasingly forceful and active role in world politics, spurred on by its oil wealth, and quickly found "friends" in the West, but this did not automatically lead to any greater successes. Such an active role was in marked contrast to its foreign policy orientation immediately after independence. While accepting a degree of generalization, it is possible and constructive to consider foreign policy through four decades to illuminate the fluctuations of style, emphasis, and content.

THE 1960s

From independence in 1960 until the outbreak of civil war in 1967, Nigeria's foreign policy emphasized caution and a low profile, with a strong reliance placed on close relations with the West, and Britain in particular. This orientation was influenced by the conservative nature of the governing elite, with its strong Islamic roots, but it was also a consciously pursued policy that sought to distance the country from the provocative radicalism of its Anglophone rival in the region, Ghana. The Ghanaian leader, Kwame Nkrumah, advocated a single continental government for Africa, but Nigeria and the majority of African states resisted this and would only support closer international cooperation. These moderate states were successful in 1963 in having the new continental association, the Organization of African Unity (OAU), established within a loose, intergovernmental framework. Such conservatism in Nigeria also led to the refusal (upon British advice) to allow the Soviet Union to establish an embassy in the country until 1962.

It would be wrong to see Nigerian policy in a completely negative and passive manner, as it contained forceful stands on a number of issues. Its relations with Britain were strained in 1961 after its successful pressure to force South Africa out of the Commonwealth. In the following year, the Anglo-Nigerian Defense Pact, which gave Britain military training rights in Nigeria, was abrogated by the federal government following student protests and active condemnation of this quasi-colonial arrangement by Obafemi Awolowo and the Action Group. This protest contributed to Awolowo's later treason trial (following alleged subversive links with Ghana) and his subsequent imprisonment, but it did little to affect the dominant economic linkages with Britain. British military instructors also continued to train Nigerian troops. Nigeria's almost instinctive suspicion of French motivations in Francophone West Africa—all of its neighbors are former French colonies and remain French-speaking today—were intensified in 1961 following France's unscrupulous action in holding atomic tests in the southern desert of its then colonial possession, Algeria. This action outraged Nigerians and led to a break in diplomatic relations with France which lasted for several years.

The civil war, which broke out in mid–1967, forced a reconsideration of both domestic and foreign policy. Western countries, hampered by their own internal pressure groups sympathetic to Biafra's suffering (and oil reserves), were reluctant to sell the large quantities of military supplies requested by the federal government. The French were openly pro-Biafra, hoping to see Nigeria split into weaker territorial units. Consequently, in its time of greatest need, the government perceived it had little option but to turn to the Eastern bloc, at least until Britain added more aid after 1967.

Following the end of the civil war in 1970, policymakers gradually returned to a more sympathetic Western orientation, although this had been undermined to some extent by the experience of the war. The burgeoning economic strength emanating from oil revenues also provided fresh impetus for a more vigorous and foreign policy outlook.

THE 1970s

The 1970s witnessed an increasingly active and committed role in African and world affairs, and this was evident at several levels. Within the African continent, Nigerian diplomats were instrumental in bringing together the majority of countries to negotiate for better terms of trade with the European Community. Nigeria's economic size, strength, and potential—and the country's willingness to use these in the bargaining process—enabled African countries, as well as others in the Caribbean and Pacific Ocean areas, to be more influential in the negotiations; thus, favorable trade arrangements for these states were agreed upon at the Lomé Convention in 1975, as well as in subsequent agreements in 1980, 1985, and 1990.

Nigeria also took the lead in organizing West African states in a grouping to boost intraregional trade and increase industrial and development opportunities through regional cooperation. These states formed the Economic Community of West African States (ECOWAS) in 1975, a 16-member organization, of which Nigeria is by far the strongest economically. Unfortunately, there have been problems in increasing the level of cooperation among the states, and Nigeria did not help matters by its expulsion of "aliens"—some 2 million unwanted West Africans in 1983 and another 750,000 in 1985. These events, combined with the smaller states' suspicions of the disproportionately stronger Nigeria, as well as residual linguistic and cultural divisions within the community, have slowed the pace of progress.

Following the removal of Gowon from office in 1975, foreign policy took on a sharper focus. The watershed event occurred in 1975 when the government decisively backed the Popular Movement for the Liberation of Angola (MPLA), a Communist movement struggling to gain control of Angola, despite the opposition of many African states and Western powers, particularly the United States. Nigerian support for the liberation

movements in Mozambique, Namibia, Zimbabwe, and South Africa also flourished at this time, and the "oil weapon"—the threat to cut supplies to Western countries to persuade them to support liberation movements—was a vocal policy. This was apparently used by Shagari in 1979 when, in an attempt to pressure Britain to allow Zimbabwe its independence, British Petroleum's operations in Nigeria were nationalized (significantly, BP was allowed back into the market in 1991).

South Africa proved to be a much tougher nut to crack, and Nigeria's attempts to pressure that country both directly and indirectly brought little success. Nigeria was a principal agitator behind the boycotts of the Olympic Games in 1976 and the Commonwealth Games in 1978 (and again in 1986), to maintain the international isolation of the South African regime. But it lacked the capability to bring dramatic results in South Africa, and partly out of frustration Nigerian policymakers and the public talked openly of acquiring nuclear weapons—both to provide stiffer support of black African claims in South Africa and to increase Nigeria's own status and bargaining position over this and other issues. Given the fact that South Africa is 80 percent black, it appeared unlikely that Nigeria could credibly plan to use nuclear weapons against the country, as its aim was to protect rather than destroy the African majority.

THE 1980s

The rise in economic fortunes and external influence in the 1970s proved transitory and was quickly countered by the country's demise in the 1980s. Economic buoyancy was replaced by a host of problems that diminished external interventions and muted antagonism toward Western powers. The government became increasingly preoccupied with trying to solve its debt problems and seeking international financial assistance and investment. With an increased dependence upon Western countries such as Britain and the United States, and faced by a global oil glut, it was impossible to talk of the oil weapon or to pursue provocative policies toward the West, as it had done in the 1970s.

The Soviet Union maintained cordial relations and still sent military advisors to Nigeria and worked (unsuccessfully) toward completing the iron and steel complex at Ajaokuta. Military leaders, however, believed that greater benefits could accrue from seeking aid and investment from the West, although they remained critical of its manipulation of the global economy. The military's policies did not resemble the docile, pro-Western approach of the 1960s. Relations with France improved significantly after the mid–1980s, as both countries agreed on the importance of preventing the expansion of Libyan interests in Chad (and further afield), and political and military cooperation greatly increased. The French were anxious to maintain their friendly contacts and position in this large Anglophone market, which remained France's most important trading partner in Africa.

The growing strength of French and West German interests in Nigeria threatened the position of the traditional dominant trading partner, Britain. Antipathy toward Britain in general, and Prime Minister Margaret Thatcher in particular, over British support for South Africa caused a stormy relationship, but Thatcher's visits to Nigeria in January 1988 and January 1989 seemed sufficient to secure Britain's position as Nigeria's largest supplier of goods.

Nigeria's relations with the United States similarly ebbed and flowed, reaching their greatest heights in the late 1970s, when President Jimmy Carter paid the only visit to the country ever made by a U.S. president. This was as much an indication of the style and preferences of Carter's foreign policy as of the economic strength of Nigeria, which was then the second largest supplier of oil to the United States. The subsequent economic downturn in Nigeria, combined with President Ronald Reagan's downplaying of regional arenas and reemphasis of global politics and neocontainment, relegated the African "giant" to a lesser role.

THE 1990s

The 1990s have been a period of mixed fortunes. On the positive side, the Gulf War boosted, at least temporarily, oil revenues and gave fleeting relief to the beleaguered economy. Nigeria's hosting in 1991 of both the annual Organization of African Unity summit and the ECOWAS summit reinforced Nigerian perceptions of the country as the "center" of Africa (see Feature 11.7). Babangida's position as chair of the OAU for 1991–1992, combined with Chief Emeka Anyaoku's promotion to the position of secretary-general of the Commonwealth in 1991, and Olusegun Obasanjo's strong run at the top job in the United Nations, enhanced this perception. Nigeria's leadership of the ECOWAS military peacekeeping force in Liberia (Ecomog)

Feature 11.7 Nigeria and ECOWAS

West Africa has traditionally received the highest priority in foreign policy. Surrounded by French-speaking countries, Nigeria has had uneasy relations with them and, partly because of this, sought to bring the region closer together within the Economic Community of West African States (ECOWAS). Founded in 1975 following diplomacy by Nigeria and Togo, ECOWAS developed some cooperative economic linkages but has not brought the region together as hoped. Nigeria dominates West Africa in terms of its economic and military strength, but it has not developed significant trade relations within the region, although smuggling and unofficial trade remain high. Nigeria has played a critical role within ECOWAS in peacekeeping efforts in Liberia and Sierra Leone during the 1990s.

Economic hardship facing all the ECOWAS countries has led them to promote national, rather than regional, agendas, and so cooperation between them seems even more difficult than before. Success of ECOWAS is integral to the ambitious plans for a continentwide African Economic Community (AEC), which is planned to develop in stages until complete integration is achieved in 2025—a goal that appears to be unattainable at this time.

showed that the country continued to be the dominant force in West Africa. All these factors did little to translate into real political power for Nigeria.[31]

On the negative side, a number of problems, both old and new, afflicted foreign policy. Despite the mini oil boom, the economy remained in dire straits, with negligible improvement in diversification. Official nonoil exports in 1994 were a paltry $244 million. The national debt of $37 billion drained the economy, and the turmoil of the transition program proved to be an equally draining political issue. But other serious fears developed because of events in Europe and Asia. The integration of the EU market in 1993, and the vast economic opportunities opening up in the markets of Central and Eastern Europe, and Asia, have left Nigeria— and most of Africa—very much on the sidelines for potential investment. The post-Cold War new world (dis)order gave little importance to sub-Saharan Africa, except perhaps to post-apartheid South Africa, which now has overtaken Nigeria in both economic and political terms as the "champion" of Africa.

The cancellation of the presidential election results of June 1993 led to increasing isolation in international circles. The United States, partly in response to pressures from TransAfrica, applied limited sanctions to Nigeria in efforts to pressure movement toward democracy. The EU also froze official contacts and arms sales to Nigeria. The imprisonment of Obasanjo, among many others, early in 1995 heightened international anxieties, but the judicial executions of nine Ogoni dissidents in November 1995 led to Nigeria's temporary dismissal from the Commonwealth and further ostracism of the regime. However, sanctions fell short of blocking Nigeria's oil trade, and Shell remained committed to investing in a future $3.6 billion gas project. Most significant, perhaps, in all this was the fact that South Africa's president, Nelson Mandela, was the most outspoken in condemning the Abacha regime and seeking sanctions against Shell, an interesting turn of events in African politics.

CONCLUSION

Nigeria has experienced dramatic changes in its political, social, and economic life since inde-

pendence in October 1960. Although it is correct to conclude that instability is a constant theme underpinning Nigerian politics, it is possible to perceive some of this as a result of the transition, via experimentation, from a country dominated by a colonial power to one searching for a system of government best suited to its needs and those of its people. The long periods of military rule can be seen as part of this trial-and-error experimentation, though in recent years the military's apparently deliberate disregard for democracy makes its rule less and less justifiable.

Critical questions are whether the military will actually withdraw in 1998, and whether the new civilian politicians will be more nationalistic, more honest, and less corrupt than previous political classes, improvements that would allow a new republic to survive and work to provide the basis for future stability. From the evidence at hand, the answers to both questions are probably in the negative.

Against this political backdrop, an agenda of crucial social and economic issues also has to be resolved, both in terms of minimizing inequalities and providing the basic human needs of the majority of Nigerians, and of restructuring the economy to put the country on a more secure footing in the new millennium. Given the current economic insecurity, gross corruption, and political volatility, the next few years are potentially more troubling than any since independence.

KEY TERMS

Anglophone
cash crops
census
devaluation
development
Economic Community of West African States (ECOWAS)
Francophone
human development index
Indigenization Decree
national debt
nuclear power
Organization of Petroleum Exporting Countries (OPEC)

population growth
privatization
revenue allocation
rural-urban migration
structural adjustment program (SAP)

Further Readings

Aluko, Olajide. *Essays in Nigerian Foreign Policy* (London: Allen and Unwin, 1981).

Forrest, Tom. *The Advance of African Capital. The Growth of Nigerian Private Enterprise* (Charlottesville: University of Virginia Press, 1994).

Forrest, Tom. *Politics and Economic Development in Nigeria* (Boulder, CO: Westview Press, 1995).

Gambari, I. A. *Party Politics and Foreign Policy: Nigeria under the First Republic* (Zaria: Ahmadu Bello University Press, 1980).

Gambari, I. A. *Theory and Reality in Foreign Policy Making. Nigeria After the Second Republic* (Atlantic Highlands: Humanities Press International, 1989).

Ihonvbere, Julius O., and Timothy M. Shaw. *Towards a Political Economy of Nigeria. Petroleum and Politics at the (Semi-) Periphery* (Aldershot: Avebury, 1988).

Okolo, Julius Emeka, and Stephen Wright, eds. *West African Regional Cooperation and Development* (Boulder, CO: Westview Press, 1990).

Olaloku, F. A., et al. *Structure of the Nigerian Economy* (London: Macmillan, 1979).

Olayiwola, Peter O. *Petroleum and Structural Change in a Developing Country. The Case of Nigeria* (New York: Praeger, 1987).

Saro-Wiwa, Ken. *Genocide in Nigeria. The Ogoni Tragedy* (Port Harcourt: Saros, 1992).

Shaw, Timothy M., and Olajide Aluko, eds. *Nigerian Foreign Policy: Alternative Perceptions and Projections* (London: Macmillan, 1983).

Shepard, Robert B. *Nigeria, Africa and the United States. From Kennedy to Reagan* (Bloomington: Indiana University Press, 1991).

Soremekun, Kayode. *Perspectives on the Nigerian Oil Industry* (Lagos: Amkra Books, 1995).

Wayas, Joseph. *Nigeria's Leadership Role in Africa* (London: Macmillan, 1979).

Williams, Gavin, ed. *Nigeria: Economy and Society* (London: Rex Collings, 1976).

Zartman, I. William, ed. *The Political Economy of Nigeria* (New York: Praeger, 1983).

Notes

1. For a general introduction to African government and politics, see Naomi Chazan, Robert Mortimer, John Ravenhill, and Donald Rothchild, *Politics and Society in Contemporary Africa* (Boulder, CO: Lynne Rienner, 1992).
2. For a detailed discussion of Nigerian history, see John Hatch, *Nigeria. A History* (London: Secker and Warburg, 1971).
3. See Robert Heussler, *The British in Northern Nigeria* (London: Oxford University Press, 1968).
4. The National "Convention" was also known as the National "Congress." The NCNC was also known before independence as the National Council of Nigeria and the Cameroons.
5. E. Wayne Nafziger, *The Economics of Political Instability. The Nigerian-Biafran War* (Boulder, CO: Westview Press, 1983).
6. Eghosa E. Osaghae, *Structural Adjustment and Ethnicity in Nigeria.* Research Report No. 98 (Uppsala: Scandinavian Institute of African Studies, 1995); Olufemi Vaughan, "Assessing Grassroots Politics and Community Development in Nigeria," *African Affairs, 94,* (1995), pp. 501–518; E. Ike Udogu, "The Allurement of Ethnonationalism in Nigerian Politics," *Journal of Asian and African Studies* 29, no. 3–4, (1994), pp. 159–171.
7. *Government's Views and Comments on the Findings and Recommendations of the Political Bureau* (Abuja: Mamser, undated), Section 53.
8. Frantz Fanon, *The Wretched of the Earth* (London: MacGibbon and Kee, 1965).
9. Billy Dudley, *An Introduction to Nigerian Government and Politics* (London: Macmillan, 1982), pp. 62–63.
10. Gavin Williams and Terisa Turner, "Nigeria," in John Dunn, ed., *West African States: Failure and Promise* (Cambridge: Cambridge University Press, 1978), p. 133.
11. See William Gutteridge, *Military Regimes in Africa* (London: Methuen, 1975); and Morris Janowitz, *Civil-Military Relations—Regional Perspectives* (Beverly Hills: Sage, 1981).
12. For a discussion of the military in this period, see N.J. Miners, *The Nigerian Army 1956–66* (London: Methuen, 1971); and Robin Luckham,

The Nigerian Military: A Sociological Analysis of Authority and Revolt 1960–61 (London: Cambridge University Press, 1971).

13. Stephen Wright, "State-Consolidation and Social Integration in Nigeria: The Military's Search for the Elusive," in Henry Dietz and Jerold Elkin, eds., *Ethnicity, Integration and the Military* (Boulder, CO: Westview Press, 1991).

14. Dudley, *Nigerian Government and Politics,* p. 70.

15. For excellent surveys of the First Republic, see K. W. J. Post and Michael Vickers, *Structure and Conflict in Nigeria 1960–1966* (London: Heinemann, 1973); and Larry Diamond, *Class, Ethnicity and Democracy in Nigeria. The Failure of the First Republic* (Syracuse: Syracuse University Press, 1988).

16. A comprehensive survey of the military between 1966 and 1979 is contained in Oyeleye Oyediran, ed., *Nigerian Government and Politics under Military Rule 1966–1979* (London: Macmillan, 1979).

17. Ladun Anise, "Political Parties and Election Manifestos," in Oyeleye Oyediran, ed., *The Nigerian 1979 Elections* (London: Macmillan, 1981), p. 89.

18. Dudley, *Nigerian Government and Politics,* p. 223.

19. The Constitution of the Federal Republic of Nigeria, 1979 (Lagos: Federal Ministry of Information, 1979), Part 1, Section 15.

20. *Government's Views and Comments on the Findings and Recommendations of the Political Bureau* (Abuja: Mamser, undated).

21. Quoted in *West Africa,* August 7–13, 1989, p. 1282.

22. Julius O. Ihonvbere, "A Critical Evaluation of the Failed 1990 Coup in Nigeria," *The Journal of Modern African Studies, 29,* no. 4 (1991), pp. 601–626.

23. William Reno, "Old Brigades, Money Bags, New Breeds, and the Ironies of Reform in Nigeria," *Canadian Journal of African Studies, 27,* no. 1 (1993), pp. 66–87.

24. *New African,* September 1993, p. 13.

25. *West Africa,* September 25–October 8, 1995, p. 1597; and October 9–15, 1995, pp. 1656–57.

26. Civil Liberties Organization of Nigeria, *Executive Lawlessness in the Babangida Regime* (Lagos, 1991).

27. Anthony Kirk-Greene and Douglas Rimmer, *Nigeria since 1970: A Political and Economic Outline* (London: Hodder and Stoughton, 1981), p. 106.

28. For a discussion of issues in the Nigerian economy, see Kirk-Greene and Rimmer, *Nigeria since 1970;* Gavin Williams, ed., *Nigeria: Economy and Society* (London: Rex Collings, 1976); and Julius O. Ihonvbere and Timothy M. Shaw, *Towards a Political Economy of Nigeria* (Aldershot: Avebury, 1988).

29. Sayre P. Schatz, "Pirate Capitalism and the Inert Economy of Nigeria," *Journal of Modern African Studies, 22,* no. 1 (1984), pp. 45–57; Nicholas Balabkins, *Indigenization and Economic Development: The Nigerian Experience* (Greenwich, CT: JAI Press, 1982); Thomas J. Biersteker, *Multinationals, the State, and Control of the Nigerian Economy* (Princeton: Princeton University Press, 1987).

30. Eghosa E. Osaghae, "The Ogoni Uprising: Oil Politics, Minority Agitation and the Future of the Nigerian State," *African Affairs, 94* (1995), pp. 325–344.

31. Julius Emeka Okolo and Stephen Wright, "Nigeria" in Timothy M. Shaw and Julius Emeka Okolo (eds.), *The Political Economy of Foreign Policy in ECOWAS* (New York: St Martin's, 1994), pp. 125–146.

CHAPTER 12

Conclusion

FOR STUDENTS OF COMPARATIVE POLITICS AND GOVERNMENT: THE LARGER QUESTIONS ON THE AGENDA OF HUMANITY

The preceding chapters introduced students to a number of major foreign powers in different parts of the world and thus to the history, cultures, and politics of much of humanity. Students will soon realize there is no royal road to knowledge or an easy shortcut to the understanding of other countries. Such understanding requires long and careful study. But students must avoid the peril of being overwhelmed by details and facts, important though they are, of foreign systems and must not lose sight of the larger questions with which this study is concerned. Three major themes that students should keep in mind are the politics and problems of modernization, the reconciliation of power and freedom in the different countries, and the relevance of the nation-state in an international system interconnected in a variety of ways.

In all of the countries presented in this book, there has been an inexorable, if uneven, march away from traditionalism and toward "modernity." In Europe the traditionalism with which we begin this study is the feudal society that existed up to the late eighteenth century, elements of which continued to exist through the nineteenth century and even up to the present. Feudal society was undermined by complex developments. The technology of warfare, especially the invention of gunpowder, deprived the feudal aristocracy of its military dominance; increased trade and commerce brought about a massive expansion of the middle classes, who could not be easily fitted into the two-way relationship between lords and serfs; and the cultural climate throughout Europe was trans-

formed by the coming of a scientific revolution. In an age of experimentation and scientific advance, the essential notions of feudalism—which based the right to rule on heredity—began to crumble. Whether one believes that science, technology, and industry represent progress or degradation is a separate question; the French Revolution and the Industrial Revolution were major facts of life that condemned feudal regimes and led to the creation of new political systems—the substance of our study.

In China and India, the traditional societies that preceded the creation of the present political systems were even less developed than the European feudal societies. By "less developed" we do not imply that there was an inferior civilization or culture in Asia (which is demonstrably false), but merely that the scientific, technological, and political movements that characterize twentieth-century societies were delayed in Asia. One measure of the distance between Europe and Asia was the relative ease with which Europeans were able to conquer and colonize the more traditional peoples of the world; and one indicator of the modernization of Asia was the ability of formerly subject peoples to overthrow European rule.

Our country studies reveal the march from the feudal to the modern condition in Britain, France, Germany, and Russia, and from the traditional to the modern in Japan, Mexico, Nigeria, China, and India. Modern political study is largely an attempt to understand why and how this march took place, why peoples have chosen different political systems to attain their objectives, and what price is paid for development as well as for stagnation.

In the nineteenth and twentieth centuries, three major types of political systems were created during rapid modernization: liberal or constitutional democracy, Fascism and Nazism, and Communism. Where a self-confident middle class emerged, mainly in Northern Europe and North America, a social base existed for systems whose political leadership was determined by free and fair elections and in which a constitutional order guaranteed protection of human and property rights. But failure of the middle class to assume political power often paved the way to authoritarian rule or to totalitarianism as in Germany and Italy.

With the Russian Revolution in 1917, Communism represented a third possibility. Under the leaders of the new state of the Soviet Union, Communism was the basis for forced industrialization under the control of the one political party that acted in the name of the proletariat. In 1989 the Soviet Union collapsed, one of the defining moments of recent years. Its command economy became too complex to be managed successfully by the centralized one-party regime. The relaxation of political controls after 1989 allowed forces of ethnicity and nationalism to become prominent.

As mentioned in the Preface, this fourth edition appears at a time of unusual flux in Russia and China, as well as in a number of countries in East Asia. This book has suggested generalizations about comparative politics and has also divided the nine countries into three groups for analytical convenience. But rapidly changing political, social, and economic factors suggest caution concerning such analytical categories.

Some "developing" counties such as Hong Kong or Singapore have a higher income per capita than some major industrialized Western European countries. Moreover, many "developing" countries are more industrialized than the "industrial" countries in which industry now accounts for less than one-third of total output. About two-thirds of the world's 5.8 billion population live in Asia and account for about a quarter of gross world product. In the developing countries, the process of economic modernization and political development has not generally resulted in democratic political systems or in respecting human rights.

Russia and China present similar problems for comparative analysis. Russia has transformed itself, at least legally, from a Communist, one-party political system to a "democratic, federative, law-governed state with a republican

form of government" according to its constitution. It is supposed to guarantee human rights—including freedom of conscience, movement, and the press and rights to private property and ownership of land. After its long autocratic past, can Russia sustain a democratic system capable of overcoming the combined forces of tradition, ethnicity, and nationalism? This will be a central concern for students of comparative politics into the next millennium.

In China, the one-party dictatorship—the self-selected group of Communist leaders—has presided over some decentralization of the economy, the movement of millions from farms to cities, an increase in consumption goods, private retailing, and a stock market. But if China has free prices it does not have a free press. It has ended central economic planning, but still has central political dictatorship. Thus, single-party rule with centralized decision making is presently combined with market competition.

At every stage of the modernizing process, all peoples confront the challenge of reconciling power and freedom. Power is necessary in order to orchestrate the activities of millions of individuals, to avoid anarchy, and to enable a people to achieve their collective goals. But the coercive state that is needed for defense, domestic tranquillity, and the general welfare may also deprive people of the fruits of their labor, their freedom, and their very lives. This is the permanent dilemma of all government—whether in primitive, feudal, or industrial societies. Is it possible to reconcile power and freedom, and, if so, under what conditions? It is not enough merely to speculate in the abstract or to dream up ideal solutions. We must review the historical developments of the major societies to be able to convert speculation into theory and theory into testable propositions.

A third theme also relates to rapid changes in the world. Is the nation-state still viable or have changing technological, economic, and military factors limited its autonomy? The ease of transport and communication within and between countries has meant a vast increase in international trade. It has also resulted in a considerable share of the world's capital being owned by multinational companies operating in different countries, and also money being easily transferred in the international financial market. Those international money flows affect interest rates and investment in the individual nation-states. The world seems a smaller place with the dramatic information revolution through which people everywhere can know a great deal about other countries through television, films, and the Internet.

Yet, in spite of these changes, the world is still divided into nation-states, each with its own interests. The members of the European Union have not yet created a superstate or a federal system. Nor have countries supposedly belonging to a particular cultural area—such as the Confucian Chinese culture, the Slavic Orthodox, the Latin American, or the African, whose members share common religious or philosophic beliefs and historical experience—combined to form a political unit transcending the individual states. After reading this volume it will be up to you, the reader and student, to make your own contribution to the understanding of these major themes and central problems on the agenda of humanity.

PHOTO CREDITS

Unless otherwise acknowledged, all photographs are the property of Scott, Foresman and Company. Page abbreviations are as follows: (t)top, (c)center, (b)bottom, (l)left, (r)right.

Page 35(b): William Strode/Woodfin Camp & Associates; **35(t):** Steve Benbow/Woodfin Camp & Associates; **36(r):** AP/Wide World; **36(l):** Superstock, Inc.; **73:** Superstock, Inc.; **86:** Stephen Lock/Gamma-Liaison; **107:** Bassignac/Gaillarde/Gamma-Liaison; **119:** Gregoire Korganow/Gamma-Liaison; **123:** AP/Wide World; **134:** AP/Wide World; **156:** Christian Vioujard/Gamma-Liaison; **178:** Patrick Piel/Gamma-Liaison; **196:** Patrick Piel/Gamma-Liaison; **198:** Corbis/Bettmann Archive; **200:** German Information Center; **235:** AP/Wide World; **238:** Corbis/Bettmann; **252:** UPI/Corbis/Bettmann; **254:** AP/Wide World; **257:** Myra McNelly; **259:** Hashimoto/Sygma; **290:** Courtesy European Union; **292:** Courtesy European Union; **295:** D. Geeraets/Gamma-Liaison; **325:** Ernest Manewal/Superstock, Inc.; **353:** Anthony Suau/Gamma-Liaison; **364:** Swersey/Gamma-Liaison; **371:** DeKeerle/Sygma; **402:** © 1989 Peter Turnley/Black Star; **404:** Corbis-UPI/Bettmann; **409:** Corbis-UPI/Bettmann; **415:** AP/Wide World; **471:** Dennis Brack/Black Star; **475:** Corbis-Reuters/Bettmann; **482:** AP/Wide World; **485:** Black Star; **503:** Superstock, Inc.; **506:** UPI-Corbis/Bettmann; **513:** Wesley Bocxe/JB Pictures Ltd.; **514:** UPI-Corbis/Bettmann; **575:** Liz Gilbert/Sygma; **579:** © 1987 Robert Reichert/Gamma-Liaison; **581:** Liz Gilbert/Sygma; **582:** Liz Gilbert/Sygma

INDEX